W9-AAD-685

It all starts here. Activate your PIN!*

*Your PIN is provided on the inside cover of every NEW copy of this textbook.

Introducing the Interactive Companion Web site for *Social Psychology: Unraveling the Mystery, 2/e*

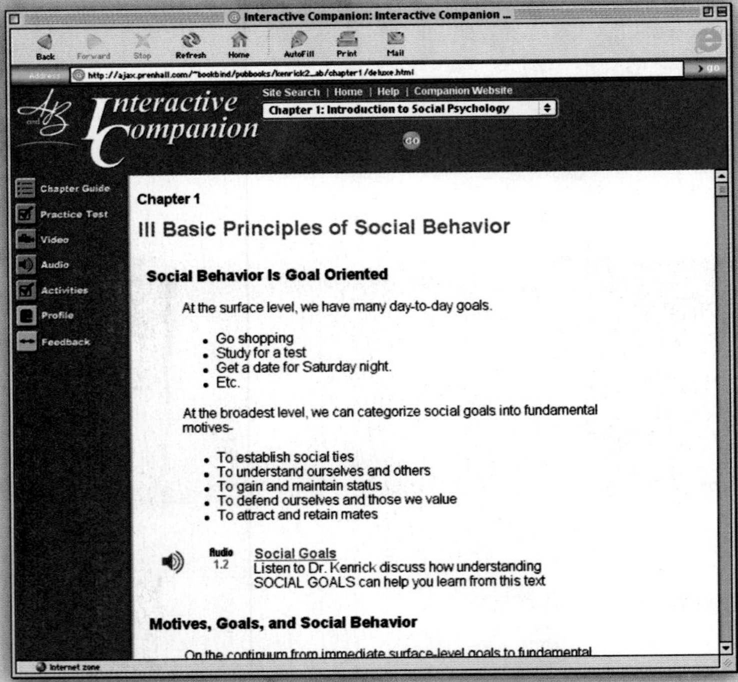

Learning has reached a whole new level with the Interactive Companion Web site – *by encouraging you to apply what you've learned through audio and video clips, Web sites, activities and practice tests.*

With the purchase of *Social Psychology: Unraveling the Mystery, 2/e*, you'll get access to this PIN-code protected Web site FREE of charge. The Allyn & Bacon Interactive Companion Web site represents an exciting new study tool that uses the latest in multimedia to review, enrich, and expand upon key concepts presented in its companion textbook.

Using chapter highlights as its organizing structure, the Interactive Companion helps you apply what you've learned by presenting you with hundreds of links to audio and video clips, Web sites, activities, and practice tests. These links are annotated with brief descriptions that help you understand the value and purpose of each type of media in the context of the chapter.

Everything you need is right here at your fingertips!

ACTIVATE YOUR PIN.

How will you benefit from using the Interactive Companion Web site?

- ✓ **Provides you with frequent feedback on your learning progress to perform better on tests.**
- ✓ **Offers highly interactive ways for you to engage with the textbook content.**
- ✓ **Adds variety to course materials and helps you study more effectively.**
- ✓ **Helps you to think critically about the information presented to you in the textbook and on the Web site.**
- ✓ **Gives you access to the latest information related to the textbook topics via the Web.**

"*A major advantage of the Web site is that it allows students to connect with a wealth of learning support any time and any place. Professors can create a vast array of assignments and projects, knowing that all students – those in dorms and those commuting from home miles away, those with easy access to libraries and those who are more isolated – have the resources to complete the assignments and projects.*"

Anita Woolfolk
Educational Psychology Professor
The Ohio State University

Easy navigation that lets you study the way you want to!

1. Each chapter begins with an attention-grabbing opener. **Click on the associated audio icon and you'll hear questions or issues framed around the chapter opener;** this allows you to hear as well as read about new concepts.
2. **Chapter learning objectives are linked to the various topic areas**, allowing you to go directly from what you need to learn in the chapter to the media assets that will help you learn this new information.
3. **Each topic area ends with an activity** that is a review of key terms. These are created as flash card exercises – allowing you to reinforce the information that you've learned from that section of the book.
4. **Every chapter ends with two items:**
   a. **Concept Check Activity** which asks you to match terms and concepts in the chapter with their definitions.
   b. **Practice Test,** which promotes self-regulation and self-monitoring, two key elements of successful learning.

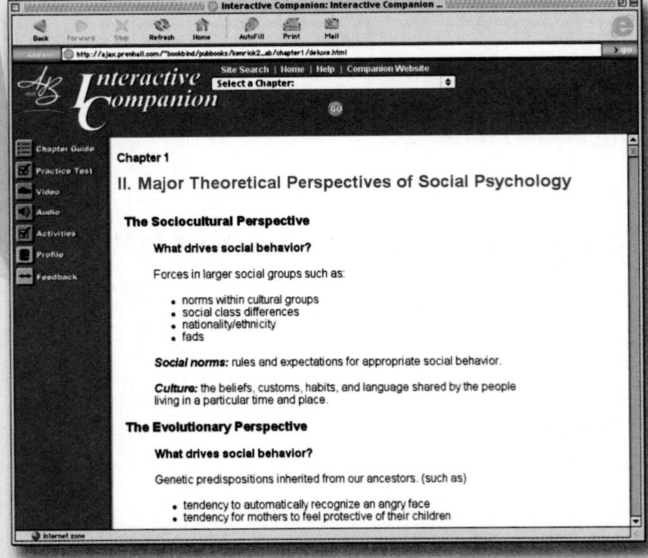

Everything you need is right here at your fingertips!

ACTIVATE YOUR PIN.

Interactive ways to prepare for that in-class exam!

Practice Test

Click on a **"Practice Test"** icon and you'll be able to test your understanding of the chapter material by completing a self-scoring practice test. Throughout the Practice Test, you are provided with hints to some of the questions. This hint will direct you to the appropriate corresponding page(s) in the textbook where you'll find the information related to the test question. You'll receive immediate results and feedback from your test, allowing you to review your weak areas in preparation for the actual in-class exam.

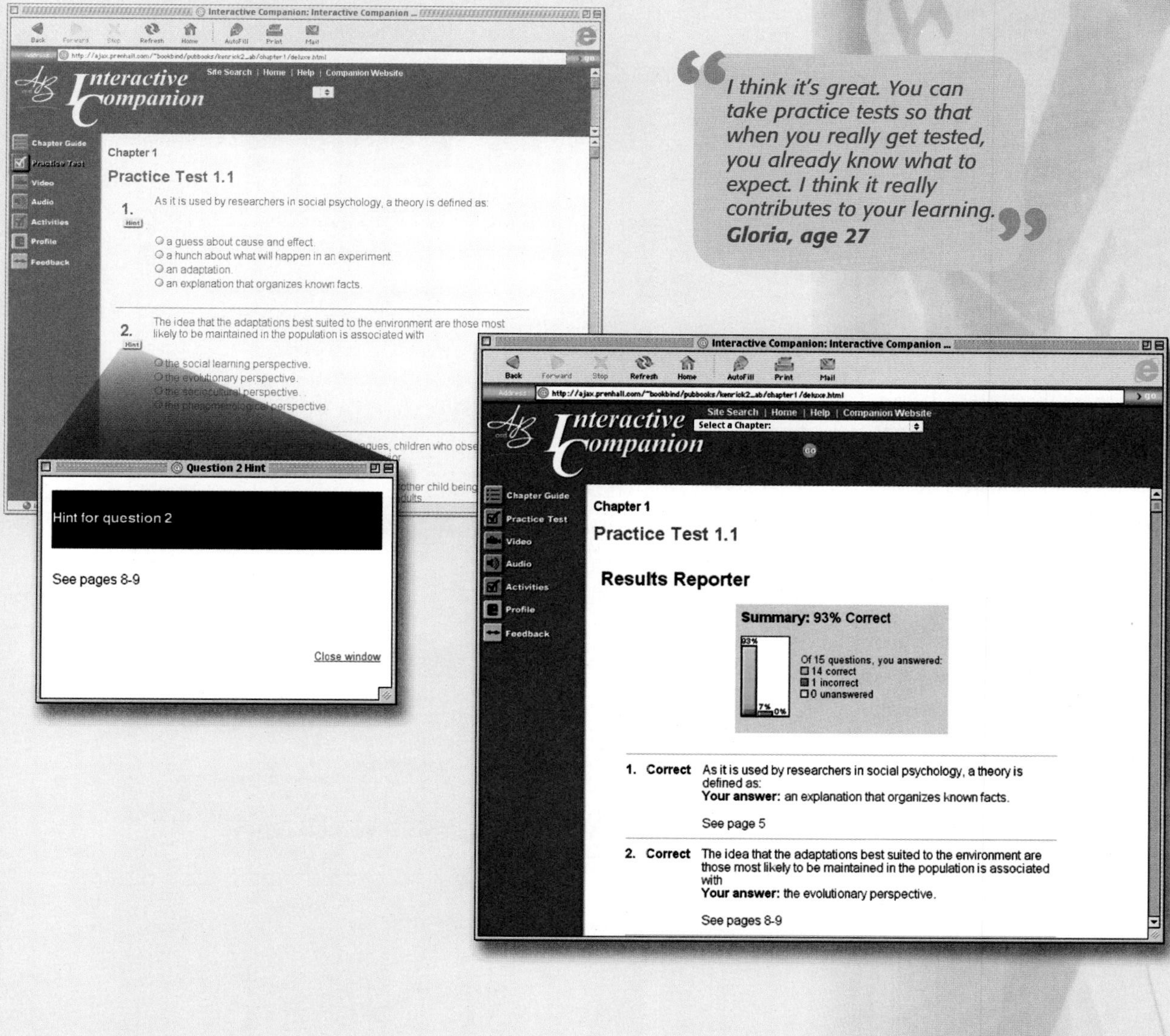

> *"I think it's great. You can take practice tests so that when you really get tested, you already know what to expect. I think it really contributes to your learning."*
> ***Gloria, age 27***

Information comes alive when you see it and hear it!

Video 

Click on a **"Video"** icon and you'll be captivated by the **sights and sounds of video segments directly related to the material you just read.** For some textbooks, these segments come from leading news sources. For others, they are part of custom videos developed to demonstrate concepts in the discipline.

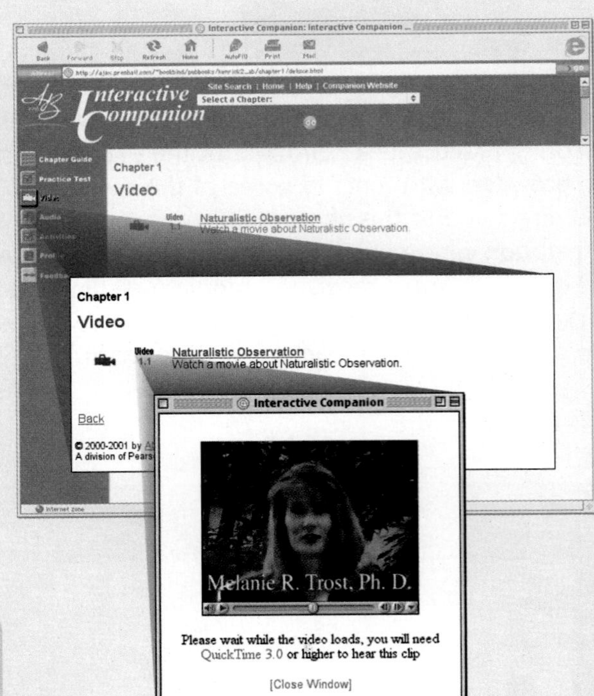

> *The audio, feedback, and videos help me understand each chapter.*
> ***Janel, age 40***

Audio 

Click on an **"Audio"** icon and you'll hear either the author of the textbook or a specialist in the field speaking directly about concepts in the book. Often **the "voice" will add background information or give examples – material that enhances and extends the chapter material.**

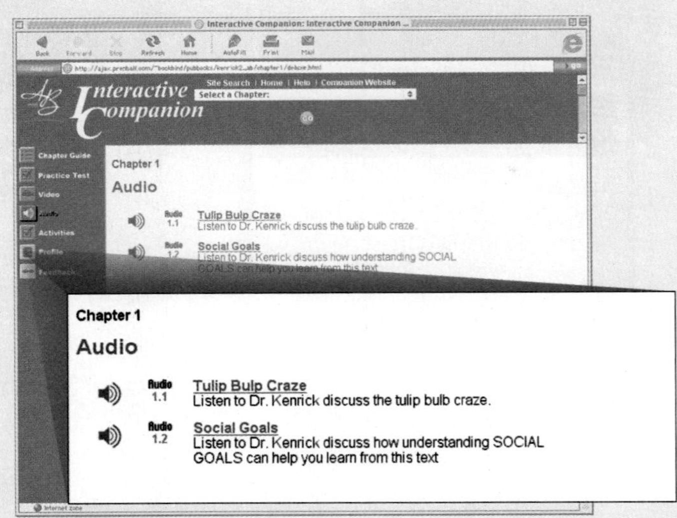

Everything you need is right here at your fingertips!

ACTIVATE YOUR PIN.

Animated activities give you more opportunities to test your level of understanding!

Activities 

Click on an **"Activities"** icon and you can complete interesting activities directly related to the information presented in the textbook. These animated activities make learning the information entertaining and informative! **You'll be asked to research, discuss, think critically, and more!**

> *I enjoyed using the Web site! The matching games and the vocabulary terms helped me the most.*
> ***Andy, age 18***

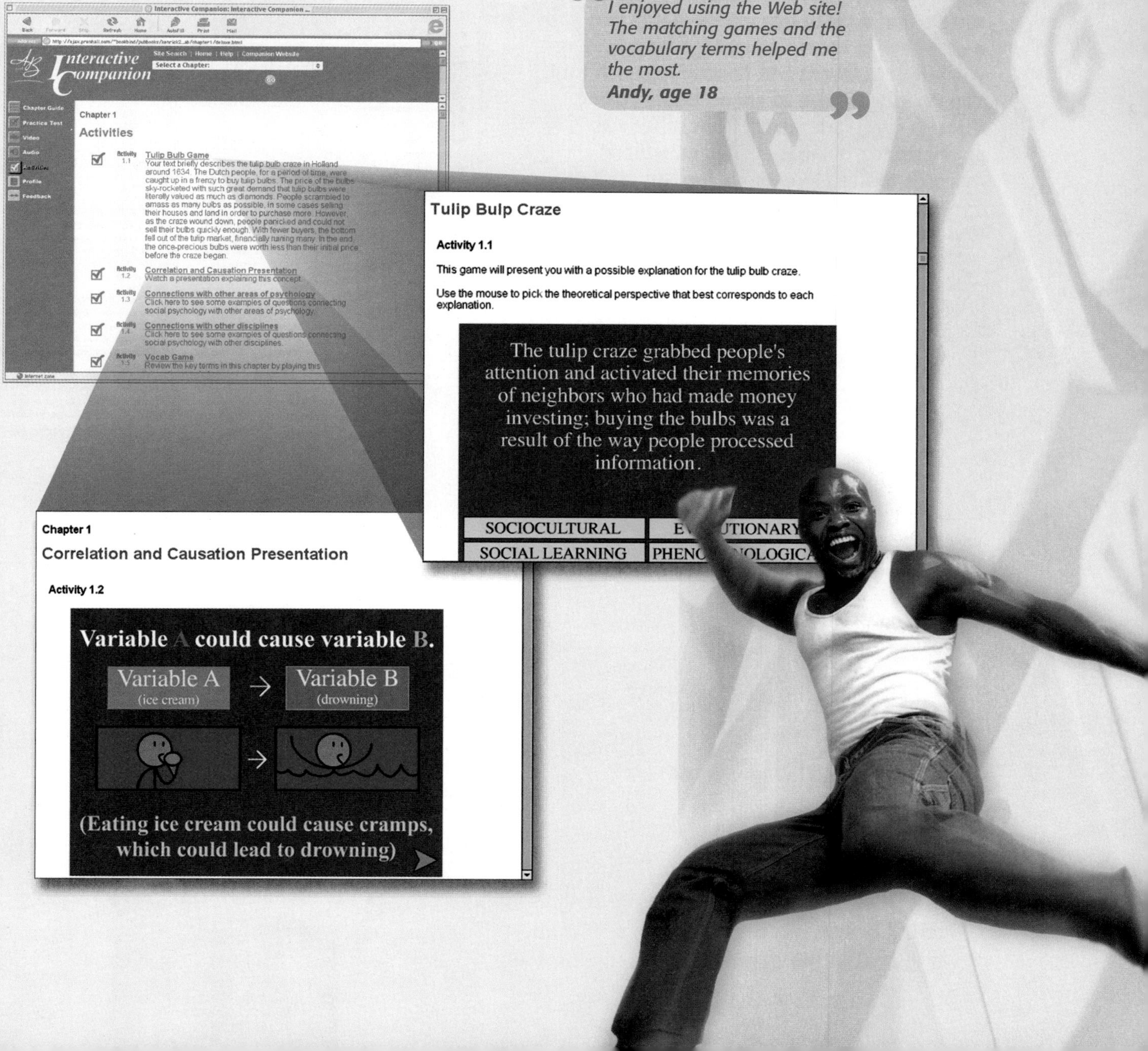

Interactive Companion

Chapter Guide
Practice Test
Video
Audio
Activities
Profile
Feedback

Chapter 1

Activities

Activity 1.1 Tulip Bulb Game
Your text briefly describes the tulip bulb craze in Holland around 1634. The Dutch people, for a period of time, were caught up in a frenzy to buy tulip bulbs. The price of the bulbs sky-rocketed with such great demand that tulip bulbs were literally valued as much as diamonds. People scrambled to amass as many bulbs as possible, in some cases selling their houses and land in order to purchase more. However, as the craze wound down, people panicked and could not sell their bulbs quickly enough. With fewer buyers, the bottom fell out of the tulip market, financially ruining many. In the end, the once-precious bulbs were worth less than their initial price before the craze began.

Activity 1.2 Correlation and Causation Presentation
Watch a presentation explaining this concept.

Activity 1.3 Connections with other areas of psychology
Click here to see some examples of questions connecting social psychology with other areas of psychology.

Activity 1.4 Connections with other disciplines
Click here to see some examples of questions connecting social psychology with other disciplines.

Activity 1.5 Vocab Game
Review the key terms in this chapter by playing this

Tulip Bulp Craze

Activity 1.1

This game will present you with a possible explanation for the tulip bulb craze.

Use the mouse to pick the theoretical perspective that best corresponds to each explanation.

The tulip craze grabbed people's attention and activated their memories of neighbors who had made money investing; buying the bulbs was a result of the way people processed information.

SOCIOCULTURAL
SOCIAL LEARNING

Chapter 1

Correlation and Causation Presentation

Activity 1.2

Variable A could cause variable B.

Variable A (ice cream) → Variable B (drowning)

(Eating ice cream could cause cramps, which could lead to drowning)

More online resources to help you get a better grade!

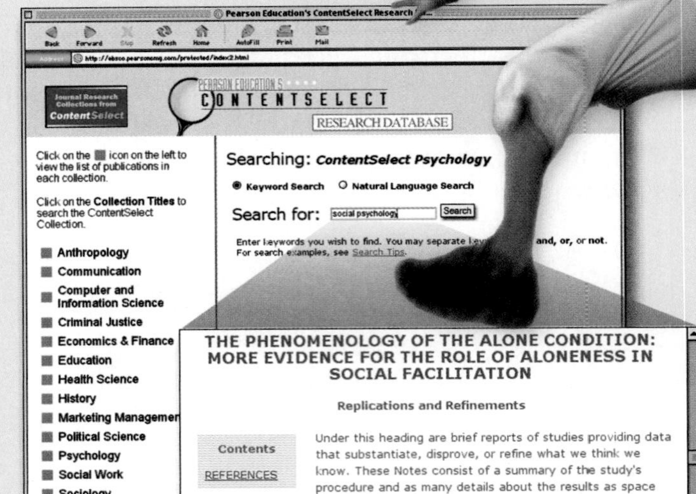

ContentSelect for Psychology

The task of writing a research paper just got much less daunting! NEW from Allyn & Bacon – customized discipline-specific online research collections. Each database contains 25,000+ articles, which include content from top tier academic publications and journals. Sophisticated keyword search coupled with a simple and easy-to-use interface will give you a competitive course advantage by providing you with a relevant and flexible research tool. You no longer have to spend hours culling through irrelevant results from other less sophisticated databases! This incredible research tool is FREE for six months, and can be accessed from the password-protected Web site available with this textbook. Visit **www.ablongman.com/techsolutions** for more details.

This powerful research tool will cut down on the amount of time you spend finding relevant information for your research papers.

Everything you need is right here at your fingertips!

ACTIVATE YOUR PIN.

Allyn & Bacon
A Pearson Education Company

Web: www.ablongman.com
Fax: (617) 848-7490
Tel: (800) 852-8024

Bookmark **www.ablongman.com/psychology** today & visit often to see what's NEW and available in the discipline of psychology!

www.ablongman.com/techsolutions

We're committed to helping instructors with their technology needs! Let us help you piece it together!

Social Psychology

UNRAVELING THE MYSTERY

Second Edition

Douglas T. Kenrick
Arizona State University

Steven L. Neuberg
Arizona State University

Robert B. Cialdini
Arizona State University

Allyn and Bacon • Boston • London • Toronto • Sydney • Tokyo • Singapore

Eexcutive Editor: Carolyn O. Merrill
Senior Editorial-Production Administrator: Joe Sweeney
Editorial-Production Service: Thomas E. Dorsaneo/Publishing Consultants
Composition Buyer: Linda Cox
Manufacturing Buyer: Megan Cochran
Cover Administrator: Linda Knowles
Text Design: rosa+wesley
Photo Researcher: Sue C. Howard
Text Composition: Omegatype Typography, Inc.

Photo credits appear on page 641, which constitutes an extension of the copyright page.

Chapter opening image credits:

page xxii: "Pueblos of Taos." Courtesy of the Anschutz Collection. Photo by William J. O'Connor; 34: Jackson Medford; 72: "Reverie" by Jamie Chase. Courtesy of The Cultural Exchange Gallery; 114: © Superstock; 150: "Harmony." © Paul Nzalamba; 190: Jackson Medford; 230: "Market Scene." © Paul Nzalamba; 262: "Love." Artist: Lan Nguyen; 296: "The Embrace." © Ludvic Attard; 334: "The Squabble." © Ludvic Attard; 376: Jackson Medford; 416: "Southern Comfort." © Matt Renard; 456: "Space Collector #3." © Luke Gray; 492: "And the Sun Came." © Paul Nzalamba.

A Pearson Education Company
75 Arlington St.
Boston, MA 02116
www.ablongman.com

Library of Congress Cataloging-in-Publication Data

Kenrick, Douglas T.
Social psychology: unraveling the mystery / Douglas T. Kenrick, Steven L. Neuberg, Robert B. Cialdini.—2nd ed.
p. cm.
Includes bibliographical references and index.
ISBN 0-205-33297-8
1. Social psychology. I. Neuberg, Steven L. II. Cialdini, Robert B. III. Title.
HM1033 . K46 2001
302—dc21 00-066389

Printed in the United States of America

10 9 8 7 6 5 4 3 2 1 RRD-OH 03 02 01

To David and Carol

To Erika, Rachel, Zachary, and Elliot

To Bobette, Christopher, and Jason

Brief Contents

Features

FOCUS ON Method

FOCUS ON Application

FOCUS ON Social Dysfunction

Contents

CHAPTER 4

Presenting the Self 114

CHAPTER 5

Persuasion 150

CHAPTER 6

Social Influence: Conformity, Compliance, and Obedience 190

CHAPTER 7

Affiliation and Friendship 231

CHAPTER 8

Love and Romantic Relationships 262

From the Authors

To students assigned a typical social psychology textbook, the field must seem like an amazing three-ring circus, where every turn of the eye reveals a dizzying assortment of attention-demanding performances. A different show unfolds in each ring—awe-inspiring acts of altruism, shocking deeds of aggression, persuasive tricks from magicians' hats, human pyramids of cooperation, and mysterious feats of self-delusion. At the center of it all stands the course instructor, the ringmaster, calling students' attention alternately to one then another facet of the spectacle—*And now, ladies and gentlemen, I invite you to shift your gaze from the clownish antics of self-deception to the daring men and women attempting to traverse the tightrope of romantic love, and then back down to the wild lion pit of aggression.*

The Need for an Integrative Approach to Social Psychology

For us, the problem with the three-ring circus presentation of social psychology is that it masks something crucial: Human social behaviors are woven together in related, interconnected patterns. To present an array of separate, disjointed chapter topics—aggression here, persuasion, prejudice, and personal relationships there, there, and there—offers a sorely inadequate view of the field. Common concepts, dimensions, and principles underlie all social behavior, and we are convinced that students will benefit greatly from knowing about them. After all, a primary rule of learning and memory is that people grasp and retain more material, more easily, when the various parts can be connected by organizing principles.

As entertaining and stimulating as a circus may be, it is not a good arena for learning. Much better, and equally engaging, is a well-constructed work of theater, cinema, or literature. The field of social psychology should be presented to students as a story, not a circus. It's an intricate story to be sure, rich in versions and variations. But it is coherent nonetheless, with recurring characters, scenes, and themes linking its elements. Our major purpose in writing this text is to offer students and instructors a cohesive framework that retains social psychology's renowned ability to captivate student interest, but that adds the more intellectually helpful (and satisfying) feature of integration.

How Do We Accomplish the Integration?

For a full year before deciding to write this book, we met for an afternoon every week to try to develop a truly integrative framework for the course. We knew that we had one ironic advantage: In a basic way, we disagreed with one another. Each of us had approached the task with a different one of the major, sometimes opposing, theoretical perspectives in social psychology today—social cognition, social learning, and evolutionary psychology. We realized that if we could find an overarching framework that would bridge our diverse approaches, it would provide an especially broad foundation for integrating the course material—one that allowed and incorporated a full range of theoretical starting points.

Those meetings were an exhilarating mix of good-natured conflicts, eye-opening insights, false starts, blind alleys, and gratifying breakthroughs... always accompanied by the shared sense that our understanding of social psychology was growing. The effort would have been worthwhile even if no book had come of it. At the end of that year of discussion and debate, not only did we have an invaluable mid-career learning experience under our belts but, as well, we had consensus on an integrative framework that we were all genuinely enthusiastic about.

The framework uses a pair of themes to tie together the text material within and across chapter topics:

1 **The goal-directed nature of social behavior.** First, we stress that social responding is goal-directed. The goals themselves may not be verbalized or even conscious, but when people obey an authority figure, begin a new relationship, or raise a fist against another, they do so in the service of some goal—perhaps to gain another's approval, verify a self-image, acquire social status, and so on. In chapter 1, we describe how everyday goals flow from fundamental social motives, such as establishing social ties, attracting mates,

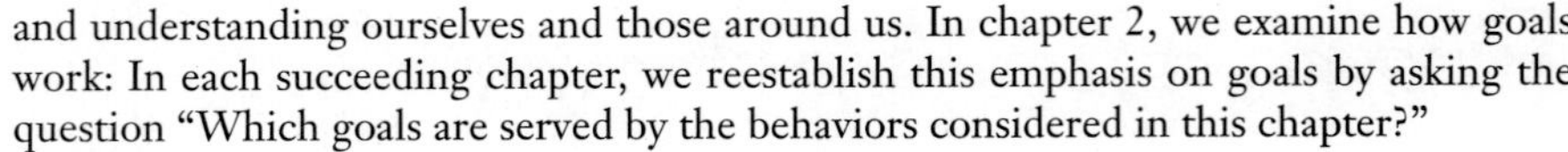

and understanding ourselves and those around us. In chapter 2, we examine how goals work: In each succeeding chapter, we reestablish this emphasis on goals by asking the question "Which goals are served by the behaviors considered in this chapter?"

2 The interaction of the person and the situation. Second, to understand fully the causes of a person's social behavior, we need to consider how aspects of that person interact with aspects of his or her situation. How do features inside the individual—attitudes, traits, expectations, attributions, moods, goals, stereotypes, and emotions—work together with features of the situation to influence social behavior? Beginning with Kurt Lewin, this interactionist theme has been prominent in our field. Unfortunately, introductory social psychology texts have rarely engaged the full explanatory power of interactionism. In contrast, we continuously invite readers to consider the interplay of influences inside and outside the person.

Interweaving Perspectives: Cognition, Culture, and Evolution

For the last two decades, social psychologists have profitably mined the cognitive perspective for insights into how humans process information about their social situations. These insights added to a foundation of findings discovered within the learning and phenomenological perspectives. In recent years, as fascinating discoveries have been made about social behavior in different human cultures and different animal species, the sociocultural and evolutionary perspectives have increasingly contributed to the mix. The sociocultural perspective has emphasized how our social thoughts and behaviors are encompassed within the larger context of the societies we live in. Cultural influences can change the answer to questions about: which techniques of persuasion will be effective, whether a person will define herself in terms of her group memberships or her individual qualities, or whether that person will marry monogamously or polygamously. The study of culture is fascinating because it often highlights differences, and reminds us that "our way" isn't always the only way. But cross-cultural research has also taught us that humans the world over have some common ways of thinking and behaving around one another. The evolutionary perspective has helped us understand why there are similarities not only across human cultures, but even across different species. Initial forays into evolutionary psychology emphasized the darker side of human nature—"selfish genes" driving aggression, sexuality, and the battle between the sexes. But evolutionary analyses have revealed that our ancestors survived not just by selfish competition, but also by forming friendships, cooperating with other members of their groups, and by forging loving family bonds.

It is becoming clearer that these various perspectives are not "alternatives" to one another. Instead, they work together to enable a fuller understanding of the social world. As long-term students of cognition, social learning, and evolutionary psychology, we have woven these threads together into the unique interactionist tapestry of this book.

The Structure of Each Chapter

After introducing social psychology (Chapter 1) and taking a closer look at the person and the social situation (Chapter 2), we organize the remaining chapters around a common structure:

1 The mystery. Each chapter begins with an account of a baffling pattern of human behavior—an incident or a set of incidents that seems beyond understanding. For example:

- Why, for example, did Reverend Moon's daughter-in-law Nansook Hong take flight from the belief system to which she had dedicated her entire life, leaving behind the immense wealth she had enjoyed as a member of the Unification Church's inner circle?
- Why did a Japanese envoy in Europe decide to disobey his superiors' repeated orders, and rescue thousands of Jews from the Holocaust?
- What features of human emotion could inspire the king of one of the world's most powerful empires to abdicate his throne, lands, and castle for the affections of a woman his family and country judged wholly unsuitable?

Later, as the chapter progresses, we introduce general principles of human behavior that, when put together properly, resolve the mystery. These mysteries represent more to us than devices for engaging reader's interest. They are designed to convey something basic about how we approach the text material: Our approach is heavily research-based, and research is akin to good detective work. Researchers, like detectives, begin their search with an interesting or perplexing question, then examine clues, gather evidence, test hypotheses, eliminate alternatives and—if things fall into place—uncover the right answer. To mine these instructive parallels, we return often in the text to the concept of researcher-as-detective.

2 The goals. Next we introduce readers to the set of goals underlying the behavior covered in the chapter, by asking "What purposes does this behavior (e.g., aggression or helping or conformity) serve for an individual?" and "Which factors lead an individual to use this behavior to achieve those goals?" Taking each goal of the set in turn, we consider factors in the person, in the situation, and in their interaction:

The person. Here we present research showing which internal factors trigger each particular goal. So, which traits motivate people to seek social approval through conformity? Which moods influence people to think deeply in order to understand themselves and others more accurately? Which beliefs lead people to discriminate against other groups in order to feel good about themselves?

The situation. Here we consider evidence of situational factors relevant to a given goal. How do personal threats engage self-protective prejudices? How do cultural norms influence the desire to seek sexual gratification through casual relationships? How does time pressure affect the inclination to think deeply before deciding what a stranger's personality is like?

The person-situation interaction. In this section, we present data demonstrating how personal and situational factors interact. Social psychologists are used to thinking about how people with different attitudes, expectations, and traits act differently in the same situation. But interactions are much richer than this: People choose their life situations, change situations they do not like, and are themselves rejected from some situations and changed by others. For example, lonely people may act in needy ways that alienate others. In turn, others may avoid them and stop inviting them to social events, further enhancing their inner feelings of social isolation. By systematically showing students the importance of person-situation interactions, we hope to illustrate the limitations of the usual single-factor explanations—such as putting all the blame for aggression or blind obedience on the person, or the converse error of viewing people as interchangeable pawns on a giant interpersonal chess board.

3 Special Features. Several of social psychology's messages and themes are highlighted in each chapter's special features:

Focus on Application. Here, we discuss how a specific experimental finding or body of findings relates to real-world issues—how research insights can be used to create less-prejudiced classrooms, help married couples stay together, or reduce violence.

Focus on Method. In chapter 1, we present research methods in terms of a detective metaphor—searching for clues by sifting through shreds of evidence. In each chapter that follows, we introduce a new tool for the researcher's detective work. For example, in describing the research findings on media violence and viewer aggression, we include a feature on how meta-analysis works. In discussing research on love, we introduce the tool of factor analysis. By introducing these tools throughout the text, we hope to show the student why methods are essential to solving fascinating riddles.

Focus on Social Dysfunction. Psychology students are fascinated by disordered behavior. In this feature, we hope to tap that fascination to demonstrate broader principles. We examine how normally healthy social behaviors can, if taken too far, produce unhealthy consequences—for example, how the usually adaptive tendency to develop strong bonds between lovers can underlie obsessive relationships.

4 Revisiting the Mystery. The final section returns to the opening mystery to help students pull together the various research findings discussed in the chapter. For example, we return to the puzzle of the fleeing daughter-in-law, the prosocial Japanese envoy, or the abdicating king, in light of research findings on social influence, altruism, and relationships (and we pull together the new clues we revealed in the chapter). In this way, we hope not only to capitalize on curiosity, but also to tap another general principle of learning and memory—the principle that students recall more facts when they are connected to vivid cases.

What We Have Left Out

A glance at the table of contents shows that we have included no separate applications chapters on such topics as health, business, or the law. This is not because of any lack of regard for their importance within social psychology. Quite the reverse. Rather than giving these topics a tagged-on, stand-alone status in the book, we want to emphasize their frequent connections to the mainstream topics of the field. Consequently, we point out these links as they occur naturally within the text discussion and (when special elaboration is appropriate) in the *Focus on Application* features found in each chapter. In this way, we hope to convey to students the inherent relationship between the principles of social psychology and the behaviors of people in workplaces, schoolrooms, and other applied settings.

For similar reasons, there is no isolated chapter or appendix on methodology. Although we do expose the reader to the major methodological issues of social psychological research in Chapter 1, we think the more valuable instruction comes in the *Focus on Method* features that appear in each subsequent chapter. There, blended with a discussion of puzzling research questions, the student learns the details of the methods that can answer them. Additionally, the student learns to appreciate that one cannot be fully confident in the results of a study without understanding how those results were obtained.

Lastly, and once again reflecting our emphasis on integration, the chapters are not grouped and divided into separate sections, such as social knowing, social influence, and social relationships. Instead, the chapter topics flow in a continuum from phenomena occurring primarily inside the individual to those occurring primarily outside. However, there is no imperative to this ordering and, with the exception of the first and last chapters, instructors may sequence the chapters to fit their own preferences without harm to student understanding.

One reason for this adaptability is that the integration we have proposed does not depend on any lock-step, building block progress through the course material. Rather, that integration comes from a pair of concepts, *goals* and the *person-situation interaction*, that apply generally to the topics of the course. Although the goals may not be the same, the ways that goals function—the mechanisms by which they develop and operate—are similar in the case of aggression or attraction or self-presentation or any of the social behaviors we consider. And, although the particular factors may differ depending on the behavior under study, understanding how factors in the person interact with factors in the situation provides the most informed insights into the causes of everyday social behaviors—whatever the behaviors, in whichever order they are considered. These two concepts, then, allow an organization that we think is both integrative and flexible.

In the pages that follow, readers will find everyday social behaviors depicted as something more tightly woven and interconnected than a three-ring circus. Beyond being "the greatest *show* on earth," social psychology may well be the greatest *story*—breathtaking, coherent, and most of all, instructive. We hope you will agree.

New in the Second Edition: A greatly revised chapter 2 (The Person and the Situation) now explores more broadly what situations are and how they influence social behavior. More generally, throughout the book we have increased coverage in many areas including dynamical systems; positive psychology, willpower and self-control; how norms and pluralistic ignorance influence student binge drinking; cultural differences in the desire for positive self-regard; the spotlight effect; the use of persuasion and social influence tactics in current advertising, marketing, and fund raising appeals; human lie detection abilities; risking health for self-presentational gain; explicit versus implicit stereotypes and prejudices; institutionalized discrimination; how technology affects social behavior; effects of social exclusion; mortality salience; the effects of video games and alcohol on aggression; evolutionary approaches to relationships; and social dilemmas.

Supplements

Our goal is to provide supplements, for students and instructors, that are a cut above the materials that usually accompany social psychology textbooks. With the help of the expert teachers and scholars who have written the supplements to accompany our book, we are confident that you will find them both useful and accurate.

Instructor's Supplements

Instructor's Resource Manual (IRM)

Prepared by Renée Bator of the State University of New York at Plattsburgh, with the assistance of the author team, the IRM contains a wealth of materials to help enrich classroom presentations. For each chapter, the IRM provides a brief and detailed chapter outline, lecture and discussion suggestions, critical thinking activities, classroom learning activities, reproducible handouts, and a list of multimedia resources (including readings, video titles, and web links).

Test Bank

A completely new test bank, prepared by Angela Bryan of the University of Colorado, and Petia Petrova of Arizona State University, contains over 1000 multiple-choice and 200 essay items.

Computerized Test Bank

This computerized version of the test bank is available in Windows, Macintosh, and DOS formats using ESATEST III, the best-selling test-generation software.

Transparencies

More than 120 full-color acetate transparencies of images taken from the text will enhance lectures and presentations.

Power Point Images

Cutting-edge PowerPoint-based electronic transparencies, prepared by author Douglas T. Kenrick and his son, David Lundberg Kenrick, a young film-maker, will add life to lectures. The new animated Powerpoints contain point-by-point graphic presentations of research, some of which go beyond those contained in the textbook presentations, are available in both text-only and graphic-enhanced formats.

Allyn & Bacon Interactive Videotape

The brief video segments that comprise this tape are ideal for helping to introduce your students to timely topics and to spark classroom discussions and critical thinking. The videotape is accompanied by a helpful user's guide.

Student Supplements

New State-of-the-Art Website

With the purchase of a new textbook, students will gain access to an exciting new website via a PIN code provided with the book. www.abacon.com/knc provides the student with a wealth of information and resources to enhance and supplement their learning: including interactive chapter outlines, animated figures, attention-grabbing computer "quiz games," as well as brief films and audio mini-lectures by the text authors. First generation websites were more of a distraction than a help, presenting disconnected pages of disorganized text and distracting weblinks to material of only remote relevance. KNC's new website was prepared by the first author working with his son, David Lundberg Kenrick, who worked his way through NYU's film school by teaching faculty and students how to use the latest technologies for film editing and computer animation. Review exercises for the student were prepared by Carol Luce of Arizona State University. We have thus taken advantage of cutting-edge multi-media tools to allow students to learn and test themselves in ways that make the process fun, and that take advantage of modern interactive technology.

Study Guide

This comprehensive study guide, prepared by Angela Bryan of the University of Colorado offers additional support and activities to help master the most important concepts in the text. It includes outlines, key terms, matching exercises, fill-in-the-blank questions, "Pro and Con" sections that compare and contrast key approaches, multiple choice practice quizzes, and discussion questions.

Practice Tests

Ten multiple-choice items per chapter, plus an answer key, are available in this handy booklet to allow students additional test-taking practice. Available only as a valuepack with the text, instructors should contact their local Allyn & Bacon representative for more information about this free supplement.

Acknowledgments

User Survey Respondents.

Jeffrey M. Adams, High Point University
Jennifer Barber, University of Michigan
Gordon Bear, Ramapo College
Frank Bernieri, University of Toledo
Nancy F. Dye, Humboldt State University
Kelli England, Virginia Polytechnic Institute
Robert Fern, Mesa Community College
Joseph R. Ferrari, DePaul University
Bryan Gibson, Central Michigan University
Kenneth J. Good, Minnesota State University, Mankato
Mark Hartlaub, Texas A & M University at Corpus Christi
Martin Kaplan, Northern Illinois University
Catherine T. Kwantes, Eastern Michigan University
Heike I. M Mahler, California State University at San Marcos
Sarah A. Meyers, Simpson College
Rowland Miller, Sam Houston State University
Roderick Neal, Bluefield State College
Joseph S. Neuschab, Roger Williams University
Felicia Pratto, University of Connecticut
Robert Reeves, Augusta State University
John W. Reich, Arizona State University
Nancy Rhodes, Texas A & M University
Bill Scott, Oklahoma State University
Charles F. Seidez, Mansfield University
Laura Sidorowicz, Nassau Community College
Jeff Simpson, Texas A & M University

Pre-revision Reviewers:

William Adler, Colin County Community College
Gordon Bear, Ramapo College
Susan E. Beers, Sweet Briar College
Martin Bolt, Calvin College
Fred B. Bryant, Loyola University Chicago
Robert Cramer, California State University, San Bernadino
Joseph R. Ferrari, DePaul University
Phillip Finney, Southeast Missouri State University
Michael R. Leippe, St. Louis University
Richard Leo, University of California at Irvine
Keith Maddox, Tufts University
Carol K. Oyster, University of Wisconsin at La Crosse
Lawrence Pervin, Rutgers University
Felicia Pratto, University of Connecticut
Todd K. Shackelford, Florida Atlantic University
David Trafimow, New Mexico State University
Anre Venter, University of Notre Dame

1st edition reviewers:

Scott T. Allison, University of Richmond
Michael L. Atkinson, University of Western Ontario
Anita P. Barbee, University of Louisville
Roy Baumeister, Case Western Reserve University
Victor L. Bissonnette, Southeastern Louisiana University
Galen Bodenhausen, Northwestern University
Nyla Branscombe, University of Kansas
Brad J. Bushman, Iowa State University
Delia Cioffi, Dartmouth College
Lisa N. Coates-Shrider, McMurry University
Diana Cordova, Yale University
Christian Crandall, University of Kansas
Cynthia Crown, Xavier University
Mark H. Davis, Eckerd College
Carl Denti, Dutchess Community College
Patricia Devine, University of Wisconsin, Madison
Joan DiGiovanni, Western New England College
Kenneth I. Dion, University of Toronto
Steve Duck, University of Iowa
Victoria Esses, University of Western Ontario
Phillip Finney, Southeast Missouri State University
Robert W. Fuhrman, University of Texas—San Antonio
Grace Galliano, Kennesaw State College
Stella Garcia, University of Texas—San Antonio
Bryan Gibson, Central Michigan University
Marti Hope Gonzales, University of Minnesota
John Harvey, University of Iowa
Cindy Hazan, Cornell University
Edward Hirt, Indiana University
David Houston, University of Memphis
Robert Hymes, University of Michigan—Dearborn
Blair Johnson, University of Connecticut
Craig A. Johnson, Hofstra University
Rich Keefe, Scottsdale Community College
Mark Leary, Wake Forest University
Larry Messé, Michigan State University
Jeffrey Scott Mio, California State Polytechnic University, Pomona
Paul A. Mongeau, Miami University
Paul Nail, Southwestern Oklahoma State University
Miles L. Patterson, University of Missouri—St. Louis
Lou Penner, University of South Florida
Pamela Regan, California State University, Los Angeles
Harry Reis, University of Rochester
Robert Ridge, Brigham Young University
Alexander Rothman, University of Minnesota
Dan Sachau, Mankato State University, Mankato
Mark Schaller, University of British Columbia
Connie Schick, Bloomsburg University, Pennsylvania
P. Wesley Schultz, California State University, San Marcos
Chris Segrin, University of Kansas
James Shepperd, University of Florida
Laura S. Sidorowicz, Nassau Community College
Dianne Tice, Case Western Reserve University
Timothy P. Tomczak, Genesee Community College
Ann Weber, University of North Carolina—Asheville
Margaret Zimmerman, Virginia Wesleyan College

Our home in the psychology department at Arizona State University is intellectually stimulating and interpersonally collegial, for which we have always been grateful. We wish to thank, in particular, our colleagues and students who commented on early drafts of this book: Terrilee Asher, Dan Barrett, Linda Demaine, Nancy Eisenberg, Rosanna Guadagno, Sara Gutierres, Carol Luce, Greg Neidert, John Reich, Kelton Rhoads, Ed Sadalla, Brad Sagarin, Delia Saenz, Melanie Trost, and Wilhemina Wosinska.

We would especially like to thank the students in our social psychology classes for providing invaluable insights from the perspective of the readers that most matter—undergraduate students.

In writing this book, we have searched for interesting real-world events and stories to help illustrate the concepts of social psychology. Several people were able to help us go beyond what was already available in published books and articles, and we greatly appreciate their efforts: Dr. Avrum Bluming, Lenell Geter, Steven Hassan, Bradley Henry, Cindy Jackson, Darlene and Bob Krueger, Eric Saul, and Rabbi Marvin Tokayer.

Turning a set of ideas into a textbook is a long, complex task, and Jim Anker was there at the beginning to offer great advice. Much thanks.

About the Authors

For over ten years, Douglas Kenrick, Steven Neuberg, and Robert Cialdini met weekly over enchiladas, shwarma, or pasta to design experiments and debate the big issues in social psychology. Over time, they came to realize that they agreed on several important things, and that these ideas could form the foundation of an integrative and exciting social psychology textbook. The authors possess over sixty years of combined experience in teaching social psychology to undergraduate and graduate students, in environments ranging from small private colleges to large public universities. They have published research in the field's most prestigious journals on a wide range of topics, including social cognition, self-presentation, persuasion and social influence, friendship and romance, helping, aggression, and prejudice and stereotyping. Each is independently recognized for integrative research that, when combined, inspire the two major themes of the book. This textbook brings together their many teaching and research interests.

Douglas T. Kenrick is a professor at Arizona State University. He received his B.A. from Dowling College and his Ph.D. from Arizona State University. He taught at Montana State University for four years before returning to ASU. His research has been published in a number of places, including *Psychological Review, Behavioral and Brain Sciences, American Psychologist, Handbook of Social Psychology, Advances in Experimental Social Psychology*, and *Journal of Personality and Social Psychology.* With John Seamon, he coauthored Psychology (1994). He has taught a graduate course on teaching psychology, and he thoroughly enjoys teaching undergraduate sections of social psychology.

Steven L. Neuberg received his undergraduate degree from Cornell University and his graduate degrees from Carnegie-Mellon University. He spent a postdoctoral year at the University of Waterloo in Canada, and has since taught at Arizona State University. Neuberg's research has been published in journals such as *Advances in Experimental Social Psychology* and *Journal of Personality and Social Psychology*, and has been supported by the National Institute of Mental Health. He has received his college's Outstanding Teaching Award and the ASU Honors College Outstanding Honors Disciplinary Faculty Award. He recently served on a federal grant review panel and as director of the ASU social psychology program, and teaches a graduate course on teaching social psychology.

Robert B. Cialdini is a Regents Professor at Arizona State University, where he has also been named Graduate Distinguished Professor. He received his undergraduate degree from the University of Wisconsin and his graduate degrees from the University of North Carolina. He is a past president of the Society of Personality and Social Psychology. His research has appeared in numerous publications, including *Handbook of Social Psychology, Advances in Experimental Social Psychology, Journal of Personality and Social Psychology*, and *Journal of Experimental Social Psychology.* His book *Influence: Science and Practice* (2001) has been translated into eleven languages.

TON HIGGINS

CHAPTER 1
Introduction to Social Psychology

The Mysteries of Social Life

On August 8, 1995, Nansook Hong tip-toed past her sleeping husband, stealthily preparing to escape a fifteen-year marriage, a $20 million-dollar mansion, and a set of religious beliefs she had cherished since childhood. Nansook's husband was the son of the Reverend Sun Myung Moon, the "divine" leader of the Unification Church (better known as the "Moonies"). As the child of two of Moon's disciples, Nansook had been raised to revere Reverend Moon and his wife as the "True Parents" of a perfect family of "sinless" children. When Moon picked her to be the bride of his eldest son, Hyo Jin, she had been humbled and honored. But when she joined the "True Family," she reports that she found her husband violating every one of the church's strict rules of conduct, lavishing worshipers' contributions on heavy drinking, drugs, and other women, savagely beating Nansook whenever she displeased him, and threatening to kill her on numerous occasions. Reverend Moon and his wife would scream at her, blaming their son's misbehavior on Nansook's

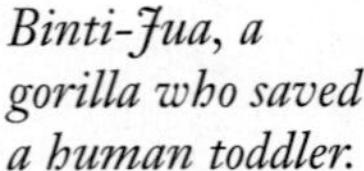

Elian Gonzales and his father

failings as a wife. Amazingly, even in the face of such abuse and hypocrisy, Nansook clung for over a decade to her belief in the sacredness of Moon and his family. It took her fourteen years to reach an epiphany—the realization that Moon was not the saint she had imagined, and that her husband would never change (Hong, 1998).

Nansook's story raises a number of puzzling questions about social behavior. For one, what causes people to cling tenaciously to their beliefs, even when those beliefs fly in the face of contradictory evidence they can see with their own eyes? For another, how does someone escape the influence of an exploitative and manipulative cult leader, or an exploitative and manipulative personal relationship?

On April 6, 2000, Juan Miguel Gonzalez boarded a private plane in Cuba. His goal was to be reunited with his son Elian (whose mother had died while bringing the boy into the United States). But Juan's goal of a father–son reunion was not to be reached easily. His relatives in Miami did not want the boy returned to Cuba, and had reportedly offered Juan $2 million to surrender his claim for his son (Contreras & Thomas, 2000). When Juan persisted in his desire to be reunited with the boy, his Miami relatives tried another tactic—they simply refused to turn Elian over. Federal troops eventually had to battle crowds of angry Cuban refugees to get the boy back to his father. A simple question raised by this episode is why Cuban Americans would oppose reuniting a man and his six-year-old son. On the other side, though, a biologist familiar with other mammals might have asked why human fathers like Juan Gonzalez care so much about their children in the first place. In 95 to 98 percent of other mammalian species, fathers contribute absolutely nothing to their offspring beyond fertilizing the mother's egg (Geary, 2000). Why are there, amongst our near and far warm-blooded relatives, so many deadbeat dads?

Binti-Jua, a gorilla who saved a human toddler.

Another intriguing instance of mammalian social behavior occurred on August 18, 1996. On that day, an energetic three-year-old boy scaled a divider at a Chicago zoo and fell twenty feet into the gorilla pit, knocking himself unconscious on the jagged rocks. Fearing the gorillas would attack the boy, zookeepers sprayed the animals with hoses to keep them away. An adult female gorilla named Binti-Jua, however, ignored the spray and snatched up the toddler. Panic stricken, the child's mother screamed, "The gorilla's got my baby!" But rather than hurting him, Binti-Jua cradled the toddler in her arms and kept the other gorillas at bay as she gently carried the tot to waiting zookeepers and paramedics.

What motivated Binti-Jua's caring and nurturant gesture? Was it her prior experience watching humans care for infants, as some observers suggested, or was it, as other observers hypothesized, a "maternal instinct" that links humans and our primate cousins? At a broader level, this episode opens up a pair of mysteries. One is the puzzle of prosocial behavior: Are any animals, even humans, capable of truly "selfless" actions, or is there always a hidden reward? Another is the puzzle of biological influences on social behavior: Could genetic factors we share with gorillas really affect behaviors such as mothering in humans, and, if so, how might those factors interact with the powerful forces of human culture?

Finally, consider a chain of social events that began on April 11, 1947, when a young man named Jackie Robinson donned a Brooklyn Dodger's uniform. As he walked out onto Brooklyn's Ebbets Field wearing the number 42, Robinson became the first African American ever to play in the Major Leagues. Before that time, African Americans had not only been denied access to professional baseball and many other jobs, but to colleges, hotel rooms, restaurants, and even drinking fountains openly reserved "for whites only." Robinson's desegregation of baseball presaged the Civil Rights movement of the 1950s and 60s, a movement that changed the fabric of American racial relations. Today, Americans of different skin colors mix openly on professional athletic fields, college campuses, and corporate boards of directors. What could have reversed so many people's opinions about acceptable and proper interracial relations in the United States? More broadly, what factors inside a person or in his or her social environment lead to racial prejudice and discrimination on the one hand, or to cooperation and tolerance on the other?

Jackie Robinson, a man who helped change the racial norms of American society

Beyond the extraordinary tales of Nansook Hong, Juan Miguel Gonzalez, Binti-Jua, and Jackie Robinson, a world of everyday social events intrigues and bedevils us all. A man and woman who have never before met marry on national television and split the next day. A six-year-old child guns down another in their first-grade classroom. A schoolteacher donates one of her own kidneys to save the life of a student. As you read the newspapers, watch TV, or talk with friends, you have likely pondered the whys and wherefores of social life—from love and kindness to betrayal and senseless aggression. These fascinating mysteries are what social psychologists hope to solve.

What Is Social Psychology?

Social life is full of mysteries. Why did Nansook Hong stay for fourteen years in a psychologically and physically abusive situation? What is the basis of the strong bonds often found between human fathers and their children? How much of human love and kindness did we inherit from our primate ancestors? What factors can lead a vast society to change its rules about racial integration? Most of us try to solve mysteries like these in our own minds, by devouring curious news stories, chatting with friends about the latest fads, or ogling the latest scandals on the supermarket checkout rack. Social psychologists go a step further in their detective work; they apply the systematic methods of scientific inquiry. **Social psychology** is the scientific study of how people's thoughts, feelings, and behaviors are influenced by other people.

Scientific Description and Explanation

We can divide the tasks of a scientific social psychology into two general categories: *description* and *explanation*. As a first step toward a scientific account of any phenomenon—bird migrations, earthquakes, or mass hysteria—we need an objective and reliable description. Part of what scientists do is to develop reliable and valid methods to help them avoid careless or biased descriptions. We discuss the methods in detail later in this chapter, and in special focus on method sections throughout the book.

Social psychology *The scientific study of how people's thoughts, feelings, and behaviors are influenced by other people.*

Careful description is a first step, but it is not, in itself, enough to satisfy scientific curiosity. Social psychologists also seek to explain *why* people influence one another in the ways they do. A good scientific explanation can connect many thousands of unconnected observations into an interconnected, coherent, and meaningful pattern. As the philosopher Jules Henri Poincaré observed, "Science is built up with facts, as a house is with stones, but a collection of facts is no more a science than a heap of stones is a house." Scientific explanations that connect and organize existing observations are called **theories.**

For centuries, astronomers had carefully observed the motions of the planets. Given the old theory that the earth was the center of the universe, the movements of the planets seemed incredibly complex. Copernicus's radical new theory that the planets revolved around the sun, not the earth, simplified and organized thousands of prior heavenly observations (Zeilik, 1994). We have tried to write this text so that the reader finishes not with a compendium of thousands of disconnected facts, but with an understanding of how those facts can be organized using a much smaller number of theoretical principles.

In addition to organizing existing knowledge, scientific theories give us hints about where to look next. For instance, Charles Darwin's theory of evolution by natural selection implied that animals could transmit unique characteristics (such as long necks on giraffes or flippers on seals) to their offspring. When Darwin originally developed the theory, however, he knew nothing whatsoever about genes or chromosomes. But his theory gave later scientists direction, and research in the last century has established that genes do indeed transmit a "blueprint" for building long-necked giraffes, short-limbed seals, or dark-haired Mediterranean humans. Darwin's theory also had implications for all the sciences of living things, including social psychology—suggesting that emotions and social behaviors (such as a dog's growl or a human's smile) could be passed from one generation to the next in the same manner as long necks, fangs, and curly hair. Those implications are still being explored, as we will see in the pages that follow.

Finally, scientific theories can help us make predictions about future events and control previously unmanageable phenomena. Copernican theory eventually allowed astronomers not only to predict when the next solar eclipse will occur, but also to carefully aim space capsules at other planets. Scientific theories led to the electric light bulb, the personal computer, the airplane, and the control of diseases such as smallpox. As we will see, social psychological theories have provided useful information about the roots of prejudice, kindness, and love; about why people join rioting mobs or religious cults; and about a host of other puzzling phenomena.

Major Theoretical Perspectives of Social Psychology

Social psychological theories have been influenced by intellectual developments ranging from the birth of sociology to the emergence of artificial intelligence. Five major perspectives (or families of theories) have dominated the field: sociocultural, evolutionary, social learning, phenomenological, and social cognitive.

The Sociocultural Perspective

The year 1908 saw the publication of the first two major textbooks titled *Social Psychology.* One of these was written by Edward Alsworth Ross. Ross saw the wellsprings of social behavior as residing not in the individual but in the social group. He argued that people were carried along on "social currents," such as "the spread of a lynching spirit through a crowd…[or] an epidemic of religious emotion" (Ross, 1908, 1–2). Ross analyzed incidents such as the Dutch tulip bulb craze of 1634, in which people sold their houses and lands to buy flower roots that cost more than their weight in gold, but that instantly became worthless when the craze stopped.

Theory *Scientific explanation that connects and organizes existing observations and suggests fruitful paths for future research.*

To explain these crazes, Ross would have looked at the group as a whole rather than at the psyche of the individual group member. He viewed crazes and fads as products of "mob mind...that irrational unanimity of interest, feeling, opinion, or deed in a body of communicating individuals, which results from suggestion and imitation" (Ross, 1908, 65).

Like Ross, other sociologically based theorists emphasized larger social groupings, from neighborhood gangs to ethnic groups and political parties (e.g., Sumner, 1906). That emphasis continues in the modern **sociocultural perspective**—the view that a person's prejudices, preferences, and political persuasions are affected by group-level factors such as nationality, social class, and current historical trends. For example, compared to her working-class Irish grandmother, a modern-day Manhattan executive probably has different attitudes about premarital sex and women's roles in business (Roberts & Helson, 1997). Sociocultural theorists focus on the central importance of **social norms,** or rules about appropriate behavior (such as rules that say don't wear white after Labor Day, don't use foul language when conversing with grandma, and so on). At the center of this perspective is the concept of **culture,** which we can broadly define as the beliefs, customs, habits, and language shared by the people living in a particular time and place (Irish immigrant factory workers in Boston in 1905 versus their great-grandchildren working in offices in Manhattan today, for example).

Different cultural norms. *As part of coming of age on Pentecost Island in the New Hebrides, young males construct tall towers, up to 100 feet high, then jump off with only vines attached to their feet. The sociocultural perspective emphasizes how people are influenced by local societal norms.*

Culture includes all the human-engineered features of the environment, from subjective features like rules of etiquette to objective features like houses and clothing (Smith & Bond, 1994; Triandis, 1994). The technological features of our culture can have powerful effects on our social behaviors, as evidenced in recent years by answering machines, video camcorders, and the Internet (Crabb, 1996a, 1996b; 1999; McKenna & Bargh, 2000). For example, telephones and email allow us to keep contact with relatives and friends who may be thousands of miles away, but they open us up to interactions with unwelcome strangers (crank callers and persistent solicitors). Answering machines allow us to screen out some of those unwelcome interactions (Crabb, 1999).

Nansook Hong describes the "culture shock" she felt on her move from Korea to the United States, where every new social situation raised new challenges. On her first day, for example, she is surprised when she is told to leave on her shoes as she enters Reverend Moon's American home. "In Korea, one never enters a home without first removing one's shoes. It is a sign of respect" (Hong, 78). On the other side, she explains how some of the indignities she endured in the Moon household, though horrifying to a woman raised in the United States, were consistent with what she had learned about a young woman's role in Korean society. As you will see, the study of groups, culture, and social norms continues as a major thrust in social psychology (Fiske, Kitayama, Markus, & Nisbett, 1998; Oishi, Wyer, & Colcombe, 2000; Lickel et al., 2000). We will consider these sociocultural influences in every chapter of this text.

Sociocultural perspective *The theoretical viewpoint that searches for the causes of social behavior in influences from larger social groups.*

Social norm *A rule or expectation for appropriate social behavior.*

Culture *The beliefs, customs, habits, and language shared by the people living in a particular time and place.*

Evolutionary perspective *A theoretical viewpoint that searches for the causes of social behavior in the physical and psychological dispositions that helped our ancestors survive and reproduce.*

The Evolutionary Perspective

Researchers adopting the sociocultural perspective have been intrigued by differences in behavior from one culture to the next. But other researchers have been more interested in similarities, not only across different human cultures but also across different animal species. That focus on similarities was adopted in the other 1908 *Social Psychology* text, by William McDougall, a British psychologist originally trained in biology. McDougall took an **evolutionary perspective**—the view that human social behaviors are rooted in physical and psychological predispositions that helped our ancestors survive and reproduce. McDougall followed Charles Darwin's (1872) suggestion that human social behaviors (such as smiling, sneering, and other emotional expressions) had evolved along with physical features such as upright posture and grasping thumbs.

Similar expression of anger in two different mammalian species. *Charles Darwin believed that some human and animal expressions can be traced to common origins. A sneering expression would have served to warn off a potential competitor, thereby saving a human, or a wolf, from potential physical damage.*

The central idea of the evolutionary perspective is **natural selection,** the assumption that animals with characteristics that help them survive and reproduce will pass those characteristics on to their offspring. New characteristics that are well designed for particular environments (called **adaptations**) will come to replace less well-designed characteristics. Dolphins are mammals, closely related to cows, but their legs evolved into fins because that shape is better suited to life under water.

Darwin assumed that, just as an animal's body is designed by natural selection, so is an animal's brain. Bees need a brain that can decipher another bee's directions to the nearest flower patch, whereas wolves need a brain that can decipher another wolf's threatening signals of aggression. Although most behavioral scientists now accept the idea that animals' brains are designed by natural selection, the suggestion still excites quite a bit of controversy when the animal in question is a primate species called *Homo sapiens* (the human being).

Indeed, McDougall's evolutionary approach to social psychology was largely abandoned for fifty years, partly because early psychologists and biologists misunderstood how biological and environmental factors interact with one another. One mistake was to assume that evolution could only produce inflexible "instincts" that were "wired in" at birth and not much influenced by the environment. Most experts on evolution and behavior now understand that biological influences on humans and other animals are usually flexible and responsive to the environment (e.g., Berntson & Cacioppo, 2000; Crawford & Krebs, 1998). Even the most basic of biological needs, like hunger, are triggered by environmental events. For example, social psychologists Roy Baumeister and Mark Leary (1995) reviewed a body of evidence to suggest that human nature includes a powerful **need to belong**—an intrinsic motivation to affiliate with, and be accepted by, others. Humans the world over congregate in groups and form affectionate bonds (Brewer & Caporael, 1995). But the need to belong is only activated when the situation suggests it might be necessary. In one study, students in an experimental chat room were left out of a conversation by the other members of their group (who ignored them to talk about marching bands or a [made-up] rock group called "Hoodoo Meatbucket," for example). Students who had been ignored were later more attentive to interpersonal acceptance and rejection experiences (Gardner, Pickett, & Brewer, 2000). Just as the nonsocial need of hunger becomes more or less active depending on when we last ate, so is the need for social acceptance satiated or intensified depending on our recent social experiences (Leary, Tambor, Terdal, & Downs, 1995).

Natural selection *The assumption that animals that have characteristics that help them survive and reproduce will pass those characteristics on to their offspring.*

Adaptation *Characteristic that is well designed for survival and reproduction in a particular environment.*

Need to belong *An intrinsic motivation to affiliate with, and be accepted by, others.*

Because evolutionary theorists are interested in understanding common human characteristics and how those characteristics interact with the social environment, they are, like sociocultural theorists, interested in examining social behavior across different societies (e.g., Buss, 1989; Kenrick & Keefe, 1992). These cross-cultural comparisons have uncovered some general patterns in human social behaviors around the world. Men and women in every human society, for example, establish long-term marriage bonds in which the man helps the woman raise a family (Daly & Wilson, 1983). This might seem unsurprising until one looks at most of our furry relatives. Mothers in 95 to 97 percent of other mammalian species go it alone without any help from the male. Why are family values so rare amongst mammalian males? Probably because, after fertilization, fathers just aren't all that necessary. A mammalian mother carries the young inside her body and then nurses them afterwards. Father care becomes useful, though, in species like coyotes and human beings, that give birth to helpless young (Geary, 2000). In those cases, the offspring of fathers who helped out are better able to survive and pass the familial genes on to future generations.

Besides the broad commonalities of human nature, evolutionary psychologists are also interested in individual differences (e.g., Gangestad & Simpson, 2000). Within any species, there are often multiple strategies for survival and reproduction. For example, some male sunfish grow large, defend territories, and build nests, which attract females. Other males are smaller and impersonate females, darting in to fertilize the eggs just as the female mates with a large territorial male (Gould & Gould, 1989). Although people in all societies form some type of long-term parental bond, they also vary considerably in their mating strategies—some men and women are monogamous; some join in marriages that involve more than one husband or more than one wife. As we shall see in later chapters, social psychologists are just beginning to explore how biological predispositions and culture interact to shape complex social behaviors from violence and prejudice to altruism and love (Fiske, 2000; Janicki & Krebs, 1998).

Social learning. *While he was still in his crib, Tiger Woods watched his father practicing his golf swing, and began imitating the movement. His father encouraged him, and spent years training him to play competitively. According to social learning theory, whether a person ends up as a successful athlete, a gang member, a doctor or a thief, depends on the models he or she was exposed to while growing up.*

The Social Learning Perspective

During the decades following 1908, Ross's group-centered perspective and McDougall's evolutionary approach declined in popularity. Instead, many psychologists adopted a **social learning perspective,** which viewed social behavior as driven by each individual's past learning experiences with reward and punishment (e.g., Allport, 1924; Hull, 1934). These experiences could be direct, as when Tiger Woods, later a golf superstar, was encouraged by his father to take to the links before he even started kindergarten. Learning can also be indirect, as when people observe others and then imitate those who seem especially good at winning praise or attention. The importance of such observational learning was demonstrated in a series of experiments conducted by Albert Bandura and his colleagues, who showed how children would learn to imitate aggressive behavior after seeing another child or adult rewarded for beating an inflatable "Bobo doll" (e.g., Bandura, Ross, & Ross, 1961). Bandura expressed concern because movies and television often teach young people that violent behavior can be heroic and rewarding. On April 8, 2000, for example, the *Arizona Republic* reported the story of a group of boys in a local high school who started a "fight club" modeled after one started by Brad Pitt's character in a 1999 movie of the same name. As modeled by the characters in the movie, the teenage boys would gather together to trade gloveless punches with one another (Davis, 2000). On a more positive note, a generation of black athletes were given a boost of encouragement by Jackie Robinson's highly acclaimed success as a major league baseball player.

Social learning perspective *A theoretical viewpoint that focuses on past learning experiences as determinants of a person's social behaviors.*

The social learning perspective is similar to the sociocultural perspective in that it searches for the causes of social behavior in a person's environment. The two perspectives are slightly different in their breadth of focus over time and place, however. Social learning theorists have emphasized the individual's unique experiences in a particular family, school, or peer group. Sociocultural theorists have not been as concerned with specific individuals or their unique experiences but have instead looked at larger social aggregates, such as Mexican Americans, college students in sororities, or members of the upper class (e.g., Moghaddam, Taylor, & Wright, 1993). Also, sociocultural theorists lean toward the assumption that norms, like clothing styles, can change relatively quickly, whereas social learning theorists have generally assumed that habits learned early in life may be difficult to break.

The Phenomenological Perspective

Despite their differences, the sociocultural, evolutionary, and social learning perspectives all emphasize the objective environment. Each assumes that our social behaviors are influenced by real events in the world. During the 1930s and 1940s, Kurt Lewin brought a different perspective to social psychology, one that emphasized the individual's unique viewpoint, or phenomenology. From Lewin's **phenomenological perspective,** social behavior is driven by each person's subjective interpretations of events in the social world.

David Koresh, leader of the Branch Davidian cult. *The group's beliefs about social reality had tragic consequences, leading to a deadly shoot-out with federal agents and a mass conflagration that took eighty-six members' lives. From the phenomenological perspective, beliefs are sometimes more important than objective reality.*

For example, whether or not you decide to work toward the goal of becoming class president would depend on (1) your subjective guess about your chances of winning the office and (2) your subjective evaluation of the benefits of being class president (Higgins, 1997; Lewin, Dembo, Festinger, & Sears, 1944). If you don't *think* it would be personally rewarding to be class president or if you want to be president but don't expect to win, you wouldn't bother to run for election—regardless of whether it would objectively be a winnable or enjoyable post for you. The fate of the Branch Davidian cult suggests how interpretation can sometimes win out over objective reality. In 1993, cult leader David Koresh had convinced his followers that the end of the world was at hand and that they would die as martyrs in a fight with messengers of the devil disguised as government agents. When federal officers visited their Waco, Texas, compound to investigate their arsenal of illegal weapons, the cult members believed that the visit foreshadowed the Apocalypse. They began a battle with federal agents that ended with the death of eighty-six cult members. Several allowed their own children to die rather than surrender to what they believed were agents of the devil.

By emphasizing subjective interpretations, Lewin did not mean to imply that no objective reality existed. Instead, Lewin emphasized the *interaction* between events in the situation and the person's interpretations. Federal agents did indeed attack the Branch Davidian compound. However, Koresh's doomsaying had given the Davidians a ready misinterpretation for those objective events.

Lewin believed that a person's interpretation of a situation was also related to his or her *goals* at the time. If a teenage boy is itching for a fight, he may interpret an accidental bump as an aggressive shove.

Phenomenological perspective *The view that social behavior is driven by a person's subjective interpretations of events in the environment.*

Social constructivist view *The idea that people, including scientists, do not discover reality but rather construct or invent it.*

As we will see, Lewin's emphasis on goals, person–situation interactions, and phenomenology have all had a great impact on the field of social psychology. The emphasis on subjective interpretation taking precedence over objective reality persists in the modern **social constructivist view** (e.g., Beall, 1993; Gergen, 1985). This is the view that "people—including scientists—do not discover reality; instead, they construct or invent it based in part on prior experiences and predispositions" (Hyde, 1996). This perspective has been frequently applied to male–female differences (e.g., Hare-Mustin & Maracek, 1988; Muehlenhard, 2000; Muehlenhard & Kimes, 1999). Some aspects of the masculine and feminine roles seem completely arbitrary. Should a "real man" wear an earring or long hair or write poetry? Should a "real woman" wear pants, be a political leader, or go on mountain-climbing expeditions? The answer clearly varies from one time and place to the next.

As we discuss in chapter 6 (on social influence), there are some questions for which social reality is the only reality that matters (what you should wear to a wedding, for instance). However, there are other questions for which local popular opinion might provide the objectively wrong answer (the end of the world did not follow the 1993 federal agents' visit to the Branch Davidian compound, for example). Where to draw the line between arbitrary social reality and objective physical reality is not only an interesting philosophical question but also, as you will see in chapter 6, a question that raises problems for all of us in some situations.

The Social Cognitive Perspective

The phenomenological emphasis on inner experience led naturally to a close association between social psychology and cognitive psychology, which examines the mental processes involved in noticing, interpreting, judging, and remembering events in the environment. The study of these processes has advanced greatly since the 1950s, when the advent of computers helped lead a "cognitive revolution"—a rebirth of interest in the workings of the mind. During the 1970s and 1980s, an increasing number of social psychologists adopted a **social cognitive perspective,** which focuses on the processes involved in people's choice of which social events to pay attention to, which interpretations to make of these events, and how to store these experiences in memory (e.g., Fiske & Taylor, 1991; Gilovich, Medvec, & Savitsky, 2000).

Consider people's reactions to Martin Luther King, Jr.'s powerful "I have a dream" speech to the Washington marchers on August 28, 1963. Many Americans were profoundly moved by the televised images of King speaking to the mass of black and white faces in front of the Lincoln Monument that day. But in order for King's persuasive appeal to work, a viewer needed to pay attention to his words, interpret his arguments as legitimate, and remember the message later. If someone watching the TV news that day was unable to pay attention because of a loud distracting conversation in the next room, King's message would have had no impact on that person. Likewise, if the viewer had paid close attention to the speech but remembered reports that several march organizers were former Communists, he or she might have interpreted and remembered King's words as particularly devious bits of propaganda.

We will discuss the specific issue of cognition and persuasive communication in some detail in chapter 5. Because of the central importance of the social cognitive perspective in modern social psychology, it will provide an essential component throughout this text as we discuss the many mysteries of social behavior.

Combining Perspectives

Table 1.1 summarizes the five major theoretical perspectives in social psychology. Although these perspectives are sometimes viewed as competing, they each actually focus on different parts of the mysteries of social life.

Consider how a social psychologist might attempt to explain the mass hysteria at Frank Sinatra's 1942 concert at the Paramount Theater. Sinatra's manager had hired a dozen girls to begin screaming, and two pretended to faint on cue. But what began as a publicity stunt got out of control, as hundreds of other young women joined in the screaming and fainting, and thirty were rushed away in ambulances. A researcher adopting a social cognitive or phenomenological perspective would be interested in the processes going on inside the young women's heads at the time—how some of them were led to focus their attention on the excitement so intensely that they fainted (Pennebaker, 1982). A researcher adopting a social learning perspective might ask how the girls in Sinatra's audience had been rewarded for physical symptoms—perhaps by gaining attention from their mothers or their

Social cognitive perspective *A theoretical viewpoint that focuses on the mental processes involved in paying attention to, interpreting, and remembering social experiences.*

Table 1.1 Major theoretical perspectives in social psychology.

Perspective	What Drives Social Behavior?	Example
Sociocultural	Forces in larger social groups.	A middle-class American woman today might delay marriage and wear short hair and pants to her executive job, whereas her great-grandmother who grew up on a farm in Sicily wore traditional dresses and long braided hair, married early, and stayed home caring for children.
Evolutionary	Inherited tendencies to respond to the social environment in ways that would have helped our ancestors survive and reproduce.	An angry, threatening expression automatically grabs people's attention, and the human expression of threat is similar to the one displayed by other species (such as dogs).
Social Learning	Rewards and punishments. Observing how other people are rewarded and punished for their social behaviors.	A teenage boy decides to become a musician after watching an audience scream in admiration of the lead singer at a concert.
Phenomenological	The person's subjective interpretation of a social situation.	Branch Davidians in Waco responded violently because they believed that federal officers were agents of the devil, whose arrival signaled the impending end of the world.
Social Cognitive	What we pay attention to in a social situation, how we interpret it, and how we connect the current situation to related experiences in memory.	If you pass a homeless beggar on the street you may be more likely to help if you notice his outstretched arm, if you interpret his plight as something beyond his control, and if he reminds you of the parable of the Good Samaritan.

The heartthrob of the bobby soxers. *When Frank Sinatra's manager hired a dozen girls to begin screaming at Sinatra's 1942 Paramount concert, it led to an episode of mass hysteria, with hundreds of girls fainting and screaming, and 30 being rushed away in ambulances. Different aspects of such an episode would be considered by theorists adopting different theoretical perspectives.*

peers (Fordyce, 1988). From a sociocultural perspective, a researcher might study how fads and styles change. Though swooning over jazz singers like Frank Sinatra became passé, it later became fashionable to scream over Elvis's sideburns, then to faint over the long-haired Beatles, then to slam-dance over punk band performances, and so on. A researcher adopting an evolutionary perspective, on the other hand, might link the sexual attractiveness of high-status males such as Sinatra or the Beatles to observations from different cultures and different animal species (Cell, 1974; Miller, 1998).

Because a single traditional perspective focuses on only part of the picture, we need to combine and integrate the different approaches to see the full picture. For example, the processes of attention and memory studied by cognitive researchers are shaped by people's learning histories and cultures, which are in turn the products of an evolutionary past in which humans have created, and been created by, their social groups (Kenrick, Sadalla, & Keefe, 1998; Tooby & Cosmides, 1992). To fully understand the mysteries of social life, then, it is necessary to piece together clues from several different perspectives.

Summary

Psychologists have applied several broad theoretical perspectives to the mysteries of social life. Researchers adopting a sociocultural perspective study the influences of larger social groups, such as social norms and class differences. Researchers adopting an evolutionary perspective look for similarities across different human cultures and different animal species, searching for evidence of inherited tendencies that would have helped our ancestors survive in their social groups. Researchers who adopt the social learning perspective look for clues in the rewards and punishments that people experience directly or observe by watching others. Researchers taking a phenomenological perspective examine people's subjective interpretations of social situations. Finally, researchers using the social cognitive perspective examine how people pay attention to, interpret, and remember events in their social lives. These different perspectives can be combined for a more complete understanding of social behavior. Further, the perspectives share some common principles, as we see in the next section.

Basic Principles of Social Behavior

Despite their differences, all the major perspectives in social psychology share a pair of key assumptions. First, people interact with one another to achieve some goal or satisfy some inner motivation. Phenomenologists and cognitive psychologists emphasize conscious goals triggered by the current situation, as when an ad saying "Father's Day is just around the corner!" reminds you to rush out and buy him another one of those Hawaiian print ties he appreciated so much last year. Learning theorists emphasize how past rewards encourage us to approach some goals and avoid others. For example, if your parents smile proudly every time you share your toys with your sister, but grimace every time you talk about money, you may set the goal of joining the Peace Corps instead of a Wall Street brokerage. Evolutionary theorists emphasize social motivations rooted in our ancestral past: People who belonged to mutually helpful social groups, for instance, were more likely to survive and pass on their genes than were self-centered hermits.

A second common theoretical thread is a focus on the interaction between the person and the situation. All the major perspectives assume that motivations inside each of us interact with events in the outside situations we encounter. For example, the evolutionary perspective emphasizes how internal reactions such as anger, fear, or sexual arousal get triggered by situations related to survival or reproduction (hungry-looking predators or flirting glances, for example). Social learning theorists study how learned responses inside the individual are linked to rewards and punishments in the social setting. And cognitive theorists examine how a person's thought processes are linked with moment-to-moment changes in the social situation. Throughout this book, then, we will emphasize two broad principles shared by the different perspectives.

1. Social behavior is *goal oriented.* People interact with one another to achieve some goal or satisfy some inner motivation.
2. Social behavior represents a continual *interaction* between the person and the situation.

In the following sections, we take a closer look at these two principles.

Social Behavior Is Goal Oriented

Goals influence our social behaviors on several levels. At the surface level, we can enumerate a long list of day-to-day goals: to find out the latest office gossip, to get comfort after failing an exam, to make a good impression on a teacher, to tell off an annoying neighbor, or to get a date for next Saturday night. At a somewhat broader level, we can talk about longer-term goals: to gain a reputation as competent, to be seen as likable, to feel good about oneself, or to develop a romantic relationship. Those broader goals often tie together several other day-to-day goals: Developing a romantic relationship incorporates shorter-term goals such as getting a date for Saturday night and being comforted by our partner after an exam. A great deal of research on social behavior considers these broader goals, and they will play an important role in our search for the causes of social behavior.

At the broadest level, we can ask about fundamental motives—the ultimate functions of our social behavior. So, for example, succeeding in one's career and making connections with people in high places could both be incorporated into a fundamental motive of "gaining and maintaining status." We may not always be consciously aware of these deeper motivations, but they affect social interactions in essential ways. To better understand these fundamental motives, let's consider several that have been investigated by social psychologists.

To Establish Social Ties In the first major textbook in psychology, William James (1890, 430) wrote:

> To be alone is one of the greatest of evils for [a person]. Solitary confinement is by many regarded as a mode of torture too cruel and unnatural for civilized countries to adopt. To one long pent up on a desert island the sight of a human footprint or a human form in the distance would be the most tumultuously exciting of experiences.

If you have ever moved to a new town, changed schools, or simply spent a weekend by yourself, you may have experienced the feeling of loneliness. At such times, we are motivated to establish ties, to make new acquaintances, to visit old friends, or just to call a relative on the phone.

When psychologists have tried to enumerate the most basic motives underlying human behavior, the desire to establish ties with other people usually comes high on the list (for example, Bugental, 2000; McAdams, 1990). Several social psychologists argue that a desire to affiliate may be part of our human heritage (Baumeister & Leary, 1995; Stevens & Fiske, 1995). Our ancestors always lived in groups, as did most of the primates from which they evolved (Lancaster, 1975). Affiliating with others brings many benefits. For example, people in groups can share food and can team up for mutual safety (Hill & Hurtado, 1996). Furthermore, we need people to satisfy our other social goals. Chapter 7 will be devoted entirely to the topic of affiliation and friendship, but the goal of establishing social ties, so central to our interactions with others, will be considered at many other points throughout this book.

To Understand Ourselves and Others People gossip, they read profiles of criminal personalities in the newspaper, and they seek feedback from their friends about their chances of getting a date with a charming new classmate. People devote a great deal of attention to gathering information about themselves and others. The importance of such information is obvious—by understanding ourselves and our relationships with others, we are able to manage our lives effectively. Someone who is "out of touch" with these realities will have a harder time surviving in a social group (Stevens & Fiske, 1995). Because social knowledge is so fundamental to all human relationships, social psychologists have devoted a great deal of attention to the topic of social cognition. In chapters 2 and 3 we explore this topic in depth, and return to it in each of the remaining chapters.

The motive to gain and maintain status. *Jackie Robinson was born the son of a sharecropper in rural Georgia, and rose to the highest level of American society. Though not all have quite such high aspirations, most of us are motivated to be well-regarded in the eyes of others.*

To Gain and Maintain Status Jackie Robinson began life in poverty, as the son of a sharecropper in rural Georgia, and was raised with four siblings by a single mother who worked as a housekeeper. After high school, however, he began a meteoric rise in status—from a star college athlete to a baseball Hall of Famer, and on to a career as a director of personnel for a large corporation, political leader in the Republican party, and civil rights activist. With the status came wealth and connections to powerful people. Robinson's prestige was such that President Eisenhower once walked across a room full of celebrities just to shake his hand. Though only a few people gain the status of a Jackie Robinson, the struggle for power and status goes on at all levels: Kindergartners compete for places on the Little League, college students fight for grades, middle managers strive for executive positions, and senators campaign to win the presidency.

In studies of people's thoughts about themselves and others, status pops up repeatedly. All around the world, "dominance versus submissiveness" is one of the two primary dimensions people use to describe the people they know (White, 1980; Wiggins & Broughton, 1985). The advantages of attaining status include not only the immediate material payoffs, but also the less tangible social benefits that flow from other people's respect and admiration. There is a good deal of evidence that most of us go to great lengths not only to present ourselves in a positive light to others but also to convince ourselves that we have reason to hold our heads up high (e.g., Tesser, 1988). Throughout this book, we will see that the motivation to gain and maintain status underlies a wide range of social behaviors.

The motive to defend ourselves and those we value. *This woman and her family are escaping their burning village during the Vietnamese war. Real or perceived threats from other groups motivate a number of social behaviors, including racial prejudice and aggression.*

To Defend Ourselves and Those We Value At the local level, people build fences around their houses, put up threatening signs on their streets, join gangs, and buy attack dogs to protect themselves. At the national level, societies build armies to protect themselves against the armies of the next nation. The controversy over Elian Gonzalez was so fierce because the boy's Miami relatives believed they were protecting him from the evils of a totalitarian communist state. His father, on the other hand, feared that Elian could only suffer living without his natural parents in a society where schoolchildren have access to guns and drugs. The motivation to defend ourselves can have obvious benefits, promoting our survival and that of our family members. During the 1990s, there were, in fact, over 2,000 murders every month in the United States—many of those in Miami. In the chapters that deal with aggression, prejudice, and intergroup conflict, we will see how violence is often triggered by real or perceived attacks or threats. People get hostile when their reputations, their resources, or their families are threatened.

To Attract and Retain Mates Bhupinder Singh, seventh maharajah of the state of Patiala in India, took 350 spouses; most North Americans will take at least one. People often go to great lengths to find and keep these partners, writing long love letters, making long distance phone calls at 2 A.M., or joining computer dating services. The search for mates is one arena in which it often seems that men and women have slightly different motivations.

Imagine how you would react to the following situation: You are at a local college bar and a fairly attractive stranger tries to start a conversation with the line "You remind me of someone I used to date." Would you react favorably—smiling and maintaining eye contact—or unfavorably—perhaps turning away? What if the stranger took a more straightforward approach, saying instead, "I feel a little embarrassed about this, but I'd like to meet you." Or how about if he or she simply walked over and said something innocuous, such as "Hi"? Michael Cunningham (1989) had his research assistants—two males and two females—try such approaches in a suburban Chicago bar and then record the responses they got. What percentage of women do you think responded positively to each of the three approaches? What about the men?

If you guessed that men and women responded very differently to these opening gambits, you were right. Somewhere between 81 and 100 percent of the men responded positively to any kind of approach (see Table 1.2). And although about 70 percent of women responded positively to a simple "Hi" or a straightforward

Table 1.2 Opening lines.

	Percentage of positive responses	
Line	Female Participants	Male Participants
I feel embarrassed…	69	81
Hi	71	100
You remind me of someone…	25	90

SOURCE: *Based on Cunningham, M. R. (1989). Reactions to heterosexual opening gambits: Female selectivity and male responsiveness.* Personality and Social Psychology Bulletin, 15, *27–41.*

approach, fully 75 percent completely ignored the man who opened with the contrived-sounding line "you remind me of someone I used to date." As we will see in the chapters on attraction and relationships, there are also a number of similarities in how men and women play the mating game (e.g., Regan, 1998).

For both sexes, initial flirtations often lead to feelings of attraction, romantic love, and perhaps even lifelong family bonds. From an evolutionary perspective, these are all connected. Indeed, evolutionary theorists believe that the goal of reproduction underlies all the other social goals. We affiliate, we seek social information, we strive for status, and we act in aggressive and self-protective ways, all toward the ultimate end of reproducing our genes.

Motives, Goals, and Social Behavior

Social behaviors may satisfy multiple motives. *Marriage may most directly satisfy the motive to attract and maintain a mate, but can lead to the satisfaction of other motives for affiliation, information, protection, and status.*

It seems unlikely that many people wake up in the morning and think, "Today, I'm going to work on gaining status and finding a good mate so I can reproduce my genes." The fundamental motives behind our behaviors are not necessarily conscious. Instead, the human psyche operates so that we feel bad when we are socially isolated, ridiculed, and rejected, and good when we are warmly greeted by a friend, complimented by a coworker, or kissed by a mate. On the continuum from immediate surface-level goals to fundamental social motives, people are often consciously aware of the moment-to-moment surface-level goals (to get a date for Saturday night); they are sometimes, but not always, aware of broader underlying goals (to develop a romantic relationship); and they may rarely be conscious of the fundamental motives, or ultimate functions, that underlie their social behavior (to attract and retain a mate).

Furthermore, the links between motives and social behaviors are sometimes quite complex. For instance, aggression may serve the goal of protection, but winning a fight might also help a teenage boy achieve status or get information about himself. In fact, a given behavior can serve more than one motive at the same time; for instance, going on a date could eventually lead to a relationship that will satisfy our needs for affiliation, for social information, for status, for a mate, and even for protection.

Of course, not all of the motivations behind social behavior are themselves "social." For example, people may act friendly to get material benefits (a better tip or a sales commission) or useful information (the location of the nearest restaurant or water fountain).

Because of these complexities, the search for the motives behind social behavior is sometimes a challenging one, like that of a detective delving into a complex conspiracy. But, as in detective work, the search for underlying motives can be an intriguing and deeply informative way to solve the mysteries of social behavior.

The Interaction Between the Person and the Situation

If an attractive stranger on your left begins to flirt with you, you may stop trying to impress your boss, who is standing on your right. If you later notice that a third person dressed in black leather has started to sneer at you and to stand possessively close to the flirtatious stranger, you may shift to thoughts of self-protection. On the other hand, a coworker who is a more devoted social climber may be so desperately trying to impress the boss as to be oblivious to flirtation opportunities or physical dangers.

In other words, the fundamental motives and specific goals active at any one time reflect the continual interaction of factors inside the person and factors outside in the world. Because we will examine these interactions in some detail throughout the book, let us consider what we mean by "the person" and "the situation" and how the two become interwoven through "person–situation interactions."

The Person When we talk about the **person,** we will typically be referring to features or characteristics that individuals carry into social situations. If asked to describe yourself, you might mention physical characteristics (your height or your gender, for example), chronic attitudes or preferences (your tendency to vote Republican, Democrat, or Libertarian, for example), and psychological traits (whether you are extraverted or introverted, hardworking or easygoing, emotional or calm, and so on). These characteristics may be based on genetic or physiological factors that make you different from others, or they may be based on past learning experiences and maintained by particular ways you have of thinking about yourself, other people, or the social settings you encounter on a day-to-day basis. Other aspects of the person may be more temporary, such as your current mood or sense of self-worth.

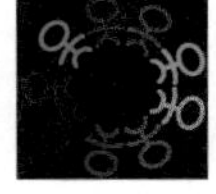

The Situation When we talk about the social **situation,** we are referring to environmental events or circumstances outside the person. These factors include features or events of the immediate social context, such as a television show you are watching or a glance from someone across the room. The situation also includes less temporary aspects of the social environment, such as family background or the norms of the culture in which you are living.

Although it is often convenient to distinguish factors in the situation from factors in the person, the two can never be completely separated. Consider a person's gender role: It is partially determined by the person's biological sex (which affects his or her physical size, distribution of muscle and body fat, capacity to bear children, and so on), but it is also affected by events in the social environment (the culture in which a particular boy or girl is raised, the norms of the current situation, and the sex of the other people around at the time) (Eagly, 1997; Kenrick, 1987). So although it often makes sense to discuss features of the person as separate from features of the situation, it is essential to understand how the two influence one another through person-situation interactions.

Person–Situation Interactions Neither the person nor the situation is a fixed entity. As William James (1890) observed, "Many a youth who is demure enough before his parents and teachers, swears and swaggers like a pirate among his 'tough' young friends" (294). Different social situations trigger different goals—sometimes we want to be liked, sometimes we want to be feared, and so on. Because there is often quite a bit going on in a single situation, your goal at any given moment may depend on what you are paying attention to. And depending on your current goals and your life-long traits, you may respond differently to a situation than others do. Think of a party where some people are dancing, some are having a philosophical discussion, and still others are listening to a joke.

As we discuss in detail in chapter 2, people and situations can change one another. When an aggressive child is let loose on a peaceful playground, for example, it

Person *Features or characteristics that individuals carry into social situations.*

Situation *Environmental events or circumstances outside the person.*

The chosen. *Some people are picked to enter certain situations not accessible to others. When a 14-year-old boy is seven feet tall, like Lew Alcindor, he is offered a different array of life experiences than his shorter friends. Alcindor later got to play basketball for a major college team (UCLA), to play professional basketball, to appear in movies and on television, and to publish his autobiography. (A few years after this photo was taken, Alcindor changed his name to Kareem Abdul-Jabbar.)*

may become a battlefield within minutes (Rausch, 1977). And, on the other side, a few years in college can change a person for life (Newcomb, Koenig, Flacks, & Warwick, 1967).

Of course, our situations do not just "happen" to us. An activity that seems like a great way to spend an afternoon to one person (bungee jumping; visiting an art museum) may have all the appeal of hanging out in a room full of Ebola virus patients for another. Thus we choose situations, and those choices reflect aspects of our personalities (Caspi & Herbener, 1990; Snyder & Ickes, 1985). There is a big difference between a bright student whose two top choices for college are West Point and Annapolis, and another whose top choices are the University of British Columbia and U.C. Berkeley.

Just as people choose their situations, so social situations may choose certain types of people to enter them. The high school freshman who is taller than average may be recruited for basketball training, for example, whereas a friend who is better than average at math and science may be recruited for honors classes. And small initial differences between people may get even larger as situations (such as basketball training sessions and honors classes) exaggerate them. At the end of their senior year, the differences between the students are likely to be much greater than they were originally. Thus situation and person mutually shape and choose one another in a continuing cycle.

Summary

Looking across different theoretical perspectives yields two general principles we will use to understand social behavior. First, social behavior is goal-oriented. People have short-term immediate goals such as getting a particular person to agree to a date on Saturday night, broader long-term goals such as feeling good about themselves, and fundamental motives such as gaining status and attracting mates. Second, motives and other aspects of the person continually interact with features of the situation. To understand fully why we do the things we do, it is important to consider the complex ways in which people and situations choose, respond to, and alter one another over time.

How Psychologists Study Social Behavior

Scientific research is a bit like detective work. A detective begins with a mystery and a set of procedures for solving that mystery: interview witnesses, look for a motive, try to rule out various suspects, examine the material evidence, and so on. There are pitfalls at every step: witnesses may lie or base their testimony on unfounded assumptions, some motives may be hidden, and the evidence may have been tampered with. Like other scientists, social psychologists begin with mysteries. We opened this chapter with several, including: What causes someone to cling to their belief in another, even when, like Nansook Hong, he or she is faced with contradictory evidence? What can lead people to change racially prejudiced beliefs and behaviors, as many did after Jackie Robinson entered the Major Leagues? Like detectives, social psychologists have a set of procedures for solving such mysteries and, like detectives, they must also be aware of certain potential pitfalls involved in using these procedures.

Descriptive method *Procedure for measuring or recording behaviors, thoughts, and feelings in their natural state (including naturalistic observations, case studies, archival studies, and surveys).*

The methods used by social psychologists can be roughly divided into two categories: descriptive and experimental. **Descriptive methods** involve attempts to measure or record behaviors, thoughts, or feelings in their natural state. When psychologists use descriptive methods, they hope to record behaviors without changing them in any way. **Experimental methods,** on the other hand, are attempts to uncover the causes of behavior by systematically varying some aspect of the situation.

Descriptive Methods

How does one go about carefully describing social behavior? Social psychologists use five major types of descriptive methods: naturalistic observation, case studies, archives, surveys, and psychological tests.

Naturalistic Observation Perhaps the most straightforward descriptive method is **naturalistic observation.** It involves, quite simply, observing behavior as it unfolds in its natural setting. As one example, Irenäus Eibl-Eibesfelt (1975) visited numerous cultures around the world and used a hidden camera to observe women flirting with men. In another study of nonverbal communication between the sexes, psychologist Monica Moore (1985) went to a setting where she expected women to naturally show a lot of nonverbal flirtation behaviors—a singles' bar. There she found several patterns of behavior not likely to be seen in comparison settings (a library or women's center meeting). For instance, a woman in the bar would frequently glance at a man for a few seconds, smile, flip her hair, and tilt her head at a 45-degree angle so her neck was exposed.

Naturalistic observation has a number of advantages as a research method. Behavior in a natural setting is spontaneous, for example, rather than artificial and contrived. In contrast, imagine the difficulties of asking students to demonstrate flirtation gestures in a laboratory. For one thing, people might not be aware consciously of how they behave when they are actually flirting. For another, people might feel too uncomfortable to flirt when they know they are being observed by researchers.

Despite its strengths, naturalistic observation also has its pitfalls. Researchers need to ensure that their subjects do not know they are being observed. Otherwise, they might not act normally. As we discuss in chapter 6, researchers have discovered some clever ways to observe behavior without arousing people's self-consciousness.

Another problem with naturalistic observation is that some interesting behaviors are rare. Imagine waiting around on a street corner for a homicide to occur. Even in the worst of neighborhoods, you would spend a long time waiting for your first observation.

A final problem is that, unless the observation is conducted very systematically, biased expectations may lead the observer to ignore some influences on behavior and exaggerate others. A **hypothesis** is a researcher's hunch or guess about what he or she expects to find. A hypothesis may lead that researcher to search for supportive information but to fail to notice inconsistent evidence. This problem is called **observer bias.** For instance, if you expected to see flirtatious behaviors in a bar, you might misinterpret a woman's hair-flip as flirtation when all she was really trying to do was keep her hair from falling into her beer mug.

Case Studies Another observational method is the **case study,** an intensive examination of one individual or group. A researcher could study a completely normal individual or group, but often selects a case because it represents some unusual pattern of behavior. Imagine that you were interested in homicidal violence resulting from "road rage." Although it would (one hopes) be fruitless to drive around in your car and wait for such an event to occur naturally, you could study the individuals involved in an event that has already occurred. You might interview the murderer and others present at the scene of the crime, read the police reports, and so on. As we see next, this approach has strengths and weaknesses.

Experimental method *Procedure for uncovering causal processes by systematically manipulating some aspect of a situation.*

Naturalistic observation *Recording everyday behaviors as they unfold in their natural settings.*

Hypothesis *A researcher's prediction about what he or she will find.*

Observer bias *Error introduced into measurement when an observer overemphasizes behaviors he or she expects to find and fails to notice behaviors he or she does not expect.*

Case study *An intensive examination of an individual or group.*

FOCUS ON Social Dysfunction

The Case of a Mass Murderer and His Family

In the late 1960s, a young man named Charles Manson went to the Haight–Ashbury district of San Francisco, where the new "hippie" subculture was beginning to emerge. In that setting, the norms and values of traditional U.S. society (derisively dubbed "the establishment") were considered outdated and even evil, responsible for such injustices as racial discrimination and the war in Vietnam. Because Manson had been in and out of prisons for most of his life, he found it easy to adopt an antiestablishment attitude; and because he was gifted with a charming and manipulative personal style, he was able to attract a group of young people to live in a commune that he called "the Family." Taking advantage of the respect and fear these young people felt for him, as well as the local norms of "free love" and drug experimentation, Manson was very successful in manipulating them to his will. He eventually convinced several of his followers to commit a series of ritual mass murders in the Los Angeles area. These gruesome killings, committed by a group of young people who had gone to San Francisco to be part of the "generation of peace and love," made such an impact on the American public that Manson and his followers could still make the news more than thirty years later (when Manson went up for parole in 1997).

A strange case like this can raise interesting questions about otherwise normal processes. For instance, do the specific events and group processes that led Manson's followers to commit a series of multiple murders shed any light on everyday acts of violence (an issue we consider in some detail in chapter 10)? Do the events in Manson's own life shed any light on the factors that lead a child to become a vicious and psychopathic adult?

Social disorder—the case of Charles Manson. *An unusual case can often elucidate otherwise normal processes. Mass murders ordered by Charles Manson and committed by several members of his communal "family" may help us understand more normal processes of aggression and intergroup hostility. But case studies have limits in making cause-effect inferences.*

When we examine Charles Manson's life, we find that, from the beginning, he was exposed to neglect, violence, and criminal role models (Bugliosi & Gentry, 1974). His mother drank excessively while she was pregnant with Charles and had a series of unstable relationships after he was born. She would leave young Charles with neighbors, saying she was going shopping, then not return for several days. At other times, she abandoned him to her relatives for long periods. Then, when Charles was five, his mother was imprisoned after she and her brother robbed a gas station and knocked out the attendant with a Coke bottle. Charles stayed with a strict but loving aunt during the three years his mother was in prison, but his mother reclaimed him when she got out. When he was twelve, she sent him to a boy's school. He ran away after ten months, but when he tried to return to his mother, she refused to take him in. By the time he reached age thirteen, Charles had begun committing crimes with the delinquent friends he made in his institutional placements. During one escape, he and another boy went to visit the boy's uncle, who put the lads to work slipping through skylights during robberies. Before reaching age twenty, Manson had been imprisoned several times for crimes ranging from armed robbery to transporting women across state lines for prostitution.

Case studies like Manson's can be rich sources of hypotheses. Manson's case suggests a number of possible hunches about the causes of his violent, antisocial behavior. Did the social norms of the antiestablishment counterculture perhaps contribute to Manson's bizarrely violent behavior, or was it the fact that he took massive doses of mind-altering drugs? Going further back in his life, could his antisocial inclinations be traced to the influences of other delinquents he met in institutions or to the lack of a stable family structure during his childhood? Or, noting the criminal tendencies in his mother and uncle, could the cause go even further back in time—to a shared genetic tendency that ran in the family?

Unfortunately, the very abundance of hypotheses we could generate from a case study gives us a clue about one of the chief limitations of the method. We simply have no way of telling which events in the case are causal and which are irrelevant. Indeed, Manson's eventual criminality might stem from an interaction of all the causes we have considered, from only one or two of them, or from a factor we did not mention (such as exposure to unusual hormones or brain damage while he was in the womb). The point is this: A case study can suggest any number of interesting possibilities for later tests with more rigorous methods, but it cannot give us grounds for confidence about cause-and-effect relationships. ■

Because case studies like that of Charles Manson are open to so many interpretations, they are, like naturalistic observations, susceptible to the problem of observer bias. Someone interested in the effects of drugs on antisocial behavior might focus on Manson's exposure to alcohol in the womb or his later use of LSD, yet fail to pay attention to the potential contributions from his social environment. Another problem has to do with **generalizability,** the extent to which a particular research finding applies to other similar circumstances. After examining only a single case, we simply cannot know which of its specifics generalize to other similar cases.

Archives One solution to the problem of generalizability is to examine a number of similar cases. Consider a study of police reports for 512 homicides committed in Detroit during 1972. Here is one:

> Case 185: Victim (male, age 22) and offender (male, age 41) were in a bar when a mutual acquaintance walked in. Offender bragged to victim of "this guy's" fighting ability and that they had fought together. Victim replied "you are pretty tough" and an argument ensued over whether victim or offender was the better man. Victim then told offender "I got mine" (gun) and the offender replied "I got mine too," both indicating their pockets. The victim then said "I don't want to die and I know you don't want to die. Let's forget about it." But the offender produced a small automatic, shot the victim dead, and left the bar. (Wilson & Daly, 1985, p. 64)

Although the details of this particular case may be unique, Margo Wilson and Martin Daly found a number of similar details across the hundreds of homicide cases they examined. First, consistent with the cross-cultural data we discussed earlier, offenders and their victims tended to be males, particularly males in their early twenties. Second, the homicides were often instigated by a conflict over social dominance.

Wilson and Daly's study of homicides is an example of the **archival method,** in which researchers test hypotheses using existing data originally collected for other purposes (police reports, marriage licenses, newspaper articles, and so on). The advantage of archives is that they provide easy access to an abundance of real-world data. The disadvantage is that many interesting social phenomena do not get recorded. Both the beginning and end of a two-month-long marriage make the public records. On the other hand, a five-year-long live-in relationship that breaks up over an argument about who to invite to the wedding never registers in the archives.

Surveys Some very interesting behaviors are unlikely to be recorded in public records or to be demonstrated in natural settings. For instance, back in the 1940s, biologist Alfred Kinsey became curious about the prevalence of sexual behaviors such as masturbation and premarital intercourse. Because these behaviors are rarely demonstrated in public, naturalistic observation would not do. Likewise, individual case studies of convicted sex offenders would be uninformative about normal sexual behavior. Kinsey therefore chose the **survey method,** in which a researcher simply asks respondents a series of questions about their behaviors, beliefs, or opinions.

The survey has one very important advantage: It allows a researcher to collect a great deal of data about phenomena that may rarely be demonstrated in public. Like other methods, surveys have drawbacks. First, the respondent may not give accurate information, because of either dishonesty or memory biases. For instance,

Generalizability *The extent to which the findings of a particular research study extend to other similar circumstances or cases.*

Archival method *Examination of systematic data originally collected for other purposes (such as marriage licenses or arrest records).*

Survey method *A technique in which the researcher asks people to report on their beliefs, feelings, or behaviors.*

it is puzzling that men answering surveys often report more heterosexual experiences than do women. Men in Britain, France, and the United States report ten to twelve sexual partners in their lives, whereas women in all these countries report just over three (Einon, 1994). The discrepancy could be due to **social desirability bias,** or the tendency for people to say what they believe is appropriate or acceptable. Sexual activity is more socially approved for men (Hyde, 1996). Because of this, men may be more inclined to talk about their sexual escapades or more likely to remember them.

Another potential problem with the survey method is obtaining a **representative sample.** A sample is representative when the participants, as a group, have characteristics that match those of the larger population the researcher wants to describe. A representative sample of North American executives would include percentages of men, women, blacks, Hispanics, Canadians, midwesterners, and southerners that reflect the total population of executives on the continent. A small group of male executives who fly regularly between San Francisco and Los Angeles or of female Hispanic executives in the New York fashion industry would not represent North American executives as a whole. The sample for Kinsey's sex survey was composed largely of volunteers from community organizations, which means that many segments of U.S. society were not well represented.

Many potential respondents are simply unwilling to volunteer to discuss topics such as their sex lives. If those who do not participate are different from the norm in their sexual activities, the researcher might draw erroneous conclusions about the whole population. Carefully constructed surveys can reduce some of these problems. But not all surveys are to be trusted, particularly when they allow subjects to select themselves for participation. For example, newspapers now ask readers to call in their opinions about controversial topics. In August 1998, readers of the Phoenix *Tribune* were asked to call in with their opinions about whether President Clinton should resign from office after admitting a sexual relationship with a White House intern. Those who called expressed extreme opinions on both sides of the issue. Perhaps many people with less extreme judgments did not call in.

Psychological Tests Are some people more socially skillful than others? Are some people inclined to think critically before allowing themselves to be persuaded by an argument? **Psychological tests** are instruments for assessing differences between people in abilities, cognitions, motivations, or behaviors. Most of us have taken a variety of psychological tests. College aptitude tests (such as the SATs) are designed to distinguish people according to their ability to do well in college. Vocational interest tests (such as the Strong Vocational Interest Blank) are designed to distinguish people in terms of their likely enjoyment of various professions.

Psychological tests are not always perfect indications of the things they are designed to measure. A test of "your ability to get along with your lover" published in a popular magazine, for example, may have very little to do with your actual skill at relationships. There are two criteria a psychological test must meet before it is useful—reliability and validity.

Reliability is the consistency of the test's results. If a test of social skills indicates that you are highly charismatic the first time you take it but socially inept when you take it a week later, your score is unreliable. To measure anything, it is essential that the measurement instrument be consistent. Some psychological tests, such as the famous Rorschach inkblots, do not provide very reliable measurements; others, such as IQ tests, yield much more consistent scores. Even if a test is reliable, however, it may not be valid. **Validity** is the extent to which the test measures what it is designed to measure. To use a rather unlikely example, we could theoretically use eye color as a measure of desirability to the opposite sex. Our test would be very reliable—trained observers would agree well about who had blue, hazel, and brown eyes; and subjects' eye color would certainly not change very much if we measured it again a month or two later. Yet eye color would probably not be a valid index of

Social desirability bias *The tendency for people to say what they believe is appropriate or acceptable.*

Representative sample *A group of respondents having characteristics that match those of the larger population the researcher wants to describe.*

Psychological test *Instrument for assessing a person's abilities, cognitions, motivations, or behaviors.*

Reliability *The consistency of the score yielded by a psychological test.*

Validity *The extent to which a test measures what it is designed to measure.*

attractiveness—it would probably not relate to the number of dates a person had in the last year, for instance. On the other hand, if judges rated the whole face, or a videotape of the person engaged in conversation, the scores might be a little less reliable but more valid as predictors of dating desirability.

Reliability and validity can be issues for all methods. For instance, archival records of men's and women's age differences at marriage are reasonably consistent across different cultures and time periods (Kenrick & Keefe, 1992). Hence, they give a reliable estimate (several times as many women as men get married in their teens, for example). Yet the marriage records from one month in one small town would probably be unreliable (perhaps two teenage men and only one teenage woman got married that particular month). With regard to validity, three different environmental surveys might agree that people are doing more recycling and driving less. Yet those survey responses, though reliable, might not be valid: people might consistently misrepresent their recycling or driving habits. It is thus important to ask about any research study: Would we get the same results if the measurement was done in a different way or by a different observer (are the results reliable)? And is the researcher really studying what he or she intends to study (are the results valid)?

Correlation and Causation

Data from descriptive methods can reveal **correlation,** or the extent to which two or more variables occur together. For instance, Leon Mann (1981) used newspaper archives to examine the puzzling phenomenon of suicide baiting, in which onlookers encourage a suicidal person to jump to his or her death. In one case, a nighttime crowd of 500 onlookers not only urged Gloria Polizzi to jump off a 150-foot water tower, but also screamed obscenities and threw stones at the rescue squad. Mann found that suicide baiting was correlated with the size of the crowd. As crowds got larger, they were more likely to taunt someone perched on the edge of life.

A correlation between two variables is often expressed mathematically in terms of a statistic called a **correlation coefficient.** Correlation coefficients can range from +1.0, indicating a perfect positive relationship between two variables, through 0, indicating absolutely no relationship, to –1.0, indicating a perfect negative relationship. A positive correlation means that as one variable goes up or down, the other goes up or down with it. As crowds got larger, for example, the amount of suicide baiting increased.

A negative correlation indicates a reverse relationship—as one variable goes up or down, the other goes in the opposite direction. For instance, the more time people spend paying attention to attractive members of the opposite sex, the less satisfied they are with their current relationship (Miller, 1997).

Correlations can provide important hints, but they do not enable a researcher to draw conclusions about cause and effect. Consider the case of crowd size and suicide baiting. Large crowds are associated with many forms of otherwise inappropriate behavior, as one can observe in New York on New Year's Eve, or in New Orleans during Mardi Gras. It seemed plausible to conclude, as Mann did in his study of suicide baiting, that large crowds led observers to feel anonymous. This in turn could reduce their concern about being identified as the perpetrators of such a cruel and nasty deed. With a correlation, however, it is always possible that the direction of causality is reversed—that B causes A rather than A causing B (see Figure 1.1). For instance, once the suicide baiting started, it may have been reported on the radio, and crowds of people came to view the spectacle (thus suicide baiting would have caused crowds, rather than the other way around). Correlations can also be found when there is no causal relationship at all, as when a third variable C is causing both A and B. For instance, Mann also found suicide-baiting to occur more frequently at night. Perhaps people are more likely to be drinking alcohol at night and drunks are more likely to be gregarious (hence to join crowds) and unruly (hence

Correlation *The extent to which two or more variables are associated with one another.*

Correlation coefficient *A mathematical expression of the relationship between two variables.*

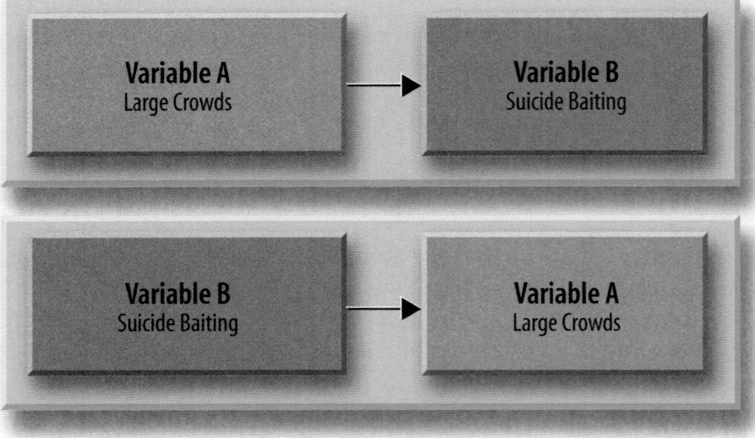

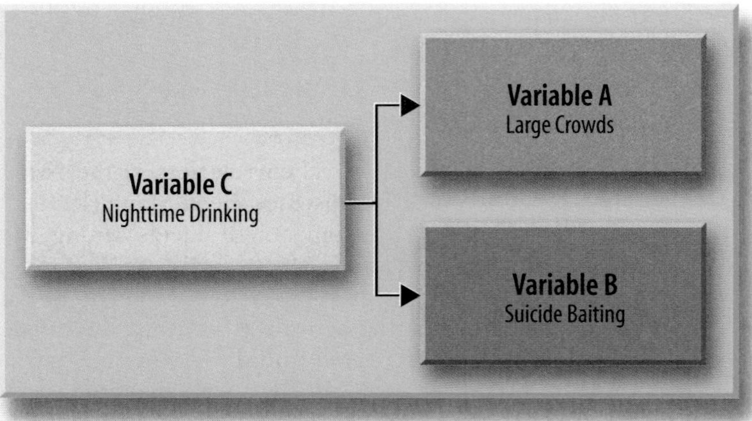

Figure 1.1
Explaining correlations.

When two variables (such as crowd size and suicide baiting) are correlated, it is possible that variable A (crowd size, in this example) leads to changes in variable B (suicide-baiting in this case). It is also possible, however, that variable B causes variable A, or that a third variable C (such as nighttime drinking, in this example) causes both A and B independently. These possibilities make it difficult to make conclusions about cause and effect relationships from correlations.

to taunt potential suicides). If so, neither darkness nor the size of the crowd was a direct cause of suicide baiting; each was related only incidentally.

Because of the different possible connections between correlated variables, it is difficult to draw clear conclusions from correlations. To track down cause and effect, researchers turn to the experimental method, in which variables are teased apart from the other factors that normally co-occur with them.

Experimental Methods

When using descriptive methods, researchers try to avoid interfering with the phenomenon they are studying. A researcher hopes that naturalistic observation does not change the usual pattern of behavior or that survey questions are not worded so as to lead people to misrepresent their true feelings or behaviors. In an **experiment,** on the other hand, the researcher actually sets out to alter people's behavior by systematically manipulating one aspect of the situation while controlling others. If a researcher wanted to know whether anonymity of the sort that occurs in large crowds actually *causes* people to act more antisocially, that researcher could vary the situation so that some people felt especially anonymous while others felt especially identifiable. In fact, Philip Zimbardo (1970) did just that, while asking students in a laboratory experiment to deliver electric shocks to a fellow student. Half the participants (non-anonymous) wore name tags and remained in their own clothes. The other half were dressed in oversized white coats with hoods that completely covered their faces. The subjects who were thus made anonymous delivered twice as much shock as did those who were left identifiable.

Experiment *A research method in which the researcher sets out to systematically manipulate one source of influence while holding others constant.*

Manipulating Variables The variable manipulated by the experimenter is called the **independent variable.** In Zimbardo's experiment, the independent variable was the different type of clothing worn (anonymous versus identifiable). The variable that is measured is called the **dependent variable.** In this case, the experimenter measured the amount of shock delivered by the subject.

Experimenting with deindividuation. *In Zimbardo's experiment, half the subjects dressed in clothing making them anonymous and the other half stayed in their normal clothes and were visible to others. That difference constituted the independent variable. The dependent variable was the amount of shock delivered to a fellow subject.*

There are several things to note about experiments. A key feature of Zimbardo's experiment is that participants were randomly assigned to the anonymous and nonanonymous conditions. **Random assignment** means each participant has an equal probability of receiving any treatment. By assigning participants to the two groups on the basis of a coin flip, for instance, a researcher reduces the chances that they are different in terms of mood, personality, social class, or other factors that might affect the outcomes. In this way, the researcher minimizes any systematic differences between the groups, such as those that might have characterized suicide observers in nighttime versus daytime crowds. Although large suicide-baiting crowds could have differed from small nonbaiting crowds in other ways related to antisocial tendencies, such systematic differences are not a problem when participants are randomly assigned. In Zimbardo's study, the only differences among subjects were due to random variations in the population (which are reduced in importance as the experimenter runs large groups of subjects).

It was also important that only the anonymity of clothing (the independent variable) varied from one group of subjects to another. All other aspects of the situation were the same—the experimenter, the setting, the victim, and the task. This also reduces the likelihood that these other variables might have influenced the antisocial behavior. Finally, aggressiveness was measured in an identical fashion for the high- and low-anonymity subjects, enabling the experimenter to quantify reliably the exact amount of shock subjects delivered in each condition.

By randomly assigning subjects and controlling extraneous variables, the experimenter gains an important advantage—the ability to make statements about causal relationships. Zimbardo could be fairly confident that it was something about his manipulation of anonymity, rather than something about the different subjects in the anonymous condition, that led to the higher level of aggression.

Potential Limitations of the Experimental Method Despite its advantage over descriptive methods in making causal statements, the experiment has its own drawbacks. For one, the laboratory settings used in most experiments are artificial. Is the anonymity created by wearing a big coat and hood really the same as that experienced in a large crowd on a dark night? Is the tendency to deliver shock really the same as the tendency to throw rocks at suicide rescue squads?

We discussed the concept of validity in psychological tests—whether a test measures what it intends to measure. The same question can be asked of experiments (Aronson, Wilson, & Brewer, 1998). **Internal validity** is the extent to which an experiment allows confident conclusions about cause and effect. Was the independent variable the sole cause of any systematic variations in the subjects' behaviors? Imagine that, in Zimbardo's deindividuation experiment, all the subjects in the anonymous condition were met by an obnoxious male experimenter while all the subjects in the nonanonymous condition were met by a pleasant female. If the subjects in the anonymous condition behaved more aggressively, we would not know whether it was because the subject was anonymous or because the experimenter was obnoxious. When another variable systematically changes along with the independent variable, it is called a **confound.** In this imaginary case, the sex and temperament of the experimenter are both confounded with anonymity. Such confounding variables are like the invisible third variables in correlations—they make it difficult to know what caused the subject's behavior.

Independent variable *The variable manipulated by the experimenter.*

Dependent variable *The variable measured by the experimenter.*

Random assignment *The practice of assigning particpants to treatments so each person has an equal chance of being in any condition.*

Internal validity *The extent to which an experiment allows confident statements about cause and effect.*

Confound *A variable that systematically changes along with the independent variable, potentially leading to a mistaken conclusion about the effect of the independent variable.*

External validity is the extent to which the results of an experiment can be generalized to other circumstances. Does delivering shock in an anonymous laboratory experiment tap the same processes as being in a large mob on a dark night, for instance? Perhaps not. Certainly, no two situations are identical, but experimenters try to pick variables that tap the same mental and emotional processes as those operating in the wider world outside.

One problem in generalizing from laboratory studies to natural behavior is that subjects know they are being observed in the lab. As we noted with naturalistic observation, people sometimes act differently when they know they are being watched. **Demand characteristics** are cues in the experiment that make subjects aware of how the experimenter expects them to behave. Experimenters try to avoid this problem by distracting participants from an experiment's true purpose. For instance, an experimenter would not tell subjects, "We are examining how long you hold down the shock button, as an index of hostility." Instead, the experimenter would offer a plausible reason for administering shock—to study how punishment affects learning, for example. This shifts attention from the participant's use of shock to the recipient's "learning responses." As you will see, social psychologists have developed some rather skillful methods of engaging subjects' natural reactions. But it is always important to be on the lookout for these possible confounds. For example, do you think that having students in the anonymity experiment wear oversized white coats and hoods (not unlike those worn by members of the Ku Klux Klan) might have communicated an expectation to act antisocially?

Field Experiments One way to overcome the hurdles of artificiality and demand characteristics is to bring the experiment out of the laboratory and into an everyday setting. This approach, using experimental manipulations on unknowing participants in natural settings, is called **field experimentation.**

Consider a study in which the researchers took advantage of a naturally occurring manipulation of anonymity—the disguises worn by Halloween trick-or-treaters (Diener, Fraser, Beaman, & Kelem, 1976). Their subjects were children in costumes who arrived to "trick or treat" at a house in Seattle, Washington. The trick-or-treaters were greeted by a research assistant who pointed in the direction of a bowl of candy alongside a bowl of pennies. She told them to take *one* of the candies each, and then she hurried off, claiming to be busy. Unbeknownst to the children, the researchers were watching from a hidden location, recording whether the little angels and super-heroes took extra candies or filched some coins from the money bowl.

Anonymity was manipulated by the way in which the experimenter greeted the children. In half the cases, she asked each child his or her name, thus removing the identity shield of the costume. In the other half, she allowed them to remain anonymous. The results supported the correlational findings obtained by Mann and the laboratory findings obtained by Zimbardo. When left anonymous, the majority of little devils grabbed more than they had been told to take. When they had been asked to identify themselves, however, most of them acted more angelically.

External validity *The extent to which the results of an experiment can be generalized to other circumstances.*

Demand characteristic *Cue that makes participants aware of how the experimenter expects them to behave.*

Field experimentation *The manipulation of independent variables using unknowing participants in natural settings.*

Why Social Psychologists Combine Different Methods

Table 1.3 summarizes the different methods and their main strengths and limitations. If each method has weaknesses, is the pursuit of social psychological knowledge hopeless? Not at all. The weaknesses of one method are often the strengths of another. For instance, experiments allow researchers to make cause-effect conclusions but have problems of artificiality. On the other hand, archival methods and naturalistic observations do not allow cause-effect conclusions (because they are correlational), but the data they provide are not at all artificial. By *combining the different methods*, social psychologists can reach more trustworthy conclusions than any single method can provide (McGrath, Martin, & Kukla, 1982).

Table 1.3 Summary of research methods used by social psychologists.

Method	Description	Strengths	Weaknesses
Descriptive Correlational Methods			
Naturalistic Observation	Inconspicuous recording of behavior as it occurs in a natural setting. **Example:** Moore's study of flirtation behavior in women.	• Behaviors are spontaneous. • Doesn't rely on people's ability to report on their own experiences.	• Researcher may interfere with ongoing behavior. • Some interesting behaviors are very rare. • Researcher may selectively attend to certain events and ignore others (observer bias). • Time consuming.
Case Studies	Intensive examination of a single person or group. **Example:** Bugliosi's study of mass murderer Charles Manson.	• Rich source of hypotheses. • Allows study of rare behaviors.	• Observer bias. • Difficult to generalize findings from a single case. • Impossible to reconstruct causes from complexity of past events.
Archives	Examine public records for multiple cases. **Example:** Wilson and Daly's study of police reports of Detroit homicides.	• Easy access to large amounts of pre-recorded data.	• Many interesting social behaviors are never recorded.
Surveys	Researcher asks people direct questions. **Example:** Kinsey's study of sexual behavior.	• Allows study of difficult-to-observe behaviors, thoughts, and feelings.	• People who respond may not be representative. • Participants may be biased or untruthful in responses.
Psychological Tests	Researcher attempts to assess an individual's abilities, cognitions, motivations, or behaviors. **Example:** Strong Vocational Interest Blank; SATs.	• Allows measurement of characteristics that are not always easily observable.	• Tests may be unreliable (yielding inconsistent scores). • Tests may be reliable, but not valid (not measuring the actual characteristic they are designed to measure).
Experimental Methods			
Laboratory Experiment	Researcher directly manipulates variables and observes their effects on the behavior of laboratory participants. **Example:** Zimbardo's study of aggression and anonymity.	• Allows cause–effect conclusions. • Allows control of extraneous variables.	• Artificial manipulations may not represent relevant events as they naturally unfold. Participants' responses may not be natural, since they know they are being observed.
Field Experiment	Same as laboratory experiment, but subjects are in natural settings. **Example:** Diener et al.'s study of "trick-or-treaters."	• Allows cause–effect conclusions. • Participants give more natural responses.	• Manipulations may not represent relevant events as they naturally unfold. • Less control of extraneous factors than in a laboratory experiment.

The psychologist's situation is analogous to that of a detective confronted with stories from several witnesses to a murder, each less than perfect. The blind woman overheard the argument but couldn't see who pulled the trigger. The deaf man saw someone enter the room just before the murder but didn't hear the shot. The child was there to see and hear but tends to mix up the details. Despite the problems presented by each witness, if they all agree the butler did it, it would be wise to check his fingerprints against those on the gun. Like the detective, the social psychologist is always confronted with bits of evidence that are, by themselves, imperfect, but that may add up to a compelling case.

Just as detectives go back and forth between evidence and hunches—using evidence to educate their hunches and hunches to lead the search for new evidence—so, too, social psychologists go "full cycle" between the laboratory and the natural world (Cialdini, 1995). Evidence from descriptive studies of the real world leads to theories to be tested with rigorous experiments. The results of these theory-testing experiments lead back to new hunches about natural events in the real world. By combining different kinds of evidence, then, it is possible to come to more confident conclusions.

Focus on Method In attempting to explain riots or cults or love affairs, the soundness of a social psychologist's conclusion depends on the validity of the methods used to generate it. As detectives, we need to distinguish incontrovertible evidence from a remote possibility. Because of the importance of evidence to all of social psychology, we will continue our discussion of research tools in later chapters in a special feature called "Focus on Method." How can we find out what subjects are secretly thinking and feeling? How can we come to trustworthy conclusions when the evidence is mixed? How can we separate cultural or family influences on social behavior from biological influences? We will discuss these issues and others in later chapters. By understanding research methods, we can hope to hone our detective skills, advancing from the level of a bumbling amateur sleuth toward that of a Sherlock Holmes.

Ethical Issues in Social Psychological Research

In reading about Zimbardo's study of aggression and anonymity, you might have wondered how the participants ended up feeling about themselves after delivering shocks to fellow students. Unlike geology or chemistry, social psychological research is conducted with living, breathing, feeling human beings (and sometimes other living creatures). This makes it important to consider another question: Is the research ethically justifiable?

Ethical Risks in Social Psychological Research Consider some of the research that we, the authors of this text, have conducted. One of us successfully induced students to give up some of their blood using a "door-in-the-face" technique: "Would you be willing to join our long-term blood donor program and give a pint of blood every six weeks for a minimum of three years? No? Then how about just a single pint tomorrow?" (Cialdini & Ascani, 1976). To study the effect of physiological arousal on romantic attraction, one of us misinformed subjects that, as part of a learning experiment, they would be receiving a series of painful electric shocks (Allen, Kenrick, Linder, & McCall, 1989). In another study, two of us misled subjects into believing that highly attractive models were other students signed up for a university dating service. We then measured whether seeing these attractive alternatives undermined participants' feelings of commitment to their current partners (Kenrick, Neuberg, Zierk, & Krones, 1994). Finally, one of us asked students whether they had ever had a homicidal fantasy, and if so, to describe it in detail (Kenrick & Sheets, 1994).

These studies yielded potentially useful information about love relationships, violence, and charitable contributions. Yet each raised the sort of ethical questions that social psychologists confront frequently. Asking people about homicidal fantasies or romantic feelings constitute potential *invasions of privacy*. The invasion may not be egregious because participants were volunteers who had the right to refrain from sharing any information they wished. But are researchers still violating social conventions by even asking? The problem of invasion of privacy becomes even more acute with naturalistic observations and field experiments, in which participants may not know that they are disclosing information about themselves. In one controversial study, subjects were approached by a private detective who offered them an opportunity to participate in an illegal "Watergate-style" break-in (West, Gunn, & Chernicky, 1975). Is this sort of invasion of privacy justified in the interest of finding out about human behavior? The general rule of thumb psychologists follow is that using unwitting subjects is acceptable if they are left completely anonymous and if they will not be induced to perform behaviors that they would not have otherwise (no actual break-ins occurred, for example).

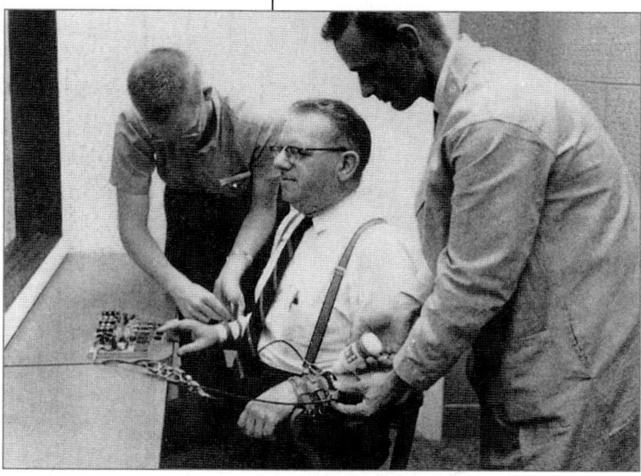

A scene from an ethically controversial experiment. *In Milgram's research on obedience to authority, subjects were led to believe that they were delivering electric shocks to a man (shown here) who said that he had a heart condition. The research raised questions about exposing subjects to psychological discomfort. Milgram argued that subjects felt that they had benefitted from the experience and that the knowledge gained, about harmful obedience similar to that occurring in Nazi Germany, made the research worthwhile.*

In experiments, people's behavior is manipulated, which raises another question: Will this research produce physical or psychological injury to the subject? Social psychological studies sometimes involve unpleasant physical manipulations, including strenuous exercise (Allen et al., 1989), injections of drugs such as adrenaline (Schachter & Singer, 1962), ingestion of alcohol (Hull & Bond, 1986; Steele & Josephs, 1990), or exposure to uncomfortable heat (Griffitt & Veitch, 1971; Rule, Taylor, & Dobbs, 1987).

Physical dangers are generally less of a problem in social psychology than in medical research (in which the manipulations may actually lead to illness or death), but there are discomforts and slight risks nevertheless. Social psychological research poses a bit more potential for psychological harm, ranging from embarrassment (from being "taken in" by a deceptive cover story, for example) through guilt (for thoughts about homicidal fantasies or alternative romantic partners) to anxiety (produced by the threat of electric shock).

In perhaps the most controversial study in social psychology, Stanley Milgram (1963) led participants to think that they were delivering painful electric shocks to an older man who had a heart condition. Partway through the experiment, the older man completely stopped responding, yet the experimenter insisted that subjects continue to deliver higher and higher levels of shock. Subjects in this study showed extreme levels of anxiety, including "profuse sweating, trembling, and stuttering" (371). Although this study was the subject of a rousing ethical controversy, Milgram (1964) defended it by pointing out that no participant showed evidence of lasting harm. In fact, 74 percent thought that they had learned something important. A year later, one subject wrote, "This experiment has strengthened my belief that man should avoid harm to his fellow man even at the risk of violating authority" (Milgram, 1964, 850). Milgram argued that researchers study controversial topics in the sincere hope that it "will lead to human betterment, not only because enlightenment is more dignified than ignorance, but because new knowledge is pregnant with human consequences" (852).

Ethical Safeguards in Social Psychological Research Social psychological research holds the promise of potential benefits—as any knowledge about love, prejudice, or homicidal violence could be used to better society. Yet the benefits must be weighed against the costs. How much discomfort for the participant is acceptable? Fortunately, there are safeguards against abuses of scientific inquiry. For one, the American Psychological Association (APA) has a set of ethical guidelines for research. These include:

Informed consent *A research participant's agreement to participate after being informed of any potential risks and of his or her right to withdraw at any time without penalty.*

1. *Obtaining informed consent from research participants.* **Informed consent** means that people agree to participate after being warned about any potential

discomfort or injury. This can pose a problem in studies that involve deception because full information would undermine people's natural responses. In the research in which participants were threatened with shock, for instance, they did not actually get shocked (because the threat was enough to produce physiological arousal and actual physical pain would have been unnecessary). In such cases, participants are told that the experiment may involve some discomfort but that they are free to withdraw at any time without penalty should they find the experience more uncomfortable than they had bargained for.

2. *Fully debriefing participants after the research is completed.* **Debriefing** involves discussing procedures and hypotheses with the participants, addressing any negative reactions they had, and alleviating any problems before they leave.
3. *Evaluating the costs and benefits of the research procedures.* Are there alternative methods of studying the problem? For instance, unless a researcher is specifically interested in fear, arousal could be induced through exercise rather than threats of shock. Does the research have the potential to produce useful knowledge that might justify temporary discomforts? For instance, Milgram argued that his study of obedience gave us insights into the horrible events in Nazi Germany.

As another ethical safeguard, any institution applying for federal research funding (as do most colleges and universities) is required to have an Institutional Review Board that evaluates the potential costs and benefits of research. Members of this board have no stake in the studies under consideration. They commonly ask researchers to revise manipulations, consent forms, or debriefing procedures. In this way, it is hoped, the trade-off between potential knowledge and subject discomfort can be optimized.

Summary

Just as a detective uses fingerprint powder and a magnifying glass to search for clues, social psychologists use research methods to help them make more accurate observations. Descriptive methods (including naturalistic observation, case studies, archives, surveys, and psychological tests) are designed to measure and record thought and behavior in its natural state. Descriptive methods can reveal correlations but cannot pin down what causes what. Experiments involve the purposeful manipulation of variables and can elucidate causes, but they may suffer from artificiality. Ethical issues in research include invasion of privacy and potential harm to subjects. Researchers and ethical review boards use a standard set of ethical guidelines to help weigh costs and benefits.

How Does Social Psychology Fit into the Network of Knowledge?

Social psychologists share many theories and methods with researchers in other disciplines. Thus you can make better sense of social psychology if you understand how it fits with other areas of knowledge.

Social Psychology and Other Areas of Psychology

Researchers in the field of *developmental psychology* consider how lifetime experiences combine with predispositions and early biological influences to produce the adult's

Debriefing *A discussion of procedures, hypotheses, and participant reactions at the completion of the study.*

feelings, thoughts, and behaviors. Social relationships are central to development. For example, social development researchers study how infants become attached to their parents and how these early experiences affect love relationships among adults (e.g., Cook, 2000; Reif & Singer, 2000; Sharpsteen & Kirkpatrick, 1997).

Personality psychology addresses differences between people and how individual psychological components add up to a whole person. Many important personality differences are intimately tied to social relationships (e.g., Caspi, 2000; Gaines, et al., 1997). For example, two of the characteristics people use most often to describe one another—extraversion and agreeableness—are largely defined by social relationships (e.g., Aron & Aron, 1997; Graziano, Hair, & Finch, 1997).

Environmental psychology is the study of people's interactions with the physical and the social environment. Environmentally oriented social psychologists study many important societal issues, including why people destroy the physical environment or how they respond to heat, crowding, and urban settings (e.g., Cohn & Rotton, 1997; Schroeder, 1995). These environmental issues will be a major focus of Chapter 13, which addresses global social dilemmas.

Social psychology also has increasingly close connections with *clinical psychology*—the study of behavioral dysfunction and treatment (e.g., Snyder & Forsyth, 1991; Snyder, Tennen, Affleck, & Cheavens, 2000). Social relationships are essential to understanding depression, loneliness, and coping with distress, for instance (Cohan & Bradbury, 1997; Jones & Carver, 1991; Reis, et al., 2000). Furthermore, many behavioral disorders are defined by their devastating effects on a person's social life. Each chapter of this text features a special "Focus on Social Dysfunction," in which we will examine problems rooted in, or causing disruptions for, social relationships. In this feature, we will consider how the social world can affect the disordered individual, and how normal group processes can sometimes go awry, from obsessive love relationships to paranoid distrust of "outsiders."

Social psychology also has direct links with two other areas of experimental psychology—*cognitive psychology* (the study of mental processes) and *physiological psychology* (studying the relation of biochemistry and neural structures to behavior). Certain types of brain damage help illustrate how the brain, cognition, and social behavior are interlinked. Prosopagnosia, for example, results from a peculiar form of brain damage that destroys a person's ability to recognize human faces (Damasio, 1985). Some modern psychologists believe that the structures of the human brain and the cognitive processes controlled by the brain have evolved primarily to deal with the problems of living in social groups (e.g., Tooby & Cosmides, 1992).

Social Psychology and Other Disciplines

Social psychology is intimately linked not only to other areas of psychology but also to other domains of knowledge. One of the first textbooks in social psychology was written by a sociologist, and the connections with the field of sociology continue to this day. For example, like sociologists, social psychologists often consider how variables such as social class and shared social norms affect behaviors such as prejudice and aggression (e.g., Cohen & Nisbett, 1997; Jackson & Esses, 1997).

Social psychology is likewise linked with anthropology, a field concerned with the links between human culture and human nature (e.g., Fiske, 2000). Anthropologists study cultures around the world for hints about human universals and the range of possible variations in social arrangements. Social psychology is also linked to several areas of biology, including genetics and zoology (e.g., Campbell, 1995; Simpson & Kenrick, 1997). In recent years, social psychologists have begun to use the methods of neuroscience to examine how hormones and brain structures affect parenting, love relationships, and responses to social stress (e.g., Berntson & Cacioppo, 2000).

In addition to its ties with other basic scientific disciplines, social psychology is closely connected to several applied sciences, including law, medicine, business, education, and political science (e.g., Harackiewicz, Barron, Carter, Lehto, & Elliot,

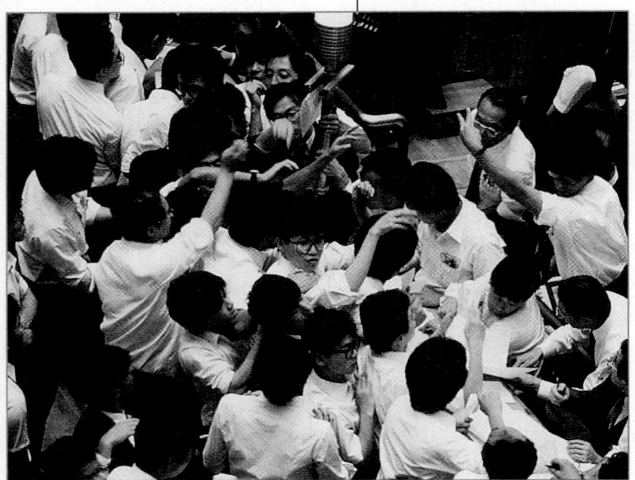

Social psychology and organizational behavior. *A classic series of studies, to be discussed in Chapter 12, examined the effects of other people on one's performance of simple and complex tasks. This work has led to other research and application in industrial/organizational psychology, an interdisciplinary field overlapping with social psychology.*

1997; Maio & Esses, 1998; McCann, 1997). Many of our interactions with other people take place in school and the workplace, and understanding social psychology can have practical payoffs in those settings. *Industrial/organizational psychology* integrates social psychology and business to understand social relationships in organizations (Pfeffer, 1998). In the political realm, many of the most pressing problems facing the world today—from environmental destruction to overpopulation to international conflict—are directly linked to social interactions. In our "Focus on Application" features, we discuss how social psychology can help us understand, and sometimes alleviate, practical problems in areas ranging from the small classroom to the global ecosystem.

These connections highlight an important point: Although each course in the curriculum considers only a few strands in the larger tapestry, all the threads are interwoven in a seamless whole. Your university education can be viewed as one long course designed to answer several big questions:

- What logical and methodological tools can we use to generate useful knowledge and to distinguish fact from fiction?
- What are the important ideas that previous thinkers have had about human nature and our place in the universe?
- How are those important ideas connected to one another?

Summary

Social psychology is closely connected to other fields of knowledge. Within psychology, developmental, personality, clinical, cognitive, and physiological psychologists often work on problems related to social behavior. Social psychology also connects to other academic disciplines, including sociology, anthropology, and biology, and to applied fields such as law, medicine, organizational behavior, education, and political science. Ultimately, all courses in the university search for methods and ideas to help us understand human nature and the universe around us.

REVISITING
The Mysteries of Social Life

At this chapter's opening, we raised several mysteries, some specific and some more general. At the specific level, we asked about the forces responsible for Nansook Hong's difficulties escaping the influence of Reverend Moon and his son, Juan Gonzalez' powerful desire to be reunited with his son, a gorilla's kindness toward a child who fell into her cage, and the changes in American norms about racism signaled by Jackie Robinson's career with the Dodgers. At the more general level, we asked why people sometimes stay in

abusive social relationships, why deadbeat dads are so common among mammals, whether common biological factors could similarly influence humans and other animals, and what general factors in the person and situation lead to prejudice versus tolerance.

In this first chapter, we have not yet delved into the evidence social psychologists have uncovered about social beliefs, relationships, prosocial behavior, or prejudice. However, the theoretical and methodological principles discussed so far have started us on the search for more informed answers. To begin with, our understanding of the limitations of case studies informs us that we can only go so far in reconstructing the causes of Nansook Hong's commitments, Juan Gonzalez' paternal inclinations, or Binti-Jua's kindness. Cases like these may inspire theoretical speculations, but hypotheses based on case studies ultimately need to be tested with more rigorous data from diverse and controlled methods. Going full circle, theoretical principles drawn from rigorous research can inspire new ways to think about particular events in the real world.

Social psychology's theories and methods also provide a set of practical detective tools to address the more general questions raised by these particular cases. Theoretical perspectives such as the sociocultural and cognitive approaches give social psychologists clues about probable places to begin their investigations. Research methods such as surveys and experiments provide tools that, like fingerprint kits to a detective, can help researchers see beyond the limitations of the unaided eye. In later chapters, we review how these different theories and methods have already yielded a wealth of information about the broader questions with which we opened the chapter. As we shall see, social psychologists have learned quite a bit about why and how people persuade and resist one another, about the motivations that draw people into bonded family relationships, how and why biological influences can affect humans and other animals in similar ways, and about the triggers of prejudice and tolerance within people and their social situations.

Not everyone who reads a social psychology text aspires to a career as a behavioral researcher. But all of us, even hermits like the Unabomber, are profoundly affected in our thoughts, feelings, and behaviors by the actions of other people. An understanding of the basic principles of social psychology can give us a new set of lenses through which to view those human beings who affect us so profoundly. As we will see, people's everyday intuitions about social behavior are often slightly biased, and sometimes deeply wrong. Trying to be aware of people's deeper motivations and of our own cognitive biases can keep us from being blinded by the seemingly "obvious" and also help us to appreciate the complexity that lies beneath the surface.

An understanding of the root motivations of social behavior is important in everyday life, providing potential clues about how to get along with coworkers, lovers, neighbors, and members of different groups whose customs might otherwise seem strange to us. Beyond that, important decisions about education, society, criminal behavior, urban development, and race relations could be better made by well-informed citizens and leaders. Finally, studying social psychology and understanding how its findings and theories are connected to other areas of knowledge can provide purely intellectual satisfaction. We are entering a century in which many of the mysteries of social life will be solved, and the educated mind will be best prepared to marvel at those discoveries.

CHAPTER 1

Summary

What Is Social Psychology?

1. Social psychology is the scientific study of how people's thoughts, feelings, and behaviors are influenced by other people. Social psychologists aim to describe social behavior carefully and to explain its causes.
2. Theories help connect and organize existing observations and suggest fruitful paths for future research.

Major Theoretical Perspectives of Social Psychology

1. Researchers who adopt a sociocultural perspective consider how behavior is influenced by factors that

operate in larger social groups, including social class, nationality, and cultural norms.
2. The evolutionary perspective focuses on social behaviors as evolved adaptations that helped our ancestors survive and reproduce.
3. The social learning perspective focuses on past learning experiences as determinants of a person's social behavior.
4. The phenomenological perspective focuses on a person's subjective interpretations of events in the social situation.
5. The social cognitive perspective focuses on the mental processes involved in paying attention to, interpreting, and remembering social experiences.

Basic Principles of Social Behavior

1. Social behavior is goal oriented. People enter social situations with short-term immediate goals, and these are linked to broader long-term goals and ultimately to more fundamental motives (such as establishing social ties, understanding ourselves and others, gaining and maintaining status, defending ourselves and those we value, and attracting and retaining mates).
2. Social behavior represents a continual interaction between features inside the person and events in the situation. People and situations choose, respond to, and alter one another.

How Psychologists Study Social Behavior

1. Descriptive methods (including naturalistic observations, case studies, archival studies, and surveys) involve recording behaviors, thoughts, and feelings in their natural state. These methods can uncover correlations but do not pin down causes.
2. Experimental methods search for causal processes by systematically manipulating some aspect of the situation (called the independent variable). Experiments allow conclusions about cause and effect but are more artificial than many descriptive methods.
3. Ethical issues for researchers include invasion of privacy and potential harm to subjects. These potential dangers must be weighed against possibly useful knowledge. Professional guidelines and institutional review boards help keep this balance.

How Does Social Psychology Fit into the Network of Knowledge?

1. Social psychology is closely connected to other subdisciplines of psychology, including developmental, personality, clinical, cognitive and physiological psychology.
2. Social psychology also connects to other disciplines, including basic research sciences like biology and sociology as well as applied fields like organizational behavior and education.

CHAPTER 1

Key Terms

Adaptation *Characteristic that is well designed for survival and reproduction in a particular environment.*

Archival method *Examination of systematic data originally collected for other purposes (such as marriage licenses or arrest records).*

Case study *An intensive examination of an individual or group.*

Confound *A variable that systematically changes along with the independent variable, potentially leading to a mistaken conclusion about the effect of the independent variable.*

Correlation *The extent to which two or more variables are associated with one another.*

Correlation coefficient *A mathematical expression of the relationship between two variables.*

Culture *The beliefs, customs, habits, and language shared by the people living in a particular time and place.*

Debriefing *A discussion of procedures, hypotheses, and participant reactions at the completion of the study.*

Demand characteristic *Cue that makes participants aware of how the experimenter expects them to behave.*

Dependent variable *The variable measured by the experimenter.*

Descriptive method *Procedure for measuring or recording behaviors, thoughts, and feelings in their natural state (including naturalistic observations, case studies, archival studies, and surveys).*

Evolutionary perspective *A theoretical viewpoint that searches for the causes of social behavior in the physical and psychological dispositions that helped our ancestors survive and reproduce.*

Experiment *A research method in which the researcher sets out to systematically manipulate one source of influence while holding others constant.*

Experimental method *Procedure for uncovering causal processes by systematically manipulating some aspect of a situation.*

External validity *The extent to which the results of an experiment can be generalized to other circumstances.*

Field experimentation *The manipulation of independent variables using unknowing participants in natural settings.*

Generalizability *The extent to which the findings of a particular research study extend to other similar circumstances or cases.*

Hypothesis *A researcher's prediction about what he or she will find.*

Independent variable *The variable manipulated by the experimenter.*

Informed consent *A research participant's agreement to participate after being informed of any potential risks and of his or her right to withdraw at any time without penalty.*

Internal validity *The extent to which an experiment allows confident statements about cause and effect.*

Natural selection *The assumption that animals that have characteristics that help them survive and reproduce will pass those characteristics on to their offspring.*

Naturalistic observation *Recording everyday behaviors as they unfold in their natural settings.*

Need to belong *An intrinsic motivation to affiliate with, and be accepted by, others.*

Observer bias *Error introduced into measurement when an observer overemphasizes behaviors he or she expects to find and fails to notice behaviors he or she does not expect.*

Person *Features or characteristics that individuals carry into social situations.*

Phenomenological perspective *The view that social behavior is driven by a person's subjective interpretations of events in the environment.*

Psychological test *Instrument for assessing a person's abilities, cognitions, motivations, or behaviors.*

Random assignment *The practice of assigning participants to treatments so each person has an equal chance of being in any condition.*

Reliability *The consistency of the score yielded by a psychological test.*

Representative sample *A group of respondents having characteristics that match those of the larger population the researcher wants to describe.*

Situation *Environmental events or circumstances outside the person.*

Social cognitive perspective *A theoretical viewpoint that focuses on the mental processes involved in paying attention to, interpreting, and remembering social experiences.*

Social constructivist view *The idea that people, including scientists, do not discover reality but rather construct or invent it.*

Social desirability bias *The tendency for people to say what they believe is appropriate or acceptable.*

Social learning perspective *A theoretical viewpoint that focuses on past learning experiences as determinants of a person's social behaviors.*

Social norm *A rule or expectation for appropriate social behavior.*

Social psychology *The scientific study of how people's thoughts, feelings, and behaviors are influenced by other people.*

Sociocultural perspective *The theoretical viewpoint that searches for the causes of social behavior in influences from larger social groups.*

Survey method *A technique in which the researcher asks people to report on their beliefs, feelings, or behaviors.*

Theory *Scientific explanation that connects and organizes existing observations and suggests fruitful paths for future research.*

Validity *The extent to which a test measures what it is designed to measure.*

CHAPTER 2

The Person and the Situation

The Enigma of an Ordinary and Extraordinary Man

According to his sister, he was an "ordinary man." He grew up in a middle-class home, where his youth was happy but uneventful (Branch, 1988; Garrow, 1986). M. L., as he was known then, was obviously intelligent, but neither his family nor his friends considered him gifted.

His college years were also unspectacular. He earned mediocre grades and even received a "laziness" award from his coworkers during a summer job. After receiving a graduate degree in theology, M. L. moved with his wife to take a job in Montgomery, Alabama. The "ordinary" young preacher had settled into an ordinary preacher's life.

But his settled life did not last long. Several weeks after the birth of his first child, the police in Montgomery arrested Rosa Parks, an African-American woman, for refusing to give up her seat on a bus to a white man. The rest, as they say, is history. This "ordinary man," the Reverend Martin Luther King, Jr., was

catapulted into fame when he led the successful Montgomery bus boycott of 1955–1956, the first of his many triumphs for the U.S. Civil Rights movement.

For the next twelve years, King endured numerous arrests, imprisonments, and attempts on his life. Despite these great obstacles, King marched on. Under his leadership the Civil Rights movement successfully dislodged longstanding legal barriers preventing blacks from having equal opportunities in education, employment, voting rights, and housing. King won the respect of people of all races for his willingness to assume huge personal burdens for the benefit of the greater good. And when an assassin's bullet cut short his life at the age of thirty-nine, King became to many a martyr, his death symbolizing both all that was wrong with race relations in the United States and the hope that the future could be so much better.

How can an "ordinary man" perform such extraordinary deeds? How can he have such a huge impact on his world?

Some argue that people's actions are determined by their personalities. From this perspective, King must have possessed a remarkable personality even before his role in the Montgomery bus boycott. Should we assume, then, that the perceptions of his family, friends, colleagues, and teachers were in error? Perhaps. But if the people who knew him best couldn't discern his true personality, who could? Moreover, if King's actions flowed from an extraordinary personality—one embodying special values and talents—how can we explain those times when these personal forces apparently abandoned him? For instance, how could a person dedicated to equality and justice run an organization so often unreceptive to the ideas and contributions of its female members? How could a person having such a strong self-identity as a preacher absent himself so frequently from his congregations on Sunday mornings? And, in light of his powerful Christian beliefs and commitment to family, how does one explain his marital infidelities? If his personality prior to the Rosa Parks incident was responsible for his actions afterwards, it surely wasn't the neatly structured personality that people so easily attribute to him.

Others argue that a person's actions are determined by the situation. Perhaps, then, we should assume that the situations in which King found himself were so powerful that virtually anyone would have responded as he did. King himself liked this explanation. He wasn't leading the movement at all, he would say. Instead, the people were pushing him along ahead of them. But, of course, this, too, is an oversimplification. After all, there were other potential leaders in Montgomery at the time who failed to assume the same burden of responsibility. And huge numbers of people throughout the nation had witnessed similar incidents of racial discrimination without taking action. The situation hadn't captured them as it had King.

It seems that, alone, neither King's personality nor his situation was enough to account for his conduct. How, then, do we explain Martin Luther King, Jr.'s, remarkable deeds?

The story of Martin Luther King, Jr., illustrates one of the fundamental principles of modern social psychology: Neither the person nor the situation alone determines social behavior. Instead, features of the person and the situation *work together* in interesting and often complex ways to influence how people relate to their social world (Snyder & Cantor, 1998). In this chapter we begin to explore this fascinating interplay of person and situation, introducing what social psychologists mean when they discuss "the person," "the situation," and "person–situation interactions."

The Person

We open our examination of social behavior by peering inside the individual, asking "Who *is* the person as he or she enters the social situation?" Our answer is that the social individual is a dynamic combination of motivations, knowledge, and feelings, all of which work with one another to produce the fascinating range of social thought and behavior we'll discover throughout this book.

Motivation: What Drives Us

Motivation is the driving force, the energy, that moves people toward their desired outcomes. Confronted with a crime to be solved, police detectives ask questions about motive, seeking to discover *why* their criminal prey might have perpetrated the dastardly deed. Of course, we all ask questions about motivation as we try to understand the everyday behaviors of those around us (Heider, 1958). Even infants as young as six months appear to understand that people do things for a reason (Woodward, 1998). Throughout this book, we provide answers to many mysteries of motivation: Why do people help others even when it places their own lives in jeopardy? Why are people prejudiced against those they don't even know? Why do people sometimes buy products they don't want and for which they have no use? Here, we begin simply by introducing the concepts of motivation more broadly.

Motives and Goals Think for a moment about what you want to accomplish over the next few weeks. Do you want to get together with your old roommate for dinner? Do you hope to catch that new blockbuster movie Saturday night? Do you want to improve your study habits? What are your **goals**?

If you're like most people, your list includes many goals having to do with everyday projects or concerns, such as looking attractive for an upcoming date, borrowing a classmate's notes for a missed lecture, or cleaning your apartment (Cantor & Kihlstrom, 1987; Emmons, 1989; Klinger, 1977; Little, 1989). Now think about why you want to accomplish these goals. Why, for example, might you want to make yourself attractive, keep up with chemistry notes, or maintain a clean apartment? Many of your goals are *subgoals*—steps toward a larger goal. For instance, making yourself attractive may help you get a date, whereas borrowing class notes may help you earn good grades. And if you ask yourself why finding a date and getting good grades are important, you might conclude that a date could lead to a desired long-term relationship, whereas doing well in school could help you achieve social and economic status. As Figure 2.1 illustrates, we have goals at multiple levels, and many of those goals enable us to reach other, more important, goals (e.g., McAdams, 1985; Murray, 1938; Vallacher & Wegner, 1987). Psychologists often use the term *goals* to refer to relatively mid- and low-level desires—like the desire to boost one's self-esteem or get good grades. They often use the term **motives** when considering goals with a broader scope, such as the desires to gain status, protect family members from harm, and so on.

Conscious and Automatic Goal Pursuit People use a wide range of strategies to reach their social goals. Some of these strategies are cognitive. If you are interested in enhancing your self-esteem, for example, you might take credit for your successes

Motivation *The force that moves people toward desired outcomes.*

Goal *A desired outcome; something one wishes to achieve or accomplish.*

Motive *A high-level goal fundamental to social survival.*

Figure 2.1
Multiple levels of goals.

A person's fundamental motive to gain status may involve the goal of getting a good job, which may have a subordinate goal of achieving high grades, which itself may have a number of subordinate goals such as wanting to attend class, go to office hours, and so forth.

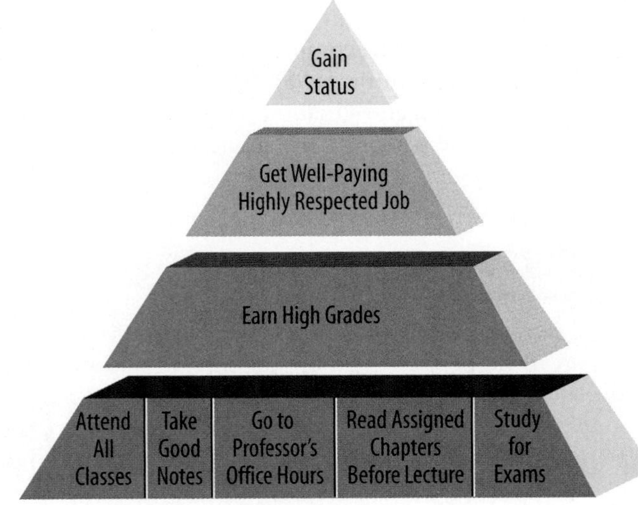

and blame others for your failures. Other strategies are behavioral. To protect an endangered family member, you might strike a tough pose and act aggressively. Thought and behavior are the tools—the strategies—people use to turn their desires into reality.

Achieving our goals sometimes requires considerable *attention*—people must contemplate alternative strategies, decide which ones to pursue, closely monitor their effectiveness, and then adjust them if necessary (e.g., Duval & Wicklund, 1972; Mischel, Cantor, & Feldman, 1996; Scheier & Carver, 1988). **Attention** is the process through which people consciously focus on what's going on within and around them. It's useful to think of attention as a spotlight that illuminates the information we need to accomplish our goals. When we are interested in romance, we shine our attentional beam on the appealing classmate and his or her reactions to us; when we are concerned about safety, we focus our attention instead on burly strangers, dark alleys, and fast-moving cars.

But sometimes our strategies are so well practiced, and used so frequently, that they become "automatized" and no longer require attention to proceed effectively (e.g., Bargh & Chartrand, 1999; Smith & Lerner, 1986). **Automaticity** refers to the ability of a behavior or cognitive process to operate without conscious guidance once it's put into motion (Bargh, 1996; Wegner & Bargh, 1998). Once an experienced driver decides to drive her car, for example, she generally does not need to pay attention to coordinating the pedals, stick shift, and steering wheel. The process of adjusting the car's direction and speed to accommodate the ebb and flow of traffic becomes relatively automatic as well. Similarly, once a well-practiced sales professional decides to start his pitch, he uses the basic strategies in his repertoire ("What cute kids you have!") without having to plan them thoughtfully in advance.

Attention *The process of consciously focusing on aspects of our environment or ourselves.*

Automaticity *The ability of a behavior or cognitive process to operate without conscious guidance once it's put into motion.*

Because attention is a limited resource—we can only pay attention to a small amount of information at any one time (e.g., Pashler, 1994)—the benefits of automaticity are great: By automatizing one task, we can devote our limited attention to other tasks. If you are an experienced driver, you have attention to spare for conversing with a passenger or for changing the radio station. Likewise, a well-trained salesman has attention to spare for better customizing his influence tactics to each individual customer. By automatizing the ways we think about and interact with others, we can move toward many of our goals with an economy of mental effort.

There are clear benefits to moving through life without having to pay close attention to every single decision we have to make. But there are costs to such automaticity as well: We sometimes make "mindless" mistakes. Picture the following: You're about to use the copy machine in the library when a stranger walks up and asks if she can jump ahead of you to copy five pages. Participants in one study, conducted by Ellen Langer, Arthur Blank, and Benzion Chanowitz (1978), were more likely to grant this favor when the person provided a reason ("May I use the Xerox machine, because I'm in a rush") than when no excuse was offered (94 percent versus 60 percent). This appears to be a sensible strategy—after all, if the request is small and the person has a justifiable rationale, why not be nice and help her out? Surprisingly, however, people were also likely to grant the request (93 percent) even when the reason offered no new information ("May I use the Xerox machine, *because I have to make copies?*"). Apparently, these subjects mindlessly activated their usual strategy, to be helpful and grant the request, as soon as they heard the person say "because." Because "because" suggests there's a reason, we may rarely register that the reason isn't really a justifiable one (after all, don't we *all* use the Xerox machine to make copies!?). Sometimes, people don't pay much attention to what they are doing and why they are doing it (Langer, 1989; Langer & Moldoveneau, 2000).

Self-Control and Willpower Moving toward goals isn't always easy. It's especially difficult when achieving one goal means ignoring other desirable opportunities—when studying for tomorrow's exam means refusing a friend's dinner invitation, when saving for a down payment on a first home means driving your old clunker for another few years, or when following doctor's orders means resisting Aunt Sylvia's wonderful cheesecake. In such cases, achieving the goal means controlling powerful counterproductive impulses. The strength needed to overcome these impulses is **willpower** (e.g., Mischel, 1996).

Mark Muraven and Roy Baumeister (2000) hypothesized that willpower works similarly to muscles—yes, muscles! Just as muscles have only so much strength to exert, people have only so much willpower they can expend. Just as muscles become tired and less effective with continuous work, willpower diminishes in strength as one uses it. Just as muscles need time to regain their full strength after exercise, it takes a while for willpower to recuperate after exerting self-control.

Consider an experiment designed to explore this last hypothesis (Baumeister, Bratslavsky, Muraven, & Tice, 1998). Thinking they were participating in a study of taste perception, hungry students—they had been asked not to eat for at least three hours before the study—were seated in a room filled with the aroma of freshly baked chocolate chip cookies. On the table in front of them sat two piles of food: a stack of chocolate chip cookies surrounded by chocolate candies, and a bowl of radishes. Participants were given one of two instructions: To eat at least two or three radishes—and no cookies or candies—during the next five minutes, or to eat at least two or three cookies (or a handful of candies)—and no radishes—during the next five minutes. The experimenter left the room. When she returned, she asked the participants to solve puzzles for an unrelated study while ostensibly waiting for their "sensory memory" of the eaten foods to fade. Unknown to the participants, the puzzles were impossible to solve. Keeping in mind the hypothesis that willpower is a limited resource that dissipates for a time after being used, who do you think quit working on the puzzles the soonest: Those participants who had to eat the radishes and resist the cookies, those who had to eat the cookies but not the radishes, or a third (control) group who were not exposed to the food at all prior to working on the puzzles?

If you guessed the first group—those who had to eat the radishes—you're correct (see Figure 2.2). Compared to the other groups, this group had to exert willpower: They had to force themselves to do what is an unpleasant task for many (eat radishes) while suppressing their strong impulse to do a pleasant task (eat cookies and candy). The expenditure of this willpower apparently left little willpower remaining for the subsequent task of working on the difficult puzzles. In contrast,

Willpower *The self-control strength used to overcome counterproductive impulses to achieve difficult goals.*

Figure 2.2
Willpower: Use it and lose it (for a while, anyway).

In one experiment, some participants had to eat radishes and suppress their urge to eat freshly-baked chocolate chip cookies, and others had to eat chocolate-chip cookies and ignore the radishes. The findings below are consistent with the hypothesis that using willpower for one task (avoiding yummy treats) reduces its availability for subsequent tasks (solving difficult puzzles).

SOURCE: *Baumeister, Bratslavsky, Muraven, & Tice (1998, Table 1, p. 1255).*

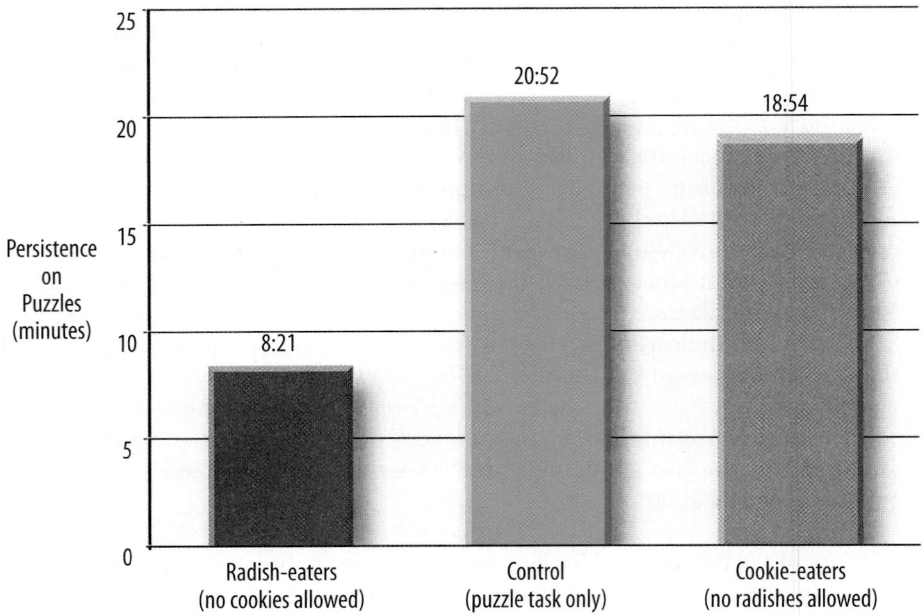

students in the "cookies" group got to do a pleasant task (eat cookies and candy) and didn't have to do an unpleasant task (eat radishes). Little willpower is required to eat tasty treats or avoid bitter foods, so they had plenty of willpower left for working on the difficult puzzles.

Perhaps some alternative explanations for these results have come to mind. You might wonder, for instance, whether the cookie-munchers were put in a better mood than the radish-crunchers, and whether people in good moods persist longer at difficult tasks. Although this is a plausible alternative, measures of participants' moods suggest that mood didn't account for these results. And other studies demonstrated similar results, making less plausible other alternative explanations (Vohs & Heatherton, 2000). For instance, concealing emotional reactions to a movie makes it more difficult, minutes later, to solve anagram puzzles or hold closed an exercise handgrip; suppressing forbidden thoughts makes it subsequently harder to control emotional reactions; and having to cope with stressful events like unpredictable loud noises, crowding, or noxious odors makes it more difficult to succeed at a range of tasks, even after the noises, crowds, and odors are gone (e.g., Baumeister et al., 1998; Glass et al., 1969; Rotton, 1983; Sherrod, 1974). In all, then, it appears that when we need willpower to achieve one goal, we will have less of it available (in the short term) to achieve later goals (Baumeister, Muraven, & Tice, 2000).

The Difficulty of Trying Not to Do Something We sometimes try to reach difficult goals by suppressing thoughts incompatible with them. Dieters may try not to think of tasty desserts, recently reformed alcoholics may try to suppress thoughts of their favorite libation, and individuals recovering from failed relationships may attempt to avoid thinking about former lovers. Unfortunately, trying *not* to do something can be quite difficult. Let's perform a short experiment: Take out a piece of paper, a pen, and a watch. Clear your mind, and don't continue reading until it feels relatively unjumbled.

Now for the next three minutes, you are *not* to think about white bears. That's right, *white bears!* Don't think about polar bears; don't think about cute, little, fuzzy-white teddy bears; don't think about any kind of white bear at all. If you *do* happen to think about white bears, scribble a little tick mark on the paper. But this shouldn't happen often, because you are going to work hard at *not* thinking about them. Ready? Remember, no white bears. Okay. Begin the three minutes now…

How did you do? Did you think of white bears at all? If you are like the participants in a study by Daniel Wegner and his colleagues (Wegner, Schneider, Carter, & White, 1987), white bears probably ambled into your mind at least several times. Some individuals even find their thoughts totally inundated with images of the furry creatures. Moreover, now that you're no longer guarding against them, white bears will likely come to mind even more often than if you hadn't tried to suppress your images of them in the first place (Wegner & Erber, 1992).

If it can be hard to stop frivolous thoughts about bears from "rebounding" back into mind, might it also be difficult to suppress other, more important thoughts? When on a diet, for example, might attempts to keep thoughts of food out of mind focus us even more on the joys of potato chips, Big Macs, and hot fudge sundaes? Might attempts to suppress thoughts of failed relationships lead us to ruminate even more about loves lost and opportunities missed? Might attempts to suppress your stereotypes of a disliked ethnic group actually increase the likelihood that you'll negatively stereotype them? The answer to these questions seems to be a resounding yes (e.g., Liberman & Förster, 2000; Macrae et al., 1996; Monteith, Sherman, & Devine, 1998; Wenzlaff & Wegner, 2000). Attempts to suppress unwanted thoughts can even contribute to serious mental health difficulties, ranging from depression to post-traumatic stress disorder (e.g., Purdon, 1999). And recent findings reveal that thought suppression can also weaken the immune system (Petrie, Booth, & Pennebaker, 1998), suggesting that it may adversely affect physical health as well. Trying not to do something can be hard.

In sum, our first peek into the person reveals that we are motivated creatures. We have goals, and we pursue them. Goal pursuit sometimes requires attention and willpower, but it often operates automatically. This automaticity frees us to focus our attention and willpower elsewhere. We turn now to explore a second key component of the person—knowledge.

Knowledge: Our View of Ourselves and the World

During his training for the ministry, Martin Luther King, Jr. studied Mahatma Gandhi's philosophy of nonviolent civil disobedience. Years later, as King led fellow black citizens in their strike against the Montgomery bus system, his knowledge of Gandhi, stored in memory, formed the foundation of his strategy—a strategy that would work time and again. Like all of us, King had turned his life experiences into knowledge, and then that knowledge into action.

Knowledge reflects our rich and varied life experiences. As Figure 2.3 illustrates, we have *sensory memories* of visual images, smells, sounds, tastes, and touches. For example, based on films you've seen, you may have an image of what Martin Luther King, Jr. looked and sounded like as he gave his rousing "I have a dream" speech at the Lincoln Memorial. We also have *beliefs* about people's behaviors, traits, abilities, goals, preferences, relationships, and usual activities (Beach & Wertheimer, 1961; Fiske & Cox, 1979). For instance, your impression of Martin Luther King, Jr. may include the beliefs that he was spiritual, wished to rid the United States of racial discrimination, and had an incredible gift of oratory. Our knowledge also includes *explanations* for why people, groups, or situations are the way they are (e.g., Kunda, Miller, & Claire, 1990; Read & Marcus-Newhall, 1993; Sedikides & Anderson, 1994). For example, we may explain King's pursuit of egalitarian goals by pointing to his religious values.

How is all this knowledge organized in memory? As an example, take out a pen and a piece of paper and list everything that occurs to you when you think about *great leaders*. Be free and open with your listing—write down everything that comes to mind.

Based on research, we suspect that your list might include some *specific examples* of great leaders—perhaps Martin Luther King, Jr., George Washington, Abraham Lincoln, Mahatma Gandhi, or Eleanor Roosevelt. We call knowledge of a specific

Figure 2.3
A mind's-eye view of Dr. King.

Mental representations hold and organize the information we have about people, objects, and events. A hypothetical mental representation of Dr. Martin Luther King Jr. might contain information of the sorts illustrated here.

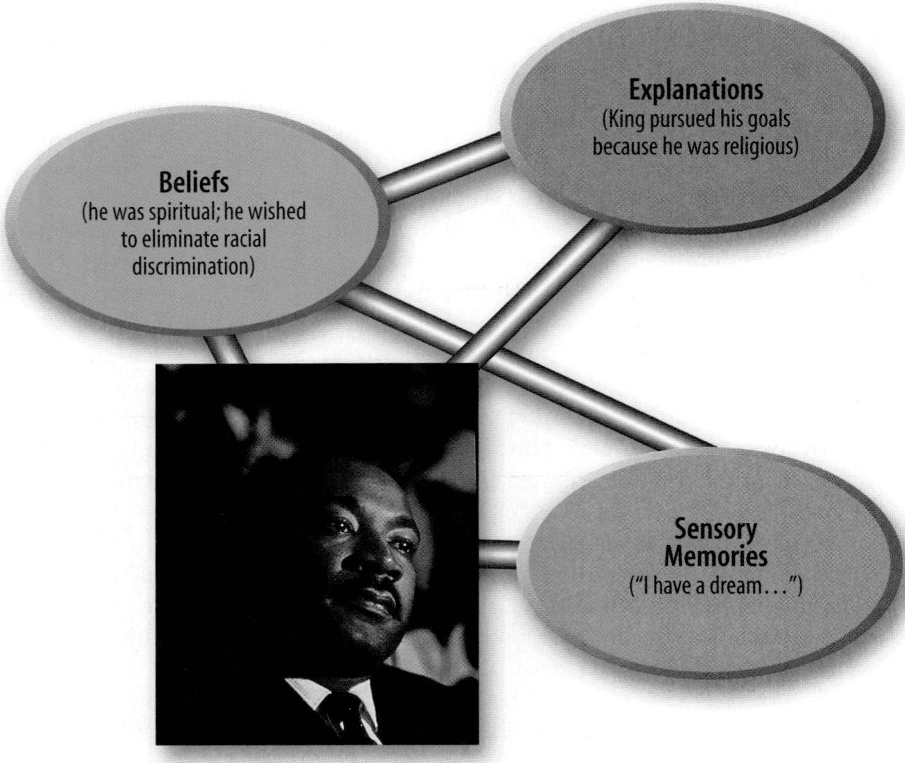

episode, event, or individual an **exemplar** (e.g., Smith & Medin, 1981; Smith & Zárate, 1992). We also suspect that your list included some *general characteristics* that great leaders, as a group, tend to possess. For example, perhaps you believe that great leaders want to better the lives of those around them and use their charisma to influence others for the better. Knowledge that represents generalized information of this sort is called a **schema** (e.g., Bartlett, 1932; Taylor & Crocker, 1981). Our views of the social world contain both exemplars and schemas. And we'll see in just a few pages that people also possess knowledge of social situations and how they fit into them. In sum, although we mentally organize our knowledge in different ways, all these organizations share a common, fundamental feature: They represent our views of the social world (Smith, 1998).

The Self-Concept The knowledge we have of ourselves is particularly important. Take a minute and list everything that comes to mind when you think about yourself.

Although the content of your list may differ from your description of great leaders, the *types* of things you listed were probably similar. You may have listed examples of past behavior, and you almost certainly listed some general characteristics you believe describe you. Indeed, just as we possess knowledge about others, we also possess knowledge of ourselves—the **self-concept,** sometimes called the *self-schema* (e.g., Kihlstrom et al., 1988; Markus, 1977). You, too, are an "object" to be understood by your mind (James, 1890).

Exemplar *A mental representation of a specific episode, event, or individual.*

Schema *A mental representation capturing the general characteristics of a particular class of episodes, events, or individuals.*

Self-concept *A mental representation capturing our views and beliefs about ourselves.*

Multiple selves. Just as our thoughts of "great leaders" include multiple exemplars, our self-view includes multiple selves. Some of our selves are linked to the roles we play (e.g., Gergen, 1971; Markus & Wurf, 1987). For instance, Martin Luther King, Jr. probably saw himself as a husband, a father, a leader, and a preacher. Other selves are linked to the future—they represent what we ideally hope to become, what we think we ought to become, and what we fear becoming (e.g., Higgins, 1987; Markus

& Nurius, 1986; Ogilvie, 1987). King hoped to be a strong, effective champion of civil rights, thought he ought to be a better husband to his wife and a better father to his children, and feared becoming a glory-seeking leader out of touch with the people. Future selves like these are important because they help define our goals and direct our actions. For example, when it becomes clear to us that our "actual selves"—who we think we actually are—fall short of our "ought selves"—who we think we ought to be—we become anxious, and this anxiety may motivate us to work harder toward our goals (Higgins, 1996). King's future selves directed him to work harder to further the rights of African Americans and other minorities, to spend more time with his family, and to avoid the intoxication of power. Finally, most of us possess, to some degree, a group or *collective self.* Just as King saw himself as being a black American, you might view yourself as being a New Yorker, a Republican, a woman, or a member of some other group (e.g., Deaux, Reid, Mizrahi, & Ethier, 1995; Markus & Kitayama, 1991; Triandis, 1989). We'll see later in the chapter that "who you are" in any moment—which of your many selves dominates—often depends on what aspect of the self is made salient by your current situation.

Knowing thyself. *How do we come to form a self-concept? By observing ourselves, by seeing how others view us, and by comparing ourselves to others, we come to know ourselves.*

Sources of self-knowledge. One way we come to understand others is by observing their behaviors and inferring what those behaviors mean about the person. For instance, if you see a neighbor viciously reprimanding his child, you might guess that he's insensitive or cruel. We sometimes learn about ourselves in a similar way, by "stepping outside ourselves" and observing our own actions (Bem, 1967, 1972). By engaging in this **self-perception process**—the process through which people observe their own behavior to infer their own internal characteristics—the neighbor may come to believe that he is not a very good parent.

Sometimes we learn about ourselves through a **reflected appraisal process**—by observing or imagining what others think of us (Cooley, 1902; Mead, 1934; Sullivan, 1953). Through this process, a child who believes that her parents view her as talented, amusing, or overweight may come to think of herself similarly. In chapter 4, we'll see that people manage their public presentations not only to influence the ways that others view them, but also—through self-perception and reflected appraisal processes—to influence the ways they view themselves.

Finally, through **social comparison**—the process of comparing one's own abilities, attitudes, and beliefs with those of others—people also come to know themselves (Festinger, 1954). For example, by seeing how well your grades compare to your roommate's, you may learn something about your academic abilities. We explore social comparison processes in chapters 3, 7, and 12.

In sum, just as we know much about others, we also know much about ourselves. We'll see throughout the book that knowledge of self, of others, and of social situations influence a great deal of social behavior.

Self-perception process *The process through which people observe their own behavior to infer internal characteristics such as traits, abilities, and attitudes.*

Reflected appraisal process *The process through which people come to know themselves by observing or imagining how others view them.*

Social comparison *The process through which people come to know themselves by comparing their abilities, attitudes, and beliefs with those of others.*

Feelings: Attitudes, Emotions, and Moods

The nasty-looking thug on a lonely street fills us with fear. The death of a beloved relative leaves us grief-stricken. A magical first encounter with that "special" person incites us to romance and desire. And Martin Luther King, Jr.'s, passionate baritone voice reverberates through us, echoing sadness and hope. Feelings are the music of life.

Social psychologists consider three general types of feelings—attitudes, emotions, and moods. **Attitudes** are favorable or unfavorable evaluations of particular people, objects, events, or ideas (Eagly & Chaiken, 1998; Petty & Wegener, 1998).

Attitude *A favorable or unfavorable evaluation of a particular person, object, event, or idea.*

You may dislike politicians, love rocky road ice cream, and be favorable toward capital punishment. Attitudes are relatively basic feelings, simple evaluations along a positive/negative continuum—we feel positively or negatively, favorably or unfavorably, approvingly or disapprovingly about something.

The specific attitude we have toward ourselves is called **self-esteem.** People who feel favorably about themselves are said to have high self-esteem; people who feel negatively about themselves have low self-esteem. Like the self-concept, self-esteem influences much of social behavior, as we'll see throughout this book.

Emotions—feelings such as fear, anger, sadness, joy, and guilt—are richer, more complex, and more intense than attitudes. In addition to their positivity/negativity component, they also possess a physiological arousal component. When people are fearful, for example, their hearts begin to pound, their respiration quickens, their facial expressions change, and their bodies manufacture key biochemicals. Moreover, complex thoughts often accompany emotions, as when gut-wrenching feelings of shame carry with them beliefs of inadequacy and self-loathing.

Finally, **moods** are feelings that are less focused and longer-lasting than emotions. When in a bad mood, everything seems gray; when in a good mood, everything is rosy; when anxious, we panic at the sight of our own shadows. A mood colors all our experiences, not just the particular event that brought it about initially.

Because social behavior is powerfully influenced by feelings, measuring those feelings is crucial. Although figuring out what goes on inside the person is difficult, psychologists have developed techniques that have proven quite successful, as we see next.

FOCUS ON Method

Assessing Attitudes, Emotions, and Moods

If you want to know how a friend feels about capital punishment or how she felt while watching the latest Hollywood tear-jerker, what would you do? To start, you might just ask her. Researchers often do the same, although in a more systematic, sophisticated way. *Self-report measures* can be as straightforward as asking a simple series of questions. Sometimes people are asked to respond to true/false or agree/disagree statements (for example, "I feel favorably toward capital punishment"). Other times, questions are asked in a way that allows for finer-grained responses. For example, "On a 9-point scale—with 1 = extremely sad and 9 = extremely happy—how do you feel right now?"

It often makes good sense simply to ask people to report their feelings. After all, feelings are personal experiences, and the person having them will usually know them best. There can be problems associated with this method, however. For instance, people may hesitate to report feelings they believe to be socially inappropriate or undesirable. As one example, politically conservative students on a liberal college campus may be reluctant to admit they favor capital punishment.

What can a social psychologist do to reduce this bias? First, a researcher can give participants a sense of anonymity by assigning them code numbers instead of having them use their names, or by having them place their unidentified questionnaires in an envelope with many others. If participants believe themselves to be anonymous, they don't need to worry about their public images. Second, the researcher can obscure the true purpose of a study by hiding the items of interest in the midst of many others, or by using a deceptive cover story suggesting that the study is exploring one question when it is really exploring another. If participants don't believe a study to be about affirmative action, for instance, they may be less likely to alter their self-reports on this issue. (See chapter 1 for a discussion of the pros and cons of deception in research.) Finally, researchers can trick participants into believing they can read the participants' true feelings—perhaps by hooking

Self-esteem *Our attitude toward ourselves.*

Emotion *A relatively intense feeling characterized by physiological arousal and complex cognitions.*

Mood *A relatively long-lasting feeling that is diffuse and not directed toward a particular, single target.*

them up to a fake, but convincing, "lie detector" machine (Jones & Sigall, 1971; Roese & Jamieson, 1993; Sigall & Page, 1971). In such a circumstance, the participant has little to gain by lying. Thus, despite the potential weaknesses of self-report techniques, researchers can make them more effective.

Because people sometimes have reason to hide their true feelings, or may have difficulty expressing feelings in words, social psychologists also look toward behavior for clues. This, of course, is similar to what nonpsychologists do when they don't trust what others are telling them. For example, you might presume that a person who smiles every time he reads of a convict being executed is in favor of capital punishment and that a person with glaring eyes, tightened jaw, and clenched fists is angry. Indeed, detailed analyses of facial expressions can often provide a fascinating window on a person's feelings (Ekman, 1982; Keltner & Ekman, 1994). Researchers can also learn about people's feelings by secretly observing how people use their environment. For example, the wear-and-tear of flooring tiles in front of the different displays at Chicago's Museum of Science and Industry revealed how much people liked the different exhibits—the tiles at the hatching-chick exhibit needed to be replaced every six weeks, whereas tiles at other displays lasted for many years (Webb, Campbell, Schwartz, & Sechrest, 1966).

Of course, not even secret observations are foolproof indicators of people's true feelings. Most behaviors are influenced by multiple factors, only some of which are related to feelings. Moreover, different people may respond to the same feeling in very different ways (e.g., Gross, John, & Richards, 2000). Whereas some people fly into a rage when angry, others become icy calm and calculating. Nonetheless, psychologists interested in assessing people's feelings can obtain very useful information by observing people's behavior.

Finally, social psychologists have several tools at their disposal that everyday people do not. For instance, in chapter 11 we will explore the *Implicit Association Test*, a computerized method that measures people's reaction times in order to assess the feelings they have toward themselves and others (Farnham, Greenwald, & Banaji, 1999; Greenwald, McGhee, & Schwartz, 1998). Social psychologists also use instruments that gather *physiological measures* of blood pressure, heart rate, respiration, sweat, and biochemical production. People who are anxious, for instance, often sweat more profusely and exhibit increases in heart rate, and specialized instruments can pick this up (Blascovich & Kelsey, 1990). Similarly, emotions such as anger, fear, disgust, and joy are characterized by particular facial expressions, which can often be assessed with the use of facial electrodes sensitive to even tiny changes in muscle activity (Cacioppo, Klein, Berntson, & Hatfield, 1993). And emotion-relevant brain activity can be observed with modern technologies such as Positron Emission Tomography (PET) scans. For example, it appears that brain activity associated with happiness occurs in a different location than brain activity associated with disgust (Davidson et al., 1990).

Physiological measures have their weaknesses, too, however. Different people often exhibit different biological responses to the same emotional state; when aroused, some people show increases in heart rate whereas others show increases in skin conductance. Moreover, physiological measures are influenced by processes other than emotion. For example, physical exertion as well as anger increase heart rate. Most important, researchers have yet to discover any physiological pattern that maps perfectly onto any particular emotion. Indeed, this problem contributes to the controversy over the effectiveness of "lie-detector" machines, an issue we explore in chapter 4.

Nonetheless, physiological instruments can be quite valuable, particularly when used in conjunction with other kinds of measures. If a person says she's afraid, exhibits the

Mapping Emotions. How do psychologists know what others are feeling? In the Positron Emission Tomography (PET) scans below, brain activation patterns differed depending on whether participants were asked to recall and re-experience events that made them feel angry or happy. Together with self report measures and behavioral observations, physiological measures like PET help researchers identify others' emotions.
SOURCE: *Damasio et al. (2000), Figure 3, p. 1051.*

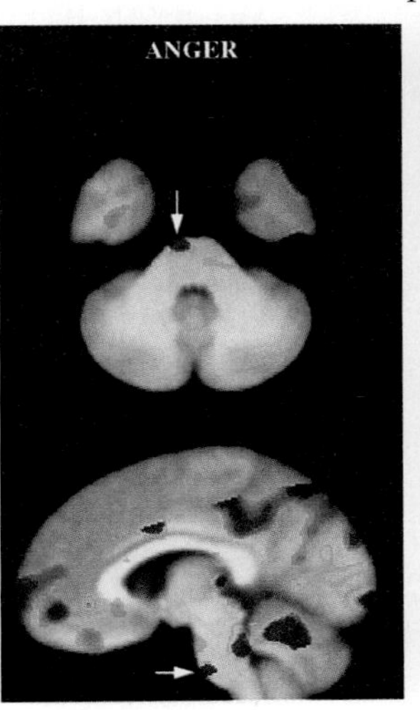

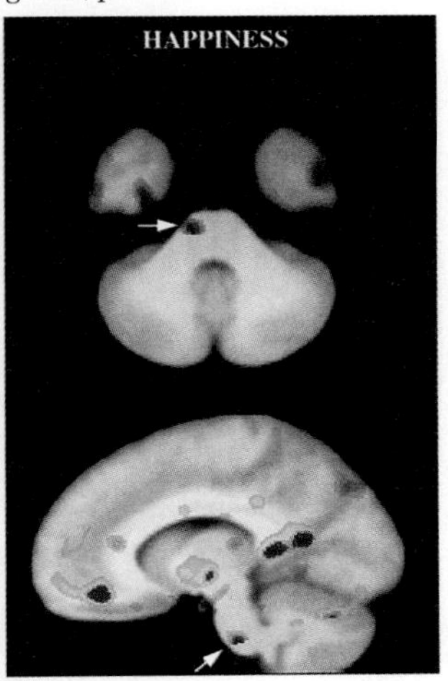

usual facial expressions and bodily postures, and has a racing heart and sweaty palms, she is probably fearful ("If it looks like a duck, walks like a duck, and quacks like a duck, it's probably a duck!"). Indeed, this seems to be the most important lesson: To the extent that self-report measures, behavioral indicators, and physiological measures all provide *converging* evidence, we can be more confident that we indeed know what the person is feeling. ■

Where Do Feelings Come From? Feelings are influenced by multiple factors, some of them relatively stable and long-lasting and others more fleeting and immediate. We begin by exploring genetic and cultural influences, and then consider physiological and cognitive processes.

Genetic and Cultural Foundations. Is there a genetic basis to what we feel and how we express those feelings? How would we know? First, we might expect many aspects of feelings to be universal, because humans share the vast majority of their genes with one another. Consistent with this hypothesis, people from many different societies express and experience emotions in surprisingly similar ways (e.g., Ekman & Friesen, 1969, 1971; Hejmadi, Davidson, & Rozin, 2000; Izard, 1971; Mauro, Sato, & Tucker, 1992; Russell, 1991, 1995). For example, people from various cultures—including nonliterate cultures unexposed to Western influences—agree strongly on which facial expressions reflect happiness, sadness, fear, disgust, and anger, and they also report very similar feelings, physiological symptoms, and emotion-related behaviors (Scherer & Walbott, 1994). Second, if there is a strong genetic component to certain feelings, they should be experienced and expressed even in individuals who haven't had the opportunity to learn how and when to experience and express them. This hypothesis is supported by the work of Eibl-Eibesfeldt (1973), who observed that even children born deaf, blind, and with brain damage—and who are thus unable to learn emotional responses from their social world—exhibit many normal emotional reactions like smiling, laughter, anger, and surprise. Finally, if genes influence feelings, then people who differ from one another genetically should differ in their feelings. This, too, is the case (e.g., Gabbay, 1992): Genetic heredity influences our emotions and moods (Lykken & Tellegen, 1996; Plomin, DeFries, & McClearn, 1990; Tellegen et al., 1988), as well as some of our everyday attitudes (e.g., Martin et al., 1986; Tesser, 1993; Waller et al., 1990). It's clear that genes contribute greatly to feelings.

It's also clear that culture and learning play a large role. For instance, in addition to cross-cultural similarities in how we experience and express our feelings, there are important cross-cultural differences as well (e.g., Ekman, 1994; Kitayama & Markus, 1994; Russell, 1994, 1995). For instance, whereas Utku Eskimos rarely express anger, even when provoked (Briggs, 1970), the men of the Awlad 'Ali Bedouin tribe of western Egypt are quick to respond angrily to even the remote appearance of an insult (Abu-Lughod, 1986). This is because cultures teach their members when and how to experience and express their feelings (e.g., Lewis, 1993; Saarni, 1993). There are three basic learning processes through which people learn about feelings—*classical conditioning*, *instrumental learning* (or *operant conditioning*), and *observational learning*. We focus here on how people learn their attitudes.

You may be familiar with the Russian physiologist Ivan Pavlov, whose dogs learned to associate the ringing of a bell with the presence of food and thus came to salivate upon hearing the bell. The process involved, called **classical conditioning,** influences the attitudes we form (Staats, Staats, & Crawford, 1962). For instance, when we associate people with uncomfortable circumstances—like a hot, humid room—we like them less (Griffitt, 1970). Even associations of which we are unaware can shape our attitudes (e.g., Cacioppo, Priester, & Berntson, 1993; Niedenthal, 1990). In one study, students viewed a series of slides of a woman going about her daily routine and were asked to form an impression of her. Just before each slide pre-

Classical conditioning *The process through which people associate new objects or events with feelings about previously experienced events.*

sentation, however, they were subliminally exposed to photos of either positive or negative objects (e.g., a bridal couple, a bloody shark). As expected, students exposed to the positive photographs formed a more favorable attitude toward the woman in the slides (Krosnick, Betz, Jussim, & Lynn, 1992). Classical conditioning processes play an important role in attitude formation. They may increase the chance we will fall in love while visiting our favorite city, develop dislikes for those we meet on cloudy days, and so on.

Instrumental learning, also called **operant conditioning,** is learning as a result of rewards and punishments (Skinner, 1938). In one experiment, students at the University of Hawaii were contacted by phone and asked about their attitudes toward the creation of a Springtime Aloha Week. Half the students were reinforced whenever they presented a favorable view; the interviewers said "good" each time a student's views supported the event. The remaining students were reinforced with a "good" each time they expressed an unfavorable view. One week later, all students completed a questionnaire on local issues, and buried within the questionnaire was an item assessing their attitude toward Aloha Week. As expected, students previously reinforced for favoring the event expressed more positive attitudes toward it than did students reinforced for opposing it (Insko, 1965).

Finally, we form attitudes via **observational learning.** We do not need to experience rewards and punishments firsthand to learn lessons from them. Instead, we often learn by observing others (Bandura, 1965, 1986). When we see others punished, we avoid their behaviors and the attitudes they represent. When we see others rewarded, we engage in those behaviors and adopt the attitudes they represent. The young Martin Luther King, Jr., watched his father win social respect for his efforts against segregation and racial discrimination, and these observations helped form King's own dislike of racism and discrimination.

Proximate Contributors to Feelings. Genes give us the capability to experience certain emotions, moods, and attitudes, and these capabilities are modified, differentiated, and developed through learning and cultural processes. What determines, however, what a person feels in any single moment? Part of this answer is relatively simple—some feelings are automatically triggered by the perception of a particular event (e.g., Zajonc, 1980). For example, the simple perception of a wasp flying rapidly toward one's head will be enough to arouse fear. We explore here two other proximate contributors to feelings: current physiological states and ongoing cognition.

Try the following: *Gently* hold the end of a pen between your teeth, making sure it doesn't touch your lips, as in Figure 2.4(a); what does this feel like? After a while, remove the pen and replace it, this time gripping the end of it firmly with your lips and making sure it doesn't droop downward, as in Figure 2.4(b); what is this sensation like?

Fritz Strack, Leonard Martin, and Sabine Stepper (1988) used this task in an experiment with student volunteers. The students (who thought the study was investigating ways for physically impaired people to perform everyday tasks like writing or phone dialing) were asked to hold a pen with their teeth, with their lips, or in their hand. While grasping the pen in the designated fashion, students performed a connect-the-dots exercise and an underlining task. Finally, the students were asked to evaluate the funniness of several cartoons by circling with the pen the appropriate number on a rating scale, still grasping the pen in the assigned fashion. This last task was what the investigators were really interested in. They expected to observe differences in the funniness ratings across the three pen-grasping conditions. What do you think they discovered? Why?

Recall your experience of holding the pen the different ways. Also, look again at the photos in Figure 2.4. Holding the pen gently between the teeth contracts the facial muscles into something like a smile; in contrast, holding the pen firmly between the lips creates a facial expression incompatible with smiling and similar to an angry grimace. Strack and his colleagues hypothesized that because different

Instrumental learning (operant conditioning) *The process through which people learn by being rewarded or punished.*

Observational learning *The process through which people learn by watching others get rewarded or punished.*

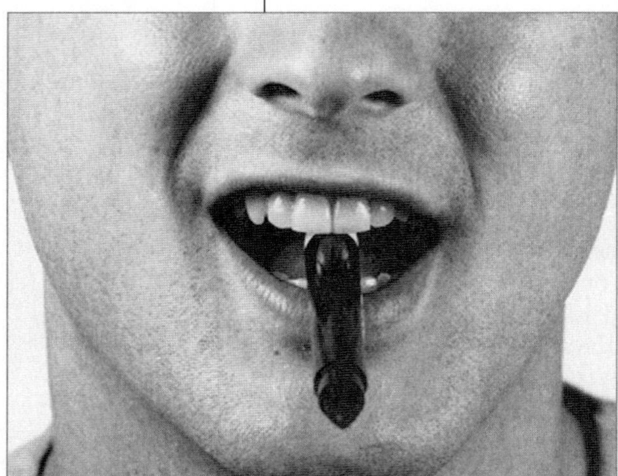

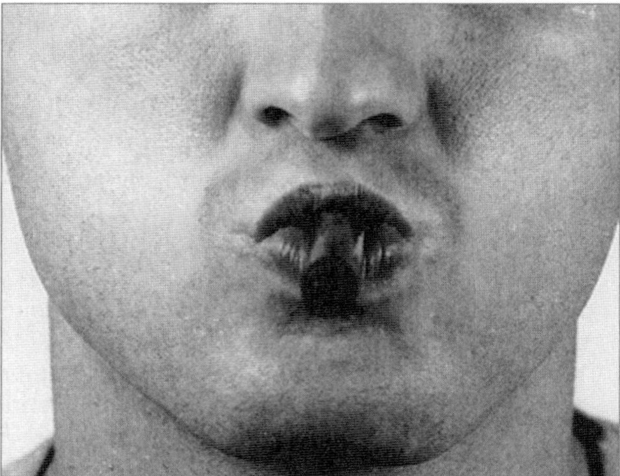

Figure 2.4
The pen-holding experiment.

Hold a pen in your mouth as the model in (a) is doing. What is this sensation like? Now hold the pen as the model in (b) is doing. What is this sensation like? Do you notice a difference between the two? How might these different facial expressions influence your feelings?

facial expressions are associated with different emotional states—for instance, we often smile when we are happy or amused—students holding the pen with their teeth (facilitating a smile) should rate the cartoons the funniest, whereas students holding the pen with their lips (inhibiting a smile) should find the cartoons less funny. These were indeed the students' reactions. Others have observed similar patterns (McCanne & Anderson, 1987), and researchers now believe that the contraction and relaxation of certain facial muscles can influence the emotions people experience (Cacioppo et al., 1993; Izard, 1990; Kleck, et al., 1976; Laird, 1974).

Just as changes in facial musculature can alter feelings, changes in other aspects of our physiology—for example, in neurochemistry and the autonomic nervous system (i.e., the heart, visceral organs, and endocrine glands)—can do the same (Lewis, 2000; Plutchik, 1994). Changes in ongoing thinking also affect our feelings. Stanley Schachter and Jerome Singer (1962) performed a complex experiment, part of which involved injecting some subjects with epinephrine, an arousing drug. These subjects were then placed in a room with a confederate who acted either unusually happy or angry. Their findings suggested that these aroused subjects paired with the happy confederate reported feeling relatively happy themselves, whereas aroused subjects paired with the angry confederate felt somewhat angry. The researchers concluded that their subjects' feelings were influenced both by physical arousal and by their *interpretations* of their present circumstance. In this case, the confederate's behaviors apparently provided subjects with useful information for understanding their own feelings.

The Schachter and Singer study had serious shortcomings, and other studies have not generally replicated its findings (Reisenzein, 1983). Nonetheless, it did focus attention on one very important point: Our feelings are influenced strongly by how we interpret—or *appraise*—our situations (e.g., Averill, 1980; Lazarus & Folkman, 1984; Neumann, 2000; Sinclair et al., 1994; Smith, Haynes, Lazarus, & Pope, 1993; Tesser, 1990). Guilty feelings, for example, arise from the perception that we have harmed a person whom we care about and who cares about us (Baumeister, Stillwell, & Heatherton, 1994; Tangney, 1992). Thus we might feel guilty when we fail to return a phone call from mom, but not when we ignore a call from the persistent salesperson who has been trying for the past three weeks to sell us unwanted magazine subscriptions. Although our action—not returning the call—is identical in both cases, our different appraisals of the two situations create quite different feelings.

The thrill of bronze, the agony of silver. *Who should be happier—athletes who finish second or athletes who finish third? Research by Victoria Medvec, Scott Madey, and Thomas Gilovich (1995) reveals that bronze medalists, such as Midori Ito, on the left, are generally happier than the more successful silver medalists, such as Nancy Kerrigan, on the right. Why might this be?*

Victoria Medvec, Scott Madey, and Thomas Gilovich (1995) cleverly demonstrated how ongoing thought can affect feelings. Before reading about their study, though, answer the following question: Who is happier following their Olympic performances: silver medalists, who finish in second place, or bronze medalists, who finish third? The researchers analyzed film of athletes from the 1992 Summer Olympics and discovered that bronze medalists were happier than the silver medalists, even though the silver medalists did better! Why? It's relatively easy for silver medalists to imagine improving their performances enough to earn the gold medal and all its associated fame and glory. As a result, they were somewhat disappointed in their performances. In contrast, it's easy for bronze medalists to imagine making even tiny mistakes that would have left them in fourth place or worse—leaving them with no medal at all. As a result, they felt relieved and happy to have won the bronze.

This kind of "what might have been" thinking—labeled **counterfactual thinking**—also influences our emotional reactions to common everyday events (e.g., Boninger, Gleicher, & Strathman, 1994; Roese & Olson, 1995). Whether we feel sad, happy, regretful, or guilty may depend on whether we imagine happier, sadder, or prouder alternatives to what really happened (e.g., Gilovich & Medvec, 1995; Niedenthal, Tangney, & Gavanski, 1994).

In sum, the foundations of our feelings are determined by our genes and culture, and our more proximate reactions are heavily influenced by current physiological states and how we interpret our surroundings and label our feelings.

Why Feelings Are Important As you walk on campus after class, thinking about your friend's upcoming wedding, you notice out of the corner of your eye a rapidly looming object. Even before you realize it's an automobile (and certainly before you're able to identify its make and model for the police report), your body tenses, you begin to lean away, your heart pumps wildly, and you shift your focus from wedding bells to the impending danger. Energized by fear, you bolt out of its path.

A case like this illustrates that one of the primary functions of emotions is to alert us when something isn't normal. When our ongoing activities are interrupted—as when the barreling car interferes with your thoughts of your friend's wedding—we become physiologically aroused, and this arousal signals us to shift our attention from our current activities to the new, emerging concern (Berscheid, 1983; Frijda, 1986; Mandler, 1975; Simon, 1967; Tomkins, 1970, 1980).

Of course, when we notice the oncoming hunk of steel, we don't become joyous, sad, or amused; none of these states help us take evasive action. Rather, we feel fear—a high-adrenaline state compatible with quick movement. This illustrates an important point: It makes little sense to sound the same emotional alarm every time something unexpected happens. Rather, different emotions accompany different circumstances (Brehm, 1999; Carver & Scheier, 1998; Frijda, 1988; Gonnerman et al., 2000; Higgins, 1996). When our security is threatened, we become fearful; when we learn of an unanticipated low grade, we are saddened; when we commit a social faux pas, we feel agitated; when we hurt a loved one, we experience guilt or shame; and when we get an even bigger raise than expected, we feel joyous.

Attitudes and moods are useful as well. Attitudes enable us to make quick approach/avoidance judgments about things, without having to think too much about them (e.g., Cacioppo, Gardner, & Berntson, 1999; Chen & Bargh, 1999). When seeing a friend, we approach her; upon encountering a burly stranger clad in leather and chains, we avert our eyes and try to pass unnoticed. And moods, often carryover feelings from emotional responses, keep us prepared to deal with our recent and current circumstances (Schwarz & Clore, 1988, 1996). If we hear of layoffs at work, we remain anxiously attuned to signs of being fired; if we've recently been praised by a

Counterfactual thinking *The process of imagining alternative, "might have been" versions of actual events.*

boss, we stay happily alert for other rewards from the company; and if we've recently lost a job, we remain sad and wary of losing other important resources.

In sum, feelings are an essential component of the person (e.g., Carver, Sutton, & Scheier, 2000; Larsen, 2000). They tell us when we're moving nicely toward our goals and when we're not. They also prepare us to deal with our circumstances and make whatever adjustments appear useful. In contrast to popular views suggesting that feelings are irrational sources of human error and misery, we see instead that they are quite functional and necessary (Zajonc, 1998).

Summary

The person is a dynamic combination of motivations, knowledge, and feelings, all of which work with one another to help produce social behavior. Motivation is the energy that moves people toward their goals. Achieving goals sometimes requires considerable attention. With practice, however, strategies for reaching some goals can become automatized, enabling us to devote our limited amount of attention to other tasks. Some goals can be reached only by exerting great willpower. When we need willpower to achieve one goal, however, we will have less of it available in the short term to achieve later goals. Trying *not* to do something may be especially difficult, as the thoughts we suppress may later rebound into awareness with even greater frequency and intensity.

Knowledge is the information we take away from our life experiences and store in memory. We organize this information in mental structures, such as exemplars and schemas. The self-concept is the knowledge we have about ourselves. We come to know ourselves by observing our own behavior (self-perception), observing or imagining how others view us (reflected appraisal), and comparing ourselves to others (social comparison).

Feelings include attitudes, emotions, and moods. Social psychologists have various ways of measuring a person's feelings, including self-report, behavioral observation, and physiological techniques. The way we experience and express our feelings is influenced by our genetic and cultural backgrounds, and the feelings we experience at any one moment are determined by proximate physiological changes and interpretations of our circumstances. One of the primary functions of emotions is to alert us that something isn't normal, so we can shift our attention from our current activities to the new, emerging concern. Attitudes enable us to make quick approach/avoidance judgments about things we encounter, and moods keep us prepared to deal with our recent and current circumstances.

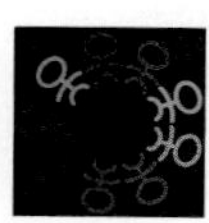

The Situation

What's going to happen to you today? Will you encounter a commuter flicking cigarette butts from his car window, a homeless person seeking a handout, or romance on the television screen? Will the weather be hot, or your neighbors noisy? Will you be insulted by a sales clerk? Complimented by a classmate? Will you interview for a job, attend a religious service, or hear musicians playing at a neighborhood coffeehouse or club? Are you under time pressure to complete a work project or term paper? As you think about your day, you'll notice that you're embedded in your physical and social world. You'll also notice that this world exerts subtle (and sometimes not so subtle) influences on you. You are *situated*, and the situations in which you find yourself greatly affect how you think, feel, and behave.

Consider your physical environment. It may be noisy or serene, clean or polluted, confined or spacious, ugly or aesthetically pleasing. And these features influence you. Noise, for example, is stressful. Long-term exposure to noise via automobile traffic, overhead flights, or poorly designed buildings can harm your health, stifle reading skills, and dampen your motivation to work hard on difficult tasks (e.g., Cohen et al., 1980; Evans, Hygge, & Bullinger, 1995; Maxwell & Evans, 2000). Or consider the interior design of your home. If its layout makes it easy for housemates to intrude on you unpredictably, you are more likely to become psychologically distressed and socially withdrawn than if you lived in a better-designed home (e.g., Evans, Lepore, & Schroeder, 1996). In one interesting experiment, Andrew Baum and Glenn Davis (1980) increased the number of friendships and the frequency of group activity among college dormitory residents merely by changing the ways their living spaces were arranged (see Figure 2.5).

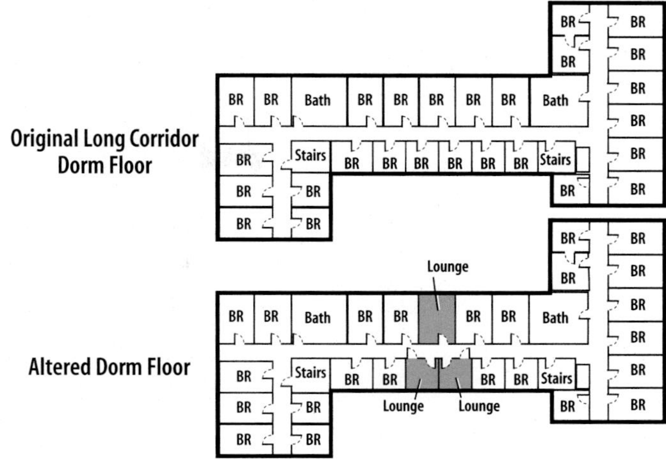

Figure 2.5
Interior design and dormitory life.

By adding just two doors to a long corridor floor, and changing three bedrooms into communal lounges, Andrew Baum and Glenn Davis (1980) altered the social life of dormitory residents: Although the residents on the two floors were initially comparable, those on the altered floor made more friends, were more social, and reported fewer problems with their floormates.

SOURCE: *Baum & Davis (1980, Fig. 1, p. 475)*

Like physical environments, social situations powerfully affect our thoughts, feelings, and behavior. Humans are a highly social species, and much of our time is spent in the presence of others. Indeed, while working on this chapter, one of us thought it would be interesting to count the number of people he encountered that day. The task quickly became overwhelming: The wife and three kids in the morning; the five people on the telephone before leaving home (not counting the computerized salesvoice pushing auto insurance!); the hundreds of folks passed during the morning drive; the hundred or so university students and employees encountered on the walk from car to office; the fourteen email and three phone messages waiting at work; the dozen or so departmental staff and colleagues met while getting the morning's mail; the forty people passed while walking to the library, the fifty or so in the library, and the thirty passed on the walk back. By 10:00 A.M., he had talked and closely interacted with over thirty people and was in a position to influence, and be influenced by, hundreds more. All by 10 A.M.! Try this yourself tomorrow. You'll be amazed.

On the surface, many social encounters appear to be of little importance. After all, how many of the hundreds of people encountered by this book's coauthor really influenced him that morning? More than you might guess, actually. Indeed, we'll see that even subtle, short-lived social encounters can have powerful consequences. People can even influence us when they're not present, as when imagined conversations with a parent or friend lead us to "do the right thing," or when the mere statue of a dictator elicits fear in the citizens of totalitarian nations.

Situations differ from one another in many ways. Some situations are fleeting, as when a billboard advertising fast-food chicken squawks for our attention as we speed by. Other situations last longer, as class periods and weddings do. Some situations are salient and stand out, as when a potential love interest approaches for a phone number. Others envelop us so fully that we barely even recognize them. For example, Americans generally fail to consciously recognize that we live in a democratic society, although this feature of our social context influences us greatly each day. Some situations are familiar and simple, and it seems we've experienced them a thousand times before. Others may be novel, and we feel challenged just to understand what's going on in them. Some situations, like funerals, lead virtually everyone to act the same. Others, like fairs in the park, provide people with flexibility to express their individuality. The range of situations in which we find ourselves is wide, and their character rich and varied. In the sections that follow, we explore the nature of situations more deeply, previewing the types of situational influence we will see throughout the book.

Persons as Situations: Mere Presence, Affordances, and Descriptive Norms

Martin Luther King, Jr., was the leader of the 1963 civil rights March on Washington, and his "I have a dream" speech deeply affected those in the large crowd. When we focus on King, however, we lose sight of the fact that the crowd was also a prominent part of the situation for him. This is the way it is in all social situations, where the influences of people on one another are to some extent reciprocal. In a classroom, your situation is defined prominently by the presence of the teacher, and the teacher's situation is defined prominently by you. When dining with a friend, your situation is defined largely by your friend and your friend's situation is defined largely by you. People are situations for one another.

Mere Presence of Others The very presence of others creates situations that affect how we think, feel, and behave. Consider how the number of students at your high school—whether it had a large versus a small student body—may have influenced your experiences there. Roger Barker and his colleagues (e.g., Barker & Gump, 1964) explored this very issue by comparing thirteen high schools in Eastern Kansas. Even though these schools were generally equivalent to one another, their students differed in interesting ways. To understand why, it helps to recognize that schools, regardless of their size, try to make similar activities and tasks available to their students. For example, even relatively small schools usually have athletic teams, language clubs, choirs, fund-raising activities, student government, and school dances. This means that schools with small student bodies are "undermanned"—they will have a difficult time getting enough students to participate in each activity. In contrast, large schools are often "overmanned"—they have more students than they need for each activity.

Because of this, each student is needed to a greater extent in a small school than in a large school, and so we might expect students in small schools to be more tolerant of differences among students and to try harder to convince and encourage their classmates to participate. In contrast, we might expect students in large schools to be less tolerant of differences and to "veto out" classmates on the social fringes, isolating them and turning them into uninvolved spectators.

Undermanned but committed. *On March 20, 1954, the boys from tiny Milan High School (enrollment 162) defeated in a shocking upset the much larger, big-city team from Muncie Central to win the Indiana state high school basketball championship—a feat so inspirational that it was immortalized by Hollywood in the film "Hoosiers." Although students in "undermanned" schools like Milan High are disadvantaged in some ways, they benefit greatly in others. In particular, they tend to participate in more school activities, have more opportunities for leadership, and take on more challenges.*

The research supported these hypotheses (Barker & Gump, 1964). Moreover, compared to students in the larger schools, students in small schools were more strongly motivated, participated in more activities, had more positions of responsibility, and felt more challenged. And it's easy to see how gaining leadership experience and participating in multiple activities might benefit students when they're older. Although there are advantages of being in larger groups, there are also advantages of being in smaller ones.

Barker's research showed that the mere number of people in one's environment creates different situations. The phenomenon of crowding makes a similar point. Being stuck in a mass of people is a very different situation than being in the midst of two or three. In particular, crowding can lead to stress (e.g., Evans, Lepore, & Allen, 2000; Sherrod, 1974). It can be especially damaging when it persists for a long time, and when life circumstances—such as poverty—provide the crowded people few opportunities to escape (Evans & Saegert,

2000). In a study of children in urban India, for instance, long-term residential crowding was linked to poor academic achievement and behavioral difficulties in school. Why? Crowded living quarters increased conflict between the children and their parents, and this conflict led to academic and behavioral problems outside the home (Evans, Lepore, Shejwal, & Palsane, 1998).

In sum, the number of people around can influence your social behaviors in important ways. We'll see two particularly prominent examples of this in chapter 12: In the first, we'll learn that the mere presence of other people can enhance a person's performance on well-mastered, simple tasks but hurt performance on unmastered, complex tasks. In the second, we'll see that the mere presence of an anonymous crowd can lead people to lose sight of their inner values and standards, and thus lead them to act in antisocial ways.

Affordances: Opportunities and Threats Different people provide us with different things. Your boss at the company picnic provides an opportunity for advancement, the attractive stranger across the quad provides an opportunity for romance, and your social psychology teacher provides an opportunity for improved grades. People are more than just positive opportunities, however. They are also possible threats (Baron & Misovich, 1993). A drunken driver may provide bodily harm, and the new budget-cutting manager at work may provide a severance check. Even the desirable stranger, who provides you an opportunity for romance, also provides the threat of an embarrassing rejection. The opportunities and threats that people and situations provide are called **affordances** (Baron & Boudreau, 1987; Gibson, 1979; McArthur & Baron, 1983).

Affordances are communicated in several ways. They may be transmitted explicitly, as when a big brother tells you he will defend you from the neighborhood bully (thereby affording you protection), or when a partygoer gives you that "come hither" look (thereby affording you romance). They may also be communicated by a person's role or position. Your boss provides an opportunity for advancement *because she is your boss.* Finally, opportunities and threats may be revealed in a person's physical characteristics and actions. For example, adults with babyish facial features—such as large round eyes, high eyebrows, and a small chin—are seen as affording warmth, submissiviness, and honesty (Berry & McArthur, 1986). In a similar vein, rounded body movements convey warmth, whereas angular body patterns convey threat (Aronoff, Woike, & Hyman, 1992).

People are pretty proficient at assessing the potential opportunities and threats others might provide (e.g., Ambady & Rosenthal, 1992; Kenny, Albright, Malloy, & Kashy, 1994; Zebrowitz & Collins, 1997). For instance, on the basis of just facial photographs or short silent videos, people are able to assess with a reasonable degree of accuracy the extent to which others are dominant, extraverted, conscientious, agreeable, aggressive, and sexually available. In one striking study, participants were able to judge accurately the effectiveness of teachers after watching just a two-second soundless film of them in action (Ambady & Rosenthal, 1993). In sum, the people we encounter provide us various kinds of opportunities and threats, which we often discern quite effectively and with little effort.

Descriptive Norms People influence others through their mere presence and through the opportunities and threats they provide. They also wield influence by communicating **descriptive norms**—information about what most people commonly do in a situation. Descriptive norms can help us make the right choices. For instance, if on the first class of your college career your classmates stop talking when the instructor approaches the lectern, there's a pretty good chance you'd do well by ending your conversation, too. Descriptive norms are powerful: Among their other effects, they influence whether we help, express our prejudices, cheat on our taxes, commit adultery, and cooperate with one another (e.g., Buunk & Baker, 1995; Komorita, Parks, & Hulbert, 1992; Latané & Darley, 1970; Steenbergen, McGraw, & Scholz, 1992).

Affordance *An opportunity or threat provided by a situation.*

Descriptive norm *A norm that defines what is commonly done in a situation.*

Descriptive norms usually represent what people really believe or feel. When customers line up outside a dance club, for instance, it usually means they think the place is worth the wait. Sometimes, however, there is a mismatch between the norm suggested by people's behavior and what they actually believe or feel. Consider a classroom lecture in which the teacher presents the material in a confusing way—no doubt a rare occurrence! Despite being confused, you may be reluctant to raise your hand and question the teacher. Why? Perhaps you will feel embarrassed to have the other students think you don't understand. So, hoping to find social validation for the belief that the lecture is dense and confusing, you scan the room for befuddled looks on the faces of your classmates—all the while masking your own befuddlement. Unfortunately, as you scan the room, all you see are faces exhibiting confident understanding. So you keep your hand down, not wanting to embarrass yourself. What you don't realize is that other students are doing the same thing: They, too, are masking their confusion while looking to see if others appear baffled. No one questions the teacher, all because you and the others have hidden your actual beliefs from one another (Miller & McFarland, 1987).

This common occurrence in the classroom is an example of **pluralistic ignorance**—the phenomenon in which people in a group misperceive the beliefs of others because everyone acts inconsistently with their beliefs. In the classroom example, the students are ignorant of the others' confusion because everyone is concealing it. We see, next, that pluralistic ignorance can contribute to a dangerous form of recreation popular on college campuses: binge drinking.

FOCUS ON Social Dysfunction

Descriptive Norms, Pluralistic Ignorance, and Binge Drinking on Campus

Scott Krueger was smart, graduating in the top 3 percent of his high school class and winning a place as an engineering student at the highly selective Massachusetts Institute of Technology. He was athletic and a natural leader, captaining his high school wrestling team and lettering in lacrosse and soccer. He was also a good citizen, volunteering to tutor less gifted students. It comes as no surprise, then, that Scott Krueger was well-liked and considered by many to be a strong role model. He was full of promise, an All-American boy.

His promise would never be realized. In September 1997, just weeks into his freshman year, Scott Krueger lay comatose in a hospital bed. An inexperienced drinker pledging a fraternity, he had consumed enough beer and rum during a mandatory hazing event to raise his blood alcohol level to a toxic 0.41 percent—more than five times the legal limit for drivers in Massachusetts. For three days medical experts heroically used all the miracle-producing technologies at their disposal, but to no avail. His brain never responded. Scott Krueger was dead.

Binge drinking—defined as consuming five or more drinks in a row for men, and four or more in a row for women—is common on college campuses (Wechsler et al., 2000). A recent survey of more than 14,000 students at 119 four-year colleges in thirty-nine states revealed that:

- Nearly 23 percent of students binged three or more times within the two-week period prior to the survey, and another 21 percent binged once or twice during that two-week period.
- Forty-five percent of students binge when they drink.
- Forty-seven percent of students drink to get drunk.
- Students in fraternities and sororities are much more likely to binge drink (79 percent) than are students living in dorms (45 percent) or off campus (44 percent).
- Male students (51 percent) are more likely than female students (40 percent) to binge drink.

Pluralistic ignorance *The phenomenon in which people in a group misperceive the beliefs of others because everyone acts inconsistently with their beliefs.*

The death of an all-American dream. *Scott Krueger's promising future ended at a fraternity hazing event, just weeks into his freshman year. An inexperienced drinker, it's likely that Scott looked to those around him for cues about how much is too much. Sadly, he never found out. Could it be that those around Scott kept their true beliefs about the dangers of binge drinking to themselves, thereby creating a state of pluralistic ignorance that contributed to his death?*

- White students are more likely to binge drink (49 percent) than are students from other ethnic groups (e.g., Hispanics 40 percent, Asians 23 percent, and African Americans 16 percent).
- Frequent binge drinkers are much more likely than nonbingers to skip class, get behind in schoolwork, do things they regret, damage property, get into trouble with police, get hurt or injured, and engage in unplanned, unprotected sexual activity.

Given the amount of drinking on campus, it would be easy for a newcomer and inexperienced drinker—someone like the eighteen-year-old Scott Krueger—to believe that the students on campus are comfortable with heavy drinking. However, research by Deborah Prentice and Dale Miller (1993) suggests that this belief may be misguided. In a series of studies, Prentice and Miller found a troubling demonstration of pluralistic ignorance. Although many of these students said they were uncomfortable with the heavy drinking on campus, they misjudged what other students were thinking. When asked about other students' beliefs, they reported that the average student was comfortable with all the heavy drinking on campus. That is, the typical student erroneously believed he or she was relatively alone in being uncomfortable with the alcohol use on campus. This misperception had especially significant implications for the men in this study: They shifted their own attitude over the course of the semester to be more in line with their mistaken perceptions of others' views. Over time, they became more comfortable with heavy drinking.

Pluralistic ignorance can be dangerous. In the case of alcohol, students may drink more than they're comfortable with. Why? "It must be safe, because others are drinking heavily." This thinking is especially likely to characterize inexperienced drinkers like Scott Krueger, who don't know how much drinking is too much. This heavy drinking then further communicates a message that few students privately endorse—that heavy drinking is safe. Thus students unintentionally encourage others to drink heavily, and the cycle of pluralistic ignorance continues.

Did pluralistic ignorance kill Scott Krueger? We'll never know for sure. There's a good chance, though, it would be convicted of being an active accomplice. ■

Rules: Injunctive Norms and Scripted Situations

Look at the grid in Figure 2.6. Along the top are several behaviors people sometimes do (e.g., talk, laugh, fight). Along the left side are a few situations in which people sometimes find themselves (e.g., own bedroom, public restroom, job interview). In each box, indicate how appropriate the relevant behavior is for the situation. How appropriate would it be, for instance, to talk in a public restroom or to fight in a house of worship?

Figure 2.6
How appropriate would it be to. . .?

In each square of the grid to the right, rate the *appropriateness* of doing the specific behavior in the specific situation. For instance, in the upper-left-hand square, assess the appropriateness of talking on a date, using a scale ranging from 0 ("the behavior is *extremely inappropriate* in this situation") to 9 ("the behavior is *extremely appropriate* in this situation").

What do you see when you look at your ratings? Are some behaviors more (or less) appropriate regardless of the situations in which they're performed? And are some situations more constraining—that is, do they "allow" fewer behaviors—than others?

Adapted from Price and Bouffard (1974), Table 1, p. 581.

Behaviors

Situations	Talk	Laugh	Fight	Cry	Belch	Read
Date						
Restroom						
Job Interview						
Religious Service						
Dorm Lounge						
Own Room						

Richard Price and Dennis Bouffard (1974) had students at Indiana University perform this task for fifteen behaviors in fifteen situations. Several of their findings stand out. First, some behaviors (e.g., talking and laughing) were seen as appropriate across many different situations, whereas others (e.g., fighting) were seen as generally inappropriate. More important, however, was the finding that situations differ in how much they limit what we can do in them. In some situations—like your own room, a park, or a dorm lounge—you are "allowed" to act in lots of different ways. In other situations—like church and job interviews—you are drastically limited in the kinds of behavior you are allowed to do.

Indeed, many situations, such as religious services and job interviews, have "rules" that tell us what we're allowed to do and what we're not. These rules are called **injunctive norms,** and they define what is typically approved and disapproved of in the situation. Injunctive norms are different than descriptive norms: Whereas descriptive norms communicate what people *typically* do, injunctive norms communicate what people *should* (and *should not*) do (Cialdini, Kallgren, & Reno, 1991). One example of an important injunctive norm is the norm of reciprocity, which obligates us to repay others for the favors they do for us. If you scratch my back, it is expected that I'll scratch yours. We'll explore the reciprocity norm in chapters 6 and 9.

Injunctive norms are sometimes *prescriptive*, in that they tell us what we ought to do in the situation (e.g., you should bathe or shower before a first date), and they are sometimes *proscriptive*, in that they tell us what we ought *not* do (e.g., you shouldn't stare at strangers in elevators). Injunctive norms are sometimes made explicit, as when a fine restaurant places a "no smoking" sign in its entryway. Sometimes, however, they are merely implied, because it's assumed that people have learned them (anyone ever seen a "no belching" sign in a nice restaurant?). In nearly all their forms, however, injunctive norms usually control people's behaviors effectively. It would be rare indeed to observe a diner burping loudly in a four-star restaurant.

Injunctive norms contribute to the extent to which particular situations are "scripted." That is, in some situations there seems to be a **script**—a list of events that happen in a predictable order. For instance, think about how people go about getting first dates. John Pryor and Thomas Merluzzi (1985) discovered that the script for getting a date in college goes something like this:

- The people notice each other.
- They get caught staring at each other, and smile.
- They find out about one another from friends.
- They attempt to "accidentally" come across one another again.
- They get a friend to introduce them.
- They begin a conversation, looking for common interests.
- One requests the other's phone number and, *finally*, asks the other out.

Injunctive norm *A norm that describes what is commonly approved or disapproved in a situation.*

Scripted situation *A situation in which certain events are expected to occur in a particular sequence.*

There are also scripts for what to do—and when to do it—on a date (e.g., Rose & Frieze, 1993). There are even scripts for breaking off a romantic relationship (Battaglia, Richard, Datteri, & Lord, 1998). Scripts are so important for some situations that people learn them quite well, cognitively representing them in memory. These mental scripts help us to both coordinate our behaviors with the behaviors of others and avoid violating the injunctive norms of the situation (Abelson, 1981; Forgas, 1979; Schank & Abelson, 1977). Indeed, to understand how frequently we rely on our mental scripts, consider how quickly and easily you notice script violations. Wouldn't you be surprised, for example, if a waitress sat down next to you and started plucking food off your plate, or if a neighbor showed up at a Presbyterian funeral in Maine wearing Bermuda shorts and a Hawaiian shirt?

In sum, injunctive norms and scripts guide people toward appropriate and expected behavior.

Strong Versus Weak Situations

Based on what we've seen so far, some situations are "stronger" than others. Whereas some situations (onrushing trucks, funerals) demand that people behave in particular ways, other situations (nightclubs, own empty living rooms) allow people to behave in many different ways. Let's consider, first, the characteristics of strong situations. They tend to afford a narrower range of opportunities and threats for the people in them. For instance, onrushing trucks provide few opportunities—except, perhaps, for heroism—and one very clear threat (to physical preservation). Strong situations also tend to have obvious injunctive and descriptive norms: For instance, it's very clear which behaviors are appropriate at funerals and which are not—and in case a mourner can't discern the norm from the actions of others, stern stares and sharp elbow nudges will correct the errors. Finally, strong situations are frequently scripted. At funerals, for instance, there's a typical sequence of events, and this sequence usually does not make much room for other activities.

In contrast, consider weak situations. Weak situations tend to afford a relatively wide range of opportunities and threats. Nightclubs, for instance, not only allow for socializing with friends, meeting new people, finding romance, dancing, listening to music, and professional networking, but also for saying something stupid to a friend, being ignored by other clubgoers, getting rejected by a desired love interest, and demonstrating clumsiness on the dance floor. Your empty living room at two o'clock in the morning affords even more possibilities—you can do nearly anything there you want. Weak situations are also characterized by a lack of clear descriptive norms, as the behaviors of others in them will vary greatly. For example, some nightclub visitors may be talking intimately, others drinking heavily, still others unashamedly flirting and flattering, and yet others dancing; this range of behaviors provides social license for an equally wide range of behavior on your part. Weak situations also communicate few injunctive norms: Nightclubs don't have as many "rules" of behavior as do funerals, and your living room has even fewer. Finally, weak situations tend not to be as scripted—in a nightclub, there is more flexibility in what you do and when you do it than there is at a funeral.

Of course, most situations provide the people in them with a reasonable amount of behavioral flexibility, falling somewhere between strong situations like onrushing trucks and weak situations like empty living rooms.

Culture

If you live in China, many of your friends are cousins, aunts, and uncles. What you do is heavily influenced by what they want you to do. In contrast, if you live in Southern California, you have many people you consider friends. Most of them are not members of your family, and the preferences of your relatives have less impact

Table 2.1 Individualistic and collectivistic nations.

Hofstede (1980, 1983) asked more than 80,000 employees of a large, multinational corporation about their work-related goals and values. As the rankings below reveal, Western nations tended to encourage greater individualism, especially compared to nations in Latin America and Asia.

Rank on Individualism	Selected National Cultures	Rank on Individualism	Selected National Cultures
# 1	United States	#32	Mexico
# 2	Australia	#34	Portugal & East Africa region
# 3	Great Britain	#40	Singapore, Thailand, & West Africa region
# 4	Canada & Netherlands	#43	Taiwan
#10	France	#44	South Korea
#15	West Germany	#45	Peru
#20	Spain	#49	Colombia
#22	Japan	#50	Venezuela
#25	Jamaica	#51	Panama
#26	Arab region & Brazil	#52	Ecuador
#30	Greece	#53	Guatemala

SOURCE: *Hofstede (1983), Figure 2, 342.*

on your life decisions. Culture—the beliefs, customs, habits, and language shared by people living in a particular time and place—can influence the circumstances we're in (how much time we spend with relatives) and how these circumstances influence us (whether our relatives strongly influence what we do).

In recent years, social psychologists have become increasingly interested in how cultures influence the ways people think, feel, and behave (e.g., Adamopolous & Kashima, 1999; Fiske, Kitayama, Markus, & Nisbett, 1998; Smith & Bond, 1994). The reason for this is straightforward: Although people from the world's cultures are clearly similar to one another in many ways—after all, we all share a common biology and basic human needs—they also sometimes differ from one another in fascinating ways. Throughout the book, we'll explore both these commonalities and differences as we unravel the mysteries of social behavior.

Much of the research on culture has focused on differences in the extent to which cultures are individualistic versus collectivistic (see Table 2.1) (Chinese Cultural Connection, 1987; Hofstede, 1980, 1983; Triandis, 1989). **Individualistic cultures** (e.g., the United States, Australia, Great Britain) predominantly socialize their members to view themselves as individuals and to prioritize their personal goals. In contrast, **collectivistic cultures** (e.g., Guatemala, South Korea, Taiwan) predominantly socialize their members to view themselves as members of the larger social group and to place the group's concerns before their own. Although cultures vary along other dimensions as well, most research has focused on this individualism–collectivism dimension, particularly as it's captured by North American and European cultures, on the one hand, and East Asian cultures on the other. So, to illustrate how cultures provide a broad situational context for their members, we'll focus in this chapter on the individualism–collectivism dimension.

Individualistic culture *A culture that socializes its members to think of themselves as individuals, and to give priority to their personal goals.*

Collectivistic culture *A culture that socializes its members to think of themselves as members of the larger group, and to place the group's concerns before their own.*

Cultural Affordances Different cultures provide different opportunities for their members. For example, individualistic cultures afford great opportunities for people to assert independence and personal control. One way individualistic cultures do this is by giving their members many choices (Fiske et al., 1998). For instance, one American belief is that each person can become president (or an astronaut, professional athlete, or famous musician): "Just work hard," the story goes, "and you can become whatever you choose to become—all opportunities are open to you." "Have it your way"—the choice is yours—advertises the popular fast food restaurant. Even the simple purchase of milk at the local market provides Americans with a myriad of choices: Whole milk, 2%, 1%, or skim? Regular milk, buttermilk, acidophilus? Lactose-free? Soy-based milk substitute? Calcium-enriched? Chocolate? Strawberry? A gallon, half gallon, quart, or pint? Paper carton or plastic jug? Amazingly, the average supermarket in our hometown of Phoenix carries more than 20,000 different items, whereas the very concept of a *super*market seems ridiculous and unnecessary to those in many collectivistic nations. By providing many choices to their members, individualistic cultures allow people to express their individuality and take personal control for meeting their own needs.

Individualistic cultures also afford easy opportunities for people to enhance themselves—to boost their images in their own eyes and in the eyes of others. Shinobu Kitayama and his colleagues (Kitayama, Markus, Masumoto, & Norasakkunkit, 1997) identified success and failure situations in both the United States and Japan. They then had American students from the University of Oregon and Japanese students from Kyoto University report how such situations would make them feel about themselves. American students tend to look for opportunities to boost their self-regard—we'll learn more about this in chapter 3—and they had no trouble doing this in the "U.S.-made" situations. They were more self-critical, however, in the "Japanese-made" situations. In contrast, Japanese students tend to be self-critical, and they demonstrated this in the Japanese-made situations. They were less self-critical, however, in the U.S.-made situations. So whereas North American situations make it easier for people to self-enhance than to self-criticize, Japanese situations make it easier for people to self-criticize than to self-enhance (Heine, Takata, & Lehman, 2000).

Finally, U.S.-made situations better enable people to exert influence and control over others, a practice consistent with the individualistic orientation of the American culture. In contrast, Japanese-made situations better enable people to relate and adjust to one another—a practice consistent with Japan's greater degree of collectivism (Morling, Kitayama, & Miyamoto, 1999). Different cultures do indeed provide different opportunities for those who live in them.

Culture and Norms "Be all that you can be," sings the catchy U.S. Army recruitment ad. "Don't be wishy-washy," people sneer at those who act inconsistently from one time to another. The norms of individualistic societies communicate a clear message: Stand out from the crowd! Be independent! Be true to your self!

On the other hand, the Malay adage warns that "one drop of indigo spoils the bucket of milk." And the Chinese maxim states that "if one finger is sore, the whole hand will hurt." These East Asian proverbs represent the very different belief of collectivistic cultures—the belief that group members ought to seek harmony and not stand out from others. And just as individualistic societies communicate norms encouraging independent behavior, collectivistic societies communicate norms encouraging interdependence and discouraging independence. In the words of the Japanese injunction, "If a nail sticks up, hammer it down!"

Consistent with this orientation toward harmony and interdependence, people in collectivistic cultures are especially likely to adjust their behaviors to fit the behaviors of others, especially if the others are people they know. Consider the famous "line judging" studies in which participants pick from a set of three lines of different length the one that matches the length of a target line (see chapter 6 for a review of this research). When alone, these length judgments are quite easy—participants almost never make a mistake. But in a group, participants often conform to obviously wrong choices (Asch, 1956). This pattern of conformity occurs in the United States and other individualistic cultures. It is even more prevalent in collectivistic societies (Smith & Bond, 1994).

Cultures may also differ in how they enforce norms. For instance, American parents often reprimand wayward children by withholding rights and privileges—"you're grounded for a week…no TV for you!" In contrast, Japanese and Chinese parents are more likely to threaten the standing of their children's social ties—"I don't like children like you," or "People will laugh at you if you behave like that" (Miller, Fung, & Mintz, 1996; Okimoto & Rohlen, 1988). These different styles of punishment make sense from the perspectives of the different cultures: People in individualistic cultures place great value on personal freedom, so punishments that take away freedom should be especially effective; members of collectivistic cultures place great value on their relationships, so punishments that threaten social ties should be especially effective.

Cultural Scripts We saw earlier that the presence of socially accepted social scripts enable people to better coordinate their behaviors with others (e.g., Forgas, 1979). How might culture influence the use of social scripts?

First, it's possible that social scripts are more pervasive in some cultures than others. For example, do you think situations are more scripted in individualistic societies or in collectivistic societies? You may have guessed that collectivistic societies would script more of their situations, because scripts help coordinate people's behavior, which is very important to cultures which greatly value social harmony. Some research suggests that your intuitions might be correct. For example, there exist formal and ritualized Japanese cultural scripts for events ranging from family meals to piano lessons to social greetings (Hendry, 1993)—events that are usually much less ordered in the United States.

Second, even when cultures script the same events, their contents may differ considerably. Consider funerals. Although funerals in most cultures share common features—disposal of the body, grieving—they also differ in fascinating ways (Matsunami, 1998). In North America, for instance, the typical funeral is a quiet, low-key affair (although there are interesting variations due to ethnicity, religion, and region). People tend to dress conservatively, speak quietly, listen respectfully to

From Britain to Bali: Funeral scripts across cultures. *The cultures in which we live greatly determine the norms we confront. Cultures also influence the contents of many of our most important social scripts, as we see in the intriguingly different funeral rituals of Great Britain and Bali.*

those speaking, and control their public expressions of grief. We might contrast this type of ceremony with the funerals held by the Berawan people of the island of Borneo (Metcalf & Huntington, 1991). The Berawan hold two ceremonies, each lasting several days and involving many people, separated by a period of at least eight months, and sometimes as much as five years. The first ceremony begins immediately after death occurs. The corpse is displayed on a specially built seat for a day or two until all the close kin have seen it, and it is then inserted in a coffin or large jar. When the time comes to perform the second ceremony, guests are summoned from far and wide to attend, and for four to ten days there is a boisterous evening party on the veranda adjacent to the jar or coffin. Drinking and socializing are encouraged, and the general hubbub from the carousings, music, games, and shotgun blasts can be heard half a mile away through the thick forest. Not exactly the type of funeral we're used to seeing!

Culture influences not only the extent to which everyday situations are governed by socially accepted scripts, but also the content of those scripts.

Summary

People are situated in their physical and social environments, and these situations affect thoughts, feelings, and behavior. The mere number of people in our environment can have a great influence, as demonstrated by research on undermanned and crowded situations. Also, different people provide us with different opportunities and threats; we generally discern these affordances effectively and with little effort. People also wield influence by communicating descriptive norms—information about what most people commonly do in a situation. Descriptive norms usually represent what people really believe or feel. When people behave in ways different from what they actually believe or feel, they can create a state of pluralistic ignorance, which can contribute to dangerous behaviors like binge drinking.

Many situations have "rules" that tell us what we're allowed to do and what we're not. These rules are called injunctive norms, and they define what is typically approved and disapproved of in the situation. Moreover, some situations are scripted, in that there is a general sequence of behaviors expected of people in them. Injunctive norms and scripts guide people toward appropriate and expected behavior. Some situations are "stronger" than others. Strong situations tend to afford the people in them fewer opportunities; they tend to have clear injunctive and descriptive norms; and they are more likely to be scripted.

Culture can influence the circumstances we're in and how these circumstances influence us. Individualistic cultures socialize members to view themselves as individuals and to prioritize their personal goals. Collectivistic cultures socialize their members to view themselves as members of the larger social group and to place the group's concerns before their own. Different cultures often provide different opportunities for their members, have different norms, and script their situations differently.

The Person and the Situation Interact

To this point, we have explored the person and the situation separately. As we mentioned in chapter 1, however, if we really want to understand how people think, feel, and behave, we need to consider the person and the situation as they *interact* with one another (e.g., Endler & Magnusson, 1976; Kenrick & Funder, 1988; Lewin, 1951; Mischel & Shoda, 1995; Ozer, 1986; Pervin, 1992; Snyder & Ickes, 1985). Here we consider six types of person-situation interaction.

Different Persons Respond Differently to the Same Situation

Imagine you've agreed to participate in an experiment studying the psychology of sports performance. The experimenter describes the "Michigan Athletic Aptitude Test," a golf-like task that correlates with performance on the physical and mental activities needed in popular sports like basketball, baseball, and hockey. The test involves putting a golf ball down a length of carpet into variable size holes placed in different, often difficult, locations. How do you think you'd do?

As Jeff Stone, Christian Lynch, Mike Sjomeling, and John Darley (1999) discovered, it would depend on your race—whether you're white or black—and on what exactly you're told the test measures. Some participants were told the test assessed natural athletic ability—the ability "to perform complex tasks that require hand–eye coordination." Other participants were told the test measured sports intelligence—the ability "to think strategically during an athletic performance." The instructions to others mentioned nothing about natural ability or athletic intelligence. As Figure 2.7 displays, these two descriptions had quite different effects on white and black participants. When the putting task was described as a test of natural athletic ability, white participants did worse than they normally do, and worse than blacks. In contrast, when the task was described as a test of sports intelligence, black participants did worse than they normally do, and worse than whites.

These findings illustrate one important type of person–situation interaction: *Different people respond differently to the same situation.* Person–situation interactions of this sort can occur because different people are attuned to different parts of a situation, or because the same situation means different things to them. In this experiment, the athletic test's apparent ability to discern natural ability was threatening only to white participants, because a poor performance would support existing stereotypes about whites ("white men can't jump") but not about blacks. In contrast, the test's apparent ability to identify sports intelligence was threatening only to black participants, because a poor performance would support negative stereotypes about blacks ("black men can't think") but not about whites. Because these two situations meant different things to the white and black participants, they responded to them differently.

Figure 2.7 Different people perform differently in the same situation.

Students in a study of "sports psychology" performed a golf-like putting task that was described as a measure of "natural athletic ability" or a measure of "sports intelligence." Control participants received no descriptive label. As the results at right reveal, white participants performed worse than usual when told the task assessed natural ability, whereas black participants performed worse than usual when told the task assessed sports intelligence. Different people respond differently to the same situation.

Data from Stone et al. (1999), Table 1, p. 1217.

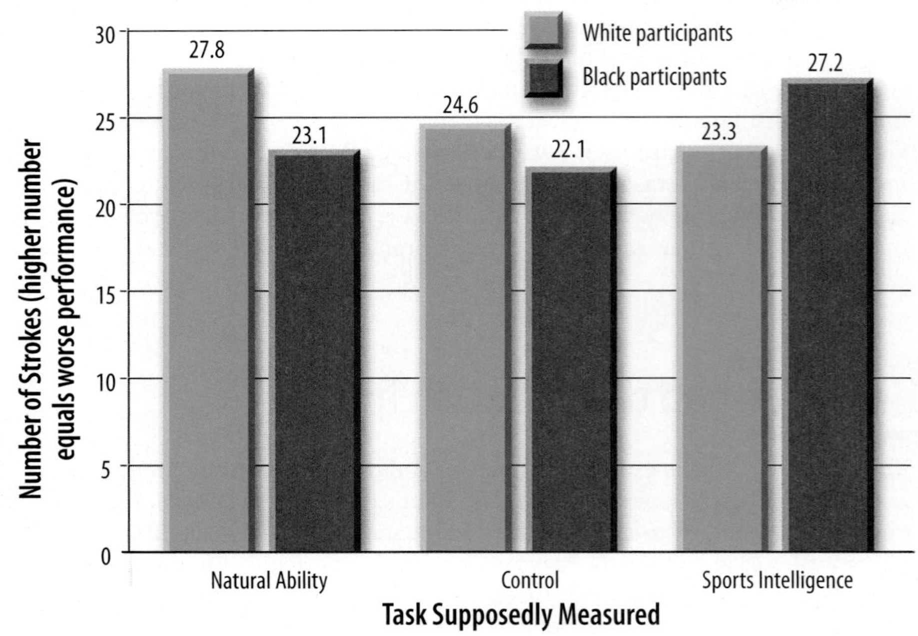

Findings like this indicate that people are better suited for some situations than for others. **Person–situation fit** refers to the extent to which a person and a situation are compatible. Just as keys don't work unless inserted into the correct locks, people can't reach their goals unless their situations provide appropriate opportunities (e.g., Baron & Boudreau, 1987; Pervin, 1992). Indeed, people who find themselves in ill-fitting situations are likely to feel dissatisfied and be unsuccessful. For example, students who see their values as fitting well with the values of their college environment tend to be more satisfied than students who perceive a poorer fit (Pervin, 1967; Pervin & Rubin, 1967; Sagiv & Schwartz, 2000). We see next that the degree of person–situation fit also has important implications for people's work lives.

FOCUS ON **Application**

Person–Situation Fit in the Workplace

Michael Ovitz was the premier deal maker in an industry known for deal making. As the agent of megastars like Tom Cruise and Barbra Streisand, and as the chairman of the Creative Artists Agency, Ovitz could make or break new films by providing or withholding star directors and actors. He was effective and powerful. So when the Walt Disney Company needed to replace its president, it recruited Ovitz as second-in-command to its chairman, Michael Eisner, a business superstar himself. With Eisner and Ovitz, Disney had created an executive Dream Team.

But the dream soon became a nightmare. The characteristics that made Ovitz such an effective power broker—his hands-on style, his ability to take command and control those around him—didn't serve him well in his role as a corporate administrator. Moreover, he wasn't used to taking orders and wasn't very good at it. Ovitz felt constrained in his new job, and was unhappy. Eisner wasn't satisfied with Ovitz's work. So a mere sixteen months after headlines had trumpeted his arrival, Ovitz admitted the mistake and resigned—with Disney's blessing (*Ovitz & Out at Disney*, 1996; *Ovitz, Hollywood Power Broker, Resigns from No. 2 Job at Disney*, 1996). Said Ovitz, "It is important to recognize when something is not working." Despite his savvy, energy, and talent, Michael Ovitz was the wrong person for the job. He didn't fit.

The Greek philosopher Plato, writing in the fourth century B.C., proposed that people should be assigned jobs according to their abilities and personalities. Because different jobs require different skills and personal characteristics, he reasoned, not everyone will be a good candidate for each job. Contemporary theorists agree (e.g., Caldwell & O'Reilly, 1990; Driskell, Hogan, & Salas, 1987; Hackman & Oldham, 1980; Holland, 1997), as do the data: When employees' personal characteristics—interests, goals, abilities, traits—fit with the demands and opportunities of their occupations, employees are happier and more likely to stay in their jobs (e.g., Meir & Hasson, 1982; Mount & Muchinsky, 1978; Spokane, 1985). In one study, first-year graduate business students whose personal characteristics better matched a profile of a "successful young manager" received more job offers upon graduating, one year later. Moreover, four years after graduating these former students were earning higher salaries, were more likely to be working full time, and had changed jobs less frequently (Chatman, Caldwell, & O'Reilly, 1999).

Other research illustrates the value of having the person fit not just the job but also the organization's culture. Organizational cultures vary in many ways, including their emphasis on innovation and risk taking, their competitiveness, and the importance they place on teamwork. Employees who fit their organization's culture tend to be more satisfied, more committed to the company, and less likely to leave for other jobs (e.g., O'Reilly, Chatman, & Caldwell, 1991).

Person–Situation fit *The extent to which a person and a situation are compatible.*

There are clear advantages, then, of creating a good fit between workers and their jobs and workplaces. Individuals can enhance their employment "fitness" and work satisfaction by identifying their personal qualities and seeking job types compatible with them. Workplaces can interview workers and attempt to screen out those whose values don't mesh with the company's. And organizations can attempt to increase fit by socializing new recruits into the workplace's values (Chatman, 1991).

Should Ovitz and Eisner have seen their mistake coming? Perhaps. In any case, this mistake was an expensive one for all parties: Personal reputations were greatly damaged, and Disney was forced to buy out Ovitz with a severance package worth nearly $90 million! All because a single worker was ill-matched to his job and work environment. ■

Situations Choose the Person

Each year, after competing to gain admission into the college of their choice, thousands of students around the world "rush" sororities, fraternities, and dining clubs. They try to win roles in the casts of theater groups, positions in student government, and spots on athletic teams. They compete for entrance into highly desirable classes and majors. They seek recognition in honors societies and deans' lists. And when they graduate, they compete for jobs and admission into graduate school.

As the great behavioral scientist Mick Jagger observed, "you can't always get what you want." Not everybody gets to enter their preferred situations. Students are rejected by their first-choice colleges, they're ignored by popular sororities, and they pound the pavement looking for jobs. This is because *situations choose the person*, another type of person–situation interaction. We'll see in chapter 8, for instance, that women across the globe prefer as romantic partners men who tend to be their age or a bit older (Kenrick & Keefe, 1992). As a result, fourteen-year-old boys will rarely get dates with twenty-one-year-old women. Much as the boys might desire such an opportunity, the women aren't going to choose them. And just as young boys don't get chosen by older women, socially awkward women don't get chosen by desirable sororities, new employees don't get chosen to lead corporations, and lazy students don't get into the best graduate programs.

Indeed, most situations limit "enrollment"—not everyone gets in. Athletic teams have slots for only so many players, and you have time and energy for only so many friends. Because of these limits, even casual situations typically have "entrance requirements" of one sort or another. To demonstrate this for yourself, stop bathing and brushing your hair for two weeks and then try to make new friends!

Persons Choose Their Situations

Just as situations choose people, *people choose their situations*. You may choose to spend next Saturday evening at the local movie megaplex; your roommate may choose the library. I may choose to grab lunch in a fast-food restaurant; you may choose to bring a bag lunch to the park. You may choose to marry and start a family; your best friend from childhood may choose to stay single. Situations don't always just happen *to* us. Rather, we play a large part in determining the situations we end up in.

We choose situations based on the opportunities they provide. If your goal is to forget about your upcoming exam, the movie theater might be a better choice than the library. If you have a migraine headache, a quiet evening at home might be better than the crowded arena rock concert. When different situations provide different opportunities, we tend to choose those whose opportunities appear to fit well with our desires and goals (Buss, 1987; Caspi & Bem, 1990; Emmons, Diener, & Larsen, 1986; Snyder & Ickes, 1985). The movie theater affords distraction, so the person hoping to escape thoughts of the upcoming exam will choose it over the library. The rock concert threatens noise, so the woman hoping to alleviate her headache will choose the living room couch instead.

Different Situations Prime Different Parts of the Person

We suspect that most of you know someone who is *bicultural*—someone who has internalized two cultures and feels like both are "alive within." You may be such a person yourself. Bicultural individuals often say that the two internalized cultures "take turns" influencing their actions (LaFromboise, Coleman, & Gerton, 1993; Phinney & Devich-Navarro, 1997): "At school…everyone was American, including me. Then I would go home in the afternoon and be Mexican again" (quoted in Padilla, 1994, 30).

Ying-yi Hong and her colleagues (Hong, Morris, Chiu, & Benet-Martínez, 2000) proposed that features of the situation *prime*, or make more ready, one cultural orientation over the other. For the Mexican–American student above, the language spoken in the different settings probably primed her different cultural orientations—the Spanish spoken at home by her parents and grandparents made her psychologically Mexican, and the English used at school made her psychologically American. In a nice demonstration of this priming process, Chinese university students in Hong Kong—who tend to possess both Chinese and western self-conceptions—were found to think more collectivistically after viewing Chinese cultural icons (e.g., a Chinese dragon or the Great Wall) and more individualistically after viewing American cultural icons (e.g., the U.S. flag, the U.S. Capitol Building) (Hong, Chiu, & Kung, 1997).

Findings such as these illustrate another type of person-situation interaction: *Different situations prime different parts of the person.* For instance, seeing an attractive person smile at us may prime thoughts of romance, whereas hearing the same person yell at us raises concerns about safety. The situations we're in bring to mind goals and beliefs that influence how we think, feel, and behave—even when we're not in the same situation anymore (e.g., Higgins, 1996). You are likely to interpret and react to an ambiguous collision with a stranger outside the movie theater differently after leaving a slapstick comedy ("How clumsy of us!") versus a blow-em-up action thriller ("He can't do that to me. I'll show him!").

Even features of the situations of which we are unaware can powerfully influence our actions (Wegner & Bargh, 1998). Students in an experiment by John Bargh, Mark Chen, and Lara Burrows (1996) were asked to create four-word sentences out of scrambled sets of five words. By design, some of the sets included words related to rudeness, others included words related to politeness, and others contained words unrelated to rudeness or politeness. After completing the task, the participants left the lab to get the experimenter so they could prepare for a second study. They found the experimenter engaged in a conversation with another subject, and the experimenter continued this conversation until interrupted by the participant (or until ten minutes had passed). Which participants were more likely to interrupt the conversation within the ten-minute time limit: Those previously primed by the rude words, the polite words, or the neutral words?

Changing situation, changing person. *Is the Asian man on the left "the same" person while dining with friends as he is in the classroom? Not likely. As circumstances change, certain features of who we are flow into prominence and others ebb into the background. Different situations prime different parts of the person.*

If you guessed those primed by the rude words, you're correct. Sixty-three percent of these participants interrupted, compared to 38 percent of those in the neutral condition and only 17 percent of those in the polite condition. Even small features of our situations can prime goals, beliefs, feelings, and habits. Because of this, we may act politely in one situation and rudely in another.

On the surface, then, "who we are" changes from situation to situation. In the classroom your "ready self" is motivated to understand and achieve, and beliefs and feelings about yourself as a student come readily to mind. In contrast, in the dorm your ready self may be interested in friendships, and beliefs and feelings about yourself as a friend may dominate. Different situations prime different parts of who we are.

Persons Change the Situation

If a clumsy person runs into a brick wall, the wall stays pretty much the same and only the person is changed. But social situations are rarely brick walls, and each person who enters a situation has the ability to change it. Add an aggressive child to a peaceful playground and it will not remain peaceful for long. Add a competitive person to a relaxed game of touch football at the company picnic and "touch" soon turns to "tackle." Add a socially skilled teacher to an awkward classroom of first-day kindergartners and the kids will soon shed their shyness and begin making friends.

Sometimes people change their situations for the same reason they might choose a situation: To better achieve their goals. A person hoping to clean up a littered neighborhood might recruit others to form a cooperative team, and the kindergarten teacher certainly wants her pupils getting along comfortably.

But people also change their situations inadvertently. Depressed college students don't desire to depress their roommates, but they may—and their roommates may start avoiding them (Joiner & Metalsky, 1996; Strack & Coyne, 1983). A boy who thinks other people dislike him doesn't intend to turn off new acquaintances, but he may—and they may become hostile (Dodge, 1986). And the cheery roommate doesn't necessarily try to raise others' spirits, but she does—and they may start looking for her when needing a boost. We'll see throughout the book many instances of people changing their situations—of leaders increasing the effectiveness of their groups, of lonely people bringing about social isolation, of people with unpopular views changing the minds of others, and the like.

Situations Change the Person

If your parents smile each time you help a stranger, or if you observe them receiving thanks for their volunteer efforts, you are more likely to develop a charitable orientation toward others. Neglectful parents can turn infants with calm dispositions into anxious toddlers. The people we marry can change our views toward politics and social issues. Watching violent pornography can desensitize you to aggression against women. Just as people change their situations, *situations can change people.*

Sometimes this change is obvious: We were one way "then" and we're different now. An infant is overwhelmed by a rambunctious Irish Setter and suddenly comes to fear dogs. But sometimes we are so embedded in a set of situations that they essentially *construct* us from the beginning, shaping our basic human and individual dispositions into the goals, beliefs, and feelings that characterize us today. This is what psychologists and sociologists refer to as **socialization.**

Socialization *The process whereby a culture teaches its members about its beliefs, customs, habits, and language.*

Socialization is the process through which a culture teaches its members about its beliefs, customs, habits, and language. In our discussion of culture, we saw that individualistic cultures socialize their children into adults who strive for independence, personal success, and high self-esteem. In contrast, collectivistic cultures socialize their young into adults who seek interdependence and relationships, group success, and harmony within their groups. How do cultures do this? Cultures have core ideas about what is good, and these values are represented in the customs, norms, politics, and institutions of the culture. For instance, the individualistic value of personal achievement is represented in American law (e.g., as an emphasis on personal property rights), in education (e.g., as the way to enable every motivated child to achieve his or her potential), and in the media (e.g., with its portrayals of entrepreneurs and their successes). And these forces influence the way people interact with one another on a day-to-day basis (e.g., American children are frequently given their own rooms from a very early age, and taught to "stand up for themselves").

Cultures exist at many "levels." In the United States, cultures differ somewhat depending on region (e.g., we'll discuss the "Southern culture of honor" in chapter 10). Cultures also differ between urban and rural areas; big cities tend to foster somewhat less collectivism than do small towns and farm country. Cultures also differ as a function of ethnicity (e.g., Latino-American culture tends to be more collectivistic than Anglo-American culture). Colleges possess their own cultures—a student who spends four years at the Naval Academy is likely to confront different norms, rules, and customs than he would at U.C. Berkeley. And there are even family cultures—the lessons taught in your house will differ somewhat from the lessons taught in your neighbor's. So even within the most individualistic country in the world, there are a wide range of cultural influences that help shape who we become.

Situations, whether they be short-lived or lasting, isolated or linked with related situations, can change who we are.

Summary

The person and the situation interact in various interesting ways to influence what we think, feel, and do (see Table 2.2). Different people respond differently to the same situation. Situations choose the people who enter them. People choose which situations to enter. Different situations bring to readiness different goals, beliefs, and feelings in each person's repertoire. People change their situations. And situations change people.

Table 2.2 Different types of person–situation interactions.

Interaction	Example
• Different persons respond differently to the same situation.	• Some students at your college think it's fun and exciting; others find it dull and nerdy.
• Situations choose the person.	• Your college doesn't admit everyone who wants to enroll.
• Persons choose their situations.	• You may choose to live in a sorority or fraternity; your dormmate may choose to stay in the dorms.
• Different situations prime different parts of the person.	• You may see yourself as studious while in class, but as fun-loving when at a party.
• Persons change the situation.	• An energetic, knowledgeable teacher can turn a quiet, passive classroom into an active, interested one.
• Situations change the person.	• If one student goes off to school at the Naval Academy, while an initially similar friend goes to U.C. Berkeley, they will likely be less similar four years later.

R E V I S I T I N G

The Enigma of an Ordinary and Extraordinary Man

Although he was indeed ordinary in many ways, Dr. Martin Luther King, Jr., arrived in Montgomery, Alabama, with several of the features that would later characterize him as the leader of the Civil Rights Movement. He wanted African Americans treated with respect, a desire instilled in him by his father, who in one instance left a lasting impression on his young son by walking out of a shoe store when the clerk refused to serve him in the "white" section. The younger Martin internalized such lessons, once quitting a job as a laborer because the white foreman insisted on calling him "nigger." We also see in King's youth evidence of another attribute. For even then, he was a natural "ladies man," nicknamed the "Wrecker" as a college student and well-versed in the art of love letters, poetry, and other courtship maneuvers.

King's motivations and beliefs were accompanied by powerful feelings. Even as a boy, he was capable of strong passions, feeling great sympathy for the poor he observed standing in Depression-era bread lines. And he felt such a love and devotion to his grandmother that he twice attempted suicide by leaping from the second floor window of his parents' home—first when he thought mistakenly that she had died and then upon her actual death. This capacity for powerful emotion later revealed itself in King's commitment to his causes and in the force of his speeches. By focusing on the person—on King's motives, beliefs, and feelings—we begin to see the makings of the Martin Luther King, Jr., the world would come to know.

These personal characteristics, however, weren't alone in setting him on his course. First, he was in the right place at the right time. Rosa Parks, the brave woman who placed herself at great personal risk by violating Montgomery's segregation ordinance, was the secretary of the local NAACP, on whose board the young Martin Luther King, Jr., served. His connection to her put him in close contact with the local controversy. Moreover, as a newcomer to town, he must have felt flattered by the request to lead his community in the boycott of the bus system. And it would have been difficult for him to refuse the request, given the local expectations that preachers be community leaders.

But these features of the situation merely placed him in an early position of leadership. They certainly didn't guarantee his success. Indeed, King's meteoric rise almost never was. His speech to announce the boycott—a speech that would set the tone for the protest, for better or for worse—began tentatively, with little of the power for which he later became known. Energized by years of inequality and discrimination, however, his audience would not allow such a performance—it would not allow King to fall short of its lofty expectations. The audience *needed* a big moment, and its responsiveness and passion pulled it from him. He began to soar:

> And you know, my friends, there comes a time when people get tired of being trampled over by the iron feet of oppression.... There comes a time, my friends, when people get tired of being thrown across the abyss of humiliation, where they experience the bleakness of nagging despair.... There comes a time when people get tired of being pushed out of the glittering sunlight of life's July, and left standing amidst the piercing chill of an Alpine November....

And the crowd's thunder drowned out King's words. The situation had demanded from King his best. King's gift of oratory took over, further energizing the crowd. The synergy between King and the people was electric, carrying all to inspirational heights and providing both King and the others the belief that he was capable of leading. The situation had chosen him. A confident man, with strong convictions, King chose to accept. King was changed into a leader, and he, in turn, gave the people increased hope.

The person and situation continued to interact throughout the boycott. The people's enthusiasm and favorable endorsements fortified him when his faith and confidence began to waver. The police department's decision to jail him for a bogus speeding violation increased his visibility and credibility, as did the firebombing of his home. And the common people's willingness to sacrifice made the boycott a success, leading to the *Time* magazine cover story on King that elevated him to national prominence.

Dr. Martin Luther King, Jr., brought to his situation a powerful commitment to egalitarian principles, the nonviolent style of protest espoused by Gandhi, and magnificent oratorial skills. The situation provided him with self-confidence and energy and bestowed upon him a wealth of opportunity. His truly extraordinary accomplishments were brought about not merely by the strength of his personality but by the interaction of that personality with the powerful situational forces in his life. Like all of us, he had his personal strengths and weaknesses. Like all of us, his actions—and his character—were shaped by the situations he encountered. And like all of us, he, in turn, shaped his world. This is the essence of social psychology.

We have thus taken the first step of our journey to understand the fascinating world of social behavior. The following chapters pick up where this one leaves off—exploring in greater depth the thought processes and behaviors people use to traverse their social landscapes.

CHAPTER 2

Summary

The Person

1. The person is a dynamic combination of motivations, knowledge, and feelings, all of which work with one another to help produce social behavior.
2. Motivation is the energy that moves people toward their goals.
3. Achieving goals sometimes requires considerable attention. With practice, however, strategies for reaching some goals can become automatized, enabling us to devote our limited amount of attention to other tasks.
4. Goals can be difficult to achieve. Some can be reached only by exerting great willpower. When we need willpower to achieve one goal, however, we will have less of it available in the short term to achieve later goals. A goal of *not* doing something may be especially difficult to achieve, as the thoughts we suppress may later rebound into awareness with even greater frequency and intensity.
5. Knowledge is the information we take away from our life experiences and store in memory. We organize this information in mental structures, such as exemplars and schemas.
6. The self-concept is the knowledge we have about ourselves. We come to know ourselves by observing our own behavior (self-perception), observing or imagining how others view us (reflected appraisal), and comparing ourselves to others (social comparison).
7. Feelings include attitudes, emotions, and moods. Social psychologists have various ways of measuring a person's feelings, including self-report, behavioral observation, and physiological techniques.
8. The way in which we experience and express our feelings is influenced by our genetic and cultural backgrounds. We partially learn how to experience and express our feelings through classical conditioning, instrumental learning (operant conditioning), and observational learning. The feelings we experience at any one moment are determined by proximate physiological changes (e.g., facial feedback) and interpretations of our circumstances.
9. Feelings are extremely functional. Emotions signal us that something isn't normal, so we can shift our attention from our current activities to the new, emerging concern. Attitudes enable us to make quick approach/avoidance judgments about things

we encounter. And moods keep us prepared to deal with our recent and current circumstances.

The Situation

1. People are situated in their physical and social environments, and these situations affect their thoughts, feelings, and behavior.
2. The number of people in our environment can have a great influence. For example, students in small, undermanned high schools were more strongly motivated, participated in more activities, had more positions of responsibility, and felt more challenged.
3. Different situations provide us with different opportunities and threats. These are called affordances, and we often detect them effectively and with little effort.
4. People communicate descriptive norms—information about what most people commonly do in a situation—and these help us make correct choices about what to do in new situations. Descriptive norms usually represent what people really believe or feel. When people behave in ways different from what they actually believe or feel, they can create a state of pluralistic ignorance, which can contribute to dangerous behaviors like binge drinking.
5. Many situations have "rules" that tell us what we're allowed to do and what we're not. These rules are called injunctive norms, and they define what is typically approved and disapproved of in the situation. Moreover, some situations are scripted, in that there is a general sequence of behaviors expected of people in them. Injunctive norms and scripts guide people toward appropriate and expected behavior.
6. Some situations are "stronger" than others. Strong situations afford the people in them fewer opportunities, have clear injunctive and descriptive norms, and are more likely to be scripted. Weak situations afford many opportunities, have less clear norms, and are less likely to be scripted.
7. Culture can influence the circumstances we're in and how these circumstances influence us. Individualistic cultures socialize members to view themselves as individuals and to prioritize their personal goals. Collectivistic cultures socialize their members to view themselves as members of the larger social group and to place the group's concerns before their own.
8. Different cultures often afford somewhat different opportunities for their members. They may also have different norms, and script their situations differently.

The Person and the Situation Interact

1. The person and the situation interact in various interesting ways to influence what we think, feel, and do.
2. Different people respond differently to the same situation. When a person "fits" well with the situation, he or she is likely to be more satisfied and effective.
3. Situations choose the people who enter them; not everyone can be in the situations of their choice.
4. People can often choose which situations to enter, and they pick those they believe provide the best opportunities to reach their goals.
5. Different situations prime different goals, beliefs, and feelings in each person's repertoire.
6. People change their situations.
7. Situations change people.

CHAPTER 2

Key Terms

Affordance *An opportunity or threat provided by a situation.*

Attention *The process of consciously focusing on aspects of our environment or ourselves.*

Attitude *A favorable or unfavorable evaluation of a particular person, object, event, or idea.*

Automaticity *The ability of a behavior or cognitive process to operate without conscious guidance once it's put into motion.*

Classical conditioning *The process through which people associate new objects or events with feelings about previously experienced events.*

Collectivistic culture *A culture that socializes its members to think of themselves as members of the larger group, and to place the group's concerns before their own.*

Counterfactual thinking *The process of imagining alternative, "might have been" versions of actual events.*

Descriptive norm *A norm that defines what is commonly done in a situation.*

Emotion *A relatively intense feeling characterized by physiological arousal and complex cognitions.*

Exemplar *A mental representation of a specific episode, event, or individual.*

Goal *A desired outcome; something one wishes to achieve or accomplish.*

Individualistic culture *A culture that socializes its members to think of themselves as individuals, and to give priority to their personal goals.*

Injunctive norm *A norm that describes what is commonly approved or disapproved in a situation.*

Instrumental learning (operant conditioning) *The process through which people learn by being rewarded or punished.*

Mood *A relatively long-lasting feeling that is diffuse and not directed toward a particular, single target.*

Motivation *The force that moves people toward desired outcomes.*

Motive *A high-level goal fundamental to social survival.*

Observational learning *The process through which people learn by watching others get rewarded or punished.*

Person–Situation fit *The extent to which a person and a situation are compatible.*

Pluralistic ignorance *The phenomenon in which people in a group misperceive the beliefs of others because everyone acts inconsistently with their beliefs.*

Reflected appraisal process *The process through which people come to know themselves by observing or imagining how others view them.*

Schema *A mental representation capturing the general characteristics of a particular class of episodes, events, or individuals.*

Scripted situation *A situation in which certain events are expected to occur in a particular sequence.*

Self-concept *A mental representation capturing our views and beliefs about ourselves.*

Self-esteem *Our attitude toward ourselves.*

Self-perception process *The process through which people observe their own behavior to infer internal characteristics such as traits, abilities, and attitudes.*

Social comparison *The process through which people come to know themselves by comparing their abilities, attitudes, and beliefs with those of others.*

Socialization *The process whereby a culture teaches its members about its beliefs, customs, habits, and language.*

Willpower *The self-control strength used to overcome counterproductive impulses to achieve difficult goals.*

chase

CHAPTER 3

Social Cognition: Understanding Ourselves and Others

Portraits of Richard Nixon

It was the spring of 1994, and the world contemplated the life of Richard Milhous Nixon, dead at the age of eighty-one. Nixon's contentious political career had been a full one, spanning five decades. He was elected to two terms as president of the United States, winning the second by a landslide. He had served in the House of Representatives, in the Senate, and for two terms as vice-president. He had played an active role in the search for U.S. Communists during the 1940s and 1950s. He had expanded, and then ended, the highly controversial Vietnam War. He had opened the relationship between the United States and mainland China. In the wake of the Watergate scandal—in which he had attempted to conceal the White House role in the bungled break-in at the offices of the Democratic National Committee—he had resigned from office in disgrace, the only president ever to do so. Later, he slowly resurrected his political life, molding for himself a respected role consulting with U.S. leaders on foreign policy issues.

Nixon's the One. *But which one? The deceiving, unscrupulous one as seen by his detractors, or the intelligent, visionary one as seen by his supporters? How can people view the same man so differently?*

Those were the facts. The facts alone, however, aren't enough to explain the vast differences in how people viewed Richard Nixon. Consider, for instance, these commentaries on his life:

> He gave of himself with intelligence and devotion to duty and his country owes him a debt of gratitude for that service.... His resilience and his diligent desire to give something back to this country and to the world provide a lesson for all of us about maintaining our faith in the future. *Bill Clinton (1994), then-U.S. President*

> He was an unscrupulous demagogue eager to inflame the fear of communism to advance his ambitions for national prominence and power.... [He] extended the war illegally and secretly.... even as he denied it to Congress and the public.... He violated his constitutional oath and broke a number of laws. *George McGovern (1994), former U.S. Senator and presidential candidate*

> In the conduct of foreign policy, Richard Nixon was one of the seminal presidents.... Richard Nixon ended a war. And he advanced the vision of peace of his Quaker youth. He was devoted to his family, he loved his country and he considered service his honor. *Henry Kissinger (1994), former U.S. Secretary of State*

> Most politicians will deceive and dissemble on occasion, but Nixon was a giant. When he felt the need to lie to the American people, he put his whole body into it.... He was merely self-indulgent, luxuriating in the petty schemes that are the poisonous logic of a paranoid mind. *William Greider (1994), political commentator*

> To tens of millions of his countrymen, Richard Nixon was an American hero—a hero who shared and honored their belief in working hard, worshipping God, loving their families and saluting the flag.... Strong, brave, unafraid of controversy, unyielding in his convictions, living every day of his life to the hilt, the largest figure of our time whose influence will be timeless. That was Richard Nixon. *Bob Dole (1994), then-U.S. Senate Majority Leader*

> He could shake your hand and stab you in the back at the same time. He lied to his friends and betrayed the trust of his family.... He was a swine of a man and a jabbering dupe of a president.... Richard Nixon was an evil man.... He was utterly without ethics or morals or any bedrock sense of decency.... He was a cheap crook and a merciless war criminal.... By disgracing and degrading the Presidency of the United States, by fleeing the White House like a diseased cur, Richard Nixon broke the heart of the American Dream. *Hunter S. Thompson (1994), political commentator*

Does his nation owe him a debt of gratitude for his selfless service, as some have suggested? Or did he defile his country by disgracing and degrading the Office of the President? Should we thank and applaud him for ending the war? Or should we instead remember him as a war criminal, responsible for tens of thousands of deaths? Was he a God-worshipping, flag-saluting hero? Or was he simply a crook, lacking any sense of morality or decency? Can it be possible these various commentators are really talking about the same person?

For nearly half a century, Richard Nixon was in the spotlight for all to observe and judge. Given this very public presence, we might guess that his many observers would have agreed on what he was like. As the comments above reveal, however, people's thoughts about Nixon diverged wildly. Indeed, even the members of his closest staff, who worked with him each day, painted contrary cognitive portraits of him. How could this be? If the impressions we form of others aren't based solely on who they are, what other factors play a role?

In this chapter, we seek to answer questions like this one as we explore the arena of **social cognition**—the ways people think about themselves and those around them.

The Social Thinker

People think about their social world. A lot. They wonder why two children would gun down their classmates in a schoolyard or why a teacher would place her own life in death's way to save others. They contemplate how to get a date with an interesting neighbor or how to win a promotion at work. They wonder, too, about themselves—about who they are and what makes them tick. Although people often think to satisfy their curiosity, much of social thought is practical. Thinking is for doing (Fiske, 1992; James, 1890). As we discussed in chapter 2, people think so that they might better attain their goals.

Most social psychologists give cognition a central role in determining behavior. They're interested not only in people's actions but also in what goes on in the mind—in that "black box" of cognition standing between the social events people encounter and their responses to them. Will you find a particular advertising campaign persuasive? It depends on what parts of the ads catch your attention, what the ads lead you to think about as you view them, and so on. Will you join with classmates to form a study group? It partially depends on whether you believe that they're smart enough to make it worth your while. How you think about your social world influences how you behave toward it.

Four Core Processes of Social Cognition

By now, most of you have had a couple of weeks to observe and interact with your social psychology professor. What do you think of him or her? How did you arrive at this impression? To begin answering questions like these, we need to consider the four core processes of social cognition: attention, interpretation, judgment, and memory.

Attention: Selecting Information What information do you have about your teacher? We learned in chapter 2 that attention—the process of consciously focusing on aspects of one's environment or oneself—is limited. People can only pay attention to a tiny fraction of the information available to them. Because different people expose themselves to different information, and because people select the information they pay attention to, you'll base your impression of your professor on a somewhat different set of information than will your classmates. Some of you have been to each lecture or class discussion, have visited your professor during office hours, and have observed him or her around campus. Some of you, in contrast, know nothing of your instructor beyond what seems apparent in the classroom. Of course, with attention to different information comes the possibility of different impressions (e.g., McArthur, 1981; Sanbonmatsu, Akimoto, & Biggs, 1993; Taylor & Fiske, 1975, 1978). If you missed the class period during which your professor talked emotionally about his new baby, you might not think of him as warm, though other students might. Throughout this chapter, we'll explore how features of the person and situation influence what we pay attention to and, thus, the impressions we form of ourselves and others.

Social cognition *The process of thinking about oneself and others.*

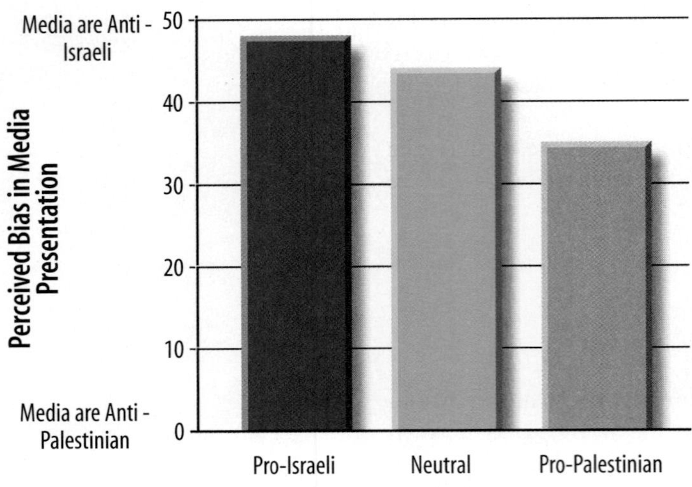

Figure 3.1
Is media bias in the eye of the beholder?

In a study conducted by Roger Giner-Sorolla and Shelley Chaiken (1994), pro-Israeli and pro-Palestinian students differed considerably in their perceptions of media presentations of the Israeli–Palestinian conflict. Compared to neutral students, pro-Israeli students thought the media was biased against Israelis, whereas pro-Palestinian students thought the identical media portrayals were biased against Palestinians. Different people may interpret the same events quite differently.

SOURCE: *Adapted from Giner-Sorolla & Chaiken (1994), Table 1.*

Interpretation: Giving Information Meaning Once we pay attention to something, we still need to determine what that information *means*—we still need to interpret it. Does your professor's upbeat style reflect a natural enthusiasm, or is it just contrived to make you more interested in the course material?

Most social behaviors can be interpreted in multiple ways. In the aftermath of Richard Nixon's death, for example, political liberals thought the media were too kind in their eulogies, whereas conservatives thought that the same media and the same eulogies were inappropriately harsh. We (the authors of this book) shouldn't have been surprised, then, that some of the professors who read an early draft of this chapter exhibited the same tendency—a few chiding us for making Nixon look too good and others criticizing us for being unfairly negative! Diverging interpretations like this aren't unusual. Strong advocates of social and political causes often believe that the mainstream media favor the opposing view (Perloff, 1989; Vallone, Ross, & Lepper, 1985). In one study by Roger Giner-Sorolla and Shelley Chaiken (1994), individuals having pro-Israeli or pro-Palestinian views watched identical news broadcasts of an Israeli–Palestinian confrontation but interpreted these broadcasts quite differently. Consistent with the researchers' expectations, pro-Israeli students thought the broadcasts favored the Palestinians, while pro-Palestinian students thought these same presentations favored the Israelis (see Figure 3.1). Throughout this chapter, we'll encounter various factors that influence how people interpret events.

Judgment: Using Information to Form Impressions and Make Decisions We gather and interpret information because we need to form impressions of people or make important decisions. We want to determine how helpful a teacher will be outside of class, whether a new acquaintance will become a trustworthy friend, or which sales strategy will work best on an unfamiliar customer. Sometimes, the decision process is straightforward and simple. For example, if you want to know how tall your professor is, you could stand him or her against a wall and pull out your tape measure. Social impressions and decisions tend to be more difficult, however, because they usually involve a fair amount of uncertainty. For instance, we rarely have all the information we'd like before forming an impression (e.g., "Has my professor been a good advisor to other students?"). Moreover, it's often unclear how to weigh the information we do have (e.g., "Is it more important to me that he or she give me a candid assessment of my chances of getting into grad school or that he or she boost my confidence so I'll work harder to get there?"). As a result, many of our impressions and decisions are "best guesses"—the best we can do given the information we have to work with. In this chapter, we explore how our goals, cognitive efforts, and previous experiences influence the social judgment process.

Memory: Storing Information for Future Use If we pay enough attention to an event, the event and our impression of it become represented in memory. Memories can directly contribute to new judgments, as when a recalled friendly encounter with a professor encourages you to seek advice from him or her in the future. Memories can also indirectly influence our impressions and decisions by affecting what we pay attention to and how we interpret it, as when the remembered encounter increases the likelihood that you will interpret future interactions with your professor as supportive. Indeed, memory influences on judgment are often *implicit*—memory can work its effects even when people fail to recognize its influence (e.g., Greenwald & Banaji, 1995; Nisbett & Wilson, 1977). Memories can even affect judgments when they are activated subliminally, as we saw in chapter 2.

To understand how people think about themselves and others, then, we need to take into account certain fundamental cognitive processes—attention, interpretation, judgment, and memory. Considering these processes may help explain the widely divergent judgments people formed about Nixon. His supporters focused their attention on foreign policy successes such as his trip to China, interpreted his long political career as reflecting his desire to serve, and were less likely to recall his failures. In contrast, Nixon's detractors focused on the debacle of Watergate, attributed his political career to selfish aims, and were less likely to bring to mind his successes. Throughout this chapter, we will return to these four processes, exploring the ways they (1) are influenced by our goals, knowledge, and feelings, and (2) influence what we think of ourselves and others.

The Goals of Social Cognition

Social thought must be flexible. It makes little sense, for instance, to devote as much mental effort to a passing stranger as to a romantic partner. Fortunately, our thought processes are well equipped to adapt to a wide range of circumstances (Higgins & Sorrentino, 1990; Kunda, 1990; Pittman, 1998; Pyszczynski & Greenberg, 1987). You'll see, for instance, that sometimes people want to be more mentally efficient, hoping to form impressions and make decisions that are both "good enough" and relatively effortless. At other times, people want to think well of themselves, wishing to boost or protect their self-image. And sometimes people want to be quite accurate in their judgments, hoping to avoid potentially costly errors and mistakes. Because these goals are very different, different "styles" of thought are sometimes needed to achieve them. People are *motivated tacticians:* As their goals change, they adopt different styles of thought (Fiske & Taylor, 1991). In the remainder of this chapter, we will explore how such goals influence the ways people think about themselves and others.

Summary

People's actions are determined largely by their social cognition—by how they think about the social events and people they encounter. There are four fundamental social-cognitive processes: attention, interpretation, judgment, and memory. *Attention* is the process of consciously focusing on features of the environment or oneself. By influencing the very information we take in, attention plays a large role in determining what we remember, what impressions we form, and what decisions we make. *Interpretation* is the process through which we give meaning to the events we experience. Because most events can be interpreted in multiple ways, the same event may lead different people to react to it quite differently. *Judgment* is the process through which we use the interpreted information available to us to form impressions and make decisions. And, with *memory*, we store and retrieve our experiences for use as guides to attention, interpretation, and judgment. Finally, our thought processes are influenced by several goals, including the desires to conserve mental effort, to manage self-image, and to gain accurate understanding.

Conserving Mental Effort

October 1973 was a difficult month for President Nixon. Spiro Agnew, his vice president, had been charged with taking bribes and was preparing to resign. Congress was restricting presidential powers. And a war broke out unexpectedly in the Middle East, raising the possibility of nuclear confrontation between the United States and

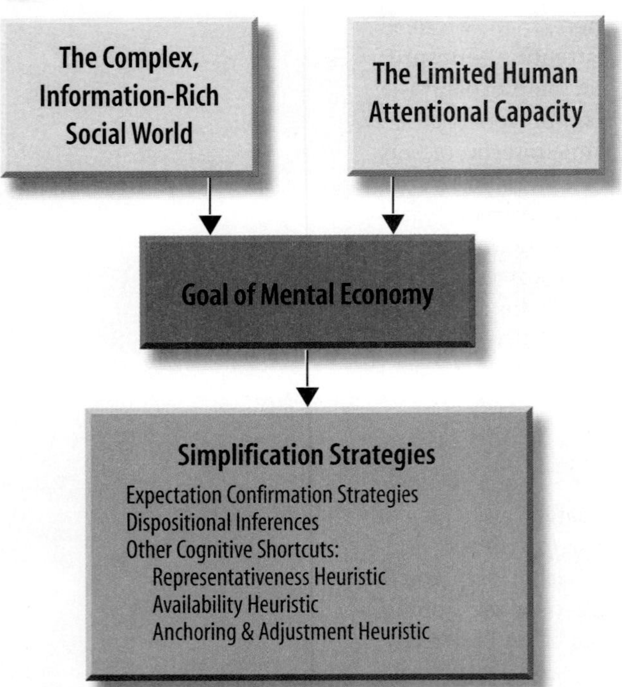

Figure 3.2
Keeping it simple.

The information-rich social environment, together with our limited attentional resources, create the need for simplifying, low-effort cognitive strategies that nonetheless let us form impressions and make decisions that are "good enough."

the Soviet Union. In the midst of all this, Archibald Cox, the special prosecutor Nixon had appointed to investigate accusations of a Watergate cover-up, demanded in court that Nixon relinquish audiotapes of White House conversations. Nixon viewed Cox's demands as an unconsitutional challenge to the presidency and had him fired. Nixon was stunned by the intensity of the public outcry that followed his decision (Nixon, 1978): Several of Cox's superiors resigned in protest; much of America—Republican and Democrat alike—was outraged; and Congress almost immediately began the process of impeachment. How could such an astute politician misjudge public reaction so badly?

To answer this question, consider the following dilemma: Given a limited attention capacity, how do you deal with the huge mass of information available in any single moment? Recall from chapter 2 that we can think consciously about at most a few things at once; we don't have the brainpower to do otherwise. This wouldn't be a limitation, of course, if we happened upon people and events slowly and sequentially—we could thoughtfully consider each new situation and, when satisfied, move on to the next. Unfortunately, the social world is not only information rich but also relentless in its pace. Social events don't wait for an invitation; they come upon us rapidly and with little concern for our present capacity to deal with them carefully.

Because of this, we need cognitive strategies that lead to effective decisions even when we don't have the mental resources for effortful, "rational" processes. We need cognitive strategies that free up scarce mental resources for other important tasks. In short, we need *simple* ways of understanding the world—strategies that help us make "good enough" judgments while expending only a minimal amount of mental effort (e.g., Gigerenzer & Goldstein, 1996). We explore several such strategies next (see Figure 3.2).

Expectation Confirmation Strategies

Our beliefs about the world function as *expectations*—they tell us what we may expect from the people and situations around us, thus saving us the effort of having to evaluate each new situation from scratch. Upon learning that a classmate belongs to a fraternity, you probably already "know" quite a bit about the person, even whether you think you'll like him. This knowledge prepares you to think about your classmate without having to expend effort to learn about the specific individual behind the label (Sedikides & Skowronski, 1991). Indeed, expectations such as these are so useful that we are reluctant to see them proven wrong. As a result, we often think about people and events in ways that maintain our expectations, thus enabling us to keep our existing views of the world relatively simple (e.g., Darley & Fazio, 1980; Miller & Turnbull, 1986; Rosenthal, 1994; Snyder, 1984).

First, people pay special attention to behaviors and events relevant to their expectations, and often even seek information that confirms their expectations (e.g., Trope & Thompson, 1997). Believing that a classmate belongs to a fraternity, you may be especially likely to notice when he arrives late to class—a characteristic likely compatible with your beliefs about fraternity brothers.

Second, we tend to interpret ambiguous events and behaviors in ways that support our expectations (e.g., Bruner, 1957; Higgins, Rholes, & Jones, 1977; Sinclair, Mark, & Shotland, 1987; Srull & Wyer, 1979). In a classic study by Harold Kelley (1950), some students were led to believe that a substitute instructor would be generally warm and friendly, while others in the same class were led to believe that he would be somewhat cold and distant. After the class period, students evaluated the teacher. Students led to expect that the professor would be nice formed quite favorable impressions of the teacher. In contrast, students led to expect that the professor would be unfriendly formed significantly less favorable impressions of the teacher. Because both sets of students viewed the same lecture, it appears that their expectations for the instructor biased the way they interpreted his actions. Findings like these reveal that we tend to interpret ambiguous events and behaviors in ways that support our expectations. You might thus presume that the tired-looking fraternity brother spent last night and a good bit of the early morning partying, as opposed to studying diligently for the upcoming midterm.

Third, we tend to remember people and events that are consistent with our expectations (e.g., Hirt, McDonald, & Erikson, 1995). Indeed, you would probably better recall the time a fraternity brother boasted of his passion for cheap beer than the time he revealed his longings for jamocha almond fudge ice cream. Participants in one study watched a videotape of a woman during an informal birthday celebration. Some were told the woman was a librarian, whereas others were told she was a waitress. They then received a surprise memory test. Consistent with their occupation-based expectations, participants in the "waitress" condition were likely to recall that she ate hamburgers and owned a bowling ball, whereas those in the "librarian" condition were likely to remember that she ate a salad and played the piano (Cohen, 1981). Although people sometimes also have very good memory for events inconsistent with their expectations—because such events can receive lots of attention—they almost always have a strong memory for events consistent with their expectations (e.g., Hirt, Erickson, & McDonald, 1993; Rothbart, Evans, & Fulero, 1979; Sherman & Frost, 2000; Stangor & McMillan, 1992).

It's not surprising, then, that expectations are so resistant to change. If people having unfavorable views toward fraternity men take special note each time a fraternity member arrives late to class, attribute his weariness to late-night partying, and recall with great clarity each boorish act, they have little reason to alter their negative beliefs. Expectations, then, not only provide a cognitively inexpensive way of understanding the people and events around us, but they also validate their own use and greatly simplify our cognitive life (Bodenhausen & Wyer, 1985; Macrae, Milne, & Bodenhausen, 1994; Macrae, Stangor, & Milne, 1994). Moreover, when our expectations are accurate, as they often are, using them enables decision making that is not only efficient but also correct (Jussim, 1991).

Regrettably, our expectations are sometimes inaccurate. For instance, although people's common stereotypes of fraternity men may indeed possess a substantial kernel of truth, they nonetheless fail to represent many fraternity members. Some fraternity members actually go on to get Ph.D.s and become second authors of social psychology textbooks. Unfortunately, acting upon inaccurate expectations can have serious consequences, as we see next.

FOCUS ON Social Dysfunction

The Self-Fulfilling Prophecy

In the early 1930s, thousands of U.S. banks went out of business—many because of irresponsible or unethical financial practices—losing billions of dollars of their customers' money. Not surprisingly, depositors in other locales became jittery, fearing that the same could happen to them. Rumors of impending bank failures were common. In some cases, hordes of customers rushed to remove their savings, a move that proved disastrous. Well-managed, responsible banks don't keep their deposits locked away in vaults but rather recirculate this money throughout the community in the form of long-term investments such as home mortgages and business loans. As a result, they're unable to meet concentrated requests for large cash withdrawals. These fearful stampedes of depositors wishing to close their accounts overwhelmed even those banks that

Getting what we expect: The self-fulfilling prophecy. *Believing that their "opponents" are likely to be competitive and unreasonable, negotiators may behave more competitively and unreasonably themselves in an attempt to avoid being exploited. Little do they know, however, that their own actions may elicit the very rigidity they initially feared. Erroneous expectations sometimes create self-fulfilling prophecies.*

were thriving and solvent the day before. Banks went broke in hours, and late-arriving depositors lost their life savings. Bank customers, in their panic, unwittingly made their initially unfounded fears a reality.

With this and other examples, sociologist Robert Merton (1948) introduced the concept of the **self-fulfilling prophecy,** in which inaccurate expectations lead to actions that cause those expectations to come true. Children erroneously expected by their teachers to be bright may perform better in school because teachers are warmer to them, challenge them with more material, and interact with them more (e.g., Harris & Rosenthal, 1985; Rosenthal & Jacobson, 1968). Job applicants inaccurately expected to be unqualified may perform less well because interviewers ask them less favorable questions, conduct shorter sessions, and "leak" negative nonverbal behaviors (Dipboye, 1982; Neuberg, 1989; Word, Zanna, & Cooper, 1974). Bargainers mistakenly expected to be competitive may actually *become* competitive because they are treated more antagonistically (Kelley & Stahelski, 1970). People in everyday social encounters who are inappropriately believed to have "cold" personalities may exhibit less warmth because they are treated more distantly (Ickes, Patterson, Rajecki, & Tanford, 1982). By acting on our inaccurate expectations, we may make them true.

When mistaken expectations are negative, the damage they create can be substantial. Imagine an intelligent, friendly fourteen-year-old, who settles with his immigrant family in a small town where everyone expects people of "his kind" to be thieves. On the streets, he is treated with suspicion by passersby and police officers; in the classroom, he is ignored by teachers, who erroneously presume he has little academic potential; and in the neighborhood, he is viewed by the local toughs as a potential recruit to their gangs. With relatively few opportunities for legitimate accomplishment, he may indeed flirt with criminal activity—thereby confirming the expectations of the community.

Are self-fulfilling prophecies inevitable? Fortunately not (Hilton & Darley, 1991; Jussim, 1991; Neuberg, 1996; Snyder, 1992). Self-fulfilling prophecies are most likely to occur when (1) the people holding the erroneous expectations control the social encounter and (2) the targets of the expectations defer to this control (Cooper & Hazelrigg, 1988; Harris & Rosenthal, 1986; Smith, Neuberg, Judice, & Biesanz, 1997; Snyder & Haugen, 1995). Men are more likely than women to create self-fulfilling prophecies, perhaps because they have generally been socialized to take control of their social encounters, whereas women are more likely to be the victims of self-fulfilling prophecies, perhaps because they have generally been socialized to be more accommodating and deferential (Christensen & Rosenthal, 1982; Nelson & Klutas, 2000). And when holders of expectations possess special power in the social encounter—as we might see in teacher–student, interviewer–applicant, and therapist–client relationships—self-fulfilling prophecies become more likely (Copeland, 1994). Indeed, recent findings suggest that low-power individuals in the educational system—students who are African American, of low socioeconomic status, or female—may be particularly vulnerable to their teachers' expectations (Jussim, Eccles, & Madon, 1995).

Self-fulfilling prophecy *When an initially inaccurate expectation leads to actions that cause the expectation to come true.*

As useful as expectations are when they're accurate, then, they can be quite dysfunctional when they aren't. Not only may they lead us to misjudge people and situations, but they can limit the achievements of others and lead us to unwittingly create the very realities we most fear. ■

Dispositional Inferences

Imagine coming home one evening to discover your roommate screaming at her father over the phone. How would you explain her behavior? Would you attribute the tantrum to her personality (perhaps she's characteristically disrespectful and spoiled)? Would you attribute her actions to a feature of the situation (perhaps her father was continuing his unfair criticism of her boyfriend)? Or might you view the behavior as caused by some interaction of the two (perhaps your friend's short temper together with her dad's negativity led to the confrontation)?

When we want to understand accurately *why* a person behaved as he or she did, we tend to consider aspects within the person and within the situation. When people desire to simplify and conserve mental effort, however, they tend to see others' behaviors as stemming primarily from their personality (Gilbert & Malone, 1995; Jones, 1990). For instance, you're likely to presume initially that your roommate was nasty to her father because she has a selfish character. Indeed, these **dispositional inferences**—judgments that a person's behavior is caused by his or her personality—seem to occur spontaneously and with little effort. That is, when we observe another's behavior, we initially assume it was caused by some characteristic within the person (e.g., Carlston, Skowronski, & Sparks, 1995; Lupfer, Clark, & Hutcherson, 1990; Moskowitz & Roman, 1992; Winter & Uleman, 1984).

Correspondence Bias: The Fundamental Attribution Error Because it's so easy to attribute others' behaviors to dispositional causes, we often underestimate the importance of situational forces. Indeed, this **correspondence bias**—the tendency to attribute behavior to a person's disposition more than is justified (Jones, 1979)—occurs so frequently that one social psychologist labeled it the **fundamental attribution error** (Ross, 1977). Participants in a study conducted by Edward Jones and Victor Harris (1967) were shown essays, ostensibly written by students on a debate team, either supporting or opposing Cuba's president, Fidel Castro. Some participants were told that the student author had freely chosen to present the viewpoint, while others were told that the student was forced by the debate coach to defend the position. When told that the essays were freely written, participants reasonably assumed that the essay reflected the writer's actual attitudes—that the writer of the pro-Castro essay was indeed strongly pro-Castro and that the writer of the anti-Castro essay was strongly anti-Castro. Surprisingly, however, participants made this dispositional inference *even when they knew the authors had no choice as to which side to take.* To a large extent, then, participants ignored the influence that the situation—the debate coach's instructions—had on the author's behavior.

Thus, not only do we have a tendency to see others' behavior as arising from their personality, but this tendency sometimes leads us to underappreciate the role of situational influences. Why? In general, it may be simpler to assume a personality influence than to assume a situational one (Gilbert & Malone, 1995). Situations that influence behavior are often "invisible" to observers. For instance, watching a teenage boy break up with his girlfriend, we may be unaware of the strong pressures placed on him by his parents. And, being unaware of this situational influence, our attributions for his behavior are likely to be dispositional ("He's cold-hearted").

One might expect, then, that as situations come into focus, people will be more likely to generate situational attributions. This is indeed the case (Krull, 1993; Krull & Dill, 1996; Trafimow & Schneider, 1994). For example, although people tend to attribute others' behavior to dispositional causes, they are somewhat more likely to attribute their *own* behavior to situational events (Jones & Nisbett, 1972; Zaccaro & Lowe, 1985). This **actor-observer difference** is partially explained by the different perspectives we have as actors and observers. As observers, it is easy to see the person but often hard to see his or her situation. As actors, however, we often see not ourselves but instead the situation—indeed, the situation is frequently of most pressing interest (Storms, 1973; Taylor & Fiske, 1978). For instance, columnist Carl

Dispositional inference *The judgment that a person's behavior has been caused by an aspect of that person's personality.*

Correspondence bias (fundamental attribution error) *The tendency for observers to overestimate the causal influence of personality factors on behavior and to underestimate the causal role of situational influences.*

Actor–observer difference *The tendency for individuals to judge their own behaviors as caused by situational forces but the behavior of others as caused by aspects of their personalities.*

Rowan wondered whether Nixon's firing of Cox reflected lunacy on the president's part, whereas Nixon himself presented a situation-based explanation: He was concerned about "how it would look to the Soviets if in the midst of our diplomatic showdown with them I were in the position of having to defer to the demands of one of my own employees" (Nixon, 1978, p. 933).

People also tend toward dispositional inferences because they're often correct. People outside the laboratory are rarely assigned randomly to social situations. Instead, as we observed in chapter 2, people choose situations that fit their personalities, and situations choose people that fit their requirements (Funder, 1987; Snyder & Ickes, 1985). Because people and situations often fit together nicely—professional athletes tend to be concerned with their physical fitness and college professors tend to be intellectually curious—the dispositional inference may be not only a simple way of understanding another's behavior but also an accurate way.

How Fundamental Is the "Fundamental Attribution Error"? In November 1991, Dr. Gang Lu went on a shooting rampage at the University of Iowa, killing five people and critically wounding another before fatally shooting himself. Lu, who had recently received his Ph.D. from the physics department, had been upset that another student had defeated him in a competition for a prestigious academic award. In a period of ten terrifying minutes, he moved through two buildings, methodically seeking his victims—the winner of the prize, the chairman of the physics department and two of its professors, the associate vice-president of student affairs, and her receptionist. The carnage complete, Lu turned the revolver on himself.

Two weeks later, outside Detroit, Michigan, Thomas McIlvane stormed into a postal service center with a semi-automatic rifle. For the next six minutes, the recently fired postal worker sprayed scores of bullets at his former colleagues, killing four supervisors and wounding five more. When the police arrived, he shot himself. McIlvane, previously dismissed for insubordination, had lost his final appeal to regain his job just six days earlier.

Why did Lu and McIlvane each embark on such a deadly path? In light of the discussion above, we might expect observers' explanations to be mostly dispositional, having to do with the killers' personal characteristics. Reporters for the *New York Times* stressed such factors in their articles: Lu was "darkly disturbed," had a "very bad

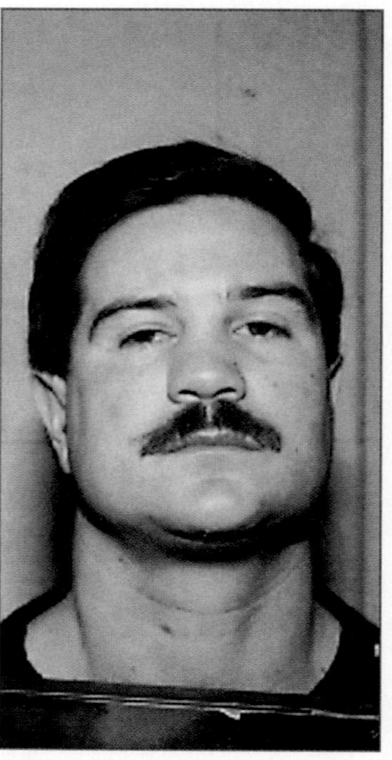

Why did they do it? *Gang Lu and Thomas McIlvane each claimed multiple victims in murderous rampages before turning their weapons on themselves. Was it something about their personalities that drove them to their crimes? Was it something about their situations? Do our explanations differ depending on the culture in which we were raised?*

temper," and had a "psychological problem with being challenged"; McIlvane was "mentally unstable," a "martial arts enthusiast," and "had a short fuse." In contrast, as Michael Morris and Kaiping Peng (1994) discovered, the causes attributed to these mass murders by writers for the *World Journal*, a Chinese-language newspaper, were quite different. According to reporters for this paper, Lu had been "isolated from the Chinese community" and his actions could be "traced to the availability of guns." Likewise, McIlvane "had been recently fired," his supervisor had been "his enemy," and he was following "the example of a recent mass slaying in Texas." Whereas writers for the American newspaper had focused on dispositional causes, as the fundamental attribution error would suggest, writers for the Chinese newspaper focused on situational causes. How do we explain these differences? And if such differences are reliable, how fundamental could the "fundamental attribution error" truly be?

In chapter 2, we learned that some cultures tend to be *individualistic* whereas others are more *collectivistic*. In highly individualistic cultures such as the United States, people are defined as individuals and are socialized to act as they wish—to take personal responsibility for their successes and failures. In collectivistic societies such as China, in contrast, people are defined in terms of their group memberships and are socialized to follow group norms—to do what is expected of them by others. Given this important distinction, we might expect people from these cultures to differ as well in their beliefs about where behavior typically comes from. Individualists should believe that aspects within a person, such as traits and attitudes, cause behavior. Collectivists should expect aspects of the situation, such as norms and social pressures, to cause behavior. Thus, the differences between cultures in the way people understand the causes of behavior may arise from broader differences in the importance that cultures place on people as individuals versus as members of social groups (e.g., Norenzayan & Nisbett, 2000).

If socialization practices indeed play a role in determining whether people prefer dispositional versus situational explanations for behavior, these different "styles" should develop as children age (Rholes, Newman, & Ruble, 1990). After all, it takes time to teach a child a culture's ways. In an important cross-cultural study, Joan Miller (1984) discovered that U.S. children tend to make more dispositional inferences for others' behaviors as they get older, a finding replicated by Leonard Newman (1991). She also discovered that Hindu children from India—a more collectivistic society—tended to make more situational inferences as they got older. The main point? As we become socialized by our cultures, we move toward their ways of thinking. In individualistic societies, people learn to prefer personality as the cause of social behavior, whereas members of collectivistic societies learn to prefer the situation. When viewed from a cross-cultural perspective, then, the fundamental attribution error seems far from fundamental.

Other Cognitive Shortcuts

To this point, we've discussed two strategies for understanding the social world while at the same time conserving mental effort—(1) people use their expectations in confirmatory ways and (2) they make dispositional inferences for others' behaviors (at least in individualistic cultures). Here, we explore several other frequently used shortcuts—known as **cognitive heuristics.**

Cognitive heuristic *A mental shortcut used to make a judgment.*

Representativeness Heuristic Jim drinks a lot of beer and spends many hours reading sports magazines. Is he more likely a member of Delta House Fraternity or of the Sierra Club? All else being equal, most people would guess Delta House. After all, people expect fraternity men to exhibit such behaviors. This use of our expectations is sometimes called the **representativeness heuristic**—because our judgment of which group Jim belongs to is based simply on how well his characteristics fit with, or represent, the different groups (Kahneman & Tversky, 1972). Because Jim's characteristics fit with belonging to a fraternity, we guess that he does.

Representativeness heuristic *A mental shortcut through which people classify something as belonging to a certain category to the extent that it is similar to a typical case from that category.*

Table 3.1 Selected causes of death.

Place a number next to each cause of death, ordering them according to the likelihood that a U.S. citizen will die from them.

Estimated Rank:	Cause of Death:
____	AIDS
____	Cancer
____	Complications in Medical Procedures
____	Diabetes
____	Falls (accidental)
____	Fire or Smoke Inhalation
____	Firearm Accidents
____	Heart Disease
____	Hernia
____	Homicide or Legal Intervention
____	Pneumonia
____	Poisoning (accidental)
____	Railway Accident
____	Traffic Accident
____	Suicide

(1) Heart Disease; (2) Cancer; (3) Pneumonia & Flu; (4) Diabetes; (5) Traffic Accident; (6) Suicide; (7) Homicide or Legal Intervention; (8) AIDS; (9) Falls (accidental); (10) Poisoning (accidental); (11) Hernia; (12) Suffocation; (13) Fire or Smoke Inhalation; (14) Complications in Medical Procedures; (15) Firearm Accidents. These estimates are based on 1998 U.S. Cause of Death data, as reported by the National Center for Injury Prevention and Control.

Availability Heuristic Let's try an exercise: see Table 3.1 above and rank order the likelihood that a U.S. citizen will die from the causes listed there. Let's see how you did. If you're like most people, you underestimated the risks for pneumonia (#3), diabetes (#4), and hernia (#11), and overestimated the threats from homicides (#7), AIDS (#8), fires (#13), and firearm accidents (#15). To understand why, think about how you performed the task. Without the statistics in hand, your guess was probably based on the ease with which you could bring to mind particular instances of each of these fatal events, a strategy psychologists label the **availability heuristic** (Tversky & Kahneman, 1973). Because the media are more likely to report impactful and visual stories, we tend to overestimate the likelihood of death by fire, AIDS, and homicide and to underestimate the likelihood of death by pneumonia, diabetes, and other less "newsworthy" events.

This tendency to overestimate the frequency of impactful events could be explained in two ways. First, it could be that people *actually remember* more instances of such events. That is, they may believe that homicides are more frequent than suicides because they recall more homicides. Alternatively, it may just *seem easier* to remember homicides than suicides—and if it seems easier, people might reasonably assume that homicides occur more frequently. But how could we determine which of these explanations is correct? As you'll see next, clever manipulations of independent variables in experiments can go a long way toward differentiating among alternative hypotheses.

Availability heuristic *A mental shortcut through which one estimates the likelihood of an event by the ease with which instances of that event come to mind.*

FOCUS ON Method

Using Experiments to Test Alternative Hypotheses

Once researchers identify an interesting phenomenon, such as people's tendency to overestimate the frequency of impactful events (homicide) and to underestimate the frequency of nonnewsworthy events (death by diabetes), they seek to learn why the phenomenon occurs. As we discussed in Chapter 1, just identifying and describing a phenomenon isn't enough. If we want to know the circumstances under which people make such errors, or if we want to be able to decrease their tendency to do so, we need to know *how* people come to make the error in the first place. In many instances, there may be multiple plausible hypotheses, and the challenge for researchers is to design studies that tease apart these alternatives.

So put on your researcher-as-detective hat and think for a moment about how you'd explore the two hypotheses for why people overestimate the frequency of impactful events relative to more pallid events. Is it because (1) people *actually remember* more impactful events (hypothesis 1) or because (2) it *seems easier* to remember impactful events (hypothesis 2)? Where would you start?

Consider the reasoning of Norbert Schwarz and his colleagues (Schwarz et al., 1991). They decided to create two experimental conditions, one in which participants would successfully recall many instances but would experience doing so as difficult (condition A), and a second in which participants would recall fewer instances but would think it easy to do so (condition B). Why these conditions? If the actual number of recalled events is most important, participants in condition A should estimate a higher homicide rate than participants in condition B. In contrast, if the felt ease of recall is most important, participants in condition B should estimate a higher homicide rate than participants in condition A. Having established the logic of the experiment, the final step is to create such differentiating conditions.

These researchers were interested not in frequency estimates of murders and diabetes, but rather in how the availability heuristic might influence people's judgments about their own personality. Through pretesting, they discovered that people can easily recall eight or nine examples of their own assertive and unassertive behaviors, but that it gets increasingly difficult when they try to remember more than ten. When you ask people, then, to describe six examples of assertive behaviors, it will feel easy to them. In contrast, when you ask them to describe twelve such behaviors, it will feel difficult to them (although they can eventually do so).

This simple finding sets the stage for a clean test of the two hypotheses. If the *number of instances actually recalled* determines people's frequency estimates, people who describe twelve instances should judge themselves to be more assertive than people who are asked to describe only six instances. Alternatively, if the *feeling of how easy it is to recall events* determines frequency estimates, then people who are asked to describe six assertive events should judge themselves as more assertive than people who are asked to describe twelve such events. As Figure 3.3 reveals, there is a winner: the felt ease of recall appears to underlie the availability heuristic.

We see, then, that a carefully done experiment can go a long way toward differentiating among alternative plausible hypotheses. Indeed, throughout this textbook, we'll encounter many studies that do just this. ■

Figure 3.3
The availability heuristic: Actual recall or the felt ease of recall?

German students were asked to recall either six or twelve examples of either assertive or unassertive behaviors. They then judged their own assertiveness. For students recalling examples of assertiveness, those who recalled six viewed themselves as more assertive than did those who recalled twelve. Likewise, for students recalling examples of unassertiveness, those who recalled six viewed themselves as more unassertive than did those who recalled twelve. These data suggest that the availability heuristic is a strategy based on the *felt ease* with which events come to mind, not on the mere number of instances remembered.

SOURCE: *After Schwarz et al. (1991), Table 1.*

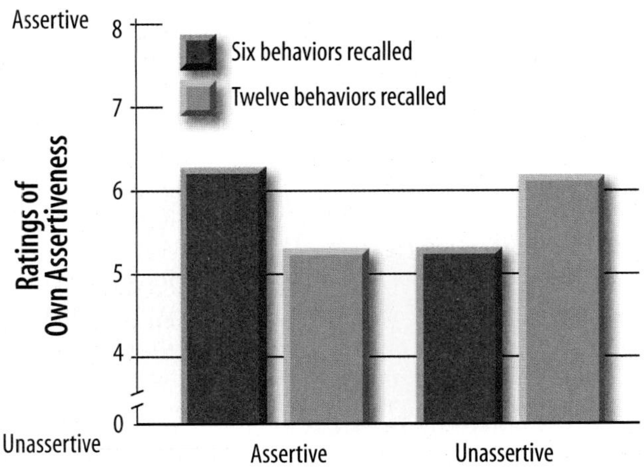

Anchoring and Adjustment Heuristic Richard Nixon was surprised by the unpopularity of his decision to fire Archibald Cox. "After all," he must have thought, "if *I* know it's the right thing to do, other people are likely to agree with me." In this case, it appears that Nixon fell victim to the **false consensus effect**—people often overestimate the extent to which others agree with them (Krueger & Zeiger, 1993; Mullen et al., 1985; Mussweiler & Strack, 2000; Ross, Greene, & House, 1977; Sherman, Chassin, Presson, & Agostinelli, 1984).

The false consensus effect results from yet another useful simplifying strategy—the **anchoring and adjustment heuristic.** When we have a novel judgment to make, we often start with a rough estimate as an *anchor*, or starting point. Once we have an anchor, we *adjust* it to account for the possibility that it is imperfect (Tversky & Kahneman, 1974). If you want to guess how well you'll do on your social psychology final exam, you may start with an estimate based on your midterm grades and then adjust it to take into account some unique characteristics of the final. (It may, for instance, have more essay questions on it; you may have two other finals that same day.) The false consensus effect is the result, then, of an anchoring-and-adjustment process in which a person uses his or her own views as the anchor (Alicke & Largo, 1995; Fenigstein & Abrams, 1993).

The anchoring and adjustment heuristic is useful because we don't have to gather lots of information before making a decision; instead, we save time and effort by starting with a useful approximation and adjusting from there. Indeed, if we select the right anchor and make the appropriate adjustments, the strategy will be both efficient and effective (Dawes, 1989; Krueger & Clement, 1997). At times, however, we may pick the wrong anchor or adjust insufficiently (Kruger, 1999). Nixon's decision about Cox seems an apt illustration: Believing himself to be representative of the U.S. citizenry, Nixon used his own view of the issue as an anchor. But because presidents and the general population are far from similar—in historical knowledge, access to present information, political views, and the like—an adjustment was necessary. That Nixon failed to make the appropriate adjustment led him to underestimate the public's reaction. Of course, he could have conducted a scientifically valid opinion poll on the matter, sampling broadly across the U.S. public, but this would have taken too much time and money. His simple intuitive estimation of public sentiment must have seemed like a good strategy at the time. Only in retrospect, when we recognize the costs of this particular decision to his presidency, does the use of this strategy in his situation seem misguided.

We've explored several strategies that people use to simplify their understandings of the social world. These strategies serve the goal of mental economy quite well: They can be implemented quickly, require relatively few cognitive resources, and generally lead to reasonably accurate judgments and decisions. In the sections below, we explore when people seek mental economy, beginning with those factors residing within the person.

Arousal and Circadian Rhythms

Jogging, riding a bicycle, and watching a horror movie all increase physiological arousal. You might be surprised to discover, however, that these activities also change the way we think. Specifically, arousal prompts us to rely on our cognitive shortcuts. For example, aroused individuals are especially likely to rely on existing beliefs and expectations (Wilder & Shapiro, 1989), to succumb to the availability heuristic (Kim & Baron, 1988), and to ignore available alternatives when making decisions (Keinan, 1987). Why?

Arousal may lead us to simplify by distracting us. If you pay attention to your pounding heart while playing tennis, for instance, you will have less attention available for understanding why your opponent is trouncing you so badly. Arousal may alternatively lead us to simplify because it narrows the beam of our attentional spotlight, making it difficult to employ more comprehensive cognitive strategies (like those we explore later in the chapter). Indeed, people who naturally possess

False consensus effect *The tendency to overestimate the extent to which others agree with us.*

Anchoring and adjustment heuristic *A mental shortcut through which people begin with a rough estimation as a starting point and then adjust this estimate to take into account unique characteristics of the present situation.*

more attentional resources tend to be more complex in how they think about things (Conway & White-Dysart, 1999). In either case, complex thinking becomes more difficult when we are aroused, leading us to rely on low-effort shortcuts.

In a related vein, Galen Bodenhausen (1990) noted that individuals lose attentional resources during certain periods of their circadian—that is, their daily, biological—cycle. He thus hypothesized that people who report reaching the peak of their cognitive functioning early in the day ("morning people") would use cognitive shortcuts more at night, whereas people who report peaking later in the day ("evening people") would rely more on these shortcuts in the morning. In studies of social judgment, subjects were randomly assigned to participate at either 9:00 A.M. or 8:00 P.M. For some of the participants, then, the experiments occurred during their peak times, whereas for the others, they occurred during their "off" times. As Bodenhausen suspected, morning people were more likely to use cognitive shortcuts at night, whereas evening people were more likely to use their shortcuts in the morning.

In sum, when we enter a situation having a shortage of attentional resources—because we're either highly aroused or because it's our circadian down time—we're more likely to rely on simplifying strategies.

Circadian rhythms and judgment. *Are you a "morning person" or an "evening person"? If you don't think it matters, think again: People are more likely to use cognitive shortcuts to make decisions during their "off" times than during the peak times of their circadian cycles.*

Positive Feelings

We're also more likely to use simplifying strategies when we're in a good mood. Imagine that a college dean is trying to decide whether a varsity football player is guilty of starting a fight with a librarian. Does the dean use her stereotypical expectations—"jocks are generally more aggressive than librarians"—and conclude that the athlete is guilty? It will depend at least partly on the dean's mood: In this case, it may be bad news for the athlete if the dean is in a good mood because people in positive moods are especially likely to rely on cognitive shortcuts (Bless et al., 1996; Bodenhausen, Kramer, & Süsser, 1994; Isen, 1987; Park & Banaji, 2000; Sinclair & Mark, 1992). Why would this be?

First, positive moods sometimes reduce attentional capacity, thereby encouraging mental shortcuts (Mackie & Worth, 1989; Stroessner & Mackie, 1992). Second, as we learned in Chapter 2, positive feelings inform us that we are doing well—that we have little reason to be especially attentive or vigilant. As a consequence, complex, effortful cognitive strategies seem unnecessary, and we rely on our cognitive shortcuts instead (Fiedler, 1988; Forgas, 1995; Schaller & Cialdini, 1990; Schwarz, 1990).

Need for Structure

It would be a mistake to think that simplifying the world is something that only other—perhaps less intelligent?—folks do. In general, when people are aroused or in a good mood, they're more likely to simplify—and, of course, all of us are aroused or happy at times. Nonetheless, there is a stable personality trait that also influences whether we use simple or more complex cognitive strategies: It's been labeled *need for structure*, and it reflects the extent to which people are motivated to organize their mental and physical worlds in simple ways. To assess this motivation, Megan Thompson, Michael Naccarato, and Kevin Parker (1989) designed the *Personal Need for Structure Scale.* People high in need for structure tend to agree strongly with items like "I enjoy having a clear and structured mode of life" and "I don't like situations that are uncertain." They are also more likely to engage in all sorts of cognitive shortcuts. For instance, they rely on preexisting expectations when judging others, form stereotypes especially easily, and attribute others' behaviors to their dispositions (Moskowitz, 1993; Neuberg & Newsom, 1993; Schaller, Boyd, Yohannes, & O'Brien, 1995; Thompson et al., 1994; Webster, 1993).

In sum, physiological arousal, positive moods, and a dispositional need for structure increase the desire for mental economy and thus encourage individuals to take cognitive shortcuts. As the next section reveals, certain *situations* also lead people to simplify.

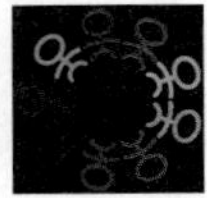

Complex Situations

It's finals week, and chaos reigns! You have four finals, a term paper, and you need to move out of your apartment. On top of it all, your boss at the restaurant wants you to interview eighteen people for two waiter–waitress openings. With all these things on your mind, are you likely to probe in great depth the past experiences, character, and background of each applicant, carefully comparing each of their strengths and weaknesses? Or might you instead rely more than usual on "quick-and-dirty" shortcuts? Research suggests the latter: Because each additional concern draws resources from the limited attentional pool, it becomes increasingly difficult for us to engage in careful thought as situations become more complex (Baumeister, Hutton, & Tice, 1989; Biesanz et al., 2001; Bodenhausen & Lichtenstein, 1987; Pratto & Bargh, 1991; Rothbart et al., 1978; Stangor & Duan, 1991).

The following study conducted by Daniel Gilbert, Brett Pelham, and Douglas Krull (1988) illustrates this overload effect nicely: Participants listened to another student make a speech about the issue of legalized abortion. Although the experimenter emphasized that the student had *no choice* of which side to take, participants believed that the student arguing for abortion rights was truly "pro-choice" whereas the student arguing against abortion was truly "pro-life." That is, they fell prey to the correspondence bias. This laboratory scenario was repeated for a second set of participants except for one feature—they expected to give a speech of their own following their evaluations of the speaker. You may have already guessed what happened to this latter group of participants: They demonstrated an even *stronger* correspondence bias. Their preoccupation with their own impending speech apparently left them with too few attentional resources to analyze the speaker's circumstances in a more comprehensive way. The more complex our situations, the more we rely on our cognitive shortcuts.

Time Pressure

We're also more likely to rely on cognitive shortcuts when we're under time pressure (Bechtold, Naccarato, & Zanna, 1986). Indeed, imagine if two of your finals and the term paper were due the following day and you had yet to finish the paper and begin studying. Would this affect your willingness to use cognitive shortcuts in evaluating those job applicants?

In one experiment, Israeli teachers read an essay presented as coming from a student of Ashkenazi descent (a high-status group in Israel) or from a student of Sephardic heritage (a relatively low-status group). Some teachers had one hour to grade the essay (low time pressure) while others had only ten minutes (high time pressure). Not only did the Ashkenazi student receive higher grades than the Sephardic student for the identical essay when time pressures were low (73 percent versus 64 percent), but this stereotyping effect was exaggerated when the teachers were rushed (80 percent versus 64 percent)—the teachers under time pressure further benefited the Ashkenazi student by two thirds of a grade level (Kruglanski & Freund, 1983).

In sum, people are more likely to use simplifying cognitive strategies when situations are complex and when time is short. This may help explain why Richard Nixon, a veteran and savvy politician, was so surprised by the outrage of the U.S. public after his firing of Archibald Cox. For as Nixon reported in his memoirs, October 1973 was a chaotic month. War had broken out in the Middle East, his vice-president was under great pressure to resign, and Congress was attempting to reduce presidential foreign policy powers. On top of everything else, he had to deal with Archibald Cox's request that he quickly turn over important presidential documents and tapes. Nixon's circumstances were almost overwhelmingly complex and time-pressured, and it's little surprise that—by his own account—he failed to see the public's perspective on Watergate, the smoldering disenchantment many Americans felt toward him, and the devastating implications of his decision to fire Cox.

Days of pressure and chaos. *President Nixon's decision to fire Archibald Cox was perhaps his worst political blunder. How did such a savvy, experienced politician make such a dramatic mistake? Might it have had something to do with Nixon's preoccupation at the time with his vice-president's imminent resignation, the war in the Middle East, and other important, pressing events?*

When the World Doesn't Fit Our Expectations

One could get the impression from our discussions thus far that people arrive on the social scene with a toolbox full of favorite cognitive shortcuts and rarely use anything more complex. It's true that we possess many simplification strategies and use them often. It's also true, however, that there's a real world out there, and to survive we must be flexible enough to go beyond such strategies when the situation calls for it. For example, when we feel accountable for our judgments—when we have to justify them to others—we're less likely to rely on simple ways of judging our social world (e.g., Bodenhausen et al., 1994; Pendry & Macrae, 1996; Schaller et al., 1995; Webster, Richter, & Kruglanski, 1996). Indeed, later in the chapter, we explore in depth those circumstances that motivate us to go beyond our cognitive shortcuts. For now, it will do merely to illustrate that people will indeed put aside their shortcuts when the situation calls for it.

Imagine that, over coffee, a friend describes a new acquaintance—Devon, an artist. You immediately envision a creative, nonconforming, somewhat idealistic individual, so you're not surprised in the least to hear her describe the funny hours he keeps and his strange style of dress. Devon fits with your expectations, so you picture him as you would many other artists. Imagine instead, however, that she describes Devon as meticulously neat, scientific, and politically conservative. This doesn't accord with your expectations. *A scientific artist? And meticulously neat?* Will you stick with your initial expectations and view him as a typical artist? Sometimes you will—if your initial expectations and beliefs are very important to you (e.g., Biek, Wood, & Chaiken, 1996; Edwards & Smith, 1996; Fiske & Neuberg, 1990). Other times, however, you'll probably search for a better way of understanding Devon, one that accounts more easily for his apparent complexities (Asch & Zukier, 1984; Fiske, Neuberg, Beattie, & Milberg, 1987; Locksley, Borgida, Brekke, & Hepburn, 1980).

Our expectations, then, don't always result in the confirming processes we've discussed. Rather, our expectations interact with the information available to us to determine whether we seek to confirm our expectations or instead seek greater accuracy. When our expectations are clearly out of sync with the world, we often go beyond them (McNulty & Swann, 1994; Swann & Ely, 1984).

Summary

When people don't want to expend much effort forming impressions and making decisions, and are satisfied with judgments that are "good enough," they can reach into their cognitive toolbox for various simplifying strategies. They can use their existing beliefs as expectations, which makes understanding new events much easier. At least in Western, individualistic cultures, people make dispositional inferences to simplify the task of understanding others' actions. And people use other cognitive shortcuts as well, including the representativeness heuristic, the availability heuristic, and the anchoring and adjustment heuristic. People are especially motivated to simplify when they're aroused or in a good mood, and when dispositionally high in need for structure, under time pressure, and in particularly complex environments. Of course, these circumstances reflect much of everyday life, suggesting that we rely on our cognitive shortcuts a great deal. There are times, however, when we go beyond these simplification strategies, as when our situational realities just don't fit with our expectations.

Managing Self-Image

How has college life gone for you? How are your grades? Have you done as well as you'd hoped? Have your relationships worked out well? If they haven't, who was to blame? As we contemplate questions like these, quick-and-easy answers—the kind of answers we seek when motivated by cognitive efficiency—may not be enough. Instead, we often seek answers that help us feel good about ourselves, that lead us to believe that we're worthy and talented people. "So some of my grades weren't so great," we think, "but I found those courses too dull to take seriously." "My relationships have worked out as well as I wanted them to," we tell ourselves, "and anyway, she was just *impossible* to get along with."

If thoughts like these come to mind, you're not alone. Few of us can rightfully claim immunity from the desire for positive self-regard, from the motivation to think of ourselves in positive, approving ways (James, 1890; McDougall, 1932). Consider, for instance, that most people report having high self-esteem, view their future prospects optimistically, and believe that they possess more favorable characteristics and abilities than the average person (e.g., Alicke, 1985; Dunning, Meyerowitz, & Holzberg, 1989; Regan, Snyder, & Kassin, 1995; Weinstein, 1980). To put it simply, most people want to feel good about themselves.

We desire positive self-regard for at least two reasons. First, with positive self-regard comes the belief that we're effective—that we can accomplish our goals—and such beliefs help us summon the energy we need in order to achieve (Bandura, 1977; Greenwald, 1980). From this perspective, positive self-regard drives us toward success. Finding ways to improve your self-regard should thus, to a point, improve your ability to accomplish important tasks (McFarlin, Baumeister, & Blascovich, 1984). Second, self-regard indicates how we're doing in our social lives. When self-regard is low, it often tells us that we need to assess our interpersonal relationships and improve them (Leary, Tambor, Terdal, & Downs, 1995). As a consequence, finding ways to boost your self-regard should also reduce your anxiety about social relationships.

This isn't to say that people want to delude themselves blindly. It certainly wouldn't be adaptive to believe that things are great when, in reality, they stink (e.g., Colvin, Block, & Funder, 1995). A somewhat weaker form of this self-deception, however, may help us work toward our goals and, at the same time, alleviate some of those distracting everyday worries. In this section, we discuss some of the cognitive strategies people use to enhance and protect their self-images and then explore the factors in the person and the situation that lead people to employ such strategies.

Cognitive Strategies for Enhancing and Protecting the Self

We'll see in other chapters that people sometimes use behaviors to affirm desired self-images. For instance, coming to another's aid can help people feel good about themselves. In this section, we focus on some of the cognitive strategies people use to enhance and protect their self-image (see Figure 3.4).

Social Comparison How smart are you? How do you know? Are your political opinions reasonable? Again, how do you know? In his landmark 1954 paper, Leon Festinger argued that people have a fundamental drive to evaluate their abilities and opinions and often do so by comparing themselves with others. To assess your intelligence, you might see how your SAT scores stack up against those of your classmates; to evaluate your opinion of the president, you may compare your views with your neighbor's. Indeed, as we saw in Chapter 2, social comparison is one way people form and develop their self-concept. Festinger's (1954) social comparison theory focused on the drive to assess one's abilities and the legitimacy of one's opinions *accurately*. We examine this part of the theory in chapters 7 and 12, when we explore who people choose as their friends and why people join groups. But people compare themselves for other reasons as well (Wood, 1989). In particular, people often compare themselves with others for the purpose of self-enhancement. How might you use social comparisons to elevate your self-image?

First, you might engage in **downward social comparison**—that is, you might compare yourself to someone who is less fortunate than yourself, has lesser abilities, and so on (Wills, 1981). For example, a study of breast cancer patients revealed that a large majority spontaneously compared themselves with others in even worse condition (Wood, Taylor, & Lichtman, 1985). As one woman said, "I just had a comparatively small amount of surgery on the breast, and I was so miserable, because it was so painful. How awful it must be for women who have had a mastectomy" (1178). Because downward comparisons can increase self-esteem and reduce stress, this woman may be better able to cope with her own difficult fate (Gibbons & Gerrard, 1989; Lemyre & Smith, 1985).

Figure 3.4
Maintaining a desirable self-image.

Social survival often requires that we assert ourselves. We need to *approach* our social environment to secure from it what we need. To believe that we are effective and have good social relationships gives us the confidence to make this approach. For this reason, people use various cognitive strategies to enhance and protect their self-images.

Downward comparisons only enhance our self-image if we can view the other person as clearly less well off than we are. Thus, we often look for ways to derogate others or to boost ourselves relative to them. In one experiment, some students at Arizona State University had their self-esteem threatened by poor performance on a creativity task; these students were especially likely to devalue their cross-state rival institution, the University of Arizona, by rating it relatively unfavorably in a survey interview (Cialdini & Richardson, 1980). Students in another study demonstrated a "self-boosting" strategy, exaggerating the frequency of their own health-oriented behaviors to convince themselves that they were indeed more fit than other students (Klein & Kunda, 1993). To feel good about ourselves, then, we not only focus on less fortunate others but we may also derogate them, or boost ourselves, to emphasize our relative favorability.

Second, people can sometimes create positive self-regard through **upward social comparison**—by comparing themselves to those better-off (Collins, 1996). This is a somewhat dangerous strategy. On the one hand, comparing yourself to the really sharp student in your math class might prove beneficial by motivating you toward self-improvement (Blanton, Buunk, Gibbons, & Kuyper, 1999; Helgeson & Taylor, 1993; Major, Testa, & Bylsma, 1991). On the other hand, such a strategy carries a risk, as you're likely to realize that you're not as smart as the other person. Indeed, if you select your upward comparisons haphazardly, the strategy may backfire. The trick is to convince yourself that you're in the *same general range* as those better off than you—if you succeed, you can focus on this connection to feel better about yourself (Wheeler, 1966).

Downward social comparison *The process of comparing ourselves with those who are less well off.*

Upward social comparison *The process of comparing ourselves with those who are better off than ourselves.*

Several threads of evidence support the idea that people want to link themselves to those who are better off. First, people often emphasize their associations with those who are already successful and worthy (e.g., Campbell & Tesser, 1985). For instance, we *bask in the reflected glory* of athletic teams more after team victories than after defeats—wearing the winners' team colors and referring to "our" successes and "their" failures (Cialdini et al., 1976; Hirt, Zillman, Erickson, & Kennedy, 1992)—and we *cut off reflected failure* by disassociating ourselves from people and events we view unfavorably (Schimel, Pyszczynski, Greenberg, O'Mahen, & Arndt, 2000; Snyder, Lassegard, & Ford, 1986).

Second, if we find ourselves "stuck" with particular associations, we do our best to enhance their status. For example, we generally enhance our views of close friends, relatives, and those social groups to which we belong (Brewer, 1979; Brown, 1986; Crocker, Thompson, McGraw, & Ingerman, 1987; Tajfel & Turner, 1986). Even when our link to another is apparently trivial—as when we merely share the same birthday with another—we tend to raise our evaluations of him or her (Finch & Cialdini, 1989). Amazingly, we even value more highly the letters that appear in our names versus those that do not (Hoorens & Nuttin, 1993; Nuttin, 1985). Indeed, we seem to boost our evaluations of just about anything or anybody we see ourselves in a "relationship" with.

In sum, the desires to enhance and protect our self-images influence to whom we pay attention and how we think about them. Using a downward comparison strategy, we focus on those less fortunate than ourselves and think of them as different from us and less worthy. We sometimes also use an upward comparison strategy, focusing instead on individuals having a somewhat higher standing than ourselves as we attempt to "hitch ourselves to their wagons."

Self-Serving Attributions People also enhance their self-image through self-serving attributions. Richard Nixon's attributions for his political successes and failures illustrate this nicely. In his first political campaign, Nixon defeated a long-time incumbent and was elected to the U.S. House of Representatives. Nixon attributed this victory to his personal values and strengths—his stand on the issues, the vigor of his campaign, and his debating skill. In contrast, when defeated by John F. Kennedy in the 1960 presidential election, Nixon's explanations focused on the external—the ruthlessness of Kennedy's campaign organization and the pro-Kennedy bias of the news media (Nixon, 1978, 225–226).

The contrast between Nixon's explanations for the two election outcomes reveals a **self-serving bias:** We tend to take personal credit for our successes and to blame external forces for our failures (Bradley, 1978; Miller & Ross, 1975; Zuckerman, 1979). One reason for the self-serving bias lies in our expectations for our performance. Because we generally expect to succeed, we're likely to interpret our successes as reflecting our abilities and efforts; because we don't expect to fail, we're likely to look for external events that "got in the way" (Miller & Ross, 1975). More fundamentally, however, the self-serving bias enhances self-image. Taking credit for our successes helps us feel good about ourselves (Miller, 1976; Sicoly & Ross, 1979; Snyder, Stephan, & Rosenfield, 1976; Weary, 1980).

This tendency is so common that it often extends beyond our individual selves, leading us to make self-serving explanations for the social groups to which we belong and the sports teams we support (Hewstone, 1989; Mullen & Riordan, 1988). Richard Lau and Dan Russell (1980) collected newspaper articles to see how players, coaches, and local sports commentators explained hometeam victories and defeats. As Figure 3.5 reveals, explanations based on internal factors (our team's ability) predominated after victories, whereas explanations based on external factors (the other team's good luck) were more likely to surface after defeats.

To enhance or protect our self-image, then, we may take credit for our successes and minimize our responsibility for failures. Research by Peter Ditto and David Lopez (1992) suggests that the self-serving bias occurs because we readily accept information that fits with our desires but vigorously challenge information incompatible with our wishes. For example, whereas we see commentaries extolling the skill level of our favorite team as "insightful," we view commentaries attributing our team's victories to mere luck as "obviously warped and misinformed."

Self-serving bias *The tendency to take personal credit for our successes and to blame external factors for our failures.*

Exaggerating Our Strengths, Diminishing Our Weaknesses Let's try an exercise (you can also try this on your friends): Rank the six traits below in order of importance. If you think it most important that people be intelligent, you should rank intelligence first; if you think it least important that people be sensitive, you should rank sensitivity sixth. And so on.

- intelligence
- sense of humor
- kindness
- creativity
- sensitivity
- industriousness

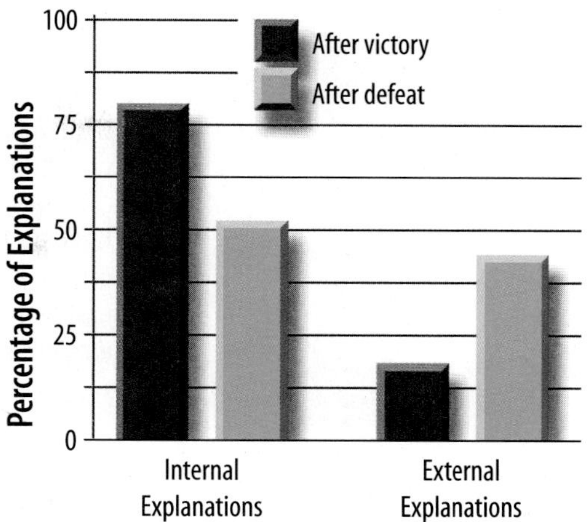

Figure 3.5
The self-serving bias in the sports pages.

In a systematic analysis of newspaper articles describing 33 major baseball and football games in the fall of 1977, Richard Lau and Dan Russell (1980) discovered evidence of the self-serving bias. Quotations from both players and coaches differed considerably depending on whether their teams won or lost: Internal explanations were most likely after victories, whereas external explanations were most likely after defeats.

SOURCE: *After Lau & Russell (1980), Table 1.*

Now rank the characteristics again, this time in terms of how well they represent you. That is, if you think creativity is your strong suit, you should rank it first. What do you find when you compare your two rankings?

If you're like most people, your two rankings will look similar. That is, if you see yourself as pretty smart, you will also place a high value on intelligence; if you believe yourself to be funny, you will put more weight on sense of humor. In general, people tend to value quite highly—in both themselves and others—those characteristics and abilities they happen to possess (Campbell, 1986; Dunning, Perie, & Story, 1991; Fong & Markus, 1982; Harackiewicz, Sansone, & Manderlink, 1985; Schmader & Major, 1999). Similarly, people tend to *de*value the traits and abilities they don't have. In one study, for instance, intellectually gifted boys who thought they hadn't done well in class minimized the importance of academics and boosted the importance of other pursuits (Gibbons, Benbow, & Gerrard, 1994).

From the self-regard perspective, the reasons for this are clear: By manipulating the relative importance of different traits and abilities, we can boost our self-image. "We have what's important," we think to ourselves, thus increasing our worth. Moreover, by using our strengths to evaluate others, we're more likely to compare favorably to them, also helping to enhance our self-image.

Just as we believe that our positive characteristics and abilities are quite important, we also believe that we possess those traits we later learn are valuable. Graduate students at Princeton who learned from a faked scientific paper that extraversion leads to career success subsequently evaluated themselves anonymously as extraverted; students who learned, in contrast, that introversion leads to success subsequently evaluated themselves as introverted (Kunda & Sanitioso, 1989). In sum, by viewing our positive traits as especially important, or by merging positive characteristics into our self-image, we can enhance and protect that self-image.

Believing We Have Control Often, enhancing or protecting our self-image involves believing we have control over certain situations and events in our lives. In the spring of 1995, the payout for the multistate Powerball lottery had reached $110 million. One of the authors of this textbook, disregarding the daunting odds, overheard the following conversation while waiting in line to buy his ticket.

Person 1: *"What are you going to do? Pick your own numbers or let the computer pick for you?"*
Person 2: *"Pick my own. I figure it gives me a better chance of winning."*

A better chance of winning?! Our "logical" minds reject such a supposition. After all, because lottery numbers are selected randomly, all numbers have an equally dismal chance of being a winner. Nonetheless, allowing the computer to pick our ticket leaves the outcome of such a potentially important event—$110 million!—totally outside our control. So what do we do? Like our tendency to roll our own dice at the craps table and to wear lucky T-shirts while watching the big game, we personally choose our lottery numbers, creating for ourselves the *perception* of control

(Biner, Angle, Park, Mellinger, & Barber, 1995; Langer, 1975; Thompson, 1999; Wortman, 1975).

To some extent, the perception of control is adaptive. Without it, we may lack the confidence needed to work toward potentially difficult goals. For instance, if you don't think you'll be able to convince a corporate recruiter to hire you, you may not even interview for the job, thus guaranteeing that you won't get it. Indeed, some have argued that a healthy self-concept and self-esteem require that we believe in our ability to control important aspects of our lives (e.g., Bandura, 1977). More than just a healthy self-concept may be at stake, however. The health of one's *body* may also hang in the balance, as we see next.

FOCUS ON Application

Control Beliefs and Health

Illness and other major life events can provoke uncertainty and the perception of having lost control. Just weeks before she was to marry, Treya Killam Wilber discovered a small lump in her right breast. The biopsy soon after the wedding revealed cancer. That night, confusion and helplessness filled her thoughts:

> I cannot sleep ... not with this terrible fear of the unknown massed densely all about me.... How many women have heard this word CANCER pounding like an endless drumbeat inside their heads, relentless, unforgiving. CANCER. CANCER. CANCER. CANCER.... These voices and stories and images around me are full of fear and pain and helplessness.... It is terrible and painful and uncontrollable and mysterious and powerful.... No way to stop it or direct it or ultimately to contain it.... After five years such-and-such percent survive, such-and-such percent die. Where will I be?.... I cannot bear this not-knowing, this groping in the dark.... (Wilber, 1993, 38–39)

And the thoughts of Ken, her new husband:

> Although everything was happening in painfully slow motion, each frame contained too much experience and too much information, which produced the bizarre sensation that things were happening both very rapidly and very slowly, somehow at the same time. I kept having the image of myself playing baseball: I am standing there with my glove on, with several people throwing baseballs at me, which I am supposed to catch. But so many balls are being thrown at me that they bounce off my face and body and land on the ground, while I stand there with a stupid-looking expression ... (36)

When people perceive a loss of control, they cope less effectively with stress and their health suffers (Thompson & Spacapan, 1991). Residents of nursing homes who perceive little opportunity to control their lives are generally worse off than those who see themselves as having more control (Rodin, 1986), and cancer patients having little sense of personal control are generally more poorly adjusted (Taylor, Lichtman, & Wood, 1984; Thompson et al., 1993).

What do we do, then, when confronted with potentially stressful events such as these? Early on, we may try to assert actual, *primary control* over the aversive events (Heckhausen & Schulz, 1995; Rothbaum, Weisz, & Snyder, 1982). For example, after discovering that she has breast cancer, a woman might exert *behavioral control*—paying special attention to diet, exercise, and rest—to prepare herself physically for the radiation and chemotherapy treatments ahead. She might exert *cognitive control*, focusing her attention on the more positive aspects of her life—for instance, on her loving children—in this way reducing the impact of the illness on her everyday mental well-being. And she might gain *information control* by seeking information about the side effects associated with treatments like chemotherapy, enabling her to cope better with the nausea and weakness. By exerting these forms of primary control, we can reduce the impact that stressful events have on us.

We may also gain some perception of control through *secondary*, less direct, means (Thompson, Nanni, & Levine, 1994). For instance, an ill person can exert *vicarious control* by believing that some other powerful person—such as a physician—can exert control over the disease on his or her behalf. This perception of control can also have its benefits for health and well-being (Taylor et al., 1984).

Control and health. *Perceptions of control can contribute greatly to one's mental and physical health. For instance, residents of nursing homes who perceive few opportunities for control are generally worse off than those who see themselves as having more control.*

Can these insights be applied? Can programs designed to increase people's perceptions of control enhance their ability to cope with stress? Apparently so. In several studies, for example, nursing home residents given greater control over their everyday lives tended to be happier, more active, and in better health than other residents (Langer & Rodin, 1976; Rodin & Langer, 1977; Schulz, 1976). Capitalizing on these ideas, postoperative hospital patients are often given responsibility for self-administering pain-killing drugs. Their ability to control the administration of these drugs generally reduces pain and may even speed recovery, even though such patients typically give themselves *less* painkiller than their physicians prescribe (Egan, 1990; Ferrante, Ostheimer, & Covino, 1990).

Are increased perceptions of personal control beneficial for all individuals? Apparently not. Rather, perceptions of control help *internals*—people who like to be in control of their environments—but may actually harm *externals*—people who like to have others in control (e.g., Reich & Zautra, 1989, 1991). In one study, middle-aged "external" women with rheumatoid arthritis became *more distressed* if their husbands encouraged them to take personal control (Reich & Zautra, 1995). The perception of personal control is only beneficial for those who want it; for those who would prefer to have others play a larger role, perceptions of personal control can be damaging.

Finally, when perceptions of control are a mere illusion—when we don't in reality have control over important events in our lives—such perceptions can be maladaptive (Baumeister, 1989; Colvin & Block, 1994; Reid, 1984). For example, unrealistic perceptions of control held by cardiac patients and rheumatoid arthritis sufferers are associated with poor adjustment (Affleck et al., 1987; Helgeson, 1992). It may be, however, that we have more control over our health than we often think. For example, even people who are HIV-positive can increase their longetivity by adhering to their difficult drug regimen, engaging in better health habits, maintaining supportive relationships, and avoiding other life stresses. And recent research indicates that positive beliefs about control can help such individuals do just that (Taylor et al., 2000). In sum, it seems that perceptions of control can be quite beneficial to mental and physical health when the exercise of control is actually possible, which is frequently the case. However, when one no longer has the ability to influence events, psychological well-being may benefit more from the acceptance of this loss.

We've seen that people have a wide range of cognitive strategies for feeling good about themselves—they compare themselves with others, are quick to take personal credit for their successes, view their strengths as being especially important, and inflate their perceptions of control. Of course, the desires for self-enhancement and self-protection are stronger for some people than others. We turn, then, to explore the person and situation factors that motivate people toward positive self-regard.

Self-Esteem

People who have high self-esteem—who feel good about themselves as individuals—are especially likely to engage in self-enhancing strategies. They're more likely than their low-self-esteem counterparts to boost themselves through social comparison, and they appear to be better skilled at using both upward and downward comparison strategies (Buunk, Collins, Taylor, Van Yperen, & Dakof, 1990). They're more likely to derogate others to improve their own feelings of self-worth (Crocker et al., 1987; Gibbons & McCoy, 1991; Wills, 1981). They're also more likely to exhibit the self-serving bias (Blaine & Crocker, 1993; Tennen & Herzberger, 1987), to inflate the importance of their own traits and successes (Harter, 1993), and to exaggerate their sense of control (Alloy & Abramson, 1979). All told, people who have high self-esteem use many cognitive strategies to improve the way they feel about themselves.

What of people who have lower self-esteem? Are they immune to such self-enhancement practices? Are they uninterested in positive self-regard? Actually, most individuals, regardless of level of self-esteem, want to feel good about themselves (Baumeister, 1993; Pelham, 1993). Self-esteem does seem to influence, however, the strategies people use to create a positive self-image. People who have high self-esteem are bold and tend to engage in direct self-*enhancing* strategies. People who have only moderate or low self-esteem, however, tend to be more cautious in how they go about gaining positive self-regard (e.g., Brown, Collins, & Schmidt, 1988; Gibbons & McCoy, 1991; Shepperd, Ouellette, & Fernandez, 1996; Wood, Giordano-Beech, Taylor, Michela, & Gaus, 1994). They focus instead on *protecting* the esteem they already possess (Baumeister, Tice, & Hutton, 1989; Spencer, Josephs, & Steele, 1993; Tice, 1993).

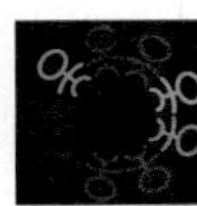

Threats to Self-Esteem

Threats to self-esteem spur people to enhance and protect their self-image (Steele, 1988; Tesser, 1988). As part of a study assessing student impressions of standardized IQ tests, participants attempted a set of problems depicted as basic to creativity and intelligence (Greenberg, Pyszczynski, & Solomon, 1982). The test was further described as an excellent predictor of future academic and financial success. Some of the participants were led to believe they had performed poorly, whereas the others were led to believe they had performed quite well. When later asked to appraise the test, the opinions of the groups diverged quite dramatically: Students who thought they had done poorly not only minimized the importance of good performance but also were likely to attribute their low scores to bad luck, unclear instructions, and the invalidity of the test—apparently everything but their own ability! This type of self-protective bias is not limited to the laboratory. Students at the University of Florida, for instance, were more likely to see the Scholastic Aptitude Test (SAT) as invalid if they had performed poorly on it (Shepperd, 1993).

Indeed, findings like these are quite common: Situational threats to self-image frequently lead to efforts to restore that self-image (e.g., Beauregard & Dunning, 1998; Pyszczynski, Greenberg, & Holt, 1985; Shepperd, Arkin, & Slaughter, 1995). In the above cases, the threat was negative performance, and the restoration attempts involved diminishing the importance of the task and derogating its fairness and validity. Self-image can also be threatened by negative interpersonal feedback ("Don't you think you could lose a few pounds?"), a serious illness like cancer, or even our own actions, as when we feel terribly about ourselves for being insensitive to someone we love. To deal with such threats, we may use the same strategies described earlier; that is, we may compare ourselves with others less fortunate, derogate those who give us negative feedback, and so forth (e.g., Aspinwall & Taylor, 1993; Dunning, Leuenberger, & Sherman, 1995; Hakmiller, 1966; Kernis, Cornell, Sun, Berry, & Harlow, 1993; Wood, Giordano-Beech, & Ducharme, 1999).

Death threat. *After thinking about death, people favor those who affirm their cherished values and derogate those who don't, seek support for their social attitudes and beliefs, and engage in other cognitive strategies to affirm their views of the world—all to protect themselves from threatening thoughts of their own mortality.*

One particularly interesting form of self-image threat is *mortality salience*—the awareness that one will, at some point, die. Tom Pyszczynski, Jeff Greenberg, and Sheldon Solomon (1999) propose that thinking about the possibility of one's own demise is extremely threatening to the self-image. Because broad spiritual and cultural views may exist partially to protect us from mortality concerns, people made aware of their mortality may seek to bolster those who validate their cherished values and derogate those who challenge them.

In one study, Christian students completing a questionnaire were made highly aware of their own mortality—they were asked to write about what will happen to them as they die and how they feel about thinking about their own death. Other Christian students completed an otherwise-identical questionnaire that made no mention of death. Later, all provided their impressions of a previously unknown person presented as either Christian or Jewish. Consistent with the hypothesis, this person was evaluated more favorably when Christian than when Jewish, thereby validating these students' religous values—but only by those subjects made aware of their own mortality (Greenberg et al., 1990). Other studies demonstrate similar effects. For example, thinking about one's death leads American students to like those who praise the United States and dislike those who criticize it, and to treat people who validate our moral values more favorably than those who morally transgress (Greenberg et al., 1990; Rosenblatt et al., 1989).

In sum, situational threats—whether in the form of apparent failure, negative feedback from others, serious illness, or thoughts of one's own mortality—potentially endanger the self-image, leading to greater self-protection efforts.

When Self-Esteem Is Fragile

The *stability* of self-views interacts with both self-esteem and threat to influence how people view themselves and others. Some of your friends probably seem very certain about who they are, whereas other friends seem much less sure (Baumgardner, 1990; Campbell et al., 1996; Pelham, 1991). Moreover, the self-esteem of some of your friends is probably very stable from day to day—they feel good about themselves today, they felt good about themselves yesterday, and they will feel good about themselves tomorrow—whereas, for others, self-esteem seems to fluctuate quite dramatically over even short periods of time (Kernis, Grannemann, & Barclay, 1989).

In general, people who have unstable self-esteem are greatly concerned with the self-implications of life's everyday events and are particularly likely to respond to these events with attempts to enhance or protect the self. In one study, for example, students possessing unstable self-esteem were more likely than their stable counterparts to generate excuses to explain their grades on a psychology exam ("I didn't care enough to study very hard for this exam"). Indeed, the tendency for high-self-esteem students to use excuses to boost their self-image and for low-self-esteem students to use excuses to protect their self-image occurred mostly for those students who had unstable self-esteem (Kernis, Grannemann, & Barclay, 1992). We see, then, that self-esteem instability interacts with level of self-esteem to influence how people maintain a positive self-regard.

Finally, these two factors interact with situational threat to determine how people create and maintain positive self-regard. Specifically, the influences of a person's self-esteem and self-esteem instability are particularly apparent when the person feels that his or her self-esteem is threatened in one way or another. In one study, subjects were given either positive or negative feedback on a speech. Individuals who had unstable high self-esteem were most likely of all subjects to generate excuses for their poor performance after receiving negative feedback ("I didn't try very hard") and least likely of all subjects to make excuses after receiving positive feedback (Kernis et al., 1993). Self-esteem, self-esteem instability, and threat all work together to influence how we go about viewing ourselves.

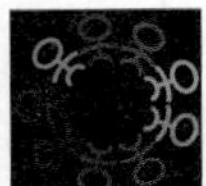

How Universal Is the Need for Positive Self-Regard?

The desire for positive self-regard has traditionally been assumed to be a universal need—everyone's interested in viewing themselves favorably, or so it seems. But is this the case? Clearly, the findings we've explored so far suggest so: People compare themselves with others, manage how they view their successes and failures, exaggerate their strengths and minimize their weaknesses, and create illusions of control—usually to feel good about themselves. You may have noticed, however, that most of the research we've explored in this section studied Americans, Canadians, and Northern Europeans. Might people from other cultures be less motivated to elevate their personal self-esteem?

Recall that people in individualistic cultures are taught to focus on the *me*—to stand out and pursue their own goals and interests. Their esteem is predominantly grounded in their personal or *in*dependent self-concepts—in their view of themselves as autonomous individuals. In contrast, people in collectivistic cultures are taught to focus on the *we*—to fit in and seek harmony with those in their groups. Their esteem is predominantly grounded in their social or *inter*dependent self-concepts—in their view of themselves in relation to others (Markus & Kitayama, 1991). People with interdependent selves should be less motivated to enhance and protect a personal self-image, for two reasons: First, "sticking out" from others is potentially damaging to harmonious relations with others, and self-enhancement promotes sticking out (recall the Japanese adage from chapter 2: "If the nail sticks up, pound it down!"). Second, people in collectivistic cultures need the approval of others to a greater extent. As a consequence, they may be especially motivated to improve themselves in the eyes of others. Self-*criticism*—not self-enhancement—is a more useful strategy for doing this.

Indeed, members of collectivistic cultures *are* less likely to demonstrate biases like the ones we've been exploring (Brockner & Chen, 1996; Heine, Lehman, Markus, & Kitayama, 1999). Consider the Japanese. Whereas Americans tend to blame their failures on the situation, Japanese attribute their failures to their own personal inadequacies (Kitayama, Takagi, & Matsumoto, 1995). Whereas North Americans tend to self-enhance and see themselves as better than others, Japanese tend to self-criticize and see themselves as worse than others (Heine, Takata, & Lehman, 2000; Kitayama, Markus, Matsumoto, & Norasakkunkit, 1997). And Canadians are more unrealistically optimistic than are Japanese (Heine & Lehman, 1995).

The evidence seems clear. The desire for favorable personal self-esteem, and the cognitive gymnastics people engage in to create it, characterizes those in individualistic cultures more than those in collectivistic cultures.

Summary

People want to create and maintain positive self-regard, and this desire affects how they think about themselves and others. The strategies we use to enhance and protect our self-regard include both downward and upward social comparison, taking credit for our successes and minimizing responsibility for our failures, magnifying the importance of things we do well and minimizing the importance of things we do poorly, and exaggerating our perception of control. Situational threats like negative feedback, failure, and mortality salience drive our desire to protect our self-image. People having different levels of self-esteem and self-esteem instability respond to these threats in somewhat different ways. Interestingly, the strong need for positive regard seems to best characterize members of individualistic cultures; members of collectivistic cultures, like Japan, tend to be self-critical instead of self-enhancing.

Seeking Accuracy

In the early hours of April 15, 1969, the recently elected President Nixon awoke to his first international crisis. A North Korean jet had shot down a U.S. plane flying a routine reconnaissance mission off the Korean coast. The initial reports were sketchy, leaving most questions unanswered: Were the men aboard killed, or had they been captured? Why was the plane shot down? Had the flight wandered mistakenly into North Korean territory? Was this an isolated incident, or was it a first move by the North Koreans to challenge the U.S. military presence in the area? Would a U.S. retaliation spark a North Korean attack on South Korea—thus forcing the United States, the Soviet Union, and the People's Republic of China toward a dangerous confrontation? If the United States did nothing, would that harm its prestige and credibility across the globe, making such incidents more likely in the future? The stakes were high, and Nixon needed to understand that night's events to predict what might happen next. An unbiased, comprehensive analysis was required.

Such an analysis may seem incompatible with what you've seen of human judgment so far—judgment that is shaded by all manner of simplifying and self-serving strategies. As useful as such strategies may be for creating mental economy and positive self-regard, however, they hardly represent the full capacities of human thought. Indeed, people can be quite accurate in their social and self-perceptions (Ambady & Rosenthal, 1992; Funder, 1999; Hastie & Rasinski, 1988; John & Robbins, 1994; Kenny, 1994; Wright & Dawson, 1988). Ironically, sometimes our shortcuts themselves lead to accuracy. For example, the simplifying use of a social stereotype will lead to pretty good judgments if the stereotype possesses a substantial "kernel of truth" (e.g., Berry, 1990; Lee, Jussim, & McCauley, 1995; Oakes, Haslam, & Turner, 1994; Swim, 1994).

Still, extreme biases toward simplicity and positive self-regard can get in the way of accurate social judgment. It's fortunate, then, that we don't simplify and self-enhance indiscriminately. After all, to survive the challenges of the social world, a good deal of *actual* understanding is necessary (Fiske, 1993; McArthur & Baron, 1983; Swann, 1984). And just as certain circumstances motivate us toward simplicity and positive self-regard, other circumstances motivate us toward accuracy in our self- and social perceptions. We begin, then, by exploring some of the strategies people use to reach a more accurate understanding of their social world (see Figure 3.6).

Figure 3.6
Seeking accuracy.

When people have a special desire to have control over their lives, or when they want to avoid making mistakes, they sometimes put aside their simplifying and self-enhancing strategies in the hope of gaining a more accurate understanding of themselves and others.

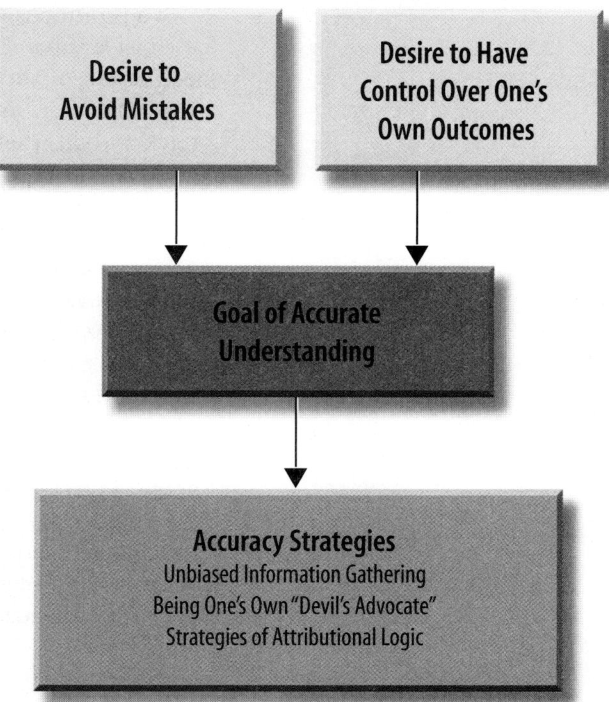

Unbiased Information Gathering

Confronted with the attack on the U.S. reconnaissance plane, Nixon began to search for accurate information, mobilizing his own intelligence services and seeking information from friendly countries. Moreover, he solicited a breadth of perspectives from his own circle of advisors: Kissinger and Agnew argued for military retaliation, while others urged caution and restraint. Nixon needed to make a good decision and wanted reliable information interpreted in an unbiased way.

Likewise, when we're motivated to be accurate in daily life, we gather more information than normal. For instance, if we want to form an accurate impression of another person, we tend to listen more and ask more questions (Darley, Fleming, Hilton, & Swann, 1988; Neuberg, 1989). We also seem to value information that will help us go beyond our initial biases. In a study by Ralph Erber and Susan Fiske (1984), student participants believed that they would be working with an education major to create new games for children and that they could win a cash reward if they did well. Before starting, they all privately completed and then exchanged personal profiles describing themselves. For half the participants, the education major—actually a confederate of the experimenters—presented herself as very creative; for the other half, she described herself as noncreative. Finally, students were given a chance to read the confederate's teaching evaluations. Half these evaluations were quite favorable and half were unfavorable, and the experimenter secretly timed how long participants read each type.

Where did the students focus their attention? Note that evaluations *in*consistent with what you expect should be particularly useful—after all, only these contain new information (Jones & McGillis, 1976). Indeed, when the confederate presented herself positively, subjects focused on the unfavorable evaluations; when the confederate presented herself negatively, they focused on the favorable evaluations. When people are motivated to be accurate—as in this case, in which participants depended on each other to win the money—they pay special attention to information that enables them to go beyond their initial conceptions (Fiske & Neuberg, 1990).

Being One's Own "Devil's Advocate"

Even after people collect a wide range of information, they may make poor decisions because they don't seriously assess alternative possibilities. This is why groups with difficult decisions to make sometimes assign a member the role of "devil's advocate." This person's task is to argue *against* the popular view, whatever it might be. Such a position is valuable because it increases the probability that alternatives will be considered and weaknesses exposed. Although there was apparently no official designation of such a role when Nixon and his advisors faced the North Korean crisis, various advisors did serve this function by disagreeing on the meaning of the attack and on what actions to take, thus providing Nixon with a broad analysis of the issues.

As individuals, we can adopt a similar orientation in our own cognitive deliberations—we can play devil's advocate for ourselves. A study by Charles Lord, Mark Lepper, and Elizabeth Preston (1984) nicely illustrates how this works. Participants read about two competing research studies—one that suggested that capital punishment deters future murders and one that indicated that capital punishment is not an effective deterrent. Consistent with research on expectation biases, participants believed the study supporting their own views to be methodologically stronger and more compelling than the study opposing their views: Proponents of capital punishment favored the study illustrating its deterrent effects; opponents favored the study showing a lack of deterrent effects.

A second set of participants underwent the same procedure, but with an important change. Prior to reading the studies, they were taught that people often interpret things in ways that fit with their expectations and desires and were instructed to counter this natural tendency by considering the opposite: "Ask yourself at each step whether you would have made the same high or low evaluations had exactly the same study produced results on the *other* side of the issue" (p. 1233). In essence, they were asked to be their own devil's advocates. As the researchers suspected, this strategy effectively reduced the bias: These participants evaluated the two studies as equally credible and convincing. When desiring to be even-handed, it will serve you well to challenge your own initial views and to consider alternative possibilities (Hirt & Markman, 1995).

Attributional Logic

People may also increase the accuracy of their judgments by working to understand the causes of others' actions. For Nixon, understanding *why* the North Koreans had shot down the U.S. reconnaissance plane was crucial, as it would determine the U.S. response. As we discovered earlier, we attribute the causes of behavior to forces either *internal* to the actor (e.g., the aggressiveness of the North Korean leadership) or *external* to the actor (e.g., the threatening military posture of the United States toward the North Koreans). When motivated to simplify, Westerners tend toward internal, dispositional attributions. When motivated to be accurate, however, people move more into the role of an impartial detective, considering more carefully both internal (dispositional) and external (situational) causes.

But how do we decide whether the cause of a behavior is internal to the actor, external to the actor, or some combination of the two? Two prominent theories designed to answer this question expanded on the ideas of Fritz Heider (1944, 1958)—the "father" of the attributional approach. First, Edward Jones and Keith Davis (1965; Jones, 1990) presented **correspondent inference theory,** which described how a person might logically determine whether a particular behavior *corresponds* to an enduring characteristic of the actor. How could Nixon know, for instance, whether the attack on the U.S. plane was due to the hostile nature of the North Korean government? Second, Harold Kelley (1967, 1973) proposed his **covariation model** of causal attribution, which proposes that people pick among several possible causes by weighting most heavily the potential cause that best *covaries*—or correlates—with the event. From these, and related, perspectives, several general principles emerged.

Analyzing Behavior in Its Social Context A good detective might begin by analyzing the circumstances immediately surrounding the behavior of interest. This was the focus of correspondent inference theory. First, then, we should ask whether the behavior was *intended* and its consequences *foreseeable.* In the absence of intention and foreseeability—if, for instance, the U.S. plane had been hit by stray bullets from a North Korean military exercise and the North Koreans had been unaware that U.S. planes would be in the area—we should probably view the event as an accident, caused by neither a stable aspect of the actor's personality nor by a powerful situational force.

Second, if we conclude that a behavior was both intended and the consequences foreseeable—for instance, if we determine that the North Koreans purposely shot at the U.S. plane, knowing that doing so would likely cause it to crash—we should consider whether the action occurred with *free choice.* In this case, we might question whether the North Koreans chose to shoot down the U.S. plane (or whether, in contrast, they were forced to fire their weapons by some more powerful nation). Only when a behavior occurs with free choice can we assume that it reflects a corresponding disposition in the actor. For instance, if we learned that the more powerful Chinese forced the North Koreans to attack the U.S. plane, we would probably attribute the action to the Chinese threat.

Based on accumulating evidence, Nixon and his advisors concluded that the attack was freely chosen, intended, and foreseeable—and thus, that it was not an accident. The third issue becomes, then, whether the behavior corresponded to some stable underlying trait or motive of the North Koreans or whether it was due to some aspect of the situation. Here the analysis gets more complicated, as there exist multiple possibilities within each of these categories. For example, perhaps the American flight had

Correspondent inference theory *The theory that proposes that people determine whether a behavior corresponds to an actor's internal disposition by asking whether (1) the behavior was intended, (2) the behavior's consequences were foreseeable, (3) the behavior was freely chosen, and (4) the behavior occurred despite countervailing forces.*

Covariation model *The theory that proposes that people determine the cause of an actor's behavior by assessing whether other people act in similar ways (consensus), the actor behaves similarly in similar situations (distinctiveness), and the actor behaves similarly in the same situation (consistency).*

In which circumstances would you be more confident that Jack's proposal is motivated by his love?

A	B
Jack loves Jill *and* Jack's buddies like Jill	Jack loves Jill *and* Jack's buddies like Jill *and* Jill is wealthy *and* Jill tolerates Jack's bad habits

You probably answered Circumstance A, because B contains many possible reasons for Jack's proposal, and as the possible reasons for Jack's proposal begin to pile up, we become less certain that Jack is motivated primarily by love. This illustrates the *discounting principle.*

Consider now the following circumstances under which Jack proposes. Again, in which case does Jack's love for Jill seem particularly influential?

A	B
Jack loves Jill *and* Jack's buddies hate Jill *and* Jill is dirt poor *and* Jill always tries to change Jack's bad habits	Jack loves Jill *and* Jack's buddies like Jill *and* Jill is wealthy *and* Jill tolerates Jack's bad habits

Again, you probably picked A. Why? Because Jack proposed despite reasons that would otherwise lead him away from such behavior. More generally, as the number of possible causes pushing against a particular action increases, we place more confidence in those causes that push toward that action. This is the *augmenting principle.*

Figure 3.7
Discounting and augmenting.

Consider the following event: Jack asks Jill to marry him. One possible cause for Jack's proposal, of course, is his love for Jill. But let's consider circumstances A and B in the figure.

wandered into North Korean airspace. Perhaps the North Koreans were testing the U.S. military commitment. Perhaps they wanted to provoke a U.S. retaliation to justify an attack on South Korea. Or perhaps it was a demonstration of military prowess by the North Korean generals to their leaders.

The large cast of possibilities makes it difficult to place great stock in any specific one of them. Kelley (1973) called this the **discounting principle:** as the number of possible causes increases, we become less sure that any particular cause is the true one. Nixon needed, then, to narrow the possibilities. Fortunately, forthcoming intelligence revealed that the plane was downed well beyond North Korean territorial airspace, reducing the likelihood that they had felt provoked. This increased Nixon's confidence that the cause of the incident was internal to the North Korean leadership, having something to do with their military plans.

In addition, the attack occurred despite strong restraining forces—for example, the inevitable condemnation by the world community and the risk of major U.S. military reprisals. This suggested to Nixon that this internal influence was pretty powerful. Such reasoning illustrates the **augmenting principle:** If an event occurs despite powerful countervailing or opposing forces, we can view the event's probable cause as especially potent (Kelley, 1973; see Figure 3.7).

Extending the Analysis: The Covariation Model Our examination to this point, then, suggests that something internal to the North Korean leadership led to the attack. Kelley's covariation model proposes that the effective detective might extend the analysis even further by considering available information from *outside* the immediate situation. For instance, we might ask whether other countries would act in the same way: If there's a lack of *consensus*—that is, if few, if any, countries besides North Korea would attack a U.S. plane flying over international waters—we might attribute more of the causal responsibility to factors within North Korea. In contrast, if there is a large consensus—that is, if many countries would mount such an attack—we should attribute more of the causal responsibility to external factors, such as U.S. foreign policies. Because few other countries have attacked U.S. military flights (low consensus), the possibility that the action had strong causes internal to the North Korean leadership is strengthened.

Discounting principle *The judgmental rule that states that as the number of possible causes for an event increases, our confidence that any particular cause is the true one should decrease.*

Augmenting principle *The judgmental rule that states that if an event occurs despite the presence of strong opposing forces, we should give more weight to those possible causes that lead toward the event.*

We might further ask whether North Korea acted similarly toward other countries. That is, if the behavior showed no *distinctiveness*—if North Korea exhibited similar military aggressiveness toward many other countries—we should view its action as coming from internal sources (North Korea's characteristic belligerence). In contrast, if the North Koreans acted distinctively toward the United States—attacking it, but not other countries—perhaps at least part of the responsibility lies externally (with the United States). Because North Korea had exhibited hostilities toward South Korea but had good relationships with mainland China and other communist countries in Asia, we might see their behavior toward the United States as being moderately distinctive, perhaps placing part of the causal influence on North Korea and part on the United States.

Finally, we might ask whether the North Koreans had acted similarly toward the United States at other times. A high level of *consistency* would suggest the stability of the underlying cause, whereas a low level of consistency would make it more difficult to draw any firm conclusions. Despite North Korean hostilities toward the United States in the past and its capture several years earlier of a U.S. navy ship, this bold, risky action was viewed by Nixon and his advisors as an isolated incident.

Putting it together, then, we see that the North Koreans were highly unusual in their unprovoked attack on the United States, making it a *low-consensus* behavior; that there existed many countries that North Korea didn't attack, making the attack a behavior of *moderate distinctiveness;* and that they hadn't made a habit of attacking U.S. military targets, suggesting *low consistency.* Such a pattern suggests an isolated incident resulting from the particular, tense interaction between the United States and North Korea. Nixon, perhaps as a consequence, decided not to retaliate, hoping to avoid an all-out war (see Figure 3.8).

We're particularly likely to infer that the proposal reflects something about Jack alone– his desparation, for example (an internal, or person, attribution)–when:

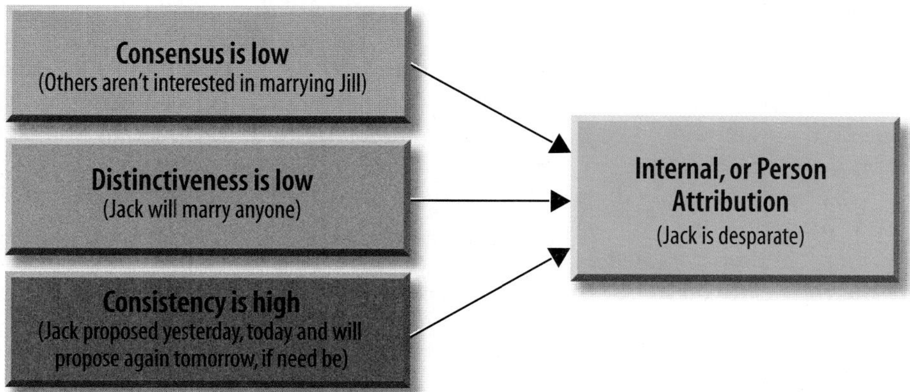

We're particularly likely to infer that the proposal reflects something special about Jill (an external, or situation, attribution) when:

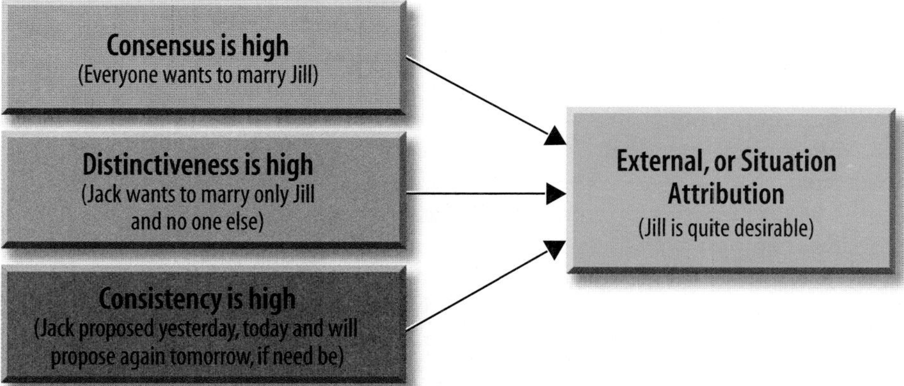

Finally, we're particularly likely to infer that Jack's proposal reflects something special about the combination between Jack and Jill–their special "magic" (an interaction attribution)–when:

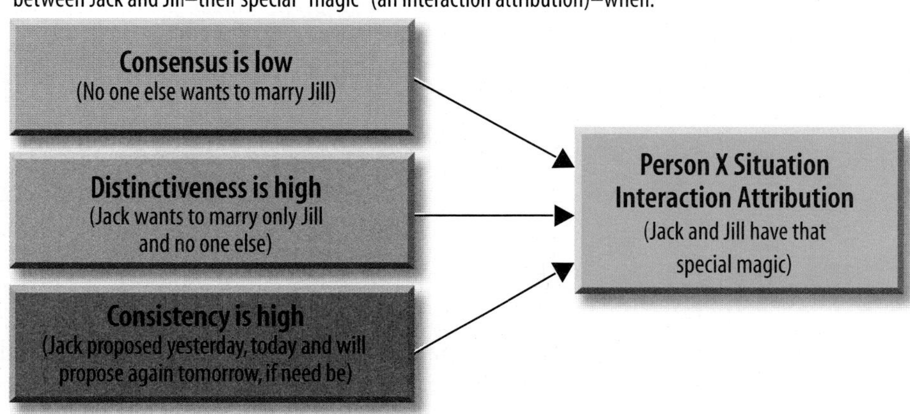

Figure 3.8
Using consensus, distinctiveness, and consistency information.

Kelley's covariation model proposes that different configurations of consensus, distinctiveness, and consistency information lead us to different conclusions about the reasons underlying a person's actions. Three configurations are particularly clear in their implications (McArthur, 1972). Consider the event in Figure 3.7: Jack asks Jill to marry him.

Explaining the Self We have focused on how people can use an attributional logic to understand the actions of others. Daryl Bem (1967, 1972) proposed, however, that people sometimes use a similar kind of reasoning to understand their own behavior. Just as we infer others' intentions, attitudes, and characteristics from their behaviors and the circumstances in which these behaviors occur, we sometimes learn about our own intentions, attitudes, and characteristics by observing how we act in different situations. Indeed, as you saw in chapter 2, such *self-perception processes* can play an important role in shaping self-concept.

Consider, for instance, an experiment conducted by Mark Lepper, David Greene, and Richard Nisbett (1973). Children attending a preschool were observed playing with various toys, games, and art materials, and those children who demonstrated an intrinsic, inherent interest in drawing with magic markers were selected for the experiment. Two weeks later, these children were individually pulled aside and asked if they would draw pictures for a visitor. The children in the *expected reward* condition were told they would get a "Good Player Award"—with a gold star and red ribbon!—for drawing the pictures, and they received the award when finished. Children in the *unexpected reward* condition did not expect the reward, but received one anyway when done. Finally, children in the *no-reward* condition knew nothing of the reward at any point.

Seven to fourteen days later, observers returned to the preschool to assess how much time the children would freely spend playing with the magic markers. Which children retained their intrinsic interest in the activity? Consider how, as an outsider, you might think about the children's interest in the magic markers after watching them play with them in the three experimental conditions. In the no-reward condition, you'd likely attribute the childrens' drawing to their actual interest, as there existed no other strong forces compelling them to draw. In the unexpected-reward condition, you'd probably do the same—after all, the children didn't know the reward was forthcoming. In the expected-reward condition, however, it could be that the kids were playing merely to get the award, thus decreasing somewhat the likelihood—via the discounting principle—that their intrinsic interest was the major cause. Self-perception theory suggests that the children might reach the same conclusions themselves. That is, by "watching" themselves draw after having been offered an award for doing so, they might infer that they really weren't very interested in drawing for its own sake.

The findings supported this reasoning: Not only did children in the expected-reward condition spend less time playing with the magic markers in the free-play period than did the other children, but their interest in the markers decreased significantly from several weeks earlier. Such findings have been replicated many times and across many domains. When we reward people for doing what they already like, we may kill their interest in the activity (Amabile, Hennessey, & Grossman, 1986; Deci, 1971; Higgins, Lee, Kwon, & Trope, 1995; Kohn, 1993; Lepper & Greene, 1978). Society's practice, then, of rewarding students for the learning that most kids naturally enjoy may actually turn them off to self-education. Of course, rewards aren't always negative in their effects. If Bobby hates to read, rewards may be needed for him to develop the much-needed skill. Even if he chooses not to read after leaving school, at least he's become literate. Moreover, positive feedback that signals outstanding performance and competence can be beneficial, increasing intrinsic interest (Boggiano, Harackiewicz, Bessette, & Main, 1985; Harackiewicz & Manderlink, 1984). Rather, it's when a reward is seen as an attempt to *control* a person's actions that it has its undermining effects (Deci, Koestner, & Ryan, 1999).

We've seen that people use a variety of strategies when they want to be particularly accurate. They can gather information in a comprehensive way, they can serve as their own devil's advocate, and they can engage in logical attributional thought.

We turn now to explore the forces within the person that lead people to think carefully about themselves and others.

Desire for Control

Do you like making your own decisions? Would you prefer a job in which you have lots of control over what you do and when you do it? People who answer yes to such questions have a strong desire for control and think about their social world differently than people who answer no (Burger & Cooper, 1979). In general, people who have a high desire for control engage in more information gathering and more complex attributional reasoning (Burger, 1992).

Students in one study read an essay promoting the use of nuclear energy. Some learned that the writer was paid $2,500 for the essay, others learned that the essay was taken from the writer's private journal, and all were asked how well the essay represented the author's personal opinions. Students who had a low desire for control exhibited a correspondence bias, equally attributing the essay to the author's personal beliefs in both circumstances. That is, they didn't seem to consider the possibility that the written opinions were influenced by the large paycheck. In contrast, subjects who had a high desire for control saw the author's beliefs as somewhat less influential when he was compensated well for presenting the opinion (Burger & Hemans, 1988).

Why should a person having a high desire for control consider more thoroughly the available information? Careful thought serves more than just to satisfy our curiosity. Rather, we think so that we may better predict, and thus control, our world. As a consequence, people who have a greater desire for control should be particularly motivated to engage in complex thought, as this study illustrated.

Sadness

As we saw in chapter 2, positive feelings can signal that "all is well"—that the world is safe and rewarding. As a consequence, we have less need to be vigilant and careful when happy. In contrast, negative feelings signal that things aren't well—that we're falling short of some important goals (Frijda, 1988). Sadness, for instance, signals the loss of something valuable, such as a friendship, a good grade, or a prized possession. As a consequence, we should become particularly aware of our social surroundings when sad. Not only have these surroundings made it difficult for us to reach our goals, but they are also our hope for reaching our goals in the future. Indeed, people experiencing mild-to-moderate sadness tend to engage in more complex thought (Forgas, 1995; Schaller & Cialdini, 1990; Schwarz, 1990; Taylor & Brown, 1988).

For instance, people who are mildly to moderately depressed are more thorough when thinking about social events (e.g., Edwards, Weary, von Hippel, & Jacobson, 2000; Flett, Pliner, & Blankstein, 1989; Gannon, Skowronski, & Betz, 1994). Consider, for instance, how carefully you might interview potential roommates after learning that your current roommate no longer wants to live with you. In a study by John Edwards and Gifford Weary (1993), moderately depressed students were less likely to rely on their academic stereotypes to form impressions of other students. Careful and comprehensive thought often helps depressed individuals deal with chronic uncertainty and lost control (Weary, Marsh, Gleicher, & Edwards, 1993).

Of course, depression does not *always* lead to more thorough thinking (Conway & Giannopolous, 1993; Lassiter, Koenig, & Apple, 1996; Sullivan & Conway, 1989). When a person's depression is severe, and when the cognitive task is difficult and unrelated to that person's present concerns, he or she is unlikely to engage in careful analysis (Hartlage, Alloy, Vázquez, & Dykman, 1993; von Hecker & Sedek, 1999).

Need for Cognition

People who are sad and who desire control are more likely to seek accurate understanding of their social world. People who are high in the need for cognition—who enjoy solving life's puzzles, view thinking as fun, and appreciate discovering the strengths and weaknesses of their arguments—also seek accurate understanding (Cacioppo & Petty, 1982). Such individuals are less likely to use simplifying heuristics and more willing to expend instead the extra effort needed to assess their circumstances fully (e.g., Ahlering & Parker, 1989; Cacioppo, Petty, Feinstein, & Jarvis, 1996; Srull, Lichtenstein, & Rothbart, 1985).

Subjects in one study read a speech either opposing or favoring legalized abortion and were told that the speechwriter was assigned to the particular position and had no choice. People low in need for cognition exhibited the correspondence bias—they believed that the speech contents matched the writer's true attitude, thus disregarding the author's lack of free choice. In contrast, people high in need for cognition correctly took into account the writer's situation (D'Agostino & Fincher-Kiefer, 1992).

Do Women and Men Think Differently?

We've seen that some people are more likely than others to seek accurate answers to their social questions. For centuries, many scientists and laypersons believed that this quest for accuracy existed primarily within men. Indeed, Gustave Le Bon—one of the founders of social psychology—shared the common view of his time that the thought processes of women were decidedly inferior in this respect:

> [The female] inferiority is so obvious that no one can contest it for a moment; only its degree is worth discussion.... They excel in fickleness, inconstancy, absence of thought and logic, and incapacity to reason. Without doubt there exist some distinguished women, very superior to the average man, but they are as exceptional as the birth of any monstrosity, as, for example, of a gorilla with two heads; consequently, we may neglect them entirely. (Le Bon, 1879, pp. 60–61; translated in Gould, 1981, pp. 104–105.)

What a striking statement! Could Le Bon be correct? Do men and women really think so differently?

If we consider the *contents* of social thought—that is, *what* people think about—the answer to this provocative question is partly yes, but mostly no. In general, because men and women share many of the same goals and enter many of the same situations, they spend much of their time contemplating similar things—whether they can afford the monthly payments on a much-needed new car, what to do about their loud and obnoxious neighbor, and so forth.

Males and females sometimes find themselves in different social roles and situations, however, and this influences what they think about. For instance, "homemakers" will spend a good proportion of their waking hours thinking about children and meals, whereas "breadwinners" will spend much of their time contemplating their occupational tasks. To the extent women are still more likely to occupy the homemaker role than are men, and men more the breadwinner role than women, the everyday thought content of the "average" man and "average" woman might reflect these differences. Moreover, although members of both sexes focus heavily on kindness, intelligence, dependability, emotional maturity, and good health when thinking about potential mates, women tend to emphasize more than men the social dominance and earning capacity of their partners while men emphasize, more than women, the physical attractiveness and youth of their partners (Buss et al., 1990; Feingold, 1990; Kenrick & Keefe, 1992); we explore these findings more fully in Chapter 8.

Several other content differences exist, as well. For instance, the vivid memories of men are more likely than women's to be related to achievement and competence

An obvious inferiority? *Marie Sklodowska Curie won Nobel Prizes in physics and chemistry—one of only three people to be doubly recognized for scientific accomplishment. Yet, many scientists disparaged her contributions, presuming that the inability of women to reason logically left them incapable of making great discoveries without male help. Even Gustave Le Bon, one of social psychology's founders, believed that the thought processes of women were obviously inferior to those of men. Madame Curie and countless other stunningly successful women have proven him—and continue to prove him—wrong.*

(White, 1988). Women's sexual fantasies tend to be more personal and emotional, whereas men's tend toward the physical and impersonal (Ellis & Symons, 1990). So although there are some gender differences in thought content, they tend to mirror gender differences in social circumstance and goals.

There are few differences, however, in the thought *processes* men and women use. That is, Le Bon's pronouncement aside, men are not more intelligent than women, nor do the sexes possess different styles of thought. Although men, on average, do have somewhat better spatial abilities (Voyer, Voyer, & Bryden, 1995), women are better at tasks requiring perceptual speed (Feingold, 1993) and have a slight advantage in verbal ability (Hyde & Linn, 1988). In any case, none of these abilities is critical to the self and social perception processes we've been exploring. Indeed, there's little evidence that men and women differ in *how* they go about understanding themselves and others. Experiments in social cognition rarely discover meaningful sex differences. Moreover, the sexes don't differ in their dispositional needs for structure, control, or cognition—the three characteristics most consistently associated with the simplifying versus accuracy-seeking styles of social thought (Burger, 1992; Cacioppo & Petty, 1982; Neuberg & Newsom, 1993; Thompson, Naccarato, & Parker, 1989). Women do, however, report themselves to be slightly lower in self-esteem than do men (Hall, 1984; Harter, 1993)—a difference that may account for the finding that women are somewhat more likely than men to accept personal blame for their own failures. If anything, then, women may use less brazen strategies to self-enhance, although the desire for positive self-regard is highly prominent for both sexes and such a difference seems quite small.

Overall, then, women and men are much more similar than different in their social thinking. Le Bon was just plain wrong—although the sexes may differ a bit in *what* they think about, they don't much differ in *how* they think.

Unexpected Events

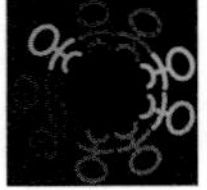

The goal of accuracy stems from a need to increase control. When personal control is taken away, people start to think more carefully (e.g., Pittman & D'Agostino, 1985; Swann, Stephenson, & Pittman, 1981). Unexpected events threaten control, and typically lead us to think in more complex ways (e.g., Clary & Tesser, 1983; Sanna & Turley, 1996; Wong & Weiner, 1981). Participants in one study read about a student who had done either well or poorly in high school and then learned about the student's college grades. For some participants, their expectations were confirmed. For example, the good student in high school received good grades in college. For others, their expectations were violated. For example, the poor student in high school did unexpectedly well in college. Participants then retold the story into a tape recorder as if they were relaying it to a friend. Those who learned of the unexpected outcome considered many more causal attributions ("perhaps he did much better than expected because he finally learned how to study") than those who simply had their expectation confirmed (Kanazawa, 1992). This study demonstrates that unexpected events increase our search for explanations. Other studies show similar influences of unexpected events (Hastie, 1984; Pyszczynski & Greenberg, 1981; Wyer, Budesheim, Lambert, & Swan, 1994).

Social Interdependence

We think carefully about others when our outcomes depend on them—when their actions have important implications for us (Berscheid, Graziano, Monson, & Dermer, 1976; Jones & Thibaut, 1958). This is the case when we're accountable to others, as we mentioned earlier (e.g., Kruglanski & Mayseless, 1988; Tetlock & Kim, 1987). For instance, if you know your boss is going to scrutinize your hiring decisions, you're likely to be quite thorough in your evaluations of the applicants. This is also the case when we're competing with people or when they have power over us (Fiske, 1993; Ruscher & Fiske, 1990). Junior managers, for example, are more likely to pay attention to their bosses than vice versa. And this is also true when we have cooperative relationships with other people. When we rely on our friends, spouses, project co-workers, and the like, we're quite thorough in our deliberations about them (Brewer, 1988; Fiske & Neuberg, 1990).

In one study, students participated in a program ostensibly designed to ease long-term, college-aged hospital patients back into everyday life. As an ice-breaker, students were told that they would work together with the former patients to create interesting games and could win cash prizes for particularly creative ideas. Some students were told they could win the prize based only on their *individual* efforts, whereas others were told that their *joint* efforts with the former patient would be critical. All students learned that their partner, "Frank," had been hospitalized as a schizophrenic. They then read a personal statement he had written, and provided their initial impressions of him.

When students' fates were tied to the patient, their impressions of him were affected less by their stereotypes of schizophrenics. Instead, they paid extra attention to his personal statement and adjusted their impressions of him accordingly

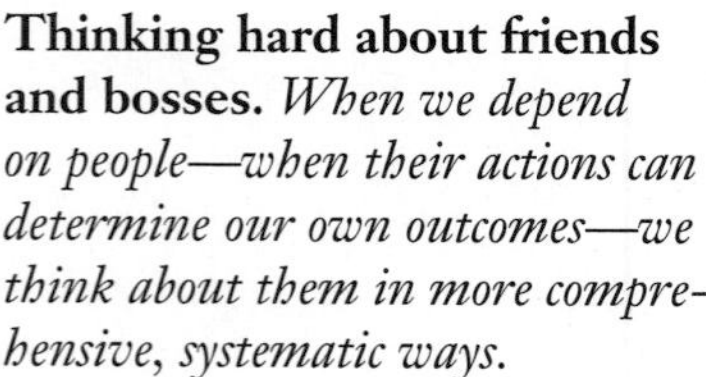

Thinking hard about friends and bosses. *When we depend on people—when their actions can determine our own outcomes—we think about them in more comprehensive, systematic ways.*

(Neuberg & Fiske, 1987). When we're interdependent on others, we think about them more thoroughly and reduce our reliance on cognitive shortcuts.

The Crucial Role of Cognitive Resources

No matter how motivated we are to be accurate, we won't be able to think deeply if we lack the necessary attentional resources (Bargh & Thein, 1985; Tetlock & Kim, 1987; Thompson et al., 1994; Wyer, Sherman, & Stroessner, 2000). Gathering a lot of information, being your own devil's advocate, and engaging in complex attributional reasoning are difficult. They require a large amount of mental resources. Even if you really want to decide on the best person for a job, for instance, you may fail if you're simultaneously distracted by a pending loan approval, dinner plans with your girlfriend's parents, or rumored layoffs at your company.

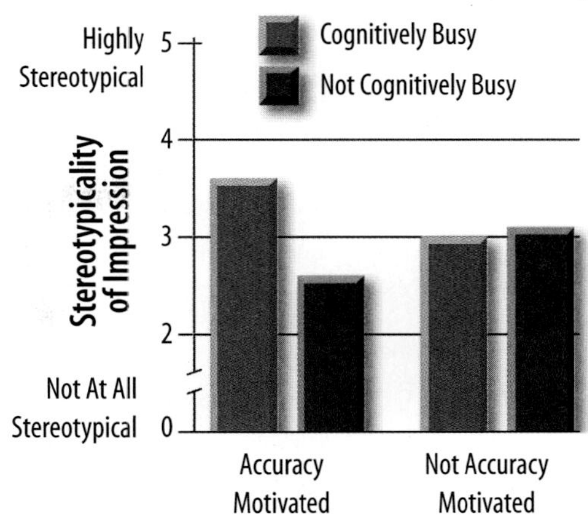

Figure 3.9
Is the desire to be accurate enough?

In the Pendry and Macrae (1994) study, participants were either motivated to form accurate impressions or not, and were either made cognitively busy or not. Only those who were both accuracy-motivated and cognitively nonbusy reduced their reliance on stereotypes.

SOURCE: *Adapted from Pendry & Macrae (1994), Table 1.*

In one study, Louise Pendry and Neil Macrae (1994) informed participants that they would be working with "Hilda," a sixty-five-year-old, on a problem-solving task. Similar to the "Frank" study described above, some participants were told that they could receive a monetary prize for working well with Hilda; they were *interdependent* with her and thus motivated to form an accurate impression of her. The remaining participants were told that they would be rewarded based solely on their own individual performance; their performance was *independent*, and so they were not especially motivated to be accurate. Moreover, because the experimenters were ostensibly interested in how people could perform multiple tasks concurrently, half the participants in each condition were asked to hold in mind an 8-digit number. All then read a personality profile that presented Hilda in a way partially consistent with stereotypes about the elderly and partially inconsistent with them. Finally, just prior to meeting her, participants provided their impressions of Hilda.

As Figure 3.9 demonstrates, the participants unmotivated by accuracy used their stereotypes of the elderly to evaluate Hilda, as did the accuracy-motivated participants who were cognitively busy. Only those who were both nonbusy and motivated to be accurate were able to reduce their reliance on the elderly stereotypes. This study demonstrates, then, that the desire to be accurate isn't enough—only when a desire for accuracy is *combined* with sufficient cognitive resources can people move beyond their tendency to simplify.

Summary

People often seek an accurate understanding of themselves and those around them. In such instances, they gather social information in a more thorough, comprehensive way and are more likely to reconsider previous impressions and judgments and to play "devil's advocate" against their current view. They are also more likely to apply attributional logic when assessing why certain events happened as they did. As people contemplate the relative contributions of forces within the person and the situation, they ask whether a person's behavior was intended and the consequences foreseeable and whether he or she behaved with free choice. They are also likely to use the discounting and augmenting principles and to use information regarding consensus, distinctiveness, and consistency. Such accuracy-motivated strategies are used more frequently by people who are sad or who have a strong desire for control or need for cognition. These strategies also tend to be instigated by unexpected events and social interdependence. Finally, because accuracy strategies are relatively thoughtful, people are less able to use them when they are under a high cognitive load (see Table 3.2).

CHAPTER 3
Summary Table

Table 3.2 Summary of the goals influencing social cognition and the factors related to them.

The Goal	The Person	The Situation	Interactions
Conserving Mental Effort	• Arousal and Circadian Rhythms • Positive Feelings • Need for Structure	• Situational Complexity • Time Pressure	• When expectations are clearly incompatible with the information available to us, we often rely on them less.
Managing Self-Image	• Self-Esteem	• Threats to Self-Esteem • Culture	• Self-esteem, self-esteem instability, and threat all work together to influence how people manage their self-image. People who possess unstable high self-esteem and who see that esteem as being threatened are particularly likely to respond strongly with self-protective strategies in defense of their selves.
Seeking Accuracy	• Desire for Control • Sadness • Need for Cognition	• Unexpected Events • Social Interdependence	• When people seek to form accurate impressions, they are often able to reduce the biasing impact of their stereotypes and expectations. The desire to be accurate is not enough, however. Only when the desire for accuracy is combined with sufficient cognitive resources can people move beyond their tendency to simplify.

REVISITING
The Portraits of Richard Nixon

We began this chapter with six widely diverging views of Richard Nixon, all written or spoken soon after his death. Can the lessons of this chapter help us understand how it was that one man was viewed so differently by those who observed him?

President Clinton, former Nixon advisor Kissinger, and Senator Dole were quite gracious and laudatory. The words of Kissinger and Dole came as no surprise. Both men shared with Nixon a common Republican political philosophy and thus probably viewed him in an expectation-confirming light. Moreover, both had self-serving reasons for thinking highly of Nixon. Henry Kissinger had been Nixon's primary foreign policy advisor; to speak glowingly of Nixon's foreign policy achievements, then, was a self-enhancing exercise, as Nixon's successes were Kissinger's successes. For Robert Dole, standard bearer of the Republican Party at the time, to praise Nixon was to raise the banner of his political party—the party that had made Nixon a member of the House of Representatives, a senator, a vice-president, and finally, a president.

Bill Clinton's affection for Nixon took many by surprise, however. Democrats had defiled Nixon for years, and Clinton's wife, Hilary Rodham Clinton, had worked for the House of Representatives committee attempting to impeach Nixon. Upon ascending to the presidency, however, Bill Clinton had grown to value Nixon's acumen in foreign policy and commitment to public service. Perhaps an appreciation for the complexities of his newly acquired position altered Clinton's perspective, motivating him to rethink his early impressions. Perhaps self-serving hopes that his own legacy would someday be a favorable one led him to discount some of Nixon's less dignified actions. After all, some of Clinton's own actions were less than dignified. Or perhaps his accountability to the voting public—who might frown deeply on anything even hinting at defamation—focused him on Nixon's positives, helping him to ignore Nixon's faults.

In contrast, the eulogies of Greider, McGovern, and Thompson were, shall we say, less charitable. George McGovern, a long-time Democratic senator from Minnesota, lost the presidential election to Nixon in 1972 by a huge margin. William Greider and Hunter S. Thompson were liberal journalists, well known for their scathing attacks on the "establishment" and its politics. Nixon's policies—particularly in Vietnam—were decidedly incompatible with the ideological values of these three commentators. It's thus not surprising that they would explain his actions in terms of an unquenchable ambition and a paranoid disposition, discounting the possibility that he had responded responsibly to powerful situational forces. And it's understandable that they focused their published eulogies on perhaps the most unambiguously negative episode of Nixon's career—Watergate—whereas Clinton, Kissinger, and Dole completely avoided the incident.

We see, then, that Richard Nixon was a canvas upon which all six commentators could paint personal portraits. The Nixon these people came to see depended a great deal on their own beliefs, goals, and social circumstances. And as you've learned, these same factors shape our own everyday observations and judgments of ourselves and others.

The lessons learned in this chapter also help you understand more about President Nixon's own thinking. We observed that he was particularly miserly with his cognitive efforts when overwhelmed by a relentless series of domestic and foreign crises. By his own account, this cognitive overload contributed to the mistakes that led to his humiliating fall from power. We observed that in the faces of both victory and defeat, he was often self-serving and egotistical. These efforts to enhance and protect his self-image were likely quite adaptive, however, enabling him to summon the confidence needed to battle back from two devastating election losses, to eventually lead the world's most powerful nation. And we observed that he was quite thoughtful when confronted with the unexpected and potentially major military crisis with North Korea—thoughtfulness that helped contribute to the favorable way so many people viewed his foreign policy decisions.

The story of how Richard Nixon viewed the social world, and of how the social world viewed him, is the story of us all. Although the content may differ a bit—each of us has our own particular combination of goals, feelings, and beliefs, and each of us presents those around us with a somewhat different canvas on which to work—the process of understanding is the same: When concerned with mental efficiency, we reach into our cognitive toolbox for those strategies that usually buy us "good enough" judgments for minimal effort. When concerned with self-image, we reach into the box for those strategies useful for enhancing and protecting our self-regard. And when circumstances become important enough, we reach in deep for those effortful strategies that we hope will lead to accurate understanding.

CHAPTER 3

Summary

The Social Thinker

1. People's actions are critically affected by their social cognition—by how they think about the social events and people they encounter. Four social-cognitive processes are fundamental: attention, interpretation, judgment, and memory.

Conserving Mental Effort

1. The social environment is amazingly complex, and humans have only a limited attentional capacity. As a result, people often use simplifying strategies that require few cognitive resources and that provide judgments that are generally "good enough."
2. People use their existing beliefs as expectations, which makes understanding new events much easier. When our expectations are accurate, using them leads to good judgments at little cost. When they are inaccurate, however, they may lead to erroneous judgments and self-fulfilling prophecies.
3. People—at least those in Western, individualistic cultures—make dispositional inferences to simplify the task of understanding the causes of others' actions. In the process, they may underestimate the impact of situational forces (the correspondence bias or fundamental attribution error), although this tendency is less prominent when people judge their own behavior (the actor–observer difference).
4. People have other cognitive shortcuts to choose from as well, including the representativeness heuristic, the availability heuristic, and the anchoring and adjustment heuristic.
5. People who are aroused, in a good mood, or dispositionally high in need for structure are particularly likely to use cognitive shortcuts.
6. When situations are particularly complex or people are under time pressure, they are also more likely to use simplifying cognitive shortcuts.
7. Sometimes people go beyond these simplification strategies, however, as when their situational realities just don't fit with their expectations.

Managing Self-Image

1. Positive self-regard is valuable because it equips us with the confidence needed to meet challenges and suggests that our social relationships are going well.
2. The strategies people use to enhance and protect their self-image include both downward and upward social comparison; taking credit for success and minimizing responsibility for failure; magnifying the importance of things they do well and minimizing the importance of things they do poorly; and exaggerating their perception of control.
3. People having high self-esteem are especially likely to engage in brazen attempts to enhance their self-regard. People having moderate-to-low self-esteem also desire positive self-regard but are more cautious in their strategies—they focus instead on protecting their existing level of self-regard.
4. Situations that threaten self-esteem increase the tendency to self-enhance or self-protect. Such situations include poor task performance, negative interpersonal feedback, a serious illness, or thinking about one's own death (mortality salience).
5. Self-esteem, self-esteem instability, and situational threat interact to promote self-enhancement and self-protection.
6. The desire for positive self-regard seems far from universal. In certain collectivistic cultures, for instance, people appear to be more motivated to be self-critical.

Seeking Accuracy

1. When seeking accuracy, people often gather social information in a more thorough, comprehensive way, reconsider previous impressions and judgments, and play "devil's advocate" against their current view.
2. The desire for accuracy may lead people to apply a "rational" attributional logic toward understanding why certain events happened as they did. As people consider the relative contributions of forces within the person and forces within the situation, they ask whether a person's behavior was intended and the consequences foreseeable and whether he or she behaved with free choice. They are also likely to use the discounting and augmenting principles and to use information regarding consensus, distinctiveness, and consistency.
3. Accuracy-motivated strategies are employed more frequently by people who are sad or who have a strong desire for control or need for cognition.
4. When events happen unexpectedly or when people's outcomes depend on the actions of others, people are more likely to seek accuracy.
5. Because accuracy strategies are relatively thoughtful, people are less able to use them when they are under a high cognitive load.

CHAPTER 3

Key Terms

Actor–observer difference *The tendency for individuals to judge their own behaviors as caused by situational forces but the behavior of others as caused by aspects of their personalities.*

Anchoring and adjustment heuristic *A mental shortcut through which people begin with a rough estimation as a starting point and then adjust this estimate to take into account unique characteristics of the present situation.*

Augmenting principle *The judgmental rule that states that if an event occurs despite the presence of strong opposing forces, we should give more weight to those possible causes that lead toward the event.*

Availability heuristic *A mental shortcut through which one estimates the likelihood of an event by the ease with which instances of that event come to mind.*

Cognitive heuristic *A mental shortcut used to make a judgment.*

Correspondence bias (fundamental attribution error) *The tendency for observers to overestimate the causal influence of personality factors on behavior and to underestimate the causal role of situational influences.*

Correspondent inference theory *The theory that proposes that people determine whether a behavior corresponds to an actor's internal disposition by asking whether (1) the behavior was intended, (2) the behavior's consequences were foreseeable, (3) the behavior was freely chosen, and (4) the behavior occurred despite countervailing forces.*

Covariation model *The theory that proposes that people determine the cause of an actor's behavior by assessing whether other people act in similar ways (consensus), the actor behaves similarly in similar situations (distinctiveness), and the actor behaves similarly in the same situation (consistency).*

Discounting principle *The judgmental rule that states that as the number of possible causes for an event increases, our confidence that any particular cause is the true one should decrease.*

Dispositional inference *The judgment that a person's behavior has been caused by an aspect of that person's personality.*

Downward social comparison *The process of comparing ourselves with those who are less well off.*

False consensus effect *The tendency to overestimate the extent to which others agree with us.*

Representativeness heuristic *A mental shortcut through which people classify something as belonging to a certain category to the extent that it is similar to a typical case from that category.*

Self-fulfilling prophecy *When an initially inaccurate expectation leads to actions that cause the expectation to come true.*

Self-serving bias *The tendency to take personal credit for our successes and to blame external factors for our failures.*

Social cognition *The process of thinking about oneself and others.*

Upward social comparison *The process of comparing ourselves with those who are better off than ourselves.*

CHAPTER 4

Presenting the Self

The Amazing Lives of Fred Demara

The air was chilly and the winds blowing hard that Valentine's Day morning in 1956, as the Maine state troopers crossed Penobscot Bay on their way to small North Haven Island. Their quarry was Martin Godgart. When not teaching high school English, Latin, and French, Godgart was leading the troop of teenage Sea Scouts, supervising Sunday school at the Baptist Church, and playing Santa Claus to the island's poor children. In his short time on the island, Godgart had earned the respect and admiration of a community normally wary of strangers. His arrest that day would shock his neighbors.

He was captured without a struggle—fighting wasn't his way—and was escorted via Coast Guard cutter back to the mainland. On the day of his trial, the courtroom was packed. What was his horrific crime? Murder? Rape? Hardly. The charge was "cheating by false premises," punishable by up to seven years in prison. The man calling himself Martin Godgart, you see, was no more Martin Godgart than you

Ferdinand Demara, Jr., The Great Imposter.

or I. He was Ferdinand ("Fred") Waldo Demara, Jr., and for the previous twenty-odd years, he had been the Great Impostor.

Consider just a few of his exploits (Allen, 1989; Crichton, 1959, 1961; McCarthy, 1952). As Robert Linton French, Ph.D., Demara was a science teacher in Arkansas; Dean of the School of Philosophy at Gannon College; and a teacher, head of the psychology center, and deputy sheriff at St. Martin's College. As Cecil Boyce Hamann, Ph.D., he entered law school at Northeastern University, trained to become a priest, and helped found LeMennais College in Maine. As Joseph Cyr, M.D., he joined the Royal Canadian Navy during the Korean War and performed heroic life-saving surgeries—despite never having before viewed the inside of a living, breathing human body. As Ben W. Jones, he got a job as a guard at the notoriously dangerous Huntsville prison in Texas and, in little more than a month, was promoted to assistant warden of the maximum security wing, where he was highly respected for his ability to peacefully defuse perilous confrontations. All this—and more—from a high school dropout who had no training or legitimate credentials in any of his adopted careers.

Demara's successes as an impostor were astounding in several ways. First, he had an extraordinary ability to present himself convincingly as someone he was not. Second, despite his lack of formal background for the jobs he assumed, he managed to avoid making job-related mistakes. Indeed, although he was uncovered many times, it was either because he was recognized as Demara (as when a prisoner in Huntsville identified him from a story that *Life* magazine had written years before) or because he had become so good in his new role that the publicity reached the ears of the owner of his borrowed identity (as when the real Dr. Cyr read in the newspaper of his wartime surgical miracles). Finally—and amazingly—so many of those duped by his lies nonetheless wanted him back. His fiancée said she loved him no matter who he really was. The warden of Huntsville said he'd be proud to hire him again if only Demara had some legitimate credentials. And the nice folks of North Haven Island convinced the judge to set him free, even urging Demara to continue teaching their children.

Why was Fred Demara willing to go to such lengths to present himself as Martin Godgart, Robert French, Joseph Cyr, Ben Jones, and the others? And how was he able to present himself so effectively under so many different guises?

The story of Fred Demara is more than just the story of an incredible impostor. It's also a dramatic, extreme example of why and how people try to manage others' impressions of them. Why do we want people to like us, fear us, or think we're smart? What sorts of behaviors make us appear likable, worthy of respect, or intelligent? In this chapter, we ask questions like these, exploring why people want to control their public images, which images they most want to present, what strategies they use to do so effectively, and when they bring these strategies to bear.

Self-presentation *The process through which we try to control the impressions people form of us; synonymous with* impression management.

Impression management *The process through which we try to control the impressions people form of us; synonymous with* self-presentation.

What Is Self-Presentation?

Self-presentation, sometimes called **impression management,** is the process through which we try to control the impressions people form of us (Jones, 1990; Leary, 1995; Schlenker, 1980). Although few people are as adventurous or successful in their self-presentations as Demara, self-presentation is pervasive in everyday life. Take yourself as an example. Why do you dress the way you do? Do you have an image, a style, you want to communicate? How do you wear your hair? Why? Do you sunbathe? Work out? For what purpose? How do you choose your friends, your hobbies, and the sports you play? Are any of these choices influenced by your desire to project a certain type of image? What kind of car do you drive? Does your car display a "vanity" license plate or a bumper sticker? Why or why not? Do you alter your posture or facial expressions when a potential love interest wanders by or when you feel threatened by a competitor or imposing stranger? For what purpose? Of course, not all public behaviors are determined by self-presentational concerns. Wearing clothes, for instance, serves functions well beyond making us look good to others. Nonetheless, most people are quite aware that their public behaviors influence the way others view them—leading most of us, for instance, to spend perhaps too much time deciding exactly *which* clothes to buy. And few people intentionally behave in ways that reflect poorly on themselves.

What images are these people trying to convey? *People frequently try to control the images others have of them by managing their public behaviors—by self-presenting.*

Why Do People Self-Present?

Sociologist Erving Goffman (1959) noted that the English word *person* derives from the Latin *persona,* meaning "mask." Apparently, the wordsmiths of ages past understood that self-presentation is an integral part of human nature. But why should people be so concerned with how others view them?

First, people self-present to obtain desirable resources from others. Because others often have what we want or need, we must "convince" them to share. The man who wants a job or who hopes to date a particular woman must convey the impression to his interviewer or love interest that he's indeed worthy. Self-presentation, then, is a way of strategically gaining control over one's life, a way of increasing one's rewards and minimizing one's costs (Jones & Pittman, 1982; Schlenker, 1980).

Second, self-presentation is a way of "constructing" a self-image. As we saw in Chapter 2, our images of ourselves—our self-concepts—are influenced partially by how we think others view us (e.g., Cooley, 1902; James, 1890; Mead, 1934). It's easier to see myself as having a good sense of humor if others validate that view by laughing, for instance, at all the right times. One interesting implication of this is that we often choose to spend time with those who see us as we see ourselves. For instance, people who have positive self-views prefer interacting with those who evaluate them favorably, and people who have negative self-views often prefer interacting with those who evaluate them unfavorably (Swann, Stein-Seroussi, & Giesler, 1992). Similarly, people are more committed to spouses who see them as they see themselves (Swann, Hixon, & De La Ronde, 1992). By managing the impressions others have of us, we are able to manage the impressions we have of ourselves.

Some researchers suggest another, more direct way in which self-presentation can influence a person's self-image. In line with the *self-perception process* (Bem, 1967, 1972) explored in chapters 2 and 3, there may be times when people serve as their own audiences—when they present not only to others but to themselves as well (Baumeister, 1982; Greenwald & Breckler, 1985; Hogan, Jones, & Cheek, 1985; Wicklund & Gollwitzer, 1982). To put it simply, if you want to see yourself in a certain way, you need to act the part (Gollwitzer, 1986). Because each time I make a witty remark I reinforce my self-image as a humorous person, I may indeed be motivated to joke a lot in public (Jones, Rhodewalt, Berglas, & Skelton, 1981; Rhodewalt & Agustsdottir, 1986; Schlenker, Dlugolecki, & Doherty, 1994; Tice, 1992).

Self-presentations, then, help us get what we want and help us create desired self-images. They also serve a social purpose: They help others know how we *expect* to be treated, enabling social encounters to run more smoothly (Goffman, 1959). Erving Goffman introduced the **dramaturgical perspective,** likening self-presentation to theater, with actors, performances, settings, scripts, props, roles, backstage areas, and the like. For the play to go smoothly—for people's interactions with each other

Dramaturgical perspective *The perspective that much of social interaction can be thought of as a play, with actors, performances, settings, scripts, props, roles, and so forth.*

The theater of everyday life. *Erving Goffman likened social interaction to theater, in which people have parts to perform, scripts to follow, and props to use. For any play to proceed smoothly, the actors must follow the script and go along with the other actors' performances. Similarly, social interactions go more smoothly when people present themselves in ways that make their roles and parts clear to others, when they follow conventional social scripts, and when they accept and respect the performances of others.*

to be comfortable—performances must follow general social scripts, and the actors must respect and go along with each other's presentations. For instance, if high-status people expect to be treated with respect, Goffman reasoned, they must do more than merely *possess* the status. They must also *play the part* by dressing appropriately, associating with the correct people, maintaining the proper distance from those of lesser status, and so forth. Demara, for example, when preparing to negotiate the book contract to tell his life story, insisted on buying a new suit, arriving by taxi instead of on foot, and meeting only with the head of the publishing house (Crichton, 1961). If he wanted to be treated as an important celebrity, Demara knew he had to play the role. His presentation also made it easier on the publishers: they now knew how he wanted and expected to be treated.

Smooth social interaction is important to all of us. Thus, we're usually reluctant to challenge others' presentations. Instead, we allow them to "save face," to get away with public presentations that may be less than perfectly true. For instance, we may publicly let slide a friend's slight boasts, knowing that to point out the exaggerations would not only embarrass the friend but make everyone else uncomfortable as well. Indeed, being sensitive to face-saving social conventions is valued in most cultures (e.g., Brown & Levinson, 1987; Cocroft & Ting-Toomey, 1994; Holtgraves & Yang, 1990), and American children as young as five years old begin to demonstrate this sensitivity by being tactful when evaluating others' work, by ignoring others' mistakes, and the like (Hatch, 1987).

In general, then, self-presentation is useful for three reasons. It helps us obtain those things we need and value; it helps us create and maintain desired self-identities; and it enables our social encounters to run relatively smoothly. Applying these lessons to Fred Demara's youth, we can begin to unravel the mystery of why he embarked on the life of an impostor. For Demara, more than most, public reputation mattered. As the gifted son of a popular and prosperous businessman, Fred not only learned the value of a favorable public image but also grew to like it. He was devastated, then, when his family's good fortune took a turn for the worse, taking with it his positive public reputation and shaking the foundations of his favorable self-image. Unable to stand the public and private humiliation of being poor, Demara ran away from home at age sixteen. He trained to be a monk, then a priest, but succeeded in neither. In frustration, he "borrowed" a car from the Catholic Boys Home where he worked, got drunk for the first time in his life, and, on a whim, joined the army. He soon realized that the army, too, was not for him, and he promptly went AWOL.

By age twenty, Fred Demara was on the run, his public reputation shattered beyond repair. To the folks in his hometown, he was the son of a failed businessman; to the Catholic Church he loved so much, he was a failure and a thief; and to the U.S. Army, he was a deserter. For a person to whom appearances mattered so much, public life was essentially over. Or was it? The logic that emerged in Demara's mind seems straightforward enough: (1) He wanted success; (2) a good reputation is central to a person's success; (3) the reputation of the man known as Demara was forever spoiled; therefore, (4) he could no longer be Demara! So he shed his tarnished identity and, assuming the reputable identities of others, began his new journey as the Great Impostor.

When Do People Self-Present?

People are more likely to present to others when they perceive themselves to be in the "public eye." When you pose for a photograph, dine in front of a mirror, or meet your lover's parents for the first time, you become aware of yourself as a public figure and become more likely to self-present, perhaps by fixing your hair, bringing out your best table manners, or being extra polite.

Interestingly, we often overestimate the extent to which we're in the public eye—a phenomenon dubbed the *spotlight effect.* In one experiment, college students were asked to don a T-shirt bearing the picture of Barry Manilow, and enter a room where others were working. When later asked to estimate how many of the observers noticed the likeness on the T-shirt, the students greatly overestimated: They predicted that nearly 50 percent noticed whereas only about 25 percent actually did (Gilovich, Medvec, & Savitsky, 2000). People often don't pay as much attention to us as we think they do.

Some people are more sensitive to how they come across than are others. Consider, for instance, a sole woman working in an otherwise male office. As a "token," she actually does stand out relative to others (McArthur, 1981; Taylor & Fiske, 1975). As a result, she's likely to be more concerned with public appearances than if she worked with other women (Cohen & Swim, 1995; Saenz, 1994). People can also stand out because of a physical disability, exceptional attractiveness, or obesity. They, too, are particularly mindful of how others view them (Frable, Blackstone, & Scherbaum, 1990). More generally, people differ in their **public self-consciousness**—in the degree to which they characteristically believe others pay attention to them. People high in public self-consciousness are especially attuned to how others view them, respond negatively to rejection, and focus to a greater degree on their reputation and appearance (e.g., Buss, 1980; Carver & Scheier, 1985; Doherty & Schlenker, 1991; Fenigstein, 1979).

Just because we see ourselves as a focus of attention, however, doesn't mean we always self-present. For example, if you don't care what a particular observer thinks of you, you have little reason to spend much effort self-presenting. We become more concerned with strategic self-presentation (1) when observers can influence whether or not we obtain our goals, (2) when these goals are important to us, and (3) when we think observers have impressions different from the ones we want to project.

First, we're more likely to self-present to observers when they control something we want. For instance, we're more interested in presenting ourselves favorably when observed by a boss than by a stranger, because our boss will usually have more power over whether we reach our goals (Bohra & Pandey, 1984; Hendricks & Brickman, 1974; Jones, Gergen, & Jones, 1963).

Second, the more important our goal, the more likely we'll step up our presentational efforts. In one study, prospective job applicants were led to believe either that they were competing with many others for just a few jobs or that there were more than enough jobs to go around. Applicants facing the greater competition reported being more likely to adjust their opinions and attitudes to conform to those of their interviewers, presumably because winning the job became increasingly important as the number of opportunities dwindled (Pandey & Rastagi, 1979).

And third, if we believe that important observers hold undesired impressions of us, we'll become motivated to disabuse them of their views. If you feel that an interviewer, for instance, sees you as unqualified for a job you really want, you will be more motivated to present yourself favorably than when you think the interviewer already believes you to be qualified (Leary & Kowalski, 1990).

Although social circumstances like these motivate most people to manage their public impressions, people identified as high in **self-monitoring** are almost always motivated to do so (see Figure 4.1). High self-monitors are adept both at assessing what others want and at tailoring their behavior to meet those demands (Gangestad & Snyder, 2000; Snyder, 1974). For instance, high self-monitors are quite skilled at reading others' emotional expressions (Geizer, Rarick, & Soldow, 1977) and detecting when others are being manipulative (Jones & Baumeister, 1976). Moreover, as you'll see in chapter 5, high self-monitors are more comfortable acting in ways inconsistent with their attitudes and beliefs. As a consequence, high self-monitors are also better at customizing their presentations to fit the situation (Danheiser & Graziano, 1982; Shaffer, Smith, & Tomarelli, 1982). Perhaps because of these skills,

Public self-consciousness *The tendency to have a chronic awareness of oneself as being in the public eye.*

Self-monitoring *The tendency to be chronically concerned with one's public image and to adjust one's actions to fit the needs of the current situation.*

1. I guess I put on a show to impress or entertain others.
2. In different situations and with different people, I often act like very different persons.
3. I'm not always the person I appear to be.
4. I may deceive people by being friendly when I really dislike them.
5. At parties and social gatherings, I do not attempt to do or say things that others will like.
6. I would not change my opinions (or the way I do things) in order to please someone or win his or her favor.

Figure 4.1 How important is self-presentation to you?

Some people are especially interested in managing their public images. The items below are from Mark Snyder's (1974) Self-Monitoring Scale. These selected items assess *other-directed self-presentation*, the extent to which people alter their behavior to influence how others view them (Briggs, Cheek, & Buss, 1980; Gangestad & Snyder, 1985). If you tend to agree with statements 1 through 4 and disagree with statements 5 and 6, you are likely a high self-monitor.

SOURCE: *Snyder and Gangestad (1986).*

high self-monitors are somewhat more likely to rise to leadership positions (e.g., Dobbins, Long, Dedrick, & Clemons, 1990).

Of course, as we discussed in chapter 2, certain behaviors can occur mindlessly, and self-presentations are no exception (Paulhus, 1993). As people shower and dress each morning, combing their hair and applying their makeup, they may be unaware that they're performing these cosmetic rituals for presentational reasons. Similarly, a city dweller who learns to carry herself so as to appear confident and in control may unintentionally walk through scenic redwood forests with the same determined gait. Finally, we should note that not all public actions are self-presentational. As you walk from one class to another, absorbed by thoughts of an upcoming exam or where to have lunch, your actions may have little or nothing to do with conveying a certain image.

The Nature of Self-Presentation

When we prepare for a date, particularly a first date, we strive to "put our best foot forward." We brush our hair and teeth, choose flattering clothes, and try to arrive on time. We steer the conversation toward our strengths (say, our knowledge of music) and try to avoid mentioning weaknesses (such as failed past relationships). As this example suggests, self-presentation generally entails the strategic "editing" of information. Because people have multiple selves—for instance, husband, father, professor, musician, sports fan—self-presentation usually takes the form of displaying those selves most appropriate to immediate goals and then, perhaps, exaggerating them a bit. The adventures of Fred Demara aside, self-presentation rarely consists of blatant fabrications of information. Few of us, after all, falsely claim to be rock 'n' roll stars or secret agents.

Despite our best efforts, self-presentation sometimes fails. Even Demara couldn't get *everyone* to like him. Sometimes we're unable to create the desired image. Other times, we accidentally acquire undesired reputations, as when a young suitor trying to impress his date with his sophistication spills his wine glass at a fine restaurant, staining himself as a klutz. When much is riding on a particular impression, self-presentational failures can carry heavy costs, especially for people who are publicly self-conscious or high in self-monitoring. Some costs are tangible, such as lost employment or dating opportunities. Other costs are psychological. For example, presentational failures threaten self-concept and self-esteem and can also be embarrassing (e.g., Miller, 1995).

The fear of self-presentational failure has been labeled **social anxiety.** Social anxiety is quite common, for example, when we're on a first date or have to speak in front of a large group (Leary & Kowalski, 1995; Schlenker & Leary, 1982b). Although some amount of social anxiety is probably useful, too much may lead people to avoid social situations entirely, to withdraw from them once there, or to inhibit their behavior if escape isn't possible (e.g., DePaulo, Epstein, & LeMay, 1990; Reno & Kenney, 1992). Thirty to 40 percent of Americans label themselves as *shy*—they experience social anxiety on a regular basis (Cheek & Briggs, 1990; Zimbardo, 1977)—and approximately 2 percent of the U.S. population experiences social anxiety severely enough to be classified as *socially phobic* (Pollard & Henderson, 1988).

Death of an admiral. *U.S. Admiral Jeremy "Mike" Boorda had always stressed the importance of honor and integrity. Imagine his state of mind, then, when the highly admired admiral was accused of improperly wearing two combat medals. Boorda committed suicide, his death shocking the nation. His suicide note to those under his command was revealing: "I couldn't bear to bring dishonor to you." By staining his reputation, the accusations would have stained the Navy's as well. To Boorda, suicide was the only way to maintain his honor.*

When people worry that simply putting their best foot forward might not be enough to achieve their goals, they may be tempted to manufacture false presentations. Demara was a master of this, going well beyond what most of us would dare even imagine. Nonetheless, most of us have at some point presented ourselves in ways that could be considered "false advertising"—perhaps "forgetting" to tell your mom or dad of a failing grade on an exam or pretending to be interested in a boss's vacation photos. Such deceptions may even be well-intentioned, as when we feign excitement over a hideous birthday gift so as not to hurt the feelings of the person giving it. Indeed, people lie to others with some frequency, and many of these lies are told for the liar's own benefit (DePaulo, Kashy, Kirkendol, Wyer, & Epstein, 1996).

Being untruthful carries with it the risk of perhaps the most devastating of unintended impressions. When one is caught "presenting" instead of just "being," people typically mark the presenter as dishonest, insincere, hypocritical, or immoral. The costs of a reputation soiled in this way are great, as people labeled as untrustworthy are avoided and isolated by others. Understanding this, Demara was horrified by the prospect of being viewed as a fraud. Indeed, despite his fiancée's desire to marry him after discovering his true identity, and despite his consuming love for her, Demara fled from her in shame. Her protestations to the contrary, Demara believed her view of him had been forever sullied.

Demara's extreme reaction sharply illustrates the importance people place on having a reputation for honesty. People will go to great lengths to present themselves as honest, and to disguise their dishonest acts. As a result, we sometimes go to equally great lengths to see if others are presenting themselves truthfully. Unfortunately, we are not very good at detecting lies.

FOCUS ON Application

Detecting Deception

Aldrich Ames was a long-time employee of the U.S. Central Intelligence Agency (CIA), and had access to top-secret, highly sensitive information. Despite this, he was viewed by his colleagues as barely competent, as an alcoholic with little ambition who would never do anything meaningful. They were wrong. On February 21, 1994, Ames was arrested by the FBI for espionage. For nine years, he'd sold information to the Soviet Union, leading directly to the deaths of at least ten CIA agents (Adams, 1995; Weiner, Johnston, & Lewis, 1995). He was a traitor to his country and, by many definitions, a mass murderer. Aldrich Ames had worked right under the noses of the very people whose job it was to stop spies like him, which raises interesting and important questions about people's ability to detect deception.

Most of us just aren't very good lie detectors, especially regarding strangers. Controlled laboratory studies reveal success rates not much better than what one

Social anxiety *The fear people experience while doubting that they'll be able to create a desired impression.*

would expect by chance (e.g., DePaulo, Zuckerman, & Rosenthal, 1980). Part of the difficulty lies in our tendency to begin by believing the words and presentations of others (Gilbert, Tafarodi, & Malone, 1993). Because we trust what people say, we often fail to pay attention to those nonverbal behaviors most useful for differentiating lies from truth—eye blinking, dilated pupils, self-touching, high voice pitch, and the like (DePaulo, 1994). It's thus instructive that *aphasics*—people who are unable to understand words—are better at detecting lies about emotion than are those of us with fully functioning language abilities (Etcoff, Ekman, Magee, & Frank, 2000). Because they focus on facial expression and tone of voice instead of what people say, aphasics are better at spotting liars. Along similar lines, less involved observers are better at detecting deceit than are more involved observers (Forrest & Feldman, 2000). Unlike aphasics, who focus on nonverbal behavior because they don't understand words, lightly involved observers focus on nonverbal behavior because they aren't interested in expending the effort needed to pay close attention to the speaker's words. In both cases, however, the resulting focus on nonverbal cues increases their ability to identify dishonesty.

This is not to say, however, that focusing on a speaker's facial expressions and tone of voice is the antidote to being deceived. Even if we focused more on these cues, we would still be imperfect lie detectors, because many factors besides lying influence these behaviors. Furthermore, some of the people most likely to lie—poker players, salespeople, and individuals with antisocial personalities, among others—are able to mask these nonverbal cues (e.g., DePaulo & DePaulo, 1989).

Are we better at detecting the lies of our intimates—friends, children, and lovers? Some studies suggest that we are, *if* we receive feedback along the way revealing which of a person's statements are truths and which are lies (e.g., Zuckerman, Koestner, & Alton, 1984). Of course, such feedback is rare in everyday life, as people who lie usually have little desire to confess afterwards. And although we seem to do a reasonable job detecting our lovers' lies, this is only when we suspect them of lying beforehand (McCornak & Levine, 1990).

So everyday people aren't very good at detecting deception. But what about people whom we'd expect to be "experts": customs inspectors, federal law enforcement agents, judges, psychiatrists, and the like? They're little better, if at all, (DePaulo & Pfeifer, 1986; Ekman & O'Sullivan, 1991; Kohnken, 1987; Kraut & Poe, 1980; Vrij, 1993). Only U.S. Secret Service agents seem to have any talent along these lines. Given these findings, it's not surprising that Ames's CIA colleagues failed to suspect his illicit activities. It's also not surprising that organizations whose job it is to catch liars and criminals often turn to technical means of assessing deceit, such as the polygraph.

The polygraph is a machine that records physiological arousal in the form of electrodermal activity, blood pressure, heart rate, and respiration. Polygraphic examiners explore whether a suspect's arousal levels increase more when he or she is questioned about potentially suspicious activities (about which a guilty suspect would likely lie) compared to when he or she is asked control questions about unrelated issues (about which even a guilty suspect would likely tell the truth). The assumption underlying the polygraph examination is that people become physiologically aroused when lying. It's interesting to note that people in earlier centuries used a similar logic. In India, for instance, suspects were forced to chew dried rice and then spit it out. Based on the assumption that guilty individuals would be anxious and thus lack saliva, suspects were deemed guilty if the rice emerged dry (Trovillo, 1939).

Unfortunately, just as no specific pattern of nonverbal behavior maps directly onto dishonesty, no specific pattern of heart rate, skin conduction, and the like does either. Fear and anger also increase arousal, and an innocent suspect may become truthfully indignant or anxious when asked about whether he or she has engaged in illicit activities. As a consequence, polygraph examinations run a great risk of inaccurately identifying innocent people as guilty. In general, studies of polygraph interrogations reveal accuracy rates running from a dismal 25 percent to highs of around 90 percent (Ford, 1996; Saxe, 1994).

The usefulness of polygraphic testing decreases further when the suspect doesn't believe that the test is effective, because such doubts reduce anxiety. Guilty suspects can also foil the test—as many intelligence officers are trained to do—by increasing anxiety levels in response to control questions by tightening their anal sphincters, biting their tongues, or pressing their toes hard against the floor (Gudjonsson, 1988; Honts, Raskin, & Kircher, 1994). Moreover, if polygraph interrogators don't have access to important information needed to fashion a well-focused series of questions or don't believe that the suspect is guilty, they're likely to interpret a lying suspect's responses as reflecting innocence. Finally, people who experience little guilt and anxiety are unlikely to be detected through these techniques. Aldrich Ames benefited greatly from these weaknesses of the test: He passed two polygraph examinations while secretly spying for the Soviet Union, enabling him to continue his deadly activities (Adams, 1995; Weiner et al., 1995).

Lie detector? *Polygraph examinations are used frequently by law enforcement and security organizations to catch murderers in their false alibis, employees suspected of selling company secrets, and spies believed to be working for the other side. Unfortunately, these "lie detector" exams often falsely identify innocent suspects as guilty and guilty perpetrators as innocent. CIA double-agent Aldrich Ames passed a polygraph examination—twice!—enabling him to continue his deadly spying for the Soviet Union.*

We see, then, that the most popular technical solution to lie detection fares badly. The polygraph exam, as typically conducted in the field by poorly trained interrogators, is a poor device for lie detection (Honts, 1994). A new approach to the technological assessment of deception measures brain waves instead of physiological arousal. Because certain brain responses occur when people recognize something they've experienced previously, a guilty suspect should exhibit these responses when an item specific to the crime is mentioned, whereas an innocent suspect should not (e.g., Boaz, Perry, Raney, Fischler, & Schuman, 1991; Farwell & Donchin, 1991). Although promising, these new techniques have yet to prove practically useful.

In all, our ability to detect lies—using intuition or mechanical devices, on everyday occasions or when trying to detect criminal wrongdoing—is mediocre at best. We are fortunate, then, that living a series of lies is very difficult to do. Each lie requires other lies to back it up, and it's easy to trip oneself up by being a bit too clever. This was Aldrich Ames's downfall, and we should be relieved. Otherwise, our lie detection abilities being what they are, he would have—literally—continued to get away with murder. ■

In light of our discussion, we hope you haven't concluded that self-presentation is always deceptive. As we mentioned earlier, self-presentation is typically more about strategically *revealing* aspects of oneself than about *manufacturing* aspects of oneself (Leary, 1995). This shouldn't be surprising. After all, because we must ultimately live up to our presentations, gross exaggeration will harm us in the long run. If your affections for another are discovered to be false, you will gain a reputation as a phony and future friendships may be difficult to come by. If you feign competence and your subsequent performance fails to meet expectations, you will find yourself searching for a new job, this time without favorable references in hand. If you pretend to be tougher than you really are and your bluff is called, you may be forced to either retreat in humiliation or fight a battle you're likely to lose. For these reasons, it usually makes little sense to create public presentations that stray far from our personal realities (Schlenker & Weigold, 1992).

In the remainder of this chapter, we'll discuss the kinds of images people frequently want to present. Most people want to be viewed as honest and trustworthy, as we've just seen. Most people also want to be viewed as stable—as consistent and predictable. Even negative self-presentations are helpful in some circumstances (Kowalski & Leary, 1990). For instance, women in bars and other nightspots who don't want men "hitting on them" may go out of their way to be dislikable, by not smiling, avoiding eye contact, and cutting conversations short (Snow, Robinson, & McCall, 1991). People may feign incompetence to avoid tedious chores or heavy responsibilities, or to lull opponents into a false sense of security (e.g., Becker & Martin, 1995; Gibson & Sachau, 2000; Shepperd & Socherman, 1997). Or they may pretend to be weak and powerless in order to receive more help from others (e.g., Jones & Pittman, 1982). Most of the time, however, we hope to be viewed favorably. Three public images are especially useful: People want to appear *likable*, to appear *competent*, and to convey *high status* and *power*. In the following pages, we describe the strategies people use to reach these goals and the person and situation factors that bring these goals to prominence.

Summary

People frequently try to manage the impressions others form of them. Self-presentation helps us obtain those things we need and value, it helps us create and maintain desired self-identities, and it enables our social encounters to run relatively smoothly. Individuals are especially likely to self-present when they see themselves as the target of others' attention, when they depend on these others to reach their goals, when these goals are important, and when they feel that these others have an undesired impression of them. Although self-presentation sometimes has a trace of falsity to it, its deceptive nature is usually quite bounded. In general, self-presentation is more about strategically revealing favorable aspects of oneself than about creating fictions.

Appearing Likable

Most cultures seriously punish impostors, and for good reason. To present oneself deceptively, to claim unearned credentials and unowned abilities, challenges the established social order and may place observers at risk. So it was to Demara's considerable credit that, despite being caught in his deceptions on numerous occasions, he served little jail time. Amazingly, the victims of his fabrications—those who should have been the most upset—frequently bailed Demara out of trouble and jail.

Fred Demara survived these unmaskings because he understood the importance of being liked. To be liked is to belong, to share the ample benefits of being tied into a social network. When we're liked, others will go the extra yard for us, excuse our mistakes, and generally make our lives easier. As a consequence, we want others to like us, and the lengths to which we go to be liked are quite impressive. Let's begin by exploring the strategies people use to get others to like them.

Strategies of Ingratiation

Ingratiation is an attempt to get others to like us. We have many ways to ingratiate ourselves with others. To ingratiate yourself with a new neighbor, for instance, you may do her a favor, become friends with one of her friends, or tell funny jokes. Four ingratiation strategies seem particularly effective (see Figure 4.2), and we explore them now.

Expressing Liking for Others "Flattery will get you nowhere," claims the cultural maxim. Untrue. Complimenting others can be an effective technique for getting others to like us, if handled delicately. For instance, having a coworker subtly mention to your boss how much respect you have for him can be a particularly successful form of flattery, because your boss is less likely to see the compliment as manipulative when it comes from a third party (Liden & Mitchell, 1988; Wortman

Ingratiation *An attempt to get others to like us.*

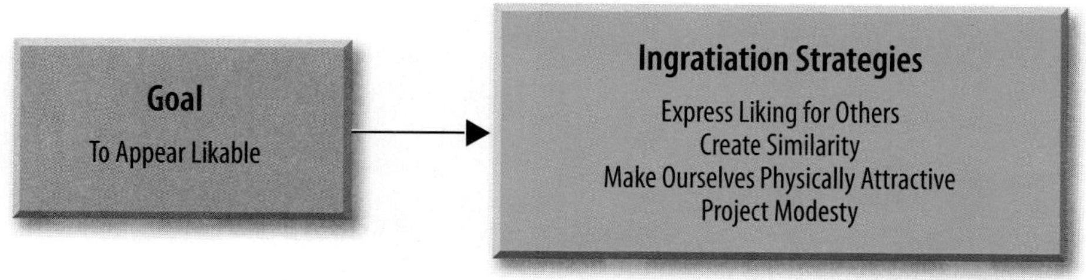

Figure 4.2
Strategies of ingratiation.

People use a variety of strategies to get others to like them.

& Linsenmeier, 1977). Asking others for advice is also often effective, as it implies respect for their expertise and knowledge.

Indeed, flattery is usually quite successful: Although we're quick to interpret as insincere the flattering statements people make toward others, we tend to accept quite readily compliments directed toward us (e.g., Gordon, 1996; Jones & Wortman, 1973). And why not? After all, in *our* particular case, the compliments are clearly well deserved!

People express their liking for others through nonverbal means as well (DePaulo, 1992; Edinger & Patterson, 1983). For instance, those of you who truly like your social psychology professor probably smile and nod more during lectures, pay focused attention, and seek more eye contact (e.g., Lefebvre, 1975; Purvis, Dabbs, & Hopper, 1984; Rosenfeld, 1966). As professors, we must admit that such behaviors make us feel good, and they probably lead us to like those students in return. Smiling, in particular, is a powerful tool for getting others to like us. In *How to Win Friends and Influence People*—over 15 million copies sold worldwide—Dale Carnegie (1936/1981) wrote, "a smile says 'I like you. You make me happy. I am glad to see you'" (p. 66). Carnegie was so taken by the impact of a well-placed smile that he even provided tips on how to smile when we don't feel like it. Is this good advice? After all, it assumes that people are able to manipulate their facial expressions without appearing insincere and fake. Are people any good at doing this? And how would we know?

FOCUS ON **Method**

The Science of Deciphering Facial Expressions

The face is a wonderful medium for self-presentation. Its complexity and flexibility—with over forty muscles that contribute to facial expression—enable us to communicate much about how we feel about ourselves, others, and our circumstances (e.g., Fridlund, 1994). With our face, we express not only anger, sadness, and shame but also surprise, disgust, relief, disbelief, and utter joy. Our face can communicate respect and awe, as well as disdain and fearlessness. Even the apparently simple smile, thought to be associated primarily with enjoyment and liking, comes in eighteen different varieties, some of which communicate fear, embarrassment, and flirtatious intent (Ekman, 1985).

Paul Ekman and Wallace Friesen (1978) developed the *Facial Action Coding System*, or *FACS*, to explore the complexity of facial expressions. FACS is a system for measuring the movement of facial muscles. Using a videotape of a face in motion, people trained in FACS are able to score these muscles for their movement, intensity, and other characteristics. The scoring process is long and tedious: Coders stop the videotape, make their measurements, advance the videotape (perhaps only a fraction of a second), code the face again, and so on, until done. Coders need 100 hours of training before they're able to use the system reliably, and it takes a trained coder around sixty minutes to score just one minute of facial activity. The difficulty of FACS seems justified by its payoff, however. In particular, this method has helped

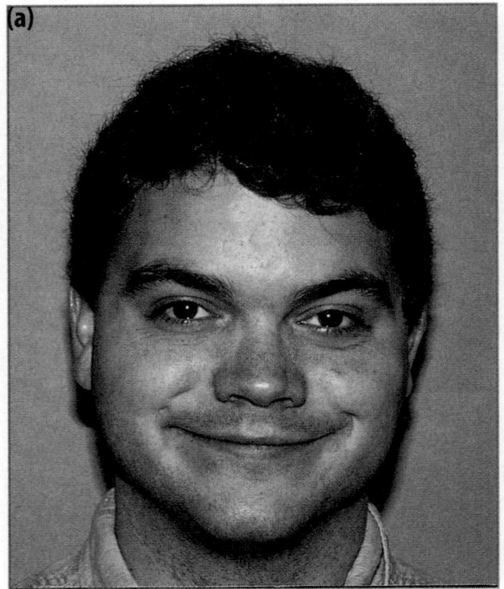

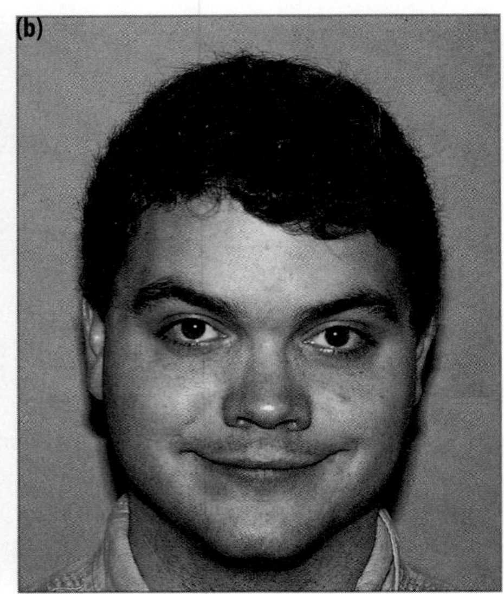

Figure 4.3
Felt and false smiles.

Not all smiles are the same. The felt, enjoyment smile is characterized by the upturning of the corners of the mouth by the zygomatic major muscles and the "crinkling" of the muscles around the eyes by the obicularis oculi muscles (a). Although most people can consciously manipulate the zygomatic major, approximately 80 percent of us are unable to contract the orbicularis oculi voluntarily. As a result, the area around the eyes can often reveal the false smile (b).

SOURCE: *D. Keltner.*

researchers learn much about how people communicate with one another and how facial expressions and emotions are related.

Which brings us back to the use of smiling as an ingratiation strategy. Researchers using FACS have discovered that false smiles indeed differ from true enjoyment smiles. The enjoyment smile—sometimes called the *Duchenne smile*, after the French scientist who first characterized its features—involves the movement of two major facial muscles: The zygomatic major pulls up the corners of the lips toward the cheekbones, while the orbicularis oculi raises the cheek, narrows the eye, and produces "crows-feet" wrinkles at the corners of the eyes, as shown in Figure 4.3 (a). This would seem easy to imitate. Not so. Although we can effectively manipulate the zygomatic major and turn up the corners of our mouths, most of us are unable to contract the orbicularis oculi voluntarily. This muscle just doesn't respond easily to our will. As a consequence, a close look around the eyes will often reveal a false smile, as shown in Figure 4.3 (b).

False smiles differ in other ways as well. They tend to be less symmetrical, meaning that the muscle movements on the two sides of the face aren't precisely the same. In addition, the muscle movements during false smiles are jerkier, less smooth. And false smiles are often held longer than natural (Frank & Ekman, 1993). Such differences make it relatively easy for a scientist using the FACS method to tell a false smile from an enjoyment smile. ■

But can people under nonscientific circumstances also discriminate between false smiles and enjoyment smiles? The answer is a qualified yes. In one study, for instance, untrained participants who viewed videotapes of people exhibiting both enjoyment and false smiles were able to guess which was which 74 percent of the time (Frank, Ekman, & Friesen, 1993). However, participants who saw each person smile just once and had to guess whether the smile was authentic or false performed only a bit better than chance—56 percent—suggesting that past experience observing another's smiles may be necessary for us to tell the two kinds apart.

Besides our unfamiliarity with others' smiles, other circumstances may also make detection of false smiles difficult (Frank & Ekman, 1993). A false smile that merely exaggerates an authentic smile is less easily detected than one that attempts to mask negative emotions such as anger or disgust. Very big, broad zygomatic movements make it more difficult to detect a false smile. And certain people (about 20 percent of the population) actually have the ability to control the orbicularis oculi, increasing their chances of escaping detection. Finally, because we generally don't expect others to lie to us and because we usually want to believe that others truly like us, we may be more susceptible to others' fake smiles than we would prefer.

Flashing a false smile to ingratiate yourself with another can be a risky strategy, then. You'll sometimes succeed—usually when you're merely exaggerating an existing enjoyment smile with people who don't know you. But, unless you're a "natural liar," you'll fail with some frequency. And when you do, the cost will be great: you'll come across as an insincere fake, perhaps the worst presentation of all.

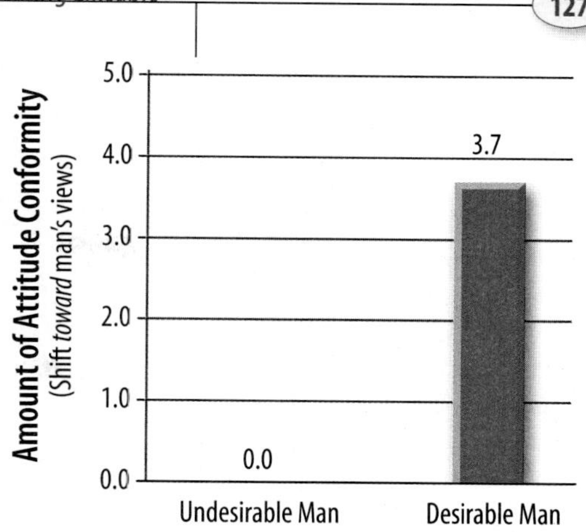

Figure 4.4
Opinion conformity as an ingratiation strategy.

In an experiment conducted by Mark Zanna and Susan Pack (1975), women anticipated interacting with men (1) who were either highly desirable or not and (2) who held either traditional or untraditional views of women. Women about to interact with the undesirable man did not shift their gender-related opinions. Women about to interact with the desirable man, however, adjusted their opinions to match his more closely. These findings demonstrate that people sometimes change their public opinions to get desirable others to like them.

SOURCE: *Adapted from Zanna & Pack (1975), Table 1.*

Creating Similarity Imagine yourself at a party, deeply engaged in a conversation with a person you want to start a relationship with. So far, the conversation has been enjoyable and safe—you've discussed common friends, the recent lousy weather, and the writing professor you both despise—and you think the person likes you. Then the topic gets political—"What do you think of traditional gender norms? Should men work while women stay home and take care of the kids?"—and your heart skips a beat. "How should I answer?" you think. "Should I tailor my response somewhat to fit with what I think the other person believes? If we disagree, will I become less desirable?"

This was the dilemma faced by female students at Princeton University in a study exploring how people form impressions of one another (Zanna & Pack, 1975). In the first stage of the study, the women received information from a male student whom they expected to meet later. The information suggested that he was either quite desirable (a tall, twenty-one-year-old Princeton senior who had a car and who was athletic, unattached, and interested in meeting women) or not (a short, eighteen-year-old, unathletic non-Princeton freshman who had a girlfriend and no car). The women additionally learned that he was either quite traditional in his beliefs about women (believing that the ideal woman is emotional, concerned with how she looks, passive, and the like) or nontraditional in his beliefs (believing that the ideal woman is independent, ambitious, and so forth).

The women then completed several questionnaires for the male student to look at, including one reporting their own attitudes about gender roles. As Figure 4.4 reveals, when the partner was desirable, the women modified their opinions to match his. A more recent study demonstrated that men did the same when presenting their views to desirable women (Morier & Seroy, 1994). We often adjust our public opinions when we want people to like us. Why?

To put it simply, we recognize that people like others who are similar to them (Berscheid & Walster, 1978; Byrne, 1971; see chapter 7). They like people who dress similarly, who have common tastes in movies and foods, and who hold similar opinions. It makes sense, then, that we often *create* similarity to ingratiate ourselves with others by altering our dress, activities, or public opinions.

Of course, people don't want to be seen as hypocrites, or as having no tastes, interests, or opinions of their own. So successful ingratiators often mix a small amount of disagreement in with their agreement (Jones, Jones, & Gergen, 1963). By disagreeing with a new acquaintance on some trivial issue such as whether we would use imagined lottery winnings to buy a Ferrari or a Lamborghini, we can now agree on an important issue without appearing insincere (Jones, 1990). Such nuances increase the probability that presenting ourselves as similar to others will indeed be an effective way of getting them to like us.

Making Ourselves Physically Attractive "I didn't have the right clothes and I didn't have the right face and I would sit back and notice how much easier it was for the girls who had those things. This is what life rewards. Life will reward you if you have the right look" ("Becoming Barbie," 1995). With this observation, and a new inheritance, Cindy Jackson decided to transform herself physically, from a woman whom no one "would look at twice" to her physical ideal, Barbie. At age

Becoming Barbie. *Cindy Jackson never liked the way she looked. So through cosmetic surgery—nearly 30 procedures in all—she began to transform herself into her physical ideal, Barbie. Is Jackson's quest to make herself physically attractive extreme? By everyday standards, yes. Is it entirely misguided? Perhaps not. Research demonstrates that, whether we like it or not, it sometimes pays to be physically attractive.*

thirty-three, she began to sculpt herself through plastic surgery: two nose jobs, a mouth enlargement, a chin reduction, breast implants (which were later removed), multiple liposuctions, cheek implants, chemical peels, hair transplants, three face lifts, and more—twenty-eight procedures in all, and still counting!

We do not know whether the benefits to Cindy Jackson of these surgeries outweighed their costs, both physical and financial (she reportedly spent $100,000). We do know, however, that physically attractive people are indeed liked more and viewed more favorably than unattractive people (Eagly, Ashmore, Makhijani, & Longo, 1991; Feingold, 1992). Attractive people are seen as more honest (Zebrowitz, Voinesco, & Collins, 1996). They are more likely to be hired for managerial positions and elected to public office, even though interviewers and voters deny any influence of physical appearance (e.g., Budesheim & DePaola, 1994; Mack & Rainey, 1990). They receive lesser fines and bail judgments in misdemeanor cases, and shorter sentences in felony cases (Downs & Lyons, 1991; Stewart, 1980, 1985). They get paid more: Compared to being of average attractiveness, there's an approximately 7 percent penalty for being unattractive and a 5 percent premium for being highly attractive (Hamermesh & Biddle, 1994). All other things being equal, this 12 percent income difference is the same gap you'd expect to find between one employee and another having an extra 1.5 years of education! Physically attractive people are more desirable for romantic relationships, as we'll see in chapter 8. Even newborn infants receive more affection from their mothers when they're cute (Langlois, Ritter, Casey, & Sawin, 1995). It clearly pays to be physically attractive.

Realizing this, most people try to make themselves more attractive. Consider the following factoids:

- In 1999, Americans had approximately 4.6 million plastic surgeries, most of them for merely cosmetic purposes (American Society for Aesthetic Plastic Surgery, 2000).
- Cosmetics and toiletries are a $20 billion-per-year industry, and perfume and cologne makers sell $10 billion worth of fragrances.
- Over 4 million Americans currently wear braces or other orthodontic devices, mostly to improve the look of their smile.

- People in the United States spend $33 billion on diet foods, weight-loss programs, and health club memberships each year.

We want others to like us, we know that being physically attractive helps, so we're apparently willing to spend our hard-earned money to buy, in Cindy Jackson's words, the "right look." The pressure to look good is so great that people roast themselves in the sun, go on severe diets, and use muscle-building steroids—all of which pose great, even life-threatening, health risks (Leary, Tchividjian, & Kraxberger, 1994).

Projecting Modesty If you aced an exam, receiving the highest grade in the class, would you immediately announce it to others? Not if you want to be liked! People who downplay their successes are generally liked more than people who boast of them (Baumeister & Jones, 1978; Rosen, Cochran, & Musser, 1990; Schlenker & Leary, 1982a; Wosinska, Dabul, Whetstone-Dion, & Cialdini, 1996). As a consequence, we often give public credit to others for aiding in our successes and gently point to weaknesses we have in other—less important—areas (e.g., Baumeister & Ilko, 1995; Jones, 1990; Miller & Schlenker, 1985).

There are risks associated with being modest, however. If people don't know of your successes, they may believe you when you profess a lack of talent. If you are too modest, people may think you have horribly low self-esteem or little self-insight (Robinson, Johnson, & Shields, 1995). And if you appear insincere in minimizing the importance of what you've done ("Oh, the award is no big deal"), people may view you as smug and arrogant (Pin & Turndorf, 1990). These risks aside, modest individuals tend to be liked.

Although modesty is a characteristic valued to some extent worldwide, there do exist some interesting cultural variations. Consider the case of Muhammad Ali, the finest heavyweight boxer of his era and perhaps of all time. His boastful claims—"I am the greatest!"—did not always endear him to boxing fans, however. In particular, Ali was disliked by many white Americans. Although some of this opposition was racist in nature, other African American boxers who fought during the 1970s and 1980s—Joe Frazier, for instance—were well liked. In part, Ali's image problem among whites was probably due to his penchant for bragging, for his immodest style of self-presentation.

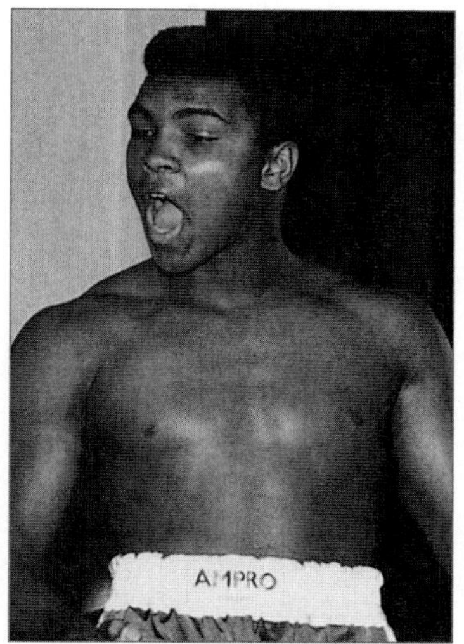

"I am the greatest!" *And perhaps he was. But Muhammad Ali's bold self-proclamations did little to endear him to many white Americans, among whom even truthful verbal immodesty is disliked.*

This illustration points to a cultural disparity between blacks and whites in the social acceptability of boastfulness. In a study exploring this difference, African American and European American college students read short biographies of three male students and then read a transcription of a conversation these students had about travel experiences, academic achievements, sports prowess, and the like. One of the students was portrayed as a *nonbragger,* who understated his strengths; a second student was depicted as an *untruthful bragger,* who boasted of things that weren't true; and the third student was presented as a *truthful bragger,* whose boasts reflected his actual accomplishments. Black and white students liked the nonbragger and disliked the untruthful bragger equally. They differed, however, in their impressions of the truthful bragger. Black students liked the truthful bragger more than the white students did (Holtgraves & Dulin, 1994). Immodesty, when truthful, is apparently tolerated more by African Americans than by European Americans.

This is not to say that European Americans are particularly modest. Indeed, compared to Americans of Asian descent, European Americans come across as quite boastful (e.g., Fry & Ghosh, 1980). Across the globe, Asians are particularly modest in their self-presentations (e.g., Farh, Dobbins, & Cheng, 1991; Kashima & Triandis, 1986), living one of Confucius's maxims: "The superior man is modest in his speech." Why do Asian Americans value personal modesty more than do European Americans, who value it more than African Americans? One explanation centers on cultural differences in individualism and collectivism. Recall that Asians, more than Europeans and Americans, tend to be collectivistic—that is, they focus on the group more than on the individual (Markus & Kitayama, 1991; Triandis, 1989). This group focus implies that it would be less appropriate for collectivistic people to present themselves as superior to other members of their groups.

The individualism–collectivism explanation cannot explain, however, why African Americans appear to be more approving of truthful immodesty than do European Americans, because these two groups do not generally differ in their levels of individualism or collectivism. One possibility, awaiting research, stems from economic differences between the groups. European Americans are historically (and currently) wealthier as a group than African Americans, and thus are able to promote themselves by casually displaying the material fruits of their successes—expensive cars, large homes, and the like. Could it be that with such display tactics historically unavailable to them, African Americans and others in relatively impoverished economic circumstances grew to rely on the self-promotional option of verbal boasting?

We should be careful not to overgeneralize from these data, however. It's unlikely that race per se can explain the differences in verbal modesty among Asian Americans, African Americans, and European Americans. For instance, in a study of Nigerians, Boski (1983) discovered a wide range of modesty norms across the different tribes: The Hausa, collectivistic in nature, stress modesty, whereas the Igbo, who are more individualistic, allow for more self-promotion. Moreover, because most of the research on modesty has explored verbal self-presentation, we know little about cultural differences in what we might call material modesty.

In sum, modesty norms are like most other norms—there exist interesting similarities and differences across cultures. Whereas all cultures appear to frown upon deceptive self-promotion, some cultures encourage modesty more than others.

To this point, we've described four tactics people use to ingratiate themselves with others: People try to convince others that they like them, using flattery and certain nonverbal expressions; they point out their similarities to others; they make themselves more physically attractive; and they act modestly. Now let's explore the characteristics of the person and situation that encourage people to be ingratiating.

Gender

On an afternoon jaunt to the library, one of us came across a collection of "advice" books for young men and women, written in the eighteenth and nineteenth centuries. In general, the recommendations for men concerned such things as industriousness, accomplishment, and status seeking. The advice for "ladies" differed considerably, focusing instead on the importance of being likable and proper. In his *Lectures on Female Education*, for example, John Barton (1794) told the students of a girls' school "to please and to captivate" (p. 72). And after extolling the benefits of cheerfulness, gentleness, modesty, and beauty, he counseled the girls that "a conduct regulated by these agreeable qualities will not only be pleasing in its appearance, but useful in its effects" (p. 162). Female writers of the time made similar suggestions, focusing in particular on the advantages of appropriate dress and manners (e.g., Farrar, 1838). The implication of such writings was clear: Women should present themselves in ways that are likable to others.

Of course, these prescriptions were written long ago, in a society different in many ways from the present one. It may surprise some of you to learn, then, that even today the desire to be liked seems generally more important to women than to men (DePaulo, 1992; Forsyth, Schlenker, Leary, & McCown, 1985). As a result, women are somewhat more likely than men to use the ingratiation tactics we just explored. In social situations, women smile more than men (e.g., Hall & Friedman, 1999; Hall, 1984), and are more likely to adjust their opinions to match those held by others (Becker, 1988; Eagly & Carli, 1981). They are more concerned with their physical attractiveness than are men (e.g., Daly et al., 1983; Dion, Dion, & Keelan,

1990; Hart, Leary, & Rejeski, 1989), and account for around 90 percent of cosmetic surgeries and procedures (American Society for Aesthetic Plastic Surgery, 2000). And women present themselves more modestly, especially in public (e.g., Berg, Stephan, & Dodson, 1981; Daubman, Heatherington, & Ahn, 1992). Not only do women focus more on getting others to like them, but they apply quite adeptly a full range of self-presentational tactics in doing so.

This doesn't mean that men are uninterested in ingratiating themselves with others. Far from it. It's important for almost everyone to be liked, and men can be as ingratiating as women. But it appears that other self-presentational goals—such as the desire to be viewed as powerful and dominant—compete more strongly for men's attention, a difference we explore later in this chapter.

Why is ingratiation relatively more important for women? One explanation suggests that women in particular are rewarded for presenting themselves in agreeable and likable ways (e.g., Deaux & Major, 1987). Consistent with this, girls become more nonverbally agreeable as they move through adolescence, presumably because they learn how society expects them to behave (Blanck et al., 1981). Biological factors may also be important. Compared to men, women usually have much lower levels of **testosterone,** a hormone responsible for important aspects of sexual development. People who have high levels of testosterone use more confrontational, hardened ways of getting what they want from others, and they are less friendly, less concerned about others' welfare, and smile less (e.g., Cashdan, 1995; Dabbs, 1997; Dabbs, Hargrove, & Heusel, 1996). In contrast, people who have lower levels of testosterone are friendlier and are more likely to use politeness and social graces to achieve their goals. Thus, both socialization and biological factors may contribute to women's greater concern with ingratiation.

Charming. *Books of etiquette have long taught young women about the value and effectiveness of presenting themselves as likable. Although the times have changed in many ways, and etiquette manuals and "charm schools" are no longer in vogue, even women today focus more on being liked than do men.*

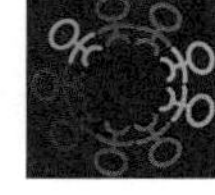

Potential Friends and Power-Holders

Personal characteristics alone don't create the desire to ingratiate oneself with others. When people hope to form or maintain friendships, or when they interact with people in positions of higher status, they're also particularly likely to be ingratiating.

Friendship Settings It almost goes without saying that we should be especially concerned with ingratiating ourselves with those people with whom we want to develop or maintain positive relationships. Participants in one study were interviewed by either a good friend or a total stranger and asked to evaluate and discuss their prospects for a successful career, satisfying relationships, and so on. The participants presented themselves more modestly to their friends than to the strangers (Tice, Butler, Muraven, & Stillwell, 1995). And just as we're careful not to toot our own horns too loudly when we are fostering friendships, we're also more likely to smile, say nice things about the other person, make ourselves more attractive, and so on (e.g., Bohra & Pandey, 1984; Daly et al., 1983).

Interacting with People in Powerful Positions Those who occupy positions of power are often less focused on getting others to like them. After all, these individuals can exercise their power to get what they want—"If your productivity doesn't improve, Smithers, you'll be out on the street collecting unemployment!" Intimidation, of course, isn't a compelling option for those having little actual power. Instead, people in positions of little power focus more on getting others to like them (e.g.,

Testosterone *A hormone present in both males and females—but usually in much greater quantities in males—responsible for important aspects of sexual development.*

Pandey, 1981; Stires & Jones, 1969). For example, members of lower social classes are especially likely to adjust their public opinions and provide socially appropriate answers to interviewer questions (Ross & Mirowsky, 1983). In another study, women modified their physical appearance to match what they thought their interviewer would like: Women interviewing with a traditional man showed up at the interview wearing more makeup and jewelry than did women expecting to interview with a man who had nontraditional views (von Baeyer, Sherk, & Zanna, 1981).

Indeed, ingratiating oneself with the holders of power is quite effective, especially in the business world (Watt, 1993; Wayne & Liden, 1995). In one study of college graduates, attempts to ingratiate themselves with supervisors—by praising them or pretending to agree with them, for instance—was the fourth largest factor contributing to career success, after hours worked per week, years of job experience, and marital status (married people are more successful) (Judge & Bretz, 1994). Similarly, workers who are liked by their supervisors tend to be paid more—according to one study, being liked was worth a pay increase of 4 to 5 percent over and beyond the impact of job performance (Deluga & Perry, 1994).

Although people in powerful positions possess more tools of influence, and thus need to rely less on ingratiation, they too want to be liked. Interestingly, they tend to use different ingratiation tactics than do their less powerful counterparts. Because they are unlikely to be perceived as "brown-nosing" their subordinates, it is less risky for them to seek affection by rendering favors and giving out compliments (Jones & Wortman, 1973). On the other hand, people in positions of power rarely seek liking by conforming their opinions to match their subordinates', as to do so might threaten their status.

Multiple Audiences

You've seen that people are pretty good at getting others to like them. You've also learned that it's not always easy, that to ingratiate oneself with others successfully requires the self-presenter to be subtle and sensitive to the possibility that others may see his or her behaviors as manipulative. Getting others to like us becomes particularly tricky when we want to simultaneously ingratiate ourselves with two audiences having opposing values. Consider, for example, the dilemma faced by the student who wants to "butter up" the professor while other students are nearby or by the politician giving a nationally televised speech who wants the support of voters on both sides of the pro-life/pro-choice divide. To flatter the professor blatantly will earn the dislike of one's peers, who frown on such behaviors, and to support the pro-life position will cost the politician the affections of the pro-choice voters. How do people manage such **multiple audience dilemmas?**

If at all possible, we segregate our different audiences. Thus, the flattering student may wait to ply his tricks until he reaches the privacy of the professor's office, while the politician may state one set of views during a meeting of pro-lifers and a different set of views at a gathering of pro-choicers. Alternatively, we might determine that one audience is more important to us than the other, as when the student decides that he'd rather have the friendship of his classmates than of his professor.

These options are sometimes unavailable, however. We can't always separate our audiences and we sometimes need the positive regard of both audiences. Even so, people are remarkably good at managing multiple audiences (Fleming & Darley, 1991). They may finesse the competing desires of multiple audiences by "moderating" their presentations—by presenting their opinions as falling somewhere between the contrasting opinions held by the two audiences (Braver et al., 1977; Snyder & Swann, 1976). Of course, an ingratiator using this strategy runs the risk of being disliked by both audiences, as might happen if a presidential candidate waffles on his or her views of the abortion issue. People may also try to present different messages on the different "channels" of communication. A student telephoning a

Multiple audience dilemma *Situation in which a person needs to present different images to different audiences, often at the same time.*

professor to request an extension on a paper may mention flattering aspects of the class while simultaneously grimacing for the benefit of his roommates (Fleming & Rudman, 1993).

Finally, we can manage the multiple audience dilemma by capitalizing on the different information the audiences may have about us. In one study, students were asked to present themselves to one conversation partner as a "nerd," and to a second partner as a "party animal." After speaking separately with each partner, the students were asked to maintain these opposing images in a conversation with both partners at once. They were able to do so effectively, partially because they made statements that would mean different things to the two partners. For example, by saying that "it's like I said before, Saturdays are good for one thing and one thing only," the students reinforced their images as nerds to the first partner and party animals to the second (Van Boven, Kruger, Savitsky, & Gilovich, 2000).

The values held by multiple audiences interact, then, to influence how we go about getting others to like us. If everyone in the audience holds the same values, we can readily sculpt our presentations to conform with them. When the audience is made up of people having differing and incompatible values, however, effective ingratiation becomes trickier, and self-presenters must become more creative to pull it off.

Summary

We frequently present ourselves so that others will like us. We can do this by expressing liking for others, pointing out our similarities with them, making ourselves more physically attractive, and presenting our achievements modestly. The desire to ingratiate oneself with others is somewhat more important for women than for men, and is especially likely to influence our self-presentations when we wish either to build a friendship or to gain influence with powerful individuals. Finally, people attempt to manage multiple audience dilemmas by segregating their audiences, moderating their presentations, or presenting different messages on different communication channels.

Appearing Competent

If Demara had posed as a postal employee, garbage collector, or waiter, his life would have been much easier—he was quite smart and socially skilled and would have learned quickly the tricks of those trades. But he decided, instead, to pass himself off as a college professor, an accountant, and a surgeon, among other learned professions. To escape detection in these more technical fields, Demara had to convince others that he was competent—that he possessed the knowledge and abilities of someone who had been trained and had received the proper certifications.

Non-impostors also have to convince others of their competence. Physicians must appear competent if they are to acquire and retain patients, salespeople must appear competent if they are to be promoted into the managerial ranks, and children must appear competent if they are to be chosen by classmates to play kickball during recess. Indeed, people are sometimes so concerned with appearing competent that they may be too distracted from the task at hand to perform it well (e.g., Baumeister, Hutton, & Tice, 1989; Lord, Saenz, & Godfrey, 1987; Osborne & Gilbert, 1992; Steele & Aronson, 1995). In this section, we explore the strategies people use to communicate their competence and the features of the person and situation that make such communications more likely.

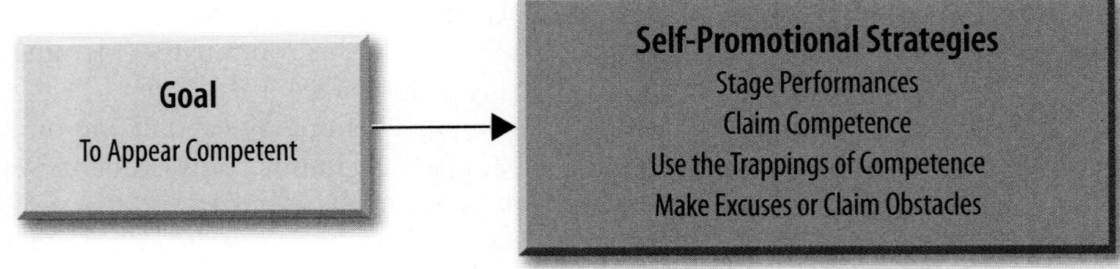

Figure 4.5
Strategies of self-promotion.

People use a variety of strategies to get others to see them as competent.

Strategies of Self-Promotion

The occupations Demara chose required years of specialized training, and we can't help but wonder why Demara's colleagues never caught him in the act, never realized that he was a fraud. It helped Demara that he was well liked, as this reduced the likelihood that people would suspect that he was incompetent (e.g., Wayne & Ferris, 1990). It also helped that he was a hard worker and a quick study. But Demara had several tricks up his sleeves as well. Although Demara's tactics for **self-promotion**—behaviors intended to create the image of competence—were, at times, outrageously bold, they usefully highlight the principles underlying the everyday strategies people employ (see Figure 4.5).

Staging Performances A legitimate reputation for competence requires that a person actually *be* competent. Unfortunately, one's achievements can go unobserved. Perhaps your dad's head was turned the moment you made that picture-perfect dive into the community pool or your mom was working in the yard when you finally mastered the difficult piano piece. Because successes are sometimes overlooked, we may seek and create opportunities to *stage* our performances, to demonstrate our competence in public (Goffman, 1959; Jones, 1990)—to subtly scream, "Lookit, Ma!" as we're about to leap off the metaphorical high dive. For instance, if you're a skilled dancer and want to impress a new love interest with your talent, you might feel tempted to arrange an evening not far from music and a dance floor.

Of course, this staging tactic has its flip side—if you're *in*competent at something (if you have the physical graces of a rhinoceros), you're likely to avoid public stagings. Demara understood both lessons well. On the one hand, he often chose professions like teaching and medicine, in which the audiences—students and patients—possessed little technical knowledge and thus could be easily impressed. On the other hand, he did his best to avoid demonstrating his dubious skills when other professionals were around by making himself scarce when necessary.

Staging performances can be as simple as moving one's body into the spotlight of public attention. In one study, participants who expected to perform well on a simulated game show chose a seat that placed them front and center. Not surprisingly, students who expected to perform poorly chose to seat themselves off to the side (Akimoto, Sanbonmatso, & Ho, 2000).

Sometimes it's not possible to stage performances of competence, nor is it possible to avoid public displays of incompetence. The boss isn't always around while we're generating valuable insights, and we may get dragged onto the dance floor against our will. So we rely on other tactics as well to convince others of our competence.

Claiming Competence Why don't we just *tell* others about our abilities? Why not just mention to a date that you're a great dancer? Our earlier explorations of modesty reveal a partial answer to this question: People who verbally self-promote are disliked by others (Godfrey, Jones, & Lord, 1986).

A second reason we rarely boast of our abilities stems from the commonly held belief that people who are truly competent don't need to claim it. Hence, to baldly state our contributions to a job-related success can imply that our role may actually have been relatively unimportant (Jones & Pittman, 1982). Because self-promoting statements come across as immodest and are only marginally credible, they can actu-

Self-promotion *An attempt to get others to see us as competent.*

ally harm one's professional success (Judge & Bretz, 1994; Wayne & Ferris, 1990).

Verbal declarations of competence are less problematic, however, when they are "invited." For instance, if you're being interviewed, verbal self-promotion is both appropriate and effective for communicating competence (Holtgraves & Srull, 1989; Kacmar et al., 1992). Moreover, we can benefit from verbal self-promotions made on our behalf by others (Giacalone, 1985). Indeed, one of Demara's favorite tricks took illicit advantage of such claims; he would forge reference letters from highly credible sources, all glowing in their praise of his competence.

Excuses, excuses. *To maintain a reputation for competence, we sometimes make excuses for our failures. Douglas Bernstein (1993) compiled a list of amazing, strange, and unusual—but actual—excuses students have used to avoid taking exams, turning in term papers, and the like: "My paper is late because my parrot crapped into my computer" (the contemporary version of "my dog ate my homework"?). "I can't finish my paper because I just found out my girlfriend is a nymphomaniac." And one from our own campus, in usually sunny Arizona: "I couldn't make the exam yesterday because it was cloudy and I drive a convertible."*

Using the Trappings of Competence Many advisors in the self-promotion industry recommend that people surround themselves with the props and habits usually associated with competence (e.g., Bly, Pierce, & Prendergast, 1986; Korda, 1975). For instance, self-promoters are advised to look busy—by writing a lot in their calendar books, by taking a while to return phone calls, or by carrying cellular phones and pagers—because very successful individuals usually have little free time on their hands. Demara was skilled at using clothing and professional-appearing stationery to convey the image of competence. If a person looks like a physician, he correctly reasoned, he or she is more likely to be accepted as such. The use of props for self-presentational purposes is frequent, and we discuss them further when we explore the ways people try to convey images of status and power.

Making Excuses, Claiming Obstacles "The sun was in my eyes," claims the outfielder after badly misjudging the lazy fly ball. "The dog ate it," pleads the sixth-grader late once again with his homework. These classic gems point to the ease with which people generate excuses after poor performances. Indeed, people may even make excuses *before* performing, anticipating for their audiences the obstacles that could get in the way of success. Although many times such excuses are valid, at other times they serve less to explain poor performance than to make the excuse-makers feel better about their performances and to help them influence the way they are viewed (e.g., Rhodewalt, Morf, Hazlett, & Fairfield, 1991).

The self-promotional value of excuses and claimed obstacles follows from the *discounting* and *augmenting* principles we discussed in chapter 3. If others believe that the sun truly was in your eyes, they may discount the relevance of your softball ability in determining your botched attempt. And if you manage to catch the ball despite the sun's glare, your reputation for competence will be augmented. So making excuses and claiming obstacles may shield us from images of incompetence following failure and create images of competence following success (e.g., Giacalone & Riordan, 1990; Quattrone & Jones, 1978; Snyder & Higgins, 1988).

It's one thing to claim an obstacle to success; it's quite another to create such an obstacle for oneself (Arkin & Baumgardner, 1985; Hirt, Deppe, & Gordon, 1991; Leary & Shepperd, 1986). However, people sometimes do just that. By **self-handicapping**—by creating circumstances for ourselves that obstruct our ability to demonstrate true competence—we may reduce the likelihood that people will attribute our failures to incompetence and increase the likelihood that people will attribute our successes to some outstanding ability.

FOCUS ON Social Dysfunction

The Paradox of Self-Handicapping

A professional athlete, successful in his first few years, signs a new, whoppingly lucrative contract and proceeds to drink his career into the gutter. A famous news anchor, successful beyond her dreams, starts abusing drugs and throws away her career in the

Self-handicapping *The behavior of withdrawing effort or creating obstacles to one's future successes.*

process. A high school student, voted "most likely to succeed," attends a prestigious university, becomes uncharacteristically negligent in his studies, and fails out.

Most of us have heard of people like this—people who after early successes begin to act in ways that make future successes less likely. This self-handicapping behavior may occur when people doubt that previous achievements accurately reflect their personal abilities and efforts (Berglas & Jones, 1978). For instance, the athlete may view his early success as arising largely from the skills of his teammates; the television anchor may believe her rapid attainment to be the result of beauty and luck; and the student may attribute his academic accomplishments to the advantages of his family's prosperous background.

The result of such beliefs is the fear that similar high-level performances will be difficult to sustain, and that the private and public esteem built upon past successes will crumble. So to maintain a public image of competence, and to preserve their fragile competence beliefs, self-handicappers withdraw effort or create obstacles to future performance. If they succeed despite the impediment, people would reasonably conclude (via the augmenting principle) that they are especially skilled; if they fail, people would reasonably conclude (via the discounting principle) that the obstacle caused the failure. In either case, by withdrawing effort or forcing themselves to hurdle daunting obstacles, self-handicappers can maintain a public and private image of competence.

Certain people are more likely than others to self-handicap. Individuals who have fragile self-esteem are especially likely to self-handicap (Harris & Snyder, 1986), as are those who have a strong desire to demonstrate their competence (Rhodewalt, 1994). Interestingly, men place more obstacles in the paths to their own achievements, although both sexes are quite adept at claiming obstacles following failures (e.g., Ferrari, 1991; Hirt, McCrea, & Kimble, 2000; Rhodewalt & Hill, 1995). And although both persons high and persons low in self-esteem self-handicap to some extent, they seem to do so for different reasons. People who have high self-esteem want to enhance their already favorable images, whereas people who have low self-esteem want to protect their less favorable images from failure (Tice, 1991).

How do college students self-handicap when confronted with difficult tasks? Let us begin to count the ways:

- by taking cognition-impairing drugs before or during the task (e.g., Berglas & Jones, 1978; Kolditz & Arkin, 1982)
- by not practicing when given the opportunity (e.g., Deppe & Harackiewicz, 1996; Ferrari & Tice, 2000)
- by consuming alcohol (Higgins & Harris, 1988; Tucker et al., 1981)
- by listening to loud, distracting music during the task (e.g., Rhodewalt & Davison, 1986; Shepperd & Arkin, 1989)
- by choosing unattainable goals (Greenberg, 1985)
- by giving a competitor a performance advantage (Shepperd & Arkin, 1991)

Our choices of self-handicaps are wide and varied, indeed.

The self-handicapping strategy carries with it heavy long-term costs. By placing significant obstacles in their paths, people reduce their chances for future success (e.g., Rhodewalt & Fairfield, 1991; Zuckerman, Kieffer, & Knee, 1998). Moreover, self-handicappers may be viewed by others as irresponsible and unmotivated (Luginbuhl & Palmer, 1991; Smith & Strube, 1991). That people will go so far to sabotage both future achievements and broader images points to the importance they place on the image of competence. And therein lies the great paradox of self-handicapping: Our great desire to appear competent leads us under some circumstances to engage in behaviors that make competent performances less likely. ■

In sum, people can project an image of competence by staging performances, making verbal claims, taking on the trappings of success, and providing excuses for their failures and claiming or creating obstacles for their success. We turn now to explore the kinds of persons for whom an image of competence is especially important, and the circumstances that create in most of us the desire to be seen as competent.

To be shy in a self-promoting world. *Shy people become anxious even imagining themselves in unfamiliar social situations. Because of this, they may miss opportunities for personal and professional advancement that staging performances, claims of competence, excuse-making, and other bold self-promotional tactics make available. Shyness hurts in more ways than one.*

Competence Motivation and Shyness

Demara hated to fail. He was determined, once he applied his considerable abilities to a task, to succeed at it. He needed to do more than just "pass"; he wanted to be among the best. He also wanted to be *seen* as one of the best. Demara was high in **competence motivation,** the desire to perform effectively (e.g., Deci & Ryan, 1985; Lewin, 1951; Murray, 1938; White, 1959). People may be high in competence motivation for intrinsic reasons, that is, because gaining mastery is interesting and challenging. This is typically called *achievement motivation* (e.g., McClelland, Atkinson, Clark, & Lowell, 1953). Alternatively, people may possess a strong competence motivation because they know that success can boost their public- or self-images. In this case, achievement is driven by the extrinsic desire to be seen (or to see oneself) as competent (Koestner & McClelland, 1990). Although only a few research studies have explored the effects of competence motivation on self-presentation, the evidence seems to support the idea that the two are associated. For instance, those who score high on measures of this second, extrinsic type of competence motivation are quick to claim personal credit for successes (Kukla, 1972). These individuals are also especially likely to display the trappings of competence by dressing professionally in their work settings (Ericksen & Sirgy, 1989). Thus, for certain people—those who are focused on public achievement—presenting a competent image may be particularly important.

Even though most people want to be seen as competent in at least some circumstances, some are unwilling to get there by adopting the competence tactics we've discussed. Some folks experience frequent or chronic **shyness**—they tend to feel tense, worried, or awkward in unfamiliar social interactions, even while merely imagining or anticipating social interaction (Cheek, Melchior, & Carpentieri, 1986; Leary, 1986b). Shy people are anxiously self-preoccupied (Cheek & Briggs, 1990; Crozier, 1979). That is, in social situations, they spend a lot of time thinking about their feelings, their behaviors, and how they come across to others ("Why am I so nervous? Is it really important what she thinks of me? I have no idea what I'm going to say next") (Cheek & Melchior, 1990).

Compared with nonshy individuals, shy people are less likely to promote their competence boldly. Instead, their self-presentations tend to be protective—rather than trying to acquire favorable public images, shy people focus on preventing unfavorable public images (Arkin, 1981). To be safe, shy people try to avoid unfamiliar social encounters (Shepperd & Arkin, 1990). They date less frequently, prefer to work alone rather than with others, and tend to occupy seats in college classrooms toward the rear and sides (Curran, 1977; Dykman & Reis, 1979; McGovern, 1976). By keeping themselves out of the attentional spotlight, they reduce the risk of coming across as incompetent. When they do find themselves in the company of others, shy people try to reduce the social pressure to appear competent. For instance, after poor performances, they're less likely to make claims of future successes (Shepperd, Arkin, & Slaughter, 1995) and may even purposely fail in order to lower the expectations others hold of them (Baumgardner & Brownlee, 1987). They are also less likely to self-handicap their performances (Shepperd & Arkin, 1990). Shy people are, however, willing to take advantage of handicaps that already exist in

Competence motivation *The desire to perform effectively.*

Shyness *The tendency to feel tense, worried, or awkward in novel social situations and with unfamiliar people.*

the situation. For instance, in the presence of an annoying distraction such as loud noise—a condition that would be expected to inhibit successful performance—shy people increase the boldness of their self-presentations (Arkin & Baumgardner, 1988; Leary, 1986a). It's not that shy people don't want to be viewed as competent. Rather, they are just particularly wary of promoting themselves when they know that they may have to prove their competence in the future.

The reluctance of shy people to promote themselves actively may carry with it significant costs. For instance, some studies suggest that shy individuals tend to be underemployed and relatively unsuccessful in their careers (e.g., Caspi, Elder, & Bem, 1988; Gilmartin, 1987; Morris, Soroker, & Burruss, 1954). Skillful self-promotion creates benefits that shy people are less likely to receive.

When Competence Matters

We are more concerned with whether we come across as competent in some settings than in others. For instance, your desire to be appreciated as a good dancer is more likely to come to mind when in a nightclub than when sitting through a psychology lecture. Similarly, certain people are more likely to arouse concerns about competence than are others. For example, you're likely to prefer being viewed as a good dancer by a romantic partner than by your chemistry professor. Of course, there are times and places where we have few self-promotional concerns of any sort, as when a father finds himself lost in the joys of playing with his child—which probably explains the goofy gestures and expressions such situations often evoke, most of which would be quite embarrassing (not to mention damaging to one's reputation) if displayed in the corporate boardroom.

Failure, or a fear of impending failure, amplifies the concern with appearing competent. If you want others to think you're smart, failing an exam will be a very noxious experience for you—one that may lead you to reach into your self-promotional bag of tricks. In one experiment, students informed they had performed poorly on a test of social sensitivity were especially likely to present themselves afterward as well adjusted. In comparison, students who had succeeded on the test engaged in a more modest self-presentation; because their social competence was validated by the test, they could focus instead on being liked (Schneider, 1969). The desire to appear competent may be particularly strong in pressure-filled, competitive circumstances. Ironically, such circumstances also increase the chance that a performer will "choke," or perform well below potential (Baumeister, 1984; Baumeister & Showers, 1986).

Competence Checks

Unlike shy individuals, socially confident people often take advantage of opportunities to promote their competence, especially after a public failure. Do these individuals self-promote with reckless abandon, without considering their present circumstances? Probably not. As James Shepperd and his colleagues (1995) demonstrated, even socially confident individuals are attuned to the riskiness of self-promotion. Participants in their study were led to believe either that they had performed poorly on an intelligence test or that they had done quite well. Moreover, some participants were told they would be tested again shortly. All then completed a short questionnaire. Regardless of conditions, shy participants were quite modest when estimating their future performance on the test and tests like it, showing no inclination to boast of future successes. Socially confident individuals, in contrast, were quick to jump at the opportunity to claim future success after they had failed. But this was only true when they wouldn't be immediately retaking the test. When they knew their second performance would be evaluated, they became more modest in their predictions. This finding illustrates, then, one kind of person–situation interaction: Certain people (those who are socially confident), when confronted with a particular situation (failure on an important test that won't be retaken), are especially likely to act in certain ways to restore the damage done to their reputations (by claiming future success).

The Interpersonal Cycle of Self-Promotion

People can change their situations. An experiment conducted by Roy Baumeister, Debra Hutton, & Dianne Tice (1989) explored how one person's self-promotions can create a social situation in which others also feel compelled to self-promote. Pairs of students were recruited for a study exploring the nature of group interviews. One of these students—labeled the "protagonist"—was instructed prior to the interview (and out of earshot of the partner) either (1) to promote him- or herself as strongly as possible, or (2) to present him- or herself modestly. The interviewer proceeded to ask the students questions about their career prospects, relationships with members of the opposite sex, and so forth, always beginning with the protagonist. As expected, protagonists instructed to self-promote provided more favorable answers than did those instructed to be modest. Interestingly, however, the *partners* of the self-promoters presented themselves more favorably than did the partners of the modest self-presenters. Illustrating the power of people to alter their situations, these self-promoters created an environment in which their partners felt compelled to self-promote as well.

Summary

People use several tactics to convey an image of competence: They stage demonstrations of their competence; they make verbal claims of their abilities and talents; they surround themselves with the physical trappings and props associated with actual competence; and they claim obstacles and make excuses to buffer the impact of their failures and boost the impact of their successes. Some people—those who have an externally driven competence motivation—seem especially likely to self-promote. Although certain settings and failure seem to evoke self-promotion in many of us, shy people tend to engage in protective self-presentation and to self-promote in only relatively subtle ways. Even socially confident individuals, however, restrain their self-promotion if their true competence can be easily checked by others. Finally, self-promoters may create situations in which others feel compelled to advertise their competence as well. Not only is a reputation for competence useful in and of itself, but it contributes strongly to an image of status and power, to which we turn next.

Conveying Status and Power

One event of his early childhood long stood out in Fred Demara's mind. His father was at that time a prosperous businessman, the owner of several movie theaters, and the well-to-do family lived in a large home in a fancy part of town. It was Demara's fourth birthday, and his father assembled the house staff in front of the large curving staircase, under the shimmering glass chandelier. "Today my son is four years old, and on this day he becomes a little man," he announced. "From this day on I shall expect all of you to address the young master with the respect due him. Beginning tonight he is to be called Mr. Demara. I will expect it of you and so shall he." And then, as if on cue, each servant stepped forward and bowed—"Happy birthday, *Mr.* Demara" (Crichton, 1959).

Seven years later, when the family was forced to vacate its glorious home after a business setback, Demara noticed the disrespect of the moving men as they unloaded the family's possessions into a rundown house on the edge of town. Young Fred was now poor, and the loss of status it implied pained him greatly. Should we be surprised, then, that as an impostor he would almost always choose to step into the shoes of men of respect and status—the physician Joseph Cyr, the famous professor Robert Linton French, and others like them?

Demara's cons were extraordinary. His desire to be held in high regard, however, was quite normal. Why *shouldn't* a person want a reputation for status and power, given the benefits that come with it? Individuals who have high status and power gain access to greater educational opportunities and material resources. They're more likely to be accepted into influential social circles that offer opportunities to make money, find desirable mates, and wield political power. And they're less likely to be bothered and hassled by others. With a reputation of high status and power comes not only the metaphorical carrot for enticing others to do your bidding but also the stick with which to intimidate them for not doing so.

Strategies of Status and Power

How do people create for themselves the appearance of high status and power? Having a reputation for competence helps, as certain kinds of status are based heavily on one's achievements. In this section, we explore a range of other tactics that people frequently use to convey an image of status and power (see Figure 4.6).

Displaying the Artifacts of Status and Power When we enter a physician's office, we immediately know where we are—thanks to the telltale waiting room, the receptionist behind the counter, and the diplomas, board certifications, and organizational stamps of approval on the walls. These are among the artifacts of the medical profession, and when in their midst, we just "know" we're at the doctor's office. Similarly, a corporate CEO is likely to occupy a top-floor corner office with large windows, imposing desk, fancy phone, and little clutter. The message? Decisions of magnitude are made here. People often display artifacts associated with high status or power so they will be accorded the respect and reputation they believe they have earned.

Unfortunately, people who have no legitimate credentials sometimes misappropriate these artifacts to gain respect. To impress upon people his worldliness and social standing, Demara traveled with a trunk he had purchased from a secondhand store—a trunk already plastered with stickers from expensive hotels and resorts across the globe, like the luggage owned by world travelers of that era. If Demara possessed such a trunk, observers reasoned, he must be a wealthy world traveler.

Conspicuous Consumption The impression of status may also be conveyed by the amounts of money and resources people are able to expend. In fact, much of material consumption serves the purpose of communicating status (Fussell, 1983; Veblen, 1899). Rich people may communicate their high status through the ability to spend

Figure 4.6 Strategies for conveying status and power.

People wield several strategies to convince others of their high status and power.

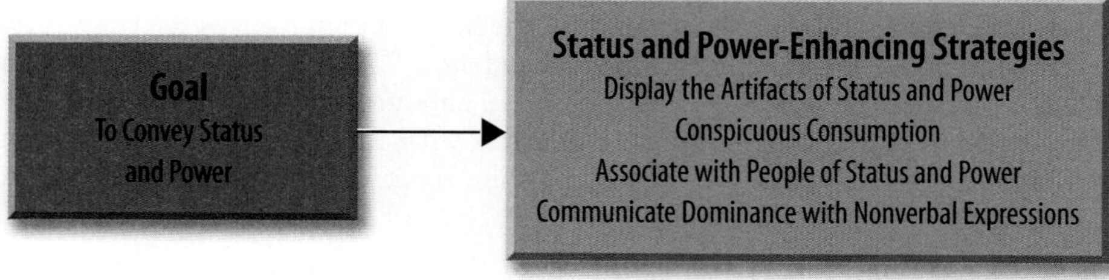

lavishly on houses in the "right" neighborhoods, automobiles, jewels, and even burial chambers for their internment following death. Less wealthy folks often do the same on a smaller scale, buying designer clothes, national-brand-name products instead of local brands or "generics," and so on (e.g., Bushman, 1993).

Giving things away and wasting money are also forms of consumption. Some wealthy people, for instance, throw grand parties. As we'll discuss in chapter 9, high-status members of some societies hold *potlatches*, ceremonial parties at which tribal leaders move up the status hierarchy by giving away or destroying valuable goods. The more the host gives away or destroys, the greater his rise in status (Murdock, 1923/1970). This connection between status and wasteful consumption may have the side-effect of deterring environmental conservation. Experiments by Edward Sadalla and Jennifer Krull (1995) demonstrated that people who dry their garments on clotheslines instead of in electrical dryers, who use a bus instead of a car to run errands, or who go out of their way to recycle aluminum cans may be viewed as being of lesser status. With such beliefs in the air, is it any surprise that many people are unwilling to engage in public displays of energy conservation or recycling?

Demara certainly understood the presentational value of material possessions. He ran scams on salesmen in clothing stores so he'd be able to dress well; he was fired from one job after exquisitely furnishing his new office at his employer's expense; and he had the expensive habit of buying drinks for strangers in bars. Conspicuous consumption, like the appropriation of high-status symbols and artifacts, can be an effective way to enhance one's social standing.

Figure 4.7
The nonverbal expression of status and power.

Which person has higher status? How can you tell? Just as people smile to convey liking for others, they adjust their bodily postures and facial expressions to communicate status and deference.

Personal Associations Managing personal associations is yet another self-presentational tool. In the fall of 1973, researchers at universities having major football teams discovered that fans were more likely to wear their team logos after victories than after defeats (Cialdini et al., 1976). Follow-up studies revealed that students were also more likely to use the pronoun *we* to describe victories ("We won!") than defeats ("They lost."). By **basking in the reflected glory** of their triumphant teams, by associating themselves with known winners, students could use the victories to strengthen their own public images. On the other side of the coin, people may **cut off reflected failure** (Snyder, Lassegard, & Ford, 1986)—that is, distance themselves from known "losers"—fearing that unfavorable public associations may leave their reputations tarnished (e.g., Goffman, 1963; Neuberg, Smith, Hoffman, & Russell, 1994). Filip Boen and his colleagues (in press) observed this very pattern among politically active citizens of Flanders, Belgium—citizens who had advertised their political preferences with posters in their front windows. After the election, nearly 60 percent of those who supported the winning parties kept their posters up, compared to only 19 percent of those who supported the losing parties. People associate themselves with winners and distance themselves from losers.

Demara understood the power of associations. For example, he always arrived at job interviews well "papered"—that is, with a handful of forged letters from men of acknowledged status and power testifying to his position and character. These letters served two purposes. First, as we learned earlier, they helped establish Demara's competence. They also, however, conferred status on him. After all, would such prestigious men write such glowing letters for a nobody? By using such connections, by linking himself to people of status or power, Demara was able to create high public regard for himself.

Basking in reflected glory *The process of presenting our associations with successful, high-status others or events.*

Cutting off reflected failure *The process of distancing ourselves from unsuccessful, low-status others or events.*

Body language *The popular term for nonverbal behaviors like facial expressions, posture, body orientation, and hand gestures.*

Status and Power in Nonverbal Expressions Much as people might smile to convey the impression that they are likable, they adopt other nonverbal signals to communicate images of status and power. Look, for example, at the people in Figure 4.7. Which of them is of higher status?

You probably picked the woman behind the desk, and quickly, too. But what led you to this conclusion? Both people are dressed well and are similarly attractive. We suspect that their **body language** (Fast, 1970)—the popular term for nonverbal expressions—tipped you off. The woman behind the desk is relaxed and seems in natural control of the situation, whereas the posture of the man on the left suggests more attentiveness.

Indeed, certain nonverbal behaviors seem to signal high status and dominance, whereas others reveal low status and submissiveness (e.g., Hall & Friedman, 1999; LaFrance & Mayo, 1978; Patterson, 1983). For instance, people who feel secure in their high status tend to adopt more relaxed, "open" postures—postures that take up more space and lay claim to greater territory (e.g., Mehrabian, 1972). High-status individuals demand attention from others but seem relatively unconcerned with others and what they are doing. This is demonstrated in *visual dominance behavior*, whereby high-status individuals maintain eye contact with their audiences when speaking but pay less attention when listening. In contrast, low-status people orient toward those who have higher status, both with their body positions and with their eyes (e.g., Exline, 1972). High-status individuals are also more likely to interrupt others (e.g., Goldberg, 1990) and to place themselves in positions of prominence, such as in the head chair in the corporate boardroom (e.g., Altman & Haythorn, 1967; Heckel, 1973; Lott & Sommer, 1967; Reiss & Rosenfeld, 1980; Russo, 1966). High-status people are also more likely to touch others and to encroach on their *personal space* (e.g., Henley, 1973), that invisible buffer or "bubble" we like to keep between ourselves and others.

Although high-status persons look relaxed when their status is secure, their posturing may change dramatically when that status is threatened. In such circumstances, they may exhibit *dominance displays* remarkably similar to those of other animals. Like the gorilla in Figure 4.8, they may puff themselves up to full size, stiffen their backs, tighten their brows, thrust their chins forward, and lean toward the challenger. These displays often suffice to convince others of their power (e.g., Keating, Mazur, & Segall, 1977; Schwartz, Tesser, & Powell, 1982).

For some people, the image of status and power is so important, the fear of being seen as weak so great, that they resort to actual aggression to communicate their power (Baumeister, Smart, & Boden, 1996; Felson, 1978; Felson & Tedeschi, 1993). For instance, a child who wants a reputation as a bruiser may beat up weaker children, especially when others are around to watch (Besag, 1989; Toch, 1969). And, unfortunately, bullying often pays: Highly aggressive boys can be among the most popular and socially connected boys in elementary school classrooms (Rodkin et al., 2000). Self-presentational aggression becomes more likely when a person's reputation for status or power is publicly insulted (Bushman & Baumeister, 1998; Felson, 1982). This may be especially true of men growing up in the American South, where unchallenged insults of honor can do great harm to one's reputation

Figure 4.8 Displaying dominance.

When threatened, many animals stretch themselves to full size, contort their faces into angry grimaces, and lean into their challengers, all with the hope of conveying their power. As the photographs of the gorilla and Richard Nixon reveal, humans and other primates share some intriguing similarities in their nonverbal displays.

(Cohen, Nisbett, Bowdle, & Schwarz, 1996). In chapter 10, we explore how self-presentational concerns contribute to aggressive behavior.

Gender Revisited

Are some people more likely than others to use strategies for conveying status and power? We learned earlier that women are more likely than men to present themselves as likable: they smile more, pay more attention to their physical attractiveness, and behave more modestly. This is not because men don't care about whether others like them. Indeed, they care a lot and often exhibit similar behaviors. Women just tend to care more. We see a similar pattern, but reversed, when we look at presentations of status and power: Men, more than women, present themselves as having status and power.

Gender, Status, and Power Men claim larger zones of personal space (Leibman, 1970) and are more likely to violate the space of lower-status others (Henley, 1973; Jourard & Rubin, 1968). Men are better at gaining control over conversations and arguments, often by interrupting and drowning out others (Frieze & Ramsey, 1976). Men are also more likely to engage in high-status visual dominance behavior. That is, they tend to maintain eye contact with their audience when speaking but pay less attention when listening. Women show the opposite pattern, minimizing eye contact when speaking and paying rapt attention when listening (e.g., Dovidio, Ellyson, Keating, Heltman, & Brown, 1988). Heterosexual men are more likely than women to present their professional status and financial standing in personal ads (Cicerello & Sheehan, 1995; Deaux & Hanna, 1984; Koestner & Wheeler, 1988). And men are more likely than women to respond to an insult with physical aggression (Felson, 1982).

What accounts for this gender difference? Socialization practices clearly play a role: males seem to be "trained" to present themselves as dominant and ascendant. In addition to learning early that the spoils of childhood go to those who have the power either to provide rewards or to inflict pain, boys also learn that girls—and, when older, women—prefer as dating and marriage partners men who have acquired social dominance and financial resources (Buss & Kenrick, 1998). We discuss this cross-cultural female preference for socially dominant males in chapter 8.

A complementary answer, however, rests in the biology of males and females. In many animal species, females choose to mate with those males best able to provide territory, food, and protection (Alcock, 1989). As a result, males in such species compete with one another, presenting themselves as strong, hardy, and powerful. Like male bullfrogs, elephant seals, and baboons, an ambitious man can't afford to have others view him as a powerless weakling, or else, the argument goes, he is likely to lose his assets and the opportunity to land the woman of his dreams (Sadalla, Kenrick, & Vershure, 1987). Further supporting the biological perspective is the fact that men who have high levels of the hormone testosterone behave more aggressively toward one another and, like male members of other primate species, generally become more dominant than those who have lower levels of testosterone (Dabbs, 1996).

We see, then, that biology and socialization each contribute to men's tendency to present themselves as having high status and power. Of course, this does not mean that such concerns are foreign to women. In some species, such as lemurs and spider monkeys, females compete with one another for dominance (Mitchell & Maple, 1985), and girls and women sometimes do the same (Savin-Williams, 1980). Moreover, there are no apparent gender differences in the human use of status artifacts, conspicuous consumption, or personal associations; women, as well as men, take advantage of these tactics. Indeed, women in one study were more likely than men to display nonverbal dominance behaviors in cross-sex conversations about pattern sewing, a domain where the women possessed much more expertise (Dovidio, Brown, Heltman, Ellyson, & Keating, 1988). In general, however, presentations of status and power are more important to men.

Aspiring women want to know. *Hillary Rodham Clinton is successful and powerful. What kinds of self-presentational difficulties have her achievements posed for her? Why is it so hard for her to maintain a favorable public image?*

The Self-Presentational Dilemma of Aspiring Women Women who seek positions of high status and power face special self-presentational roadblocks. Consider the case of Hillary Rodham Clinton, former first lady and current U.S. Senator representing New York state. Hillary Clinton had been the president of her college class. She had attended an Ivy League law school, become a partner in a prestigious law firm, and been acclaimed as one of the 100 most important attorneys in the United States. She was known to commit much of her talents to charitable work, to be religious, and to be a loving and protective mother. Why, then, has she been so disliked by so many for so long?

Hillary Clinton's problems stemmed partially from her success. Women in traditionally male fields, like the law, are often penalized for doing their jobs well—perhaps even *because* they do their jobs well (Heilman, 1995). Moreover, Clinton's communication style was direct—too direct for some! She is often blunt and to the point, wasting little time on niceties. Although this style is generally acceptable (and sometimes even desirable) in achieving men, it is not as easily accepted in similarly achieving women. For instance, although men allow themselves to be influenced by direct, assertive, task-oriented men, they remain uninfluenced by women who use this same style (Carli, 1990; Carli, LaFleur, & Loeber, 1995). Similarly, whereas assertive body language communicates status quite effectively when used by men, it is less effective when displayed by women (Henley & Harmon, 1985).

It seems unfair that some of the most effective power and status tactics used by men are unsuccessful when used by aspiring women. Indeed, the problem compounds itself when one considers the secondary impressions people form of women who use these tactics. Women who exhibit task-oriented or domineering styles are generally disliked by men and viewed as threatening; these strategies are usually less costly for men (Carli et al., 1995; Copeland, Driskell, & Salas, 1995). Moreover, women who display high-status body language run a risk of being seen as sexually aggressive (Henley & Harmon, 1985).

These research findings suggest, then, that Hillary Clinton's assertive style, in concert with her great successes, contributed to her image among some as a stereotypical "Iron Maiden"—a cold, conniving, abrasive female achiever (Ashmore & Del Boca, 1979; Deaux & Lewis, 1984; Heilman, Block, & Martell, 1995; Kanter, 1977).

You might not be surprised that men tend to dislike self-promoting women. You might also expect that women would be different—that they would easily accept other women who present themselves assertively. Some evidence suggests that this is not the case, however. In several experiments, Lauri Rudman (1998) discovered that women—more than men—disliked self-promoting women. Rudman and others suggest that women are more likely to support women who promote the causes of *others* but may be less likely than men to support women who promote *themselves* (e.g., Janoff-Bulman & Wade, 1996).

Two points stand out. First, we see again the importance of being liked: People who are liked find it easier to achieve status and power. Second, ambitious women face much greater self-presentational hurdles than do their equally ambitious male counterparts. That women still need to hide their ambitions and successes attests to the lasting power of sex-role stereotypes.

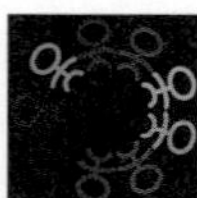

Threats to Personal and Material Resources

Certain situations are more likely to elicit displays of status and power than others. In particular, people are especially likely to display status and power when there's a threat of losing existing resources or the promise of gaining new ones.

Competition for Existing Resources Nonverbal and aggressive displays of status and power increase when people perceive a tangible threat to their existing image or hard-won resources. For instance, men who have their toughness insulted are particularly likely to respond with verbal and physical aggression (Felson, 1982). Similarly, when challenged to be brave and gutsy, people are more likely to take risks with their health (Martin & Leary, 1999). For instance, to avoid being viewed by others as "overly cautious" or "wimpy," in-line skaters often refuse to wear pads (Williams-Avery & Mackinnon, 1996), and gay men may fail to use condoms (Gold, Skinner, Grant, & Plummer, 1991). And we suspect that such challenges may also lead people to drive too fast, refuse to wear seatbelts, and drink too much at a single sitting.

Fred Demara understood the value of displaying status and power not only for pre-empting suspicions about his background but also for dealing with such threats as they arose. On those few occasions when he was accused of being a fraud, he would stretch himself to fullest size (and he was a physically formidable man), contort his large face into a mask of indignant rage, and go face-to-face with his accuser. Just as most animals impressed by the dominance display of a more powerful individual adopt a submissive posture and back down, Demara's accusers usually found this display sufficiently compelling—"such a man is not to be trifled with, especially over unconfirmed suspicions," the reasoning must have gone—to allow Demara to maintain his status, at least for the time being.

Availability of Unclaimed Resources Every two years, newly elected members of the U.S. House of Representatives arrive in Washington, D.C., to assume their posts. Their first task? To land assignments on committees that, by virtue of their importance or timeliness, confer upon them power and influence. And so, right away, the image building begins as the novice politicians jockey among themselves to convince party elders of their potential.

These public presentations reflect the tendency of individuals to display status and power when valuable resources become newly available. Bullfrogs do it by bellowing loudly upon discovering an unclaimed, nutrient-rich location in the marsh; siblings do it with threatening glances upon receiving from grandma the hottest new video game; and young men do it by adopting a high-status persona when meeting attractive, and potentially unattached, women (e.g., Shaw & Wagner, 1975). And it's often an effective strategy. Bullfrogs and children who make the most noise will usually gain special access to the marsh and new toys, while men subtly playing up their status will usually attract the attentions of desirable women.

Different Strategies for Different Audiences

Presentations of status and power can be complex. How people attempt to create such images and even whether they make such an attempt depend partially on an interaction between the gender of the presenter and the gender of his or her audience. Men, for instance, present differently to other men than to women. Although men are particularly likely to respond aggressively when insulted in front of an audience (e.g., Brown, 1968; Felson, 1978), this self-presentational aggression is strongest when the observers are also male (Borden, 1975). In fact, female audiences often inhibit male self-presentational violence. This is not because women frown upon male displays of status and power. Indeed, women greatly value status and power in their male partners and as a result, men boast of their professional status and height in personal ads (e.g., Cicerello & Sheehan, 1995; Deaux & Hanna, 1984; Gonzales & Meyers, 1993; Koestner & Wheeler, 1988), purchase more charity raffle tickets when with women than when alone (Rind & Benjamin, 1994), and so forth. Instead, women are just generally less approving than men of physical aggression. Thus, although men present their status and power to both male and female audiences, they texture their tactics to fit with the different preferences of these audiences.

Summary

People often want others to see them as holding high status and power. Four tactics—displaying status artifacts, conspicuous consumption, associating with high-status others, and expressing nonverbal dominance—help convey images of high status and power. Men are more likely than women to seek such images, and women who do seek status and power must often "soften" their apparent ambitions to avoid being disliked. People are more likely to present their status and power when their resources are threatened or when new, unclaimed resources become available. Finally, the gender of the presenter interacts with the gender of the audience to determine which tactics work best to convey images of status and power. Men typically use more direct, physical tactics when presenting to men than to women, whereas women often must "soften" their apparent ambitions to avoid being disliked.

More generally, Table 4.1 summarizes the goals of self-presentation and the person and situation variables that influence which presentations people are likely to engage in.

CHAPTER 4
Summary Table

Table 4.1 Summary of the goals served by self-presentation and the factors related to them.

The Goal	The Person	The Situation	Interactions
Appearing Likable	• Gender	• Audiences of Potential Friends • Audiences of Power-Holders	• The values held by multiple audiences interact to influence how people get others to like them. If everyone in the audience holds the same values, people can readily sculpt their self-presentations to conform with them. When the audience is composed of people having differing and incompatible values, however, more creative ingratiation tactics become necessary.
Appearing Competent	• Competence Motivation • Shyness	• Competence Settings • Impending or Actual Failure	• Compared to shy people, socially confident individuals promote themselves in exaggerated ways after their public reputation for competence has been shaken by failure but not if their true competence can be easily checked by others. • Self-promoters create social environments in which others feel compelled to self-promote as well.
Conveying Status and Power	• Gender	• Competition for Existing Resources • Availability of Unclaimed Resources	• The gender of the presenter interacts with the gender of the audience to determine which tactics work best to convey images of status and power. Men typically use more direct, physical tactics when presenting to men than to women.

REVISITING
The Amazing Lives of Fred Demara

By any standard, the accomplishments of Fred Demara were astounding. For more than twenty years, he lived a series of theatrical productions, reserving all the lead roles for himself: the famous, life-saving surgeon; the highly respected college professor; the courageous prison warden; and many others. He convinced thousands that he was someone he was not. But why? What motivated him to become an impostor? And what made him so successful?

The research findings we have presented in this chapter provide us with some useful tools for understanding Demara's life. In the small factory town where he grew up, Demara was, in his early years, a center of attention: He was physically large, he was the son of one of the town's leading citizens, and his intellect was superior. Demara learned quickly that he was special and believed himself worthy of respect. From his father, a dapper dresser and creative showman, Demara learned a second critical lesson: Appearance matters. How early these lessons took root, we cannot know, but they were firmly established by the time his father's business went bust. Image meant so much to Demara, and, in a period of just a few days—the time needed to move from the family mansion to the small hovel on the edge of town—his image was in tatters.

Demara, however, had been taught that his destiny was special, that he was the master of his own future. Rebutting the actual circumstances at home, he would show everyone—even himself—that he had "class." On the way to school each morning, he would secretly change from the practical, inexpensive workboots his mother had bought to the shiny black shoes he had surreptitiously purchased with pinched pennies. On Valentine's Day, he somehow managed to buy fancy boxed chocolates for his class. For an eleven-year-old boy, his public reputation under attack and his self-concept uncertain, an excursion into self-presentation hardly seems strange. After all, who among us hasn't wanted to prove our desirability after having a relationship end, to demonstrate our competence after a work failure, or to display our toughness when mocked?

These small presentations did little to restore Demara's reputation, however. And so on the day his father finally admitted that the family would never again be rich, that they would never move back to the big house, Demara realized that his reputation in town was forever spoiled; people would never again accord him the respect he craved. So he ran away from home, seeking, perhaps, a new audience. Still, it would be a mistake to view even this action as falling outside the range of normal social conduct. After all, seeking the opportunity to create new, unspoiled images, many students choose to attend college far from home, divorced people move to the other side of the country, and once-poor professionals retreat to the suburbs, hoping to escape their roots.

But Demara bungled his opportunities badly. Frustrated with his training for the priesthood, he stole a car, and hating the regimentation of the Army, he deserted. Demara had become a wanted man. Having a criminal record meant that he could no longer take the "Fred Demara Show" on the road. And so he took that one huge self-presentational leap that most of us would never consider and could never pull off: Demara disposed of himself, discarded his past.

In this bold choice, we see again the power of the person–situation interaction. A person with Demara's drive for public recognition but without the threat created by the failure of his father's business and the dilemma created by his crimes would probably live normally among his neighbors, recognized only for his abilities and slightly inflated ego. A person confronted with Demara's family failure and criminal predicament but without his great need to be respected would probably hide himself from others, living unobtrusively on the run. These factors converged, however, in Demara, and from them emerged someone unique—the Great Impostor.

At this fork in Demara's road it becomes too easy to pass off his actions as aberrational, as the dysfunctional behaviors of some self-presentational freak. What can a closer look at Demara possibly tell us about ourselves, we wonder? Plenty. We all share with Demara not only similar presentational goals—to appear likable, to appear competent, and to convey status and power—but also similar ways of creating these desired images. Indeed, Demara's great success as an impostor was rooted in his skillful use of common presentational strategies. When he wanted to be liked, he would flatter others, adjust his opinions, make himself attractive, and display a

The last Demara. *As the Great Impostor, Fred Demara's exploits illustrated, in extreme form, the self-presentational goals and tactics people commonly use each day. Demara eventually stopped impostoring and, returning to his religious roots, spent his last twenty-three years ministering to the ill and disadvantaged under his own name.*

dignified modesty. When he wanted people to respect his talents, he would work hard, stage performances, and get others to boast for him. And when he wanted others to respect his status, he would dress the part, surround himself with worldly objects, associate himself with high-status others, and carry himself with poise and dignity. These are precisely the self-presentational tactics we use to manage the impressions others have of us.

Demara was expert in the everyday tactics of self-presentation, and so we see in his life many lessons on how to manage one's reputation successfully. But we also see the costs. As an impostor, Demara was constantly afraid of making a mistake, of saying something that could cause his whole edifice of deception to crumble. He was also painfully aware that he was a fraud. Perhaps worse, he had begun to lose himself: "Every time I take a new identity, some part of the real me dies, whatever the real me is" (Crichton, 1959, p. 10).

In Demara's journey, then, we see much of what science has taught us about why and how people present themselves as they do. Like Demara, most of us care deeply about how others view us. Like Demara, we often find ourselves in circumstances that threaten our desired reputations. Like Demara, we reach into our oft-used presentational bag of tricks when people don't view us the way we want to be viewed. And like Demara, we fear the costs of undesired reputations. It seems fair to say that there's something of Demara in each of us.

Ferdinand Waldo Demara, Jr., died of heart failure in 1982. He was only sixty years old. The many obituaries published nationwide noted that he had lived under his own name for almost twenty-three years, trying, it seemed, to make up for his past. Returning to his religious roots, he had worked at youth camps, a rescue mission for the poor, and as a bona fide Baptist minister and hospital chaplain. We suspect that, of all people, Demara would have found comfort in the knowledge that his final reviews were favorable.

CHAPTER 4
Summary

What Is Self-Presentation?

1. Self-presentation, sometimes called impression management, is the process through which we try to control the impressions people form of us.
2. We self-present for three primary reasons: to acquire desirable resources, to help "construct" our self-images, and to enable our social encounters to run more smoothly.
3. We are more likely to focus on self-presentation when we think others are paying attention to us, when they can influence whether or not we reach our goals, when these goals are important to us, and when we think these observers have impressions of us different from the ones we desire.
4. Some people are more likely to self-present than are others. Although people generally overestimate the extent to which they're in the public eye (the spotlight effect), individuals who are high in public self-consciousness are especially aware of how they are coming across to others. People who are high self-monitors care about how others view them and often adjust their actions to fit the behaviors of the people around them.
5. Self-presentation is sometimes deceptive, but usually not. Instead, our self-presentations typically focus on emphasizing our strengths and minimizing our weaknesses.
6. Because liars threaten the trust needed to maintain social relationships, people often go to great lengths to detect them. Unfortunately, people are mediocre lie detectors at best. Polygraph exams don't fare much better.

Appearing Likable

1. Perhaps more than any other self-presentational goal, we want others to like us.
2. To create an image of likability, we may express our liking for others, using both verbal flattery and nonverbal behaviors such as smiling; point out or create similarities with others; make ourselves physically attractive; and act modestly.
3. Women, more than men, focus on getting others to like them.
4. We are generally interested in being liked by people with whom we want to start or maintain a friendship and by people who are in positions of power.

5. We sometimes find ourselves in circumstances in which we want to be liked by multiple audiences, who differ in what they value. These multiple audience dilemmas are difficult, and we try to manage them by segregating the audiences, moderating our presentations, presenting different messages on different communication channels, or texturing messages so they mean different things to the different audiences.

Appearing Competent

1. We frequently want others to view us as competent.
2. To create an image of competence, we may stage performances so that others have an opportunity to view our skills and abilities, make verbal claims of competence, surround ourselves with the trappings of competence, and make excuses for our failures or claim obstacles to possible success. People may even self-handicap by withdrawing effort or placing real obstacles in the way of future successes.
3. People high in extrinsic competence motivation are especially concerned with how they come across in public. Shy people are less likely than nonshy individuals to engage in bold self-promotion.
4. Competitive settings such as workplaces, classrooms, and athletic fields often increase our desires to appear competent.
5. Recent failures increase the desire to appear competent.
6. Compared to shy people, socially confident individuals are especially likely to promote themselves in exaggerated ways after their public reputations for competence have been shaken by failure, but not if their true competence can be easily checked by others. Also, self-promoters often create a social environment in which others feel compelled to self-promote.

Conveying Status and Power

1. We sometimes want others to view us as having status and power.
2. To create an image of status and power, we may display the artifacts of status and power, conspicuously consume material resources, associate ourselves with others who already possess status and power, use body language to convey status and power, and even behave aggressively.
3. Men, more than women, focus on presenting themselves as having status and power.
4. Women face an especially difficult self-presentational dilemma: When presenting their status and power, they are frequently disliked by both men and women.
5. People try to present themselves as having status and power when existing resources are threatened and when newly available resources lie unclaimed.

CHAPTER 4

Key Terms

Basking in reflected glory *The process of presenting our associations with successful, high-status others or events.*

Body language *The popular term for nonverbal behaviors like facial expressions, posture, body orientation, and hand gestures.*

Competence motivation *The desire to perform effectively.*

Cutting off reflected failure *The process of distancing ourselves from unsuccessful, low-status others or events.*

Dramaturgical perspective *The perspective that much of social interaction can be thought of as a play, with actors, performances, settings, scripts, props, roles, and so forth.*

Impression management *The process through which we try to control the impressions people form of us; synonymous with* self-presentation.

Ingratiation *An attempt to get others to like us.*

Multiple audience dilemma *A situation in which a person needs to present different images to different audiences, often at the same time.*

Public self-consciousness *The tendency to have a chronic awareness of oneself as being in the public eye.*

Self-handicapping *The behavior of withdrawing effort or creating obstacles to one's future successes.*

Self-monitoring *The tendencies to be chronically concerned with one's public image and to adjust one's actions to fit the needs of the current situation.*

Self-presentation *The process through which we try to control the impressions people form of us; synonymous with* impression management.

Self-promotion *An attempt to get others to see us as competent.*

Shyness *The tendency to feel tense, worried, or awkward in novel social situations and with unfamiliar people.*

Social anxiety *The fear people experience while doubting that they'll be able to create a desired impression.*

Testosterone *A hormone present in both males and females—but usually in much greater quantities in males—responsible for important aspects of sexual development.*

CHAPTER 5

Persuasion

The Changing Story of Peter Reilly

In 1973, Peter Reilly was a sensitive and intelligent eighteen-year-old whose life changed forever when he returned home after an evening church meeting to find his mother lying on the floor, murdered. Though reeling from the sight, he had the presence of mind to phone for help immediately.

At five feet seven inches and 121 pounds, and with not a speck of blood on his body, clothes, or shoes, Peter Reilly seemed an unlikely killer. Yet from the start, when they found him staring blankly outside the room where his mother lay dead, the police suspected that Reilly was responsible for her murder. The reason for that suspicion had less to do with what they knew about him than with what they knew about the victim. She took delight in irritating the people she met—men especially—belittling, confronting, and challenging them. By any measure, she was a difficult woman to get along with. Thus it did not seem unreasonable to police officials that Reilly, fed up with his mother's constant antagonisms, would fly off the handle and slaughter her in a spasm of rage.

"Harmony," © Paul Nzalamba

Peter Reilly being taken away after his conviction.

At the scene and even when taken in for questioning, Reilly waived his right to an attorney, thinking that if he told the truth, he would be believed and released in short order. That was a serious miscalculation. Over a period of sixteen hours, he was interrogated by a rotating team of four police officers, including a polygraph operator who confidently informed Reilly that, according to the lie detector, he had killed his mother. The chief interrogator told Reilly, falsely, that additional evidence proving his guilt had been obtained. He also suggested to the boy how he could have done the crime without remembering any such thing: Reilly had become furious with his mother, had erupted into a murderous fit during which he slaughtered her, and now had repressed the horrible memory. It was their job, Reilly's and the interrogator's, to "dig, dig, dig" at the boy's subconscious until the memory was recovered.

Dig, dig, dig they did, exploring every way to bring that memory to the surface, until Reilly did begin to recall—dimly at first but then more vividly—slashing his mother's throat and stomping on her body. Analyzing, reanalyzing, and reviewing these images convinced him that they betrayed his guilt. Along with his interrogators, who pressed him relentlessly to break through his "mental block," Reilly pieced together from the scenes in his head an account of his actions that fit the details of the murder. Finally, a little more than twenty-four hours after the grisly crime, though still uncertain of many specifics, Peter Reilly formally confessed in a signed, written statement. That statement conformed closely to the explanation that had been proposed by his interrogators and that he had come to accept as accurate—even though he believed none of it at the outset of his questioning and even though, as later events demonstrated, none of it was true.

When Reilly awoke in a jail cell the next day, with the awful fatigue and the persuasive onslaught of the interrogation room gone, he no longer believed his confession. But he couldn't retract it convincingly. To almost every official in the criminal justice system, the confession remained compelling evidence of his guilt: A judge rejected a motion to suppress it at Reilly's trial, ruling it voluntarily made; the police were so satisfied that it incriminated Reilly that they stopped considering other suspects; the prosecuting attorneys made it the centerpiece of their case; and the jury members who ultimately convicted Reilly of killing his mother relied on it heavily in their deliberations.

To a one, these individuals did not believe that a normal person could be made to confess falsely to a crime without the use of threats, violence, or torture. And to a one, they were wrong: Two years later, evidence was found hidden in the chief prosecutor's files that placed Reilly at a time and in a location on the night of the crime that established his innocence and that led to the repeal of his conviction and to the dismissal of all charges.

What happened in that interrogation room that was so powerful that it manufactured an admission of murder yet was so elusive that police, prosecutors, judge, and jury did not grasp its impact? Through what mysterious methods and extraordinary circumstances could the police convince a wholly innocent man of his guilt? The methods were not so mysterious nor the circumstances so extraordinary. They embodied the features of everyday persuasion—and they are all the more alarming for it. In the remainder of this chapter, we will consider how those features generate attitude and belief change, how that change can be measured, and what goals are served by the change.

What Is Persuasion?

If we are to place the blame for Peter Reilly's false confession within the workings of the persuasion process, we had best establish what we mean by the concept. Although social scientists have defined **persuasion** in a variety of ways (Perloff, 1993), we view it as change in a private attitude or belief resulting from the receipt of a message. So, if a discussion with your supervisor at work about her favorite political candidate caused you to change what you said publicly about the candidate or even to sign a petition supporting the candidate, you would not necessarily have been persuaded by her comments. Your public statements might reflect just an attempt to get your boss's approval, not a genuine shift in your thoughts or feelings about the politician. It's only when a message brings about inner change in your views on a topic that we can say that it persuaded you. As we discussed in chapter 2, *attitudes* are favorable or unfavorable feelings toward particular things. *Beliefs*, on the other hand, are thoughts (cognitions) about these things. In this chapter, we will examine how both can be changed through the persuasion process.

Pervasive persuasion. *Persuasive appeals are everywhere in our daily lives.*

While you are awake today, you will likely be the target of hundreds of persuasive messages. Many will come from total strangers, as conservative estimates suggest that you'll receive 300 to 400 persuasive appeals from marketers alone (Rosselli, Skelly, & Mackie, 1995; Turnkuist, 2000). Some will be delivered through the mail or over the phone; others will appear on billboards or in magazine, radio, or television advertisements; still others will ambush you on the Internet. In face-to-face interactions, your friends, family, neighbors, and acquaintances will try to change your mind, too. And you'll try to move them toward your own point of view.

What is plain, then, is that persuasion efforts are everywhere in daily life. What is not so plain is why sometimes they succeed while other times they fail. We will spend the rest of this chapter seeking out the reasons that persuasive appeals succeed and fail. Fortunately, our efforts will be aided greatly by a large body of research into the factors that make for an effective persuasive message. Indeed, beginning in earnest with government information and propaganda programs enacted during World War II (Hovland, Lumsdaine, & Sheffield, 1949; Lewin, 1947; Stouffer, Suchman, DeVinney, Star, & Williams, 1949), social psychologists have been studying the persuasion process for over half a century. We will tap that rich body of information to answer four major questions: What kinds of attitudes resist persuasion? How can persuasion be measured? Which are the most direct causes of persuasion? And finally, what are the goals that persuasion serves?

Strong Attitudes Resist Persuasion

Strong attitudes resist change (Bassili, 1996; Petty & Krosnick, 1996). This is true in two senses. First, strong attitudes are more stable than weaker ones; they are more likely to remain unchanged as time passes. Second, they are less pliant than weaker attitudes in that they are better able to withstand persuasive attacks or appeals specifically directed at them. Let's say you now hold a strong attitude toward gun control. Not only is your attitude likely to be the same next month, but also if someone tried to change your mind on the issue at that point, you would probably not be influenced.

What are the components of a strong attitude that make it unlikely to change? Research by Eva Pomeranz, Shelly Chaiken, and Rosalind Tordesillas (1995) suggests that there are two main reasons that strong attitudes resist change: *commitment* and *embeddedness.*

People are more *committed* to a strongly held attitude. That is, they are more certain that it is correct, they are more sure that they won't change it, and their position is more extreme. In addition, a strongly held attitude is more *embedded in* (connected to) additional features of the person, such as the individual's self-concept,

Persuasion *Change in a private attitude or belief as a result of receiving a message.*

values, and social identity (Boninger, Krosnock, & Berent, 1995). For example, officers of the National Rifle Association are committed to an anti-gun-control position, and typically make that position a central part of their social identities. Consequently, they are unlikely to change their attitudes on this topic.

It appears that both commitment and embeddedness make strong attitudes more resistant to change (Visser & Krosnick, 1998). But, they do so in different ways (see Figure 5.1) Being committed to a particular attitude causes people to review relevant information in a biased fashion and to intensify their opinions. All this leads them to dismiss evidence that goes against their initial attitude. For example, in one experiment, participants who already had strong attitudes about capital punishment were shown an essay and a research study that opposed their position on the issue. They reacted by rejecting this information, deciding that the essay's arguments were weak and the study's methods were flawed (Pomeranz, Chaiken, & Tordesillas, 1995).

The embeddedness of the attitude did not cause participants to reject contradictory information, however. Embeddedness restricted change in another way—by simply tying the attitude to so many other features of the person (beliefs, values, additional attitudes) that it became difficult to move in any direction. That is, because changing an embedded attitude would mean changing all sorts of other aspects of the self, people are reluctant to undertake the process (O'Brien & Jacks, 2000).

On the surface, the evidence that people are unlikely to change strong attitudes and beliefs makes the phenomenon of persuaded false confessions—such as Peter Reilly's—even more mystifying. Surely, a blameless person has strongly held attitudes and beliefs regarding his or her own innocence. Indeed, because this is the case, experienced criminal interrogators typically do not try to attack such a belief directly until they have first weakened it.

A favorite tactic used to weaken a belief of innocence is to convince suspects that they don't remember doing the deed because they were powerfully affected by alcohol or drugs or, in the case of Peter Reilly, a blind rage, while performing it (Ofshe &

Figure 5.1 Why strong attitudes resist change.

Commitment—one quality of strong attitudes—shields attitudes against contradictory information, whereas embeddedness—a second quality of strong attitudes—anchors them to a variety of other change-resistant features of the self.

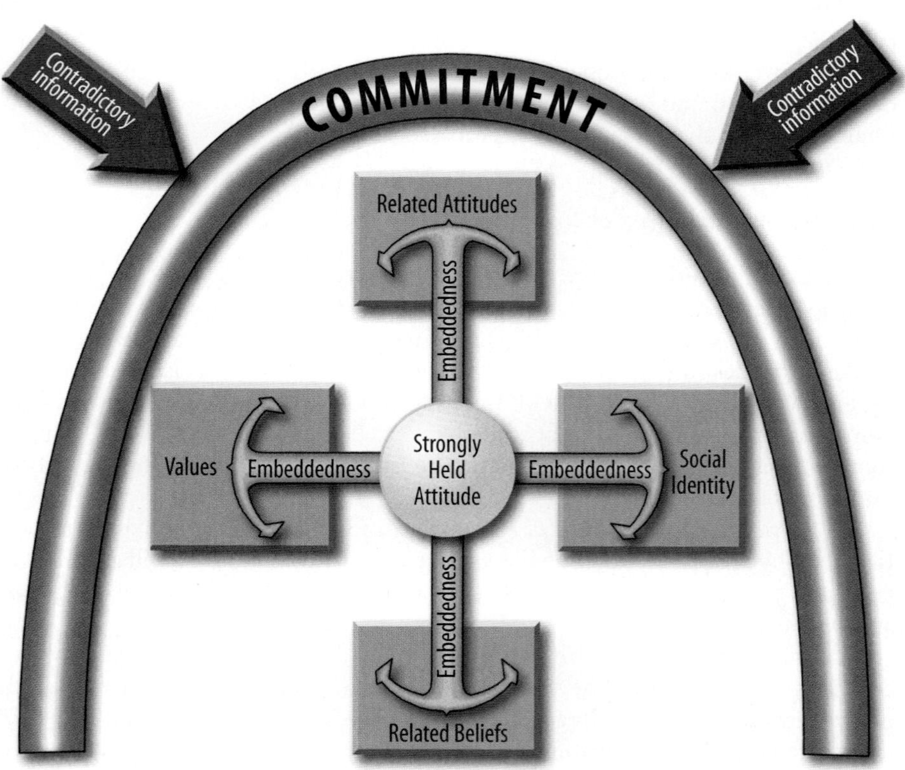

Leo, 1997). During his interrogation, Reilly reported being greatly alarmed by the idea—planted well before the interrogation began—that he could have suppressed the memory of his murder of his mother, because that idea sent the first tremors of self-doubt through him.

This tactic works so well for interrogators because it undercuts both of the aspects of strong attitudes and beliefs that resist change. First, it reduces suspects' commitment to their innocence by undermining the certainty and intensity of their belief in that innocence: suspects cannot be sure that they haven't perpetrated the crime if it is possible that they don't remember it. Second, the tactic decreases the embeddedness of the belief by unhooking the crime from the self-concept of the person who committed it: the view of oneself as someone who could not have done such a thing simply does not apply if it was the alcohol or drugs or blind rage that did it.

Measuring Attitude Change

As should be apparent, clever persuaders have developed many techniques for changing attitudes and beliefs, even initially strong ones. In the process of trying to understand whether and when these various techniques are effective, researchers have had to confront the knotty question of how to measure persuasion accurately. After all, we can't claim that a persuasion tactic works if we can't tell how much change it creates. And correctly measuring change is often no simple task. You've no doubt recognized that your actions change if someone is recording them. Of course, scientists studying persuasion want to record it in its truest, least altered form. Consequently, they frequently rely on certain proven methods for reducing the impact of the act of measurement on their data.

We briefly discussed one such method in chapter 2, in which we described how researchers sometimes measure attitudes unobtrusively (covertly), without asking subjects to give self-reports of these attitudes. In these cases, the researcher judges the attitude in question by simply observing an attitude-relevant behavior. For instance, using the *lost letter technique* (Milgram, Mann, & Harter, 1965), researchers can learn the neighborhood attitude toward racial integration by recording the percentage of people there who will mail a "lost" letter secretly placed on the street and addressed to the Council for Racial Integration. The more letters that are mailed, the more favorable is the presumed attitude.

In general, researchers have found that these covert techniques are more accurate than self-report measures only when people have a good reason to be less than honest about their true feelings—for example, when they want to appear more fair-minded or unprejudiced than they actually are (Fazio, Jackson, Dunton, & Williams, 1995; Nowicki & Manheim, 1991). Under these circumstances, covert techniques are preferred because they are a more **nonreactive measurement** than are self-reports; that is, using them to record a response is less likely to distort the response. When there is no good reason for people to hide their feelings, however, self-reports are usually preferred because they inquire about attitudes more directly (Dunton & Fazio, 1997).

Research using the littering of handbills as a covert measure of attitude illustrates when covert tactics are especially useful (Cialdini & Baumann, 1981). An initial study found that after voting in a presidential election, people were less likely to litter handbills they found on the windshields of their cars if the handbills' message supported their favored candidate. In fact, before the official voting totals were announced, this measure correctly predicted the winning candidate at all nine of the voting locations where it was used—but so did a simple exit poll that asked people how they had voted. Thus, when there was little reason for individuals to conceal their actual attitudes, a self-report measure was just as accurate as the covert one. However, in a follow-up study using the politically sensitive topic of increased women's rights, the pattern was quite different. When asked by a college-age female

Nonreactive measurement
Measurement that does not change a subject's responses while recording them.

survey taker whether they supported or opposed the Equal Rights Amendment for women, the great majority (75 percent) of male undergraduates said that they supported it. But when attitude was measured covertly, by how likely male undergraduates were to litter a handbill that either supported or opposed this amendment, fewer than half (46 percent) were found to be supportive.

Assessing attitude through secret observation isn't the only way scientists have tried to make their studies nonreactive. To help achieve this goal, they have also identified a particular research design, the *after-only design*, which assesses persuasion by measuring attitude only after the persuasion attempt.

FOCUS ON **Method**

The After-Only Design

Suppose that you belong to a group that wants to save lives by reducing the speed limit on state highways and that you have been assigned the job of writing a persuasive letter on this issue that will be mailed to all the citizens of your town. Suppose further that after reading the rest of this chapter, you devise a letter full of persuasive tactics. But before authorizing the funds for a full mailing, the treasurer of your group, who is skeptical of your persuasive skills, requires that you first do a test on a small sample of people to see if your letter is genuinely effective. What could you do to best test your letter's ability to change citizen attitudes?

Chances are that your first answer to this question would be wrong. Many students assume that the best—or only—way to perform such a test properly is by doing a *before-after design* study of attitude change, in which the attitudes of the intended audience are measured both prior to and then again following the persuasive message. Let's say you do such a study. First, you go door to door surveying the attitudes of a randomly selected set of citizens toward highway speed limits; this would be your *before-measure*. Then, a week later, you send your persuasive letter to each of these people. Next, you wait another week and survey their attitudes door to door again; this would be your *after-measure*. And, because you are a careful researcher, you include a randomly selected control group of people who didn't get the letter but did get surveyed twice—just to assure that it was truly your letter that caused any change between the before- and after-measures. The top part of Table 5.1 shows the design of your study. If you found that the attitudes of the people who got your letter changed more than did those of the people who didn't receive it, would you then be in a position to go to your group's treasurer with convincing evidence of the persuasiveness of your message?

Not if the treasurer—we can call him Donald—is knowledgeable about research design. He might complain that your findings may not have been due solely to the impact of your letter but, instead, to the combination of your before-measure *plus* your letter. That is, Donald could say that maybe getting surveyed about highway speed limits the first time *sensitized* the people in your study to this issue so that when they got your letter, they were more receptive to its message. For example, after being surveyed initially, perhaps they began to notice how many cars travel at unsafe speeds on the highways or perhaps they paid more attention to news reports of high-speed accidents. Then, when your letter came, they may have been uniquely ready to be persuaded by it. If so, your study did not provide good evidence that just sending out your letter alone—which the group planned to do—would be effective. Donald might insist that until you showed him that evidence, he wouldn't feel justified in releasing funds for the full mailing of your letter; and he would have a legitimate point.

How could you design your study differently to avoid this criticism? Because the before-measure was the culprit in your study's design, you could simply eliminate it and measure attitudes only once, the week after your letter arrived. Fortunately, a

Table 5.1 **The before-after and the after-only designs for studying attitude change.**

In both kinds of designs, subjects are first randomly assigned to either receive a persuasive message (experimental group) or not to receive it (control group). In a before-after design (top), successful persuasion is assumed if the difference between the before- and the after-measures is significantly larger in the experimental group than in the control group. In an after-only design, successful persuasion is assumed if, on the after-measure alone, the experimental group is significantly more favorable to the message than the control group.

Random Assignment to Groups	Before-Measure	Message	After-Measure	Conclusion
		Before-After Design		
Experimental Group	Measure attitude	Send message	Measure attitude	If the difference between the before- and the after-measure is significantly greater in the experimental group than in the control group, the message was likely effective.
Control Group	Measure attitude	Do not send message	Measure attitude	
		After-Only Design		
Experimental Group		Send message	Measure attitude	If the attitudes on the after-measure alone are significantly more favorable to the message in the experimental group than in the control group, the message was likely effective.
Control Group		Do not send message	Measure attitude	

before-measure is not necessary to establish persuasiveness, provided that a basic but powerful research procedure is used: *random assignment,* in which participants are placed in one or another condition of the study completely by chance. Random assignment works to equate the groups of participants in each condition so that before the study begins, the groups are equivalent to one another (on average) in every way, including their initial attitudes. With groups that start out the same, we can be confident that any after-measure difference in attitude is due to the message.

Take your study. If you randomly assign people to be in the group that gets your letter or to the control group that does not, randomization will work to assure that the two groups have the same average attitude toward highway speed limits before you send the letter. (The larger the number of participants in each group, the more confident you can be that the randomization process has done its job.) Now, when you survey the attitudes of both groups a week after sending your letter, if you find a difference between the two groups on attitude toward highway speeds, you will be able to claim confidently (to Donald or anyone else) that it was most likely your letter that did the trick—because the letter was the only prior difference between the groups.

The bottom part of Table 5.1 illustrates this streamlined design for your study. The logic of this approach is used by most scientists who study persuasion. Thus you will see that the majority of studies in this chapter employ this research design—called the *after-only design*—to draw conclusions about attitude change even though no actual change is measured. ■

Cognitive Responses: Self-Talk Persuades

Now that we have considered how to measure attitude change effectively, let's move to the question of how change happens. Although social psychologists have provided many important insights into what motivates people to change, one of the most valuable was offered by Anthony Greenwald (1968) in the **cognitive response model** of persuasion, which represents a subtle but critical shift in thinking about attitude change. According to this model, the best indication of how much change a communicator will produce lies not in what the communicator says to the persuasion target but, rather, in what the target says to him- or herself as a result of receiving the communication.

Earlier approaches to attitude change emphasized the importance of the message itself—its clarity, logic, memorability, and so on—because it was thought that the target's comprehension and learning of the message content were critical to persuasion (Hovland, Janis, & Kelley, 1953; McGuire, 1966). Although this is often true, the cognitive response model added an important insight by suggesting that the message is not directly responsible for change. Instead, the direct cause is the *self-talk*—the internal cognitive responses—people engage in after being exposed to the message. A great deal of research supports the model (Eagly & Chaiken, 1993; Killeya & Johnson, 1998).

Positive Self-Talk What are the implications of this view for the way you should fashion a persuasive attempt? Let's take as an example the letter supporting lower highway speed limits that you imagined writing to citizens of your town. The most general implication is that you would be foolish to structure the attempt without simultaneously thinking about what your audience members would say to themselves in response to the letter. You want to find ways to stimulate positive cognitive responses to your letter.

This means that besides considering features of your intended message (for example, the strength and logic of the arguments), you should take into account an entirely different set of factors that are likely to enhance positive cognitive responses to your message. For instance, you may want to delay the mailing of your letter until your local newspaper reports a rash of highway speeding deaths; that way, when your letter arrives, its message will gain validity in the minds of the recipients because it will fit with prominent, other information (Anderson, 1991; van der Plight & Eiser, 1984). Or you might want to increase the favorability of cognitive responses to your letter by printing it professionally on high-quality paper because people assume that the more care and expense a communicator has put into a persuasion campaign, the more the communicator believes in its validity (Kirmani, 1990; Kirmani & Wright, 1989).

Counterarguments Besides trying to ensure that your message creates positive cognitive responses in your audience members, you should also think about how to avoid negative cognitive responses—especially **counterarguments,** which weaken the impact of a persuasive message by arguing against it, thereby reducing attitude change (Brock, 1967; Ruscher & Hastings, 1996). Thus, you might want to include in your letter a quotation from a traffic safety expert asserting that higher speed limits increase automobile fatalities because, typically, people generate fewer counterarguments against a position if they learn that an expert holds it (Cook, 1969; Sternthal, Dholakia, & Leavitt, 1978). Other tactics for reducing counterarguing have also proven effective: Giving audience members little time to formulate counterarguments or giving them distracting or overburdening tasks that drain their ability to counterargue makes audience members more susceptible to persuasion (Gilbert, 1991; Hass & Grady, 1975; Romero, Agnew, & Insko, 1996). In one study, subjects who could not counterargue (because their cognitive capacities were overburdened by a taxing task) were persuaded by information even though they knew the information was false (Gilbert, Tafarodi, & Malone, 1993).

Cognitive response model *A theory that locates the most direct cause of persuasion in the self-talk of the persuasion target.*

Counterargument *An argument that challenges and opposes other arguments.*

Peter Reilly's interrogators employed each of these tactics to persuade a wholly innocent young man that he was a murderer. First, Reilly was informed that the polygraph operator who saw "scientific evidence" of Reilly's guilt in his lie detector results was an expert in his field and that the polygraph machine could not be wrong in implicating him.

Reilly: *Does that actually read my brain?*
Polygraph operator: *Definitely. Definitely.*
Reilly: *Would it definitely be me? Could it have been someone else?*
Polygraph operator: *No way from these reactions.*

In fact, as we discussed in chapter 4, the results of polygraph examinations are far from infallible, even in the hands of practiced operators; because of their unreliability, they are banned as evidence in the courts of many states and countries (Gudjonsson, 1992).

Second, Reilly was never given the time to form counterarguments to the theories and accusations of guilt directed at him incessantly during eight consecutive hours of interrogation; a tag-team of four interrogators took turns peppering him in rapid succession with questions, allegations, and denunciations. Third, even if he had been afforded the time to generate counterarguments, events before the interrogation had probably drained him of the ability to do so: At the start of formal questioning, he was mentally and emotionally spent and hadn't eaten or slept in twenty-four hours. During the interrogation, Reilly's repeated claims of exhaustion and an inability to think straight went unheeded.

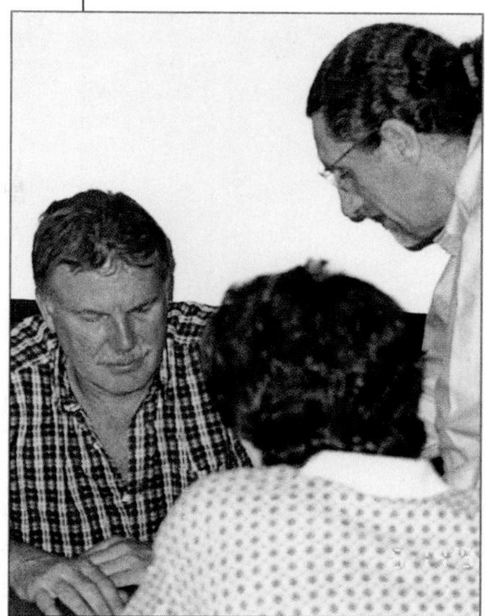

Exhaustive questioning. *Pushing suspects to defend themselves when they are physically and cognitively depleted is a notorious practice among some criminal interrogators. In one case in England, police arranged for a dog to bark through the night to keep the suspects awake until questioning could begin (Mullin, 1989).*

Reilly: *I'm so damned exhausted. I'm just gonna fall asleep.*
Interrogator: *No you won't.*
Reilly: *I wish I wasn't so tired because things come into my head and go right out again.*
Interrogator: *What else Peter? Run through the whole picture again.*

In sum, the same counterargument-suppressing factors that have increased persuasion in scientific research—communicator expertise and insufficient time and ability to formulate counterarguments—were used by Peter Reilly's interrogators. Peter eventually came to believe their message, even though he knew it to be false at the time.

Defeating a Message through Inoculation and Counterarguing Factors that stimulate counterarguing decrease persuasion (Jain, Buchanan, & Maheswaran, 2000; Killeya & Johnson, 1998). You can use this fact to neutralize an opponent's message. One clever way to stimulate counterarguing in an audience is to send an unconvincing message favoring your opponent's position, which will cause the audience to think of all sorts of arguments against that rival position. Then, when your opponent delivers a stronger version of his or her message, the audience will already have a set of counterarguments to attack it. William McGuire (1964) has named this the **inoculation procedure** because of its similarity to disease inoculation procedures in which a weakened form of a virus is injected into healthy individuals.

You might use this technique in your campaign to reduce highway speed limits by including in your persuasive letter a few of your opponents' weaker arguments and asking recipients to consider the validity of those arguments. This should lead recipients to develop counterarguments against your opponents' view and should protect them from stronger attacks by your rivals.

Inoculation procedure *A technique for increasing individuals' resistance to a strong argument by first giving them weak, easily defeated versions of it.*

Although the inoculation procedure offers an ingenious and effective approach (Eagly & Chaiken, 1993), by far the most common tactic for reducing the persuasiveness of an opponent's message is simply to give audience members direct counterarguments against the strongest versions of that message. In the advertising arena, this tactic can be highly effective, as we will see in the following section.

FOCUS ON Application

Smoking the Tobacco Companies with Counterarguments

Something extraordinary happened on July 22, 1969, during U.S. Congressional hearings on tobacco regulation: Representatives of the tobacco industry argued vigorously in favor of a proposal to ban all advertising of their own products on radio and television. The unexpected tobacco company support for the ban enabled legislation that has prohibited tobacco advertising on the airwaves in the United States since 1971.

What could account for this unprecedented action on the part of Big Tobacco? Could it be that in the aftermath of the 1964 Surgeon General's Report on the frightening health consequences of smoking, tobacco company executives became concerned about the health of the nation? Hardly. They didn't reduce their intensive ad campaign for smokers after the ban. They simply shifted their advertising dollars from the airwaves to other places such as magazines, sports sponsorships, promotional giveaways, and movie product placements. For example, secret documents of one tobacco firm included a letter from movie actor/director Sylvester Stallone agreeing to use its cigarettes in several films in return for $500,000 (Massing, 1996).

So, it was only on the airwaves that the tobacco industry wanted to bar the advertising of its products. But this deepens the mystery of their motives even further: In the year they proposed the ban, tobacco executives had been spending four out of five advertising dollars on television because advertisers recognized it as "by far the most effective way to reach people, especially young people" (White, 1988, p. 145). What could have made them want to abandon their most persuasive route to new customers?

The answer lies in something equally remarkable that occurred two years earlier: Against all odds, a young attorney named John Banzhaf successfully argued to the Federal Communications Commission (FCC) that it should apply its "fairness doctrine" to the issue of tobacco advertising. The fairness doctrine acknowledged the power and importance of counterargument in a free society by requiring that when positions on controversial topics of public importance are broadcast, free air time must be made available to citizens wishing to state opposing views. The FCC's ruling made an enormous difference, allowing antitobacco forces such as the American Cancer Society to air ads that punctured and parodied the tobacco ads' images of health, attractiveness, and rugged independence—often by satirizing the tobacco company's own ads and showing that, in truth, tobacco use led to ill health, damaged attractiveness, and addictionlike dependence. In one, tough Marlboro Man–like characters were rendered weak and helpless by spasms of hacking, wheezing, and coughing.

Coughing up the truth. *Counterarguments like this one can be very effective against the persuasive appeals of tobacco companies.*

From their first appearance in 1967, the counterads began to devastate tobacco sales. After a quarter-century climb, per capita cigarette consumption dropped precipitously in that initial year and continued to sink (nearly 10 percent) during the three years that the counterads were aired; the great majority of the decline has been traced to the counterads (McAlister, Ramirez, Galavotti, & Gallion, 1989; Simonich, 1991). The tobacco industry reacted predictably by increasing its television advertising budgets to meet this new challenge, but to no avail—because, by the rules of the fairness doctrine, the more ads they ran, the more time had to be given to the counterarguing messages.

When the logic of the situation finally hit them, the tobacco companies maneuvered masterfully. They supported a ban on the advertising of their products on the air—*only* on the air—where the fairness doctrine applied. With these ads prohibited, the antitobacco forces could no longer receive free air time for their counterads. In the first year after the ban on tobacco ads went into effect, cigarette consumption in the United States jumped more than 3 percent, even though the tobacco companies were able to reduce their advertising expenditures by 30 percent (Fritschler, 1975; McAlister et al., 1989). ■

Tobacco opponents found that they could use counterarguments to undercut tobacco ad effectiveness. But the tobacco executives learned (and profited from) a related lesson: One of the best ways to reduce resistance to a message is to reduce the availability of counterarguments to it. Of course, the counterarguments that people have at their disposal don't come only from others. People are sometimes spurred to think about a message and to generate their own counterarguments. When they are willing and able to do so is the topic of the next section.

Dual Process Models of Persuasion: Two Routes to Change

In studying cognitive responses to persuasion, researchers have recognized that people don't always process the information carefully after receiving a message; sometimes they accept or reject it without much thought at all (Chaiken & Trope, 1999). This recognition led to the development of **dual process models of persuasion,** which incorporate two basic kinds of attitude change processes—those that involve hard thinking about message arguments and those that do not (Smith & DeCoster, 2000). Two key dual process models are the **elaboration likelihood model** of Richard Petty and John Cacioppo (1986) and the **heuristic-systematic model** of Shelly Chaiken (1987).

Although the models are somewhat different, they have much in common. Most important, each addresses the question of when it is that people are likely to think deeply versus superficially about a communication. And each proposes the same answer: Message recipients will consider a communication deeply—paying close attention to the quality of its arguments—when they have both the *motivation* and the *ability* to do so. If either of these conditions is missing, recipients will pay only superficial attention to the message. Instead, they will focus on some factor other than quality, such as the mere number of arguments or the status or attractiveness of the communicator (see Figure 5.2).

Motivation Two factors influence a person's motivation to process a message deeply. The first is the personal relevance of the topic: The more an issue directly affects people, the more willing they are to think hard about it. The second is the tendency to think hard about *any* topic, called one's need for cognition. Let's examine these factors in turn.

Personal Relevance. Suppose that in tomorrow's edition of your campus newspaper you read an article describing a plan by university administrators that would require each student to pass a comprehensive exam covering all prior class work before graduation. Suppose as well that the administrators were proposing that the plan go into effect immediately so that, if approved, it would apply to you! Because of this direct personal relevance, you would be motivated to consider the administrators' arguments carefully before deciding whether to support or oppose the plan, no doubt mulling over those arguments and analyzing them in terms of their quality. Now, imagine the same set of events with one change: the policy is designed to go into effect not this year but in ten years; so it would not apply to you. Under these conditions, the dual processing models would predict that you would respond quite differently to the article. No longer would you be motivated to pore over its points, working up arguments and counterarguments in response. Instead, you might process the administrators' arguments lightly, deciding whether to support or

Dual process model of persuasion *A model that accounts for the two basic ways that attitude change occurs—with and without much thought.*

Elaboration likelihood model *A model of persuasive communication that holds that there are two ways attitude change can take place—deeply or superficially.*

Heuristic–systematic model *A model of persuasive communication that holds that there are two ways attitude change can take place—the message recipient uses heuristic shortcuts or processes information systematically.*

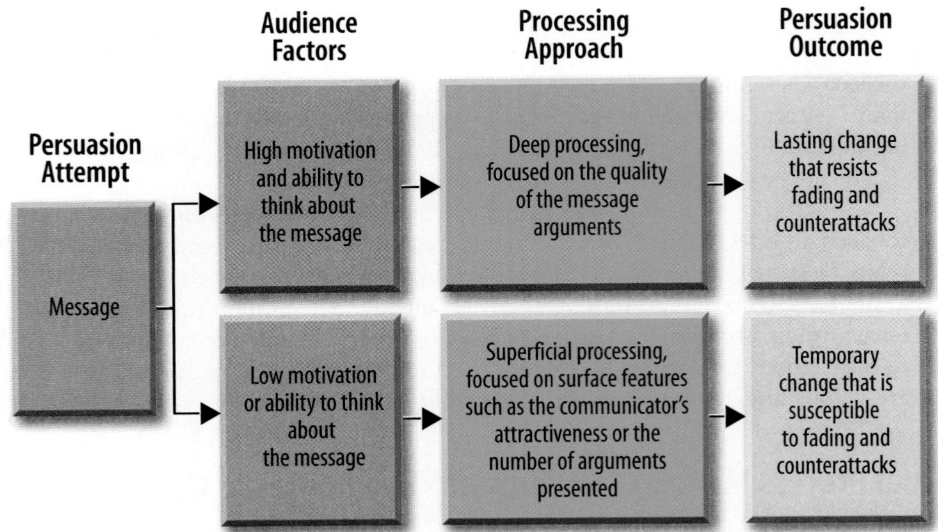

Figure 5.2
Dual routes to successful persuasion.

Depending on whether they have the motivation and ability to think hard about a message, people will process it either deeply or superficially. Although both processing approaches can lead to persuasion, deep processing produces more enduring change.

oppose the proposal based on something as superficial as the number of arguments the administrators listed favoring their plan.

A study done by Richard Petty and John Cacioppo (1984) confirmed these predictions. College students read either three or nine arguments favoring comprehensive exams. Those arguments were either of high quality ("Average starting salaries are higher for graduates of schools with exams") or of low quality ("The exams would allow students to compare performance against students at other schools"). Figure 5.3 shows the outcome of the study. When students thought the policy would apply to them, they processed the message deeply, becoming more favorable after reading strong arguments and less favorable after reading weak ones. However, when they thought the policy would not cover them, because it would not go into effect for ten years, students based their opinions on the number rather than the quality of the arguments.

Need for Cognition. Another motivating factor resides less in the topic than in the individuals themselves: **need for cognition.** As we discussed in chapter 3, some people simply prefer to think more fully and deeply than others about almost any issue. These people have a high **need for cognition,** the preference for engaging in deliberative thinking. This need can be measured by questions inquiring how much a person likes to think deeply about things in general (Cacioppo, Petty, Feinstein, & Jarris, 1996). Individuals who have a high need for cognition are motivated to think hard even about issues that are not personally relevant to them. For example, in one study, University of Iowa undergraduates read a communication containing either strong or weak arguments in favor of a tuition increase that would go into effect a decade later. Thus, the issue was not personally relevant to these students. Yet, those who had a high need for cognition expended more effort thinking about the communication's points and were more swayed by the quality of those points than were those who had a low need for cognition (Cacioppo, Petty, Kao, & Rodriguez, 1986).

Need for cognition *The tendency to enjoy and engage in deliberative thought.*

In sum, people can be motivated to think deeply about a topic by such factors as the personal relevance of the topic and their natural preference for thought (need for cognition). When this motivation is high, people base their opinions on a careful analysis of the quality of the arguments for and against the issue. When this motivation is low, people don't focus so much on the strengths and weaknesses of the arguments; rather, they often base their opinions on surface-level considerations—simply counting the number of arguments, for example. Although these surface-

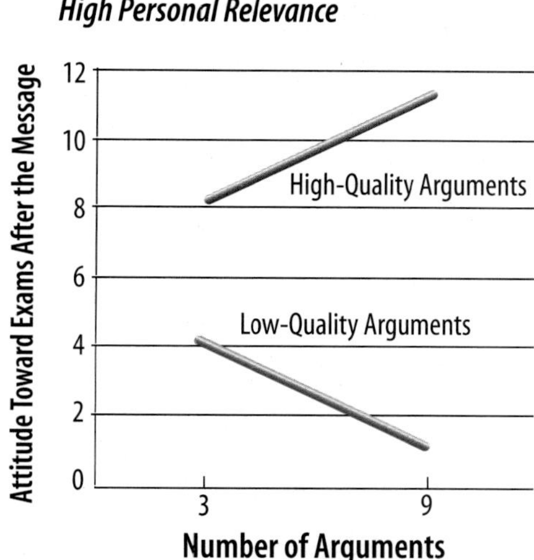

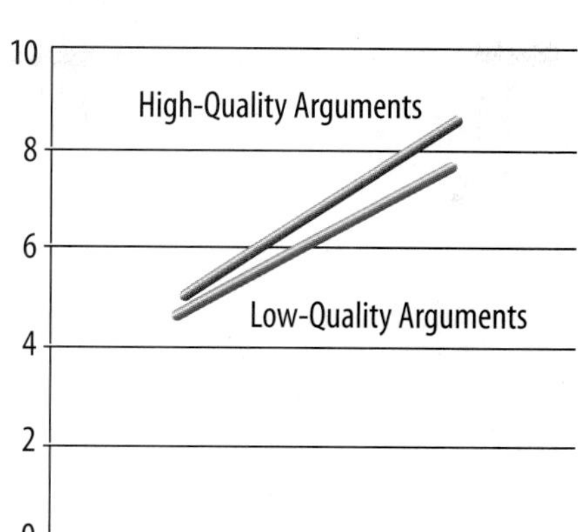

Figure 5.3
The effects of personal relevance.

When the topic was personally relevant, students responded to a message by taking into account the quality of its arguments. When the topic was not personally relevant, the students processed the message superficially, responding not to the quality of the arguments but to the sheer number. Thus, both deep and superficial message processing can lead to persuasion, but in different ways.

SOURCE: *Adapted from Petty & Cacioppo, 1984.*

level factors can produce as much initial attitude change as strong arguments, the change fades more quickly and is more vulnerable to persuasive attempts to change the attitude back again (Haugtvedt & Petty, 1992).

Thus, in your letter designed to convince people to support lower speed limits, you would be well advised not just to provide strong arguments favoring your position but to motivate recipients to consider the arguments thoroughly, perhaps by explaining at the outset how relevant this issue is to their own safety. ("Studies show that lowered highway speed limits would prevent hundreds of deaths next year. Yours could be one of them.") That way, the change your letter generates is more likely to last.

Ability Having a strong desire to process a message deeply may not be sufficient. A person must also have the ability to follow through. If you were motivated to think thoroughly about a communication—let's say an ad for a camera you wanted to buy—what could prevent you from weighing the points of the ad carefully? Researchers have uncovered several ways of limiting your ability to do so: providing distractions to take your mind off the ad (Petty, Wells, & Brock, 1976); providing you with information insufficient to let you know what to think about the ad's points (Wood, Kallgren, & Preisler, 1985); and providing insufficient time for you to consider those points fully (Ratneswar & Chaiken, 1991).

A study conducted by Joseph Alba and Howard Marmorstein (1987) showed how this last factor, insufficient time, can affect consumers' reactions to camera advertisements. Subjects were given information about two comparably priced camera brands, A and B. The information described twelve separate features that the cameras had in common. Brand A was described as superior to brand B on just three of these features, but they were the most important features to consider in purchasing a camera (those involving the quality of the camera and pictures). Brand B, on the other hand, was described as superior on eight of the features, but they were relatively unimportant aspects of a camera purchase (for example, the presence of a shoulder strap). In one condition of the study, subjects were exposed to each feature for only two seconds. In a second condition, subjects were given five seconds to consider each feature. Finally, a last group of subjects had as much time as they wanted to study the information about the twelve features. Later, subjects rated their favorability toward the cameras.

The results were striking. When given only two seconds per feature to evaluate the cameras, few subjects preferred the higher quality camera (17 percent); the majority opted for the camera that had a greater number of unimportant advantages. When given five seconds per feature, this pattern changed somewhat; but, still, fewer than half (38 percent) preferred the quality choice. It wasn't until subjects had unlimited time to consider the alternatives that the pattern reversed and the majority of subjects (67 percent) favored the camera that had fewer but more important advantages.

Does the idea of having insufficient time to analyze the points of a communication remind you of how you have to respond to typical, rapid-fire advertisements? Think about it for a second (better still, think about it for an unlimited time): Isn't this the way radio and television commercials operate? In contrast to print ads, the points in their messages speed past in a stream that can't be slowed or reversed to give you the chance to process any of it deeply. As a result, you focus not on the quality of the advertiser's case but on superficial aspects of the case, such as the likability or attractiveness of the people in the ads. This is also true of much of the other information you receive through the broadcast media (political opinions, interviews with public figures, and so on).

To explore the possibility that people would respond to the more superficial facets of a message when the message was presented in a television or radio format as opposed to a print format, Shelly Chaiken and Alice Eagly (1983) did a study of University of Toronto students. The students received a communication advocating that their school switch from the semester system to the trimester system. For half, the communicator was made to seem unlikable; he said that he didn't like the city, the university, or its students very much. For the other half of the subjects, the communicator was made likable; he said that he did like these things. Students who saw him deliver his comments in television format or heard him in radio format changed their opinions on the topic much more in his direction if he was likable than if he was unlikable. However, those who read a transcript of his comments in print format weren't persuaded by his likability at all (see Figure 5.4). Thus, it was only those individuals receiving broadcast information who couldn't process its arguments deeply and who, therefore, had to rely on aspects of the communicator in making their decisions. It is perhaps for this reason that popular U.S. presidents affect public opinion more than do unpopular presidents only when they state their positions on television (Jorden, 1993).

In summary, dual processing models of persuasion recognize two ways in which people process persuasive communications. Deep processing involves paying attention to the quality of the arguments in the communication, which results in focused thinking about those arguments and in change that is based on their strengths and weaknesses. Superficial processing involves paying attention to other aspects of the communication besides argument quality, such as the mere number of arguments

Figure 5.4 The medium affects the message.

Recipients of a message were more persuaded by a likable communicator only when it was delivered in radio (audio) or TV (video) format. When information is presented in these ways, recipients don't have the ability to think about it carefully—the way they do when it is presented in written format. Therefore, they must rely more heavily on the features of the communicator than on those of the communication.

SOURCE: *Adapted from Chaiken & Eagly, 1983.*

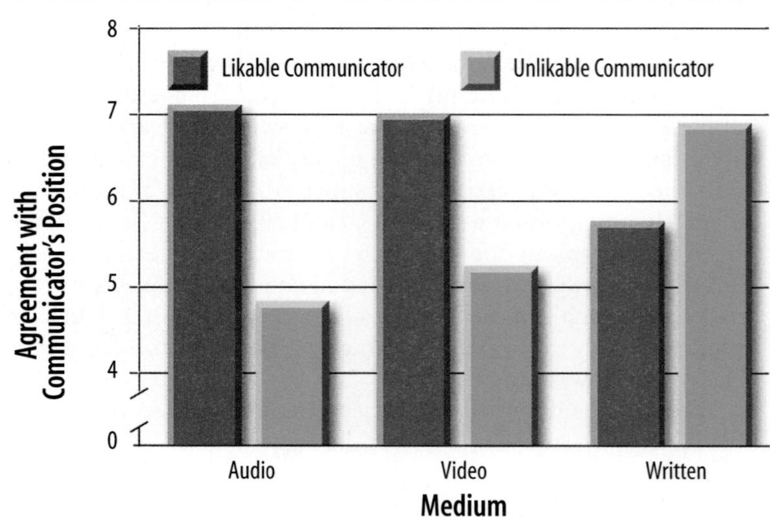

or the communicator's likability. This leads people to change their attitudes and beliefs on the basis of these secondary factors. People are likely to engage in deep processing of a message when they have both the motivation and the ability to do so. If either is missing, they are more likely to process the message superficially.

No matter which kind of processing is used, people change their attitudes and beliefs to achieve personal goals. Let's consider what they are.

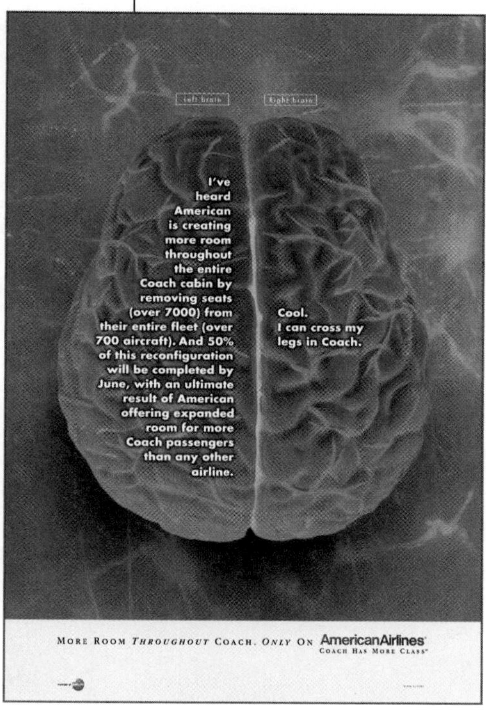

A dual-brainer. *This advertiser has cleverly arranged to appeal simultaneously to both deep and superficial information processors in the market.*

The Goals of Persuasion: Why People Change Their Attitudes and Beliefs

Without much strain, you could probably think of several reasons why one person might want to persuade another, as all manner of goals can be realized by changing another's attitudes and beliefs. But why would an individual choose to *become* persuaded? What goals would be served by such change? This seems the more intriguing and instructive question (Snyder & DeBono, 1989).

To understand the functions of attitude change, we should first consider what the functions of attitude might be. Psychologists have proposed several: through their attitudes, people can gain rewards and avoid punishments, organize information efficiently, express themselves to others, maintain self-esteem, and fit in with their groups (Herek, 1986; Katz, 1960; Shavitt, 1990; Smith, Bruner, & White, 1956).

Combining these various functions and applying them to the issue of attitude change, we can see three major persuasion goals. Individuals may yield to a persuasive message in order to

1. hold a more accurate view of the world,
2. be consistent within themselves, or
3. gain social approval and acceptance.

Sometimes, more than one goal can be achieved by the same attitude shift. For example, when one moves closer to a friend's position on an issue after the friend makes an excellent point, this move should promote both accuracy and social approval. Although these three goals don't always operate consciously, in the remainder of this chapter, we will consider how they motivate people to change.

Summary

Persuasion refers to a change in a private attitude or belief produced by a message. Strong attitudes and beliefs are resistant to change because (1) people are more committed to them; and (2) they are embedded in an array of other attitudes, beliefs, and values. Researchers often use methods designed to make the measurement of change as nonreactive as possible. One way they do so is by assessing individuals' attitudes and beliefs covertly rather than by asking for a self-report. A second way they do so is to use after-only designs that measure attitudes and beliefs only after the persuasion attempt.

Although the features of a message affect persuasion, according to the cognitive response model, the self-talk that the message generates is more directly related to the change. Persuasion can occur either when a person processes a communication deeply or superficially. Deep (versus superficial) processing is associated with (1) higher levels of motivation and ability to analyze the message, (2) greater personal relevance of the topic, (3) stronger need for cognition, (4) more time to consider the message, and (5) more enduring change. People may yield to a persuasive appeal to achieve the goals of being accurate, being consistent, or gaining approval.

Seeking Accuracy

Silver-tongued politicians, smooth-talking salespeople, and sensationalizing advertisers can often mislead their audiences. It should come as no surprise, then, that in order to avoid costly mistakes, people want to orient themselves to the world as it truly is. Holding accurate attitudes and beliefs offers one way to do so. In this section, we will explore some of the shortcuts people use to try to achieve accuracy. We will then examine those features in the person and those in the situation that influence the accuracy goal.

Good Shortcuts

As we have already seen, when individuals want to be accurate in their views of an issue—for example, when the issue is personally important—they spend considerable time and effort analyzing the relevant evidence (Petty & Cacioppo, 1979). But we must be careful not to suppose that only those thinking deeply about a topic want to hold accurate views of it (Chaiken, Liberman, & Eagly, 1989). Frequently, people want to be accurate but don't have the time or ability to analyze the evidence closely. What then? They often rely on a different kind of evidence to help them choose correctly—shortcut evidence of accuracy. This shortcut evidence can be gathered from three sources: credible communicators, others' responses, and ready ideas.

Credible Communicators When circumstances don't allow a thorough examination of a persuasive communication, people striving for accuracy can base their opinions on the credibility of the communicator (Chaiken & Maheswaran, 1994; Petty, Cacioppo, & Goldman, 1981). What are the characteristics of a credible communicator? Over many years of research, two have emerged: A credible communicator is expert and trustworthy (Perloff, 1993).

Expertise. Two thousand years ago, the great Roman poet Virgil offered simple advice to those seeking a shortcut to accuracy, "Believe an expert." Today, most people follow that advice. For instance, when the media present an expert's views on a topic, the effect on public opinion is dramatic. A single expert opinion news story in the *New York Times* is associated with a 2 percent shift in public opinion nationwide; when the expert's statement is aired on national television, the impact nearly doubles (Jorden, 1993; Page, Shapiro, & Dempsey, 1987).

What does this tell you about how to increase the effectiveness of your highway speed reduction letter? If there are public statements by transportation safety experts that support your position, you would make a mistake not to search for and include them, especially when your intended audience doesn't initially favor your proposal (Aronson, Turner, & Carlsmith, 1963). Still, you won't be optimally persuasive by just convincing your audience that you are a source of expert information. Research conducted around the world indicates that you must also demonstrate that you are a trustworthy source of that information (McGuiness & Ward, 1980).

Trustworthiness. Whereas expertise refers to a communicator's knowledge and experience, *trustworthiness* refers to the communicator's honesty and lack of bias. How can communicators appear to be honest and unbiased when delivering a persuasive message? They can do so by conveying the impression that their message is intended not to change attitudes in order to serve the communicators' own interests but instead to serve the audience members' interests by informing them accurately about the issues (Campbell, 1995). Advertisements promising "straight talk" about a problem or product illustrate one approach often taken to establish trustworthiness. Another is trickier: Rather than arguing only in their own favor, communicators sometimes make a show of providing both sides of the argument—the pros and the cons—which gives the impression of honesty and impartiality. Researchers have long known that communicators who present two-sided arguments and who appear to be arguing against their own interests can gain the trust of their audiences and become more influential (Eagly, Wood, & Chaiken, 1978; Smith & Hunt, 1978), especially when the audience initially disagrees with the communicator (Hovland, Lumsdaine, & Sheffield, 1949).

Advertisers have hit on one particularly effective way of seeming to argue against their own interests. They mention a minor weakness or drawback of their product in the ads promoting it. That way, they create a perception of honesty from which they can be more persuasive about the strengths of the product (see Figure 5.5). Advertisers are not alone in the use of this tactic. Attorneys are taught to "steal the opponent's thunder" by mentioning a weakness in their own case before the opposing lawyer does, thereby establishing a perception of honesty in the eyes of jury members. Experiments have demonstrated that this tactic works. When jurors heard an attorney bring up a weakness in his own case first, jurors assigned him more honesty and were more favorable to his overall case in their final verdicts because of that perceived honesty (Williams, Bourgeois, & Croyle, 1993).

Figure 5.5
When something bad makes something good.

Forty years ago, the advertising firm of Doyle, Dane, Bernbach was given the task of introducing a small German car to the U.S. market, where no little cars were selling and no import had ever thrived. It responded with legendary success in a series of ads that imparted overall credibility to the car and to the company by pointing to small liabilities. You may have to strain to see it, but in the ad copy, a negative comment precedes each set of positive comments.

Others' Responses When people want to react correctly to a persuasive message but don't have the motivation or ability to think about it deeply, there is another kind of shortcut they can take. They can observe the responses of others to the message. For example, if under such conditions you heard a political speech and everyone in the audience around you responded enthusiastically to it, you might well conclude that the speech was a good one and become persuaded in its direction (Axsom, Yates, & Chaiken, 1987). In addition, the more consensus you witnessed among audience members, the more likely you would be to follow their lead, even if you didn't initially agree with them (Betz, Skowronski, & Ostrom, 1996).

Although consensus among audience members increases the impact of their responses, a lone other's response to a message can sometimes greatly influence an observer's response to it as well. Criminal interrogators understand this and often support their claim that a suspect is guilty by telling the suspect that they have an eyewitness who agrees with them. What is worrisome about this tactic is that interrogators frequently employ it when no such witness exists. Not only is the use of false evidence in police interrogations legal, according to sociologist Richard Leo (in press), who watched 182 interrogations, but also, after false evidence was presented, suspects made incriminating admissions in the majority of these cases. Is it possible that some of these admissions were made by suspects who were truly innocent but convinced of their guilt by the falsified evidence? And, if so, what would be the circumstances that would lead to this remarkable form of persuasion?

Saul Kassin and Katherine Kiechel (1996) devised a study to answer precisely these questions. They constructed a situation in which college students who were performing a computer task in an experiment were accused by the researcher of a wrongdoing that they had not committed—pressing a specific key that they had been warned to avoid, which erased all of the data. Upset, the researcher demanded a signed confession from the student. How many of the students signed even though not one was guilty? That depended importantly on two features of the study. First, those individuals who had been cognitively overloaded while performing the computer task (they had to process information at a frenzied pace) were more likely to admit guilt than were those who were not overloaded by the task (83 percent versus 62 percent). As we have seen before, when people are made to feel confused and uncertain, they are more vulnerable to influence.

Second, half of the students heard a fellow subject (actually an experimental confederate) claim that she had seen the student press the forbidden key. The individuals implicated by the bogus eyewitness testimony were significantly more likely to confess than were those who were not (94 percent versus 50 percent). So powerful was the combination of these two factors that those students who were both overloaded by the situation and falsely accused by a witness admitted their guilt 100 percent of the time!

An even more frightening aspect of these particular students' mental states is that, apparently, most of them truly believed their confessions. When waiting alone outside the laboratory afterward, they were approached by another student (actually a second experimental confederate) who asked what had happened. Sixty-five percent of them responded by admitting their guilt to this unknown person, saying such things as "I hit the wrong button and ruined the program." Obviously, the impact of others' views—even the views of a single other—can greatly affect our susceptibility to persuasion, especially when we have first been made to feel unsure of ourselves. These factors fit disturbingly well with Peter Reilly's confession. During his interrogation, he was cognitively overloaded to the point of confusion and was then assured by others that he was guilty.

Ready Ideas According to the availability heuristic we discussed in Chapter 3, one shortcut people use to decide on the validity or likelihood of an idea is how easily they can picture it or instances of it (Bacon, 1979; Tversky & Kahneman, 1973).

This gives communicators a subtle way to get an audience to accept an idea—by making the idea more *cognitively ready,* that is, easier to picture or to bring to mind.

Communicators can use two methods to make an idea more cognitively ready. The first is to present the idea several times. Much research shows that repeated assertions are seen as more valid (Hertwig, Girerenzer, & Hoffrage, 1997). Moreover, much research shows that repeated assertions are seen as more valid (Hertwig et al., 1997). After an idea is encountered several times, it becomes more familiar and easier to picture, which makes it seem more true (Arkes et al., 1989; Boehm, 1994).

Asking an audience to imagine an idea or event is a second method for increasing its readiness and believability (Garry & Polaschek, 2000). After you have once imagined something, it becomes easier to picture the next time you consider it, thus appearing more likely. The impact of the act of imagining isn't limited to beliefs; it influences behavior too. In one study (Gregory, Cialdini, & Carpenter, 1982), homeowners were asked to imagine themselves experiencing certain benefits of cable TV; other homeowners only read about these benefits. Weeks later, the homeowners were given the opportunity to subscribe to cable TV. Those who had imagined themselves enjoying the benefits of cable TV were more than twice as likely to subscribe (47 percent versus 20 percent).

In another study, after imagining themselves in a car accident, students at New Mexico State University became significantly more willing to support traffic safety initiatives (Gregory, Burroughs, & Ainslie, 1985). You no doubt see the relevance of these findings to your letter advocating lower speed limits: you might ask readers to take a minute and *just imagine* how easy it would be to get involved in an accident when traffic is traveling at high rates of speed.

Thus, ideas can be made to seem more valid by increasing their cognitive readiness, which can be accomplished by presenting the ideas more than once and by arranging for the audience to imagine or picture the ideas. In retrospect, it is clear that Peter Reilly's interrogators used both of these methods. He was assaulted by repeated assertions that he had murdered his mother and was incessantly pushed to imagine how he could have done it. By the time the interrogation was over, these imaginations had become reality for both the interrogators and Reilly.

Interrogator: *But you recall cutting her throat with a straight razor.*
Reilly: *It's hard to say. I think I recall doing it. I mean, I imagine myself doing it. It's coming out of the back of my head...*
Interrogator: *How about her legs? What kind of vision do we get there?... Can you remember stomping her legs?*
Reilly: *You say it, then I imagine I'm doing it.*
Interrogator: *You're not imagining anything. I think the truth is starting to come out. You want it out.*
Reilly: *I know...*

What Affects the Desire for Accuracy?

The desire for an accurate perspective on a topic is not always the same. At some times and in certain people, it can be particularly intense. At other times and in other individuals, it can drop drastically. Let's explore a set of factors that affect when and how the goal for accuracy operates to influence persuasion.

Issue Involvement You probably have an opinion on thousands of issues. Although it would be nice to hold accurate views on them all, you are more motivated to be correct concerning those that involve you directly. Political differences in a remote part of the world may spark important events there—war, revolution, and social change. But you would probably be less motivated to hold informed opinions on such issues than on a plan for a local sales tax increase. As a rule and as we've

seen, you'll want to have more accurate attitudes and beliefs on issues that are *personally* important. Consequently, you'll be more likely to think hard about messages concerning these issues, becoming persuaded only when the arguments are strong (Petty & Cacioppo, 1979).

One study showed how easy it is for advertisers to get you more involved with a topic so that you will pay careful attention to their messages. The researchers wrote advertising copy—for disposable razors—that either used the self-referencing pronoun *you* exclusively ("You might have thought that razor technology could never be improved") or did not. Individuals who saw the self-referencing ads thought more thoroughly about the information and were only influenced by it when it contained strong arguments (Burnkrant & Unnava, 1989). Can *you* see how *you* could incorporate this device into *your* letter concerning highway speed limits—and that it would be wise to do so only if *you* had good arguments to support *your* cause? Of course, textbook writers would never stoop to using this tactic.

Mood Being in a happy or sad mood does more than give you a positive or negative feeling; it also gives you information about the nature of your immediate situation (Schwarz & Clore, in press). If you are feeling happy at the moment, it is likely that your current environment has recently been receptive and rewarding. If you are feeling sad, on the other hand, chances are that the environment has recently yielded something unfortunate; it will seem a riskier place, and you will feel more vulnerable (Salovey & Birnbaum, 1989). No doubt you would want to make sure that you react correctly to a persuasion attempt in this insecure environment. Thus, when in a sad versus a happy mood, you will be especially motivated to acquire accurate attitudes and beliefs that pertain to the situation at hand—because of what your mood says about the potential danger of making errors in the immediate environment (Bless, Bohner, Schwarz, & Strack, 1990; Schwarz, Bless, & Bohner, 1991).

Suggestibility Suggestible individuals are particularly likely to believe what others tell them. An examination of their personality traits helps explain why: They tend to score low on self-esteem and high on interpersonal trust, showing less confidence in themselves than in others (Gudjonsson, 1992). It makes sense, then, that when striving for accuracy in their attitudes and beliefs, these individuals rely less on what they think than on what others tell them to think. Hence, they can be easily misled by false information, even about the events they have seen. In one study, participants watched a film of a bank robbery and were later given a written summary of the events that was erroneous in several respects. Those who had been previously rated as suggestible on the basis of personality tests were much more likely to be influenced by this erroneous information, coming to believe not what they had seen in the film but what the summary told them they had seen (Lampinen & Smith, 1994).

Does this information help reduce the mystery of why Peter Reilly admitted to a murder he did not commit? It well might, in that expert psychological opinions given during and after his trial characterized Reilly as "a classic case of an impressionable personality" who possessed low self-esteem and a high degree of trust in others, especially authorities.

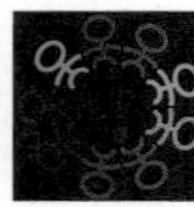

Done Deals The Bible says that there is a time for all things, "a time to every purpose under heaven." The goal of accuracy is not excused from this rule. For example, Peter Gollwitzer and his coworkers have shown that there is a particular time when people are most motivated to be accurate—when they are deciding what to feel, believe, or do. *After* that decision is made, however, the desire to see things as they really are can give way to the desire to get on with the now-made decision (Gollwitzer, Heckhausen, & Steller, 1990).

In one study demonstrating this effect, German college students were asked to consider a personal project for which they had not yet chosen a course of action.

Other students were asked to consider a project for which they had chosen a course of action but hadn't yet begun. Both groups were then asked to report their thoughts about the projects. Those students who hadn't yet decided what to do thought more evenhandedly about the project than did those who had already made a decision: They had just as many positive thoughts as negative thoughts, whereas those who had made a decision had many more positive than negative thoughts about the project (Taylor & Gollwitzer, 1995). Thus, the desire to be unbiased and accurate in their thinking was strongest before these students had made a decision; after the decision, the accuracy motive faded in favor of the desire to feel good about it so that they could confidently begin steps to carry out their plans.

Unwelcome Information Under certain circumstances, people choose to believe only what they want to believe, usually what fits with their self-interests and personal preferences (Johnson & Eagly, 1989; Kunda, 1990). This tendency can affect persuasion. For example, people see information that contradicts what they prefer to believe as less valid than information that supports these beliefs; as a result, such evidence is less persuasive (Lord, Ross, & Lepper, 1979; Pyszczynski, Greenberg, & Holt, 1985). Other research has revealed how this process works. People who receive persuasive information that fits with their personal interests, preferences, and positions feel content and typically don't expend the cognitive effort needed to look for flaws. However, those who encounter information that doesn't fit become upset and search it for weaknesses they can use to form counterarguments (Giner-Sorolla & Chaiken, 1997; Liberman & Chaiken, 1992; Munro & Ditto, 1997). Although it is not necessarily harmful to scrutinize and resist information at odds with one's preferred traits and beliefs, it can be self-destructive if overdone, as we see in the following section.

FOCUS ON Social Dysfunction

Defensiveness and Denial

Do people take a biased approach, trying to challenge and undermine negative (but not positive) information, even when the information concerns the vital matter of their own health? Indeed they do (Ditto, Scepansky, Munro, Apanovitch, & Lockhart, 1998; Kunda, 1987). For example, drivers with a history of hospitalization for auto accidents nonetheless continue to believe that they are better and safer drivers than most (Guerin, 1994; Svenson, 1991).

Suppose you were participating in an experiment using a new saliva test to detect an enzyme deficiency that predicted pancreatic disease in later life. How much would you believe in the accuracy of the new test? According to a study done by Peter Ditto and David Lopez (1992) on Kent State University students, that would depend on whether the test identified you as possessing the worrisome deficiency. Like the majority of those students, you would likely downgrade the accuracy of the test if it informed you that pancreas problems were in your future. A second study showed how you might go about it. Ditto and Lopez asked subjects if there were any irregularities in their diet, sleep, or activity patterns over the last forty-eight hours that might have affected the accuracy of the test. Those who got health-threatening results listed three times more "irregularities" than did those receiving health-confirming results. Thus, they searched for ways to undercut evidence contradicting their preferred image of healthiness.

On the surface, this tendency seems potentially harmful. And it can be, as it involves finding fault with information that can warn of physical danger. However, a study by John Jemmott and his coworkers (1986) suggests that most people are not so foolish as to ignore the warning entirely. Participants in that experiment were told that an enzyme deficiency test either did or did not identify them as candidates for future pancreatic disorders. Those who were informed that they had the deficiency judged the test's validity as significantly lower than did those informed that they were deficiency-free. Nonetheless, 83 percent of the deficiency-present individuals asked to receive information about services available to people who had the deficiency. Thus, although they tried to defend against the threat in the test results, the great majority did not simply brush the matter aside; instead, they made arrangements to get more information and, if need be, assistance.

This may represent an especially effective overall orientation to evidence that disputes existing or preferred beliefs about the self. An initial tendency to minimize such evidence would help manage the anxiety the evidence produced (Gibbons, Eggleston, & Benthin, 1997). A second, allied tendency (to seek more information and stay alert to the need to change one's beliefs) is in keeping with the goal of seeing the world accurately and would assure that no genuine danger is ignored. Hence, for most people, the tendency to reject unwelcome information is normally not harmful in such situations because it is tempered by the accuracy motive, especially when important aspects of the self are at stake.

It is when people place no reasonable limits on their desire to view the world according to their beliefs and preferences that a serious problem arises (Armor & Taylor, 1998). Take the 17 percent of threatened subjects in the Jemmott et al. study who did not ask for further information about the enzyme deficiency. Not only did they resist the unwelcome message but also they resisted the chance to protect themselves if it proved true. This sort of reaction is more than healthy skepticism toward incongruous information. It might be characterized as *denial,* and it can be self-destructive (Gladis, Michela, Walter, & Vaughn, 1992; Lazarus, 1983).

Who are these individuals who engage in denial when confronted with troubling information? They are not merely optimists—individuals who believe that, as a rule, good things are likely to happen to them (Scheier & Carver, 1992). They are better termed *chronic unrealistic optimists*—individuals who refuse to believe that they are vulnerable to bad events in general and who, therefore, fail to take precautions against them (Davidson & Prkachin,1997; Weinstein, 1987). Apparently, such individuals are so upset by the possibility of harm that they repress relevant information and deny that they are vulnerable to the harm (Taylor, Collins, Skokan, & Aspinwall, 1989). The irony is that by repressing and denying the existence of distressing dangers, these individuals make the very same dangers more real.

This tendency to deal with threat by ignoring or denying the problem can appear in normal individuals, too, but only under certain conditions. For the most part, fear-arousing communications usually stimulate recipients to take actions to reduce the threat (Boster & Mongeau, 1984; Robberson & Rogers, 1988). For instance, a lecture to French teenagers about the dangers of alcohol was significantly more effective in changing attitudes and behaviors toward drinking when accompanied by fear-arousing versus neutral pictures (Levy-Leboyer, 1988). However, there is an exception to this general rule: When the danger described in the fear-producing message is severe but the recipients are told of no effective means of reducing the danger—self-restraint, medication, exercise, diet, or the like—they may deal with the fear by "blocking out" the message or denying that it applies to them. As a consequence, they may take no preventive action (Rogers & Mewborn, 1976).

This helps explain why it is important to accompany high-fear messages with specific recommendations for behavior that will diminish the danger: The more clearly people see behavioral means for ridding themselves of the fear, the less they will need to resort to psychological means such as denial (Leventhal & Cameron, 1994) (see Figure 5.6 on the opposite page). The lesson: Don't try to persuade people through fear without giving them specific steps to handle the fear. This applies to your letter designed to convince citizens of the dangers of high speed limits. Vividly describing the highway mayhem these high speed limits allow should be effective as long as you also describe specific steps recipients can take to reduce the danger, such as contributing to relevant political action groups or calling relevant legislators (whose phone numbers you should provide). ■

Expertise and Complexity Suppose you are sitting on a jury deciding how much money to award a man who claims that he contracted cancer as a result of exposure to a chemical while on the job. His employer, a manufacturing firm, admits that he was exposed to this chemical but disputes that it caused his cancer. One piece of evidence you hear is the testimony of an expert witness, Dr. Thomas Fallon, who states that scientific data show that the chemical does indeed lead to cancer in a variety of species, including humans. How swayed are you likely to be by this expert? According to a study done by Joel Cooper, Elizabeth Bennett, and Holly Sukel (1996), that would depend not just on how expert you think he is but also on how complex his testimony was.

In that study, mock jurors heard Dr. Fallon described as either highly expert or only moderately expert on the topic. Some of the jurors then heard him give his testimony in ordinary language, saying simply that the chemical causes liver cancer, several other diseases of the liver, and diseases of the immune system. Other jurors heard him give his testimony in complex, almost incomprehensible language, saying that the chemical led to "tumor induction as well as hepatomegaly, hepatomegalocytosis, and lymphoid atrophy of the spleen and thymus." The most interesting finding of the study was that the highly expert witness was more successful in swaying the jury only when he spoke in complex, difficult-to-understand terms. Why? The study's authors think that when Dr. Fallon used simple language, jurors could judge the case on the basis of the evidence itself. They didn't need to use his expertise as a shortcut to accuracy. However, when his testimony was too obscure to understand, they had to rely on his reputation as an expert to tell them what to think. These results suggest an interesting but discomforting irony: Acknowledged experts may be most persuasive when people can't understand the details of what they are saying!

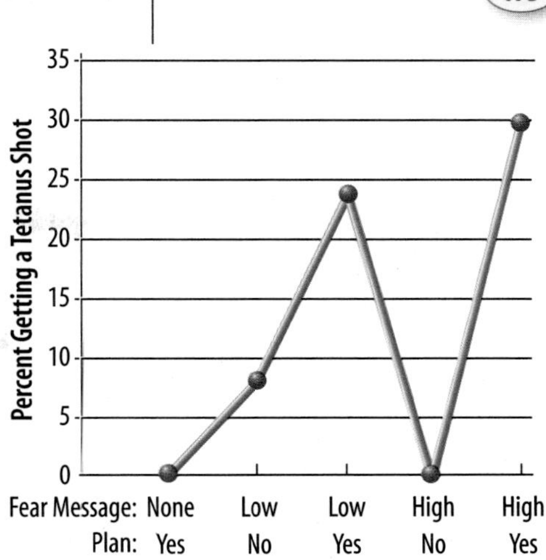

Figure 5.6
Fear is not enough. You have to have a plan.

Students read a public health pamphlet on the dangers of tetanus infection that either was or was not laden with frightening images of the consequences of contracting tetanus. In addition, they either did or did not receive a specific plan for how to arrange to get a tetanus shot. Finally, there was a control group of students who got no tetanus message but did get a plan. The high-fear message spurred recipients to get a shot only if it included a plan identifying the specific actions they could take to secure a shot and thereby reduce their fear of tetanus.

SOURCE: *Adapted from Leventhal & Cameron, 1994.*

Trustworthiness and Need for Cognition If expertise is more persuasive primarily when the audience is taking a mental shortcut, does the other component of credibility—trustworthiness—work the same way? Some research suggests that it does. We have already seen that there are certain individuals (those low in need for cognition) who, as a rule, prefer to take shortcuts in their thinking (Cacioppo et al., 1996). These individuals should be especially likely to use a communicator's reputation for trustworthiness in deciding whether to accept his or her arguments. Those high in need for cognition, on the other hand, should focus on the strength of the arguments themselves rather than on the reputation of the person presenting them. That is exactly what one experiment found: An audience of low-need-for-cognition individuals was persuaded by a trustworthy communicator even when he gave weak reasons for his position. But an audience of high-need-for-cognition individuals was not influenced by his reputation for trustworthiness, changing attitudes primarily when he had strong arguments to give (Priester & Petty, 1995).

Summary

Most people want to hold accurate attitudes and beliefs. But when and how they seek to achieve this goal varies. One path to accuracy follows the deep processing route, in which people think carefully about the arguments in a message. However, a second path to accuracy follows a more superficial, shortcut route: People frequently decide to change for accuracy's sake when the source of a persuasive message is credible, when others have accepted the message, and when the ideas in the message are cognitively ready (easy to picture).

Several accuracy-related factors reside inside the person and affect reactions to persuasive appeals. People directly involved with the issue want to be accurate because their self-interests are at stake; people in a sad mood are also likely to be more motivated to see things accurately because they feel more threatened by the possibility of mistakes; and people who are suggestible accept many persuasive messages as accurate because they trust others more than themselves. Additional accuracy-related factors arise from the situation. Accuracy motives can become less prominent when a decision has already been made or when the content of a message conflicts with what a recipient wants to hear. When taken to extremes, the tendency to repress or deny unwanted information can be dangerous. People are most likely to use communicator credibility as a shortcut to accuracy when the communication is complex or their need for cognition is low.

Being Consistent

The giant of nineteenth-century British science, Michael Faraday, was once asked about a long-hated academic rival, "Is the professor always wrong, then?" Faraday glowered at his questioner and replied, "He's not that consistent."

In Faraday's dismissive description of his opponent's intellect, we find a pair of insights relevant to the goal of consistency. The first is straightforward: Like most people, Faraday considered consistency an admirable trait that ought to appear in one's behavior. When it doesn't, there is cause for scorn (Allgeier et al., 1979). Finding the second insight requires a bit more digging. Why did Faraday feel the need to deflate his rival's occasional accomplishments at all? A social psychologist might answer the question by suggesting that Faraday himself was a victim of the workings of the **consistency principle,** which states that people are motivated toward cognitive consistency and will change their attitudes, beliefs, perceptions, and actions to achieve it. To maintain consistency within his unfavorable view of his rival, Faraday had to find a way to negate the successes of the man—hence, the characterization of his opponent's accomplishments as inconsistencies.

Although we can't be certain that a desire to be personally consistent motivated Faraday's response (he's been unavailable for questioning since 1867), we can review the evidence for the causes of similar responses in modern-day individuals. In the process, we will first examine the two main consistency theories—balance and cognitive dissonance—that have guided the investigations of persuasion researchers. Then, we will consider the features in the person and in the situation that affect the goal of being consistent.

Balance Theory

According to Fritz Heider (1946, 1958), who proposed **balance theory,** we all prefer to have harmony and consistency in our views of the world. We want to agree with the people we like and disagree with those we dislike; we want to associate good things with good people and bad things with bad people; we want to see things that are alike in one way as alike in other ways, too. Heider says that such harmony creates a state of cognitive balance in us. When we are in a state of balance—perhaps finding ourselves agreeing on a political issue with someone we truly like—we are content; there is no need to change. But if our cognitive system is out of balance—for example, when finding ourselves disagreeing on an issue with the person we like so much—we will experience uncomfortable tension. To remove this tension, we will have to change something in the system. Let's take a closer look at balance theory to see how this pressure to change can affect persuasion.

Name your favorite movie actor. Now, suppose you heard this person advocating a political position that you opposed. The theory states that your cognitive system would be out of balance because you would be disagreeing with someone you liked—recall, balance exists when you agree with a person you like or disagree with one you dislike. What could you do to relieve the resulting tension and bring

Consistency principle *The principle that people will change their attitudes, beliefs, perceptions, and actions to make them consistent with each other.*

Balance theory *Heider's theory that people prefer harmony and consistency in their views of the world.*

the system into balance? One maneuver would be to change your feelings about the actor; that way you would then disagree with someone you dislike. A second approach would be to change your attitude toward the topic; that way you would then agree with someone you like. In both instances, harmony would again reign.

Which approach you would take would likely depend on the strength of your attitudes. For example, if you had very deep feelings about the political topic—let's say gun control—you would probably achieve balance by changing your opinion of the actor who disagreed with you. If, however, you didn't have a strong attitude toward the topic, you would be more likely to achieve balance by changing that attitude to agree with the liked individual. A great deal of research has supported the predictions of balance theory as it applies to attitude change (Eagly & Chaiken, 1993; Insko, 1984; Judd & Krosnick, 1989). In general, people do change their views in order to keep the connections involving themselves, communicators, and communication topics in harmony.

Advertisers frequently try to make use of this tendency in their choice of famous spokespeople for their products. By the logic of the communicator expertise effect we discussed earlier, it makes sense for the Nike Corporation to hire basketball star Michael Jordan to promote their basketball shoes. But by what logic would the McDonald's Corporation want to pay him millions of dollars to promote their fast food restaurants? By the logic of balance theory. Because people like Michael Jordan, they should come to like whatever he is advocating (or just associated with). According to balance theory, one doesn't have to be expert to be convincing, just liked.

Scoring points, scoring profits. *Although it's unlikely that many have studied balance theory, advertisers recognize something that the theory predicts: If you like Mike, you should like what Mike likes. This is why he is paid to promote products—such as cellular phones, cologne, and underwear—that are unrelated to his athletic talents.*

The willingness of manufacturers to pay enormous sums to celebrities (whose talents may be unrelated to their products) suggests that the business community has determined that the pull of cognitive balance makes the investment worthwhile. Evidence of the potential return on investment to business of being associated with positive people and things can be seen in the results of a poll indicating that 76 percent of consumers would switch to a corporate brand or product connected to favorably viewed causes such as the Olympics (Kadlec, 1997). According to the credit card company, Visa, which is an Olympic sponsor, if a store displays a Visa sign featuring the Olympics rings symbol, Visa card purchases rise by fifteen to twenty-five percent (Emert, 2000).

Cognitive Dissonance Theory

By far, the theoretical approach that has generated the most evidence for the motivation to be consistent is Leon Festinger's (1957) cognitive dissonance theory. Like balance theory, its basic assumption is that when people recognize an inconsistency among their attitudes, beliefs, or behaviors, they will feel a state of uncomfortable psychological arousal (termed **cognitive dissonance**) and will be motivated to reduce the discomfort by reducing the inconsistency. In addition, Festinger stated that people will be motivated to reduce an inconsistency only to the extent that it involves something important. For example, if you perceive an inconsistency in your beliefs about the wisdom of riding motorcycles—on the one hand, they seem economical but, on the other, dangerous—you should feel strong dissonance only if riding motorcycles is a real and important issue for you, perhaps because you are thinking of buying one. This helps explain why strong dissonance effects rarely occur unless the self is involved (Aronson, 1969; Thibodeau & Aronson, 1992).

Cognitive dissonance *The unpleasant state of psychological arousal resulting from an inconsistency within one's important attitudes, beliefs, or behaviors.*

Dogbert does dissonance. *Although dissonance rarely works as dramatically as depicted here, cartoonist Scott Adams has accurately captured several of the conditions (low pay, insufficient justification, free choice) that the theory says lead to self-delusion.*

When the inconsistency includes something about the self, it becomes more important and the need to resolve it increases.

Before dissonance theory came to prominence, persuasion theorists had focused mainly on changing attitudes and beliefs first, assuming that these shifts would then cause behavior change. Although this sequence often occurs, one of the valuable contributions of dissonance theory has been to show that the reverse can also occur—changing a behavior first can spur an individual to change related attitudes and beliefs in an attempt to keep them consistent with the action (Cooper & Scher, 1994).

There have been many dissonance experiments performed through the years, but the one published by Leon Festinger and J. Merrill Carlsmith in 1959 is easily the most famous. In the study, subjects who had performed a boring task (turning pegs on a board) were paid either $1 or $20 to tell the next subject that the task was interesting and a lot of fun. When later asked their attitudes toward the boring task, those receiving the $1 payment had come to see it as more enjoyable than had those receiving $20, who hadn't changed their attitudes at all.

How can we explain this strange result? Dissonance theory offers an answer. Subjects paid only $1 had to confront two inconsistent cognitions about themselves: "I am a generally truthful person" (something that almost everyone believes) and "I just told a lie for no good reason." The easiest way for them to reduce the inconsistency was to change their attitudes toward the enjoyableness of the task; that way, they would no longer have to view themselves as lying about its being fun. In contrast, subjects paid $20 had no dissonance to reduce because they had a good reason (*sufficient justification*) for what they did—the $20. After all, even a generally truthful person will tell a white lie for $20. So, because of the $20, what they did was not inconsistent with their views of themselves as generally truthful; hence, they didn't feel any pull to change their attitudes toward the task.

Counterattitudinal Behavior This explanation of the Festinger and Carlsmith study underscores a fundamental assertion of dissonance theory: A **counterattitudinal action**—behavior that is inconsistent with an existing attitude—will produce change in that attitude only when the actor sees no strong external justification for taking the action. It is for this reason that contrary behavior leads to attitude change principally when the actor feels that he or she has had *free choice* in performing it (Brehm & Cohen, 1962). For example, if you signed a petition supporting a disliked politician because your boss at work insisted on it, you would not likely feel a strain

Counterattitudinal action *A behavior that is inconsistent with an existing attitude.*

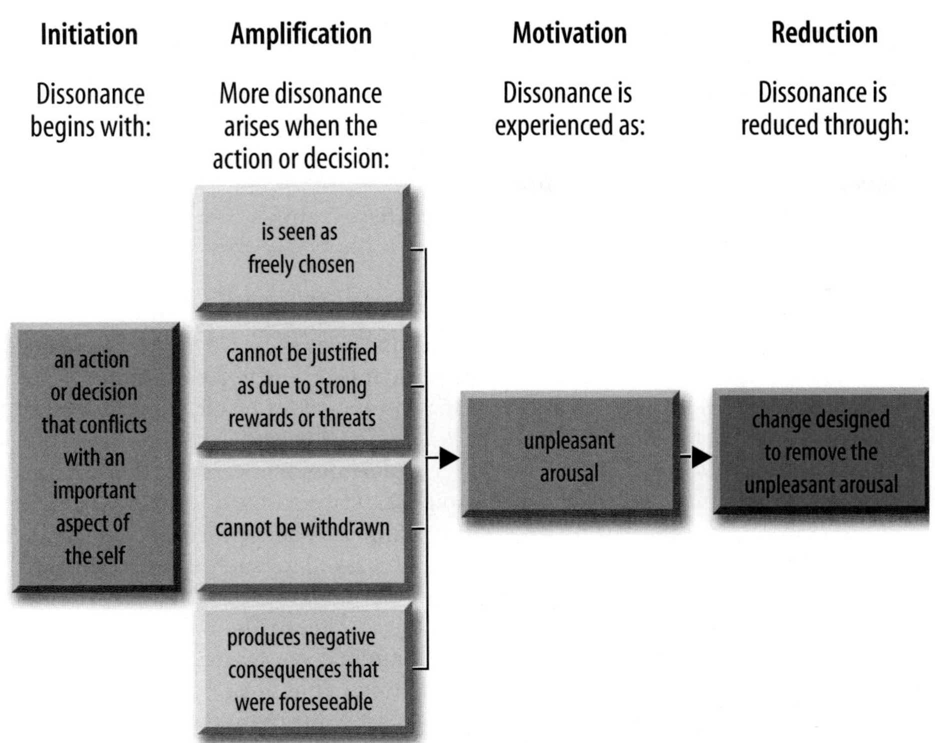

Figure 5.7
From dissonance induction to dissonance reduction.

A number of factors initiate, amplify, motivate, and reduce cognitive dissonance.

to become more positive toward the politician because you would probably see yourself as having little choice in the matter, given your boss's strong pressure. When potent external forces (threats, bribes, requirements) take away one's sense of personal choice in counterattitudinal behavior, dissonance rarely results (Eagly & Chaiken, 1993).

Postdecisional Dissonance Counterattitudinal behavior isn't the only way that dissonance is produced. Another source of dissonance was examined in a study conducted at a Canadian racetrack, where bettors at the $2 window were approached and asked what chance they thought their favored horse had to win (Knox & Inkster, 1968). Half were asked immediately before placing their bets and half were asked immediately after. In two separate studies, those asked after laying down their money were significantly more confident of their horse's chances. How odd. After all, nothing about the race, field, track, or weather had changed in the few seconds from before to after the bet. Perhaps not, but according to dissonance theory, something about the bettors had changed: They had experienced **postdecisional dissonance,** which is the conflict one feels between the knowledge that he or she has made a decision and the possibility that the decision may be wrong. To reduce the unpleasant conflict, the bettors persuaded themselves that their horses really would win.

In general, soon after making a decision, people come to view their selections more favorably and all the alternative selections less favorably; this is particularly so when they feel highly committed (personally tied) to the decision (Brehm & Cohen, 1962; Eagly & Chaiken, 1993). In the case of the racetrack bettors, they became committed once they placed their bets and could no longer change their choices. At that point, they became irrevocably tied to their selections and had to reduce their postdecisional dissonance by convincing themselves that they had chosen correctly. Recall that, earlier in this chapter, we said that after an irreversible decision, the desire to see things accurately is no longer paramount (Taylor & Gollwitzer, 1995); dissonance theory tells us that it is replaced by the desire to see things consistently (see Figure 5.7).

Postdecisional dissonance *The conflict one feels about a decision that could possibly be wrong.*

What Affects the Desire for Cognitive Consistency?

The goal of achieving (or simply maintaining) cognitive consistency has been the subject of considerable research within social psychology (Albarracin & Wyer, 2000). That research has uncovered several features of the person and of the situation that play a role in determining how the desire for consistency affects persuasion. Most of the evidence for the impact of these features comes from explorations of dissonance theory.

Arousal Festinger (1957) claimed that inconsistency produces unpleasant arousal and that people will frequently change their attitudes to be rid of the discomfort. In general, research has supported both components of Festinger's claim.

First, there is good evidence that inconsistency does result in increased arousal (Elkin & Leippe, 1986; Harmon-Jones, Brehm, Greenberg, Simon, & Nelson, 1996). In one study, researchers set up a typical dissonance procedure: Princeton University students were given free choice to write an essay contrary to their attitudes toward a total ban of alcohol on campus. The researchers said that they needed an essay that was in favor of the ban and asked for such an essay, saying, "We would appreciate your help, but we want to let you know that it's completely up to you." When these students agreed to write the counterattitudinal essay, their arousal (as measured by physiological recordings) jumped compared to similar students who were given no free choice in the matter. Thus, just as dissonance theory would expect, individuals who freely chose to act contrary to their existing attitudes experienced elevated tension as a result of the personal inconsistency (Croyle & Cooper, 1983).

Second, there is also good evidence to support the other part of Festinger's claim—that people will modify an inconsistent attitude as a way of reducing the accompanying unpleasant arousal (Fazio, Zanna, & Cooper, 1977; Zanna & Cooper, 1974). In one experiment, subjects who freely wrote a counterattitudinal essay but did not experience any arousal, because they had secretly been given a tranquilizer, did not alter their attitudes toward the topic; thus, eliminating the arousal eliminated the need to change (Cooper, Zanna, & Taves, 1978). Other studies have found that it is not just general arousal that is crucial to the change process but rather the particular variety that Festinger first suggested—*unpleasant* arousal (Elliot & Devine, 1994; Losch & Cacioppo, 1990). It is the annoying quality of that arousal that motivates change, discomforting inconsistent individuals until they do something to restore consistency. In all, research has implicated uncomfortable arousal as a critical factor in inconsistency-based attitude and belief shifts.

Preference for Consistency In introducing the consistency goal, we reported a quotation from Michael Faraday that indicated his value for consistency. Most people would agree, but not everyone. Consider the following statements by various other famous persons: Ralph Waldo Emerson: "A foolish consistency is the hobgoblin of little minds"; Oscar Wilde: "Consistency is the last refuge of the unimaginative"; and our favorite, Aldous Huxley: "The only truly consistent people are dead." Obviously, the concept of consistency is not held in universally high regard (Staw & Ross, 1980).

This insight led one of the authors of this textbook and two colleagues to develop a Preference for Consistency scale by asking subjects to agree or disagree with such statements as "It is important to me that my actions are consistent with my beliefs" (Cialdini, Trost, & Newsom, 1995). They found that individuals who scored low on preference for consistency didn't show typical consistency effects. For instance, in a standard dissonance procedure, participants were given high or low levels of choice in writing an essay that favored raising tuition on their campus. Although those scoring high in preference for consistency showed the usual dissonance effect, becoming more positive toward a tuition increase only if they had free choice in writing the essay, those scoring low on the scale did not show this effect. They were equally positive toward an increase whether they had high or low choice in advocating it. As one might expect, the motive to be self-consistent doesn't apply to those who don't value consistency (Bator, 1998).

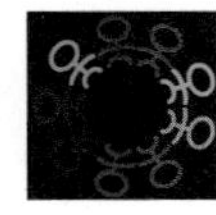

Consequences The outcomes of a counterattitudinal act affect the amount of attitude change it creates. Because no one wants to perform *consequential* behaviors that conflict with an existing attitude, it stands to reason that the more impact a person's behavior has had on the world, the more he or she will feel motivated to change attitudes to fit that behavior. For example, if after agreeing to write a counterattitudinal essay favoring big tuition hikes at your school, you learned that your essay persuaded administrators to schedule a large increase, you should be especially likely to convince yourself of the need for the increase. Research generally supports this view (Collins & Hoyt, 1972). Although strong negative consequences of inconsistent actions don't seem necessary for attitude change, they do enhance it (Harmon-Jones et al., 1996; Johnson, Kelly, & LeBlanc, 1995).

However, there is an important qualification: negative consequences will spur more change only when they are foreseeable. Imagine that after being given a free, in-home demonstration by a vacuum cleaner salesman, you declined to buy his model because you thought it had done a mediocre job on your rugs. But before leaving, he asked if you would sign a statement that he could show his boss saying that you liked the machine and had enjoyed the demonstration. Thinking that you should give him something in return for spending an hour cleaning your carpets, you agree. Imagine further that later you learned that your action had some unwelcome consequences: The salesman had gone next door and sold your neighbor a vacuum cleaner, partly on the basis of your signed recommendation.

Now, to justify your actions, you might try to convince yourself of the quality of the vacuum cleaner—*if* you felt that you should have foreseen the consequences of what you did, perhaps because you recalled that you had heard of this tactic before. If the tactic was a complete surprise to you, however, something you could not have foreseen, you probably wouldn't accept personal responsibility for what happened and probably wouldn't become more favorable toward the machine (Cooper, 1971; Goethals, Cooper, & Naficy, 1979). Once more, then, we see that factors that link an inconsistent act—or its consequences—to the self are more likely to motivate change.

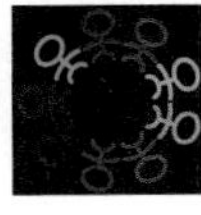

Salience of the Inconsistency If, as we have suggested, people change their attitudes and beliefs to be rid of an inconsistency, then aspects of the situation that make the inconsistency salient (prominent) to them should produce greater change (Blanton, Cooper, Skurnik, & Aronson, 1997). One way to make an inconsistency salient is through the use of the *Socratic method*, an approach for shifting a person's position on a topic by posing questions that reveal hidden contradictions between it and the person's position on related topics. Socrates, the author of the method, felt that once the discrepancies were made obvious, the person would try to eliminate them. Research on persuasion has supported Socrates' prediction: Most people react to messages that reveal their inconsistencies by moving toward consistency (McGuire, 1960; McGuire & McGuire, 1996).

In fact, an effective way to get people to perform socially beneficial acts is to make salient the discrepancy between what they value and what they do. Suppose that a survey-taker called and inquired into your attitude toward recycling and that you expressed a high opinion of it. Suppose that she then asked you to recall the times in the past month that you had failed to recycle (a newspaper or soft drink can). Most likely, after being confronted with this mismatch between your beliefs and actions, you would resolve to be more supportive of recycling in the future. This tactic of getting people to express their commitment to a good cause and then pointing out that they have not always lived up to that commitment has successfully reduced energy consumption in Australian households (Kantola, Syme, & Campbell, 1984). In the United States, Elliot Aronson and his coworkers have employed the tactic to increase water conservation, recycling, and condom use (see Fried & Aronson, 1995).

Think how a salient inconsistency could have pushed Peter Reilly to admit to a murder someone else committed. At first, he had no memory of the crime. But, after hours of mind-draining interrogation, he began to accept the "expert" evidence against him in his polygraph test, began to defer to the assurances of authority figures that he was guilty, and began to see the imagined scenes of his involvement as real. Is it any surprise that his failure to recall any specifics, which had become the single, salient inconsistency in the case, couldn't stand for long? Soon thereafter, he began not simply to admit to the killing but to add details. When these specifics didn't match with the facts the interrogators knew, they would claim that Reilly was being evasive, and he would offer different specifics. In one instructive exchange, after being chastised for remembering incorrect details, he plaintively asked his interrogator for "some hints" so he could make everything fit.

What happened to Reilly is remarkably similar to what happened in the earlier-discussed Kassin & Kiechel (1996) study, in which innocent people were accused of hitting a computer key that ruined data. Many of those who came to believe (on the basis of false evidence) that they were guilty remembered details of how and when the (non)event occurred, saying such things as, "I hit it with the side of my hand right after you called out the A." Evidence like this aligns well with a conclusion drawn by psychologists studying other kinds of responding (for instance, eyewitness testimony in court and "recovered" memories in therapy sessions): So wide-ranging is the desire for consistency that it can reach into one's memory and change the features of recalled events to make them conform to a newly installed belief (Bowers & Farvolden, 1996; Loftus & Ketcham, 1994).

Consistency with What?

Although most people strive to be consistent with their prevailing self-concept, this can lead to different behaviors because not everyone shares the same view of self. For instance, the desire for consistency often results in different behaviors in different cultures, because what people want to be consistent with differs in these cultures.

Successful Ads in Different Cultures When advertisements for the U.S. military tempt recruits by challenging them to become "All that you can be" and when ads for L'Oreal cosmetics urge women to ignore the products' high prices because "You're worth it," they are appealing to a type of personal self-enhancement that would seem foreign to many people in non-Western cultures. That is so because, as we first discussed in chapter 2, in North America and Western Europe, the prevailing sense of self is different from that of much of the rest of the world. Primarily, it involves the individual, the single person; hence, it is this individualized version of the self that is enhanced or protected by attitude and belief change.

In many other cultures, however, the prevailing conception of the self is not so narrow. Rather, it is a collective self, expanded to include one's group (Markus & Kitayama, 1991; Triandis, 1989). For citizens of these cultures, performing an act that doesn't fit with a personal belief doesn't necessarily threaten the most important (collective) conception of self. Consequently, such personal inconsistencies may not be especially motivating. This may explain why residents of Eastern communal cultures appear to show traditional dissonance effects much less often than do Westerners: Traditional dissonance procedures typically engage only the individualized self (Heine & Lehman, 1997).

This is not to say that citizens of communal societies fail to enhance or protect important aspects of themselves through attitude and belief change. However, the emphasis is on the collective version of self. For example, a message should be more effective in a communal society if it promises group rather than personal enhancement. But the opposite should be true in an individualistic society. To test this reasoning, Sang-Pil

I am the one. We are the world. *Ads like that on the left, which connect to an individualized sense of self, are more successful in the United States. Ads like that on the right, which connect to a collective sense of self, are more successful in Korea.*

Han and Sharon Shavitt (1994) examined advertisements in two nations characterized by either an individualized or a collective sense of self—the United States and Korea, respectively. First, they evaluated the advertisements that appeared in popular U.S. and Korean magazines over a two-year period. They found that in Korea, the ads appealed more to group and family benefits and harmony, whereas in the United States, they appealed more to individual benefits, success, and preferences.

But, just because advertisers in the two cultures use different kinds of appeals, does that mean that they work as intended? To answer this question, Han and Shavitt conducted a second study. They created ads for products (for instance, chewing gum) that emphasized either personal or group benefits ("Treat yourself to a breath-freshening experience" versus "Share a breath-freshening experience"). Next, they showed the ads to potential consumers of the products in Korea and the United States and asked for reactions. In Korea, people were more positive toward the ad, the product, and a purchase when the ad focused on group gain; in the United States, the reverse occurred (see Figure 5.8). Thus, ads that emphasized advantages to the group or to the individual were more successful when the emphasis matched and promoted the culture's predominant version of self.

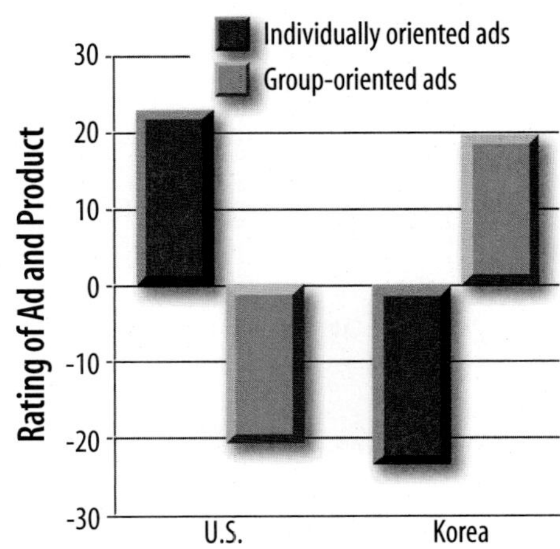

Figure 5.8
Selling the self in two cultures.

Citizens of the United States and of Korea rated magazine advertisements that emphasized the achievement of either personal or group goals. In the United States, where an individualized sense of self predominates, raters had more favorable reactions to ads appealing to individual benefits. But in Korea, where a collective sense of self predominates, the group-oriented ads were better received.

SOURCE: *Adapted from Han & Shavitt, 1994.*

Summary

According to balance theory and dissonance theory, when most people experience an inconsistency within their attitudes, beliefs, or actions, they feel unpleasant arousal, which motivates them to reduce the inconsistency. An inconsistent action is most likely to bring about attitude change when it is freely chosen, incongruent with an important aspect of the self, difficult to change, and not easily justified as due to strong external pressures such as rewards, punishments, or requirements. In addition, the action is especially likely to create change when it produces negative and foreseeable consequences. People don't experience the desire for consistency equally. In fact, a measure of preference for consistency indicates that some individuals prefer to be inconsistent. Finally, people around the world seem more receptive to messages consistent with their culture's prevailing view of self.

Gaining Social Approval

If you learned that a close friend was offended by your opinion on gun control, would you consider changing your position somewhat? People sometimes shift their positions to gain approval from those around them. Holding the right position can project a public image that opens doors to desired social exchanges, whereas holding the wrong position can lead to social rejection. The motivation to achieve approval is called **impression motivation,** because its goal is to make a good impression on others (Chaiken et al., 1989; Chaiken, Giner-Sorolla, & Chen, 1996). This tendency can sometimes conflict with the pursuit of the other two persuasion-related goals we have discussed—those of accuracy and consistency. Let's explore which features of the person and situation tend to make the third goal, social approval, rise above the others.

What Affects the Desire for Social Approval?

Self-Monitoring If social gains motivate attitude change, we might expect those who are most attuned to relationships and interpersonal settings to change their attitudes most in response to such rewards.

Certain individuals are especially adaptable in their opinions as they move from situation to situation. Like attitudinal chameleons, they are able to adjust their "colors" to those that are favored in each new environment. As we discussed in chapter 4, these individuals are called high self-monitors because they constantly monitor and modify their public selves (how others see them) to fit what is socially appropriate (Snyder, 1987). In contrast, low self-monitors are much more likely to rely on their own standards in deciding how to respond in a new situation. Thus high self-monitors are more motivated by the social approval goal than are low self-monitors, who are more motivated by the consistency goal (DeBono, 1987).

If high self-monitors are especially sensitive to what others think of them, might they be especially susceptible to advertising that promises a desired image in the eyes of others? That is what one study found. High self-monitors were more persuaded by ads that promoted socially appealing images (prestige, sophistication) associated with particular brands of coffee, whiskey, and cigarettes than they were by ads touting the quality of the same brands (Snyder & DeBono, 1985). In sum, high self-monitors, who pay special attention to the social rewards of the situations they enter, pay special attention to persuasive arguments that show them how to maximize those social rewards.

Gender: Women, Men, and Persuasion Like high self-monitors, women tend to be sensitively attuned to relationships and interpersonal issues. This sensitivity affects the way they respond to persuasive appeals. When Wendy Wood and Brian Stagner

(1994) examined the research investigating differences in persuadability between men and women, they reported a surprising conclusion: Women seem to be more readily influenced than men. What might account for this tendency in women? One hint comes from evidence that the tendency is strongest in group pressure contexts, in which a person's position is out of line with those of the rest of the group. Under these conditions, women are most likely to yield to influence attempts (Eagly & Carli, 1981). An even more instructive insight comes from work showing that if others in the situation cannot observe whether change has taken place, women don't change any more than men (Eagly & Chrvala, 1986; Eagly, Wood, & Fishbaugh, 1981). Thus, you shouldn't expect your letter concerning highway speed limits to generate more change in women, as there is no evidence that women are more persuaded than men under private circumstances.

Why would the presence and surveillance of others in the situation affect women's willingness to agree? Wood and Stagner think the reason lies in the approved gender role for women in most societies. In social contexts, it often falls to women to cultivate positive relationships, to build interpersonal bridges, and to assure social harmony—all of which can be accomplished by shifting toward agreement. To do less is to risk the social disapproval that goes with failing to live up to societal expectations. After all, if women are expected to perform the vital task of fostering cohesiveness and consensus, they are likely to be rewarded for finding ways to agree rather than disagree, especially in social contexts (Carli, 1989; Stiles et al., 1997).

Social scientists have noted that this tendency for women to try to build and maintain connections in their important groups is reflected in the language they use to respond to the statements of disagreeing others (Tannen, 1990). In contrast to men, who are more direct in staking out a position ("that's the opposite of my view"), women respond with more questions and bridging phrases ("that's interesting"), which allow them to stimulate more discussion and find opportunities for accord. In the view of most of these scientists, the linguistic differences flow from the distinct gender roles approved for men and women. These contrasting roles can lead to contrasting views of the world. According to Tannen (1990), life for men is a *contest* in which one struggles to preserve independence. For women, on the other hand, it is a *community* in which one struggles to preserve harmony. It should be no surprise, then, that in a man's search for independence he would be more likely to disagree, whereas in a woman's search for harmony, she would be more likely to agree.

The Role of the Audience If people sometimes allow themselves to be persuaded in order to gain the acceptance of others, it follows that they ought to change in ways that they think those others would approve (Tetlock, Skitka, & Boettger, 1989). What would you think of the intelligence of someone who was easily persuaded to your position? The answer depends on who had done the persuading. If you had delivered the argument, you would assign greater intelligence to anyone who could so quickly see the "wisdom" of your point of view. But if you had only witnessed the other readily persuaded to your position, you would assign less intelligence to anyone who could be so easily "sold." Do people understand that persuaders elevate but observers diminish the intelligence of an easily persuaded other? A study by Sanford Braver and his coworkers (1977) showed that indeed they do; in addition, they use this information to gain others' respect.

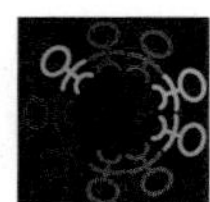

College students heard a persuasive message from another student on the topic of shortening the number of years of medical training for doctors. They were then asked to say aloud whether and how much they had changed their opinions due to the message. For one set of students, this opportunity occurred in the sole presence of the persuader. For a second set, it occurred in the sole presence of an observer. A third set stated their positions in front of both the persuader and the observer. Just as would be expected if people shift their positions to garner the respect of those around them, those students reporting to the persuader alone announced the most

Impression motivation *The motivation to achieve approval by making a good impression on others.*

change, whereas those reporting to the observer alone announced the least change. Moreover, when the students recorded their opinions later, this time anonymously, they showed the same pattern as in their public statements. Thus, not only do people alter their positions tactically to gain esteem and approval from others, but also those tactical shifts can sometimes create genuine attitude change.

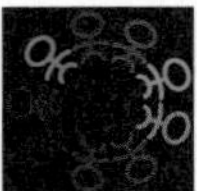

The Expectation of Discussion Earlier, we reviewed research showing that when an issue is personally relevant, people think hard about it and are persuaded only by messages containing strong arguments (Petty & Cacioppo, 1984, 1986). These tendencies reflect the desire for accuracy in one's opinions: If an issue affects you personally, you will want to change your position only if provided with good reasons. Persuasion researchers Michael Leippe and Roger Elkin (1987) wondered what would happen if they pitted this accuracy goal against the goal of gaining social approval.

To find out, they gave Adelphi University undergraduates a communication arguing for the implementation of comprehensive exams at their school in the next year. Half heard strong arguments and half heard weak arguments in the message. Just as had been found in prior research, these personally involved students thought deeply about the message arguments and were much more persuaded when its arguments were strong versus weak. Other subjects in the study were treated similarly except for one difference: They were told that, after hearing the message, they would have to *discuss* their views on the topic with another student whose position was unknown. With this difference, the researchers introduced another consideration to their subjects. Not only did they have to be concerned about the accuracy of their opinions but also they had to consider the impression their opinions would make on their future discussion partner. Among these subjects, the strength of the message arguments made much less of a difference in determining their attitudes. Rather than changing a lot when the arguments were strong and very little when they were weak, these subjects chose to hold moderate opinions no matter which arguments they heard.

Why would expecting to discuss a topic lead people to become more moderate in their views? The middle position on an issue offers a pair of advantages to someone concerned about making a good impression. By seizing the middle, one not only gets to appear broadminded, a socially desirable trait, one gets to hold an especially flexible and defensible position in the upcoming exchange. From the center, one can use arguments on both sides of the issue—without the appearance of inconsistency—to counter any attacks from the other discussant; this reduces the chance of an embarrassing discussion performance, especially when the other's position is unknown (Snyder & Swann, 1976; Tetlock, 1983).

When do these admissions of persuasion reflect actual changes in attitude? It appears that opinion shifts designed to create a good impression on another can become lasting when the process of shifting causes people to think about the topic in a different way than before—for example, by taking the perspective on the topic of the person one is trying to impress. If, instead, the shifts don't cause people to think differently or deeply about the issues, the changes don't last, and people "snap back" to their original positions as soon as they think they don't have to impress anyone any longer (Cialdini, Levy, Herman, Kozlowski, & Petty, 1976; McFarland, Ross, & Conway, 1984).

As we have seen, the goal of social approval becomes more relevant when people expect to have to discuss their views with another. However, this expectation does not have equally powerful effects in all people and all situations. In the next section, we see how it interacts with other factors to alter persuasion.

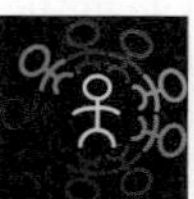

Self-Monitoring and Expectation of Discussion Earlier, we differentiated high self-monitors, who focus on the goal of social approval in deciding when to be persuaded, from low self-monitors, who focus more on the goal of self-consistency. One team of researchers (Chen, Schechter, & Chaiken, 1996) reasoned that it should be the approval-oriented, high self-monitors whose attitudes would be most affected by the expectation of discussion. In an experiment testing this reasoning, subjects received a communication arguing that the media should reduce its coverage of terrorist hijackings. Half expected that, after reading the communication, they would have to discuss their views on the topic with another subject whose opinion was unknown. The other half also read the communication but anticipated no subsequent discussion. As predicted, only the high self-monitoring subjects were influenced by the expectation of discussion, becoming significantly more moderate in their positions when they thought they would have to defend those positions. Thus, making approval relevant to the persuasion situation influenced the attitudes of just those individuals who act primarily to achieve the social approval goal.

The Other's Position and Expectation of Discussion In a second study, these same researchers asked a related question: What would happen to the attitudes of social approval–oriented people who expected a discussion not with someone whose position was unknown but with someone whose position they *did* know? The researchers predicted that, under these conditions, such individuals would not have to move toward the center (in an attempt to defend a position ably) but could gain their discussion partner's approval by moving toward his or her known position. In this study, subjects were oriented toward the approval goal or the accuracy goal by first reading a series of essays that emphasized the importance of being accepted or of being accurate. All subjects expected to discuss the topic of whether the media should be allowed to broadcast election returns before all votes were in. Half thought that their discussion partner strongly favored the idea and half thought their partner strongly opposed it. The finding: Only those who had been oriented toward others' acceptance moved their attitudes to conform to their discussion partner's; those who had been oriented toward accuracy ignored their partner's position in deciding their own positions on the topic.

In these two studies, we see that individuals oriented toward social approval adjusted their attitudes prior to a discussion (in which social approval would be relevant) but that individuals oriented toward either the goals of consistency or accuracy were not much influenced by this opportunity to manage others' impressions. Here we see more evidence of a striking feature of human behavior that we have discussed before: The goal most likely to guide a person's actions in a situation is not necessarily the most potent or productive. It's the one that is most prominent in the person's mind at the time.

Our consideration of the impact of the desire for approval on attitude change provides yet another way to understand Peter Reilly's baseless confession. At the time he made it, he had a strong respect for the police (hoping himself to become an officer someday), had just lost his only family, and had been informed, falsely, that his friends had expressed no interest in his well-being—all of which were likely to make him crave the approval of those in that room. Tragically for Reilly, they were his persuaders, and the one sure way to gain their approval was to agree with them.

Summary

The desire for social approval influences willingness to change. Two social approval–related aspects of the person can affect persuasion. The first is the personal trait of self-monitoring. High self-monitors are more attuned to interpersonal rewards such as those that come from holding socially appropriate or admired attitudes. As a result, they are more likely to be influenced by advertisements that emphasize socially appealing images. Women, too, seem more responsive to interpersonal considerations in changing their attitudes, but not for reasons of image. Rather, the feminine gender role assigns them the task of creating social cohesion, which they can often accomplish by finding ways to agree, especially in groups.

Two features of the situation also affect persuasion through their impact on the desire for social acceptance. First, the nature of the audience to whom one reports persuasion influences the amount of persuasion reported; the most occurs when reported to a persuader and the least when reported to an observer. These reports of persuasion can actually reflect true attitude change when, in the process of shifting a position, one is inspired to think differently or more deeply about the issue. Second, when one expects to discuss a topic after receiving a persuasive message, the social appropriateness of one's position becomes more relevant, and people are more likely to change to gain social approval. Both of these tendencies are amplified when the goal of social approval is salient. Table 5.2 provides an overall summary of the factors influencing the persuasion goals of accuracy, consistency, and social approval.

CHAPTER 5
Summary Table

Table 5.2 Summary of the goals served by persuasion and the factors related to them.

Goal	The Person	The Situation	Interactions
Seeking Accuracy	• Issue Involvement • Mood • Suggestibility	• Done Deals • Unwelcome Information	• One component of credibility is expertise. When striving for accuracy, people rely on the expertise of a communicator principally when the message is highly complex. • A second component of credibility is trustworthiness. Those who characteristically rely on it as a guide to accuracy are low in need for cognition.
Being Consistent	• Arousal • Preference for Consistency	• Consequences • Salience	• People are more likely to be persuaded by messages that are consistent with the predominant sense of self in their culture.
Gaining Social Approval	• Self-Monitoring • Gender	• Role of the Audience • Expectation of Discussion	• High self-monitors (who pay more attention to social rewards) shift their attitudes and beliefs more than do low self-monitors when expecting a discussion. • People who have been reminded of the importance of social approval shift their attitudes and beliefs more when expecting a discussion.

REVISITING

The Story of Peter Reilly

When Peter Reilly was interviewed about his life twenty years after the murder, much damage was still evident. At thirty-eight, he was disillusioned, divorced, unemployed, and recently back in Connecticut after bouncing through a series of low-paying jobs in other states (O'Brien, 1993). At the end of that interview, Reilly revealed what it was about the entire affair that most puzzled and distressed him.

Interestingly, it was not the puzzle of how he could be persuaded to confess falsely to a murder. Comments he made at a conference two years later demonstrated that he understood quite well how it could and did happen:

> To be kept awake for many hours, confused, fatigued, shocked that your only family was gone, in a strange and imposing place, surrounded by police who continue to tell you that you must have done this horrible thing and that nobody cares or has asked about you,...assured by authorities you don't remember things, being led to doubt your own memory, having things suggested to you only to have those things pop up in a conversation a short time later but from your own lips...under these conditions you would say and sign anything they wanted. (Reilly, 1995, p. 93)

If Peter was aware of precisely how he was led to confess, what was the mystery that still confounded him twenty years after the fact? It was the puzzle of why the police had never changed their minds about him. Despite strong evidence of his innocence, those who extracted his admission of guilt and who used it to convict and imprison him still believed it, insisting that, "The subsequent reinvestigation did nothing to change the fact [of Reilly's guilt] as far as we are concerned" (Connery, 1995, p. 92).

Why haven't the police and prosecutors in the case been swayed by the uncovered evidence pointing clearly to Reilly's innocence? Consider the intense cognitive dissonance they would feel if they permitted themselves to believe that they had trapped, convicted, and imprisoned an innocent boy who never fully recovered from the ordeal, while the real killer roamed free. Because that belief would be so inconsistent with the central conception of themselves as champions of fairness and justice, it makes sense that they would deny validity to the idea and to any evidence that supported it. To do otherwise would invite heavy psychological costs.

Does psychological self-protection really explain the inflexibility of these individuals? Perhaps any police official or prosecutor looking at the totality of the evidence would judge Reilly guilty. However, that possibility does not fit with the answer to the last mystery we will consider in the Reilly case: How did information hidden for years in the chief prosecutor's files surface to exonerate Reilly after the verdict? Death led to Reilly's rebirth. The prosecutor died of a heart attack, and his successor (who had not been involved in the conviction) came across some startling evidence in the case files—eyewitness reports of two people, including an off-duty state trooper, placing Reilly in another location at the time of the crime. He quickly recognized the need to serve justice by disclosing the evidence and freeing Reilly.

Indeed, every court officer who has seen the evidence and who was not part of the prosecution team decided similarly. It is telling that those officials who were in some way responsible for the harm to Reilly remain adamant that the evidence implicates him. But those looking at the same evidence and having no personal responsibility for past harm see things very differently.

Peter the wiser. *At a conference more than twenty years after his interrogation, Peter Reilly demonstrated that he understood very well how the police once persuaded him of his guilt. But he's never understood why they won't concede their error. If Peter asked you for help in resolving this question, what would you tell him?*

What can we think about the motives of the first prosecutor? By all accounts, he believed fervently in Reilly's guilt until the day he died, sure that he was acting fairly and righteously (Connery, 1977). He no doubt dismissed the critical evidence as unreliable and a hindrance to true justice. And what should we say about the character of the other officials involved who have committed and recommitted themselves to their initial positions in the face of contrary information? If terms such as *immoral* or *malevolent* don't seem appropriate, what label would best apply? We can offer a suggestion: *Human.*

CHAPTER 5

Summary

What Is Persuasion?

1. Persuasion is a change in a private attitude or belief resulting from the receipt of a message.
2. Strongly held attitudes are resistant to persuasion because of two properties: commitment and embeddedness.
3. Researchers use two methods to try to measure persuasion in a nonreactive manner: covert measures and after-only designs.
4. According to the cognitive response model, the most direct determinant of persuasion is not the persuasive message itself but what the recipient says to him- or herself in response (self-talk).
5. Dual process models of persuasion recognize that attitude change can occur through either deep or superficial processing of the message arguments.
6. Recipients of a message process it deeply when they have both the motivation and the ability to do so; otherwise they process it superficially.

Seeking Accuracy

1. Most of the time, people want to hold accurate attitudes and beliefs. One way to achieve this goal is to process persuasive messages deeply, thinking carefully about the arguments. However, a second path to this goal is a superficial route in which recipients use shortcut evidence of accuracy.
2. Three sources of shortcut evidence are credible communicators, the responses of others to the message, and ready ideas.
3. People are more motivated to be accurate in their views when the issue involves them personally and when they are in a sad mood.
4. When striving for accuracy, suggestible individuals are particularly likely to accept persuasive messages because they trust others' views more than their own.
5. People most want to hold accurate attitudes and beliefs before a decision. After the decision is made, they may prefer to be biased in favor of their choice.
6. Sometimes people resist information because it conflicts with what they prefer to believe. When individuals take this to an extreme by denying the validity of threatening information, they put themselves at risk.
7. People are most likely to use communicator credibility as a shortcut to accuracy when the communication is complex or their need for cognition is low.

Being Consistent

1. According to the consistency principle, we are motivated toward cognitive consistency and will change our attitudes and beliefs to have it.
2. Heider's balance theory and Festinger's dissonance theory both propose that inconsistency produces an uncomfortable tension that pushes people to reduce the inconsistency.
3. Heider asserted that individuals want to experience balance in their cognitive systems and will change their attitudes and opinions to keep the systems in harmony.
4. According to Festinger, inconsistencies on important issues lead to dissonance (a state of uncomfortable psychological arousal). Research has shown that dissonance is most likely to occur when a counterattitudinal action conflicts with an important aspect of the self, is viewed as freely chosen, cannot be justified as due to strong rewards or threats, cannot be withdrawn, and produces negative consequences that were foreseeable.
5. Not everyone desires consistency. In fact, those who have a low preference for consistency try to avoid it.

Gaining Social Approval

1. People sometimes change their attitudes and beliefs to gain approval.
2. High self-monitors are focused on making a good impression; consequently, they are more likely to be persuaded by advertisements that promise a desirable image in the eyes of others.
3. Women, too, seem more responsive to interpersonal considerations in changing their positions, but not for reasons of image. Instead, the feminine gender role assigns them the task of creating social

harmony, which they can often accomplish by finding ways to agree, especially in groups.

4. The nature of the audience influences how much change people report after receiving a persuasive message. The most change is reported in the sole presence of a persuader, and the least in the sole presence of an observer.
5. When expecting to have to discuss one's position on an issue, individuals move toward the center if the position of their discussion-partner is unknown; if it is known, they move toward the partner's position. These tactical shifts, designed to achieve social approval, can lead to genuine, lasting attitude change when the shifts cause people to think differently or more deeply about the issue than before.
6. When the goal of social approval is salient, people are more likely to use attitude and belief change to achieve it rather than to achieve the goals of accuracy or consistency.

CHAPTER 5
Key Terms

Balance Theory *Heider's theory that people prefer harmony and consistency in their views of the world.*

Cognitive response model *A theory that locates the most direct cause of persuasion in the self-talk of the persuasion target.*

Consistency principle *The principle that people will change their attitudes, beliefs, perceptions, and actions to make them consistent with each other.*

Counterargument *An argument that challenges and opposes other arguments.*

Counterattitudinal action *A behavior that is inconsistent with an existing attitude.*

Cognitive dissonance *The unpleasant state of psychological arousal resulting from an inconsistency within one's important attitudes, beliefs, or behaviors.*

Dual process model of persuasion *A model that accounts for the two basic ways that attitude change occurs—with and without much thought.*

Elaboration likelihood model *A model of persuasive communication that holds that there are two ways attitude change can take place—deeply or superficially.*

Heuristic–systematic model *A model of persuasive communication that holds that there are two ways attitude change can take place—the message recipient uses heuristic shortcuts or processes information systematically.*

Impression motivation *The motivation to achieve approval by making a good impression on others.*

Inoculation procedure *A technique for increasing individuals' resistance to a strong argument by first giving them weak, easily defeated versions of it.*

Need for cognition *The tendency to enjoy and engage in deliberative thought.*

Nonreactive measurement *Measurement that does not change a subject's responses while recording them.*

Persuasion *Change in a private attitude or belief as a result of receiving a message.*

Postdecisional dissonance *The conflict one feels about a decision that could possibly be wrong.*

CHAPTER 6
Social Influence: Conformity, Compliance, and Obedience

The Extraordinary Turnaround (and Around) of Steve Hassan

Steve Hassan claims that a high-speed collision with a semitrailer truck battered, hospitalized, nearly killed...and saved him.

At the time, Hassan was a member of the Unification Church—an organization better known as the Moonies—whose leader is the Reverend Sun Myung Moon. Although critics describe Moon as a multimillionaire Korean businessman intent on creating a religious cult to enrich and empower himself and his family, his followers consider him the new Messiah whose mission is to establish a kingdom of God on Earth. As Hassan drove headlong toward the collision that would shatter and "save" him, he was one of Reverend Moon's most fervent followers.

It hadn't always been so. Barely two years earlier, he was a normal nineteen-year-old college student who had never heard of the Moonies. His parents, a hardware store owner and a junior high school teacher, had provided a supportive, loving

Wedding masses. *By the time this mass wedding of Moon followers occurred in Madison Square Garden, Steve Hassan was no longer in the organization. Otherwise, he may have been part of this 2,075-couple ceremony, dutifully encountering his bride for the first time.*

home life and middle-class upbringing. Although not intensely religious, he participated regularly in his Jewish faith along with his family. He was doing well in school, loved to read, and intended to become a teacher and writer after graduation. Despite a desire to improve the world, he was neither obsessed with the idea nor depressed by an inability to make a big difference. In all, there seemed little about him to predict the startling turnaround he would soon make.

After a breakup with his girlfriend left him feeling lonely, things changed quickly. Hassan was approached on campus by three attractive young women who invited him to a discussion group—dinner made up of young people like himself. He agreed, and in the course of a few days was recruited, indoctrinated, and inducted into Moon's organization.

Over the next two years, he became wholly dedicated to the group and to his role in it—so dedicated that he moved in with the Moonies, turned over his bank account to them, and renounced all sexual relations until his marriage, which would occur only at a time and to a woman (possibly a stranger to him) chosen by Reverend Moon. He broke off contact with his family and quit school to work full time raising funds for the organization by selling candles, mints, and flowers on the streets. He allowed himself to be relocated to distant cities, where he labored without pay for long periods on three to four hours of sleep a night. He never informed his parents or former friends of his whereabouts because he had come to see them, like most other outsiders, as carriers of Satan's message. The work itself was tedious, arduous, and dangerous: Twice, he fought and escaped armed robbers on dark city streets rather than give up the night's proceeds—because, as he explained, "I would never let anyone steal God's money" (Hassan, 1990, p. 24).

Ironically, Hassan's devotion to the Unification organization led to his separation from it. Exhausted from forty-eight hours of nonstop efforts, he fell asleep at the wheel of the Moonie-owned van he was driving to his next task. After crashing into an eighteen-wheel truck, he was pinned in the wreckage for nearly an hour while rescue crews struggled to free him. Through the searing pain, he still thought only of his shame at failing his mission. Chanting over and over, "Father, forgive me," he blamed himself and worried about the effect of the crash on the group's finances. But a delayed—and revolutionary—reaction to the accident was about to occur.

Following extensive surgery and a week in the hospital, he was released to visit his sister's home, where he encountered his father and several strangers who said they wanted to discuss his association with the Unification Church. From the start, Hassan knew that the strangers were "deprogrammers" retained by his family to convince him to desert the Messiah. He resisted fiercely. In one harrowing incident, while being driven to an apartment where the deprogramming would take place, he considered reaching over and snapping his father's neck, thinking it better to kill the father who had raised him than to betray the one who had inspired him. Hassan decided against this course of action only because he was sure he could never be moved from his new father's side.

He was entirely mistaken. Within days, he had rejected Moonie doctrine, expressing deep embarrassment that he had embraced it so completely. He felt bewildered that he had been willing to give up everything—faith, family, and future—to a wealthy businessman who claimed to be the new Messiah. Hassan's turnabout is now complete. Today, he is an active opponent of the Unification movement, making his living counseling families on how to help their loved ones escape the control of the Moonies and similar groups. How could Steve Hassan have been so quickly influenced to join and devote himself to this strange religious sect? And, after years of escalating commitment, how was he just as quickly influenced to abandon his deep personal investment in it?

The answers to both puzzles lie in the same set of psychological principles. They are the principles of social influence that we consider in this chapter. **Social influence** can be defined as a change in behavior caused by real or imagined pressure from others. Defining influence as a change in behavior distinguishes it from *persuasion*, which, as we discussed in chapter 5, refers to a change in private attitudes and beliefs and which may not necessarily lead to behavior change.

The most effective social influence attempts succeed in changing a person's attitudes and behavior, as in Steve Hassan's experience with the Moonies. But shifting someone's attitude isn't necessary for social influence to occur; all that's required is behavior change. For example, a pair of your friends might influence you to come with them to a particular movie without even trying to persuade you that the movie is one you'll enjoy. Instead, they might make you feel obligated to comply simply by pointing out that you chose the movie last week. Although a feeling of obligation is a powerful tool of social influence (Howard, 1995), it's hardly the only one. We will encounter many equally powerful tools in the process of examining, first, the major categories of social influence (conformity, compliance, and obedience) and, next, the major goals of social influence (choosing correctly, gaining social approval, and managing self-image).

Categories of Social Influence: Conformity, Compliance, and Obedience

Social psychologists have considered three major categories of social influence: conformity, compliance, and obedience. The amount of overt social pressure associated with these categories escalates as one moves from conformity to compliance and, finally, to obedience. **Conformity** involves changing one's behavior to match the responses or actions of others, to fit in with those around us. Before a party or concert, you might ask, "What will people be wearing?" Imagine showing up in shorts and a T-shirt when everyone else is wearing formal clothing, or imagine appearing in formal wear when everyone else is dressed casually. The discomfort most of us would feel in such situations gives you some sense of the strength of the desire to fit in. Conformity can occur without overt social pressure; no one may ever have to take you aside to say, "You're dressed inappropriately," but you may still voluntarily leave to change into an outfit that looks less out of place.

Compliance refers to the act of changing one's behavior in response to a direct request. The request may come from sources as distinct as friends ("C'mon, have a beer and forget your studying!"), salespeople ("You should sign now because we can't guarantee this model will be here tomorrow."), charities ("St. Mary's Food Bank needs your contributions to feed the poor this Thanksgiving. Please give."), or panhandlers on the street ("Hey buddy, can you spare $3.75 for a cup of cappucino?"). As in the case of a restroom sign asking you to wash your hands before leaving, the requester need not be physically present to exert pressure to comply.

Obedience is a special type of compliance that involves changing one's behavior in response to a directive from an authority figure. A boss may require employees to work overtime, a military officer may command soldiers to attack the enemy, or a police officer may order drivers to take a detour. In directing others to obey, authority figures typically exert the most overt attempts at influence.

Before considering the factors that motivate us to yield to social influence pressures, let's explore conformity, compliance, and obedience in greater depth by examining a classic piece of research into each process. These pieces of research are noteworthy in that each revealed more impact of social influence than nearly anyone expected and each stimulated a tradition of investigation that continues today (Blass, 2000; Cialdini, 2000; Levine, 1999).

Social influence *A change in overt behavior caused by real or imagined pressure from others.*

Conformity *Behavior change designed to match the actions of others.*

Compliance *Behavior change that occurs as a result of a direct request.*

Obedience *Compliance that occurs in response to a directive from an authority figure.*

Together forever. *Being surrounded by like-minded people can have a powerful effect on interpretations of reality. Members of the Heaven's Gate cult were required to disassociate from all family and friends and to consult only with other group members before making any decision. The group's unanimity led members to accept their leader's belief that a spaceship was coming to "take them to the next level." The group was so united, and thereby confident, in this belief that in March 1997, 39 members committed joint suicide to allow their spirits to board that ship.*

Conformity: Asch's Research on Group Influence

When Steve Hassan joined the Unification organization, he was pressured to separate himself from the dissenting views of his family and friends and he was surrounded constantly by believers, a practice common to many extreme religious sects:

> In many cults people eat together, work together, have group meetings, and sometimes sleep together in the same room. Individualism is discouraged. People may be assigned a constant "buddy" or be placed in a small unit of a half dozen members. (Hassan, 1990, p. 60)

It may be understandable that a group's unanimity might influence something as subjective as a person's religious beliefs. After all, whether Reverend Sun Myung Moon is or is not the Messiah can't be tested with hard data. What seems more remarkable is that group pressure can lead people to conform even when contradictory evidence is right before their eyes. This phenomenon was investigated in a series of experiments conducted by Solomon Asch (1956). Asch was interested not only in the submission of individuals to group forces but also in the capacity of people to act independent of conformity pressures.

To investigate these processes of conformity and independence, Asch asked college students in groups of eight to match the lengths of different lines. A typical line-matching problem is shown in Figure 6.1. The task was not difficult. In the control condition, in which there was no group pressure pushing toward wrong choices, 95 percent of the participants got all of twelve line matches right. For those in the experimental condition, however, the situation changed. They were faced with a social consensus that contradicted their own eyes. Before making their own judgments, they heard five other students (who were actually confederates of the experimenter) unanimously agree on an answer that was clearly wrong. Did they stick to their guns and give the right answers or did they go along with the crowd? As shown in Figure 6.2, only 25 percent of these participants ignored the group's obvious errors and gave only correct answers. The other 75 percent went against the evidence of their senses and conformed to some extent. Although no one went along every single time, one individual conformed on eleven of the twelve choices.

What was going on in the minds of the participants when they heard the whole group make judgments that seemed plainly wrong? One participant, who stayed independent of group pressure, became embarrassed, whispering to a neighbor at one point, "I always disagree, darn it." When the experiment was over and he was asked whether he thought the entire group was wrong, he turned to them and said,

Figure 6.1 Asch's line-judging task.

In Asch's conformity studies, subjects were shown a standard line like that on the left and three comparison lines like those on the right. Their task was to choose the comparison line that matched the length of the standard line. It was an easy task—until the other group members began choosing incorrectly.

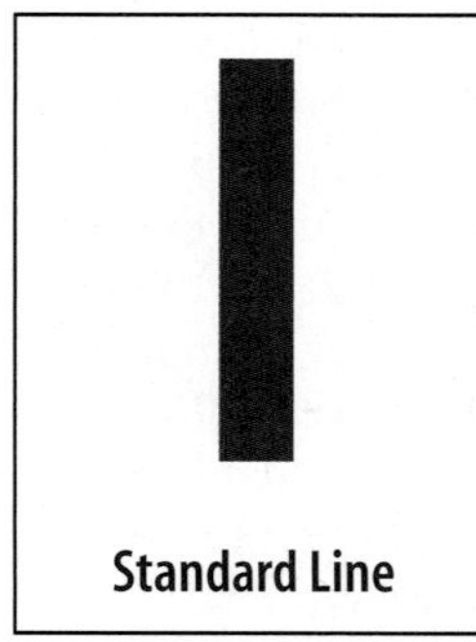

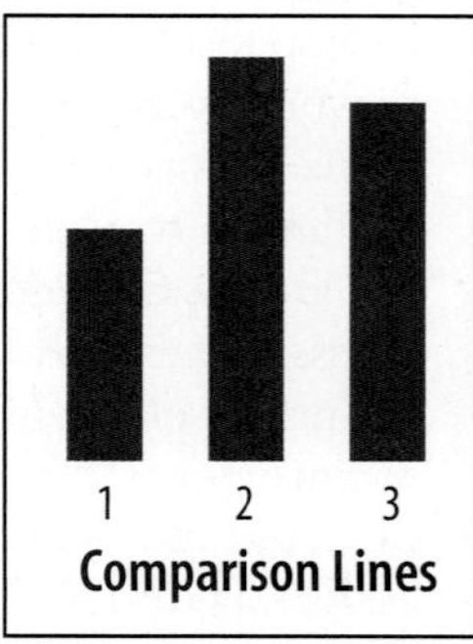

"You're *probably* right, but you *may* be wrong!" He was "exultant and relieved" when the true nature of the experiment was disclosed to him. Although he hadn't buckled under group pressure, even he had been led to doubt his own judgment. The participant who conformed eleven out of twelve times (more than any other participant) claimed later that he was swayed by the seeming confidence of the other group members. He said he actually came to believe that they were right, thinking that he alone had fallen victim to some sort of "illusion." Asch's research demonstrated that people faced with strong group consensus sometimes go along even though they think the others may be wrong. In addition, they sometimes believe that the others are right, doubting the evidence of their own senses if the members of their group seem confident enough.

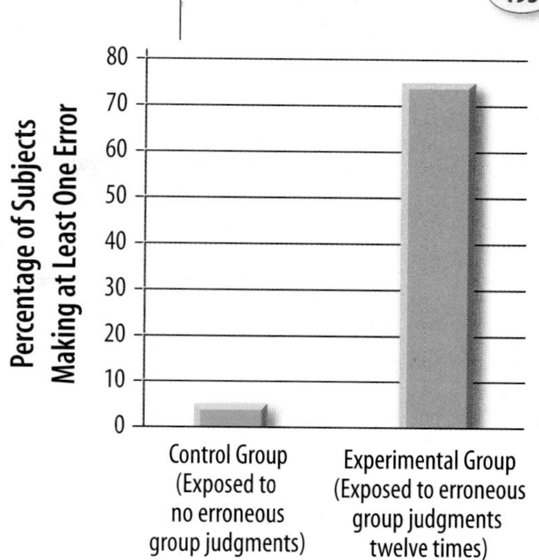

Figure 6.2
Effects of incorrect group judgments on conformity.

Subjects estimated the length of lines either after the other group members had made no errors in their own estimates (control group) or after the other group members had all judged the line lengths incorrectly (experimental group). Only 5 percent of control group subjects made any errors. But 75 percent of experimental group subjects made at least one mistake.

SOURCE: *Adapted from Asch, 1956.*

Asch obtained his results among students who were strangers convened for a short experiment. Think how much more potent the social pressure might be when those confident others are members of one's own circle, whose goodwill is treasured. And imagine how much more potent the pressure might become within groups like religious cults, in which the members are often taught to suppress their individuality and are counseled daily on the importance of blind faith in the group's beliefs. Two months before the Heaven's Gate commune members committed suicide in 1997, they spent several thousand dollars for a high-powered telescope because they had heard rumors about a small object (which they suspected was a spaceship) that appeared to be trailing the Hale-Bopp comet. When they complained to the salesman that the telescope showed them no trace of the mysterious object, he explained that there never was a trailing object, only a rumor based on a blip of static in one very early and poor-quality image of the comet. How did they respond to this direct evidence against their group's unanimous and firmly held beliefs about a spaceship carrying their extraterrestrial contacts? They decided to continue believing in the spaceship's

Say what? *The only true subject (#6) assesses for himself the length of lines (top) and reacts with puzzlement and dismay when other group members answer incorrectly (bottom).*

existence but to stop looking at the evidence: They turned in the telescope for a refund (Ferris, 1997).

Compliance: The "Foot-in-the-Door" Technique

It seems unlikely that a recruiter for the Unification Church would have had much success if he had walked up to Steve Hassan on campus and asked, "How would you like to drop out of school, break off all ties to your family, and dedicate yourself entirely to collecting money for a cultlike group led by a Korean multimillionaire?" Hassan was recruited through an approach much more subtle than that. First, he was invited to meet a group of other young people interested in "combating social problems." Next, he was invited to what he was told was a weekend workshop, only to learn later that it went on for three days. Following the more intense recruiting efforts at the workshop, he was urged to attend another workshop, and later—in lock-step order—he was encouraged to become a full member, live in the church house, and donate his bank account to the Church. This approach—starting with a small request and advancing to larger requests—is the basis of a commonly used compliance technique called the **foot-in-the-door technique**.

The term *foot-in-the-door* refers to door-to-door salespeople getting one foot in the door as a way to gain full entry. The psychological underpinnings of this technique were investigated in a clever series of experiments by Jonathan Freedman and Scott Fraser (1966). To address their question, "How can a person be induced to do something he would rather not do?" Freedman and Fraser left the laboratory to conduct field experiments.

In one experiment, 156 housewives in Palo Alto, California, were called on the phone and asked to do something the researchers guessed that most people would rather not do: allow a team of six men from a consumer group to come into their home for two hours "to enumerate and classify all the household products you have." The women were told that the men would need full freedom to go through the house exploring cupboards and storage spaces. Few women (only 22 percent) complied if this was all they were asked. However, another group of women was contacted twice, once with a small request designed simply to get a "foot in the door"—they were asked to answer a series of eight questions about household soaps (such as "What brand of soap do you use in your kitchen sink?"). It was such a minor favor that nearly everyone agreed. Three days later, these women were contacted by the same consumer group, but now with the larger, home-visit request. Under these circumstances, 52 percent of the women agreed to allow the team of men to rummage through their cupboards and closets for two hours.

So, agreeing to something as innocent sounding as answering an eight-question survey may have a big impact on your later willingness to make larger and larger commitments to the same cause. Freedman and Fraser noted that a similar "start small and build" approach was used on U.S. prisoners of war captured by the Chinese in the early 1950s during the Korean War. A prisoner might first be asked to make anti-American statements so minor as to seem inconsequential, such as "The United States is not perfect." Once a prisoner agreed, he might be asked by an interrogator to elaborate on why the United States is not perfect, then later to make a list of the "problems with America" he had identified and to sign it. The Chinese might then use his statement in an anti-American radio broadcast, and the prisoner would come to label himself as a "collaborator" and to act in ways consistent with this label (Schein, 1956).

Foot-in-the-door technique *A technique that increases compliance with a large request by first getting compliance with a smaller, related request.*

Can people be influenced like this in everyday life? And how can social psychologists find out? Most of social psychology's knowledge of human behavior comes from controlled laboratory experiments, which offer an excellent way to understand the *causes* of that behavior (see chapter 1). But these experiments have their drawbacks. For instance, laboratories are artificial settings where responding might not occur as it would in daily life. Therefore, social scientists sometimes employ other methods that are better able to capture behavior as it normally takes place. One such method is the field experiment, in which researchers perform controlled experimentation in naturally occurring settings, as Freedman and Fraser did to study the foot-in-the-door tactic. A second method doesn't require controlled experimentation at all. Instead it involves the careful observation of people as they act and interact in natural situations.

FOCUS ON Method

Participant Observation

Suppose you had a friend who was a terrific salesperson, better than anyone else in the clothing store where she worked. To learn what she did to get people to buy, you could follow along one day to watch her operate. By systematically observing what she did to make sales, you might well increase your understanding of the social influence process.

But what if you were interested in how the social influence process worked beyond clothing sales in that particular shop? What if you were interested in why people comply with requests in general, ranging from requests to vote for a certain candidate to requests to contribute to a certain charity? Under these circumstances, you'd have a problem because you'd be unlikely to have friends in each of these compliance professions willing to let you watch and record their most effective techniques.

A few years ago, this was the dilemma facing one of your textbook authors, Robert Cialdini. He was interested in the reasons people comply with requests of all sorts. Furthermore, he thought that studying the tactics of a wide variety of *successful* "compliance pros" would be especially instructive because these individuals have learned what makes people say yes to requests—otherwise, they wouldn't be successful. But he recognized that few influence practitioners would want him tagging along to record their secrets and perhaps interfere with their effectiveness. To resolve his dilemma, Cialdini engaged in a distinct type of systematic natural observation: **participant observation.** Rather than simply watching from the side, the participant observer becomes an internal spy of sorts. Often with disguised identity and intent, the researcher infiltrates the setting of interest to examine it from within.

To study the compliance professions from the inside, Cialdini (2001) enrolled in the training programs of a broad range of these professions—sales, advertising, fund raising, public relations, recruitment, and so on—learning the same lessons that successful influence practitioners regularly pass on to trainees. Through it all, he looked for parallels, common principles of influence that rose to the surface and persisted in each of the professions. Six widely used and successful principles of influence, to which we'll refer throughout this chapter, emerged from this program of participant observation:

- *Reciprocation.* People are more willing to comply with requests (for favors, services, information, and concessions) from those who have provided such things first. Because people feel an obligation to reciprocate, Cialdini found that free samples in supermarkets, free home inspections by exterminating companies, and free gifts through the mail from marketers or fund raisers were all highly effective ways to increase compliance with a follow-up request. For example, according to the Disabled American Veterans organization, mailing out a simple appeal for donations produces an 18 percent success rate, but enclosing a small gift—personalized address labels—boosts the success rate to 35 percent (Smolowe, 1990).
- *Commitment/consistency.* People are more willing to be moved in a particular direction if they see it as consistent with an existing or recently made

Participant observation *A research approach in which the researcher infiltrates the setting to be studied and observes its workings from within.*

commitment. For instance, high-pressure door-to-door sales companies are plagued by some buyers' tendency to cancel the deal after the salesperson has left and the pressure to buy is no longer present. In training sessions Cialdini attended, several of the door-to-door sales companies claimed that they had significantly reduced this problem with a trick that heightens the customer's sense of personal commitment to the sale: Rather than having the sales representative write in the details of the contract, they have the customer do it.

- *Authority.* People are more willing to follow the directions or recommendations of someone they view as an authority. So automatic is the tendency to follow an authority, Cialdini noted, that many times advertisers try to—and do—succeed merely by employing actors dressed to look like experts (scientists, physicians, police officers, and so on).
- *Social validation.* People are more willing to take a recommended step if they see evidence that many others, especially similar others, are taking it. Manufacturers make use of this principle by claiming that their products are the fastest growing or largest selling in the market. Cialdini found that the strategy of increasing compliance by providing evidence of others who had already complied was the most widely used of the six principles he encountered.
- *Scarcity.* People find objects and opportunities more attractive to the degree that they are scarce, rare, or dwindling in availability. Hence, newspaper ads are filled with warnings to potential customers regarding the folly of delay: "Last three days." "Limited time offer." "One week only sale." One particularly single-minded movie theater owner managed to load three separate appeals to the scarcity principle into just five words of advertising copy that read, "Exclusive, limited engagement, ends soon."
- *Liking/friendship.* People prefer to say yes to those they know and like. If you doubt that this is the case, consider the remarkable success of the Tupperware Home Party Corporation, which arranges for customers to buy its products not from a stranger across a counter, but from the neighbor, friend, or relative who has sponsored a Tupperware party and gets a percentage of its profits. According to interviews done by Cialdini, many people attend the parties and purchase the products, not out of a need for more containers that go *pffft* when you press on them, but out of a sense of liking or friendship for the party sponsor.

Question authority. *Because people respond automatically to the appearance of authority, advertisers feel that they can successfully portray this TV quiz show host as credible source of information.*

Before we can feel secure in the conclusions of participant observation studies, we usually need to find support for their conclusions elsewhere—for example, in experimental research or in additional natural observations by other scientists. Fortunately, as we'll see in this chapter, experimental evidence and additional observations have validated the role of each of these principles in compliance decisions. For instance, in one study, each of the principles, when applied in the sales presentations of department store clerks, produced a significant increase in retail clothing purchases (Cody, Seiter, & Montagne-Miller, 1995). ■

Obedience: Milgram's Shock(ing) Procedure

In July 1983, 2,075 identically dressed couples were married by Reverend Sun Myung Moon in Madison Square Garden. Most partners were strangers to one another. Why marry a total stranger? In this case, it was because Reverend Moon had chosen the partners and directed them to marry each other. They obeyed. Obeying such an unusual command may make more sense when we realize that Moon's followers regard him as the greatest spiritual being on earth. For most of us, however, effective orders can come from decidedly lesser authorities than such beings: Political leaders, military commanders, police officers, high school principals, store managers, and parents issue commands that produce obedience on a daily basis. Social psychologist Stanley Milgram wanted to see how far the obedience-inducing power of authority could be extended. Would you obey orders from a researcher you had never before met if he or she asked you to deliver painful, potentially deadly electric shocks to an innocent victim? And if so, what would the victim have to say to get you to stop obeying such orders?

Mean machine. *Milgram's subjects delivered shocks by operating the levers of this intimidating piece of equipment.*

In a well-known series of studies done decades ago, Milgram (1974) placed advertisements in local newspapers to solicit participants for a "memory experiment" at Yale University. Suppose that one of those studies was being conducted today and that you signed up to participate. Here's what you'd encounter: Upon your arrival at the laboratory, you'd be introduced to another subject (actually a confederate of the experimenter). After hearing that the research would examine the effects of punishment on memory, you'd be assigned to the Teacher role and the other participant to the Learner role in the study. You'd be informed that, as part of your duties, you'd have to deliver a series of electric shocks to the Learner. At this point, the Learner would mention that he had been treated for a heart condition and express concern about the dangers of receiving electric shocks. To this, the experimenter would reply that, although painful, the shocks would produce "no permanent tissue damage."

The experimenter would then take you both to the next room, where the nervous Learner would be strapped into an apparatus looking eerily like an electric chair. That accomplished, you'd be ushered into an experimental room and shown a menacing shock-delivery machine with shock levers ascending from 15 to 450 volts. Each group of four shock levers would be assigned a progressively more frightening label, ranging from "Slight shock" through "Moderate," "Strong," "Very strong," "Intense," "Extreme intensity," to "Danger: Severe shock." A final pair of levers (for the 435- and 450-volt shocks) would apparently deliver shocks so intense that the English language had no words to describe them adequately, as they carried only the stark label "XXX."

Before beginning, you would receive an unpleasant sample shock of 45 volts to give you an idea of what the Learner would be experiencing. You'd then be instructed to deliver a shock to the Learner every time he erred on a memory task, advancing to the next higher shock lever with every new mistake. With each error and each more punishing shock, the confederate would voice increasingly desperate cries of pain. At first, he'd simply cry out, "Ugh." At 120 volts, he would shout out, "Hey, this really hurts!" At 150 volts, he'd plead to be released:

> That's all! Get me out of here. I told you I had heart trouble. My heart's starting to bother me now. Get me out of here, please. My heart's starting to bother me. I refuse to go on. Let me out.

Would you continue or stop? If you tried to stop, the experimenter would prod you by saying, "Please continue." If you failed to obey, the experimenter would insist, "The experiment requires that you continue." If you persisted in your disobedience, he'd state, "It is absolutely essential that you continue." Finally, he would demand, "You have no choice; you must go on."

If you continued to follow orders and deliver the shocks, the Learner's appeals would become more agonized and desperate. Finally, he'd burst into a litany of pleas, demands, and shrieks:

> Let me out of here. Let me out of here. My heart's bothering me. Let me out, I tell you. Let me out of here. Let me out of here. You have no right to hold me here. Let me out! Let me out! Let me out! Let me out of here! Let me out! Let me out!

Should that not be enough to convince you to resist the experimenter's orders, things would suddenly change. When you delivered the next shock, you'd hear nothing from the Learner's chamber. If you asked the experimenter to see if the Learner was all right, he'd refuse, saying instead, "Treat no response as a wrong response, and deliver the next higher level of shock." For the final eight shocks—into the "Danger" category and the region marked "XXX"—the Learner, once so vocal in his pain, would be deadly silent.

How likely would you and other participants like you follow orders to go all the way to 450 volts? Before publishing his study, Milgram described the procedures to 40 psychiatrists at a leading medical school and asked them to predict the results. They expected that fewer than 4 percent of Milgram's subjects would continue once the Learner stopped answering and that only 0.01 percent would go all the way to the end. Sadly, the psychiatrists greatly underestimated the power of obedience to authority. More than 80 percent of the participants continued past the Learner's refusal to answer. Even more remarkably, 65 percent persisted to the end—defying an innocent victim's repeated screams and enduring his subsequent ominous silence—simply because the "boss" of the study commanded it (see Figure 6.3). What's more, these high levels of obedience have remained steady when researchers have repeated Milgram's procedures in more recent years (Blass, 1999).

Milgram conducted an elaborate series of follow-up studies. In one, he explored the extent to which his results were due to the scientific credibility of Yale University, where the study took place. He rented office space in a rundown section of Bridgeport, Connecticut, and ran the same procedures again. Surprisingly, a large proportion of participants (48 percent) obeyed the researcher's orders even under these questionable circumstances, indicating that his findings were not limited to university-based authorities. But how do we know that it was authority influence rather than some other factor—the desire to release pent-up aggression, for instance—that caused Milgram's subjects to behave so cruelly?

The evidence supporting the obedience to authority explanation is strong. First, it's clear that, without the researcher's directive to continue, the participants would have ended the experiment quickly. They hated what they were doing and agonized over their victim's agony. They implored the researcher to let them stop. When he refused, they went on, but in the process they trembled, perspired, shook, and stam-

Figure 6.3 Obedience in the Milgram study.

Despite predictions to the contrary from psychiatrists at Yale Medical School, the majority (65 percent) of subjects obeyed a researcher's commands to deliver every available shock, up to 450 volts, to an innocent fellow subject.

SOURCE: *Adapted from Milgram, 1963.*

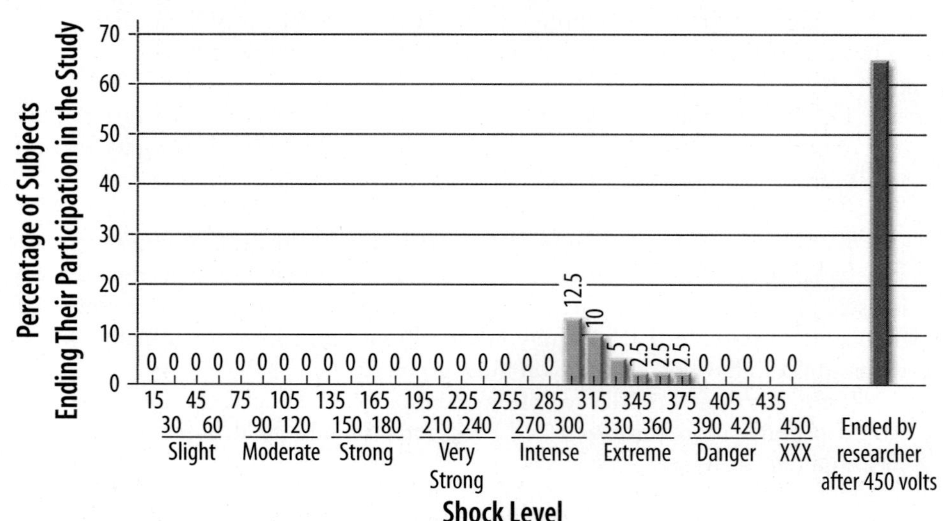

mered protests and additional pleas for the victim's release. In addition to these observations, Milgram provided even more convincing evidence for the interpretation of his results in light of obedience to authority. In a later experiment, for instance, he had the researcher and the victim switch scripts so that the researcher told the Teacher to stop delivering shocks to the victim, while the victim insisted bravely that the Teacher continue. The result couldn't have been clearer: 100 percent of the participants refused to give one additional shock when it was merely the fellow participant who demanded it. These results would hardly be expected if participants' principal motive was to release aggressive energy rather than to follow an authority.

If, as Milgram's research indicates, a majority of people will deliver painful shocks to a heart patient on the orders of a research scientist who has no real authority over them, it becomes less surprising that soldiers will kill innocent civilians and that cult members will kill themselves at the direction of more personally relevant authority figures. But *why* do people obey? What goals are served by this and the other forms of social influence?

The Goals of Social Influence

Notice that conformity, compliance, and obedience all refer not to the act of wielding influence but to the act of yielding to it. When it comes to understanding human motivation, yielding questions are more interesting—and more instructive—than wielding questions. Think of the obvious, self-serving reasons Moonie leaders had for wanting to get Steve Hassan to conform, comply, and obey: He could be made to give them all of his money, time, energy, and support. In general, it's not difficult to imagine why people would want to influence others to do their bidding. Much more intriguing is why people would agree to *be* influenced. Consequently, that is the question we address. Just as in chapter 5, in which we emphasized the goals of individuals who choose to alter their attitudes and beliefs, in this chapter we emphasize the goals of those who choose to conform, comply, and obey. As we will see, people yield to social influence to achieve one or more of three basic goals: choosing correctly, gaining social approval, and managing self-image.

Summary

Social influence refers to behavior change resulting from real or imagined pressure from others. Traditionally, social psychologists have studied three main kinds of social influence: conformity, compliance, and obedience. Conformity occurs when one matches one's actions to those of others. The research of Solomon Asch demonstrated that, when faced with a strong group consensus, people often conform even if they believe that the group may be in error. Compliance occurs when one agrees to a request of another. One compliance tactic, the foot-in-the-door technique, increases compliance with a large request by first getting compliance with a smaller, related request. Obedience occurs when one follows the directives of an authority. The famous Milgram studies revealed a surprising willingness of average citizens to obey authority commands, even to the point of harming an innocent victim. People yield to social influence to achieve three major goals: choosing correctly, gaining social approval, and managing self-image.

Choosing Correctly

According to Robert W. White (1959), we all have a motive for *competence*, a motive to master our environments so that we consistently gain desired rewards and resources. Of course, consistently succeeding in any environment doesn't occur by accident. To do well, we must choose well. From a profusion of possibilities, we must make the choices most likely to bring us the rewards and resources we seek. It's for this reason that influence professionals are forever trying to convince us that, if we select their products or services—from hair care to health care—we will have chosen well and gotten a "good deal." The problem when encountering influence attempts of this sort lies in recognizing when the offered deal is in fact a good one.

How can we know beforehand whether a choice for a particular toothpaste or restaurant or political candidate will prove wise and effective? Frequently, we rely on two powerful principles to steer us correctly in our influence decisions—authority and social validation.

Authority

The most striking research evidence for the influence of legitimate authority comes from the Milgram obedience study. But the tendency to defer to an authority arises in many more situations than the laboratory setting that Milgram constructed (Blass, 1991; Miller, Collins, & Brief, 1995). What's more, the behaviors influenced in these situations range from the ordinary to the dramatic (Sabini & Silver, 1982). In the realm of ordinary behaviors, we can find deference to authority in something as commonplace as the tone of voice one uses in a conversation. Communication researchers who study what happens in conversations have learned that people shift their voice and speech styles toward the styles of individuals in positions of power and authority (Giles & Coupland, 1991; Pittam, 1994). One study explored this phenomenon by analyzing interviews on the *Larry King Live* television show. When King interviewed guests having great social standing and prestige (for instance, George Bush, Bill Clinton, and Barbara Streisand), his voice style changed to match theirs. But when he interviewed guests of lower status and prestige (for instance, Dan Quayle, Spike Lee, and Julie Andrews), he remained unmoved, and their voice styles shifted to match his (Gregory & Webster, 1996).

As Milgram's findings demonstrated, people also follow an authority's lead in situations involving much more dramatic consequences than changes in voice. Consider, for example, the catastrophic consequences of a phenomenon that airline industry officials have labeled "captainitis" (Foushee, 1984). Accident investigators from the Federal Aviation Administration have recognized that an obvious error by a flight captain often goes uncorrected by other crewmembers and results in a crash. It seems that, because of the captain's authority position, crewmembers either fail

The catastrophic consequences of captainitis. *Minutes before this airliner crashed into the Potomac River near National Airport in Washington, D.C., an alarming exchange occurred between pilot and copilot concerning the wisdom of taking off with ice on the wings. Their conversation was recorded on the plane's "black box."*

to notice or fail to challenge the mistake. They appear to assume that if the captain said it, it must be right.

In light of the remarkable power of authority over human behavior, we can better understand Steve Hassan's actions as a member of the Unification organization. To devoted members, the Reverend Moon is the wisest being on earth, and high-ranking officials are viewed as intermediaries carrying out his wishes. To fail to follow the directions of any of these individuals would be to disobey ultimate authority. Indeed, when anthropologist Geri-Ann Galanti (1993) secretly infiltrated a Moonie introductory weekend, she found that the group's authoritarian structure was instilled in recruits from the outset:

> We were continually made to feel like children rather than adults. Lecturers take on a position of authority because they are the ones in possession of the knowledge. Until we've learned it all, we must remain unquestioning children/students. (p. 91)

It's clear that authorities have a potent impact on the choices and actions of others. What is it about authorities that makes them so influential? The teacher role assumed by leaders at the Moonie recruitment weekend provides some clues.

Think back. Throughout your schooling, when your English teachers corrected your writing style, you probably took their criticisms into account in your next paper. That was no doubt the case for multiple reasons. First, like many authorities, teachers have power over you. They can affect your grade in the class, your standing in school, your chances for a good position after graduation, and so on. For such reasons alone, it makes good sense to follow their directions. But there's a second reason. Like many authorities, teachers are experts on the subject at hand. If they say that a sentence you've written is awkward, you're likely to *believe* it and to change in order to improve your writing in general. In short, just as we learned in chapter 5, following the advice of authorities helps us choose rapidly and correctly. Although some authorities are in a position to force us into obedience, it's more interesting to consider how effective they can be without the power to reward or punish—when what they have instead is **expert power,** the power that comes from acknowledged competence in the matter at hand (French & Raven, 1959).

Authorities as Experts An authority's expert power can have a strong effect on compliance because it serves our strong motivation to choose correctly. Milgram (1965, p. 74) claimed that his subjects' obedience occurred not simply through overt pressure but, as well, "by the uncritical acceptance of the experimenter's definition of the situation." When authorities are presumed to know best, following their lead becomes a sensible thing. This helps explain why less educated individuals are more obedient to authority figures (Hamilton, Sanders, & McKearney, 1995; Milgram, 1974): They tend to presume that authorities know more than they do.

Because following an expert's direction is normally wise, and because authorities are frequently experts, we often use authority as a decision-making heuristic (shortcut). Assuming that an authority knows best can be an efficient way of deciding, because we don't have to think hard about the issues ourselves; all we have to do to be right is accept the authority's advice. But unthinking reliance on authority can be dangerous, too. This shortcut approach can lead us to respond to the symbols rather than the substance of genuine authority (Bushman, 1984).

The results of a study conducted by a team of physicians and nurses revealed the force that one such symbol—the mere title Dr.—has in the medical arena. Hospital nurses received a phone call from a man they'd never met but who identified himself as the doctor of a patient on their floor. He then ordered them to give twice the maximum acceptable dosage of a drug to that patient. Ninety-five percent obeyed and had to be stopped on their way to the patient's room with the unsafe drug dosage in their hands (Hofling, Brotzman, Dalrymple, Graves, & Pierce, 1966). A

Expert power *The capacity to influence that flows from one's presumed wisdom or knowledge.*

follow-up study asked nurses to recall a time when they'd obeyed a doctor's order that they considered inappropriate and potentially harmful to a patient. Those who admitted such incidents (46 percent) attributed their actions to their beliefs that the doctor was a legitimate and expert authority in the matter—the same two features of authority that appear to account for obedience in the Milgram procedure (Blass, 1999; Krackow & Blass, 1995). Incidents of this deference to the symbols of authority continue to occur. A seventeen-year-old convinced nurses at a Virginia hospital to carry out twelve treatments on six patients by misrepresenting himself as a doctor on the phone (Teenager, 2000).

Authorities as Agents of Influence It should come as no surprise that influence professionals frequently try to harness the power of authority by touting their experience, expertise, or scientific recognition—"Fashionable clothiers since 1841," "Babies are our business, our only business," "Four out of five doctors recommend the ingredients in...," and so on. There's nothing wrong with such claims when they're real, because we usually want to know who is an authority on a topic and who isn't; it helps us choose correctly. The problem comes when we are subjected to phony claims of this sort. When we aren't thinking hard, as is often the case when confronted by authority symbols, we can be easily steered in the wrong direction by false authorities—those who aren't authorities at all but who merely present the aura of authority. For instance, people are more willing to perform a variety of unusual actions (to pick up a paper bag on the street, stand on the other side of a Bus Stop sign, put money in someone else's parking meter) if directed to do so by someone wearing a security guard's or firefighter's uniform; moreover, they are more likely to do so unquestioningly (Bickman, 1974; Bushman, 1984).

In sum, authorities are formidable sources of social influence. One reason is that they are often expert. Consequently, following their directions offers us a shortcut route to choosing correctly. However, when we defer to authority orders or advice too readily, we risk performing actions that may be unethical or unwise. Let's turn now to a second major principle that people use to help them achieve the goal of choosing correctly, social validation.

Social Validation

Just as following the advice of an authority is normally a shortcut to good decisions, so is following the lead of most of one's peers. If all your friends are raving about a new restaurant, you'll probably like it, too. Therefore, we frequently decide what we should do in a situation by examining what others, especially similar others, are doing there. We use the actions of these others as a means of **social validation,** as an interpersonal way to locate and validate the correct choice (Festinger, 1954).

Because the desire to choose correctly is powerful, the tendency to follow the crowd is both strong and widespread. Studies have shown that, based on evidence of what their peers are doing, bystanders decide whether to help an emergency victim (Latané & Darley, 1970), citizens decide whether to pay their taxes fully (Steenbergen, McGraw, & Scholz, 1992), juveniles decide whether to commit a wide range of crimes (Kahan, 1997), spouses decide whether to "cheat" sexually (Buunk & Baker, 1995), and homeowners decide whether to recycle their trash (Schultz, 1999). In this last study, residents of a Los Angeles suburb received information describing the regular curbside recycling behavior of many of their neighbors. This information produced an immediate increase in the amount of material the residents recycled. In addition, when observed up to a month later, they were recycling more trash than ever. These improvements did not occur, however, for residents who received only a plea to recycle.

Social validation *An interpersonal way to locate and validate the correct choice.*

Whenever influence practitioners identify a psychological principle that people use to reach their goals, the practitioners are sure to use it to advance their own goals. We saw that this was the case for the authority principle, and it is no less the

FOR THE SECOND YEAR IN A ROW, YOU VOTED DINERS CLUB #1 REWARDS PROGRAM.

THANK YOU, THANK YOU.

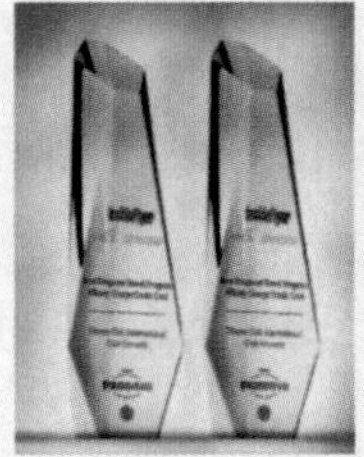

BREAKING THE PLASTIC MOLD.℠

Social validation. *If people like you think it's good, it must be good.*

case for the principle of social validation. Sales and marketing professionals make a special point of informing us when a product is the "largest selling" or "fastest growing" in its market. Bartenders are known to "salt" their tip jars with dollar bills at the start of their shifts to give the impression that previous customers tipped with folding money. Church ushers sometimes prime collection baskets for a similar reason and with a similar effect on proceeds. Television commercials depict crowds rushing into stores and hands depleting shelves of the advertised item. Consider the advice offered more than 350 years ago by the Spaniard Balthazar Gracian (1649/1945) to anyone wishing to sell goods and services: "Their intrinsic worth is not enough, for not all turn the goods over or look deep. Most run where the crowd is—because the others run" (p. 142). This tendency to run because others are running affects more than product sales. Indeed, it accounts for some of the most bizarre forms of human conduct on record. In the Focus on Social Dysfunction feature, we examine one such form, mass hysteria.

FOCUS ON Social Dysfunction

Mass Hysteria

Throughout history, people have been subject to extraordinary collective delusions—irrational sprees, manias, and panics of various sorts. In his classic text on "the madness of crowds," Charles MacKay listed hundreds that occurred before the book's first publication in 1841. It is noteworthy that many shared an instructive characteristic—contagiousness. Often, they began with a single person or group and then swept rapidly through whole populations. Action spread to observers, who then acted and thereby validated the correctness of the action for still other observers, who acted in turn.

For instance, in 1761, London experienced two moderate-sized earthquakes exactly a month apart. Convinced by this coincidence that a third, much larger quake would occur in another month, a soldier named Bell began spreading his prediction that the city would be destroyed on April 5. At first, few paid him any heed. But those who did took the precaution of moving their families and possessions to surrounding areas. The sight of this small exodus stirred others to follow, which, in cascading waves over the next week, led to near panic and a large-scale evacuation. Great numbers of Londoners streamed into nearby villages, paying outrageous prices for any accommodations. Included in the terrified throngs were "hundreds who had laughed at the prediction a week before, [but who] packed up their goods, when they saw others doing so, and hastened away" (MacKay, 1841/1932, p. 260).

After the designated day dawned and died without a tremor, the fugitives returned to the city furious at Bell for leading them astray. As MacKay's description makes clear, however, their anger was misdirected. It wasn't the crackpot Bell who was most convincing. It was the Londoners themselves, each to the other.

A similar, though less historic incident took place in modern Singapore when, for no good reason, the customers of a local bank began drawing out their money in a frenzy. The run on this respected bank remained a mystery until much later, when researchers interviewing participants discovered its peculiar cause: An unexpected bus strike had created an abnormally large crowd waiting at the bus stop in front of the bank that day. Mistaking the gathering for a crush of customers poised to withdraw their funds from a failing bank, passersby panicked and got in line to withdraw their deposits, which led more passersby to do the same. Soon illusion had become reality and, shortly after opening its doors, the bank was forced to close to avoid ruin ("News," 1988).

In all, most people feel that behaviors become more valid when many others are performing them. In instances of mass delusion, this social validation extends to wildly irrational acts that seem to reflect correct choices not because of any hard evidence in their favor but merely because multiple others have chosen them. ■

Although the tendency to follow the lead of our peers can lead to misguided behavior, most of the time it doesn't. Most of the time it sends us in right directions, toward correct choices. Which are the factors that spur people to use the actions of others in the process of trying to choose correctly? Social psychologists have uncovered several. We begin with one that resides in the person.

Uncertainty

When people don't trust their own judgments, they look to others for evidence of how to choose correctly (Wooten & Reed, 1998). This self-doubt may come about because the situation is ambiguous, as it was in a classic series of experiments conducted by the Turkish social psychologist Muzafer Sherif (1936). Sherif projected a dot of light on the wall of a darkened room and asked subjects to indicate how much the light moved while they watched it. Actually, the light never moved at all; but, because of an optical illusion termed the *autokinetic effect*, it seemed to shift constantly about, although to a different extent for each subject. When participants announced their movement estimates in groups, these estimates were strongly influenced by what the other group members estimated; nearly everyone changed toward the group average. Sherif concluded that when there's no objectively correct response, people are likely to doubt themselves and, thus, are especially likely to assume that "the group must be right" (p. 111). Many studies have supported his conclusion (Bond & Smith, 1996; Tesser, Campbell, & Mickler, 1983).

Despite initial uncertainty, once a group has agreed on a response, members can hold onto it fiercely (Jacobs & Campbell, 1961). In one study, group members who had undergone Sherif's autokinetic effect procedure returned many months later to be tested again, but this time with no other group members present. When placed in the darkened room once more, these individuals saw the light move a distance that fit with the group answer formed a year earlier (Rohrer, Baron, Hoffman, & Swander, 1954).

People also feel unsure of themselves when the task they face is difficult. Richard Crutchfield (1955) gave college students the opportunity to conform to the majority position on a variety of tasks, ranging from perceptual problems to opinion items. The one that generated the most conformity (79 percent) was a numerical problem that was the most difficult of all the tasks—because it was actually impossible to solve. In many cults, knowing what to believe at any given moment is also an impossible problem to solve because the answers are based on the ambiguous and constantly changing views of the leadership. In addition, cult groups often add to their members' sense of disorientation by using tactics such as exhaustion and sleep deprivation that create mental confusion (Baron, 2000). As Steve Hassan (1990) reports, "In such an environment, the tendency within most people is to doubt themselves and defer to the group" (p. 68).

When people feel unsure of their grasp on reality, they're more likely to defer to authority figures, too. In field tests of combat artillery units, teams that are fully rested often refuse to fire on hospitals and other civilian targets, but after 36 sleepless hours, they obey orders to fire at anything without question (Schulte, 1998).

Consensus and Similarity

While Steve Hassan was a group member, he and other Moonies used a tactic during their introductory recruitment weekends that increased the chance that at least some first-time visitors would return for more training. Likely candidates for Church membership were grouped with similar likely candidates; they were labeled "sheep." Others, who asked too many questions or showed signs of stubborn individualism, were labeled "goats" and were quickly separated from the sheep so as not to contaminate them with doubt. Various cultlike groups around the world do the same thing at their introductory sessions. This particular tactic is effective because it incorporates two factors that people rely on to choose correctly: consensus and similarity.

Consensus Remember Asch's (1956) conformity research? It showed that people would make obvious errors on a line-judging task merely because everybody in their group had already chosen to make that error. Imagine the pressure you would feel in such a situation if *everyone* else chose an answer that looked wrong to you. With perfect agreement among the others, you'd probably trust the group more and yourself less. In your desire to choose correctly, you might well conform because you believed that the group was right. In addition, the more group members who were in agreement, the stronger would be your tendency to conform (Bond & Smith, 1996; Insko, Smith, Alicke, Wade, & Taylor, 1985) (see Figure 6.4).

In contrast, imagine a slightly different situation: Before you have to give your answer, the consensus of the group is broken by one individual who chooses the line that looks right to you. Now, when it's your turn to speak, what would you do—go along with the majority or join the rebel? Most likely, you'd become much less likely to agree with the majority. Even a single visible dissenter from the group's position emboldens others to resist conformity (Morris & Miller, 1975). Why should that be? One reason is that a dissenter reduces confidence that the group has *the* right answer (Allen & Levine, 1969); therefore, people seeking to select accurately begin looking beyond the group's choice to other possibilities.

Because of the conformity-cracking power of diverse points of view, nearly all cultlike groups try to suppress communication with outside sources of information, including family and friends (Singer & Lalich, 1995). According to Steve Hassan (1990), the factor that separates those who leave such groups on their own ("walk-aways") from those who stay is that only the walk-aways have managed to maintain contact with outsiders. For the most part, though, cult members are enveloped by consensus

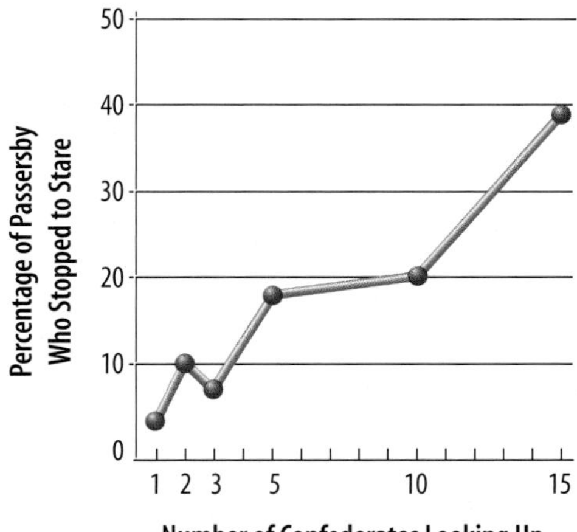

Figure 6.4
Looking up.

What could motivate pedestrians on a wintry day in New York City to stop, stand, and stare at little of obvious interest or importance? Researchers had sent confederates to stare upward for 60 seconds. The more confederates staring upward at nothing in particular, the more passersby joined the group.

SOURCE: *Adapted from Milgram, Bickman, & Berkowitz, 1969.*

about the teachings of the group, making even wrongheaded beliefs appear correct. Margaret Singer, who has spent a lifetime studying cults, frequently asks former members why they remained in their often-abusive groups for as long as they did. Here's a typical answer: "I'd look around and I'd think, 'Well, Joe's still doing it. Mary's still doing it. It must be me; it must be me. *I* just don't get it'" (Singer & Lalich, 1995, p. 273).

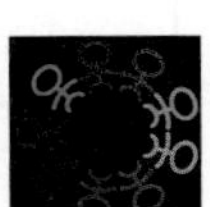

Similarity If people follow the lead of others to make good choices for themselves, it stands to reason that most of the time they would want to follow the actions of individuals similar to themselves. Suppose you were trying to decide which of two classes to take next term. Wouldn't you be more likely to seek out and accept the advice of individuals like you, who match your background, interests, and goals? If they think one class is better than the other, the chances are good that you would too (Suls, Martin, & Wheeler, 2000).

Heightened sensitivity to the responses of similar others appears in a wide variety of situations. For example, in one study, New Yorkers were strongly influenced to return a lost wallet after learning that a similar other had first tried to do so. But evidence that a dissimilar other—a foreigner—had tried to return the wallet had no effect on the New Yorkers' decisions (Hornstein, Fisch, & Holmes, 1968). In a different study, children watched a film depicting another child's positive visit to the dentist. Did watching this film reduce the children's dentist office anxieties? Yes, but that was so principally when the child in the movie was the same age as those viewing it (Melamed et al., 1978).

Although similar others can take us in positive directions, they can lead us down dark, deadly paths as well. Take the phenomenon of copycat suicides. After highly publicized suicide stories appear in the media, the suicide rate jumps in those areas that have been exposed to the stories (Phillips, 1989). Apparently, certain troubled individuals imitate the actions of other troubled individuals in the act of suicide. What's the evidence that this increase in self-inflicted deaths comes from the tendency to look to similar others for direction? Copycat suicides are more prevalent among people who are similar in age and sex to the victim in the previously publicized suicide story. For instance, following a German television story of a young man who killed himself by leaping in front of a train, railway suicides increased dramatically, but only among other young German men (Schmidtke & Hafner, 1988).

In sum, we are more likely to match our actions to those of others when those others are in agreement with one another and akin to us. Both of these factors—consensus and similarity—stimulate conformity because they give us confidence that the others' choices represent good choices for us, too. Combining both consensus and similarity in the same procedure creates a highly effective fundraising technique, called the **list procedure** (Reingen, 1982). Researchers went door to door collecting money for charity, showing residents a list of others in the vicinity who had already given. The longer the list of neighbors (similar others) that residents saw, the more likely they were to give a donation.

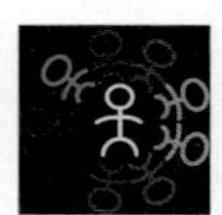

Uncertainty and the Desire for Accuracy

Now that it seems clear that one reason people conform to the majority is to choose accurately, wouldn't you agree that the more someone wants to be accurate, the more he or she will conform to what everyone else has decided? If you do agree, you would be right. But, sometimes, you would be wrong because another factor interacts with one's desire for accuracy, and it can change everything. It is a factor we have already discussed—uncertainty. We concluded that when people don't trust their own judgments, they rely on the group's judgment. If so, we should expect that when individuals are uncertain, the more important accuracy is to them, the more they will follow the crowd. However, if they are highly certain of their judgments, they won't have to seek the truth in the actions of others. Thus, when individuals are

List procedure *A technique that seeks to gain compliance with a request by displaying a long list of others, especially similar others, who have complied.*

already certain, the more important accuracy is to them, the less they will simply follow along.

To test this reasoning, Robert S. Baron, Joseph Vandello, and Bethany Brunsman (1996) created a variation of the Asch line-judging procedure. Instead of choosing correct line lengths, University of Iowa undergraduates had to choose the correct suspect in criminal lineups. First, they saw a picture of a single criminal suspect. Then, they saw a picture of a lineup containing four suspects, including the one they had previously seen. Their task was to pick out of the lineup the previously seen suspect. This was repeated thirteen times with thirteen different pairs of pictures. To make accuracy especially important for one group of students, the researchers promised a $20 prize to those who made the most correct choices. But, for some students, there was an added complication—the pictures were flashed on a screen so quickly (half a second each) that they couldn't be very certain of their judgments. Other students did not encounter this uncertainty because, for them, the pictures were left on the screen for five seconds each.

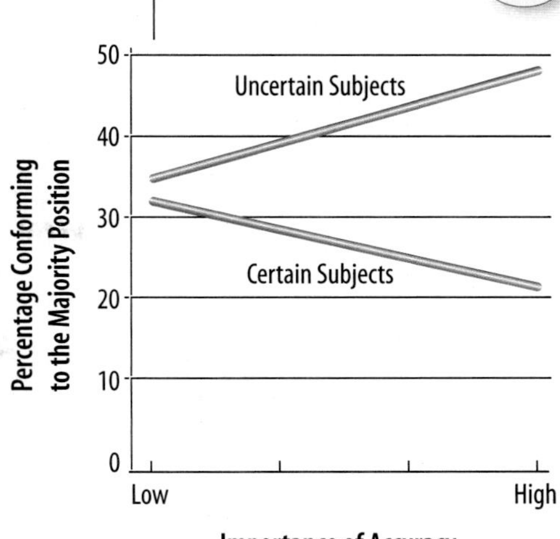

Figure 6.5
Conformity and uncertainty.

Subjects who were uncertain of their judgments on a face-identification task (because the faces were presented very rapidly on a screen) conformed to the unanimous majority position more often when being accurate was especially important to them. However, those who were certain of their judgments (because the faces were left on the screen for five full seconds) conformed less often when accuracy was especially important. Thus, only the uncertain individuals chose conformity as the best route to accuracy.

SOURCE: *Adapted from Baron, Vandello, & Brunsman, 1996.*

How did the students choose when, on seven separate occasions, they heard confederates unanimously identifying the wrong suspects in the lineups? Did they conform to the majority or stay with their own judgments? That depended on how uncertain they were of their private judgments and on how important accuracy was for them on the task. Those who were unsure of their judgments became more likely to conform to the majority when accuracy was important; but those who were sure of their judgments became less likely to conform when accuracy was important (see Figure 6.5). Although the sure and unsure individuals moved in opposite directions, their movement was motivated by the same goal: to choose correctly. The critical difference between them was whether they felt that relying on themselves or on others offered the best route to choosing correctly. The motivation to be accurate pushes us toward conformity only when we are unsure of our own judgments.

Summary

People use two sources of external information to help them choose correctly—authorities and peers. One good reason for paying special attention to authorities is that they are often experts. Because experts typically possess valuable information, it makes sense to follow their recommendations. Hence, people sometimes defer to authorities without thinking much about the issues. Although this shortcut (heuristic) route normally steers people correctly, it can also lead to poor choices (such as following a false authority) because of its automatic, unthinking character. Besides authorities, people frequently look to peers for help in making wise decisions. People feel that behaviors are more valid if many others are performing them. Although following the actions of peers can lead to misguided behavior (as in cases of mass hysteria), it normally does not. When motivated to be accurate, we are likely to use others' choices as a guide when we feel uncertain about our own judgments or competence, when the others are unanimous in their judgments, and when the others are similar to us.

Gaining Social Approval

Most everyone wants to be correct. But it's not easy. Part of the difficulty comes from the fact that the term *correct* can have two different and sometimes opposing meanings. So far in this chapter, we've emphasized just one of these meanings—accuracy.

We've focused on the willingness to be influenced in order to be *right.* But the second meaning of being correct—being socially appropriate or approved—can also leave people open to influence (Insko, Drenan, Solomon, Smith, & Wade, 1983). Frequently, people change to be more accepted in their group or culture—in other words, to belong (Baumeister & Leary, 1995).

Take, for example, the account by Irving Janis (1997) of what happened in a group of heavy smokers who came to a clinic for treatment. During the group's second meeting, nearly everyone took the position that, because tobacco is so addicting, no one could be expected to quit all at once. But one man disputed the group's view, announcing that he had stopped smoking completely since joining the group the week before and that others could do the same. In response, the other group members banded against him, delivering a series of angry attacks on his position. At the following meeting, the dissenter reported that, after careful thought, he had come to an important decision: "I have gone back to smoking two packs a day; and won't make any effort to stop again until after the last meeting" (p. 334). The other group members immediately welcomed him back into the fold, greeting his decision with applause.

This account illustrates the old dictum that "it's easier to get along if you go along." In a classic set of studies, Stanley Schachter (1951) observed how groups pressure members who deviate from the consensus. In newly formed discussion teams, Schachter planted a male confederate who asserted an opinion different from the other members'. The group's reaction typically followed a three-step sequence. First, the others directed a large number of comments to the deviate, arguing heatedly with him. Next, when he failed to come into line with the group mind, the other members began to ignore him and to treat him with disdain. Finally, when he held firm through the shift from hot attack to cold shoulder, he was rejected outright with a vote to expel him from the group.

However, Schachter found that groups can respond with affection to opinion deviates, provided the dissenters admit the error of their ways and adopt the group's view. In some discussion groups, the confederate was programmed to be a "slider"—someone who began by disagreeing, but who gradually yielded to group pressure. What happened to the slider? He, too, received an initial barrage of comments designed to convert him to the group position. But, because he yielded, he never experienced the disdain and rejection that the unbending deviate did. In fact, the slider was embraced as fully into the group as any other member. For a deviate in a group, then, the unforgivable sin is not to be different; it is to *stay* different. As a result, many dissenting individuals shift toward group consensus to be accepted and to avoid rejection.

These twin needs to foster social acceptance and escape social rejection help explain why cults can be so effective in recruiting and retaining members. An initial showering of affection on prospective members, called "love bombing," is typical of cult induction practices. It accounts for some of the success of these groups in attracting new members, especially those feeling lonely or disconnected. Later, the threatened withdrawal of that affection accounts for the willingness of some members to remain in the groups: After having cut their bonds to outsiders, as the cults invariably urge, members have nowhere else to turn for social acceptance.

Social Norms: Codes of Conduct

How can people know which behaviors will lead to social acceptance? The message is carried in the social norms of the group or culture. Cialdini, Kallgren, and Reno (1991) have differentiated two kinds of social norms: descriptive norms, which define what is typically done; and injunctive norms, which define what is typically approved and disapproved. Although what is usually done and what is usually approved are frequently the same, this is not always so. For instance, the great majority of holiday shoppers may pass by a Salvation Army charity kettle without giving a donation, but that same majority may still approve of giving to the organization.

Descriptive norms can inform people of what is likely to be effective action for them. Thus, these norms connect to the first goal we discussed in this chapter, the goal of choosing correctly (accurately). By following what most people do in a setting, one can usually make an accurate choice. Injunctive norms, on the other hand, inform people of what is likely to be acceptable to others. These norms connect to the second goal of social influence, the goal of social approval. If you want to enhance the extent to which you are appreciated and wanted in a group, you would be best advised to pay special attention to injunctive norms.

One particular injunctive norm that is renowned for its favorable effect on social relationships is the norm for reciprocity. It produces potent forms of social influence. According to the sociologist Alvin Gouldner (1960), every human society abides by the **norm of reciprocity,** which obligates people to give back the type of behavior they have received.

The norm of reciprocity creates one of the great benefits of social life. If you do me a favor today, you have the right to expect a favor from me tomorrow. Those traded favors allow us to accomplish tasks we could not do alone (moving a heavy dresser, for example) and help us all survive through uneven times (buy me lunch today when I'm broke, and I'll buy you lunch when my paycheck comes in). Through the exchange and repayment of gifts, favors, and services, people become connected to one another in ongoing relationships. Anyone who violates the norm by taking without giving in return invites social disapproval and risks the relationship (Cotterell, Eisenberger, & Speicher, 1992; Meleshko & Alden, 1993). Most people feel uncomfortable receiving without giving in return because they don't want to be labeled as "takers" or "moochers."

Reciprocal Favors The reciprocity norm is often exploited by influence professionals who begin by giving us something before asking for compliance with their request. For example, the Hare Krishna Society is an Eastern religious sect that experienced tremendous growth in wealth and property during the 1970s. Dressed in ill-fitting orange and white robes with sandals and leg wrappings and wearing beads and bells while chanting and beating tambourines, members provided a bizarre sight to the average citizen. Yet they managed to solicit millions of dollars in contributions from such average citizens who were walking down the street, shopping at the mall, or waiting to catch a plane in the airport. How did they do it? Shrewdly, they profited by first giving things away. A business traveler walking through the airport would be approached by someone in robes and given a "gift" (often a flower quickly pinned onto a jacket or thrust into a hand). If the airport visitor tried to give back the gift, the fundraiser would refuse to take it: "No, it is our gift to you." After mumbling, "Well, thank you," and preparing to move on, the unsuspecting recipient would be asked for a contribution. Even though the traveler did not want the gift, the powerful rule to exchange one favor for another had now been engaged. In response, the traveler would frequently reach into a pocket or purse and make a donation (Cialdini, 2001).

It is not only fundraisers who have discovered how to exploit the powerful principle of reciprocity. Businesses do it all the time by offering "free gifts" for simply listening to a sales pitch, "free workouts" at health spas, "free weekends" at resorts, "free inspections" in the home, and so on. Such techniques are often effective in getting people to buy products and services that they would not have purchased without the powerful social pressure produced by having accepted a gift (Gruner, 1996; Regan, 1971). Perhaps this explains why Tupperware parties normally begin with a round of games that have small Tupperware items as prizes. Those guests who don't win a prize get to reach into a grab bag for theirs so that all have received something from the company before the buying begins. Waiters and waitresses can significantly increase the size of their tips by giving diners something as small as a single piece of candy (Lynn & McCall, 1998).

Norm of reciprocity *The norm that requires that we repay others with the form of behavior they have given us.*

Buenos nachos. *Gifts of food seem especially obliging first favors. Small samples of food products are often given away in supermarkets. Some food manufacturers no longer wait until customers are in the store to provide a free sample.*

Reciprocal Concessions Gifts, favors, and services are not the only actions governed by the reciprocity norm; so, too, are the *concessions* people make to one another in negotiations. After receiving a concession from another, most people feel an obligation to make a concession in return. A compliance tactic designed to exploit this felt obligation is called the reciprocal concessions or **door-in-the-face technique** (Cialdini et al., 1975). Rather than starting with a small request designed to get a yes and then advancing to the desired favor (as occurs in the foot-in-the-door technique), someone using the door-in-the-face technique begins with a large request intended, of all things, to get the target person to say no! After the target rejects the first request, however, the requester *retreats* to the desired favor. By retreating from a large first favor to a smaller one, the requester appears to make a concession to the target, who—through the norm of reciprocity—feels obligated to provide a return concession by agreeing to the reduced favor. Several years ago, a resourceful Boy Scout selling tickets to the circus used the technique on one of this text's authors:

> He asked if I wished to buy any tickets at $5 apiece.... I declined. "Well," he said, "if you don't want to buy any tickets, how about buying some of our big chocolate bars? They're only $1 each." I bought a couple and, right away, realized that something noteworthy had happened. I knew this to be the case because: (a) I do not like chocolate bars; (b) I do like dollars; (c) I was standing there with two of his chocolate bars; and (d) he was walking away with two of my dollars. (Cialdini, 2001, p. 36)

Although it cost $2, the episode with the Boy Scout did have a payoff. It led to a series of experiments exploring the door-in-the-face technique (Cialdini et al., 1975). In one study, researchers approached college students on campus and asked them if they would like to help the County Youth Counseling Program by chaperoning a group of juvenile delinquents on a day trip to the zoo. That request, by itself, was mostly ineffective. Only 17 percent complied. However, the results changed when this request was preceded by a much larger one: "Would you be willing to spend two hours a week as a counselor for a juvenile delinquent for a minimum of two years?" After the students said no to this initial, huge request (as all did), the researchers retreated to the smaller one: "Oh, well, if you can't do that, would you be willing to chaperone a group of delinquents on a day trip to the zoo?" Now fully 50 percent complied. By presenting the zoo request as a concession—a retreat from the earlier request—the researchers spurred the students to reciprocate with a concession of their own.

Of special interest to university students and faculty is evidence that the door-in-the-face technique can greatly increase a professor's willingness to spend time helping a student. In one study, only 59 percent of faculty members were willing to spend fifteen to twenty minutes to meet with a student on an issue of interest to the student—when that was the only request the student made. However, significantly more faculty members (78 percent) were willing to agree to that same request if they had first refused the student's request to spend two hours a week for the rest of the semester meeting with the student (Harari, Mohr, & Hosey, 1980).

Related to the door-in-the-face technique but somewhat different, is the **that's-not-all technique.** An important procedural difference between the two techniques is that in the that's-not-all tactic, the target person does not turn down the first offer before a better second offer is provided. After making the first offer but before the target can respond, the requester betters the deal with an additional item or a price reduction.

Jerry Burger (1986) found this approach useful for selling bakery goods during a campus bake sale. After first citing a price of $1 apiece for cupcakes and before customers responded, the salesperson added two cookies to the deal at no extra cost. This produced more purchases than simply offering a cupcake and two cookies at a $1 price from the outset (76 percent versus 40 percent). One reason this technique

Door-in-the-face technique *A technique that increases compliance by beginning with a large favor likely to be rejected and then retreating to a more moderate favor.*

That's-not-all technique *A technique that increases compliance by "sweetening" an offer with additional benefits.*

"How much would you pay for all the secrets of the universe? Wait, don't answer yet. You also get this six-quart covered combination spaghetti pot and clam steamer. Now how much would you pay?"

Figure 6.6
The "that's-not-all" technique.

SOURCE: *Drawing by Maslin © 1981 The New Yorker Magazine, Inc.*

works is that the target person feels a need to reciprocate the receipt of the improved deal. See Figure 6.6 for an extreme illustration.

Norms of Obligation Across Cultures Although the obligation to reciprocate what one has received exists in all human societies (Gouldner, 1960), it may not apply with the same strength in each. In its strictest form ("I am obligated to return to you precisely the kind of favor you gave me"), the rule for reciprocation involves a kind of economic exchange between two individuals (Clark & Mills, 1993). Thus, this strict form of the rule should be most powerful in a society such as the United States, in which people are most likely to define themselves as free-standing individuals rather than as parts of groups. But in other cultures in which people see themselves as more embedded in family, friendship, and organizational networks, other norms of obligation may predominate.

To test these ideas, Michael Morris, Joel Podolny, and Sheira Ariel (2001) gained access to a multinational bank (Citibank) that had branches in 195 countries. Two features of Citibank's business operation lent themselves to a controlled investigation of the impact of cultural norms. First, the bank's policy was to minimize differences in the organization and structure of its branches around the world. That is, the services and products offered, the job categories and organizational charts, and even the physical aspects of the branch offices were highly similar in each location. Second, it was also bank policy to hire personnel almost exclusively from the local countries. Of course, these employees could be expected to carry with them the norms of their respective nations. Thus, if differences were observed in patterns of obligation among employees in the various countries, they could be traced to different cultural norms rather than to differences in the organizational structure of the workplace.

The researchers selected four societies for examination: the United States, China, Spain, and Germany. They surveyed multiple Citibank branches within each society and measured employees' willingness to comply voluntarily with a request from a coworker for assistance with a task. The main reason employees felt obligated to comply differed in the four nations. Each of these reasons reflected a different normative approach to obligation.

- *In the United States.* Employees in the United States took a *market-based* approach to the obligation to comply. They offered assistance on the basis of the norm for a reciprocal exchange of favors between two individuals. In deciding to comply, they asked, "What has this person done for me recently?" They felt obligated to comply if they owed the requester a favor.

- *In China.* Employees in China took a *family-based* approach. They offered assistance on the basis of ingroup/outgroup norms that encourage loyalty only to those within one's small group. In addition, they felt especially loyal to those of high status within their small group. In deciding to comply, they asked, "Is this requester connected to someone in my unit, especially someone of high ranking?" If the answer was yes, they felt obligated to yield to the request.
- *In Spain.* Spanish personnel took a *friendship-based* approach. They offered assistance on the basis of friendship norms that encourage loyalty to one's friends, regardless of the friend's position or status. They decided to comply by asking, "Is this requester connected to my friends?" If the answer was yes, they felt obligated to say yes.
- *In Germany.* German employees took a *system-based* approach to obligation. They offered assistance on the basis of the existing norms and rules of the organization. Rather than feeling obligated to specific individuals or groups, they felt obligated to support the system that governed these individuals and groups. They decided to comply by asking, "According to official rules and categories, am I supposed to assist this requester?" If the answer was yes, the obligation to grant the request was high.

Clearly, different norms of obligation to comply with requests predominate in different cultures. This is not to say that these cultures are entirely different from one another in this regard. No doubt, obligations to prior benefactors, to ingroup members, to friends, and to legitimate systems exist in all four of the cultures studied by Morris, Podolny, and Ariel. But, as their findings make clear, the relative potency of these different norms of obligation varies from culture to culture.

Approval

Imagine that before going to dinner with friends, there is divided opinion about whether to eat Mexican or Italian food. At the restaurant, opinions diverge in a discussion of a hot political topic. After dinner, there is another difference of opinion, this time over whether to go to a crowded bar for a drink or to a quiet coffee shop for intellectual conversation. Do you have a friend who would be especially likely to go along with the group in each instance to keep things operating smoothly? Can you think of another friend who would be willing to argue every disagreement to the bitter end? What might be the psychological differences between the two people? In other words, what factors inside the person affect the tendency to "go along to get along," the willingness to be influenced in order to be socially approved? Let's explore three person factors that affect whether an individual is likely to accommodate to the group position—approval, collectivism versus individualism, and rebelliousness—beginning with approval.

Certain individuals are very concerned with social approval and seem highly motivated to gain the respect of those around them. In an early study of personality and conformity, researchers measured people's need for social approval before observing how these same people responded to group pressure to make incorrect choices (as in the Asch line-judging experiments we described earlier). Just as would be expected if need for social approval motivates people to yield to others, those whose personality test scores indicated a high need for approval were more likely to go along with the group (Strickland & Crowne, 1962). Other researchers found a similar effect when measuring voice patterns among people having a discussion. High-need-for-approval speakers were especially likely to adopt their partner's vocal intensity and pause lengths (Giles & Coupland, 1991).

Treating the preference for approval as a need frames it in a somewhat negative way, implying that going along with others is based in some personality weakness. However, there is another way to view it. The desire for approval is at the center of the "nicest" of the major personality factors—agreeableness. Agreeableness is made up of a host of positive characteristics, including warmth, trust, and helpfulness. In addition, agreeable people are described as accommodating and compliant. They are inclined to go along with others in their groups to avoid conflict (Suls, Martin, & David, 1998). Psychologists who have studied personality and social behavior have suggested that agreeableness may have been vitally important to our ancestors' survival in groups (Graziano & Eisenberg, 1997; Hogan, 1993). According to this perspective, yielding in order to be agreeable should be regarded positively, as a valued personal trait. After all, it would be impossible for groups to function efficiently without a substantial amount of member conformity (Tyler & Degoey, 1995).

Collectivism versus Individualism

Earlier, we said that the injunctive norms of a group or culture tell people which of their behaviors will be met with social approval. However, some individuals in these groups and cultures are more likely than others to live up to these norms. What determines this tendency to respond to social norms rather than to personal preferences? One cause is a person's definition of self. Some people characterize themselves in personal and individualized terms, focusing on features that distinguish them from others: "I am an avid outdoors person with a strong spiritual nature." Other people characterize themselves in collective terms, identifying themselves by the groups to which they belong: "I am a member of the Sierra Club and am active in the Campus Interfaith Council." David Trafimow and Krystina Finlay (1996) found that people who defined themselves in individualistic ways made their decisions on the basis of their personal attitudes rather than group norms. However, those who defined themselves through their groups were more affected by what they thought others felt than by what they felt. Cultures that differ in the extent to which they are individualistic or collectivistic also produce this effect. In the Asch line-judging procedure, citizens of the more collectivistic societies of the East conform to a greater extent than do citizens of the more individualistic societies of the West (Bond & Smith, 1996).

Rebelliousness

How would you react if your taste in art was scorned by those around you? The British psychologist Michael Argyle (1957) examined how male high school students responded in such a situation. After expressing an opinion about the artistic value of a Marc Chagall painting, the boys heard their opinions belittled by classmates. When asked their opinions of the painting again, some shifted to agree with the others, while another group remained unchanged. However, a third group of boys did something surprising. They moved in the direction opposite to the others' position—not merely withstanding the social disapproval but defying it by becoming more extreme in their original opinions. Who are these rebellious individuals? Clearly, they are not conformists, who yield to the influence of others. But neither are they nonconformists, who simply resist social influence. Instead, they appear to be *anticonformists*, who react to social influence by reacting against it (Nail & Van Leeuwen, 1993; Nail, MacDonald, & Levy, 2000).

This tendency to react against social influence exists to some degree in most people. According to **reactance theory** (Brehm, 1966; Brehm & Brehm, 1981), we all value our freedom to decide how to act. When something (such as social pressure) threatens to take away that freedom, we often respond by doing the opposite of what we are being pressured to do. For instance, one study found that drivers who returned to their parked cars were slower at leaving their parking spaces if another driver was waiting to take the space. In addition, they moved even more slowly if the waiting driver honked to pressure them to leave faster (Ruback & Jwieng, 1997).

Reactance theory *Brehm's theory that we react against threats to our freedoms by reasserting those freedoms, often by doing the opposite of what we are being pressured to do.*

Of course, some people respond against threats to their freedoms more strongly than do others. These reactant individuals can be identified by a personality scale that includes items such as "If I am told what to do, I often do the opposite" (Bushman & Stack, 1996; Dowd, Milne, & Wise, 1991). Studies have found that highly reactant individuals are more likely to defy the advice of even their therapists and physicians (Dowd et al., 1988; Graybar, Antonuccio, Boutilier, & Varble, 1989).

Because cultlike groups are in the business of suppressing personal freedoms, they want nothing to do with highly reactant individuals. Remember Steve Hassan's description of how the Moonies sized up and split up recruits at introductory sessions? Those who seemed to be going along with the program were called "sheep" and were separated from those who showed signs of rebelliousness, the "goats." It is instructive that physical isolation of the goats was just the first step; if they spoke out again, they were quietly directed to leave (Hassan, 1990).

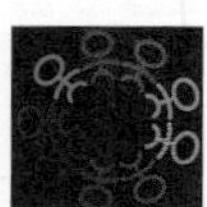

Personal Appeal

Which features of a person's social situation are likely to alter the motivation to go along to get along? One factor is the appeal of the group or individual pressuring for change. For example, if you found yourself among people you didn't much care for, you would be unlikely to try to dress like them, comply with their requests, or obey their directives. In contrast, you would be much more receptive to the influence efforts of people you liked or valued (Hackman, 1992).

Would you choose a political decision maker simply because he or she was good-looking? Although you might think not, candidates' looks have a deceptively strong impact on elections (Budesheim & DePaola, 1994; Zebrowitz, 1994). For example, voters in a Canadian federal election gave physically attractive candidates several times as many votes as they gave unattractive ones—while insisting that their choices would never be influenced by something as superficial as appearance (Efran & Patterson, 1974, 1976). Looks are influential in other domains as well. Good-looking fundraisers for the American Heart Association generated nearly twice as many donations (42 percent versus 23 percent) as other requesters (Reingen & Kernan, 1993). Likewise, physically attractive salespeople are more effective at getting customers to part with their money (Reingen & Kernan, 1993). It is not surprising, then, that when Steve Hassan accepted an invitation to his first Unification Church weekend, it was at the urging of three attractive young women he met on campus.

In addition, we are more attracted to—and more influenced by—those with whom we share connections and group memberships, especially when these similarities have been made prominent (Burn, 1991; Turner, 1991). Thus, salespeople often search for (or fabricate) a connection between themselves and their customers: "Well, no kidding, you're from Minneapolis? My wife's from Minnesota!" Fundraisers do the same, with good results. In one study (Aune & Basil, 1994), donations to charity more than doubled when the requester claimed a shared group identity with the target person by saying, "I'm a student, too" (see Figure 6.7).

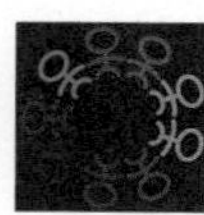

Observability

Just as we would expect, if social influence is sometimes based on the desire for acceptance and approval, conformity is less prevalent in private. When people can keep their decisions secret, they don't have to worry about the loss of connection and respect that an independent opinion might create.

Chester Insko and his colleagues (1985) demonstrated this point by presenting groups of University of North Carolina students with an ambiguous problem: judging whether a blue-green color was more blue or more green. When the students had to announce their judgments aloud and in public (rather than writing them down privately), they conformed more to what the other group members had said.

Figure 6.7
Hat trick.

Influence professionals of all sorts recognize the compliance-producing power of common group membership.

SOURCE: *Drawing by Levin © 1978. The New Yorker Magazine, Inc.*

Other studies have shown similar effects with judgments as trivial as evaluations of the taste of coffee and as serious as decisions about how to handle racist propaganda on campus (Blanchard, Lilly, & Vaughn, 1991; Cohen & Golden, 1972). After learning what others have said, people are especially likely to go along if their own responses are observable to the group (Campbell & Fairey, 1989). Cults appear to recognize that conformity is stronger when behavior is observable: Many such groups keep members under the unrelenting gaze of other members. For example, the Heaven's Gate cultists, who committed joint suicide in 1997, were required to perform their daily activities with a "partner" from the group.

In sum, people are more likely to go along with the influence attempts of appealing individuals because they are more motivated to gain the approval of those individuals. Two important situational sources of personal appeal are physical attractiveness and common group membership. Because the increased yielding comes from a desire to get along with these others, their influence is most pronounced when they can see whether yielding occurred.

Who's Strong Enough to Resist Strong Group Norms?

Norms don't always steer people in beneficial directions. What the people in one's group typically do and approve can be unhealthy. For example, among certain subgroups of young people, peer norms may support such dangers as alcohol and tobacco use. When these potentially harmful norms are strong, is there any psychological factor that will help resist them? Alan Stacy and his coworkers (1992) investigated several possible factors that might reduce high school students' vulnerability to peer norms for cigarette smoking. Only one proved effective: the students' belief that they possessed the ability to resist their peers' influence. A student who held this belief was significantly more likely to withstand even strong normative influence—for example, when most of the student's small group of friends smoked and approved of smoking. Other research has found similar results among students in every ethnic group examined: white, black, Hispanic, and Asian (Sussman, Dent, Flay, Hansen, & Johnson, 1986). Thus, even strong normative pressure doesn't sway everyone.

These findings may offer a way to reduce negative social influence in schools. If the belief in one's own capacity to resist peer pressure can protect a person from such pressure, instilling this belief in schoolchildren should safeguard them from dangerous peer norms, right? Right, but research suggests that the way in which this belief is instilled is crucial to the success of the strategy, as the Focus on Application feature shows.

Figure 6.8
Message pollution.

In an attempt to dramatize the problem of littering, the developers of this public service announcement have contaminated their message with a potentially harmful countermessage: "Littering is what we Americans do."

FOCUS ON Application

Doing Wrong by Trying to Do Right

In many schools, it has become common to give students resistance training intended to equip them with the skills necessary to reject the influence efforts of peers who try to tempt them into unhealthy habits. The resistance-skills education often takes the form of "just say no" training, in which students repeatedly practice how to deflect the negative influence of classmates. These resistance-skills-only programs have produced an entirely unexpected result: Despite coming to see themselves as more able to resist peer influence, the students in the programs often become more likely to engage in the unhealthy habits!

How could this be? A study done in the Los Angeles and San Diego County public school systems offers an answer. It examined the impact of junior high school programs for limiting adolescent alcohol use. After participating in multiple "just say no" skits and exercises intended to bolster their resistance to peer pressure to drink, students came to believe that drinking was more common among their peers than they had previously thought (Donaldson, Graham, Piccinin, & Hansen, 1995). By giving students resistance skills through repeated "just say no" trials, the program inadvertently conveyed an unintended message—"A lot of your peers do this and want you to do this." Thus, although these students became more able to resist peer influence, they became less motivated to do so because they perceived that drinking was the norm for people their age.

Alcohol reduction programs are not the only ones that have backfired in this way. After participating in an eating disorder program at Stanford University, college women exhibited more eating disorder symptoms than before. Why? A key feature of the program was the testimony of classmates about their own harmful eating behaviors, which made such behaviors seem more prevalent to participants (Mann et al., 1997). Similarly, a suicide prevention program administered to New Jersey teenagers informed participants of the alarmingly high number of teenage suicides. As a consequence, participants became more likely to see suicide as a possible solution to their problems (Shaffer, Garland, Vieland, Underwood, & Busner, 1991).

In all, there seems to be an understandable but misguided tendency of health educators to call attention to a problem by depicting it as regrettably frequent. It is easy to forget that the statement "Look at all the people like you who are doing this *unhealthy* thing" contains the powerful and potentially undercutting message "Look at all the people like you who *are* doing it" (see Figure 6.8).

What can program designers do to avoid these boomerang effects? Health educators must structure their programs so participants see the unwanted behavior as the exception rather than the rule. That way, the power of norms will work for the program rather than against it. Indeed, when resistance-skills training is included as part of a program that shows participants that healthy behavior is the norm, the resistance-skills training no longer reduces program effectiveness but instead enhances it (Donaldson et al., 1995). Under these circumstances, young people acquire both the ability to resist a peer's unhealthy influence and the desire to do so, because they recognize that *most* of their peers prefer the healthier route. As a result, the program is more likely to be successful. ■

A second factor interacts with norms to affect their impact on group members' behavior: the degree to which the member identifies with the group. Chances are, if you are reading this book, you are a college student. But not everyone who is taking college classes identifies him- or herself primarily in that way. If asked "Who are you?" many college students would describe themselves first in terms of religious, family, or ethnic group memberships. For these individuals, college student norms may not be especially influential because they don't identify strongly with the group, even though they are members of it.

Deborah Terry and Michael Hogg (1996) found good support for this idea in a study of Australian university students. The researchers measured subjects' views of the strength of the student norm on campus for regular exercise by asking them to estimate the amount of approval for regular exercise among their peers at the university. The students also indicated how much they identified themselves with their university peer group. When asked about their own intentions to exercise regularly during the upcoming weeks, only those individuals who identified themselves strongly as university students planned to follow the norms of the group. Those who held little identification with the group didn't let the approval of other group members affect their exercise plans at all. In sum, even strong group norms won't guide the behavior of members of the group who don't identify themselves psychologically as group members.

Summary

Most people are motivated to gain social acceptance and approval. As a result, they often allow themselves to be influenced by others whose acceptance and approval they value. The injunctive norms of a group, organization, or culture inform people of the actions that are likely to be approved and disapproved by its members. One such norm is that for reciprocation. To gain acceptance and avoid social disapproval, people change their actions to conform to the norms of the group. This is especially true of individuals who have a high need for approval, who hold a collectivistic view of themselves, and who do not possess a rebellious nature. In addition, the tendency to go along with group norms in order to get along with group members is heightened when the group is highly valued and when the norm-relevant behavior is observable to the group. However, even strong group norms can be resisted when members believe that they have the power to withstand group influence or when members don't feel highly identified with the group.

Managing Self-Image

Restaurant owners typically face a big problem with callers who make reservations but fail to appear. Tables that could have been filled by paying customers stand empty, causing substantial economic loss. The problem has become so severe that some restaurateurs have begun requesting the credit card numbers of callers and charging a fee if they don't honor their reservations. However, Gordon Sinclair, the proprietor of Gordon's restaurant in Chicago, has hit on a highly effective tactic that doesn't bruise the egos of his customers when they call for reservations. He has instructed his receptionists to stop saying, "Please call us if you change your plans," and to start asking, "Will you call us if you change your plans?" and to wait for a response. As a result, his no-show rate has dropped from 30 percent to 10 percent (Grimes, 1997).

What is it about this subtle shift that leads to such a dramatic difference? The receptionist specifically asks for and waits for the customer's affirmative response. By inducing customers to make a personal commitment to a behavior, this approach increases the chance that they will perform the behavior.

A **personal commitment** ties an individual's identity to a position or course of action, making it more likely that he or she will follow through. This is so because most individuals prefer to be consistent and have a strong desire to see themselves as the kind of person who lives up to promises and commitments (Baumeister, Stillwell, & Heatherton, 1994; Kerr, Garst, Lewandowski, & Harris, 1997). Indeed, students at Boston University behaved almost as consistently with a commitment they made to a computer as to another person (Kiesler, Sproull, & Watters, 1996). As a consequence, even seemingly insignificant commitments can lead to large behavior changes. For instance, getting people to answer a five-question survey about organ donation increases their willingness to become organ donors (Carducci, Deuser, Bauer, Large, & Ramaekers, 1989).

Commitment-Based Tactics

Because of the desire to be consistent with their existing behaviors, promises, and self-images, people are often vulnerable to a simple request strategy. This basic strategy—first obtaining a commitment and then making a request that is consistent with it—is at the core of numerous compliance techniques used regularly by influence professionals. Let's look at several that differ primarily in the way they obtain the initial commitment.

The Foot-in-the-Door Technique Earlier in this chapter, we described the foot-in-the-door technique, which increases compliance with a particular request by first gaining compliance with a smaller, related request. The power of the technique can be seen in a study in which Israeli researchers went to a local apartment district, knocked on half the doors, and asked residents to sign a petition favoring the establishment of a recreation center for the mentally handicapped. Because the cause was good and the request was small, almost everyone agreed to sign. Residents in the other apartments did not receive a visit and, consequently, did not make a commitment to the mentally handicapped. Two weeks later, on National Collection Day for the Mentally Handicapped, all neighborhood residents were approached at home and asked to give money to this cause. Only about half (53 percent) of those who had not been previously asked to sign a petition made a contribution, but nearly all (92 percent) of those who had signed two weeks earlier gave a donation (Schwartzwald, Bizman, & Raz, 1983).

What is it about saying yes to a minor charity request that causes people to say yes to a larger, related one? According to Jonathan Freedman and Scott Fraser (1966), who first investigated the foot-in-the-door technique, compliance with the initial request changes people's self-images: They come to see themselves as more helpful, public-spirited individuals. Then, to be consistent with this modified self-identity, they are more willing to comply with other charitable requests. A study by Jerry Burger and Rosanna Guadagno (2000) offers support for the idea that the foot-in-the-door technique works by changing self-concept. They found that the technique was successful only on individuals who scored high on *self-concept clarity*, which reflects the extent to which people alter their self-concepts on the basis of new information. Thus, the more a person was likely to change self-concept as a result of agreeing to a small charity request, the more that person was then likely to agree to a larger charity request.

Personal commitment *Anything that connects an individual's identity more closely to a position or course of action.*

Low-ball technique *Gaining a commitment to an arrangement and then raising the cost of carrying out the arrangement.*

The Low-Ball Technique Someone using the **low-ball technique** first gets a commitment from another by offering a good deal, then—after the commitment is obtained—raises the cost of completing the deal (Cialdini, Cacioppo, Bassett, & Miller, 1978). The tactic can be surprisingly effective. For example, French cigarette smokers were asked to participate in a study in which they would fill out a short questionnaire. After committing to a date and time, they were informed that the study required them to refrain from smoking for eighteen hours before the experiment. Even though they were given the chance to back out after hearing of the nonsmoking requirement, an astounding 85 percent agreed to participate anyway—many more than the 12 percent who agreed to participate if informed of the nonsmoking requirement before they committed to a date and time (Joule, 1987).

Automobile salespeople "throw the low-ball" regularly: First, they induce a customer to choose a particular car by offering a low price on that model. After the selection has been made—and, at times, after commitment to the car is enhanced by allowing the customer to take it home overnight or arrange financing with the bank—something happens to remove the attractive price before the final papers are signed. Perhaps a calculation error is "discovered" or the sales manager disallows the deal because "we'd be losing money at that price." By this time, though, many customers have experienced a strong internal commitment to that automobile. Consequently, they often proceed with the purchase.

How could it be that car shoppers would forge ahead with a purchase after the reason they decided for it had been removed? After making an active choice for something, people see it more positively and are reluctant to relinquish it (Cioffi & Garner, 1996; Kahneman, Knetsch, & Thaler, 1991). This is especially the case when they think they have come to own it, because once they have taken "mental possession" of an important object, it becomes part of self-concept (Ball & Tasaki, 1992; Beggan & Allison, 1997). Hence, the behavior of car buyers who fall for the low-ball technique makes good psychological, if not good economic, sense. Despite the increased cost, many car shoppers decide to buy anyway, saying, "It's worth a few hundred dollars extra to get the car I really like because it fits who I am." Rarely do they realize that it wasn't these positive feelings toward the car that caused their commitment to it. Instead, it was their commitment to the car (launched by the low-ball technique) that caused the positive feelings.

The Bait and Switch Technique A somewhat similar practice sometimes employed by car dealers is called the **bait and switch technique.** Initially, an automobile is advertised at a special low price to get customers to decide that they can afford to purchase a new car. They make the commitment to buying a car by visiting the dealership to secure the deal. When they arrive, however, they find that the advertised model is sold and no longer available or is of low quality, possessing none of the features people typically want. However, because they have made an active commitment to getting a new car from that dealer, they are more willing to agree to examine and buy a more expensive model there. Vehicles are not the only merchandise sold through the bait and switch tactic; appliance and furniture stores are notorious for relying on it.

French researchers Robert Joule, Fabienne Gouilloux, and Florent Weber (1989), who called it the "lure" procedure, demonstrated how the technique worked at their university. Students were recruited for an interesting study involving movie clips that would pay 30 francs (about $6) for their participation. However, when they appeared for the experiment, they were informed that it had been cancelled. They were also told that, as long as they were there, they could volunteer for a different experiment, which offered no pay and was less interesting than the first one—it involved memorizing lists of numbers. The researchers knew that the second experiment was not attractive enough to get many volunteers by itself: When it was described to another group of students, only 15 percent agreed to participate without pay. But the bait and switch procedure tripled the number of volunteers: About 47 percent of the students who had made a commitment of time and effort to come to participate in an attractive experiment that was cancelled were then willing to take part in a much less attractive experiment.

Like the low-ball tactic, the bait and switch works by first getting people to commit to a desirable arrangement. Once the commitment is in place, they are willing to accept a less attractive arrangement—one they would have likely bypassed before being tricked into making the commitment.

Bait and switch technique *Gaining a commitment to an arrangement, then making the arrangement unavailable or unappealing and offering a more costly arrangement.*

The Labeling Technique Another way to induce a commitment to a course of action is to give a person a label that is consistent with the action, a procedure called the

labeling technique. For instance, elementary school children who were told by an adult "You look to me like the kind of girl (or boy) who understands how important it is to write correctly" became more likely to choose to work on a penmanship task three to nine days later in private (Cialdini, Eisenberg, Green, Rhoads, & Bator, 1998). Alice Tybout and Richard Yalch (1980) demonstrated how labeling tactics could be used to spur adults to vote. They interviewed 162 voters and, at random, told half that, according to their interview responses, they were "above-average citizens likely to vote and participate in political events." The other half were told that they appeared to be average in these activities. As a result, those given the above-average label not only saw themselves as better citizens than those given the average label, but also they were more likely to vote in a local election held a week later.

Savvy politicians have long understood the committing character of labels. Former secretary of state Henry Kissinger was renowned as one of the most capable negotiators of his time. Yet, even he was impressed by the international bargaining skills of then-president of Egypt Anwar Sadat. Before negotiations began, Sadat would assure his opponents that they and citizens of their country were widely known for their cooperativeness and fairness. With this sort of flattery, he not only created positive feelings, he also connected his opponents' identities to a course of action that served his goals. According to Kissinger (1982), Sadat was a successful negotiator because he understood how to get others to act on his behalf by giving them a reputation to uphold.

In sum, because of a desire in most people to live up to their commitments, it is possible to increase a target person's performance of an action by using any of several commitment-based techniques. Although these techniques differ in the way they bring about the commitment, they have in common the establishment of an early commitment that ties the target person's identity to the desired action. In the process of performing the action, the target person achieves the goal of managing (that is, enhancing, confirming, or protecting) self-image. Let's look more closely at some of the factors of the person and of the situation that affect when and how people live up to their commitments so as to manage their self-images.

Existing Values

So far, we have focused on commitments that have been created by outside pressures—requests for small favors, induced choices or decisions, and external labels. But certain commitments reside within a person in the form of existing values. Sometimes people can be influenced toward a course of action because they recognize that the action is consistent with a value—let's say politeness—that they already possess or wish to possess. Thus, those who value politeness may go along with something not because they want what is being offered but because they want to be polite.

One of your textbook authors, Robert Cialdini, once took training in several phone sales operations to learn their influence strategies. He was surprised that two of the companies included breath exercises in the sales skills taught to new recruits. Why breath exercises? The companies had learned that many people consider it discourteous to interrupt a caller while he or she is speaking. Instead, they wait for a pause, feeling that it would be impolite to break in—even to say, "Sorry, not interested"—as long as the salesperson is talking. By learning to hold their breaths for long periods, the salespeople could achieve the goal of delivering more product information before they paused and prospects felt entitled to speak.

Labeling technique *Assigning a label to an individual and then requesting a favor that is consistent with the label.*

People often align their behaviors to fit with values such as good health, world peace, religious faith, and so on. These deep-seated values keep individuals working at the important personal projects in their lives, causing them to persevere through time, toil, and adversity (Lydon & Zanna, 1990; Sheldon & Elliot, 1999). Thus,

Table 6.1 Commitment-based compliance techniques.

Technique	The First Step		The Second Step	
	Inducing the Initial Commitment by:	Example:	Taking Advantage of the Initial Commitment by:	Example:
Foot-in-the-Door	Gaining the target person's compliance with a small request.	Getting the target to sign a petition for a charitable cause.	Requesting compliance with a related, larger request.	Asking for a donation to support the cause.
Low-Ball	Obtaining the target person's agreement to a specific arrangement.	Negotiating a deal with the target on a new car.	Changing the terms of the arrangement.	Saying that the original deal contained a calculation error.
Bait and Switch	Spurring the target person to take a course of action.	Getting the target to decide to buy a new car by advertising a very low price.	Describing the chosen action as impossible or unwise and suggesting a related action instead.	Referring to the advertised car as sold or inferior and offering a more expensive model.
Labeling	Assigning the target person a trait label.	Describing the target as above average in citizenship.	Seeking compliance with a request that is consistent with the label.	Asking the target to vote in the next election.

marketers who can create a link between our personal values and their products or services will likely have us as long-term customers. This form of influence can be quite ethical and beneficial, but it can also be used to bind people to activities and organizations that are not in their best interests. Cultlike groups, for instance, recruit and retain members by linking the group's (declared) purposes to such widely held values as spiritual salvation, personal enlightenment, and social justice (Zimbardo, 1997). Steve Hassan says that before he joined the Unification Church, he felt committed to reducing social problems but didn't know how to go about it. During his first visit to a Moonie gathering, he was assured that the group was dedicated to combating "just such social problems as the ones I was concerned about" (Hassan, 1990, p. 13).

Internal Focus

If people try to manage their self-concept by being consistent with their personal values, then those who are clearly aware of their values should behave especially consistently with them. The *private self-consciousness scale* (Fenigstein, Scheier, & Buss, 1975) measures this tendency to pay attention to one's personal values, attitudes, and beliefs. Research has determined that individuals scoring high on private self-consciousness do indeed act more consistently with these internal factors than with external factors such as social norms or preferences (Froming & Carver, 1981; Chapman, Symons, & Caya, 1994). For instance, two weeks before Spanish parliamentary elections, voters answered questions about the extent to which the opposing political parties possessed characteristics that fit with the voters' values concerning such things as diversity, equality, and social change. Four days after the election, they were asked to name the party for which they had voted. Those highest in private self-consciousness were most likely to have cast a ballot for the party that fit their personal values (Echebarria & Valencia, 1994). Other research indicates that even a temporary increase in the tendency to focus inside oneself produces a similar effect (Ybarra & Trafimow, 1998). Thus, people who typically or temporarily focus inside themselves on their values appear to use these values to steer their actions and, hence, to confirm their identities.

In sum, to manage their self-concepts, people try to act in concert with the personal values that help make up these self-concepts. Thus, influence professionals can increase compliance by establishing links between their requests and the values to which people feel committed. Individuals who are especially likely to focus inside themselves on their personal values (for example, those scoring high in private self-consciousness) will be particularly vulnerable to this approach.

Active and Public Commitments

When it comes to spurring future consistent behavior, not all commitments are created equal. The most enduring commitments are those that most clearly connect a desired course of action to an individual's self-concept. Two situational features of commitments work successfully in this regard: Lasting commitments are active and public.

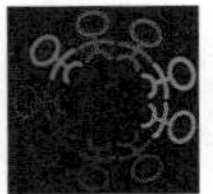

Active Commitments According to *Consumer Reports* magazine ("Rock 'n' ripoff," 1997), an important piece of information has been disappearing from ads for popular rock music concerts—ticket prices. Why should concert promoters try to hide the cost of a ticket from fans? Even if the figure is high, people will find out the price of a seat as soon as they call or visit a ticket outlet, right? True, but promoters have recognized that potential concertgoers are more likely to purchase tickets after that call or visit than before. Even making a phone call to inquire about ticket prices constitutes an active personal commitment to the concert, which makes the caller more favorable to the idea of attending.

The impact of action on future action can be seen in research investigating the effect of active versus passive commitments (Allison & Messick, 1988; Fazio, Sherman, & Herr, 1982). For instance, in a study by Delia Cioffi and Randy Garner (1996), college students volunteered for an AIDS education project in the local schools. The researchers arranged for half to volunteer actively by filling out a form stating that they wanted to participate. The other half volunteered passively by failing to fill out a form stating that they didn't want to participate. Three to four days later, when asked to begin their involvement in the project, the great majority (74 percent) who appeared as scheduled came from the ranks of those who had actively agreed to participate.

What was it about active commitment that caused these individuals to follow through? One way people come to perceive and define themselves is through an examination of their actions (Bem, 1967; Vallacher & Wegner, 1985). The evidence is strong that we think our actions tell us more about ourselves than do our non-actions (Fazio, 1987; Nisbett & Ross, 1980). Indeed, compared to those who volunteered passively for the AIDS education project in the Cioffi and Garner (1996) study, those who volunteered actively were more likely to explain their decisions by implicating their personal values, preferences, and traits. Thus active commitments give us the kind of information we use to shape our self-images, which then shape our future behavior (Dolinski, 2000).

Public Commitments In addition to active commitments, public commitments to a course of action increase the chance that people will maintain that course of action into the future. Morton Deutsch and Harold Gerard (1955) performed a classic experiment that examined how both types of commitments operate. The researchers had subjects estimate the lengths of lines in an Asch-type procedure. One group of subjects left these length judgments in their minds, not committing to them either actively or publicly. A second group wrote down their estimates privately for just a second—thereby making the commitment active—and then immediately erased them. A third group wrote down their judgments and turned them over to the experimenter, making an active and public commitment to their decisions. At this point, all subjects received information that their judgments were wrong—they learned that the other subjects in the study (actually confederates) had estimated the lines differently. Deutsch and Gerard wanted to find out which of the three groups would be most inclined to stay with their initial choices after receiving feedback that the choices were incorrect. The results were clear. Those whose judgments had never left their heads, having been neither written down nor made public, were least loyal to them. Those who had made an active commitment to their initial choices were less willing to change their minds when confronted with contradictory evidence. But, by far, it was those who had connected themselves publicly to their first estimates who most resolutely refused to shift from those positions later (see Figure 6.9).

Percentage of Subjects Remaining Loyal to Their Initial Judgments
100
80
60
40
20
0
Neither Active nor Public
Active Only
Active Plus Public
Commitment

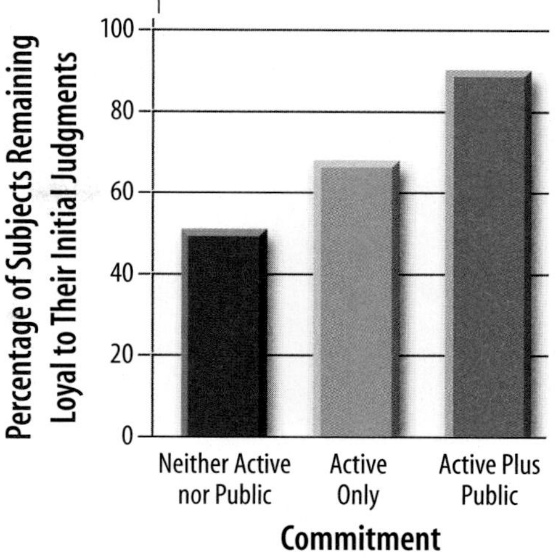

Figure 6.9
The staying power of different types of commitments.

Individuals who made active and public commitments to an initial set of judgments were most likely to stay loyal to those judgments when they were later attacked. Those who made neither active nor public commitments were least loyal.

SOURCE: *Adapted from Deutsch & Gerard, 1955.*

We can think of two reasons why public commitments were the most resistant to change. First, participants who had gone on record may not have wanted to be seen by the experimenter as easily influenced or inconsistent. This is a real possibility, as most people prefer to be seen as resolute and stable (Baumeister, 1982). But there is a second reason as well. Once people have made a public pronouncement, they come to believe it more (Schlenker, Dlugolecki, & Doherty, 1994; Schlenker & Trudeau, 1990). For example, in research conducted by Diane Tice (1992), subjects agreed to play the role of an extraverted person and then did so under either public or private circumstances. Much more than subjects in the private condition, those who played the extraverted role in public incorporated extraversion into their real self-concepts, describing themselves later as truly more outgoing and sociable. This new extraverted identity showed itself in subjects' behavior after the study was over and they were left in a waiting room with a confederate: Those who had publicly portrayed themselves earlier as extraverted sat closer and talked more to the confederate. Tice also found that the effect of public self-presentations was strongest when subjects felt that they had free choice in deciding to make them. In sum, like active commitments, public commitments—especially when freely chosen—alter self-image (Kelly, 1998; Kelly & McKillop, 1996; Schlenker, 1980). These altered self-images then guide further actions accordingly.

Men, Women, and Public Conformity

Because public pronouncements have the ability to change not just social image but also self-image, people may try to protect their self-concepts by being careful about when they publicly admit that they have been influenced. But which aspects of self-concept people choose to protect in this way can differ for men and women.

The Deutsch and Gerard (1955) experiment demonstrated that, in the face of conformity pressures, people are more loyal to their public decisions than to their private decisions. However, one study showed that men may be especially reluctant to conform under public conditions (Eagly, Wood, & Fishbaugh, 1981). In that study, male and female participants conformed to the group opinion to about the same extent when their responses were privately made, but males conformed less than females to the group opinion when they had to do so in public.

Why would men resist public conformity more than women? The researchers suggest that the males' nonconformity may have represented conformity at a higher level—with an image of independence that is socialized into the identity of most men (Eagly, 1987). Men prefer to see themselves as independent, unique, and self-sufficient. Election surveys over the last 40 years have found that men are even more likely than women to announce their political category as Independent (Norrander, 1997). A man who expresses nonconformity communicates a picture of himself as self-reliant, as a leader rather than a follower. To whom is he communicating this picture? It appears that he is sending the message as much to himself as to others.

One series of studies found that men base self-esteem on factors that make them unique and independent, whereas women are more likely to base self-esteem on factors that connect them to members of their groups (Josephs, Markus, & Tarafodi, 1992). Thus, because of the potent impact of public pronouncements on private image, men may resist public conformity in an effort to stay true to a view of themselves as possessing independence.

Roy Baumeister and Kristin Sommer (1997) have suggested a further twist to the plot: men's public nonconformity might be motivated not by a desire to be independent of the group but by a desire to belong. They contend that men want to be accepted by their groups as much as women do; however, women seek acceptance from close cooperative relationships, whereas men aim to be accepted by demonstrating a unique ability or by showing the potential for leadership. After all, a leader is importantly interconnected with group members. In all, it appears that women and men don't differ much in their basic social influence goals—for example, to be accepted and to validate their self-images—but that they do differ in the routes they take to reach those goals.

Summary

One way to achieve the goal of managing self-image is through the social influence process. People can enhance, validate, and protect their identities by yielding to requests for action that fits with their self-concepts. Several influence techniques (the foot-in-the-door, the low-ball, the bait and switch, and labeling techniques) work by establishing an early commitment that links the target person's identity to a desired course of action. In addition, people have existing commitments in the form of personal values that spur them to comply with requests that are consistent with these values. Therefore, influence practitioners can increase compliance by establishing connections between their requests and the values to which targets feel committed, especially when these values are prominent in consciousness. The values to which a target feels committed can differ for men and women. The factors affecting the goal of managing self-image, as well as those affecting the other social influence goals, are presented in Table 6.2.

CHAPTER 6
Summary Table

Table 6.2 Summary of the goals served by social influence and the factors related to them.

The Goal	The Person	The Situation	Interactions
Choosing Correctly	• Uncertainty	• Consensus • Similarity	• The desire for accuracy increases conformity only when people are unsure of their judgments.
Gaining Social Approval	• Desire for Approval • Collective Sense of Self • Rebelliousness	• Others' Appeal • Public Observability	• Even strong forms of group approval and disapproval can be resisted by people who: believe they can withstand group pressure are not highly identified within the group
Managing Self-Image	• Existing Values • Internal Focus	• Active Commitments • Public Commitments	• When conformity threatens one's identity as an independent person, one may conform less in public situations. This is especially true of men who see independence as an important part of self-concept.

REVISITING

The Turnaround of Steve Hassan

We promised at the beginning of this chapter that by the end, you'd understand the causes of Steve Hassan's remarkably rapid switch from normal college student to fully committed follower of the Reverend Moon. Furthermore, we promised that, in the process, you'd also understand the causes of his subsequent, equally rapid shift away from the Unification organization—because the causes are the same. They are the principles of social influence that drive all of us to conform, comply, and obey. They may get us to vote for a candidate, purchase a product, or donate to a cause. In Hassan's case, they got him to change his life dramatically, twice.

Let's examine how these principles worked in terms of the three goals of social influence that we've described. Like the rest of us, in making any important changes, Hassan wanted to achieve the goal of *choosing correctly*. The Unification organization accommodated him by providing information from both of the sources people normally use to make correct decisions—authorities and peers. The authorities were Reverend Moon himself, the new Messiah, and officials of the group who took the role of teachers. The peers were young people just like Hassan who had decided to devote themselves to the purposes of the organization because, just like him, they shared similar concerns about the world. Among these peers, the consensus about the correctness of their actions was total. Moreover, Hassan was pressured to cut off contact with voices from outside the group that could undermine this consensus. Under these conditions, the opinions and norms of the group forged a compelling sense of reality for him.

When Hassan was deprogrammed out of the Unification organization, the deprogrammers relied on these same principles. They, too, portrayed themselves as experts and teachers on the matter at hand, demonstrating intricate knowledge of the group's doctrines, dynamics, and deceptions. They, too, revealed themselves to be just like him, recounting how each had been subjected to the same recruitment and persuasion tactics that he had experienced and exhibiting an unshakable consensus that they were right in their decisions to leave the group. And by hiding him from the Unification organization for five days in a secret apartment, they, too, cut him off from his customary reference group.

In recruiting and retaining Hassan as a member, the Moonies also saw to it that he could achieve the goal of *gaining social approval* by yielding to the group's wishes. At the beginning, he was approached by appealing young people whose acceptance he found desirable. Not long after, at recruitment workshops, he was the focus of great positive attention and affection. Then, once he was a full-fledged member, his only approval came from those who shared his group membership; and, of course, that approval came exclusively for doing things that advanced the group's purposes. Hassan's deprogramming experience proceeded similarly. He was quickly impressed with how personally appealing the deprogrammers were, describing them as warm, caring, and spiritually minded individuals. He was also gratified by the sympathetic and respectful attention they gave him. And, in the isolation of the apartment where he was being held, his only approval came from responses that fit the deprogrammers' purposes.

As the world turns. *As he was when he joined the Moonies, Steve Hassan is still striving to make the world a better place. Today, he does so not as a cult member but as a cult fighter.*

When members of the Unification organization tried to influence Hassan toward the group, they made certain that by yielding, he could achieve the goal of *managing his self-image*, assuring him that his inner commitment to solving social problems could be met by joining the group. His deprogrammers did the same, except that they allowed him to see that leaving the group was the way to achieve this goal. They pressed him to get in touch with his deep-seated values for honesty, family, and freedom—all of which were incompatible with what he had experienced in the Unification organization. But most tellingly, after he recognized for himself that the group had deceived and trapped him into an unhealthy environment, he saw how he could recommit himself to a life of social service: He could help others extricate themselves from these prisonlike organizations. He could become a cult exit counselor and reduce the social problems that cults create in our world. In all, the deprogramming experience was successful because it provided Hassan with a substituted reference group, set of values, and sense of purpose—just as the Moonie recruitment and indoctrination experience had done years before.

Hassan has since remained committed to his vision, emerging to become one of the country's leading cult exit counselors and explaining his effective techniques (Hassan, 2000) in ways that rely on insights from the scientific study of social influence—insights that you, too, now possess, at a fraction of the cost.

CHAPTER 6

Summary

1. Social influence is defined as a change in behavior caused by real or imagined pressure from others. It is different from persuasion in that it refers to shifts in overt actions rather than in private attitudes and beliefs.

Categories of Social Influence: Conformity, Compliance, and Obedience

1. Social psychologists have investigated three major types of social influence: conformity, compliance, and obedience.
2. Conformity refers to behavior change designed to match the actions of others.
3. Compliance refers to behavior change that occurs as a result of a direct request.
4. Obedience is a special type of compliance that occurs as a result of a directive from an authority figure.

Choosing Correctly

1. People often rely on two powerful psychological principles to help them choose correctly: authority and social validation. Thus, they are more willing to be influenced by authority figures, on the one hand, and similar peers on the other.
2. One reason authorities are influential is that they are often expert, and, by following an authority's directives, people can usually choose correctly without having to think hard about the issue themselves.
3. Just as following an authority is normally a shortcut to choosing correctly, so is following the lead of most of one's peers. The choices of these others provide social validation for the correctness of that choice.
4. People are most likely to allow themselves to be influenced by others when they are uncertain about how to respond in the situation—because when uncertainty and ambiguity reign, people lose confidence in their own ability to choose well.
5. When others share a consensus about the correct way to act, they are especially influential to observers.
6. In addition, observers are more likely to be influenced by others who are similar to them and who, therefore, provide better evidence about what the observers should do.
7. When choosing accurately is important, only uncertain individuals are more likely to follow the crowd; those who are already sure of the validity of their judgments are less willing to conform.

Gaining Social Approval

1. Frequently, people change in order to be more accepted and approved by their groups and to avoid the social rejection that often comes from resisting group pressure for change.
2. Injunctive norms of a group or culture inform people as to the behaviors that are likely to get them accepted or rejected there.
3. One such norm is that of reciprocity, which obligates people to give back to those who have given first. Anyone who violates this norm risks social disapproval and rejection, which makes people more willing to comply with requests of those who have provided an initial favor or concession.
4. The door-in-the-face technique engages the tendency to reciprocate concessions. It begins with a large favor likely to be rejected and then retreats to a smaller favor.
5. The desire for social approval and a collective self-definition both increase one's willingness to submit to social influence in order to gain acceptance. But a tendency for rebelliousness decreases one's susceptibility to social influence, especially when the influence is seen as threatening one's freedom to decide.
6. Two features of a person's social situation increase the motivation to go along to get along: the appeal

of the group or individual pressing for change and the public observability of the person's actions.

7. Even strong group norms can be resisted when members feel that they have the ability to withstand group influence or when members don't feel highly identified with the group.

Managing Self-Image

1. People can manage their self-image by yielding to requests for action that fits or enhances their identity.
2. Influence professionals can increase compliance by linking their requests to the values to which people feel committed, especially when these values are prominent in consciousness.
3. Several influence techniques (foot-in-the-door, low-ball, bait and switch, and labeling) work by establishing an early commitment that links a person's identity to a desired course of action.
4. These commitments are most effective when actively and publicly made, particularly when they are also made with free choice.
5. In order to maintain the image of self-reliance, men are less likely than women to conform publicly to the group opinion.

CHAPTER 6
Key Terms

Bait and switch technique *Gaining a commitment to an arrangement, then making the arrangement unavailable or unappealing and offering a more costly arrangement.*

Compliance *Behavior change that occurs as a result of a direct request.*

Conformity *Behavior change designed to match the actions of others.*

Door-in-the-face technique *A technique that increases compliance by beginning with a large favor likely to be rejected and then retreating to a more moderate favor.*

Expert power *The capacity to influence that flows from one's presumed wisdom or knowledge.*

Foot-in-the-door technique *A technique that increases compliance with a large request by first getting compliance with a smaller, related request.*

Labeling technique *Assigning a label to an individual and then requesting a favor that is consistent with the label.*

List procedure *A technique that seeks to gain compliance with a request by displaying a long list of others, especially similar others, who have complied.*

Low-ball technique *Gaining a commitment to an arrangement and then raising the cost of carrying out the arrangement.*

Norm of reciprocity *The norm that requires that we repay others with the form of behavior they have given us.*

Obedience *Compliance that occurs in response to a directive from an authority figure.*

Participant observation *A research approach in which the researcher infiltrates the setting to be studied and observes its workings from within.*

Personal commitment *Anything that connects an individual's identity more closely to a position or course of action.*

Reactance theory *Brehm's theory that we react against threats to our freedoms by reasserting those freedoms, often by doing the opposite of what we are being pressured to do.*

Social influence *A change in overt behavior caused by real or imagined pressure from others.*

Social validation *An interpersonal way to locate and validate the correct choice.*

That's-not-all technique *A technique that increases compliance by "sweetening" an offer with additional benefits.*

CHAPTER 7
Affiliation and Friendship

The Woman "Everybody Loved" and the Man Who Hated Her

At the age of four, Elliot Roosevelt's daughter announced that she "loved everybody and everybody loved her" (Cook, 1992; p. 52). Lovable little Eleanor grew up to be internationally famous for her sociability and extraversion. Her circle of friends included many wealthy "blue bloods" such as her rough-riding uncle Teddy and her husband Franklin D. But the circle was too wide for some of her aristocratic associates, one of whom commented that if Eleanor was invited to dinner, "You would never know quite who she would bring along—Blacks, Jews, Sapphists in slacks, rude communist youths" (p. 1).

She was known for the passionate and kind quality of her relationships with other people. For instance, two other commentators said of her, "She changed my life, just by caring," and "Her very presence lit up the room" (1).

Eleanor Roosevelt

One woman described running to catch a bus in Greenwich Village:

> ... there was this long-legged woman with quite a stride running for the bus. She was much faster than I was.... She hopped on just as the bus pulled out, and held out her long arm and with a very firm grip pulled me aboard. And I got on right into the smiling face of Eleanor Roosevelt (2).

But Eleanor Roosevelt was not loved by all. One man didn't even *like* her. In fact, according to his biographer, FBI Director J. Edgar Hoover literally "despised" Eleanor Roosevelt (Gentry, 1991). He took sadistic pleasure, for example, in leaking scandalous stories about her love affairs with various men and women. When she was appointed U.S. representative to the United Nations and referred to as "first lady of the world," Hoover "flew into a towering rage" (p. 391). And when, as U.N. ambassador, she received a series of threatening letters, Hoover simply, and scornfully, refused to investigate the matter.

In contrast to Eleanor Roosevelt's gregariousness, Hoover's biography describes a "peculiarly private man" who "shrank from human contact" (Gentry, 1991). His long-time chauffeur referred to Hoover's suspiciousness of "outside people" (20). Hoover never married, and his niece said he was afraid of personal involvements. One aide described Hoover's behavior at the funeral of a man with whom he had worked closely for years:

> He looked the way he always did when he was in public: irritated, put upon, as if his being here was a great imposition. No, there was no emotion. I've never known Mr. Hoover to really care about anything or anybody, except maybe his dogs. He was a very cold man. (699)

Eleanor Roosevelt wasn't the only person to feel the sting of Hoover's bitterness. Indeed, he kept a long list of personal enemies. And Hoover wasn't above abusing his official powers to place illegal wiretaps and hidden microphones in the hopes of uncovering dirty secrets about the private lives of the people he disliked (Martin Luther King, Jr., like Eleanor Roosevelt, was a favorite target for such practices).

The social relationships of Eleanor Roosevelt and J. Edgar Hoover raise a number of questions we'll consider in this chapter. What factors draw people into friendly relationships, and, conversely, what factors lead some people not to care for one another? Why is it that some people, such as Eleanor Roosevelt, are generally sociable and well liked, whereas others, such as J. Edgar Hoover, are generally withdrawn or disliked by others?

Why do people seek friendships? Most of us take social relationships so much for granted this question may seem ridiculous. But though all animals need to eat, not all hunger for the social life. Indeed, members of many species live a hermit's existence. Consider our close relatives, the orangutans: "Social relationships among the orangutans are few...[T]hey are virtually limited to relations between mothers and their offspring and the brief, simple encounters between adult males and females (only in order to copulate)" (E. O. Wilson, 1975, 257).

To explain why many animals prefer the solitary existence, zoologist John Alcock (1993) points out that sociality has serious costs associated with it. Animals of the same species compete with one another for the same food, for home sites, and for other scarce resources. They also bring contagious diseases and parasites. Worse yet, they may cheat, and even kill, one another. All these costs also apply to *Homo sapiens.* So it is perhaps a wonder that people are not generally more like the suspicious and solitary J. Edgar Hoover and less like the gregarious and trusting Eleanor Roosevelt. As we'll see, though, there are a number of potential rewards that motivate us to associate with others. But first, let's define what we mean by affiliation and friendship.

Friendship. *When students are asked to describe what friends are, they include mutual enjoyment, support, openness, trust, and equality. Although the dictionary distinguishes friends from relatives and lovers, actual friendships do not involve such a neat distinction.*

What Is a Friend?

Since the time of William James (1890) and McDougall (1908), psychologists who have probed the roots of human motivation have agreed that an **affiliation motive**—a desire to be near others and to have pleasant and affectionate interactions with them—is fundamental (e.g. Baumeister & Leary, 1995; Murray 1938). And research has supported the importance of this motive in human affairs (McAdams, 1990; Winter, 1996).

Affiliative behavior can include interactions with complete strangers—people we don't know at all—such as the outgoing stranger in line at the supermarket who makes a comment about the latest tabloid news. It can extend to relationships with acquaintances—people we know only slightly, such as the familiar clerk in the supermarket, to whom we may only say hello. Beyond these casual relations, we also affiliate with intimates—with friends, relatives, and lovers.

Webster's dictionary defines a **friend** as "someone on terms of affection and regard for another who is neither relative nor lover." When researchers have gone a step beyond Webster and asked students about the ideal characteristics of a friend, they find a reasonable amount of agreement (Bukowski, Hova, & Boivin, 1994; Sharabany, 1994). For instance, when Keith Davis and Michael Todd (1985) asked groups of students to list the characteristics of friendship, most of them generated lists that included such items as:

1. Friends participate as equals.
2. Friends enjoy each other's company.
3. Friends trust one another to act in their best interest.
4. Friends help each other in times of need.
5. Friends accept one another and are not inclined to mold one another into new people.
6. Friends respect one another.
7. Friends act themselves around one another and do not "wear masks".
8. Friends understand one another.
9. Friends confide in one another.
10. Friends share similar interests and values.

Of course, these are ideal characteristics. Indeed, if you consider the people you regard as friends, you realize that real friendships don't usually contain all of these features all of the time (Davis & Todd, 1985).

Relationships with friends are more voluntary than relationships with relatives (Adams & Bleiszner, 1994). We pick our friends, and we can switch them for others, but this isn't true for our relatives. Although Webster excludes relatives from the category of friends, the line real people draw is fuzzier than the one in the dictionary. In many societies, including many subcultures in North America, your closest friends are frequently genetically related to you in some way (Daly, Salmon, & Wilson, 1997; Rushton, 1989). Indeed, our ancestors tended to live in groups composed of fairly closely related individuals, so that one's friends were virtually always one's relatives. The modern industrialized world is different from any other period in history in that people spend less time in the company of their relatives (Adams & Bleiszner, 1994).

Affiliation motive *The desire to be near others and to have pleasant interactions with them.*

Friend *Someone with whom we have an affectionate relationship.*

The distinction between friends and lovers is based on the presence of romantic or sexual feelings (Rawlins, 1992). Again, the distinction sometimes gets a bit fuzzy, and love and friendship can shade into one another (Oliker, 1989). In fact, the majority of married people pick their spouse as their "best friend" (Myers, 2000). Nevertheless, because marriages involve legal rules, exclusive "rights," and inherent role differences between the partners, they do not meet all the ideals of friendship (Rawlins, 1992). And there is generally a big jump between the degree of passion one feels for the person one defines as a "best friend" and for the person one defines as a "lover." There has been an explosion of research into romantic relationships in the last two decades, so we'll devote a separate chapter—chapter 8—to exploring love and romance. In this chapter, we focus mainly on the "platonic" aspects of friendship and affiliation.

Studying Real-Life Relationships

Take a minute to think back over the last month. During that time, how many satisfying interactions have you had with close friends? Although that may seem like a simple enough question, your answer might not provide reliable scientific data, for a number of reasons (Reis & Wheeler, 1991; Schwarz, 1990). For one thing, different people might use a different criterion for deciding what "a close friend" is. For another, there are all the normal cognitive biases we discussed in chapter 3 that distort your memory. If you had an unpleasant interaction with your roommate this morning, for instance, that might cast a negative light over your memories, making it difficult to remember pleasant interactions from two weeks ago (Forgas, Levinger, & Moylan, 1994; Schwarz & Clore, 1983). Simply sitting in a room with a foul odor leads people to recollect more unpleasant memories (Ehrlichmann & Halpern, 1988).

So to study people's actual interactions, what's a researcher to do? One possibility is naturalistic observation—follow people around as they go about their daily lives. Unfortunately, this can change the very interactions a researcher is interested in studying. With an eavesdropping researcher on the scene, conversations would probably stick to socially desirable topics and avoid extremes of anger or intimacy (Reis & Wheeler, 1991). In the "Focus on Method" feature, we consider an approach that has many of the advantages of naturalistic observation, without the disadvantage of an experimenter standing around with a tape recorder and notebook.

FOCUS ON Method

Studying Intimate Relationships Without Really Being There

Scientists interested in finding out about real relationships while avoiding the problems of a lurking researcher have hit on a simple but elegant idea: Skip the observer, and ask people to record their own behaviors as they naturally occur during the course of their everyday lives (e.g., Lydon, Jamieson, & Holmes, 1997; Suls, Martin, & David, 1998). Researchers using one such approach, called the **experience sampling method,** supply subjects with portable beepers. When the beeper sounds, the participants fill out a short description, detailing who they are with and what's going on (Czikszentmihalyi, Larson, & Prescott, 1977).

Experience sampling method
An observational technique in which subjects fill out frequent descriptions of who they are with and what is going on.

Another technique is to have subjects fill out a short questionnaire after every meaningful social interaction (e.g., Berry & Landry, 1997; Pietromonaco & Feldman-Barrett, 1997). This method has been developed most extensively by a team of researchers at the University of Rochester, and their technique is called the Rochester Interaction Record (Gable & Reis, 1999; Reis & Wheeler, 1991).

If you were a participant in a study using the interaction record method, you would, in exchange for $20 or class credit, fill out a brief questionnaire after every significant social interaction you had during a two-week period. You'd be told that "interactions" might include working together or having a conversation. Merely being in the presence of another, as in watching television without talking, would not be counted as an interaction.

To get an idea of what it's like to participate in this research, think back to the last interaction you had that lasted at least 10 minutes. Then fill out the interaction record in Table 7.1.

By having people record their own interactions right after they occur, researchers gain several advantages. They get information about real, ongoing behavior, without the problem of having an observer there to interfere with the actual interaction. An intimate conversation with a troubled friend, for instance, simply would not be the same if there were a researcher in a white coat sitting nearby taking notes. By waiting until the interaction naturally ends, the recording process is less likely to change the normal course of events. At the same time, having people record the interactions right after they occur reduces many of the memory biases that would enter in if they filled out a questionnaire a month later.

These experience sampling methods have helped researchers paint a more realistic picture of everyday social interactions. For instance, the average college student reports seven interactions lasting ten minutes or longer each day. That means 210 interactions to remember over the course of a month. Small wonder, then, that people have some difficulty accurately remembering them. One team of researchers asked people to record all the lies they told during their interactions (DePaulo, Kashy, Kirkendol, Wyer, & Epstein, 1996). Although most people might be inclined to forget their "little white lies," they reported a surprisingly large number when they were asked to record each interaction immediately. Many everyday lies were designed to make other people feel better ("No, I really like the new hairdo!"),

Table 7.1 A typical Rochester Interaction Record.

Instructions: Record the last significant interaction you had with another person. A significant interaction is defined as any situation involving two or more people responding to one another. A conversation is the most obvious example of a significant interaction, but there are other sorts of interactions as well—working on a task together or just hanging out, for instance. Merely being in another person's presence isn't enough. For example, if you watch television without talking to the person, that isn't an interaction. In order to count, you must be responding to one another, such as by talking about what you're watching.

Date: _______ Time: _______ A.M./P.M. Length: _______ hours _______ minutes

List the initials, and sex, of up to 3 main participants _______ _______ _______

If there were more than 3 people, how many: Males _______ Females _______

Now rate the interaction on the following dimensions:

How **intimate** was it?	*superficial*	1 2 3 4 5 6 7	*meaningful*
Did **you disclose:**	*very little*	1 2 3 4 5 6 7	*a great deal*
Did **others disclose:**	*very little*	1 2 3 4 5 6 7	*a great deal*
Did you **feel** like **part of a group?**	*did not feel like part of a group*	1 2 3 4 5 6 7	*felt like part of a group*
The **quality** was?	*unpleasant*	1 2 3 4 5 6 7	*very pleasant*
How **satisfied** were you?	*less than expected*	1 2 3 4 5 6 7	*more than expected*
Who **initiated** the interaction?	*I initiated*	1 2 3 4 5 6 7	*someone else initiated*
Who had more **influence?**	*I influenced more*	1 2 3 4 5 6 7	*other influenced more*

Circle the **type of interaction:** Job Task Pastime Conversation Date

SOURCE: *Reis & Wheeler (1991).*

although the majority were self-serving ("My grandmother in Tulsa died the night before the exam, Professor."). The average college student in this study reported about two lies a day. In another study, the researchers found that strangers were likely to tell self-serving lies, whereas friends incline toward lies that made the other person feel better (DePaulo & Kashy, 1998).

Researchers using the experience-sampling methods have gotten a boost from the computer revolution. Students in these studies can now be given their own hand-held computer, which is like sending out an invisible robotic interviewer. Several times a day, regardless of where the student is, the computer signals with a beep. When a student responds, a questionnaire pops onto the screen (e.g., Parkinson, Briner, Reynolds, & Totterdell, 1995; Stone, Broderick, Porter, & Kaell, 1997). Beep. "How are you feeling right now?" In this chapter and the next, we describe results from various studies that have used these everyday experience sampling methods. ■

Agreeableness and Dominance

When people think about themselves and others, questions about affiliation and friendship, such as How likable am I? and How outgoing and socially dominant is this person? are foremost in our minds (McCrae & John, 1992). Research conducted around the world, in fact, reveals that people's thoughts about themselves and other people can be well described along two dimensions: agreeableness and dominance (White, 1980; Wiggins & Broughton, 1985). Figure 7.1 shows how these two dimensions provide the framework of an interpersonal circumplex, or circular arrangement of the words commonly used to describe others (Wiggins & Broughton, 1985). Take a minute to see if you can place yourself within the circle, and then pick a close friend and do the same for him or her.

Eleanor Roosevelt and J. Edgar Hoover stood at very different points on this circle. On the horizontal dimension, Eleanor Roosevelt was clearly at the warm-agreeable end. The headmistress of her high school said, "It is impossible to wish for oneself a more delightful companion.... She is ... never out of sorts" (Cook, 1992, p. 116). Hoover, on the other hand, struck most people as defining the cold-hearted end of the horizontal dimension. According to FBI assistant director William Sullivan, Hoover "didn't have affection for one single solitary human being around him" (Summers, 1993, 24).

On the other hand, both Hoover and Roosevelt were closer to the assured-dominant end of the vertical continuum. Both, for instance, began commanding great respect in their high school years; Hoover was class valedictorian, and Roosevelt inspired admiration in both teachers and fellow students. As adults, both were quite ambitious and went on to earn prominent social positions, one as FBI director and the other as a U.N. delegate and prominent crusader for human rights. The combination of characteristics would place Hoover in the upper-left quadrant, arrogant-calculating, and Roosevelt in the upper-right quadrant, gregarious-extraverted.

Figure 7.1
The interpersonal circumplex.

Note that the two main dimensions people use to describe one another are *assured-dominant vs. unassured-submissive* (the vertical dimension) and *warm-agreeable vs. cold-hearted* (the horizontal dimension). Extraverted people (upper right) tend to be both agreeable and dominant.

SOURCE: *Adapted from Wiggins, et al. (1989).*

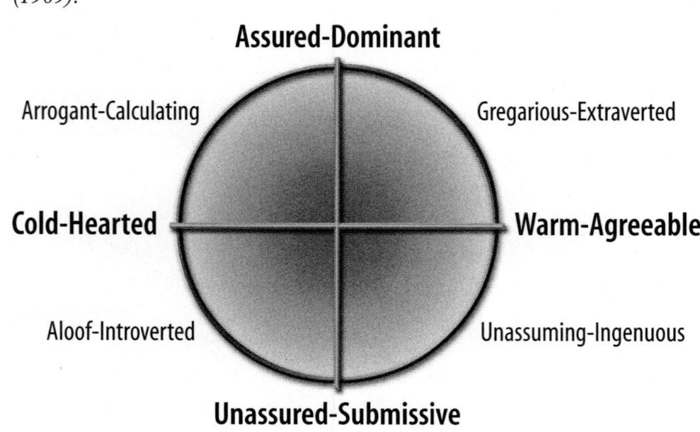

The dimensions of agreeableness and dominance apply to the lives of everyday people as well. Knowing how agreeable and dominant a person is tells us a lot about the kind of relationship we will have with him or her (c.f., Berry, Willingham, & Thayer, 2000; Graziano, Jensen-Campbell, & Hair, 1996; Shiner, 2000). Everyone prefers agreeable associates, but people seem to prefer interacting with others who complement their dominance levels. Dominant people like being with submissive others and vice versa (Dryer & Horowitz; 1997).

Relational Problems and the Interpersonal Circumplex Affiliating with other people has many benefits, but it isn't free, and it isn't painless (Duck, 1994). Being agreeable and cooperative takes time and attention away from other tasks, and there's always the danger that if you're dominant you'll be perceived as exploitative or if you're agreeable you'll be taken for a sucker.

These relational problems can be understood in terms of the same two dimensions of the interpersonal circumplex (Gurtman, 1992). Take a moment to consider yourself in terms of some sample items from a test of interpersonal problems (Table 7.2), and then do the same thing for the friend you rated a few minutes ago. Finally, consider where you both stand in the circle of problems in Figure 7.2. Is your position in the earlier interpersonal circumplex similar to your position in Figure 7.2?

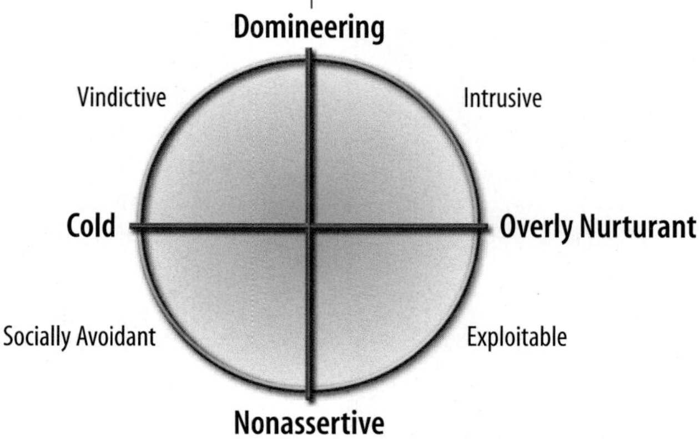

As we'll discuss below, these same two dimensions of agreeableness and dominance may be helpful in understanding the differences between men's and women's relationships with one another. And the dimensions are also centrally relevant to the goals of affiliative behavior.

Figure 7.2
A circumplex for interpersonal problems.

This circumplex is based on the same two dimensions used in the interpersonal circumplex and describes the problems people have in their relationships with others.

Goals of Affiliative Behavior

What makes us want to affiliate with others? Social psychologists once thought this question could be answered in terms of a simple and powerful model.

Liking Those Who Make Us Feel Good The **reinforcement–affect model** assumes that people are motivated by one very simple goal—the desire to feel good (Byrne & Clore, 1970). The central premise of the reinforcement-affect model is that we

Table 7.2 Sample items tapping interpersonal problems.

Interpersonal Problem	Sample Items
Domineering	"It is hard for me to take instructions from people who have authority over me." "I am too independent."
Vindictive	"It is hard for me to be supportive of another person's goals in life." "I am too suspicious of other people."
Cold	"It is hard for me to show affection to people." "It is hard for me to feel close to other people."
Socially Avoidant	"It is hard for me to introduce myself to new people." "I feel embarrassed in front of other people too much."
Nonassertive	"It is hard for me to let other people know what I want." "It is hard for me to be self-confident when I am with other people."
Exploitable	"I am too gullible." "I let other people take advantage of me too much."
Overly Nurturant	"It is hard for me to set limits on other people." "I am overly generous to other people."
Intrusive	"It is hard for me to keep things private from other people." "I tell personal things to other people too much."

Reinforcement–affect model
The theory that we like people with whom we associate positive feelings and dislike those with whom we associate negative feelings.

J. Edgar Hoover as a teenager. *Hoover is shown here in uniform as company commander of his high school Cadet Corps. Hoover's relationships were generally hierarchical, and his problems with others were in the upper left quadrant of the circumplex of interpersonal problems: He was domineering, vindictive, cold, and not overly nurturant or exploitable. Unlike Eleanor Roosevelt, Hoover did not maintain contact with his high school friends after he moved on in life.*

affiliate with, and come to like, people we associate with positive feelings. Conversely, we come to dislike, and to avoid, people we associate with negative feelings.

The reinforcement–affect model has been used to explain a wide range of findings: why people are drawn to others who agree with their attitudes and are repelled by those who disagree with them, why people are drawn to others who possess desirable characteristics such as physical attractiveness, and even why we may come to like other people who just happen to be around when we hear good news (Byrne, London, & Reeves, 1968; Lott & Lott, 1974; Veitch & Griffitt, 1976). According to simple principles of classical conditioning, good or bad feelings in any situation will automatically rub off on any person who happens to be there. Just as salivation was elicited by the bell that Pavlov's dogs heard when they were fed, so a good feeling is elicited by someone who was around when something nice happened.

Although the general principle underlying the reinforcement–affect model of attraction is a powerful one, it may be a bit too simple to explain fully the complexities of human attraction. For instance, sometimes we like people more when we meet them under unpleasant circumstances, provided they're in the same boat and aren't the cause of the unpleasant feelings (Kenrick & Johnson; 1979). And we may judge someone as very physically attractive, independent of whether the person's attractiveness makes us feel good or bad (Kenrick, Montello, Guttierres, & Trost, 1993). Thus, our attraction to other people is not simply a function of the positive or negative feelings we experience when they're around.

Social Rewards May Be Domain-Specific The reinforcement–affect model of attraction is a "domain-general" model of behavior. A domain-general model attempts to explain all behavior using some simple rule—in this case, Do it if it feels good. The problem with such a general rule is that it doesn't tell us why sometimes the very same behavior may make one person feel good while it makes another person feel bad. Modern approaches to social relationships are increasingly likely to ask more "domain-specific" questions (Bugental, 2000). What is the person motivated to do at this time in this particular relationship (Laursen & Bukowski, 1997; Sedikides & Skowronski, 1997)? Sometimes it feels good to get a hug from someone else, sometimes we prefer their advice rather than their affection, and at still other times it feels best to be left completely alone. In line with our focus on the adaptive functions of social behavior, we will consider affiliation and friendship in terms of four specific, and sometimes competing, social goals that help us understand when and why people seek the company and affection of others: getting social support, getting information, gaining status, and exchanging material benefits.

Summary

Friendships are distinguished from other relationships by being voluntary and lacking passion. Across cultures, two prominent dimensions—agreeableness and dominance—characterize people's thoughts about relationships. The reinforcement–affect model posits a domain-general goal of feeling good. Domain-specific models assume different relationships have different goals at different times. We will consider four main goals people have for affiliating with others and forming friendships: to get social support, to get information, to gain status, and to exchange material benefits.

Getting Social Support

At 8 P.M. on the evening of October 30, 1938, a massive panic swept across the United States. The panic followed radio reports of a strange object that had landed in Grover's Mill, New Jersey. Listeners heard commentators describe a strange, humming, cylindrical object that suddenly began to unscrew itself. They then heard blood-curdling screams as a strange creature reportedly emerged and began to shoot flames at onlookers. At this point, radio contact was interrupted, only to be followed later by emergency reports of thousands of deaths as the creature made its way toward New York. The later broadcasts included reports of other aliens, now landing up and down the East Coast.

Princeton University psychologist Hadley Cantril (1940) reported that over a million people were taken in by the realism of the radio broadcasts. These panicking multitudes had tuned in too late to know that the reports were actually a dramatic presentation of a Martian invasion depicted in H. G. Wells's novel, *War of the Worlds.*

How did the panic victims respond when they thought that the earth was being invaded by spaceships? According to Cantril's report on the incident, it was very common for people to want to be near their loved ones. He recorded accounts such as the following:

> I wanted to be together with my husband and my nephew so I ran out of the house—I stood on the corner waiting for a bus and I thought every car that came along was a bus and I ran out to get it.... When I got home my husband was not there so I rushed in next door and warned the neighbors that the world was coming to an end.
>
> The girls in the sorority houses and dormitories huddled around their radios trembling and weeping in each other's arms. They separated themselves from their friends only to take their turn at the telephones to make long distance calls to their parents, saying goodbye for what they thought might be the last time. (Cantril, 1940, pp. 53, 54, 95)

Although most of us have never had to endure threats of a Martian invasion, Cantril's (1940) report illustrates an important general point: When we are under stress, we often turn to others for support. **Social support** can be defined as the emotional, informational, or material assistance provided by other people in one's social network. Because unique factors affect how people exchange material resources and information, we will focus in this section on emotional support—the affection, caring, and nurturance that people provide for one another (Gottlieb, 1994). In later sections, we address informational and material support.

The tendency to turn to others when we are emotionally distressed may be linked to a basic feature of human nature: humans, like the members of other species, are safer in numbers (Bowlby, 1969; Trivers, 1985). People in groups can protect one another in times of trouble. And having another shoulder to huddle against may even have medical benefits.

FOCUS ON Application

Health Psychology and Social Support

Is having friends good for your health? This is the sort of question that might be asked by a health psychologist. **Health psychology** is the study of behavioral and psychological factors that affect illness (Gatchel, Baum, & Krantz, 1989; Salovey, Rothman, & Rodin, 1998). Health psychologists assume that the physical condition of our bodies is intimately connected with how we think and how we behave. One of the more intriguing conclusions to emerge from health psychology research is that nurturant contact with other people is linked to a longer and happier life (Reif & Singer, 2000).

Social support *Emotional, material, or informational assistance provided by other people.*

Health psychology *The study of behavioral and psychological factors that affect illness.*

A human's best friend in times of stress. *Research discussed in the text suggests that, under some circumstances, the company of a pet dog may be more stress-reducing than the company of a friend.*

Consider first the harmful properties of social isolation. Loneliness has been tied to depression, drug and alcohol abuse, sleep disturbances, headaches, visits to medical doctors, and even mortality in nursing homes (Jones & Carver, 1991; Takahashi, Tamura, & Tokoro, 1997). Loneliness is also associated with a lowered immune response (Kiecolt-Glaser et al., 1985).

Over time, the increased vulnerability of loneliness can take a serious toll. One team of researchers searched out medical doctors who had, during medical school, described themselves as "loners." Several decades later, those lone wolves had significantly higher rates of cancer than did their more gregarious classmates (Shaffer, Graves-Pirrko, Swank, & Pearson, 1987). Another study found that after a heart attack, 16 percent of patients living alone versus 9 percent of those living with someone else had relapses (Case, Moss, & Case, 1992). In contrast, people who have strong social ties are less upset by stressful life events, are more resistant to disease, and live longer, even after being diagnosed with life-threatening diseases (e.g., Buunk & Verhoeven, 1991; Sarason, Sarason, & Gurung, 1997). Just having someone to talk to about stressful events can enhance your emotional well-being (Lepore, Ragan, & Jones, 2000; Reis et al., 2000).

Studies showing a relationship between stress resistance and social support are correlational. That is, they highlight a statistical association between having nurturant friends and being healthy but do not prove a causal link. Perhaps people who have certain types of personalities are both more likely to have friends and to be physically healthy. For instance, maybe extraverts are more likely to exercise or less likely to sit around and dwell on every unpleasant event that happens to them. The reverse might be true of those who are highly anxious by nature. Niall Bolger and John Eckenrode (1991) attempted to eliminate these sources of confusion by testing students the month before they took medical entrance examinations. The researchers measured the students' standings on personality tests tapping extraversion and neuroticism (emotional instability), and they also measured the students' daily stress as well as their contacts with others. Even when students' pre-existing traits were taken into account, contact with other people served as a buffer against experiencing anxiety: Students with more social contacts were less traumatized by the exams.

Some research suggests that the best source of emotional support may come not from other people but from "man's best friend," the dog. Karen Allen, Jim Blascovich, Joe Tomaka, and Robert Kelsey (1991) subjected women to stressful tasks under one of three conditions—alone, with a friend, or with their pet dogs. The researchers measured the women's heart rate, blood pressure, and skin conductance. To induce stress, subjects were asked to count backwards by thirteens and seventeens rapidly. The physiological measures indicated that having a human friend present only served to increase anxiety. (The anxiety-arousing effect of friends in this experiment was probably due to the particular type of task, which involved possible public embarrassment. As we describe below, embarrassment is one stressor that may be made worse rather than better by the presence of others.) However, having their dogs at their sides significantly reduced physiological signs of distress. And the helpful canine effects are not limited to short-term experiments. Over a period of years, elderly people who have dogs are less likely to visit doctors and more likely to survive heart attacks (Friedmann, Katcher, Lynch, & Thomas, 1980; Siegel, 1990). ■

As you can see, research suggests that companionship is generally good for your mental and physical health. But this is not equally true for all people all of the time. The consequences of social support depend on the situation and on the person. Who turns to others for social support, and which situations arouse the need for such support? Logic would dictate that people prone to insecurity or anxiety would need more emotional support and that this need should be provoked by situations evoking insecurity, anxiety, or loneliness. In the following sections, we discuss research that supports such logic.

Birth Order

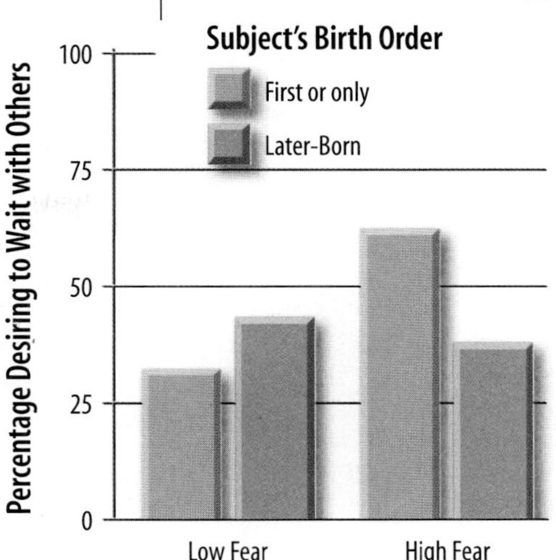

Figure 7.3
Fear and affiliation.

When they were not frightened, firstborns were not particularly eager to associate with others. However, when threatened by a painful electric shock, firstborns were substantially more eager to affiliate. Schachter suggested that firstborns not only respond more to threat but also are more likely to have parents who responded attentively to their fears.

Imagine that you've just arrived for a laboratory experiment and are confronted by a serious-looking researcher dressed in a white lab coat with a stethoscope hanging out of his pocket. Standing in front of a formidable array of electrical equipment, he introduces himself as Dr. Gregor Zilstein of the Medical School's Departments of Neurology and Psychiatry. Looking at you ominously, he explains that the experiment will investigate the effects of electrical shock:

> I feel I must be completely honest with you and tell you exactly what you are in for. These shocks will hurt; they will be painful. As you can guess, if, in research of this sort, we're to learn anything at all that will really help humanity, it is necessary that our shocks be intense.

After showing you the shock apparatus, Zilstein "reassures" you that although the shocks will be "quite painful," they will do no "permanent damage." There will be a ten-minute delay while the machinery is set up, so he gives you the choice of waiting by yourself or together with some of the other participants. Would you choose to wait alone or in the company of the others?

Stanley Schachter (1959) actually gave this choice to groups of women. Other participants were given the same choice, but without the threat of a painful shock.

Schachter found that whether participants chose to wait alone or in groups depended not only on the fear of shock, but also on the subjects' birth order. His results are depicted in Figure 7.3.

As you can see, women who were firstborns or only children had the strongest desire to affiliate. But they were not generally more affiliative; they craved companionship only in the highly stressful condition. Schachter speculated that the reason for the difference is that firstborns and only children learn to turn to others to soothe their feelings of anxiety. Such children have parents who, because they are new to the parenting game, are more likely to worry about their children's every sigh of distress and to readily console them for the slightest discomfort. Thus, at an early age, firstborns learn to associate the presence of others with stress reduction. By the time a later-born child comes along, mommy and daddy may be jaded to the whimperings of these children, who therefore do not learn to turn to others to reduce their distress.

In keeping with these laboratory findings, Schachter also reported that firstborns were more likely to seek the emotional support of psychotherapy when they were troubled, whereas later-borns were more likely to turn to the nonsocial chemical comforts of alcoholism.

In case you were wondering, no one actually received any shock in these experiments. Because only the threat of actual shock was necessary to arouse fear, the researcher chose to deceive subjects rather than actually deliver on the threat of shock (which would have been more honest but ultimately less ethical).

Threats: Why Misery (Sometimes) Loves Company

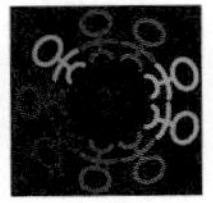

The term *emotional support* is implicitly tied to certain situations: people seek the support of others when they are feeling threatened or isolated, as when they are by themselves and hear reports of Martians invading New Jersey. Impersonal dangers and social isolation both increase our motivation to get solace from others.

Impersonal Danger In the original Schachter experiments, the threat was the impersonal danger of an electric shock. Later research by Brooks Gump and James Kulik (1997) suggests that, under such threat, we are especially desirous of the company of similar others. For example, pairs of female undergraduates in one study were told that the experiment had to do with ischemia, the restriction of normal blood flow. Some were led to believe that the experiment would be relatively painless—a blood pressure cuff would be partially inflated around their arms. Other women were led to expect being strapped into a tortuous device that would squeeze around the arm and below the rib cage, presumably to produce a sharp pain similar to the angina felt by heart patients. The researchers measured affiliative tendencies by recording the time spent looking at another woman in the room. When both women expected to suffer the same torturous pain, they spent twice as much time looking at one another as when they were expecting no suffering.

Social Isolation As we noted in chapter 1, William James (1890) noted social isolation as the cruelest of tortures. "To one long pent up on a desert island," James observed, "the sight of a human footprint or a human form in the distance would be the most tumultuously exciting of experiences" (Vol. II, 430). Warren Jones and his colleagues (1985) have summarized a number of factors that boost those feelings of social isolation. These include having recently moved (Cutrona, 1982), starting college (Weiss, 1973), losing a job (Bahr & Harvey, 1979), living alone (DeJong-Gierveld, 1980), and having inadequate means of transportation (Kivett, 1978). On the other side of the coin, Evans and Lepore (1993) found that people from crowded homes are less likely to seek support from others or to offer support in an unpleasant situation. Apparently, social isolation makes us crave the company of others, but social inundation makes us long to be alone.

Pushing Support Away

If it's so good for your health, then doesn't everyone invite as much social support as possible? Not quite. Some people actively reject support from others (Buunk, Doosje, Jans, & Hopstaken, 1993). For one thing, we don't always perceive social support as a good thing, especially when we can't reciprocate (e.g., Greenberg & Westcott, 1983). As we discuss more fully in chapter 9, when someone does you a favor you can't return, it may be a source of embarrassment, marking you as a "charity case."

The potential for embarrassment in fact tends to decrease the motivation to seek support from others.

Imagine that, like subjects in a classic experiment conducted by Irving Sarnoff & Philip Zimbardo (1961), you were told that you were about to participate in an experiment in which you would have to suck on various objects related to the "oral" period of development, including pacifiers and nipples from baby bottles. Would you want to wait with others or alone? If you are like the subjects in this study, you would choose to wait alone under these potentially embarrassing conditions. Friends' supportive function seems to disappear when their presence might lead you to feel evaluated. When female students in one experiment worked on a stressful math test, their blood pressure was lower if they had a close friend around, unless the friend was in an evaluative role, in which case it was just as well to be alone or among strangers (Kors, Linden, & Gerin, 1997). As we noted earlier, at times like these, a better companion would be a dog, who is unlikely to make any snide evaluative comments.

Some people push away support inadvertently. As we see next the very people most in need of emotional support may unintentionally shut off the flow of social nurturance they crave.

FOCUS ON Social Dysfunction

The Self-Perpetuating Cycle of Loneliness and Depression

Researchers have discovered that depression and loneliness may work hand-in-hand to drive away social support. To begin with, depressed individuals are less effective in coping with stress in their lives (Marx, Williams, & Claridge, 1992). And then they make things worse by acting in ways that may increase the stress. When they turn to their friends and roommates for help, their depressive focus on the negative aspects of their lives tends to alienate the very people who could provide support. Even the most sympathetic friends eventually tire of hearing repetitions on the theme of "life is miserable, nothing ever goes my way, it's all hopeless." To further compound matters, depressive individuals may seek out relationships with people who view them unfavorably (Swann, Wenzlaff, Krull, & Pelham, 1992). When friends of depressed people do try to help, they themselves may become depressed (Joiner, 1994). In the long run, other people find the interactions unpleasant enough that they begin to avoid the depressive individual (Joiner, Alfano, & Metalsky, 1992; Strack & Coyne, 1983).

Loneliness shows some of the same self-perpetuating characteristics, and is sometimes directly linked to depression (see Figure 7.4). Lonely students are, compared to their more gregarious counterparts, more nervous, more depressed, and more likely to criticize themselves (Russell et al., 1980). They tend to think about themselves in self-defeating ways—making internal and stable attributions for interpersonal problems ("I can never do anything right") even when there are obvious external explanations for their problems (Peplau, Russell, & Heim, 1979). For instance, a student who has just moved away to college and who lacks a car to visit friends may ignore his problematic situation and decide he is lonely only because others find him unattractive and boring.

Instead of inviting others over or going out to a public event, lonely students tend to cope with their isolation in counterproductive ways, for instance, by eating,

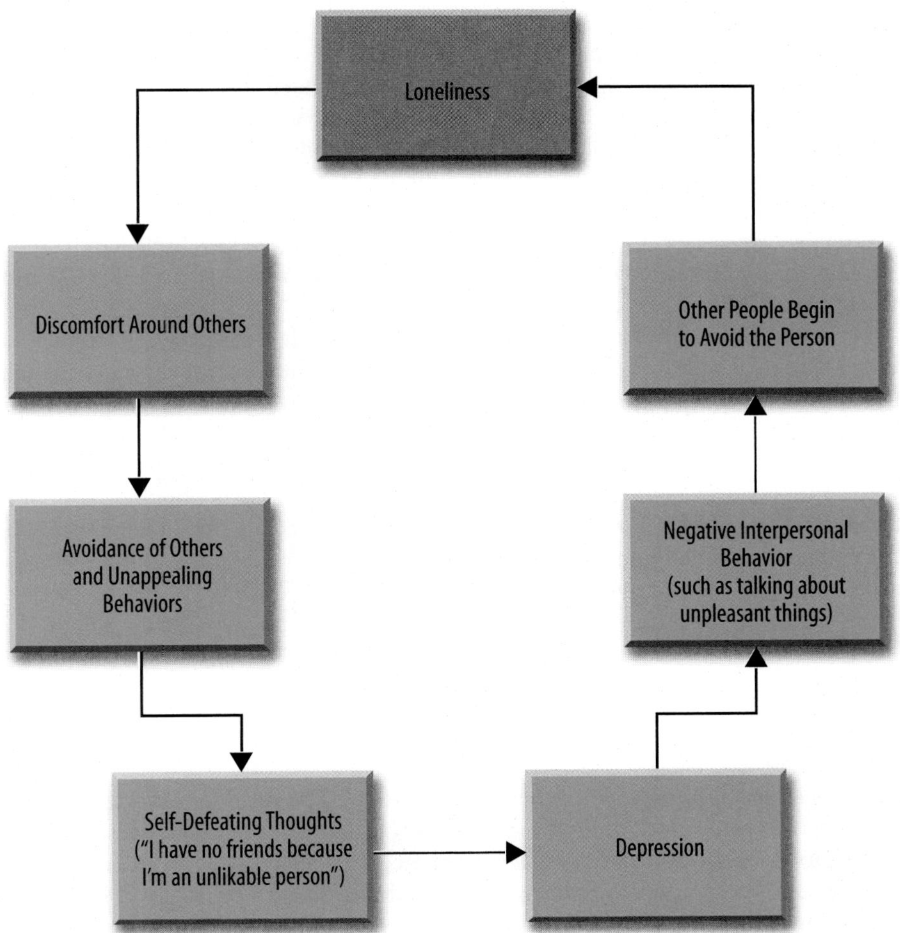

Figure 7.4
The self-perpetuating cycle of loneliness.

Although loneliness and depression are not always linked, they can be connected as parts of a cycle of self-defeating thoughts and behaviors. Lonely people are uncomfortable around others and act in ways that reduce their sources of social support. This may in turn lead not only to more feelings of loneliness, but also to self-defeating thoughts and, in turn, to depression. Depression itself leads to behaviors that further act to turn off others, thereby contributing to additional loneliness.

taking drugs, or watching TV (Paloutzian & Ellison, 1982). When lonely students do get around others, they may act in ways that make them less attractive—they may talk more about themselves, change the topic more frequently, ask fewer questions about their conversational partners, and make more inappropriate self-disclosures than students who are not lonely (Jones, Hobbs & Hockenbury, 1982; Solano, Batten, & Parish, 1982).

To make things worse, lonely people set unrealistically high expectations for both themselves and others (Rawlins, 1992). After talking to others, lonely students rate themselves and others more negatively and show less interest in seeing the partners again (Gable & Reis, 1999; Jones, Freemon, & Goswick, 1981; Jones, Sansone, & Helm, 1983). Based on a number of studies, Warren Jones and his colleagues (1985) concluded that "lonely individuals are self-absorbed, non-responsive, negativistic, and ineffective in their interactions with strangers" (223). And even when their conversational partners perceive them positively, the lonely students walk away from the interaction feeling as if they've done poorly (Christensen & Kashy, 1998). ■

Attachment and Social Development

Not all of the cycles involving interaction and social support are negative though. In his book *Attachment*, British psychologist John Bowlby (1969) suggested that people whose parents provided a secure relationship are better suited to handle stresses later in life. This may be because those who had secure attachments to their mothers are better equipped to get support. In one longitudinal study, researchers followed children from infancy through their later experiences in preadolescent summer camps (Shulman, Elicker, & Sroufe, 1994). Compared to those whose maternal attachments had been insecure, children who had been securely attached to their mothers later showed more skill in dealing with their peers. Thus, those with the least need may be the most able to get what they need! In chapter 8, we consider the role of attachment in adult romantic relationships.

As children grow into their teenage years, they may rebuff their parents' offers of emotional support. Adolescents increasingly turn from their parents to their peers for social support (Aseltine, Gore, & Colten, 1994). The trend continues in college (Fraley & Davis, 1997). In fact, contact with their parents does not seem to reduce feelings of loneliness in college students; only contact with friends helps (Cutrona, 1982; Davis, Morris, & Kraus, 1998).

On the other hand, parental support is not irrelevant, even for college students. People who have reassuring relationships with their parents have less negative moods and get better grades in school, whereas friends aren't particularly helpful in these domains (Cutrona, Cole, Colangelo, Assouline, & Russell, 1994, Davis et al., 1998). So, if you someday find yourself in the role of a parent with a teenager who spurns your well-intended offers of support, you will probably help him or her most by keeping the offer open. And if you are on the other side, it is probably best for your mental health and happiness (not to mention your grade point average) to accept the offer of a parental shoulder to lean on.

Summary

Who seeks social support, and when do they do so? The need for emotional support is especially pronounced in firstborns. Certain situations (such as impersonal threats and feelings of social isolation) trigger the need for social support, whereas others (such as embarrassing settings) suppress the desire to turn to others. Finally, some people intentionally or unintentionally act in ways to cut off the very support they need. In the next section, we consider another goal of affiliating with others—to get information.

Getting Information

On top of their shoulders (useful to cry on), other people also have heads full of potentially useful facts, ideas, and alternative opinions. If you want to find out quickly how to fix a leaky faucet, hem a pair of slacks, or prepare a good spaghetti sauce, a friend or neighbor can be more helpful than any book in the public library. And when we put our heads together with others, our communal IQ often goes up (Wegner, 1987; Thompson & Fine, 1999). People working with friends tend to do better on any number of tasks, from memorizing words to solving complex problems (Andersson & Roennberg, 1997; Zajac & Hartup, 1997). One reason friends work well together is that they share a similar base of knowledge and are better equipped to "read" one another's feelings and intentions (Colvin, Vogt, & Ickes, 1997).

Our friends can provide a wealth of facts about the physical world and problem-solving strategies. But when it comes to *social* realities (such as "how likable am I?"), other people's opinions are more or less all that matters. During the 1960s and 1970s, "encounter groups" became a fad (Rogers, 1970). The goal of the groups was to have direct and honest "encounters" with other people in which the normal social façades could be dropped and participants could share their frank reactions to one another and disclose their own inner selves. In one common exercise, group members would pair up and discuss their honest first impressions of one another, each one sharing a positive and a negative impression. Humanistic psychologist Carl Rogers, a prominent advocate of encounter groups, noted that the central, and most beneficial, goal of these groups was not simply to have people "feel good" but for them to receive honest feedback about how others perceived them. According to Rogers, a key to mental health is having a genuine and honest relationship, within which you can share your thoughts and feelings without fear of rejection. James Pennebaker and his colleagues have provided substantial evidence that the simple opportunity to discuss unpleasant experiences with others can be beneficial to your health (e.g., Pennebaker, Barger, & Tiebout, 1989; Pennebaker, Hughes, & O'Heeron, 1987).

Besides information about ourselves, other people also provide us with information about others. Despite the fact that J. Edgar Hoover had less than flattering things to say about Franklin D. Roosevelt's wife and friends, President Roosevelt kept up a friendly relationship with Hoover. Why? Probably because Hoover was a valuable source of information about friends and enemies alike—he was the consummate gossip. Indeed, Roosevelt turned to Hoover several times to pick up confidential behind-the-scenes information about people who opposed him.

Social Comparison and Liking for Similar Others

In chapter 3, we mentioned Leon Festinger's (1954) classic social comparison theory. According to Festinger, people have a drive to evaluate their opinions and abilities, and frequently the best way to do so is to compare themselves with others. Some questions (such as whether we can run a mile in five minutes) can be answered by checking the physical rather than the social world. However, to answer many questions about our abilities and opinions, we must turn to others. Are you being unreasonable in your relationship with your boyfriend or girlfriend? Do others perceive you as friendly or unfriendly? Are your opinions about the death penalty and abortion sensible ones, or do they make you seem eccentric?

Festinger's theory included an additional assumption—that we prefer to compare our opinions and abilities with similar rather than dissimilar others. To know

Similarity and friendship. *Research suggests that we like people whose looks and ages are similar to ours, who think like us, whose interests overlap with ours, and whose personal habits are similar to ours. Part of the appeal of similar others is that they affirm our beliefs and attitudes.*

whether you are a decent intramural basketball player, for instance, you wouldn't compare with NBA all-stars. The relevant comparison group is other intramural players. Likewise, if you are a liberal Democrat and you want to know whether your opinions about abortion and the death penalty are reasonable, you don't turn to members of the American Nazi Party for feedback, but to other liberal Democrats. This aspect of Festinger's theory was an important historical influence on one of the most heavily researched topics in social psychology—the attraction toward similar others (Byrne, 1971; Tan & Singh, 1995).

Our motivation to obtain information from others is partly driven by a desire for accurate information. But most of us want our accurate information served with a spoonful of sugar, so we gravitate toward information that makes us feel good or that validates our view of the world (Baumeister, 1998; Sedikides, 1993). Our attraction to similar others stems partly from the fact that they often agree with us, which makes us feel good (Clore & Byrne, 1974; Orive, 1988). Conversely, we tend to respond negatively to others who disagree with us (Rosenbaum, 1986). Part of the attraction to similar others is the simple expectation that they will like us more than dissimilar others (Condon & Crano, 1988). But another part is that they confirm our views about ourselves and the world (Pittman, 1998).

Not everyone is equally drawn to similar others and repulsed by those who are different though. Biographers note that Eleanor Roosevelt found it stimulating to expose herself to different perspectives (recall the comment about how this wealthy white Anglo-Saxon Protestant befriended "Blacks, Jews, and rude communist youths"). J. Edgar Hoover, on the other hand, was intolerant of disagreement, and surrounded himself with others having very similar beliefs, habits, and backgrounds (Gentry, 1991). J. Edgar Hoover's friend Clyde Tolson, for instance, was not only remarkably similar to Hoover in attitudes, personality, and his dedicated approach to work, but also was described as "the ultimate yes-man."

Self-Disclosers and Non-Disclosers

Your friends probably differ in the tendency to consult others for information. On the input side, some people need the feedback of others to come to decisions about appropriate behavior, whereas others seem happy making up their own minds. On the output side, some people openly disclose information about themselves, while others play it close to the vest. Indeed, a key aspect of being a friend is **self-disclosure,** sharing intimate information about oneself (Harvey & Omarzu, 1997). Mutual disclosure is so important that complete strangers can be made to feel like friends after just half an hour of mutual disclosure of intimate details (Aron, Melinat, Aron, Vallone, & Bator, 1997). You can often get others to like you just by opening up to them (Collins & Miller, 1994). But people differ widely in their proclivity for self-disclosure. Women are more likely than men to disclose information about themselves (Dindia & Allen, 1992).

Self-disclosure *The sharing of intimate information about oneself.*

What are men talking about while women are disclosing intimate details about personal relationships? If you guessed sports and politics, you have probably overheard one or two conversations between men (Aries & Johnson, 1983; Rawlins, 1992). The difference in conversational content is so pronounced that people can reliably distinguish a transcript of a conversation between two men from a conversation between two women, even with all the obvious clues taken away. As the researcher who found this observed, "Girls don't talk about garages" (Martin, 1997).

The greater levels of self-disclosure among women may help explain findings, which we will discuss below, that females have more satisfying friendships than do males.

Other factors in the person affect how some of us transmit information and receive information from others (DePaulo & Kashy, 1998; Kenny & DePaulo, 1993). For instance, people high in the need for social approval are likely to selectively transmit positive information to others (Crowne & Marlowe, 1964). Rather than telling Steve that his classmates think he is relentlessly argumentative, if you are high in the need for approval you might tell Steve that people find him a thought-provoking conversationalist. Presumably, those high in the need for approval understand the principle that people sometimes dislike the bearers of bad news (Rosen & Tesser, 1970).

On the reception side, people who are socially anxious tend to make negative interpretations of the feedback they receive from others (Pozo, Carver, Wellens, & Scheier, 1991): "She said my haircut was 'distinctive,' sure! She probably means I look like a weirdo." Thus, anxious people may interpret neutral news as bad news, at least when the news is about them.

Some people's reluctance to transmit negative information goes further than mere censorship. To avoid making another feel uncomfortable, people sometimes simply make up something more pleasant. In other words, they lie. More lies come out of the mouths of people who are sociable, manipulative, and highly concerned with self-presentation. As we discussed earlier, some everyday lies are designed to serve the other person ("I told my roommate I was having a wonderful time at his party"); others are more self-serving ("I lied to appear honest"). Manipulative people, and those with chronically poor relationships, on the other hand, tell more self-serving lies (Kashy & DePaulo, 1996).

Uncertainty

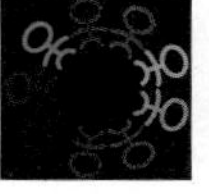

Are there circumstances that lead us to seek others as sources of information? According to social comparison theory, the motivation to compare our opinions, abilities, or reactions with others will increase when we are feeling uncertain about something important (West & Wicklund, 1980). We don't need to check with others concerning topics about which we already know the answer (Is Christmas going to be on December 25 this year?) or about which we aren't very concerned (Was the 1992 fava bean harvest larger in Iran or Turkey?). And some circumstances are more likely to arouse uncertainty than others. For instance, rumors (like the stories about witches in Salem that spread during 1692) tend to spread more rapidly when an event is important and when actual facts are difficult to obtain (Allport & Postman, 1947). In one experimental study of uncertainty and affiliation, students were threatened with painful shock. Some saw physiological recording gauges informing them how other students were responding to the same threat. Other students watched their own physiological responses, and still others were given no information (Gerard & Rabbie, 1961). When the students thought that they knew how other students were responding, they were less interested in affiliating than when they were given no information or information only about their own responses. This is consistent with the notion that part of the motivation for affiliation under fear is to compare one's own reactions with others.

Similarity

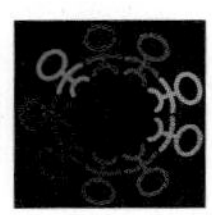

Other studies support a second assumption of social comparison theory—that people in a state of uncertainty want to compare themselves with others who are similar to themselves, either by virtue of being "in the same boat" or by virtue of having similar interests and personality (Gump & Kulik, 1997; Miller & Zimbardo, 1966). But more recent research also suggests that people's need to compare with similar others has its limits. When the issue is highly important to our welfare, we prefer affiliating with others who can give us accurate information whether they are similar or not. For instance, coronary bypass patients waiting for surgery prefer sharing a room with someone who has already had the operation over someone who is, like them, awaiting surgery (Kulik & Mahler, 1990). Likewise, students imagining waiting for a strong electric shock say that, if talking were allowed, they would rather wait with someone who has already experienced the shock (Kirkpatrick & Shaver, 1988).

The main goal of affiliation in truly threatening situations is often cognitive clarity: People whose welfare is on the line are not interested in affiliating simply to know whether their reactions are "socially appropriate"; they want to get the most useful information they can (Kulik, Mahler, & Earnest, 1994).

When Dissimilarity Can Save Self-Esteem

Whether we seek information from similar others may depend on our self-concepts. Jennifer Campbell and Abe Tesser (1985) propose that one important goal of social interaction is to maintain a positive evaluation of one's self. From the perspective of their *self-esteem maintenance theory*, comparing oneself with similar others can be a double-edged sword. If a person is similar to you, and very successful, you may be able to "bask in their glory" (Cialdini et al., 1976; Hirt, Zillman, Erickson, & Kennedy, 1992). To say "My brother just won an award for his writing!" is to subtly suggest that you are part of a family of geniuses. However, if the similar person's triumphant performance is in an area you regard as a special skill of your own, it may lead you to feel bad about your own performance (Beach et al., 1998). For instance, if you also fancy yourself a writer, your brother's prize may remind you that you have never won any writing awards. Campbell and Tesser (1985) note that, as a consequence, people prefer others whose performance is good and similar to their own but not better.

On the other hand, we aren't bothered if we find that another is better than us at something we don't regard as centrally relevant to how we define ourselves. As the pioneering psychologist William James noted:

> I, who for the time have staked my all on being a psychologist, am mortified if others know much more psychology than I. But I am content to wallow in the grossest ignorance of Greek. My deficiencies there give me no sense of personal humiliation at all. (1907, p. 310)

Figure 7.5
Blissful ignorance of social comparison information.

Students in one study estimated their skill at solving anagrams both before and after seeing another student do either worse or better than they had. Unhappy people upped their self-estimates after beating out the opponent and lowered them after being beaten. Happy people likewise upped their self-estimates after beating the other student, but they also raised self-estimates when the other student did better.

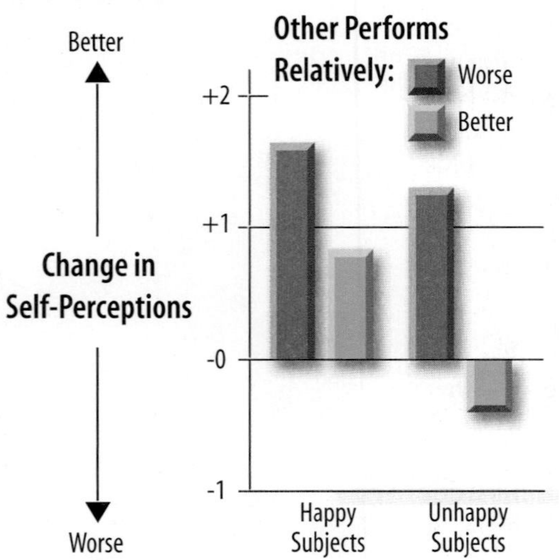

To avoid comparisons that provoke envy in long-term relationships, people are very good at making fine distinctions. A husband and wife in Tesser and Campbell's research were both political science professors, yet they expressed surprise when the researchers inquired whether there were problems of social comparison posed by their being in the same field. They were hardly in the same field, they pointed out, since one studied international relations while the other studied comparative politics!

A recent study suggests that the ignorance resulting from selective social comparisons may indeed be associated with bliss. Sonja Lyubomirsky and Lee Ross (1997) found that chronically unhappy students responded sensibly to social comparison information. As shown in Figure 7.5, the unhappy students raised their estimates of their own skill when they did better than a partner and lowered their estimates when they did worse. Happy students also raised their estimates when they outperformed the other student, but when the other student outperformed them, they were oblivious to the feedback and raised their self-appraisals anyway.

Summary

We are sometimes motivated to affiliate with others because they can share information with us. But not all of us want to share all the information all the time. Some people disclose more personal information in their conversations, and women generally disclose more than men. We look to others for information in situations that lead us to feel uncertainty, and we generally prefer information from similar others. If the circumstances require the unadulterated truth, however, we may prefer to check with dissimilar others. We are reluctant to dig too deeply for information that someone else excels on a characteristic we see as central to our self-esteem, especially when that person is a close personal friend. Indeed, chronically happy people's self-appraisals seem oblivious to information that another has done better than they have.

Gaining Status

J. Edgar Hoover shared one feature with Eleanor Roosevelt, that ensured neither would want for companionship. Both were politically powerful—so powerful, in fact, that being in their good graces could mean the difference between success and failure. For instance, Clyde Tolson's close friendship with J. Edgar Hoover had a very favorable impact on his career. Indeed, Hoover even created a special position, of associate FBI director, for his buddy. Tolson's rise supports the folk wisdom that "it's not what you know, but who you know."

People at the highest social ranks are often quite conscious of this relationship. Although he wasn't an elected delegate, young Franklin Delano Roosevelt (then a state representative living in Albany) attended the 1912 Democratic convention and "worked the crowd," promoting himself as Woodrow Wilson's biggest supporter from New York state. When Wilson won the nomination, and later the national election; Roosevelt was rewarded with an influential political post, that of assistant secretary of the Navy. Once they moved to Washington, Eleanor began assisting Franklin's political rise by befriending the members of powerful families:

> ...she devoted almost every afternoon to the tedious tradition of "calling." She left her calling cards at the door or in the hands of Cabinet wives, Supreme Court wives, congressional wives. There was not a notable wife she missed.... [S]he met everybody, looked for potential friends and allies, kept a detailed record in a calling journal, and reported it all to FDR. (Cook, 1992, 207)

Washingtonians aren't the only ones who form bonds to increase their status. In fact, the same political power alliances are found in other primate species (de Waal, 1989). Social status in chimpanzee troupes, as in humans, is related to "who you know," and the top positions of dominance are often occupied by coalitions of friends, who, in tandem, can outrank even the largest and most domineering single chimps.

Overly zealous attempts to move up in the dominance hierarchy can defeat the goal of being liked. As Oscar Wilde put it, "People will forgive you anything but your success." Of course, as we just noted in discussing self-esteem maintenance theory, Oscar Wilde's dictum may apply only when your success reflects badly on other people. We promote the success of those who are loyal to us, as Tolson was to J. Edgar Hoover, and we want those who are teamed up with us to succeed, because it can reflect positively on us. On the other side of the coin, we are attracted to powerful people whose alliance can serve us well, as Franklin and Eleanor Roosevelt were attracted to the power elite of Washington. In the next section, we will

Teaming up for status. *Humans aren't the only primates who form alliances to gain power. The two male baboons at the left have formed a coalition to compete for a female with the larger, more dominant, male at the right. By forming this coalition, both of the less dominant males may gain access to mating opportunities that neither would have on his own.*

consider how men and women sometimes strike a different balance between dominance and likability in their relationships.

Sex Differences in Friendships

Elizabeth Read was an attorney and friend of Eleanor Roosevelt. She was also a high-ranking member of the League of Women Voters. Every week, she scanned the Congressional record and published an influential newsletter called *City, State, and Nation.* Despite her dedicated interest in political causes, however, she had this to say in a letter to another friend:

> ...we did not get down to the real issue: Whether a cause, or one's human relationships, is the more important.... I know that for myself the human relationships are.... You could work fifty years for a cause, and find your life too dreary and barren to be endured. If a person is lucky enough to meet a human being that is worth devotion, that—in the absence of a crisis, or an all-compelling call—is the important thing. (Cook, 298)

Elizabeth Read's evaluation of the relative importance of intimate relationships over career demonstrates a common difference between men and women. Interviews with college juniors and seniors suggest that males are more likely to base their personal identity on career advancement, whereas females' identities are more likely to blend career and intimate relationships (Maines & Hardesty, 1987). These sex differences begin early in life (Rawlins, 1992). Among adolescents, female friendships are more intimate and involving than males', and a female's self-esteem is tied more closely to having an intimate friend (Townsend, McCracken, & Wilton, 1988). Social inclusion is so important to them that excluding a girl from a social group is the primary method teenage girls use to hurt one another (Owens, Shute, & Slee, 2000).

Friendships among male adolescents are less intimate and more likely to involve discussion of activities, such as competitive sports (Martin, 1997; Shulman, Laursen, Kalman, & Karpovsky, 1997). In their interactions with their parents, adolescent males are relatively more likely to discuss careers and colleges, while females are relatively more likely to discuss friends and family problems. In college, females are also closer to their same-sex friends than males are (Wheeler, Reis, & Nezlek, 1983). Perhaps as a consequence of these differences, college females have more friends than do males (Nezlek, 1993). In later life, men have more relationships with coworkers, while women have more with people outside work (Rawlins, 1992).

Anita Barbee and her colleagues (1993) noted another consequence of gender differences in friendship styles. Because the female role emphasizes nurturance and emotional expressiveness, they argue, females may have an easier time getting and giving social support. Males, on the other hand, whose role emphasizes achievement and independence, have a relatively more difficult time giving and obtaining social-emotional support, though they may be better at dealing with instrumental support (such as helping a friend fix his car).

A number of research findings support Barbee's analysis of the sex differences in social supportiveness. For instance, females tend to be more agreeable, more empathic, more skilled in nonverbal communication, and better at smoothing interactions in social groups (Bank & Hansford, 2000; Eagly & Wood, 1991). Women tend to smile more than men, to be more attentive and agreeable than men, and to show their appreciation of their friends more directly (Carli, 1989; Hall & Halberstadt, 1986; Helgeson, Shaver, & Dyer, 1987). Males are more concerned that they will be scorned by their friends for being unable to solve minor problems on their own (Bruder-Mattson & Hovanitz, 1990). In approaching problems in their romantic relationships, males are more likely to take a logical and unemotional approach (Kelley et al., 1978). For instance, they are more likely to use dismissive statements such as "Don't get so excited" or "It's not that important." Finally, men emphasize social hierarchy in relationships more than women do (McWilliams & Howard, 1993). Clearly, this distinction applied better to J. Edgar Hoover than to Eleanor Roosevelt.

In sum, men's relationships are marked more by hierarchy and instrumentality—components of status-seeking—and women's more by an emphasis on emotional support and intimacy. As a consequence, men may get more respect in their relationships, but women tend to get more affection. Is it any surprise, then, that both sexes place more value on friendships with women?

Status by Association

What circumstances might trigger the desire to affiliate with others for the sake of gaining status? When status is salient, as in relationships on the job, people ought to try to associate with the higher-ups. On the other side of the coin, when another person has a socially undesirable characteristic that could lead to stigma by association, people may be motivated to distance themselves.

Kissing Up to High Status Concern about status in relationships comes to the fore when the social hierarchy is prominent. Indeed, relationships at work are likely to develop along status lines (Kanter, 1977). Graduate students who attend professional meetings become painfully aware of an annoying tendency of their conversational partners to break eye-contact to read the name tags of passers-by. The lowly graduate student is often deserted in mid-conversation if he or she is talking to a name-tag reader who spots a famous person walking by: "Excuse me. I need to run.... Ah, Doctor Zilstein, I noticed your name tag. I've read so many of your papers, and find them so inspiring...." When people in organizations were surveyed about office politics, they frequently mentioned aligning themselves with powerful others as a way of getting ahead (Allen, Madison, Porter, Renwick, & Mayes, 1979). Like Clyde Tolson and other FBI officials in their "yea saying" attitude toward J. Edgar Hoover, people in organizations commonly agree with their superiors in the hopes of getting the boss to like them (Greenberg & Baron, 1993; Liden & Mitchell, 1988).

Friendship and status seeking. *J. Edgar Hoover curried the favor of presidents, upon whom he was dependent for continued appointment as head of the FBI. In turn, he helped them by passing on confidential information about potential enemies. Hoover spotted Nixon as a potential ally during Senator McCarthy's Communist hunt in the 1950s, and he assisted Nixon in his rise to power.*

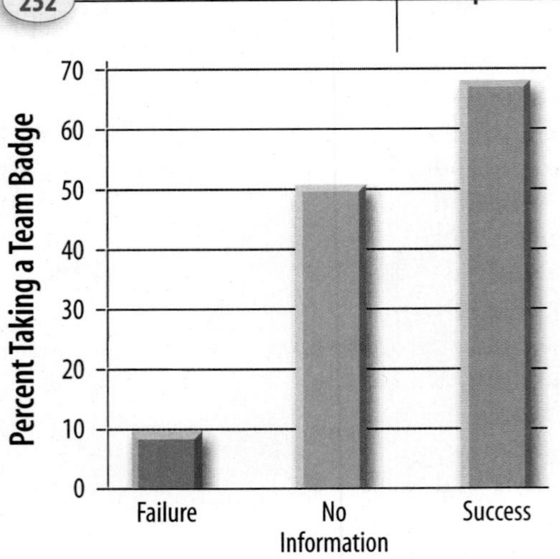

Figure 7.6
Cutting off reflected failure.

Students in one experiment were told that their team had done either splendidly or very poorly. Compared to those who got no information, those who thought the team had failed were substantially less likely to take a team badge.

This desire to form friendships with higher-ups is particularly strong in highly status-oriented cultures, such as in Japan. In one study, office workers in a U.S. organization and workers in a Japanese organization ranked the other office members and indicated how much they liked them. The Americans most liked workers at their own level, but the Japanese most liked those of higher status (Nakao, 1987).

Kissing Off Stigmatic Associations On the other side of the coin, there is some evidence that people sometimes seek to break social connections that could reflect poorly on them. For example, students in one experiment filled out the "Johnson Anger and Hostility Scale," and were later told their scores indicated a person who "has tendencies toward hostility and repressed anger but is usually unaware of these tendencies." Others filled out "Johnson's Dishonesty Scale," and were led to believe that they had high levels of "repressed dishonesty." Afterward, they saw another student's personality questionnaire, and read a note from that student. In the note, the other person confessed either to becoming violent with a little nephew or to stealing some cash from a gym locker. Finally, the students rated themselves on the same personality questionnaire. Students who were feeling defensive about their own "repressed hostility" distanced themselves from the angry person, rating their own personality as very dissimilar. On the other hand, students who had been made defensive about their own "repressed dishonesty" placed more distance between themselves and the thief (Schimel et al., 2000). Male undergraduates in another study similarly distanced themselves from a man who was similar to them, but whose best friend was a homosexual (Neuberg, Smith, Hoffman, & Russell, 1994).

In a sense, this distancing phenomenon is the converse of "basking in reflected glory" (broadcasting one's associations with successful others), which we discussed in chapter 4. C. R. Snyder, MaryAnne Lassegard, and Carol Ford (1986) studied this distancing phenomenon in small groups of students assigned to "the Blue team" to work together on intellectual problems. Students were informed that their teams had either failed (scoring below 70 percent of people their age) or succeeded with flying colors (scoring above 90 percent of people their age). Afterwards, students were told, "There is a box of team badges by the door, you may take one and wear it if you like." Compared to students who got no information, those told their group had failed were far less likely to pick up the badge (see Figure 7.6). The researchers explained the results in terms of Heider's (1958) balance theory, which, as we discussed in chapter 5, assumes that people manage their associations to maintain consistent (and preferably favorable) images of themselves.

Seeking Status May Erode Social Support

As we noted earlier, there may be an inherent conflict between the motive to get emotional support and the motive to gain status through friendship. There is, in fact, some evidence that mixing work and play may, in the long run, damage one's social support networks. Highly motivated students, for example, often talk with their friends about how they're doing in school. Because your friends have only so much interest in what you're doing to get ahead, that may be a formula for losing friends. Less motivated students keep their social support networks stronger in part by talking about things that their friends find more interesting (Harlow & Cantor, 1994).

Over the lifespan, men's status orientation may make them less desirable as friends. This has interesting implications for cross-sex friendships. As it turns out, men value the company of women, but women do not always reciprocate and would often rather hang out with other women (McWilliams & Howard, 1993). Women find their same-sex friendships more meaningful and more enjoyable than relationships with men (Reis, Senchak, & Solomon, 1985). As we noted earlier, women show their appreciation of their friends in very direct ways. Men are not so directly appreciative (Helgeson, Shaver, & Dyer, 1987). Women send a thank you note saying "That was really fun! I really value having you in my life! Let's have lunch again next Friday!" Men say, "I think I can find it in my heart to help you work on your pathetic golf swing again. Let's get together next Friday so you can watch how a master does it!" Small wonder that both sexes search for females in times of stress. Here's an example of the person changing the situation. Males' sex-typical emphasis on status and competition often leads them to create a somewhat different (and less supportive) social environment than the one in which females dwell.

Summary

One motive for affiliating with others is to gain status. Men tend to play out power motivations in their relationships more than do women. In settings where social hierarchies are prominent, people are more likely to seek friends who can enhance their status. Pursuing status motives in our relationships may reduce social support, and men in particular may create social worlds that are status-oriented but not as socially supportive as the worlds created by women.

Exchanging Material Benefits

Imagine you were living 1,000 years ago in a small group of people in the deepest jungles of South America. Imagine further that food is sometimes abundant but other times quite scarce. You have a lucky day at the local fishing hole and come home with a twelve-pound fish. Do you hoard it for yourself and your immediate family, or do you share? For most of the history of the human species, our ancestors spent their time in just such small groups (Caporeal, 1997; Sedikides & Skowronski, 1997). Research on modern hunter-gatherers reveals that if they did not share goods and services with one another, they would often perish (Hill & Hurtado, 1993).

Hunters in the Ache tribe, living in the Paraguayan jungle, for example, have a lot of ups and downs in their success at the hunt. Some days they bring home much more food than they could possibly eat; other days they come home empty-handed. If a man caught a wild pig and hoarded it for himself and his family, much of it would go to waste (there are no deep-freeze refrigerators in the Paraguayan jungle). During unlucky periods, individual hunters and their families would starve. Instead of living by a philosophy of "rugged individualism," however, hunters who have a lucky day share their meat with other families. And they don't just share a little; they share a lot—fully 90 percent. In exchange for this generosity, their neighbors share with them on days when the luck runs the other way. By exchanging resources in this way, the group provides a mutual insurance policy against starvation (Hill & Hurtado, 1993).

Because of the importance of sharing resources, all societies have strong rules about who shares what with whom (Haslam, 1997). We discuss those rules in the next section.

Ache Indians. *By generously sharing resources when they are in the luck, families ensure reciprocity when the luck runs the other way. In this way, everyone stands a better chance of survival.*

Fundamental Patterns of Social Exchange

Although we may not have recently shared wild pig with our friends and neighbors, most of us frequently exchange material benefits including rides to the store, Thanksgiving dinners, and inside tracks on job opportunities. The exchange of goods and services is so important to social life that some social psychologists believe it is at the very heart of our relationships with others (e.g., Foa & Foa, 1980).

One of the most influential theories of friendship assumes that we are most drawn to relationships in which we experience **equity**—a state of affairs in which your benefits and costs from the relationship are proportional to the benefits and costs incurred by your partner (e.g., Hatfield, Traupmann, Sprecher, Utne, & Hay, 1985). To understand how equity works, pick one friend and list the rewards and benefits that each of you gets from your relationship. Your friend may benefit you by being a good study partner, a source of compliments, and host to some really fun parties. You may provide the same benefits for your friend, minus the parties, but he may also get to borrow your car when his old junker is in the repair shop.

Next try to list the costs you both incur from being in the relationship. As costs to you, perhaps your friend occasionally distracts you with irrelevant jokes during study sessions, beats you mercilessly at tennis, and criticizes your choice of romantic partners. As costs to your friend, you may occasionally make him feel dumb by getting better grades on the same exams or go into dark moods whenever you lose at tennis. If you add up all your benefits and costs, and compare them to his, the relationship is equitable if you both seem to get a similar value. If, on the other hand, you feel that he gets somewhat more out of the relationship, you will feel underbenefitted. If you feel that you get more out of the relationship, you will feel overbenefitted.

Equity is not the only form of **social exchange** in relationships. Nick Haslam and Alan Fiske (1999) categorized social relationships into four models, each characterized by a different set of social exchange rules (see Table 7.3).

In **communal sharing** relationships, all members of a group share a pool of resources, taking when they are in need and giving when others are in need. Families often share according to a communal rule. In **authority ranking** relationships, goods are divided according to a person's status in the group. In a business, for instance, the boss gets a higher salary, a personal secretary, a reserved parking spot, and the freedom to come and go as she chooses. **Equality matching** involves exchange in which no one gets more than the others. Friends in a Chinese restaurant often share according to this sort of rule: everyone gets one spring roll and a bowl of sweet and sour soup, and no one takes a second serving of the Kung-Pao shrimp until everyone else has had their first. Finally, **market pricing** is a form of exchange in which everyone gets out in proportion to what they put in. If a waiter provides good service, he expects a good tip, and if you pay a lot for a meal, you expect cuisine that is above the ordinary. Market pricing is roughly equivalent to equity exchanges.

As implied by this more complicated view of social exchange, people aren't always motivated by the same exchange rules in their relationships with others. The form of exchange depends on who's involved in the interaction and what type of interaction it is. We return to this topic in chapter 8, in which we discuss love and family relationships. We now turn to a consideration of some factors in the person and in the situation that affect decisions about exchange.

Equity *A state of affairs in which one person's benefits and costs from a relationship are proportional to the benefits and costs incurred by his or her partner.*

Social exchange *The trading of benefits within relationships.*

Communal sharing *A form of exchange in which members of a group share a pool of resources, taking when they are in need and giving when others are in need.*

Authority ranking *A form of exchange in which goods are divided according to a person's status in the group.*

Equality matching *A form of exchange in which each person gets the same as the others.*

Market pricing *A form of exchange in which everyone gets out in proportion to what they put in.*

Individual Differences in Communal Orientation

When you think about the people you know, are there some who are always "counting"—keeping close tabs on what they give to and what they get from others? Whether someone is bothered by being underbenefitted or overbenefitted seems to depend in part on his or her personal orientation toward social exchange (Buunk, Doosje, Jans, & Hopstaken, 1993; Clark, Ouellette, Powell, & Milberg, 1987). People who take a communal orientation tend to believe that each person in a re-

Table 7.3 Different models of social exchange.

Model of Social Relations	Rules of Exchange	Example of Relationship Using this Rule
Communal Sharing	All members of a group share in the group's resources as needed and depend on one another for mutual care.	A tight-knit family
Authority Ranking	Higher-ranking individuals are entitled to loyalty, respect, and deference; lower-ranking individuals are entitled to protection, advice, and leadership.	Military squad
Equality Matching	No one gets more than others; people take turns, share equally, and reciprocate benefits.	Children playing a game at summer camp
Market Pricing	Individuals trade according to rational rules of self-interest, taking goods and services in proportion to what they put in, and seeking the best possible "deal."	Customer–shopkeeper

lationship should give whatever is necessary to satisfy the needs of the other. Those low on this dimension, on the other hand, take a more market-oriented view—that what you give to another should be equal in value to what you get from him or her. As indicated in Figure 7.7, Bram Buunk and his colleagues (1993) found that people who are low in communal orientation (the market-value people) feel best when they are treated equitably and unhappy when they are getting either too much or too little. Those high in communal orientation, on the other hand, are not particularly troubled if there is a discrepancy between what they are giving and what they are getting in a relationship. In fact, they seem to be quite happy even when they are putting more into a relationship than they are getting out of it.

Thus, people who have a communal orientation are less concerned with keeping careful track of inputs and outputs in their relationships with others. As we discuss in the next section, a communal orientation can characterize not only people, but also particular relationships and particular social situations.

Are there certain circumstances in which we are more or less likely to pay attention to rewards and costs in our relationships? We consider two such circumstances here—the type of relationship and the proximity of the players.

Figure 7.7
When we get more—or less—than we deserve.

Bram Buunk and his colleagues found that people high in communal orientation are not particularly troubled by situations in which they are underbenefitted or overbenefitted. However, those who are low in communal orientation experience negative feelings if they are either under- or overbenefitted.

SOURCE: *Buunk et al. (1993).*

Communal and Exchange Relationships

Margaret Clark and Judson Mills and their colleagues have drawn a distinction between communal and exchange relationships (e.g., Clark & Chrisman, 1994; Clark, Mills, & Corcoran, 1989). Exchange relationships are based on rewards and benefits traded in the past or that the person expects to trade in the future. Communal relationships, on the other hand, are relationships based on mutual concern for one another's welfare. A mother's relationship to her child is a good example of a communal relationship: the mother is likely to provide benefits based on the child's needs, not keep a mental checklist of benefits and costs to be used to decide whether to put the kid out on the street if the "deal" gets too costly for her.

A number of studies support the utility of a distinction between exchange and communal relationships. For instance, when young children share rewards with casual acquaintances, they use an equity principle—giving benefits depending on deservingness. When they share with friends, however, they are more inclined to distribute rewards equally—keeping less track of who deserves what (Pataki, Shapiro, & Clark, 1994). People in long-term relationships, or who want to establish long-term relationships, stop keeping track of the rewards they provide for the other. Instead, they pay closer attention to what the other person needs (Clark, Mills, & Corcoran, 1989; Mills & Clark, 1994).

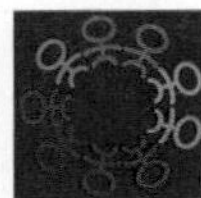

Proximity

Another simple principle is that we are more likely to exchange rewards with another person when it is easy to do so. One factor that reduces the cost of sharing is physical proximity. If I need a cup of sugar or an egg, for instance, it is a whole lot less costly to borrow one from my next-door neighbor than to go down the block to the house of someone I know better. The same principle holds if I want to invite someone to play a game of chess or to share a pizza.

Research conducted over several decades demonstrates a powerful **proximity-attraction principle**—we tend to choose our friends from those who live or work nearby. For instance, a classic study of friendships in a student housing project found that when residents were asked to name the person they most liked in the complex, the next-door neighbor headed the list (Festinger, Schachter, & Back, 1950). This was not because people had chosen to live near friends—residents were randomly assigned to apartments. Another study found that police cadets developed friendships with other cadets whose last names started with the same letter (Segal, 1974). Why? Cadets had been assigned to classroom seats and dorm rooms by alphabet, so they spent their time in the proximity of those with similar last names.

Neighbors are attractive not only because there are low costs to interacting with them, but also because they are simply more *familiar.* Whereas people are a bit wary of strange stimuli, including other people's faces, frequent exposure generally leads to liking (Bornstein, 1989; Zajonc, 1968). The tendency to feel positively toward people, places, or things we've seen frequently is called the **mere exposure effect.**

Besides being familiar though, neighbors have an even more obvious advantage. Physical proximity makes it easy to engage in those everyday social exchanges.

Are Exchange Relationships Different in Western and Non-Western Cultures?

We noted earlier that the rules of exchange vary for different relationships; there are different rules for relatives, friends, and strangers. These rules also seem to interact with culture. When asked to distribute grades within a group of strangers, both Chinese and U.S. students preferred equity, giving grades based strictly on performance. Even when the group was composed of friends, however, Americans still gave some weight to deservingness. However, when Chinese were dividing rewards with friends, they were, compared with Americans, much more likely to switch the allocation rule so that everyone was treated equally, regardless of how deserving they were (Leung & Bond, 1984). Why the difference? One explanation for this difference in exchange rules is that Chinese traditionally spend more time in groups of relatives and close neighborhood friends. That is, the cultural divergence may depend not on some vast discrepancy in how Americans and Chinese think but rather on a discrepancy in the composition of their friendship groups.

Let's consider a more detailed example of how culture can affect friendship. Iris is eight years old and lives in a thatched hut with her parents and five brothers and sisters in a small village in Papua, New Guinea. Her grandparents live in a house ten feet away, and her paternal uncles and their families live in the other neighboring houses. She refers to her cousins as brothers and sisters and plays with them every day. Every day, the family exchanges food with relatives, further strengthening the bonds between them. As part of her play, she learns to babysit her relatives. Iris knows that when she gets older, she will marry one of her more distant relatives, who lives in a nearby village.

Erika, on the other hand, lives in an apartment with her parents and one younger brother in a suburb of a Swedish city with a population of over a million. Her family has lived there for only two years, and although she has made several friends in the complex, they frequently move away and lose contact. Erika visits her mother's parents about six times a year and her father's parents and her only aunt and two cousins

Proximity-attraction principle *The tendency to become friends with those who live or work nearby.*

Mere exposure effect *The tendency to feel positively toward people, places, or things we have seen frequently.*

twice a year. She is one of 90 second graders in her school, and after school, she goes into the city for music lessons, where she meets girls who live many miles away from her. When she grows up, she plans to study medicine at a university and perhaps live in another country (Tietjen, 1994).

The differences between the social lives of Iris and Erika illustrate three important distinctions noted by cross-cultural psychologists Fathali Moghaddam, Donald Taylor, and Stephen Wright (1993):

1. Relationships in Western society tend to be freely chosen; those in more traditional cultures tend to be involuntary. As the saying goes, "You can choose your friends, but you can't choose your family." In farming communities or jungle villages, there is little choice indeed. Your acquaintances are limited to members of your family and your tribal and religious group. Extended families may limit one another's freedom, but also seem to buffer their members against extremes of stress (Diener, 2000).
2. Relationships in traditional cultures tend to be more permanent and continuous than those in Western cultures. In a modern urban setting, you may never see a first-time acquaintance again, many of your friends will move away and be replaced by new ones, and even your marriage may be temporary. In a small farming community or a jungle village, your relationships with the members of your small community will last your whole life.
3. Relationships in urban Western society tend to be individualistic; those in traditional societies tend to be collective. Relationships with first-time acquaintances (like the person you talk to in the check-out line), with good friends, and with lovers are one-to-one, and the form of such relationships is determined by the personalities, attitudes, beliefs, and desires of the two individuals involved. In a small community, a person's relationships with neighbors and relatives are determined by the groups they belong to.

Exposure and attraction. *Research suggests that we generally come to like those people and things to which we are frequently exposed. This may help us to understand why political campaigns often involved repeated exposure to the candidate's name and face, without any mention of the issues. The politician hopes that you will simply come to like him or her due to simple exposure.*

A number of features of traditional society disfavor voluntary, temporary, and individualistic relationships. Some are based simply on technology. A man living in the mountains of Nepal may be "only" twenty miles away from a potential friend in the next village, but to cover that twenty miles, he must hike along a footpath through the mountains, and it would take all day to travel one way. In the same time it takes the Nepalese villager to hike the twenty miles up the mountain footpath, and with less effort, a New Yorker can visit a friend in Los Angeles, Seattle, or even London. And telephones, fax machines, and email make it easy for modern urban dwellers to stay directly in touch with people all around the world.

The extended rural American family. *Researchers studying relationships have generally emphasized voluntary, short-term relationships such as those found in large urban areas. But cross-cultural researchers note that involuntary extended family relationships are characteristic of people living in most of the world's rural cultures. Perhaps college-educated researchers living in large European and American cities have lost touch with the world's most common relationships.*

Another source of such relationship differences comes from societal norms about collectivism versus individualism. As discussed in chapter 2, collectively oriented societies see the social group as more important than the needs of the individual and value interdependence as opposed to independence (Hsu, 1983; Triandis, 1994). Individualistic societies such as the United States and Canada, however, place more emphasis on individual rights, freedom, equality, and personal independence (Hofstede, 1980; Triandis, 1994).

The reason modern urban societies such as the United States and Canada are relatively more individualistic and less collectivist may be inherently connected to the types of relationships likely to occur in these mobile and highly democratic societies. When one's network consists largely of short-term, interchangeable acquaintances, a market-based distribution of resources makes more sense than when one's network consists of close family members.

The insight that different relationships have different exchange rules is a very important one for understanding the social psychology of friendship. Early research in the field was conducted mostly in laboratories at large urban universities and was mostly concerned with relationships between strangers. As researchers began to study closer, more intimate, relationships, they realized that the old models, based solely on "market-based" rules of exchange, may not always apply (Berscheid & Reis, 1998). In the next chapter, we focus on long-term love and family relationships. As we will see, those relationships hardly follow the same rules that apply to a business.

Summary

One important goal of affiliation is to exchange material benefits. People high in exchange orientation are uncomfortable being underbenefitted or overbenefitted in a relationship and seek relationships where contributions are relatively equal. People are more likely to adopt a needs-based rule in communal relationships. We are likely to befriend those who live near us, partly because it is easier to exchange material benefits with them. Finally, people tend to adopt different rules of exchange with different people, and in different cultures. Table 7.4 summarizes the factors relevant to this and the other goals discussed in this chapter.

CHAPTER 7
Summary Table

Table 7.4 Summary of different influences on friendship and affiliation.

The Goal	The Person	The Situation	Interactions
Getting Social Support	• Birth order	• Impersonal threats • Feelings of social isolation	• Potential embarrassment or loss of face may lead people to reject social support. • Depressed or lonely people may act in ways that cut off needed support. • People often reject social support from parents as they grow older.
Getting Information	• Gender • Need for approval	• Uncertain situations • Similarity of others	• When someone close is better than us on a feature central to our self-concepts, we avoid comparing with them. • Happy people are oblivious to information that others have outperformed them.
Gaining Status	• Gender	• Prominence of social hierarchy • Importance of status in culture • Stigmatization of others	• Mixing work and play may weaken supportive relationships. • Because women are less hierarchical and more supportive, men tend to value friendships with women more than women value friendships with men.
Exchanging Material Benefits	• Communal orientation	• Anticipated length of relationship • Physical proximity	• Compared to Americans, Chinese de-emphasize equity and favor equality amongst close friends. • Voluntary, impermanent, and individualistic relationships in modern societies may favor equity over traditional communal exchange.

REVISITING

The Beloved Roosevelt and the Hate-filled Hoover

Can the research on affiliation and friendship provide any clues about the infamous antipathy between Eleanor Roosevelt and J. Edgar Hoover? As we noted, the two occupied very different locations on the interpersonal circumplex. Roosevelt was extremely agreeable—smiling, warm, humble, and supportive of her friends. Hoover was unusually disagreeable—scowling, critical, suspicious, and willing to stab even his closest associates in the back. Their personal differences played out in self-perpetuating interactions. Eleanor Roosevelt created a world where it was easy for others to befriend her. Hoover's style alienated even the people who worked alongside him for years. Having thus inspired others to dislike him, Hoover had more reason to be suspicious. Indeed, several presidents plotted to remove him from office. Hence, Hoover created an environment in which he had good reason not to trust others, providing a good example of the self-fulfilling prophecy we discussed in chapter 3.

We also noted that concern over embarrassment could lead people to avoid seeking social support. Fear of embarrassment was a lifelong issue for Hoover, in part because his father had been hospitalized for a stigmatizing mental illness. As for social support, Hoover apparently pushed it away, and did so actively. As his niece noted, he seemed to fear getting too close to people. Eleanor Roosevelt, on the other hand, spent her life surrounded by supportive others.

We also discussed how male status-seeking can sometimes undermine social relationships. Hoover certainly fit the extreme male prototype in this regard. He had an extraordinary need for power and wielded it mercilessly inside his self-made kingdom at the FBI. For her part, Roosevelt did not let power come between her and her friends. Despite her great status, she did not worry about losing status by associating with "stigmatized" others. Before, during, and after her term as first lady, she persistently associated with minority group members, lesbians, and outspoken leftists.

In discussing social exchange across cultures, we noted that the rules of exchange may change depending on who is nearby. The lives of Eleanor Roosevelt and J. Edgar Hoover tell an interesting story in this regard. Roosevelt came from a large, extended family and grew up in country homes around her cousins. Like the girl in the small village we discussed earlier, she actually married one of these cousins (her name was already Roosevelt before she married Franklin D.). The Roosevelts had several of their own children, and they remained close to the extended family all their lives. Eleanor thus grew up in an environment conducive to a communal orientation. Hoover, on the other hand, grew up in a large city (Washington, D.C.), lived alone with his mother, had no siblings, no wife and no children.

Thus Hoover's family background, early experiences, and isolated cultural milieu led him to adopt an extremely individualistic and self-centered interpersonal style. But why did he take such a fervent dislike to someone as pleasant as Eleanor Roosevelt? The powerful similarity-attraction principle, and its converse, the dissimilarity-repulsion principle, undoubtedly provide part of the answer. On issues central to their respective views of the world, Hoover and Roosevelt were polar opposites. Hoover was conservative and isolationist—concerned about foreigners and insidious socialist influences in the United States, disdainful of human rights activists, and obsessed with law and order. Roosevelt was extremely liberal, internationally educated and connected, concerned with human rights, and favorable toward the political left.

Eleanor Roosevelt and her family. *Part of the difference between Eleanor Roosevelt and J. Edgar Hoover may be linked to the fact that she spent her life surrounded by members of a large, extended family, whereas he spent his life in an urban setting without a close-knit, extended family.*

In one very direct confrontation, she publicly criticized Hoover for using "Gestapo tactics" after learning that he was spying on her friends. When he was later asked to investigate threats against her life, he refused by sarcastically expressing concern about the "human rights" of her harassers.

Perhaps because of his father's history of mental illness, Hoover was particularly obsessed with stigma by association. During the House UnAmerican Activities trials, he and Senator Joseph McCarthy exploited any remote association with Communists to blackmail people into betraying their friends and acquaintances. Interestingly, Hoover shared a stigma with Eleanor Roosevelt, one that he went to great lengths to keep secret. Recall that he kept files on the sex lives of his enemies and had helped spread rumors about Eleanor's sexual relationships with men and women. After his death, biographers uncovered evidence that Hoover himself may have had a rather unconventional private life. Thus, Hoover's public attacks on the sex lives of figures such as Eleanor Roosevelt and Martin Luther King, Jr., may have been designed to distance himself from his own secret stigma. We will leave the exact details of Hoover's secret life a mystery for now, since they will elucidate the "Focus on Social Dysfunction" topic of the final chapter of this book.

CHAPTER 7

Summary

What Is a Friend?

1. The affiliation motive is the need to be near others and to have pleasant and affectionate interactions.
2. Relationships with friends are voluntary, unlike those with relatives (although people often see relatives as friends). Relationships with friends differ from love relationships in the lack of romantic or passionate feelings.
3. Because people's memories of their relationships can be biased and incomplete, researchers have developed techniques such as experience sampling, in which subjects record and rate their own interactions several times daily.
4. Around the world, people think about relationships in terms of two dimensions—agreeableness and dominance. These dimensions combine to form a circumplex that can also map relational problems.
5. According to the reinforcement–affect model, relationships have one overriding goal: to increase pleasant feelings and decrease unpleasant ones. Domain-specific models assume that different goals characterize different relationships at different times.

Getting Social Support

1. Social support is defined as the emotional, material, or informational assistance others provide.
2. Health psychology is the study of behavioral and psychological factors affecting illness. Having adequate social support is linked to reduced psychological and physical symptoms, better immune response, and quicker medical recoveries. Such support can come from pets as well as people.
3. Compared with later-born children, first-borns are more likely to seek emotional support under stress.
4. People seek out social support when threatened by impersonal dangers or feeling socially isolated, but avoid social support if stress comes from crowding or fear of embarrassment.
5. People may reject social support if they do not think they can reciprocate. Lonely and depressed people think and behave in ways that ultimately drive away the very support they seek.

Getting Information

1. Other people can provide useful information about objective reality, social norms, and the self.
2. According to social comparison theory, people desire to measure themselves against similar others to evaluate their opinions and abilities.
3. Women are more likely to disclose personal information and elicit self-disclosures from others. People high in need for social approval bias their transmission of information toward the positive, while those high in social anxiety bias their reception of information toward the negative.
4. We seek information from others when we are uncertain about consequential issues and when the others are similar to us.
5. According to self-esteem maintenance theory, we avoid comparisons with very close others when they excel in the same domains we do. Chronically happy people ignore information that others have outdone them but are attentive to information that they have outdone others.

Gaining Status

1. Compared to women, men place less emphasis on intimacy and more on power in their relationships. Consequently, men get more respect from their friends and acquaintances, whereas women get more affection.
2. People seek affiliations with high-status individuals in contexts in which status is salient, more so in some cultures than others. Conversely, people sometimes distance themselves from others who may damage their status.
3. Pursuing status in our relationships may reduce social support.

Exchanging Material Benefits

1. Sharing material resources is essential for survival in small, self-sufficient groups of the sort in which our ancestors lived.
2. Equity occurs when your benefits and costs from a relationship are proportional to those of your partner. Different exchange rules apply in different relationships: In communal sharing, everyone takes freely from a common pool as they need. In authority ranking, resources are distributed according to status. In equality matching, everyone gets the same share. In market pricing, people trade goods and services according to rules of self-interest, seeking the best possible "deal."
3. Some people characteristically adopt a communal orientation and keep less careful track of inputs and outputs in relationships.
4. When people expect long-term interactions they tend to adopt rules of communal exchange. People living or working near one another are especially likely to become friends, partly because they share resources and rewarding experiences.
5. A person's typical orientation toward exchange may depend on cultural factors affecting who they spend time around. In cultures and places where relatives interact frequently, people adopt more communal norms.

CHAPTER 7

Key Terms

Affiliation motive *The desire to be near others and to have pleasant interactions with them.*

Authority ranking *A form of exchange in which goods are divided according to a person's status in the group.*

Communal sharing *A form of exchange in which members of a group share a pool of resources, taking when they are in need and giving when others are in need.*

Equality matching *A form of exchange in which each person gets the same as the others.*

Equity *A state of affairs in which one person's benefits and costs from a relationship are proportional to the benefits and costs incurred by his or her partner.*

Experience sampling method *An observational technique in which subjects fill out frequent descriptions of who they are with and what is going on.*

Friend *Someone with whom we have an affectionate relationship.*

Health psychology *The study of behavioral and psychological factors that affect illness.*

Market pricing *A form of exchange in which everyone gets out in proportion to what they put in.*

Mere exposure effect *The tendency to feel positively toward people, places, or things we have seen frequently.*

Proximity-attraction principle *The tendency to become friends with those who live or work nearby.*

Reinforcement–affect model *The theory that we like people with whom we associate positive feelings and dislike those with whom we associate negative feelings.*

Self-disclosure *The sharing of intimate information about oneself.*

Social exchange *The trading of benefits within relationships.*

Social support *Emotional, material, or informational assistance provided by other people.*

CHAPTER 8

Love and Romantic Relationships

The Puzzling Love Lives of the British Monarchs

The amorous affairs of British royalty have inspired gossip for centuries. Consider King Henry VIII. His notorious troubles with marital commitment started around the same time a disgruntled Catholic priest named Martin Luther began the protests that split Europe into Protestant and Catholic states. The two seemingly unrelated chains of events linked together after the Pope refused to invalidate Henry's first marriage to Catherine of Aragon. Defying the Pope, Henry divorced Catherine, married Anne Boleyn, and turned England to the new Protestantism. After thus disrupting the course of European history, Henry soon divorced Anne, and went on to marry four more women.

The web of questions surrounding Henry's string of marriages is intimately related to many of the issues we will pose in this chapter, but let's begin with one simple question. Of Henry's six wives, five were quite a bit younger than he, but one was several years older. Which of his wives was the older woman—the first, second, third, fourth, fifth, or last? You could answer this even if you knew nothing

Henry VIII

about British history but did know something about the patterns of human love and marriage around the world.

Henry ruled England in the 1500s, but his wasn't the last romantic scandal in the British royal family. For several years before Princess Diana's death in 1997, the media trumpeted her marital problems with Prince Charles. Despite their success in having two sons to assure the continuity of the royal line, and despite the potentially great rewards for maintaining their marriage, Charles and Diana had grown unable to bear each other's company within the confines of the same castle.

The problems of Charles and Diana were almost exactly opposite those faced several decades earlier by Charles's uncle, Edward VIII. According to Wallis Simpson, the woman Edward fell in love with, "His slightest wish seemed always to be translated instantly into the most impressive kind of reality. Trains were held; yachts materialized; the best suites in the finest hotels were flung open; aeroplanes stood waiting." Yet, Edward VIII gave it all up on December 10, 1936, when he made the following momentous radio announcement:

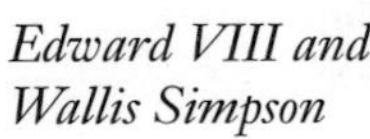

Edward VIII and Wallis Simpson

> You must believe me when I tell you that I have found it impossible to carry the heavy duty of responsibility and discharge my duties as King as I would wish to do, without the help and support of the woman I love. I now quit altogether public affairs...

With these words Edward abdicated England's throne and all the wealth, lands, power, and privilege that accompanied it. He did this because the woman he loved was considered unacceptable as a member of the British royal family. But why did Edward give up his throne for Wallis when he could have married any number of intelligent, beautiful, socially appropriate partners?

In this chapter, we will consider research that sheds light on some of these puzzling questions about romantic relationships. What is the nature of love? Why are some people willing to change their whole lives, and even the course of history, in the service of love? What forces draw people into love affairs with partners often much younger or older than themselves? And why does love disappear, so that people who once cared deeply for one another later have difficulty even staying in the same house (or castle) together?

Our first task is to consider how romantic relationships differ from the other forms of attachment considered in chapter 7. We can then examine romantic relationships by exploring the goals they serve and the characteristics that influence whether and how people seek to attain those goals.

Defining Love and Romantic Attraction

What is love?

The question was once regarded as outside the realm of science, but researchers have found that love's complex array of feelings, thoughts, and behaviors is amenable to scientific research. Like many natural phenomena, though, it is not as simple as one might think at first blush. For one thing, love is multifaceted; there is no single

Table 8.1 Commonly listed features of love.

Feature	Percentage of Subjects Listing It	Feature	Percentage of Subjects Listing It
Caring	44	Contentment	10
Happiness	29	Euphoria	10
Want to be with other	28	Put other first	9
Friendship	23	Sexual passion	9
Feel free to talk about anything	20	Supportiveness	9
Warm feelings	17	Attachment	8
Accept other the way s/he is	16	Closeness	8
Trust	15	Concern for other's well-being	8
Commitment	14	Empathy	8
Sharing	14	Heart rate increases	8
Think about the other all the time	14	Helping	8
Sacrifice	14	Feel good about self	7
Understanding	13	Forgiveness	7
Honesty	12	Have a lot in common	7
Respect	12	Miss other when apart	7

SOURCE: *Based on Fehr, 1988.*

defining characteristic of love (Fehr & Russell, 1991; Fletcher, Simpson, & Thomas, 2000). For another, there's more than one variety of love (Shaver, Schwartz, Kirson, & O'Connor, 1987). We will deal with each of these issues in turn.

The Defining Features of Love

Beverly Fehr (1988) gave students at the University of British Columbia three minutes to list as many features of love as they could. Table 8.1 shows the thirty features mentioned most frequently. Notice that some of the features listed in Table 8.1—such as "Caring," "Accept other the way s/he is," "Understanding," and "Supportiveness"—reflect different aspects of the same emotional state. Can the different features of love be boiled down to a smaller set of feelings? Robert Sternberg (1986) proposed that love could be reduced to three essential components: passion, intimacy, and commitment.

- The **passion** component consists of physiological arousal and a longing to be united with the other.
- The **intimacy** component includes feelings that promote a close bond with the other. These include a desire to promote the lover's welfare, a feeling of happiness being with the other, mutual sharing, and emotional support.
- The **decision/commitment** component consists in the short term of a decision to love the other person and, in the long term, of a commitment to maintain that love.

How can we tell whether Sternberg's three-component theory is a valid one or whether there should really be six or seven or ten components to love? One answer comes from factor analysis, a statistical technique that sorts test items or behaviors into conceptually similar groupings.

Passion *The factor on love scales composed of items tapping romantic attraction and sexual desire.*

Intimacy *Factor on love scales composed of items tapping feelings of close bonding with another.*

Decision/commitment *Factor on love scales composed of items tapping decision that one is in love with and committed to another.*

FOCUS ON Method

Uncovering the Different Factors of Love

One of the goals of the scientific enterprise is to simplify complexity. Psychologists often discover that a dazzling array of characteristics masks a simpler underlying structure. For example, people use literally thousands of words to describe one another (from *altruistic* and *anal* through *petty* and *pusillanimous* to *zany* and *zealous*). **Factor analysis** is a statistical technique for examining the correlations between items in long lists and for using those correlations to sort the items into piles that "go together" (Fletcher, Simpson, Thomas, & Giles, 1999). If you describe a coworker as agreeable, you would probably also describe this person as warm, friendly, and nice. Hence, the words *warm*, *friendly*, and *nice* are found to correlate with one another in descriptions of others, and factor analysis sorts them into a common category (or factor). Likewise, if you describe a friend as conscientious, you are also likely to describe this person as neat, orderly, and hard-working. So, a factor analysis sorts these words into another conceptual pile (Donahue 1994; McCrae & John, 1992).

Are there common factors underlying the many attributes of love? When Arthur Aron and Lori Westbay (1996) subjected all 68 of Fehr's love features (the thirty listed in Table 8.1 and thirty-eight others) to factor analysis, they found that the features could be organized into three groups. One group includes items such as trust, caring, honesty, supportiveness, and forgiveness. A second group includes loyalty, devotion, and sacrifice. The third group includes butterflies in the stomach, heart rate increases, mutual gazing, sexual passion, and excitement.

Thus, Aron and Westbay's factor analysis supports Sternberg's theory that love has three core ingredients—intimacy, decision/commitment, and passion. (In fact, Sternberg also used factor analyses in developing and testing his theory.) Some researchers find that feelings tapped by the intimacy factor often overlap quite a bit with feelings tapped by the other two (Acker & Davis, 1992; Fletcher, Simpson, & Thomas, 2000). That is, feelings of deep intimacy with another person are often closely linked to feelings of passion and commitment.

Like all statistical techniques, factor analysis is a tool rather than a magical pathway to truth. It simply explores the correlations between whatever items the researcher examines. A researcher who neglected to include items tapping a passion factor, for instance, might find only two factors. Also, because a factor analysis summarizes correlations over a large group of people, it does not tell us about individual variations in approaches to love.

Despite these limitations, factor analysis is helpful to researchers in finding patterns underneath complexity. And factor studies of love do agree on several conclusions (Aron & Westbay, 1996). For most people, for example, there is more than one component to love, and for most people, intimacy is a central component. ■

Are There Different Varieties of Love?

Research on the components of love (such as passion, intimacy, and commitment) asks the question: How do different feelings inside one person combine within one love relationship? Research on the types of love addresses a different question: How do those different elements get combined in different kinds of relationships (e.g., Hendrick & Hendrick, 1986; Lee, 1977)?

To appreciate this distinction, think for a minute about different relationships for which you might use the word *love*. Not all of them involve equal parts of passion, intimacy, and commitment. If you are infatuated with an attractive person who has winked at you several times, you may feel passion without intimacy or commitment. On the other hand, consider your feelings about a close family member. You may be committed to maintaining a close relationship with your brother for the rest of your life but not experience increased heart rate or "magic" in his presence.

In one attempt to study the different types of love, Beverly Fehr and James Russell (1991) asked students the following question:

> If asked to list types of the category CHAIR, you might write: rocking chair, recliner, lawn chair, kitchen chair, stool, bean bag chair, and so on. The category we're interested in is LOVE. Please list as many types of LOVE as come to mind.

Factor analysis *A statistical technique for sorting test items or behaviors into conceptually similar groupings.*

The students mentioned many different types of love, including love of pets and love of life, but the most frequently mentioned types of love involved other people. The top-10 list included friendship, sexual love, parental love, brotherly love, sibling love, maternal love, passionate love, romantic love, familial love, and puppy love.

These types of love can be further divided into two broad groups, with parental love, maternal love, familial love, and brotherly love in one group and passionate love, romantic love, and puppy love in the other. Indeed, several researchers have argued for a central distinction between companionate and passionate love (Sprecher & Regon, 1998). Hatfield and Rapson (1996) define **passionate love** as "a state of intense longing for union with another" and **companionate love** as "the affection and tenderness we feel for those with whom our lives are deeply entwined" (p. 3).

The goal of forming a family bond. *Strong attachments between parents and children almost certainly contributed to the successful survival of our ancestors.*

The different types of love are intimately connected to the different types of close relationships in our lives. Fehr and Russell (1991) speculate that our different conceptions of love are organized around several central types of relationships. The two most central appear to be the love of a parent for a child and the love between romantic partners. Those different feelings may serve different goals in different types of relationships, as we discuss in the next section.

The Goals of Romantic Relationships

What purposes are served by falling in love and maintaining romantic relationships? Why are people so interested in passion, intimacy, and commitment?

One motivation that distinguishes romantic relationships from friendships is the desire for sexual gratification. The passion factor is composed of interconnected feelings of physical attraction, romance, and the desire for sexual union. In fact, research suggests passionate love to be almost synonymous with sexual attraction (Hatfield & Rapson, 1996). Hence, the first motive we consider in this chapter is the desire for sexual gratification.

From an evolutionary perspective, sexual gratification is necessary but not enough to ensure the survival of human offspring. The survival of a human child has probably always depended on parents who were bonded together and could count on one another for long-term fidelity and shared resources (Zeifman & Hazan, 1997; Geary, 2000). Human females do not simply deposit their eggs under a leaf and move on, as do many nonmammalian species. Instead, they spend years caring for their children. And unlike males in over 95 percent of mammalian species, who contribute little more than sperm, the human male generally stays around to help the female care for their young (Miller & Fishkin, 1997; Zeifman & Hazan, 1997). Hence, a second important goal of romantic relationships is to form a family bond.

To some extent, romantic relationships also bring all the benefits of intimacy with close friends. A lover, like a friend, can provide information and a ready source of social support. As one of our students said when asked why she would want to be in a romantic relationship: "You can depend on a lover more than on a friend" when you need a ride to the airport, emotional support, or someone with whom to do things. Indeed, when Ellen Berscheid and her colleagues asked students to name the one person to whom they felt closest in their lives, more people named a romantic partner than any other category (Berscheid, Snyder, & Omoto, 1989). Thus, much of the research discussed in chapter 7 regarding the rewards of friendship also applies to many romantic relationships. In this chapter, we'll consider some unique

Passionate love *A state of intense longing for union with another.*

Companionate love *Affection and tenderness felt for those whose lives are entwined with our own.*

ways in which romantic relationships can serve the goal of gaining resources and social status. Lovers share resources and status in very direct ways, and pass those benefits to their children in ways most friends never do. As we will see, there are interesting sex differences in the role played by resources and social status in love relationships (Gutierres et al., 1999).

Summary

Researchers have uncovered three factors underlying various feelings of love: passion, intimacy, and decision/commitment. These feelings combine differently in different types of love relationships, such as familial/companionate and passionate love. These different relationships share certain goals but differ in others. This chapter will consider three major goals of love and romantic relationships: to obtain sexual satisfaction, to form a family bond, and to gain resources and social status.

Obtaining Sexual Satisfaction

The drive to satisfy a passionate sexual attraction can wreak havoc in human affairs. Henry VIII was powerfully smitten with Anne Boleyn, but she refused to yield to his sexual advances until he abandoned his first wife. Centuries later, Prince Charles's reputed refusal to end an affair with an old lover contributed to his divorce from Princess Diana. And in the months after Diana's death, sex and history again commingled as President Clinton's opponents used an alleged sexual affair with a White House intern to call for his impeachment.

How fundamental is the desire for sexual satisfaction to human love relationships? Sexual desire is usually listed as the most important ingredient distinguishing passionate love from other forms of love (Jacobs, 1992; Sprecher & Regán, 1998). And that desire arises frequently in everyday life. Sexual fantasies enter the mind of the average college man or woman several times a day (Ellis & Symons, 1990; Leitenberg & Henning, 1995). And when more than 4000 people were asked, "Did you think about sex or were your thoughts sexually colored even for a moment during the last five minutes?" One in two men and four in ten women under the age of twenty-five said, "Yes." Thoughts cooled down for older people, but one in four men and one in seven women between the ages of twenty-six and fifty-five still said yes to the same question (Cameron & Biber, 1973).

The strength of human sexual motivation is revealed by the risks people will run to satisfy their sexual desires. If a Comanche man and woman were caught in an act of sexual infidelity, the man could be whipped and the woman's husband could cut off her nose and slash the bottom of her feet (Hatfield & Rapson, 1996). In many societies, sexual infidelity was considered grounds for justifiable homicide, and such homicides were legal in the state of Texas until 1974 (Daly & Wilson, 1983). Nonetheless, these harsh sanctions did not stop sexual infidelity. Despite the terrible consequences, everyday people, royal monarchs, and elected presidents continue to act on their sexual impulses.

Not everyone is equally dominated by these passions, however. When Alfred Kinsey and his colleagues conducted their surveys of sexual activity, they encountered one man who, despite apparently sound health, had ejaculated only once in thirty years. But they also found another who claimed to have ejaculated over thirty times a week for thirty years (Kinsey, Pomeroy, & Martin, 1948). Sexual behavior also varies with transitory aspects of a situation—such as the thrill of a dance or the gestures of the person sitting across the table in a nightclub—and with the norms of the wider culture. Why might people differ so immensely in their sexual behaviors? A number of factors may enter the equation, beginning, most obviously, with the physiological.

Hormones

Most other mammals are sexually active only when the female is ovulating, but human beings feel sexual desire at all phases of the female's menstrual cycle. Does this mean that human desire is disconnected from biological factors? No. Human sexual desire is still linked with mammalian physiology. Numerous studies find a connection between sexual desire and the production of testosterone in both men and women (Leitenberg & Henning, 1995; Regán, 1999). For instance, injecting testosterone into men who have malfunctioning testes leads them to increase their sexual fantasies, and stopping the injections leads to a drop in fantasy (Regán & Berscheid, 1999). Likewise, injections of testosterone increase sexual desire and fantasy in women (Sherwin, Gelfand, & Brender, 1985). Sexual fantasies in developing teenage boys are also linked to rises in testosterone levels (Udry, Billy, Morris, Groff, & Raj, 1985). Studies of girls between the ages of thirteen and sixteen found similar results; that is, levels of androgen (of which testosterone is the most prominent hormone) predicted how much the girls fantasized about sex (Udry et al., 1985).

Sociosexual Attitudes

Some people feel very positively about sex; others associate it with negative feelings. Feelings of guilt inhibit sexual behavior for some individuals. In particular, people who have what one team of researchers called **erotophobia** tend to have sex lives influenced by guilt and fear of social disapproval, to have intercourse infrequently with few partners, to be shocked by sexually explicit films, and to avoid information about sex (Byrne, 1983; Fisher, Byrne, White, & Kelley, 1988).

Individuals also vary in their attitudes about how sexual feelings should be expressed within a relationship. Jeffry Simpson and Steve Gangestad (1991; 1992) developed a scale that measures a dimension they call **sociosexual orientation,** which refers to the tendency to prefer either unrestricted sex (without the necessity of love) or restricted sex (only in the context of a long-term, loving relationship). The scale includes questions about sexual behavior, such as: "How often do (did) you fantasize about having sex with someone other than your current (most recent) dating partner?" The scale also measures agreement with statements such as "Sex without love is OK" and "I would have to be closely attached to someone (both emotionally and psychologically) before I could feel comfortable and fully enjoy having sex with him or her."

On the basis of responses to their scale, Simpson and Gangestad distinguish between people who are relatively restricted and those who are unrestricted in approaching sexual behavior. Compared to people who have a restricted orientation, individuals who have an unrestricted orientation had relatively more partners in the past, including one-night stands. They also intended to have relatively more partners in the future; began having sex earlier in the relationship; were more likely to carry on more than one relationship at a time; and felt less investment, commitment, love, and interdependence with their current partners (Simpson & Gangestad, 1991). Moreover, unrestricted and restricted individuals seek different types of partners. Unrestricted people choose partners who are socially visible and attractive. Restricted individuals prefer partners who show traits linked with good parenting, such as responsibility, affection, stability, and faithfulness (Gangestad & Simpson, 2000).

Do restricted people simply have a lower sex drive, or do they have more guilt over sex? Surprisingly, no. Sociosexual orientation is not tied to the frequency of sex within a relationship (Simpson & Gangestad, 1991). Once they are involved in a satisfying relationship, restricted individuals want sex just as much as unrestricted individuals do, and they are just as satisfied with sex. And restricted individuals are not particularly prone to feeling guilty about sex or to be shy around the opposite sex.

Wallis Simpson, the American woman who was responsible for Edward VIII's abdication of the British throne, displayed many features of an unrestricted individual. Friends from high school described her as "boy crazy" and "daring" in her interactions with the opposite sex. For her first husband, she chose a man who was

Erotophobia *Tendency to feel guilt and fear of social disapproval for thoughts and behaviors relating to sex.*

Sociosexual orientation *Individual differences in the tendency to prefer either unrestricted sex (without the necessity of love) or restricted sex (only in the context of a long-term, loving relationship).*

An individual who adopted an unrestricted approach to sociosexuality. *Wallis Simpson showed a number of features of an unrestricted approach. She was extraverted, flirtatious, and "wild" in high school; she then married a good-looking and charming "ne'er do well." She later divorced him and began a whirlwind life of international affairs. One of her lovers between marriages was Felipe Espil, South American ambassador and international playboy.*

handsome and charming, though quite irresponsible. After that marriage broke up, she had a mad affair with an international playboy before marrying her second husband, whom she left for the prince of England—himself a rather attractive and socially visible man who had had several notorious affairs by the time Wallis swept him off his feet.

Social Attractiveness and Sexual Desirability

Whatever their sexual motives and attitudes, two individuals may differ in sexual behavior because one has more opportunities for sexual relationships than the other, perhaps because of characteristics making him or her attractive as a sexual partner. One such feature might simply be social skill. Consistent with this possibility, high *self-monitoring* individuals, who are skillful at gauging social situations and crafting their performances to fit what others expect, have more sexual partners (Snyder, Simpson, & Gangestad, 1984). Physical attractiveness is also linked to sexual opportunities, as good-looking people are treated more warmly by the opposite sex, date more frequently, and are more sexually experienced (Feingold, 1992; Reis et al., 1982; Speed & Gangestad, 1997). In fact, when they were led to believe that a prospective date was good-looking, college students in two experiments conducted by Wade Rowatt, Michael Cunningham, and Perri Druen (1999) were willing to lie about themselves to increase their chances of having that person choose them.

What is considered attractive? To some extent, the answer changes across time and place. For example, trends toward thinness in women have varied during this century in our culture and across cultures (Anderson, Crawford, Nadeau, & Lindberg, 1992). However, research by Devendra Singh (1993) indicates that one feature of female attractiveness has remained constant—a low waist-to-hip ratio. Men prefer an average-weight woman with a low waist-to-hip ratio (large hips, small waist) to the other possibilities. In men, a higher waist-to-hip ratio (hips and waist similar) is considered relatively more attractive (Singh, 1995).

Other features that make a woman sexually attractive include large eyes and a small nose. On the other hand, a man having a medium-sized nose and a large jaw is more attractive to women (Cunningham, Druen, & Barbee, 1997).

Another feature that tends to be linked to physical attractiveness is bodily symmetry, the degree to which the left and right sides of the body are matched (e.g., Langlois & Roggman, 1990). Psychologist Steven Gangestad and biologist Randy Thornhill (1997) measured students' right feet, ankles, hands, wrists, elbows, and ears, and compared those with the same measurements taken on their left sides. Having a symmetrical appearance had different effects on the sexual behaviors of men and women. Symmetrical men began having sex earlier and had had more sexual partners than had asymmetrical men, whereas the effects were negligible for women.

Gender Differences in Sexuality

Why don't symmetrical females, like symmetrical males, have more active sex lives? Gangestad and Jeffry Simpson (2000) suggest that attractive women, unlike attractive men, are not motivated to "cash in" their good looks for access to many different sexual partners. Why? As we discuss next, men and women tend to have different goals for sexual behavior and different attitudes toward casual sex.

What is the lowest level of intelligence you would be willing to accept in a spouse? What about a single date? A sex partner? What if it were a one-night stand and you would never see the person again?

When students at Arizona State University were asked these questions, men and women often expressed similar standards (Kenrick, Sadalla, Groth, & Trost, 1990).

When asked about their standards for a single date, for instance, both men and women wanted a person of at least average intelligence. For a steady partner or marriage partner, both sexes wanted someone well above average in intelligence. But when they were asked about their criteria for a sexual partner, the sexes diverged, as shown in Figure 8.1. Whereas women wanted more intelligence in a sexual partner, men were willing to have sex with a woman who did not meet their minimum standards for a date.

When the researchers asked students specifically about a "one-night stand," in which no one would ever know and you would never see the person again, the differences between men and women were even greater (Kenrick, Groth, Trost, & Sadalla, 1993). These sex differences were replicated at other universities, and they fit with results of an extensive review based on 177 studies, which suggested that the difference in attitudes toward casual sex is among the largest gender differences ever found (Oliver & Hyde, 1993; Regán, 1998; Wiederman & Hurd, 1999).

Of course, attitudes are not always perfectly indicative of actual behaviors. Would the two sexes really differ if they were offered an opportunity for a one-night stand? Consider a field experiment conducted by Russell Clark and Elaine Hatfield (1989). In this experiment, college women walked up to a man on campus and said, "I have been noticing you around campus. I find you to be very attractive." Then they asked the man one of three questions: "Would you go out tonight?" "Will you come over to my apartment?" "Would you go to bed with me?" As part of the same experiment, men walked up to women and asked them the same questions.

The results of this research are depicted in Figure 8.2. About half of men and women said yes to a request for a date, but the numbers radically diverged for the other requests. In fact, not one of the women said yes to an invitation to go to bed. Males, on the other hand, said yes in more than 70 percent of the cases. Men were even more willing to have sex than to go on a date.

Is it simply fear of pregnancy that leads women to prefer less wildly active sex lives? Studies of homosexuals suggest that the answer is no. Although homosexual behavior presents women with absolutely no danger of becoming pregnant and no risk of dealing with potentially aggressive males, lesbians prefer to, and actually do, lead less active sex lives than do heterosexual women (Bailey, Gaulin, Agyei, & Gladue, 1994).

Opportunities for sexual encounters with strangers simply do not fulfill women's goals for satisfying sexual relationships. When Hatfield and her colleagues asked 189 undergraduate students and 53 couples to describe their desires in the sexual realm, women, compared with men, emphasized love and intimacy as prerequisites of good sex (Hatfield, et al., 1989). Consistently, other research indicates that, for the majority of women (but only a minority of men), emotional involvement is an absolute prerequisite for sex (Carroll, Volk, & Hyde, 1985). This difference is not limited to European American cultures: when Chinese women fantasize about sex, they imagine pulling men into intense, emotional, enduring relationships, whereas Chinese men fantasize about the physical seduction (Jankowiak, 1988).

For sexuality outside a committed relationship, then, sex differences are hard to miss. When it comes to long-term relationships, however, the two sexes look very much alike. Recall that although women were uninterested in having sex with a stranger, they were

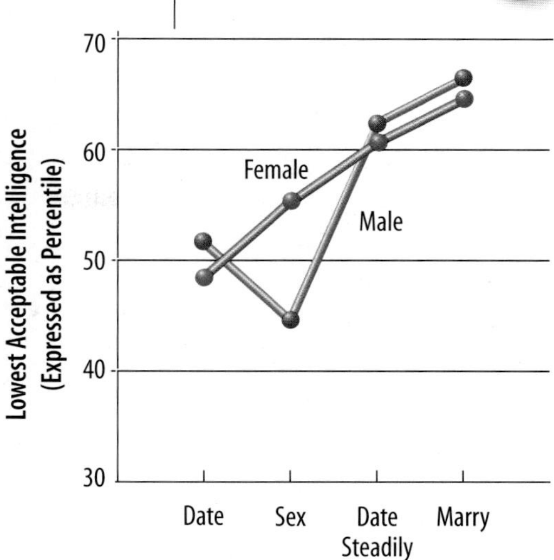

Figure 8.1
Minimum standards for partners.

When asked about the minimum intelligence acceptable for a dating or marriage partner, men and women have similar standards. The sexes differ, however, in that men report that they are willing to have sex with someone who does not meet their intelligence criteria for a single date, whereas women are more particular about sexual partners.

SOURCE: *Kenrick, Sadalla, Groth, & Trost, 1990.*

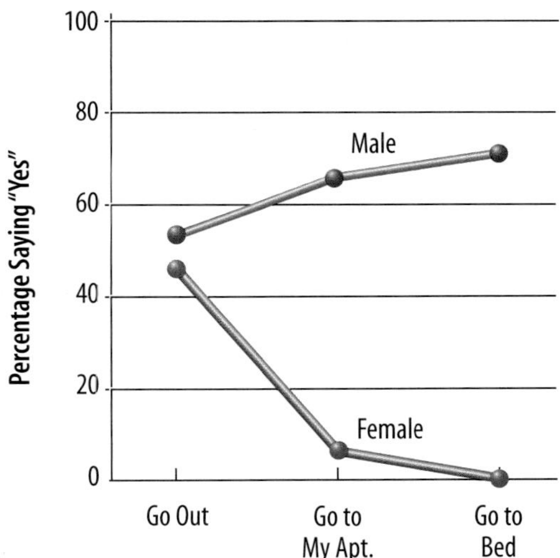

Figure 8.2
Men's and women's responses to a stranger's overtures.

Students at Florida State University were approached by students of the opposite sex and invited to go out, to go to the other student's apartment, or to go to bed. Men and women were both equally receptive to offers to go out but differed greatly in their responses to sexually toned overtures.

SOURCE: *Based on Clark & Hatfield, 1987.*

The Romeo and Juliet effect. *Shakespeare intuitively understood a phenomenon that was corroborated by social psychological research centuries later. Obstacles to a love affair can produce arousal, which can sometimes fan the flames of love.*

just as interested in going on a date as were males. And men and women were virtually identical in their selectiveness about intelligence in dates and long-term partners. Men and women in long-term relationships experience love and attachment in ways much more similar than different (Hazan & Shaver, 1994a). Hence, the large gender differences found in relationships with strangers change to very small, and often nonexistent, differences in longer relationships. Although these gender similarities are less attention-grabbing, they are just as important, and we will return to them when we discuss the motivation to form family bonds.

Arousing Settings

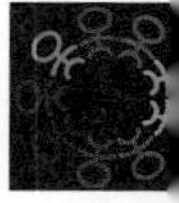

Think back to the last time you felt a sexual impulse or feeling. Where were you? What was going on? Who else was there, and what were they doing?

For some insights into the situational determinants of passionate arousal, consider the world's most celebrated tale of whirlwind passion. The setting is a dance in the noble house of Capulet in Verona, Italy. Young Romeo, son of Capulet's enemy, enters and spies a girl whose beauty inspires an immediate craving to touch her hand. She is likewise taken with him, and after the touch, they talk flirtatiously for a moment and then steal a kiss. Only moments after first sight, however, they learn that they belong to rival families. This unpleasant news does nothing to squelch their ardor. Indeed, it seems to inflame their desire to be together. Shakespeare's classic depiction of this encounter between lovers beautifully captures several of the crucial elements of similar events in the real world.

Throughout the world, dances, like the one at which Romeo and Juliet fell in love, are important settings for meeting potential mates (Rosenblatt, 1974). Paul Rosenblatt speculated that the "excitement of activity, rhythm, and anticipation of possible liaisons...may be mistaken for sexual or romantic excitement" (84). This possibility is consistent with the social psychological theory that people sometimes mistakenly attribute their generalized arousal to members of the opposite sex (Berscheid & Walster, 1974; Rosenblatt & Cozby, 1972).

The Two-Factor Theory of Love Romeo and Juliet had more than just the dance to fuel the fires of passion. Their families were embroiled in a bitter feud. Researchers have found a "Romeo and Juliet effect" among modern-day lovers, that is, parental interference can fuel romantic passion. As parents increasingly complain about a young couple's relationship, for example, the partners increase their feelings of love for one another (Driscoll, Davis, & Lipetz, 1972).

To explain findings that parental interference—as well as fear, social rejection, and sexual frustration—could enhance passionate attraction toward another person, Ellen Berscheid and Elaine Walster (1974) proposed a **two-factor theory of love.** According to this theory, love, like other emotions, consists of general physiological arousal (racing heart, butterflies in the stomach) and a label (love, fear, excitement, depending on the situation in which one experiences the arousal). To the extent that arousal from other sources could be misattributed to a potential lover, any arousing situation could enhance passion. For example, one set of studies showed that the fear of a painful electric shock or of standing on a narrow, shaky suspension bridge over a rocky canyon fueled men's attraction to an attractive woman in the same situation (Dutton & Aron, 1974).

Two-factor theory of love *The theory that love consists of general arousal (factor one), which is attributed to the presence of an attractive person (factor two—the cognitive label that the feeling is "love").*

Other studies suggest that any form of arousal can fuel passion. Simply exercising strenuously for a few minutes can enhance a man's attraction to a good-looking woman (White, Fishbein, & Rutstein, 1981; White & Kight, 1984). So can sexual arousal from another source (Carducci, Cozby, & Ward, 1978; Stephan, Berscheid, & Walster, 1971). In one amusing study, couples were brought into a laboratory and put through a rather unusual and arousing task together. The couples were velcro-strapped together at the wrist and ankle on one side. The interlaced pairs were then timed while they made several tries at crawling on their hands and knees across a gym mat and over a three-foot-high barrier. They had to do all this while carrying a cylindrical pillow between their heads, and racing to finish in under one minute. The participants found this game arousing and exciting; and, compared to other couples who shared a more mundane activity, the exhilarating game enhanced their feelings about the quality of their relationship (Aron et al., 2000). According to two-factor theory, the arousal from such activities can be mistaken for passionate attraction.

A flirtation gesture. *Not all flirting is done with words. When a woman flirts with a man, she demonstrates a number of telltale nonverbal gestures—including hair flipping, neck exposure, and direct eye contact.*

Arousal-Facilitation Theory The two-factor theory assumes that arousal from other sources such as parental interference is mistakenly attributed to a potential lover. However, there are some problems with this theory. For one thing, arousing situations can lead to increases in positive feelings for a person of the *same sex*, even in a cross-section of college students (Kenrick & Johnson, 1979; Riordan & Tedeschi, 1983). Because the vast majority of these students are heterosexual, their increased liking for a same-sexed person is hard to explain as misattributed passionate attraction. An additional problem with misattribution theory is that students may increase their attraction for an attractive member of the opposite sex even when it is made clear to them that their arousal is not due to that person (Allen, Kenrick, Linder, & McCall, 1989).

One explanation that can incorporate all these findings is called **arousal-facilitation theory** (Allen et al., 1989). According to this theory, arousal from any source is simply a burst of energy that adds fuel to whatever fire is burning at the time. Just as the caffeine in a cup of strong coffee may cause a runner to run a bit faster, or a speaker to talk a little more rapidly, so a burst of arousal can lead to more sexual attraction toward someone to whom you are already attracted. According to this theory, you do not have to make a cognitive mistake for arousal to have its intensifying effect. For whatever theoretical reason, however, it is clear that a burst of arousal, even from an irrelevant source, can fuel passion for a sexually attractive partner (Foster, Witcher, Campbell, & Green, 1998).

Nonverbal Cues

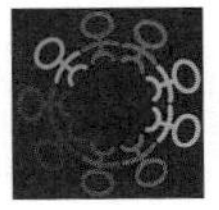

People frequently find themselves in arousing situations, from dances to horror movies, yet do not feel any sexual passion for an attractive person they observe there. Something else about the person is necessary to trigger sexual responsiveness.

Good looks are often a cue for sexual approach, as we discussed earlier. But beyond appearance, a person's behaviors may also serve as sexual cues. How someone acts toward us can be either like an aphrodisiac or like a bucket of cold water. Before they exchanged a single word, Romeo gently touched Juliet's hand. Although men, like Romeo, usually take the first overt step, nonverbal cues from the woman often start things rolling. Monica Moore (1985) observed women in singles' bars and found an extensive repertoire of gestures that appeared designed to attract men—such as a head toss followed by flipping the hair and exposing the neck or an eyebrow flash followed by a smile. Women who displayed more of these gestures were more likely to be approached by men.

Arousal-facilitation theory *The theory that general arousal will enhance any ongoing behavioral or cognitive process, including attraction for another.*

Another very simple gesture associated with attraction is staring. Opposite-sex strangers who simply stare at one another for two minutes in a laboratory (actually a long time to stare, if you try it) are likely to report feelings of passionate love for one another (Kellerman, Lewis, & Laird, 1989). Of course, staring is a double-edged gesture, since it is also part of hostility and threat displays in many primates, including humans (de Waal, 1996). In order for it to enhance attraction, it needs to be mutual.

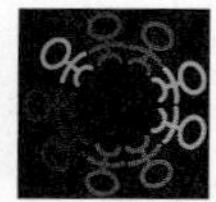

Cultural Norms About Sexuality

Wallis Simpson's romantic escapades may have reflected the norms of her time and place. The 1920s were a time of sexual experimentation, during which magazines discussed open marriages and nymphomaniacs were heroines of literature (Martin, 1973).

There are important cultural differences in the age at which people begin sex, the acceptability of premarital and extramarital sex, and the association between love and sexuality (Hatfield & Rapson, 1996). For instance, the Silwa of Egypt had very strong taboos against premarital sex, and young people did not violate those taboos (Ammar, 1954). In contrast, on the Pacific island of Mangaia, young children openly practice intercourse, and everyone has multiple sex partners before marriage (Marshall & Suggs, 1971). The norms among North Americans about expressing sexual motivations are somewhere in between. Americans, on average, begin kissing at around age fourteen or fifteen and have intercourse at seventeen or eighteen (DeLamater & MacCorquodale, 1979). Japanese, on the other hand, begin kissing at an average age of twenty and intercourse at age twenty-two or twenty-three (Hatano, 1991). Alongside these variations in norms regarding premarital sex are cultural differences in attitudes about extramarital sex. Compared with North Americans, for instance, Dutch men and women have more positive attitudes toward extramarital sex (Buunk, 1980).

In North American and European society, there have been dramatic changes in attitudes about sexuality during this century, and these variations have been accompanied by changes in sexual behavior. For instance, Kinsey's classic surveys of sexuality conducted around 1950 found that 71 percent of men and 33 percent of women had had premarital intercourse by age twenty-five (Kinsey et al., 1948, 1953). Two decades later, another large survey found that by age twenty-five, 97 percent of males and 67 percent of females had had premarital intercourse (Hunt, 1974).

Variations in Perceptions and Reactions

Sexual motivation is thus related to features of the person, such as sociosexual orientation and gender, and features of the situation, such as eye contact and irrelevant arousal. To understand sexual motivation fully, however, we must also consider how person and situation variables interact. In this section, we consider how different types of people may interpret the same situation in more or less sexual ways and how combinations of cues in the same situation can trigger different aspects of the same person's sexual persona.

An experiment conducted by Antonia Abbey (1982) illustrates how the same situation can be perceived as more sexual by some people than by others. Male and female students watched a man and woman carry on a five-minute conversation. Afterwards, the eavesdroppers and the conversationalists rated the interaction. Men and women perceived the same interactions somewhat differently. Compared to females, males viewed female actors as more promiscuous and seductive. Obviously, these perceptual differences can lead to unpleasant misunderstandings between the sexes (Abbey, Ross, McDuffie, & McAuslan, 1996; Sheets & Braver, 1999).

A later study found that, compared with women, men are more likely to interpret a woman's compliments, gifts, or touches as a signal for sexual intent. But if the woman in question is the man's sister, he agrees with the female interpretation of those behaviors as platonic. Compared with men, on the other hand, women in this study were more skeptical about interpreting a man's compliments, gifts, or touches as evidence of commitment. The authors interpreted these various interpretational biases as adaptive. Because a woman can become pregnant, it is not in her interest to be too naïve about a man's honorable intentions. On the other hand, because women are reticent about jumping into bed, it is in a man's interest not to miss any possible signs of sexual interest (Haselton & Buss, 2000).

When it comes to sexual attraction, the person and the situation interact on a much broader level. There is some evidence that human nature and culture can interact in ways that undermine sexual attraction between people who might otherwise fall for one another (Walter, 1997). How this works was illustrated in a natural experiment conducted with Israeli children raised on a kibbutz. Instead of being raised by their parents, they were raised in pods of several children from different families. When they grew up, Josef Shepher (1971) examined their social relationships and found a fascinating anomaly. The former podmates had stayed close friends, but did not marry one another. This is directly contradictory to classic findings that people tend to marry their neighbors (e.g., Bossard, 1932). What made it even more interesting is that there were no social norms prohibiting sexual attraction between podmates.

Friendliness or sexually toned flirtation? *Research suggests that men perceive more sexuality in situations that women perceive as friendly.*

What happened? Shepher suggested the cause was an interaction between an unusual feature in the cultural environment (unrelated children living together) and an internal mechanism designed to reduce sexual feelings between brothers and sisters. Over the course of evolutionary history, this would be a problem because harmful recessive genes show up much more frequently when brothers and sisters mate. One way to prevent sexual attraction between siblings is to develop a natural aversion to strong sexual relationships between people raised under the same roof who, in the past, were usually brothers and sisters (van den Berghe, 1983). This may help explain why men, who see sexuality in other women's behaviors, make an exception for their sisters, who they perceive as innocent (Haselton & Buss, 2000).

Thus the situation in the kibbutz seemed to trigger an innate mechanism normally invisible in other societies. This mechanism may help explain why Romeos and Juliets throughout history are likely to find someone from the family down the street more attractive than another family member. These findings also remind us that asking whether sexual behavior is a function *either* of evolved genetic mechanisms *or* of sociocultural norms *or* of learning experiences is the wrong question. Instead, the more productive questions ask how biological influences interact with culture to affect learning and how those processes affect our thoughts and motivations.

Summary

Sexual motivation is triggered partly by features of the person, ranging from momentary hormone levels to dispositions or gender; and partly by specific features of the situation, ranging from momentary arousal potential to the norms of the broader society. At an interactive level, men and women may perceive the sexual possibilities in the same situation differently. Finally, internal mechanisms that may have reduced incest in the past might be activated by the unusual cultural practice of raising unrelated children in the same family units.

Establishing Family Bonds

A woman from the !Kung hunting and gathering society in the Kalahari desert observed, "When two people come together their hearts are on fire and their passion is

Long-term relationships are good for your health. *Research suggests that having a spouse is associated with disease resistance and longevity.*

very great. After a while, the fire cools and that's how it stays" (quoted in Jankowiak & Fischer, 1992, p. 152). Kalahari hunter-gatherers are not the only people to experience the cooling of passion's fire. Research conducted in North American society also reveals that passionate sexual attraction is frequently intense at first but fades over time (Acker & Davis, 1992; Sprecher & Regán, 1998). Along with passionate feelings, sexual intercourse also declines over time (Hatfield & Rapson, 1996). After only a year, the average rate of intercourse between husbands and wives slows to half its original frequency.

If passion is bound to fade, why do people stay in long-term relationships? Sometimes married couples answer that they are staying together "for the sake of the kids." But most frame the answer in a more positive light—our long-term partners become inextricable threads in our daily lives, and a feeling of intimacy and commitment grows during the years that passion fades (Cimbalo, Faling, & Mousaw, 1976). As D. H. Lawrence put it, "Fidelity and love are two different things, like a flower and a gem. And love, like a flower, will fade, will change into something else or it would not be flowery."

The increasingly solid "gem-like" feelings come partly from sharing many of the relational benefits discussed in chapter 7, such as material resources and social support. But long-term love relationships are different from even the closest of friendships. If a best friend of the same sex moves to another town or goes on a trip for a few months or a year, we hope he or she will write, but usually accommodate quickly to the absence. Separation from a long-term lover, on the other hand, is often emotionally torturous. Losing a spouse to either divorce or death seems to wreak more psychological and physical havoc than almost any other life event (Diener, 2000). Divorce, for instance, is followed by increased alcohol abuse, violence, admissions into psychiatric facilities, and even suicide (Brehm, 1992). And after one spouse dies, the surviving partner's chance of dying skyrockets (Kaprio, Koskenvuo, & Rita, 1987). Conversely, having a marriage partner around seems to protect a person against major diseases, including cancer (Goodwin, Hunt, Key, & Samet, 1987).

So, there are many reasons why lovers stay together after early passion subsides—it feels good to stay in those relationships and bad to leave them. But saying that something feels good begs the question. *Why* are love relationships so much more intensely central to one's life, and painful to sever, than other relationships? Social psychologists, increasingly moving beyond research on encounters between strangers to focus on long-term relationships, are beginning to speculate that the answer may indeed be "for the sake of the family."

The Importance of Attachment

After reviewing a host of studies on relationships of all types, Roy Baumeister and Mark Leary (1995) posited that all humans have a general **need to belong.** They suggested that a desire for strong and stable relationships serves several functions. The same feeling that keeps a romantic couple bonded together to raise their children, they posit, also keeps them attached to the children. Indeed, there is evidence that the bonds between committed lovers may be based on the same psychological mechanisms that link a mother and her infant (Zeifman & Hazan, 1997).

One of the parallels is that separated lovers seem to go through the same **three-stage pattern of separation distress** shown by infants separated from their mothers (Hazan & Shaver, 1994a). Those stages are *protest* (crying, active searching, and reluctance to be soothed), *despair* (passivity and obvious sadness), and, finally, emotional *detachment* (including coolness toward the mother or former lover when reunited).

Where does the attachment bond come from? A strong bond between mother and child is characteristic of all mammalian species and probably served to promote the newborn's survival (Bowlby, 1969). The bond leads the young child to stay close to the mother and to cry out when the two are separated. The mother's presence reduces the child's stress and provides a **secure base** from which the child can safely explore the environment. Adult love relationships can also provide a secure base

Need to belong *The human need to form and maintain strong, stable interpersonal relationships.*

Three-stage pattern of separation distress *The reaction sequence shown by infants or adults separated from those to whom they are intimately attached: (1) protest (attempts to reestablish contact), (2) despair (inactivity and helplessness), (3) detachment (lack of concern and coolness toward the parent or lover).*

Secure base *Comfort provided by an attachment figure, which allows the person to venture forth more confidently to explore the environment.*

of confidence from which to explore the world and work productively (Green & Campbell, 2000). Another parallel is that infants and adult lovers, although capable of enjoying the company of several different people, tend to feel emotionally powerful attachments to only one primary person (Hazan & Shaver, 1994b).

Bringing the Male into the Bond The bond between a mammalian mother and her offspring serves an obvious purpose—it helps the offspring survive (Bowlby, 1969). For 95 percent of mammals, the adult male is out of the attachment loop, contributing little more than sperm to his offspring (Geary, 2000). But human males are different—they normally show a great deal of interest in, and care for, their offspring. A recent study found that husbands mirror the hormonal changes of their expectant wives (Storey et al., 2000). Just before birth, for example, they show increases in prolactin (a hormone linked to parenting in other animals). And just after birth, they decrease their secretion of testosterone (a hormone linked to dominant and sexual behaviors). In species with helpless young, family bonds motivate the parents to merge their interests with those of their needy offspring (Bowlby, 1969).

The Psychological Consequences of Being Attached People in close relationships often perceive a merging of their selves with those of their partners, so that their partners' well-being becomes their well-being (e.g., Aron, Avron, Tudor, & Nelson, 1991). Hence, it feels almost as good to give your partner a back rub as to get one. The relationship between parent and child clearly demonstrates how one person can merge another's interests with his or her own (Clark & Chrisman, 1994). Few parents expect to be repaid in kind for the years spent feeding and caring for their young children or for the money spent on automobiles and college educations. The only "payoff" desired by many parents is an unselfish one indeed—that their children be happy.

Attachment Style

Like the desire to drink when we are thirsty or to bundle up against the cold, the need to form deep attachments may be fundamental to the human condition (Baumeister & Leary, 1995). But not everyone finds it as simple to form a deep attachment as to reach for a glass of water or a warm jacket. Some people run from love, others drive potential lovers away by demanding too much affection too soon, and some seem to rush into casual affairs as a way to avoid long-term commitments (Brennan & Shaver, 1995). Even after negotiating all the difficulties of finding someone to love and making a mutual commitment, many people, like Prince Charles and Henry VIII, find themselves unable to maintain the bond.

Take a moment to think about your own affectionate relationships, and choose one of the following descriptions:

1. I find it relatively easy to get close to others and am comfortable depending on them and having them depend on me. I don't often worry about being abandoned or about someone getting close to me.
2. I am somewhat uncomfortable being close to others; I find it difficult to trust them completely, difficult to allow myself to depend on them. I am nervous when anyone gets too close, and, often, love partners want me to be more intimate than I feel comfortable being.
3. I find that others are reluctant to get as close as I would like. I often worry that my partner doesn't really love me or won't want to stay with me. I want to merge completely with another person, and this desire sometimes scares people away.

Cindy Hazan and Phillip Shaver (1987) used those self-descriptions as part of their research on romantic love and attachment styles. They based the three categories on developmental studies of mother–infant relationships (Ainsworth, Blehar, Waters, & Wall, 1978; Bowlby, 1969, 1973). Developmental researchers had found that some children had a **secure attachment style**—they easily expressed affection

Secure attachment style *Attachments marked by trust that the other person will continue to provide love and support.*

toward their mothers, and did not seem to worry about being abandoned. Their mothers acted consistently warm and responsive. Other children had an **anxious/ambivalent attachment style**—they became visibly upset at any separation from their mothers and seemed preoccupied with possible abandonment. Their mothers acted inconsistently—alternately ignoring the children and intruding into their activities. Finally, children who had an **avoidant attachment style** showed a defensive detachment, disregarding their mothers and refusing their affection if they returned after a brief absence. Mothers of avoidant children often rebuffed their infants' overtures for attention and comfort (Ainsworth et al., 1978).

Hazan and Shaver (1987, 1994a) speculated that these early mother–infant experiences might translate directly into different styles of loving in adults. Adults who chose category 1 above, for instance, were classified as "secure," those who chose category 2 were classified as "avoidant," and those who chose category 3 were classified as "anxious/ambivalent." People who scored themselves as secure also reported staying in love relationships longer than those who scored themselves as either anxious/ambivalent or avoidant. Avoidant lovers were not only fearful of intimacy but also more prone to jealousy. Anxious/ambivalent lovers, on the other hand, reported not only more emotional highs and lows in love but also more relationships that would be classified as "obsessive." In another study of 144 dating couples, Jeffry Simpson (1990) found that people having avoidant or anxious styles were more critical and suspicious of their relational partners.

Temperament

A recent study of the personality traits of 3,147 married twins found that problems maintaining long-term bonds may stem from genetically based differences in temperament (Jockin, McGue, & Lykken, 1996). First, twins in unstable marriages tended to be unconventional and extraverted. Because unconventional and extraverted people are likely to adopt an unrestricted sociosexual orientation, their relationships are less stable. Rock stars and actors, for example, have the social skills to flirt well and are inclined to ignore social rules against infidelity. Second, twins in unstable marriages were prone to negative moods. Although moody individuals may want to be in long-term relationships, their grouchiness leads their partners to feel more dissatisfied (Caughlin, Huston, & Houts, 2000; Shackelford & Buss, 2000).

An impressive longitudinal study found additional support for the importance of temperament to the maintenance of long-term relationships. Lowell Kelly and James Conley (1987) followed the life course of 300 couples who became engaged in the 1930s. Twenty-two broke their engagements, and fifty got divorced between 1935 and 1980. The researchers found that, among both men and women, emotional stability in the 1930s predicted a stable marriage over the next half century. Men who had difficulties controlling their impulses were also likely to get divorced. As in the study by Jockin et al. (1996), extraverted and unconventional individuals were more prone to breakups than were introverted and conventional people.

Self-esteem is also linked to emotional stability and is tied to relationship longevity in an interesting way. People who have low self-esteem tend to feel stronger romantic love. However, those who have high self-esteem have longer relationships (Dion & Dion, 1975). It appears that low self-esteem may fuel the ups and downs of passion but, in the long run, may lead to an anxious/ambivalent attachment style. People with low self-esteem, for example, underestimate how much their partners like and respect them (Murray, Holmes, & Griffin, 2000). In the long run, their insecurities could undermine the very supportive relationships they need to feel better about themselves.

Anxious/ambivalent attachment style *Attachments marked by fear of abandonment and the feeling that one's needs are not being met.*

Avoidant attachment style *Attachments marked by defensive detachment from the other.*

Exchange/Communal Orientation

As we discussed in chapter 7, Margaret Clark and Judson Mills and their colleagues found important differences between the *exchange* orientation in relationships between strangers (in which "costs" and "benefits" are accounted carefully) and the *communal* feeling characterizing close relationships (in which benefits are given freely according to the partner's needs) (Clark, Oullette, Powell, & Milberg, 1987; Mills & Clark, 1982).

In research conducted in the Netherlands, Bram Buunk and Nico VanYperen (1991) measured individual differences in *exchange orientation.* Individuals high in exchange orientation agreed with statements such as "I am apt to hold a grudge if I feel a friend or loved one has not fulfilled an obligation in our relationship" and "I feel resentment if I believe I have spent more on a friend's present than he/she has spent on mine." Such exchange-focused individuals are, as one might expect, likely to be especially dissatisfied when they perceive that their partners are getting a better bargain. Given the general tendency people have to make self-serving attributions—to view themselves in the best possible light—it is probably no surprise that people having high exchange orientations were generally more unhappy with their relationships.

As you can see, then, several personality traits are linked to the tendency to form and maintain stable long-term relationships. Some of these characteristics affect relationship stability because they affect the motivation to stay in a long-term relationship. Individuals who find intimacy uncomfortable, who are outgoing and unconventional enough to find easy replacement partners, and who are selfish about what they give and take from others may simply be unmotivated to work to maintain a committed relationship. However, some of these personal characteristics may reflect skill as well as motivation. Anxious/ambivalent individuals desire stable relationships as much as stable individuals, for example, but have failed to learn that being clingy and emotionally demanding works against them in the long run.

But the stability of our relationships isn't just a function of our personalities. Feelings of attachment wax and wane over time, for example. When Henry VIII married his first wife, Catherine of Aragon, he was deeply in love with her. Yet toward the end of their marriage, he could think of nothing but Anne Boleyn. Several years later, his attachment to Anne Boleyn had frayed sufficiently that he sent her to the gallows. Edward VIII cried like a baby when he was separated from his long-term lover, but he later ended that affair without a tear, instructing a servant to inform the woman that he would no longer be seeing her. Many of us have experienced the ebb and flow of our attachments to others. Are there certain factors in the situation that are reliably linked to increases or decreases in the motivation to stay in deeply bonded relationships?

Threats

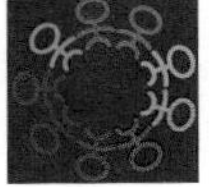

On a moment-to-moment level, situations that trigger fear, anxiety, or insecurity intensify people's need to be near their primary attachment objects (Hazan & Shaver, 1994a). Developmental research on attachment suggested that mothers provide children a safe haven from a stormy environment (Ainsworth et al., 1978). The secure-base phenomenon was also demonstrated in infant rhesus monkeys separated from their real mothers and given soft, terry cloth "mother substitutes" (Harlow, 1971). When the researchers frightened a young monkey with a large plastic insect, the panicked primate ran directly to his cloth mother and clutched at her desperately. After a few minutes of contact comfort, he was emboldened, and began a series of reconnaissance missions toward the strange object, darting back to the secure base of the cloth mother whenever he became frightened again.

Adult humans are not above the behavioral equivalent of shouting, "I want my mommy," as they turn to their partners for safe haven. And on the giving end, signs of emotional need in our partners can move us to cradle them in nurturance (Hazan & Shaver, 1994a).

The threat that may be most critical in sparking the need to be with our partners is a threat to our relationships themselves. Indeed, there may be a well of latent passion in long-term relationships, invisible to the partners until they perceive a

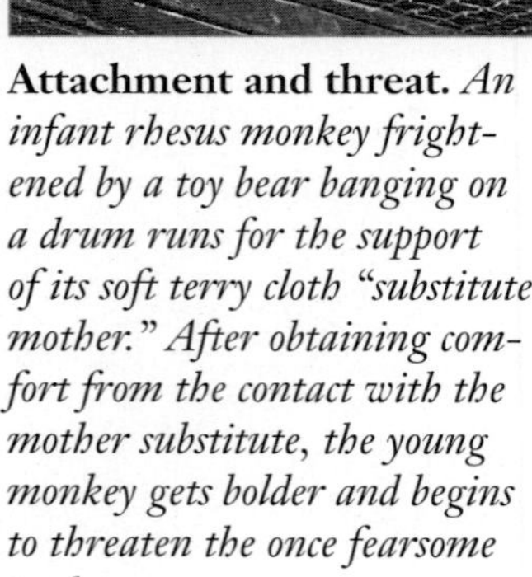

Attachment and threat. *An infant rhesus monkey frightened by a toy bear banging on a drum runs for the support of its soft terry cloth "substitute mother." After obtaining comfort from the contact with the mother substitute, the young monkey gets bolder and begins to threaten the once fearsome toy bear.*

danger of separation. Richard Solomon (1980) compared a long-term love relationship to drug addiction. Both experiences lose their ability to trigger the momentary "high" over time, but once either habit is formed, there are withdrawal symptoms if the supply is cut off. Those symptoms are painful enough to motivate people to do almost anything to obtain a "fix." Indeed, the grief of separation feels very much like drug withdrawal and is influenced by the same opiatelike chemicals in the body (Panskepp, Siviy, & Normansell, 1985).

The passionate drive to be reunited with a lost partner may be generally adaptive, helping us to maintain healthy relationships. But it may misfire in certain instances, as we see next.

FOCUS ON Social Dysfunction

Obsessive Relationships and Unrequited Love

- In Israel, a taxi driver had a brief casual relationship with a rabbi's daughter. She rejected his attempts to continue the relationship, but he clung to a belief that she really loved him and was simply testing the strength of his feelings. He was finally jailed after kidnapping her at gunpoint, but even that did not stop his obsessional harassment (Goldstein, 1987).
- In Manhattan, a medical writer was imprisoned because, after eight arrests, she refused to stop pursuing a renowned surgeon. During her trial, she described the relationship as passionate and romantic, while he described a nightmare in which she appeared suddenly in the seat next to him on international airline flights, unexpectedly showed up half-dressed at his apartment, and sent letters to his friends. She even threatened to kill him, saying, "I can't live while you are alive on this earth" (Anderson, 1993).

Some such cases end up even more painfully. Tatiana Tarasoff was murdered by fellow university student Prosenjit Poddar to avenge his hurt feelings because she did not reciprocate his passionate love for her. When such obsessions become extreme, they are labelled **erotomania**—a disorder characterized by the fixed, delusional belief that one is passionately loved by another. The goal of erotomanic fantasies is typically an "idealized romance or spiritual union" rather than sexual desire (Anderson, 1993).

Erotomania *A disorder involving the fixed (but incorrect) belief that one is loved by another, which persists in the face of strong evidence to the contrary.*

More common than clinical erotomania are cases of former spouses or lovers who, though nonviolent, make their ex-partners miserable with incessant attempts to restore the relationship. Indeed, "the large majority of stalking cases in the United States involve a terminated relationship or marriage" (Anderson, 1993).

Like infants separated from their mothers, people who find their love unrequited go through a sequence of protest, despair, and detachment (Baumeister, Wotman, & Stillwell, 1993). During the stage of protest (when the infant cries out in distress and actively refuses to accept rejection), "would-be lovers complained, cried, made further demands, requested explanations, persisted unreasonably, occasionally went berserk, and generally refused to accept the message of rejection" (Baumeister et al., 1993, 391). A stage of despair sometimes followed, in which would-be lovers reported feelings of sadness, depression, passivity, and damaged self-esteem. In the third phase of separation (defensive detachment), spurned lovers derogate the rejectors and proclaim that they would now refuse a relationship even if it were offered.

Most well-functioning people can recognize the agony of unrequited love. When social psychologists Roy Baumeister, Sara Wotman, and Arlene Stillwell (1993) asked students about experiences of romantic attraction to someone not attracted to them, 93 percent recalled at least one such experience that was either moderately strong or "powerful, intense, and serious." The experiences were generally regarded as negative on both sides. As targets of unrequited affection, students reported guilt, confusion, and annoyance. As would-be lovers, they reported damage to their self-esteem and often felt the rejector had led them on or had hidden stronger reciprocal feelings of attraction than they had admitted.

Why would people become enmeshed in such nonreciprocal romances? Partly because the experiences were not completely negative. Both the rejected and the rejector often retain warm feelings afterwards. Some of the unpleasantness follows because an initially mutual attraction grows for one while it dies for the other. Because the target isn't always completely clear in breaking the bad news, the other may be left with false hopes. Furthermore, movies and literature frequently depict lovers who persist in the face of rejection only to win their desired lovers in the end. Finally, those being rejected often distort reality slightly in order to protect their own self-esteem (Baumeister et al., 1993). It is hard to admit, even to ourselves, that another person finds us unacceptable as a love object. ■

Competition Within Each Sex

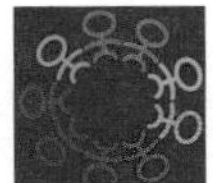

Several other situational factors work against the motivation to stay in long-term relationships. One of these—a partner's infidelity—is often listed as the primary precipitant of a divorce. Both men and women get jealous when interlopers threaten their relationships. However, there are some fascinating gender differences in sensitivity to infidelity. One such difference showed up when students who had been in committed sexual relationships were asked to make the following rather unpleasant choice:

> Imagine that you discover that the person with whom you've been seriously involved has become interested in someone else. What would distress or upset you more:
>
> 1. Imagining your partner falling in love and forming a deep emotional attachment to that person.
> 2. Imagining your partner having sexual intercourse with that other person.

Othello: the pain of jealousy. *In Shakespeare's tragedy, Othello is driven to homicidal rage when the treacherous Iago deceives Othello into believing that his wife is being unfaithful. Research suggests that men are more troubled by a wife's sexual infidelity, women more by a husband's emotional infidelity.*

The majority of the men reported they would be more distressed by the sexual infidelity. However, approximately 80 percent of the women said they would be more upset by the emotional attachment (Buss, Larsen, Westen, & Semelroth, 1992). Similar sex differences in the triggers of jealousy have since been found in Korea, Japan, Germany, Netherlands, and Sweden (Buss, Shackelford, Kirkpatrick et al., 1999; Buunk et al., 1996; Wiederman & Kendall, 1999).

Keeping an eye out for the competition makes sense because your partner may leave if there are a lot of available alternatives

(Greiling & Buss, 2000; Rusbult, Zembrodt, & Gunn, 1982). The effects of a pool of alternatives show up at the level of whole populations, in the relative ratio of available men and women. Marcia Gutentag and Paul Secord (1983) found that when there was a surplus of women of marriageable age, men were less likely to commit to marriages, and the societal norms shifted toward sexual permissiveness and delayed marriage. On the other hand, when there were more marriageable men than women, norms shifted toward domestic values, with earlier marriages and less sexual permissiveness. Gutentag and Secord viewed the phenomenon as an economic one: when there are surplus marriageable men, women are in a buyer's market and can demand more of the family values they traditionally tend to desire. When there is a surplus of marriageable women, on the other hand, men can demand more of the sexual permissiveness they traditionally prefer before marriage.

The Give and Take of Marital Relationships

It takes two personalities to tango. No matter how pleasant your personality may be, you can't guarantee a harmonious relationship with your partner. Marital interactions are a continual two-way street—each partner's jokes, barbs, purrs, and growls create the situation for the other, and ultimately for themselves as well. If we could understand how couples communicate in ways that escalate or de-escalate conflict, would it be possible to teach dysfunctional couples how to avoid letting a disagreement over what movie to see turn into the emotional equivalent of thermonuclear war?

FOCUS ON Application

Studying Healthy Communication to Save Marriages

Imagine that you're married and that your spouse returns from work in a bad mood. To cheer him or her up, you suggest dinner at your favorite restaurant, but you get a testy response: "I really DON'T feel like eating Chinese again for the fifth time this month, thank you!" Do you drop the conversation and slam the door on your way out to eat alone—to let your partner know you don't enjoy being snapped at. Or do you point out how short-tempered snappiness led his or her parents to divorce last year, or perhaps use the opportunity to bring up a few problems in the relationship that have been on your mind of late? Though none of these responses sounds good on paper, it's often difficult not to strike back at our partners' unpleasantness. Over time, though, such tit-for-tat, negative communications can destroy the fabric of a relationship. One team of psychologists working at the interface of social and clinical psychology has carefully studied the interaction styles of happy and unhappy couples and used their findings to help couples in trouble (Markman, Floyd, Stanley, & Storaasli, 1988; Notarius & Pellegrini, 1984).

The research team began by videotaping couples discussing problems in their relationships. To discover how well-functioning couples resolve their differences, the researchers also invited happy couples to discuss their problems and videotaped those performances. In addition, they tracked couples over the first ten years of marriage to discover what differentiated those who stayed together from those who eventually split. From twenty-five separate research investigations conducted over a twenty-year period, the researchers discovered some key differences between healthy and unhealthy communication patterns. They then used those discoveries to intervene in troubled marriages (Notarius & Markman, 1993).

Couples in the program began with a list of potential problem areas, including alcohol and drugs, careers, children, home chores, money, relatives, religion, and sex. They were asked to discuss any problems that pertained to their own relationships. One finding was that members of unhappy couples were likely to respond to conflict with "zingers"— negative statements about their partners that could erase twenty acts of kindness and that often bring on counter-attacks. An irony of intimate relationships is that people who are normally polite and diplomatic in dealing with strangers and acquaintances are often quite rude to their partners—the very people who expect tender loving care from them. Thus the researchers developed a "guide to politeness" for couples. The guide included the following rules, to be used particularly when you are thinking of throwing a zinger:

1. When your partner asks you to do something, say what you can do or want to do rather than what you can't or don't want to do. If your partner suggests a movie but you're feeling tired, you might say, "I'd love to go to the movies tomorrow," rather than, "I'm too tired."
2. When your partner does a chore, show appreciation rather than finding the aspect that doesn't meet with your approval. Say, "Thanks for washing the counter," rather than "You missed a spot." If you routinely don't like the way your partner does a task, discuss it at a time specially set aside for the purpose.
3. Always greet each other with a warm hello and leave with a tender goodbye. Don't come home, go to bed, or leave the house in silence.
4. Avoid being a "psychopest," analyzing your partner's behavior under the guise of being helpful when in fact you are merely being critical. Don't say things like "You're behaving just like your mother" or "Do you know you're being anal retentive about the den?"
5. Always speak for yourself, not your partner. Say, "I really want to go to the picnic," rather than, "I know you will have a good time at the company picnic."
6. When you have an opinion, say it rather than fishing around with questions to get your partner to guess what it is. Try "I'd really like to eat Mexican food tonight" instead of "Do you want to eat out tonight?"
7. If you don't have anything nice to say, try keeping quiet. (Based on Notarius & Markman, 1993, 77–78)

As another part of couples training, partners learn techniques for controlling their cognitions to de-escalate conflict. One technique is the "stop-action" tactic: Whenever you feel the impulse to sling a hostile barb, tell yourself, "Stop!!! If I say this negative thing, I will only make things worse."

Can such techniques work, or are the individual partners' personalities usually too overwhelming to change communication over the long haul? The answer is an optimistic one. In one longitudinal study, premarital couples in the effective communication program had a 50 percent lower rate of breakup and divorce than a comparison group of nonparticipant couples (Notarius & Markman, 1993). ■

Relationships Change Our Personalities We've been discussing how your behaviors can change your relationships. On the other side of the equation, long-term relationships are situations that can eventually change your personality (Cook, 2000). Lee Kirkpatrick and Cindy Hazan (1994) found that some people switched from anxious/ambivalent to avoidant attachment styles over a four-year period. The switch to a standoffish approach may have been a way to control the unpleasant arousal of obsessing over whether "she loves me" or "she loves me not."

Over the long haul, some partners change their personalities to fit with one another. From two long-term studies of people born during the 1920s, Avshalom Caspi and Ellen Herbener (1990) discovered that those married to dissimilar partners were more likely to have changed their personalities. On the other hand, individuals who married partners with similar personality traits were happier in their marriages. The researchers argued that the choice of a spouse is one of the more important ways in which we choose life situations to match our own dispositions. In the long run, those choices can also allow us to remain more like ourselves.

Commitment Changes the Perception of Alternative Relationships Social psychologists have uncovered another interesting way in which aspects of the situation interact with internal aspects of the person to affect the stability of a relationship. People in committed relationships seem to reduce threats to their bonds by changing their perceptions of attractive alternative partners (Johnson & Rusbult, 1989).

In one study of this phenomenon, Jeffry Simpson, Steven Gangestad, and Margaret Lerma (1990) asked students to judge advertisements from magazines such as *Cosmopolitan*, *Gentleman's Quarterly*, and *Time*. Included in the series were several photographs of attractive members of the opposite sex. College men and women who were involved in dating relationships, in contrast to those not involved, rated those attractive persons as significantly less physically and sexually attractive. In another study, participants saw a profile of a highly attractive member of the opposite sex, and learned that this person was currently available (Lydon et al., 1999). Half were also told that this person had expressed a romantic interest in them. How the participants responded depended on how committed they were to their current relationship. When the attractive person expressed a romantic interest, the less committed participants increased their interest, but the more committed actually became less attracted. These findings indicate that being in a loving relationship leads to a defensive change in perception—seeing potentially threatening alternatives as less desirable. And people who are inattentive to the alternatives are, as you might expect, more content with what they've got (Miller, 1997).

Summary

The motivation to form a family bond is affected by several personality characteristics, including attachment style, conventionality, moodiness, and exchange orientation. That motivation is also influenced by factors in the situation, including outside threats, and the pool of competitors. At an interactive level, each partner's behavior is also a response to, and a stimulus for, the behaviors of the other. Over the long haul, a good or a bad relationship can change our personal characteristics: some partners make it easy to adopt a secure attachment style; others make it easy to feel anxious and ambivalent. Finally, commitment to a relationship can influence one's perception of the available alternatives.

Gaining Resources and Social Status

Henry Kissinger was Richard Nixon's secretary of state. Kissinger looked more like a well-fed grocer than a chiseled movie star, yet he dated the most desirable women in the world. When a movie actress was asked by a puzzled talk show host what women could possibly see in Kissinger, her response was quick and certain: "Power!"

The appeal of power and status in a mate seems obvious. With power and status often comes access to material rewards (Turke & Betzig, 1985). The simple economics of this equation have been laid bare in numerous studies of other animal species (Daly & Wilson, 1983; Gould & Gould, 1989). In several species of birds, for example, dominant males flock to the breeding area first to compete for the richest territories. Females arrive later and choose among the males. Males with poor territories may attract no mates, whereas those with rich territories may attract multiple mates. Why do some females share the same mate when there are unattached males available? Because a resource-rich territory translates directly into surviving chicks (e.g., Pleszczynska & Hansell, 1980). In other species, when resources are so scarce that even dominant males cannot provide enough resources to feed the offspring, the rules of the game change, and one female may share several males (Gould & Gould, 1991).

How do these harsh economics of status, resources, and mating choice apply to human beings? The answer depends on the sex of the person, the social and economic conditions in his or her culture, and the level of involvement in his or her current relationship.

Gender and Sexual Orientation

Several factors in the person are linked to seeking status in a mate. We will focus on the interconnected links with gender and sexual orientation.

Women's Preference for Status Numerous studies reveal that women are, compared with men, more motivated to seek a mate high in social dominance or status (e.g., Townsend & Roberts, 1993; Wiederman, 1993). For instance, students in one study rated the attractiveness of potential partners dressed in either high- or low-status garb. In one case, this individual was dressed as a Burger King employee, wearing a blue baseball cap and a polo shirt displaying the company logo. In another case, he or she wore an upper-class ensemble including a blue blazer and a gold Rolex wristwatch. Sometimes the person was physically unattractive, and sometimes he or she was good-looking. Men preferred the good-looking woman regardless of her apparent social class, but women preferred a homely, well-dressed man to a handsome burger flipper (Townsend & Levy, 1990). Likewise, women are more sexually attracted to men who show nonverbal signs of self-assurance and confidence than to men who act meek and humble, whereas men don't care either way, about a woman's dominance (e.g., Sadalla, Kenrick, & Vershure, 1987).

In singles' advertisements, men are more likely to advertise any status or wealth they have, whereas women are more likely to request it in a man (Rajecki, Bledsoe, & Rasmussen, 1991; Wiederman, 1993). And women actually respond more to men who advertise their income and educational levels, whereas men reading women's ads pay no attention to it (Baize & Schroeder, 1995). A study of 37 different cultures found the same trends around the world (Buss, 1989). Like American women, Japanese, Zambian, and Yugoslavian women rate good financial prospects in a mate as more important than do men in those countries (Buss & Schmitt, 1993).

Who makes a more desirable date? *Women presented with a man dressed in a suit and tie find him more desirable than the same man dressed as a fast-food clerk. Even if the man in the suit is unattractive, he is regarded as more desirable. Men pay less attention to the status of a woman's clothes and prefer a physically attractive woman in a fast-food outfit to a physically unattractive woman dressed in fancy clothes.*

Older men and younger women. *Why would two people separated by decades of age get together in a romantic relationship? The fact that women around the world are attracted to older men with status, and that very young men are attracted to relatively older women, is consistent with the different resources each sex contributes to the offspring.*

Men's Preference for Reproductive Resources Age and social status are linked differently for men and women. Women around the world tend to seek and to marry somewhat older men, who generally have more resources and social status (Buss, 1989; Kenrick & Keefe, 1992). Men, on the other hand, show a more complex pattern—older men are attracted to younger women, men in their 20s are attracted to women around their own age, and teenage men are attracted to slightly older women (Kenrick, Gabrielidis, Keefe, & Cornelius, 1996; Otta et al., 1999). Given the obvious benefits of having a resourceful partner, why do men pay so much less attention to the potential resources an older woman could provide and opt instead for women in their twenties? One part of the answer may come from a biological inequity between the resources males and females provide for their offspring.

Throughout the history of our species, females have always provided direct physical resources to the offspring—carrying them inside their bodies, nursing them, and taking primary care of them for years afterwards. Hence, it would have been advantageous for ancestral men to emphasize health and reproductive potential as the resource they sought in a mate (Cunningham et al., 1997). One of the cues to health and reproductive potential would be a woman's age and physical attractiveness (Pawlowski & Dunbar, 1999). Because men do not contribute their bodies to the offspring, biological theorists posit that ancestral females sought high-status men who could provide either direct care and resources or good genetic material (Gangestad & Thornhill, 1997). Men's and women's ages were thus linked in a different way to the resources they provided for the offspring.

We noted that men advertise, and women request, financial resources in singles' advertisements. On the other side of the bargain, men evaluating potential dates place more emphasis on physical appearance (Shaw & Steers, 1996). One illustration of the differential exchange is the finding that being seen with a physically attractive member of the opposite sex improves the social impression made by a man but has no effect on the impression made by a woman (Bar-Tal & Saxe, 1976; Sigall & Landy, 1973).

Indeed, to say that a man is physically attractive is to say he shows signs of social dominance, such as a strong chin and mature features, whereas a physically attractive woman shows signs not of dominance but of youthfulness and fertility (Cunningham et al., 1997; Singh, 1993; Wade, 2000).

One possible alternative explanation of these sex differences focuses on the media. Perhaps women of all ages tend to prefer older, high-status men and men of all ages tend to prefer good-looking women in their twenties and thirties because of the sex-biased images presented in the media (Kenrick, Trost, & Sheets, 1996). The media explanation, however, cannot explain why the age difference is found in cultures remote from modern television and movie images, including a small island in the Philippines during the 1920s and Amsterdam during the 1600s (Kenrick & Keefe, 1992; Kenrick, Nieuweboer, & Buunk, 1995).

Are Homosexuals Different? Because homosexuals are attracted to members of their own sex, they provide an ideal "control group" for examining some theories of mate choice (Bailey et al., 1994). Consider the theory that women's attraction to wealthy, attractive men is caused by exposure to media. Homosexual men in the United States also grow up watching powerful older men on television and in the movies. If the media determines what people find attractive in their sex partners, homosexual men ought to be attracted to these high-status, older men. The research shows, however, that homosexual men are relatively uninterested in a partner's wealth and social status. They are more interested in physical attractiveness (Bailey et al., 1994). And instead of seeking older men, homosexual males have age preferences just like those of heterosexual men (Kenrick, Keefe, Bryan, Barr, & Brown, 1995). Older homosexuals show a strong attraction toward men in their twenties, despite the fact that the younger men do not reciprocate the interest. Like the older men, young homosexual men are interested in young men. Very young homosexual men, like very young heterosexual men, have some interest in slightly (but not much) older men.

The homosexual data, although puzzling at first, may actually be quite scientifically informative. The findings fit with the theory that human mating behavior, like human vision or hearing or problem solving, is not simply a "one-switch" mechanism (cf. Tooby & Cosmides, 1992). Although the switch for sexual preference is reset, for whatever reason, homosexual men's whole pattern of preferences suggests that most other switches are set at the same settings as in heterosexual men. Homosexual women, on the other hand, show a complex combination of the preferences expressed by heterosexual men (some preference for youthful partners, for example) and heterosexual women (less emphasis on physical attractiveness and more inclination toward sexual fidelity, for example). These complexities suggest that homosexual choice is not simply an inverted form of heterosexuality but instead a complex pattern in which some aspects of mating behavior, but not others, are altered.

What Happens When Women Gain Status and Resources? Throughout most of history, women have had less access to status and resources than have men. Although sex differences remain, some groups of modern women are wealthier and higher in status than most men. If one examines the singles' advertisements in the *Washingtonian* magazine, for example, one finds advertisements by independent, professional women who are doctors, lawyers, business executives, and college professors and who often mention that they are wealthy and propertied (Kenrick & Keefe, 1992). When women achieve their own wealth and social status, do they shift to an emphasis on "traditionally male" considerations in a mate, such as youth or physical appearance?

This possibility has been examined by looking at the mate preferences of women who have high professional status, such as careers in medicine or law. Somewhat surprisingly, wealthy and high-status women place just as much emphasis on traditional preferences as do poorer, lower-status women, continuing to be relatively more interested in older, higher-status men as partners (Kenrick & Keefe, 1992; Townsend & Roberts, 1993; Wiederman & Allgeier, 1992).

Culture, Resources, and Polygamy

High in the Himalayan mountains along the border of Tibet and Kashmir, where cold winters and lack of rain make for rough survival conditions, a single woman may marry not one man but several. These men pool their resources to help raise the children as one family under the same roof. Just a couple of hundred miles south of Tibet, in the state of Patiala in northern India, the great maharajah Bhupinder Singh married 350 women.

Are these variations in marriage patterns completely random? Cross-cultural research suggests that the simple answer is no. Marital arrangements are linked to the distribution of status and resources within a society, which are in turn linked to the larger physical environment in which that society exists. A closer examination of the economics of marriage arrangements also teaches a broader lesson: When we go beyond gawking at how "they" are strangely different from "us," cross-cultural research can help us see the common threads that tie all of us together as a species.

Looking across cultures, the first thing we notice is that marriage patterns are not randomly arrayed at all. **Monogamy** is the practice of one man marrying one woman; **polygamy** includes both **polyandry** (one woman marrying more than one man) and **polygyny** (one man marrying more than one woman). Only about half of 1 percent of human societies allow polyandrous unions between a woman and

Monogamy *Marital custom in which one man marries one woman.*

Polygamy *Marital custom in which either one man marries more than one woman (polygyny) or one woman marries more than one man (polyandry).*

Polyandry *Marital arrangement involving one woman and more than one husband.*

Polygyny *Marital arrangement involving one man and more than one wife.*

multiple men, whereas the vast majority allow a man to marry multiple wives. Nevertheless, most of the individual marriages in all societies are monogamous. But why then, if our species is generally inclined toward monogamy, are any societies and any marriages within those societies nonmonogamous?

Let's take another look at the polyandrous Tibetans. A woman does not simply choose any random group of men to marry. In fact, in all cases, the group is made up of brothers. Why does this happen? The answer is linked to resources in the environment. The harsh conditions of life in the high Himalayan desert have made it difficult for a single man and a woman to survive alone. Even in the modern era, Tibetan families in which one man marries one woman have fewer surviving children than do families in which brothers pool their resources (Crook & Crook, 1988). By sharing one wife, brothers can preserve the family estate, which would not even support one family if it were subdivided each generation. If all the children are girls, the polyandrous pattern will switch to a polygynous one, and several sisters may marry one man, passing the family estate on to the sons of that marriage. Hence, Tibetan polyandry appears to be an economically based strategy—a limited pool of resources must be channeled into a very focused family line.

Societies in which one man marries several women demonstrate another economic reality: the monogamy rule is broken only for men having high social status or economic wealth. Laura Betzig (1992) studied marital arrangements across different societies and historical epochs, and notes:

> In Mesopotamia and Egypt, India and China, Aztec Mexico and Inca Peru, and in many empires that came later, powerful men kept hundreds, or thousands, or even tens of thousands of women—along with one, or two, or three at most, legitimate *wives;* lesser men kept progressively fewer women. (310)

Again, economic resources provide the link between social status and polygynous marriage. Men are especially likely to take multiple wives when several conditions converge: (1) a steep social hierarchy, (2) a generally rich environment so one family can accumulate vast wealth, (3) occasional famines so the poor face occasional danger of starvation (Crook & Crook, 1988). Under these circumstances, a woman who joins a large wealthy family reaps benefits, even if she would have to share her husband with other women. Although a poor man might shower her with attention, a wealthy family provides a better buffer against famine and the chance of great wealth for her children in times of plenty.

A polygynous family. *One man is likely to marry multiple women only when he is able to accumulate a relatively high level of wealth and status.*

A polyandrous family. *One woman marries more than one man only rarely, and generally when resources are scarce.*

Cross-cultural studies thus suggest that the links between marriage, wealth, and status have been forged by survival needs. How strong those links are in any particular society depends on the social and economic milieu.

Increasing Levels of Involvement

People want different resources in long-term versus short-term partners. In considering the abstract qualities they would like for a partner, students of both sexes expect more earning capacity and social status in a long-term mate than in a casual partner (Kenrick et al., 1990). Women considering a man for a short-term relationship value someone who is willing to spend money freely and extravagantly and to give them gifts early in the relationship. For long-term partners, women emphasize ambition and a promising future career (Buss & Schmitt, 1993). Both men and women considering a partner for a long-term relationship seek a partner whose status and value to the opposite sex is similar to their own. But there is one exception to this similar-value rule. Men considering a partner for a short-term sexual relationship tend to be unconcerned with their own status and value relative to the woman's. In short-term contexts, then, men, but not women, seem to turn off their "comparison shopping" mechanisms (Kenrick et al., 1993; Regán, 1998).

Status, resources, and social "market value" may have an important influence on who will be chosen as a partner in the first place. But once the couple has passed into an intimate relationship, the accounting process may change. Studies in which partners are asked to count the benefits and costs they give and receive in their romantic relationships do not find such accounting to be a terribly important predictor of happiness (Clark & Reis, 1988; Clark & Chrisman, 1994). Once we have fallen in love, we may become as interested in our partner's benefits as in our own (Aron, Aron & Smollan, 1992; VanLange & Rusbult, 1995).

Economic issues and perceived inequities can resurface, however, when couples are considering a separation (e.g., Notarius & Markman, 1993). This suggests that people (or at least some people) never completely lose track of the economic considerations but push them to the back of their minds in successful relationships. After considering research on these issues, Margaret Clark and Kathleen Chrisman (1994) suggested that once in a communal relationship, only gross violations of "fair exchange" will get long-term partners counting costs and rewards. Consistent with this reasoning, Mikula and Schwinger (1978) found that the "accounting" process depended on the degree of good feeling between partners. Relationships in which people feel neutral about one another follow an **equity rule**—you get out benefits based on what you put in. Relationships in which people feel fairly positively about one another follow a slightly different rule—everybody shares equally. Finally, those characterized by very positive feelings, as found in smoothly functioning marriages, follow a **need-based rule**—you give what your partner needs, without counting. Thus, increasing feelings of love lead to a decrease in the nickel-and-dime accounting of who gave what to whom.

Flipping things around, paying undue attention to the accounting process can undermine intimate feelings. One experimental study found that simply asking romantic partners to focus on the external benefits they get from their partners led to a decrease in feelings of love (Seligman, Fazio, & Zanna, 1980). Hence, it seems wisest not to pay too much attention to the external resources you are getting from your partner once you have committed yourself.

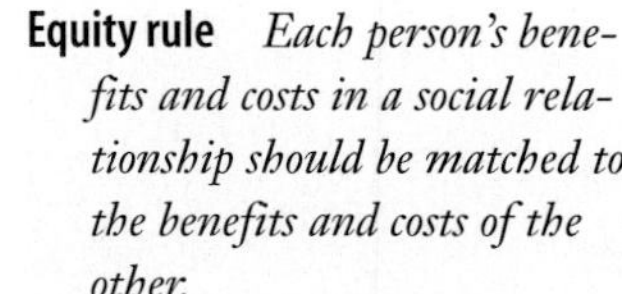

Equity rule *Each person's benefits and costs in a social relationship should be matched to the benefits and costs of the other.*

Need-based rule *Each person in a social relationship provides benefits as the other needs them, without keeping account of individual costs and benefits.*

When Dominance Matters

Like most influences on social behavior, the importance of social dominance involves an interaction between the person and his or her situation. We discuss two interesting types of interactions here. First, dominance may be desirable or

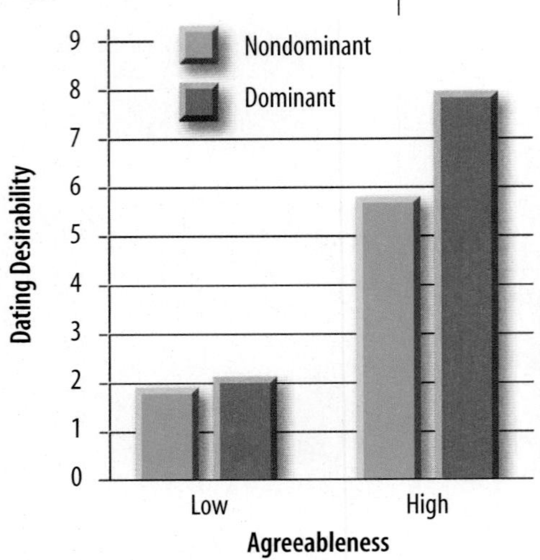

Figure 8.3
Nice guys don't finish last, after all.

Female students judging men who are not agreeable pay little attention to whether the man is dominant or not. Dominance only matters when the man is agreeable.

SOURCE: *Based on Jensen-Campbell, Graziano, & West, 1995.*

undesirable in a mate, depending on other features of that person's personality. Second, our feelings about where we rank in the social dominance hierarchy depend on an interaction of our sex, and the characteristics of other competitors.

Dominance by Itself Isn't Enough We have discussed several findings suggesting that women seek socially dominant and competitive men. These characteristics are part of the traditional male role, which emphasizes attaining social rank over others, in contrast to the traditional female role, which emphasizes communal links with others (Sidanius, Cling, & Pratto, 1991). But what happens over the course of a relationship between a traditionally competitive male and a traditionally communal female?

After observing ongoing social interactions between traditional and nontraditional men and women, William Ickes (1993) suggested a paradoxical problem for traditional partners. Although women are initially attracted to socially dominant and competitive men, such traditional men are not particularly pleasant to live with. Women in long-term relationships with traditionally masculine men are less satisfied than women in relationships with more "feminine" or **androgynous** men (who combine traditionally masculine and feminine characteristics) (Antill, 1983). As Ickes (1993) notes, although dominant men may be attractive to women, they are less likely to be loving, kind, and considerate in long-term relationships.

Additional research suggests that, rather than being drawn to men who demonstrate pure "machismo," women most prefer partners high in *both* masculine assertiveness and feminine nurturance (Green & Kenrick, 1994). Indeed, though women are relatively more attracted to traditionally masculine characteristics, both sexes will take a pass on competitive characteristics if it means getting a partner who lacks nurturance or expressiveness.

A series of studies by Laurie Jensen-Campbell, William Graziano, and Stephen West (1995) further elucidates the interactive combination of masculine dominance and nurturant qualities. Students read a description of an opposite-sexed person and tried to form a mental image of that person. They read about someone who manifested one of four combinations of dominance and agreeableness. For example, some students read about someone who was both dominant ("assertive," "bold," "talkative") and agreeable ("considerate," "cooperative," "sympathetic"). Others read about someone who was dominant but disagreeable ("rude," "selfish," "uncooperative"), and so on. Students then rated the targets on several characteristics, including desirability as a date.

For male subjects, it made no difference whether the woman was dominant, but they strongly preferred agreeable women to disagreeable women. Female subjects preferred men who were dominant, but only if they were also agreeable (see Figure 8.3). If a man was not agreeable, he was not considered desirable as a date, regardless of how dominant he was.

Thus, socially dominant characteristics may be initially attractive in a partner (particularly a man), but they are not, by themselves, predictive of a satisfying long-term relationship in either sex. Perhaps sensitive to this problem, people of both sexes are inclined to place little value on dominant characteristics if they are not accompanied by nurturant characteristics (Cunningham, Barbee, Graves, Lundy, & Lister, 1996).

Androgynous *Demonstrating a combination of masculine and feminine characteristics in one's behaviors.*

Who's on Top? Whether I will be able to attract the mate I desire depends on the competition. A TV show called *The Dating Game* made the rivalry explicit, asking contestants to compete with one another for a date with a member of the other sex. One team of social psychologists brought this game into the laboratory. Contestants were videotaped and their tactics were correlated with their physical and psychological traits. The researchers found that symmetrical men with an unrestricted sociosexual orientation were more likely to use direct competitive tactics than were less symmetrical and restricted men. These sexy men tried to dominate their opponent with statements like: "You'd have a lot more interesting time with me than with that other guy." Restricted men took a softer approach, focusing on their own positive qualities, and presenting themselves as "nice guys" (Simpson, Gangestad, Christensen, & Leck, 1999).

Dominance and attraction. *Women are only attracted to dominant men if the men are also kind and understanding.*

Women were less likely to try to dominate their opponents (Simpson, et al., 1999). But this doesn't mean women are immune to feelings of status competition in the mating arena. It simply shows up in different ways. Consider the findings of a recent study conducted by Sara Gutierres and her colleagues. Participants were shown profiles of eight members of their own sex who had presumably signed up for a campus dating service. In some cases, the other students were all highly socially dominant. One was former editor of a university newspaper who had published articles in *Runner's World* on what it takes to achieve excellence, and another was a youthful proprietor of a successful business. In other cases, the profiled students were low in social dominance (one listed a letter to the editor of the campus newspaper as his or her major accomplishment, for example). Attached to each profile was a photograph. Half the students saw very attractive members of their sex (actually models from a local agency). The other half saw average-looking people. When later asked to rate their own desirability as a marriage partner, the men downgraded themselves after seeing a pool of potential competitors full of socially dominant high-roller types. The women, on the other hand, were affected by the other women's physical attractiveness, downgrading their own mate value when the other women were all good looking (Gutierres, Kenrick, & Partch, 1999).

Along the same lines, researchers in the Netherlands found that men were more jealous if they imagined their partner flirting with a socially dominant man; whereas women were more jealous if the interloper was a beautiful woman (Dijkstra & Buunk, 1998). Other findings suggest these sex differences in concern about the competition may be justified. Women's commitment to their current relationships was weakened after seeing a group of socially dominant men, whereas men's commitment was undermined by seeing physically attractive women (Kenrick, Neuberg, Zierk, & Krones, 1994).

In a related study, students filled out a scale measuring bodily self-esteem (from Franzoi & Shields, 1984). Men's bodily self-esteem was linked to features of strength and dominance (like broad shoulders and muscularity). Women's was linked to features associated with fertility (such as waist-to-hip ratio and breast size) (Wade, 2000). As we noted earlier, men place relatively more emphasis on a woman's physical appearance (Shaw & Steers, 1996). Though men are optimistic about improving their financial or social status, women feel more helpless to change the physical features that men look for in mates (Ben-Hamida, Mineka, & Bailey, 1998). This may contribute to women's feeling more embarrassed and objectified in circumstances that draw attention to their bodies, like being seen in a bathing suit (Frederickson, Roberts, Noll, Quinn, & Twenge, 1998).

Summary

The motivation to seek social status in a relational partner is markedly higher in women than in men. Women seek older, higher-status, wealthier partners, whereas men seek the resources of youth and fertility in a partner. Rather than reversing the preferences of heterosexuals, homosexuals show a complex pattern consistent with the notion that different aspects of mating behavior are controlled by different cognitive and affective mechanisms. People of both sexes expect more social status and wealth in long-term partners, but once committed to a relationship, other issues come into play. Masculine dominance is attractive, but more in the short term and not at the cost of agreeableness and nurturance. The person and situation factors associated with the different motives involved in love relationships are summarized in Table 8.2.

CHAPTER 8
Summary Table

Table 8.2 Summary of the goals served by romantic relationships and factors related to each goal.

The Goal	The Person	The Situation	Interactions
Obtaining Sexual Satisfaction	• Testosterone • Restrictedness of sociosexual orientation • Opportunities provided by social attractiveness • Gender	• Arousing settings • Nonverbal cues in potential partners • Societal permissiveness toward sexual expression	• Men may perceive sexuality in a situation women see as friendly. • Raising children under the same roof may trigger a mechanism designed to prevent incest.
Establishing Family Bonds	• Attachment style (secure, anxious/ambivalent, avoidant) • Temperament • Exchange orientation	• Threats • Partner infidelity • Sex ratio in population	• One partner's communications shape the situation for the other. • Over time, marital situation can affect partners' traits. • Commitment to a long-term relationship changes perceptions of the available alternatives.
Gaining Resources and Social Status	• Gender • Homosexuals' choices often match those of their biological sex	• Resources affect cultural rules about marriage • Anticipated length of relationship • Once involved, economics become less important	• Social dominance is attractive to women only if it is combined with kindness. • Women's feelings about their position in the social hierarchy are linked to their appearance and that of their competitors; men's are based more on status and economic resources.

REVISITING
The Love Lives of the British Monarchs

We opened this chapter with some questions raised by the love lives of British royalty. Having read the chapter, can you venture a guess as to which of Henry VIII's six wives was older than he was? The answer follows directly from the cross-cultural findings that men, as they age, tend to prefer first older and then progressively younger women. It was his first wife—Catherine of Aragon. All his other marriages took place after he reached his late thirties, when men tend to marry younger women. Given the cross-cultural tendency for women to place high value on powerful, high-status males, it also makes sense that Henry, with all his wealth and power, would have fared well in the exchange of status for age. Henry could attract women in their twenties when he was a teen and could still do so when he was approaching fifty. Less powerful teenagers and older men would have more difficulty.

For several of the other questions we raised, we cannot offer certain answers, but we can now take more educated guesses. Why did Charles and Diana's marriage fail, despite the fact that, unlike Henry and his first two wives, they had produced a male heir? One reasonable guess comes from research suggesting that women are particularly likely to be jealous of strong emotional commitments on the part of their partners. Indeed, a central marital problem was that Charles continued a long-term relationship with a woman who had been his lover before he met Diana. Just as Catherine of Aragon learned centuries earlier when Anne Boleyn came along to dislodge her as queen, a man's emotional attachments to other women are a sign that his support may soon disappear.

Why did Edward VIII abdicate his throne for Wallis Simpson, when he could have had any one of a number of more socially appropriate partners? Again, we can only offer an educated guess based on what we know of his life, but many of the facts fit with research-based generalizations. For one thing, Edward demonstrated the classic anxious/ambivalent attachment style. Such individuals are often profoundly upset at the thought of any separation from their lovers and willing to go to extreme lengths to maintain those relationships. It may seem irrational to abandon such an exalted social position for any relationship. But throughout most of our evolutionary history, it made sense for our ancestors to put their love relationships first, before other "rational" considerations. Indeed, wealth and power would have mattered little if our ancestors had not developed mating bonds and thereby produced descendants who could inherit that wealth. The historical importance of providing for one's descendants is certainly obvious in Henry VIII's life—he showered benefits and titles on his illegitimate son, he fought to make it possible for his eldest daughter to ascend to the throne if there were no male descendant, and he divorced his first two wives because they did not bear a male heir.

Love and romantic relationships nicely demonstrate two aspects of the interplay between persons and situations—how our personal characteristics alter, and are altered by, the life situations we choose to enter. Henry VIII, for example, was socially dominant, extraverted, and impulsive. These characteristics make a person charming in the short term but may later disrupt a marriage. On the other hand, even the most powerful personality can be affected by the marriage situation. Despite his hardy temperament backed by all the power of the British throne, Henry's wives shaped his life in ways he could not completely control. Catherine of Aragon, who was highly religious and conventional, steadfastly refused to grant his wish to let him leave the marriage. And his second wife, Anne Boleyn, was hardly putty in the hands of this powerful king. Before they married, she refused to yield completely to his sexual advances until he made her queen. Later, she lobbied hard for Henry to push England toward the Protestant Reformation.

The relationships between long-term lovers and between parents and children are perhaps the central "situations" of most of our lives and, as with Henry and Catherine, Charles and Diana, and Edward and Wallis, our behaviors and personalities not only shape those relationships but also are in turn shaped by them.

CHAPTER 8

Summary

Defining Love and Romantic Attraction

1. Feelings of love involve a number of components, which can be organized into three factors. Passion consists of romantic attraction and sexual desire. Intimacy consists of close bonding with the other. Decision/commitment consists of a decision that one loves another and a commitment to maintain that love.
2. Factor analysis is a statistical technique for sorting items or behaviors into conceptually similar groupings.
3. The feelings associated with love combine differently in different varieties of love, such as love for a family member or for a passionate lover. Passionate love is characterized by intense longing for another, whereas companionate love is composed of feelings of affection and tenderness.
4. Major goals of romantic relationships include sexual satisfaction, forming family bonds, and gaining resources and social status.

Obtaining Sexual Satisfaction

1. Individual differences in sexual desire have been linked to the hormone testosterone in both sexes. Erotophobes tend to feel guilt about sex and to avoid sexual situations. Individuals having an unrestricted sociosexual orientation have more sexual partners and choose partners who are socially attractive. Restricted individuals choose partners who give evidence of potential for good parenting.
2. Individuals who are socially skillful and physically attractive may have more opportunities to express their sexual desires. Some features of physical attractiveness, including waist-to-hip ratios and bodily symmetry, are widely regarded as attractive across cultures.
3. Women are less interested in casual sexual opportunities and more selective about sexual partners. The two sexes tend to be more similar in approaching long-term relationships.
4. Situations that increase general physiological arousal can increase passionate attraction. According to two-factor theory, arousal from any source can be mistakenly attributed to the lover. According to an arousal-facilitation alternative, arousal can boost attraction even when the person is aware the arousal did not come directly from the lover.
5. Women display a number of nonverbal gestures to signal interest in a man. Direct eye contact can facilitate attraction in both sexes, but must be mutual.
6. Different people perceive potentially sexual situations differently. Compared to women, for example, men generally tend to perceive more sexuality in an interaction between a man and a woman, unless the woman is his sister.
7. Culture and evolutionary mechanisms may interact in influencing sexual attraction. Boys and girls raised under the same roof are less likely to later become passionately attracted, suggesting a mechanism blocking strong sexual attraction between siblings.

Establishing Family Bonds

1. Adult attachments show many features of the attachment bond between mother and child, including a similar pattern of distress at separation. Unlike typical mammals, human adult males also bond with their offspring. Close bonds change the normal rules of social exchange.
2. Individuals differ in their styles of attachment. Some are secure and confident of their lovers' support. Others are anxious/ambivalent; still others are avoidant. Individuals who are conventional, introverted, and well adjusted tend to have more satisfying and stable marriages.
3. People oriented to exchange rather than to communal benefits experience more dissatisfaction with their marriage partners.
4. Threatening situations increase the desire to be near those to whom we are attached. Erotomania is a disorder in which the individual persists in believing that another person is deeply in love with him or her despite strong evidence to the contrary. It may involve a misfiring of a normal reaction to a threatened love bond.
5. Men are somewhat more upset by a partner's sexual relationship than by a deep emotional bond whereas women tend to be relatively more troubled if their partners form a deep emotional bond with someone else.
6. When there are relatively many available women and few men, norms shift toward sexual permissiveness and later marriage. When there is a relative surplus of men, societal norms shift toward earlier marriage and less permissiveness.
7. Harmonious relations between a couple depend on more than a pleasant personality in one individual, because negative communications by the other can change the situation and lead to an unpleasant cycle.
8. Marriage itself is a situation that can affect personal traits over time. Commitment to a relationship changes the perception of alternatives, leading people to see members of the opposite sex as less attractive.

Gaining Resources and Social Status

1. A mate's status, wealth, and dominance are more important to a woman considering a man than to a man considering a woman.
2. Although men do not place high value on economic resources and social status in a woman, a woman's "resources" may be related to her reproductive

potential, and signs of youthful maturity and attractiveness are universally valued by men as signs of this potential.
3. Homosexual men act like heterosexual men in preferring relatively young attractive partners and paying relatively little attention to a partner's status.
4. Even women having wealth and status continue to seek long-term male partners having still greater status and wealth.
5. Polygamy involves more than two partners, and includes polyandry, in which one woman marries more than one man, and polygyny, in which one man marries more than one woman. Polyandry often involves a woman marrying brothers and is found in areas where resources are scarce and families would not survive if their land holdings were divided between children. Polygyny is more common and has been found in extreme when a steep social hierarchy combines with a generally rich environment to allow one family to accumulate vast wealth.
6. Both sexes seek long-term partners whose status and market value are similar to their own, but once people are involved in long-term relationships, accounting of relative contributions decreases and the partner's needs become more merged with one's own.
7. Dominance is only attractive in combination with kindness.
8. Women's feelings about their place in the social dominance hierarchy are linked to their feelings about physical appearance; men's to status and resources.

CHAPTER 8
Key Terms

Androgynous *Demonstrating a combination of masculine and feminine characteristics in one's behaviors.*

Anxious/ambivalent attachment style *Attachments marked by fear of abandonment and the feeling that one's needs are not being met.*

Arousal-facilitation theory *The theory that general arousal will enhance any ongoing behavioral or cognitive process, including attraction for another.*

Avoidant attachment style *Attachments marked by defensive detachment from the other.*

Companionate love *Affection and tenderness felt for those whose lives are entwined with our own.*

Decision/commitment *Factor on love scales composed of items tapping decision that one is in love with and committed to another.*

Equity rule *Each person's benefits and costs in a social relationship should be matched to the benefits and costs of the other.*

Erotomania *A disorder involving the fixed (but incorrect) belief that one is loved by another, which persists in the face of strong evidence to the contrary.*

Erotophobia *Tendency to feel guilt and fear of social disapproval for thoughts and behaviors relating to sex.*

Factor analysis *A statistical technique for sorting test items or behaviors into conceptually similar groupings.*

Intimacy *Factor on love scales composed of items tapping feelings of close bonding with another.*

Monogamy *Marital custom in which one man marries one woman.*

Need-based rule *Each person in a social relationship provides benefits as the other needs them, without keeping account of individual costs and benefits.*

Need to belong *The human need to form and maintain strong, stable interpersonal relationships.*

Passion *The factor on love scales composed of items tapping romantic attraction and sexual desire.*

Passionate love *A state of intense longing for union with another.*

Polyandry *Marital arrangement involving one woman and more than one husband.*

Polygamy *Marital custom in which either one man marries more than one woman (polygyny) or one woman marries more than one man (polyandry).*

Polygyny *Marital arrangement involving one man and more than one wife.*

Secure attachment style *Attachments marked by trust that the other person will continue to provide love and support.*

Secure base *Comfort provided by an attachment figure, which allows the person to venture forth more confidently to explore the environment.*

Sociosexual orientation *Individual differences in the tendency to prefer either unrestricted sex (without the necessity of love) or restricted sex (only in the context of a long-term, loving relationship).*

Three-stage pattern of separation distress *The reaction sequence shown by infants or adults separated from those to whom they are intimately attached: (1) protest (attempts to re-establish contact), (2) despair (inactivity and helplessness), (3) detachment (lack of concern and coolness toward the parent or lover).*

Two-factor theory of love *The theory that love consists of general arousal (factor one), which is attributed to the presence of an attractive person (factor two—the cognitive label that the feeling is "love").*

CHAPTER 9

Prosocial Behavior

The Strange Case of Sempo Sugihara

The years of Nazi ascendancy in Europe bear awful witness to the worst of human nature. More than 11 million civilians—including Gypsies, homosexuals, and political dissidents, but the majority of them Jews—were uprooted, degraded, brutalized, and finally murdered in the Holocaust. It is ironic, then, that this period gives simultaneous evidence of the best of human nature: Remarkable acts of kindness, heroism, and self-sacrifice were undertaken on behalf of those victims by individuals who, for the most part, hardly knew them. Yet what may have been the single most effective helping action taken during the time of the Holocaust has gone virtually unrecognized in the years since.

It began near dawn on a summer day in 1940, when 200 Polish Jews crowded together outside the Japanese consulate in Lithuania to plead for help to escape the sweeping Nazi advance through eastern Europe. That they'd choose to seek the aid of Japanese officials is a puzzle. At the time, the governments of Nazi Germany and

Sugihara's Lifeline. *A line of men waits for life outside Sempo Sugihara's office while another line of men waits for death in a Nazi concentration camp. It's likely that without Sugihara's help, those in the first line would have soon become like those in the second.*

imperial Japan had close ties and shared interests. Indeed, those ties and mutual interests were so strong that they would soon lead the countries to join in a wartime alliance against much of the rest of the world. Why then would these Jews, the hated targets of the Third Reich, throw themselves on the mercy of one of Hitler's international partners?

The answer requires that we look back a few years to the mid-1930s. At that time, before its close strategic associations with Hitler's Germany developed, Japan had begun allowing displaced Jews easy access to its settlement in Shanghai as a way of gaining some of the financial resources and political goodwill that the international Jewish community could provide in return. The paradoxical result was that in the prewar years, as most of the countries of the world (the United States included) were turning away the desperate prey of Hitler's Final Solution, it was Japan—Hitler's ally—that was providing them sanctuary (Kranzler, 1976).

By July 1940, then, when 200 of the "prey" massed outside the door of the Japanese consulate in Lithuania, they knew that the man behind that door offered their best and perhaps last chance for safety. His name was Sempo Sugihara and, by all appearances, he was an unlikely candidate for their savior. A midcareer diplomat, he'd become Japan's Consul General in Lithuania by virtue of 16 years of committed and obedient service in a variety of earlier posts. His rise within the diplomatic corps was facilitated by the right credentials: He was the son of a government official and a samurai family, Japan's warrior class known for loyalty, skill, and ferocity in battle. He'd set his professional goals high, dreaming of someday becoming the Japanese ambassador to Russia. Sugihara was also a great lover of entertainments, parties, and music. On the surface, therefore, there was little to suggest that this fun-seeking, life-long diplomat would risk his career, his reputation, and his future to try to save the Jews who woke him from a sound sleep one morning at 5:15. That, though, is precisely what he did—with full knowledge of the potential consequences for him and for his family.

After speaking with members of the crowd outside his gate, Sugihara recognized the depths of their plight and wired Tokyo for permission to authorize travel visas for them. Although some aspects of Japan's lenient visa and settlement policies were still in place for Jews, his request was summarily denied, as were his more urgent second and third petitions when he persisted in pressing the case for help. It was at this point in his life—at age 40 with no hint of prior disloyalty or disobedience—that this comfortable, professionally ambitious, career official did what no one could have anticipated. He decided to begin writing the needed travel documents in outright defiance of his clearly stated, and twice restated, orders.

It was a choice that cost him his career. Within a month, he was transferred from his Consul General post to a lesser position in Berlin, where he could no longer maintain a free hand. Ultimately, he was expelled from the Foreign Ministry for his insubordination. In dishonor after the war, he was reduced to selling light bulbs for a living. But in the weeks before he had to close the consulate in Lithuania, he stayed the course he'd set for himself, interviewing applicants day and night and authoring the papers required for their escape. Even after the consulate had been shut and he'd taken up residence in a hotel, he continued to write visas. Even after the strain of the task had left him thin and exhausted, even after the same strain had left his wife incapable of nursing their infant child, he wrote without respite. Even on the platform for the train taking him to Berlin, even on the train itself, he wrote and thrust life-granting papers into life-grasping hands, eventually saving thousands of innocents. And at last, when the train began to draw him away, he bowed deeply and apologized to those he had to leave stranded—begging their forgiveness for his deficiencies as a helper (Watanabe, 1994).

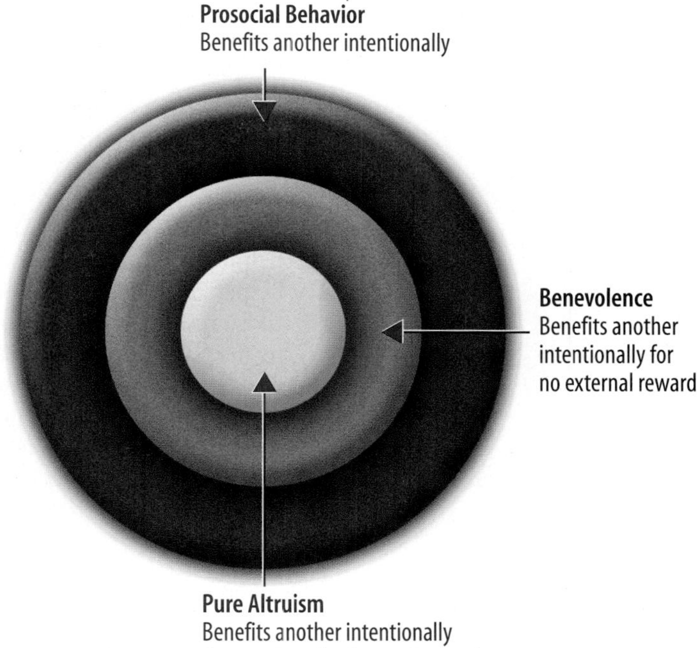

Figure 9.1
Types of prosocial behavior.

Within the general category of prosocial behavior we can locate two increasingly exclusive (and increasingly interesting) subtypes: benevolence and pure altruism.

To understand Sugihara's decision to help thousands of Jews escape to Shanghai—and, as we will see, the subsequent decision of the Japanese High Command to maintain and protect them there for the entire course of the war—it's important to recognize a fundamental truth about prosocial action: It rarely arises from any single factor. A variety of forces act and interact to bring about help. Before we encounter these forces—and, in the process, try to solve the puzzle of Sempo Sugihara's actions—we should be clear about what prosocial behavior is. In addition, we should recognize that helping can serve the goals of the helper: there are advantages, both tangible and intangible, to giving aid. Therefore, in this chapter, after defining and illustrating what we mean by prosocial behavior, we identify the major goals of prosocial action and examine how they can account for various types of help giving, including that of Sempo Sugihara.

Defining Prosocial Behavior

Prosocial behavior takes place in a wide range of sizes and forms, all involving assistance of some sort. There are three different types of prosocial action that differ primarily in the motivation for providing assistance (see Figure 9.1).

Types of Prosocial Behavior

At its most basic level, **prosocial behavior** refers to action intended to benefit another. This label applies even when the helper also stands to benefit. So, if on your way to a movie, you put a $20 bill into a Salvation Army kettle to impress a friend, that would still be prosocial action. Within this broadest category, however, there's a more limited type of prosocial behavior. We can call it **benevolence,** action intended to benefit another but not to provide external reward or recognition to the helper. Suppose that instead of dropping $20 into a Salvation Army kettle to impress a friend, you sent it anonymously to that organization because you knew it would make you feel good inside. The crucial difference between these two kinds of assistance is whether you expected the reward to come from outside or inside yourself. Psychologists have long seen the importance of this distinction between external

Prosocial behavior *Action intended to benefit another.*

Benevolence *Action intended to benefit another but not to gain external reward.*

and internal sources of reward for helping and have assigned more moral value to prosocial acts that are motivated only by internal rewards. In fact, some theorists have defined such internally motivated helping as *altruistic* (Bar-Tal & Raviv, 1982; Eisenberg & Fabes, 1998).

Other theorists (Batson & Shaw, 1991), however, want to reserve the concept of altruism for an even more limited type of prosocial behavior—something that we can label *pure altruism.* **Pure** (or **true**) **altruism** refers to conduct intended to benefit another for no other reason than to improve the other's welfare. In this category of helping actions, the help occurs without regard for external *or* internal rewards for the helper. There may well be rewards for helping but, for the act to be truly altruistic, those rewards cannot have *caused* the decision to help. Thus, if you were to send $20 to the Salvation Army and you felt better about yourself afterward, you would have nonetheless engaged in pure altruism, provided you didn't make the donation *in order* to feel better or for any other self-oriented reason. At present, the most controversial question confronting helping researchers is whether there ever is a purely altruistic act, untouched by self-interest. Toward the end of this chapter, we'll consider a program of research that has pursued the answer to this fundamental question.

The Goals of Prosocial Action

It's reasonable to ask why we should expect anyone to be helpful. After all, helping usually involves giving away resources—time, energy, funds, and so on. Yet prosocial action occurs regularly in all human societies (Fiske, 1991), and helpfulness is a heritable trait, one that is passed on genetically (Rushton, Fulker, Neale, Nias, & Eysenck, 1986). It seems likely, then, that helping serves some valuable functions, not just for societies but for individuals as well. Indeed, significant bodies of research in social psychology point to several goals that prosocial action can serve. We can help (1) to improve our own basic welfare, (2) to increase social status and approval, (3) to manage our self-image, and (4) to manage our moods and emotions. Let's first consider the most basic of these reasons for helping someone else—to help ourselves.

Gaining Genetic and Material Benefits

The question of why people help has always been a prickly one from the standpoint of the theory of evolution. On the surface, giving away resources to aid others presents a problem for the Darwinian view that we always operate to enhance our *own* survival. In seeming contradiction to this idea, we know that people help regularly in a variety of ways, from holding open a door, to sending money to a legitimate charity, to pulling a child from a burning building (McGuire, 1994; Pearce & Amato, 1980). Besides appearing in impressively varied ways, helping also appears impressively often in modern society. In the United States alone, approximately 70 percent of all households make monetary charitable contributions, and almost 110 million Americans volunteer in a public service organization (Tax-Smart Charity Gifts, 1998; Giving and Volunteering in the U.S., 1999). Even relatively intense forms of aid, such as blood donations, take place with notable frequency: Americans—nearly 10 million of them—give 14 million units of blood a year (Piliavin & Callero, 1991). Such other-oriented tendencies make more evolutionary sense when we add two insights to traditional evolutionary accounts of behavior.

Pure (true) altruism *Action intended solely to benefit another and thus not to gain external or internal reward.*

Insights into the Evolution of Help

The first insight was provided by the biologist W. D. Hamilton (1964), who recognized that, from an evolutionary standpoint, the actions of an individual are de-

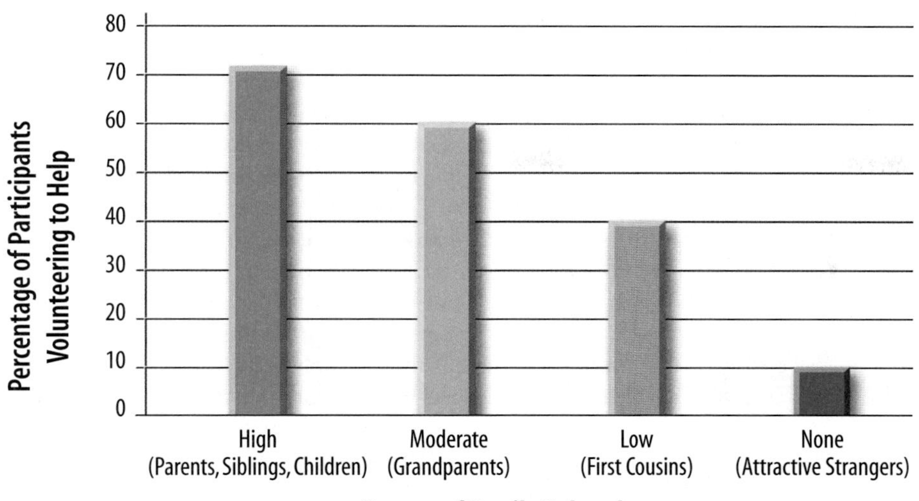

Figure 9.2
Helping relatives and nonrelatives.

Participants indicated whether they would help certain others in a wide variety of situations. Their willingness to help closely reflected their genetic relatedness to the others.

SOURCE: *Adapted from the results of Cunningham et al., 1995.*

signed not so much to ensure that the individual will survive as to ensure that the *genes* making up that individual will do so.

Protecting Our Kin This distinction between personal survival and genetic survival is incorporated in Hamilton's concept of **inclusive fitness,** the likelihood that one's genetic makeup will be preserved not just in one's own offspring, but also in the offspring of any relatives. The distinction is a profound one for understanding and predicting when helping will occur because it implies that people may well accept personal risks and losses if, in the process, they increase their inclusive fitness—the chance that their genes will survive. Consequently, we should be willing to risk even our own survival, if it increases the chance that more copies of our genes will survive in any relatives we help.

The evidence is overwhelming that individuals prefer to help those to whom they are genetically related. Many animal species aid their relatives—feeding, defending, and sheltering them—in direct relation to their degree of relatedness: An animal tends to help most those with which it shares the largest percentage of genes through ancestry—its offspring, parents, and siblings (on average, 50 percent of these genes overlap). Next come aunts, uncles, nieces, and nephews (25 percent overlap), followed by first cousins (12.5 percent overlap), and so on; unrelated animals are helped least (Greenberg, 1979; Sherman, 1981). In large measure and in a large number of cultures, we humans show the same pattern (Burnstein, Crandall, & Kitayama, 1994; Cunningham, Jegerski, Gruder, & Barbee, 1995; Essock-Vitale & McGuire, 1985); see Figure 9.2. This tendency to help genetically close relatives holds true for such diverse forms of aid as donating a kidney in the United States or intervening in an ax fight in the jungles of Venezuela (Borgida, Conner, & Manteufal, 1992; Chagnon & Bugos, 1979).

The tendency to help kin is so strong that, for the common good, societies have had to take action to curb this response. Take a look inside yourself and answer the following question: If you were caught in a natural disaster—an earthquake or flood—whom would you try to help first? If you're anything like those individuals who have actually lived the experience, the answer would be clear: You'd render aid first to family members, and only then to others (Form & Nosow, 1958; Kaniasty & Norris, 1995). Regrettably for many victims, rescue workers typically come to the same answer. For example, when a notoriously destructive tornado hit Xenia, Ohio, in 1974, two thirds of designated health care providers went or stayed home until they had tended to their families' needs (Laube, 1985).

Inclusive fitness *The survival of one's genes in one's own offspring and in any relatives one helps.*

You de-louse my back, and I'll de-louse yours. *Reciprocal aid, in the form of mutual grooming, often occurs among animals. This cooperation benefits all involved.*

Reciprocal Aid Hamilton's notion of inclusive fitness gives us a way to understand self-sacrifice among kin. But how can the logic of evolution explain the fact that in both animal and human groups, aid is regularly directed toward nonrelatives? Here's where the second important insight of modern evolutionary theory applies, in the concept of **reciprocal aid,** as outlined by Robert Trivers (1971). He pointed out that helping is often mutual and cooperative, so that helpers benefit by being helped in return. Recall that in Chapter 6, you learned that all human societies have a norm for reciprocity that obligates people to give in return for the benefits they've received. Trivers showed that mutual helping often takes place among animals, too. Those whose genes encouraged such interactions would have a survival advantage.

In the case of reciprocal aid among unrelated individuals, the survival advantage comes from the material advantage that cooperators would have over noncooperators. Indeed, cooperators do frequently enjoy this advantage in the long run because their mutual assistance gives them access to rewards and continuingly profitable relationships that wouldn't otherwise be available (Bendor, Kramer, & Stout, 1991). Take, for example, the findings of European economists who studied the impact of cooperative approaches in long-term employer–employee relationships. They found that when firms reciprocated by providing benefits to employees whose work helped the firm, the employees expended more effort and reduced the amount of shirking on the job. All of which greatly improved profits, ensuring the survival of the firm and the employees' jobs (Fehr, Gachter, & Kirchsteiger, 1997). In sum, then, the benefits of reciprocal helping can not only provide a material advantage to those who engage in it skillfully, but that material advantage can then lead to a genetic advantage for those individuals who profit from it.

Double duty. *The special connection—genetic and otherwise—between identical twins makes them feel particularly helpful to one another.*

FOCUS ON Method

Using Behavioral Genetics to Study Helping

The investigation of how much of human conduct can be explained by heredity versus environment has a long history in the annals of science (Galton, 1875). Most recently, scientists called behavioral geneticists have made important new inroads into this question by using special methods for disentangling these two fundamental causes of behavior. One of these methods involves the study of twins (Segal, 2000).

For example, behavioral geneticists contrast two kinds of twins: identical twins, who share all their genes, and nonidentical twins, who share only half their genes. On the great majority of traits, identical twins have proven to be more similar in their personalities than have nonidentical twins (Tellegen et al., 1988). But do studies of identical versus nonidentical twins give us evidence about what motivates the tendency to help? Yes they do, in two ways. First, for both adults and children as young as fourteen months, identical twins are more alike in their helping patterns than are nonidentical twins (Rushton et al., 1986; Zahn-Waxler, Robinson, & Emde, 1992). The size of these differences led the researchers to estimate that the tendency to help is due about equally to genetic and nongenetic factors.

Second, other studies have asked whether identical twins are especially likely to act prosocially toward each other. Nancy Segal (2000) found that on a task requiring subjects to earn points, identical twins worked harder to win points for each other than did nonidentical twins. Furthermore, on a puzzle-solving task, 94 percent of the identical twins helped each other but only 46 percent of nonidentical twins did so. Finally, in a bargaining game, the identical twins cooperated to benefit each other significantly more often than the nonidentical twins did (Segal, 2000). Of course, these results are consistent with the concept of inclusive fitness and the idea

Reciprocal aid *Helping that occurs in return for prior help.*

that individuals will act to increase the welfare of their genes, even if those genes are in someone else's body.

In sum, it appears from studies of twins that there is a strong genetic impact on the tendency to help. At the same time, there is also a strong impact due to learning and environment—an optimistic finding for those who hope to be able to instill a prosocial orientation in others, especially children. ■

Learning to Help

Which features of the person might spur an individual to help in order to gain genetic and material benefits? Two stand out: instilled beliefs and an expanded sense of "we."

Instilled Beliefs If helping others—even unrelated others—can produce genetic and material gains for the helper, then those individuals who most strongly believe this to be the case should be most likely to help. This is precisely what one survey of U.S. corporations found: Those whose executives viewed self-interest as a reason for charity were especially likely to be big donors (Galaskiewicz, 1985).

Where does this view that helping is a way to promote one's own interests come from? One place is the learning process. Even relatively late in their development, people can be educated to believe that prosocial behavior is—or is not—personally prudent. Take, for instance, training in classical economic theory. A basic assumption is that people will neglect or exploit others to maximize their own outcomes. Research has demonstrated that economics students, more than students in other disciplines such as psychology, do follow the expectations of classical economic theory. They're more likely to take advantage of a partner in a bargaining game (Marwell & Ames, 1981). They're more likely to demand a lopsided payment for themselves in a negotiation (Kahneman, Knetsch, & Thaler, 1986). And, especially pertinent to the topic of helping, they're less likely to make donations to charities (Frank, Gilovich, & Regan, 1993).

Of course, it is possible that this unhelpful orientation to the world isn't trained into economics students but is there, full-blown, before they set foot in an economics class. But research by Robert Frank, Tom Gilovich, and Dennis Regan (1993) suggests not. They discovered that these kinds of differences between students in economics and those in other fields grew with greater training in their respective majors, suggesting that these tendencies are learned to a significant extent.

The Expanded Sense of "We" There is another way a learned orientation to the world can influence the extent to which individuals will act prosocially for a direct benefit. That learned orientation—an expanded sense of "we"—develops in the home, well before a person encounters a college curriculum, and it involves genetic rather than material benefit. As you've already seen, people prefer to help those to whom they're genetically related, presumably to enhance the survival of their own genes. It isn't really possible, though, for individuals to look inside one another and determine how many genes they share. Instead, people have to rely on *cues* of genetic relatedness—features that are normally associated with relatives (Krebs, 1989). One such cue is the early presence of particular others or types of others in the home. Humans as well as animals react to those who were present while they were growing up as if they are relatives (Aldhous, 1989; Wells, 1987). Although this clue to genetic relatedness can occasionally steer us wrong, it's normally accurate because people in the home typically *are* true family members—a group nearly everyone views as "we."

An interesting upshot of this logic is that those individuals whose parents regularly opened their homes to a wide range of people—of varying backgrounds, customs, and appearances—should be more likely, as adults, to help strangers. That would be so because their conception of "we" will have been broadened to include more than just the immediate or even the extended family. For them, the help-inspiring sense

The outsiders. *This photo shows Sugihara's wife, son, and sister-in-law in Nazi-held territory some months after he'd been relieved of his duties in Lithuania. Note the sign on the park gate, which reads "No Jews allowed." It's unknown whether the sign was an incidental or purposive part of the picture. We do know, however, that Sugihara himself took the photograph and that he positioned his family* outside *the gate. What do you think? Was the sign an incidental feature of the shot or a consciously included piece of bitter irony? For a suggestive bit of evidence, see if you can locate the sister-in-law's right hand.*

of "we-ness" should extend more fully to the *human* family (Hornstein, 1982; Piliavin, Dovidio, Gaertner, & Clark, 1981).

One source of support for this idea comes from cultures having different norms for inviting others, especially mere acquaintances, into the home. In many Asian societies, such invitations are rare, and an outsider who receives one should feel greatly honored. In Western society, however, get-togethers in the home with a variety of acquaintances—for casual dinners, to watch sporting events on TV, and so forth—are much more commonplace. Consistent with the notion that diverse home environments will lead to help for strangers, Americans are more willing to help people outside their own groups than are Japanese or Chinese individuals. But the Japanese and Chinese are more willing to help individuals from within their own groups than are Americans (Leung, 1988).

Evidence like this further deepens the mystery of Sempo Sugihara's actions to help Jewish refugees before the outbreak of World War II. Why would a member of Japanese society, noted for its reluctance to embrace outsiders, be so dedicated to the welfare of a group of foreigners? Our first hint comes from an experience in Sugihara's youth. His father, a tax official who had been sent to Korea for a time, moved the family there and opened an inn. Sugihara recalled being greatly impressed by his parents' willingness to take in a broad mix of guests—tending to their basic needs for food and shelter, even cleaning their hair and clothing of lice—despite the fact that some were too impoverished to pay (Watanabe, 1994). From this perspective, perhaps we can see one reason for Sugihara's later helping efforts toward thousands of European Jews—an expanded sense of "we" flowing from exposure to diverse individuals in the home. As he stated in an interview forty-five years after the fact, the nationality and religion of these victims didn't matter to him, it only mattered that "they were *human*, and they needed help" (Craig, 1985).

Of course, it's always risky to try to generalize from a single case to a broader conclusion. In this instance, however, we know that Sugihara wasn't the only notable rescuer of that era whose early home life incorporated human diversity. Samuel and Pearl Oliner (1988) found large differences in this regard between European Gentiles who harbored Jews from the Nazis and those who did not: Rescuers reported close childhood associations with more people of different social classes and religions. Moreover, while growing up, they felt a sense of similarity to a wider and more varied group of people than did nonrescuers. Not only was this expanded sense of "we" related to their decisions to aid people different from themselves during the war, but also, when interviewed half a century later, rescuers were still helping a greater variety of people and causes (Midlarsky & Nemeroff, 1995; Oliner & Oliner, 1988). All this suggests a piece of advice for prospective parents who want their children to develop a broadly charitable nature: Give them positive contact in the home with individuals from a wide spectrum of backgrounds.

Similarity and Familiarity

Just as prior learning history can influence one's sense of "we," so can certain features of the immediate situation. For instance, people feel a greater sense of unity toward others with whom they have recently shared intimate information (Aron, Melinat,

Aron, Vallone, & Bator, 1997). According to an evolutionary account of helping motivation, those situational factors associated with an especially important category of "we"—relatives—should lead to increased helping. Evidence regarding two such factors, similarity and familiarity, is consistent with the evolutionary view.

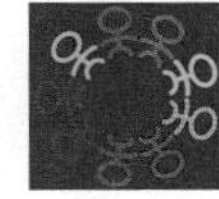

Similarity One way two people can estimate their degree of genetic relatedness is by assessing their degree of similarity (Rushton, Russell, & Wells, 1984); this seems to be true not only for physical characteristics but also for certain personality traits and attitudes (Martin et al., 1986; Waller et al., 1990). If prosocial action is motivated by a (no doubt nonconscious) desire to promote one's own genetic survival, then people ought to assist others who are similar to them in appearance, personality, and attitudes. For example, people report that they would assign higher priorities for life-saving medical treatment to those who share their political attitudes (Furnham, 1996). More generally, Dovidio (1984) looked at all the tests of the similarity-helping relationship that he could find and discovered that in 29 of the 34 cases, similar others got significantly more help than dissimilar others. This tendency to benefit similar others occurs even within families, where greater helping occurs between family members who resemble one another (Leek & Smith, 1989, 1991). According to these results, when deciding which of several individuals to call on for help, all other things equal, your best choice would be the one most similar to you in personality and appearance.

Oddly, though, one dimension on which genetic similarity should be relatively clear, race, has not produced the typical similarity-leads-to-aid finding. When Faye Crosby, Stephanie Bromley, and Leonard Saxe (1980) examined the research literature, they found that fewer than half the studies showed more helping for someone of the same race. How do we account for these conflicting patterns? A beautifully crafted set of experiments by Samuel Gaertner and John Dovidio (1977, 1986) seems to have provided the answer: When people think they may be seen as prejudiced for not assisting a member of another race, they help that individual as much as a member of their own race. However, if they think they can fail to help and yet not appear prejudiced, the usual pattern reappears and they are more likely to assist a racially similar person. These results demonstrate that although genetic factors may play a significant role in helping decisions, so do social factors (Sommers & Ellsworth, 2000).

If it's true that similarity leads to helping, then it ought to be possible to convince others to help us by convincing them that we're alike. Indeed, there's evidence that one such approach may have saved many lives: At the outset of this chapter, after recounting Sempo Sugihara's baffling benevolence toward thousands of European Jews, we alluded to a related mystery—the puzzling decision of the Japanese military government to shelter and sustain the Jews within their borders for the length of the war, against the protests of their Nazi allies. The events surrounding that decision, as described by a variety of scholars (Kranzler, 1976; Ross, 1994; Tokayer & Swartz, 1979), offer fascinating corroboration of the similarity-helping relationship and indicate how victims can—with great personal benefit—arrange to include themselves in the helper's sense of "we."

FOCUS ON Application

Getting Help by Adjusting the Helper's Sense of "We"

Although the best evidence on the subject indicates that Sugihara's visas saved thousands of Jews (Levine, 1997), when they arrived in Japanese-held territory, they became part of an even larger contingent of Jewish refugees concentrated in the Japanese-controlled city of Shanghai. After the attack on Pearl Harbor, all refugee passage in and out of Shanghai ended abruptly and the situation of the Jewish community there quickly became precarious. Japan, after all, was by then a full-fledged

Combatants in the battle to influence Japanese policy toward Jews. *Colonel Josef Meisinger (pictured after his capture by Allied forces) was unsuccessful in persuading the Japanese High Command to treat the Jews under its control as the Nazis wished. One reason may be the recognition, highlighted at a crucial meeting with Jewish leaders, of the common Asian origins of the Japanese and the Jews. Those Jewish leaders, Rabbis Kalisch and Shatzkos (pictured with their translators on the day of the meeting) sought to include their people in the Japanese officials' sense of genetic "we" and to exclude the Nazis in this respect.*

wartime conspirator with Adolph Hitler and had to avoid steps that might threaten the solidarity of its alliance with this virulent anti-Semite. Yet, despite the potentially damaging impact on its relations with Hitler, the Japanese government resisted Nazi pressures to annihilate the Shanghai Jews in early 1942 and remained adamant in that resistance through the end of the war. Why?

According to Marvin Tokayer (Tokayer & Swartz, 1979, 178–181), the former chief rabbi of Tokyo, the answer may well have to do with a little-known set of events that took place several months earlier. The Nazis had sent to Tokyo Gestapo Colonel Josef Meisinger, known as the "Butcher of Warsaw" for ordering the execution of 16,000 Jews there. Immediately upon his arrival in April 1941, Meisinger began agitating for a policy of brutality toward the Jews under Japan's rule—a policy that he stated he'd be happy to help design and enact. Uncertain at first of how to respond and wanting to hear all sides, high-ranking members of Japan's military government called on the Jewish refugee community to send two leaders to a meeting that would importantly influence their future. The chosen representatives were both highly respected religious leaders, but they were respected in different ways. One, Rabbi Moses Shatzkes, was renowned as an intensely studious man, one of the most brilliant religious scholars in Europe before the war. The other, Rabbi Shimon Kalisch, was much older and was known for his remarkable ability to understand basic human workings—a social psychologist of sorts.

When the two entered the meeting room, they and their translators found themselves in the company of some of the most powerful members of the Japanese High Command, who wasted little time in asking a pair of fateful questions: Why do our allies the Nazis hate you so much, and why should we resist their attempts to harm you? The scholar, Rabbi Shatzkes, was speechless. But Rabbi Kalisch's knowledge of human nature had equipped him to give, in one reply, the consummate answer to both questions. "Because," he said calmly, "we are Asian ... *like you.*"

Although brief, this assertion was inspired because it made prominent two notions that stood to help the Jews by reshaping the Japanese officers' reigning sense of "we." First was a long-debated theory in Japan that tried to account for the remarkable resemblance between the characteristics of ancient Judaism and the Shinto religion of Japan. The theory was that at least some of the 10 "lost tribes" of Israel had traveled across Asia to Japan and had intermarried, mixing their beliefs and their blood, with the Japanese. The second point that Rabbi Kalisch's statement was designed to underscore was that, according to the Nazi's own racial claims, the German Master Race was genetically different from the "inferior" Asian peoples. With a single, penetrating observation, then, he sought to reframe the officers' conceptions of "we"—so that now it was the Jews who were included and the Nazis who were (self-proclaimedly) not.

Witnesses to the meeting report that the old rabbi's assertion had a powerful effect on the Japanese officers. After a lengthy silence, they conferred among themselves briefly and announced a recess. When the meeting reconvened two hours later, it included a pair of high-ranking Shinto priests who spent the next four hours discussing intently with the rabbis the uncanny similarities of their religions and the possibility of common origins. Here is where the scholar, Rabbi Shatzkes, became invaluable. With his deep and vast religious knowledge, he was able to point to parallels that even the priests had not previously recognized.

At the conclusion of the afternoon-long session, the most senior military official rose and granted the reassurance the rabbis had hoped to bring home to their community: "Go back to your people. Tell them...we will provide for their safety and peace. You have nothing to fear while in Japanese territory." And so it was. ■

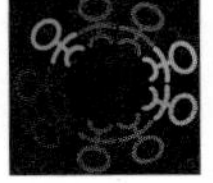

Familiarity Because individuals typically live with their relatives or have had frequent contact with them, familiarity can also serve as a cue for similar heredity. Consider, for instance, that the word *familiar* is virtually the same as *familial.* Of course, a great deal of prior exposure to another doesn't guarantee genetic overlap. But, it doesn't have to in order to be useful in the selfish decision of whom to help. By the logic of evolutionary psychology, if familiarity with another is just roughly associated with shared genes, assisting that other should benefit the helper's genes and should result in increased aid (Rushton, 1989; Schroeder, Penner, Dovidio, & Piliavin, 1995). Support for this idea exists on both fronts.

First, in both human and animal societies, the more related individuals are, the more contact they have with one another (Greenberg, 1979; Hames, 1979; Rushton, 1989). Second, people are more willing to help the others—even the *type* of others—they are familiar with. Once again, we can look for evidence to the rich data of Samuel and Pearl Oliner (1988) on rescuers of Jews during World War II. Compared to those who did not help, rescuers were more likely to have had contact with Jews before the war in their neighborhoods, at work, and in their friendships. Fundraisers report a similar phenomenon: People are much more willing to help with a problem if they know someone afflicted with it. This may help explain why charity agencies are so intent on personalizing victims of a disorder, developing ad campaigns that feature a specific poster child or that tell the story of a particular victim. They know that donations are less likely to flow to an anonymous group of stricken individuals than to a single, familiarized representative of that group (Redelmeier & Tversky, 1990). As Thomas Schelling (1968, p. 130) has said, "If we know people, we care." This may be the case because, as social psychologists have shown, the more we know another, the more similarity we assume (Cunningham, 1986; Kenny & Kashy, 1994).

This relationship between familiarity and aid may provide another clue to the causes of Sempo Sugihara's helping actions. In the months before his decision to sacrifice his career to assist Jewish refugees, Sugihara came into contact with an 11-year-old Jewish boy, Solly Ganor, whose aunt owned a shop near the Japanese consulate. During those months, Sugihara befriended Solly, giving him a coin or contributing to the boy's stamp collection whenever they met. On one such occasion, Sugihara dismissed Solly's expression of thanks, telling the boy to just "consider me your uncle." To this Solly responded, "Since you are my uncle, you should come Saturday to our Hanukkah party. The whole family will be there." At that party, Sugihara met not only Solly's immediate family but also a distant relative from Poland who described the horrors of Nazi occupation and asked for Sugihara's assistance in getting out of Europe. Sugihara replied that he was not then in a position to help but that perhaps he would be in the future. That opportunity to save his new friends came eight months later: The first exit visas Sugihara authorized were those of Solly's family (Ganor, 1995, p. 35).

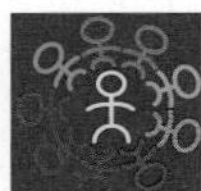

Types of Helpers, Victims, and Need

Of course, the motive to help others in order to help oneself won't lead to prosocial activity in all people and circumstances. The Helping Orientation Model proposed by Daniel Romer, Charles Gruder, and Terri Lizzadro (1986) predicts that the opportunity to get something in return will motivate only certain kinds of people to help. These are labeled receptive givers—because they want to receive when they give—and are differentiated from people Romer, Gruder, and Lizzadro call altruists, whose desire is to give for others' sake and not for material benefit to themselves. As a test of their model, the researchers called the two kinds of helpers on the phone and asked them to participate in an experiment for which they were told they either would or wouldn't receive class credit as compensation. As predicted, when compensation was offered, receptive givers were much more likely to agree to help if they'd get credit in return. Just the reverse was true for the altruists, however, who volunteered more frequently when helping would be uncompensated.

The evolutionary perspective on helping also predicts some intricacies in the ways aid is provided. That is, the tendency to favor kin isn't expected to be equal under all circumstances. For instance, if people help closely related others to ensure the survival of more of their own genes, the preference for helping close kin should be strongest when survival is at issue. In a test of this hypothesis, Eugene Burnstein, Chris Crandall, and Shinobo Kitayama (1994) asked U.S. and Japanese college students how willing they would be to help others when the help involved either rescuing them from a burning building or picking up an item for them at the store. Generally, the closer the relative, the greater the willingness to help. However, in both cultures, this tendency to favor close relatives was much more pronounced when the need was life threatening.

Summary

Primitive personal gain—of both the genetic and the material kind—can spur people to help, especially those who believe that they should get something back for their helping efforts. In addition, it appears that we try to secure a genetic advantage by helping individuals who give evidence of being related to us, such as those who seem similar, familiar, or like those with whom we have had early contact in the home. This tendency to assist related others is particularly strong when the others' survival is threatened.

Gaining Social Status and Approval

Besides genetic and material advantages, a less direct kind of benefit can flow to helpers. Because helpfulness is viewed positively across human cultures (Schroeder et al., 1995), those who help can elevate their image in the eyes of others. Donald Campbell (1975) argued that, to encourage assistance in situations that don't offer material or genetic rewards to the helper, all human societies provide *social* rewards to those who help. These social rewards usually take the form of increased liking and approval. In addition, prosocial acts can also enhance the helper's perceived power and status in the community (Nowak & Sigmund, 1998). For instance, corporations that give larger charitable contributions are viewed as more successful by the leaders of other corporations (Galaskiewicz, 1985).

Potlatch power. *By giving away vast stores of goods, highborn members of Northwest Pacific Coast tribes got something they wanted more—legitimacy for their claims to rank and status. At one Kwakiutl potlatch, blankets were piled and ready for giving.*

The tactic of giving to increase social standing is not unique to corporate cultures. In his monumental work, *The Gift*, French anthropologist Marcel Mauss (1967) detailed the importance and universality of gift giving in human social organization. However, despite the pervasiveness of the process, it can appear in a striking variety of forms. One of the most spectacular occurs in the practice of *potlatching*—a ritual celebration in which the host gives away enormous quantities of goods to his guests, often going broke or into debt in the process. Although known in certain other parts of the world, such as Melanesia, it has been found primarily among the Native American cultures of the Northwest coast, especially in the Kwakiutl tribe.

A flourishing institution in the latter part of the nineteenth century, potlatching was eventually banned by the Canadian government. By 1951, when the "potlatch law" was officially repealed, there was hardly any need for the government's action, the tradition having long before lost its function for the tribal peoples. But that hasn't stopped social scientists from wondering and arguing about what that function was (Morris, 1994). Some have contended that the primary purpose of the potlatch was to give physically separated individuals (from distinct families and tribes) the regular opportunity to establish and strengthen social ties in a positive environment of feasting and celebration. However, while such opportunities were no doubt present, participants always saw them as minor, as mere prelude to the grand finale of giving. Other explanations, correctly taking into account the centrality of the process of giving, emphasized economic functions such as the redistribution of wealth or the creation of obligations that could be called upon in the future. But economic explanations of this sort don't fit with evidence that the most glory came to the host who destroyed rather than distributed much of his property—often in great fires fed by furniture, wooden canoes, and barrels of valuable candlefish oil, until the flames spread to the walls and incinerated the host's house and remaining possessions (Woodcock, 1977).

If none of these speculations seems to capture the essential purpose of potlatching, what might? The answer currently favored by most anthropologists is that the custom functioned to establish and validate rank in the societies. They note that wealth among these tribes was highly esteemed and, along with family lineage, was the basis for social standing. Thus, anyone who could accumulate and afford to *expend* great wealth could rightfully assert a claim to distinguished social status (Cole & Chaikin, 1990; Rosman & Rubel, 1971). What was actually valued, then, was not wealth but rank, privilege, and title, all of which could be claimed and legitimated by the giving away of wealth. When viewed in this light, the Kwakiutl chiefs of old were not so different from today's business chieftains who give generous corporate donations so that they and their companies will be perceived as more powerful and successful by their own rivals (Galaskiewicz, 1985).

Social Responsibility: The Helping Norm

The norms of a society often influence behavior powerfully. As we discussed in chapter 6, there are two kinds of social norms. *Descriptive norms* define what's typically done, whereas *injunctive norms* define what's typically approved and disapproved.

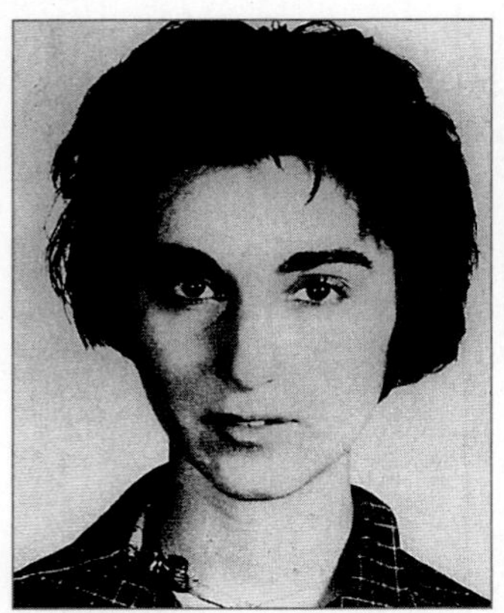

Catherine Genovese. *Prior to Catherine Genovese's murder on a dark New York City street, social psychologists had spent relatively little time in the investigation of helping. But the special circumstances of her death—thirty-eight people had watched it occur over a span of thirty-five minutes without lifting a finger to help—brought a new research question into prominence: What are the factors that enhance and inhibit the tendency to help?*

Both kinds of norms affect helping: People are more likely to give assistance when they have evidence that others help and that others approve of help (Warburton & Terry, 2000). However, it's the approval of prosocial action that seems most relevant to the goal of gaining status and social approval. The Polish social psychologist Janusz Reykowski (1980) demonstrated the power of expected social approval in an experiment done on Bulgarian college students who were told, falsely, that admiration for altruists at their school was low. Later, when asked for assistance, they were far less likely to comply than those who had not received this information about their school's norms.

The most general helping norm is the **social responsibility norm** (Berkowitz, 1972). It states, rather broadly, that we should help those who need—who are dependent on—our help. As we'll see, several factors affect when the social responsibility norm guides a person's decision to help. One of the most heavily researched is whether others (bystanders) are present when a helping opportunity arises, especially if the opportunity involves emergency aid. These bystanders can influence the action of the social responsibility norm—and, consequently, the decision to help—in three ways: by serving as sources of help, as sources of information about whether helping is required, and as sources of approval or disapproval of helping action.

Bystanders as Sources of Help In the early years of experimental social psychology, the study of antisocial behavior (prejudice, conflict, aggression) was given more weight than the study of prosocial activity. Perhaps because of the still-vivid horrors of World War II, social psychologists appeared more concerned with understanding and reducing the evil within human conduct than in understanding and enhancing the good. That changed decisively in the mid-1960s, however—due, in no small measure, to a single event. At 3:00 A.M. on March 13, 1964, a young woman named Catherine Genovese was knifed to death by a man she didn't know on the street outside her apartment in New York City. News of the killing created a national uproar (Rosenthal, 1964).

What was it about this particular crime that left the country horrified? It wasn't that it involved murder—killings were, and still are, commonplace in New York. It wasn't that it was especially brutal—though the victim was stabbed repeatedly while she begged for life. It wasn't even that the assailant, who was later caught and convicted, had killed two women previously. Rather, it was that the crime had been a long, loud, *public* event, observed by thirty-eight of Genovese's neighbors who, roused from their beds by the commotion, peered down on it from the safety of their apartment windows. Thirty-eight people had witnessed the emergency and not one had helped, not even to call the police.

In the swirl of publicity that followed a front page *New York Times* story, social scientists found themselves pressed—by students in classrooms, by reporters in interviews, even by friends at cocktail parties—for the answer to the same question: With thirty-eight people watching, why didn't someone help? After one such party, two New York–based social psychologists, Bibb Latané and John Darley (1970), sat down to analyze the mystery. In the process, they hit upon an explanation that everyone else had missed: Although previous accounts had stressed that no action was taken *even though* thirty-eight people had looked on, Latané and Darley suggested that no one had helped precisely *because* there were thirty-eight witnesses. With so many observers on the scene, it was possible for each to think that someone else, perhaps someone more qualified, would help. According to Latané and Darley, responsibility for aid may become spread so thinly among a group of onlookers—a process called **diffusion of responsibility**—that no one of them feels the obligation to act, and so no one does.

Social responsibility norm *The societal rule that people should help those who need them to help.*

Diffusion of responsibility *The tendency for each group member to dilute personal responsibility for acting by spreading it among all other group members.*

To test their idea, Darley and Latané (1968) did the first of many studies examining how the number of bystanders to an emergency affects the likelihood that anyone would help. Over an intercom system, New York City college students heard another student having what seemed to be an epileptic seizure. The percentage of subjects who left their private cubicles to give help declined dramatically with the number of other subjects who could help. If subjects thought they alone had heard the seizure, 85 percent of them tried to help. However, if they knew that just one other subject had heard the seizure, assistance dropped to 62 percent; adding four fellow subjects to the intercom network suppressed helping even more, to 31 percent.

What does diffusion of responsibility have to do with the norm of social responsibility? Recall that the norm obliges us to help those who are dependent on *us* for help. So if the presence of others diffuses helping responsibility to those others, the victim automatically becomes less dependent on *us* for aid, which weakens our obligation to help according to the norm. Support for this view comes from research showing that it's not the mere presence of others that inhibits emergency assistance, it's the presence of others who could reasonably be expected to help (Bickman, 1971).

Bystanders as Sources of Information About Helping Besides diffusion of responsibility, Latané and Darley suggested another reason that onlookers might suppress emergency assistance: They may reduce the chance that a genuine emergency will be interpreted as one. In many cases, it is not clear to observers that an emergency is occurring; and when people are uncertain, they are reluctant to act (Tversky & Shafir, 1992a, b; Bastardi & Shafir, 1998). Instead, they look around for information to help them define the situation. In a developing emergency, bystanders become sources of information for one another. Each looks at the others for clues about how to react, but does so quickly and subtly, with unconcerned glances, so as not to appear flustered or alarmist. As a result, everyone notices that everyone else is calmly *failing* to act, which leads all to the conclusion that there must be no real emergency. This, according to Latané and Darley (1968) is the phenomenon of *pluralistic ignorance*, in which each person in a grouping decides that because nobody is concerned, nothing's wrong. Could this state of affairs contribute to what—on the surface—appear to be shameful levels of bystander "apathy" in modern society? It appears so.

In one study, researchers pumped smoke through a vent into a laboratory where subjects were filling out a questionnaire (Latané & Darley, 1968). Subjects who were alone left the room to report the smoke 75 percent of the time, whereas subjects in groups of three did so only 38 percent of the time. But, by far, the danger was reported least often, only 10 percent of the time, by groups of three that contained one true subject and a pair of experimental confederates instructed to act as though there was no cause for alarm. The behavior of the true subjects was remarkable: even as clouds of smoke filled the air, they worked dutifully at their questionnaires, coughing, rubbing their eyes, and waving the fumes away from their faces—but not reporting the problem. When asked why not, they indicated that they were sure the smoke signaled no fire, no real crisis. Instead, they defined the smoke in nonemergency terms: steam, smog, air conditioning vapor, or, in one case, "truth gas" intended to extract honest answers to the questionnaire!

It appears, then, that multiple bystanders, especially if they're passive, can reduce emergency aid by creating a shared illusion that nothing's wrong. Opposite-hand support for this conclusion comes from studies showing that onlookers who act alarmed, rather than placid, increase the likelihood of such aid (Staub, 1974; Wilson, 1976). The pluralistic ignorance phenomenon is most powerful when the existence of an emergency is not clear. It's in ambiguous situations that people look to others to try to understand what's going on. And it's in these situations, then, that this phenomenon can fool them into inaction (Clark & Word, 1972, 1974).

Bystanders as Sources of Approval or Disapproval There's a third way others can influence the workings of the social responsibility norm: by approving or disapproving of the decision to help. An individual who conforms to the norm and helps another

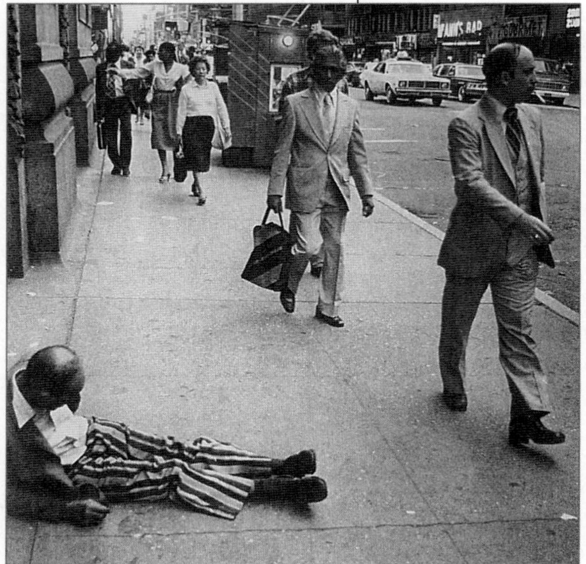

Victim? *At times like this one, when the need for emergency aid is unclear, even genuine victims are unlikely to be helped in a crowd. Think how, if you were the second passerby in this picture, you might be influenced by the first passerby to believe that no aid was called for.*

in need usually gets the approval of observers. That is why in most cases, people assume that their helping acts will be socially rewarded (Bickman, 1971; Schwartz & Gottlieb, 1976). It is also why people are more likely to help when they think that others can identify them and their helping efforts (Schwartz & Gottlieb, 1976, 1980). But, as we've seen, some situations contain cues—for example, visibly passive bystanders—that make it appear that aid may not be appropriate. In these situations, helping is reduced, especially if the potential helper is identifiable to bystanders (Schwartz & Gottlieb, 1980). Thus being identifiable can either increase or decrease the tendency to help depending on whether others in the setting do or don't seem to favor the idea of aid.

Fear of social disapproval frequently suppresses assistance in one especially troubling type of potential emergency—a physical confrontation between a man and a woman. Lance Shotland and Margret Straw (1976) suspected that witnesses to such confrontations may not help because they think their intervention might be unwelcome interference in a "lovers' quarrel." Indeed, this was how some of the bystanders in the Catherine Genovese incident explained their inaction (Rosenthal, 1964). To test their hypothesis, Shotland and Straw exposed study participants to a staged fight between a man and a woman. When there were no cues as to the sort of relationship between the pair, the great majority of male and female participants (nearly 70 percent) assumed that the two were romantically involved; only 4 percent thought they were complete strangers. In other experiments in which there were cues that defined the combatants' relationship—the woman shouted either "I don't know why I ever married you" or "I don't know you"—Shotland and Straw uncovered an ominous reaction on the part of participants. Although the severity of the fight was identical, observers were less willing to help the married woman because they thought it was a private matter in which their intervention would be unwanted and embarrassing to all concerned.

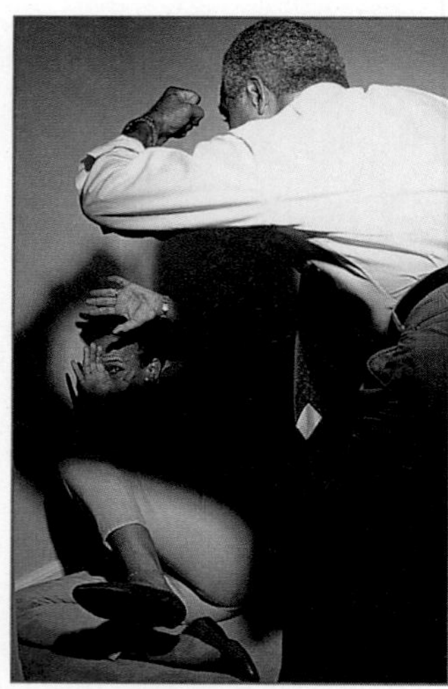

To get help, you have to say the right thing. *Observers of male–female confrontations often assume that the pair is romantically involved and that intervention would be unwanted or inappropriate. To combat this perception and get aid, the woman needs to shout "I don't know you!"*

Thus a woman caught up in a physical confrontation with a male stranger should not expect to get bystander aid by simply shouting for release. Observers are likely to define the event as a domestic squabble, and with that definition in place, may well assume that helping would be socially inappropriate. Fortunately, Shotland and Straw's data suggest a way to overcome this problem: By loudly labeling her attacker a stranger—"I don't know you!"—a woman should greatly increase her chances for aid.

A more general piece of advice for anyone in need of emergency assistance is to recall the fundamental lesson of bystander intervention research: Observers fail to help not so much because they are unkind as because they are unsure. They are often unsure of whether helping is appropriate. If they decide that it is, they are often unsure that they are responsible for providing it. And if they decide that they are, they are often unsure of how to help. If you were to find yourself in a crisis surrounded by onlookers, your best strategy would be to dispel these basic uncertainties for them. State clearly that you need aid, assign the principal responsibility for helping to one person, and describe the kind of assistance you require: "I need help! You, sir, in the blue jacket, call an ambulance."

In sum, bystanders can influence the social responsibility norm and, hence, the decision to help in an emergency via the three routes depicted in Figure 9.3. First, others can serve as sources of potential aid; therefore, with more observers present, any one of them will feel less personal responsibility for providing that aid, thereby reducing helping. Second, others can serve as sources of information about whether aid is called for; therefore, when others seem passive in the face of a possible emergency, the situation is frequently assumed to be a nonemergency and no one helps. Third, others can serve as sources of approval or disapproval for aid; therefore, the

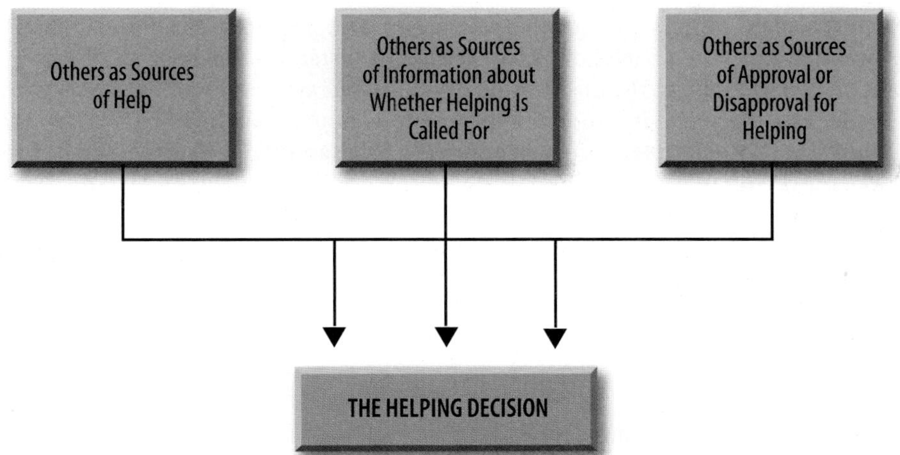

Figure 9.3
Effects of onlookers on decisions to help.

Others can affect the decision to provide assistance in three ways.

presence of others can either increase or decrease prosocial action, depending on whether helping seems appropriate or inappropriate for the situation.

Need for Approval and Awareness of the Helping Norm

Need for Approval If Campbell (1975) is right that, in order to heighten prosocial activity, human societies reward altruists with praise and honor, those individuals who desire such approval should be more likely to help. In one study, college students first completed a personality scale measuring their need for approval then had a chance to donate money to a good cause (Satow, 1975). Overall, the students who most desired approval from others gave more money. There was an important exception, however: When the donation was given in private, those who valued approval were no longer more generous. It seems that people having a high need for approval aren't especially kind. Rather, they are simply more desirous of the esteem that comes with the appearance of kindness.

Awareness of the Helping Norm Because it takes a while to learn the rules of one's culture, we might expect that children would help to gain social approval only after they understand that adults favor helpers. Very young children have no good appreciation of the social responsibility norm and, consequently, their prosocial behavior is unrelated to social approval (Eisenberg, 1992; Eisenberg-Berg & Hand, 1979). However, between six and nine years of age, they become aware that adults value and praise helpfulness toward those in need (Bryan & Walbek, 1970; Eisenberg-Berg, 1979); as a result, it is at these ages that children help more when an adult is present to evaluate their actions (Froming, Allen, & Jensen, 1985). Thus, it was probably around the age of six that you first came to recognize that adults would approve of your helping actions, and it was probably at this age that you began helping more in their presence in order to win their approval.

Effects of Those Around Us

Although norms are said to be always in place within a culture, they're not always in force. That is, an individual is more likely to obey a norm immediately after something has made the norm salient or prominent (Kallgren, Reno, & Cialdini, in press). Several studies have shown that this is the case for helping: The more people are put in mind of the social responsibility norm, the more they help (Berkowitz, 1972; Harvey & Enzle, 1981; Rutkowski, Gruder, & Romer, 1983).

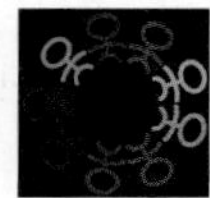

Helping Models The sight of others acting in a socially responsible manner—by dropping money in a Salvation Army kettle, for instance—can spur an observer to help in two ways. First, the observation of others' behavior is frequently the way that people, especially children, learn appropriate conduct (Bandura, 1977). Exposing children to prosocial television programming, for example, teaches them to be more cooperative and generous (Forge & Phemister, 1987; Hearold, 1986). In addition to this teaching function, a prosocial model can also serve as a reminder, bringing the norm to consciousness in adults who may not have been thinking about helpfulness until they came across an instance of it. In a classic study by James Bryan and Mary Ann Test (1967), Los Angeles motorists were more likely to stop and help the driver of a disabled car if they'd witnessed another motorist doing so a quarter mile before.

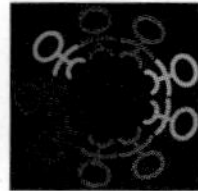

Population Density Compared to rural areas, cities are decidedly less helpful places—true around the world (Amato, 1983; Korte & Kerr, 1975; Smith & Bond, 1998). Robert Levine and his coworkers (1994) assessed helping tendencies in thirty-six U.S. cities, using a helping index that included six separate measures of aid. They found that it was the density rather than the sheer size of a city that crucially affected helping. The more closely packed the population, the less assistance was given. One reason this is the case is that, to deal with the stimulus overload and stress caused by a dense population, urbanites often close themselves off and fail to see the needs of those around them (Evans & Lepore, 1993; Krupat, 1985; Milgram, 1970). As a result, the helping norm, which requires them to give assistance to those *in need*, doesn't stimulate aid.

Gender and Help

Helping often takes place as a result of interactions between factors in the person and in the situation that are associated with the goal of gaining status and approval. Research on gender and helping offers one such illustration.

Most people view women as the more helpful sex; they're rated as kinder, more compassionate, and more devoted to others' welfare than men (Ruble, 1983; Spence & Helmreich, 1978). What's more, there's good agreement on this point around the world; in over 90 percent of cultures studied, the traits of kindness, softheartedness, and helpfulness are more associated with women than with men (Williams & Best, 1990). It seems odd, then, that two sources of evidence suggest the reverse.

The first type of evidence comes from the lists of helpers in our society who have exerted heroic efforts on behalf of others (Huston, Ruggiero, Conner, & Geis, 1981). For example, beginning in the early 1900s the Carnegie Hero Commission has regularly awarded medals to ordinary citizens who distinguish themselves "in saving, or attempting to save, the life of a fellow being." Although women have been eligible from the outset, more than 90 percent of the over 7,000 Carnegie medalists have been men. The second kind of evidence comes from social psychological studies of aid. Extensive reviews of these studies have found a decided tendency for men to help more often (Eagly & Crowley, 1986; Piliavin & Unger, 1985). What are we to make of the seeming inconsistency between what most people believe and what these two sources of information reveal about the helpfulness of men and women?

To solve the puzzle, we have to recognize first that, besides biological differences that may affect how helping takes place (Dabbs, 2000), males and females are socialized differently from one another (Burn, 1996; Gilligan, 1982). From childhood, men and women learn that different kinds of behavior are expected and admired in them—for example, men should be gallant and strong whereas women should be caring and gentle. These expectations about what's masculine and feminine constitute the gender roles of a society, and they can lead women and men to help under different sets of conditions. It's expected, for instance, that men will engage in typically male activities. This is one reason men are more likely to help others with car trouble (Penner, Dertke, & Achenbach, 1973; Pomazal & Clore, 1973; West, Whitney, & Schnedler, 1975), even when the aid only involves making a phone call for assistance (Gaertner & Bickman, 1971). Conversely, it is expected that women will engage in typically female activities. John Dovidio (1993) and his students provided a simple but telling illustration of this general point when, at a laundromat, they asked for help either carrying or folding some clothes: Women were more willing to fold the laundry, and men were more willing to carry it.

In addition, gender roles specify which *traits* are considered masculine and feminine, and these traits can affect when and how helping occurs. According to Alice Eagly and Maureen Crowley (1986), masculine helping traits are quite different from feminine helping traits. To fit with gender roles, masculine assistance should be daring, forceful, and directed toward anyone who's deserving—strangers included; feminine assistance, on the other hand, should be nurturing, supportive, and focused primarily on the needs of relationship partners such as family and friends. From this perspective, we can see why many more men than women are honored by the Carnegie Hero Commission: Heroism fits with the masculine—but not the feminine—gender role, as a hero is courageous and bold and willing to rescue nameless victims. Indeed, the Commission's bylaws specifically discriminate against anyone who saves a family member—that's not seen as heroic enough.

But does this gender-role explanation account for why men help more than women in social psychological experiments? Eagly and Crowley (1986) think it does. They point out that most helping experiments, especially those done in the early years, exposed subjects to emergency situations and victims with whom they had no prior relationship. No wonder, Eagly and Crowley say, that men help more than women in these studies: assistance under these conditions requires bold, direct action on behalf of strangers, which is consistent principally with the masculine gender role.

Good support for this analysis comes from studies of types of aid more consistent with the feminine gender role, such as the willingness to provide emotional support and informal counseling on personal problems (Aries & Johnson, 1983; Johnson & Aries, 1983; Otten, Penner, & Waugh, 1988); in these studies, women helped more than men. Even studies of emergency aid—which show the usual tendency for men to help (strangers) more than do women—find the reverse when the person in need is a friend (McGuire, 1994). However, the way that women provide emergency assistance is likely to be more indirect (summoning help) than for men, who tend to provide the help themselves (Senneker & Hendrick, 1983). Thus, the answer to the question "Who is likely to help more, women or men?" depends on whether the required help conforms to the socially approved feminine or masculine gender role.

Summary

Because helping is admired, people can use it as a way to gain social status and approval. This is why individuals high in need for approval are more likely to help in public than in private. This is also why prosocial behavior is greatly affected by the norm of social responsibility, which promises social approval if we help needy others and social disapproval if we don't. In emergencies, the presence of multiple bystanders can diminish the impact of the social responsibility norm by diffusing responsibility for help, by creating the impression that no help is needed (pluralistic ignorance), and by framing helping as inappropriate. Factors that increase the awareness of the social responsibility norm—seeing a helpful model, for instance—

usually increase assistance. Conversely, factors that decrease awareness of the norm—very young age, for instance—typically decrease assistance. Finally, consistent with socially approved gender roles, men help more than women when strangers require bold, direct action, and women help more than men when friends and family need emotional support and assistance.

Managing Self-Image

Any meaningful action we take can influence how we think of ourselves (Schlenker & Trudeau, 1990; Vallacher & Wegner, 1985). Prosocial action is no exception to this rule. For example, 50 years after the fact, Elizabeth Midlarsky and Robin Nemeroff (1995) found that the self-esteem of people who had been rescuers during the Holocaust was still being elevated by the help they had provided. Less extreme types of aid show a similar pattern. In one study, elementary school students who privately agreed to give up their recess time to work for hospitalized children came to see themselves as more altruistic immediately, and they still thought of themselves as more altruistic a month later (Cialdini, Eisenberg, Shell, & McCreath, 1987).

Because prosocial behavior can affect how we view ourselves, we can use it to manage self-image (self-concept) in two principal ways: We can use it both to *enhance* and to *verify* our self-definitions (Swann, 1990). For instance, if you felt in need of an ego boost, you could decide to do someone a good turn and—like the students who gave up their recess time—you could improve your self-image in the process. Or, if your sense of self already included an altruistic component—let's say you've always thought of yourself as charitable or generous—you might help a needy person to confirm that view; here, the goal would not be to enhance your self-concept but to verify it (Penner & Finkelstein, 1998; Grube & Piliavin, 2000). Beth Stark and Kay Deaux (1994) found support for this self-verification process in a study of volunteer workers in a prisoner rehabilitation program. The factor that best predicted whether a worker wanted to continue in the program was how much he or she felt volunteering was "an important reflection of who I am." In the following section, we explore a pair of factors in people that help them define who they are and that affect prosocial actions accordingly.

Personal Norms and Religious Codes

Helpful individuals frequently cite their personal beliefs and values as spurring their decisions to help. A study of charitable giving and volunteering in the United States found that 87 percent of the people surveyed said that a reason they contributed was that it was consistent with their existing personal values; no other factor was cited as often (Hodgkinson & Weitzman, 1990); see Figure 9.4. A similar pattern emerged when Mark Snyder and Allen Omoto (1992) asked 116 volunteer workers at an AIDS center why they decided to help; by far the largest number of volunteers (87 percent) cited the connection of the work to their existing personal values. Finally, researchers who have studied the rescuers of Jews during the Holocaust report that many of the rescuers explained their actions in terms of a desire to live up to their humanitarian beliefs and values (Anderson, 1993; Oliner & Oliner, 1988).

If, as it appears, the beliefs and values that form a person's self-image can motivate that person toward prosocial behavior, it should be the case that those who have most fully internalized (incorporated) prosocial beliefs and values into their self-image should be most motivated to help. For evidence in this regard, let's examine the influence of two kinds of internalized beliefs and values on helping: personal norms and religious codes.

Personal Norms According to Shalom Schwartz (1977), internalized beliefs and values link together to form an individual's **personal norms,** which represent the individual's internal standards for particular conduct. A personal norm differs from a social norm in two crucial ways. First, in the case of personal norms, the standards for what is appropriate behavior are inside the individual, not outside in moral rules of the culture. Second, approval and disapproval of relevant behavior also come from inside rather than outside the person; that is, the "pats on the back" (for behavior that meets the standards) and the "slaps on the wrist" (for behavior that violates the standards) are self-administered. So, if your personal norm for helping influenced whether you gave a dollar to a homeless person, it would be because you first looked inside rather than outside yourself for guidance; and, afterward, your reward would come from acting in accord with your own rules, not the society's. In general, research has supported Schwartz's thinking. People who have strong personal norms regarding such actions as giving blood, tutoring blind children, or engaging in curbside recycling programs are more likely to engage in these behaviors (Guagnano, Dietz, & Stern, 1994; Hopper & Nielsen, 1991; Schwartz & Howard, 1982).

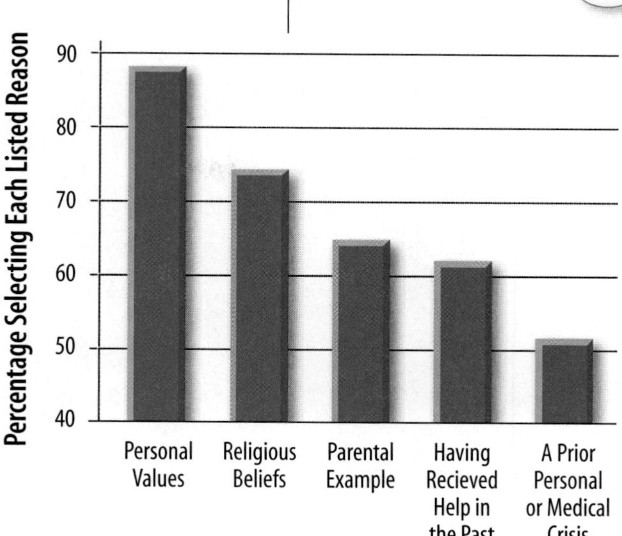

Figure 9.4
Reasons givers give for giving.

Hodgkinson and Weitzman (1990) gave charitable individuals a list of personal background reasons for helping and asked them to indicate all that applied to them. The most frequently cited reasons involved personal values and religious beliefs.

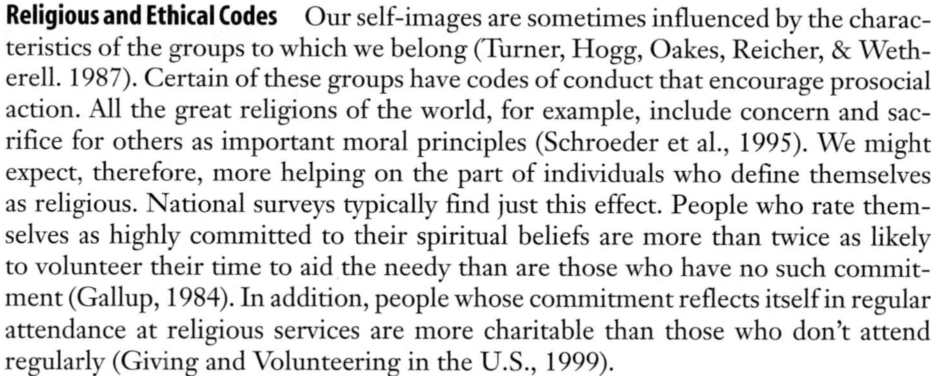

Religious and Ethical Codes Our self-images are sometimes influenced by the characteristics of the groups to which we belong (Turner, Hogg, Oakes, Reicher, & Wetherell. 1987). Certain of these groups have codes of conduct that encourage prosocial action. All the great religions of the world, for example, include concern and sacrifice for others as important moral principles (Schroeder et al., 1995). We might expect, therefore, more helping on the part of individuals who define themselves as religious. National surveys typically find just this effect. People who rate themselves as highly committed to their spiritual beliefs are more than twice as likely to volunteer their time to aid the needy than are those who have no such commitment (Gallup, 1984). In addition, people whose commitment reflects itself in regular attendance at religious services are more charitable than those who don't attend regularly (Giving and Volunteering in the U.S., 1999).

More dramatic evidence of the role that religious self-definition can play in the decision to help comes from the simultaneously sobering and uplifting story of Reginald Denny. On April 29, 1992, a Los Angeles jury acquitted of all charges four white police officers who had dealt a severe, much publicized, videotaped beating to a black man, Rodney King. The jury's decision hit the streets of South Central Los Angeles like a torch, igniting a seventy-two-hour riot among the area's mostly minority-group residents, who felt that justice had been perverted. Roving gangs looted, burned, and terrorized. Especially targeted were white residents or motorists who had, unknowingly, driven into this violent, racially charged environment. Reginald Denny, a truck driver, was one. Pulled from his eighteen-wheel rig, he was relentlessly kicked and beaten by a group of young black men who left him lying unconscious in an intersection—all of which was recorded by a news helicopter team hovering directly above, beaming live pictures of the scene into thousands of homes.

Ten minutes' drive from that intersection, Lei Yuille, an African-American woman, saw the televised events and rushed to Denny's aid. There she was joined by two other rescuers, both African-American men, spurred to help by the same broadcast images. One, Titus Murphy, was a burly engineer, big enough to defend Denny from further battering. The other, Bobby Green, was a fellow trucker who knew he would be needed to drive Denny's eighteen-wheeler to the hospital—which

Personal norms *The internalized beliefs and values that combine to form a person's inner standards for behavior.*

Harm versus help—not a black-and-white choice. *Reginald Denny lies unconscious beside his truck while two attackers taunt a helicopter pilot photographing his plight. Lei Yuille is shown at a subsequent press conference, where she explained that her decision to help flowed from her religious self-conception.*

he did at speeds up to 55 miles per hour with Yuille in the cab and Murphy clinging to the running board while holding Denny fast. If we can partially interpret Murphy's and Green's decisions to intervene in terms of their physical abilities (Cramer, McMaster, Bartell, & Dragra, 1988; Huston et al., 1981), how are we to account for the actions of Lei Yuille, a slender, 38-year-old dietitian? What could have caused her to transcend the us-versus-them antagonisms of that day and speed herself to the aid of one of "them"? When asked, she described something about herself and her family that she felt provided the only answer necessary: "We are Christians," she said (Deutsch, 1993).

The mobilizing power of self-definition also contributes to a deeper understanding of Sempo Sugihara's benevolence toward the victims of Nazi persecution. Like Lei Yuille, Sugihara was once asked by an interviewer to explain his noble actions; and, like her, he answered by identifying a group membership that helped define him. "You must remember," he told the interviewer, "I come from a samurai family." Perplexed, because the samurai tradition in Japan had always been a warrior tradition, the interviewer pressed Sugihara further. He conceded that, yes, the samurai were noted for the destructive fury of their attacks on battlefield combatants, but that the beleaguered Jews who appeared at his door in July 1940 were hardly that. They were defenseless prey; consequently, there was a rule in the samurai code of conduct, *bushido*, that applied: "When a wounded bird flies into a samurai's coat, he is honor-bound to protect it. He must not throw it to the cat" (M. Tokayer, personal communication, May 19, 1994). In sum, our actions often flow from our conceptions of who we are or who we wish to be. When these existing or desired self-concepts require helpfulness, people in need frequently benefit.

Labeling and Self-Focus

If it is true that a prosocial self-image spurs people to help, it ought to be the case that any situational factor that reminds or convinces people of their prosocial nature should raise their motivation to help. Two such factors have been shown to work in this fashion: labeling and self-focus.

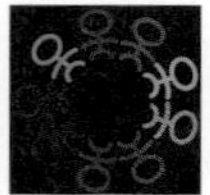

Labeling Effects Social theorists have long recognized that one way we decide who we are on the inside is to look outside ourselves to the reactions of others. Charles Horton Cooley (1922) proposed the notion of the "looking glass self," the idea that our self-images are greatly influenced by how others see us. Sociologists have used this perspective to explain how negative social labels—calling someone a deviant or a criminal—could create future antisocial behavior (Becker, 1963; Schur, 1971). Psychologists, however, have been more interested in examining the impact of positive social labels on prosocial behavior. For example, Joan Grusec and her coworkers (1978) found that labeling children as kind and helpful led these children to donate, anonymously, more of their experimental prizes to other children; furthermore, three weeks later, children labeled in this manner were still more willing to aid others (Grusec & Redler, 1980). Prosocial labels work on adults, too. One to two weeks after hearing themselves described as generous and charitable, New

Haven, Connecticut, residents were more willing to give a donation to the Multiple Sclerosis Society (Kraut, 1973).

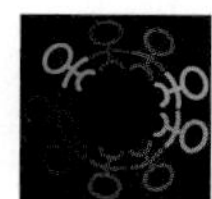

Self-Focus Because most of us value helping (Schroeder et al., 1995), it stands to reason that situational factors that focus us inside, on that personal value, should increase our helping efforts. Researchers have devised several creative techniques for getting subjects to focus on themselves—filling out a biographical questionnaire, posing for a photograph, watching themselves on closed-circuit TV, claiming personal responsibility for their emotions, looking in a mirror—all of which have led these self-focused subjects to help more (Duval, Duval, & Neely, 1979; Gibbons & Wicklund, 1982; Rogers, Miller, Mayer, & Duval, 1982). For instance, Claudia Hoover, Elizabeth Wood, and Eric Knowles (1983) found, first, that pedestrians who were stopped and asked to pose for a photograph (as part of a student's photography project) became more self-focused, as measured by the number of first-person pronouns *(I, me)* they used in an interview afterward. Second, after posing for the photograph, people were more helpful in picking up envelopes dropped by a passerby.

Oddly, though, some research has shown that self-focusing procedures can also decrease helping (Gibbons & Wicklund, 1982; Rogers et al., 1982). How can we explain this seeming contradiction? The key is to recognize that focusing on oneself doesn't guarantee that, when looking inside, one's value for helping will stand out. Suppose you just failed a test and something—let's say the presence of a mirror—caused you to focus attention on yourself. Chances are that, even if a helping opportunity arose, your internal focus would not be concentrated on your personal value for helping; more likely, it would be concentrated on your concern and frustration at failing the test. Thus, we might expect that when you're preoccupied with a personal problem, self-focus would orient you to your problem and away from your value for helping, making aid less likely. However, if you had no major personal problem to deal with while you were self-focused, and you encountered a salient, legitimate helping opportunity, you should orient to your internal helping values, making aid more likely (Froming, Nasby, & McManus, 1998). In fact, this is exactly the pattern of results found in a study done at the University of Texas by Frederick Gibbons and Robert Wicklund (1982). The presence of a mirror decreased the helpfulness of subjects who thought they had scored poorly on a test; but it increased the helpfulness of those who thought they had done fine and who, consequently, had no absorbing self-concern to distract them from helping issues.

Overall, what Gibbons and Wicklund's (1982) research demonstrates is that assistance is more frequent when self-focus is combined with the presence of a prominent, legitimate need for aid—because such a need will direct the internal focus toward one's helping values. When the need for aid is not salient or legitimate, however, or when there is some absorbing personal problem, self-focus will not lead to helping because the focus—although internal—will not be directed toward one's helping values (see Figure 9.5).

Deciding Not to Help Friends or to Seek Their Help

Frequently, to manage our self-images optimally through helping, we have to take into account features of the person we're helping and of the situation we're in. An illustration can be seen in a study done by Abraham Tesser and Jonathan Smith (1980), who began with the hypothesis that we will try to help our friends succeed as long as that success doesn't damage how we view ourselves. They reasoned that our self-esteem is determined by comparing ourselves to those we feel are similar to us—friends rather than strangers. Therefore, although we won't mind if our friends do better than us on unimportant tasks, we won't want them to do better than us on dimensions that are important to our self-esteem.

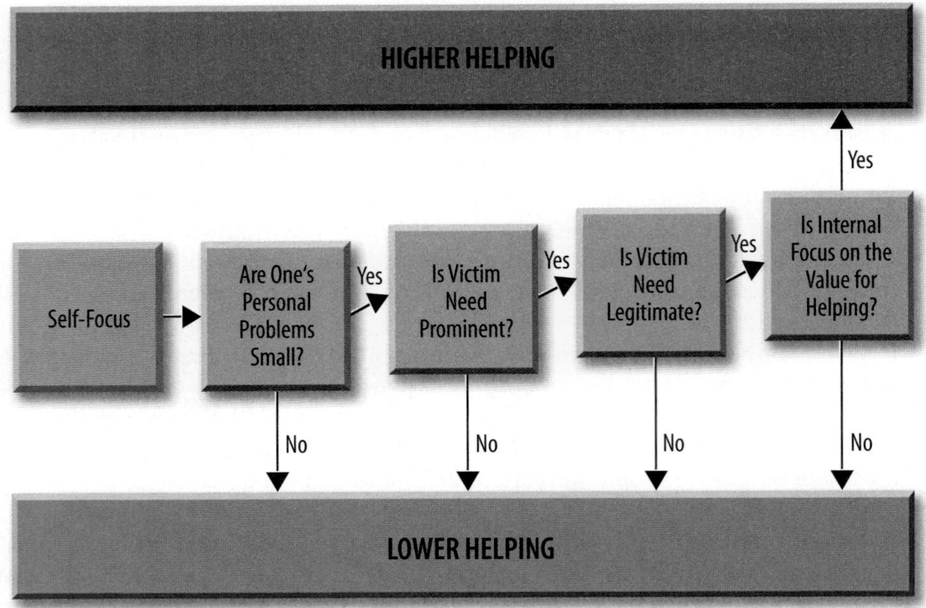

Figure 9.5
Self-focus and the decision to help.

Self-focus is likely to lead to greater assistance primarily when that focus is directed to one's internal value for helping. The presence of a large personal problem or the lack of a prominent, legitimate need for aid in the situation will channel the internal focus away from one's internal value for helping, and, consequently, may well reduce aid.

To test this reasoning, Tesser and Smith first arranged for participants to do somewhat poorly on a verbal skills task, which was described either as a good indicator of "how well people can do in school" or as just a game "that doesn't tell us anything about the person." Next these participants got the chance to give clues to help a friend and a stranger perform the verbal skills task. As predicted, when the task was described as just a game—and, hence, was mostly irrelevant to participants' self-concepts—friends were given better clues than were strangers. Just the reverse occurred, however, when they thought the task measured intellectual ability and was relevant to self-esteem; in that case, friends got the poorer clues. Thus we don't always try to support a positive self-image by helping more. Depending on who the recipient is and on how we wish to view ourselves, we may actually try to maintain self-esteem by helping less.

As we see next, when taken to extremes, this desire to maintain self-esteem within the helping process can lead to self-damaging decisions.

FOCUS ON Social Dysfunction

Failing to Seek Needed Help

Consider the following peculiar findings: In one study, male participants were given the opportunity to request help on a mechanical task they could not solve, but fewer than 10 percent did (DePaulo, 1982). In Japan, Sweden, and the United States, individuals who received money from another liked that person more when he asked for repayment than when he did not (Gergen, Ellsworth, Maslach, & Seipel, 1975). Rather than appearing thankful, the citizens and governments of countries that receive foreign aid often respond with resentment and hostility toward the donor nation (Gergen & Gergen, 1983).

What are we to make of these curious tendencies to avoid asking for needed assistance, to prefer those who require repayment of their gifts, and to risk future help by criticizing the actions and intentions of current helpers? Although the answer is complex, much of it is captured in the single, instructive comment of French anthropologist Marcel Mauss (1967, 67), "Charity wounds him who receives." The work of a trio of social psychologists, Jeffrey Fisher, Arie Nadler, and Bella DePaulo, has detailed the nature and location of the "wound"—it is to the self-concept and, more specifically, to the sense of self-esteem. These researchers have stressed that the receipt of aid, even much-needed aid, isn't always wholly positive (DePaulo & Fisher, 1980; Fisher, Nadler, & Witcher-Alagna, 1982; Nadler & Fisher, 1986). In the process of relieving the immediate problem, assistance may, under certain circumstances, threaten self-esteem by implying that the recipient is incompetent, inadequate, or dependent. It is under these circumstances that—to maintain a positive self-concept—an individual may reject offers of needed help or minimize the value of that help. What are these circumstances? Nadler (1991) lists several.

Gender. Beginning in elementary school and proceeding through adulthood, in the majority of settings, males are less willing than females to request assistance (Barbee et al., 1993; Barnett et al., 1990; Corney, 1990). Most observers explain this difference in terms of socialization rather than biology (Nadler, 1991; Schroeder et al., 1995). That is, being independent and in control is more congruent with the traditional masculine (versus feminine) gender role. Differential training in self-sufficiency starts quite early, as a mother is typically less willing to respond to the cries of her own baby if it is a boy than if it is a girl (Ruddy & Adams, 1995). Thus, while still in infancy, children are socialized into traditional gender-role behavior, and little boys begin learning to be "little men." To avoid violating this learned conception of masculinity, then, males may refrain from requesting aid. Support for this view comes from research showing that the help-seeking difference between the sexes is especially strong in men and women who subscribe to traditional gender roles (Nadler, Maler, & Friedman, 1984).

Some evidence suggests that the desire to be in control leads men to perceive more frequently that they have no real need for assistance (Bruder-Mattson & Hovanitz, 1990); thus, they see less reason to request it. This may help explain the infamous reluctance of men to ask for directions when traveling and women's consternation in the face of it: What women define as a problem requiring assistance ("I think we're lost. Let's pull over and ask for directions."), men do not ("Lost? We're not lost. We're not lost at all.").

Age. At two points in our lives, the tendency to seek help drops. The first occurs relatively early, around the age of seven or eight. According to Rita Shell and Nancy Eisenberg (1992), one reason for this shift is the development at that time of cognitive abilities that allow an enduring sense of self to be formed and threatened. It's not until after age seven or eight that children possess the mental capacity to recognize that the receipt of aid may imply lessened self-worth (Rholes & Ruble, 1986; Ruble, Feldman, & Boggiano, 1976). Consequently, it's not until after that age that they begin protecting their self-worth by resisting some opportunities for help.

The second drop in help seeking occurs much later, after the age of 60. It seems strange that just as people enter a time when they may become more needful of assistance, they become particularly unwilling to ask for it (Brown, 1978; Veroff, 1981). Once again, however, we can solve the puzzle by recognizing the sometimes-threatening impact that assistance can have on self-esteem. The elderly report being especially concerned about maintaining personal control and self-sufficiency (Lieberman & Tobin, 1983; Ryff, 1995). It makes sense, then, that they may reject opportunities for assistance that jeopardize their confidence that they still possess these qualities. Should you find yourself in the position of wishing to help the elderly, the existing research and thinking on the topic suggests that you do so in a way that preserves their independence and choice in the matter. Don't try to assume full control; instead, especially when their capacities are still intact, give elderly individuals responsibilities and options for managing the assistance (Reich & Zautra, 1995). Not only should they be more likely to accept the aid but also they are likely to be happier and healthier as a result than those given little control (Heckhausen & Schulz, 1995; Langer, 1989; Langer & Rodin, 1976).

Self-esteem. If you had to guess, would you say that high self-esteem or low self-esteem individuals are more reluctant to ask for assistance? Your first thought might be that those having low self-esteem would be more reluctant, in order to protect what little self-esteem they have. But research indicates the reverse. On academic tasks, in counseling groups, in alcohol treatment, and for a variety of other needs, it is high self-esteem people who avoid help seeking (Nadler, 1991; Wills & DePaulo, 1991). Why? Arie Nadler (1986) explains these findings in terms of the desire of such individuals to maintain their images of themselves as highly competent. In support of this explanation, studies have shown reduced help seeking among high self-esteem persons only in situations in which getting help would threaten a competent self-image—for example, when needing aid reflects low intelligence (Tessler & Schwartz, 1972). ■

Summary

It appears that people can and do use prosocial activity to support their self-image. Therefore, when prosocial beliefs and values are important to one's self-concept, helping is more frequent. For example, people having strong religious beliefs and values—which typically favor prosocial action—are more helpful than those whose self-concept is not tied so closely to religious beliefs and values. Similarly, individuals who have strong personal norms toward helping are more likely to engage in prosocial action. Situational influences that reinforce a person's prosocial self-definition also increase assistance. For instance, individuals who hear themselves labeled as generous or kind become more helpful as a result. And people who are made to focus inward after seeing a prominent helping opportunity are more likely to provide aid because the inward gaze will make their helping values more salient. An exception to this finding occurs when the potential helper has an absorbing personal problem—because the internal focus is likely to fall on the problem rather than on any personal value for helping. Finally, the way people use helping to manage their self-concept often depends on an interaction between person and situation factors. We can see examples of this in the decision to accept or reject aid. Individuals who have high (but not low) levels of self-esteem tend to refuse assistance if the features of the situation threaten their view of themselves as competent and self-sufficient.

Managing Our Emotions and Moods

Help can be rewarding—and not just for the one who receives it. As we've seen, helpers can use it to produce material or genetic gain, to get social approval, and to support their self-image. There's another, even more direct way that help can benefit the helper—by removing the unpleasant state of arousal that comes from witnessing a victim's suffering. Think of the agitation and alarm you would feel if you came upon a family trapped and crying for rescue from the window of a burning building. The sight of their terrified faces, the sounds of their agonized pleas would no doubt trigger a powerful negative emotional reaction in you. Helping might be the most straightforward way for you to eliminate the emotional distress because it would eliminate the cause, the victims' plight.

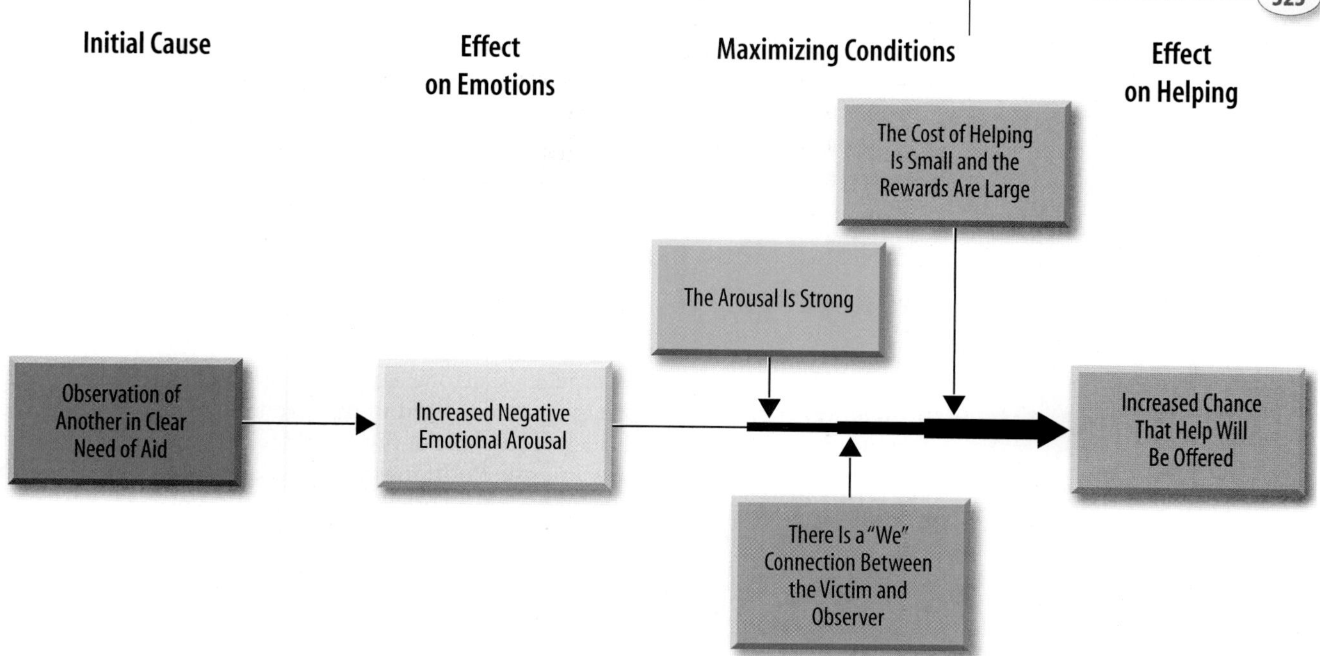

Figure 9.6
The arousal/cost–reward model of emergency helping.

According to the arousal/cost-reward model, people who observe another in clear need of emergency aid will experience negative emotional arousal and will want to help to relieve this personal distress. There are three conditions under which assistance will be maximized: when the arousal is strong, when there is a "we" connection between the victim and the observer, and when the cost of helping is small while the rewards are large.

Managing Emotional Arousal in Emergencies: The Arousal/Cost–Reward Model

This motivation for helping—to reduce the aversive arousal (distress) that we feel when observing substantial suffering or need—is the cornerstone of the **arousal/cost–reward model** developed by Jane Piliavin and her colleagues (Dovidio, Piliavin, Gaertner, Schroeder, & Clark, 1991; Piliavin et al., 1981) to explain helpfulness in emergencies. It proposes that observers of an emergency victim's plight will experience negative emotional arousal and will want to lend assistance in order to relieve this personal distress. According to the model, there are several conditions under which assistance should be most likely, all of which have received research support (see Figure 9.6).

1. *When the arousal is strong.* If negative arousal stimulates helping, the more an emergency generates such arousal in observers, the more helping it should produce. Several studies, using both physiological and verbal measures of arousal, have supported this prediction (Cramer et al., 1988; Gaertner & Dovidio, 1977; Krebs, 1975). In fact, when John Dovidio (1984) examined six studies of emergency aid that measured arousal, he found in each instance that as arousal rose in lone bystanders, so did their tendency to leap to the aid of victims.
2. *When there is a "we" connection between the victim and helper.* People are more willing to help those with whom they share an identity or similarity (a sense of "we-ness"), and this is especially so in life-and-death or emergency situations involving decisions about whom to rescue from a burning building (Burnstein, Crandall, & Kitayama, 1994). One reason this seems to be the case is that observers are more aroused by the plight of someone they feel connected with (Krebs, 1975).
3. *When reducing arousal through helping involves small costs and large rewards.* Because negative emotional arousal is unpleasant, those who can end it by helping will be motivated to do so. However, this should not be true, according to the model, if the helping act itself is even more unpleasant (costly) than the emotional distress—for example, if helping means having to make contact with the victim's blood (Piliavin & Piliavin, 1972). In sum, to the

Arousal/cost–reward model
The view that observers of a victim's suffering will want to help in order to relieve their own personal distress.

extent that helping is a low cost–high reward activity, people will relieve their negative emotional arousal prosocially. As the net cost of helping escalates, however, they are increasingly likely to choose other ways to reduce their emotional distress, such as leaving the scene (Dovidio et al., 1991).

Managing Mood in Nonemergencies: The Negative State Relief Model

The arousal/cost–reward model has proven very successful at explaining how and why helping occurs in emergencies: strong emotional arousal is typically part of an emergency and, thus, helping can be used to manage that arousal. In nonemergency situations, in which such arousal is not normally present, individuals may still use helping to manage less intense emotional states: their moods. The idea that helping is a tactic that people sometimes use to influence their moods is called the **mood management hypothesis,** a part of the *negative state relief model* of helping (Cialdini, Kenrick, & Baumann, 1982; Schaller & Cialdini, 1990), which holds that people use helping to manage one particular mood—temporary sadness.

According to the negative state relief model, people often help to relieve their sadness because helping can be a reinforcing, mood-enhancing experience for them. One reason that prosocial activity may be reinforcing is that it has frequently been associated with reward in the past. Think about it. Hasn't it been the case that, since early childhood, you've gotten smiles, praise, or approval from your parents and teachers when you've shared with those around you? And hasn't it been the case as well that those you helped were more likely to do something nice for you in return? By virtue of the process of conditioning, this repeated pairing of prosocial activity with reward has likely worked to make you experience helping as pleasant and rewarding in itself (Aronfreed, 1968; Grusec, 1991).

Good support for the idea that giving assistance can pick up a person's spirits comes from laboratory studies showing that the act of helping can raise a helper's mood (Harris, 1977; Williamson & Clark, 1989; Williamson, Clark, Pegalis, & Behan, 1996) and from national surveys showing that, after the act, donors to charity feel better (Hodgkinson & Weitzman, 1994) and volunteers report feeling a "helper's high" (Luks, 1988). In the following sections, we examine the personal and situational factors that affect when people use aid to dispel their own sadness.

Presence of Sadness The most basic principle of the negative state relief model is that, because prosocial action can raise one's mood, temporarily saddened individuals will use it to feel better again. If this is so, people who respond with sadness to another's plight should help more, as indeed they do. For instance, in a pair of experiments, subjects watched as a young woman received electric shock as part of a "learning task." After recording their moods, they had the chance to volunteer to take some additional shocks for her. In both studies, those conditions that generated the most sadness also generated the most volunteers (Batson et al., 1989; Cialdini et al., 1987).

The more interesting prediction of the negative state relief model, however, is that helping can be used to raise a mood that was lowered by an event unrelated to a victim's plight. So, suppose you were feeling sad because something caused you to recall the death of a childhood pet and, while in that mood, you were asked to help a stranger. According to the model, you might be especially inclined to do so because the pleasurable effect of doing someone a good turn could counteract your sadness. In fact, con artists frequently employ a tactic that relies on just such a tendency. They first look in the obituary column of the local newspaper to identify relatives of recently deceased residents. Then, after waiting a few days for the emotional turmoil to subside—but not so long that the sadness has drained away—they visit these relatives' homes with a hard-luck story; a favorite is that they are selling magazine

Mood management hypothesis
The idea that people use helping tactically to manage their moods.

subscriptions to earn enough money to reenroll in college. Under these conditions, the bereaved are said to be "easy marks"—presumably because by doing good they can make themselves feel better, at least for a while. In keeping with this logic, research has demonstrated that helping levels can jump significantly in people exposed to techniques that increase temporary sadness, such as reminiscing about unhappy events, reading a series of depressing statements, failing at a task, and doing or just witnessing harm to another (Cialdini, Kenrick, & Baumann, 1982).

Age Recall that the negative state relief model says that helping becomes gratifying in itself by being repeatedly associated with various kinds of approval and reward throughout childhood and that, after coming to be pleasurable in this way, it can be used to counteract temporary sadness. If this is true, the tendency to give assistance when sad should depend to some degree on age. Young children should be the least likely to help when sad because for them, helping hasn't been paired with reward often enough to have acquired a rewarding quality. But as children age and experience a longer history of such pairings, they should be increasingly willing to help when sad to elevate their mood. Research has generally supported this prediction (Cialdini & Kenrick, 1976; Perry, Perry, & Weiss, 1986). In one study, students of three age groups (six to eight, ten to twelve, and fifteen to eighteen) were given prize coupons for performing a task and then were allowed to donate some of their winnings to other students at their school. Before they got the chance to share their coupons, however, some were put in a sad mood by having them think about sorrowful experiences. Sadness increased donations primarily among the oldest students, suggesting that only they were employing sharing as a way to make themselves feel better (Cialdini & Kenrick, 1976). These data suggest that it is not until their early teens that children experience the good feeling that accompanies prosocial choices and, consequently, make those choices to adjust their moods.

Costs/Benefits of Helping Suppose that while feeling a bit depressed, you had the chance to be helpful. Under which situational conditions would your sadness lead you to grasp the opportunity? If, as the negative state relief model suggests, managing mood is one motivation for prosocial action, the answer is clear: those conditions that would allow helping to elevate your mood.

It stands to reason that if you want to relieve a negative mood through helping, you should try to find the most painless route. After all, aid that costs you great amounts of time, energy, or resources might make you feel even worse rather than better for it. Therefore, those who start out in a saddened state ought to be especially sensitive to the cost/benefit aspects of helping opportunities.

James Weyant (1978) investigated this idea using a clever experimental procedure. First, he put Florida State University students into a happy, neutral, or sad mood. Then, he gave them a chance to volunteer for a nonprofit organization—either an organization that would generate a relatively large personal benefit by allowing them to feel they had supported an important cause (the American Cancer Society) or one that would produce a relatively small such benefit (Little League Baseball). Finally, half of the students were told that if they decided to help, they would have to collect donations in a personally costly fashion, by going door to door; the other half were told that they could collect donations in a way that didn't involve much personal cost, by sitting at a donations desk. Although students in a happy mood volunteered more than those in a neutral mood, these two kinds of participants weren't much affected by the costs and benefits of the helping opportunity. However, those in a sad mood were dramatically affected, helping most when the benefits outweighed the costs and helping least when the costs outweighed the benefits (see Figure 9.7). It appears, then, that saddened individuals are particularly choosy about the prosocial activities they select, volunteering for those likely to dispel their negative mood and avoiding those likely to deepen it.

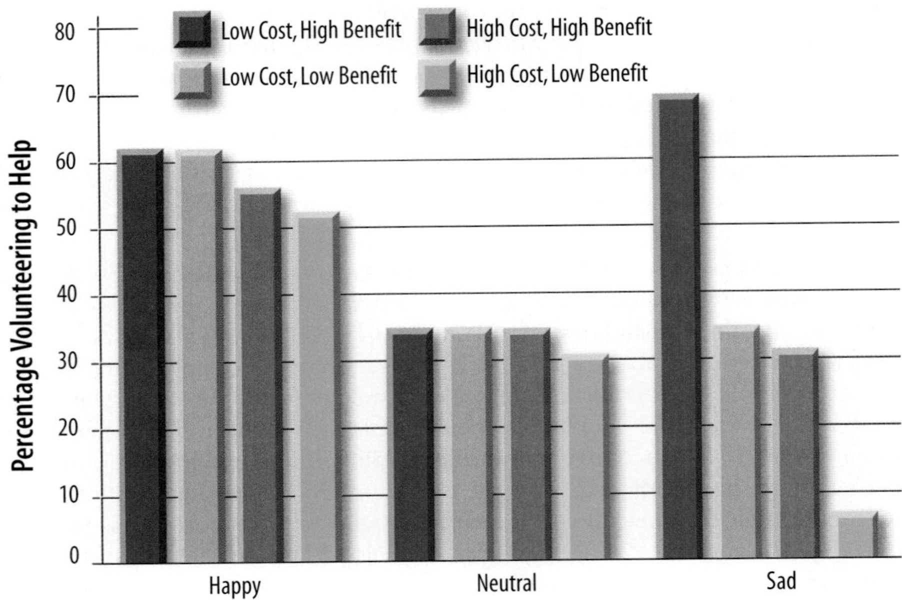

Figure 9.7
Sad and selective.

Subjects put into a happy, neutral, or sad mood got the chance to assist a nonprofit organization in a way that promised either high or low personal benefit and either high or low personal cost. Only the saddened individuals took the cost/benefit factors into account in deciding to volunteer. In this sense, saddened individuals seem to take a discriminating approach to helping opportunities, choosing sensitively among those likely to provide high-versus-low quality experiences.

SOURCE: *From Weyant, 1976.*

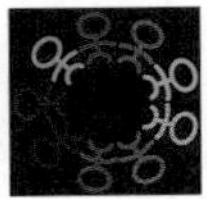

Ability of the Helping Act to Influence Mood For anyone interested in relieving sadness, a prosocial act should be attractive to the extent that it is able to change mood. Hence, if you were feeling so low that you thought nothing could cheer you up, helping wouldn't be especially likely because, under those circumstances, you couldn't use it to manage your mood. This is one reason that deeply depressed people, who don't believe that pleasurable activities can make them feel better, don't show elevated helping levels (Morris & Kanfer, 1983).

To test the idea that saddened individuals will help more only when they think their moods are changeable, one study put participants into a sad, neutral, or happy mood and then gave them a placebo drug (tonic water). Half were told the drug would "freeze" their current mood so that normal activities would not change it for the next thirty minutes. The other half thought their present mood was changeable. Finally, all got the chance to volunteer to contact blood donors by making phone calls. Although the placebo drug information didn't affect the helping decisions of those in a neutral or happy mood, this wasn't so for the saddened participants, whose helping increased solely when they thought their moods could be changed by it (Manucia, Baumann, & Cialdini, 1984).

Gourmets and Gourmands There is a French word used in the English language that simultaneously implies restraint *and* indulgence, reticence *and* enthusiasm, fastidiousness *and* passion, apathy *and* intensity. Before reading on, think for a moment about what it might be and about how a single word could possibly incorporate so many opposites. The word is *gourmet*, which refers to a person who reacts with uncommon disdain or uncommon relish to an item (usually food), depending on its quality. If it is unappealing or subpar in some way—an overcooked meal, perhaps—a gourmet, even a hungry one, is more likely than most to sniff and walk away. But if the offering promises great pleasure, the gourmet will partake fully and zealously. Much evidence indicates that saddened individuals confronted with a helping opportunity take a gourmet's approach: Because mood management is a goal, they are selective and discriminating, choosing those opportunities that offer the prospect of an especially rewarding experience and avoiding those that do not (Cunningham, Shaffer, Barbee, Wolff, & Kelley, 1990; Manucia et al., 1984; Weyant, 1978).

But this tendency to manage mood by taking advantage of only the most personally rewarding prosocial activities isn't equally strong in all people. In fact, it interacts with the kind of mood (happy or sad) a person is in. Although temporarily elated people are usually helpful (Salovey, Mayer, & Rosenhan, 1991), they don't seem to use helping to manage their moods in the gourmet fashion of temporarily sad people. Rather, they approach helping situations in the manner of the *gourmand*—a person of hearty appetite but indiscriminate taste, eager to partake robustly of whatever the environment provides. Thus, we find elated individuals especially willing to help whether the helping act promises to be rewarding or not. To understand why, let's examine some of the earliest evidence that happiness does indeed lead to benevolence.

Alice Isen and her coworkers have demonstrated the powerful impact of positive mood on helping in natural settings. For example, in a study done in San Francisco and Philadelphia shopping malls (Isen & Levin, 1972), shoppers were made to feel happy when, after making a call from a public phone, they found a coin that the researchers had secretly placed in the return slot. Other shoppers found no such coin. After completing their calls, all of the shoppers passed a female confederate who dropped a manila envelope filled with papers. Whereas very few people who had found no coin stopped to help pick up the papers (12 percent), almost all of those who had found a coin did so (96 percent).

What is it about positive mood that increases a person's benevolence? The answer seems to lie in the tendency of elated people to see themselves and their environments in exceptionally rosy terms. They like others more than do neutral mood individuals (Forgas & Bower, 1987). In addition, they feel more competent (Alloy, Abramson, & Viscusi, 1981) and more optimistic about their future fortunes (Forgas & Moylan, 1987). For each of these reasons, then, we can see why happy individuals would be willing to give some of their resources to a needy other.

Finally, elated people tend to think about and remember the positive rather than negative features of almost anything they consider, including helping situations (Isen, Shalker, Clark, & Karp, 1978). That is, when encountering a helping opportunity, happy individuals will be especially likely to recall the positive aspects of past helping situations and to focus on the positive aspects of the present one. With so upbeat a view of the rewards and costs of aid, it's not surprising that happy people are helpers. In support of this account, Margaret Clark and Barbara Waddell (1983) found that a helping opportunity evoked significantly more positive thoughts from happy (versus neutral mood) individuals. This explanation for the greater prosocial activity of happy individuals may also explain their rather unselective, gourmand-like approach to helping situations of differing quality. It may not be that they aren't concerned about managing their mood, it may just be that, because of their sunny, confident orientation, it rarely occurs or appears to them that helping could damage that mood (Mayer & Gaschke, 1988).

Summary

People try to manage their emotions and moods through prosocial actions. In the case of emergencies, in which the emotion involved is usually an intense form of unpleasant arousal (distress), there are three conditions under which people are particularly likely to aid another as a way of reducing their distress: when the arousal is strong, when there is a "we" connection between the victim and the helper, and when reducing the arousal through helping involves small costs and large rewards for the helper. Less intense states, such as temporary sadness, can also be managed through helping. However, certain circumstances reduce the helpfulness of sad individuals: when they are too young (below teenage) to recognize and experience aid as personally rewarding, when the helping act looks too costly, or when it seems unable to change the mood. By contrast, temporary elation increases assistance in a wider range of helping situations, probably because it causes an overly positive view of the world, including helping opportunities. See Table 9.1 for a summary of each of the major goals of prosocial behavior.

CHAPTER 9
Summary Table

Table 9.1 Summary of the goals served by prosocial action and the factors related to them.

The Goal	The Person	The Situation	Interactions
Gaining Genetic and Material Benefits	• Instilled beliefs regarding prosocial action • An expanded sense of "we"	• Similarity of victim to helper • Familiarity of victim to helper	• Those who think of prosocial activity as a way to benefit themselves are more helpful only when they can be compensated for the help. • The tendency to aid relatives over nonrelatives is especially strong when the need is life-threatening.
Gaining Social Status and Approval	• Need for approval • Awareness of the helping norm	• Helping models • Population density	• Whether males or females help more depends on whether the helping action fits more with the masculine or feminine gender role.
Managing Self-Image	• Self-concept • Personal norms • Religious codes	• Labeling • Self-focus	• The decision to help a friend over a stranger depends on the impact on one's self-concept. • High self-esteem can lead one to refuse needed aid if the aid threatens self-concept.
Managing Our Emotions and Moods	• Sadness • Age	• Costs/benefits of helping • Ability of helping to influence mood	• People in a sad mood approach helping selectively, choosing opportunities that appear rewarding; but people in a happy mood are much less selective, choosing to help in a wide range of situations.

Does Pure Altruism Exist?

It is rare for a common English word to have been coined by a psychologist, but that is the case for *empathy*. The great figure of American experimental psychology, Edward Bradford Titchener (1909), first fashioned it out of a German art term that referred to the tendency of observers to project themselves into what they saw—the way we might mentally place ourselves in the scene of a painting or into the shoes of another. This process of putting oneself in the place of another is called **perspective taking.** It's one reason that most researchers find a strong connection between empathy and prosocial action, as people who assume the perspective of a needy other are more likely to help (Davis, 1994; Krebs & Russell, 1981; Underwood & Moore, 1982). It seems that when you put yourself in a victim's shoes, they will likely take you to their owner's aid.

This appears to be true even among individuals who provide help for a living. In one study, those professional psychotherapists who possessed a strong, natural tendency for perspective taking were especially willing to help a young woman who needed assistance with an article she was writing on psychotherapy (Otten, Penner, & Altabe, 1991). Although perspective taking (a cognitive activity) has been seen as a feature of empathy from the time of Titchener, modern theorists have added a second component to the mix, an emotional component that involves sharing the feelings of another (Eisenberg & Miller, 1987). Hence, empathy is best viewed as including both the cognitive process of putting oneself in another's position and the emotional result of experiencing what the other is feeling (Davis, 1994).

Perspective taking *The process of mentally putting oneself in another's position.*

What's noteworthy about empathy is the claim, made most forcefully by C. Daniel Batson and his associates, that when one empathizes with a suffering other, a special form of helping can result that is purely altruistic, that is, motivated only by a concern for the other's welfare. Although Batson (1991) concedes that help is often designed for personal gain—to make a good impression, to bolster self-concept, to relieve distress or sadness, and so on—he says that when empathy enters the picture, the basic motivation for helping can shift from self*ish* to self*less*. In other words, the goal of improving another's welfare can become dominant, suppressing—even supplanting—the goal of improving one's own welfare.

Perspective taking: Putting yourself in another's blues. *If you came upon this scene, what are the chances that you would help? They would jump significantly if you first imagined yourself in the needy person's position.*

The Empathy–Altruism Sequence

What's the sequence of events that can turn us from egoistic (selfish) to altruistic (selfless)? Batson and Laura Shaw (1991) think it proceeds as follows: The process of perspective taking, in which we try to put ourselves in another's position, can first be stimulated by perceived similarity between ourselves and the other, or by an attachment (kinship, friendship, prior contact) we have to the other, or simply by instructions to take the other's perspective (Batson, Turk, Shaw, & Klein, 1995). Second, provided that the other is needy or suffering in some way, the perspective taking will cause us to experience **empathic concern**—feelings of warmth, tenderness, and compassion toward the other. Empathic concern, which some theorists label *sympathy* (Wispé, 1991), is the key element of Batson's model because, unlike such emotional responses as personal distress and sadness, it is said to orient helpers away from a focus on their own welfare and onto a focus on the other's welfare. According to Batson, empathic concern leads directly to altruistic motivation—the desire to better another's welfare for its own sake—and, thus, to pure altruism (see Figure 9.8).

To support the idea of pure altruism, Batson and his associates have done a series of experiments attempting to show that various egoistic motivations can't explain the pattern of helping that occurs when people feel empathic concern for another. In one study (Batson, Duncan, Ackerman, Buckley, & Birch, 1981), for instance, they wanted to demonstrate that participants experiencing empathic concern for a victim—"Elaine," a fellow participant who was receiving electric shocks—would help in a way that couldn't be explained simply as a selfish attempt to reduce their own unpleasant arousal at seeing her suffer.

Empathic concern was instilled in certain participants by telling them that they were very similar to Elaine in values and interests. Reasoning that individuals observing suffering could reduce their resulting arousal either by ending the victim's plight or by leaving the scene, the researchers gave subjects the chance to volunteer to take a set of eight remaining shocks for Elaine after they had seen her react badly to an initial pair of shocks. Half of the participants (Difficult Escape) were told that if they decided not to help, they would nonetheless have to stay and continue to watch Elaine suffer the remaining shocks; the rest (Easy Escape) were told that if they decided not to help, they could leave immediately. You would think that people motivated primarily to reduce their unpleasant arousal as painlessly as possible would help less in the Easy Escape condition, in which they could quickly leave the source of the arousal without having to endure any shocks. That is exactly what happened—*except* when they felt empathic concern for Elaine. Under those circumstances, it didn't matter whether escape was easy or difficult for them; they stayed and helped.

Empathic concern *Compassionate feelings caused by taking the perspective of a needy other.*

Batson (1991) has interpreted these findings as indicating that egoistic motives, such as the desire to reduce unpleasant arousal, may often determine whether an individual helps but that these reasons may no longer play a decisive role once the individual feels empathic concern for the victim. This is because, then, the crucial

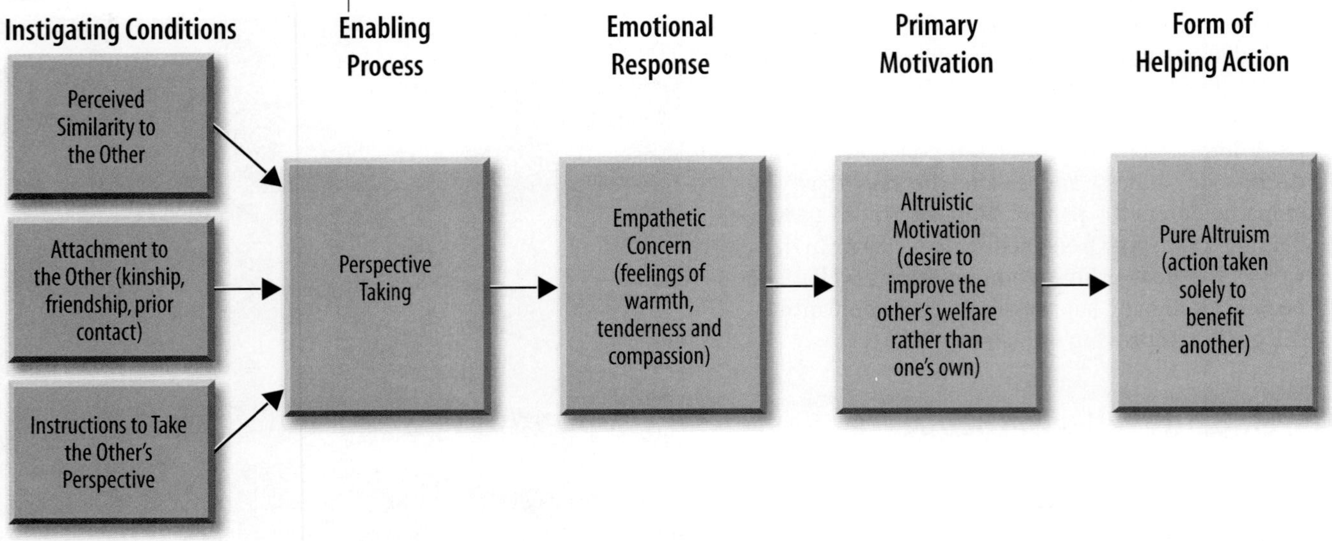

Instigating Conditions	Enabling Process	Emotional Response	Primary Motivation	Form of Helping Action
Perceived Similarity to the Other; Attachment to the Other (kinship, friendship, prior contact); Instructions to Take the Other's Perspective	Perspective Taking	Empathetic Concern (feelings of warmth, tenderness and compassion)	Altruistic Motivation (desire to improve the other's welfare rather than one's own)	Pure Altruism (action taken solely to benefit another)

Figure 9.8
Batson's model of the road to altruism.

Pure altruism requires special circumstances, according to Batson's empathy–altruism model.

motivation to help is no longer selfish but is truly altruistic. Using a similar logic, he and his coworkers have attempted to show that empathic concern overwhelms the influence of many of the other possible egoistic motives for helping: to gain social approval (Archer, 1984; Fultz, Batson, Fortenbach, McCarthy, & Varney, 1986), to bolster self-concept (Batson et al., 1988), to relieve sadness (Batson et al., 1989; Cialdini, Schaller, et al., 1987; Schroeder, Dovidio, Sibicky, Matthews, & Allen, 1988), and to make oneself feel happy (Batson et al., 1991; Smith, Keating, & Stotland, 1989). By examining and discounting the impact of each of these egoistic motives when empathy is present, Batson's research has added provocatively to the evidence suggesting that pure altruism can exist.

An Egoistic Interpretation

You might notice, however, that one important selfish reason for prosocial behavior hasn't been tested in Batson's work. It is the first motive we considered in this chapter—to ensure the survival of one's genes. Furthermore, in looking back at that section of the chapter, you might also notice that the factors that Batson says lead a person to feel empathic concern for another are identical to the factors that signal shared genes with another—kinship, similarity, friendship, and prior contact (familiarity). It may be, then, that feelings of empathic concern stimulate helping because they inform us that the recipient of that concern is likely to possess a greater than normal percentage of our genes (Kenrick, 1991; Krebs, 1991). This leads to the ironic possibility that when we feel empathy for another, we may be helpful not because of the most elevated motive—pure altruism—but because of the most primitive one—genetic advantage.

How could it occur that empathic feelings would be associated with shared heredity? During the thousands of years when human behavior patterns were first developing, we lived in small bands—roving tribal villages—of genetically similar individuals who learned to communicate with one another in very basic ways, including the communication of emotion that comes from perspective taking (Buck & Ginzberg, 1991; Hoffman, 1984). Because this kind of empathic communication took place most frequently with members of one's family and tribe, the experience of empathy for another was linked with genetic similarity. What could have easily evolved, then, is a tendency to aid those with whom one empathizes (kin, friends, similar or familiar others) because they are likely to be one's relatives and that aid is therefore likely to increase the survival of one's own genes.

Of course, most people aren't likely to be conscious of such a process when deciding to help someone whose perspective they've taken. Instead, all they are likely to feel is a greater sense of identity or oneness with another (Galinsky & Moskowitz, 2000). This might explain why, in one study, college students who were asked to take the perspective of a fellow student came to see more of themselves in that person (Davis, Conklin, Smith, & Luce, 1996). This tendency to immerse ourselves in those with whom we empathize raises a crucial question about the existence of pure altruism: If empathy causes us to see our*selves* in another, can the decision to help that other be truly selfless?

Although there can be debate on that question (Batson et al., 1997; Cialdini, Brown, Lewis, Luce, & Neuberg, 1997), there's little doubt that when we do take another's perspective, the impact on helping can be dramatic.

Summary

According to the empathy-altruism model, empathic concern for a needy other can spur pure altruism—helping intended simply to improve the other's welfare. Furthermore, perspective taking, which produces empathic concern, can be brought about by instructions to take another's perspective or by perceived attachments to the other (similarity, kinship, familiarity, friendship). In support of this model, those who take another's perspective do feel empathic concern and do appear to want to help for reasons having to do with the other's welfare rather than their own. A nonaltruistic explanation exists, however, for why perspective taking leads to seemingly selfless aid: The factors that lead naturally to perspective taking (similarity, kinship, familiarity, friendship) are traditional cues of common genetic make-up. Thus, perspective taking may stimulate feelings of shared heredity, and the resultant helping may serve the goal of promoting one's own (genetic) welfare rather than the purely altruistic goal of promoting another's welfare.

REVISITING
The Case of Sempo Sugihara

We began this chapter with an account of Sempo Sugihara's decision to assist Jewish refugees in Lithuania while knowing that this assistance would destroy his long-cherished diplomatic career. The decision was bewildering on its surface because there seemed nothing about the man that could have predicted his actions. But below the surface, we promised, there were features of Sugihara and of his situation that, like uncovered clues, could resolve the mystery. Let's revisit and summarize those features.

First, during his childhood, Sugihara witnessed memorable acts of kindness by his parents. Although such kindness likely had a general influence on his prosocial nature, there was something special about it that may have had a specific impact on his decision to help the Jews: those whom his parents assisted were often foreigners—strangers and travelers given shelter and care. This early experience may well have led Sugihara to include a wider-than-normal range of individuals in his sense of "we." Indeed, from his subsequent comments, it appears that he expanded the boundaries of "we" beyond the immediate or extended family to the human family.

Second, Sugihara developed a personal attachment to an eleven-year-old Jewish boy, which provided the opportunity for social contact with the boy's family. If, as research evidence suggests (Batson et al., 1995), attachment and contact of this sort led him to empathize more readily with the plight of these individuals, it is not surprising that the boy's family would have received the first exit visa Sugihara wrote. Nor is it surprising that, after once committing himself to such a rescue effort, he would continue to assist similar others in a similar fashion (see chapter 6 for a discussion of the role of initial commitments in producing consistent later behavior).

Finally, Sugihara's willingness to sacrifice himself for the benefit of defenseless victims is consistent with his samurai background and self-image. To have "thrown a wounded bird to the cat" would have violated a code of conduct that was central to an important component of his self-definition. And, as we have seen, individuals will often go to great lengths to assure that their actions coincide with their preferred or existing self-concept.

When viewed beneath the surface, then, Sempo Sugihara's puzzling behavior seems not so puzzling after all. Rather, it appears quite compatible with the action of three factors—an expanded sense of "we," a prior attachment to the victim, and a helping-relevant self-image—that have been shown to stimulate prosocial acts in a wide variety of individuals. But, one might ask, "Well, which one of the three factors did it? Which spurred him to begin writing the visas?" This seems a poor question. It presumes that there's only one cause of any particular act. It's naive to suppose that a helping decision as complex as Sugihara's—or most helping decisions, for that matter—could be attributed to a single cause. More likely, it was an interaction of factors—perhaps all three that we've described plus others we haven't uncovered—that pushed him to action.

One last question deserves consideration. Now that we think we know why Mr. Sugihara made his self-sacrificial choice, now that we can explain it in terms of ordinary influences on prosocial activity, should we find it any less awe-inspiring, any less noteworthy? Not in the least. Too often, observers treat human mysteries resolved like magic tricks revealed: Once the unknown is dispelled, wonder decays and attention drifts, as if there's nothing left to marvel at. But this is a superficial view, because what remains after the unknown is dispelled is the known, the marvelously systematic known. Perhaps the most awe-inspiring aspect of Sugihara's astonishing decision is that it can be traced to a set of recognized and rather commonplace motives for helping.

CHAPTER 9

Summary

Defining Prosocial Behavior

1. Prosocial behavior is action intended to benefit another.
2. There are two more limited types of prosocial behavior: benevolence, which is action intended to benefit another but not for external reward, and pure altruism, which is action intended solely to benefit another, thus not for internal or external reward.

Gaining Genetic and Material Benefits

1. People sometimes help to improve their own inclusive fitness (the survival of genes in offspring and relatives). This goal can be achieved by such means as aiding relatives or giving to nonrelatives who are likely to help in return (reciprocal aid).
2. People will be more likely to help another when early childhood experiences, similarity, and familiarity lead them to see the other in terms of family (the genetic "we").
3. Behavior geneticists, who use such methods as twin studies to determine how much of a behavior is due to heredity versus environment, typically find that both genetic and environmental factors are important causes.

Gaining Social Status and Approval

1. Because helping is typically valued in a culture, people may help to gain prestige and social approval.
2. Individuals having a strong need for approval are more likely to help under public circumstances.
3. The most general helping norm is the norm of social responsibility, which states that we should help those who are dependent on us for assistance. Once children become aware of this norm, they are more likely to help in the presence of adults who can give them approval for the aid.
4. Factors that draw attention to the social responsibility norm (for example, helping models) lead to more helping.
5. Bystanders observing possible emergencies influence the decision to help in three ways: by serving as sources of potential aid, by serving as sources of information about whether aid is required, and by

serving as sources of approval or disapproval for helping.

6. Consistent with the socially approved masculine gender role, men help more when the situation requires heroic, direct assistance of the needy, including strangers. Consistent with the socially approved feminine gender role, women help more when the situation calls for nurturant, supportive help for relationship members.

Managing Self-Image

1. Because prosocial behavior can affect how people view themselves, they can use it to both enhance and verify their self-definitions.
2. Persons possessing strong religious codes and personal norms toward helping appear to help in order to act in accord with their self-images.
3. The labels others apply to us affect our self-images. Therefore, when we are labeled as generous or kind, we become more helpful.
4. Because most people value helping, they become more prosocial when they are made to focus inside on these values.
5. Not only does giving aid affect self-concept, so does accepting aid—by implying to the recipient that he or she may be incompetent, dependent, or inadequate.

Managing Our Emotions and Moods

1. Because helping is experienced as rewarding, it can be used to relieve an unpleasant state in the helper.
2. In emergencies, this unpleasant state is aversive arousal (distress), which, according to the arousal/cost–reward model, leads to assistance principally when (1) the arousal is strong, (2) there is a "we" connection between the victim and helper, and (3) reducing the arousal involves small costs and large rewards.
3. In nonemergency situations, helping can relieve the unpleasant state of sadness. According to the negative state relief model, temporarily saddened individuals help more when they (1) are old enough (early teens) to experience helping as self-rewarding, (2) see the personal benefits of aid outweighing the costs, and (3) view the help as able to influence their moods.
4. Elated individuals help in a wide range of situations, probably because they have an overly positive view of helping opportunities.

Does Pure Altruism Exist?

1. According to the empathy–altruism model, people who experience empathic concern for a needy other are willing to help simply to improve his or her welfare (pure altruism). Furthermore, perspective taking, which produces empathic concern, can be brought about by perceived attachments to another (similarity, kinship, familiarity, friendship).
2. In support of this model, those who take another's perspective do feel empathic concern and do appear—at least on the surface—to want to help for reasons having to do with the other's welfare rather than their own.
3. A nonaltruistic explanation exists, however, for why perspective taking leads to seemingly selfless aid: The factors that lead naturally to perspective taking (similarity, kinship, familiarity, friendship) are traditional cues of shared genetic makeup. Thus, perspective taking may spur feelings of shared heredity, and the resultant helping may serve the goal of promoting one's own (genetic) welfare.

CHAPTER 9
Key Terms

Arousal/cost–reward model *The view that observers of a victim's suffering will want to help in order to relieve their own personal distress.*

Benevolence *Action intended to benefit another but not to gain external reward.*

Diffusion of responsibility *The tendency for each group member to dilute personal responsibility for acting by spreading it among all other group members.*

Empathic concern *Compassionate feelings caused by taking the perspective of a needy other.*

Inclusive fitness *The survival of one's genes in one's own offspring and in any relatives one helps.*

Mood management hypothesis *The idea that people use helping tactically to manage their moods.*

Personal norms *The internalized beliefs and values that combine to form a person's inner standards for behavior.*

Perspective taking *The process of mentally putting oneself in another's position.*

Prosocial behavior *Action intended to benefit another.*

Pure (true) altruism *Action intended solely to benefit another and thus not to gain external or internal reward.*

Reciprocal aid *Helping that occurs in return for prior help.*

Social responsibility norm *The societal rule that people should help those who need them to help.*

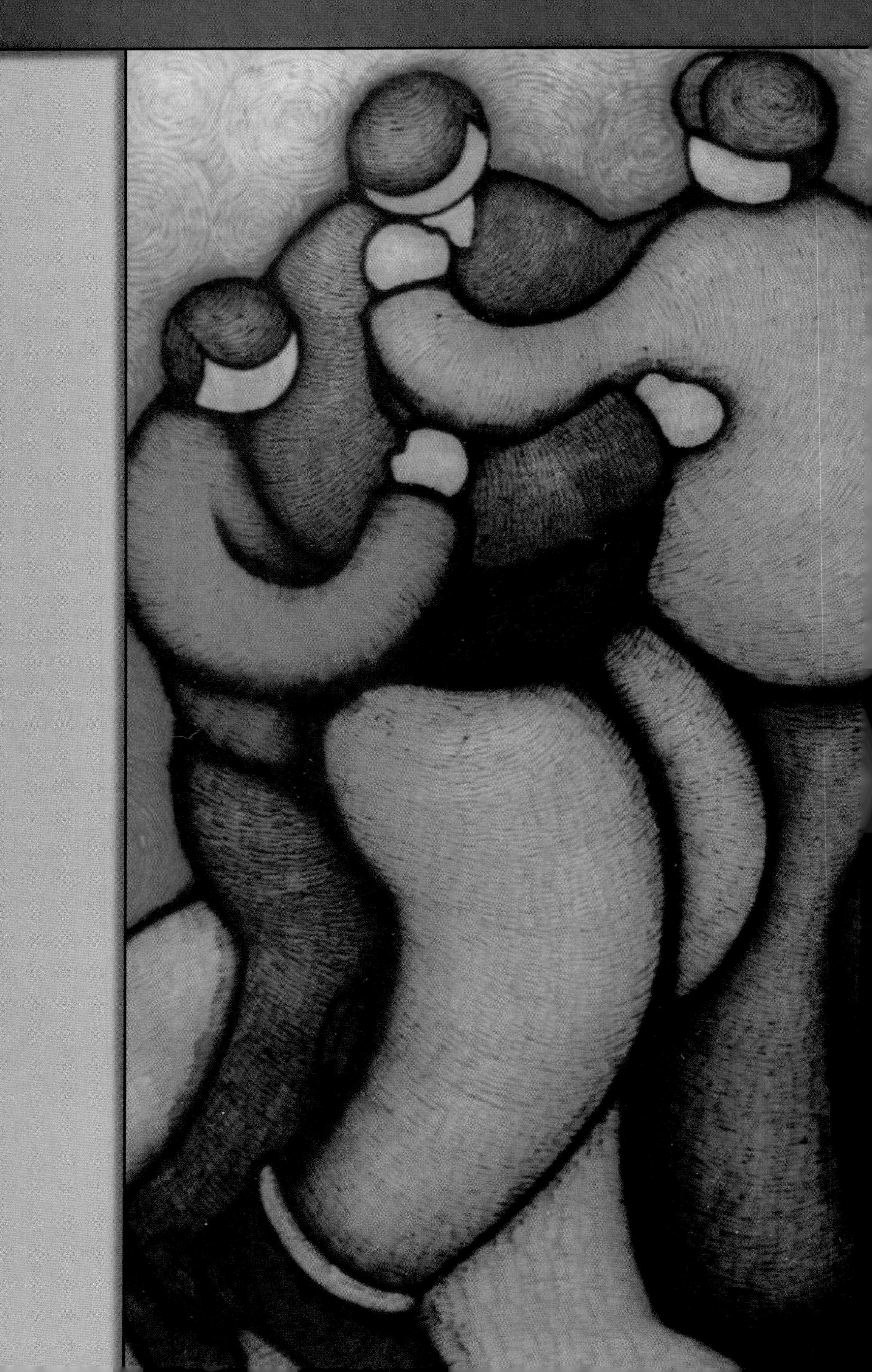

CHAPTER 10

Aggression

A Wave of Senseless Violence

Patricia Krenwinkel had been a Campfire Girl, a singer in the church choir, and a member of the Audubon Society. In the comfortable, middle-class neighborhood where she grew up, she was described as a "very normal child" who was "very obedient." After high school, she attended a Catholic college in Alabama before moving out west to be with her sister. In California, however, the former Campfire Girl's life took a new turn. She moved into a commune, where drugs and free love were the everyday leisure activities and conventional society was scorned. Then, on a hot August night in 1969, she accompanied three of her new friends (a man and two women) to a house in a wealthy area of Los Angeles. There, she and her friends proceeded to brutally murder five complete strangers. Patricia was reluctant to participate in the killing at first, but after one intended victim tried to escape, Krenwinkel chased her and stabbed her several times with a knife (Bugliosi & Gentry, 1974).

Patricia Krenwinkel

Krenwinkel's male accomplice was Charles Watson. Charles had been an A student in high school and an all-around athletic star who had set the Texas state record for the low hurdles. After his arrest, those who knew him refused to believe he was guilty, describing him as "the boy next door," and "a nice guy" who had "no temper." Yet he was by far the most vicious of this murderous pack. That night, he began the killing outside the house, repeatedly shooting a teenage boy as he begged for mercy. Once inside, Watson shot, stabbed, and beat three more people, hitting one man over the head with a blunt object thirteen times and stabbing him fifty-one times. One of his victims was a pregnant woman. As she pleaded for the life of her unborn child, Watson plunged a knife into her body.

Unlike the clean-cut Krenwinkel and Watson, Susan Atkins seemed bound for trouble. She'd dropped out of high school, becoming a topless dancer and a prostitute, and she'd hung out with violent gangster-types. After a previous arrest, her own father had asked police not to let her back into society. After the killings, she wrote "Pig" on the wall in the victims' blood. She later bragged about the murders, claiming to have enjoyed them.

Charles Watson

Linda Kasabian was the third woman who drove to the scene of the murder. Like Susan Atkins, she had a troubled background: she was a product of a broken home and had had two unsuccessful marriages. Unlike Atkins, however, she was unwilling to participate in the killings. Instead, she stayed outside the house. When she heard screams, Linda ran to ask her friends to stop but was too late. She was met by a wounded victim staggering out of the house, to whom she said, "Oh, God, I'm so sorry." After unsuccessfully begging the others to stop, she ran back to the car.

And this wasn't the end of their murderous spree. On the very next night, Krenwinkel, Watson, Atkins, and Kasabian again drove together into a well-to-do neighborhood. This time, they were joined by Charles Manson and two other members of his now-notorious "Family." Again the victims were complete strangers to their assassins, and again, Linda Kasabian refused to do any killing. Soon afterwards, Kasabian escaped from the group, eventually becoming the chief witness for the prosecution. She was the only member of the group to show remorse during the trials.

Susan Atkins

Kasabian reported that, while the other Family members gleefully watched the news reports of the killings after the first night, "in my head I kept saying, 'Why would they do such a thing?'" This was a question many others would also ask. Were the killings completely random and senseless, or did the group have some motives that might connect these killings to the "everyday" violence that leaves tens of thousands of people dead or injured every year? Were these killers products of the powerful situational pressures Manson had arranged within the Family, as their defense attorneys would later claim? If so, why did Linda Kasabian, and later several other members of the circle, refuse to participate?

Most of us will never be involved with anything remotely as violent as the Manson Family's mass murders. In the normal course of our lives, however, we may confront fistfights, family violence, purposeful shoves on the basketball court, heated arguments, or thinly veiled insults designed to do psychological harm. Adolescents in one recent study reported an average of 1.5 conflicts a day, ranging from verbal insults between friends to angry arguments with parents and fistfights with siblings (Jensen-Campbell & Graziano, 2000). What causes these outbursts of hostility? And why do people differ in their proclivity for such conflicts, with some managing to skillfully avoid any violence in their lives and others seeming to seek it out?

Linda Kasabian

As you'll learn in this chapter, aggression, like other social behaviors, results from a decipherable pattern of interactions between the person and the situation. And you'll see that aggressive acts—from a mischievous taunt to a mass murder—make more sense when you understand the social psychological motives that underlie them.

What Is Aggression?

In everyday life, we use the word *aggression* to cover a range of behaviors, from snide comments to violent murders. The word is sometimes even used to describe assertive behavior, as when we talk of "an aggressive sales pitch." Most social psychologists, however, define **aggression** as behavior intended to injure another (e.g., Baron & Richardson, 1994; Berkowitz, 1993a). There are three crucial components of this definition:

1. Aggression is *behavior.* It is not the same as anger, an emotion that is often, but not always, associated with aggression. It is possible to be angry and not to act on those feelings. It is also possible to act aggressively without being angry. When Manson's followers later talked about their murderous spree, none of them indicated feelings of anger toward their victims.
2. The behavior is *intended,* or purposeful. You could hurt, even kill, someone else by accident, and it would not qualify as aggressive behavior. Indeed, people respond very differently to being hurt, depending on whether they believe they were harmed on purpose or inadvertently. A teasing comment, for example, often hurts the recipient when the teaser meant only to make a friendly joke (Kowalski, 2000). If the harm were truly unintended, this would not qualify as aggression.
3. The behavior is aimed at *hurting* another person. Social psychologists distinguish aggressiveness from **assertiveness,** which is behavior intended to express dominance or confidence. They also distinguish real aggression, with its malicious intent, from playful aggression (Boulton, 1994; Gergen, 1990). Play fighting can range from rough-and-tumble wrestling between children to pinching between lovers. It can be distinguished by frequent smiling and laughter, in contrast to the staring, frowning, and baring of the teeth that often accompany malicious aggression (Fry, 1990).

Different Types of Aggression

Social psychologists often distinguish between indirect and direct aggression (e.g., Bjorkvist, Osterman, & Lagerspetz, 1994; Walker, Richardson, & Green, 2000). **Indirect aggression** involves an attempt to hurt another person without obvious face-to-face conflict. Malicious gossip is an example of indirect aggression. **Direct aggression** is behavior aimed at hurting someone to his or her face. It may be either physical—striking, kicking, pushing, or shoving—or verbal—insulting, cursing, or threatening another person.

Another important distinction involves whether the aggression is emotional or instrumental. **Emotional aggression** is hurtful behavior that stems from angry feelings that get out of control. If someone throws a chair at a coworker in a blind rage, that would be an example of emotional aggression. **Instrumental aggression** is hurting another person to accomplish some other goal—to punish someone or to increase one's status, for instance. Instrumental aggression would also include a soldier's killing an enemy to protect his own life or an assassin's killing for money (Berkowitz, 1993a). Table 10.1 gives examples of each of the different types of aggressive behavior.

Aggression *Behavior intended to injure another.*

Assertiveness *Behavior intended to express dominance or confidence.*

Indirect aggression *Behavior intended to hurt someone without face-to-face confrontation.*

Direct aggression *Behavior intended to hurt someone "to his or her face."*

Emotional aggression *Hurtful behavior that stems from angry feelings.*

Instrumental aggression *Hurting another to accomplish some other (nonaggressive) goal.*

Gender Differences in Aggression May Depend on Your Definition

In their classic *The Psychology of Sex Differences,* Eleanor Maccoby and Carol Jacklin (1974) reviewed research that strongly supported a common assumption—that males are more aggressive than females. Twenty years later, Kaj Bjorkqvist, a prominent Finnish aggression researcher, argued instead that "[t]he claim that human

Table 10.1 Examples of different categories of aggressive behavior.

	Direct	Indirect
Emotional	An angry driver starts a fistfight with another driver who was tailgating him.	Under cover of night, an irritated tenant deflates the tires on the landlord's car.
Instrumental	A bank robber shoots a guard who attempts to thwart the robbery.	A woman interested in dating a man asks her sister to tell the man a vicious rumor about his current girlfriend's infidelity.

males are more aggressive than females...appears...to be false, and a consequence of narrow definitions and operationalizations of aggression in previous research" (Bjorkqvist et al., 1994 p. 28).

Supporting Bjorkqvist's view, a number of studies find no sex differences in aggression and related tendencies, and still other studies find higher levels of aggression in women than in men. When people are asked about their feelings of anger, there is no clear sex difference (Averill, 1983; Buss & Perry, 1992). Studies conducted in the Netherlands and the United States have found that women are more prone to feel jealousy in relationships than are men (Buunk, 1981; 1982; DeWeerth & Kalma, 1993; Paul, Foss, & Galloway, 1993). And when it comes to actual violence within relationships, some studies suggest that women are actually more likely than men to use physical aggression against their partners (e.g., Stets & Straus, 1990). Finally, girls, compared with boys, are more likely to use indirect aggression—hurting others through gossiping, spreading vicious rumors, and rejecting them socially (Owens, Shute, & Slee, 2000).

In light of such findings, some researchers have suggested that, perhaps due to the feminist movement, gender differences in aggression have been decreasing since the 1960s, along with a number of stereotypes about the sexes (Goldstein, 1986; Hyde, 1990). Back in the 1960s, women committed only about 15 percent of homicides. Was the first Manson Family murder, committed in 1969 by a group of three women and one man, part of the beginning of a trend toward "equal time" in the violent role?

Gender and aggression. *In an argument about excessive violence in his son's hockey game, this man beat another man to death. Every year, American men commit the vast majority of homicides and assaults.*

No, according to a recent reanalysis of the studies on this topic (Knight, Fabes, & Higgins, 1996). On reexamining the studies used to argue that sex differences are disappearing, George Knight and his colleagues found some serious flaws in the case. Consider the most unambiguous act of aggressive behavior—murder. Since the 1960s, the percentage of U.S. homicides committed by women hasn't increased at all. In fact, it's been decreasing. Whereas men committed 85 percent of homicides in the 1960s, they committed 90 percent during the 1990s (see Figure 10.1). The FBI statistics for aggravated assault are very similar to those for homicide—men commit the overwhelming majority of nonfatal acts of violence as well.

What's going on here? Are there sex differences in aggression or not?

The answer appears to be linked to one's definition of aggression. If researchers ignore the different types of aggression and lump physically violent acts such as homicide together with gossiping, verbal insults, and reported feelings of jealousy, the sex differences are obscured. Women indeed get angry, they indeed get jealous, and they even resort to physical violence. And in annoying situations, men may be the more restrained sex—at first (Ramirez, 1993).

If a woman imagines her partner being unfaithful, she considers how to do emotional harm, while a man is more likely to think about physically hurting someone (Paul et al., 1993).

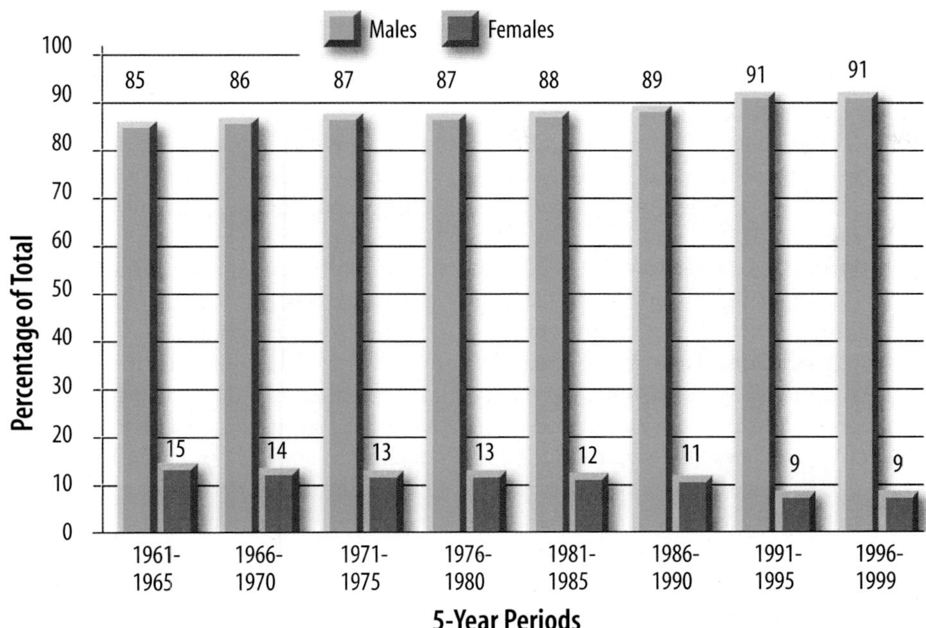

Figure 10.1
Percentage of homicides committed by each sex (1962–1991).

Males in the United States, as in all societies, commit most of the homicides. Changes in sex role norms since the 1960s have not been followed by a tendency for American women to commit a greater proportion of homicides.

SOURCE: *Statistics based on Department of Justice, FBI Uniform Crime Reports.*

And the sexes differ in their inclination toward emotional versus instrumental aggression. Women view aggression as a way to vent their angry emotions, whereas men are more likely to view it as a means to an end, that is, as a way to exert control over others (Campbell & Muncer, 1994).

Thus, it seems that, if we define aggression in terms of emotional expressions of jealousy and anger, or if we include indirect attempts to hurt another, women are at least as aggressive as men. If, on the other hand, we limit our definition to physically assaultive or murderous behavior, men are substantially more aggressive (Archer, 1994).

That explains many of the inconsistencies, except one. What about findings showing that females are more physically violent in relationships (e.g., Stets & Straus, 1990)? Again, the apparent discrepancy begins to evaporate if we make some important definitional distinctions. Women may be more likely to slap or hit their partners than men, but the damage they do is considerably less severe (Archer, 1994). When a 120-pound woman strikes a 180-pound man, the act is simply not as physically damaging as when the reverse occurs. And as we discuss in more detail later, female violence in relationships is often motivated more by self-defense (Dobash, Dobash, Daly, & Wilson, 1992). When one considers that female relational violence generally does less damage and that it is often motivated by self-defense, their greater aggression in relationships may be more apparent than real.

Thus one's definition of aggression is important. Depending on how you define aggression, women are either less aggressive, equally aggressive, or more aggressive than men. To say that the differences depend on definitions doesn't mean that they're arbitrary or meaningless. On the contrary, the difference between physical violence and indirect aggression is a real one indeed, as real as the difference between being beaten with a baseball bat and being called a jerk behind your back (Harris, 1992). As you'll see, the differences between men's and women's aggressiveness are often linked to different motivations. So we now ask, why are people aggressive?

The Goals of Aggressive Behavior

Aggressive behavior may serve a wide range of motivations (Baumeister & Campbell, 1999). Even violent criminal aggression may serve very different motives—some hurt others to defend their public image, some hurt to exploit others for their own satisfaction, and still others simply blow up from too much frustration (Toch, 1984). Based on several decades of research on the topic, Leonard Berkowitz (1993a) suggested a number of goals that aggression might serve, including the desire to influence other people, to gain power and dominance over others, to create an impression of toughness, to gain money or social approval, or simply to discharge unpleasant feelings. Some, such as Sigmund Freud, have suggested that aggressive behavior may serve as a goal in itself. This is a philosophically interesting idea, but could it really be true?

Instincts: Drives Toward Death and Destruction? Freud's view of human motivation had originally included only "life instincts"—selfish drives that contributed to the individual's survival and reproduction. After viewing the ravages of World War I, though, the founder of psychoanalysis added the new idea of a "death instinct"—an innate pull to end one's own life. At one level, the idea of a death instinct was based on a sensible assumption. Psychologists have long accepted that living organisms often strive toward "drive reduction": when there is a source of irritation, we try to reduce it. If we are happiest when nothing is irritating us, then perhaps we all seek the ultimate drive reduction—death. A problem with postulating a death instinct, of course, is that it would conflict with the life instincts. Realizing this problem, Freud postulated that, rather than killing ourselves, we redirect our self-destructive instinct toward the destruction of other people.

Dizzying logic, yes. But correct? Probably not. One basic problem with Freud's idea of a death instinct is that it flies in the face of the most powerful theory in the life sciences—Darwin's theory of evolution by natural selection. Evolutionary theorists find it hard to imagine how a "death instinct" could ever have evolved, because any animals having even the slightest tendency *not* to act self-destructively would survive more successfully than those bent on annihilating themselves.

On the other hand, some evolutionary theorists have speculated that an "aggressive instinct" could have evolved through natural selection, to the extent that aggression pays off for survival or reproduction. Those animals willing to fight for their territories, their mates, or their resources would survive better than those that simply turned and ran (e.g., Lorenz, 1966; Tinbergen, 1968). The Nobel Prize–winning ethologist Konrad Lorenz (1966) proposed that humans, like animals, have an innate urge to attack. Like hunger or sexual desire, these aggressive urges will build up over time until they are discharged.

Lorenz postulated that animals need to release aggressive energy in some way. When the energy is expressed indirectly, as when a bird preens its feathers during a face-to-face conflict with another bird, or when a teenage human begins to stroke his hair in a face-to-face argument with another teenage human, it is called **displacement.** The idea that aggressive impulses build up inside the individual and need to be released is a key component of a social psychological theory called the catharsis-aggression theory (Feshbach, 1984). **Catharsis** refers to the discharge of pent-up emotion—aggressive energy in this case.

In the past, when psychologists thought about an "aggressive instinct," they often assumed that the environment would not affect such an inner destructive drive. But although Lorenz's evolutionary model of aggressive drive is like Freud's theory of the "death instinct" in assuming an inherent tendency to be aggressive, it is different in presuming an interaction between that drive and events in the environment (Tinbergen, 1968). Animals (including humans) will not be inclined to act aggressively unless the drive is triggered by something outside (such as a threat, an attack, or a frustration).

Displacement *Indirect expression of an aggressive impulse away from the person or animal that elicited it.*

Catharsis *Discharge of aggressive impulses.*

Aggression and Adaptive Goals According to modern evolutionary analyses, humans are not "programmed" to be blindly aggressive (Buss, 2000; Gilbert, 1994). Aggressive behavior is one strategy for survival and reproduction, useful in some situations but not in most others. After reviewing the research on aggression across a wide range of animal species, J. P. Scott (1992) notes that aggression can serve a number of goals, allowing animals to control their territorial boundaries, to divide limited resources, and to defend their young. But any thoughtless tendency to commit random acts of aggression to let off steam would make little survival sense. Aggression always bears the risk of retaliation and could result in injury or death. Although it makes survival "sense" to act aggressively when it might lead to status or might help oneself or one's family members, then, pure aggressiveness vented in the absence of an immediate, useful goal would probably hurt an animal's chance to survive and reproduce (Gilbert, 1994).

This analysis suggests that aggressive behavior is never a goal in itself. However, it would be incorrect to assume that each act of aggression is perfectly chosen to lead to some sensible adaptive goal. As we will see, aggressive behavior is often a very inexact and imperfect means of attaining a goal. As we shall also see, different motivations can sometimes flood over into one another, so that an act of aggression can be boosted by generally unpleasant feelings, sexual arousal, or even just the energy produced by exercising (Jo & Berkowitz, 1994; Zillmann, 1994).

What functions does aggression serve? We consider four here: to cope with feelings of annoyance, to gain material and social rewards, to gain or maintain social status, and to protect oneself or the members of one's group.

Summary

Aggression is behavior intended to injure another. It can be direct (undisguised and "in the person's face") or indirect (nonconfrontational and ambiguous). Some aggression is emotional (motivated by anger); some is instrumental (motivated by some other goal). Although Freud posited that aggression could be motivated by a "death instinct," modern theorists generally hold that aggression, like all social behavior, is motivated by adaptive goals that, on average, are designed to serve survival and reproductive functions.

Coping with Feelings of Annoyance

Before committing their notorious mass murders, the Manson Family was living a somewhat impoverished lifestyle. Manson had been sending them on "garbage runs" to collect food from dumpsters behind supermarkets. For those like Krenwinkel and Watson, who came from solid, middle-class backgrounds, the perception of hardship must have been magnified. To make the contrast even worse, Manson and several other members of the group had lived for a time in the elegant home of Brian Wilson (leader of the highly successful Beach Boys musical group). During their stay with Wilson, they drove around in his Rolls Royce and lived quite splendidly (Wilson estimated that their short stay had cost him $100,000).

Manson, having spent most of his life in prisons and foster homes, got his hopes up about joining in this wealthy lifestyle. He had come to believe that Wilson's friend Terry Melcher, a wealthy record producer, would sign him to a recording contract. Ultimately, however, Wilson put them out, Melcher spurned Manson, and the group was reduced to stealing garbage. This detail is one clue to the first gruesome mass murder—the house that Manson and his Family picked was not a random choice, as it first seemed. In fact, it had belonged to Terry Melcher. The prosecuting attorney believed that the victims were chosen because they represented the fame and wealth that Manson and his associates felt they had been denied (Bugliosi & Gentry, 1974).

The Frustration–Aggression Hypothesis

In 1908, William McDougall proposed that aggression is an evolved instinct designed to remove obstacles to the satisfaction of other biological drives. This was an early version of the **frustration–aggression hypothesis**—the theory that aggression is an automatic response to any blocking of goal-directed behavior. The idea was later expanded by John Dollard and his colleagues (1939). In the book *Frustration and Aggression*, they argued that "aggression is always a consequence of frustration" (p. 1). By this, they meant two things: (1) whenever you see someone acting aggressively, you can assume that the person was previously frustrated, and (2) whenever someone is frustrated, some act of aggression will surely follow. Hence, if you get a flat tire that makes you an hour late for work, you'll need to take it out on someone, perhaps your passenger, another innocent driver, or the office clerk who greets you as you walk through the door. On the other side, if your boss begins the day by yelling at you, a frustration–aggression theorist would guess that something had frustrated him on the way to work.

Social psychologists have raised a number of objections to the original frustration–aggression hypothesis (e.g., Baron & Richardson, 1994; Zillmann, 1994). One objection is that some aggressive acts, particularly those we categorized earlier as instrumental, don't seem to follow any particular frustration. During the 1930s and 1940s, a group of Brooklyn mafiosi ran a business called Murder Incorporated, whose employees were paid handsome salaries to assassinate complete strangers—people who had not frustrated them in the least. Such cold-blooded instrumental aggression does not fit the assumption that aggression must be preceded by frustration. A second objection is on the other side of the equation—frustration doesn't always lead to aggression. If a travel agent tells you that all the economy flights to Hawaii are booked, and you believe she tried her best to help you, you may feel frustrated, but you are unlikely to get angry at her.

Despite the problems with the original frustration-aggression hypothesis, Leonard Berkowitz (1989; 1993a) argued that completely rejecting the idea would be like throwing out the baby with the bathwater. He postulated a **reformulated frustration–aggression hypothesis.** According to Berkowitz's revision, frustration is linked only to emotional (or anger-driven) aggression, not to instrumental aggression (of the Murder Incorporated type). Further, he suggested that frustration leads to aggression only to the extent that it generates negative feelings. If you think that the travel agent is purposefully frustrating you, and you were strongly anticipating a low fare to Hawaii, then you'll feel a lot of negativity and be more prone to snap aggressively at her. There is another key implication of Berkowitz's reformulation: *any* event that leads to unpleasant feelings, including pain, heat, or psychological discomfort, can lead to aggression. The unpleasant feeling need not result from frustration per se. The original and reformulated frustration–aggression hypotheses are depicted in Figure 10.2.

According to the reformulated theory, unpleasant feelings may or may not lead to overtly aggressive behavior, depending on a number of factors—some in the person, some in the situation (Berkowitz, 1989; 1993a). We now turn to a consideration of these factors.

Frustration–aggression hypothesis (original) *The theory that aggression is an automatic response to any blocking of goal-directed behavior.*

Reformulated frustration–aggression hypothesis *The theory that any unpleasant stimulation will lead to emotional aggression to the extent that it generates unpleasant feelings.*

Excitation-transfer theory *The theory that anger is physiologically similar to other emotional states, and that any form of emotional arousal can enhance aggressive responses.*

Feelings of Arousal and Irritability

What internal factors stimulate people to act aggressively when they are annoyed? Two sets of factors have been examined, one related to temporary arousal states and the other to chronic irritability.

General Arousal Berkowitz's (1989) modified frustration–aggression hypothesis assumed that aggression can be fueled by any form of unpleasant arousal, whether or not it results from frustration. Dolf Zillmann (1983, 1994) went one step farther, arguing that any internal arousal state can enhance aggressive activity, including the arousal generated by exercising or even by watching an erotic film. According to Zillmann's **excitation-transfer theory,** the emotional reaction of anger has the same symptoms that one feels during any arousing emotional state, including in-

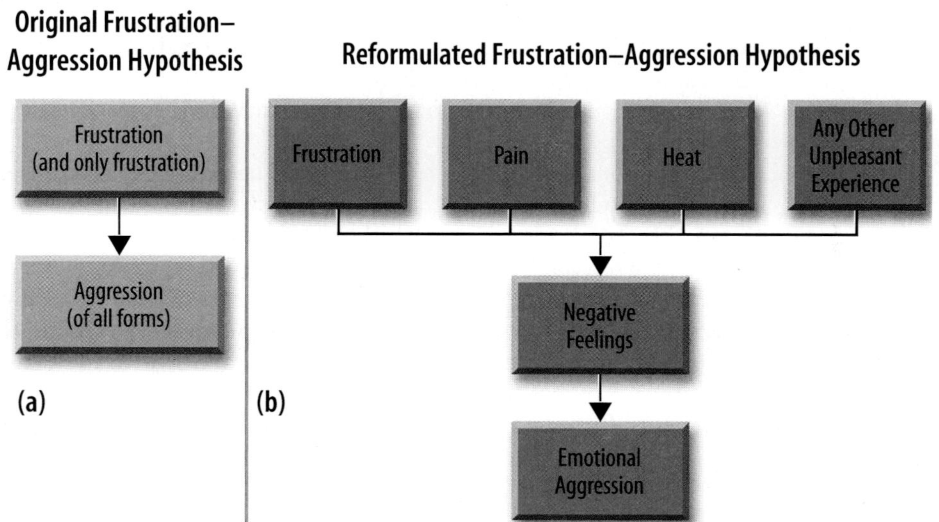

Figure 10.2
The original and revised frustration–aggression hypotheses.

According to the original hypothesis (a), frustration always leads to aggression, and conversely, aggression is always preceded by frustration (Dollard et al., 1939). According to the revised hypothesis (b), frustration is one of many unpleasant conditions that could lead to negative feelings and subsequent emotional aggression (Berkowitz, 1989). Instrumental aggression, according to the revision, is not necessarily preceded by unpleasant circumstances or negative feelings.

creased heart rate, sweaty palms, and elevated blood pressure. If a person is emotionally aroused for any reason and is later annoyed, the residual arousal may be mistaken for anger.

In one test of the excitation-transfer theory, women were annoyed by another woman, and some were then shown a nonviolent erotic film (Cantor, Zillmann, & Einseidel, 1978). When they later got a chance to retaliate at their tormentor, women who had viewed erotica were more aggressive than women who had seen a neutral control film. The researchers noted that the women who had watched the erotic film were more physiologically aroused than women who had seen the control film and suggested that, consistent with excitation-transfer theory, the physiological arousal had been transferred into feelings of anger. In another experiment, students who had strenuously pedaled an exercise bike retaliated against a provoker more than did subjects who had sat quietly and not become physiologically aroused (Zillmann, Katcher, & Milavsky 1972).

Chronic Irritability and the Type A Personality Can you think of someone you know who's particularly likely to get annoyed if things start to run behind his or her tight deadlines or when there's a line at the restaurant or a traffic jam? **Type A behavior pattern** is a group of personality characteristics including time-urgency and competitiveness that is associated with higher risk for coronary disease (Gilbert, 1994; Rhodewalt & Smith, 1991). Type As are often distinguished from Type Bs, who take a more laid-back approach to deadlines and competition and who are at lower risk for heart problems.

Type A behavior pattern *A group of personality characteristics, including time-urgency and competitiveness, that is associated with higher risk for coronary disease.*

Because of their competitiveness, Type As tend to work harder and to rise higher in their professions (Matthews, Scheier, Brunson, & Carducci 1980). On the other hand, their hostility can sometimes get in the way on the job. Robert Baron (1989) studied managers and technical employees for a large food-processing company, comparing the Type As and Type Bs. He found that Type As had more conflicts with their subordinates and were less accommodating in conflicts with their fellow workers. Another study found that Type A bus drivers on the crowded streets of India are more likely to drive aggressively—passing other vehicles, slamming on their brakes, and honking their horns. Compared with Type B drivers, Type As have more accidents and get more reprimands for bad driving (Evans, Palsane, & Carrere, 1987).

The fact that Type As are also more likely to die of heart attacks is consistent with the fact that they are more prone to physiological arousal when they are annoyed (Matthews et al., 1992). Over the years, the physiological correlates of angry arousal apparently take a toll on their cardiovascular systems. Research suggests that hostility is the Type A component most associated with heart disease (Rhodewalt & Smith 1991; Williams, 1984). For instance, Redford Williams (1984) found that physicians who had been hostile and cynical in medical school were, compared with their less antagonistic colleagues, five times more likely to die or to have a heart attack during the twenty-five years following school.

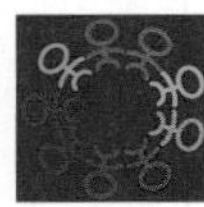

Unpleasant Situations

In one study, almost 1,000 Swedish teenagers described situations in which they had gotten angry. Researcher Bertil Torestad (1990) categorized the anger-inducing situations and found that many were directly connected to frustrating and annoying situations. One major category, for instance, was "thwarted plans" (such as "my parents don't allow me to go out in the evening"). Another category was "environmental frustrations," (such as "I go to see a film listed in the paper, but when I get there it isn't playing"). Many of the situations that annoyed teenagers were social—they involved frustrations caused by other people. Consistent with the revised frustration–aggression hypothesis, researchers have found that many unpleasant situational factors, ranging from physical pain and unpleasant heat to long-term economic hardship, can all fuel hostility (Lindsay & Anderson, 2000).

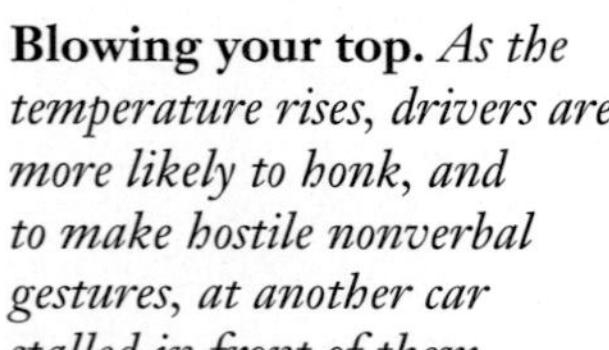

Blowing your top. *As the temperature rises, drivers are more likely to honk, and to make hostile nonverbal gestures, at another car stalled in front of them.*

Pain Leonard Berkowitz and his colleagues have conducted a series of experiments in which some students, assigned to the role of "supervisors," administered shocks and rewards to other students working under them (Berkowitz, 1993b). The supervisors were asked to place a hand in a tank of water (presumably to investigate the influence of harsh unpleasant conditions on supervision). In some cases, the water was painfully cold ice water; in other cases, the water was closer to room temperature. The supervisors made to feel uncomfortable became more aggressive—recommending more shocks and fewer rewards for the students they were supervising (e.g., Berkowitz, Cochran, & Embree, 1981; Berkowitz & Thome, 1987). This research supports the folk wisdom that when the boss is having a bad day, you should stay out of his or her way.

Sweltering Heat The Manson Family murders we described earlier were committed during a heat wave in August. During the previous night, the temperature hadn't dropped below 90 degrees Fahrenheit, and during the day it soared to over 100. Could this unpleasant weather have contributed to the Family members' violent inclinations? A reasonable amount of evidence suggests that the answer is yes—violent behaviors of all sorts are more likely during hot weather (Anderson, Bushman, & Groom, 1997). For instance, Alan Reifman, Richard Larrick, and Steven Fein (1991) investigated how many times pitchers in major league baseball games threw balls that hit batters. Sometimes, pitchers hit batters on purpose—to intimidate them, for instance. This can be dangerous, because professionals fire a hard ball at speeds approaching 100 miles per hour. Reifman and his colleagues found that the hotter it got, the more batters were hit (see Figure 10.3).

Can we attribute this pattern of battered batters to aggression? Perhaps pitchers just got less accurate as the temperature went up, or maybe the games during the hotter part of the season were more important. To rule out these alternative explanations, Reifman and his colleagues statistically controlled for factors such as the number of wild pitches, walks, and errors (related to inaccuracy), as well as the attendance at the game (related to the game's importance). None of these factors could account for the relationship between temperature and the number of hit batters. The overheated pitchers weren't just throwing the ball anywhere; they were taking dead aim at the batters, and the hotter it got, the deadlier their aim got.

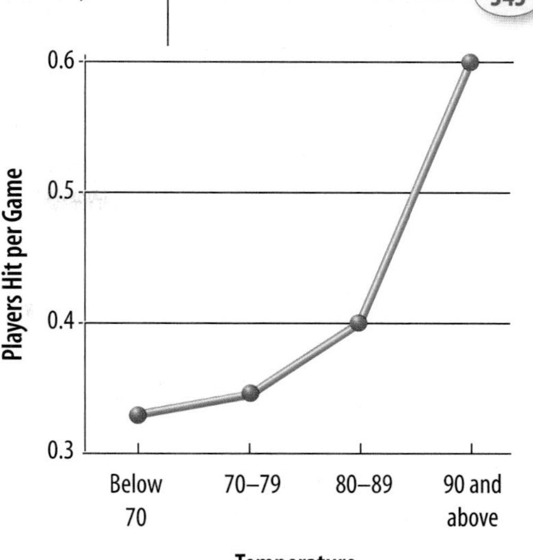

Figure 10.3
Heated competition.

The figure depicts the number of players hit by pitches during major league baseball games, as a function of temperature. Note that above 90 degrees, more than twice as many batters were hit. Analyses suggest that this is done purposely, and not because of heat-induced errors, or other confounding factors.

SOURCE: *Reifman, Larrick, & Fein, 1991.*

A very similar relationship was found between heat and horn honking (Kenrick & MacFarlane, 1986). In this study, a car stopped at a light blocked other drivers from entering an intersection, as the driver of the stopped car simply sat there ignoring the green light. The researchers recorded the number of times that drivers behind the stopped vehicle honked their horns and the amount of time they spent leaning on the horn. The study was conducted at an intersection in Phoenix, Arizona, where temperatures soar well above 100 degrees during the summer. At lower temperatures, drivers either didn't honk, or they tapped lightly on the horn as a gentle reminder that the light had changed. As the temperatures rose, however, so did the tempers of the drivers, who became increasingly likely not only to honk but also to lean continuously on the horn as the green light went unheeded. Several accompanied their honking with other signs of hostility—some cursed at the driver of the stopped car and others used hand signals unlike any they teach in driver's ed.

The effect of heat on aggression isn't limited to baseball pitches and horn honks. For instance, assaults, wife-beatings, rapes, murders, and even urban riots are all more likely to occur during hot periods (Anderson & DeNeve, 1992; Anderson et al., 1997). One possible explanation is that unpleasantly hot weather in itself fuels aggressive feelings. Even within the same city, aggressive crimes increase more than nonaggressive crimes as the mercury rises (Anderson, 1987). Likewise, the heat–hostility relationship holds even among subjects randomly assigned to different temperature conditions in a laboratory experiment (Anderson, Deuser, & DeNeve, 1995). Another contributing factor may be the fact that there are simply more people (including violence-prone criminals and their potential victims) out on the streets when it gets warm. This would explain why crime is reliably found to drop when it gets very cold. Although people do find cold weather to be unpleasant, most people stay home and huddle up by the fireplace. This would also explain why, under at least some circumstances, aggressive crimes have been found to drop again at very high temperatures, when aggressors and potential victims are likely to stay indoors (and comfy) in front of the air conditioning vent (Rotton & Cohn, 2000).

The research on heat and aggression suggests a bit of practical advice. When you start getting irritable on a sweltering day, it's a good idea to cool off with a shower, a swim, or simply a move into a shadier, breezier place. The worst way to handle your frustrations is to drive out into traffic and to honk at some guy who has his car windows rolled down (a signal that he has no air conditioner).

Poverty In line with the original frustration–aggression hypothesis, Carl Hovland and Robert Sears (1940) reasoned that economic hardship, presumably associated with a long-term diet of frustration, would lead to increased aggression. To test the hypothesis, they examined the correlation between the price of cotton and the number of lynchings in fourteen states of the American South during the years 1882 to 1930. Consistent with their predictions, they found a negative correlation—the lower the price (meaning worse times for the agricultural economy), the higher the number of lynchings. Using more sophisticated statistical techniques available four decades later, Joseph Hepworth and Stephen West (1988) re-examined these data, controlling for various possible confounding variables. The new analyses corroborated the earlier findings—economic hardship was indeed correlated with increased lynching. Lynching was highest when a recession followed a period of rising economic well-being, suggesting that dashed hopes of continued growth were most frustrating. Additional research has shown a link between economic threats and violent crimes of many types (e.g., Landau, 1988; Landau & Raveh, 1987)

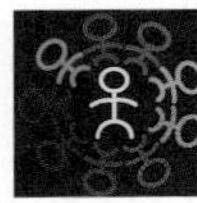

Frustration, Perception, and Personal Choices

Unpleasant circumstances interact with factors inside the person in several interesting ways. We will consider two here. First, when people get annoyed, they change their way of thinking. Circumstances look different to us when we're stuck in traffic on a hot and muggy day. Second, certain types of people may contribute to their own frustrations by going out of their way to end up in annoying circumstances.

Annoyance Leads to Changes in Perception of Situations Leonard Berkowitz went a step beyond just reformulating the old frustration–aggression hypothesis. He proposed a more elaborate theory of the relationship between unpleasant feelings and aggression. According to his **cognitive-neoassociation theory,** an unpleasant situation triggers a complex chain of internal events (see Figure 10.4). The first step in this process is that the unpleasant event unleashes negative feelings. For instance you smash your shin on a cinderblock while searching for your lost car in a hot, humid parking lot, and it brings on a flood of negative feeling. Once you're in a negative mood, a second step occurs—your thoughts turn to other negative experiences you've had in the past. Berkowitz's (1990) model envisions our memories as stored in interconnected networks of associated ideas, images, and feelings. Once a negative feeling or thought occurs, it activates a host of related negative memories, feelings, and behaviors.

Whether that chain of associations leads to aggressive behavior or to flight depends again on factors in the person that interact with factors in the situation. For example, participants in one laboratory experiment were provoked by an obnoxious experimenter who acted disgusted with their performance on an anagram task. Following this, they evaluated a woman who gave them another test as part of her job interview for a research assistant's position. Participants who had been insulted were kind in evaluating the assistant, unless she made a few mildly annoying mistakes. In this case, they seemed to unleash their resentment towards the obnoxious experimenter onto her, rating her significantly more negatively than did other, non-provoked, participants (Pedersen, Gonzales, & Miller, 2000). Other research suggests that this displacement of hostility from one person onto another is especially likely when the second person provides any kind of triggering excuse to unleash the hostility, or when the second person resembles the first one in some way (Marcus-Newhall, Pedersen, Carlson, & Miller, 2000).

A key finding Berkowitz relied on in developing his neoassociation theory was what he dubbed the weapons effect. The **weapons effect** refers to the tendency for weapons, such as guns, to enhance aggressive thoughts and feelings (e.g., Lindsay & Anderson, 2000). In the classic demonstration of this effect, male students were told that they were participating in a study of physiological responses to stress (Berkowitz & LePage, 1967). If you were a subject in this experiment, you would meet another student, and the experimenter would explain that you were both going to take turns working on several problems. Your particular problem would be to list ideas a publicity agent might use to improve a popular singer's public image. Your fellow subject would be asked to think of things a used car salesman might do to improve sales.

Cognitive-neoassociation theory *The theory that any unpleasant situation triggers a complex chain of internal events, including negative emotions and negative thoughts. Depending on other cues in the situation (such as weapons), these negative feelings will be expressed as either aggression or flight.*

Weapons effect *The tendency for weapons, such as guns, to enhance aggressive thoughts, feelings, and actions.*

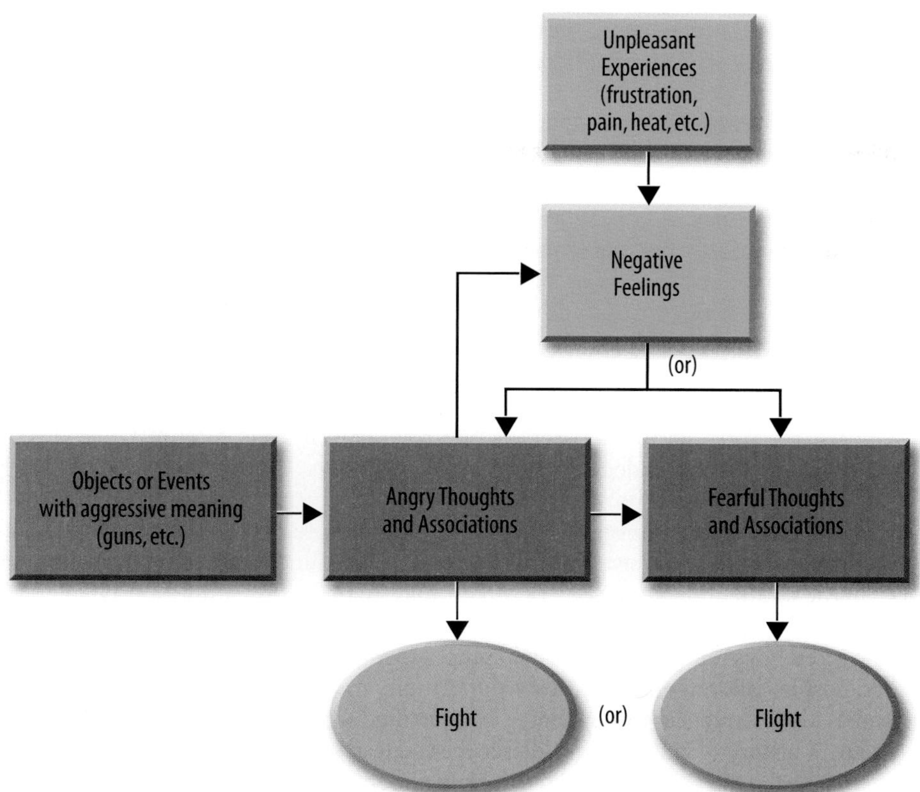

Figure 10.4
Cognitive neoassociation theory.

According to Leonard Berkowitz, unpleasant stimulation leads to negative feelings and negative thoughts. The negative thoughts follow the negative feelings but can also feed back into increased negative feelings. Other cues in the situation, such as the presence of guns, may tilt these negative thoughts toward the consideration of aggressive behavior.

After you wrote down your ideas for the publicity campaign, the other student would judge the quality of your suggestions and give you feedback on your performance. This is where annoyance entered the picture—the "feedback" came in the form of electric shocks, anywhere from one to ten of them. If you were lucky, you would be in the nonangered condition—your partner would deliver only the minimum single shock (indicating that your solutions were "very good"). If you were unlucky, your partner would blast you with not one, two, or three shocks but seven of them (simultaneously hurting you and expressing a harsh evaluation of your creativity). In that condition, as the experimenters planned, subjects tended to become angry.

Following this, though, you'd get a chance to retaliate. The experimenter would bring you to the control room. In one control condition, you'd view an empty table with a shock key on it. In another, there were two badminton racquets on the table. In the crucial experimental condition, there was a 12-gauge shotgun and a .38 caliber revolver lying on the table. If there were sports equipment or weapons on the table, the experimenter would explain that it was part of another experiment, and instruct you to disregard them. Next, the experimenter would give you a sheet on which your partner had supposedly written his used-car sales ideas (in reality, all students saw the same suggestions prepared by the experimenter). Finally, you'd be asked to read the suggestions and to deliver "feedback" to the other student in the form of one to ten shocks. What do you do? Figure 10.5 depicts the main results of the study.

As Figure 10.5 shows, the presence of guns in this experiment did not increase aggression if the person wasn't annoyed to begin with. In fact, nonangered subjects in the presence of weapons delivered very few shocks, and the shocks were very brief. But everything changed when the subjects were annoyed; now the presence of guns increased both the length and the number of shocks given. In line with his cognitive neoassociation theory, Berkowitz (1993a) believes that the mere

Figure 10.5
The weapons effect.

In a study by Berkowitz and LePage (1967), students were given the chance to deliver shocks to another student who had either treated them positively or annoyed them. As shown on the left, weapons didn't increase aggression when subjects weren't annoyed. As shown on the right, however, annoyed subjects delivered more shocks when guns were present.

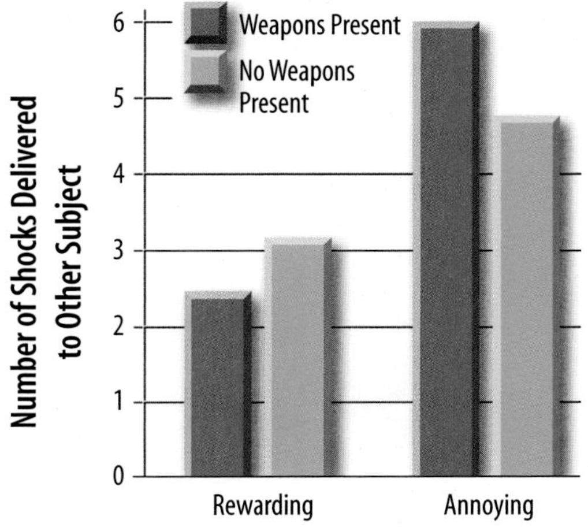

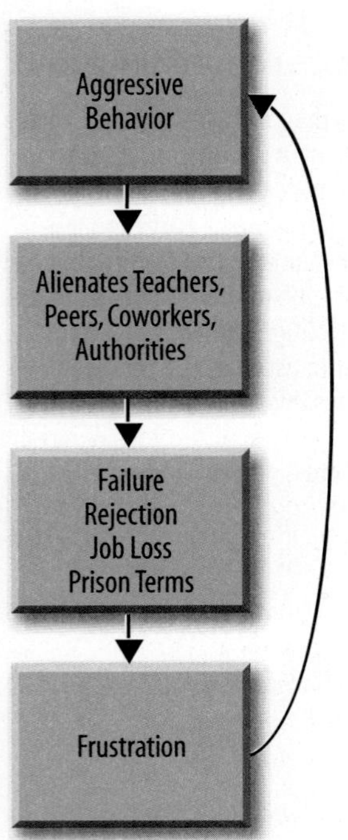

Figure 10.6
The cycle of frustration and aggression.

People who are aggressive elicit negative reactions from others, including teachers, peers, and authority figures. Consequently, they suffer more setbacks, including expulsion from school, social rejection, and incarcerations. These experiences increase frustration in their lives and lead to more aggressiveness.

presence of guns increases aggressiveness by "priming" aggressive associations. When the person is already angry, these associations increase the likelihood of retaliation.

Some People Create Their Own Annoying Situations Another type of interaction occurs when people choose situations to match their personal characteristics. In one study, Canadian students were given the choice between different working conditions (Westra & Kuiper, 1992). Type A students seemed to go out of their way to choose the very situations that engage their competitiveness and time urgency. Would you enjoy working on the stock exchange, where traders need to stay constantly alert for the chance to win, or to avoid losing, hundreds of thousands of dollars? Or would you rather run a snowboarding shop, where you'd encounter laid-back customers and no particular deadlines? If you're a Type A, these findings suggest that you'd pick a job having unrealistic deadlines and time pressure. By seeking out competitive and frustrating situations, Type As seem to create the very circumstances likely to set off their hostile tendencies.

Similarly, people who are prone to act aggressively may create life experiences that add to their own frustrations. These, in turn, elicit more aggressiveness. On a moment to moment basis, aggressive children begin to incite counteraggression from other children the moment they walk onto a playground (Rausch, 1977). A hostile child can turn a peaceful play session into open warfare in a matter of minutes. In the long term, hot-tempered boys tend to fare poorly in school (Moffitt, 1993). By alienating their teachers, hostile children miss out on the opportunity to learn basic math and writing skills, and as a consequence, they are later less qualified for jobs and suffer more unemployment. A history of violence in adolescence can lead to other irrevocable consequences, such as disfiguring injuries or time spent in prison. Partly because of persisting personality traits and partly because of the different environments they create for themselves, aggressive children get trapped in a cycle of frustration, which in turn leads to more aggression (Caspi, 2000; Moffitt, 1993). This cycle is depicted in Figure 10.6.

The discussion of person–situation interactions should help make one thing clear. Frustration doesn't inevitably lead to aggression. Some people are able to cope with frustrating situations nonaggressively by avoiding those situations in the first place or by acting to reduce conflict when they're confronted with annoyances. Type Bs, for instance, seem to go out of their way to cool down potentially hostile interactions (Baron, 1989). Just as frustration does not invariably lead to aggression, we shall see in the sections that follow that frustration is not necessary to produce aggression—some people act aggressively even when they are not frustrated.

Summary

One goal of aggression is to cope with feelings of annoyance. Within the person, annoyance-triggered aggression can be instigated by momentary states of arousal or by a chronic inclination towards Type A competitiveness. Within the situation, short-term annoyances such as pain or heat and long-term frustrations such as poverty have been linked to aggression. At the interactive level, feelings of annoyance or the presence of weapons may lead to cognitive associations that bring on more aggressive and unpleasant feelings. Over the lifespan, aggression-prone people may fill their own lives with the very annoyances that lead them to act aggressively.

Gaining Material and Social Rewards

Vikings marauding across the countryside, modern soldiers plundering villages, urban gang members controlling lucrative drug territories, muggers shaking down subway riders, and schoolyard bullies taking children's lunch money have one thing in common—they reap rewards from aggressive behavior.

Al Capone. *A man who used violence and antisocial behavior to gain immense material benefits, he came from a culture where this path to success had a long history.*

FOCUS ON Social Dysfunction

Gangland Violence

Al Capone may be the best-known gangster who ever lived, and his reputation was, in part, linked to his aggressive behavior. In one of his more notorious acts, Capone invited three men to a banquet in their honor and served them a lavish meal and several bottles of fine wine. After wining and dining the men, however, Capone had his henchmen tie them to their chairs. He then personally proceeded to beat each of the three men with a baseball bat before having each one shot in the back of the head.

Despite his occasional capacity for extreme violence, Capone was in many ways a pleasant fellow to be around. His wife regarded him as an ideal husband, and many who knew him regarded Capone as a warm and benevolent friend. What, then, would prompt an otherwise friendly man to such extremes of violence? One answer is that it was part of his job description: Capone was an ambitious member of a profession that was, in his culture, a common path to material and social success.

Al Capone grew up just after the turn of the century in a poor immigrant family in Brooklyn. Because Capone was a tough and ambitious kid, he won the attention of a local mobster named Frankie Yale. When he was only sixteen, Yale put him to work collecting "protection" money from local businessmen. At age eighteen, Capone killed his first man during a robbery.

After killing a second man, who belonged to a rival gang, Capone was forced to move to Chicago, where he began to earn big money and work his way to the top of the local mob. During his rise, Capone killed several other men, mostly during struggles to control lucrative alcohol-distribution territories. Once he rose to the top, most of his murdering was done by others. However, he did occasionally do his own killing, to make a point. In the case of the men he beat with a baseball bat, Capone had learned that the three, hoping to advance their own careers, were plotting against him. To maintain his position as a powerful mafioso, he was expected to punish such disloyalty with death.

The payoffs for Capone's aggressiveness were by no means small. The president of the Chicago Crime Commission once said, "Al Capone ran the city. His hand reached into every department of the city and county government" (Kobler, 1971, 13). By age twenty-nine, he controlled a syndicate reaping profits in the hundreds of millions of dollars, owned a beautiful estate in Florida, and wore diamonds that cost more than most men earned in a lifetime.

Partly because of the enormous economic opportunity opened by the combination of Prohibition laws and the continued demand for alcohol, Capone became richer and more infamous than most mafiosi. However, he wasn't the first, nor the last, to play the role of Mafia don. Indeed, local thugs had wielded immense political and economic power in Southern Italy and Sicily for centuries (Servadio, 1976). Because the region had been almost continually occupied, and exploited, by foreign armies, including Greeks, Romans, Arabs, Normans, and Spaniards, the native residents inherently disliked and distrusted government. Instead, they were loyal to local powerful men, who would protect them, get them jobs, and at the same time, demand payment for that protection. These local thugs ruled with a dominant and violent hand and would use their own wealth and power to bribe or threaten government officials. If push came to shove, the mafiosi were expected to act violently to protect their power and their territory from other thugs. Given such a history, the behavior of Capone and other U.S. mafiosi seems less of a puzzle.

As one former gang member noted, street gangs in modern U.S. cities are hardly anarchies (Rodriquez, 1994). Instead, they are often highly structured groups having codes of honor and discipline. Consider the U.S. Cosa Nostra, formally organized in 1931 by a Sicilian immigrant named Salvatore Maranzano (also known as Little Caesar). Maranzano was no street punk like Capone; he was college educated and had even studied for the priesthood. Well read and fluent in six languages, Maranzano had carefully studied the writings of Julius Caesar. Indeed, he organized the U.S. mafia along the lines of Caesar's legions (Davis, 1993).

Two points about the mafia and associated organized criminals are important to remember. First, underneath what appears to outsiders to be a breakdown of societal structure is a clear and organized set of social structures and rules, derived from a particular military and political history. Second, like international conflict, a good deal of mafia violence has been about controlling wealth and lucrative territories. Once again, then, we see that social dysfunctions are often rooted in otherwise functional processes. For mobsters, the usual competition for material rewards gets magnified into a serious malady for the rest of society. ■

According to one theory of aggression, payoffs maintain aggression at all levels. Just as a mafia don acts violently to maintain a lucrative drug, alcohol, or gambling business, so the local schoolyard bully may act violently to win some reward, if only a candy bar or praise from the other bullies. Let's look now at this reward-based view of aggression.

The Social Learning Theory of Aggression

The dangers of encouraging aggression in children. *Andrew Golden, several years before he and Mitchell Johnson systematically massacred a teacher and four of their schoolmates.*

One of the most influential psychological theories of aggression is the **social learning theory,** developed by Albert Bandura (1973, 1983). According to this model, aggressive behavior is influenced by rewards associated with aggression. These rewards can come directly, as when a boy's father buys him an ice cream sundae after the boy has been in a fight or gives the boy a firearm as a Christmas present. The accompanying photo depicts young Andrew Golden, posed in combat fatigues, and holding a rifle. The smile and pose suggest that his parents encouraged this early play with firearms. Several years later, Andrew, now eleven, and Mitchell Johnson, age thirteen, systematically gunned down four fellow students and a teacher. Like Andrew, Mitchell had been encouraged to shoot guns from earliest childhood by his parents and grandparents.

Rewards can also come indirectly, in the form of observation. By watching movies and television programs in which attractive and sympathetic characters punch, kick, beat, and shoot those who frustrate them, Bandura believes, children learn that violence is an acceptable way of handling conflicts with others. Just a few months before Johnson and Golden's killing spree, fourteen-year-old Michael Carneal similarly shot eight of his classmates in Paducah, Kentucky. Carneal had recently watched a movie in which movie star Leonardo DiCaprio committed a similar act of mayhem.

In a classic series of studies, Bandura and his colleagues examined the processes by which children come to imitate such depictions of violent behavior. In one study, children were exposed to a model who engaged in a series of unusual violent acts towards a "Bobo Doll" (an inflatable, life-size clown with a red nose that honks when Bobo is punched). The researchers found that, if the children observed the aggressive person receiving a reward, they were likely to spontaneously imitate the aggressive behavior when they themselves were later placed in the room with the Bobo Doll. They didn't do so if they'd watched the model being punished. However, even if the model was punished, the children learned the unique aggressive behaviors, as demonstrated when the experimenter later offered the children a reward to imitate what they'd seen earlier (Bandura, Ross, & Ross, 1963a, 1963b).

Social learning theory *The theory that aggression is learned through direct reward or by watching others being rewarded for aggressiveness.*

Bandura argues that, when children observe modeled violence, it can result in learning at several levels. First, the observer may learn new techniques of aggression (regardless of whether the model is rewarded). After watching a movie that depicted a man being doused with gasoline and burned, for instance, one band of teenagers set fire to a woman walking home with her groceries. Second, the observer may learn the rules about whether aggression is likely to be rewarded (if the model is punished, the child learns not to act aggressively in the present situation; if the model is rewarded, the child learns that aggressiveness is now appropriate). Similarly, even if you learn to play the piano, you may not tickle the ivories at a given party if you are not encouraged to do so or if you expect the other people at the party to be annoyed with your playing. Likewise, people who have learned to shoot a gun or to hurt someone using martial arts will generally not do so unless they expect it will lead to positive, rather than negative, consequences for themselves.

Bandura also notes that a person need not be particularly angry or upset to engage in reward-motivated aggressive behavior. Hired assassins and trained soldiers often act aggressively with no feelings of anger at all. Thus, social learning theory is particularly applicable to instrumental aggression.

Who Finds Rewards in Violence?

Are some people more likely to act aggressively for personal gain? Even if the position of mobster were offered, not every struggling immigrant could be as cold-blooded as Al Capone in his willingness to kill others who stood in the way of business success. On the other hand, if a person had little empathy for others and a magnified sense of self-worth, it would be easier for him or her to hurt others for personal gain. Similarly, if a person were less sensitive to punishment, the potential costs of retaliation by victims or society would loom less large as deterrents.

Psychopathy A **psychopath** is an individual characterized by a lack of empathy for others, grandiose self-worth, and a lack of sensitivity to punishment (Hare et al., 1990; Mealey, 1995). Psychopathy is also called antisocial personality disorder or sociopathy. Robert Hare (1993) has described psychopaths as "below the emotional poverty line." To make things worse, psychopaths' indifference to the pain of others is accompanied by impulsiveness and a tendency to deny responsibility for their own misdeeds. In a study comparing criminal violence in psychopaths and nonpsychopaths, Hare and his colleagues found that psychopaths' violent acts were three times more likely to have been motivated by personal gain and over ten times less likely to have been motivated by emotion (Williamson, Hare, & Wong, 1987). Thus violence perpetrated by psychopaths is cool and calculated for personal reward. Capone showed many of the classical characteristics of psychopathy, as in his cold-hearted willingness to beat men to death and to assassinate his business competitors. And like Capone, many psychopaths are quite socially charming (except to those who stand in their way).

Like the violence of adult psychopaths, the aggression of schoolyard bullies also tends to be focused more on personal gain rather than on other motives such as retaliation or self-defense (Olweus, 1978). In a study of young adolescent boys in Sweden, researchers found that about 5 percent of them were viewed by their teachers and classmates as bullies. These boys were typically cool and deliberate in their bullying, picking targets whom they could easily beat in a fight. As Berkowitz (1993a) notes, the aggressiveness of such bullying boys wasn't designed just to injure their victims, but was a tool used to gain other rewards.

Empathy Feelings of empathy—sharing the emotions of another—seem to make aggressive behavior unrewarding (Baumeister & Campbell, 1999; Miller & Eisenberg, 1988). If, like most people, you cannot help feeling distressed when you watch someone else in pain you would probably take little pleasure in the life of a henchman for the mob. Highly empathic people put themselves "in the other person's shoes," and are likely to be consumed with guilt over hurting another (Leith & Baumeister, 1998). On the other hand, psychopaths, with their general tendency

Psychopath *Individual characterized by impulsivity, irresponsibility, low empathy, and lack of sensitivity to punishment. Such individuals are inclined toward acting violently for personal gain.*

to feel less emotional arousal, and their particular lack of empathy (Harpur, 1993; Williamson et al., 1987), feel less compunction about hurting others spontaneously in the course of committing other crimes.

Alcohol Intoxication Although empathy for another's pain can keep most nonpsychopaths from using violence, alcohol may temporarily turn off those normal empathic feelings. Participants in one study were given either an alcoholic or a nonalcoholic beverage to drink. Then they were asked to recall a conflict they had had in their romantic relationship. Those who were intoxicated expressed more blame—they were less able to see their partner's side of things—and they felt more anger at their partner (MacDonald, Zanna, & Holmes, 2000). This helps explain the strong association between spouse abuse and alcohol consumption (Coker et al., 2000). One study found that wife-beaters drank, on average, 120 drinks per month—more than 13 times as many as a control group and twice as many as a group taken from the same pubs attended by the spouse abusers (Lindeman et al., 1992). The researchers considered the possibility that alcohol abuse is simply correlated with antisocial behaviors of all sorts. If so, then maybe alcohol itself does not cause spouse abuse. However, spouse abusers are generally intoxicated at the time of the offense (Lindeman et al., 1992). This suggests that it's the state of being intoxicated, rather than a trait of the drinker, that stimulates the aggressiveness.

It seems that one effect of alcohol is to remove the normal restraints against aggressive behavior—the concerns about the punishing negative consequences that will follow from hurting another. Fifty percent of the assailants in violent crime cases are drunk at the time they commit their misdeeds (Bushman, 1993). Indeed, alcohol leads to aggressiveness even in nonalcoholics, sometimes even when they're unprovoked (Gantner & Taylor, 1992; Gustafson, 1992).

The lowered empathy and lack of concern about consequences may explain why alcohol is commonly involved in date rape (Abbey, Ross, McDuffie, & McAuslan, 1996). Antonia Abbey and her colleagues (1996) reviewed research suggesting that date rape may be increased by "alcohol myopia"—a narrow focus of attention on whatever seems most important to the person at that moment (Steele & Josephs, 1988). Under the influence of alcohol, a sexually aroused man may become narrowly focused on his own sexual gratification and ignore or misinterpret his date's efforts to resist his advances.

Glamorizing Violence

According to social learning theory, children learn from watching others that aggression can sometimes lead to rewards. They also learn that reward is more likely to follow aggressive behavior in particular situations. Although extremes of violence are not common in everyday life, children can observe aggressive models being rewarded for violence every day on movies and TV. These days they can even practice being a violent "super-hero" in graphic computer games.

Violence is glamorized in the media. *Movies and television programs expose children to thousands of acts of "justified" violence, from fistfights to mass murders.*

Media Effects One Manson Family member explained their violent spree by saying: "We were brought up on your TV" (Bugliosi & Gentry, 1974). A key assumption of Bandura's (1983) social learning theory is that the media can teach us that aggressive behavior may lead to rewards. The lessons are certainly there in abundance. Turn on the television set during prime time, tune in to a children's cartoon show, or go to a movie house, and chances are that neither you, nor your innocent little niece or nephew, will have to wait long to witness mayhem. Indeed, by the time an American child reaches age eighteen, he or she is likely to have witnessed 200,000 acts of violence on television (Plagens, Miller, Foote, & Yoffe, 1991).

Even among the "normal" characters portrayed on television, 40 percent are portrayed as violent and 10 percent as homicidal (Gerbner, Gross, Morgan, & Signorelli, 1981).

After conducting his early research on observational learning and aggression, Bandura (1973) became concerned. If watching a few minutes of aggression in a lab can inspire a child to act aggressively, what about the long-term effects of watching so much glamorized violence on television? Correlational studies indicate that children, especially boys, who watch a lot of aggressive television are more aggressive toward other children (Belson, 1978; Friedrich-Cofer & Huston, 1986). Of course, such correlations do not prove causality. Perhaps children predisposed toward violence simply choose to watch more aggressive television. Or, maybe some third factor, such as poverty, leads independently to both violent behavior and a preference for "shoot-em-up" television programs. If so, poor people would continue to act violently even without the influence of violent television. One researcher investigated twenty-two different "third factors" that might have accidentally produced an association between violent behavior and television viewing. Even when all those other possible causes were measured and statistically removed, the connection between violent behavior and TV watching still remained (Belson, 1978).

These findings support the theory that televised violence spurs real-life violence. Additional support comes from experimental studies in which researchers controlled the amount of aggressive television to which observers are exposed (Wood, Wong, & Chachere, 1991). In general, such studies suggest that more violent TV leads to more aggressive behavior in children (e.g., Leyens, Camino, Parke, & Berkowitz, 1975; Parke, Berkowitz, Leyens, West, & Sebastian, 1977).

Not all the research on media aggression yields the same conclusion, however (e.g., Freedman, 1984; Friedrich-Cofer & Huston, 1986; McGuire, 1986; Wiegman, Kuttschreuter, & Baarda, 1992). Confronted with seemingly contradictory findings, researchers need not throw up their hands in exasperation. To help bring order to the confusion, researchers in this area have turned to **meta-analysis**—the statistical combination of results from different studies of the same topic. In the next section, we consider this technique and how it has helped researchers come to a clearer conclusion about media effects on aggression.

FOCUS ON Method

Using Meta-Analysis to Examine the Effects of Violent Media

When a researcher conducts any experiment, say manipulating exposure to violent TV, that researcher doesn't expect everyone to respond identically to the experimental manipulations. Although the majority of people exposed to a violent film might use a higher level of shock, on average, than those exposed to a nonviolent control film, some subjects, perhaps those who entered the experiment in a bad mood or who were chronically grouchy, would be highly aggressive even in the control condition. Others, perhaps those who entered the experiment in a good mood or who were fundamentally opposed to violence, would refuse to use high levels of punishment even after being exposed to a violent film. Random variations due to peoples' moods, personalities, daily experiences, and even social class add enough "noise" that some experiments fail to discover an effect that is actually there.

What does a researcher do when studies contradict one another? Returning to the detective analogy used in chapter 1, what would a detective do if a group of witnesses, none of them perfectly reliable, gave different versions of a crime they had witnessed? Rather than ignore all the testimony, a good detective would likely put all the accounts together and look for recurring themes or story elements common to several witnesses.

Meta-analysis is a statistical technique for discovering the commonalities across a number of different studies. In the same way that variations between subjects in

Meta-analysis *The statistical combination of results from different studies of the same topic.*

a single experiment are treated as random error and taken into account when an experimenter conducts a test of statistical significance, so the variations between research studies on the same question are taken into account in a "meta-test" of statistical significance across all the studies. By using a number of studies, each with a large number of subjects, the chances increase dramatically that various random effects will cancel themselves out, and that any true effects of the particular experimental variable will shine through.

Consider the imaginary findings depicted in Table 10.2. In both cases, subjects delivered an average of seven shocks in the nonviolent control conditions and ten shocks in the violent media conditions. On the left, the results are depicted as they would be if there were absolutely no sources of error affecting the results. On the right, the results are depicted more like they would be in the real world, complete with various sources of error. Note that in both cases, the overall means are the same. If one looks at only the first and second comparisons in the naturally noisy data set (rows 1 and 2 on the right side), one could mistakenly conclude that exposure to violent media *reduced* aggression, whereas the comparison in row 4 would lead to a conclusion of no differences. Other comparisons, such as the last one, would exaggerate the size of the media effect. By comparing across a large number of studies, however, the various sources of random error tend to cancel one another out, and we're able to get a better idea of the "true" effect of violent media on the number of shocks delivered. In essence, this is what is involved in a meta-analysis—statistically averaging across a number of studies on the same question.

Because a number of researchers have examined the relationship between violent media and aggression, several meta-analyses have been conducted in this area (e.g., Andison, 1977; Hearold, 1986; Wood, Wong, & Chachere, 1991). For example, Wendy Wood and her colleagues Frank Wong and Gregory Chachere (1991) examined twenty-eight experimental studies—in which children or adolescents were observed after watching an aggressive (or a nonaggressive) film and in which observers later recorded whether the subjects spontaneously acted aggressively (for instance, by hitting another child on the playground). As expected in the normally noisy world, the researchers found the results were mixed. In about a third of the comparisons, in fact, the control subjects were more aggressive than the experimental subjects. In those reversals, however, the effects tended to be relatively small. Many more studies found higher aggression in the subjects exposed to aggressive media, and more of those positive aggression effects were large. When the data were averaged across all the studies, the overall statistics were powerful enough that the researchers could be confident in concluding that "media

Table 10.2 A hypothetical example of ten studies measuring number of shocks delivered by subjects exposed to violent, as opposed to nonviolent, media.

	Results if no chance factors operated		More typical results	
	Violent media	Nonviolent media	Violent media	Nonviolent media
	10	7	5	10
	10	7	7	9
	10	7	10	7
	10	7	8	8
	10	7	12	13
	10	7	9	6
	10	7	15	7
	10	7	11	1
	10	7	10	5
	10	7	13	4
(Average)	10	7	10	7

violence enhances children's and adolescents' aggression in interaction with strangers, classmates, and friends" (380).

Why do some studies fail to find an effect of violent media if there is one? Wendy Wood and her colleagues noted that, although the impact is real, it is small to moderate in size. The effect is equivalent to that of a training program for the SATs that increased scores from an average of 1000 to 1050 rather than to that of a program that moved everyone from 1000 up to 1200 (which would be a very large effect). With a small effect, not all children would be affected all of the time. For example, media violence seems to have little effect on young girls, and even less as they move into adolescence (Friedrich-Cofer & Huston, 1986; Hearold, 1986). But even a so-called small effect might be worth worrying about. Wood and her colleagues provide another way to think about this: 13 percent of those exposed to a violent program will become more aggressive than normal. In most experimental studies, children are exposed to only one or two episodes of media violence. If such a brief exposure can increase violence even slightly, what are the effects of the 200,000 acts of violence a child will watch before finishing high school? ■

As you can see, conclusions from meta-analyses of media and aggression support Bandura's social learning theory of aggression. If people are exposed to models who act aggressively and get rewarded, they will learn to imitate that aggressive behavior. This research has not tended to support an alternative, catharsis theory, which postulated that watching aggression is one way of discharging aggressive energy (Bushman, Baumeister, & Stack, 1999).

Pornographic films and magazines often glamorize a particularly troubling form of violence—rape. In some such films, the victim is depicted as resisting the rapist at first but later rewarding the man's coerciveness by enjoying herself and wanting more sex. Donnerstein and Berkowitz (1981) found that, after watching such films, even nonangered men delivered more electric shocks to a woman. Men who were angry at the woman delivered more shocks after watching a violent erotic film, whether the woman in the film ended up enjoying herself or not. Research on violent pornography thus supports the social learning position, and again fails to support the catharsis theory.

Violent Computer Games Teenagers Eric Harris and Dylan Klebold enjoyed playing a graphically violent video game called *Doom*, which had been licensed by the U.S. military to train soldiers to kill effectively. On his Web site, Harris had a customized version in which two shooters, equipped with extra weapons and unlimited ammunition, gun down helpless opponents. As a school project, they made a videotape in which they acted the game out, wearing trenchcoats and pretending to shoot school athletes. On April 20, 1999, Harris and Klebold turned their gory fantasies into reality, slaughtering thirteen of their Columbine High School classmates, and wounding twenty-three others. Did their experience winning points for killing opponents on the computer screen teach them that murder could be rewarding? Social psychologists Craig Anderson and Karen Dill (2000) gathered data that suggest the answer may be yes. In a correlational study, Anderson and Dill found that real-life videogame play was associated with a record of aggressive and delinquent behaviors such as destroying property and hitting other students. As with all correlations, this does not establish cause-and-effect. Perhaps the violent video game choices merely reflect delinquent tendencies, rather than causing them. However, college students randomly assigned to play a graphically violent game (*Wolfenstein*) later had more aggressive thoughts and feelings than a comparable group who

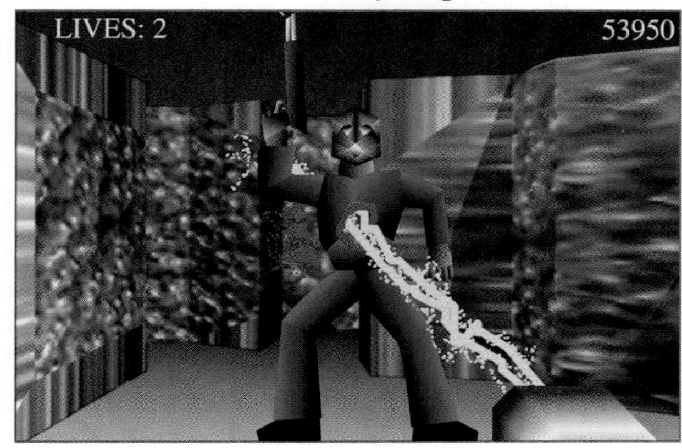

Graphic violence. *Children who spend more time playing violent video-games are more likely to get into trouble for violent behaviors in school or the neighborhood, and college students who play violent games in a lab experiment increase their violent thoughts and feelings.*

played a nonviolent game. The researchers concluded that violent video games can provide a forum in which youngsters learn and practice aggressive solutions to conflicts.

Glamorized Military Violence Further evidence that glamorized violence can make violence more rewarding comes from a fascinating study of twenty-nine countries involved in World Wars I and II (Archer & Gartner, 1984). In nineteen of these countries, homicide rates were at least 10 percent higher in the five years after than in the five years preceding the war. There were no comparable changes in fifteen control nations not involved in war. The researchers found that the more citizens who had been lost in battle, the higher the postwar homicide rate. But it was not the losing nations whose homicide rates went up. Instead, homicides increased most dramatically in the victor nations (Archer & Gartner, 1984). These changes were not due to downturns in the economy or unemployment. One possible explanation is that during and after a war, risky violent behaviors are glamorized as heroic, and are rewarded with medals, parades, and social praise. In the country that wins, this positive view of violence gets especially reinforced.

Watching Violence Magnifies Violent Inclinations

Glamorized public violence may make aggression seem more rewarding, but it is not likely to affect everyone in the same way. As we noted, females are less influenced by media violence as they grow older. Further, not everyone finds it rewarding to expose themselves to such depictions of violence. Many people will go well out of their way to avoid watching a movie such as *Pulp Fiction* or a bloody boxing match. Others seem to relish such experiences.

Researchers in Montreal caught moviegoers either before or after they watched a violent film (*Missing in Action*, which contains 61 depictions of death by machine-guns, bayonets, knives, and explosions) or a nonviolent film (*A Passage to India*, which contained no violent deaths). All participants were asked to fill out a short aggression questionnaire. The researchers found that the violent film increased aggressive tendencies in viewers, whereas the nonviolent one produced no change. More interesting, though, is that those who chose the aggressive film were substantially more aggressive to begin with (Black & Bevan, 1992). Thus, aggressive films make people more violent, but it is violence-prone people who choose to expose themselves to the aggression in the first place. Once again, we see a form of dynamic interaction between person and situation. Some people are prone to find violence pleasurable, and they choose situations in which violence is glamorized; others find it unpleasant, and they choose to avoid such situations. Over a series of such choices, as people make one person-consistent choice after another, small initial differences between people may get magnified.

Summary

Some forms of aggression, particularly instrumental aggression, are motivated by the potential for material and social rewards. According to social learning theory, a reward can enhance aggression when it is direct or when the person observes others being rewarded for hostility. Psychopaths are particularly likely to hurt others for instrumental rewards; people high in empathy are unlikely to do so. Alcohol intoxication may reduce the perceived costs of aggression by inhibiting feelings of empathy for a victim. At the situational level, observation of violent media, graphic video games, or glorification of military violence can increase aggressiveness. At the interaction level, people who are initially favorable toward violence are more likely to choose situations that further enhance those violent tendencies.

Gaining or Maintaining Social Status

Male animals competing for dominance. *The combination of differences in parental investment and sexual selection generally leads male mammals to compete more for status.*

In describing his adolescent fistfights, a Scottish man said, "The one giving out the most stitches got the reputation" (Archer, 1994, 127). Across many cultures, aggressive behavior is used to win the respect of others. Indeed, many societies hold high regard for the "warrior status," a role which includes the enjoyment of aggression and the readiness to fight for one's "honor" (McCarthy, 1994). Amongst the Yanomamö of Brazil and the Masai of Eastern Africa, only warriors can win positions of respect. Likewise, young men on the island of Truk who avoid the frequent brawls there are disdained and ridiculed by the young women. And in societies such as the Dodoth of Northern Uganda, a man isn't permitted to marry and have children until he has proven himself as a warrior.

At one level, acting aggressively to gain status is a subset of acting aggressively to gain material and social rewards. Indeed, to keep the bootlegging profits rolling in, Al Capone needed to use violence to maintain his status as a mob boss. But the goal of gaining and maintaining status has another unique connection with aggression—people may fight for status even when it brings no tangible material rewards. Indeed, some people will fight for status even when they know they'll be punished for it. Some psychologists believe that the goal of gaining social status has a unique role in determining aggression, a role connected to our evolutionary past.

Aggression and Sexual Selection

Why is the association between aggression and status so prevalent from the jungles of Brazil to the streets of Glasgow? Canadian psychologists Martin Daly and Margo Wilson (1988; 1994) believe that the link can be traced to the powerful evolutionary principles of **differential parental investment** and sexual selection. According to the principle of differential parental investment, discussed in chapter 8, females have more to lose from a rash mating decision (they can become pregnant). Hence, they will take care in choosing the males with which they mate, giving preference to those whose traits suggest better quality genes.

What does female selectivity have to do with aggression? The answer lies in **sexual selection**—the process whereby any tendencies that help in reproduction are passed on to future generations (Miller, 2000). To win the attentions of selective females, males can do one of several things. They can display positive characteristics: a beautiful peacock's tail or an ability to build a sturdy nest or to defend a rich territory. Or they can beat out the competition directly—by fighting their way to the top of the local dominance hierarchy. Whether the game is defending a territory or winning a place at the top of the hierarchy, it helps to be larger and more aggressive (Alcock, 1993). When the shoe is on the other foot and males invest more in the offspring, females compete with one another (Ridley, 1993). For example, the phalarope is a bird species in which males are small and drab. Females are larger and more aggressive, and they do the courting. Why? The males are the ones who brood and rear the chicks. They are therefore more choosy about the females with whom they will mate.

Hence, evolutionary theorists assume an inherent link between successful reproduction and competing for status. In this equation, aggression is only an incidental by-product. Sexual selection theory makes several assumptions that apply to humans. Because humans are mammals and female mammals always invest heavily in their offspring, males will generally be more likely to compete for status and territory (Buss & Duntley, 1999; Campbell, 1999). That relationship should hold across the human race. We mentioned earlier that the vast majority of homicides in

Differential parental investment *The principle that animals making higher investment in their offspring (female as compared to male mammals, for instance) will be more careful in choosing mates.*

Sexual selection *A form of natural selection favoring characteristics that assist animals in attracting mates or in competing with members of their own sex.*

the United States during recent decades have been committed by males. Consistent with the evolutionary perspective, the same gender difference holds up worldwide (see Figure 10.7).

If aggressive competition between males is about mating, then it should rise and fall with particular conditions. When males have little access to other resources with which to attract females, competition with other males should be harsher. Likewise, as males enter the years of reproductive competition, the aggressiveness should increase. Once a male has attracted a long-term mate, on the other hand, he has less need to be butting heads with other males. We consider the evidence for these predictions below. In addition to the reproduction-based gender differences, assumed to hold up across cultures, there are also independent cultural differences in status-linked aggression, which we will also consider.

Sex and Testosterone

Zoologists have observed that the male proclivity for violent competitiveness is found widely among mammals (Boulton, 1994). You don't need to tromp off to study the antelopes of Uganda or the chimpanzees of Tanzania to see the mammalian sex difference in aggressiveness. Go out to the nearest farm and observe the differences between bulls and cows or stallions and mares, or stay in the neighborhood and observe the differences between male and female dogs.

We just considered evidence that in human societies around the world, males are more homicidally violent than females. The sex difference in physical aggressiveness appears even in young children in different societies (Ahmad & Smith,

Figure 10.7 Percentage of same-sex homicides across various cultures and time periods.

Homicides committed by adult members of the same sex (men killing men, women killing women) have been committed predominantly by men across different cultures and periods of history.

SOURCE: *Daly & Wilson (1988).*

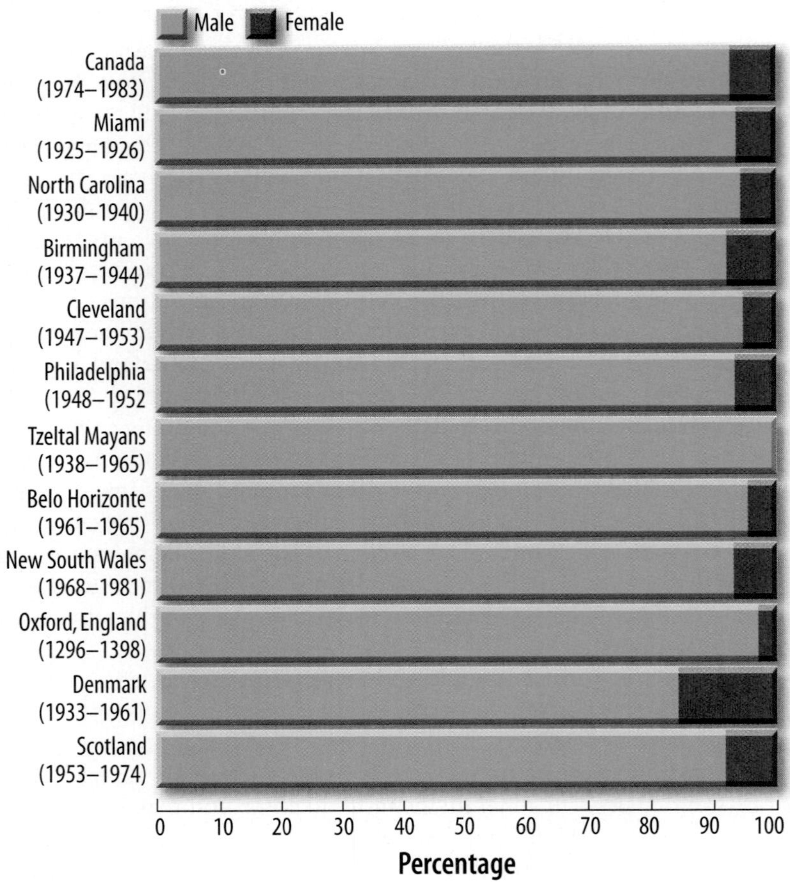

1994; Munro et al., 2000). Consistent with the perspective of sexual selection theory, even playful fighting amongst boys often gets dangerous and appears to be motivated by the desire to win status (Boulton, 1994; Fry, 1990).

The biological motivation to compete for status may be linked to the distant evolutionary past, but the driving mechanism is still in our bodies today. Testosterone is a hormone linked to masculine bodily development and behavior in a wide range of animal species. It flows in greater quantities through male than female bloodstreams and has been directly linked to both aggressiveness and social dominance. In an early study of its effects, researchers injected testosterone into low-ranking hens. The hens began to act aggressively, to crow like roosters, and to rise up in the status hierarchy (Allee, Collias, & Lutherman, 1939). Later research found similar effects in other animals. From rats to monkeys, injections of testosterone boost aggressiveness and dominance over other group members (Ellis, 1986; Monaghan & Glickman, 1992). What about human beings? Social psychologist Jim Dabbs and his colleagues have conducted an extensive series of investigations into the links between testosterone and social behavior. Some of their findings are:

High-testosterone males. *Researcher Jim Dabbs has found that men with high testosterone are more likely to have showy tattoos and to engage in a variety of antisocial behaviors. Southern men with records of delinquency had higher testosterone levels than a comparison group of college students.*

- Measures of testosterone taken from over 600 prison inmates have revealed that those having high testosterone levels are viewed as tougher by other prison inmates. They also have more confrontations with prison authorities. Additionally, the crimes committed by these high-testosterone prisoners were, on average, more violent (Dabbs et al., 1987, 1991, 1995).
- A study of delinquent men and women living in a southern city revealed them to have higher testosterone levels than a comparison group of college students (Banks & Dabbs; 1996) (see photo).
- An examination of records for 4,462 military veterans in their 30s and 40s revealed that those having high testosterone levels were more likely to have had trouble with the law, to have been violent, to have abused drugs and alcohol, to have gone AWOL while in the service, and to have an unusually large number of sexual partners (Dabbs & Morris, 1990).
- Testosterone levels are associated with aggressive behaviors even in boys aged nine to eleven (Chance, Brown, Dabbs, & Casey, 2000).

All of these findings are correlational, making it difficult to determine whether high testosterone was a cause or a consequence of aggressive and antisocial behavior. The causal picture is muddied because testosterone can be raised by competition or sexual behavior (Mazur & Booth, 1998). For example, male college students in one study were insulted and pushed by another student (Cohen, Nisbett, Bowdle, & Schwarz, 1996). When subjects' testosterone levels were measured after this face-off, they had risen significantly.

Experimental studies in which testosterone is administered to some subjects and not to others, however, suggest that this hormone is a cause, and not just a correlate, of increased competitive behavior. In one study, a small group of normal men were given increasingly higher doses of testosterone, doubling every two weeks over a six-week period (Kouri, Lukas, Pope, & Oliva, 1995). During the course of the testosterone treatment, they were placed in a laboratory with another subject who they believed was penalizing them by pressing a button that would reduce cash paid to them. Those given the testosterone injections were more likely to retaliate than men given an inert placebo.

A fascinating series of studies by Dutch psychologists examined a group of fifty individuals as they were undergoing medical sex change procedures. Stephanie VanGoozen and her colleagues (1995) were able to track changes in both directions. Thirty-five of the transsexuals were females receiving testosterone as part of their desired transformation into males. Fifteen were men receiving testosterone-suppressing drugs as part of their desired transformation into females. The researchers measured changes in sexual motivation and aggressive behavior. Administration of testosterone to women increased their aggression proneness and their sexual arousability. The effects on men deprived of testosterone were just as dramatic in the opposite direction: they showed decreases in aggression and sexual arousability.

It is important to note that both males and females produce testosterone and that testosterone may affect females in some of the same ways that it affects males (Dabbs, et al., 1998; Glickman, et al., 1993). But adult males produce about seven times as much testosterone as do females (Mazur & Booth, 1998). Even in men, though, the effects of testosterone on aggression, like the effects of watching violent media, are not overwhelming, and researchers sometimes need to examine a large number of subjects to find clear effects (Dabbs & Morris, 1990).

In any individual, then, heightened testosterone is hardly an automatic trigger for violent or antisocial behavior. Instead, it may be more closely linked to competitive behaviors including chess playing, tennis playing, debating, and even watching Olympic soccer games (Mazur & Booth, 1998; Mazur, Booth, & Dabbs, 1992). After reviewing a number of studies, Allan Mazur and Alan Booth (1998) conclude that high levels of testosterone in humans encourage "behavior intended to dominate—to enhance one's status over—other people" (353). They note that sometimes this behavior is aggressive or rebellious, but sometimes it is not. Thus, it seems that testosterone does not have a direct effect on aggressiveness, but only an indirect one via its enhancement of dominance motivation.

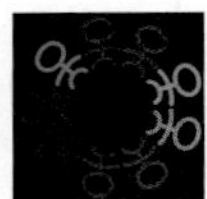

Insults and Other "Trivial Altercations"

Many situations that elicit aggressive behavior trigger the motive to enhance one's status (or to avoid losing status). Consistent with the assumption that status-linked aggression is more crucial to males than to females, a greater percentage of male murderers are motivated by a desire to retaliate for a previous insult or "put-down" (Daly & Wilson, 1988).

Consider the brutal Manson Family murders with which we opened the chapter. Although the crime scene appeared at first to have been randomly chosen, further investigation revealed otherwise. Manson had been insulted not once but three times by people connected to that house. Shortly before the murders, he had gone to the house looking for Terry Melcher, the Hollywood agent who had previously spurned him. It turned out that the property had been purchased by another Hollywood agent, and when Manson tried to approach this man, he was again rebuffed, this time quite rudely. On the same visit, a friend of one of the residents saw Manson wandering on the property, and, in an insulting tone, asked him what his business was.

The power of a personal put-down to elicit aggression has been harnessed in a number of laboratory studies of aggression. Compared to those treated with respect, experimental subjects are more likely to deliver electric shocks or other unpleasant consequences to another participant who insults them (e.g., Buss, 1963; Carver & Glass, 1978). Outside the laboratory, teenagers who are asked about what makes them angry often mention others insulting or teasing them (Torestad, 1990). And college students' fantasies about killing others often follow incidents in which the other person humiliates them in some way (Kenrick & Sheets, 1994). Furthermore, urban gang fights are often triggered by the members of one gang insulting the status of another (Archer, 1994; Chin & Lee, 1993).

Concern about saving face often gets carried to extreme lengths. In a classic study of homicides in Philadelphia, Marvin Wolfgang (1958) categorized 37 percent of the causes as "trivial altercations": disputes started over relatively petty issues, such as an insult, a curse, or one person bumping into another. Yet trivial altercations were the most common motives for murder. As one Dallas homicide detective put it: "Murders result from little ol' arguments about nothing at all. Tempers flare.

A fight starts, and somebody gets stabbed or shot. I've worked on cases where the principals had been arguing over a 10 cent record on a jukebox, or over a one dollar gambling debt from a dice game" (quoted in Wilson & Daly, 1985, 59).

Only men seem to get involved in homicides over trivial altercations. Why? After an extensive examination of police reports of Detroit homicides, Wilson and Daly (1985) suggested that what was at stake was actually nontrivial:

> Violent male-male disputes are really concerned with "face," dominance status, and..."presentation of self" in a highly competitive social milieu.... [In] the typical, almost tragic, progression of events,...neither victim nor offender finds it possible to back down.... (59–60)

Not every man responds to a put-down by running for the nearest gun. Whether such status confrontations turn violent depends on a feature of the broader situation—the culture in which a person is raised, as we see next.

The Culture of Honor The McCoys were convinced that Floyd Hatfield had stolen one of their hogs. So they felt it necessary to retaliate. What followed was a decade of violence. Forty members on each side were drawn into the famous Hatfield–McCoy feud, and over a dozen of them were dead before it was over (Waller, 1988).

The Hatfields and the McCoys were agricultural families whose feud may illustrate a general principle linking geography, history, economics, and cultural norms. According to Richard Nisbett (1993), those who reside in the southern and western United States are socialized into a "culture of honor." One of the key elements of the **culture of honor** is the need to defend one's honor with violent retaliation if necessary (Cohen & Nisbett, 1997).

The Southern culture of honor (and violence). *William Anderson Hatfield (seated) was the patriarch whose family became enmeshed in a feud with the relatives of Ranel McCoy. The Hatfields and McCoys were agricultural families from the Kentucky/West Virginia border who showed many of the characteristics associated with the "Southern culture of violence."*

In developing their theory about the culture of honor, Nisbett and his colleagues reviewed a number of interesting findings. For one, the South has a long history of violence, including feuds, duels, and bushwhackings, and a peculiar game called Purring, in which two opponents grasped each other by the shoulders and kicked each other in the shins until one released his grip. Andrew Jackson was involved in more than 100 violent quarrels in his lifetime and even killed one political opponent. In the old South, according to Nisbett, it was impossible to get a conviction for murder when the perpetrator had been insulted and had warned the victim of his intention to kill if the insult wasn't retracted or compensated.

And the laws still reflect that culture. For example, some states have laws requiring that a person try to retreat from a conflict situation before resorting to the use of deadly force. These "retreat rules" are seen by some to require cowardly and dishonorable behavior inconsistent with the image of a "true man" (Cohen, 1996). Indeed, such retreat rules have often been struck down by courts in southern and western states. Consistent with the culture of honor hypothesis, these rules exist in nine of ten northern states but only in about half of southern states and in fewer than one in five western states (Cohen, 1996).

Of course, no geographical area is without a history of human violence. Is the South any more violent than other areas? Consistent with Nisbett's thesis, homicide rates tend to be higher in southern states. Along with Gregory Polly and Sylvia Lang, Nisbett found that the increased homicide rate couldn't be completely explained by various differences between southern and northern cities (such as temperature, racial composition, or city size). Even after controlling for these other factors, whites living in the South had a homicide rate more than twice as high as that for other regions, such as New England (Nisbett et al., 1995). Indeed, one social

Culture of honor *A set of societal norms whose central idea is that people (particularly men) should be ready to defend their honor with violent retaliation if necessary.*

psychologist has argued that the southern culture of violence, and not the heat, may explain the high homicide rates in cities such as Houston (Rotton, 1993).

Another feature of the homicide data is consistent with Nisbett's thesis that Southern violence is linked to a culture in which face saving requires retaliative aggression. The North–South difference holds true only for argument-related homicides. Southerners aren't generally more violent or more criminally oriented; they're simply more likely to kill as part of an argument. In survey studies, there is a similar pattern—Southerners do not generally approve of violence, but they are more inclined to condone violence as a reasonable response to an insult.

Dov Cohen, Brian Bowdle, and Norbert Schwarz joined Nisbett to conduct a fascinating, and slightly dangerous, series of experiments examining these regionally based differences in aggression (Cohen et al., 1996). The experimental setting was arranged so that the subject had to crowd past another student working at a filing cabinet, forcing that other student to move out of the way. The subject was then required to return past the same tight spot, at which point the other student slammed the file drawer shut, pushed his shoulder against the subject, and called the subject an "asshole." The confederate then quickly retreated behind a locked door—which turned out to be a good idea, as one subject actually pursued the confederate and aggressively rattled the door knob. Two confederates were stationed nearby to record the subject's reactions to this insult. In response to this provocation, 65 percent of Northerners responded with more amusement than anger. This was true for only 15 percent of Southerners, however, who generally indicated much more outrage than humor.

Nisbett, himself born in Virginia, argues that the culture of honor is rooted in the economy and history of the early South. He notes that the South was settled by "swashbuckling Cavaliers of noble and landed gentry status, who took their values not from the tilling of the soil and the requirements of civic responsibility but from the knightly, medieval standards of manly honor and virtue" (442). The descendants of these southern pioneers later populated the western states and brought the norms of the "culture of honor" with them. Although residents of the region no longer live the same lifestyle as their swashbuckling forebears, the norms of honor apparently live on.

Different Opportunity Paths

Testosterone appears to stimulate a motivation towards dominance in men (Mazur & Booth, 1998). If that motivation can be satisfied without resort to violence, presumably it will. From the perspective of sexual selection theory, the male tendency to struggle for dominance is itself only a path to a more important goal—successful reproduction. This suggests that male status-linked aggressiveness will appear only in those circumstances when less dangerous paths to social status are blocked. Status-driven aggression should also be enhanced when females are hard to come by, but reduced when a man has succeeded in the goal of attracting a mate. Research supports each of these interactive predictions.

Blocked Pathways to Success Violence and competitiveness are most pronounced in certain groups, particularly poor men during late adolescence and early adulthood (Wilson & Daly, 1985). David Rowe (1996) argues that delinquency may be a strategy that young men adopt only when their other options are limited. Rowe notes that the combination of criminal violence and early sexual behavior is high amongst those having low intelligence. For more intelligent individuals, who can accumulate greater wealth and resources through safer, conventional means, it makes more sense to work hard, stay in school, and delay starting a family.

Using their sample of 4,462 U.S. military veterans, James Dabbs and Robin Morris (1990) were able to examine the different correlates of high testosterone in high- and low-status men. Their results are depicted in Figure 10.8. Whereas high testosterone did not boost antisocial behaviors in men of high status, it substantially boosted the risk of adult delinquency in men of lower status.

Why the difference? Dabbs and Morris explain it in terms of the different paths to status. For men in both the upper- and the lower-class groups, testosterone probably stimulated the same drive for competition and dominance. However, upper-class men did not need to beat someone up to act on that drive—they could vent it during vigorous and risky activity on the tennis court, chess board, or stock exchange. For men in the lower-class group, though, who may have been unemployed or working in menial jobs, these pathways to respect were not available, so they were more likely to answer the drive for respect and status by hitting someone or thwarting the law.

One popular view suggested that low self-esteem leads to aggressiveness. After reviewing the evidence for this claim, however, social psychologist Roy Baumeister and his colleagues concluded that it is false. Instead, people with high self-esteem (particularly men) are more likely to act aggressively (Baumeister, Bushman, & Campbell, 2000). However, it is not people who are comfortable with themselves that we most need to watch out for. Instead, it is those with an inflated and unstable high appraisal of themselves that is currently being threatened (e.g., Bushman & Baumeister, 1998; Kernis, Grannemann, & Barclay, 1989).

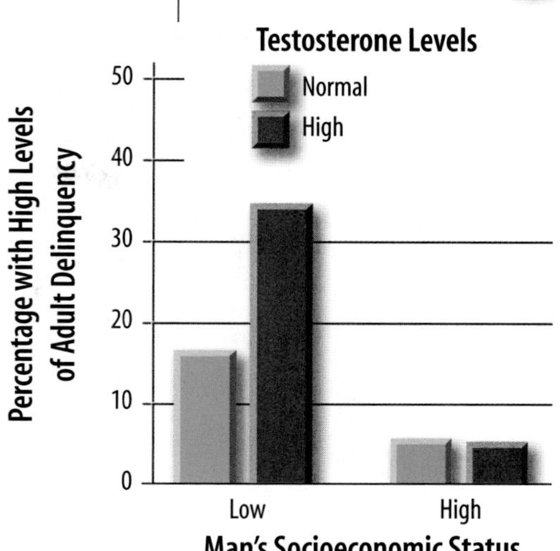

Figure 10.8

Testosterone contributes to risk of antisocial behavior only in lower class men.

As shown on the right side of the figure, testosterone has no relationship to adult antisocial behavior in men who are above average in education and social class. As shown on the left, however, high testosterone is associated with substantially greater risk in lower-class men, who presumably have limited resources with which to achieve social dominance.

Competition for Mates Several lines of evidence suggest that status-linked aggressiveness ebbs and flows along with competition for mates. In other animal species, male aggressiveness increases just before the mating season, when territories and females are being contested (Gould & Gould, 1989). In humans, boys increase their dominance competitions at puberty, when successful competitiveness (such as being a sports star) begins to lead to popularity with the opposite sex (Weisfeld, 1994). More serious violence also occurs during men's late teens and twenties when their testosterone levels are highest (Daly & Wilson, 1988). Daly & Wilson point out that these are also the years when males are competing most vigorously for mates.

Craig Palmer (1993) observed aggressive behavior among amateur hockey players in Canada. Young, unmarried males acted aggressively in 42 percent of their games, compared with only 15 percent for the older, married hockey players. When the researcher categorized the aggressive acts, he found young players less likely to use humorous aggression and more likely to use the hostile types. Young players not only got angry more easily, they also acted aggressively toward other players even when they didn't appear angry (see Figure 10.9). Palmer (1993) views this "cool overaggression" in terms of the evolutionary model of aggression we discussed earlier. For younger males who have not attracted a permanent mate, aggressive interactions with other males are made more serious by the importance of gaining and maintaining social status (and the consequent enhancement of attractiveness to women). Older, married men are in a better position to laugh it off.

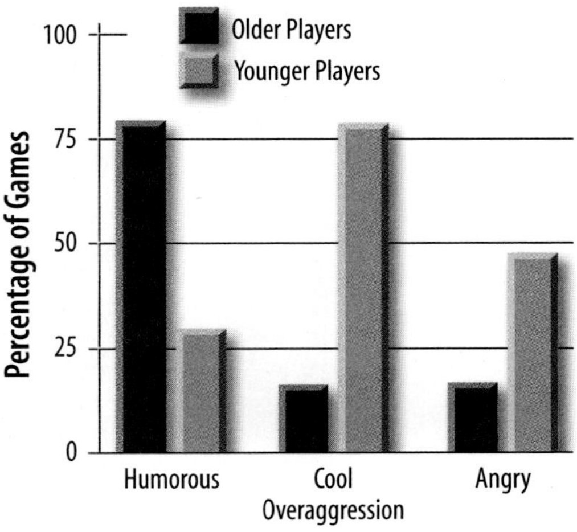

Figure 10.9

Aggressiveness in male hockey players.

One researcher kept records of various types of aggression committed by younger single hockey players and older married players. The older, more established men were generally less aggressive, and if they were aggressive, it was more likely to be humorous. Younger players were more likely to show angry aggression or cold, instrumental hostility.

Summary

Social status is a goal of aggression that, according to an evolutionary perspective, applies more to males than to females. According to sexual selection theory, this is because our female ancestors were more likely to mate with males who dominated their competitors. Males across species, including humans, are more likely to compete aggressively for status, and this sex difference appears to be linked to the hormone testosterone. Status-linked violence can be elicited by insults to a person's honor, even when they appear trivial. Face-saving aggressiveness is more acceptable in "cultures of honor" such as those of the Old South and the Wild West. Status-linked aggressiveness interacts with social opportunity and is found more in those whose paths are blocked. High testosterone interacts with social class and is associated with antisocial behavior only in those of lower socioeconomic status. Finally, men are more likely to act aggressively when they have not yet successfully attracted a mate.

Protecting Oneself or Others

A jury is likely to have little sympathy for someone who murdered because of annoyance at the hot weather or a desire to collect hit money or win the respect of fellow gang members. But the final motive for aggression we'll consider can serve as a legitimate excuse, even for homicide. J. Martin Ramirez (1993) surveyed people in Spain, Finland, and Poland about the circumstances under which aggression might be justified. In all three countries, people rated "self-defense" and "protecting others" at the top of the list of justified causes of aggression.

When cornered, even the most pacific creature may turn violent, as one of the authors of this text learned when, as a young child, he tried to pick up a cute little squirrel in New York City. After letting out an ear-piercing squeal, the furry rodent attacked with razor sharp teeth, sending a sadder but wiser young naturalist to the emergency room. Even the hoodlums in street gangs often join because, like squirrels surrounded by potential predators, they feel threatened. In discussing the gangs prevalent in New York during Al Capone's childhood, one historian observed that "slum kids had to belong to a gang for protection and survival" (Schoenberg, 1992). As we discuss in upcoming chapters, the perception of threat to oneself or to one's group may play a deadly role in intergroup violence ranging from local racial attacks to international war.

Of course, not everyone protects himself or herself from violence by acting aggressively. As we discuss below, some people are more likely to engage in self-defensive aggression, and some circumstances are more likely to turn defensive feelings into self-protective violence.

Self-Defenders

In Hans Toch's (1984) classic attempt to classify violent criminals, one of his murderous types was what he called the "self-defender." Such people "react to other persons as sources of physical danger. They are afraid that if they don't strike first, they'll become victims themselves" (Bertilson, 1990, 459).

Two features of the person might contribute to the tendency to resort to this type of self-defensive aggression, one related to attributional style, the other related to one's relative size and strength.

Defensive Attributional Style Most aggressive children, rather than being heartless little psychopaths, are actually frightened of being attacked (Dodge, Price, Bachorowski, & Newman, 1990). These little aggressors are often characterized by two key features: (1) a tendency to be overly emotional, and (2) a tendency to believe that others are threatening them. Based on their studies of schoolyard aggressiveness, Kenneth Dodge and his colleagues have developed a social-information processing model of aggressive behavior in children (Dodge, 1982; Dodge et al., 1990; see Table 10.3).

Table 10.3 Differences in social information processing by defensive and nondefensive children.

			Response of:	
			Nondefensive Child	Defensive Child
Step 1	Search the situation for possible threats.	Is anyone threatening me in any way?	Less likely to notice if another child bumps against him or her in a game.	More likely to notice other child bumping against him or her.
Step 2	Interpret the cues.	Why did that kid bump into me?	More likely to interpret ambiguous bump as an accident.	More likely to interpret bump as attempt to push him or her around.
Step 3	Consider possible ways to respond.	What should I do about the kid repeatedly bumping into me?	More likely to consider a peaceful solution, such as making a joke.	More likely to consider an aggressive solution, such as hitting or retaliating in another way.
Step 4	Select a response.	Which possibility will best solve the problem?	More likely to rule out an aggressive response even if he or she considers it.	More likely to rule out a peaceful response.
Step 5	Carry it out.	How do I do what I've decided on?	More skilled at carrying out peaceful options.	More skilled at carrying out aggressive options.

Emotional children tend to have a **defensive attributional style**—a tendency to notice threats and to interpret other children's behavior as intentionally meant to harm them (Dodge & Coie, 1987). Out of fear of such harm, hostile children are more likely to consider, and to choose, aggressive responses to situations that other children would ignore. And older children and adolescents who are incarcerated for violence often show the same defensive pattern. Rather than simply beating up others for the fun of it, they act aggressively in response to what they perceive as threats from others (Dodge et al., 1990).

The Effect/Danger Ratio and Abusive Relationships Because of their relatively small physical size, females are more likely to be on the receiving end of bullying in their relationships with males (Ahmad & Smith, 1994). One survey of women waiting in doctors' offices revealed a startling fact: More than 40 percent had been physically abused by a husband or boyfriend at some time in their lives, and almost half that number were currently in an abusive relationship (Coker et al., 2000). Indeed, of the women killed in the United States, more than half are killed by their own partners.

Women also kill their partners, but for very different motives (Browne, 1993; Daly & Wilson, 1988). Whereas men are likely to kill their partners as part of a pattern of harassment and attempted control, women are likely to kill their partners in self-defense. Thus, women resort to violence only in extreme circumstances—when they have been repeatedly threatened and abused.

Given that females feel angry as frequently as men do, why does it take more extreme circumstances to trigger serious physical violence in them? Finnish psychologist Kaj Bjorkvist and colleagues (1994) suggest that part of the answer may come from what they call the "effect/danger ratio." The **effect/danger ratio** is a person's assessment of the likely beneficial effect of aggressiveness, balanced against the likely dangers. If you are truly angry at another person, a punch in the face may deliver more of the desired effect than a verbal insult. However, the punch in the face is more likely to elicit physical violence in return. If your opponent is sixty pounds heavier than you and has twice the upper body strength, you are likely to think twice about using physical aggression as a persuasive tool. Ironically, for

Defensive attributional style *A tendency to notice threats and to interpret other people's behavior as intended to do one harm.*

Effect/danger ratio *Assessment of the likely beneficial effect of aggressiveness balanced against the likely dangers.*

women who live under constant threat from a larger, abusive man, killing him may seem less dangerous than a milder counterattack, which might just provoke more violence on his part.

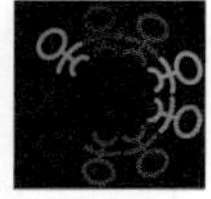

Perceived Threats

In the movie *The Paper*, a character who had begun to carry a gun to work is asked by a colleague, "When did you start getting so paranoid?" His response: "When people started plotting against me." It makes sense that "pre-emptive" aggression is more likely to occur when there is a perception of actual threat. When one of the authors of this textbook taught a course at the local state prison, an inmate wrote an essay describing how, upon entering prison, he severely beat the first inmate who threatened him. The rationale was that if fellow prisoners don't see you as dangerous, they will harass you relentlessly.

When one researcher asked teenagers what triggered their everyday feelings of anger, they most frequently mentioned someone else's intentionally acting unreasonably towards them, insulting them, teasing them, or physically harassing them (Torestad, 1990). And when college students were asked about homicidal fantasies, most could remember at least one, and it was often triggered by a threat to oneself or to a valued other (Kenrick & Sheets, 1994).

Simply showing up at school can be a threatening experience for some U.S. teenagers. The combination of being African American and being a teenager drastically increases the chance of encountering threats on a daily basis. Teenagers are 2.5 times more likely to be victims of violent crime than are people over twenty years of age, and blacks are 10 times more likely to be murdered than whites (Hammock & Yung, 1993). Among African American male adolescents, homicide is, in fact, the most common cause of death.

If the perception of retaliation is removed, on the other hand, people become less concerned with protecting themselves. As we discussed in considering the effect/danger ratio, females may avoid acting aggressively because they fear an aggressive counterattack (Eagly & Steffen, 1986). What happens when the dangers of retaliation are removed? Jenifer Lightdale and Deborah Prentice (1994) conducted two studies in which men and women played an aggressive computer game under conditions of anonymity or identifiability. When they could be identified, women acted less aggressively than did men. However, when they could act aggressively without being identified, the gender difference disappeared. Although these experiments involved a relatively nonhostile form of aggressiveness—attacking another in a computer game—the female members of the Manson Family demonstrated that there are circumstances under which women can lose their concerns about even extreme violence towards strangers.

Self-Protective Aggression Can Increase Danger

As we noted earlier, children who view the world in hostile terms are most likely to strike out first (Dodge & Frame, 1982). When a child makes a preemptive strike against even an imagined threat, however, the world actually becomes more dangerous, as the child's preemptive strike is likely to elicit retaliation. This finding indicates a reciprocal interaction involving cognition and the social environment. In this case, a belief becomes a self-fulfilling prophecy—the child who views the world as more aggressive actually acts to create a world that is more aggressive.

Because of the real threats to their safety, adolescents in inner-city schools are highly fearful of attack, and some carry weapons to protect themselves. In fact, one survey found that one of every five students in U.S. high schools reported having carried a weapon to school during the preceding thirty days (Center for Disease Control, 1991). Unfortunately, as more young people carry dangerous weapons, the likelihood of serious violence goes up, and, in a vicious circle, so does the felt need to carry a weapon.

Like frightened teenagers, adults often purchase guns for self-defense (Kellermann et al., 1993). Unfortunately, those guns are much more likely to be used against friends or acquaintances than against criminals. In fact, compared to non-gun owners, those who purchase guns increase, rather than decrease, their own likelihood of being killed. Ironically, the increased danger comes from the fact that another person is now likely to use the gunowner's own gun against him or her (Sugarmann & Rand, 1994). Having a gun in the home increases one's chance of being killed almost threefold (Kellerman et al., 1993).

Summary

Aggression is seen as most justified when it is motivated by defense of oneself or others. Aggressive youngsters are more likely to interpret other people's behaviors as threatening, and women, because of their relatively smaller size, are more likely to avoid aggressive self-defense except in extremely threatening circumstances. Women are likely to kill their husbands only after a history of threats and brutality by their husbands. Adolescents, especially African American teenagers, are commonly threatened with violence and may begin to carry weapons for self-defense. Unfortunately, this feeds into a cycle of violence which only increases the danger to people who have weapons.

Reducing Violence

As you've seen throughout this chapter, even apparently senseless violence begins to make sense when you examine the surrounding events. Though some theorists once suggested that we had "instincts" to act aggressively for aggressiveness's own sake, evidence now suggests that any biological tendencies toward aggression play themselves out in continual interaction with events in the environment.

Given all we've learned about these environmental triggers of aggressive motivation and their connection to factors inside the person, is there anything we can do to reduce violence? A number of psychologists believe the answer is yes, and several of them have put their ideas into action by setting up programs to reduce and prevent violence. One psychological program successfully reduced bullying in elementary school children (Olweus, 1991). Another reduced fighting and arrests among violent teenagers (Hammock & Yung, 1993). How do aggression-reduction programs work? There are several different approaches, each of which focuses on different motives for aggression. Some teach alternative techniques for gaining reward, some teach ways of handling annoyance and unpleasant arousal, others punish aggressive behavior, and still others propose to prevent aggression by reducing the threat of guns.

Rewarding Alternatives to Aggression

One of the best-known treatment programs for aggressive children was established by Gerald Patterson and his colleagues (Patterson, Chamberlain, & Reid, 1982; Patterson, 1997). The program's main assumption is simple and consistent with much of the research we've reviewed: that the goal of aggressive behavior is often to attain rewards. From this social learning perspective, aggression can be reduced if the rewards that follow hostility are extinguished and if other means of attaining rewards are put into place. The essential components of this program involve training parents in the principles of behavior modification, teaching them to recognize how they reward aggressive behavior in their children, and encouraging them to begin rewarding more acceptable alternative behaviors.

As part of the program, the parents and their child establish a contract in which the child wins points for appropriate behavior and loses points every time he or she acts aggressively. If a child earns enough points in a given day, he or she is permitted some reward. The reward is chosen to match what the child finds most desirable; it might be staying up late to watch television, a special dessert, or having mom read a story at bedtime. Patterson's group has conducted rigorous research on the program and concluded that it is effective, for most children.

Another approach to reducing aggression aims at cognition—by trying to teach people to control their own anger-arousing thoughts. We discuss this approach next.

FOCUS ON Application

Using Cognition to Manage Angry Arousal

Earlier, we discussed Dolf Zillmann's (1983) theory of cognitive processes and aggressive feelings. In recent years, Zillmann (1994) has expanded his theory to consider the mutual influence of angry feelings and thought processes in the escalation of hostility. Zillmann's model of these mutual influences is presented in Table 10.4.

According to his model, people go through three stages as they become progressively more angry. At each stage, there is an interaction of thoughts, feelings, and behaviors. Imagine a woman discussing the volume of music with her hard-rock-loving upstairs neighbor. At Stage 1, she is not highly emotionally aroused, her thought processes are careful and balanced, and her behaviors are cautiously assertive ("Sorry to bother you, but since it's after midnight, I wonder if you could turn down your Black Mega-Homicide album a few decibels. I'm getting a little nervous at the way my ceiling fan is vibrating dangerously over my head."). If the neighbor jokingly responds, "Hey, we're having a 'Thank God it's Wednesday party.' Try to loosen up a little bit!" she may move to Stage 2, in which her arousal goes up, her thought processes are more selective and self-concerned, and her behaviors are more unyielding and hostile ("Turn the damn thing down or I'll call the police and get you and your drugged-out zombie friends evicted from this place!"). Because such hostile behaviors often trigger retaliations, the upstairs neighbor may simply slam the door in her face and turn the music up. At this point, she is likely to

Table 10.4 Zillmann's model of the interdependencies between cognition and emotional excitation in escalating aggressive behavior.

	Stage 1	Stage 2	Stage 3
Cognition	Judgment is balanced. The person appraises the situation carefully and exhaustively.	Judgment begins to tip toward increased self-concern and lower empathy for the other's position. Appraisal of the situation is more selective.	Judgment highly biased—excessive self-concern and illusions of invulnerability. Empathy for the other is gone. Spiteful thoughts predominate.
Affect (excitation)	Physiological arousal is low to moderate.	Arousal in the moderate range.	Arousal is high.
Behavior	Cautious, but assertive.	Unyielding and hostile.	Impulsive, explosive, irresponsible, reckless, violent.

SOURCE: *Based on Zillmann, 1994.*

move to Stage 3, in which her arousal levels are quite high, her cognitive processes are narrowly focused on spiteful counterattack, her capacity to empathize with the neighbor's reaction to her screaming insults is gone, and her choice of actions leans toward reckless and explosive behavior (perhaps returning with a baseball bat). In this cycle, the ability to think clearly becomes increasingly compromised as emotional arousal increases. It's just when cool-headed rationality is most needed that it goes out the window.

Given that we understand how arousal and cognition work together to escalate aggression, is there anything we can do to short-circuit the cycle? One successful aggression reduction program trained people to short-circuit this escalating process by using cognition to block the runaway negative arousal. Raymond Novaco's (1975, 1995) cognitive approach focuses on training people to modify their own thoughts and feelings with well-rehearsed "self-statements."

Participants are taught to speak to themselves (silently) as they imagine situations that particularly annoy them. The self-statements deal with four stages of provocation:

- **Preparing for provocation.** For times when they find themselves in situations likely to make them angry, participants rehearse statements such as "I can manage this situation. I know how to regulate my anger."
- **Confronting the provocation.** For times when they're face-to-face with an upsetting event, they rehearse statements such as "You don't need to prove yourself" and "It's really a shame that this person is acting the way he is."
- **Coping with the arousal and agitation.** If subjects find themselves getting upset, they are trained to say things such as "Time to relax and slow things down."
- **Reflecting on the provocation.** After the subject has been in a provoking situation, during the time that people often continue to fume, he or she is taught to say things such as "These are difficult situations, and they take time to work out" and "It could have been a lot worse."

The treatment was used for people who had problems controlling their anger. The cognitive approach was compared with two control conditions: one group was trained in deep-muscle relaxation techniques, and another was instructed only to pay attention to their anger experiences. Comparing the groups on feelings of anger and on physiological measures such as blood pressure, Novaco found that both relaxation and cognitive treatments had positive effects. Combining the two—teaching people both to control their thoughts and to relax—was the most effective treatment. ■

The cognitive and behavioral treatments we've discussed so far have met with some success in reducing aggression at the individual level. But some psychologists believe that to reduce aggressiveness in any true sense will require intervention at the societal level. Some researchers have therefore examined the effects of various legal punishments on aggressive behavior.

Legal Punishments

In general, psychologists believe that punishment may not always be effective in training people to be nonaggressive. Punishing children often increases their feelings of anger and frustration, and, if it's corporal punishment, it may teach a child that it's all right to be aggressive when in a position of power. Further, as we noted earlier, psychopaths, who are overrepresented among violent criminals, do not seem to learn from threats of punishment. Nevertheless, punishment, if it's immediate, strong, and consistent, may suppress some aggressive behavior (Berkowitz, 1993a).

Unfortunately, it is impossible for police and courts of law to catch every act of aggression and to punish it swiftly. Studies have revealed no clear effects of capital punishment on murder rates. There are, for instance, no differences in homicide rates in states with and without capital punishment, and, comparing across different countries, those employing capital punishment actually have slightly higher homicide rates (Bedau, 1967; Nathanson, 1987; Shin, 1978). David Phillips (1985), examined British press coverage of notorious executions between 1858 and 1921. He found that when an execution was intensively covered in the press, it was followed by a brief reduction in the number of homicides in London. Unfortunately, these brief downswings were followed by upswings about two weeks later. Hence, the bottom line is that capital punishment doesn't seem to have much effect on overall homicide rates.

Another study suggested positive effects from a much less extreme form of deterrence—arrest for spousal abuse (Sherman & Berk, 1984). Unfortunately, later research hasn't generally replicated these positive effects of arrest on spousal abuse, and even when positive effects have been found, they are short-lived (Sherman et al., 1991).

Prevention by Removing Threats

If deterrence isn't an entirely effective strategy in reducing violent crime, what about prevention? David Johnson (1993) has recently argued that violent crime, which leads to over 20,000 Americans dead and 70,000 wounded each year, is a topic for which preventive psychological interventions should be receiving massive research attention. Compared with the amount of money and resources aimed at capturing and punishing violent criminals after they've done their harm, however, our society invests almost nothing in trying to prevent violence before it happens.

One form of prevention would be gun control, now favored strongly by law enforcement officials and social scientists alike (Berkowitz, 1993a). Opponents of gun control argue that "guns don't kill people, people kill people." That argument sounds sensible, until one checks the FBI crime reports to see exactly how people in the United States kill other people. Seven times out of ten, people killing people use guns. So, of the roughly 250,000 people murdered in the United States during the last ten years, over 180,000 of them were done in with firearms.

Another fear is that armed criminal types will terrorize unarmed citizens. The response to this fear is the belief that good citizens are safer if armed with their own weapons: "If guns are outlawed, only outlaws will have guns." But when nonoutlaws buy guns, rather than increasing their chances of protecting themselves against the bad guys, they instead dramatically increase their own chances of being killed or of having a family member killed (Kellermann et al., 1993).

In no other industrialized nation besides the United States are the citizens so "well protected" with handguns and automatic weapons. This doesn't make the United States safer, though; homicide rates in the United States are several times higher than those of any other major industrialized nation. If one compares the crime rates in Seattle, Washington, with those in nearby Vancouver, British Columbia (where handguns are rare), one finds that most crime statistics are similar in the two cities, with the exception of homicide, which is several times lower in Vancouver (Kellermann et al, 1993). Thus studies comparing homes with and without guns and countries with and without gun control suggest that serious gun-control interventions could result in dramatic decreases in the most frightful form of violence.

Summary

Psychologists have developed and tested a number of different interventions designed to reduce aggressiveness. Different approaches are connected to different goals (as summarized in Table 10.5). One approach is to train aggressive children in nonaggressive ways of obtaining rewards. Another is to train aggressive people to short-circuit the cognitive associations that escalate aggressive interactions. A third is to punish the aggressive person, an approach that has some dangers associated with it. Some psychologists advocate prevention, including removing the tool used in most U.S. homicides—the gun.

CHAPTER 10
Summary Table

Table 10.5 A summary of the goals served by aggression and the factors related to each goal.

The Goal	The Person	The Situation	Interactions
Coping with Feelings of Annoyance	• General physiological arousal • Type A tendencies toward time urgency and competitiveness	• Pain • Heat • Poverty (especially following short economic upswings)	• Unpleasant feelings or the presence of guns can prime a network of aggression-related thoughts and feelings • Type As choose work situations that contribute to their own frustration. • Hot-tempered children get trapped in a lifetime cycle of missed opportunities and self-induced frustrations.
Gaining Material and Social Rewards	• Psychopathic tendencies • Low empathy • Alcohol intoxication	Factors that glamorize violence, including • Media violence • Violent computer games • Winning a war	• People who choose to watch violent media are more aggressive to begin with, and watching it further increases their aggressive proclivities.
Gaining or Maintaining Social Status	• Gender • Testosterone	• Insults • "Trivial altercations" • Culture of honor	• Older males having mates and good social position become less hostile. • Testosterone increases antisocial behavior only in low-status males.
Protecting Oneself or Others	• Defensive attributional bias • Effect/danger ratio	• Perceived threats • Threatening neighborhoods • Proliferation of weapons	• Viewing the world in hostile terms leads to pre-emptive aggression, which in turn makes the world more hostile. • Possession of guns for self-protection increases one's chances of being killed.

REVISITING
Senseless Violence

Thirty years after their notorious murders, the Manson Family members still fascinate the U.S. public. Logging onto the Internet, one finds a Charles Manson "home page," complete with access to photos of Manson, paintings by Manson, recordings of his music, and updates about recent parole hearings for him and other Family members. One learns here that Manson, Krenwinkel, Atkins, and Watson have all been denied parole in the last few years.

In the transcript of his most recent parole hearing, Manson continues to express absolutely no remorse and to claim that he is a victim, innocent of wrongdoing—on the legal technicality that he was never convicted of murdering anyone with his own hands.

Charles Manson, still unrepentant after three decades. *Manson's aggressive behaviors, unlike those of his followers, seemed to stem more from deeply rooted personality characteristics than from transient situational factors.*

Another Internet item reports that he has stopped answering mail from a new generation of "fans" unless they include at least $200 with their letters. Manson's lifetime pattern of self-centered exploitation fits with the description of psychopaths—individuals who feel little remorse or empathy and who often use violence and other antisocial acts as instrumental means to an end (Hare et al., 1990). While at the head of his "family" of young devotees, he used threats and sexuality to manipulate them to commit crimes for him. And, although he chose the victims and planned out the murders, his statements then and now indicate that he would have been more than satisfied to have his followers pay the price for these crimes while he went free.

Manson's penchant for aggressiveness, social dominance, and sexuality fits with the picture of a high-testosterone male painted in our discussion of status-based aggression. Furthermore, Manson came from a poverty-stricken, low-opportunity background. His own mother deserted him, he never knew his father, and while other children were getting a formal education, Manson was in and out of reform schools. That pattern is consistent with research findings that it is the combination of low social opportunity and high testosterone levels that is most deadly (Dabbs & Morris, 1990).

Patricia Krenwinkel, on the other hand, who began life as an obedient Campfire Girl, apparently returned to her former ways while serving a life sentence in prison. Now over fifty years old, she has reportedly been quiet, reclusive, and repentant for her crimes for decades. She was described as "a model prisoner." Charles Watson, the former high school athlete and all-around "good guy" from Texas, went a step further in his repentance. He studied religion in prison, became ordained as a minister, and now works to save the souls of his fellow inmates. Susan Atkins also repented for her former murderous ways and writes about her love of Jesus on a Christian Web page.

It's easy to attribute Manson's involvement in such awful crimes to a lifetime history of antisociality and lack of opportunity. But of Family members such as Krenwinkel and Watson, who were nonviolent before and after that period, we must still ask, with Linda Kasabian, "Why would they do such a thing?" Here the research literature on aggression may again provide some clues to make the murders seem a little less random. We discussed how aggression is increased by unpleasant circumstances, including heat and poverty. As we noted, the August days of those gruesome murders were a time of sweltering heat and of poverty for Manson's followers. To middle-class youths like Krenwinkel and Watson, these times must have seemed especially harsh, particularly after having been exposed to the abundant wealth of Beverly Hills during the previous months.

In discussing the motive of self-protection, we considered evidence that attributions can be important in inspiring aggressive behavior. If another person is perceived as a potential threat or the source of one's unpleasant experiences, aggression may follow. Although it's unlikely that Manson and his followers viewed their victims as immediate threats, Manson apparently used the spirit of the times to create just the sort of embattled "us versus them" mentality found in cults such as those in Waco and Jonestown (discussed in chapter 6). In the late 1960s, U.S. society was clearly split into two embattled camps, characterized at one extreme by long-haired, drug-experimenting, free-loving hippie types (such as Manson and his group) and at the other by traditional and financially comfortable "establishment" types. During the year preceding the murders, young people were dying in increasing numbers in a war many regarded as unjust, police were brutally clashing with college students protesting that war, and two heroes of the counterculture (Martin Luther King, Jr., and Robert Kennedy), both of whom had spoken out against that war, had been assassinated. Many young people talked openly of a revolution against a society perceived as materialistic, capitalistic, imperialistic, and downright evil. Manson, like many charismatic leaders, masterfully manipulated this sense of group threat and self-righteousness in his young hippie followers. As we'll discuss in chapter 11, on prejudice, and in chapter 13's treatment of international conflict, self-righteous hatred of outgroups has fueled brutal acts from individual lynchings to systematic programs of genocide.

To summarize the lessons of this chapter, most aggression is "senseless" to the extent that it exploits others and is likely to elicit counter-aggression in return. On the other hand, even acts as seemingly senseless as mass murder can be demystified by analyzing how factors in the person and the situation interact to trigger fundamental social motivations.

CHAPTER 10

Summary

Defining Aggression

1. Aggression is defined as behavior intended to injure another. Angry feelings, unintentional harm, assertiveness, or playful aggression would not qualify as aggression under this definition.
2. Direct aggression involves an undisguised attempt to hurt another to his or her face. Indirect aggression is nonconfrontational and ambiguous.
3. Emotional aggression is hurtful behavior that stems from angry feelings. Instrumental aggression is hurting another to accomplish some other goal.
4. Women are as aggressive as men if one counts indirect aggression and mild physical aggression within relationships. Men are more aggressive if one considers serious physical assault and homicide.
5. Freudian ideas about a "death instinct" don't fit with powerful general principles of evolution. Modern evolutionary theorists believe that aggressive drives would only evolve if they were linked to adaptive survival or reproductive goals.

Coping with Feelings of Annoyance

1. The original frustration–aggression hypothesis presumed that aggression was always a consequence of frustration and that all frustration always led to aggression. The reformulated hypothesis presumes that emotional aggression can be increased by any unpleasant stimulus.
2. According to the excitation-transfer theory, annoyance-linked aggression can be increased by any emotionally arousing experience that could be mistaken for anger, including watching an erotic film.
3. Type A behavior pattern is characterized by time-urgency and competitiveness and an inclination to become angry at job-related frustrations.
4. In the short term, annoyance-linked aggression can be increased by unpleasant stimulation, including pain or heat. Over the long term, poverty is also associated with more violence.
5. According to the cognitive-neoassociation theory, either unpleasant stimulation or the presence of aggression-related cues (such as guns) can prime a network of negative thoughts and feelings.
6. Aggressive people, such as Type As, often make their own lives more frustrating.

Gaining Material and Social Rewards

1. In some subcultures, a willingness to act violently has been a ticket to wealth and success. Much of organized criminal violence has been about the control of wealthy business territories.
2. According to the social learning theory of aggression, rewards for violence can come either directly (from parents or friends) or indirectly (from watching other people get rewarded for aggression). Anger is not necessary when aggression is motivated by rewards.
3. Psychopaths have a lack of empathy for others, a high sense of self-worth, and an insensitivity to punishment. These individuals are especially likely to engage in cool and calculated aggression. Alcohol is likely to suppress feelings of empathy that normally make it unpleasant to hurt others.
4. Media such as television and movies often depict heroes being rewarded for violent behavior. Studies of the effects of violent media on observers don't always yield strong results, but meta-analyses of many studies lead to a clear conclusion: Across the many acts of violence shown in the media and the many people watching that violence, there is a reliable increase in aggression in viewers. Violence also goes up after playing graphic video games and after successful wars.
5. Violent people choose to watch more violence, and their violent tendencies are increased by watching it.

Gaining or Maintaining Social Status

1. According to sexual selection theory, female animals often choose to mate with males who have demonstrated their ability to compete successfully with other males. This selection led, over time, to increases in status-oriented aggressiveness in males.
2. Testosterone is associated with heightened aggressiveness and antisocial behavior in delinquents, prison inmates, and military veterans. Experimental administrations of this hormone increase aggressiveness in college students and transsexuals. It appears to motivate dominance-oriented behaviors, which may or may not turn into aggressiveness.

3. Even trivial insults to honor can lead to violence. In cultures of honor, such as the Old South, honor-related violence among men is more tolerated than in other regions.
4. Status-linked violence is found in men whose paths to success are blocked, such as younger, poorer men. Consistently, high levels of testosterone are associated with aggressive and antisocial behavior only in men of lower socioeconomic status. Males are also more likely to act aggressively when they are competing for mates.

Protecting Oneself or Others

1. Across countries, aggression in the defense of oneself or others is considered justified.
2. Children having a defensive attributional style are more likely to perceive potential threats and often act aggressively as a preemptive defense. Women fear more dangers in response to their own aggressive behavior and are likely to resort to it only in situations of extreme self-defense.
3. Adolescents are more likely to be threatened in school, and the dangers go up for African American adolescents.
4. When the dangers of retaliation are removed, women may act more aggressively.
5. Preemptive or defensive aggression may actually increase threats in the long run. Simply buying a gun increases the chance of being killed threefold.

Reducing Violence

1. Psychological interventions have had some success in reducing aggression at the individual and group levels. One type of intervention teaches aggressive children nonaggressive alternative strategies for winning rewards.
2. Cognitive interventions teach aggressive people self-statements designed to short-circuit escalations of angry arousal and hostile thought patterns.
3. Punishment may suppress aggressive behavior in the short run but has the downside of teaching aggression over the long run. At the societal level, legal punishments have not been found to be particularly effective deterrents to violence.
4. Some psychologists have argued for preventive approaches, including reducing the numbers of guns. Other countries in which people have limited access to handguns, such as Canada, have substantially lower homicide rates than the United States.

CHAPTER 10 Key Terms

Aggression *Behavior intended to injure another.*

Assertiveness *Behavior intended to express dominance or confidence.*

Catharsis *Discharge of aggressive impulses.*

Cognitive-neoassociation theory *The theory that any unpleasant situation triggers a complex chain of internal events, including negative emotions and negative thoughts. Depending on other cues in the situation (such as weapons), these negative feelings will be expressed as either aggression or flight.*

Culture of honor *A set of societal norms whose central idea is that people (particularly men) should be ready to defend their honor with violent retaliation if necessary.*

Defensive attributional style *A tendency to notice threats and to interpret other people's behavior as intended to do one harm.*

Differential parental investment *The principle that animals making higher investment in their offspring (female as compared to male mammals, for instance) will be more careful in choosing mates.*

Direct aggression *Behavior intended to hurt someone "to his or her face."*

Displacement *Indirect expression of an aggressive impulse away from the person or animal that elicited it.*

Effect/danger ratio *Assessment of the likely beneficial effect of aggressiveness balanced against the likely dangers.*

Emotional aggression *Hurtful behavior that stems from angry feelings.*

Excitation-transfer theory *The theory that anger is physiologically similar to other emotional states, and that any form of emotional arousal can enhance aggressive responses.*

Frustration–aggression hypothesis (original) *The theory that aggression is an automatic response to any blocking of goal-directed behavior.*

Indirect aggression *Behavior intended to hurt someone without face-to-face confrontation.*

Instrumental aggression *Hurting another to accomplish some other (nonaggressive) goal.*

Meta-analysis *A statistical combination of results from different studies of the same topic.*

Psychopath *Individual characterized by impulsivity, irresponsibility, low empathy, and lack of sensitivity to punishment. Such individuals are inclined toward acting violently for personal gain.*

Reformulated frustration–aggression hypothesis *The theory that any unpleasant stimulation will lead to emotional aggression to the extent that it generates unpleasant feelings.*

Sexual selection *A form of natural selection favoring characteristics that assist animals in attracting mates or in competing with members of their own sex.*

Social learning theory *The theory that aggression is learned through direct reward or by watching others being rewarded for aggressiveness.*

Type A behavior pattern *A group of personality characteristics, including time-urgency and competitiveness, that is associated with higher risk for coronary disease.*

Weapons effect *The tendency for weapons, such as guns, to enhance aggressive thoughts, feelings, and actions.*

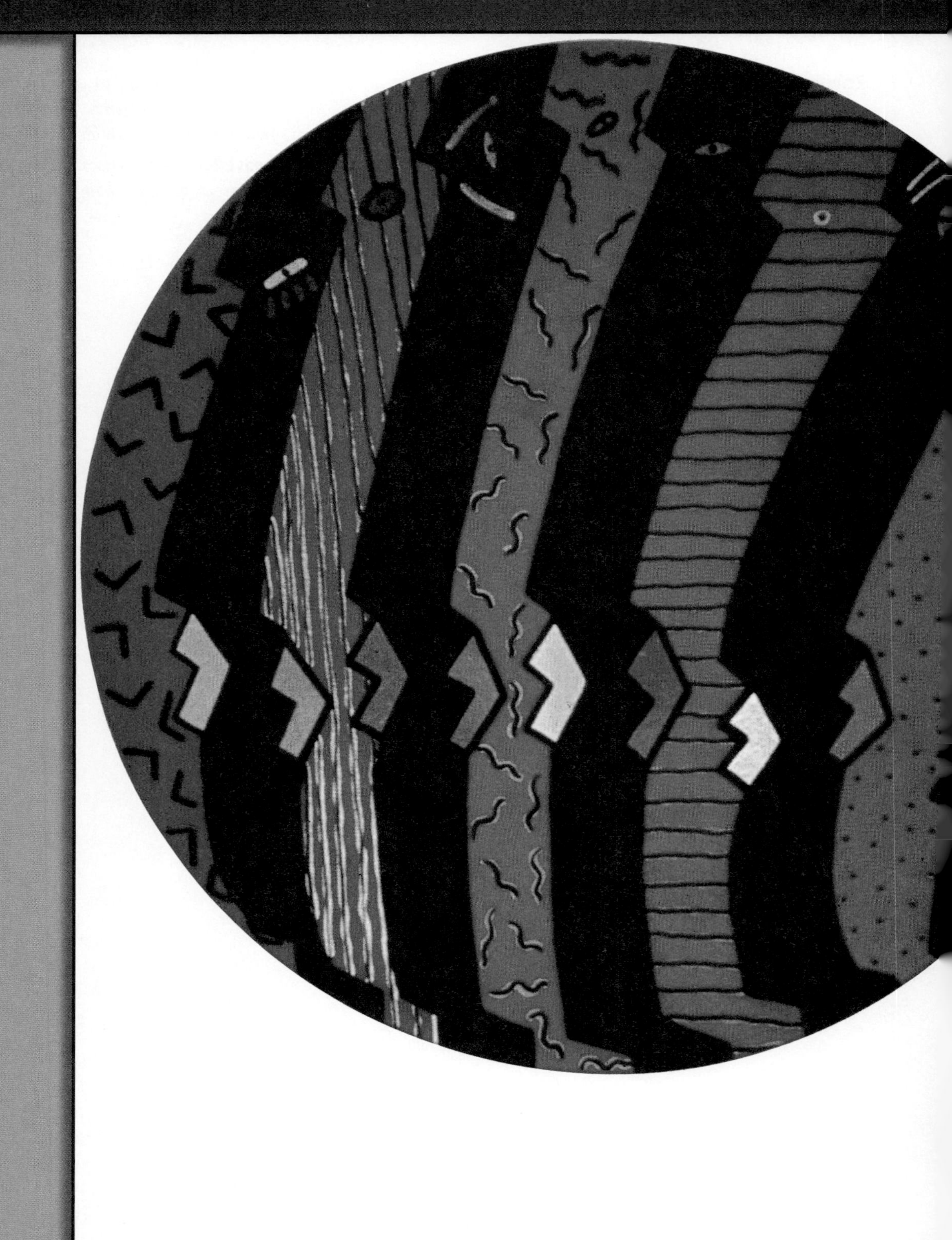

CHAPTER 11

Prejudice, Stereotyping, and Discrimination

The Unlikely Journey of Ann Atwater and C. P. Ellis

The place was Durham, North Carolina, and tensions were mounting. Challenging the centuries-old institutions of racial discrimination, African Americans had taken to the streets, boycotting businesses that would not employ them, staging sit-down strikes in restaurants and theaters that refused to serve them, and marching to protest unfair housing practices. These protests angered many in Durham's white population, who considered their city a model of good race relations and fair treatment. On several occasions, demonstrators from the two sides clashed violently.

Against this backdrop of confrontation, officials called a public meeting to address perhaps the most contentious issue of all—school desegregation. In 1971, a full seventeen years after the Supreme Court had ruled that separate public schools for black and white children violated the U.S. Constitution, Durham's school system was still almost entirely segregated. The black community wanted to desegregate the schools and increase funding for black students; most of the white community wished to maintain the existing system.

The meeting began quietly, but the peace wouldn't last. Claiborne Paul "C. P." Ellis and Ann Atwater were soon, once again, at each other's throats. "If we didn't have niggers in the schools, we wouldn't have any problems. The problem here today is niggers!" the white man shouted. The black woman leaped to her feet: "The problem is that we have stupid crackers like C. P. Ellis in Durham!"

Public showdowns were nothing new for these two (Davidson, 1996; Hochberg, 1996; Terkel, 1992). C. P. Ellis was the Exalted Cyclops of the Durham chapter of the Ku Klux Klan. He regularly attended city council and other public meetings and frequently rallied his members against the civil rights marchers. He distributed racist literature and taunted blacks on the streets. He threw an impromptu celebration party on the day of Martin Luther King, Jr.'s, murder, toasting the assassin. And, carrying a loaded gun, Ellis had once shot a black youth in the back. He was willing to use violence to achieve his goals.

Ann Atwater was a community activist who often found herself face to face with C. P. Ellis, fighting for everything he opposed. Her expert knowledge of bureaucratic regulations made her an effective warrior against governmental discrimination. Her persuasive abilities and powerful personality made her a dynamic grass-roots leader. And the sheer magnitude of her presence—she was a large woman, unafraid to throw her bulk around if necessary—made "Roughhouse Annie" a person to be reckoned with.

With their strong personalities and opposite goals, Ellis and Atwater collided with some frequency. Indeed, at one city council meeting, Ellis's racist epithets outraged Atwater to the point that she was ready to commit murder: Pulling a knife from her purse, she climbed over the rows of chairs toward her unsuspecting target. Fortunately—for both her and Ellis—she was intercepted without incident by several friends who quietly disarmed her. Not surprisingly, her animosity toward Ellis was matched by his toward her: He "hated her guts."

It seemed inevitable that Ellis and Atwater would always be at odds. So what followed the first school desegregation meeting was astonishing. Within just weeks of their shouting match, they developed a mutual respect and within months had become real friends—to the shock of both black and white communities. Now, decades later, the former leader of the KKK and the militant civil rights activist continue to share a special bond. Says Ann Atwater, "I don't know of anything that could change us from being friends.... We don't shake hands. We hug and embrace." C. P. Ellis feels the same. And perhaps even more amazing, this former Klansman—this man who excitedly celebrated the assassination of Martin Luther King, Jr.—now claims as his greatest achievement his role in winning the first union contract in Durham to include Martin Luther King, Jr.'s, birthday as a paid holiday.

How do we explain the fascinating journey of these former foes? Why at one time were their lives so utterly consumed by powerful racial prejudices and stereotypes? And what changed their long-standing hatred into true respect and friendship?

Open the newspaper or turn on the evening news and you're likely to observe hostilities like those that once bound C. P. Ellis and Ann Atwater. A Los Angeles delicatessen owned by an Arab American is torched after the hateful words "Arab go home" are scrawled on a wall. At the University of Wisconsin, "Think extinction" is spray-painted on the Jewish Student Center. At the University of New Mexico, journals on women's studies are stolen from the library and replaced with books on Nazism and Hitler. Walking to their New York City school, two African-American children are assaulted by four white teenagers, who spray their faces with a white substance: "You'll turn white today," one attacker tells his young victims. In Bangor, Maine, three teenagers attack a man, throwing him off a bridge to his death; later, they boast to friends that they "jumped a fag and kicked the shit out of him and threw him in the stream." Lone gunmen in the Midwest and Southern California drive through neighborhoods on killing rampages, targeting Jews, blacks, and

Asians. And wars between people of different ethnicities and religions litter the landscape—Jews and Arabs in the Middle East, Catholics and Protestants in Northern Ireland, Turks and Kurds in Turkey, Christians and Muslims in Indonesia, Muslims and Hindus in India and Pakistan…and on and on and on.

Many of us would like to believe that hate crimes are infrequent deviations from societal norms of intergroup respect and tolerance. We may fool ourselves into believing that negative prejudices exist only in easily identifiable "rednecks" or "extremists." Or we may say to ourselves that large-scale interethnic conflicts occur only elsewhere, in less "civilized" places—conveniently forgetting our own history of slavery and institutionalized laws discriminating against ethnic minority groups, women, and homosexuals. Unfortunately, as the research explored in this chapter suggests, most of us hold at least a few negative prejudices and stereotypes, and these feelings and beliefs often lead us to discriminate against others. In this chapter, we explore the consequences of negative prejudices, stereotypes, and discrimination; why they exist so powerfully; when they come into play; and what we can do about them.

Planet Prejudice

"But aren't things getting better?" you ask. This is a fair question. Indeed, compared to recent U.S. history, the present social atmosphere *is* more tolerant. Not only are most types of group-based discrimination now illegal, but fewer people are likely to express the simple, old-fashioned views common to past generations—that blacks are inherently lazier than whites, that women are genetically less intelligent than men, and so forth (e.g., Schuman, Steeh, & Bobo, 1985). Instead, people's feelings toward other groups tend to be more complex than in previous decades. For instance, racial prejudices held by whites are often accompanied by feelings of guilt, owing to the belief that blacks have been treated unfairly (Devine, Monteith, Zuwerink, & Elliot, 1991; Gaertner & Dovidio, 1986; Katz, Wackenhut, & Hass, 1986; Myrdal, 1944; Swim & Miller, 1999).

Although the movement away from old-fashioned views reflects, in part, an authentic shift toward tolerance, it also reflects contemporary societal norms that frown upon expressions of bigotry. As a result, people are less likely to *present themselves* as prejudiced, particularly to strangers (Crosby, Bromley, & Saxe, 1980; Dovidio & Gaertner, 2000). Instead, bigoted views are usually expressed more subtly, under the cover of arguments that can be defended on nonprejudicial grounds (McConahay, 1986; Sears, 1988; Swim, Aikin, Hall, & Hutner, 1995; Tougas et al., 1995). "It's not that I'm sexist," a man might say, "I just think that affirmative action is discrimination in reverse." Because there are ideological reasons for opposing policies like affirmative action that may have nothing to do with negative prejudice (Sniderman & Tetlock, 1986), bigoted individuals can use such issues to stealthily express and act upon their negative sentiments. In sum, although bigoted feelings, beliefs, and behaviors still exist throughout our society and throughout the world, they're somewhat more complex and expressed more subtly than in the past (see Figure 11.1).

Prejudice and Stereotypes

The attitude we have toward members of a particular group—how we *feel* about them—is known as **prejudice.** Ask yourself how you feel when you meet for the first time someone you know to be homosexual, Muslim, or Mexican. If your initial reaction is one of dislike, or if you desire to avoid or withdraw from that person, you harbor a negative prejudice against that group. Although our focus in this chapter is on negative prejudices, people also have positive prejudices toward certain

Prejudice *A generalized attitude toward members of a social group.*

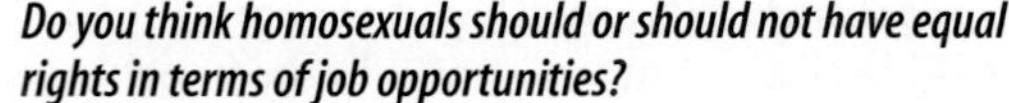

Figure 11.1
The times they are a'changin'. Or are they?

Americans' stated beliefs about homosexuals have become more favorable over the past 20-odd years (Herek, 2000). Despite this general change, however, old stereotypes concerning homosexuals still stand, as revealed by people's relative discomfort regarding homosexual schoolteachers and clergy.

SOURCE: *Data from Gallup Poll, November 1996. From Internet, "Americans growing more tolerant of gays," by Lydia Saad. http://www.gallup.com/poll/news/961214.html.*

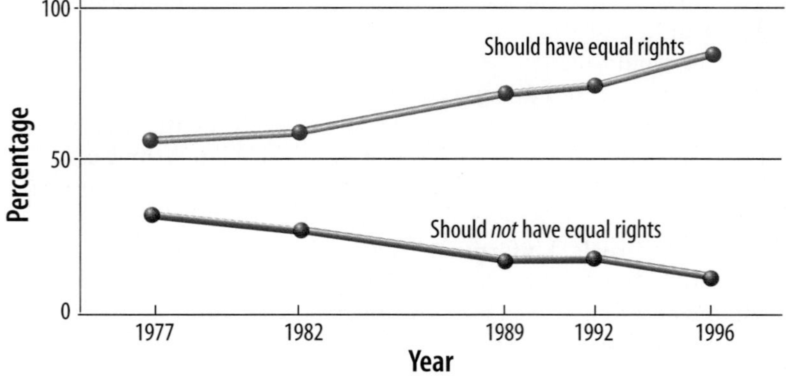

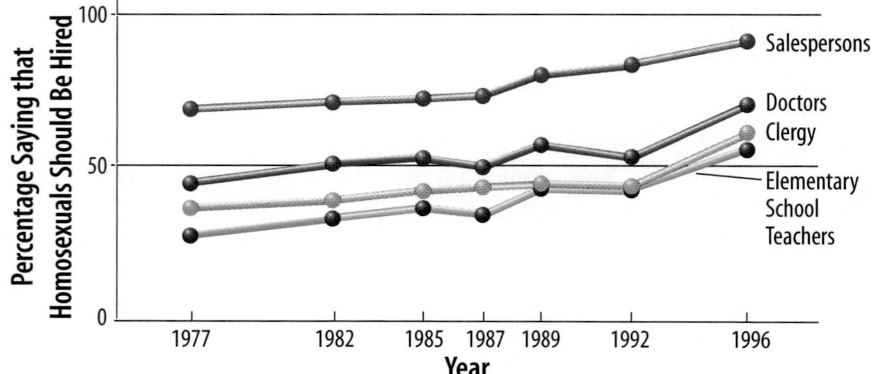

groups. In one study, for instance, American college students liked Canadian and Swiss people nearly as much as they liked Americans, and they liked Swedes even more (Stapf, Stroebe, & Jonas, 1986).

Walter Lippman (1922), a journalist, coined the term **stereotypes** to refer to the generalized *beliefs* we hold about groups—beliefs that reflect what we think members of a particular group are like. For instance, common stereotypes held by people in the United States include the beliefs that European Americans are achievement oriented, egotistical, and racist; that African Americans are loud, lazy, and antagonistic; that Asian Americans are shy, well mannered, and intelligent; and that Mexican Americans are family oriented, lower class, and hard working (e.g., Niemann et al., 1994). Not only can stereotypes be positive or negative, but people also hold positive stereotypes for groups against whom they are negatively prejudiced. People who dislike Asians, for instance, may nonetheless believe them to be intelligent and well mannered.

Stereotype *Generalized belief about members of social groups.*

Social psychologists often distinguish between *explicit* and *implicit* stereotypes and prejudices (e.g., Banaji & Greenwald, 1995; Devine, 1989; Dovidio, Kawamaki, Johnson, Johnson, & Howard, 1997; Fazio, Jackson, Dunton, & Williams, 1995; von Hippel, Sekaquaptewa, & Vargas, 1997). For example, if you ask yourself how you feel toward members of Group X, the attitude you're aware of is your explicit prejudice toward the group. You can directly state this prejudice, and researchers measure it using surveys and questionnaires. But you also have implicit attitudes toward Group X—prejudices you're not aware of and that you can't directly report. Implicit prejudices and stereotypes can only be measured indirectly, often by assessing how long it takes to make certain judgments. To experience one currently popular method for assessing implicit prejudice, go to http://www.yale.edu/implicit/ and take the Implicit Association Test (e.g., Greenwald, McGhee, & Schwartz, 1998; Rudman et al., 1999).

Discrimination

The term **discrimination** refers to *behaviors* directed toward others because of their group membership. If we treat two people differently and they're identical in all respects except for, say, their religion, we could rightly be accused of discriminating on the basis of religion. Consider, for instance, the following study conducted in Northern Ireland (Kremer, Barry, & McNally, 1986): Randomly selected Catholic and Protestant residents of a town known for its religious conflict were mailed questionnaires surveying their transportation habits. A stamped return envelope was provided, and the scientist ostensibly conducting the study was given a "Catholic name" (Patrick Connolly) on some questionnaires and a "Protestant name" (William Scott) on others. Protestants from this town were just as likely to return the questionnaires whether the researcher was believed to be Protestant or Catholic. They did not discriminate. In contrast, the Catholics were twice as likely to complete the questionnaire if the researcher was believed to be Catholic. Because the questionnaires were identical, the different completion rates could only reflect discrimination by the town's Catholic participants.

This case from Northern Ireland is an example of personal discrimination—the discrimination is performed by an individual. Some discrimination is performed not by individuals, however, but by society's institutions. *Institutionalized discrimination* is discrimination that has been built into the legal, political, economic, and social institutions of a culture (e.g., Feagin & Feagin, 1999). It may be direct and hostile, as when laws prohibit certain groups of people from living in certain neighborhoods or working in certain occupations. Certainly, the United States has a long history of direct institutionalized discrimination (e.g., as in slavery-supporting laws and practices, laws discriminating against women, and so on). Although direct, hostile discrimination of this sort is generally illegal today, some forms of it remain. The U.S. military, for instance, is required to discharge homosexuals upon discovering their sexual orientation.

Institutionalized discrimination is usually more subtle and unintentional than this, however. As one example, consider that members of disadvantaged minority groups often have a more difficult time competing for employment because they have poorer educational backgrounds. Although the system that creates higher quality educational opportunities for wealthy white students in the suburbs isn't explicitly designed to make life difficult for poor black or Hispanic job seekers, that is one of its consequences. Ironically, institutionalized discrimination may even sometimes be well intentioned, as when a paternalistic desire to keep women safe and "on a pedestal" may make a business reluctant to hire women for jobs in a coal mine. Individuals discriminate against members of other groups, and society's institutions do so too.

Sexual Harassment as Gender Discrimination As many as 50 percent of American women are sexually harassed at one time or another during their academic or working lives (Fitzgerald, 1993), and the U.S. Army alone spent in just one year an estimated $250 *million* to deal with problems associated with sexual harassment, including the costs of replacing effective soldiers who retired because of it (Faley et al., 1999). Sexual harassment is a common and costly form of discrimination, in both economic and psychological terms (e.g., Woodzicka & LaFrance, in press).

But what constitutes sexual harassment? Disagreements abound. If a manager repeatedly asks his secretary for a date despite her persistent rejections, is that sexual harassment? If he graphically describes pornographic movies and brags about his sexual prowess, is that harassment? As with other forms of discrimination, labeling a

Discrimination *Behaviors directed toward people on the basis of their group membership.*

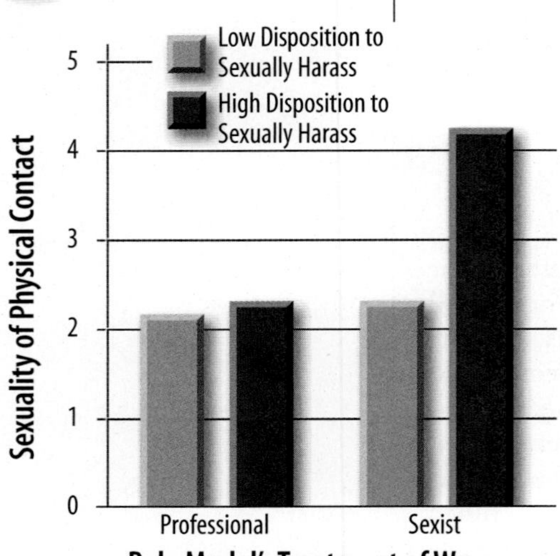

Figure 11.2
Who sexually harasses and when?

Sexually harassing behavior usually results from an interaction between personality dispositions and salient social norms. In one experiment, male participants predisposed toward sexual harassment were more likely to touch a female confederate in sexual ways, but only when they had first observed the male experimenter behave toward her in a sexist manner.

SOURCE: *Data from Pryor, LaVite, and Stoller (1993), Figure 1.*

behavior "sexual harassment" often depends on who's doing the behavior, who's targeted by the behavior, and who's doing the labeling (Frazier, Cochran, & Olson, 1995).

Behaviors are generally viewed as more sexually harassing when performed by a person of relative power, such as a boss (e.g., Pryor & Day, 1988), and as less harassing when performed by attractive, single individuals (Sheets & Braver, 1993). Moreover, women are more likely than men to characterize behaviors like staring and flirting as sexually harassing (e.g., Gutek, 1985; Terpstra & Baker, 1986; U.S. Merit Systems Protections Board, 1988). Americans tend to agree, however, that overt sexual bribery, unwanted physical advances, and sexual propositions at work or school are sexually harassing (e.g., Frazier et al., 1995).

Of course, not every harassing behavior is illegal. In the eyes of the law, illegal sexual harassment takes two forms. *Quid pro quo* (from the Latin for "something for something") *harassment* refers to attempts by the perpetrator to exchange something of value—a job, a good grade—for sexual favors. *Hostile environment harassment* refers to creating a professional setting that is sexually offensive, intimidating, or hostile. Furthermore, to qualify as illegal discrimination, sexual harassment must be directed at members of only one gender.

Who are the harassers? The great majority of sexual harassment is directed by men at women (e.g., Fitzgerald et al., 1988). In particular, men who view themselves as "hypermasculine," and who perceive strong connections between power and sex, are more likely than others to become sexual harassers (Bargh, Raymond, Pryor, & Strack, 1995; Pryor, 1987; Pryor & Stoller, 1994). Whether they actually harass, however, depends on the situation. In an experiment ostensibly researching teaching skills, male participants previously assessed as having a disposition toward quid pro quo harassment were especially likely to touch female "learners" (actually, confederates) in a sexual way, but only when the task could legitimately involve touching—teaching, for instance, a woman how to putt a golf ball (Pryor, 1987).

In another study, male students were asked to train a young woman to perform a computer word-processing task. These men were introduced to the female trainee (again, a confederate) by a male graduate student who acted either in a very sexist, harassing way toward the woman (putting his arm around her shoulders, fondling her hair, and visually checking out her body) or in a respectful, professional manner. As Figure 11.2 reveals, men having a disposition favoring sexual harassment were more likely to touch the women in sexual ways, but only when they were exposed to the harassing model (Pryor, LaVite, & Stoller, 1993).

In general, then, sexual harassment is more likely to be perpetrated by men who see a strong connection between power and sex and who are placed in settings where harassing opportunities are both available and implicitly condoned.

In sum, *prejudices*, *stereotypes*, and *discrimination* refer to how we feel toward, think about, and behave in relation to members of groups. Often, negative prejudices, stereotypes, and discriminatory tendencies cluster together, forming syndromes we know as racism, sexism, anti-Semitism, heterosexism, ageism, and the like.

The Costs of Prejudice, Stereotyping, and Discrimination

The targets of negative prejudices often bear large burdens. In a nationwide experiment, white, black, and Hispanic "customers" met with realty and leasing agents to inquire about homes or apartments. Even when researchers matched these trained actors on all relevant characteristics except ethnicity, presented the minority-group customers as having *higher* incomes, and had them inquire about the same houses and apartments within just hours of each other, agents discriminated in favor of white customers: They informed white customers of more available homes, followed them up more frequently with phone calls, and steered black and Hispanic customers to minority-group areas of town (Yinger, 1995).

Not only is it harder for blacks and Hispanics to find adequate housing, but they also pay more when they do—on average $3,000 more than whites for the same house. This amounts to a "discrimination tax" totaling $4.1 billion per year for the U.S. African American and Hispanic communities (Yinger, 1995). Other kinds of discrimination abound as well.

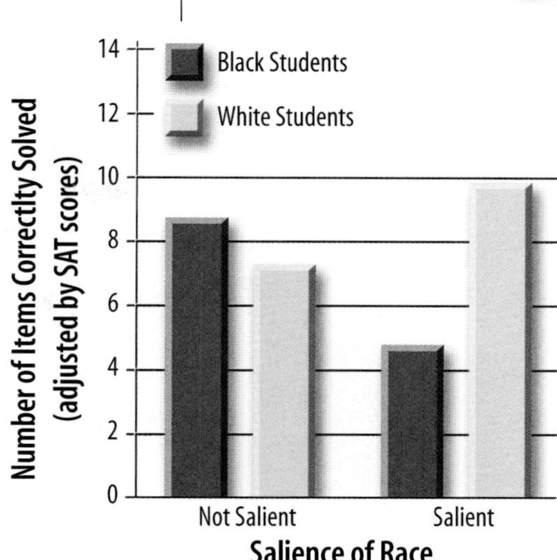

Figure 11.3
When negative stereotypes are in the air.

Just knowing that one's group is looked upon negatively can make it difficult to live up to one's potential. In one study, both black and white students performed well on a difficult exam (relative to their abilities, as assessed by SAT scores)—except when asked beforehand to report their race. When race was made salient, black students underperformed whites.

SOURCE: *Adapted from Steele and Aronson (1995), Figure 4.*

- An audit of the auto industry revealed that white men were offered better deals on cars than were white women (who were asked to pay $109 more), black women ($318 more), and black men ($935 more) (Ayres & Siegelman, 1995).
- An experiment conducted on physicians revealed that they were only 60 percent as likely to order the top-rated diagnostic test for heart disease for black patients than for white patients, even though these "patients" (actually, confederates of the researchers) described identical symptoms and provided identical information about themselves (Schulman et al., 1999).
- Women and members of minority groups tend to receive less pay for the same work, even after controlling for job type, educational background, and the like (e.g., Stroh, Brett, & Reilly, 1992).
- Even when accused of the same crime, black, Hispanic, and Native American youths are more likely to be detained by the criminal justice system than are white youths ("And justice for some," 2000).
- Overweight women, compared to thinner women, receive less financial help from their parents for attending college (Crandall, 1995).

The direct, tangible implications of these forms of discrimination are clear. Less noticeable, but perhaps as powerful, are the effects of *merely knowing* that others hold negative prejudices and stereotypes concerning one's group (Pinel, 1999). For example, "tokens" in a group—a lone woman in a group of men, for instance—often worry that they will be stereotyped by the others (Cohen & Swim, 1995). As a result of this increased self-consciousness, tokens are less able to concentrate on their tasks (e.g., Lord & Saenz, 1985; Saenz, 1994). Claude Steele and Joshua Aronson (1995) hypothesized that **stereotype threat**—the fear of confirming others' negative stereotypes about one's group—also makes it more difficult for people to perform up to their potential. In a series of studies exploring this idea, undergraduate students answered difficult questions taken from the verbal section of the Graduate Record Exam (GRE). Black students performed below their abilities—but only when race was made salient and they believed that a poor performance would confirm the cultural stereotype that blacks are less intelligent than whites (see Figure 11.3). Indeed, the findings of recent studies suggest that individuals from many groups may perform beneath their potential when they fear confirming the negative stereotypes held of their groups. As a few examples, consider the following:

- Women performed worse on math tests when gender was made salient than when it was not (Shih, Pittinsky, & Ambady, 1999; Spencer, Steele, & Quinn, 1999).
- White men performed worse on a math test when they thought they were being compared to Asian men than when they thought otherwise (Aronson et al., 1999).
- White men performed relatively poorly on an athletic task when they thought it was related to "natural ability," whereas black men performed relatively poorly on the task when they thought it was related to "athletic intelligence" (Stone, Lynch, Sjomeling, & Darley, 1999; see Figure 2.7, p. 62).
- French-speaking Canadian undergraduates from lower social classes performed more poorly when they thought a test was diagnostic of intellectual

Stereotype threat *The fear that one might confirm the negative stereotypes held by others about one's group.*

ability than when they thought it was unrelated to intellectual ability (Croizet & Claire, 1998).

- Asian-American women performed worse on a math test after their gender had been made salient, but better on the same test after their Asian identity had been made salient (Shih, Pittinsky, & Ambady, 1999).

When negative stereotypes about our group are "in the air," we are often less able to perform up to our potential.

In addition to creating poorer performance, stereotype threat may also lead targets of negative stereotypes to **disidentify** with those arenas where society expects them to fail—to decide that the arena is no longer relevant to their self-concept and self-esteem (Crocker & Major, 1989; Steele, 1992). For instance, afraid of confirming the stereotype that they are unintelligent, African American students may, over time, disconnect academic performance from their self-images (Major, Spencer, Schmader, Wolfe, & Crocker, 1998). Results from one study are consistent with this: The self-esteem of black children was less tied to school performance in the tenth grade than in the eighth grade—a pattern not found for white children (Osborne, 1995). In the short term, disidentifying with academics may be adaptive, helping these children maintain positive feelings about themselves in the face of negative social stereotypes. In the long run, however, distancing themselves from academic development leaves these children ill prepared to compete successfully in a world where knowledge and the ability to learn are critical.

Other problems exist when negative stereotypes and prejudices are "in the air": The targets of negative stereotypes and prejudices can never be sure *why* others are behaving as they are. Consider, for instance, a woman who is not hired for a job. "Did I lose the job because I'm less qualified than the others," she might wonder, "or is it because they don't want a woman?" Of course, even if she does get the job, certain attributional ambiguities remain: "Did I get the job because I'm the most qualified applicant, or just to fill some quota?" For most people, social feedback is a valuable source of information about one's abilities, skills, and character. For members of groups targeted by negative stereotypes and prejudices, however, the meaning of social feedback is more ambiguous and less useful (Crocker, Voelkl, Testa, & Major, 1991; Major & Crocker, 1993).

In sum, being the target of negative prejudices and stereotypes has both material and psychological costs (Swim & Stangor, 1998). Less research has explored the costs borne by those who themselves discriminate and by members of societies where negative prejudices play—or have historically played—a prominent role. Nonetheless, these costs are significant as well (Bowser & Hunt, 1996; Simpson & Yinger, 1965). At the individual level, people who discriminate are likely to lose important opportunities, miss out on potentially valuable friendships, fail to employ highly qualified individuals, and so on. When people derogate other groups in order to feel better about themselves—a process we'll discuss later in this chapter—they impede their own efforts toward real self-improvement (Pettigrew, 1973). Moreover, when negative stereotypes and prejudices are in the air, they harm even nonbigoted people, whose social encounters may be hampered by concerns that they will be inaccurately perceived as prejudiced ("Will she assume from my comment about affirmative action that I'm sexist?" "Will he think that I'm not hiring him because he's Hispanic?"). Nonbigoted people may also be disliked by others for having friends who are themselves targets of prejudice (e.g., Goffman, 1963). In several experiments, for instance, heterosexual men were viewed less positively when they were believed to have homosexual friends (Neuberg, Smith, Hoffman, & Russell, 1994; Sigelman et al., 1991).

Finally, negative prejudices and stereotypes cost society. Current and even past prejudices can keep members of targeted groups from bettering themselves, creating an "underclass" that detracts from the community's economic welfare. Moreover, remedying the problems created by discrimination requires huge amounts of money. And when prejudices develop into aggression, the level of human tragedy

Disidentify *To reduce in one's mind the relevance of a particular domain (e.g., academic achievement) to one's self-esteem.*

can be staggering, as illustrated by the atrocities occurring during the last decade in Rwanda, the Middle East, Northern Ireland, and the former Yugoslavia.

The Goals of Prejudice, Stereotyping, and Discrimination

In light of the great damage that negative stereotypes, prejudices, and discrimination wreak on victims, perpetrators, and societies alike, one might reasonably wonder *why* people think, feel, and behave in such ways. After all, to paraphrase Rodney King—the black Los Angeles motorist beaten by white police officers following a high-speed car chase in 1991—wouldn't we all be better off if we could just get along?

If the answer to this question is yes, it's certainly not a simple yes. Prejudicial feelings, stereotypical thinking, and discriminatory actions serve several important goals. They can help obtain material benefits for one's own group, they can provide social approval, they can bolster personal and social identities, and they can help us navigate complex, information-rich social environments with an economy of mental effort. We explore each of these possibilities in turn.

Summary

Prejudice, stereotypes, and discrimination permeate the world's cultures. Prejudices are the generalized attitudes we have towards members of particular social groups, stereotypes are the beliefs we have about members of social groups, and discrimination is behavior directed towards people on the basis of their group membership. Individuals targeted by negative prejudices, stereotypes, and discrimination incur significant economic, social, and psychological costs. Intolerance toward members of other groups is also costly for those holding the prejudices and stereotypes, as well as for societies in which discrimination exists.

Gaining Material Benefits for One's Group

Ann Atwater longed for her "piece of the pie." She and other members of the black community wanted to share in the American Dream. She wanted to obtain a well-paying job, to live in a clean and safe neighborhood, and to send her children to good schools. The laws and practices of white America denied her these opportunities.

C. P. Ellis wanted the same for his family. Although white, he was poor, like Ann Atwater. To Ellis, the black call for increased opportunity was a declaration of economic war. The pie is only so big, he thought. If the blacks get a piece, his thin slice, and the thin slices of whites like him, would become but slivers.

Like many others, Ellis believed that blacks and whites were competing for a limited pool of economic resources. Of course, logic tells us that Ellis's ability to get a well-paying job was obstructed as much by white competitors as by black competitors. Why, then, was it so easy for him to see blacks, but not whites, as the competition? Why wasn't Ellis equally resentful and antagonistic toward his white rivals? And why did he band together with other whites to hinder the progress made by blacks?

Creating and Maintaining Ingroup Advantage

Imagine yourself in the following laboratory experiment: You're seated with other students, and the researcher projects a series of dot patterns onto the screen at the front of the room. Each slide is presented for only a short time, and your task is to estimate the number of dots on each. You make your guesses quietly and privately.

When the slide show is complete, the researcher ushers you into an individual cubicle where you're told that, on the basis of your guesses, you're an "overestimator." (Other participants are told instead that they are "underestimators." In reality, your designation is randomly assigned on the basis of a coin flip.) Of course, you have no preconceived notions of what it means to be an overestimator or underestimator, and the researcher explicitly tells you that neither type is better than the other.

You find the next task more interesting. You remain in your private cubicle, and your job is to allocate monetary rewards and penalties to the other people in your session. These other folks are identified in only two ways: by a code number, to hide each person's identity, and by a group designation that labels each person as either an overestimator or an underestimator. Your allocations will remain entirely confidential, and you'll never have any contact with the other participants. How would you split the money?

Henri Tajfel and his colleagues (1971) placed British teenagers in this very situation and labelled it the **minimal intergroup paradigm** because the groups (of overestimators and underestimators) were randomly determined, artificial, short-term, and involved no contact between the members. Would participants allocate more money to members of their own groups (i.e., *ingroups*) than to members of other groups (i.e., *outgroups*)? The answer was yes. Indeed, even when groups are minimally defined, people tend to display an **ingroup bias,** benefiting members of their own groups over members of other groups (e.g., Brewer, 1979; Mullen, Brown, & Smith, 1992; Tajfel, 1982).

The Nature of Group Living and Intergroup Conflict The roots of the ingroup bias may lie in our evolutionary past (Campbell, 1965; Eibl-Eibesfeldt, 1989; Fishbein, 1996; Fox, 1992; van der Dennen & Falger, 1990). Group living was necessary for our ancestors' survival. Within small communities, humans cooperated with each other and developed norms of reciprocity to further strengthen the group bonds (Axelrod & Hamilton, 1981; Trivers, 1971). Moreover, because these communities consisted primarily of biological relatives, behaviors that strengthened the group usually also benefited the genes of each individual member—increasing the likelihood that he or she (and his or her relatives) would survive and reproduce (Hamilton, 1964). It would have been advantageous, then, for humans both to think in terms of groups and to value the groups to which they belonged. Indeed, the ingroup bias seems a cross-cultural feature of human social life, and the inclination to favor one's own group may even operate automatically (Otten & Wentura, 1999; Perdue, Dovidio, Gurtman, & Tyler, 1990).

This alone doesn't explain, however, why people so often *dislike* members of other groups. Why, for instance, have Californians at times exhibited such fervent sentiments opposing immigrants to their state? **Realistic group conflict theory** proposes that intergroup conflict emerges when groups find themselves competing for the same resources (e.g., Bonacich, 1972; Brewer & Campbell, 1976; Sherif, Harvey, White, Hood, & Sherif, 1961/1988). Not only should such conflicts increase people's positive feelings of solidarity toward their own group, but they should also lead people to develop strong dislikes for other groups. After all, "they" are trying to deny "us" the resources we need to survive and prosper. As a result, group members may act in ways that aid their group and harm other groups.

Minimal intergroup paradigm *An experimental procedure in which short-term, arbitrary, artificial groups are created to explore the foundations of prejudice, stereotyping, and discrimination.*

Ingroup bias *The tendency to benefit members of one's own groups over members of other groups.*

Realistic group conflict theory *The proposal that intergroup conflict, and negative prejudices and stereotypes, emerge out of actual competition between groups for desired resources.*

Justifying Group Advantage Whereas proponents of realistic group conflict theory propose that negative prejudices and stereotypes naturally *emerge* from economic conflict between groups, others have suggested that powerful people and institutions sometimes strategically *manipulate* stereotypes and prejudices to give themselves an advantage (Cox, 1959; Reich, 1971). For instance, some have argued that white Europeans invented the concept of black racial inferiority to justify their exploitative incursions into Africa. Hitler is said to have encouraged anti-Semitism to bring Germans together as a unified force under his command. And C. P. Ellis eventually came to believe that Durham's businessmen encouraged and financed the KKK's racist activities to keep the poor whites and poor blacks fighting each other so that neither would notice the enormous wealth the town's leaders were accumulating.

Are systematic, economically motivated attempts like these to create or amplify negative stereotypes and prejudice common or powerful? Given that they would involve presumably secretive conspiracy, it's hard to know for sure. Existing research does tell us, however, that most of us want to believe that the world is *just*—that good things happen to good people and that bad things happen to bad people (Lerner, 1980). It makes sense, then, that successful individuals would want to believe that they're entitled to their economic successes—that they've earned their positions in life "fair and square." As a result, people may indeed use stereotypes and prejudices to justify existing social and economic inequalities (Jost & Burgess, 2000; Sidanius & Pratto, 1993). For instance, by stereotyping African Americans as unintelligent and lazy, white Americans can justify their own group's relatively high economic status.

In sum, the desire to benefit the ingroup helps to create and maintain intergroup tensions. We see next that certain features of the person and situation increase this desire, thereby leading to negative stereotypes and prejudices.

Our resources for us, or our resources for them? *Group competition for economic resources can create or magnify negative prejudices and discrimination. In the 1990s, Californians fought to eliminate state expenditures for immigrants. More than 50 years earlier, Californians fought to slow the migration to their state of farmers from Oklahoma, Arkansas, and Texas, fearing that these "Okies" would take their jobs. In both cases, economic concerns led many Californians to stereotype the potential competitors as inferior people with enormous families who would threaten their valued way of life.*

Social Dominance Orientation

"Some groups of people are simply not the equals of others." "It's sometimes necessary to step on others to get ahead in life." "Some people are just more worthy than others." Such are the statements of persons high in social dominance orientation. **Social dominance orientation** describes the extent to which a person wants his or her own group to dominate and be superior to other groups (Pratto, Sidanius, Stallworth, & Malle, 1994; Sidanius & Pratto, 1999). Unlike individuals who believe that all people should be treated equally, individuals high in social dominance orientation prefer social systems in which groups are ordered according to their worth. They believe that superior groups (often their own) ought to be wealthier and more powerful.

People having a strong social dominance orientation are particularly likely to hold negative stereotypes and prejudices against lower-status groups, perhaps because such stereotypes and prejudices help justify the existing social hierarchy. For instance, Americans having strong social dominance orientations are more prejudiced against blacks and Arabs, disapprove more of interracial marriages and gay and lesbian rights, are more sexist, and are more supportive of governmental policies through which the United States could dominate other nations (Pratto et al., 1994).

The prejudice-creating influences of social dominance orientation are not limited to Americans. Most large societies have a social hierarchy in which a powerful group wields considerable influence over groups of lesser status (e.g., Murdock, 1949). In Canada, for instance, the majority white population controls most of the wealth, and indigenous Indian tribes and Asian immigrants seek to increase their political, social, and economic status. In Taiwan, "Mainlanders" (immigrants from the Chinese civil war in the mid-20th century) hold most of the power; the "Taiwanese" (descendants of mainland Chinese who arrived on the island 13 centuries ago) are next in rank; and the island's aboriginal people are the poorest of the three groups. In Israel, Ashkenazi Jews—having origins in Europe—are more powerful than Sephardic Jews—whose origins lie in Northern Africa and the Middle East. Israeli Arabs compose only 18 percent of the population and have little real power, and the Palestinians have even less. We might hypothesize that, to justify such power differentials, people in these and other countries having strong social dominance orientations would be particularly likely to hold negative stereotypes and prejudices against members of the lower-power groups (Jost & Banaji, 1994).

Social dominance orientation
The extent to which a person desires that his or her own group dominate other groups and be socially and materially superior to them.

To explore this hypothesis, Felicia Pratto and her colleagues (1998; Sidanius & Pratto, 1999) measured social dominance orientation in Canada, Taiwan, China, and Israel. Then they asked citizens about their views toward women and their country's low-status groups. The commonality across nations was striking. In all countries, individuals having a strong social dominance orientation demonstrated greater levels of sexism. Moreover, in most countries, social dominance orientation was associated with increased prejudices. In Canada, those high in social dominance orientation are biased against indigenous Indian groups and homosexuals; in Taiwan, those having strong social dominance orientations are prejudiced against aboriginal Taiwanese; and in Israel, these individuals dislike Sephardic Jews, Israeli Arabs, and Palestinians. Only in China, where the low-power ethnic groups live at some distance from native Chinese (e.g., in Tibet or Mongolia) and pose little challenge to the existing status structure, was there no evidence for a link between social dominance orientation and negative prejudice.

We see, then, that social dominance orientation operates similarly across the globe: In all cultures explored to date, individuals high in social dominance orientation are more sexist and, in most cultures, more racist as well.

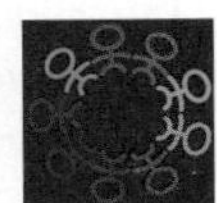

Intergroup Competition

When economic times are tough, acquiring resources for one's group takes on special urgency. We should thus expect increased ingroup favoritism and outgroup hostility when people believe they're competing with other groups for land, housing, jobs, and the like.

Carl Hovland and Robert Sears (1940) gathered data on the U.S. South between 1882 and 1930, correlating economic conditions with the number of lynchings—illegal hangings—of black people. As we noted in Chapter 10, economic pressures were clearly linked to outgroup hostility: When economic times were rough, white southerners lynched more blacks (Hepworth & West, 1988). This tendency wasn't confined to the South, as difficult economic times in northern cities also led to increased white violence against blacks, as well as to violence against immigrant Chinese (Olzak, 1992).

Competition and animosity at Robbers Cave. *The tug-of-war and other competitive events created powerful antagonisms between the Eagles and Rattlers, culminating in near-warfare.*

To explore the role of intergroup competition more closely, Muzafer Sherif and his colleagues (1961/1988) designed an intriguing field experiment. They began by selecting twenty-two well-adjusted, white fifth-grade boys with above-average intelligence, average-to-good school performance, and Protestant, middle-class, two-parent family backgrounds. All the boys attended different schools in the Oklahoma City area and didn't know each other prior to the study. The researchers then split the boys into two essentially identical groups and sent them to camp at Robbers Cave State Park in rural Oklahoma.

During the first days of the study, each group took part in typical camp activities—sports, hiking, swimming, and the like—unaware that the other group existed across the park. Soon, these two collections of strangers became real groups, with leaders, norms, favorite activities, and even names—the Rattlers and the Eagles. The experiment was now ready to proceed.

The researchers began a four-day tournament of contests—baseball games, tugs-of-war, touch football, tent pitching, a treasure hunt, and cabin inspections. To the winning group would go a trophy, individual medals, and highly appealing camping knives. To the losing group...nothing. Consistent with realistic group conflict theory, animosities between the groups grew quickly during the first baseball game and fiercely escalated throughout the competition. The Eagles burned the Rattlers' flag. The Rattlers raided the Eagles' cabin, turning over beds and scattering possessions. Derogatory name-calling increased in frequency and intensity. Several fist fights broke out. And when the Eagles won the tournament and went off to celebrate their victory, the Rattlers raided their cabin and stole the hard-won camping knives. The Eagles confronted the Rattlers, the two groups began skirmishing, and the researchers had to physically separate the boys to avoid a full-scale fight.

Two days later, after a cooling-off period during which the Rattlers and Eagles were kept apart, the boys rated the characteristics of each group. These findings corroborated the researchers' observations. Whereas the campers saw members of their own group as brave, tough, and friendly, they viewed members of the other group as sneaky, smart-alecky stinkers! These data are particularly striking when we recall that the boys had been selected for the study because of how similar they were to one another.

Indeed, whether it be U.S. whites disliking blacks, the British disliking West Indians, the Dutch disliking Turks and Surinamers, or the French disliking Asians, we see that negative prejudices and stereotypes often "target the competition": People direct their hostilities toward those groups they see themselves competing with at the moment (Pettigrew & Meertens, 1995). Because economic competition in different locales often involves different "players"—British "versus" West Indian workers in London, Korean business owners "versus" black consumers in south-central Los Angeles—each society possesses a somewhat distinct set of cultural stereotypes and prejudices. Thus, although intergroup competition is a cross-cultural phenomenon, we find that the groups stigmatized by it differ in different cultures.

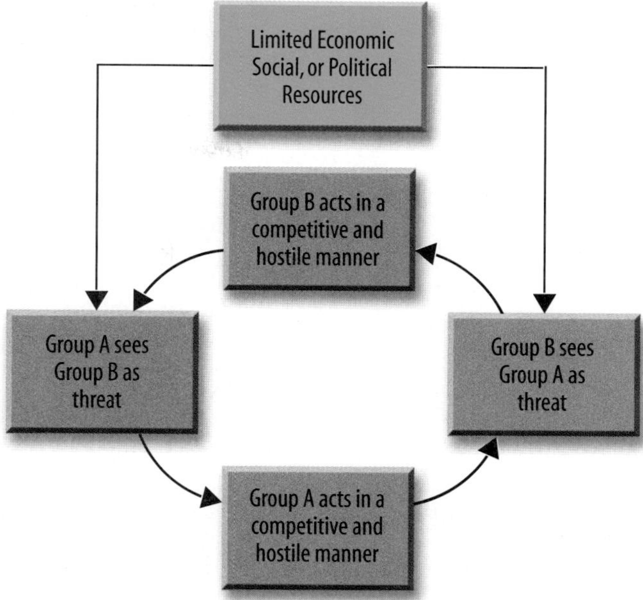

Figure 11.4
The competitive spiral.

As groups see one another as competitors for common resources, they may begin to behave in ways that bring about or exaggerate the very competition they feared. This self-fulfilling spiral can rapidly escalate, creating stubborn and intense intergroup hostilities.

The Self-Fulfilling Spiral of Intergroup Competition

As blacks like Ann Atwater took to Durham's streets to protest the discrimination that confined them to inadequate housing, low-paying jobs, and lousy schools, poor whites like C. P. Ellis worried that any black gains would come at their expense. As the black calls for equal opportunity were generally dismissed by whites, blacks increased the frequency and vigor of their protests. In turn, the views of many of Durham's white citizens became harder and even more fixed. The conflict spiraled. Ann Atwater developed from a respectful housekeeper into "Roughhouse Annie," the militant civil rights activist. C. P. Ellis changed from being a quiet man struggling to keep his family afloat to the reactionary leader of the KKK.

Competition and hostility breed increased competition and hostility. As people view others as competitors, they themselves begin to compete, inadvertently bringing about or amplifying the competition they initially feared (Kelley & Stahelski, 1970; see Figure 11.4). This *self-fulfilling prophecy* can quickly spiral into increasingly intense forms of competition, as those involved become even more convinced of the others' malicious designs. This process is particularly pronounced at the group level, because groups compete more intensely against each other for resources than do individuals (Insko et al., 1994; Schopler & Insko, 1992).

In this self-fulfilling spiral of intergroup competition, we see two fundamental forms of the person–situation interaction: First, competitive situations create competitive people and groups who possess little trust for one another, illustrating once again that *situations can change people* in important ways. Second, competitive, untrusting people and groups create ever more competitive and hostile situations, an example of how *people change their situations.* It's easy to see how such competitive spirals can create stubborn intergroup hatreds such as the ones between Israelis and Palestinians in the Middle East.

Summary

Because people want economic, social, and political resources for their groups, they may create competitive advantages for their own groups and come to dislike and believe negative things about other groups. Individuals who are high in social dominance orientation view the world as a place where groups compete with each other for scarce economic and social resources; as a result, they are more likely to hold negative stereotypes of and prejudices against other groups. Moreover, when times are tough and people perceive themselves as struggling for economic and social security, they are more likely to adopt and express negative stereotypes and prejudices. Finally, intergroup competition can rapidly spiral in a self-fulfilling manner, as each group increasingly distrusts the other and behaves in an increasingly hostile manner. We turn, next, to explore the role that social approval plays in creating and maintaining stereotypes, prejudice, and discrimination.

Gaining Social Approval

Like Durham, the city of Little Rock, Arkansas, experienced considerable turmoil over the issue of school desegregation. As the school year began in September 1957, the nation watched as Governor Orval Faubus had Arkansas National Guardsmen turn away at gunpoint the nine black students wanting to attend Central High School. To enforce the Supreme Court's ruling outlawing racial segregation in public education, President Eisenhower sent 1,000 troops from the Army's 101st Airborne Division to escort the nine students to and from classes. Faubus responded the following year by closing the city's high schools to all students, black and white.

Most of Little Rock's clergymen believed that allowing black students equal educational access was not only fair but morally right as well. Beyond pleading for patience and peace, however, most of the city's white clergymen avoided taking a public stand on the issue. How do we explain the discrepancy between the ministers' private moral beliefs and their public behaviors?

To answer this question, Ernest Campbell and Thomas Pettigrew (1958) went to Little Rock and observed the consequences for those few pro-integration clergymen who did speak their minds. These ministers were insulted and snubbed, and Sunday morning church attendance dropped significantly. Some were even dismissed or transferred against their will. What all the ministers of Little Rock knew, and what the outspoken ministers chose not to heed, was that the white church-goers did not want black students attending school with their white sons and daughters. And because clergy cannot effectively tend to their congregations in the absence of social approval and respect, many of the ministers felt they had no choice but to make their actions conform to their congregation's segregationist views.

Showdown at Central High. *Defying the Supreme Court, the Arkansas National Guard turned away, at gunpoint, the nine black students registered to attend classes at Little Rock's Central High School. Several weeks later, by order of President Dwight Eisenhower, 1,000 Army paratroopers arrived to escort the students past the dangerous mob into and away from school each day.*

The plight of the Little Rock ministers highlights the influence of social approval on intergroup relations. As we saw in chapters 4 through 6, people want the approval of others and can get it by adjusting their opinions and behaviors to match those held by others. If those we care about view a particular group negatively, we may conform to these views in the hope of "fitting in" and gaining their approval (Blanchard, Crandall, Brigham, & Vaughn, 1994; Pettigrew, 1958). Most of us, for instance, have at some point forced a smile at a prejudiced remark or joke we privately found offensive, fearing social rejection if we were to express our disapproval publicly. In one experiment, for example, nonsexist women publicly conformed to the sexist opinions of three other participants, demonstrating that even nonprejudiced people may express prejudiced views to gain social approval (Swim, Ferguson, & Hyers, 1999). More often, a prejudiced social environment provides permission for bigoted people to express the views they already hold (Wittenbrink & Henley, 1996). Participants in one study evaluated sexist events as being less offensive after hearing a series of sexist jokes—but only if they held sexist beliefs to begin with (Ford, 2000).

Of course, social norms and expectations do more than lead us to *pretend* that we hold certain stereotypes and prejudices. Because social norms deeply infiltrate our everyday lives, and because we spend so much time around those from whom we seek approval, we can also *internalize* these messages, accepting them as our own (e.g., Guimond, 2000). Just as it must have been quite easy for C. P. Ellis to pick up the racist messages of the pre-civil-rights South, it's easy for us today to internalize the stereotypic and prejudicial messages we hear in our homes, communities, and media.

Conformity Seeking, Self-Monitoring, and Perceived Social Standing

In his classic study of white college students in South Africa, Thomas Pettigrew (1958) discovered that strongly racist students scored particularly high on a scale measuring *conformity* tendencies, agreeing with statements like "a good group member should agree with the other members" and "to become a success these days, a person has to act in the way that others expect him to act." Similarly, individuals who are *high self-monitors*—who use the beliefs and actions of others to guide their own social behaviors (Snyder, 1974)—are also especially likely to express stereotypical and prejudiced views if they believe them to be socially appropriate (Fiske & Von Hendy, 1992; Sheets & Bushardt, 1994). People who, as a rule, want to fit in are more likely to adopt their community's prejudices, stereotypes, and discriminatory habits.

People's perceptions of their *social standing* also influence whether they conform to prejudiced norms. Recall, for example, a time when you were a newcomer—the new kid on the block, the new employee on the job, or the new student in the dorm. As a peripheral member of the group, you probably wanted to fit in and demonstrate your worth to the others. As a consequence, you were more likely to conform to the group's norms.

Jeffrey Noel, Daniel Wann, and Nyla Branscombe (1995) provided a nice demonstration of how the desire for social approval can lead peripheral group members to become especially hostile toward outgroups. Their subjects were fraternity and sorority members and pledges (members "in training"). As Figure 11.5 illustrates, full-fledged members exhibited similar amounts of prejudice against outgroup members regardless of whether their opinions were to be kept private or made public. In contrast, the pledges belittled other fraternities and sororities more when their evaluations were about to be made public to their fraternity brothers or sorority sisters. In an attempt to gain social approval, pledges strongly conformed to the norm of derogating other fraternities and sororities.

Figure 11.5
Pledging one's dislike for other groups.

Fraternity and sorority pledges at the University of Kansas were especially disparaging of other fraternities and sororities when they believed that members of their own groups would see their opinions. Peripheral members of groups—such as pledges—want to be accepted, even to the point of boldly proclaiming their outgroup prejudices.

SOURCE: *Data from Noel et al. (1995), Figure 3.*

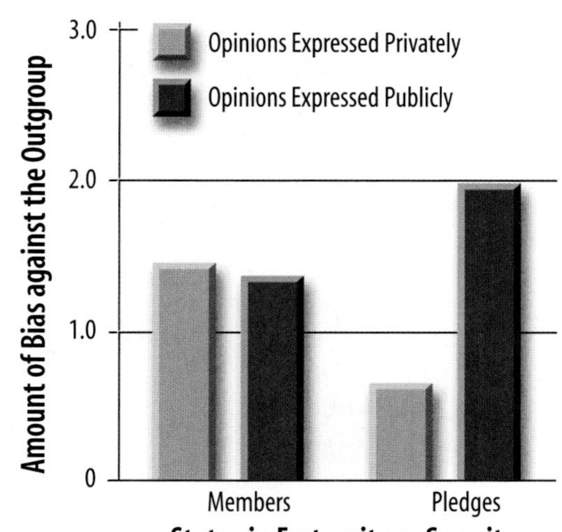

The Time and the Place

Conformists, high self-monitors, and people with a peripheral group standing have a greater need for social approval and, thus, are more willing to adopt a group's prejudicial norms. Norms, however, change over time and differ across locations. With these changes should come attendant shifts in people's expressions of stereotypes and prejudices.

Religious racism? *Many of the most virulently racist hate groups have religious beliefs at their foundations. For example, members of Aryan Nations ("Church of Jesus Christ Christian") see themselves as serving the principles of Christianity. Are groups such as Aryan Nations cynically constructing a facade of religiosity to justify racial ideologies that might otherwise seem reprehensible? Or do they truly believe they are doing the work of God? It seems puzzling, indeed, that people having strong religious beliefs can be so bigoted.*

Over the past forty years, white people report increasingly favorable views toward issues such as racial integration, interracial marriage, and black presidential candidates (Gallup, 1997). Do findings like these reflect actual changes in people's prejudices and stereotypes, or do they merely reveal people's desire to answer such surveys in socially appropriate ways? We've seen that the desire for social approval may lead people to adopt negative prejudices when they believe that others are bigoted. This same desire for social approval, however, may also lead people to adopt tolerant views when they believe that tolerance is the societal norm. For example, among high school students in North Carolina, white students' views of blacks were more favorable if they believed that their friends and parents approved of interracial friendships (Cox, Smith, & Insko, 1996).

If findings like these don't represent changes in actual attitudes, they surely reflect changes in the culture's injunctive and descriptive norms. As we discussed in earlier chapters, *injunctive norms* tell us what we *ought* to do and feel, and changes in U.S. laws and policies now communicate the message that discrimination against people on the bases of race, sex, ethnicity, religion, and age is inappropriate and counter to American beliefs. *Descriptive norms* tell us what people *actually* do and feel, and because the coercive power of the new laws has reduced the amount of observable discrimination, people are likely left with the impression that their peers are less bigoted now than before. Across the United States as a whole, then, changes over time in the injunctive norms have probably led to similar changes in the descriptive norms. As a result, people are not only less willing to express bigoted views in public but also may be less likely to hold them.

Norms also differ from place to place, and people adjust accordingly. For example, observations of coal miners in West Virginia revealed that most white workers would mingle comfortably with black workers in the mines but would avoid them in town, where cross-race friendships were frowned upon (Minard, 1952). Newly jailed inmates randomly assigned to live in a racially tolerant cell block became less racist during a one-month period, as compared to prisoners randomly assigned to live in a more bigoted cell block (Foley, 1976). As a last example, southerners who migrated to the North and nonurbanites who migrated to cities became increasingly tolerant after their moves (Tuch, 1987). As people move from work to play, from town to city, and from region to region, their expressions of prejudice tend to shift as well.

Intrinsic Religiosity and Prejudice

Many of the world's major faiths ascribe to the principle that people should accept others unconditionally, without regard to their race or ethnicity. It is thus puzzling that people who report being religious tend to be more prejudiced than those who do not (Allport & Kramer, 1946; Batson & Ventis, 1982). Why might this be?

People are religious for different reasons, and understanding these reasons can help us understand the association between religion and prejudice (Allport & Ross, 1967; Batson & Burris, 1994). Some people possess an **extrinsic religiosity**—that is, they see religious worship as an opportunity to make friends, gain status, or find support during difficult times. From this perspective, religion is used to get something else and is merely a means to some other end; its messages are not adopted as a life standard. Individuals who are religious for extrinsic reasons tend to be more negatively prejudiced than nonreligious people (e.g., Batson & Ventis, 1982).

A second form of spirituality has been labeled **quest religiosity** (Batson & Ventis, 1982). From this perspective, religion is a never-ending personal journey toward truth. People who are primarily quest-oriented are open-minded about

Extrinsic religiosity *An orientation toward religion that sees it as a means of gaining other things of value, such as friendships, status, or comfort.*

Quest religiosity *An orientation to religion that sees it as a journey taken to understand complex spiritual and moral issues usually accompanied by a belief that quick, simple answers are wrong.*

spiritual matters and don't expect to find simple answers to complex spiritual and moral issues. Quest-oriented individuals are open-minded about other things as well, which may explain why they exhibit few prejudices in either their self-reports or their actions (Batson & Burris, 1994).

Finally, people may adhere to an **intrinsic religiosity,** hoping to live their religion and internalize its teachings (Allport & Ross, 1967). From this perspective, religion is neither a means to some other goal nor a journey but rather an end in itself. Because most organized religions teach tolerance, and because intrinsically religious people hope to integrate their religious creeds into their identities and actions, we might expect intrinsically religious individuals to be low on prejudice. Indeed, intrinsically religious people seem less prejudiced than extrinsically religious people and no more prejudiced than those who report themselves to be nonreligious (Batson & Ventis, 1982; Donahue, 1985; Gorsuch, 1988). But are they?

Most of the studies exploring the link between religiosity and prejudice rely on self-report data. Daniel Batson and his colleagues have investigated the public *behavior* of intrinsics, however, and suggest that the true attitudes of intrinsically religious people may not be as they appear. In one study, white subjects reported their views of blacks on a questionnaire. Afterwards, they were asked to choose one of two people to interview them about their opinions; one of the interviewers was white, the other black. Subjects who scored high on scales of intrinsic religiosity presented themselves as particularly unprejudiced on the questionnaire but later preferred to discuss their views with the white interviewer (Batson, Naifeh, & Pate, 1978).

White subjects in another study were given a choice of watching a movie in one of two rooms; in one room sat a white student, and in the other room sat a black student. In a condition in which avoiding the black student could easily be seen as reflecting racial prejudices—when the movies presented in the two rooms were identical—intrinsically religious subjects were especially likely to choose the room with the waiting black student. In contrast, when avoiding the black person could be justified on nonprejudicial grounds—when *different* movies were shown in the two rooms—the instrinsically religious subjects no longer showed this preference for the black student (Batson et al., 1986). Batson and his colleagues suggest that intrinsically religious people may be more concerned with *appearing* tolerant—with presenting themselves as righteous in the eyes of others—than with actually *being* tolerant.

These findings reveal, then, an interesting interaction: In circumstances in which others can straightforwardly identify prejudice, intrinsically religious whites express and claim tolerant racial views. However, when it is difficult for observers to conclude anything about one's racial attitudes, intrinsically religious whites are as racist as people who make no claims of religiosity. Only people who see religion as a quest tend to be less prejudiced than people who see themselves as nonreligious. Note, however, that almost all research on religion and prejudice has focused on white Christians. Whether these findings generalize to other groups is a question yet to be thoroughly explored.

In light of such findings, it's perhaps less surprising that places of worship are the most racially segregated institutions in the United States (Gallup, 1997). And they may also help us understand better the powerful pressures placed on the Little Rock ministers by their congregations: Although the ministers' religiosity may have been of the unprejudiced, quest-oriented variety, their parishioners—even the intrinsically religious ones—did not want their children mixing with black students.

Intrinsic religiosity *An orientation to religion in which people attempt to internalize its teachings, seeing religiosity as an end in and of itself.*

Summary

Social approval concerns contribute to prejudice, stereotyping, and discrimination. People having conformist tendencies, high-self-monitors, and those of uncertain group standing are especially likely to adopt the society's existing prejudices.

Because norms regarding prejudice and discrimination change over time and differ across locations, attitudes and behaviors—at least as they are publicly expressed—change as well. Finally, members of organized Christian religions are generally more prejudiced than are nonreligious people. Only those who view religion as a quest for truth and meaning tend to be unprejudiced.

Managing Self-Image

C. P. Ellis was eight years old, playing football with his white neighbors against a team of black children from the other side of the railroad tracks. The black team won and, as the kids wandered toward their respective homes, one of C. P.'s teammates, frustrated by the loss, yelled back at the departing victors, "You niggers get back across the track." Given the time and place, these were far from fighting words, and the black children returned to compete the following weekend. For the young C. P., however, it was a defining moment—an awakening. Blacks were not just "blacks" or "colored," he realized. They were "niggers." And although he recognized that he was poor and that his family was looked down upon by many, he knew in that instant that he could never be a *nigger*—that there would always be someone beneath him on the social ladder. "Yeah," C. P. enthusiastically chimed in, "you niggers need to get back home!" With those words, he felt the security that comes from believing yourself better than someone else (Davidson, 1996, 64–65).

Twenty-five years later, C. P. Ellis discovered a second, related sense of security. As the ritual-laden induction ceremony ended with a ringing ovation from the assembled audience and the Exalted Cyclops of the Durham Ku Klux Klan welcomed him into the fold, an emotional Ellis felt for the first time that he was no longer an outsider. He now belonged to something important—a brotherhood—and with his membership gained an enhanced self-identity (Davidson, 1996, 123). Before the ceremony, he could take refuge in knowing that he *was not* a "nigger"; afterwards, he could also take pleasure and pride in knowing that he *was* a Klansman.

Personal and Social Identities

Social behavior is often motivated by the desire to feel good about oneself, and people are quite creative in the ways they accomplish this (see chapter 3). For example, confronted by personal failure, we may attempt to preserve a favorable self-image by blaming other groups for our inadequacies—that is, by **scapegoating** them. Scapegoating is usually directed toward easily identifiable groups against whom socially acceptable prejudices already exist. For example, it was a simple matter for C. P. Ellis to blame his financial failures on blacks. As he stated years later, "I had to hate somebody. Hatin' America is hard to do because you can't see it to hate it. You gotta have something to look at to hate. The natural person for me to hate would be black people, because my father before me was a member of the Klan" (Terkel, 1992). By blaming other groups for our own misfortunes and frustrations, we are better able to deal with our self-doubts and to feel good about ourselves.

Alternatively, by linking ourselves to successful others and distancing ourselves from unsuccessful others—by *basking in reflected glory* and by *cutting off reflected failure*—we can boost our self-images (e.g., Cialdini et al., 1976; Snyder, Lassegard, & Ford, 1986). These strategies reveal that self-image is influenced by more than just a sense of ourselves as individuals. Rather, self-image is also influenced by our **social identity**—by our opinions of, and feelings about, the social groups with which we identify. Like C. P. Ellis, whose self-image was elevated when he embraced the Klan and its white Christian heritage, many of our self-images are elevated by the pride we have in our groups and ethnic backgrounds.

Scapegoating *The process of blaming members of other groups for one's frustrations and failures.*

Social identity *The beliefs and feelings we have toward the groups to which we see ourselves belonging.*

The observation that social identities contribute to self-esteem forms the foundation of social identity theory (Tajfel & Turner, 1986). Just as individuals manage their personal identities by comparing themselves to other individuals, people manage their social identities by comparing their groups to other groups. Specifically, by positively differentiating your group from other groups—by engaging in *downward social comparison*, seeing your group as better than "them"—you can create a positive social identity, which in turn can increase your sense of self-worth (e.g., Hunter et al., 1996; Lemyre & Smith, 1985; Oakes & Turner, 1980; Rubin & Hewstone, 1998). To create this positive differentiation, you might directly enhance your own group, perhaps through positive stereotypes. C. P. Ellis, for instance, was able to enhance his social identity by seeing the KKK as unique in its moral code of honor, chivalry, and desire to defend Christian America. Instead, you might actively derogate other groups, thereby making your own group look positive in contrast (Cialdini & Richardson, 1980). For example, by enthusiastically endorsing his culture's negative stereotypes of blacks as unintelligent and lazy, Ellis was better able to view the members of his own group as smart and hard-working. You might also discriminate against the other group by taking away its opportunities, thus giving your group a *real* advantage. Of course, you could do all of these things. By exaggerating the KKK's favorable characteristics, by labeling blacks with strong negative stereotypes, and by effectively fighting to block economic and educational gains by blacks, Ellis was able to boost his social identity and, thus, his broader self-image.

Ethnic pride. *How we view the social groups to which we belong influences how we view ourselves. For this reason, we look to celebrate our social identities. Unfortunately, positive social identities sometimes come at the expense of other groups, because we derogate them so that our group can look good by comparison.*

Ingroup Identification

C. P. Ellis immersed himself in Klan activities and soon established a reputation as an energetic and effective worker. Committed to the organization from the very beginning, Ellis's identification with it grew as he rapidly moved up in the group's hierarchy, first to chaplain and then to Exalted Cyclops—the top position in the Durham klavern. His identity as a Klansman became an increasingly important part of his self-image, and his desire to act on his racist prejudices grew stronger as well. This is as we might expect. When people identify strongly with their groups, they have more to gain from their groups' favorable standings and more to lose should their groups' positions weaken.

Indeed, research indicates that people who are highly identified with their group are especially quick to discriminate in favor of it (Branscombe & Wann, 1992). In one experiment, for example, students at a French-Canadian university had the job of anonymously allocating extra-credit course points to fellow students. Some of the possible recipients were members of the students' own groups and some were not. Students who felt no strong identification with their ingroups allocated points equally across the two groups. As predicted, however, high identifiers gave more points to their own groups (Gagnon & Bourhis, 1996). Ingroup identification leads to increased discrimination.

Authoritarianism

Authoritarianism *The tendency to submit to those having greater authority and to denigrate those having less authority.*

The tendency to use negative prejudice and discrimination as tools for managing self-image is also tied to a personality characteristic called **authoritarianism**—the tendency to submit to those having greater authority and to denigrate those having less authority. When people around the world learned of mass extermination in the Nazi concentration camps, they faced troubling questions: Where do prejudices this powerful come from? What kind of person participates in such killings? And what kind of person stands idly by and does nothing? One group of psychologists proposed that a psychologically flawed personality must be part of the answer, as we see next.

FOCUS ON Social Dysfunction

The Authoritarian Personality

Auschwitz-Birkenau was the most notorious death camp of all. Built by the Nazis in southern Poland, its function was to incarcerate political prisoners, house slave laborers for nearby factory work, and exterminate Jews and other "undesirables." Rudolf Höss, the camp's commandant, carried out these orders with extraordinary efficiency. In less than four years, Höss and his troops murdered 1.5 to 2.5 million people. Höss provided a very simple explanation for his leading role in Hitler's "final solution": he was merely following orders. "I did not reflect on it at the time," he later said. "I had been given an order, and I had to carry it out.... What the Führer, or in our case his second-in-command, the Reichsführer SS, ordered was always right" (Höss, 1960, 160–161). After the war, Höss was captured, tried, and hanged for his crimes.

How do we explain the actions of Rudolf Höss and those like him? Theodor Adorno, Else Frenkel-Brunswik, Daniel Levinson, and Nevitt Sanford (1950) proposed that blind obedience and negative prejudices find root in families in which parents severely punish and shame their young children for even small transgressions. As a result, the children feel hostile toward their parents and other authority figures. But they do not want to express or acknowledge their hostility because doing so may (1) bring even more punishment and (2) create a powerful internal conflict between hating their punitive parents and believing that they ought instead to love and respect them. As a result, said the researchers, these children learn to repress their antagonisms toward their parents and other authorities and to displace their aggressive impulses onto weaker members of society.

And thus is created the *authoritarian personality* (Adorno et al., 1950). Those who have this personality are characterized by the following features: They readily submit to authorities but are aggressive against those perceived to be lower than they are on the social ladder; that is, they "kiss ass" above and "kick ass" below. They readily adopt and conform to society's conventions and rules. They are tough-minded toward people who challenge society's conventions. They view the world in simple black–white terms, abhorring shades of gray. And, most important for our purposes, they are hypothesized to be strongly prejudiced against members of minority groups.

Merely following orders. *Rudolf Höss, pictured here (second from left) being transported to his war-crimes trial in Poland, had millions executed at the Auschwitz-Birkenau concentration camp. A true authoritarian, Kommandant Höss provided a simple explanation for his leading role in Hitler's "final solution" for the Jews: He was merely following orders.*

This view of prejudice quickly became prominent, perhaps because it seemed to explain why the German people—perceived to be very orderly, disciplined, and respectful of authority—not only allowed the dictatorial Adolf Hitler to come to power but also went along with his program to annihilate the Jews and others. But other researchers found weaknesses in the explanation offered by Adorno and his colleagues (e.g., Christie & Jahoda, 1954). For one thing, much of the support for their view of the role of punitive families in creating authoritarianism was based on case studies (Ackerman & Jahoda, 1950; Adorno et al., 1950; Hopf, 1993). As we discussed in chapter 1, the case study method has important weaknesses. Later research has given some support to other explanations for how people become authoritarian. According to one alternative view, adolescents simply learn to be authoritarian by observing their authoritarian parents (Altemeyer, 1988, 1998). According to another account, tendencies toward authoritarianism are passed along genetically (Scarr, 1981). All three views have received some empirical support.

Still, Adorno and his colleagues turned out to be quite correct about many things, including the relationship between authoritarianism and negative prejudice. People who view the world through authoritarian lenses are more negatively prejudiced toward outgroups than are people who do not (e.g., Bierly, 1985; Cunningham, Dollinger, Satz, & Rotter, 1991; Haddock, Zanna, & Esses, 1993; Wylie & Forest, 1992). This holds true for authoritarians in the United States, Canada, England, South Africa, Russia, and many other countries (e.g., Altemeyer, 1988; Duckitt & Farre, 1994; Heaven & Furnham, 1987; McFarland, Ageyev, & Abalakina, 1993; Stephan et al., 1994; Van Staden, 1987).

It would be reassuring to believe that authoritarian tendencies are confined to monstrous individuals like Rudolf Höss. It would also be a mistake. We have seen, for example, how easy it is for everyday folks to obey the extreme commands of others (chapter 6). Moreover, the bulk of the studies demonstrating ties between authoritarianism and prejudice used college students as participants—people like you. Finally, even though authoritarianism is a relatively stable personality characteristic, formed largely as a result of childhood experiences, it tends to increase when we experience frustrating negative events (Sales & Friend, 1973). Because many of us possess some degree of authoritarianism, we also possess the capacity to do real damage to members of lesser-status groups under certain circumstances. ■

Failure

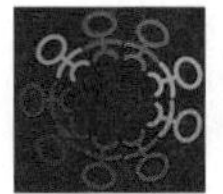

The bakery where C. P. Ellis worked as a deliveryman was closing down and C. P. needed a job. It was a stroke of luck, then, that a local gas station was up for sale, and better luck yet that a neighboring store owner offered to co-sign the mortgage. Seeing this as his big chance to create a better life, Ellis jumped at the opportunity and put his heart, soul, and sweat into the business. Despite his considerable skills as an auto mechanic, however, his third-rate education left him woefully unprepared to run a business. With great disappointment and frustration, he would arrive at the end of each month only to discover that, after paying his bills, he was no better off than before. Around this time, C. P. Ellis attended his first KKK rally and just weeks later became a member. Was this a coincidence? Probably not.

When our self-images are shaken by frustration and failure, we are more likely to derogate members of stigmatized groups (e.g., Crocker et al., 1987; Miller & Bugelski, 1948; Sinclair & Kunda, 2000; Spencer, Fein, Wolfe, Fong, & Dunn, 1998). Consider an experiment in which University of Michigan students first took an intelligence test and were given bogus feedback that they had either performed quite well or quite poorly (Fein & Spencer, 1997). They then went to a second study where they evaluated a job candidate's personality and job qualifications. Some subjects learned that the female job candidate was Jewish, activating for them stereotypes of the "Jewish American Princess." In contrast, other students learned that the candidate was Italian, activating no negative stereotypes for this population. Students who thought they did well on the intelligence test evaluated both candidates equally well. In contrast, students who thought they did poorly on the test evaluated the Jewish applicant much less favorably than the Italian candidate. Interestingly, the students who derogated the Jewish candidate subsequently showed increases in their personal self-esteem, suggesting that people can sometimes restore threatened self-esteem by derogating members of negatively stereotyped groups.

As these studies show, failure motivates us toward discrimination and prejudice. With the Klan's message of honorable white Christian purity, Ellis was able to counteract the esteem-threatening effects of his business difficulties.

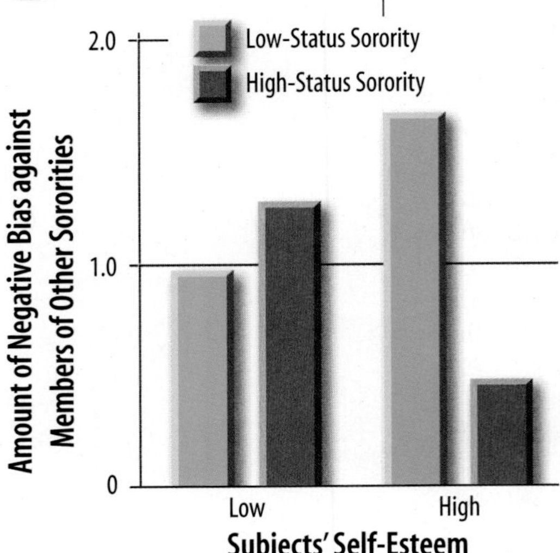

Figure 11.6
Self-esteem and threat on sorority row.

In a study of sorority women at Northwestern University, those with low self-regard derogated members of other sororities. The views of women who thought highly of themselves, however, depended on the prestige of their own affiliations: Those in a prestigious sorority showed little bias against other sororities, whereas those in a low-status sorority showed the greatest amount of bias of all. Apparently, belonging to a sorority "beneath them" was quite threatening, leading these women to derogate members of other houses in an attempt to restore their damaged self-image.

SOURCE: *Data from Crocker et al. (1987), Table 2, p. 913.*

Self-Esteem and Threat

If boosting ingroups or derogating outgroups can help restore threatened self-esteem, a person with a chronically threatened sense of self—with relatively low self-esteem—should readily partake of such strategies (Wills, 1981; Wylie, 1979). This is indeed the case: Individuals having low self-esteem tend to be negatively prejudiced against outgroup members, and they show consistent favoritism toward the ingroup (Crocker & Schwartz, 1985; Crocker et al., 1987). You might be surprised to learn, however, that people who have high self-esteem also favor their own groups, often to an even greater extent than do people who have low self-esteem (Aberson, Healy, & Romero, 2000). The ingroup bias displayed by high self-esteem individuals may be especially pronounced when they are threatened by personal failure.

What happens, for example, when a woman who has high self-esteem ends up in a low-status sorority? Jennifer Crocker and her colleagues (1987) suspected that these women would find the low prestige of their sorority threatening to their self-regard. After all, these women likely believe that they deserve better. If so, the researchers reasoned, they should be especially likely to derogate members of other sororities. To explore this hypothesis, Crocker and her colleagues recruited sorority women from Northwestern University and assessed their views of sororities on campus. As Figure 11.6 reveals, most sorority women evaluated the members of other sororities more negatively than they did members of their own. For women who had low self-regard, the status of their own sororities made no difference: They derogated the members of other sororities, regardless. In contrast, sorority prestige made a large difference for women who had high self-esteem. Those in prestigious sororities showed little bias against other sorority women, whereas those in low-status sororities strongly derogated other sororities. Apparently, belonging to a low-status sorority threatened the positive self-image of these high-self-esteem women. Level of self-esteem and the presence of a social threat interact, then, to determine the amount of ingroup favoritism. Challenges to self-image are particularly threatening to people who hold themselves in high regard. As a result, these people are likely to demonstrate more pronounced ingroup favoritism.

Summary

We can use negative prejudices, stereotypes, and discrimination to manage our personal and social identities. By scapegoating members of weak minority groups or by elevating our groups over other groups, we can view ourselves in a more favorable light. People who are strongly identified with their groups or who have authoritarian personalities are particularly likely to use stereotypes and prejudices to manage their self-images. Moreover, after failing at something important to them, people are especially likely to demonstrate ingroup biases and discrimination. Finally, individuals who have high self-esteem are particularly likely to derogate members of outgroups, but only when their high self-regard is threatened.

Seeking Mental Efficiency

> My wife was driving down the street in a black neighborhood. The people at the corners were all gesticulating at her. She was very frightened, turned up the windows, and drove determinedly. She discovered, after several blocks, she was

> going the wrong way on a one-way street and they were trying to help her. Her assumption was that they were blacks and were out to get her. Mind you, she's a very enlightened person. You'd never associate her with racism, yet her first reaction was that they were dangerous. (Gilbert Gordon, in Terkel, 1992, 289)

Stereotyping is a cognitively inexpensive way of understanding others: By presuming that people are like other members of their groups, we avoid the effortful process of learning about them as individuals (Allport, 1954; Hamilton, 1981; Lippman, 1922; Tajfel, 1969). Moreover, because stereotypes are rich and vivid expectations of what group members will be like, we feel as though we know much about a person as soon as we identify the groups to which he or she belongs. Because stereotypes provide ready *interpretations* of ambiguous behaviors, the driver described above presumed that the black pedestrians were trying to harm her (e.g., D'Agostino, 2000; Duncan, 1976; Dunning & Sherman, 1997; Sagar & Schofield, 1980). Because stereotypes provide ready *explanations* for why certain events occur, people might guess that a boy's poor score on a math exam reflects either bad luck or insufficient effort but that a girl's identically poor score reflects a lack of ability (Deaux & LaFrance, 1998; Frieze et al., 1978; Swim & Sanna, 1996). And because stereotypes provide different *standards* for evaluating members of different groups, we think little of a solid basketball performance by a black player but assume that a similarly performing white player is highly talented (Biernat & Manis, 1994). Stereotyping provides a lot of information for little effort.

The Characteristics of Efficient Stereotypes

In the long run, stereotypes are most useful as simplifying tools when they are reasonably accurate—when they do a pretty good job describing what group members are truly like. Although many stereotypes are badly inaccurate, others contain a substantial kernel of truth (e.g., Biernat, 1993; Brigham, 1971; McCauley, 1995; Oakes, Haslam, & Turner, 1994; Ottati & Lee, 1995; Ryan, 1996). For example, Janet Swim (1994) compared actual sex differences with college students' estimates of these sex differences. Although students' stereotypes sometimes underestimated the sex differences and sometimes overestimated them, Swim found that they were generally reasonably accurate. Most telling, the students rarely got the *direction* of the sex differences wrong. For example, they almost never erroneously believed that women are generally more aggressive than men.

Ironically, highly accurate stereotypes—those that fully reflect the complexity of real social groups—would be too complex to save us much time or effort. As a result, stereotypes tend to exaggerate the reality a bit by "sharpening" the differences between groups and "softening" the differences within groups, as we see in Figure 11.7 (Dijksterhuis & van Knippenberg, 1999; Krueger & Rothbart, 1990; Secord, Bevan, & Katz, 1956; Tajfel, Sheikh, & Gardner, 1964). Recent research has focused on how this "softening" process leads people to see members of other groups as being overly *homogeneous*, or similar to each other (Mullen & Hu, 1989; Ostrom & Sedikides, 1992; Park, Judd, & Ryan, 1991). For example, although women are on average less aggressive than men, some women are extremely aggressive and others are extremely peaceful. Men in particular tend to underappreciate this variety, however, believing instead that most women are similar in their lack of aggressiveness.

The "they all look the same to me" phenomenon is one form of this **perceived outgroup homogeneity** effect—the tendency to overestimate the extent to which members of other groups are similar to one another. Because we generally fail to appreciate the variety of facial features possessed by members of other racial groups, we are not very good at accurately recognizing them (e.g., Anthony, Copper, & Mullen, 1993; Brigham & Malpass, 1985). Consider, for instance, the case of Lenell

Stereotyping *The process of categorizing an individual as a member of a particular group and then inferring that he or she possesses the characteristics generally held by members of that group.*

Perceived outgroup homogeneity *The phenomenon of overestimating the extent to which members within other groups are similar to each other.*

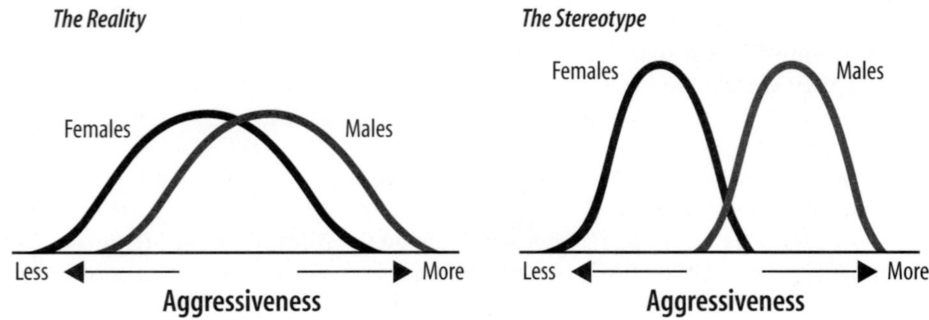

Figure 11.7
Sharpening and softening to create efficient social categories.

To save us time and cognitive effort, we often *sharpen* the distinctions between groups and *soften* the differences within groups. For example, although males and females differ in their aggressiveness, we tend to exaggerate this difference in our minds.

Geter. Geter was a young engineer working at a research center in the Dallas area when he was identified from a photograph as the armed robber of a fast-food restaurant. There was no physical evidence linking Geter to the crime, he had no criminal record, and his coworkers testified that he had been working fifty miles away at the time of the theft. Nonetheless, convinced by the confident testimony of white and Hispanic eyewitnesses, the all-white jury found Geter guilty of the $615 robbery and sentenced him to life in prison. His case received a thorough second look only after persistent efforts by his coworkers and the NAACP brought it to the attention of local and national media. But only after the police arrested another man for the crime—a man implicated for a string of similar robberies and identified by the same witnesses who fingered Geter—did the Dallas prosecutor's office declare Geter's innocence. After sixteen months behind bars, Geter again became a free man (Applebome, 1983, 1984).

The tendency to overestimate the homogeneity of other groups serves a useful purpose: It makes it easier for us to stereotype others. If a woman believes, for instance,

A case of mistaken identity. *Do these men look similar to you? White and Hispanic witnesses to a string of robberies thought so. As a result, Lenell Geter, on the left, was convicted of a crime for which the man on the right was eventually arrested. Given the difficulty people have identifying others of different races—one manifestation of the perceived outgroup homogeneity effect—it seems fair to question whether Geter would have been misidentified had the eyewitnesses also been black. After all, as Geter assured one of the authors, "I'm much better looking than the other guy!"*

SOURCE: *L. Geter, personal communication, August 1997.*

that virtually all men are sports fans, she can comfortably assume that the next man she encounters will be sports-minded as well. If she believes, however, that men vary widely in this respect, she'll be less confident that the next man she encounters will be sports-minded, forcing her to form an effortful impression of him based on his individual characteristics (Linville, Fischer, & Salovey, 1989; Ryan, Judd, & Park, 1996).

We see, then, that forming and using simple, homogeneous stereotypes is cognitively efficient, especially if they're reasonably accurate; it enables us to allocate our limited cognitive resources elsewhere. Stereotypes are even more efficient because they come to mind easily (e.g., Banaji & Greenwald, 1995; Devine, 1989; Locke, Macleod & Walker, 1994; Macrae, Milne, & Bodenhausen, 1994; Perdue & Gurtman, 1990). That is, once you categorize an outgroup member, you'll quickly begin to see him or her as you see members of that group in general. Next, we explore one method researchers use to investigate the automatic activation of stereotypes.

FOCUS ON **Method**

Exploring the Automatic Activation of Stereotypes

When you hear the word *bread*, what other words come to mind? The word *butter* was probably near the top of the list. Because *bread* and *butter* are linked in memory, thinking about one leads us to think about the other. Indeed, thinking first about *bread* increases the speed with which *butter* comes to mind. This observation underlies the *semantic priming method* for discovering which ideas are linked together in memory: If after seeing one concept (e.g., *dog*) we recognize a second concept (e.g., *cat*) more quickly than we would otherwise, we know that the two ideas are closely associated in memory (Meyer & Schvaneveldt, 1971; Neeley, 1991).

Several teams of social psychologists have used this technique to demonstrate that thinking about a person's gender or race can easily, and sometimes automatically, activate stereotypes (e.g., Banaji & Hardin, 1996; Blair & Banaji, 1996; Dovidio, Evans, & Tyler, 1986). One study went a step further, showing that racial stereotypes and prejudices can be automatically activated in people who aren't even consciously thinking about race or social groupings (Wittenbrink, Judd, & Park, 1997):

White American college students at the University of Colorado were asked to decide quickly and accurately whether strings of letters presented on a computer screen were words or not. If the target letters formed a word, the students were to press a "yes" button; if the letters didn't form a word, they were to press a "no" button. The participants made these word/not-word decisions about negative black stereotypes (e.g., *dangerous*), positive black stereotypes (e.g., *musical*), negative white stereotypes (e.g., *materialistic*), positive white stereotypes (e.g., *educated*), words unrelated to race stereotypes (e.g., *sunny*), and random strings of letters. The computer measured the time participants needed to make the decisions. Unknown to the participants, however, these words were sometimes preceded by subliminal presentations of the words *BLACK* and *WHITE*. How did the words *BLACK* and *WHITE* influence the speed with which participants reacted to the stereotypical target words?

If characteristics such as *dangerous* and *musical* are stereotypically associated in white Americans' minds with African Americans, and if stereotypes can be activated even when people are not consciously thinking about people or race, then white Americans should be particularly quick to identify the black stereotype words after being subliminally exposed to the word *BLACK*. Similarly, if characteristics such as *materialistic* and *educated* are stereotypically associated in white Americans' minds with their own group, then white Americans should more rapidly identify target words related to their ingroup stereotypes after being subliminally exposed to the word *WHITE*.

This was indeed the case, but only when the stereotypes were consistent with the prejudices held by the participants: The word *BLACK* facilitated decisions about words related to *negative* black stereotypes, and the word *WHITE* facilitated decisions about words related to *positive* white stereotypes. That is, the word *BLACK* made it easier to recognize words such as *dangerous*, but not *musical*, and the word *WHITE* made it easier to recognize words such as *educated*, but not *materialistic*. This study demonstrated that even when people aren't focused on forming impressions of others, stereotypes and prejudices can be automatically activated in their minds. ■

It's clear that stereotyping can be an efficient—if often damaging—way of understanding others. We turn now to explore those factors within the person and the situation that lead people to stereotype others for reasons of cognitive efficiency.

Need for Structure

Some people like their lives to be relatively simple and well organized. They dislike interruptions and unexpected events, and, as we learned in chapter 3, strive for simple ways to view the world. These individuals have a high *need for structure* (Thompson, Naccarato, & Parker, 1989). Because stereotypes are one way to simplify the world, such persons are more likely to use their existing stereotypes to understand others (Naccarato, 1988; Neuberg & Newsom, 1993). They are also more likely to form stereotypes of new groups.

Consider, for instance, an experiment conducted by Mark Schaller, Carrie Boyd, Jonathan Yohannes, and Meredith O'Brien (1995). Participants were asked to determine the relative intelligence of two groups—labeled As and Bs—based on the group members' abilities to solve easy and difficult anagram (scrambled letter) puzzles. Participants learned about 25 members of each group and were told whether each member had successfully solved his or her assigned anagram. Overall, members of Group B solved more anagrams than did members of Group A. The information also revealed, however, that members of Group A had been assigned many more of the tough anagrams. Indeed, even though members of Group A were actually better at solving both the easy and difficult anagrams, their *overall* success rate wasn't as good because they had been given tougher puzzles to solve. Participants seeking the simplest way to stereotype the two groups could rely on the total number of puzzles solved. Doing so, however, would lead them mistakenly to view the members of Group A as less intelligent than the members of Group B. As the researchers predicted, participants identified as higher in need for structure focused primarily on the easily available, simple information, thus creating the erroneous stereotype.

These findings provide an interesting insight into several common stereotypes. For instance, some whites believe that blacks are inherently unintelligent and disposed to criminality. Might it be, however, that those possessing these stereotypes fail to account sufficiently for situational forces known to influence intelligence and criminal behavior—like poor educational opportunities and poverty (Fairchild, 1984)? Similarly, might the stereotype that women are inherently more communal than men be due partially to the failure to consider fully the differences in family and work roles that women and men fill (Cejka & Eagly, 1999; Eagly & Steffen, 1984; Hoffman & Hurst, 1990)? The findings of Schaller and his colleagues suggest that the answers to these questions may be yes—that some people, particularly those high in need for structure, form mistaken or exaggerated stereotypes about the innate nature of certain behaviors because they fall prey to the *correspondence bias* discussed in chapter 3—they don't adequately account for the situational influences on people's behavior.

Moods and Emotions

Feelings influence the motivation and ability to think about things thoroughly. They also influence which ideas come to mind. As a result, our moods and emotions can powerfully influence whether and how we stereotype others.

First, recall from chapter 3 that people in good moods are less motivated to think about things thoroughly. Whereas certain negative moods, such as sadness, signal that we need to pay close attention to the people around us, positive moods signal that we can go about our business with relatively little worry that we'll be troubled in the near future (Schwarz, 1990). People in positive moods, then, should be less concerned with being perfectly accurate and should be more willing to rely on simplifying cognitive shortcuts like stereotypes. Indeed, positive moods do increase stereotyping (e.g., Bodenhausen, Kramer, & Susser, 1994; Mackie et al., 1989; Park & Banaji, 2000; Stroessner & Mackie, 1992).

Second, emotions that are arousing—like anger, fear, and euphoria—reduce the amount of cognitive resources available to us, limiting our ability to think about things thoroughly and thus making stereotyping more likely. For instance, anger and anxiety make people particularly likely to stereotype others (Bodenhausen, Sheppard, & Kramer, 1994; Wilder, 1993). Indeed, even when the physiological arousal is unrelated to feelings—as occurs after exercise—stereotyping is still more likely (Kim & Baron, 1988; Paulhus, Martin, & Murphy, 1992).

Moods and emotions also influence which categories people use to understand others. Most of us fall into numerous categories, and how we are categorized by others may depend on how they're feeling at the time. One of this text's authors, for instance, is Jewish and a college professor. People who like college professors but dislike Jews are more likely to see him as a college professor if they're in a good mood when they meet him. If they're in a bad mood, however, they may be more likely to categorize him as a Jew.

In a related vein, most groups can be characterized by both positive and negative stereotypes, and a person's mood will influence which stereotypes are more likely to come quickly to mind (e.g., Erber, 1991). For instance, Jews are stereotypically seen by many as both intelligent and materialistic. When people are in a good mood, they're more likely to see a particular Jew as intelligent, and when they're in a bad mood, they're more likely to see him or her as materialistic.

Finally, moods influence how specific stereotypes are framed, as even normally favorable characteristics like intelligence can be viewed negatively—as sly or cunning, for instance. An experiment by Victoria Esses and Mark Zanna (1995) demonstrated this nicely: Canadian students put into a negative mood were not only more likely to view Native Indian, Pakistani, and Arabic people unfavorably but also were more likely to further devalue the characteristics (e.g., dark-skinned) stereotypically associated with these groups.

Thus both positive and negative moods can be problematic if one wants to avoid stereotyping others or evaluating them negatively (see Figure 11.8). Although

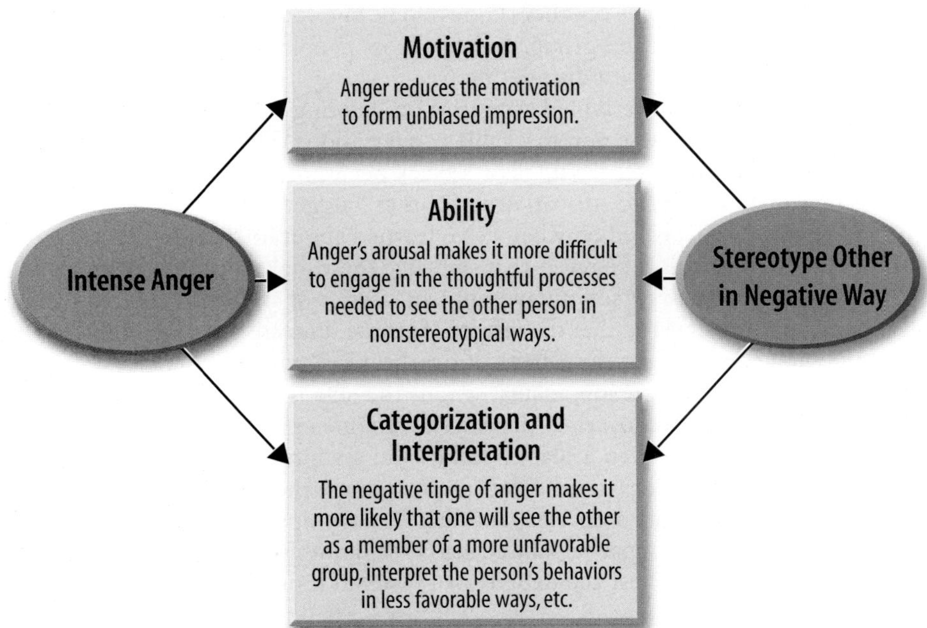

Figure 11.8
Feelings and stereotyping.

Our moods and emotions influence how we view others: They can alter (1) how motivated we are to go beyond our stereotypes and prejudices, (2) our ability to go beyond our stereotypes and prejudices, and (3) how we categorize and interpret the information available to us. For example, experiencing intense anger increases the likelihood that we will negatively stereotype others because it reduces our motivation to be fair, reduces our capacity to think carefully, and makes unfavorable social categories and interpretations more accessible.

people in negative moods are more motivated to go beyond their stereotypes to understand others, they tend to think about others in less favorable ways. Those in positive moods, on the other hand, view others more favorably, but they are also more likely to be cognitively lazy and to use their stereotypes. Finally, when highly aroused, either positively or negatively, people may not have the cognitive resources to go far beyond their stereotypes.

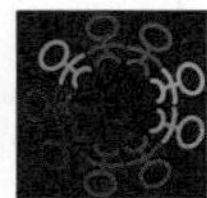

Cognitively Taxing Circumstances

Certain situations limit the amount of attention we have available for forming impressions of others, thereby increasing our reliance on simple, efficient thought processes such as stereotyping. For example, we are more likely to stereotype in situations that are complex—that have many things going on (Bodenhausen & Lichtenstein, 1987; Rothbart, Fulero, Jensen, Howard, & Birrell, 1978; Stangor & Duan, 1991). We are also more likely to stereotype when circumstances require us to perform other cognitive tasks at the same time. In one study, participants were asked to form an impression of an elderly woman. Even when they were motivated to form an accurate impression of "Hilda," participants who also had to keep in mind an 8-digit number were unable to avoid using their stereotypes of the elderly (Pendry & Macrae, 1994). Finally, sometimes we need to form impressions of others under time pressure, as when an interviewer knows that she has only 15 minutes to devote to each of 30 job applicants. Because time pressure reduces the amount of attention one can devote to understanding others, it increases the use of stereotypes (Bechtold, Naccarato, & Zanna, 1986; Dijker & Koomen, 1996; Kruglanski & Freund, 1983; Pratto & Bargh, 1991).

In sum, when circumstances tax our attentional capacity—either because they are particularly complex, require us to perform multiple tasks, or put us under time pressure—we rely more on stereotypes. This may explain why the generally nonracist white woman driving through the black neighborhood was so quick to misperceive the helpful intentions of the black pedestrians: Cognitively burdened by the task of navigating through unfamiliar streets, she may have been unable to go beyond the easily activated, culturally transmitted stereotype that blacks are dangerous (Devine, 1989).

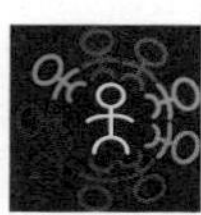

Overheard Ethnic Slurs

Some names for groups are so derogatory and hurtful that most people dare speak them only in the presence of others known to be bigoted or when they hope to insult a member of the targeted group. Indeed, most people have difficulty just talking *about* such words. Yet, with disquieting frequency, we hear ethnic slurs yelled from passing cars, see them scribbled as graffiti on building walls, or encounter them in the midst of an otherwise unremarkable conversation. What are the consequences? How do you think whites would view a black person, for instance, soon after overhearing someone refer to African Americans as "niggers"?

One possibility, based on what we've learned about how easily negative stereotypes can come to mind, suggests that slurs like these make it more likely that whites would view the black person unfavorably. In a series of studies, Jeff Greenberg and his colleagues discovered that the effects of ethnic slurs are not so straightforwardly simple, however. Rather, the effects of overheard ethnic slurs depend on both the characteristics of the person against whom the slur is directed and on the prejudice level of the person overhearing the slur. In one experiment, white participants watched a debate between a black speaker and a white speaker. For some participants, the black speaker won the debate; for others, the white speaker won. Afterward, as the participants prepared to evaluate the two speakers anonymously, a white confederate posing as a participant either (1) said nothing, (2) gave his opinion that the black speaker had lost the debate, or (3) salted his opinion with a racial slur—

"There's no way that nigger won the debate." The ethnic slur interacted with the black speaker's success to determine how he was evaluated. The black speaker was evaluated as less skillful by participants hearing the slur *only when he lost the debate.* When he won, the black speaker was not denigrated (Greenberg & Pyszczynski, 1985).

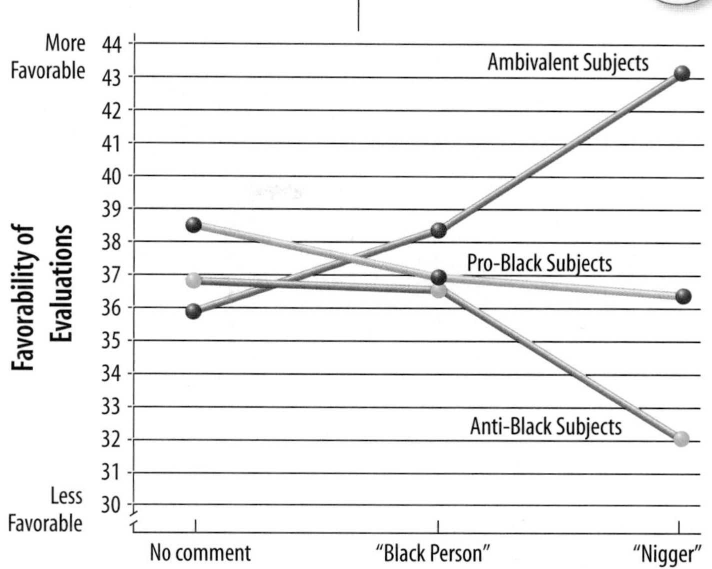

Figure 11.9
Overhearing an ethnic slur.

How does hearing or seeing an ethnic slur influence the way we judge those victimized by it? In one study, a slur against a black team member led white participants having anti-black views to evaluate her poorly; it had no influence on white participants who had pro-black views; and it led white participants who had ambivalent views toward blacks to evaluate her positively. The effect of overhearing an ethnic slur depends on our initial attitudes toward the victimized group.

SOURCE: *Data from Simon & Greenberg (1996), Table 1.*

This finding makes an important point: Even though overhearing the slur likely activated in most white participants' minds negative stereotypes about blacks, only those participants evaluating the poorly performing speaker relied on these stereotypes for their judgments. In contrast, when the speaker's good performance suggested that the negative stereotypes did not apply to him, the participants were less likely to use them. Indeed, much research shows that people rely less on their stereotypes when they appear to be inconsistent with the personal characteristics of the individual they are judging (Fiske & Neuberg, 1990; see chapter 3).

A second experiment demonstrated that the effects of overhearing an ethnic slur also depend on the views of the person overhearing them (Simon & Greenberg, 1996). Three groups of subjects, differing in their prejudices, participated in a study of "group processes." Upon arriving at the lab, white participants and one black confederate first worked individually on a problem and then passed their solutions around to the other participants working in different cubicles. Unknown to the participants, however, the researchers replaced these solutions with others, attaching to one either (1) a comment stating that "I can't believe they stuck us with this black person!", (2) a comment stating that "I can't believe they stuck us with this nigger!", or (3) no comment at all. Later, participants rated each other's characteristics.

As Figure 11.9 reveals, the ethnic slur had a negative effect on evaluations of the black team member, but only for participants who had strong negative prejudices to begin with. Participants who had strong pro-black attitudes were uninfluenced by the ethnic slur. And, perhaps most interesting, participants who had ambivalent feelings toward blacks—who held both strong positive and strong negative views—evaluated the black team member more *positively* after hearing the ethnic slur. For these ambivalent participants, the slur cast against a team member who had done nothing wrong may have reminded them of their own more virulent views—views inconsistent with their egalitarian self-images. Perhaps to protect themselves from an undesirable self-image, the ambivalent participants "bent over backwards" to evaluate the team member positively (Katz, Wackenhut, & Hass, 1986).

These findings illustrate that not all people are influenced the same way by overheard ethnic slurs. In particular, ethnic slurs are more likely to activate negative stereotypes in those who are negatively prejudiced than in those who are not (Lepore & Brown, 1997; Wittenbrink et al., 1997). We see again, then, the interactive nature of persons and situations.

Summary

Stereotyping allows us to gain a lot of potentially useful information for relatively little cognitive effort. Among other cognitive benefits, stereotypes help us interpret ambiguous behavior, provide ready explanations for why others act as they do, and suggest standards for how we should evaluate members of different groups. People are more likely to rely on their stereotypes when they have a high personal need for

CHAPTER 11
Summary Table

Table 11.1 A summary of the goals served by prejudice, stereotyping, discrimination, and the factors related to them.

The Goal	The Person	The Situation	Interactions
Gaining Material Benefits for One's Group	• Social dominance orientation	• Intergroup competition	• As groups view one another as potential competitors, they begin to compete, inadvertently bringing about the hostile competition they initially feared. This self-fulfilling prophecy can spiral into an increasingly intense conflict, as those involved become even more convinced that the others are hostile.
Gaining Social Approval	• Conformity seeking • Self-monitoring • Perceived social standing	• The time • The place	• People who are extrinsically religious tend to be more prejudiced than nonreligious people, but people who are religious in a quest-oriented way exhibit few strong prejudices. • People who are intrinsically religious tend to publicly adopt their religion's social norms. Privately, however, they do not appear to be less prejudiced than nonreligious people.
Managing Self-Image	• Ingroup identification • Authoritarianism	• Failure	• People with low self-esteem tend to devalue members of other groups. People with high self-esteem do so as well, but primarily when their self-image is threatened by failure.
Seeking Mental Efficiency	• Need for structure • Moods and emotions	• Cognitively taxing circumstances	• Overhearing an ethnic slur can lead a person to discriminate against the target of the slur, particularly when the slur seems consistent with the target's personal characteristics and when the slur fits with the listener's existing prejudices.

structure and when their moods and emotions leave them unmotivated or unable to process information about others thoroughly. Situations that demand a lot of cognitive resources also encourage stereotyping. Negative stereotypes brought to mind by overhearing an ethnic slur can induce people to evaluate the targeted person less favorably, but not when the person's individual characteristics appear incompatible with the stereotypes. Illustrating another kind of interaction, ethnic slurs are particularly likely to lead only those already possessing strong negative stereotypes to use them when evaluating others.

To this point, we have seen that stereotypes, prejudices, and discrimination serve multiple functions (see Table 11.1). It's no wonder, then, that stereotypes, prejudices, and discrimination are so resistant to change, a topic we explore next.

Reducing Prejudice, Stereotyping, and Discrimination

For Ann Atwater and C. P. Ellis, racial antagonism was a part of everyday life. It is thus remarkable that within just weeks of their hostile confrontation at the school meeting, they began to respect each other, and, within just months, had developed a true friendship. How can we explain such a dramatic turnaround? In this final section, we build on what we've learned to explore ways of effectively reducing negative prejudices, stereotyping, and discrimination.

Interventions Based on the Ignorance Hypothesis

If you ask passersby on the street to explain why negative prejudices and stereotypes exist, a good many will propose that people "just don't know any better." We might call this the *ignorance hypothesis:* If people only learned what members of other groups are truly like, they wouldn't stereotype, be prejudiced, or discriminate against them. This perspective suggests that after simply putting individuals from different groups together or simply teaching them what members of other groups are really like, they would discard their stereotypes and prejudices (Stephan & Stephan, 1984).

Indeed, there are some reasons to believe that simple contact and education could help reduce intergroup antagonisms. Both contact and education could teach people that they are similar to members of other groups. This should make outgroup members more likable, decrease the usefulness of the ingroup–outgroup distinction, and reduce the anxiety people sometimes feel when interacting with outsiders (Stephan & Stephan, 1985). People might also learn that members of other groups are *not* all the same, which would limit the usefulness of broad, simple stereotypes.

Unfortunately, research demonstrates that merely putting individuals from antagonistic groups in contact does little to reduce hostility (Miller & Brewer, 1984; Stephan & Stephan, 1996). Similarly, simply teaching people what other groups are like is an ineffective way to brush away intergroup hostilities (Stephan & Stephan, 1984). Both simple contact and fact-based education alone are inadequate, for two reasons. First, such approaches assume that prejudices and conflict emerge from a straightforward logical assessment of outgroup characteristics. Although people may sometimes reason in this way, intergroup hostilities are generally linked less strongly to "facts" we have about other groups than to our emotional reactions to them (Haddock, Zanna, & Esses, 1994; Jussim, Nelson, Manis, & Soffin, 1995; Stangor, Sullivan, & Ford, 1991; Stephan et al., 1994). Moreover, these approaches assume that people will easily accept information that disconfirms their stereotypes—an assumption that does not reflect the efforts most people go through to avoid changing their stereotypes.

Consider, for example, the many ways that sexist physics students might dismiss the outstanding test performance of a female classmate. By attributing her excellent class grades to luck, extraordinary effort, or special advantage—to anything but intelligence—they can maintain their belief that women naturally lack science and math abilities (Pettigrew, 1979). Alternatively, by simply assuming that the woman's great grade is counterbalanced by poor performances in other math and science classes, her classmates again have no need to change their stereotyped views (Seta & Seta, 1993). And even if the students acknowledge her superior scientific acumen, they may retain their unflattering stereotypes of female students in general by "fencing her off" as a remarkable exception to the rule (Allport, 1954; Kunda & Oleson, 1995; Rothbart & John, 1985; Weber & Crocker, 1983).

By assuming, then, that prejudices and conflict emerge from a straightforward logical assessment of outgroup characteristics and that people actually want to rid themselves of erroneous stereotypes, the ignorance hypothesis fails to appreciate that stereotypes, prejudices, and discrimination serve important needs. This isn't to say that contact and education are useless. Indeed, as we discuss below, interpersonal contact *can* effectively reduce intergroup prejudices and stereotypes—but only under the right conditions. Moreover, certain educational programs—like those that teach perspective-taking and reasoning skills—may be useful for increasing tolerance or reducing stereotyping (Landis & Brislin, 1983; Schaller, Asp, Rosell, & Heim, 1996). But simple contact and fact-based education play only a limited role in reducing intergroup conflict.

The Goal-Based Approach

A goal-based strategy for reducing prejudice, stereotyping, and discrimination, in contrast, may be more effective. Such an approach incorporates two established points: First, prejudice, stereotyping, and discrimination serve important goals for people. As we've learned, for example, discriminating against members of other groups can help us gain economic resources for our own group. Second, specific features of the person and situation bring these goals into prominence. For instance, the desire to benefit the ingroup is stronger for certain people (e.g., those high in social dominance orientation) and under certain circumstances (e.g., intergroup competition for limited economic resources).

This approach to understanding prejudice, stereotyping, and discrimination suggests several logical steps we might take to reduce them. First, we might attempt to *change features of the person.* For example, because people who are anxious are particularly likely to stereotype others, we might try to reduce their anxiety before they encounter members of easily stereotyped groups.

Second, we might try to *change features of the situation.* For instance, if people are more likely to form and express prejudices when it is socially acceptable to do so, a community concerned with intergroup conflict might focus some of its energies on creating and advertising social norms that disapprove of prejudice and approve of intergroup tolerance and appreciation.

Third, we might *give people alternative ways to satisfy their goals.* For instance, we've learned that people sometimes derogate members of other groups to boost their own self-regard. Steven Fein and Steven Spencer (1997) hypothesized that if people had other ways to feel good about themselves they would have less reason to derogate others. Participants in their study evaluated a female job candidate who was presented as either Jewish American or Italian American; in this particular student population, only the Jewish females were targets of unfavorable stereotypes. Before evaluating her, however, some of the participants had an opportunity to affirm their self-worth by writing about the things important to them; the other participants were not given this opportunity. The researchers' findings supported their predictions: The Jewish candidate was evaluated less favorably than the otherwise-identical Italian candidate *only* by participants given no chance to validate their self-worth. Findings like this suggest that interventions aimed at providing people with alternative ways of satisfying their needs may be effective in the fight against negative prejudices and stereotypes.

Fourth, we might try to *activate goals incompatible with prejudice, stereotyping, and discrimination.* Three goals may be especially influential—*accuracy*, *fairness*, and *empathy.* As we learned in chapter 3, people who are motivated to be accurate often go beyond their stereotypes and prejudices to form more individualized impressions of others (e.g., Neuberg & Fiske, 1987). Moreover, because many people like to view themselves as fair and egalitarian—as the kind of people who treat members of all groups equally—they are more likely to renounce their prejudices when they see themselves or their community acting unfairly (e.g., Dutton & Lake, 1973; Monteith, 1993). Milton Rokeach (1971) had a subset of white college freshmen at Michigan State University confront the inconsistency between their prejudices and their value for equality. The intervention was strikingly successful: The students in the self-confrontational conditions increased their support for black equal rights, were more likely to join the NAACP when solicited months later, and were even more likely to choose ethnic relations as their major. When treating others equally becomes a prominent value, commitment to negative prejudices and stereotypes weakens. Indeed, for white people with extremely prominent egalitarian values, seeing a black person brings to mind these values and not negative stereotypes (Moskowitz, Salomon, & Taylor, 2000).

Finally, people become more tolerant when they adopt the goal of empathizing with other groups—when they try to view the world from the other group's perspective (Galinsky & Moskowitz, 2000; Stephan & Finlay, 1999). Daniel Batson and his colleagues (1997) found, for example, that people instructed to empathize with a particular person with AIDS subsequently viewed people with AIDS, as a group, more favorably.

The feelings of empathy that arise from taking another's perspective may underlie the success of some role-playing interventions (McGregor, 1993). For instance, in Jane Elliot's famous "Blue Eyes—Brown Eyes" technique for reducing racial prejudices, some participants are targeted for discrimination and humiliation because of their eye color. After a stressful few hours as a victim of discrimination, participants appear to be both less prejudiced (Byrnes & Kiger, 1990) and more sensitive to interracial issues. When circumstances lead us to see things from the perspective of unfairly disadvantaged groups, we are more likely to challenge our own stereotypes and prejudices.

In sum, the goal-based approach suggests four broad intervention strategies (see Figure 11.10). We see next that the circumstances that improve the effectiveness of intergroup contact do so, in part, because they implement at least one of these four strategies.

When Contact Helps

In the landmark civil rights case *Brown v. Board of Education*, the Supreme Court heard arguments for and against desegregating the Topeka, Kansas, public schools. Many of the country's most well-respected social scientists proposed that schooling black and white children together would decrease racial prejudices and hostilities, particularly if certain conditions were met (e.g., Allport, 1954; Watson, 1947; Williams, 1947). Unfortunately, little attention was paid to these conditions, and many of the early

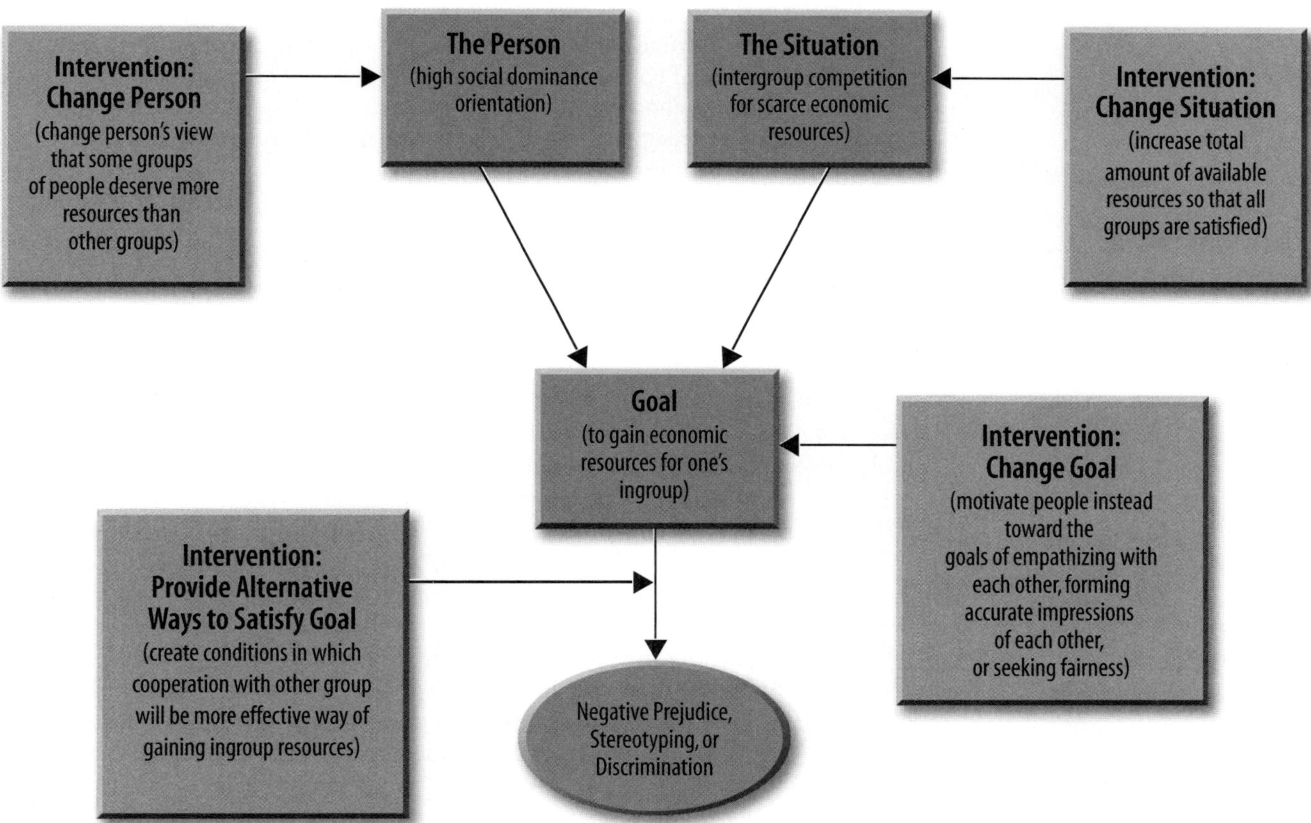

Figure 11.10
Goal-based strategies for reducing negative prejudices, stereotyping, and discrimination.

Features of the person and situation activate goals that may be satisfied by negative prejudices, stereotyping, or discrimination. Most effective interventions will thus include at least one of the following strategies: (1) change features of the person; (2) change features of the situation; (3) give people alternative ways to satisfy their goals; or (4) give people alternative goals incompatible with prejudice, stereotyping, and discrimination.

desegregation attempts actually fueled racial tensions (Stephan, 1978). Today, research has much to tell us about when contact is likely to reduce intergroup conflict (Miller & Brewer, 1984; Pettigrew & Tropp, 2000; Stephan & Stephan, 1996).

- *Outgroup members must possess traits and abilities that challenge the negative stereotypes of their group* (Blanchard, Weigel, & Cook, 1975). For example, prejudice-reduction interventions such as school desegregation and equal employment programs will be most effective when they put men and whites in contact with well-prepared women and members of minority groups.
- Because people are more likely to be accepting of other groups when they believe that tolerance is socially appropriate, intergroup *contact should be supported by local authorities and norms* (Cook, 1978). When school districts voluntarily hire more minority-group teachers, for example, and when teachers form interracial friendships, students will be more likely to view contact with students from other groups as legitimate.
- *The groups should be of equal status, at least within the contact setting* (Aronson, Blaney, Stephan, Sikes, & Snapp, 1978; Weigel, Wiser, & Cook, 1975). If a teacher treats white students better than black students, or if a company hires women for only low-status clerical positions, there is little chance that intergroup contact will lead to changes in stereotypes and prejudices.
- *The contact should occur at the individual level*—person-to-person—thus allowing people to notice that they are similar in important ways to members of other groups and that the others *aren't* all alike (Amir, 1976; Herek & Capitanio, 1996; Pettigrew, 1997). Person-to-person contact also makes possible the formation of friendships, and people with friends from other groups are more likely to feel favorably toward those groups (Pettigrew, 1998). A lack of contact at the individual level—as when students in desegregated schools separate into race-based groups at lunchtime and during other free periods—makes it more difficult to reduce negative stereotypes and prejudices.
- *The contact should be rewarding* (Blanchard et al., 1975). If men and women work together on a project that fails, for instance, neither group is likely to change their negative stereotypes of the other.
- Finally, contact in which members of different groups *work together toward common goals* is especially likely to encourage intergroup tolerance (Cook, 1985).

Figure 11.11
From hostility to friendship.

The hostility between the Rattlers and the Eagles eventually turned to friendship and acceptance after the two groups stopped competing and began cooperating with each other.

SOURCE: *Data from Sherif et al. (1961/1988), Tables 7.5 and 7.6, pp. 194–195.*

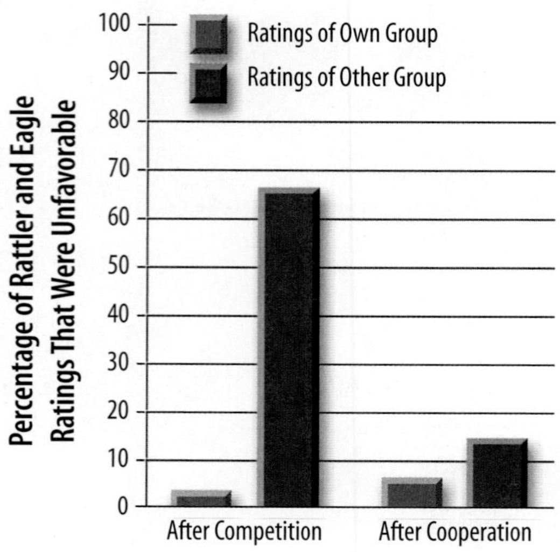

This last point is illustrated nicely by the experience of the rival residents of the Oklahoma boys' camp we discussed earlier in this chapter. When we last visited the Rattlers and Eagles, the two groups were on the verge of warfare. And the situation progressively worsened, as contact between the two groups brought forth increasingly intense name calling, food fights, and physical skirmishes. Having successfully created intensely hostile groups, Muzafer Sherif and his colleagues (1961/1988) turned their attentions toward discovering a way to eliminate the hatreds. Their strategy was an elegantly straightforward one: If competition between groups creates hostility, they reasoned, then eliminating the competitive orientation and replacing it with a cooperative orientation should reduce hostility. And so the researchers placed the two groups in circumstances that required them to cooperate to get what they wanted. In one case, the engine of the truck used to transport the campers "broke down." The campers eventually realized that they could pull the truck to a rolling start, but only by working together (using, ironically, the very same rope from their earlier tug-of-war competition). Through cooperative activities like this one, the two groups began to abandon their hostilities and, by the end of camp, had pooled their money and voted to share a bus on the return trip home (see Figure 11.11). By replacing a competitive orientation with a cooperative one, Sherif and his colleagues reduced the hostilities between the two groups.

Cooperation between members of different groups works for a variety of reasons. It replaces competition as a way of gaining economic and social resources. It motivates people to be more accurate in their understanding of outgroup members, reducing the tendency of competing groups to view each other in simplified ways (Ruscher, Fiske, Miki, & Van Manen, 1991). And when we cooperate with others, we are more likely to include them in our sense of "we"—to see them as part of us (Dovidio et al., 1997; Gaertner et al., 1990, 1993). As we discussed in chapter 9, people sometimes expand their sense of "we" to include many others and they sometimes contract it to include just a few (Allport, 1954; Brewer, 1991). Regardless of where people draw this boundary, however, they tend to prefer those inside the boundary to those outside it. So when working together with members of other groups—producing a "we are all in this together" mentality—people begin to see others as they see themselves, thus breaking down intergroup prejudices and stereotypes.

Working together at Robbers Cave. *After being forced to cooperate with each other, as in their tug-of-war against the truck, the Eagles and the Rattlers came to like each other more.*

Sherif's intervention did more than just capitalize on the beneficial effects of cooperation, however. It also implemented the other five principles of effective contact. Because all the boys were selected to be highly similar to one another, the erroneous stereotypes held of the two groups were relatively easy to disconfirm. Cooperation between the groups was supported and approved by the camp authorities. The two groups were accorded equal status by the camp staff. The cooperative tasks required members of the two groups to interact with each other on an individual level. Finally, the cooperation was successful, making the contact a rewarding experience. By carefully crafting the correct set of conditions, Sherif and his colleagues were able to turn intergroup hostilities into acceptance and friendship.

FOCUS ON Application

Cooperation in the Classroom

Do you remember what classes were like when you were in elementary school? In most classrooms, the teacher stood in front, spouting facts and calling on students to answer questions. "So who was the sixteenth president of the United States?" Some students—those eager to show the teacher how smart they are—nearly leapt from their chairs, hands reaching for the sky, hoping to attract the teacher's attention. Others—those afraid of making a mistake—slouched behind their desks and classmates, expressionless, striving for invisibility. The eager students not called on were visibly disappointed and, still seeking an opportunity to impress their teacher and classmates, may have secretly hoped that the student called on got the answer wrong. The avoidant students, in contrast, breathed a great sigh of relief—only to look at the clock and realize that the class was far from over and that they'd have to make themselves invisible yet again (Aronson et al., 1978).

Within this competitive context, it's not surprising that many early attempts to desegregate the schools did little to reduce negative prejudices and stereotypes. The young black students, victimized throughout much of their education by inadequate schools, were generally ill prepared to compete against their white counterparts and soon seemed to confirm the negative stereotypes held of them. In addition, the anxieties common to the competitive classroom reduced their cognitive resources, making it difficult for black students to perform well and for white students to think beyond their stereotypes. Finally, many teachers unhappy with desegregation resegregated their classrooms—whites over here, blacks over there. Confronted by the failure of school desegregation to reduce interracial prejudices, several teams of researchers and educators imported the lessons learned from studies like Sherif's and began to restructure the classroom environment (DeVries & Slavin, 1978; Johnson & Johnson, 1975; Weigel, Wiser, & Cook, 1975).

Consider, for example, the *jigsaw classroom* designed by Elliot Aronson and his colleagues (1978) and first implemented in the Austin, Texas, school district. In it, each student is assigned to mixed-race and mixed-gender teams of six or so students. Not coincidentally, the lessons are also divided into six parts (e.g., Lincoln's childhood, his career as a lawyer, his election to the presidency, and so forth). Each student is first given one part of the lesson and meets with an "expert" group made up of students from other teams who share the same assignment (e.g., Lincoln's childhood). Students then return to their home teams and convey their new knowledge to the other students. Because each student's information is only one piece of the puzzle, he or she depends on the five teammates to learn the whole lesson.

Classroom structures like this take advantage of the six principles of effective contact. First, by splitting off first into expert groups, all students are better prepared to teach their own teams effectively, which helps minority students disprove stereotypes of incompetence. Second, because the teacher assigns students to teams, the interracial, cross-gender contact has the clear support and approval of an important authority. Third, the students are accorded equal status in the classroom—they're not segregated by race or gender, and they're all given equal responsibilities. Fourth, the contact is at the individual level, allowing students to see each other's favorable characteristics and to dispel illusions of outgroup homogeneity. Fifth, the students work cooperatively with each other toward the common goal of learning the day's lesson. And sixth, because the performance of students tends to improve within such structures—particularly the performance of students who had previously been doing poorly—the contact can be rewarding for all students if grades are designed to benefit from the improvement of teammates.

Indeed, students learning in cooperative classrooms are more likely to form close cross-ethnicity friendships, even with other students outside their classrooms (Johnson, Johnson, & Maruyama, 1984; Slavin & Cooper, 1999). Moreover, the achievement levels of students rise in such classrooms (Johnson & Johnson, 1994; Stevens & Slavin, 1995). Given the documented gains—reduced intergroup hostility and better overall educational achievement—cooperative classrooms can be an important weapon in the fight against negative prejudices, stereotypes, and discrimination. ■

Summary

The ignorance hypothesis suggests that people would change their prejudices and stereotypes if only they knew the true facts about members of other groups. Facts alone, however, are not sufficient. Rather, because prejudice, stereotyping, and discrimination serve several useful functions, only intervention strategies that take these functions and their causes into account will be successful. Under certain conditions, contact between members of different groups can be useful for creating cross-group friendships and reducing intergroup conflict: Members of negatively stereotyped groups need to disconfirm these stereotypes; the contact should be supported by local norms and institutions; members of the different groups should interact as equal status participants; the contact should be at the individual, person-to-person level; the contact should be rewarding; and the contact should be cooperative, with members of the different groups working toward common goals.

REVISITING

The Journey of Ann Atwater and C. P. Ellis

The conflict between Ann Atwater and C. P. Ellis was fierce and unwavering. They despised each other, and each would have been happy to see the other dead. How can the research we've explored help us explain the white-hot intensity of their hatred for each other and the power of the prejudices from which this hatred flowed?

Recall, first, that both were poor. Each needed more if their families were ever to realize the American Dream. As the civil rights movement gained momentum, the concerns and prejudices of poor whites like Ellis intensified: Black gains were likely to come out of poor white pockets, they thought, and this belief was reinforced by those who held the true wealth and power. At its core, then, the conflict between Atwater and Ellis rested on their common desire to gain economic and social resources for their own groups.

But this is only part of the reason for their hostilities, for prejudices and stereotyping serve other important functions as well. In light of the social norms of their time, Atwater and Ellis gained social approval for expressing their prejudices. In particular, the racist norms of the Old South influenced C. P. Ellis early in his life, his father being a member of the Ku Klux Klan. Moreover, negative prejudices and stereotypes helped Atwater and Ellis maintain favorable self-images. By viewing whites as immoral, Ann Atwater could better claim virtue for herself. By derogating blacks in response to personal frustrations and failure, C. P. Ellis could see himself as more worthy, and by joining the Klan, he could associate himself with what he saw as a gallant and chivalrous attempt to preserve white Christian culture. Finally, the simplifying nature of stereotyping would certainly have been valuable for both Atwater and Ellis, given their work-filled, overwhelming, anxiety-laden lives.

So their prejudices grew. And as they found themselves working against each other with increasing frequency, Ellis came to represent for Atwater all that was wicked about whites, and Atwater came to represent for Ellis all that was base and threatening about blacks. It's astounding, then, that within weeks of the first school desegregation meeting the two began to respect each other and not long after became true friends. How do we explain such a dramatic turnaround?

It began when the organizer of the meetings—in a stroke of genius, or perhaps just by good fortune—convinced Atwater and Ellis to co-lead the group in its search for solutions to the desegregation problem. To say they were reluctant partners would be an understatement. But their agreement to work together—or perhaps, more accurately, to keep a wary eye on each other—provided a critical first step toward reconciliation, as their new responsibilities required that they *cooperate*. This step had been voluntary. Their second step was not. "How could she agree to work together with the Ku Klux Klan?" hissed the black community. "How could our leader even contemplate dealing with that woman?" spat Ellis's followers. For Ellis, in particular, the rejection was devastating: He'd only wanted to protect the interests of the poor white community, and, in response, it would no longer accept him as one of its own. He was alone. And so Ellis and Atwater started drifting toward each other, pushed together by the very extremists who had hoped to keep them apart.

As they began to evaluate each other more closely, with an eye, this time, toward accuracy, they began to notice their many similarities. They were both hard-working but poor, both passionate in their desire to create better opportunities for their children, both brutally straightforward in their style, and both people of principle. Atwater was surprised to learn that Ellis feared entering black neighborhoods, just as she feared entering white neighborhoods. Ellis noticed that the black schools were in appalling condition, not because blacks didn't care about keeping them up, as he had once thought, but because, just like the school his children attended, they received

few financial resources. It was natural for them to empathize with each other. Perhaps they were not one another's enemy, they began to think. Perhaps, instead, they had a common enemy—the rich who hoped to deny poor folks, black *and* white, a rightful "place to stand." Ellis's and Atwater's circles of "we" began to expand to include the other.

They'd never be the same. As the meetings continued, their connection grew stronger, and now, thirty years later, they still call each other "friend." Although the story of Ann Atwater and C. P. Ellis is extraordinary in one sense, it is unremarkable in another. For not only are the social forces that led them to hatred the very same forces that underlie our own prejudices and stereotypes, but the forces that inspired them to overcome their antagonisms are the very same ones that can help us do the same.

CHAPTER 11

Summary

Planet Prejudice

1. Prejudice, stereotypes, and discrimination permeate the world's cultures and exact significant economic, social, and psychological costs from their targets. Intolerance toward members of other groups is also costly for those holding these prejudices and stereotypes, as well as for societies in which discrimination exists.

Gaining Material Benefits for One's Group

1. To gain resources for our groups, we may create competitive advantages for our own groups and come to dislike and believe negative things about other groups.
2. People high in social dominance orientation want their own groups to dominate other groups and to be socially and materially superior to them. As a result, they are more likely to hold negative prejudices against and stereotypes of other groups.
3. When economic times are tough—when groups are competing for material resources—people are more likely to adopt and express negative prejudices and stereotypes.
4. By viewing one another as competitors, groups may bring about or amplify the competition they initially feared. This self-fulfilling prophecy can quickly spiral into increasingly intense forms of competition.

Gaining Social Approval

1. We often express or adopt the prejudices, stereotypes, and discriminatory tendencies held by those whose social approval we seek.
2. Individuals with conformist tendencies, who are high-self-monitors, or who are uncertain of their group standing are especially likely to adopt their group's existing prejudices.
3. Because norms regarding prejudice and discrimination change over time and differ across locations, attitudes and behaviors—at least as they are publicly expressed—change as well.
4. Those who consider themselves to be religious for intrinsic reasons overtly present themselves as relatively nonracist. When it is difficult for an observer to conclude anything about their racial attitudes, however, these individuals are as racist as people who make no claims of religiosity. Only people who view religion as a quest for truth and meaning tend to be less prejudiced than people who consider themselves to be nonreligious.

Managing Self-Image

1. Negative prejudices, stereotypes, and discrimination can help us manage our personal and social identities. For example, by scapegoating members of weak minority groups or by elevating our groups over other groups, we can view ourselves in a more favorable light.
2. Those who are strongly identified with their groups or who are high in authoritarianism are particularly likely to use prejudices and stereotypes to manage their self-images.
3. When people fail at something important to them, they are especially likely to demonstrate ingroup biases and discrimination.
4. Persons with high self-esteem are particularly likely to derogate members of outgroups, but only when their high self-regard is threatened.

Seeking Mental Efficiency

1. Stereotyping allows us to gain potentially useful information for relatively little cognitive effort.
2. Stereotyping others helps us interpret ambiguous behavior, provides ready explanations for why certain others act as they do, and suggests standards

for how we should evaluate members of different groups.

3. People are more likely to rely on their stereotypes when they have a high need for structure and when their moods and emotions leave them unmotivated or unable to process information about others thoroughly.
4. Situations that demand a lot of cognitive resources also make stereotyping more likely.
5. Negative stereotypes brought to mind by overhearing an ethnic slur can lead people to evaluate the targeted person less favorably, but not when the target's individual characteristics appear incompatible with the stereotypes. Illustrating another kind of interaction, only persons already possessing strong, unfavorable stereotypes tend to be negatively influenced by ethnic slurs.

Reducing Prejudice, Stereotyping, and Discrimination

1. The ignorance hypothesis suggests that people would change their prejudices and stereotypes if only they knew the true facts about members of other groups. Facts alone, however, are not sufficient.
2. Because prejudice, stereotyping, and discrimination serve several useful functions, intervention strategies that take these functions and their causes into account will be most successful.
3. Under certain conditions, contact between members of different groups can create cross-group friendships and reduce intergroup conflict: Members of negatively stereotyped groups should behaviorally disconfirm these stereotypes; the contact should be supported by local norms and authorities; members of the different groups should interact as equal status participants; the contact should be at the individual, person-to-person level; the contact should be rewarding; and the contact should be cooperative, with members of the different groups working toward common goals.

CHAPTER 11

Key Terms

Authoritarianism *The tendency to submit to those having greater authority and to denigrate those having less authority.*

Discrimination *Behaviors directed toward people on the basis of their group membership.*

Disidentify *To reduce in one's mind the relevance of a particular domain (e.g., academic achievement) to one's self-esteem.*

Extrinsic religiosity *An orientation toward religion that sees it as a means of gaining other things of value, such as friendships, status, or comfort.*

Ingroup bias *The tendency to benefit members of one's own groups over members of other groups.*

Intrinsic religiosity *An orientation to religion in which people attempt to internalize its teachings, seeing religiosity as an end in and of itself.*

Minimal intergroup paradigm *An experimental procedure in which short-term, arbitrary, artificial groups are created to explore the foundations of prejudice, stereotyping, and discrimination.*

Perceived outgroup homogeneity *The phenomenon of overestimating the extent to which members within other groups are similar to each other.*

Prejudice *A generalized attitude toward members of a social group.*

Quest religiosity *An orientation to religion that sees it as a journey taken to understand complex spiritual and moral issues usually accompanied by a belief that quick, simple answers are wrong.*

Realistic group conflict theory *The proposal that intergroup conflict, and negative prejudices and stereotypes, emerge out of actual competition between groups for desired resources.*

Scapegoating *The process of blaming members of other groups for one's frustrations and failures.*

Social dominance orientation *The extent to which a person desires that his or her own group dominate other groups and be socially and materially superior to them.*

Social identity *The beliefs and feelings we have toward the groups to which we see ourselves belonging.*

Stereotype *Generalized belief about members of social groups.*

Stereotype threat *The fear that one might confirm the negative stereotypes held by others about one's group.*

Stereotyping *The process of categorizing an individual as a member of a particular group and then inferring that he or she possesses the characteristics generally held by members of that group.*

CHAPTER 12

Groups

The Surprising Rise and Fall of Margaret Thatcher

The obstacles she faced seemed insurmountable. In the 600-year history of Britain's parliamentary system, no political party had chosen a woman as its leader. The Conservative Party, in particular, was not fond of female politicians. Indeed, at the time of her run for its leadership position, only seven of the 276 Conservative members of Parliament (MPs) were women. She was atypical of Conservative politicians in other ways as well. In a party in which privilege and old-boy networks were valued, she came from a middle-class background and had few high-level political connections. In a party in which appearances of effort were often seen as undignified, she had a penchant and reputation for hard work. In a party in which traditional institutions were cherished, she was willing to dismantle any institution, traditional or not, that impeded the progress of her political ideals. And in a party that had moved toward the moderate political center, she was unabashedly right-wing in her views. By all appearances, she was out of step with the very people whose votes she sought.

An unlikely victor.

These same people also worried about her lack of experience. She'd played almost no role in formulating policy in the areas of foreign affairs and national defense and hadn't held one of the three major government positions traditionally seen as qualifying a politician for national leadership. She wasn't particularly well liked. Many of her colleagues saw her as rigid, blunt, and humorless. She was perhaps even less popular outside Parliament, where her decision as education minister to end a free-milk program for Britain's children had earned her the unflattering nickname Milk Snatcher and made her "the least popular woman in England." In all, there seemed little reason to view her as a serious candidate.

Few were thus surprised when an informal poll taken three weeks before the leadership election indicated that only two of the 276 Conservative MPs would vote for her, or when London bookies stacked the odds 50 to 1 against her campaign. When other polls taken just the day before the election predicted that more than 60 percent of the MPs planned to vote against her, her detractors were confident that she'd be handily defeated.

Their confidence was misplaced. Stunning the British political establishment, she defeated the incumbent Edward Heath on the first ballot and additional challengers on the second, becoming the new leader of the Conservative Party. And when, four years later, her Conservatives defeated the Labour Party in the 1979 general election, Margaret Roberts Thatcher became the first female prime minister in British history.

Those who saw Thatcher's triumph as an aberration were to be shocked again, and yet again, as she went on to win reelection as prime minister twice more. In all, she led her country for almost 12 continuous years, longer than any other British prime minister of the twentieth century. Contemporary historians count Margaret Thatcher as one of the most prominent leaders in British history.

But then, when it seemed that Thatcher could lead her nation for years to come, her own Conservative Party—the very party she had brought to power over a decade earlier—ungraciously dumped her from its leadership position, thereby ousting her from office and removing from the political stage one of the world's most influential leaders. The tide had turned against Thatcher, bringing to a quick end her amazing and, some would say, implausible political career (Mayer, 1979; Ogden, 1990; Thompson & Thompson, 1990).

How do we explain the startling twists and turns of Margaret Thatcher's political life? How was it that, in only three weeks' time, the Conservative Party shifted its allegiances from its powerful and experienced leader to this improbable, upstart challenger? Why were the British people so willing to return her to power, time and time again? And what group processes led to her rapid and unceremonious downfall, a downfall as unlikely perhaps as her initial ascent to power?

The story of Margaret Thatcher's rise and fall is in itself a fascinating one. Thatcher's story is also fascinating for what it tells us about how groups work and function. You've seen throughout this textbook that people are "group beings" who are born into families, play with friends, learn with fellow students, cheer with strangers at sporting events, toil with coworkers to earn a living, and join forces with their comrades against common enemies. From the family room to the schoolyard, from the stadium to the workplace to the military base, we live in groups.

In this chapter, we examine how groups influence individuals and how individuals influence groups. We'll see that crowds often bring forth the worst and best of human propensities—aggression and compassion, indifference and help, laziness and team spirit. We'll see how random collections of individuals can merge into unified groups. We'll see that groups are sometimes surprisingly effective and sometimes stunningly incompetent. And we'll explore the dynamic relationships between leaders and their followers, discovering how leaders are chosen, what makes them effective, and what makes them fail. In sum, we will take a close look at the group processes that influence your life each and every day.

The Nature of Groups

In its broadest sense, a **group** consists of two or more individuals who influence each other. This, of course, is a minimal definition, encompassing both collections of people who just happen to be in the same place at the same time (such as people waiting at a city bus stop) and highly structured organizations whose members share goals and identities (such as sororities and fraternities). Although a gathering of strangers awaiting the cross-town express seems like less of a "real" group than does a sorority, each can influence our actions. We begin, then, by exploring "groupings"—mere collections of individuals—and later turn our attentions to the characteristics and workings of "real" groups.

The Mere Presence of Others and Social Facilitation

Norman Triplett was a fan of bicycle racing. He also happened to be a psychologist. So when he observed that cyclists exhibited faster times competing against other cyclists than when competing singly against the clock, he headed for his laboratory to conduct one of the first experiments in social psychology. Triplett (1897–1898) asked children to wind fishing reels as quickly as possible. Like the bicycle racers, the children performed faster in the presence of others than when working alone.

Triplett attributed this phenomenon to a competitive instinct aroused by other people. What Triplett didn't know, however, was that performance can improve even when other people are not competitors and even when they just happen to be milling nearby. Why might the *mere presence* of others improve performance? Robert Zajonc (1965) noted that being around other people is physiologically arousing; their presence increases our heart rate, quickens our breathing, and so on. Zajonc also recalled the well-known finding that people who are aroused are more likely to exhibit *dominant responses*—familiar, well-learned behaviors (Spence, 1956). He reasoned that the presence of others, by simply arousing us, should lead us to exhibit dominant responses.

If Zajonc's logic is correct, being around others should sometimes improve performance and sometimes make it worse. When a dominant response advances a task, the presence of others should improve performance. Consider, for example, an experienced assembly-line autoworker who installs front-left fenders, a job that requires the worker to align the fender to the frame and then push it hard into place. For the autoworker, installing fenders is a well-mastered, simple task, meaning that the dominant response—first align, then push—enables the worker to complete the job successfully. As a result, as others wander the workfloor and increase the worker's arousal, he or she should become even more productive than usual.

But what would happen if a design change required a different installation procedure—first align the fender, then *hook* it into place? Would the presence of others still improve the worker's performance? Probably not, argued Zajonc, because the worker's dominant responses would no longer be appropriate to the task. As more people wander past the autoworker, the dominant response—pushing with enough force to pop the fender in—would interfere with the ability to hook the fender gently onto its fasteners. When our well-practiced, dominant responses don't

Group *Minimally, groups are two or more individuals who influence each other. Collections of individuals become increasingly "group-like," however, when their members are interdependent and share a common identity, and when they possess structure.*

Figure 12.1
Performing in the presence of others.

Being around other people is arousing, and when we are aroused, we are more likely to behave in well-learned, familiar ways. These dominant responses tend to be correct for well-mastered, "simple" tasks. As a result, we tend to perform better on mastered tasks when others are around. In contrast, dominant responses tend to be incorrect for unmastered, "complex" tasks. Consequently, we tend to perform more poorly on unmastered tasks when others are around.

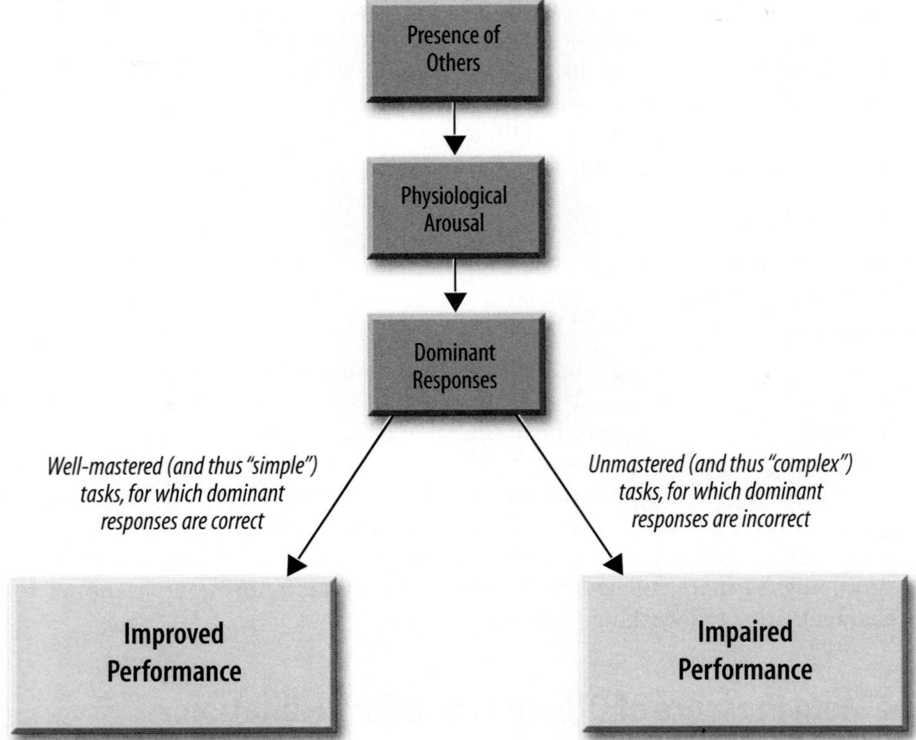

advance a task—as with most new, unmastered tasks—the presence of others should impair performance.

Numerous studies support this theory of **social facilitation:** The presence of others indeed improves performance on well-mastered, simple tasks and hinders performance on unmastered, complex tasks (Bond & Titus, 1983; Guerin, 1993) (see Figure 12.1). As one example, consider the experiment performed by James Michaels and his colleagues (1982). After spying on pool players at Virginia Polytechnic Institute and assessing their shot-making ability, four confederates sauntered over to observe them. As predicted by social facilitation theory, the good players—for whom pool was a relatively well-learned game—performed even better when watched, improving their shot-making rate from 71 percent to 80 percent. In contrast, the less talented players—who had not yet mastered the game—got worse, dropping from a 36 percent to 25 percent success rate.

Social facilitation *The process through which the presence of others increases the likelihood of dominant responses, leading to better performance on well-mastered tasks and worse performance on unmastered tasks.*

The mere presence of others seems to be enough to facilitate dominant responses (e.g., Schmitt, Gilovich, Goore, & Joseph, 1986). Indeed, even simple creatures such as cockroaches have their dominant responses enhanced by the presence of other roaches (e.g., Zajonc, Heingartner, & Herman, 1969). In humans, *evaluation apprehension* and *distraction* can each intensify this effect. First, when people believe that observers are explicitly assessing their performances, they become increasingly aroused, and this arousal further facilitates their dominant responses (Cottrell, 1968; Seta & Seta, 1992; Seta, Crisson, Seta, & Wang, 1989). For example, observers in a position to evaluate the autoworker's job performance will elicit dominant responses more than will blindfolded people who are in no position to judge (Cottrell, Wack, Sekerak, & Rittle, 1968). Second, as anyone studying for an exam in a busy dorm lounge knows all too well, being around others can be distracting, forcing people to struggle just to focus on the task at hand. Consider the arousal experienced by our autoworker as he or she tries to suppress now-obsolete dominant responses while also trying to ignore the hordes of noisy people wandering in and out of the workspace (Baron, 1986; Sanders, 1981). The distracting nature of people, and our tendency to believe that others are often evaluating us, together increase our arousal and thus facilitate our dominant responses.

In sum, just being around others makes it more likely that people will perform the behaviors they are most familiar with. As we see next, random groupings of individuals influence people in other ways as well.

In a crowd, you can lose more than just your wallet. *The presence of others may mask our identities and relax our inhibitions, leading us to lose contact with our values and to do things we would never consider doing otherwise.*

Crowds and Deindividuation

Imagine yourself in a gathering crowd at the base of a tall building, watching a man who is perched high above and contemplating suicide. Would you scream at him, challenging him to jump? Perhaps not, but don't be so sure. Just as white lynch mobs in the early 1900s became more vicious toward their black victims as their crowds grew in size (Mullen, 1986), urban crowds are more likely to bait potential jumpers as they grow larger (Mann, 1981). In one case reported by Leon Mann (1981), angered onlookers shouted obscenities and hurled rocks at rescue workers trying to avert the suicide. Actions that would rarely come from a lone individual—like daring a suicidal person to jump from a building—become more likely when that same individual is immersed in a group. Why?

In groups, people lose their senses of individual identity and, as a result, relax their inhibitions against behaving in ways inconsistent with their normal values—a process called **deindividuation** (Festinger, Pepitone, & Newcomb, 1952; Le Bon, 1895/1960; Zimbardo, 1969). Groups deindividuate their members in two ways. First, crowds sometimes mask the identities of their individual members, making them anonymous and less accountable for their actions (Prentice-Dunn & Rogers, 1980). Consider the results of the clever field experiment we briefly described in chapter 1 (Diener et al., 1976). One Halloween night in Seattle, as thousands of costumed children roamed the streets in search of candy and other treats (and perhaps some tricky mischief as well), researchers awaited their arrival at twenty-seven homes scattered throughout the city. In the foyer of each home stood a table with two bowls—one filled with candy, the other with pennies and nickels. After greeting the children, the adult experimenter told the children to take *one* candy, and she then exited the room, leaving only the children and an observer hiding behind a colorful screen. Fifty-seven percent of the trick-or-treaters arriving in groups stole extra candy or money, as compared to only 21 percent of the children arriving alone. Consistent with hypotheses, the anonymity provided by being in a group clearly contributed to this increased theft: When children in groups were first asked their names and addresses by the researcher—thus eliminating their anonymity—they transgressed only 21 percent of the time.

Crowds also deindividuate by distracting members' attention away from their individual selves and their personal values (Prentice-Dunn & Rogers, 1982). In a second Halloween study, Arthur Beaman and his colleagues (1979) found that older children (aged nine and above) who had been asked their names and addresses were even less likely to steal extra candy when a mirror had been propped up behind the candy bowl. Apparently, seeing themselves in the mirror made these children *objectively self-aware* (see chapter 8) and thus less able to cast aside their personal values forbidding theft.

The Halloween studies illustrate one of the potentially problematic consequences of being among others: People may become deindividuated. These studies also tell us something about how "real" groups may begin to emerge out of mere collections of individuals. In each study, the behavior of the first group member had a large influence on the behaviors of those who followed: If the first child stole, the others were more likely to steal; if the first child took just the single allowed candy, the others followed this more positive example (Beaman et al., 1979; Diener et al., 1976). These findings support the conclusions drawn from a recent review

Deindividuation *The process of losing one's sense of personal identity, which makes it easier to behave in ways inconsistent with one's normal values.*

of sixty studies of deindividuation. According to Tom Postmes and Russell Spears (1998), people's actions in crowds result not from their diminished sense of personal values and identity, but from their greater sensitivity to the actions of others in their immediate surroundings. In this way, *norms* begin to emerge, turning crowds into real groups.

Indeed, the actions of even a single individual can begin to provide structure to an initially haphazard collection of strangers. Just as one impulsive individual can turn an assembly of strangers at a bus stop into a group of jeering suicide baiters, one prosocial individual can turn the same strangers into a helpful rescue squad. The ways in which influence flows through groups are complex, however, a topic we turn to next.

Groups as Dynamic Systems: The Emergence of Norms

Imagine living in a new neighborhood development of, say, 100 homes. One day, you receive a flier announcing a meeting in two weeks to consider forming a neighborhood council. There would likely be a wide range of initial opinions: some community members would see the council as a waste of time, others would see some value in it, and yet others wouldn't care much either way. Regardless of your initial inclinations, however, most of you would remain at least slightly open to well-reasoned, persuasive arguments. So as you discuss the issue with your neighbors, you might find yourself changing your mind a bit. Of course, your neighbors are in the same boat, so they, too, are probably being influenced by each other. In all, with each of 100 households interacting with a host of friends and acquaintances in the neighborhood, it is likely that opinions throughout the community will change in numerous, and seemingly chaotic, ways.

Under such circumstances, do you think you'd be able to predict your community's final decision or the patterns of opposition and approval that would emerge? Although social psychologists know quite a bit about the general factors that determine influence in large groups (e.g., Festinger, Schachter, & Back, 1950; Latané, Liu, Nowak, Bonevento, & Zheng, 1995), circumstances like these are stunningly complex and it's extremely difficult to keep track of everything: There are just too many interconnected people having too many opinions influencing too many others over too long a time. But before you throw up your hands in despair, you should know about some fairly simple tools for studying complicated group interactions like these, tools as close as the nearest personal computer.

FOCUS ON Method

Using Computer Simulation to Explore Complex Group Processes

Researchers trying to understand group influence aren't the only scientists confronting astounding levels of complexity. Consider the complicated problem of predicting the weather, with warm fronts and cold fronts moving in every direction, affected by everything from tidal variations and the earth's rotation to the proverbial butterfly fluttering its wings in Brazil. Or ponder how an economy stays in balance as thousands of businesses and millions of separate individuals buy and sell goods and services for a multitude of personal reasons. These problems were once thought so complicated as to inspire little more than awe in scientific researchers. All that has changed in recent years, however, with the arrival of high-speed computers. Scientists have not only developed more complicated models of such **dynamical systems**—systems that possess many interconnected elements and that change and evolve over time—but also have discovered something quite unexpected: Order often emerges out of apparent chaos (Lewin, 1992; Lorenz, 1963; Waldrop, 1992).

Dynamical system *A system (e.g., a group) made up of many interacting elements (e.g., people) that changes and evolves over time.*

To illustrate this, let's step back a moment to the days well before the advent of the personal computer. As World War II ended, American soldiers returned to the United States to begin or continue their college educations. To accommodate the rush of new students, the Massachusetts Institute of Technology (MIT) quickly constructed Westgate, the first university housing project dedicated to married veteran students and their families. To MIT students returning from the war, it was a unique opportunity to find affordable housing in an expensive city. To social psychologists, however, it was a unique opportunity to explore how real groups form and develop. And so, in the summer of 1946, Leon Festinger, Stanley Schachter, and Kurt Back (1950) of MIT's Research Center for Group Dynamics began what became a classic study in the psychology of groups.

For our purposes here, one of their findings stands out: Over time, residents living near one another began to hold similar attitudes toward their community council. Westgate's 100 single-family homes were arranged in nine courts, with most houses within each court facing each other. Because MIT randomly assigned families to homes, it's safe to assume that attitudes toward housing associations were at first distributed haphazardly throughout the whole community. Over time, however, these scattered views began to cluster together—not because people relocated to be closer to those holding similar beliefs but because people influenced, and were influenced by, those living near them. Because residents communicated most often with members of their own courts, the courts began to emerge as unique groups, with their own attitudes toward the Westgate Council and their own norms either supporting or opposing it. From chaos, then, emerged organization.

Without the necessary tools, it was impossible for Festinger and his colleagues to explore in great depth how clustering of group attitudes like this might come about. But with the help of a desktop computer and a simple spreadsheet program, we can watch structure emerge out of disorder (Latané & Bourgeois, 1996). In Panel A of Figure 12.2, we approximate the layout of Westgate and randomly distribute across it opinions on the issue of a neighborhood council. We then let the computer "assume" that the 100 "residents" will communicate primarily with residents of their own courts, as Festinger and his colleagues found. We also add a second simple presumption—that residents will be influenced by the opinion of the majority of the neighbors they talk to. Finally, the computer has the residents communicate with their immediate neighbors twice a "week" for two weeks. Although it would keep a chess grand master busy for some time trying to predict how residents in our make-believe community will mutually influence one another on a day-by-day basis, it is a simple matter to have a computer do the calculations.

In Figure 12.2, Panel B, we see that with just a few rounds of computer simulation, opinions toward the Westgate Council cluster together substantially. Whereas the Tolman and Richards Courts support the council unanimously, and the Miller, Freeman, Williams, and Rotch Courts are now generally supportive of the council, the Carson, Howe, and Main Courts are generally opposed. Although some individuals within most courts buck the trend, residents in the courts have generally come to agree with one another. From an initially scattered collection of individuals having equally scattered views emerge groups having coherent norms.

Computer simulations like these are valuable not only because they may help us explain existing findings but also because they can help us generate novel predictions. For example, what would have happened if a few residents holding opposing views had instead been assigned to each other's courts? By changing just a few of the initial values we give the computer, we see that our simple model predicts that Richards Court would move from being unanimous in support of the council to being unanimous in opposition to it, that Carson Court would have changed its predominant view, and that Tolman and Main Courts would have been influenced as well (Panels C and D). The complexity of interpersonal influences means that even small changes like this one—moving merely four people in a community of 100—can have large effects. You will also notice, however, that even though the

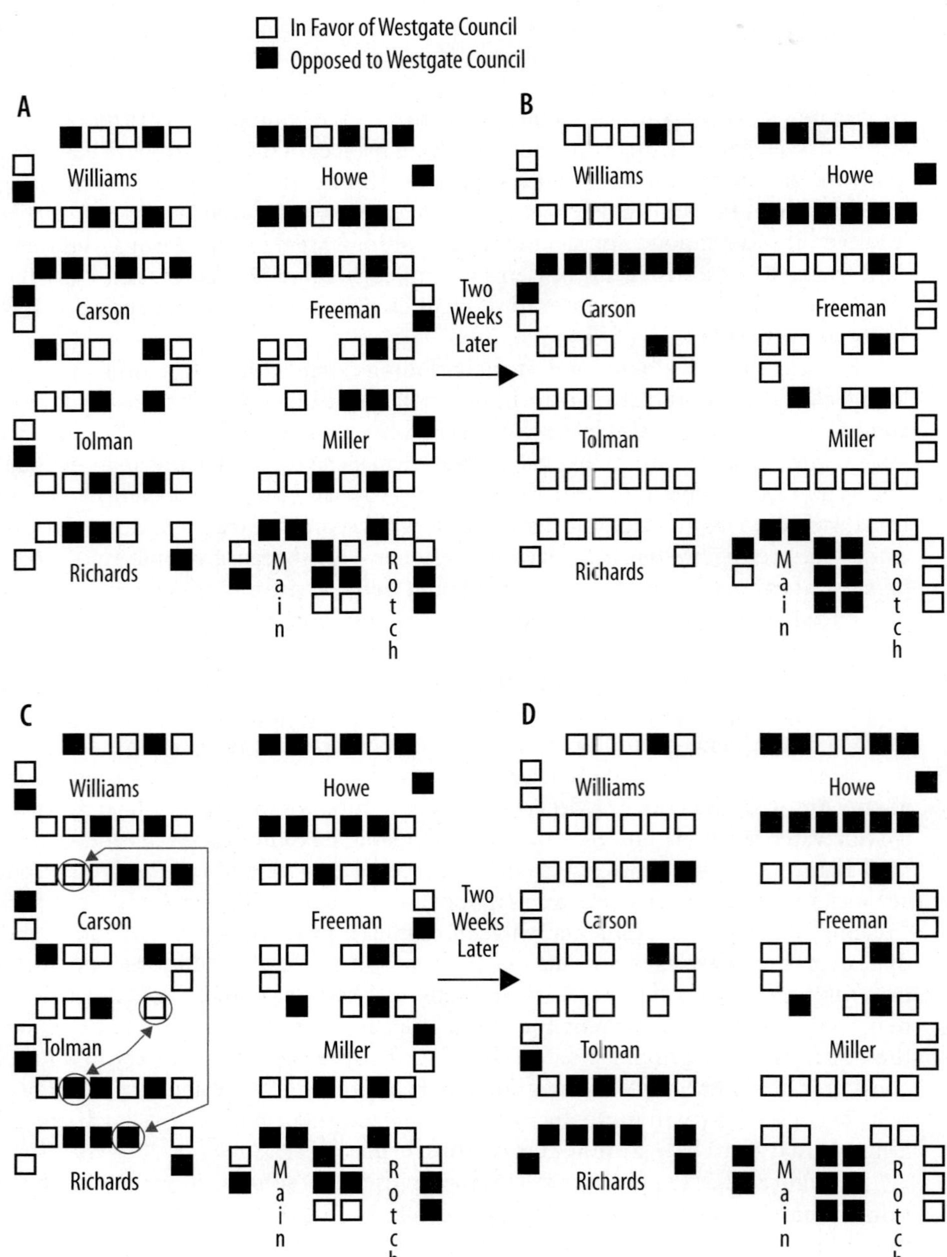

Figure 12.2
The emerging group norms in Westgate.

In our computer simulation of Westgate, we start with various attitudes toward the Westgate Council scattered throughout the community (Panel A) and see that most of the courts soon adopt common norms (Panel B). What happens if we make a small change to the community, assigning just four of the residents to different houses (Panel C)? Although the residents' attitudes again cluster together, the norms held by some courts change dramatically. For instance, Richards Court, unanimously in favor of the Westgate Council (Panel B) becomes unanimously opposed to it (Panel D). Even small changes in groups can lead to very different outcomes.

particular pattern has changed, there is still obvious clustering. Organization still emerges out of chaos.

Computer simulations are beginning to prove quite useful for understanding group dynamics and other areas of social psychology (e.g., Hastie & Stasser, 2000; Ilgen & Hulin, 2000; Tesser & Achee, 1994; Vallacher & Nowak, 1997). These simulations become particularly valuable when researchers "go full cycle" to test the novel predictions created by the simulations against real human behavior (e.g., Latané & Bourgeois, 1996). So just as computer simulations help meteorologists predict weather patterns over Europe and economists comprehend stock market crashes on Wall Street, they assist social psychologists in clarifying the intriguing but complicated interactions that take place among people in groups. ■

"Real" Groups

A crowd of strangers dancing at a concert is different from a crowd of strangers streaming past one another on a busy street. The concert-goers influence one another, thereby showing the first signs of being a group. Mutual influence, however, is just one feature of "groupness." Indeed, when we think of corporations, social clubs, community associations, and families, it becomes clear that groups have other important features as well. In particular, real groups are likely to have a stable structure and to have members who are interdependent and share a common identity.

Sororities are "real" groups. *Sororities have all the features we commonly attribute to real groups. They have structure, in the form of roles (president, treasurer) and injunctive norms (not to date motorcycle gang members). Their members depend on one another to reach shared goals, as when they want to host social functions and philanthropic events for the community. And their members share a common group identity—they view themselves as being a group.*

Interdependence The members of "real" groups tend to be interdependent: They need each other to reach their shared goals. To say that group members are interdependent means more than does saying that they are all aimed in the same direction. Although the millions of British citizens registered as members of the Conservative Party share the goal of electing representatives to implement their preferred policies, they can independently do their business—by casting their ballots—without having much interaction with one another. In contrast, the Conservative members of Parliament (MPs), of whom Thatcher was one, are interdependent: they need to work with one another each day to increase the likelihood that their policies become law. The Conservative MPs constitute more of a real group than do Britain's Conservative voters.

Group Identity Do the students at your college constitute a real group? The answer depends partly on whether you all *perceive yourselves* to be a group (Campbell, 1958; Lickel et al., 2000). On an average day in the middle of the semester, as students on campus wander to and from class, probably few of you are aware that you share a common identity. On the day of the annual football contest against your cross-state rivals, however, this identity becomes salient and interactions among students become more grouplike. Although some group identities wax and wane in this way, others are a salient part of everyday life. Sorority members, who live, eat, and party together, probably are conscious of their affiliation most days, often going so far as to advertise it proudly with big Greek letters emblazoned across their clothing.

Group Structure Many groups develop stable structures. They may possess *injunctive norms*—shared expectations for how group members *ought* to behave if they wish to receive social approval and avoid disapproval (Levine & Moreland, 1998) (see chapters 2 and 6). For instance, members of a particular sorority may expect one another to dress conservatively, to stay away from men sporting nose rings and tattoos, and to get good grades. Groups may also create **roles** for their members. Whereas injunctive norms describe how *all* members ought to behave, roles are shared expectations for how *particular* group members should behave. For example, a sorority president may be expected to set the agenda for chapter meetings and confer regularly with other Greek organizations, whereas a treasurer may be expected to collect dues and balance the sorority's bank account. Roles often make groups more efficient, because it is rarely desirable for every member to contribute in the same way (Barley & Bechky, 1994; Bastien & Hostager, 1988). Just imagine, for example, the chaos that would reign if every sorority sister tried to run the weekly meetings or collect the dues.

A group may also have a **status hierarchy,** in which members are ranked in terms of their social power and the influence they have over other members (Kipnis, 1984). In a sorority, for instance, the president has more official status than the other officers, who in turn have more official status than the remaining members. A structured group usually also has a stable **communication network** through which

Role *Expectation held by the group for how members in particular positions ought to behave.*

Status hierarchy *A ranking of group members by their power and influence over other members.*

Communication network *The pattern of information flow through a group.*

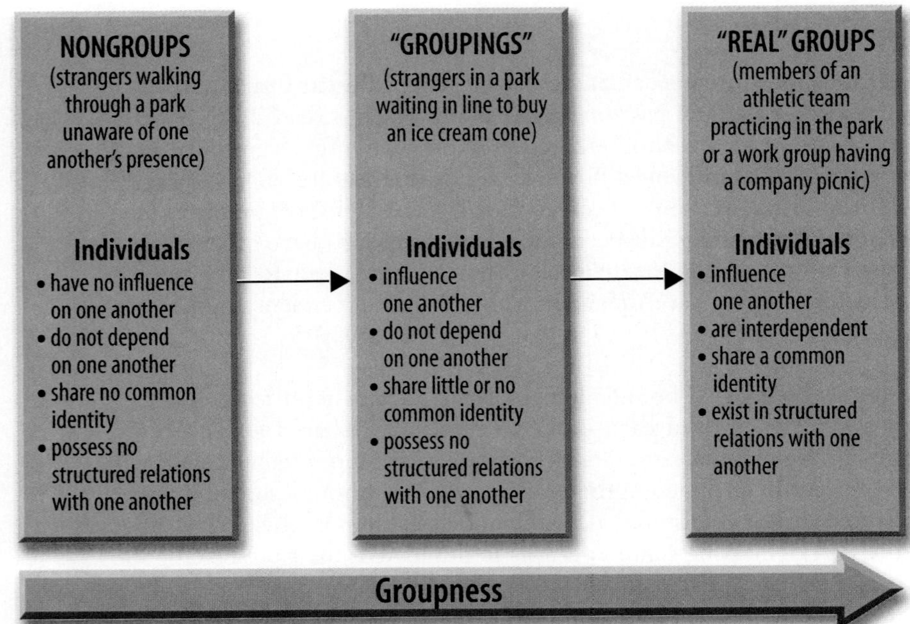

Figure 12.3
A continuum of groupness.

At the minimum, groups are two or more individuals who influence each other. Collections of individuals become increasingly "group-like," however, when their members are interdependent and share a common identity and when they possess structure (roles, injunctive norms, status hierarchies, communication networks, cohesiveness).

information flows to its members. For example, in highly *centralized* networks, information tends to flow from one member (usually the leader) to all other members simultaneously, as when a sorority president makes an announcement during a chapter meeting. In *decentralized* networks, information passes among members without having to go through one particular person. In many businesses, instructions from senior officers are often passed, chainlike, through managerial layers until they finally reach the workers on the factory floor.

A final feature of group structure is **cohesiveness,** or the strength of the bonds among group members. Groups can be cohesive, or close-knit, because their members enjoy being with one another *(interpersonal cohesiveness)* or because they are all committed to the group's task *(task cohesiveness)*. When a job requires communication and coordination, cohesive groups work particularly well (Gully, Devine, & Whitney, 1995; Mullen & Copper, 1994; Zaccaro, 1991). But cohesion isn't always good. Interpersonally cohesive teams sometimes have difficulty staying focused on their tasks (e.g., Zaccaro & Lowe, 1988) and are more susceptible to certain decision-making errors (e.g., Mullen, Anthony, Salas, & Driskell, 1994), as we will see later.

In sum, stable groups are often structured by injunctive norms, roles, status hierarchies, stable communication networks, and cohesiveness. More broadly, we see that structure, interdependence, and a common group identity distinguish real groups from groupings—collections of individuals who merely influence one another. This distinction is a fuzzy one, however. For example, real groups can exist without having well-defined structures, as in the case of chanting fans at a football game. It seems best, then, to view "groupness" as a continuum (see Figure 12.3): Groups having structure, interdependence, and shared common identity are "groupier" than groups possessing fewer of these features (Levine & Moreland, 1998). In the remainder of this chapter, we focus primarily on these more "groupy" groups.

Why Do People Belong to Groups?

Cohesiveness *The strength of the bonds among group members.*

Margaret Thatcher was an unrelenting individualist, emphasizing throughout her political life the need for self-reliance and personal responsibility: "The only thing I'm going to do for you is to make you freer to do things for yourself. If you can't do it, I'm sorry. I'll have nothing to offer you" (Thatcher, cited in Gardner, 1995, 236).

Yet even she found it valuable, even necessary, to belong to groups. People seem to have a basic "need to belong" (Baumeister & Leary, 1995; McDougall, 1908), a proposition supported by cross-cultural findings revealing the universality of group living (Coon, 1946; Mann, 1980). But *why* are groups so important that we seek to spend so much of our lives in them? What do groups do for us?

People seek groups for various reasons (Mackie & Goethals, 1987; Moreland, 1987). We sometimes join groups because they allow us to express our values publicly, as when opponents of capital punishment pray together in candlelight vigils on the nights of planned executions. Other times, we join groups because they provide needed emotional support, as when cancer patients attend support groups (see chapter 7). This chapter focuses on two other primary reasons people belong to groups: to accomplish tasks they can't effectively accomplish otherwise and to acquire and share information in especially potent ways. We also explore a more secondary goal, that of gaining the material and social benefits of leadership. Although few people join groups with the aim of becoming leaders, many begin to seek leadership as they become aware of its rewards.

Summary

In its broadest sense, a group is a mere collection of two or more individuals who influence one another. Even these simplest groupings can have a large impact on a person's behaviors. The mere presence of others is arousing, leading people to think and behave in well-learned, familiar ways. As a result, the presence of others tends to facilitate performance on well-mastered, simple tasks and hinder performance on unmastered, complex tasks. Moreover, people sometimes become deindividuated in crowds, losing their sense of individual identity and relaxing their inhibitions against behaving in ways inconsistent with their normal values. Random groupings of communicating individuals are dynamic systems, however, and over time may begin to evolve injunctive norms—an important characteristic of stable, structured groups, along with roles, status hierarchies, communication networks, and cohesiveness. Moreover, the members of stable groups tend to be interdependent and to share a common group identity. Participating in such groups can satisfy several goals. Groups can help people get things done and make better decisions and can provide enhanced social and material resources through leadership opportunities.

Getting Things Done

Your family and the North Atlantic Treaty Organization. Kappa Kappa Gamma sorority and the Westgate community council. The high school chess club and the United States of America. Margaret Thatcher's Conservative Party and General Motors. Although these groups differ in many ways, they have one important thing in common: They help their members accomplish tasks that would be difficult—if not impossible—to accomplish alone.

Lightening the Load, Dividing the Labor

Our ancestors discovered long ago that their chances of personal survival increased dramatically when they grouped themselves with others. In groups, they were better able to hunt, gather, and cultivate food; they were better able to build shelters and defend themselves; and they had others to care for them when they fell ill (Brewer, 1997; Caporael & Baron, 1997). The philosopher Baruch Spinoza was right when he noted that "because no one in solitude is strong enough to protect himself

Working together. *As in many agricultural communities, the Amish pool their labor when tasks are too large for any individual or family to do alone easily, as we see in this traditional barn raising.*

and procure the necessities of life, it follows that men by nature tend toward social organization" (Durant & Durant, 1963, 651).

Of course, the benefits of groups extend to less fundamental tasks as well. The chess club provides its members with practice partners and competition. Political parties and social action groups help people influence public policy. Certainly, by getting herself elected to Parliament and to the group of Conservative MPs, Margaret Thatcher placed herself in a much stronger position to change British social policy. Even groups themselves often see advantages of banding together to get things done: Families join with other families to create small communities. These communities band together to form states, which form nations, which work together in alliances and even larger organizations such as the United Nations.

Group performance is potentially more effective than individual performance for two reasons. First, "many hands make light work": In groups, individuals can share common burdens. In many agricultural communities, for example, families help one another bring in the crops, herd livestock to market, and build new barns. Although a single family alone might be able to raise a barn, helpful neighbors make the task much easier. Second, people in groups can divide their labor: With multiple people on the job, different people can perform different tasks. As a result, individuals can specialize—some becoming architects, others carpenters, and still others surveyors and landscapers. And because specialists are typically more proficient than generalists, groups often accomplish tasks better and faster than any individual could.

This is not to say that groups always outperform individuals. Moreover, groups rarely perform to their full potential (Davis, 1969; Laughlin, 1980; Steiner, 1972). Ironically, a major threat to efficient group performance is closely tied to one of the very reasons people belong to groups to begin with—their desire to lighten their personal loads.

FOCUS ON Social Dysfunction

The Social Disease of Social Loafing

The New England pickle factory was in…well, a pickle. It appeared that its pickle packers—the workers responsible for stuffing pickles into jars—had become a bit careless. Instead of stuffing only correct-sized pickles into the jars, some had begun to plop in pickles that were too short. Short pickles float and bob around unattractively in the brine, and the inspectors in quality control (the pickle police?) had to reject jar after jar of packed pickles. Pickle-packing productivity was proceeding poorly (Turner, 1978).

But why, you might ask, should you give a gherkin about pickle packing? To answer this question, let's step back to the late 1800s, to the laboratory of Max Ringelmann, a French agricultural engineer. Ringlemann researched farming productivity and observed that extra workers rarely increased output as much as one might expect. In one set of experiments, Ringlemann had men pull carts as hard as they could, either alone or working together in groups. He discovered something curious: As the number of men working together increased, the average pulling power of each man decreased. In two-person teams, each man was, on average, 93 percent as productive as he was working alone; in four-person teams, each man was only 77 percent as productive; and in eight-person teams, each man was merely 49 percent as productive (Kravitz & Martin, 1986; Ringelmann, 1913).

Ringelmann attributed part of the inefficiency to the difficulty of coordinating the efforts of many people, of getting them all to pull at the same time. Other research, however, has since revealed that decreased coordination is only one reason why groups can lose efficiency (Steiner, 1972). Most notably, as Ringelmann himself suspected, individual group members often exhibit **social loafing:** They decrease their personal efforts as their groups grow larger (Ingham, Levinger, Graves, & Peckham, 1974; Latané, Williams, & Harkins, 1979).

For some tasks, social loafing isn't much of a problem: If five people could push a car out of a ditch, there seems little reason for a team of ten individuals to exert themselves fully. After all, the goal is not to break a sweat but merely to get the car rolling again. For other tasks, however, social loafing can be quite a problem. The goal of the pickle company, for instance, wasn't merely to produce some minimum number of jars each day. Instead, it wanted to pack as many pickles as possible. Managers probably didn't suspect, however, that by hiring many pickle packers to increase overall productivity, they also increased the propensity of each packer to *free-ride* on the efforts of the others—to take it easy and rely on the efforts of his or her coworkers (Kerr & Bruun, 1983). They probably also didn't realize that once employees saw able-bodied coworkers beginning to free-ride, they would reduce their own efforts so as not to be "suckered" into unfairly carrying the load for others (Kerr, 1983). The pickle company was paying individual workers for effort it never received, and consumers were paying for the factory's inefficiency. As Bibb Latané and his colleagues (1979) put it, social loafing can be a social disease.

Group members are more likely to loaf when their contributions are unidentifiable—when they and others are unable to tell whose contributions are whose (e.g., Williams, Harkins, & Latané, 1981). It is worth noting that the pickle-packing assembly line was configured so that conveyer belts deposited the packed jars into a common hopper for inspection. Inspectors were thus unable to identify those particular pickle packers responsible for the poorly packed jars. There were few direct costs to those individual workers who chose to pack their pickles poorly.

How, then, is a pickle purveyor to promote productivity? What would *you* do to limit social loafing when working on a group project? Based on a meta-analysis of almost 80 studies, Steven Karau and Kipling Williams (1993) provide several suggestions. First, make each group member's contributions identifiable (Kerr & Bruun, 1981; Williams et al., 1981). Coaches of football teams typically film and score the performance of individual players. When other group members can evaluate our contributions, we are less likely to loaf (Harkins & Jackson, 1985; Szymanski & Harkins, 1987). We generally don't want to view ourselves—or to be viewed by others—as slackers.

People are also less likely to loaf when the task is meaningful, challenging, or important to them (Brickner, Harkins, & Ostrom, 1986; Harkins & Petty, 1982; Zaccaro, 1984) and when they believe that their personal efforts will lead to a better group performance (Shepperd & Taylor, 1999). People are less likely to loaf when they believe they can make a unique contribution to the group goal (Kerr & Bruun, 1983). If group members each have a somewhat different job, they cannot easily presume that the work of others will hide their own laziness. Social loafing also decreases in cohesive teams: People loaf less when working with friends than with strangers. Finally, people who are collectivistic—such as women and residents of "Eastern" societies such as Japan—are less prone to loaf than are those who are more individualistic—men and residents of "Western" societies such as the United States (e.g., Earley, 1989; Gabrenya, Wang, & Latané, 1985; Karau & Williams, 1993).

In sum, you can increase productivity on your group projects (or in pickle factories) in the following ways: Select persons committed to the work and frame their tasks as a challenge; make their individual efforts identifiable and assign each person to a unique aspect of the project; and create an environment in which all members feel committed to the group (Shepperd, 1993). ■

Social loafing *Reducing one's personal efforts when in a group.*

Expectations of Individual Failure and Group Success

Have you ever joined other students to study for an exam? Why? We suspect that your decision to do so—or not—was influenced by two straightforward considerations: (1) how well you thought you'd do on the exam if you studied alone and (2) how well you thought you'd do on the exam if you studied with others. When you believe that you'll better accomplish your tasks when working with others than when working alone, you're more likely to form or join a group (Zander, 1985).

People are more likely to join a group when they worry that they may fail as individuals—when they hold low expectations for personal success (Loher, Vancouver, & Czajka, 1994). Jeffrey Vancouver and Daniel Ilgen (1989) tested this hypothesis at Michigan State University by allowing male and female students to choose whether to work alone or with another student on six different tasks. Some of the tasks were stereotypically "male," such as changing a car's oil or designing a tool shed. The others were stereotypically "female," such as designing a store window or taking a quiz on flowers. Vancouver and Ilgen presumed—quite correctly, it turned out—that men would be less confident in their abilities to do well on the female tasks and that women would be less confident in their abilities to do well on the male tasks. As a result, they predicted that the students would much prefer to work alone on gender-consistent tasks and with others on gender-inconsistent tasks. This is indeed what they found. As students' expectations of individual success went down, their desire to work with others went up.

We suspect that these uncertain students preferred working with others because they also believed that their partners would be more skilled at the task, or that at least "two heads would be better than one." This brings us to the second part of the formula: People are more likely to join a group when they believe it will effectively move them toward their goals. In a study at the University of Delaware, Edgar Townsend (1973) found that students who viewed organizations as fruitful paths to their own personal and community goals were especially likely to be active in off-campus volunteer groups. Not surprisingly, people who've had success working in groups in the past are more likely to prefer working in groups in the future (Eby & Dobbins, 1997; Loher et al., 1994).

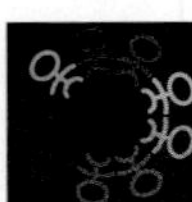

Current Needs, Individualistic Societies

Joining a group is a more attractive strategy for getting things done under some circumstances than others. Sometimes there is just no choice, as when a worker must join a labor union to get a job at the local factory. More frequently, however, people join performance groups when current circumstances make it hard to succeed alone.

Reviewing the history of performance groups, Alvin Zander (1985) observed that they typically emerged to address societies' needs at the time. Trade guilds formed in China around 300 B.C. to enforce levels of professionalism, maintain high prices of goods, and arbitrate disputes. In Rome around 50 A.D., slaves organized into collectives to provide aid and emergency funds to one another. In the second century A.D., Jewish communities in Eastern Europe and the Middle East formed philanthropic societies to finance hospitals, homes for the aged, schools, and other charitable causes. In the twentieth century, the nations of Western Europe and North America formed the North Atlantic Treaty Organization (NATO) to deter aggression by the Soviet Union, while American citizens formed groups such as the National Association for the Advancement of Colored People (NAACP) and the Sierra Club to further their social causes. When interpersonal or societal circumstances become undesirable—when they make it difficult for people to reach their goals—individuals are more likely to create or join performance groups (Zander, 1985).

Some societies more than others seem to "breed" performance groups. Who participates in more performance groups—members of individualistic societies or members of collectivistic societies? You may have guessed collectivistic societies. After all, we've seen that collectivism is essentially *about* groups—about being interdependent with others, subordinating one's needs to the group's needs, and being loyal and committed. But, in an interesting paradox, people in these societies participate in fewer performance groups: People in collectivistic societies are generally so committed to their existing groups that they don't look elsewhere when they need help getting things done. Alternatively, consider prototypical individualists. Because they are less tied to their current groups, they feel free to "shop around" for other groups to fit their particular needs of the moment. In individualistic societies, then, people are quick to join many groups, although their commitment to these groups may often be shallow and transitory (Triandis, 1995).

Protecting the environment. *Some needs are so great, and the task so large, that only coordinated effort by many individuals will be successful. Millions of people worldwide believe that the threats to the earth's natural ecology create such a need, and they have formed together into thousands of groups to clean parks and rivers, slow the harvesting of rain forests, reduce automobile and factory emissions, and encourage recycling.*

Citizens of individualistic societies join multiple performance groups for other reasons as well. Individualistic societies tend to be wealthier, more literate, and are often more urban than collectivistic societies, and these factors make it easier to join multiple groups (Meister, 1979; Stinchcombe, 1965). Urban living brings strangers together in the same place, providing a large pool of people who could work together for common goals. Moreover, residents of highly literate societies are exposed to many links with others—through newspapers, magazines, bulletin boards, and, these days, the Internet. Residents of nonliterate societies can only learn about potentially useful groups through personal contact, television and radio, or word of mouth.

When Are Groups Most Productive?

Margaret Thatcher won stunning majorities in several election campaigns and steered her nation through severe economic hardships and to victory against Argentina in the Falkland Islands War. These and other successes were attributable, in large measure, to the effective performances of the campaign committees and advisory teams she formed and led. But what are the characteristics of effective groups? Are group members who have certain personality types more valuable than others? Are large groups more productive than small groups? Are groups composed of similar individuals more effective than groups of individuals who have varying backgrounds, experiences, or skills?

The answers to these and similar questions almost always come back the same: It depends. In particular, it depends on the type of task the group is hoping to accomplish (Davis, 1973; Hackman & Morris, 1975; Holland, 1985; McGrath, 1984; Steiner, 1972). Different tasks require different skills. What is needed to pull a bus from a ditch is different from what is needed to manage a nation's economic policy. In this section we explore how features of the group interact with requirements of the task to affect a group's productivity.

Who Should Be in the Group? After her surprising victory in the Conservative Party leadership election, Margaret Thatcher faced an important first task—appointing an advisory team (or "shadow cabinet" as it is known in British politics). She needed to put the right person in the right job (Thatcher, 1995). This, of course, is an issue that faces managers of all sorts, from those leading nations to those running fast-food restaurants: What kinds of people work together best for what kinds of tasks? Robert Hogan and his colleagues (Driskell, Hogan, & Salas, 1987; Hogan, Raza, Sampson, Miller, & Salas, 1989) have proposed a framework to explore this question.

By classifying tasks by the skills required to complete them successfully and by classifying workers in terms of fundamental personality characteristics, they have hypothesized which people are best for different jobs. For example, team members who are prudent and conforming should perform well at conventional, routine tasks such as accounting but poorly at artistic tasks in which originality, nonconformity, and risk taking are valuable. In contrast, a team made up of socially skilled individuals should do particularly well on tasks such as teaching but poorly on conventional tasks in which their desires to socialize would interfere with the need to follow routines carefully and to pay close attention to detail. Early research supports the framework (Hogan et al., 1989).

Along similar lines, most problem-solving teams require at least one member who is achievement motivated and energetic (otherwise the team doesn't do any work), one member who is imaginative and curious (otherwise the team doesn't generate any good ideas), and one member who is agreeable and tolerant (otherwise the team doesn't get along) (Morrison, 1993). Moreover, teams that have too many highly sociable members often have problems staying on task, whereas teams that have too few sociable members never develop the rapport needed to generate new ideas freely (Barry & Stewart, 1997). The overall lesson, then, is this: Groups that are most productive tend to have members who complement one another and whose personality characteristics closely match the requirements of their tasks.

How Big Should the Group Be? Because different tasks have different requirements, we would expect small groups to be better for some tasks and larger groups to be better for others. An **additive task** is one that requires each group member to do the same thing. For these tasks, productivity is determined simply by summing the contributions of all members (Steiner, 1972). For example, each worker in the pickle-packing line packs pickles, each member of a tug-of-war team pulls on the rope, and each fan in the stands cheers for his or her team. If we add together the number of pickle jars packed by each packer, the pulling force exerted by each rope puller, or the decibels of noise generated by each fan, we arrive at the total productivity of each group. With additive tasks, then, the more people, the greater the group's overall productivity. Of course, as we learned earlier, large groups can have problems achieving their full potential. Not only do people in groups sometimes loaf (Karau & Williams, 1993; Shepperd, 1993) but it is also more difficult to coordinate the efforts of many individuals effectively (Diehl & Stroebe, 1987; Latané et al., 1979).

In a **disjunctive task,** the group's product must be selected from just one of its members' individual efforts (Steiner, 1972). As a result, group success is determined by the productivity of the group's most successful member. Imagine that a number of advertising agencies are competing for a highly lucrative account. With a tight deadline, each agency gives its employees a few days to generate ideas, knowing that they'll need the rest of the time to put together a compelling presentation. At the end of the three days, which agencies will have generated the best idea, all else being equal: The smaller or the larger ones? If you thought the larger agencies would win, you are correct. By simple virtue of their size, they are more likely to employ at least one individual who will generate an exceptionally good idea. They will also generate a few exceptionally lousy ideas, but because each agency gets to present its best idea, the larger agencies are more likely to get the account (Frank & Anderson, 1971). To compete successfully on disjunctive tasks, then, smaller groups need to have, on average, better-skilled and more creative workers than their larger counterparts.

Additive task *A job in which each member performs the same duties; group productivity is thus determined by summing the contributions of all members.*

Disjunctive task *A job in which the group's product is selected from just one member's performance; group productivity is thus determined by the performance of the group's most successful member.*

Finally, let's consider tasks that can be completed only if each group member does his or her job effectively: If one person fails, the whole group fails. For example, a string of mountain climbers can move only as fast as its slowest member, and the district attorney's office will get the criminal behind bars only if the investigating detective *and* the lab technician *and* the prosecuting attorney all do their jobs successfully. For these **conjunctive tasks,** the performance of a group is determined by its weakest member. Because large groups are more likely to have a member or two whose performance is particularly weak, larger groups will tend to be less successful than smaller groups on conjunctive tasks (Frank & Anderson, 1971; Steiner, 1972). What do smart managers do when they have weak team members working on conjunctive tasks? If they cannot remove them from the team or train them to perform more effectively, managers try to assign the least competent individuals to the easiest tasks, in this way minimizing the extent to which these individuals slow down everyone else.

In sum, larger groups are generally beneficial for additive and disjunctive tasks, but problematic for conjunctive tasks.

Is Diversity Valuable? As we've just seen, one of the advantages of large groups—at least for some tasks—is that they are more likely to include individuals having notable and diverse talents, perspectives, and life experiences. That is, they are more likely to be heterogeneous. Of course, a group doesn't need to be large to be diverse. Indeed, two groups of equal size may also differ in their heterogeneity. Consider, for instance, two basketball teams whose starting players average 6 feet 8 inches in height. On Team A, all five starters are 6 feet 8 inches, making this team homogeneous on height. On Team B, one of the starters is 7 feet 1 inch, a second is 6 feet 10 inches, a third is 6 feet 9 inches, a fourth 6 feet 6 inches, and the fifth is 6 feet 2 inches; this team is heterogeneous on height. All else being equal, which team would you rather coach?

We suspect you'd choose Team B, because its greater diversity in height would makes it easier for you to satisfy the functions of the different basketball positions—to find the right person for the job. The more heterogeneous Team B can better cover the different needs of the game of basketball. Indeed, not only is team heterogeneity often valuable in sports (Widmeyer, 1990) but heterogeneous groups also may have important advantages over homogeneous groups in other domains as well (Jackson, 1992; Levine & Moreland, 1998; Milliken & Martins, 1996).

Like the value of different personalities or the value of different group sizes, the value of group diversity depends greatly on the task (Laughlin, 1980; Steiner, 1972). Group heterogeneity helps on disjunctive tasks, in which a group needs only *one* member to get the correct answer. More generally, heterogeneous groups seem to do best on tasks requiring new solutions, flexibility, and quick adjustments to changing conditions (e.g., Hoffman, 1959; Nemeth, 1992). For example, scientists—whose jobs require innovation and creativity—perform better when their collaborators span a wider range of scientific disciplines (Pelz, 1956). Similarly, management teams whose members have different kinds of expertise and educational backgrounds are more innovative (Bantel & Jackson, 1989; Wiersema & Bantel, 1992).

This is not to say that diversity comes without costs. Diversity in experience can often hurt performance on conjunctive tasks, in which groups succeed only if *each* of their members performs his or her role well. Moreover, business teams varying widely in personalities, values, or backgrounds often have high turnover (Cohen & Bailey, 1997; McCain, O'Reilly, & Pfeffer, 1983), and communication within highly diverse groups tends to be less frequent and more formal (Zenger & Lawrence, 1989). The benefits of heterogeneous groups must be weighed, then, against their costs.

Cultural Diversity and Group Performance The issue of group heterogeneity has crucial implications for today's U.S. workplaces, which are becoming more demographically diverse each year. By the year 2005, women will make up 48 percent of the workforce and ethnic minorities over 25 percent (Fullerton, 1995). Moreover, ethnic minorities are estimated to provide 57 percent of the growth in the labor market, and 20 percent of new workers are immigrants (Jackson, 1992). Given that

Conjunctive task *A job in which success is achieved only if each member performs successfully; group productivity is thus limited by the performance of the group's least successful member.*

today's businesses are more culturally diverse and more likely to operate globally, it is important to understand how cultural diversity influences business productivity.

Like other kinds of diversity, racial and ethnic diversity have both advantages and disadvantages for group productivity (Maznevski, 1994; Milliken & Martins, 1996; Pelled, 1996). Culturally diverse groups may generate a wider range of solutions to problems, especially if the diversity is related to the task. In one experiment, researchers created four-person groups that were either all-white or ethnically mixed and had them generate ideas on how to get more foreign tourists to visit the United States (McLeod & Lobel, 1992). The ideas generated by the ethnically mixed group were judged to be both more effective and more feasible than the ideas generated by the all-white group.

As we saw earlier, however, diversity can have costs. These costs may be especially great when the diversity is racial or ethnic. People tend to be prejudiced against members of other racial and ethnic groups and often don't understand them very well. As a consequence, racially and ethnically diverse workplaces are prone to communication problems and a lack of cohesion. Moreover, employees working on diverse teams tend to be less committed to the group and to miss work more often. Workers on culturally diverse teams are also more likely to seek other jobs. It seems that the costs of ethnic and racial diversity in the workplace can be great, often outweighing its advantages (Maznevski, 1994; Milliken & Martins, 1996; Pelled, 1996).

This need not be the case. Warren Watson, Kamalesh Kumar, and Larry Michaelsen (1993) created four- and five-member student work teams as part of an upper-level management course. About half of these teams were homogeneous, consisting only of white Americans. The remaining teams were culturally diverse, consisting of a white American, a black American, an Hispanic American, and a foreign national from a country in Asia, Latin America, Africa, or the Middle East (the five-member diverse teams had an additional Hispanic American or foreign national). The teams were challenged to generate solutions to four different business problems over the course of a semester. As Figure 12.4 reveals, the diverse groups initially had problems: Their performance was worse than the homogeneous groups', perhaps because the diverse groups had more difficulty getting along. As the semester wore on, however, the members of the diverse groups learned how to work with one another and, by the last assignment, were getting along as well as members of the homogeneous groups. More important, their overall performance was also as good by this last assignment.

Figure 12.4 Overcoming the potential difficulties of cultural diversity.

In a study of management students assigned to work together in either ethnically homogeneous (all white) or ethnically diverse groups, researchers found that diverse groups initially had problems getting along with one another and performed relatively poorly. By the end of the semester, however, these problems had disappeared and performance had improved considerably.

SOURCE: *Data from Watson et al., 1993, Table 2.*

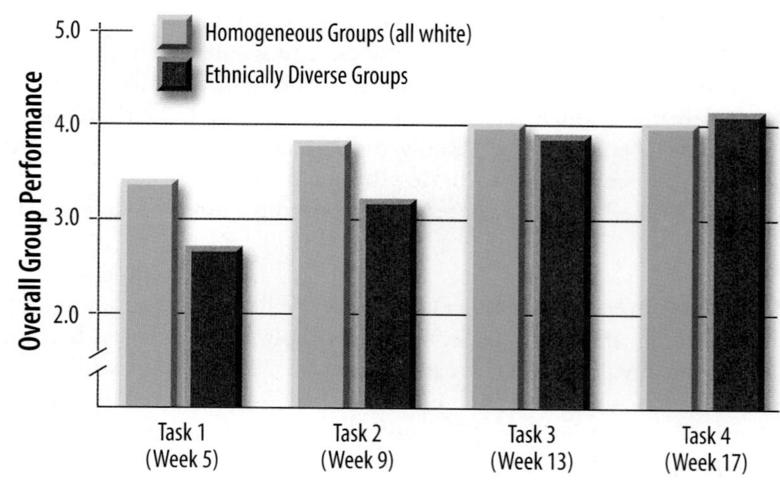

These findings suggest that culturally diverse groups can overcome their initial difficulties and become more productive if they have the sufficient motivation and opportunity. The benefits of cultural diversity can be great, if managers find ways to improve group communication, coordination, commitment, and cohesion.

Summary

Groups help people accomplish tasks they can't easily accomplish alone. Not only do "many hands make light work" but working together in groups enables members to learn specialized skills, potentially increasing both task quality and efficiency. Groups sometimes fall short of their potential productivity because their members engage in social loafing. People seek groups when they fear they will fail working alone or when they believe the group is particularly likely to be successful. Certain tasks can be accomplished only through group action, and the values promoted in individualistic societies encourage people to use numerous performance groups to reach their goals. Finally, features of the group—such as its members' personalities, its size, and its diversity—interact with the demands of the task to determine how productive it becomes. Groups become more productive when (1) their members have skills, knowledge, and perspectives that complement one another; (2) these skills, knowledge, and perspectives are effectively communicated among group members, and (3) these skills, knowledge, and perspectives mesh with the requirements of the task.

Making Accurate Decisions

Margaret Thatcher was widely acclaimed for her victorious handling of the Falkland Islands War; time and again, she seemed to make the right decisions. Yet she had no experience in foreign affairs or defense policy and had never served in the military. How could she have been so successful?

The answer to this question rests on a second important feature of groups: They often possess a great deal of useful information (Festinger, 1954; Schachter, 1959). Even small, casual circles of friends can be extremely informative. They can recommend good pizza parlors, interesting psychology courses, or lucrative investment opportunities. They can tell you whether your political views are based on faulty information, whether your fears of an impending tuition increase are justified, or whether you are as attractive, smart, and creative as you think you are.

When group members freely share information, they may make better decisions than when alone (Resnick, Levine, & Teasley, 1991; Stasser, 1992; Thompson, Levine, & Messick, 1999; Tindale & Kameda, 2000; Weick & Roberts, 1993). Take Margaret Thatcher's circle of advisors. Their expertise ranged widely—some knew foreign policy, others knew defense, and still others knew about health care, labor relations, and the like. As a result, when Argentina attacked the Falkland Islands, Thatcher didn't need to be an expert herself on the logistics of warfare or South American diplomacy. Rather, she just needed access to people who possessed this knowledge and were willing to communicate it to her. In social psychological terms, Thatcher's government had a **transactive memory:** Knowledge located within the minds of its individual members and ways to spread it through communication (Wegner, 1987, 1995). Many groups have transactive memories, each possessing more knowledge as a group than any individual member has alone (e.g., Hollingshead, 2000; Liang, Moreland, & Argote, 1995; Wegner, Erber, & Raymond, 1991).

Transactive memory *A group memory system made up of (1) the knowledge held by individual group members and (2) a communication network for sharing this knowledge among the members.*

Because a transactive memory provides such rich information, group decisions can be more accurate than individual decisions. An experiment conducted by Larry

Michaelsen, Warren Watson, and Robert Black (1989) illustrates this nicely. Students in 25 organizational behavior classes were assigned to small teams to work on various problems over the semester. In addition, students took six exams, first as individuals and then, after they had turned in their answer sheets, as a group. Both individual and group test scores contributed to students' course grades. Not only did the groups score higher than their average individual members but they also scored higher than their *best* individual members. Indeed, in only 3 of the 222 groups did the best member outperform the group. In certain circumstances, then, virtually all members gain from the group's knowledge (Watson, Michaelsen, & Sharp, 1991).

Of course, groups don't always lead their members to make better decisions. Sometimes groups just don't possess accurate information. For example, the three-member military junta ruling Argentina was advised by its intelligence and diplomatic services that Britain didn't have the military capability to retake the islands by force. Obviously, this was poor information: The British routed the Argentinians upon arriving on the scene. Moreover, useful information doesn't always get shared effectively, even when someone in the group does have it (Stasser, 1992; Stasser & Titus, 1985). Finally, even when knowledge is effectively shared within a group, that information may still be processed in a biased, unsatisfactory manner. Like individuals thinking alone, for example, groups may favor information confirming their initial views (Frey, Schulz-Hardt, & Stahlberg, 1996). Later, we explore how being in a group influences how people make decisions. First, however, we consider the factors in the person and the situation that lead people to use groups as sources of information and as aids to decision making.

The Need to Know

Individuals who have a thirst for knowledge often quench it in groups. Indeed, there are thousands of groups and organizations dedicated to providing information. Interested people gather in study groups to prepare for upcoming exams, in investment clubs to pool financial analyses, and in astronomy clubs to share notes on the cosmos. The computer revolution has created an explosion of *chat rooms*. Reminiscent of European "café society," where interested people would gather to discuss art, philosophy, literature, and the events of the day, cybergroups now gather on the Internet to discuss topics of common interest. People who "need to know" often seek answers in groups.

From café society to the Internet. *Just as writers and artists of nineteenth century Paris gathered to share, discuss, and critique their art and the trends of the time, students today gather in "cyberspace" to share, discuss, and critique areas of current interest.*

This need to know may go well beyond intellectual curiosity. A person facing a lifetime illness, for example, may turn to a self-help support group for information. Although such groups can serve other functions—such as providing emotional support or friendship—some people join these groups primarily for information. A recent study of gay men who have HIV/AIDS, for example, revealed that a significant subset of members stopped attending meetings when their support groups stopped providing new information (Sandstrom, 1996).

Uncertain Circumstances

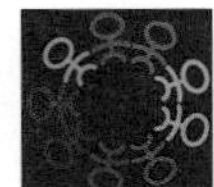

Uncertain circumstances activate this need to know in most of us. It's not difficult to place yourself in the following scene: As your appointment nears its end, your physician reenters the examination room looking concerned and says, "I've got bad news. You have a brain tumor and need neurosurgery." In stunned shock, you ask a few questions but, in the days that follow, new ones relentlessly interrupt your thoughts. You wonder what the operation will be like and how it's going to feel afterwards. You wonder whether your fears are reasonable or whether you are overreacting. Faced with uncertainty, you want information.

In chapter 7, we explored a series of classic studies by Stanley Schachter (1959) that investigated whether uncertain situations increase the desire to affiliate with others. Experimental participants anticipated electrical shocks that were either "quite painful" (the high-fear condition) or "not in any way painful" (the low-fear condition). While the equipment was ostensibly being readied, participants were allowed to choose whether to wait alone or with others. The high-fear participants generally preferred waiting with others, as long as the others were in the same boat—that is, as long as they were also waiting to be shocked. As Schachter put it, "misery doesn't love just any kind of company, it loves only miserable company" (24). He proposed that this preference served an informational goal for his experimental participants: By being with these potentially "miserable" others and observing their behaviors, the fearful subjects could assess whether their own fears were reasonable. Uncertain circumstances motivate people to seek information from others—to engage in the *social comparison* processes (Festinger, 1954) we have explored in various chapters of this textbook.

Of course, as we also discussed in chapter 7, people facing uncertainty also want to know exactly what the upcoming event is going to be like. As a result, they often prefer to group themselves not just with others who are in the same boat but with those who have already completed the journey—those who have already experienced the event and who can thus reveal to them what lies ahead (e.g., Kirkpatrick & Shaver, 1988). For instance, hospital patients awaiting severe medical procedures such as coronary bypass surgery prefer to share a room with patients who have already had the procedure than to share a room with those who, like them, still await it (Kulik & Mahler, 1989). Indeed, the information helps: awaiting bypass surgery in a room with patients who have already had it can reduce anxiety (Kulik & Mahler, 1987). An experimental study tells us why this might be: People facing uncertain, fearful events can get more useful answers to their questions from those who have already experienced the event than from those who haven't (Kulik, Mahler, & Earnest, 1994).

Discussion and Decision-Making

We've seen that groups can provide people with information useful for making important decisions. For many decisions, however, information is not enough. Even after Margaret Thatcher was briefed on the logistical difficulties of fighting a war eight thousand miles from home and on the strength of the Argentinian military forces, she still needed to decide what the British response should be and how it

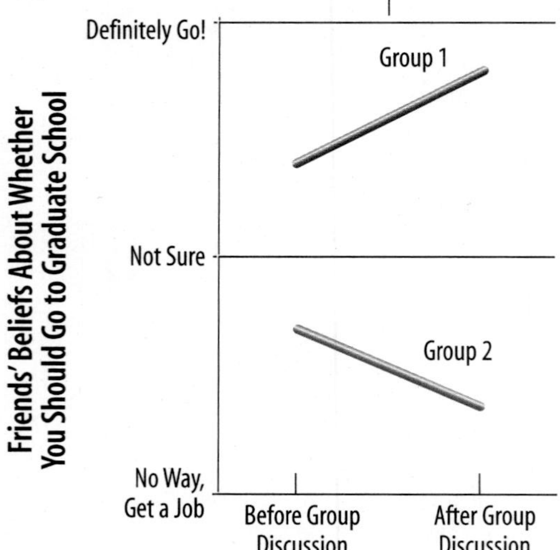

Figure 12.5
The polarizing effects of group discussion.

Discussion enhances the initial views of group members. If one group of friends believes, on average, that you ought to go to graduate school, they will believe so even more strongly after discussing it among themselves. In contrast, if a second group of friends believes, on average, that graduate school would be a waste of your time, they will be even less enthusiastic about it after discussing it among themselves.

should be carried out. Fortunately, groups can help in a second way—by providing opportunities to discuss the available information and ways of using it. Depending on a host of interacting factors, group discussions can influence individuals' decisions in various ways.

Majority Influence and Group Polarization In January 1998, President Bill Clinton was accused of instructing a twenty-four-year-old former White House intern to deny in legal proceedings that they had had a sexual affair. The accusation created a national uproar. If true, Clinton could be removed from office. If false, the tactics used by Clinton's detractors would stand as a low point in American politics. For months, the controversy dominated the radio and television airwaves. Do you remember talking with your friends or coworkers about it? How did these discussions influence your opinions about Clinton and about the American political process?

Let's say you hadn't yet formed a strong opinion when you found yourself with four friends discussing the latest developments over lunch. Let's also say that three friends believed that Clinton should resign or be removed and one did not. We discussed in chapter 5 how our desires to be accurate and to receive social approval often push our beliefs and attitudes toward the majority view (Wolf & Latané, 1985). The odds are pretty good, then, that your personal opinion would have shifted at least a little bit toward the anti-Clinton side of the issue.

You wouldn't have been alone. The opinions of your friends would probably have shifted further toward the anti-Clinton end of the continuum as well, resulting in what social psychologists call **group polarization:** After discussing an issue, the average judgment of group members tends to become more extreme than it was prior to the discussion (Isenberg, 1986; Lamm & Myers, 1978; Moscovici & Zavalloni, 1969). Because the members of your hypothetical group were, on average, moderately anti-Clinton prior to the lunchtime discussion, they would likely become, on average, more extremely anti-Clinton afterwards (see Figure 12.5).

Early researchers observed that discussions led group members to make riskier decisions than they would as individuals, a phenomenon they labeled the *risky shift* (e.g., Stoner, 1961; Wallach, Kogan, & Bem, 1962). Subsequent studies discovered, however, that this shift toward risky decisions occurs only when the initial group tendency is toward risk taking; when the initial tendency favors caution, discussion leads to even safer decisions (e.g., Wallach et al., 1962; Knox & Safford, 1976). Group discussion polarizes decisions about risk. And it polarizes other kinds of decisions as well. Groups of relatively prejudiced individuals become even more prejudiced after discussing racial issues (Myers & Bishop, 1970), groups of moderately profeminist women become even more profeminist following discussion (Myers, 1975), and so on. Discussion exaggerates and enhances the group's pre-discussion views.

Group polarization *When group discussion leads members to make decisions that are more extremely on the side of the issue that the group initially favored.*

Why might this be? First, members of groups are likely to hear more arguments favoring the group inclination than arguments opposing it. If most of the people in your group are anti-Clinton, you are going to hear a lot of anti-Clinton arguments. Some of these will be persuasive and new to you, pushing you further in the anti-Clinton direction. Of course, others in the group will also hear new anti-Clinton arguments, so they, too, will move even further toward the anti-Clinton position. As a result of this *persuasive arguments* process, the group view, on the whole, becomes more extreme than it was prior to the discussion (e.g., Burnstein & Vinokur, 1977).

Second, discussion also illuminates the group norm. In your hypothetical group of friends, for instance, you would probably discover quite early the anti-Clinton norm. If you liked the members of the group and were motivated to gain their positive regard, you would be tempted to shift your judgments toward theirs. Moreover, people tend to feel better about themselves when they compare favorably to others, and the group discussion provides a wonderful opportunity to boost your self- and social-regard by adopting a strong anti-Clinton position. After all, if the group values anti-Clinton views, you could become an even more treasured member of the group by becoming even more anti-Clinton. If most group members are similarly motivated, the overall group position quickly becomes extremely anti-Clinton as each member tries to gain even more of the valued anti-Clinton position. Through *social comparison* processes, too, then, groups tend to polarize during discussion (Baron & Roper, 1976; Blascovich, Ginsburg, & Howe, 1975; Goethals & Zanna, 1979; Myers, 1978).

In sum, majority views in groups often have powerful influences on the judgments of group members—influences that can lead to extreme decisions. Before exploring the factors that make majority views especially influential, however, we consider the possibility that minority views may also influence people's decisions, at least under certain circumstances.

Minority Influence How could Margaret Thatcher's scant initial support build into the groundswell that eventually carried her to the leadership of her party? And how were Thatcher's few backers not only able to resist the powerful majority influences of the incumbent Edward Heath's supporters but also able to convince Heath supporters to switch their allegiances to Thatcher? After all, we've seen throughout this textbook how powerful majority influence can be.

Indeed, **minority influence** is difficult to accomplish, for several reasons. First, opinion minorities are generally less able to exert social pressures on others. The rewards of social acceptance, and the punishment of social isolation, can be doled out in much greater measure by opinion majorities. After all, if you'd been a Conservative MP, wouldn't you rather be socially valued by the vast majority of your colleagues than by just a few, all else being equal? And wouldn't you be more fearful of being socially rejected by the many than by the few? Second, as we discussed in chapter 6, opinions expressed by larger numbers of people gain credibility and validity. "If all these people believe that Edward Heath would make a better leader," you might think, "perhaps he really *is* better."

Without the sway of the crowd on their side, individuals who want to convince others of minority opinions must marshall high-quality arguments and come across as especially credible. Consistent with this, research reveals that opinion minorities are most persuasive when

- *they hold steadily to their views* (Maass & Clark, 1984; Moscovici, Lage, & Naffrechoux, 1969). By consistently espousing their opinions, minorities demonstrate that these views are clearly convincing to them and should be to others as well. Thatcher's few initial supporters were steadfast, partially because they agreed with her policies and partially because they saw her as the only real alternative to Heath.
- *they originally held the majority position* (e.g., Clark, 1990; Levine & Ranelli, 1978). Thatcher had supported Heath in the past and had even served in his cabinet. As a result, her view that he had become too liberal gained the credibility that observers perceive when they see someone on their own side change an opinion. After all, "if *she* became convinced that his views were mistaken," they might think, "maybe there's something to it."
- *they're willing to compromise a bit.* Even while holding steadily to their views, minorities who demonstrate a willingness to negotiate will come across as reasonable and nonrigid (Mugny, 1982). Because no view is perfect, we find individuals who are rigid in their beliefs less credible, and thus we are persuaded less by them. Although we will see that a growing unwillingness to compromise contributed to Thatcher's eventual downfall, she was more flexible in her early years.
- *they have at least some support from others* (Asch, 1955; Morris & Miller, 1975; Mullen, 1983; Tanford & Penrod, 1984; Wolf & Latané, 1985).

Minority influence *When opinion minorities persuade others of their views.*

Several individuals holding a minority position are more influential than is a lone voice of dissent, partially because several dissenters can't be as easily dismissed as "out of touch." Indeed, Thatcher's big break came when Airey Neave, an MP who had little formal clout but a great deal of respect, endorsed her candidacy and brought with him the support of 15 of his colleagues. These votes added much-needed credibility to Thatcher's minority campaign, making it easier for others to come over to her side as well.

- *they appear to have little personal stake in the issue* (Maass, Clark, & Haberkorn, 1982). Thatcher presented her run for the party leadership as one based on ideological commitment and not on personal ambition. Indeed, she made clear early on that she'd step aside in her challenge if another ideologically conservative candidate would run in her place.
- *they present their views as compatible with the majority view but just a bit "ahead of the curve"* (Kiesler & Pallak, 1975; Maass et al., 1982; Paicheler, 1976, 1977). Thatcher presented her views as both consistent with traditional British values and as the wave of the future. "My views build on yours in a way that will make our nation stronger," she seemed to tell the voters.
- *the audience wants to make an accurate decision*, for this is when the audience will pay closest attention to the *quality* of arguments the two sides present (Laughlin & Ellis, 1986) (see chapter 5). Thatcher benefited from this focus on accuracy, as the leadership campaign was viewed as a critical one for the party's future. As a result, party members focused carefully on the quality of the arguments presented by the two candidates, and quality of argument was Thatcher's clear strength.

Even when minorities are persuasive, however, their influences may remain indirect or hidden (e.g., Alvaro & Crano, 1997; Wood, Lundgren, Ouellette, Busceme, & Blackstone, 1994). For instance, people may be privately swayed by minority arguments but still go along with the majority in public (Maass & Clark, 1984). Why? By concealing their shifts toward the minority view, individuals may avoid social disapproval. In addition, movement toward the minority view doesn't always take the form of a dramatic, all-or-nothing conversion. Although well-presented minority arguments may not be immediately convincing, they do lead people to reassess their views and think harder and more creatively about the issues (Legrenzi, Butera, Mugny, & Perez, 1991; Nemeth, 1986; Nemeth, Mayseless, Sherman, & Brown, 1990). Over time, this reevaluation may lead people to shift their opinions.

We see, then, that a host of interacting factors within group discussions influence members' decisions. Majority views are powerful, especially when people are worried about social approval, when the majority is big, or when people are making decisions about opinion rather than fact. In contrast, because people who hold minority views are less able to rely on the powers of social reward and punishment, they face an uphill battle, as Thatcher did: They must have strong arguments to make *and* present these arguments credibly *and* have an audience motivated to find the best answer.

FOCUS ON Application

Majority and Minority Influence in the Jury Room

Imagine for a moment that you're a prosecuting attorney about to present your closing arguments to a twelve-person jury. To get a conviction, you need a unanimous verdict. How many jurors do you need to convince?

If you answered twelve, you're formally correct; unanimity means "everyone agrees," and there are twelve members of this jury. In reality, however, a prosecuting attorney's case is a bit easier than that. Although estimates vary, a prosecutor who is able to convince just eight of the twelve jurors has as much as a 90 percent chance to win a conviction (Davis et al., 1975; Kalven & Zeisel, 1966; MacCoun & Kerr, 1988). How could this be?

What you need to remember is that the jury is a group—a group that deliberates before rendering its decision. Although jurors come to immediate consensus in around 30 percent of cases, the remaining 70 percent of decisions require conversation and debate (Kalven & Zeisel, 1966). And like members of other decision-making groups, jurors try to persuade one another. So even when prosecuting attorneys can convince only eight jurors, they can be pretty confident that their side will be represented well in the jury room. After all, opinion majorities are powerful: Given their numerical advantage, they possess not only a greater arsenal of persuasive arguments but also the powers of social pressure.

The near-fiction of the lone, but persuasive, hold-out. *Cultural myths and popular fiction bring us the rational and fiercely independent dissenter, able to withstand the arguments and pressures of the majority to persuade them of the truth, as Henry Fonda's character did in* Twelve Angry Men. *In reality, however, such steadfastness is unusual. Only in limited circumstances do single individuals holding minority views successfully convert majority members to their cause.*

Of course, majority views don't always win out. As the relative size of the minority faction increases, so does its resistance to majority influence and its ability to influence majority jurors (e.g., Tindale et al., 1990). Moreover, because jurors tend to exhibit a *leniency bias*—a greater willingness to acquit defendants than to convict them—a minority of jurors standing on the "not guilty" side of the issue has a somewhat easier time than does a minority voting to convict (MacCoun & Kerr, 1988; Tindale & Davis, 1983). Nonetheless, the power of minority jurors isn't great, and two legal trends appear to decrease it even further. First, in many jurisdictions, juries are getting smaller—down to as few as six members. This makes it more likely that a juror holding a minority position will be alone in his or her views, and we know that lone jurors are less able to hold fast to their positions (Kerr & MacCoun, 1985; Saks, 1977). Second, some courts no longer require juries to reach unanimous decisions but instead allow verdicts based on only three-quarters or two-thirds agreement. In such circumstances, jurors in the majority have less reason to take minority positions seriously (Hastie, Penrod, & Pennington, 1983; Kerr et al., 1976). The prospects of jurors holding minority views are not good.

Counter to the idealized notion that jury verdicts emerge from group discussion, then, we see instead that they are often determined before deliberations begin. When even a small majority of jurors initially shares a preferred verdict, it's very likely that the group's ultimate verdict will unanimously go that way. And the likelihood that a single disagreeing juror will persuade the rest toward his or her view is quite slim. In the classic film *Twelve Angry Men,* Henry Fonda plays a dedicated juror who converts all eleven others to his minority opinion. In North American cultures, we presume that a lone, rational juror will likewise stand fast against mistaken colleagues and perhaps even convert them to the truth. After all, jurors are the keepers of justice. Alas, such individuals are more likely to be found on your local movie screen than in your local courtroom. ■

As we've seen, the research on majority and minority influence provides some clues for unravelling the mystery of how Margaret Thatcher overcame such great odds to become the leader of Britain's Conservative Party. For example, when Airey Neave and his colleagues joined Thatcher's cause, it gained much-needed credibility. And the leadership campaign was viewed as critical to the party's future, thus focusing the MPs on the quality of the arguments presented by the two candidates, a clear strength for Thatcher. Although opinion minorities are usually less influential than opinion majorities, that can change with the right combination of interacting factors.

Groupthink and Defective Discussion The jury system exists because people believe that, through discussion, a group of individuals can better sift through the evidence to find truth and justice. Corporations form managerial teams because they believe that, through discussion, such groups can create more effective business strategies. Leaders of democratic nations assemble circles of advisors because they believe that, through discussion, they will create more informed social policies. People discuss important problems with groups of friends because they believe that doing so leads to better personal decisions.

Unfortunately, groups don't always make better decisions than individuals. This is partly because discussion isn't always *discussion* as we like to think of it—as an open, thoughtful, sharing of information and viewpoints. Irving Janis (1972, 1983) reviewed the history of presidential decision fiascoes, including John F. Kennedy's decision to launch the ill-fated Bay of Pigs attack on Cuba and Richard Nixon's decision to cover up the bungled Watergate break-in. Janis suggested that these and other disastrous decisions shared certain common features. Most fundamentally, these decisions were characterized by what he labelled **groupthink**—a style of making group decisions driven more by members' desires to get along than by their desires to evaluate potential solutions realistically. Due to excessive pressures toward agreement, group members failed to engage each other in effective discussion, which often resulted in avoidable mistakes.

Figure 12.6 illustrates how certain characteristics of the group and circumstances can lead members to turn their focus toward agreeing with one another and maintaining group collegiality, which, in turn, can lead to poor decisions. For example, when powerful leaders reveal their own views at the beginning of the discussion, group members are less likely to engage in the kinds of critical discussion needed to ferret out bad ideas (Flowers, 1977; Leana, 1985; McCauley, 1989; Shafer & Crichlow, 1996; Tetlock et al., 1992). Kennedy's stated preference for the Bay of Pigs invasion stifled thorough debate on the issue, with calamitous results. To his credit, Kennedy learned from his mistake. In future meetings (such as those regarding the Cuban Missile Crisis) he refrained from presenting his own positions until his advisors had discussed their own views (Janis, 1983). Tightly knit groups may also be somewhat more susceptible to poor decision making, primarily when their leaders are highly directive (Mullen et al., 1994).

As group members get overconfident and begin to believe (perhaps falsely) that everyone agrees on the proper course of action, their discussions fall prey to a variety of defective processes (Tetlock et al., 1992). They fail to consider their objectives thoroughly, to survey alternative solutions, to examine the risks associated with the preferred choice, or to plan for the possibility that their solution will go wrong. As a result, they're more likely to make poor decisions (Herek, Janis, & Huth, 1987).

We see, then, that group discussions in and of themselves don't lead individuals to make better decisions. Rather, many factors *interact* to determine when group discussions create good decisions and when they create poor decisions (Aldag & Fuller, 1993; Whyte, 1989). Decisions are better when group members are focused on the task rather than on social harmony, when leaders encourage people to air alternative perspectives, and when groups have procedures to ensure that members critically evaluate all proposals and gather outside feedback. Such characteristics increase the likelihood that the group members will share the best available knowledge and that the perspectives of dissenting minority members will be heard. Under such circumstances, the information value of groups can be great indeed.

Groupthink *A style of group decision making characterized by a greater desire among members to get along and agree with one another than to generate and critically evaluate alternative viewpoints and positions.*

Summary

Groups provide much valuable information. People who have a great "need to know" are especially likely to join with others to share information. Moreover, when circumstances are uncertain, we seek others to gain clarity on what we ought to expect. Groups can also be quite useful for making decisions, especially when members freely share good information. Group discussion frequently moves members

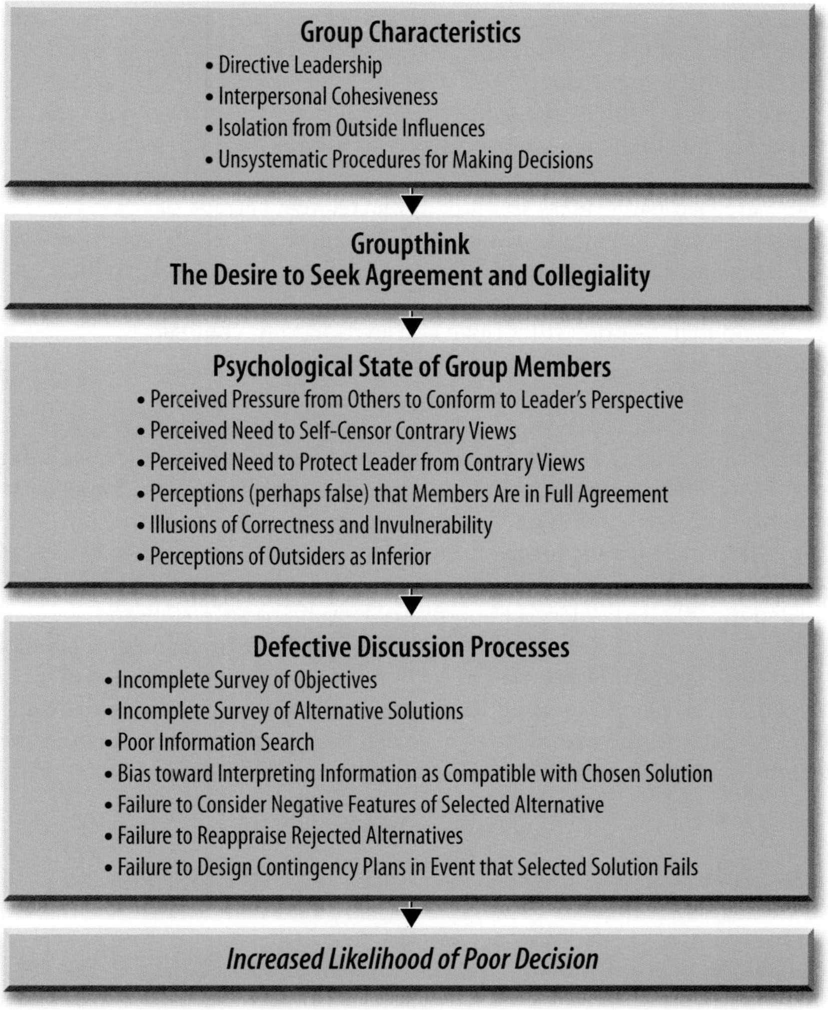

Figure 12.6
When group discussion interferes with good decision making.

Inspired by Janis's (1972, 1983) classic research on "groupthink," social and decision scientists understand more about how the desire for group agreement can create discussion processes harmful to good decision making.

SOURCE: *Adapted from Janis & Mann (1977).*

toward the majority view, as they become persuaded by the others' arguments and try to win their approval. Sometimes, however, minority opinions sway the views of others, although the circumstances in which this occurs are more limited. Finally, group discussions lead to poor decisions when members are more concerned with maintaining group harmony than with generating and critically evaluating alternative viewpoints and positions.

Gaining Positions of Leadership

After the fact, many observers of the British political scene were quick to remark that any number of candidates could have successfully defeated the incumbent, Edward Heath. They may have been correct. Yet it was Margaret Thatcher, and not the others, who seized the opportunity. Why was she compelled to step in where others feared to tread? Many of the same observers, viewing her ascendancy as a piece of luck, expected her turn at the helm to be unsuccessful and short-lived. Again, they were mistaken, as Thatcher's tenure lasted fifteen years. Why was Thatcher such an effective leader for so long? And why would she seek leadership in the first place?

It seems clear why groups would want, even need, leaders. As they grow in size, groups tend to become unwieldy and disorganized. To combat this, groups select individuals to lead—to coordinate the group's multiple tasks, to channel relevant information appropriately, to inspire members to achieve the group's goals, and so on. Indeed, leadership is so important that all known societies have leaders as part of their social organizations (Lewis, 1974; Mann, 1980; Zamaripa & Kreuger, 1983).

What is perhaps less clear is why people would *want* to lead. Leaders must invest large amounts of their time, take responsibility for the group's outcomes, and sometimes even put their personal security and life on the line. Prime ministers, presidents, and popes have all been targeted by assassins in recent years. Even when they're not being shot at, leaders are often subjected to a barrage of criticisms, complaints, and personal intrusions. Although Bill Clinton was easily reelected to the U.S. presidency in 1996, he had to endure probing inquiries not only about his politics but also about his character, personal finances, and sexual relationships. Oscar Wilde once said that "people will forgive you anything but your success," and when it comes to their leaders, people are often very unforgiving.

If the costs of leadership are so great, why would anyone want the job? The simple answer is that the rewards of leadership are also great. When groups are successful, their leaders gain a great deal of personal satisfaction for a job well done. Moreover, groups tend to distribute many resources to their leaders, compensating them not only with recognition and high social status but also with the more material rewards of larger salaries, special business opportunities, and the like. Consider the case of Charles Wang, chairman of Computer Associates International, who was compensated in 1999 with salary and bonus to the tune of $655 million ("Executive Pay," 2000). As Table 12.1 reveals, others in similar positions are compensated nicely as well, and the average CEO earned in 1999 *475 times* the average wage of a blue-collar worker. Even people in small leadership positions—an assistant manager at a fast-food restaurant, the president of a sorority—receive social or financial benefits greater than those received by individuals lower in the group's status hierarchy.

Table 12.1 The top ten compensation packages for corporate leaders, 1999.

	1999 Salary and Bonus	Long-Term Compensation (e.g., stock options)	Total Pay
1. Charles Wang *Computer Associates Intl.*	$ 4,600,000	$650,824,000	$655,424,000
2. L. Dennis Kozlowski *Tyco International*	4,550,000	165,446,000	169,996,000
3. David Pottruck *Charles Schwab*	9,000,000	118,900,000	127,900,000
4. John Chambers *Cisco Systems*	943,000	120,757,000	121,700,000
5. Stephen Case *America Online*	1,575,000	115,510,000	117,085,000
6. Louis Gerstner *IBM*	9,266,000	92,983,000	102,250,000
7. Jack Welch *General Electric*	13,325,000	79,813,000	93,138,000
8. Sanford Weil *Citigroup*	10,181,000	80,049,000	90,230,000
9. Peter Karmanos Jr. *Compuware*	2,200,000	85,321,000	87,521,000
10. Rueben Marle *Colgate Palmolive*	4,200,000	81,117,000	85,318,000

SOURCE: *Business Week, 4/17/00, p. 101.*

When asked why he robbed banks, ace criminal Willie Sutton gave a straightforward answer: "Because that's where the money is!" Why do people want to become leaders? To a large extent, the same holds: Because that's where the money and social status are. And leaders can reap these rewards without even carrying a gun!

For some people, acquiring the fruits of leadership is a primary reason for belonging to groups: They join (or create) groups so they may have followers to lead and resources to acquire. For others, however, gaining the benefits of leadership is only a secondary goal of group membership: People may first join a group to get things done, to acquire useful information, or to gain emotional support, but once inside they may see the benefits that accrue to leaders and pursue such positions for themselves.

We explore here two primary issues: (1) Who becomes a leader, and why? That is, what person and situation factors trigger an individual's desire to seek leadership, and what factors lead a group to accept that individual as its leader? And (2) when are leaders effective? When are they able to motivate their groups to follow their direction and perform well?

Who Wants to Lead?

Because leadership has significant costs as well as benefits, it makes sense that not everyone aspires to leadership. What kind of person, then, is motivated to lead?

Leadership provides power and status, enables goal achievement, and is a sign of accomplishment. Logically, then, people ought to seek leadership when they are ambitious—when they have a strong desire to exercise power over others or when they have a strong urge to do great things (McClelland, 1984; Winter, 1973). As we saw in chapter 7, the *need for power* is the desire to attain prestige, status, and influence over others. For example, as measured by their own public statements and the judgments of biographers, U.S. presidents Harry S. Truman and John F. Kennedy rated particularly high in the need for power (Simonton, 1994), and such presidents have been more likely to lead the country into military conflict (Winter, 1987). On the other hand, the *need for achievement*, introduced in chapter 4, is the desire to do something exceptionally well for its own sake (McClelland, 1984). Jimmy Carter and Herbert Hoover were the presidents judged highest in the need for achievement, and achievement-oriented presidents are more likely to initiate new legislation or try out innovative approaches to leadership. Regardless of whether they are driven by power or achievement, however, leaders tend to be highly ambitious (Hogan & Hogan, 1991; Sorrentino & Field, 1986).

Ambition is not enough, however. Indeed, we all know individuals who have lofty ambitions who never ascend to positions of leadership. Beyond their ambitions, leaders tend to be highly energetic, which enables them to turn their ambitions into reality (Hogan & Hogan, 1991; Simonton, 1994). The self-made multimillionaire Andrew Carnegie, who ran steel mills and became one of America's great philanthropists, attested to the importance of effort when he observed that the average person "puts only 25 percent of his energy and ability into his work" and that the world "stands on its head for those few and far between souls who devote 100 percent." Systematic studies of leaders in many different fields bear out the importance of both ambition on the one hand, and the ability and willingness to work hard on the other (Simonton, 1994).

Margaret Thatcher demonstrated both ambition and energy. Since childhood, she had lofty goals. She won a scholarship to a prestigious grade school and went on to earn a degree in chemistry from Oxford. Not yet satisfied, she proceeded to get a law degree and then ran for Parliament at the tender age of twenty-six, braving defeat twice before finally being elected. Her need for achievement was perhaps matched by her desire for power; her biographers commonly described her as domineering and forceful. She was also stunningly energetic, establishing a lifetime pattern of working long hours. Coupled with her ambitions, this energy enabled her to rise to the top of the British political system.

Thatcher had one characteristic that goes against the general rule of leadership, however, and against Thomas Carlyle's (1841; in Simonton, 1994) dictum that "the history of the world is but the biography of great men": She was a woman! All British prime ministers before and after her have been men, as have the vast majority of members of Parliament. Likewise, in the United States, there has never been a female president or vice-president, and over 90 percent of seats in both houses of Congress have always been occupied by men. With the exception of some notable female leaders, such as India's Indira Gandhi and Israel's Golda Meir, the leaders of nations have been overwhelmingly male.

One reason for this is that men, in general, are somewhat more interested in becoming leaders than are woman (Konrad et al., 2000). For example, in a cross-cultural study of IBM employees in 40 different countries, Hofstede (1980) found that male workers around the world tended to be interested in power, leadership, and self-realization, whereas female workers tended to stress quality of life and relationships between people. The male preference for leadership is no doubt influenced by the ways males and females are socialized (Geis, 1993). This preference may also be linked to a more fundamental sex difference, however: The hormone testosterone, present in higher concentrations in males, motivates competition for status (Mazur & Booth, 1998), as we saw in chapter 10. Of course, the greater average desire that men have to lead says nothing about how *effective* men and women are as leaders, a topic we consider later.

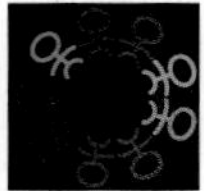

When Opportunity Knocks

Margaret Thatcher surprised everyone when she stepped up to challenge Edward Heath. Indeed, she may have surprised even herself: just six months earlier she had told a British newspaper that "it will be years before a woman either leads the party or becomes prime minister. I don't see it happening in my time" (Ogden, 1990, 119). But circumstances change. We will explore in this section two situational factors that can trigger one's desire to pursue a leadership role. The first we call "voids at the top." When the position carries with it great rewards, leadership openings can fuel one's ambitions. Such openings can also evoke one's sense of responsibility toward the group, especially if no other qualified candidate steps forward. Second, people are sometimes well situated for leadership opportunities by virtue of being "in the right place at the right time" or because of their personal connections.

Voids at the Top In certain fish species, only large, dominant males control territories and get to mate. As long as the dominant male is around, other local males remain small and colorless—fading into the background. When the dominant male dies, however, the smaller submissive males begin to secrete more testosterone, leading them to become larger and more competitive. The one that wins out continues to grow larger and more colorful, taking over as the prince of pond (Fernald, 1984). As far as we know, humans rarely change their size or coloration in response to leadership openings. They do, however, often quietly bide their time in more servile positions until a higher-status position opens up. In the case of Margaret Thatcher, she drew relatively little attention to herself while serving under Edward Heath in subsidiary posts in the Conservative party; she bit her tongue when she disagreed with his policies. As dissatisfaction with Heath grew, however, and leadership became a possibility, Thatcher burst forth as a vocal critic. When there are openings at higher levels of a status hierarchy, the leadership ambitions of some individuals come to the fore.

Leadership opportunities open up when current leaders die or depart the group. They also become available as groups grow larger (Hemphill, 1950; Mullen, Salas, & Driskell, 1989). As more people try to work together, problems of coordination, administration, and communication increase, and members seek leaders to organize them and pull things together. Furthermore, groups cry out for leadership more when they face a crisis than when things are calm (e.g., Hamblin, 1958; Helmreich & Collins, 1967). Admiral William Halsey, referring to military leadership during the Second World War, noted that "there are no great men, only great challenges that ordinary men are forced by circumstances to meet" (Simonton, 1994, 404). Important problems lead groups to call out for leaders, and such calls are more likely to inspire ambitious or responsible individuals.

Connections People sometimes just happen to be well situated for leadership—they're in the right place at the right time. For example, by virtue of being at the center of a communication network or at the head of a table, some individuals have more links to others and are thus more likely to be asked to lead (Forsyth, 1990; Nemeth & Wachtler, 1974). Connections of a more personal sort are also important. Indeed, many would argue that "it's not what you know, but who you know" that determines getting ahead in this world. Franklin Delano Roosevelt was doubly related to the earlier president Theodore Roosevelt, both by blood (he was TR's fifth cousin) and by marriage (Franklin's wife Eleanor was TR's niece). Although Margaret Thatcher had a much longer road to travel and often described her father as a simple grocer, that simple grocer also spent several years as the mayor of her hometown. And when Thatcher later made her successful bid for the Conservative party leadership, she succeeded partly because she was backed not only by Airey Neave and his coalition of backbenchers but also by Keith Joseph, the ideological leader of the party's right wing.

Who Gets to Lead?

Before becoming prime minister, Margaret Thatcher had a vision of how England ought to be governed. But so did a lot of other people, and the political ambitions of most never got beyond debating current events with their spouses over supper. Not every energetic individual having a high need for achievement gets to be a prime minister, president, or even captain of the local field hockey team. Groups don't give the same opportunity to everyone who wants to lead. Instead, they try to choose individuals who possess the characteristics that fit best with the group's needs (Fiedler, 1993; Hollander, 1993).

Consider the findings of Stewart McCann (1997). Interested in presidential leadership, he investigated the extent to which victory margins of presidents were determined by their personal strength (their power motivation, forcefulness, and activeness), their political conservatism, and the amount of socioeconomic threat during the election year. In years when things weren't going well for the country, presidents who were strong and conservative won by larger margins than did those who were less strong and more liberal. When things were going well, however, presidents who were less dominant and more liberal won by larger margins than did presidents who were strong and conservative. In different circumstances, voters sought different kinds of leaders.

More generally, people have images and beliefs of what good leaders are like and try to find leaders who fit those images (Chemers, 1997; Lord, Foti, & De Vader, 1984). First, good leaders are usually seen as possessing relevant skills. Not surprisingly, individuals who have high levels of expertise are more likely to be chosen to lead (e.g., Rice, Instone, & Adams, 1984; Stogdill, 1974). Second, leaders are expected to be self-confident. Indeed, political leaders whose speeches suggest confidence are more likely to win elections than are those who give speeches sprinkled with doubt and concern (Zullow, Oettingen, Peterson, & Seligman, 1988). Third, good leaders are expected to be invested in the group, which may be why people who speak a lot and participate during group meetings are especially likely to be chosen to lead—even when their participation isn't particularly useful or illuminating (Bavelas, Hastorf, Gross, Kite, 1965; Mullen et al., 1989; Sorrentino & Boutillier, 1975; Stein & Heller, 1979).

Finally, in people's minds, leaders have a certain "look" to them. For instance, leaders are expected to have physically mature facial features—narrow eyes, a broad jaw, and an angular face; people with "baby-faced" features—large eyes, a small chin, and a round face—are seen as more submissive and naïve, and therefore are less well suited for certain kinds of leadership (Zebrowitz, 1994; Zebrowitz, Tenenbaum, &

Trying to look the part. *Concerned that voters viewed him as weaker than George Bush, his war-hero opponent, the short and meticulously neat Michael Dukakis donned a fighter's uniform and hopped on the M1 tank for a photo opportunity. Dukakis knew that, when choosing U.S. presidents, appearances matter.*

Goldstein, 1991). And in U.S. society, the right look also means being tall. For example, the five greatest presidents according to historians were Lincoln (6 feet 4 inches), Washington, Jefferson, and Franklin D. Roosevelt (all around 6 feet 2 inches), and Andrew Jackson, the shortest of the bunch at only 6 feet 1 inch (Simonton, 1994). And twenty-two of the last twenty-six U.S. presidential elections have been won by the taller candidate.

This tendency to evaluate potential leaders against our stereotyped images of what good leaders are like can have unfortunate consequences, because our images may be shallow and only partially attuned to the characteristics that actually make for effective leadership. For example, otherwise highly qualified individuals who don't fit our images are likely to be passed over for important leadership positions. This may partially explain why women are so underrepresented as leaders (Bartol & Martin, 1986; Eagly, 1983). It's not simply that men are more motivated to seek positions of leadership, as we discussed before. Rather, women just don't "look" like leaders in the stereotypical sense and so are less likely to be chosen to lead (Kenny, Blascovich, & Shaver, 1994; Lord, De Vader, & Alliger, 1986; Zebrowitz, 1994). Indeed, even when highly qualified women step forward as candidates, men are, on average, more likely to win. In one study, characteristically dominant individuals were placed together with characteristically submissive individuals. As expected, when dominant individuals interacted with submissive individuals of their own sex, the dominant individuals rose to leadership three fourths of the time. When dominant men interacted with submissive women, this pattern was more pronounced, with the men becoming leaders nine times out of ten. But when dominant women interacted with submissive men, the pattern reversed itself: The submissive men were more likely to become leaders than were the dominant women (Nyquist & Spence, 1986). To many individuals, women look less like leaders. As a result, women's leadership talents may go unrecognized and untapped.

In sum, leaders emerge through an interactive process in which groups try to select leaders whose characteristics match the groups' needs. It was thus quite important to Margaret Thatcher's success that she possessed characteristics people believed leaders should possess. Most important, she was quite skilled and her personal style exuded confidence.

When Are Leaders Effective?

Just because a person is a leader doesn't mean he or she is an *effective* leader. Indeed, the histories of nations, corporations, and athletic teams—virtually all kinds of groups—are littered with the ruins of poor leadership. What factors, then, influence whether a leader will successfully move a group toward its goals? The answer depends on how the personal characteristics of the leader mesh with, and engage, the motivations of the group members. Just as people with certain personalities are better equipped for some tasks than for others, some leadership styles are more effective in some groups than are others. Leadership success is thus *contingent* upon the group's needs (Fiedler, 1967, 1993). For example, workers in conventional occupations (such as accountants) respond well to task-oriented and authoritative leadership, whereas workers in investigative occupations (such as college professors) much prefer to manage themselves (Hogan, Curphy, & Hogan, 1994).

Moreover, as a group's circumstances change, the leader's style usually must change as well if he or she hopes to remain effective (Fiedler, 1993; Hersey & Blanchard, 1982). Whereas new workers tend to appreciate leaders who assign them to clear, structured tasks, more expert workers do not take as well to directive leadership. Finally, whether a particular leadership style is effective may depend on the other resources available to the leader. In a classic early experiment conducted by Kurt Lewin, Ronald Lippitt, and Ralph White (1939; White & Lippitt, 1960), children meeting in groups to work on hobbies were led by adults who adopted either autocratic or democratic leadership styles. The autocratic leaders were instructed to decide dictatorially what the groups would do and how they would do it. The democratic leaders were instructed to encourage the groups to make their own decisions. When the leaders were there to watch over them, groups having autocratic leaders spent more time working than did groups having democratic leaders. Does this mean that a dictatorial leadership style is more effective than a more democratic one? Not necessarily. When the leaders were absent, the groups with autocratic leaders decreased their efforts, whereas the groups with democratic leaders did not. Autocratic leadership may be effective only when leaders can supervise their members closely (see Figure 12.7).

It's clear, then, that the effectiveness of leaders depends on the nature of the task. With this in mind, we return to the issue of gender differences in leadership, asking this time whether men are indeed more effective leaders, as stereotypes suggest.

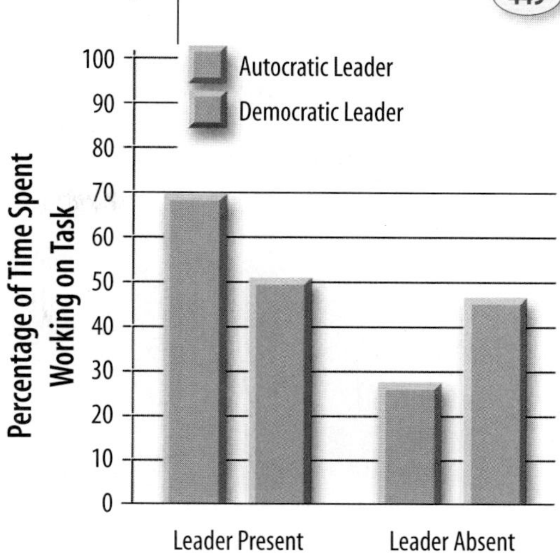

Figure 12.7
Autocratic and democratic leadership.

Children working on hobbies were supervised by either autocratic or democratic leaders (Lewin, Lippitt, & White, 1939; White & Lippitt, 1960). Whereas the autocratic leaders told the groups what to do and how to do it, the democratic leaders encouraged the groups to determine their own paths. Groups assigned to autocratic leaders spent more time working than groups with democratic leaders, but only when their leaders were there to supervise their activities. When their leaders were absent, they drastically decreased their efforts. Autocratic leaders may be effective only when they can keep their group members under close surveillance.

SOURCE: *Data from White & Lippitt (1960) p. 65.*

Gender and Leadership

> ...more nonsense was written about the so-called "feminine factor" during my time in office than about almost anything else. I was always asked how it felt to be a woman prime minister. I would reply: "I don't know: I've never experienced the alternative." (Thatcher, 1993, 18)

When Margaret Thatcher was growing up in the 1930s, the division of labor in society was fairly clear-cut: Women stayed home as full-time homemakers, and the men went off "to work." This began to change during World War II, and continues to change now, as women make up an increasing percentage of the workforce. Although women in positions of world leadership and top management are still the exception, more and more women are leading their groups, and this trend is likely to continue. How do women fare in leadership positions? The question has practical importance. If women are as effective as men in leadership roles but are denied access to those roles because they don't match people's images of what a leader should be, then organizations are losing a valuable pool of talent, and women are being unfairly treated.

Alice Eagly, Steven Karau, and Mona Makhijani (1995) explored the question of sex differences in leader effectiveness using the technique of meta-analysis. The researchers first gathered seventy-four organizational studies and twenty-two laboratory studies that compared male and female leadership effectiveness. Combining these results, they discovered that the average sex difference in leadership was zero—men and women did not differ in their effectiveness as leaders. They delved a bit deeper, however, and rated each of the occupations in terms of its compatibility with the male and female gender role. That is, positions such as grade-school principal were coded as "female," whereas jobs such as drill sergeant were coded as "male." They also rated whether the position required the ability to connect well with others and whether it required an ability to control and influence others. Considering these additional factors, a sex difference emerged from the data: Women were more effective in jobs that were viewed as feminine or that required interpersonal skills; men were more effective in jobs that were viewed as masculine or that required a hard-nosed task orientation.

Eagly and her colleagues (1995) explained their results in terms of *social role theory*. According to this perspective, we are all encouraged to behave in ways that are congruent with culturally defined gender roles. Because the culturally appropriate behavior for a man is to be controlling and directive, men will tend to be particularly effective leaders when the group's task requires someone to ride its members hard. In contrast, because the culturally appropriate behavior for a woman is to be relationship-oriented, women will tend to be particularly effective leaders when the group's task requires someone to attend to the members' needs and feelings.

In sum, to ask simply whether men or women make better leaders prompts the oversimplified conclusion that the sexes are equally effective. When one takes the requirements of the leadership situation into account, however, we see that the typically male orientation toward leadership is particularly effective in some occupational settings, whereas the typically female orientation toward leadership is particularly effective in others. Highly effective leaders are those able to use either "female" or "male" strategies as circumstances warrant.

Transformational Leaders We've seen that leaders can be effective by matching their styles to the needs of the group. There are special exceptions to this rule, however: Some leaders are effective not because they change themselves but because they transform the group (Bass, 1985; Burns, 1978; House & Shamir, 1993). Have you ever had a teacher, a coach, or a boss who inspired you to rise above your everyday personal concerns, to put forth your best efforts for the good of your group or even of your whole society? Over a decade ago, Bernard Bass and Bruce Avolio of the Center for Leadership Studies at the State University of New York began an extensive program of research by addressing a similar question to South African business executives and U.S. Army colonels. From the participants' responses, they developed the Multifactor Leadership Questionnaire (MLQ) and, in the years since, have tested it on numerous groups around the world, including managers in New Zealand, India, and Japan; executives and middle managers in a Fortune 500 firm; and military officers in Canada and Germany. Based on this research, they have concluded that there are certain characteristics of leaders that inspire not only high satisfaction among followers but also high productivity (Bass & Avolio, 1993; Geyer & Steyrer, 1998). They label individuals who have several of these characteristics **transformational leaders,** because, like John F. Kennedy, Martin Luther King, Jr., and even Adoph Hitler, these leaders significantly altered the motivations, outlooks, and behaviors of their followers. Transformational leaders engage the aspirations and self-concepts of followers so that the successes of the group become the followers' own personal successes and the leader's mission becomes their own (House & Shamir, 1993). Such leaders intellectually stimulate their followers, getting them to examine their values and approaches to life, and make them feel that they are personally important and have important contributions to make. In Table 12.2, we list the features of transformational leadership.

We've seen, then, that leaders can be effective in two general ways: They can fit their styles to the existing needs of the group, or they can inspire the group toward their own goals. Like the emergence of leadership itself, we see that leadership effectiveness is determined by an interaction between the person (the potential leader) and the situation (the group).

Summary

Considerable benefits can be gained from group leadership. Because leading a group often requires significant sacrifices, groups reward their leaders in social and material ways. Those who have a need for power or a need for achievement tend to be ambitious in their leadership aims. Individuals who have high energy levels are more likely to see their ambitions to fruition, and men are somewhat more likely to seek leadership positions than are women. The inclination to lead increases when leadership positions become available and when one has connections to past and current leaders. Of course, not everyone who wants to become a leader indeed becomes one. Groups select their leaders based on how well they see potential candidates fitting with their images of what good leaders are like. Because women don't tend to match traditional leadership prototypes, they are less frequently chosen to lead. Finally, leaders are effective when they match their styles to the needs of the group or when they transform the group into one that adopts their own goals and aspirations. We summarize the factors associated with leadership, and with the other goals, in Table 12.3.

Transformational leadership
Leadership that changes the motivations, outlooks, and behaviors of followers, enabling the group to reach its goals better.

Table 12.2 The characteristics of transformational leadership.

The Characteristic	How Leader Manifests It
Idealized Influence or "Charisma"	Communicates a sense of a "joint mission" in followers. Expresses dedication to his or her followers. Appeals to the hopes and desires of followers. Is willing to sacrifice his or her self-gain for the good of the group.
Intellectual Stimulation	Creates an openness to new ways of thinking. Creates a "big picture" that connects different views of the problem. Is willing to entertain even seemingly foolish ideas.
Inspirational Motivation	Convinces followers that they have the ability to accomplish more than they previously thought possible. Sets an example for others to strive for. Presents an optimistic view of the future.
Individualized Consideration	Recognizes individual strengths and weaknesses. Shows interest in the well-being of others. Supports worker's efforts to better themselves on the job.

SOURCE: *Bass & Avolio, 1993.*

CHAPTER 12
Summary Table

Table 12.3 Summary of the goals served by belonging to groups and the factors related to them.

The Goal	The Person	The Situation	Interactions
Getting Things Done	• Expectations of Individual Failure and Group Success	• Current Needs • Individualistic Societies	• Groups are particularly productive when certain characteristics—member personalities, size, and diversity—fit well with the demands of their tasks.
Making Accurate Decisions	• The Need to Know	• Uncertain Circumstances	• Group discussion often leads members to adopt the majority view. In limited circumstances, however, group members holding minority views are influential. • When group members are more concerned with maintaining their social relationships than with generating and critically evaluating alternative decisions, group discussion can lead to very poor decisions.
Gaining Positions of Leadership	• Ambition (Need for Power and Need for Achievement) • Energy • Gender	• Voids at the Top • Connections	• Groups select leaders who fit their "prototype" of what a good leader is for the circumstances they face. • When a leadership style fits well with the current needs of the group, groups perform better.

REVISITING

The Rise and Fall of Margaret Thatcher

Because she was a woman in the male world of British politics, and a right-wing thinker in a party and country that had been moving toward the left, the likelihood that Margaret Thatcher would ever lead her country was slim. But as research informs us, special things can happen with the right leader and the right kind of leadership at the right moment. Furthermore, even minority factions can grow to become majorities. Thatcher, partly by design and partly by good fortune, captured her opportunities and made the most of them.

Concerned about her tenuous position as a woman in the Conservative party, Thatcher generally kept her more controversial views to herself. But when the opportunity came to challenge the incumbent Conservative leader Edward Heath, she spoke up, daring to do what others dared not. In the aftermath of Thatcher's victory, it became clear that several potential candidates would likely have defeated Heath had they decided to run. But only Thatcher saw the void at the top and was willing to risk all to fill it. Perhaps she better understood the circumstances: that Heath's long-time support was broad but shallow; that her enthusiasm for communicating her message would create an interconnected network of pro-Thatcher sentiment that Heath's more distant, elitist strategy would be unable to contain; and that her direct, strong style would counteract the fact that, as a woman, she didn't fit with people's images of what a leader should be. In addition, she took advantage of fortunate circumstances. After announcing her candidacy, she still had little support. Airy Neave's backing came unexpectedly and was crucial to her eventual success because, as we've discussed, minority positions usually fizzle quickly without committed support from at least a few others. And without the coincidental scheduling of parliamentary debates in which she took part, few would have seen her great potential, for she convincingly trounced her debate opponent from the ruling Labour Party.

Of course, neither her character nor her circumstances alone produced her success. Rather, it was an interaction of the two. To put it simply, Thatcher was the right leader at the right time. Indeed, this special confluence of forces characterized most of her political career. Mired in a horrible financial slump, the British people were receptive to new economic approaches, and her emphasis on self-reliance and belt tightening seemed worth a try. And so she became prime minister. During her first term, with her popularity at a record low, Argentina attacked the Falkland Islands; Thatcher's style again fit the situation perfectly. She was strong and determined, Britain won the war, and Thatcher easily won reelection. And so it went, through her second term as well. Her country needed decisive leadership, and decisive she was.

But, slowly, the job began to change. Now that many people were financially better off, they worried that her tough economic policies were leaving the poor behind. They wanted a more compassionate stance. Others thought that Thatcher's opposition to the emerging European Union would weaken Britain's trading status in Europe and elsewhere. Some leaders don't need to change with the times, but can rather define the times for their followers. This, however, was not Thatcher's strong suit. She was more a debater—a master of facts and argument—than a charismatic, transformational motivator. Other leaders respond to changing circumstances by altering their styles and strategies. But adaptation was not Thatcher's way, either. And so it came to pass that, in her third term, her effectiveness began to wane.

Like Heath's downfall a decade and a half earlier, Thatcher's descent was surprising and rapid (Watkins, 1991). Ironically, it was similar to Heath's in other ways as well. As had Heath, Thatcher distanced herself from many followers and antagonized others. She had always been tough and reluctant to contemplate opposing views, but with victory after victory, she came to see herself as invincible—more a monarch, some thought, than an elected official who would need the support of others. Leaders and followers are in an interactive relationship, and without loyal followers, it is difficult to lead effectively.

The fallen Margaret Thatcher. *Margaret Thatcher's rapid fall from leadership was as surprising as her ascent to it. Ironically, her strong, self-confident, decisive leadership style became her greatest liability, as she was unable or unwilling to adapt to the new demands of the times.*

Moreover, just as Heath had failed to recognize that his policies were sure political losers, Thatcher began to make similar mistakes. Laying the groundwork for groupthink and ineffective decision making, she had increasingly filled her cabinet with politicians of like mind, and it had become a place where alternative positions were scorned and where "oppositional" individuals were unwelcome. The "Iron Lady" ran the show with an iron fist. In frustration, one of the dissenting voices—a long-time Thatcher colleague—resigned his post and warned in a bold parliamentary speech of the dangers of following Thatcher's course. Just as the early deserters from Heath's camp had given Thatcher's minority campaign crucial credibility and momentum, this defection did the same for one of Thatcher's ambitious rivals. She was ousted within days. Ironically, that very same strong, self-confident, decisive leadership style that brought her to the top also brought her down (Thompson & Thompson, 1990).

For many of us, seeing the social world means seeing a collection of apparently independent individuals. Margaret Thatcher's journey is thus particularly instructive, for if the story of such a committed individualist can be understood only within the contexts of the groups in which she lived, it is easier to see how our own lives, too, are so intertwined with the lives of others.

CHAPTER 12

Summary

The Nature of Groups

1. The mere presence of others can facilitate performance on well-mastered tasks and impair performance on unmastered tasks. Social facilitation is enhanced when task performers think others are evaluating them and when the others are distracting.
2. People can become deindividuated in groups, losing their sense of identity and relaxing their inhibitions against behaving counter to their normal values.
3. Although the flow of influence within groups is complex, order generally emerges from the chaos, as communicating group members begin to share attitudes and beliefs. Computer simulations help investigators explore complex group interactions.
4. Minimally, groups are two or more individuals who influence one another. Collections of individuals become increasingly "grouplike" when their members are interdependent and share a common identity and when they develop structure (i.e., injunctive norms, roles, status hierarchies, communication networks, and cohesiveness).

Getting Things Done

1. Performance groups help people accomplish tasks that would be difficult to accomplish alone.
2. Although groups are frequently more productive than individuals, they are rarely as productive as they could be. People often loaf, decreasing their personal efforts as their groups grow larger.
3. People who expect to have difficulty reaching their goals as individuals or who expect to reach their goals easily as group members are particularly likely to join groups to accomplish their tasks.
4. When societal circumstances are difficult, people are particularly likely to create or join performance groups.
5. Although members of both collectivistic and individualistic societies join together to get things done,

people in individualistic cultures belong to more performance groups, albeit with less commitment to each.

6. Productive groups have members whose personalities closely match the requirements of their tasks.
7. Large groups outperform smaller groups on additive and disjunctive tasks but underperform smaller groups on conjunctive tasks.
8. Diverse groups are especially productive on disjunctive tasks and tasks requiring new solutions, flexibility, and quick adjustments to changing conditions. They are less productive on conjunctive tasks and tasks in which interpersonal cohesion and communication are important.

Making Accurate Decisions

1. When groups effectively share useful information, members usually make better decisions.
2. Individuals who need to know about things are especially likely to create and join information groups.
3. Uncertain, threatening circumstances lead people to seek others for informational purposes.
4. Group discussions frequently influence members toward the majority view. One implication of this is group polarization, which occurs for two reasons: Group members tend to hear more arguments supporting the majority view of the issue and thus are more likely to be authentically persuaded, and group members may try to make themselves look good by adopting a more extreme version of the group's preferred position.
5. Minority influence is difficult because individuals holding minority views are less able to rely on the powers of social reward and punishment. To be persuasive, minorities must possess quality arguments, present these arguments credibly, and have an audience motivated to find the best answer.
6. Group decisions are better when members are task focused and not excessively interpersonally focused, when leaders encourage alternative perspectives, and when groups have explicit procedures to ensure that members critically evaluate all proposals and gather outside feedback. Such features reduce "groupthink" and increase the likelihood that decisions will be informed by the best available knowledge.

Gaining Positions of Leadership

1. Because leading a group often requires personal sacrifices, groups reward leaders with social status and material gain.
2. People who want to lead tend to be ambitious, energetic, and male.
3. People are more likely to seek leadership when there is a void at the top. People also become interested in leadership by virtue of being "in the right place at the right time" or of having personal connections.
4. Leaders emerge through an interactive process in which groups try to select leaders whose characteristics match their needs. Partly because women often don't fit people's stereotypes of what an effective leader is, they are underrepresented in high-level leadership positions.
5. Effective leadership depends on how the personal characteristics and style of the leader mesh with the group's needs. Men tend to be more effective leading jobs requiring "masculine" skills and a hard-nosed task orientation; women are more effective leading jobs requiring "feminine" skills and interpersonal sensitivities.
6. Certain leaders are transformational, changing the motivations, outlooks, and behaviors of their followers.

CHAPTER 12

Key Terms

Additive task *A job in which each member performs the same duties; group productivity is thus determined by summing the contributions of all members.*

Cohesiveness *The strength of the bonds among group members.*

Communication network *The pattern of information flow through a group.*

Conjunctive task *A job in which success is achieved only if each member performs successfully; group productivity is thus limited by the performance of the group's least successful member.*

Deindividuation *The process of losing one's sense of personal identity, which makes it easier to behave in ways inconsistent with one's normal values.*

Disjunctive task *A job in which the group's product is selected from just one member's performance; group productivity is thus determined by the performance of the group's most successful member.*

Dynamical system *A system (e.g., a group) made up of many interacting elements (e.g., people) that changes and evolves over time.*

Group *Minimally, groups are two or more individuals who influence each other. Collections of individuals become increasingly "group-like," however, when their members are interdependent and share a common identity, and when they possess structure.*

Groupthink *A style of group decision making characterized by a greater desire among members to get along and agree with one another than to generate and critically evaluate alternative viewpoints and positions.*

Group polarization *When group discussion leads members to make decisions that are more extremely on the side of the issue that the group initially favored.*

Minority influence *When opinion minorities persuade others of their views.*

Role *Expectation held by the group for how members in particular positions ought to behave.*

Social facilitation *The process through which the presence of others increases the likelihood of dominant responses, leading to better performance on well-mastered tasks and worse performance on unmastered tasks.*

Social loafing *Reducing one's personal efforts when in a group.*

Status hierarchy *A ranking of group members by their power and influence over other members.*

Transactive memory *A group memory system made up of (1) the knowledge held by individual group members and (2) a communication network for sharing this knowledge among the members.*

Transformational leadership *Leadership that changes the motivations, outlooks, and behaviors of followers, enabling the group to reach its goals better.*

CHAPTER 13
Social Dilemmas: Cooperation Versus Conflict

Contrasting Future Worlds

In 1971, Italy and Bangladesh were both densely populated countries. Italy, with a population of about 54 million, had fifty people for every one in the state of New Mexico (whose area is similar to Italy's). Bangladesh, on the other hand, had an even denser population, with 66 million people crammed into an area less than half Italy's size (see Figure 13.1).

Over the next three decades, Bangladesh doubled its population. This tiny country is now home to 132 million human beings. As many people now live in Bangladesh as populated the continental United States in 1940. Although Bangladesh is a fertile country, its farms are insufficient to feed so many people. Per capita grain production, for example, once as high as that of the United States, has dropped to a third of what it once was. As a consequence, two out of every three Bangladeshi children cannot find enough food to eat (Brown, 1999). And if you've felt strapped for cash lately, consider trying to make ends meet on the average Bangladeshi's income—twenty-four times less than the average American's. The unemployment

Figure 13.1
The People's Republic of Bangladesh is about the size of Wisconsin.

If everyone in California, New York, Texas, Pennsylvania, Illinois, Ohio, Florida, Michigan, New Jersey, and Indiana (the ten most heavily populated states of the United States) were suddenly to migrate to Wisconsin, it would then have a population roughly equivalent to that of Bangladesh.

rate (at 35 percent) runs about six or seven times higher than that in the United States, and the literacy rate for adults is a scant 38 percent (compared to 97 percent in the United States).

In response to these dismal conditions, Bengalis have flocked into neighboring India, where they've hardly been welcome. In 1983, 1,700 Bengalis were slaughtered in five hours when the residents of one Indian village went on a rampage against them. This event illustrated how overpopulation has contributed to longstanding international conflicts on the Indian subcontinent. At the beginning of the twentieth century, Bangladesh was part of India. But after a series of gruesome and bloody revolutions, the predominantly Muslim areas of Pakistan and Bangladesh split first from India, and then from each other. Like Bangladesh, the populations of India and Pakistan have exploded. And the conflicts between these overpopulated countries have taken a dangerous turn. In 1998, ignoring the lessons of the costly cold war between the United States and the Soviet Union, and turning a deaf ear to threats of economic repercussions, India exploded five nuclear bombs. Viewing the tests as a veiled threat, Pakistan responded by unleashing its own nuclear tests. In addition to destabilizing the political climate of these regions, nuclear weapons development sucks away tremendous economic resources that could be used to feed and educate the underfed masses in these countries.

Italians, on the other hand, have gone in a completely different direction. The Italian population has stabilized at 57 million, with a growth rate that is currently negative. At the same time, the Italian economy is one of the world's great success stories. During the second half of the twentieth century, Italy moved from the status of a third-world country to one of the word's wealthiest (with per capita incomes similar to those in Japan or the Netherlands). At 97 percent, Italy's literacy rate is identical to that in the United States.

Meanwhile, Italy's alliances with its fellow European countries have completely turned around the conflicts of the early twentieth century. Indeed, the Italians have joined with their former foes in a European equivalent of the United States, where common passports and a shared currency are erasing old national boundaries. Like Italy, the other Western European nations have seen a decrease in population growth along with an increase in economic prosperity. And European countries are leading the rest of the world in efforts to protect the environment (Hawken, Lovins, & Lovins, 1999).

The Indian and European subcontinents hold out two contrasting images of the world's future. If the population explosion in third-world countries like Bangladesh and India continues, the world's forests, oceans, and rivers will continue to be depleted, other species will continue to be driven to extinction, and international conflicts will continue to increase (Homer-Dixon et al., 1993; Oskamp, 2000). If, on the other hand, the revolutionary changes now taking place in Italy and the rest of Europe continue, the human population explosion and its vast toll on the earth's fragile ecosystems could be halted or even reversed. Indeed, some economic theorists envision a coming revolution in which quiet and efficient vehicles exhaust only water vapor, industrial waste is nearly eliminated, unemployment disappears, efficient houses produce their own energy, the world's disappearing forests are renewed, and the waste from coal, nuclear reactors, and petroleum is largely eradicated (Hawken, Lovins, & Lovins, 1999).

Overcrowding in Bangladesh. *This view of Bangladesh shows the overcrowding that overpopulation can create.*

On paper, it hardly seems like a difficult choice. So why doesn't the whole world follow the European example? With overpopulation, environmental degradation, and international conflict placing such obvious costs on the people in Bangladesh, India, and Pakistan, why don't they do something about it?

The puzzles of unrestrained population growth, destruction of the earth's resources, and international conflict, are probably the most important questions facing humankind today.

We consider these puzzles together in this chapter for two related reasons. First, these group-level social phenomena complete our progression from the psychology of the individual through ever more complex interactions of the person and the environment. Second, each of these global social dilemmas vividly demonstrates how the thoughts and feelings inside single individuals can combine into unexpected patterns at the group level. Indeed, the problems of overpopulation, environmental destruction, and international conflict emerge only at the level of very large groups—so large that they strain the limits of our individual cognitive capacities (Gardner & Stern, 1996).

First, we define social dilemmas and examine what these three social problems have in common. Then we analyze the goals that underlie these grand dilemmas and the factors in the person and situation that may tell us how to resolve them.

Defining Social Dilemmas

In his 1908 text, *Social Psychology*, William McDougall argued that effective political and economic policies must be grounded in an understanding of the psychology of the individual. In keeping with McDougall's viewpoint, later social psychological research suggests that the modern problems of overpopulation, environmental destruction, and international conflict are all connected to the psychology of individual minds. Each builds on self-serving psychological mechanisms originally designed for life in small groups. Unfortunately, these same mechanisms have disastrous consequences at the global level. Indeed, each global problem pits single individuals, with all their self-serving and self-deceiving tendencies, against the greater good of their larger groups. As such, each qualifies as a form of **social dilemma**—a situation in which an individual profits from selfishness unless everyone chooses the selfish alternative, in which case the whole group loses (Allison, Beggan, & Midgley, 1996; Komorita & Parks, 1995; Schroeder, 1995).

Research on social dilemmas is rooted in a very simple game called the *prisoner's dilemma* (Rapoport, 1960; VanVugt, 1998). Imagine that you're a professional crook and that you and your partner in crime have been arrested for trespassing and suspicion of a recent string of heists. Your lawyer confronts you with the following choice: Admit the string of heists and testify against the other crook, and you'll walk completely free; or keep your mouth shut, and let your fellow brigand testify against you. If that happens, he walks off with the light sentence while they throw the book at you and send you up to the state penitentiary for several years. If you both come clean on the heists, then neither of you will get any brownie points, but you'll each get a moderate sentence. And if you both keep your mouths shut, they'll press the relatively minor charge of trespassing, but you'll both evade justice on the actual robberies. You and your partner are now caught in the dilemma depicted in Figure 13.2. When students in laboratory experiments play variants of this game, solitary defection leads to the best outcome for one player but the worst for the other. Mutual defection leads to slightly negative outcomes for both, whereas cooperation results in the greatest mutual gain (moderately positive for both cooperators) (e.g., Sheldon, 1999; Tenbrunsel & Messick, 1999).

International conflicts sometimes take the one-on-one character of the prisoner's dilemma, as the leaders of two opposing nations try to face each other down. However, a more common type of social dilemma pits the individual's immediate interest against that of the larger group (Foddy et al., 1999; Probst, Carnevale, & Triandis, 1999). These group-level dilemmas confront billions of human beings every day, and underlie the problems of overpopulation and environmental destruction. The prototype of these insidious social dilemmas is the "tragedy of the commons," which we discuss next.

Social dilemma *A situation in which an individual profits from selfishness unless everyone chooses the selfish alternative, in which case the whole group loses.*

Figure 13.2
The Prisoner's Dilemma.

Imagine you are one of two burglars who have been arrested while trespassing at the scene of a potential heist, and you are being held on suspicion of a string of burglaries. You have two options: Remain silent (thereby cooperating with the other crook in evading prosecution), or confess to the district attorney (thereby defecting on your pact of silence with the other burglar). If only one person confesses, thereby providing the D.A. with solid evidence against the other, the one who confesses goes free. For the pair of you, the best outcome is if you both remain silent. But the decision poses a dilemma: if you remain silent, while the other crook confesses, things will turn out really badly for you.

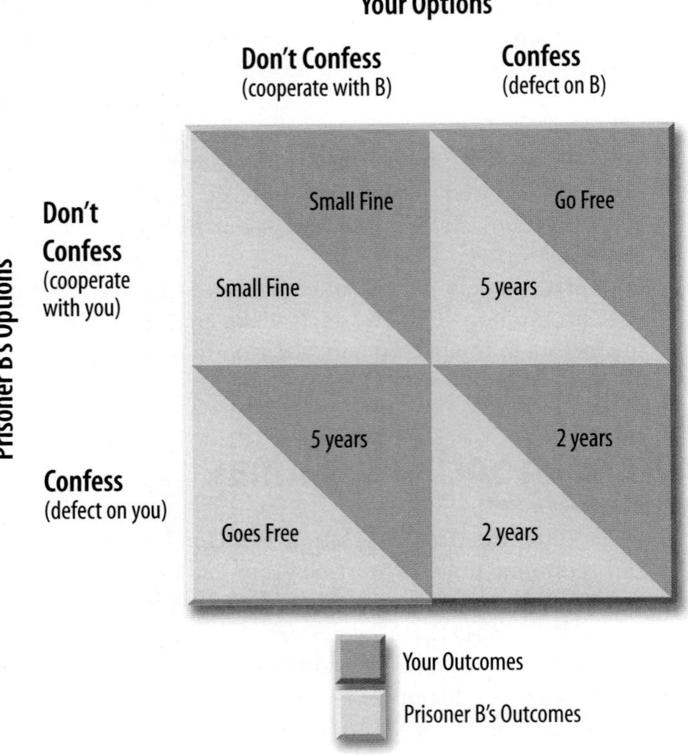

FOCUS ON Social Dysfunction

The Tragedy of the Commons

The great economic philosopher Adam Smith argued that if all individuals were given free rein to seek their own self-interests, an "invisible hand" would lead from all this selfishness to a greater public good (Smith, 1776). Smith's theory that the selfish needs of different individuals would balance out for the public good became the rallying cry for a laissez-faire approach to economics—an approach in which government does not interfere with individual freedom.

When it comes to protecting the environment, however, the laissez-faire approach can lead to disastrous consequences. To illustrate how individual selfishness can lead to ruinous consequences for the group, ecologist Garrett Hardin (1968) described the overgrazing of common pastures in New England. Those pastures were public areas where sheepherders were free to graze their animals. On their own private pastures, herders would graze only as many animals as the land could support, aware that overgrazing would destroy the grass and starve their whole herd. On the commonly shared areas, however, herders showed no such restraint. Consequently, the commons were frequently destroyed by overgrazing.

What caused the tragedy of the commons? According to Hardin, the same individual selfishness that delicately controlled the "invisible hand" of the economic marketplace became the "invisible fist" that crushed the commons. The immediate benefit of adding one more animal was paid directly to the individual sheepherder. However, the cost of that surplus animal was shared by all users of the commons. Thus, the most self-interested action an individual could take, in the short run, was to add an additional animal. When large numbers of herders followed that short-sighted strategy, however, the long-range cost was the destruction of the grazing area for the whole group.

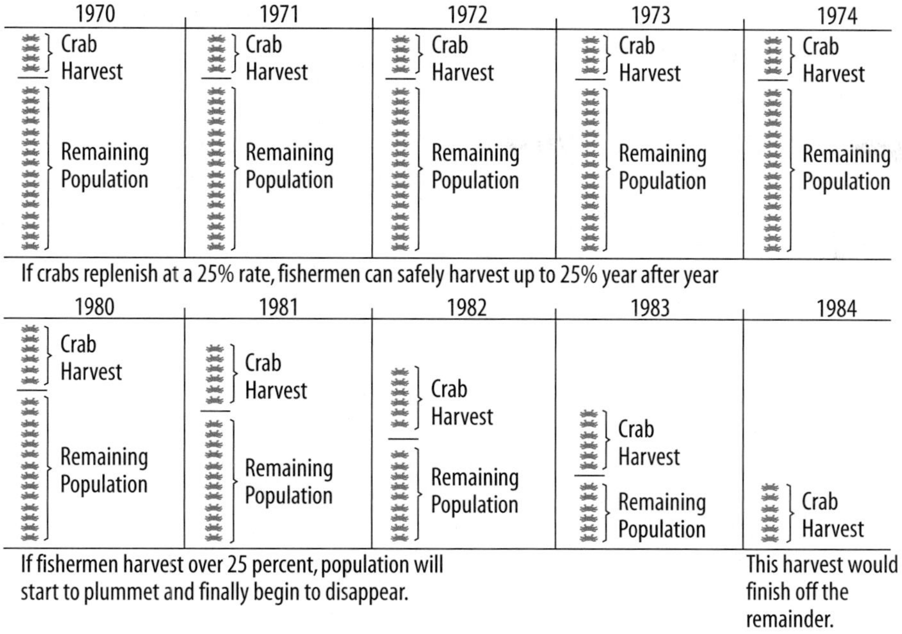

1970	1971	1972	1973	1974
Crab Harvest	Crab Harvest	Crab Harvest	Crab Harvest	Crab Harvest
Remaining Population	Remaining Population	Remaining Population	Remaining Population	Remaining Population

If crabs replenish at a 25% rate, fishermen can safely harvest up to 25% year after year

1980	1981	1982	1983	1984
Crab Harvest	Crab Harvest	Crab Harvest	Crab Harvest	
Remaining Population	Remaining Population	Remaining Population	Remaining Population	Crab Harvest

If fishermen harvest over 25 percent, population will start to plummet and finally begin to disappear.

This harvest would finish off the remainder.

Figure 13.3
When taking a little extra leads to a lot less.

If crab fishermen harvest slowly, the population continues to replenish itself, allowing continued profit in the future. Although conservation is in the interest of the industry as a whole, the immediate interest of individual crab fishermen tempts them to take as many as they can now. But if all do so, they destroy most of the breeding population, as happened during the 1980s. This is an example of a replenishing resource management dilemma.

The commons dilemma is an example of a particular type of dilemma, called a **replenishing resource management dilemma** (Schroeder, 1995). In this type of dilemma, group members share a renewable resource that will continue producing benefits if group members don't overharvest it. The case of the Alaska king crab is a perfect example (see Figure 13.3). In the four years between 1980 and 1984, the Alaska king crab harvest went down 92 percent, despite an increasing number of boats searching for crabs with more and more sophisticated equipment. Fearing a total extinction, the Alaska state government completely closed down the king crab industry (Gardner & Stern, 1996). If crab fishermen as a group harvested crabs at the same rate that the crab population replenished itself, they could have continued to reap the same profits year after year. Each individual crab fisherman, however, makes the highest short-term profits by harvesting as many crabs as possible in a given year. If all individuals try to maximize their profits in a given year, there won't be enough crabs to replenish the population, and the remainder will quickly disappear.

Social psychologist Kevin Brechner (1977) was interested in simulating the commons dilemma in the laboratory. He offered groups of three students a chance to earn a semester's worth of experimental credit (normally three hours) in just half an hour if they could succeed in winning 150 points in a game. To win the points, the students simply pressed a button that took a point from a common pool and put it into their own personal accounts. The common pool was displayed on a board with twenty-four lights. When any of the players took a point, one of the lights in the common pool went out. Like a field of grass for common grazing or a breeding population of king crabs, the pool of points replenished itself. When the pool was near the top, it replenished rapidly—every two seconds. If it went below three-quarters full, it replenished more slowly (every four seconds). Below half, the replacement rate slowed to every six seconds. And if it was "grazed" down to one-fourth of its original size, points were replaced only every eight seconds. Once the last point was "grazed," the game was over, and the pool stopped replenishing completely (see Figure 13.4).

Replenishing resource management dilemma *A situation in which group members share a renewable resource that will continue to produce benefits if group members do not overharvest it but also whereby any single individual profits from harvesting as much as possible.*

To succeed, students needed to cooperate in keeping the pool at a high level so it could replenish itself at the maximum rate. When students were not allowed to com-

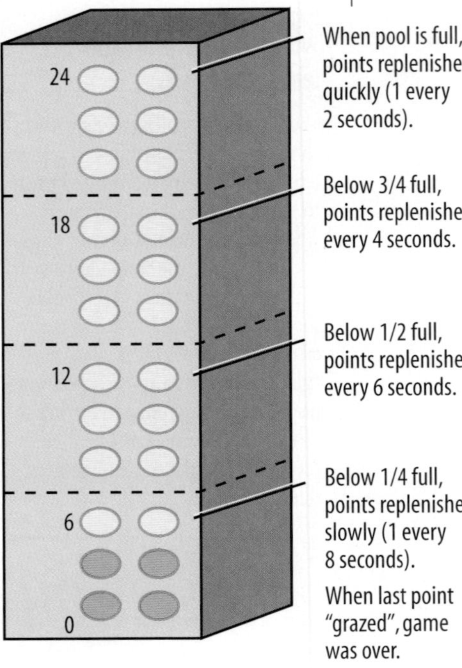

Figure 13.4
Social traps in the laboratory.

Groups in Kevin Brechner's (1977) experiment were faced with a resource that, like a crab population, replenished more rapidly if harvested slowly. Because of individual selfishness, the pools were very rapidly depleted, especially when group members could not communicate with one another.

municate, they tended to do very poorly. In fact, most noncommunicating groups ran the pool dry in less than one minute. Those students earned an average of only fourteen points each. When students were allowed to communicate with one another, they did quite a bit better, although they still usually failed to optimize, averaging about seventy points per person. Like the disappearing crab problem, then, controlled laboratory research shows that people often have great difficulty maintaining common resources (e.g. Seijts & Latham, 2000). Even though the whole group benefits when its individual members restrain themselves from taking too much of the resource too quickly, individual temptations to be selfish often lead to group ruin. ■

In dilemmas like the tragedy of the commons, each individual can *take* something from a limited common pool. It's worth distinguishing this type of dilemma from a public goods dilemma. A **public goods dilemma** is a situation in which the whole group can benefit if some of the individuals *give* something for the common good, but in which individuals profit from "free riding" if enough others contribute (Allison & Kerr, 1994; Dawes, 1980; Larrick & Blount, 1997). An example is when public broadcasting stations appeal for money. If some minimum number of listeners contributes, the station can continue to provide broadcasts for all to enjoy. If too few people contribute, though, the public good will be lost. The dilemma arises because no single individual is essential to providing the public good. Indeed, the most self-serving thing to do, from a purely economic perspective, is to ignore the requests and hope someone else will be more socially responsible. In this way, an individual gets the benefits without incurring any of the costs.

Like resource management dilemmas, public goods dilemmas have been studied in the laboratory (e.g., Sell, Griffith, & Wilson, 1993; Van Dijk & Wilke, 2000). In public goods dilemmas, the outcomes aren't nearly so dismal as in replenishing resource dilemmas—between 17 percent and 60 percent of the individuals faced with this dilemma choose to contribute, and 45 percent to 65 percent of the groups have enough contributors to obtain the public good (Braver, 1995). In the outside world, not everyone contributes to the public television station, but enough usually do to keep the operation afloat. Nevertheless, many groups do lose public benefits because the majority of their members choose the selfish alternative.

Findings on social dilemmas are reminiscent of the research on emergency helping (Latané & Darley, 1970). As we noted in chapter 9, people in crowds are apt to shirk their individual responsibility to help a needy victim. It seems that when people share responsibility for conserving a resource, they tend to look out for themselves and leave it to "someone else" to conserve. Unfortunately, other people often operate on the same self-serving principle, and everyone loses in the long run.

The key global problems are all grand-scale social dilemmas. As we'll describe in detail throughout this chapter, each pits simple mechanisms of individual self-interest against the good of the global community. Those global problems are also linked to one another (Howard, 2000; Oskamp, 2000).

Public goods dilemma *A situation in which (1) the whole group can benefit if some of the individuals give something for the common good but (2) individuals profit from "free riding" if enough others contribute.*

Interlocking Problems and Solutions

What could possibly have led villagers in Assam, India, to go on a five-hour rampage and massacre 1,700 Bengali immigrants? A team of 30 researchers was assembled to study this and related incidents around the world (Homer-Dixon et al., 1993). They found a common pattern: Overpopulation is leading to dwindling natural resources in a number of countries, which in turn puts a tremendous strain on their economies. Short-term solutions to these economic problems (such as extensive logging of rainforests for quick profits) only make the problems worse in the long run.

Given the dramatic increases in world population (see Figure 13.5), the research team concluded that more environmental destruction and international conflict will likely follow. Population growth in areas such as Bangladesh, Central America, or Africa, for example, has damaged local environments and food sources, leading the local residents to migrate away in search of livable habitats. This migration in turn leads to international conflicts as whole populations come into conflict over the remaining valuable lands and resources. The murderous spree against Bengali immigrants wasn't a historical anomaly. Such genocidal incidents have become more common in Africa, Central America, and Europe in recent years.

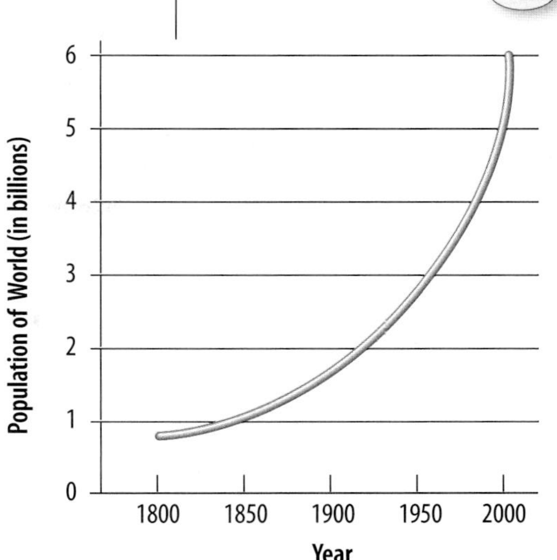

Figure 13.5
The population explosion.

For over 1 million years, the human population was relatively low (below 10 million). There have been dramatic increases in the last 200 years, however, and a population of almost 10 billion is projected within the next several decades. This increase is leading to serious environmental damage and, in turn, to international political conflicts.

Goals Underlying Global Social Dilemmas

Why do people get trapped in these escalating dilemmas? Few of us wake up in the morning with the intentional goal of contributing to global overpopulation, environmental destruction, or international conflict. Instead, most of us contribute unintentionally, simply by going about our lives with the goals that have always served human beings well. Indeed, global problems are "dilemmas" partly because each is rooted in motivations that were useful for our ancestors living in small groups. Many of the motivations we've discussed throughout this book come into play in influencing the individual decisions that add up to global social problems. For example, the goal of reproduction, discussed in chapter 8, no doubt underlies the population problem. And the general goal of simplifying complex information, discussed in depth in chapters 2 and 3, often causes people to cling to a simple political or economic solution without analyzing how it would play out in the complexities of the real world (Gardner & Stern, 1996; Gilovich, 1981). However, our discussion of global social problems will focus on two goals that take on very special characteristics in large groups of people—the desire to gain immediate satisfaction and the desire to defend ourselves and valued others.

Gaining Immediate Satisfaction The desire to gain immediate satisfaction is a good example of a goal that serves individual needs but leads to problems at the group level. Our ancestors didn't stand around helpless and immobile in the rain and snow, or search for the most difficult way to catch a fish or cut down a tree. Instead, they survived because they always had an eye out for special advantages: warmth in the winter and coolness in the summer, convenient ways to get around, more abundant supplies of fruit, fish, and meat, and technologies that would save time and labor. The irony is that the hard-won knowledge gathered by our ancestors could end up creating an intolerable life for our descendants.

Fortunately, another feature of human beings is our capacity to (at least occasionally) delay short-term gratification for long-term benefits (Insko et al., 1998; Yamagishi & Cook, 1993). Understanding the circumstances under which we seek short-term versus long-term satisfaction could suggest solutions to the great problems of the modern age.

Defending Ourselves and Valued Others The goal most directly related to international conflict is the desire to defend ourselves and valued others. There are again opposing forces at work here, and protecting our special interests may require a delicate balance. As we learned in chapter 11, groups sometimes compete with one another over scarce resources, and this competition escalates as those resources become scarcer. Hence, nations and groups within those nations have inherent conflicts of interest (Mitchell, 1999). On the other hand, if that competition leads to outright warfare, the competitors place themselves and those they value in great danger, particularly in a world armed with abundant and dangerous weapons.

We will thus organize our discussion of global social dilemmas around these two basic goals: to satisfy drives for immediate comfort and resources and to protect ourselves and those we value.

Summary

Social dilemmas pit individual selfishness against group good. Replenishing resource dilemmas involve situations in which group members share a resource that will continue producing unless overharvested. It is most profitable for the group to underharvest, but there is a motivation for the individual to cheat. Public goods dilemmas are situations in which the whole group will benefit if enough people contribute but also in which there is an individual incentive to "free ride." Overpopulation, environmental destruction, and international conflict are interlocked dilemmas pitting short-term individual interests against the long-term good of humanity. The goals of gaining immediate satisfaction and defending ourselves and valued others underlie these dilemmas.

Gaining Immediate Satisfaction

During the 1960s, a popular expression was "If it feels good, do it!" Physiological psychologists James Olds and Peter Milner (1954) actually discovered an area of the mammalian brain that seemed to be especially designed to control "feeling good." Olds and Milner implanted electrodes into a region of the brain's hypothalamus that was later dubbed the "pleasure center." Animals would press a lever for hour after hour just for a jolt of stimulation there. It makes biological sense that a good feeling would follow any behavior that satisfies an animal's needs. Under ordinary circumstances, such a feeling would be the body's way of saying "Whatever you just did, do it again!" But the desire for short-term satisfaction can sometimes lead us into traps, as you'll see next.

Social Traps

Several decades ago, behavioral psychologist John Platt (1973) provided some fascinating insights into how the drive for immediate self-gratification could lead to social dilemmas. According to Platt, the desire for quick gratification leads people into **social traps,** which he defined as

> Situations in society that contain traps formally like a fish trap, where men or organizations or whole societies get themselves started in some direction or some set of relationships that later prove to be unpleasant or lethal and that they see no easy way to back out of or to avoid. (641)

Social trap *A situation in which individuals or groups are drawn toward immediate rewards that later prove to have unpleasant or lethal consequences.*

Platt noted that social traps, far from being mysterious, operated according to the most basic of reinforcement principles: We repeat those behaviors that lead to immediate reinforcement. Unfortunately, the trap occurs when behaviors that are reinforcing in the moment have hidden costs. Those costs can be hidden for several reasons.

Differences Between Short-Term and Long-Term Consequences Sometimes, the short-term consequences of our behaviors are positive but the long-term consequences are negative. If you drive to work alone or adjust your household thermostat to 75 degrees F. regardless of the outside temperature, you get immediate and personal payoff. The costs of shrinking energy supplies come only after years, and most of us don't think about them when we take the comfortable shortcut today. In the opposite direction, the costs of spending an extra half hour on the bus, wearing sweaters indoors, or sweating a bit in the summer are also immediate and personal. Although these behaviors lead to the benefits of more abundant fuel and cleaner air, these payoffs are far removed.

Sliding into smogland. *For years, Los Angeles has had record high levels of smog. When only a few Los Angelitos drove cars, they were simply a convenient means of transportation, and made no substantial contribution to air quality problems. However, the millions of automobiles on the road now bring relatively fewer rewards, and many greater punishments, including massive traffic jams and a perennial cloud of smog.*

Ignorance of Long-Term Consequences Automobiles produce emissions that contribute to lung cancer, cardiovascular disease, hypertension, and mental retardation (Doyle, 1997). The original designers of internal combustion engines had no idea of these consequences. Likewise, the designers of the Soviet Union's Chernobyl nuclear plant probably did not foresee that their plant's meltdown would one day cover Europe with toxic radiation. Thus, we sometimes get trapped in behavior patterns because they provide great rewards in the short term and costs that do not become obvious until much later.

Sliding Reinforcers A **sliding reinforcer** is a stimulus that brings rewards when used in small doses, but punishments when used in large doses. For some time, Los Angeles has had the most polluted air of any major metropolitan area in the United States. A substantial portion of that pollution comes from automobile exhaust fumes. When the first automobiles were introduced into the Los Angeles area, though, they provided convenience without much impact on air quality. If there were only a few cars on the road, there would still be no atmospheric problem in Los Angeles. Unfortunately, when several million of them went on the road, the machines turned the city's sunny skies into a cloud of gray smog.

Thus, social traps are based on rules that are, in other circumstances, adaptive. The individuals who get trapped aren't pathological or abnormal in their behavior. Indeed, each individual is making a rational decision—to seek immediate self-interest! The problem arises when individuals join together in groups, and individual selfishness becomes a problem for the group as a whole. The idea of a social trap can help us understand not only the destruction of the environment but also overpopulation and international conflict, each of which gets worse as individuals or groups seek short-term selfish rewards that sometimes mask long-term shared costs (Howard, 2000; Linder, 1982; Lynn & Oldenquist, 1986).

Social traps have two components. The first is the problem that David Messick and Carol McClelland (1983) called a "temporal trap"—payoffs that come soon have more control over our behavior than consequences that come later. The second component of the problem has nothing to do with time pressure but comes from the social dilemma component—each self-centered individual is inclined to hope that all the other members will act unselfishly. Messick and McClelland (1983) noted that even when individuals play a resource dilemma game by themselves, with no one else to compete with, they still don't graze optimally, as they are sucked into the temporal trap of immediate reinforcement. In groups, however, people do much worse. This suggests that social selfishness greatly compounds the problem of the individual's need for immediate gratification.

Sliding reinforcer *A stimulus that brings rewards in small doses, which change to punishments when they occur in large doses.*

What factors influence people to seek immediate personal self-gratification over long-term benefits to the group? These tendencies should be related to personal and situational factors that (1) enhance egotistic self-centeredness, (2) focus the person on immediate gratification versus long-haul benefits, (3) decrease feelings of social responsibility and interdependence, and (4) promote competitiveness rather than cooperation. We will now consider research that has explored a number of these factors.

Egoistic versus Prosocial Orientations

What factors inside the person are likely to lead him or her to look out for "number one" instead of the group's long-term benefits? A great deal of research in recent years has focused directly on this question, attempting to distinguish people who have different values about benefiting themselves versus others (e.g., VanLange, Agnew, Harinck, & Steemers, 1997; VanLange & Visser, 1999).

Distinguishing Different Value Orientations Imagine that you're playing a game in which you and the other players can earn real money. Which of the following four outcomes would you prefer?

1. You sacrifice your own rewards, enabling the other people in the group to make a lot more money.
2. You and the other players work together so that, although none of you get the highest possible reward, you all do slightly better than most would do on their own.
3. You cooperate with the group if it is in your own personal interest but compete if you see a way to make more personal profits.
4. You compete to win, even sacrificing some of your own winnings if it helps you do better than the other players.

After presenting people in different countries with a standard series of questions in which they allocate benefits to themselves and their groups, social psychologists have concluded that people tend to take one of these four approaches to these problems (e.g., Liebrand & Van Run, 1985; McClintock, Messick, Kuhlman, & Campos, 1973). **Altruists** value the group benefits, even if it means that they must make personal sacrifices. **Cooperators** value working together to maximize the joint benefits to themselves and the group. **Individualists** try to maximize their own personal gains, without regard to the rest of the group. Finally, **competitors** strive to come out relatively better than other players—to "win" regardless of whether their personal winnings are high or low in an absolute sense. Most people fall into the cooperative and individualistic categories, with smaller numbers falling into the altruistic and competitive types (Liebrand & VanRun, 1985; VanLange et al., 1997). Hence, some researchers conveniently categorize altruistic and cooperative people into a "prosocial" category and individualists and competitors into an "egoistic" category (Biel & Garling, 1995; VanLange & Liebrand, 1991). See Table 13.1.

Altruist *An individual oriented toward bringing the group benefits, even if it means personal sacrifice.*

Cooperator *An individual oriented toward working together to maximize the joint benefits to the self and the group.*

Individualist *An individual oriented toward maximizing personal gains, without regard to the rest of the group.*

Competitor *An individual oriented to come out relatively better than other players, regardless of whether personal winnings are high or low in an absolute sense.*

In one experiment, students from the Netherlands or California played a game involving "energy conservation." Groups of seven students started with a pool of about $100. Over five rounds, each player could win the amount of money he had taken for himself, provided the total taken by the whole group did not exceed what was left in the pool. Subjects could choose to take money for themselves in $1.50 increments ranging from $1.50 to $9. With seven people playing the game across five trials, the group could win only if most people took very small amounts on any trial (choosing $1.50 or $3 would usually be the safest strategy).

On the first trial of the game, altruists were the only ones who were even close to the mark for obtaining the group good, taking just over $3 for themselves. Cooperators took around $4, individualists around $5, and competitors over $5. As the game progressed, all subjects realized that the money would run out, and so tended to reduce the amounts they took. However, competitors and individualists, even though they got information that they had taken far too much on the first trial, never reduced their takings enough to make up for their big initial self-helpings. Even on

Table 13.1 Social value orientations.

General Orientation	Specific Approach	Description
Egoistic	Individualist	Motivated to maximize their own outcomes, with no regard for the costs or benefits to others.
	Competitive	Motivated to do relatively better than others, even if it increases their costs.
Prosocial	Cooperative	Motivated to maximize joint profits for themselves and group members.
	Altruistic	Motivated to help others, even at a cost to themselves.

the last trial, when resources were nearly gone, competitors still took slightly more than anyone else (Liebrand & VanRun, 1985).

Consistent with these results, other studies also find that people having prosocial (altruistic or cooperative) value orientations cooperate more than those having egoistic (individualistic or competitive) orientations (Allison & Messick, 1990; Biel & Garling, 1995). Highlighting the dilemma of short-term self-interest, groups of self-centered individuals end up with fewer goodies than groups of less greedy, community-oriented individuals (Sheldon & McGregor, 2000).

Outside the lab, egoists are less willing to inconvenience themselves by cutting back on their driving or supporting a pro-environmental carpooling program (Cameron, Brown, & Chapman, 1998; Van Lange, Van Vugt, Meertens, & Ruiter, 1998).

Development of Prosocial and Egoistic Orientations Why do people differ in their orientations? Paul VanLange and his colleagues speculated that the differences are rooted in experiences of interdependence with others, beginning in childhood and further shaped by interactions during adulthood and old age (VanLange, Otten et al., 1997). The researchers examined these hypotheses in several ways. In one study, they asked 631 Dutch men and women about their families: how many brothers and sisters did they have, and what was their position in the family? Prosocial individuals (altruists and cooperators) had more siblings than egoists (individualists and competitors). In particular, prosocial individuals had more *older* siblings. VanLange and his colleagues reasoned that growing up in a home with several siblings required people to develop norms of sharing and that older siblings were better at modeling and enforcing those sharing rules. The researchers also found that prosocial individuals had more sisters than did egoists. Because sisters are somewhat more likely to adopt a prosocial orientation, having a sister means that you will see more cooperativeness and less competitiveness in your home as you are growing up.

Sisterhood and prosocial orientation. *Researchers in the Netherlands found that growing up in a home with several siblings was associated with a more cooperative orientation, particulary when those siblings were older sisters.*

The researchers also examined the relationship between prosocial orientation and attachment style (as discussed in chapter 8). They found that prosocially oriented people were more likely to have a secure attachment style in their romantic relationships. In other words, prosocials, compared with egoists, feel relatively less fear of abandonment in their relationships and are comfortable being close to others. Related research suggests that individual differences in trust are important in a social dilemma (VanLange & Semin-Goosens, 1998). In laboratory social dilemmas, people who generally trust others are more likely to cooperate with other group members (Parks, Henager, & Scamahorn, 1996; e.g., Yamagishi, 1988b).

Changing the Consequences of Short-Sighted Selfishness

What factors in the social situation can reverse people's tendency to go for quick self-gratification over long-term benefits to the group? Platt (1973) suggested that the timing of rewards and punishments for selfish versus group-oriented behaviors was crucial. Other research suggests that the activation of social norms may also play a key role.

Timing Rewards and Punishments As we discussed earlier, John Platt (1973) suggested several ways in which the timing of rewards and punishments is crucial to social traps. Capitalizing on those insights, he suggested several ways to use these same selfish reward-seeking tendencies to draw people out of social traps. Platt's solutions have enormous practical utility, as they suggest ways in which each of us can help. Let us consider several of them.

1. *Using alternative technologies to change long-term negative consequences.* When science writer Brad Lemly tested the new Honda Insight for the April 2000 issue of *Discover* magazine, he was amazed to find that a car with a tiny three-cylinder engine was peppy enough to negotiate speedy entries onto the freeway. One of a new generation of "hybrid" cars that combine lightness, sleekness, and a computerized electric engine that supplements the gas motor and recharges itself with the energy used in braking, Honda's new car gets over seventy miles to the gallon. By the year 2003, Honda promises to release a similar car that uses no gas at all, but runs off a hydrogen cell whose only emission will be water! By mid-year 2000, Toyota had already sold 30,000 hybrid vehicles in Japan, and American auto companies such as GM, Ford, and Chrysler were racing to develop even more efficient models.

Buying one of the new hyper-efficient cars is just one of the things you can do to enjoy the conveniences of modern life with less destructive impact on the environment. Solar panels, which extract free energy from the sun, likewise allow low-impact comfort seeking. Insulating one's home is another such solution. Although home insulation seems less futuristic than solar panels and electric cars, it's one of the most important changes people can make to cut down energy waste (Gardner & Stern, 1996). In fact, using solar panels, insulating, covering windows, and tuning furnaces could save more than 75 percent of the energy used to heat homes (Yates & Aronson, 1983). Technological changes are often quite effective because they can be done on a "one-shot" basis—buying an energy-efficient car, for example, will lead to energy conservation for years to come (Stern, 2000).

2. *Moving the future negative consequences into the present.* If you turn your air conditioner to a chilly 68 degrees during the first week in August, meanwhile leaving your back porch door open for the cat, you might not have to pay any consequences for your inefficient decisions until the second week in September, when the August electric bill arrives. Alternatively, a household thermostat could be fitted with a bright, digital printout that gave household members continual feedback in dollars and cents about how much energy they were using. In this way, keeping doors tightly closed and covering the windows during the day would have a visible and immediate rewarding effect—whereas turning the air conditioner on would have a visible and immediate punishing effect. Indeed, research supports Platt's suggestion that immediate feedback about energy consumption is an effective means to encourage conservation (Seligman, Becker, & Darley, 1981; Van Vugt & Samuelson, 1999).

Using new technology to save the environment. *New technologies, like this hybrid gas/electric car, can sometimes reduce the long-term negative consequences of previously damaging reward-seeking behaviors. One obstacle is that people must be convinced to adopt new technologies, many of which, like better home insulation and solar panels, are not as glamorous as sleek new cars.*

3. *Adding immediate punishments for undesirable behaviors.* If an individual gets a stiff fine for littering, or if a company is penalized for pollution, that takes away the immediate pleasure of environmentally destructive behaviors. Such an approach is consistent with Garrett Hardin's (1968) suggestion that global social dilemmas can be solved only if the citizens of the modern

world agree to live with "mutual coercion, mutually agreed upon" (1247). If punishments are large enough, and if people believe they will get caught, aversive consequences could work to decrease environmentally destructive behaviors (Yamagishi, 1988a; DiMento, 1989). On a broader level, environmental psychologists believe that dramatic benefits would follow from simply requiring industrial polluters to pay the costs of cleaning up their own toxic and harmful waste products instead of spewing them out into the air and water (Howard, 2000; Winter, 2000). As things are currently done, most polluting industries leave their mess for the public to clean up after it has already damaged the environment. Indeed, industries now pollute vastly more than all private citizens combined, and technologically developed countries like the United States are the worst offenders (Stern, 2000). On the other hand, in countries like Denmark, industrial leaders are discovering that, by emulating the recycling loops found throughout nature's ecosystems, they can dramatically reduce costs and consequently increase profits (Hawken et al., 1999).

4. *Reinforcing more desirable environmental alternatives.* Rewards for desirable behaviors work without triggering negative emotional reactions. Many North American cities now support recycling programs that allow people to conveniently place all their glass, plastic, and paper in bins outside their homes. And these programs work (McKenzie-Mohr, 2000). Easy recycling makes environmentally sound behaviors more rewarding, and thus helps boost recycling in more of the population (Howenstine, 1993; Vining & Ebreo, 1992). A similar approach is to offer rewards (such as lottery tickets) for using public transportation or for reducing energy use (Geller, 1992). Research suggests that such approaches, though sometimes expensive, can be successful (Gardner & Stern, 1996). Their costs can be reduced because people respond better to intermittent rewards, and it is neither necessary nor efficient to reward someone every time he or she acts for the collective good (Neidert & Linder, 1990).

Most of the social trap solutions suggested by Platt (1973), such as adding punishments or alternative rewards, were designed to work by triggering alternative selfish motivations in single individuals. Platt also suggested the use of social pressures. These socially based solutions often involve the activation of social norms about proper behavior (Kerr, 1995; Oskamp, 2000).

Activating Social Norms As we've noted, norms can be *descriptive* or *injunctive* (Kallgren, Reno, & Cialdini, 2000). A descriptive norm, as described in chapter 6, is simply what most people do in a given situation, with no necessary implication of right or wrong. For example, most students at Arizona State University wear running shoes at least once a week, and the majority of Mexican Americans living in New Mexico eat more spicy food than do the majority of Swedish Americans living in North Dakota. There would be nothing immoral about an ASU student who didn't wear running shoes, a Swede who ate spicy foods, or a Chicano who preferred unspiced mashed potatoes to salsa. On the other hand, an injunctive norm is a social expectation about what people *should* do in a particular situation. Throwing litter in a trash receptacle rather than out the car window is considered right and proper, regardless of how many other people do or don't behave that way. Both descriptive and injunctive norms influence people's inclinations to act unselfishly in social dilemmas.

Descriptive Norms—"Everybody's Doing It." Demonstrating the importance of descriptive norms, people adjust their own cooperativeness to match the rest of their group. For instance, students in one social dilemma study contributed more to the public good when a greater percentage of the rest of the group did so (Komorita, Parks, & Hulbert, 1992). Moreover, our beliefs about what others would do in the same situation influence our cooperativeness in social dilemmas. For example, economists, whose models of human behavior assume rampant individual selfishness, are substantially more selfish than other groups (Braver, 1995; Miller, 1999). If you expect

The norm of social responsibility. *One powerful injunctive norm in society specifies that individuals are responsible for helping solve the world's problems. Organizations such as Greenpeace and the Nature Conservancy try to appeal to that sense of social responsibility.*

that everyone else will do the selfish thing, it may make sense to act selfishly. On the other hand, when students in the Netherlands and the United States were led to expect that the other parties involved in a social dilemma were highly moral, they were more likely to cooperate (VanLange & Liebrand, 1991).

Injunctive Norms—"Doing the Right Thing." Several types of injunctive norms influence people to act more or less selfishly in social dilemmas. These include the norms of commitment, reciprocity, fairness, and social responsibility (Kerr, 1995; Lynn & Oldenquist, 1986; Stern, Dietz, & Kalof, 1993). According to the norm of commitment, if you have said you will do something, the proper thing to do is to carry through with it. Indeed, people do stick by their commitments to work for the group good, even when it turns out to be costly to them personally (e.g., Braver, 1995; Neidert & Linder, 1990).

In one study of the commitment process, students confronted a public goods dilemma. Each person in a group of five received $10 to start and could choose either to keep the $10 or to contribute it to the group pool. Contributing one's own money to the group pool increased the possibility that all players could win $15, but this choice also opened up two negative possibilities—losing $10 if not enough others cooperated and allowing other players to be "free-riders"—sharing in the benefits without contributing.

Half the students were allowed to communicate with one another before beginning the game. During most of those discussions, students joined as a group in expressing their commitment to contribute. When the researchers examined actual contributions, the results were clear—individual students in groups that spent more time discussing their mutual commitment followed through with the cooperative choice (Kerr & Kaufman-Gilliland, 1994).

If injunctive norms control greediness in social dilemmas, people ought to act more responsibly when they can be identified. Indeed, people cooperate more when they think that other group members will be able to observe their individual choices (Messick & Brewer, 1983; Neidert & Linder, 1990). These findings, based on studies of U.S. college students, suggest that even in an individualistic and capitalistic society, people are aware that "looking out for number one" is socially undesirable. There are, however, cultural differences: Americans are more likely to act selfishly than people raised in more communal cultures. For example, Craig Parks and Anh Vu (1994) compared the cooperativeness of Americans and South Vietnamese in social dilemmas. South Vietnam is a collectivist culture, in which people are more likely to define themselves in terms of their group memberships, whereas the United States, as discussed in earlier chapters, is a highly individualist culture. Consistent with these differences in cultural norms, Vietnamese made less selfish individual choices in the social dilemmas.

Different Strokes for Different Folks

In designing social interventions to prevent the environmental damages of wholesale selfishness, it is important to consider how different motivations inside individuals interact with different types of intervention policies. David Karp and Clark Gaulding (1995) divided environmental interventions into three categories, which they dubbed "command-and-control," "market-based," and "voluntarist."

Command-and-control policy *A prescriptive legal regulation that uses police power to punish violators.*

Command-and-control policies are prescriptive legal regulations that use police power to punish violators. Historically, this approach has been most common. The U.S. Environmental Protection Agency (EPA) frequently uses command-and-control approaches. For example, the Corporate Average Fuel Efficiency regulations threaten automobile manufacturers with fines if they don't produce enough fuel-

Table 13.2 Interaction between different environmental interventions and different motivations within individuals.

Type of Intervention	Motive Activated	Example
Command-and-Control	Fear	Penalties for automobile manufacturers who produce too many gas-guzzling cars. Loss of educational benefits for families having too many children (as in China).
Market-Based	Greed	Tax rebates for consumers who purchase solar heating panels. Payments for voluntary sterilization (as in India).
Voluntarist	Social Responsibility	Sierra Club's appeal to members to write to Congress in favor of a new wilderness area. Planned Parenthood's appeals for volunteers to work delivering birth control in poor countries.

efficient cars. As noted in Table 13.2, command-and-control policies appeal to fear motivations. **Market-based policies,** on the other hand, offer rewards to those who reduce their environmentally destructive behaviors. Examples are financial rebates for consumers who buy energy-efficient refrigerators or who install solar panels. Market-based approaches appeal to a different motive—greed (or "enlightened self-interest," to put it another way). Finally, **voluntarist policies** use neither threats nor economic rewards but rather appeal directly to people's intrinsic sense of social responsibility. In 1990, for example, William Reilly, a top administrator of the EPA, argued that "we must engage the heart, which is not reached by appeals to law or economics." As part of that effort to engage "heart-felt" environmentalism, he asked for voluntary commitments from U.S. companies to cut production of toxic compounds in half. Within three years, 1,135 companies responded to his appeal. Although the government is only recently beginning to appeal to social responsibility motives, many private environmental groups, such as the Sierra Club, Greenpeace, and the Nature Conservancy, have done so successfully for decades. It may bode well for the world's future that the membership in those organizations now numbers in the millions (Winter, 2000).

As Karp and Gaulding (1995) note, there are different societal implications of policies that appeal to these different motives. For instance, command-and-control policies are likely to elicit resistance. Automobile manufacturers, for example, have fought punitive regulations every step of the way. Fear-based policies won't work if the violators don't expect to get caught or if the punishment costs less than the benefits of noncompliance. Punitive policies also require a great deal of policing effort.

Market-based approaches (such as tax rebates for energy efficiency) have several advantages over command-and-control policies. Because they involve rewards, they don't trigger resistance, and don't require policing (people will readily identify themselves when they can get goodies for doing so). In dilemma games, rewards for cooperation work more effectively than punishments for selfishness (Komorita & Barth, 1985). The problem is that market-based strategies can be costly and, in cases such as the destruction of the rainforests, it may not be economically feasible for the government to pay enough to counterbalance the short-term financial benefits of the destructive behaviors (Rice, Gullison, & Reid, 1997).

Voluntarist approaches can capitalize on norms of environmental concern or social responsibility (Stern et al., 1993). They have several advantages—requiring no coercive governmental laws or costly administration and policing agencies. Voluntarism goes against the economic model of self-interest, but that model may paint an overly pessimistic picture of human nature (Miller, 1999). Research on social dilemmas demonstrates that people often do cooperate for reasons that aren't simply egoistic (Braver, 1995; Larrick & Blount, 1997). Michael Lynn and Andrew Oldenquist (1986) suggest several such motivations, including some we've already discussed: prosocial motivation, as when people send food to strangers starving somewhere

Market-based policy *An offer of rewards to those who reduce their socially harmful behaviors.*

Voluntarist policy *An appeal to people's intrinsic sense of social responsibility.*

Social responsibility appeals work better for some individuals than others. *Not everyone is willing to lay their time or money on the line in response to "volunteered" appeals from organizations such as Sierra Club or Greenpeace. Government programs are more likely to appeal to fear motivation, although recently, market-based appeals have been used to appeal to "enlightened self-interest" as a motivation.*

halfway around the world; group-egoistic motivation, as when people act to improve the community of which they are a part (Knowles, 1982; Kramer & Brewer, 1984); and moral motivation, as when people recycle because they think it's the "right thing to do," regardless of what others are doing (Dawes, 1980; Zuckerman & Reis, 1978).

Summary

Individual orientations toward social dilemmas can be divided into egoistic and prosocial approaches. Egoistic individuals are more likely to seek their own immediate reward over the group benefit. Compared to prosocial individuals, those having an egoistic orientation tend to have fewer siblings, particularly sisters. Situational triggers for self-centered versus group-centered behavior include the timing of rewards and punishments and the activation of descriptive and injunctive norms. Different interventions designed to reduce selfishness appeal to different motivations in people and will work better in some situations than in others. Coercive command-and-control policies appeal to fear motivations and work only among people who expect to be caught and punished. Market-based interventions use rewards to appeal to economic self-interest but may be expensive to administer and might ultimately undermine people's intrinsic motivation to act prosocially. Voluntarist interventions appeal to norms of social responsibility and will work better among prosocially oriented individuals.

Defending Ourselves and Valued Others

Thus far, we've been discussing how large-scale problems can flow from primitive urges to seek positive gratification. On the other side of the coin, serious social problems can also stem from a primitive motivation to avoid being exploited or harmed by members of outgroups.

Outgroup Bias and International Conflict

In 1913, an anthropologist described a curious custom he'd observed in the aboriginal tribes of Australia (Radcliffe-Brown, 1913). Before entering a camp, the anthropologist's native interpreter would stand on the outskirts until the village elders approached him. The elderly men would inquire about the interpreter's father's father and then discuss his genealogy for a few minutes. When they could find a common relative, he would enter. In one case, however, the interpreter could find absolutely no links. Frightened by this turn of events, he slept far outside the village that night. The interpreter explained that he was a Talainji and that these men, members of the Karieria tribe, were not his relatives. In this land, he explained to the puzzled anthropologist, "the other must be my relative or my enemy. If he is my enemy, I shall take the first opportunity of killing him, for fear he will kill me" (164).

Outgroup hatred and distrust. *Around the world, people tend to distrust other groups and regard them as inferior. These Arab protesters are defacing an American flag, which they regard as a symbol of evil. On the other side, many Americans regard Arabs and their culture as vastly inferior to that of the United States.*

Unfortunately, the tendency to favor the members of one's own group and dislike outsiders is universal (LeVine & Campbell, 1972). Indeed, anthropological evidence suggests that human groups have been fighting with one another since the dawn of history (Baer & McEachron, 1982). Chapter 11 considered how this outgroup bias creates local problems within modern society, such as the conflicts between civil rights workers and Klan members in North Carolina. When the outgroup is made up of people from a foreign country competing with our own, it can seem especially alien and threatening. During the Cold War, for instance, President Ronald Reagan once referred to the Soviet Union as an "Evil Empire," and his predecessor Richard Nixon said that it helped to clarify the world struggle to think of Russia as evil, darkness, and the devil. Conversely, Soviets at the time viewed Americans as evil and greedy imperialists who used their power to prop up dictators around the world.

All the factors discussed in chapter 11 concerning prejudice against other racial and ethnic groups apply to international outgroups as well. Different countries, for example, are often in conflict over real benefits, including territory and natural resources, and disdain of foreigners may be one way to raise group self-esteem. In this section, we will explore the larger political arena, but remain grounded in psychological processes, examining specifically how factors in the person and situation trigger the motivation to defend ourselves and those we value.

Some of Us Are More Defensive Than Others

What factors inside the person might lead to a tendency to be alert to threats from an international outgroup? This question is important for two reasons. Knowing which individuals are especially sensitive to such threats could help individual leaders deal with each other and perhaps help them tailor negotiation tactics to avoid triggering dangerous feelings of outgroup hostility. Second, examining such individual differences might help us understand decision making by both powerful citizens and the less powerful people who indirectly affect international policy through "public opinion."

Gender and social dominance orientation. *Men across groups tend to score higher in the motivation for social dominance. This man's t-shirt suggests that he believes that his groups—Christians, Americans, heterosexuals, gun owners, and conservatives—are superior to the alternatives.*

Social Dominance Orientation In chapter 11, we discussed the relationship between social dominance orientation and intergroup prejudice. Social dominance orientation refers to the desire that one's ingroup dominate other groups (Sidanius, Levin, Liu, & Pratto, 2000). In addition to its links to intergroup prejudice within a society, social dominance orientation is also tied to attitudes about military strength and international conflict (Nelson & Milburn, 1999).

People who score high on social dominance orientation tend to favor increased military spending and more aggressive approaches to international conflict. In 1990, Iraq's leader, Saddam Hussein, invaded neighboring Kuwait. The United States led a massive military counterattack in which tens of thousands of Iraqis were killed. During the conflict, Felicia Pratto and her colleagues (1994) measured Stanford undergraduates' social dominance orientation and asked the students how they thought Iraq should be handled. Compared to those having low scores, students high in social dominance orientation said they were more willing to sacrifice personally for the war, and favored more military force and restriction of civil liberties (such as freedom of the press) for the war effort.

Gender Differences in Ethnocentrism and Militarism Would there be fewer international conflicts if more women were world leaders? Some research suggests that the answer might be yes. The researchers who developed the social dominance scale have found that it is centrally linked to a person's gender (Sidanius et al., 2000). In a wide range of countries, including Sweden, India, England, and the United States, men are more militaristic, politically conservative, ethnocentric, and punitive than are women (Sidanius et al., 1994).

In one study, Jim Sidanius, Felicia Pratto, and Lawrence Bobo (1994) surveyed a random sample of 1,897 men and women from Los Angeles about their social dominance orientation. Because Los Angeles is a very culturally diverse city, the sample included people of different ethnicities, religions, and places of origin. The researchers found that men were more dominance-oriented than women across all of the social groupings they investigated. Whether young or old; rich or poor; well educated or poorly educated; Republican or Democrat; Asian, European, or Latino, men tended to have higher social dominance scores. The difference between men and women wasn't large and was sometimes smaller than the differences across groups. For example, Republican women had higher social dominance scores than did Democratic men. Nevertheless, within any group, men reliably tended to score higher in social dominance orientation. And a larger sample of 7,000 respondents from 6 different countries corroborated the sex differences (Sidanius et al., 2000).

What accounts for this gender difference in social dominance orientation? Sidanius and Pratto think neither biological nor sociocultural factors tell the whole story. They instead favor a *biocultural interactionist* position. Pratto (1996) observes that the distinction between natural and cultural factors is a false dichotomy because humans evolved to live in social groups in the first place. According to their biocultural perspective, men in all human cultures have tended to gravitate to positions involving "ranking" (such as chiefs, lords, and in modern times, government officials) and competition with outgroups (warriors, or in modern times, soldiers).

The researchers believe that this difference in social dominance orientation is cross-culturally universal because in all ancestral societies, there was a correlation between a man's social status and his reproductive success. They base this argument on the theory of sexual selection, which, as discussed in chapters 8 and 10, is itself based on findings from a wide range of species. If the members of one sex have characteristics that help them compete with the members of their own sex, or to win the affections of the opposite sex, those characteristics will increase over generations. Modern biological theorists believe that *female choice* is most often the central force in sexual selection. Because females are often more selective in choosing mates, males must compete amongst themselves for females' attentions. In human

Gender-typed cultural roles. *Across cultures, men are likely to choose roles emphasizing social dominance, such as military and warrior roles. According to the biocultural interactionist theory, ancient inclinations interact with the roles and norms created by current societies (which are themselves built around those ancient inclinations).*

groups throughout history, men who were successful as warriors, protecting the group against opposing groups, reaped direct and indirect rewards.

Sidanius and Pratto's biocultural interactionist theory of social dominance doesn't stop with biological differences in sexual selection and assume that it is "all in our genes." Instead, they note how males' competitive tendencies influence their choice of occupations and political groups. For instance, 84 percent of police officers are men, as are 86 percent of people in the military. At the highest levels of such occupations, the sex differences are even greater—98 percent of the highest ranking people in the U.S. Department of Defense are men. This is partly because of the choices made by men and women, and partly because of the aspects of the culture that encourage the existing sex differences. In most countries, women still aren't permitted in the military and female police officers are rare (Pratto, Stallworth, Sidanius, & Siers, 1997).

Authoritarianism and Sense of Threat As discussed in chapter 11, authoritarianism reflects the tendency to respect power, obey authority, and rigidly cohere to society's conventions (Adorno et al., 1950; Altmeyer, 1981; Feather, 1998). Authoritarians, compared to their nonauthoritarian counterparts, are likely to favor a "Rambo-like crusade" against drug pushers and a national quarantine for people with AIDS and to be unfavorable toward protection of the environment (Peterson, Doty, & Winter, 1993). In the international arena, authoritarians are generally more favorable toward a strong military and more hostile toward foreigners (Doty, Peterson, & Winter, 1991; Tibon & Blumberg, 1999). Students scoring high in authoritarianism wanted more use of force against Iraq during the war in the Persian Gulf, even to the point of using nuclear weapons. And afterwards, they expressed less regret about the deaths of Iraqi civilians and more gloating over the U.S. victory (Doty et al., 1997).

Timothy McVeigh, the man convicted of killing 168 people in the 1995 bombing of the federal building in Oklahoma City, demonstrated a number of features of the authoritarian personality. He was reportedly strongly racist and suspicious of a "New World Order" undermining the U.S. government, and he reputedly believed that the bombing was morally justified as a retaliation for offenses by the federal government. He quit the National Rifle Association because he thought them "too soft," and his favorite piece of literature was a racist and anti-Semitic book popular among the far right (Morganthau & Annin, 1997). McVeigh's profile fits with findings of a study by Marina Abalakina-Paap and her colleagues Walter Stephan, Traci Craig, and Larry Gregory (1999). These researchers studied the distinctive characteristics of people who accept conspiracy theories. The typical believer in conspiracy theories tends to be high in authoritarianism and in feelings of alienation, powerlessness, and hostility.

Other studies corroborate that authoritarians are especially prone to feeling threatened (Lambert, Burroughs, & Nguyen, 1999; Lavine et al., 1999). Consequently, they tend to be low in openness to new experiences, and to strike observers as defensive and prejudiced (Butler, 2000; Lippa & Arad, 1999; Saucier, 2000).

Although social dominance orientation and authoritarianism overlap to some extent, an important distinction is that authoritarianism is believed to be based on personal threat, whereas the male tendency to be more inclined toward social dominance is believed to be somewhat universal and not as directly linked to unpleasant personal experiences (Sidanius et al., 1994). Social dominance orientation also lacks the moralistic components of authoritarianism (Whitley, 1999). In the section on situational triggers of defensiveness, we will consider evidence that authoritarian tendencies in general become more pronounced in individuals and in societies when people feel threatened.

Simplified Images of International Conflict Political psychologist Philip Tetlock (1983) examined the speeches made by policymakers involved in international conflicts. He noted that, in making important decisions, national leaders often fall back on overly simplified images of the world. During the Cold War relationship between the United States and the Soviet Union, for example, two very simple images of the conflict were dominant. One of these was the **deterrence view**—that any sign of weakness would be exploited by the opponent and that leaders needed to show their willingness to use military force, even to the point of the "mutually assured destruction" that would follow a nuclear war. From a deterrence perspective, some demonstration of aggressiveness is often necessary as a preventive measure to stop the other side from aggressing against one's group. The other prominent view was a **conflict spiral view,** which presumed that every escalation of international threat leads the opponent to feel more threatened, and that leaders need to demonstrate peaceful intentions in order to reduce the opponent's own defensive hostilities. Research involving common citizens has found that people who hold a deterrence view—that demonstrations of weakness would be exploited—are less likely to support nuclear disarmament (Chibnall & Wiener, 1988).

Tetlock (1983) noted that each of these cognitive frames was correct in some circumstances and incorrect in others. Against an opponent such as Hitler, a deterrence viewpoint might have been more effective than a view that led to conciliation. With regard to the Cold War between the United States and the Soviet Union, Soviet premier Gorbachev's attempts to thaw out relations were probably tied to a conflict spiral view. As we will discuss in more detail below, Gorbachev used a technique designed to defuse conflict spirals by challenging the opponent to match increasingly bolder acts of disarmament.

Deterrence view *The belief that signs of weakness will be exploited by the opponent and that leaders need to show their willingness to use military force.*

Conflict spiral view *The belief that escalations of international threat lead an opponent to feel more threatened and that leaders should thus demonstrate peaceful intentions to reduce the opponent's own defensive hostilities.*

Competition and Threat

During the first half of the twentieth century, the citizens of Italy, Germany, France, and England were twice embroiled in massive world wars that killed millions. As the twenty-first century dawns, those same nations not only have stopped threatening one another but are now joined in a cooperative union. A passport from Italy is now interchangeable with a passport from France, Great Britain, Holland, Belgium, Luxembourg, Denmark, Ireland, Spain, Portugal, Finland, Sweden, and Austria (all the countries that have combined into the new European Community). How did mutual cooperation replace mutual threat and hostility? Examining the situational factors that trigger the motivation to protect one's ingroup may provide part of the answer.

In this section, we consider two related factors linked to escalations and de-escalations in outgroup hostility—competition over resources and threat. We discussed how these factors relate to intergroup prejudice in chapter 11 and now consider how they extend beyond local prejudices to international conflicts.

Group Competition Over Resources At the chapter's opening, we discussed the bloody conflict between Bengali immigrants and the natives of Assam, India. This incident was linked to competition over scarce resources—fertile land in areas of rapid population growth. It demonstrates how realistic group conflict theory can be directly applied to international relations.

Although international conflicts sometimes trace directly to realistic conflict, the economic motivations aren't always explicitly recognized by the participants. Instead, competition may simply lead people to alter their perception of the members of the other group and to lower their threshold for becoming annoyed with the others (Kemmelmeier & Winter, 2000). As we discussed in chapter 11, the boys in the Rattlers and the Eagles at the Robbers Cave summer camp came to perceive outgroup members more negatively after competing for scarce rewards. But the former enemies shifted to a more positive view after the groups joined together to work toward common goals (Sherif, Harvey, White, Hood, & Sherif, 1961).

At the population level, militaristic and punitive authoritarian tendencies tend to increase when the economy turns down and people face unemployment and hunger (McCann, 1999). Sales (1973), for example, found higher ethnocentrism, patriotism, and punitive aggressiveness (as judged by increasing budgets for police and harsher punishments for crimes) during the Great Depression of the 1930s as compared to the preceding economic boom of the "Roaring 20s." Another study compared the period of 1978 through 1982 (a time of increasing unemployment, rising interest rates, and economic dissatisfaction) with the period 1983 through 1987 (a time of increasing personal income, decreasing interest rates, and economic hopefulness). This study revealed higher levels of racial prejudice and some signs of a heightened emphasis on power and toughness (such as more registrations for attack dogs) during the economic hard times (Doty et al., 1991). Historically, the clearest example of increased authoritarianism following economic hard times was the rise of Nazism in Germany after the terrible depression and international humiliation Germans suffered following their loss in World War I. During such difficult times, Hitler's plans to expand German territory and simultaneously restore international respect for Germany fell on receptive ears amongst the German populace.

A number of researchers have found that simply placing people into groups increases competitiveness, even though that competition may result in losses for all concerned (e.g., Bornstein & Ben-Yossef, 1994; Insko et al., 1994; Schopler et al., 1995). For example, subjects in one experiment played a social dilemma game in which they could choose between cooperation and competition. To make it a dilemma, the game was arranged so that cooperation led to the best outcomes, but only if both sides agreed to cooperate. If one side chose to cooperate while the other chose to compete, the cooperator would take a large loss and the competitor a large win. Finally, if both chose to compete, neither would do as well as if both cooperated (Insko, Schopler, Hoyle, Dardis, & Graetz, 1990). Over a series of ten trials, individuals playing against other individuals fared well, making predominantly cooperative choices. Groups playing against groups, on the other hand, lost out because they were too competitive.

Economic threat and authoritarianism. *Hitler and the Nazi Party rose to power at a time when Germans had suffered intense economic depression and international humiliation after the loss of World War I.*

Students in another study recorded their daily interactions and categorized them as either group or individual activities. More of the interactions involving groups were competitive, particularly when males were involved (Pemberton, Insko, & Schopler, 1996) (see Figure 13.6). Other research supports this general pattern; people in groups are more likely to respond to annoyances by escalating from mild complaints through threats and physical harassment (Mikolic, Parker, & Pruitt, 1997).

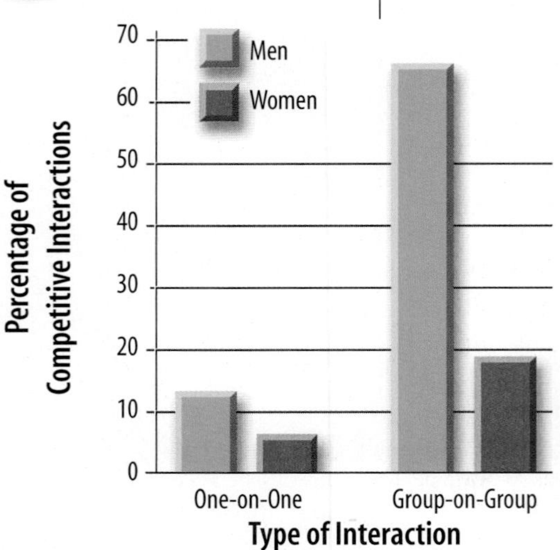

Figure 13.6
Group competitiveness in everyday life.

Michael Pemberton, Chester Insko, and John Schopler asked students to record and categorize their daily interactions. Students recorded more competitive interactions involving groups than during one-on-one meetings with others. The pattern held for both sexes, but women were less likely to have competitive interactions, even in groups, whereas men in groups had predominantly competitive interactions.

Why are group interactions more competitive? Part of the problem, according to Insko and his colleagues, is that individuals, assuming that large groups bring out the worst in people, simply expect the members of the *other* group to act more competitively, which leads both sides to act competitively in a self-perpetuating cycle. When the researchers analyzed the content of discussions between group members, they found a positive relationship between competitiveness and distrust of the other side's intentions (Pemberton et al., 1996).

How can groups move from distrust to trust? For one thing, individual experiences that encourage two groups to cooperate with each other can reduce outgroup biases (Gaertner, Mann, Dovidio, Murrell, & Pomare, 1990; Thompson, 1993). If an individual in Group A is given the chance to negotiate one-to-one with an individual in Group B, and they manage to come to a satisfactory settlement, both individuals walk away with more positive opinions of the other group as a whole (Thompson, 1993). These positive one-on-one experiences teach group members that the individuals on the other side have motivations similar to those of the individuals on "our side." Simply reminding people that their two groups are interconnected in some way can also reduce the "us versus them" mentality (Kramer & Brewer, 1984). When the members of the United States Olympic team play against other countries, for example, they forget the former rivalries between their "home teams" in Michigan, Nebraska, and California.

Herbert Kelman and his associates have directly applied many of the social psychological findings on intergroup competition and cooperation to international conflict resolution (Kelman, 1998, 1999; Rouhana & Kelman, 1994). During official negotiations, both sides often face pressures that enhance competition. These include the need to bargain for terms that benefit one's own side, to satisfy sometimes angry constituencies who will read about the negotiations in the newspapers, and so on. Over the last few years, Kelman has brought together groups of influential Israelis and Palestinians for noncompetitive, interactive problem-solving workshops. These workshops involve political leaders, parliament members, influential journalists, former military officers, and government officials from the two sides. Participants get together not to negotiate, but simply to familiarize one another with the viewpoints of the other side and to brainstorm potential solutions that could later be brought to official negotiations. In these noncompetitive group settings, participants develop more complex images of the other side. This helps them overcome their prejudicial oversimplifications. The nonhostile norms of the group settings also promote new ideas for solutions. And the participants form new coalitions that cut across the lines of conflict (Kelman, 1998).

Participants in these interactive problem-solving workshops have gone on to become members of actual negotiating teams, such as the group that developed the 1993 "Oslo agreement" (a major step forward after years of total stagnation in Israel–Palestine relations). Thus, the insights of social psychological research may have the potential for the most useful of applications—promoting international harmony.

Besides reducing international aggression, cooperation between nations may, over the long haul of history, have other positive consequences. We consider these as we examine the effects of Japan's historical fluctuations between international withdrawal and openness.

FOCUS ON Method

Time-Series Analysis and International Cooperation

As social psychologists have begun to explore the political realm, they have had to grapple with interesting problems in isolating cause-and-effect relationships from uncontrolled historical data. Researchers can't conduct retrospective experiments—to discover what would have happened if Britain had attacked Germany first instead of trying to appease Hitler, for example. Single incidents in history have all the causal ambiguities of case studies, which we discussed in chapter 1. As we noted there, case studies are open to numerous interpretations because there are so many factors leading up to any particular event. Historians, however, are fond of saying that "history repeats itself." When similar events occur again and again in history, a careful search can uncover recurrent patterns among the circumstances leading up to, or following from, those events. In examining those events over time, researchers can take advantage of a method called time-series analysis.

Time-series analysis is, quite simply, a method in which two or more recurring events are examined for linkages over time—a search for history repeating itself. For example, we know that downturns in the economy are often linked with increases in racial violence (Hepworth & West, 1988). If economic hard times are causing the racial violence, we ought to find that racial violence follows economic downturns. But if racial violence precedes economic downturns as frequently as it follows them, then it seems unlikely that the economic downturns are causing the violence.

Dean Keith Simonton (1997) was interested in the cultural consequences of national **xenophobia** (fear and distrust of foreigners) versus openness to foreign influence. To study this issue, he examined the history of creative accomplishments in Japan. Japan is a homogeneous nation that, until World War II, had not been occupied by outsiders for over 1,000 years. Over the centuries, Japanese openness to outsiders has varied quite a bit. At some times, the exchange of ideas and goods with the outside has been openly encouraged; at other times, Japanese citizens have faced the death penalty for exposing themselves to foreign influence. Simonton noted that xenophobic tendencies are often driven by a feeling that a country's well-being is threatened by an intrusion of alien ideas on traditional ideas and social norms.

Using a time-series analysis, Simonton asked the question: Has the influx of foreign ideas and people had a positive or negative effect on the national achievements of Japan? Simonton looked for historical fluctuations in achievements in art, medicine, business, politics, and military affairs during the period from 580 to 1939. He examined whether those achievements had been reliably preceded by changes in openness to foreign influence (as measured by such variables as Japanese travel abroad or foreign teachers visiting Japan).

To address these questions, Simonton divided the years between 580 and 1939 into sixty-eight consecutive twenty-year generations. Thus the years 1880 through 1899 would constitute one generation. He then looked at the number of important historical achievements by prominent politicians, artists, entrepreneurs, and military figures during each generation, asking whether those achievements were linked to national openness in other generations. If the country was open to foreign influence during the 1860s and 1870s, for example, did that lead to more, or less, national achievement during the 1880s and 1890s?

Simonton found that openness to foreign influence was related to increased Japanese achievements in a number of domains. Figure 13.7 shows some of his results for the artistic domain. There was a time lag in the beneficial effects of openness to foreign influence on achievements in the creative arts. That is, the positive effects of outside influence took two generations to show up. A similar time-lagged effect was found for achievements in medicine. In the business domain, on the other hand, the beneficial effects went the other way—if Japanese business leaders accomplished a lot in a particular generation, that tended to lead to greater Japanese openness to foreign influence during the generation that *followed* the achievements.

Why would cultural openness have positive effects on national artistic creativity? Simonton (1997) suggests that, because creative accomplishments often involve the fusion of different ways of thinking, creative insights of other cultures provide novel elements to be mixed with the existing ideas in one's own culture. Furthermore, people exposed to a wide range of perspectives are better able to throw off the

Time-series analysis *A method in which two or more recurring events are examined for linkages over time.*

Xenophobia *Fear and distrust of foreigners.*

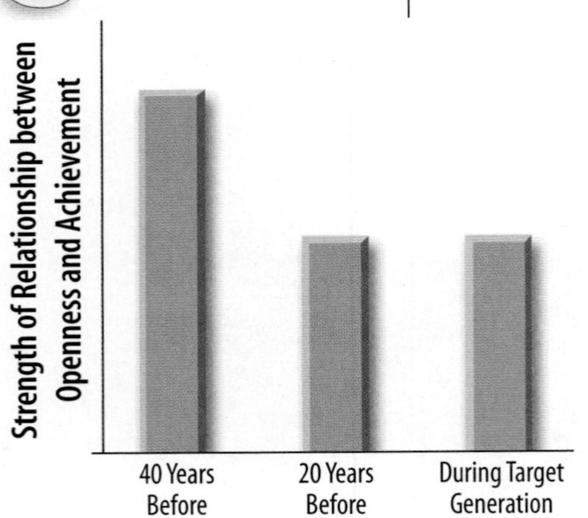

Figure 13.7
Japanese artistic achievements and openness to outside influences.

Using a time-series analysis, Dean Keith Simonton discovered that Japanese artistic accomplishments were most strongly related to Japan's openness to influence forty years before. In other words, there is a time lag in the effect of foreign influence. This effect would have been invisible without a more complex time-sensitive analysis.

usual restrictions on their own creative imagination (Simonton, 1994, 1997). As Simonton (1997) notes, the time-series data from Japan are consistent with less rigorous historical observations, such as the fact that the Golden Age of Greece came after the Greeks absorbed the rich cultural heritages of Persia, Egypt, and Mesopotamia.

Simonton's (1997) time-series analyses of Japanese national achievement illustrate how rigorous research methods can supplement the qualitative understanding of history. Moreover, his results suggest an additional reason for international cooperation—openness to other cultures can fuel the achievements of one's own culture. ■

Threats During the Cold War, the United States and the Soviet Union amassed over 40,000 weapons, any one of which was capable of destroying a city the size of New York or Moscow. Leaders at the time used the term "mutually assured destruction"—the certainty of everyone being destroyed presumably created the ultimate deterrence force. Indian prime minister Behari Vajpayee apparently believed that nuclear weapons could prevent wars between India and its neighbors. In response to world outrage over India's renewed underground nuclear tests in May 1998, he claimed that the weapons had been developed solely to promote peaceful coexistence and not to attack Pakistan. Unfortunately, Pakistan took it as a threat and exploded its own nuclear weapons as a counter-threat. After the fact, we can never know whether the huge stockpile of nuclear weapons prevented the United States from attacking the Soviet Union, or vice versa. But research suggests, in general, that threats tend to increase rather than decrease conflict.

For several decades, Morton Deutsch and his colleagues have studied the effects of threats on cooperation and conflict in laboratory simulations (Deutsch, 1986; Deutsch & Krauss, 1960). In one classic study, students played the "Acme Trucking Game," in which the goal was to win points by making as many truck deliveries as possible (Deutsch & Krauss, 1960). In the game, player A has two possible routes to take—a long circuitous route that only A controls or a shorter route shared with player B. Using the quicker route requires A and B to take turns. In one variation of the game, called "unilateral threat," one of the players has the means to threaten the opponent—a gate can be shut down to prevent the opponent from using the faster route. In another variation, both players have a gate. And in a final variation, neither player has a gate to use as a threat. Players won the most points when neither one had the potential for threatening the other. Under these circumstances, they most often took turns using the common road. Under conditions of mutual threat, players often got involved in aggressive and counteraggressive use of the gate and spent most of the game unable to use the most efficient route.

In a more complex dilemma-type game, subjects were told by the experimenter:

> There are two of you who are going to play a game in which you can either win money or lose money. I want you to earn as much money as you can regardless of how much the other earns. This money is real and you will keep whatever you earn. (Deutsch, 1986, 164)

The game consisted of a series of trials. Players picked one of several plays on any trial, ranging from cooperation to attack or defense.

Unbeknownst to the real subjects, their opponents were actually confederates of the experimenter. Deutsch's experimental confederates tried out several different strategies for inducing cooperation from a partner. One of these was a *punitive deterrent* strategy in which the accomplice used the cooperative reward strategy on the first trial, and responded with an attack if the real player did not cooperate. Another strategy was the *nonpunitive deterrent* strategy. In this case, the accomplice responded to an attack with a defense, and otherwise cooperated. Finally, some accomplices used a *turn the other cheek* strategy. In this case, the accomplice started out playing cooperatively and kept cooperating. If attacked by the opponent, he would get even more cooperative.

Figure 13.8 shows the results from this experiment (Deutsch, 1986). Note that the most successful strategy was the nonpunitive deterrence approach. The least successful was the totally cooperative turning of the other cheek. The punitive deterrence strategy started out somewhat successfully but dropped in effectiveness as it made the opponent increasingly angry and elicited counterattacks.

Deutsch argued that the principles of conflict and cooperation found in these laboratory dilemmas apply to interactions between nations. When one nation uses coercive pressure on another, as when the United States escalated the war in Vietnam with antipersonnel bombs and defoliation, it tends to elicit anger and counterattacks from the opponent. When one nation consistently "turns its other cheek" to another nation's aggressions, as when the Allies "appeased" Hitler when he first began invading his neighbors, it is likely to lead to exploitation. The best approach for a country is generally to choose cooperation unless it is attacked.

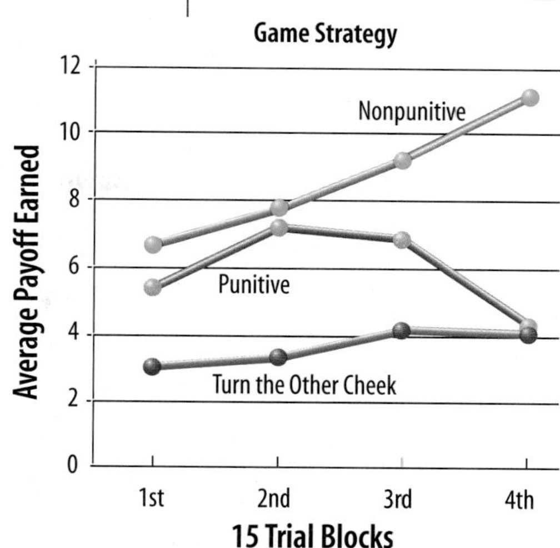

Figure 13.8
Winning and losing strategies.

In Morton Deutsch's laboratory dilemma game, confederates of an experimenter played one of three strategies against subjects in a laboratory dilemma. A punitive deterrent strategy was less effective over time, often eliciting angry retaliations. A strategy of turning the other cheek was consistently exploited by opponents. A nonpunitive deterrent strategy won the most points over the course of the game.

SOURCE: *Deutsch, 1986.*

Another fascinating series of investigations at the interface of psychology and political science examined how international threat affects decision-making in national leaders and their political constituencies (e.g., Mandel, Axelrod, & Lehman, 1993; Satterfield, 1998; Tibon, 2000). In one study, Canadian psychologists Peter Suedfeld, Michael Wallace, and Kimberly Thachuk (1993) analyzed over 1,200 statements made by national leaders before, during, and after the Persian Gulf crisis of 1991. Suedfeld and his colleagues examined the "integrative complexity" of leaders' public statements. **Integrative complexity** is the extent to which the leaders' statements demonstrate simplified "black-and-white," categorical thinking as opposed to acknowledgment of all sides of a conflict. A simple statement, for example, might state repeatedly that Iraq acted in an evil way and describe the evils of Iraq's leader, Saddam Hussein. A complex statement might express disapproval of Iraq while discussing the different historical facets of the conflict, including Kuwait's refusal to negotiate with Iraq about a secure Persian Gulf outlet and Kuwait's violation of OPEC price-control agreements. The researchers found that leaders of the nations most directly involved in the conflict (such as U.S. President Bush and Iraqi President Saddam Hussein) made less complex statements than those who were less involved. Furthermore, the statements got simpler and simpler as the stressfulness of the situation increased.

According to Suedfeld and his colleagues, cognitive complexity goes down during international crises because anxiety strains cognitive resources. Under stress, leaders rely on heuristics rather than systematic and complex decision making (see chapter 3). That's not always bad; the right heuristic may lead to a quick and correct decision. But the simplified thinking of leaders under stress can be disastrous if it leads them to ignore crucial information about their opponents or to stick rigidly to a failing plan. Leaders under stress also take more black-and-white moral positions. This is sometimes appropriate, but in other cases, simplified moralistic thinking interferes with the flexibility that may be needed to deal with a quickly changing crisis situation (Suedfeld & Tetlock, 1991).

The problems of simplified thinking are further exaggerated when members of different nations don't even understand their opponents' view of the world.

Integrative complexity *The extent to which a person demonstrates simplified "black-and-white," categorical thinking as opposed to acknowledgment of all sides of an issue.*

Intercultural Misperception and International Conflict

Just days before George Bush unleashed the force of more than 500,000 troops and a massive technological attack on Iraq, a news correspondent had this to say:

> Five months ago George Bush refused to believe that Saddam would carry out his threats against Kuwait. But the threats turned out to be true, and the Iraqi dictator marched in his troops almost unopposed. Today Saddam hesitates to believe that Bush will carry out his promise to use force against him. (McDaniel & Thomas, 1991)

According to social psychologist Paul Kimmel (1997), George Bush and Saddam Hussein both misunderstood the threats made by the other side because of gaps in intercultural communication. Before Saddam Hussein invaded Kuwait, he had met with U.S. ambassador April Glaspie and indicated his intentions. Based on his interactions with the U.S. ambassador, he believed that Washington wouldn't get involved if he invaded. Later, he apparently didn't believe that the United States would lead a counterattack but instead interpreted the military preparations as a bluff.

These misunderstandings were costly ones, eventually leading to the deaths of thousands of Iraqis and hundreds of Americans. What could have caused such miscommunication? Part of the problem is that communications between Westerners and Arabs are often confusing for both sides. According to one Western diplomat stationed in the region at the time of the war, "In the Middle East everyone lies. If you tell the truth you are considered hopelessly naive and even dangerous because people find the truth the most difficult of options to understand" (Lane, 1991, 18).

When U.S. troops were dispatched to Saudi Arabia, they were given a training booklet to help them avoid insulting local Arabs. It included the advice that "It is natural for an Arab to speak with double meanings—and the American who fails to watch for these can make foolish mistakes" (Dickey, 1991, 27).

Arabs themselves apparently experience frequent difficulties with communications from the other side. Hussein's negotiators reported feeling that U.S. leaders were insulting them rather than negotiating sincerely. After those negotiators refused even to accept a letter from Bush to Hussein, which they said contained

Saddam Hussein. *The Iraqi leader who led the invasion of Kuwait in 1990 and elicited a costly counterattack by the United Nations. An analysis of statements made by leaders, including Saddam Hussein and U.S. president George Bush, revealed more simplified thinking at times of intense conflict. Peter Suedfeld and his colleagues (1993) suggest that anxiety puts a strain on cognitive resources and leads to simplified, heuristic thinking.*

"language that is not compatible with language between heads of state," one Iraqi negotiator said, "I never thought that you Americans could be so arrogant. Such a free and open country you have and still you refuse to see our viewpoint" (quoted in Kimmel, 1997, 408).

Based on his own work with international negotiators, Kimmel (1997) recommends that they include a period of "intercultural exploration" in their negotiations. Intercultural exploration involves identifying each side's cultural assumptions and communicating them clearly before moving on to collaborate in finding a solution. He notes, for instance, several basic differences between the assumptions of American and Iraqi negotiators. Americans were task oriented, impersonal, definite in their demands, and fast paced. Iraqis, on the other hand, prefer slower-paced, personal negotiations in which the two groups get to know one another. Another important difference is that Americans tend to focus on the future, whereas Arabs have a much stronger sense that the past should be considered. An Egyptian diplomat observed, "You have to remember you're in a region where people talk about the Crusades as if they were yesterday" (quoted in McGrath, 1991, 24).

Kimmel distinguishes several levels of cultural awareness, ranging from

- *Cultural chauvinism:* A complete unawareness of other cultures, which leads negotiators to attribute ignorance and bad intentions to the other side.
- *Ethnocentrism:* An awareness of ethnic, religious, racial, or national differences, accompanied by a conviction that one's own way is the "right" one.
- *Tolerance:* Awareness of, and appreciation of, differences, but still accompanied by a feeling that one's own culture is more effective and realistic. Leads negotiators to try to "educate" or "develop" those who differ.
- *Minimization:* Awareness of cultural differences, but a focus on the many similarities across human cultures, which could lead to ignoring important differences at critical points in negotiation.
- *Understanding:* Realization that one's own way of doing things is only one of many, and that others are not abnormal in any way.

Kimmel notes that most negotiators have a hard time operating consistently at the level of "understanding." This is partly because negotiators prefer the familiar norms of their own group and partly because the constituents back home may not trust them if they seem too chummy with the other side. Nevertheless, negotiations based on an awareness of the important differences in cultural assumptions are bound to go more smoothly.

One of the key goals of intercultural awareness on the part of international negotiators, according to Kimmel (1997), is to move from a focus on "us" versus "them" to "we." When two groups focus on their shared goals, deception and threats become less necessary.

The Reciprocal Dynamics of Cooperation and Conflict

Negotiation dilemmas involve dynamic interactions—complex interconnected patterns of change over time. Looking back at Figure 13.7, we can see the effects of a punitive strategy getting worse over time, whereas the effects of a nonpunitive deterrence strategy tended to improve (Deutsch, 1986). Opponents in laboratory dilemmas often "lock in" on either a cooperative or a competitive pattern (Rapoport, Diekmann, & Franzen, 1995). Let's consider three areas of research on such dynamic interactions: tit-for-tat strategies, dollar games, and perceptual dilemmas.

Tit-for-tat strategy *A negotiating tactic in which the individual responds to competitiveness with competitiveness and to cooperation with cooperation.*

Tit-for-Tat Strategies The most "stable" strategy in reciprocal negotiations over time is called a **tit-for-tat strategy** (Axelrod, 1984; Komorita, Hilty, & Parks, 1991). A player using the tit-for-tat strategy responds cooperatively when the opponent is cooperative. When the opponent is competitive, the player responds competitively and then switches back to a cooperative strategy to "bait" the opponent back to the mutually beneficial cooperative pattern. According to social psychologist Samuel Komorita and his colleagues (1991), the tit-for-tat strategy works by doubly relying on the powerful norm of reciprocity (discussed in detail in chapter 9). It reciprocates cooperation with cooperation and returns competition for competition. It thus combines the "you scratch my back, I'll scratch yours" reciprocation with "an eye for an eye" retaliation. Indeed, experience playing against someone who uses a tit-for-tat strategy can even lead intrinsically competitive people to get the message, and begin cooperating (Sheldon, 1999).

The Dollar Game The nuclear arms race between the United States and the Soviet Union also showed characteristics of a reciprocal social dilemma, and in fact illustrated a special type of social trap. The entrapping quality of this type of competitive escalation is shown nicely in a dilemma called the "dollar game" (Teger, 1980).

Could you imagine otherwise intelligent college students bidding several dollars to win a $1 prize? Each of the authors of this textbook has played the game in class and watched it happen again and again. The game begins by offering a dollar to the highest bidder. The game initially appeals to greed—if the highest bid is 4 cents, then the dollar would go for 4 cents, and the bidder would gain 96 cents. However, other students who see one of their number about to get a dollar practically for free join the fray with higher bids. The feature of the game that makes it a social trap is this: the second-highest bidder must also pay up. Thus if one student bids 4 cents, and another bids a dime, the top bidder wins 90 cents, but the second bidder loses 4 cents. Because of this feature, no one wants to come in second, so it may actually become profitable to bid over a dollar if you have made the second-highest bid (of say 90 cents) and your opponent bids the full dollar. As the game progresses, the initial greed motivation is replaced with increasing fear of loss. In classes, we have often watched students get caught up in the action and once saw the bidding go over $20. Those same excessive bids have repeatedly been found in laboratory subjects playing the game in smaller groups (Teger, 1980).

In the actual Cold War, the Soviets and Americans also started by thinking they might get an easy benefit (when the United States developed the first nuclear weapon, one Senator called it a "gift from God"). Building a few nuclear weapons to use as a deterrent seemed at first a guarantee for peaceful relations. But like the players in the dollar game, leaders of the two nations soon got trapped by a fear of loss if the other side got ahead in production of weapons. Losses for players of the dollar game involve small investments of cash and potential loss of face, and both of these motivations, on a much larger scale, played a role in driving the United States and the Soviet Union to such immense investments in nuclear weaponry.

Perceptual Dilemmas Despite all the evidence that hostility will be reciprocated with hostility, history keeps repeating itself with failed attempts to use aggressive coercion as a negotiating technique. For example, the Nazi bombing of civilian areas in London was designed to force the British to surrender. Instead, it had the effect of strengthening the British determination to fight. Nevertheless, when the Americans joined with the English against the Germans, they repeated history by bombing German civilian areas in the hopes of weakening German resolve. Again, the bombing did little to weaken the German will to resist (Rothbart & Hallmark, 1988). If threats and coercive manipulations fail so often in the laboratory and in the real world, why are they used so frequently? Social psychologists Myron Rothbart and William Hallmark (1988) suggest that part of the answer has to do with simple cognitive tendencies toward "ingroup favorability" and "outgroup bias."

In a pair of laboratory experiments, Rothbart and Hallmark asked students to role-play a defense minister from either "Takonia" or "Navalia"—two hypothetical nations sharing the same island and a history of conflict. "Defense ministers" were asked to judge the effectiveness of several strategies for dealing with the opponent. The strategies ranged from cooperative (for example, unilaterally cutting back your production of submarines by 20 percent, with the expectation that your opponent will then make similar cutbacks in artillery) to coercive (building more submarines and threatening to use them if your opponent does not cut back its long-range artillery forces). Although Takonian and Navalian ministers read about the same conflict, their ideas about effective strategies were the mirror-opposite of one another. Students acting as Takonian ministers believed that their own country would respond to cooperative strategies but that the Navalian opponents would probably have to be coerced. Navalians, however, believed that Navalia would respond best to cooperative overtures but that the Takonians would require coercion to bring them into line.

Because students role playing Navalian and Takonian ministers couldn't have felt the same sort of punitive anger that might have motivated the bombings of North Vietnam or Germany, Rothbart and Hallmark (1988) argue that their results are a simple extension of the "minimal group" findings, discussed in chapter 11 on prejudice. Merely putting people into two groups leads them to judge their own side in positive terms (as generally "cooperative," for example) and the other side in negative terms (as "stubborn" and "noncompliant").

Ingroup biases of students role-playing Takonians and Navalians in a laboratory simulation are harmless. However, similar ingroup biases show up in the real world of international relations, where they can have disastrous consequences. Scott Plous (1985) found evidence that American and Soviet leaders both wanted mutual disarmament but perceived the other side as wanting nuclear superiority. Plous argued that both sides were locked in a **perceptual dilemma**—an unfortunate combination of a social dilemma and an outgroup bias. In a perceptual dilemma, each side in a conflict believes that its best outcome would be for both sides to cooperate, while simultaneously believing that the other side will gladly exploit, but not offer, cooperative gestures.

To test his idea that Soviet and American leaders during the 1980s were locked in a perceptual dilemma, Plous sent questionnaires to United States senators. He asked the senators to rate the desirability of America's continued arming or disarming if the Soviets either armed or disarmed. The senators were also asked what they thought the Soviets would prefer. The results (shown in Figure 13.9) show that U.S. senators thought it best for the United States if both sides disarmed. They strongly opposed either continued escalation or U.S. disarmament in the face of continued Soviet armament. Unfortunately, the senators thought that Soviet leaders viewed things very differently. Although they believed that the Soviets would also like mutual disarmament, they thought the Soviets would most prefer to continue arming while the United States disarmed. Under those circumstances, the United States would be left with no alternative but to keep building arms reluctantly. A survey of Soviet leaders, however, showed that Soviets thought exactly the opposite (Guroff & Grant, 1981). The Soviets themselves viewed arms control as essential but firmly believed that the Americans preferred to keep building the U.S. arsenal.

These findings suggest that neither the Soviets nor the Americans had purely aggressive intentions in stockpiling nuclear weapons. Instead, they were mainly trying to communicate their threat potential to the other side. Unfortunately, coercive threats take on a life of their own when two sides use them against one another. As we discussed in the preceding section, laboratory studies suggest that threats tend to escalate conflict (Deutsch, 1986). One analysis of ninety-nine serious international disputes (involving troop movements, port blockades, withdrawn ambassadors, and so on) found that, if they were not preceded by an arms race, only 4 percent led to war. Of those that were preceded by an arms race, on the other hand, fully 82 percent resulted in war (Wallace, 1979).

Perceptual dilemma *The combination of a social dilemma and an outgroup bias, in which each side in a conflict believes that it is best for both sides to cooperate, while simultaneously believing that the other side would prefer that "we" cooperated while "they" defected.*

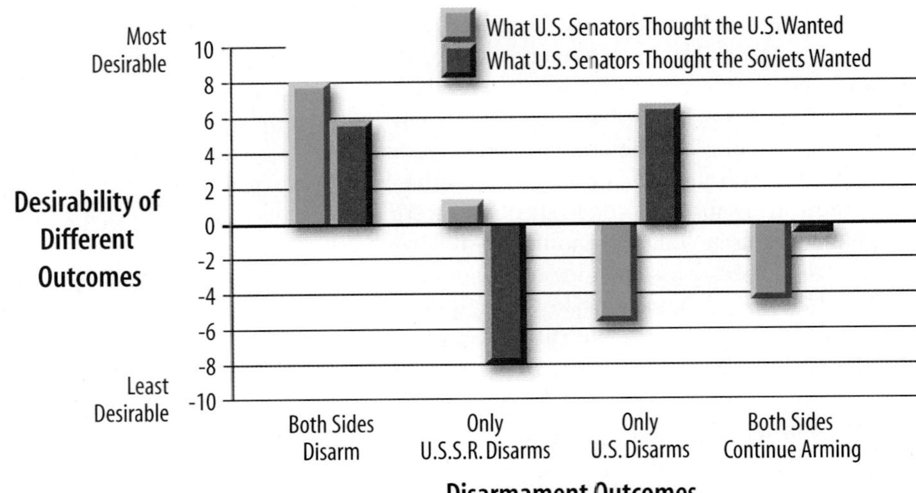

Figure 13.9
A perceptual dilemma.

U.S. senators surveyed during the Cold War correctly perceived that neither side wanted to disarm while the other side continued to get stronger. However, they believed that the "ingroup" (the United States) most wanted mutual disarmament while the "outgroup" (the Soviet Union) slightly preferred the "sneaky" alternative of continuing to prepare for nuclear war while the United States disarmed. Analyses of Soviet leaders' statements indicated that the Soviets wanted to disarm but believed that the United States most wanted to continue building nuclear weapons while the Soviets got weaker.

Although the Cold War is over and the Soviet Union has been largely disbanded, most of the nuclear weapons built by the Soviets and Americans still exist. Because they are so abundant, there is a remaining danger of an accidental nuclear war. In addition, several other countries, such as China, India, Israel, and Pakistan now have their own nuclear weapons, or the technology to build them. Can advances in social science help us solve the problems that advances in physical science have wrought in the field of military technology?

FOCUS ON Application

Increasing Intergroup Cooperation with the GRIT Strategy

We have considered several obstacles to international cooperation. People naturally divide themselves into beloved ingroups and despised outgroups (Krebs & Denton, 1997; Tajfel & Turner, 1979). Once conflicts begin, they tend to escalate (Deutsch, 1986). Arms races between nations often lead to war (Wallace, 1979). Fortunately, though, the upward spiral of conflict isn't inevitable: it can be reversed.

In chapter 11, we discussed the warring summer campers at Robbers Cave (Sherif et al., 1961). When forced to work together toward common goals, the Rattlers and Eagles overcame their rivalry and even started to like one another. These findings suggest that countries in conflict could promote peace by working together toward mutually beneficial goals (such as finding a cure for cancer or AIDS). Replacing international competition with cooperation may be easier said than done however. While two sides are still locked in conflict, each side distrusts the other's motives and fears exploitation. And as we mentioned earlier, laboratory studies do show that unconditional cooperation will often be exploited (Deutsch, 1986).

As a way out of the two-sided dilemma of increasing threat versus exploited appeasement, psychologist Charles Osgood (1962) suggested the GRIT strategy. **GRIT** (short for "Graduated and Reciprocated Initiatives in Tension Reduction") is a strategy for breaking conflict spirals by publicly challenging the opponent to match de-escalations. To break a conflict spiral, Osgood proposed that one side of the conflict begin with a peaceful initiative. To avoid appearing or actually becoming weaker with such a conciliatory move, Osgood suggested the first step be a small one. Along with the small initial peace offering, the peace-promoter using GRIT makes a public statement that larger and larger reductions in conflict will follow if the other side follows suit with peaceful initiatives of its own. By reciprocat-

GRIT (Graduated and Reciprocated Initiatives in Tension Reduction) *A strategy for breaking conflict spirals by publicly challenging the opponent to match de-escalations.*

ing gradually larger reductions in armaments, both sides can thereby avoid ever getting into a highly disadvantaged position. The beauty of the GRIT strategy is that, instead of challenging one another toward increasing competition, the opponents begin to challenge one another toward increased cooperation.

The GRIT strategy has been effective in laboratory conflict simulations (Lindskold, 1983). Does it work in the real world of international relations? Apparently, John F. Kennedy used just such a strategy to slow down the escalating conflict with the Soviet Union after the Cuban Missile Crisis (Etzioni, 1986). A fierce dispute over the Soviet Union's placement of missiles in Cuba led to widespread concern about an actual nuclear war. Eight months after the crisis, Kennedy called for an end to the conflict between the United States and the Soviet Union and offered a unilateral act of disarmament—the United States would stop open-air testing of nuclear weapons and would not resume them until another country did. In this way, he offered the Soviet Union the chance to follow his lead. Five days later, Soviet premier Nikita Krushchev followed with a speech welcoming Kennedy's proposal and calling for an end to the stockpiling of nuclear weapons. Krushchev also raised Kennedy's offer by halting the production of strategic bombers. A month later, the two countries began negotiating, and they signed a nuclear weapons treaty later that summer.

GRIT and the end of the Cold War. *Soviet premier Gorbachev used a variation of the GRIT strategy—graduated and reciprocated initiatives in tension reduction—to help spin down the conflict spiral of nuclear weapons production. He won the Nobel Peace Prize for his efforts. He is pictured here with former presidents Reagan and Bush.*

During the 1980s, Soviet premier Mikhail Gorbachev used a very similar strategy to bring U.S. president Ronald Reagan to the bargaining table. Gorbachev first proposed a one-sided weapons test ban in the Soviet Union and offered to continue it if the United States would follow suit. When the United States didn't reciprocate, Gorbachev showed his resolve by beginning weapons tests again. However, his first gesture had warmed up American public opinion, so Gorbachev tried again the following year by offering to have American inspectors verify Soviet arms reductions. This time he was successful, and Reagan agreed to a treaty that required reductions in nuclear armaments on both sides. Gorbachev's policy of reciprocal concessions had indeed led to a happy outcome and may have been a key to ending the Cold War.

The GRIT strategy, like the tit-for-tat and the punitive deterrence strategies, leads competitors into a pattern of dynamic interaction. It differs in a very important way, however. Instead of stimulating conflict or stabilizing an already peaceful situation, it leads to a pattern of escalating peacemaking.

Summary

The goal of defending the ingroup is linked to several factors in the person: dominance orientation, authoritarianism, and simplified images of conflict. It can be triggered by competition between groups or by the use of threats by the other side. At an interactive level, the motivation can lead to "locked in" patterns of competition or cooperation. The tit-for-tat strategy, which reciprocates either competition or cooperation, can be most effective in stabilizing negotiations over time. Escalating competitive interactions, such as the Cold War, are a type of social trap, which engages participants in more and more costly interactions over time. Such dilemmas are made worse by outgroup prejudices that lead participants to believe that their opponents, but not themselves, are more responsive to coercive strategies and less interested in a cooperative solution. The GRIT strategy is a technique designed to reset interaction patterns from competitive escalation to cooperative escalation. The person, situation, and interactional factors linked to both goals discussed in this chapter are summarized in Table 13.3.

CHAPTER 13
Summary Table

Table 13.3 Summary of goals affecting social dilemmas and of related person, situation, and interactional factors.

The Goal	The Person	The Situation	Interactions
Gaining Immediate Satisfaction	• Personal value orientation: prosocial (altruistic and cooperative) vs. egoistic (individualist and competitive)	• Timing of positive and negative consequences for selfishness. • Descriptive and injunctive norms about selfish vs. group-oriented behavior.	• Command-and-control policies appeal to fear. They may trigger resistance and only work if violators expect to get caught. • Market-based policies appeal to greed. They elicit less resistance but may be economically infeasible. • Voluntarist policies appeal to social responsibility. They require no government policing but fail if people are truly selfish.
Defending Ourselves and Valued Others	• Social dominance orientation • Gender • Authoritarianism • Deterrence vs. conflict spiral • Simplified images of conflict	• Competition over scarce resources. • Interacting at group vs. individual level. • Threats. • Stressful decision-making context for leaders. • Culturally biased communication.	• Groups and individuals can "lock in" to repeated cooperative or competitive patterns. • Tit-for-tat strategy reciprocates cooperation and competition and stabilizes interactions. • Escalating competitions such as "dollar game" are a form of social trap. Outgroup biases create perceptual dilemmas in which opponents are seen to desire more competitive outcomes. • GRIT strategy replaces escalating competition cycle with escalating cooperation cycle.

REVISITING
The Future

We opened this chapter with the contrast between two possible pathways for the world's future. One is unfolding on the Indian subcontinent, as Bengalis, East Indians, and Pakistanis continue to multiply their numbers and magnify the conflicts that have driven them apart for most of the last century. Another is unfolding in Western Europe, where population growth has slowed to a standstill, environmental consciousness has blossomed, and former foes have united into a cooperative union. Down one path, humans will continue to destroy the planet's resources, fight over the dwindling remainders, and do irreversible damage to the oceans, the atmosphere, and the earth's other species. Down the other, humans will live in quieter, greener, and more harmonious conditions, and literally save the planet.

In this chapter, we saw how overpopulation, environmental destruction, and international conflict are all conceptually linked to the phenomenon of social traps—situations in which immediate selfishness leads, in the long run, to group disaster. In the case of overpopulation, individuals act on the most primary of individual selfish motives—the inclination to reproduce one's genes. As the growing population demands more food, those who harvest the oceans and the forests are daily drawn into a classic social dilemma—although it is in the larger group's interest to harvest slowly, it is in the selfish interest of any individual fisherman or logger to take as much as possible now. The result, as in the case of the Alaska king crab, is often disastrous for all concerned. Likewise, international conflicts often demonstrate the features of another sort of trap, illustrated in the "dollar game." In this type of trap, an initial desire for what seems like a good outcome (winning a dollar or scaring off a potential adversary) is replaced by a fear of losing face and an escalating commitment of resources.

Social traps are intellectually fascinating because they illustrate how order can emerge in complex systems. "Locked in" cyclic patterns emerge from the individual motivations of a handful of international leaders, or thousands of crab fishermen, or billions of individuals making decisions about family planning or recycling. One of the most fascinating features of such complex systems is that they can often be pulled in a completely different direction by a small input (Nowak & Vallacher, 1998). Just as a few threats can lead to a locked-in pattern of conflict, a few trusting acts done as part of a GRIT strategy can get two nations locked into a pattern of cooperation.

Although the momentum of overpopulation and international conflict sometimes seems unstoppable, the example of Italy and Western Europe suggests that the tide can be turned. Demographers suggest one very simple solution—the wide dissemination of family planning knowledge and technology. Family planning technology could provide an elegant solution because it does not require convincing billions of people to suppress their primitively selfish sexual desires. Instead it short-circuits the natural system, and simultaneously appeals to another general human motivation—to control family size when density goes up. The remaining problem, however, is not a technical one, but a social one: people need to use existing knowledge and technologies to limit their family sizes and use the world's resources more wisely (e.g., Bryan, Aiken, & West, 1996; Oskamp, 2000).

To move towards the brighter of the two possible futures, we will need to better understand the different sources of motivation that drive different people. Most government interventions have involved "command-and-control" approaches, punitive policies that only work when violators expect to get caught and punished. Moreover, when nations try these sorts of coercive manipulations on one another, they trigger primitive ingroup protection and social dominance motivations, which often make the problems worse. In contrast, appeals to material self-interest can lead to more voluntary group-oriented behavior. Reward-based appeals may even work at the international level, as in the case of the emerging European community or the two centuries of (mostly) successful cooperation between the separate states of the United States. Finally, appeals to social responsibility engage the noblest levels of human motivation, as when environmental groups work to save the rainforest or when the United Nations steps in to help starving populations in Africa or to distribute free family planning information to the world's poor.

The discovery of the simple dynamics of social traps underlying these complex global problems raises an optimistic possibility. Perhaps social scientists might uncover solutions to problems that cannot be solved by technological innovations. These great problems are rooted in behavior, emotion, and cognition, and their solution may well stimulate the most important and exciting scientific discoveries of the dawning century.

CHAPTER 13

Summary

Defining Social Dilemmas

1. A social dilemma is a situation in which an individual profits from seeking personal benefits, unless everyone chooses selfishly, in which case the whole group loses.
2. The "tragedy of the commons" is an example of a replenishing resource management dilemma, in which group members share a renewable resource that continues producing benefits unless members overharvest it.
3. A public goods dilemma is a situation in which the whole group can benefit if some of the individuals give something for the common good, but in which the public good will be lost if too few people contribute.
4. Overpopulation, environmental destruction, and international conflict are special dilemmas emerging at the level of nations and global populations. Each pits short-term individual interests against the long-term good of humankind. The global dilemmas are interconnected and contribute to one another.

Gaining Immediate Satisfaction

1. A social trap is a situation in which individuals or groups are drawn in by immediate rewards but ultimately get caught in unpleasant or lethal consequences. Social traps are caused by differences between short-term and long-term consequences, ignorance of long-term consequences, or sliding reinforcers.
2. Person factors affecting the goal of immediate satisfaction include value orientations. Altruists and cooperators have a prosocial orientation, whereas competitors and individualists have an egoistic orientation. Egoists tend to have fewer siblings, whereas prosocial individuals have more older siblings, particularly sisters. Egoistic orientation in adulthood is associated with less trust and relationship security.
3. Situation factors affecting this goal include short-term and long-term consequences of conservation or wasteful behaviors. To increase conservation, one could change long-term negative consequences with alternative technologies, move future negative consequences to the present, add immediate punishments for undesirable behaviors, and reinforce desirable alternatives. Social solutions include the activation of descriptive and injunctive norms, including commitment.
4. Command-and-control policies appeal to fear of punishment to coerce less short-sighted behavior. Market-based policies appeal to individual self-interest. Voluntarist policies appeal to norms of social responsibility and work better with people who have a prosocial orientation.

Defending Ourselves and Valued Others

1. Social dominance orientation refers to desires that one's own group dominate other groups. Across cultures, men tend to have higher social dominance orientations than do women. Authoritarians are deferential to authority, highly respectful of power, moralistically aggressive, and ethnocentric. Leaders adopting a deterrence view believe that signs of weakness will be exploited and that one must show willingness to use military power. Those holding a conflict spiral view believe that demonstrations of peaceful intent reduce opponents' defensiveness.
2. Authoritarian tendencies tend to increase under conditions of economic threat. Simply placing people into groups can trigger competitiveness. Intergroup cooperation can lead to decreases in outgroup prejudices.
3. Time-series analyses examine two or more recurring events for historical links. A time-series study of Japan found that openness to foreign influence led to an increase in artistic creativity two generations later.
4. Threats increase competition in laboratory conflicts. Although unconditional cooperation is exploited, punitive deterrent strategies anger opponents and escalate conflict. Nonpunitive deterrence strategies seem to minimize conflict and help players maximize gains. International leaders show decreased cognitive complexity during conflicts, perhaps because anxiety strains cognitive resources.
5. Threats and cooperative gestures between nations are sometimes misinterpreted due to cultural differences in communication.
6. The tit-for-tat strategy, which reciprocates both competition and cooperation, is most effective in stabilizing conflict situations. The dollar game is a social trap that mimics international conflicts such as the Cold War. International conflicts are worsened by perceptual dilemmas, in which opponents believe the other side desires not a reduction in conflict but an unfair and one-sided solution.
7. The GRIT strategy is a technique that replaces conflict escalation with cooperative escalation.

CHAPTER 13

Key Terms

Altruist *An individual oriented toward bringing the group benefits, even if it means personal sacrifice.*

Command-and-control policy *A prescriptive legal regulation that uses police power to punish violators.*

Competitor *An individual oriented to come out relatively better than other players, regardless of whether personal winnings are high or low in an absolute sense.*

Conflict spiral view *The belief that escalations of international threat lead an opponent to feel more threatened and that leaders should thus demonstrate peaceful intentions to reduce the opponent's own defensive hostilities.*

Cooperator *An individual oriented toward working together to maximize the joint benefits to the self and the group.*

Deterrence view *The belief that signs of weakness will be exploited by the opponent and that leaders need to show their willingness to use military force.*

GRIT (Graduated and Reciprocated Initiatives in Tension Reduction) *A strategy for breaking conflict spirals by publicly challenging the opponent to match de-escalations.*

Individualist *An individual oriented toward maximizing personal gains, without regard to rest of the group.*

Integrative complexity *The extent to which a person demonstrates simplified "black-and-white," categorical thinking as opposed to acknowledgment of all sides of an issue.*

Market-based policy *An offer of rewards to those who reduce their socially harmful behaviors.*

Perceptual dilemma *The combination of a social dilemma and an outgroup bias, in which each side in a conflict believes that it is best for both sides to cooperate, while simultaneously believing that the other side would prefer that "we" cooperated while "they" defected.*

Public goods dilemma *A situation in which (1) the whole group can benefit if some of the individuals give something for the common good but (2) individuals profit from "free riding" if enough others contribute.*

Replenishing resource management dilemma *A situation in which group members share a renewable resource that will continue to produce benefits if group members do not overharvest it but also whereby any single individual profits from harvesting as much as possible.*

Sliding reinforcer *A stimulus that brings rewards in small doses, which change to punishments when they occur in large doses.*

Social dilemma *A situation in which an individual profits from selfishness unless everyone chooses the selfish alternative, in which case the whole group loses.*

Social trap *A situation in which individuals or groups are drawn toward immediate rewards that later prove to have unpleasant or lethal consequences.*

Time-series analysis *A method in which two or more recurring events are examined for linkages over time.*

Tit-for-tat strategy *A negotiating tactic in which the individual responds to competitiveness with competitiveness and to cooperation with cooperation.*

Voluntarist policy *An appeal to people's intrinsic sense of social responsibility.*

Xenophobia *Fear and distrust of foreigners.*

CHAPTER 14
Integrating Social Psychology

Public Spectacles, Hidden Conspiracies, and Multiple Motives

On August 28, 1963, more than 200,000 Americans stood in sweltering heat before the Lincoln Memorial. They listened to rousing folk songs and speeches. But the crowning moments of their great march on Washington came at 3:30 in the afternoon, when Reverend Martin Luther King, Jr., stepped to the podium. He delivered a speech that was to be a turning point in U.S. race relations.

King began his rhetorical masterpiece with a reference to Abraham Lincoln: "Five score years ago, a great American, in whose symbolic shadow we stand today, signed the Emancipation Proclamation." The promises of that "great beacon light of hope," King declared, along with those of the U.S. Constitution and the Declaration of Independence, were like bad checks when black Americans tried to cash them in for their guarantees of freedom. King announced ominously that "the whirlwinds of revolt will continue to shake the foundations of our nation until the bright day

"And the Sun Came." © Paul Nzalamba

of justice emerges," and he added that "we cannot be satisfied as our children are stripped of their selfhood and robbed of their dignity by signs stating 'for whites only.'"

King's most potent words came toward the end of his speech, when he declared,

> I have a dream that one day on the red hills of Georgia, sons of former slaves and the sons of former slave owners will be able to sit down together at the table of brotherhood.... I have a dream that my four little children will one day live in a nation where they will not be judged by the color of their skin but by the content of their character. I have a dream that one day...right there in Alabama, little black boys and black girls will be able to join hands with little white boys and white girls as sisters and brothers.

As he approached his conclusion, King repeated a phrase from a patriotic American hymn: "Let freedom ring from the prodigious hilltops of New Hampshire. Let freedom ring from the mighty mountains of New York.... Let freedom ring from every hill and molehill of Mississippi, from every mountainside, let freedom ring!" King closed his great speech on a note full of hope, looking to "that day when all of God's children—black men and white men, Jews and Gentiles, Protestants and Catholics—will be able to join hands and sing in the words of the old Negro spiritual, 'Free at last, free at last; thank God almighty, we are free at last.'"

Top: Martin Luther King, Jr., at the March on Washington.

Bottom: President John F. Kennedy and Attorney General Robert F. Kennedy with FBI Director J. Edgar Hoover.

Behind the scenes of this great unifying event, however, King's personal world was being torn apart. Just before the march, President John F. Kennedy and his brother Robert, the attorney general, had persuaded King to break off his friendships with Stanley Levison and Jack O'Dell, two whites prominent in the civil rights movement. Why would the Kennedys, who were becoming more committed to solving the race problem, try to split up the movement's leaders? This is a mystery linked to another prominent man we discussed earlier—FBI Director J. Edgar Hoover. Hoover had informed the Kennedys that Levison and O'Dell were affiliated with the Communist party.

Hoover and his agents were also behind a press release designed to undermine the civil rights march. The FBI had strategically leaked information about march organizer Bayard Rustin's earlier arrest for homosexual behavior. And just before the march, between friendly meetings with King, Robert Kennedy had secretly approved FBI wiretaps of King. The electronic eavesdropping caught King bragging about his extramarital sexual exploits, unwittingly providing ammunition for Hoover's vicious crusade against the black preacher.

Why would Hoover mastermind such a strong personal attack on King, a vendetta matched only by his campaign decades earlier against Eleanor Roosevelt? Why would the Kennedys cooperate with Hoover? Why would King yield to Hoover's plot to tear him from his close friends? And how could immense societal change arise out of all the self-focused personal motivations of everyone involved in this intrigue, from the handful of great leaders to the many thousands of marchers torn between "the whirlwinds of revolt" and the dream of interracial peace and harmony?

The social interactions surrounding the march on Washington illustrate many of the mysteries of social life. In this chapter, we'll try to integrate the pieces of the puzzle that we've discussed throughout this book. We'll see that the many separate clues do fit together to yield some "take-home" lessons about gender, about culture, about dysfunctional social behavior, and about how to apply the findings and methods of social psychology to everyday life. In the course of fitting these puzzle pieces together, we'll reconsider the fundamental motives underlying social behavior and the ever-important interactions between the person and the social situation.

Self-presentation and public life. *Just as revelations about President Clinton's alleged affair with a White House intern were reaching a fever pitch in 1998, Clinton gave a masterful State of the Union message with apparent calmness and cool confidence. As his opponents called for his impeachment, his popularity ratings rose. In the politics of everyday life, most of us occasionally face the task of presenting different aspects of our selves to different audiences.*

What Ground Have We Covered?

We began this book by defining social psychology as the scientific study of how people's thoughts, feelings, and behaviors are influenced by other people. We proceeded from the simplest level, considering the individual person's motives, feelings, and thought processes and how these parts fit together with his or her situation. In that chapter, we used the example of Martin Luther King. Around the time of the march on Washington, we can see King's different motives again coming sharply into conflict as he faced a very difficult situation: the choice between personal friendships and the good of the civil rights movement. In chapter 3, we examined the mental processes people use to understand themselves and others, highlighting the vastly differing perceptions people held of former President Richard Nixon. Martin Luther King, Jr. had been on both sides, first regarding Nixon as "absolutely sincere" about civil rights but later viewing Nixon as "a moral coward" who had "no real grounding in basic convictions."

We went on to reflect on how people present themselves to others, considering the case of the great imposter Ferdinand DeMara and noting that we all manage our self-presentations to help meet important personal goals. At the time of the march on Washington, John and Robert Kennedy were caught in a complex self-presentational dilemma. Their goal of being seen by the U.S. public as promoting civil rights inspired them to befriend King, but their goal of being seen as hard on Communism worked at cross-purposes by motivating them to cooperate in Hoover's attack on King.

In chapters 5 and 6, we examined how people persuade and influence one another. King's 15-minute speech to the marchers in Washington was certainly one of history's masterpieces of social influence. Borrowing the credibility of Abraham Lincoln and the U.S. Constitution, he conjured up images of freedom and justice that eventually led millions of people to reconsider their attitudes about race relations.

We next considered affiliation and friendship. With the support of social networks, people can climb Mt. Everest or go to the moon. Without them, it would be impossible to get almost anywhere in life. Even with his great rhetorical powers, Martin Luther King, Jr. couldn't have brought hundreds of thousands of people to Washington. He needed the support of powerful politicians and an army of civil rights workers. Nor could J. Edgar Hoover have carried out his campaigns against people like King and Eleanor Roosevelt without the cooperation of powerful allies and a vast network of federal agents.

From friendship, we moved on to consider love and romantic relationships—social interactions that have the power to change the course of history, as the focus on King's extramarital affairs may have done. We noted how our own personal satisfactions in relationships with lovers and family members are often served by promoting another's well-being. This theme continued in chapter 9, where we considered such prosocial behaviors as Sempo Sugihara's great personal sacrifices on behalf of the Jews in Nazi Germany—not unlike King's dedication to the cause of civil rights.

In chapter 10, we discussed a troubling side of human social life—aggression. We saw how brutality could arise even in otherwise normal people and also how it could, ironically, be triggered by some of the same positive group-based motives that stimulated the march on Washington. Some of these themes came up again in chapter 11, in which we considered stereotyping, prejudice, and discrimination, using the case of the Klansman and the civil rights worker to demonstrate how normal processes of cognition and motivation can lead either to bitter bigotries or sweet harmonies.

Finally, we moved beyond the individual level to consider processes that arise only in groups, such as Margaret Thatcher's cabinet, the workers in a factory, or the great crowd of marchers on Washington. It would seem that the interactions of so many people, with so many individual motives, would lead to an unpredictable and chaotic state of affairs, but we saw instead that a more regular pattern of dynamic self-organization often emerges within the group. We discussed how one of those self-organizational patterns—the social trap—may underlie global social problems such as overpopulation, environmental destruction, and international conflict—processes that came together in the five-hour-long massacre of 1,700 Bengali immigrants by the residents of Assam, India.

Thus we began our exploration by searching inside the individual's head. Step by step, we've moved outward to explore increasingly complex interactions—people presenting themselves to others, negotiating webs of social influences, loves and hatreds, and finally coming together in organizations, crowds, and nations.

Findings and Theories

In our broad survey of social psychology, we encountered a great many intriguing research findings. Here are just a few examples:

- If people are arbitrarily divided into two groups whose members have little or nothing in common, they may begin within minutes to believe that the members of "our" group are smarter and more deserving than "them" (Tajfel & Turner, 1979).
- People will obey authority figures such as research scientists or medical doctors, even if the authority asks them to do something that may hurt, or kill, another human being (Hofling, Brotzman, Dalrymple, Graves, & Pierce, 1966; Milgram, 1992).
- The majority of North Americans and Europeans rank themselves within the top few percent in terms of leadership skills, friendliness, and driving ability, but East Asians view themselves in more humble terms (Heine, Takata, & Lehman, 2000).
- People are generally drawn to others who live and work nearby. Yet men and women who were raised in the same house on an Israeli kibbutz do not find one another highly sexually desirable (Shepher, 1971).
- A lone individual trusted with a small share of a replenishing resource will take care not to exhaust it, but placed into a group of people sharing a larger resource, he or she will join in a greedy rush to deplete it (Neidert & Linder, 1990; Schroeder, 1995).

Social psychologists have uncovered thousands of other research "facts," but as Poincaré observed, "a collection of facts is no more a science than a heap of stones is a house." Instead of finishing your study of social psychology with a loose heap of colorful trivia nuggets, you should come away with an interconnected set of theoretical principles that lay a foundation for understanding your social interactions on the job, in your family, out on the streets, or during your travels.

Major Theoretical Perspectives of Social Psychology

In chapter 1, we described five historically important theoretical perspectives. Let's revisit those perspectives to see how they are woven through the field of social psychology. More important, let's explore the links among them.

The different perspectives are not incompatible alternatives. Instead they're interlinked views of the same social phenomena. One way to appreciate these links is to look at the perspectives along a continuum of **proximate** to **ultimate** levels of explanation (see Figure 14.1). A proximate explanation focuses on immediate causes in the here and now (an accusation of Communist ties led Robert Kennedy to approve the FBI wiretap of King). By contrast, a relatively more ultimate explanation focuses on background or historical causes (Communists had been secretly involved in major social movements in the United States for decades). Proximate and ultimate explanations aren't alternatives. Instead, they're intimately woven together—the historical background factors, for example, affect the perception of the immediate situation (fear of Communist ties only made sense when considered in historical context).

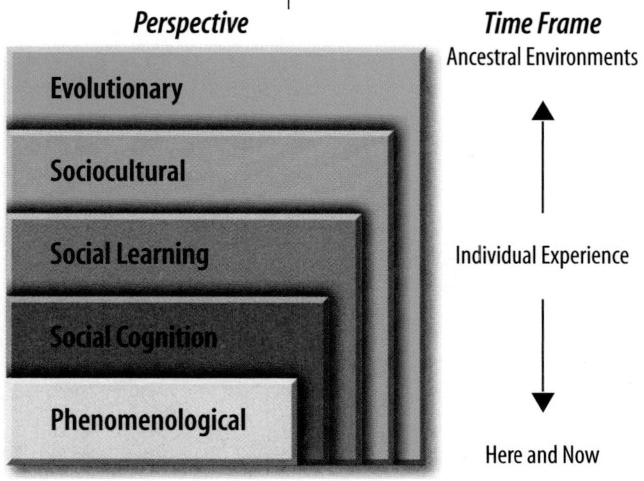

Figure 14.1
Theoretical perspectives are interconnected.

The different theoretical perspectives are not incompatible but instead provide different perspectives on the same phenomena. Phenomenological approaches tend to take very "proximate" glimpses of behavior, examining causes in the immediate present. Cognitive and learning perspectives connect momentary interpretations to long-term memory and the individual's past experiences with reward and punishment. Sociocultural and evolutionary perspectives consider how background factors in the broader culture and the evolutionary past affect learning and ongoing thought and perception.

As we indicate in Figure 14.1, relatively proximate questions are narrower in focus (Why did the story of Elián Gonzales and his father consume so much media coverage?), and they are nested within broader, more ultimate, questions (Why are people generally so concerned about children and families?). Now let's explore the connections among these different levels of explanation.

The Sociocultural Perspective

In chapter 1, you read about E. A. Ross (1908), who viewed social psychology as the study of fads, crazes, riots, and other group phenomena. In surveying social psychology, you've seen many social processes that emerge only in groups. One example is minority influence, a process in which a small part of a group changes the opinions of the larger group (Moscovici, Mucchi-Faina, & Maass, 1994; Nemeth, 1994). The civil rights movement is a good example: an initially small band of people eventually brought together hundreds of thousands of others from "the red hills of Georgia… the prodigious hilltops of New Hampshire…and every hill and molehill in Mississippi" to change the norms of U.S. society.

Until recently, these mutual influences between several hundred individuals in a mob or several hundred thousand individuals in a larger society seemed too complex to study scientifically. In the last few years, however, scientists working in fields from ecology to economics have begun to develop powerful new mathematical and conceptual tools for studying complex dynamical systems, such as crowds and social movements, which involve many mutually interacting elements (Nowak & Vallacher, 1998; Nowak, Vallacher, Tesser, & Borkowski, 2000). Why aren't hairstyles and attitudes more randomly distributed across different groups instead of clustered together? It is, for example, as unlikely that you'll see someone with multiple tattoos and purple hair at the Republican women's luncheon as that you'll see a clean-cut man wearing a business suit dancing at a Pearl Jam concert. The new conceptual tools are allowing researchers to study *how* attitudes and behaviors spread and cluster within large groups (Latané, 1996; Latané & L'Herrou, 1996).

A central legacy of the sociocultural approach is the focus on norms—social expectations about appropriate behavior that vary between and within different societies (Smith & Bond, 1994). In the late 1990s, business organizations and their employees sometimes clashed over different norms for multiple body piercings (one Canadian woman was fired by a Starbuck's coffeehouse for wearing a tiny barbell through her tongue). In the corporate business subculture of North American society today, it's socially appropriate to sport body piercings only on one's earlobes. In other subcultures (artistically oriented youth, for example), it's considered socially desirable to pierce multiple chunks of metal through ears, noses, eyebrows, tongues, nipples, and even genitalia. In yet other societies, people have indulged in even

Proximate explanation *A focus on relatively immediate causes.*

Ultimate explanation *A focus on background or historical causes.*

Cultural influences on bodily ornamentation. *In different cultures, at different times in history, the norms about the appropriateness and placement of body piercings have varied widely for women and for men.*

more extreme forms of bodily mutilation, placing giant objects in their lips and ears, stretching their necks to twice their normal lengths, and wrapping the bones of their feet so tightly that they crippled themselves. These wide variations illustrate the powerful influence of norms on social behavior.

In each chapter of this book, we've discussed the influences of culture, such as the individualistic norms of North American society and the collectivist norms of China and Japan (Ji, Schwarz, & Nisbett, 2000; Oishi, Wyer, & Colcombe, 2000). Taking this cross-cultural focus helped us see things that would otherwise be invisible. The self-serving biases so prominently displayed by Europeans and Americans, for example, are not found among Asians, who may instead go out of their way to belittle their own accomplishments (Heine et al., 2000; Kitayama, Markus, Matsumoto, & Norasakkunkit, 1997).

The Evolutionary Perspective

The evolutionary perspective views social behavior through the lens of Darwin's theory of evolution by natural selection (Kenrick & Luce, 2000; Ketelaar & Ellis, 2000). The central assumption is that, along with an opposable thumb and an upright posture, we inherited a brain designed partly to help us deal with the problems of living in human social groups. Researchers are beginning to adopt this perspective in examining many topics in social psychology, including aggression, altruism, love, prejudice, gender, and emotion (e.g. Crabb, 2000; Crawford & Krebs, 1998; Ketelaar & Clore, 1997; Taylor et al., 2000).

Like sociocultural theorists, evolutionary psychologists look across cultures, but they search more for human commonalities than for differences between people (e.g., Buss, 1989; Daly & Wilson, 1988; Kenrick & Keefe, 1992). Explorations of varying cultures reveal not only fascinating differences but also fundamental similarities in humans around the globe.

Seeing Our Commonality Through the Many Societal Differences We've discussed many differences in social rules from culture to culture. Bringing along dessert or gently refusing another helping of the main course may indicate graceful manners in Toledo but boorish rudeness in Tokyo. A woman marrying two brothers at the same time would be loathsome in Topeka but wholesome in Tibet. Learning about such cultural differences can reduce our ethnocentrism by making us aware that there are many other ways of being social than the one we learned as children. And an even closer look at other cultures can teach us another lesson: Beneath all the cultural differences, there is a core of similarity connecting all human beings with one another.

We've encountered many such similarities through the course of this book. Recall, for example, that although societies vary widely in their homicide rates and in their cultural norms about the appropriateness of violence (e.g., Cohen & Nisbett, 1997), males commit over 80 percent of the homicides in every society. Further, these homicides are often committed for similar reasons, with threats to a man's honor at the top of the list everywhere in the world (Daly & Wilson, 1988). Similarly, despite wide variations in marriage patterns around the world, including one woman marrying several men and one man marrying several women, we also saw that these differences are accompanied by some underlying universals. All human cultures have some form of marriage, for example, and even in societies that allow multiple spouses, most people nevertheless pair up monogamously, with one woman marrying one man (Daly & Wilson, 1983).

Universals and particulars. *The particular norms about marriage vary from culture to culture, but long-term bonds between parents are a universal feature, found across all human societies.*

Likewise, we've seen cross-cultural variations in rules for gift giving alongside universal rules about reciprocity, cross-cultural variations in individualism alongside a universal tendency toward communalism in family groups, and so on. Thus, as we meet people from different societies and from different subcultures within our society, we should expect that these people will play by rules that are sometimes shockingly different from ours. But we also expect to find that, beneath sometimes dazzling differences, human beings everywhere have basic goals and concerns much like our own.

Culture and Evolution Interacting Although evolutionary psychologists and sociocultural theorists have differed in their emphasis on universals versus differences, it would be an oversimplification to say that sociocultural theorists have ignored universals or that evolutionary psychologists have ignored differences (Buss & Kenrick, 1998; Triandis, 1994). Indeed, the two perspectives are looking at two sides of the same coin, and it would be a mistake to try to draw a line between culture and evolution (Janicki & Krebs, 1998). Cultural social psychologist Alan Fiske and his colleagues (1998) argue that, just as the human mind is designed to learn a language, so, too, it is designed to learn a set of cultural norms. And just as human language is, in turn, shaped by the human mind, so, too, is human culture. That is, culture develops within the potentialities and limits set by human evolution, and human evolution develops within the possibilities and limits set by culture (see Figure 14.2).

In addition to observing similarities across cultures, evolutionary researchers have searched for parallels in social behavior across different species (e.g., Low, 1998; Sadalla, Kenrick, & Vershure, 1987). For example, the behavior of males and females is generally more similar in species in which males help care for the offspring—as do many birds and human beings—than in species in which males make minimal investments—as do baboons (Gould & Gould, 1989). Paying attention to similarities across cultures and species in amorous, aggressive, and altruistic behaviors can help us see our own social behavior in broader perspective.

Social psychologists who adopt an evolutionary perspective don't buy pith helmets and set off for Africa to dig up hominid bones or live among gorillas. Those studies are relevant to human evolution, but they fall into the domain of anthropology and zoology. Instead, social psychologists use evolutionary principles to derive

Figure 14.2 Evolutionary and sociocultural factors are not independent.

Human beings have always lived in cultural groups, and the norms of those groups have affected the evolution of our species. Conversely, cultural norms are adopted or changed based on how successfully they fit human nature. The process is a continual loop of biological and cultural forces.

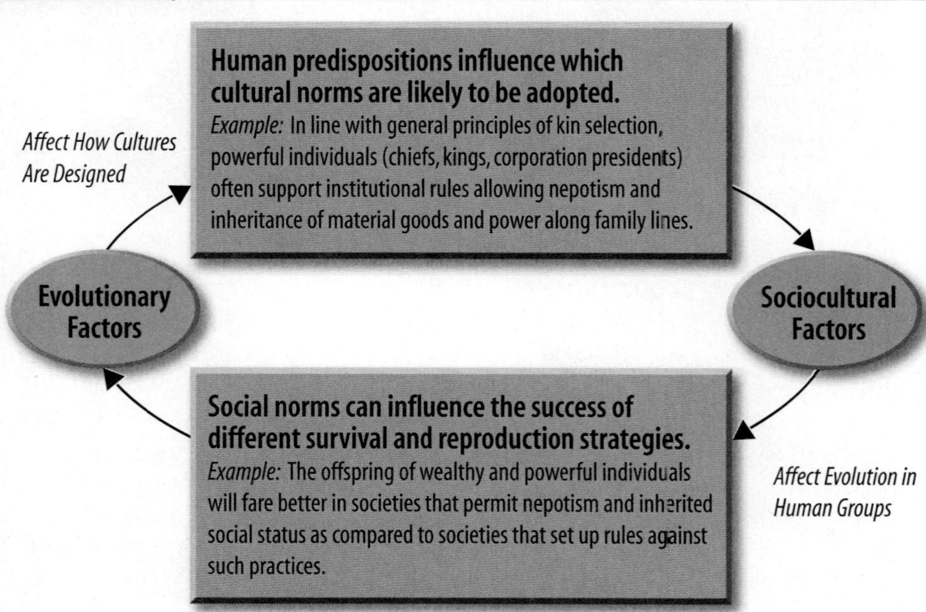

hypotheses about ongoing social interactions that can be tested in laboratory or field experiments, surveys, or behavioral archives (e.g., Graziano, Jensen-Campbell, Todd, & Finch, 1997; Haselton & Buss, 2000; Schaller & Conway, 1999). For example, we discussed in chapter 8 how researchers used evolutionary models to make different predictions about how men and women would evaluate their relationships after viewing attractive or socially dominant members of the opposite sex (Kenrick, Neuberg, Zierk, & Krones, 1994; Dijkstra & Buunk, 1998). The "fossils" that psychologists hunt for are not bones buried in the ground but the inherited psychological mechanisms we still carry around inside our heads (Buss & Kenrick, 1998).

The Social Learning Perspective

The social learning perspective brings us down from the grand levels of society and evolutionary history to a smaller scale, that of the individual person responding to rewards and punishments in a particular environment. We saw, for example, that people feel positively about another person or group if first exposed to that person or group while their mood is boosted by something as simple as eating tasty food (reason enough to enhance one's appreciation of cultural diversity by taking a tour of various Middle Eastern, Asian, and Latin American restaurants). Martin Luther King, Jr.'s speech at the march on Washington masterfully used this principle of association to connect his cause to powerful patriotic symbols and images of happy little children. In chapter 10, we saw how playing graphic computer games can reward violent thoughts and impulses (Anderson & Dill, 2000).

There's a direct linkage between the social learning and the sociocultural perspectives. Indeed, we learn different cultural norms (whether to feel uncomfortable about eating beef or horse or dog, for example) from years of such conditioning and modeling experiences. We've also discussed evidence that social learning sometimes follows tracks laid down by the evolutionary history of our species. For example, children raised together in a kibbutz pod learn to like one another, yet they don't marry each other. Apparently, the normal processes leading to sexual attraction among people in the same neighborhood are inhibited by being raised under the same roof. This suggests that a mechanism may have evolved to prevent siblings from learning to feel strong, passionate attraction to each other (Shepher, 1971). In this case, a unique cultural learning environment may have "tricked" that mechanism.

The Phenomenological Perspective

Whereas the social learning perspective is concerned with events in the objective world, such as a parent threatening to take away a misbehaving child's dessert, the phenomenological perspective is concerned with the subjective world, as when the rowdy child doesn't believe the parent's threat. In this view, the psychological environment isn't always the same as the physical environment, and the person's view of the environment may be affected by his or her needs at the moment. An affectionate lover may be seen as a saviour when you're stranded alone in a room full of strangers but as a nuisance when you're trying to study for tomorrow's exam.

We've seen numerous examples of the ways personal goals can affect subjective interpretations of the world. For instance, the fact that second-place winners in the Olympics are less happy than third-place winners shows how subjective interpretations can sometimes overwhelm objective reality (Medvec, Madey, & Gilovich, 1995). As another example, people who enter a committed relationship begin to tune out attractive members of the opposite sex, who could threaten the relationship (Drigotas & Rusbult, 1992; Simpson, Gangestad, & Lerma, 1990). In viewing one's actual partner, on the other hand, positive illusions may help the relationship survive (Murray & Holmes, 1997). Persistent social illusions are found in several areas of social life and can sometimes be pathological (e.g., Sanna, 1998; Taylor & Brown, 1988). As we saw in chapter 8, for example, obsessive relationships are usually based on a radical misperception of another person's feelings. Unless one is mentally unbalanced, however, one's views of reality usually correlate with actual reality.

The Social Cognitive Perspective

What processes create one's subjective phenomenology? Interpretations of the social world depend on the mental processes of noticing, interpreting, and remembering—processes that are the focus of the social cognitive perspective, probably the most influential perspective in modern social psychology (e.g., Gilovich, Medvec, & Savitsky, 2000; Malle, 1999; Sherman & Frost, 2000).

Adopting a social cognitive perspective helps us make sense of one FBI agent's response to King's speech at the march on Washington. The agent stated that the "powerful demagogic speech" convinced him "that Communist influence is being exerted on Martin Luther King, Jr.," and that "we must mark him…as the most dangerous Negro…from the standpoint of Communism…and national security." How could a speech full of references to the U.S. Constitution and the Battle Hymn of the Republic be so interpreted? A social cognitive perspective would focus on the cognitive cues made salient by the FBI investigation of possible Communist connections to the Civil Rights movement and by Director Hoover's almost obsessive concern with Communist conspiracies.

Because it forms a crucial part of our own interactionist model, a social cognitive perspective has been woven throughout every chapter of this book. For example, the distinction between "automatic" and "thoughtful" cognitive processing has been central in research on persuasion and attitude change. Processes of social attribution (as in deciding whether a compliment is sincere or manipulative) were central to our discussion of friendship, love, prosocial behavior, aggression, and stereotyping. Indeed, the goal of seeking information is one that we found to underlie a great many social interactions.

The social cognitive perspective has important links to the other perspectives. Consistent with the phenomenological perspective, research adopting the cognitive perspective has historically been concerned with momentary changes in attention, judgment, and memory triggered by changes in the immediate social situation (Fiske & Taylor, 1991; Wegner & Bargh, 1998). However, without cognitive processing on a moment-to-moment basis, there would be no learning, and without past learning or a brain that evolved to organize complex information about the social world, there would be no causal attributions, social schemas, heuristic judgments, or group stereotypes. Figure 14.3 depicts just one example of such links by highlighting some of the interconnections between social cognition and social learning.

There's a similar two-way street between any of the perspectives (as shown in the earlier connection between the sociocultural and evolutionary perspectives). The importance of considering more than a single perspective reveals itself in different approaches to gender.

Gender schemas. *Our attention is easily drawn to people who cannot be easily classified as male or female, in line with research suggesting that gender schemas are powerful and primary mental categories.*

Are Gender Differences in Our Genes, in Our Cultural Learning Experiences, or All in Our Minds?

If you can't tell from the accent whether a person is from Boston or New York, you may not care enough to even comment on it. If you can't immediately tell whether the person is a man or a woman, on the other hand, this uncertainty will probably capture your attention and interest.

Why are people so fascinated by these rare gender ambiguities? Social psychologists Susan Cross and Hazel Markus (1993) suggest that it's because gender is such a vivid social category. Whether someone is a male or a female is immediately

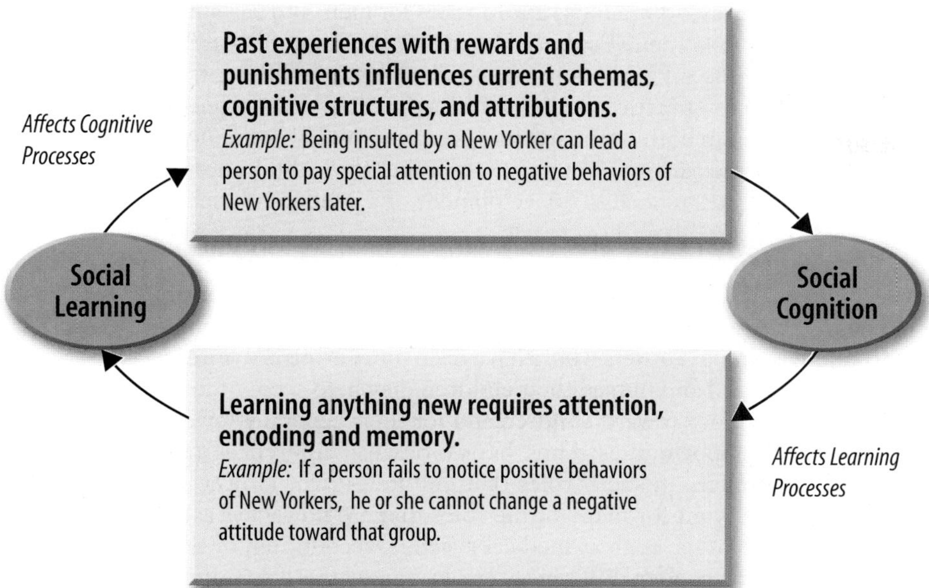

Figure 14.3
The interplay of cognition and learning.

To learn to like or dislike another group, for example, we must notice that group and register our experience with them in long-term memory. Once we have learned a habitual way of responding to others, it will affect our later tendency to notice and remember them. Thus, learning and cognition go hand in hand.

visible to the naked eye and relevant in many everyday situations. These researchers adopted the cognitive perspective that gender stereotypes function like other categories, including racial stereotypes. Once we put someone into a simple category, we don't need to expend extra cognitive effort to understand or interact with him or her.

Consistent with this perspective, young children who see someone act out of line with their gender stereotypes may mentally distort the behavior to bring it back into line. For instance, five- and six-year-old children shown a girl sawing a piece of wood may misremember it as a boy doing the sawing (Martin & Halverson, 1983). And adults also bend their perceptions to fit gender-role schemas. Adults in one study judged a baby's reaction when a jack-in-the-box pops open. Was the baby's cry fearful or angry? Observers who thought the baby was a girl were more likely to see fear; those who thought it was a boy were more likely to see anger (Condry & Condry, 1976).

Findings such as these suggest gender biases in social judgment. But do they mean that gender is "all in the head"? Carol Martin (1987) suggested that gender stereotypes, like some other stereotypes, are based on at least a kernel of truth. Canadian subjects reported large gender differences between the typical "North American male" and the typical "North American female." Men were perceived as substantially higher in dominance, aggressiveness, and willingness to take a stand; women were perceived as much more gentle, tender, compassionate, and warm. People rating themselves on the same dimensions reported the same stereotypical differences, but to a much lesser degree. Thus, cognitive biases can lead us to magnify small actual gender differences (Martin, 1987).

Alice Eagly (1995) reviewed a large number of studies examining actual gender differences in behavior as well as stereotypes about those differences and concluded that laypeople have a reasonably good feel for which differences are large (such as physical violence and attitudes about premarital sex) and which are small (such as feelings of anger and attitudes about long-term relationships). Why do people, despite all their cognitive biases, still end up with a fairly good idea about the size of gender differences? Eagly suggests that it is precisely because gender is such a salient cognitive category—people pay a lot of attention to the similarities and differences between men and women.

Why do men and women act in line with gender stereotypes? That's still a controversial question to be resolved by research. Undoubtedly, young children learn that certain behaviors are more appropriate for men, and certain behaviors are more appropriate for women (Eagly & Wood, 1999). Some of these gender role norms are similar across different cultures, while others are different. For example, more women than men practice medicine in Russia, but the reverse is true in the United States. Women in both countries, however, commit fewer homicides and spend relatively more time caring for infants. Observing these differences and similarities no doubt contributes to a child's development of a gender-role schema, and informs a young boy or girl about how to act.

At another level, we can ask where the societal differences and similarities come from in the first place (Kenrick & Li, 2000). From an evolutionary perspective, some types of division of labor would have naturally arisen from gender differences in reproductive biology; others would have been more arbitrary. The fact that our female ancestors carried and nursed their children may help account for women's generally greater nurturance toward children and for their generally lower enthusiasm about casual sexual opportunities. Thus, basic biological differences may contribute to the gender differences in social roles that children learn. However, our reproductive history is irrelevant for many of the roles that are nowadays arbitrarily assigned to one sex or the other, such as medical practice, accounting, or social work. In short, asking whether gender differences are in our genes, our cultural learning experiences, *or* in our minds may be the wrong question. All these forces work together to produce social behavior (Kenrick & Luce, 2000).

As our discussion of gender illustrates, each of the different perspectives helps us understand social behavior, and putting the different perspectives together elucidates more of the whole picture (see Figure 14.4). The interactionist framework we've used to organize this book is a synthesis of the different historically important perspectives. In the next section, we reprise the main points of our framework.

Summary

Different perspectives are interconnected views of the same phenomena. Evolutionary and sociocultural perspectives provide historical explanations for the roots of

Figure 14.4 Different perspectives on gender.

The similarities and differences between men and women can be considered from each of the different major perspectives, and doing so helps us to see the connections between those perspectives.

Perspective	*Gender Differences*
Evolutionary	Women bear children, men do not.
Sociocultural	Some social roles are assigned to women (such as nurse), some roles are assigned to men (such as military leader).
Social Learning	Boys are punished for playing with dolls. Girls are rewarded for playing house.
Social Cognition	People remember a man's behavior in line with a stereotype including "aggressiveness"; they remember a woman's in line with a stereotype including "nurturance".
Phenomenological	A woman may not try for a position of leadership because she believes it is impossible for her to attain it.

social behavior in human biology and cultural norms. Social learning and social cognitive perspectives focus on more immediate causes in individual learning history and processes of attention, interpretation, judgment, and memory. Learning and cognitive processes combine with each other and are influenced by biological and cultural background. Phenomenological perspectives focus on immediate subjective interpretations. All the perspectives are tightly interlinked, as each set of factors influences, and is influenced by, the others.

Combining the Different Perspectives

In chapter 1, we derived two broad principles from the different historical perspectives: (1) social behavior is goal oriented, and (2) social behavior represents a continual interaction between the person and the situation. Now that we've reviewed the field of social psychology, let's revisit these two broad principles and the essential lessons about them that have emerged.

Social Behavior Is Goal Oriented

For each topic in social psychology, we began with a simple question: What goals or motives underlie this particular sort of behavior? Why did Nansook Hong cling to an abusive marriage for over a decade? Why did Sempo Sugihara sacrifice his own career to save Jews from the concentration camps when so many others failed to help? Why did Klansman C. P. Ellis give up his prejudices to befriend a black civil rights worker he previously despised? And what clues about everyday motivation can we draw from these exceptional cases?

With regard to the question of why people like Sugihara help others, for example, we considered four general goals: to gain genetic and material advantages, to enhance social standing and approval, to manage self-image, and to manage moods and emotions. We discussed the question of why people like Charles Manson and Al Capone act violently in terms of four likely goals: to cope with feelings of annoyance, to gain material or social benefits, to gain or maintain status, and to protect oneself or others. And we considered the question of why people affiliate with their friends in terms of four goals: to get social support, to get information, to gain status, and to exchange material benefits.

In looking back over the different goals, we can see that the same goals sometimes underlie very different social behaviors. For example, we discussed how the goal of improving or maintaining status influenced self-presentation, social influence, friendship, helping, love, aggression, and prejudice. With our discussion of the broad range of social behavior behind us, it's time to consider the commonalities between the goals behind different social behaviors. Can we derive a smaller number of fundamental motivations that, taken together, underlie most of our social interactions?

In chapter 1, we discussed several examples of broad motives underlying social behavior: (1) to establish social ties, (2) to understand ourselves and others, (3) to gain and maintain status, (4) to defend ourselves and those we value, and (5) to attract and retain mates. We chose these particular motives for a reason. After looking over the broad field of social psychology, we concluded that one or more of these motives are related directly or indirectly to almost all the social behaviors discussed throughout this book. In a sense, these broad motives give us hints about the ultimate function of many of the things we do with, to, and for other people.

Let's consider these fundamental motives again, with an eye to two questions: How do these broad motives shed light on the function of social behaviors ranging from altruism to xenophobia? And how do these broad motives connect to more specific day-to-day and moment-to-moment goals that arise in our interactions with other people?

To Establish Social Ties A central purpose of social behavior is to form and maintain friendly associations with other people (Baumeister & Leary, 1995; Taylor et al., 2000). With other people on our side, we can accomplish tasks we would never dream of on our own, as Martin Luther King, Jr., drew strength from his supporters to help focus America's attention on civil rights problems. And with others against us, the simplest task can turn into a nightmare. In looking back, we see that the motivation to establish social ties reveals itself in various forms: to be seen as likable (chapter 4), to fit in (chapter 5), to conform to the preferences of others (chapter 6), or to gain approval (chapters 9 and 11). And chapter 7 was dedicated entirely to the topic of affiliation and friendship.

The list of goals we discussed in chapter 7 (getting social support and information, improving one's social status, and exchanging material benefits) tells us something important about the different goals of social behavior. They are often interdependent. In particular, when you establish social ties you open the gate to satisfying your other social goals. To understand ourselves and others, to gain and maintain status, to attract and retain mates, and to defend ourselves and those we value, it is crucial that we seek and maintain the company of others. When that goal is blocked, as when King was asked by the Kennedys to break off two important friendships, it can be a painfully difficult experience. Indeed, King tried to get Attorney General Robert Kennedy to tell him which of his phones was being tapped so he could continue his friendship with Stanley Levison, even when continuing that friendship could damage the very cause to which King had dedicated his life.

Mark Leary and his colleagues (1995) argued that social ties underlie another important goal—to maintain self-esteem. When students were excluded from a work group, for instance, or when they merely thought about doing something likely to lead to social rejection (causing an accident or cheating on an exam), they reported feelings of lowered self-esteem. In all, these researchers conducted five studies supporting their hypothesis that self-esteem is a *sociometer*—an index of whether we feel included or excluded by other people (Leary & Baumeister, 2000).

To Understand Ourselves and Others Was Martin Luther King, Jr., really a Communist-influenced, rabble-rousing hypocrite, as J. Edgar Hoover claimed? Did your sister's new coworker bring her coffee and a doughnut because he's a genuinely nice guy, an obsequious schmoozer, or a lecherous wolf in sheep's clothing? Are you charming and likable, as your best friend says you are, or a socially awkward klutz, as you felt when you went on that blind date? It's hard to get through any social interaction without giving some thought to who the players are, why they're doing what they're doing, and what they're thinking and expecting of you (Stevens & Fiske, 1995). Hence, the motivation to understand ourselves and others has come up again and again throughout this book. It was the focus of chapter 3, and it was central to several other chapters. For instance, we included the goal of gaining or organizing social information in our discussions of attitudes, friendship, prejudice, and groups, and we discussed the goal of developing and managing self-concept in one form or another in the chapters on attitudes, self-presentation, social influence, prosocial behavior, and prejudice.

Our discussion in chapter 3 highlighted another important point about broad social motives: they can be broken down into component subgoals. Sometimes we search for information to simplify the world, sometimes to protect our views of ourselves, and sometimes to gain a detailed and accurate picture of ourselves and others (Pittman, 1998). Which informational goal is active depends on other aspects of the situation. Sometimes it's enough to take a cognitive shortcut, as when we assume that the next person driving a yellow car with a light on top will give us a ride to the airport. Sometimes we need to search more deeply for accurate information, as when we lose a game of chess to someone we classified as a ditzy airhead. And sometimes we need to protect our self-regard, as when we refuse a phone call from a former lover who's calling to read us a long list of our personal flaws.

For the family. *King's speech at the march on Washington made reference to his own children, and his desire to make a safer world for those he held dear no doubt contributed to his zeal in fighting for civil rights.*

To Gain and Maintain Status As we noted earlier, the goal of gaining and maintaining status was central to several topics, including self-presentation, social influence, affiliation and friendship, love and romantic relationships, aggression, prejudice, and group dynamics. Self-esteem is linked not only to whether we feel liked by others but also to whether we feel respected by others. We feel better about ourselves when others look up to us. As we noted in chapter 3, for example, North Americans and Europeans are motivated to see themselves as, compared to others, more competent, more intelligent, and otherwise more worthy of respect (e.g., Steele, 1988; Tesser, 1988). Likewise, in chapter 11, we saw that people sometimes make themselves feel better by focusing on how another person or group is below them in status (Brewer & Brown, 1998).

Status carries not only the benefits of direct access to rewards. As we discussed in chapter 8, it also brings the indirect benefits of attracting mates and promoting the survival of our offspring. As we discussed in chapter 7, people all around the world think about themselves and others along two prominent dimensions—agreeableness and social dominance (White, 1980; Wiggins & Broughton, 1985). We want to know not only whether someone else is nice but also whether he or she is above or below us in the status hierarchy.

Psychologists Robert and Joyce Hogan (1991) note the occasional conflict between the two basic motives to be liked and to gain status. If you're too eager to move ahead of others in the social hierarchy, you may lose points for agreeableness. At the same time, if others like you, trust you, and feel like part of your family or team, they will not only help you succeed, but also share in your glory (Tesser, 1988).

To Defend Ourselves and Those We Value Violence and prejudice, as we saw in chapters 10, 11, and 13, are often triggered by the goal of defending ourselves and our group members. On the other hand, this same motive can contribute to prosocial behaviors, because risking yourself to save another often means fighting for him or her. King's interwoven images of angry, unsatisfied blacks and children victimized by prejudice made it clear that he believed his quest was, in some way, a battle for his own children's future. Indeed, such connections help illustrate the link between the goals of ingroup protection and reproduction.

At the beginning of the chapter, we discussed J. Edgar Hoover's vendetta against King. On closer examination, Hoover's antagonism toward King and the civil rights movement was linked to an exaggerated goal of self- and group defense. In the next section, we discuss the fine line between paranoid suspicion and normal social skepticism and self-protection.

FOCUS ON Social Dysfunction

The Thin Line between Normal and Abnormal Social Functioning

Historian Arthur Schlesinger (1978), a former special assistant to President Kennedy, described J. Edgar Hoover as suffering from "incipient paranoia." Likewise, a recent biography of Hoover described him on the book's jacket as "paranoid" (Gentry, 1991). Was the man who headed the FBI for almost fifty years actually paranoid?

Hoover certainly did not suffer from the hallucinations or disorganized speech patterns that qualify a person for a diagnosis of paranoid schizophrenia. However, he did have beliefs that others regarded as delusions, and he met several of the criteria for the milder diagnosis of paranoid personality disorder. According to the *DSM-IV-R,* the manual used by clinicians to diagnose mental disorders, paranoid personality disorder involves a pervasive distrust and suspiciousness that others are acting in malevolent ways. Its symptoms include unjustified suspicion that others are deceiving you; preoccupation with unjustified doubts about the loyalty of friends or associates; a tendency to bear grudges; hypersensitivity to being slighted by others; an obsession with sexual infidelity; and a tendency to counterattack against perceived slights or assaults (based on Barlow & Durand, 1995).

Hoover showed several symptoms of a paranoid personality. He kept a list of personal enemies, amongst whom Martin Luther King, Jr., and Eleanor Roosevelt were prominent. Both of them had angered Hoover by speaking out against the FBI. King's slight was merely to mention to a reporter that he agreed with a *New York Times* article critical of the FBI's handling of one particular civil rights case. Hoover kept detailed information about his enemies' sex lives, which he released to the press whenever he felt anyone might become a threat to him. Former agents who disagreed with Hoover about policy were referred to as "Judases." One former assistant to Hoover stated that "If he didn't like you, he destroyed you." When a book critical of the FBI was published in 1950, Hoover had the publisher called before the House Un-American Activities Committee and slandered as having links with Communists.

Hoover was unquestionably a defensive, suspicious, and hostile man, but was he insane? In fact, his behaviors indicate the sometimes fine line between normal and abnormal social processes. Consider a few other facts about his situation. Most observers, including Attorney General Kennedy and many members of the FBI, believed that the Communist party had very little influence on the civil rights movement. Communist party membership in the United States had been dwindling for decades and virtually disappeared after revelations about Stalin's reign of terror. However, the party had been popular around the time of the Great Depression. Socialists and Communists were active in the growth of organized labor unions, and they helped promote poverty-buffering policies such as unemployment insurance. Several of King's associates, including Jack O'Dell, Stanley Levison, and Bayard Rustin, had indeed been members of Communist or socialist groups at that time. Hoover had uncovered those associations and released a book, called *Masters of Deceit,* discussing how Communists had infiltrated social action groups. And there was, in fact, a true "Communist conspiracy" to foment worldwide revolution, which included spies and covert Communist operations which Hoover and the FBI had uncovered inside the United States.

Hence, Hoover's tendency to interpret ambiguous associations as links to the Communist conspiracy demonstrates normal cognitive biases discussed in earlier chapters, such as the availability heuristic (overestimating the probability of events that come easily to mind) and the confirmation bias (seeking to affirm the truth of our theories without considering other possibilities). These types of cognitive biases plague us all, so it makes sense that a man who spent most of his life searching for hidden conspiracies would be on red alert for any remotely suspicious ties between people. Because Hoover saw Communism as a serious threat to the United States, his defensive attitude toward anything associated with Communism is a natural outgrowth of ingroup protective tendencies.

Hoover's particular proclivity for collecting damaging evidence about his enemies' sex lives also makes a bit more sense when considered in light of reports of another allegation—that Hoover was himself a homosexual. If the U.S. public had been informed that the crime-fighting defender of American values was a homosexual, his powerful position (which depended on continual reappointment by elected politicians) would have been seriously jeopardized. By maintaining extensive intelligence on the sex lives of powerful people, including senators, congressmen, presidents, and their wives, and by demonstrating a willingness to use that information, he managed to hold his position as head of the FBI for five decades. The inherent political power of sexual secrets is immense, as the case of President Clinton and Monica Lewinsky has more recently illustrated.

Hoover's case thus demonstrates the central lesson of the Focus on Social Dysfunction features throughout this book. Disordered social behavior often reveals normal psychological mechanisms in bolder relief. Conversely, understanding normal psychological mechanisms can often help us understand the function of apparently disordered behavior. ■

J. Edgar Hoover and Clyde Tolleson. *Hoover was alleged to have had a homosexual relationship with his assistant, Clyde Tolleson. Here they are shown on one of their semiannual vacations together in Miami Beach. Hoover's inclination to collect secrets about other people's sex lives may have been motivated in part by the knowledge of the damage he would suffer if his own private life were made public.*

Hoover did more than spy on powerful leaders; he also did them numerous favors, such as providing useful secrets about their political opponents. This demonstrates another important point: the motivation to protect ourselves and our group members doesn't always lead to hostility. Sometimes defense involves circling the wagons; sometimes it involves inviting the enemy in for dinner. We saw in chapter 11 that the most satisfactory solution for the intergroup hostilities among boys in the Robber's Cave summer camp was to have the two groups work together toward a common goal (Sherif, Harvey, White, Hood, & Sherif, 1961). In this way, the motivation toward group defensiveness can be linked to the kinder and gentler motivation to form social alliances.

To Attract and Retain Mates From an evolutionary perspective, the social behavior of all animals, including humans, is influenced by behavioral mechanisms that ultimately serve one central motive—successful reproduction. As we noted in chapter 8's discussion of love and romantic relationships, however, to say that animals are designed to reproduce doesn't mean simply that everything they do is ultimately designed to result in sex. Reproduction involves much more than just sexual intercourse. All mammals, and humans in particular, are designed to have only a few offspring, on which they lavish a great deal of care (Zeifman & Hazan, 1997). Whereas some species of fish produce hundreds of offspring every season, more than five human children is considered a large family. John and Robert Kennedy came from a relatively large family. There were nine children, but those children were born over a period of 17 years, and their parents spent another three decades caring for them. So compared with most other species, humans demonstrate very strong "family values" and devote tremendous resources to child care.

As we noted in discussing the case of Elián Gonzales in chapter 1, humans differ from most mammals in another important way. Good parenting is a goal not only of the human female but also of the male (Geary, 2000). And human mothers and fathers give their offspring not only food and shelter but also years of psychological support and social survival training. In many cases, parents even set their children up with jobs and marriages when they reach adulthood. John and Robert's father, Joseph Kennedy, used his considerable wealth and power to help them survive and succeed. As we discussed in chapter 8, men and women join together to raise the children in every human culture. These parental bonds are a part of our biological heritage, although, like language, they are flexible and sensitive to the environment.

The goal of attracting and retaining mates demonstrates two other important points about goals. First they aren't necessarily conscious. Second, they involve imperfectly tuned mechanisms. Biological theorists assume that all animals in the world today, including modern humans, are here because their ancestors reproduced more efficiently than their competitors. But biologists don't assume that ants or geese or humans had ancestors that were conscious of the goal of reproducing their genes. Nor were those ancestors infallible in making the most adaptive choices. Ants sometimes commit mindless suicide by attacking a human who has a can of insect spray in hand, and geese raised by humans sometimes try to mate with the wrong species. In so doing, these animals are enacting programs that, in most other circumstances, helped their ancestors survive and reproduce. In the case of human beings,

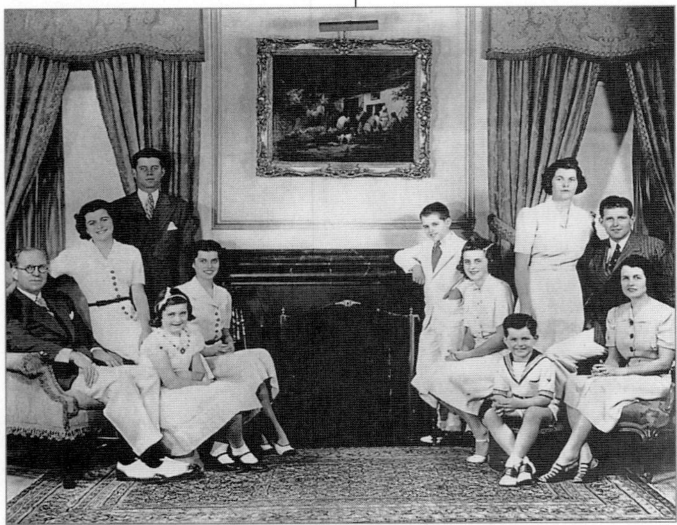

Family values. *The motive to attract and maintain mates is ultimately linked to successful reproduction. Unlike the males in most other mammalian species, human males, like Joseph Kennedy (shown here with his wife, Rose, and their children), contribute considerable time and resources to their children. [John and Robert (in white suit) are standing; Edward (later a senator) is the youngest boy in front.]*

we saw that our choices of mates are, in many cases, motivated neither by a conscious drive to reproduce nor by any other obvious "rational" strategy. The avoidance of unrelated members of the opposite sex raised together in a kibbutz "family," for example, wasn't based on a conscious adaptive choice. Instead, it seemed to reflect a mechanism that helped most of our ancestors avoid the harmful genetic consequences of incest.

Are There Other Basic Motives Underlying Social Behavior? We believe most of the particular goals that we've addressed in this book can be linked to one of five basic social motives: to form alliances, to gather social information, to gain status, to protect oneself and one's group, and to mate. In many cases, a particular social behavior can simultaneously serve more than one motive—joining a group can result in social support, social information, increased status, and self-protection, for instance, and finding a mate can likewise further many objectives besides the direct goal of starting a family.

On a moment-to-moment basis, however, our movement through the social world is rarely driven by an awareness of these grand-scale "ultimate" motives. Instead, we guide our life toward shorter-term, proximate goals (Little, 1989). When Martin Luther King, Jr., and J. Edgar Hoover finally met, the two were quite cordial to each other (Gentry, 1991). King probably turned on the charm with the very narrow goal of getting this potentially dangerous man to form a more favorable impression of him, not the goal of benefitting his children or of promoting racial equality. Likewise, each of the fundamental motives we've discussed can be subdivided into several more immediate goals. Attracting a mate, forming a relationship, responding to a competitor's flirtation with one's partner, and sharing child care are all part of the ultimate goal of successful reproduction, but we need to do very different things to achieve the various subgoals.

In several cases, we discussed social goals that don't serve social ends but instead serve the more general motivation to seek rewards or avoid unpleasant feelings. For some time, psychologists tried to reduce all behavior to one or two content-free motivations, such as "seeking reward." However, many psychologists now search for more specific goals aimed at solving particular problems (Pinker, 1997; Sedikides & Skowronski, 1997). There are no doubt certain categories of resources that are generally rewarding, such as increases in status or access to food. But particular social situations may change everything. Whether an M&M, a handshake, a bit of gossip, a kiss, a compliment, or a victory is reinforcing, punishing, or neutral critically depends on the social context in which it occurs and on the goals that are activated at the time. A handshake from someone we desire as a mate, a kiss from someone we regard as an enemy, or a smashing victory in a game of chess against one of our own children, for instance, may be more punishment than reward. Hence, when we want to understand the root causes of social behavior, it's often more fruitful to consider goals at a more specific level and to consider how those goals interact with the situation the person is in, as we discuss in the next section.

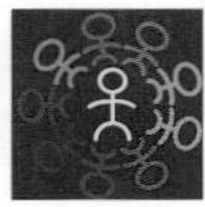

The Interaction Between the Person and the Situation

As we've seen, people differ in their desires for social support, social information, status, sex, and personal security. They also vary in other ways that affect social relationships—in their beliefs, in their attributional strategies, in their self-esteem, and so on. Some people, like Hoover, are defensively hostile much of the time; others, like King, are more often self-sacrificially altruistic. These differences between people have been studied from all the different perspectives (see Figure 14.5).

Perspective	Person	Situation
Evolutionary	• Genetic predispositions • Human nature	• Features in our ancestors' environments linked to survival or reproduction
Sociocultural	• Internal social standards	• Societal norms
Social Learning	• Habits • Conditioned preferences	• Rewards • Punishments
Social Cognition	• Schemas • Remembered episodes • Attributional strategies	• Attention-grabbing features of the social environment
Phenomenological	• Current goals • Social constructions	• Immediate situation (as perceived or misperceived)

Figure 14.5
Different perspectives on the person and situation.

Each of the theoretical perspectives takes a slightly different (but compatible) view of factors in the person and in the situation.

We've also seen that situations vary in the extent to which they trigger different motivations. Some situations, such as a personal insult or another person's flirting with one's lover, bring out the defensive vindictiveness in most of us. Other situations, such as the sight of a starving child, bring out the altruistic tendencies in most of us. These situational factors range from momentary changes in the social situation to childhood experiences to broad cultural norms about appropriate behavior.

Finally, we have seen that there is a continual interaction between those factors inside the person and those in the social situation. The many ways in which person and situation factors interact can be summarized in terms of six general principles.

Different Persons Respond Differently to the Same Situation As we noted in chapter 2, Gordon Allport observed that "the same fire that melts the butter, hardens the egg." Two people may focus on the same details of the same situation and nevertheless respond differently to it. Threats to our lives would stop many of us from persisting in most courses of action, but for Martin Luther King, Jr., who had built his life around the teachings of dedicated martyrs such as Jesus Christ and Mahatma Ghandi, such threats seemed to make him fight harder. Likewise, we've seen that how people respond to persuasive arguments, orders from authority, hostile insults, and attractive members of the opposite sex can vary as a function of differences in their personalities.

Situations choose people. *Someone like John F. Kennedy Jr., who was tall, dark, handsome, intelligent, and wealthy (even if he were not also the son of an American hero) had very few doors closed in his face but instead was frequently chosen to enter situations such as parties, dates, friendships, and jobs.*

Situations Choose the Person Other people could have led the Montgomery bus boycott, but Martin Luther King, Jr. was drafted by his peers. Other people would have loved to direct the FBI, but J. Edgar Hoover was appointed. And other people dreamed of being president of the United States in 1960, but John F. Kennedy was the one elected. Obviously, not everyone gets to enter every situation he or she would like. We are sometimes chosen, sometimes overlooked, and sometimes rejected by potential dates, potential friends, potential athletic teams, potential colleges, and potential jobs. Those choices are themselves a function of our enduring characteristics and our self-presentations—how others perceive our likeability, our competence, and our social dominance. In this final way, then, the social situation and the person become inseparable from each other, so that it becomes meaningless to ask where one ends and the other begins. Our personalities and our situations can truly be said to cause one another.

People choose situations. *Robert Kennedy's son Michael seemed to relish dangerous situations that would make others cringe—kayaking through the Snake River rapids and leaping off seventy-five-foot cliffs, for instance. Despite warnings from the local ski patrol, he continued to play football while racing downhill on skis, an activity that led to his death in 1997.*

Why delve so deeply into the complex interactions between persons and situations? Why not just keep our explanations simple? The answer is that simplistic explanations are often incorrect. Although the cognitive misers within us are often satisfied with simple black or white answers, the truth is usually a much more thought-provoking blend of checkerboards and swirls in various shades of gray. Searching carefully through these complexities helps us avoid placing too much blame on the single individual or making the converse error of viewing people as passive pawns of their situations. Charles Manson's neglect by a delinquent mother and Martin Luther King, Jr.'s, happy childhood in the home of a successful Baptist minister were different enough to have shaped them in important ways. But not every neglected child turns out to be a vicious mass murderer, and not every child of a happy religious home turns out to be a great social crusader.

Persons Choose Their Situations Most of us are aware of the power of the situation. Parents warn their children to beware of the bad influences of unsavory friends and lovers, high school counselors advise students to select just the right college, and religious leaders counsel us to avoid places of temptation. Although we don't always follow such counsel, most of us do avoid certain situations and actively seek out others. We saw, for example, that gender-typed males will volunteer to watch erotic films whereas gender-typed females will not. Likewise, violence-prone people are more likely to choose a violent film to watch, whereas those having a more pacific nature won't. In this way, the relationship between person and situation gets magnified—delinquent teens choose to hang out with other ruffians; well-behaved teens choose the church group; intellectuals, the science club. As a consequence, their respective delinquent, well-behaved, and highbrow tendencies will be further enhanced.

Different Situations Prime Different Parts of the Person Sometimes, we want people to like us; other times, we want them to respect us; still other times, we want them to fear us. In some circumstances, we want another person to be completely frank with us; in others we prefer the person be polite and diplomatic. These motives rarely just pop out of thin air—they are more often triggered by the situations in which we find ourselves. For example, most of us can be driven to obsession by a decision about buying a new car or a choice between two potential mates. We've shown at several points in the book that situations having important personal consequences motivate most people to search for accurate and thorough information (Neuberg

Different situations activate different parts of the self. *In the photo at the left (smiling), Hillary Rodham Clinton is preparing to speak to a group of women leaders in Dublin. In the photo at the right, she is listening to questions during the confirmation hearing for George W. Bush's nominee for EPA administrator, Christie Whitman, whose poor record on environmental protection was seen by Democrats as antithetical to the EPA's goals.*

& Fiske, 1987). Situations in which we're mentally overloaded, or in which our decisions don't have important consequences, on the other hand, such as buying a Christmas present for Uncle Herbert late on December 24, tend to trigger a motivation to take cognitive shortcuts—to trust an authority, to go along with the crowd, or to buy from the friendliest salesperson. In short, personal motives are almost always connected to triggers in the social situation.

Persons Change the Situation In our discussion of groups, we saw that a single individual could change the direction of a whole group of others, either from the top down, in the case of leaders such as Margaret Thatcher, or from the bottom up, as in the case of minority influence. During the course of his years as director, J. Edgar Hoover transformed the Federal Bureau of Investigation into a much more powerful, and more paranoid, organization than it had been before. These changes influenced the behaviors not only of several presidential administrations but also of thousands of other U.S. citizens.

Situations Change the Person Although we may do our best to choose situations that match our personal dispositions, we often end up in circumstances we couldn't perfectly predict. A reserved woman may have chosen a certain liberal arts college because she wanted to avoid the crowds of a large, urban university and found an unexpectedly nonconformist social climate. At the end of the college experience, that person is more likely to be politically liberal (Newcomb, 1961). Throughout this book, we've shown how social behavior can be influenced by cultural norms that vary across societies or within one society over time. Martin Luther King, Jr.'s, role as a neighborhood pastor was forever changed by the pressure on him to lead the Montgomery bus boycott, and each one of us is likewise changed in smaller ways by the jobs we take, the people who befriend us, and sometimes even by a chance event such as the glance of an attractive stranger at a party.

Summary

Much of our social behavior is driven by motives to establish social ties, to understand ourselves and others, to gain and maintain status, to defend ourselves and those we value, and to attract and retain mates. These motives are interdependent and can be broken into more immediate subgoals. Persons and situations continuously interact in that different situations and different facets of situations trigger different motivations, different people respond differently to the same situation, people change and choose their situations, and situations change and choose people.

Why Research Methods Matter

If the social world were simpler, we could just trust our eyes and ears to tell us why people act the way they do. But research on self-presentation and social cognition teaches us that our eyes and ears don't always take in the full story. Not only do other people try to hide their own motives in very skillful ways, but also our own minds often distort, oversimplify, or deny what we see and hear. Even if we could clear away all these cognitive and motivational biases, there would still be our limited perceptual capacities and the constraints of reality to add confusion. Even a microscope won't allow us to see how different genes interact with one another and with earlier life experiences to affect how different people respond to their everyday social encounters. As we've just discussed, persons and situations interact in highly complex and reciprocal ways that can make the search for causal relationships boggling to the unaided mind.

The search for scientific explanations of social behavior, then, requires a very special sort of detective work. Research methods are the tools that allow that detective work to be done. For this reason, understanding research methods is important not only to the social scientist but also to every one of us. After all, we're all the consumers of social science information. Can we trust the conclusions of a magazine article or a television documentary about the causes of gang violence or teen pregnancy or racial conflict? Just because a conclusion is offered confidently by a well-spoken, attractive news commentator doesn't mean it's right. Without research to back up his or her conclusion, the expert's opinion is subject to all the same biases of social perception and social cognition that can lead you or your father or your great-aunt Ginger astray.

FOCUS ON Method

Some Conclusions for Consumers of Social Science Information

Throughout this book, we've discussed a number of detective tools that psychologists use to overcome their own perceptual and cognitive limitations. These included general-purpose tools, such as meta-analysis and unobtrusive measures, and specialized tools, such as facial action coding and behavior genetic studies of twins separated at birth. Looking over these methods yields some general conclusions for amateur and professional social psychological detective work.

1. *Look for good descriptions to accompany explanations.* Before considering motives for a crime, a detective needs an accurate picture of what happened. Experiments help uncover cause-and-effect relationships but cannot paint a complete picture of real-world behavior. Descriptive methods such as surveys and archives help fill out the picture. Ideally, research programs go "full cycle" between experimentation—used to unravel causal mechanisms—and field work—used to keep the researcher tracking phenomena that really matter in the outside world (Cialdini, 1995).

Good observation requires more than just the naked eye. Like a telescope to an astronomer, some techniques can help psychologists examine otherwise invisible social phenomena. For example, factor analysis taps the capacities of computers to help researchers discern statistical patterns among attitudes, feelings, and behaviors, such as the five factors of personality or the three factors of love (Aron & Westbay, 1996; McCrae & John, 1992). Not all such methods require fancy technology. Analyses of emotional expression exploit simple, slow-motion videotape technology, and thought-listing techniques involve merely asking people to make their private ruminations public (Ekman & Friesen, 1971; Petty & Wegener, 1998).

2. *Don't trust everything people say.* The butler may claim innocence with an earnest face, but the jury should still review the evidence. As we noted, people's reports can be biased or dead wrong. You may not be willing or able to say if your angry outburst was affected by feelings of insecurity, for example, or if your empathy for a hungry child was based on a general human inclination toward nurturance. Several techniques, including unobtrusive measurement and behavior genetic methods, are designed to see beyond people's limited views.

As an information consumer, you don't need to be a methodological expert, but when you hear about research relevant to you, you ought to ask if the conclusions are based on people's reports about things they cannot, or will not, describe accurately. Again, like a good detective, you must examine the whole picture. When survey respondents admit behaviors such as masturbation or homicidal fantasies, we can guess that, if anything, they are underestimating. But if they describe themselves in desirable ways—that they harbor no racial prejudices, for example—it's best to look for covert measures to corroborate their stories.

3. *Beware of confounds.* Just because the butler was at the crime scene and owned a gun doesn't mean he did it. In experiments, confounding variables are factors accidentally varied along with the independent variable, as when children who watch an aggressive film encounter a hostile-looking male experimenter with a large tattoo, while children in the control condition encounter a saintly looking, grandmotherly experimenter. Maybe the grandma in this poorly designed imaginary study suppressed children's expressions of hostility or the tattooed man instigated them, or maybe not. But if the same experimenters didn't run both conditions, we can't tease apart the effects of the film, versus the experimenter's demeanor, on the children's aggression.

Confounds also plague descriptive studies, as when a researcher finds a correlation between property crimes and ethnicity but fails to consider social class. Social class is a potential confound because it's systematically linked with both race and property crimes (the wealthy have less need to burglarize hubcaps). Without measuring social class, we can't tease out (or unconfound) its effects.

Behavior genetic methods, discussed in chapter 9, incorporate several techniques for teasing apart confounds. Children resemble their parents and siblings in social behaviors ranging from altruism to violence. These similarities could be due to either shared family environment or shared genes. Without special methods, we can't tell. By examining adopted siblings (who share an environment but not genes) or identical twins separated at birth (who share genes but not an environment), we can begin to pull apart the normally confounded factors.

4. *Ask for converging evidence.* Just as a detective wouldn't trust an individual witness without checking other sources, so we shouldn't place too much confidence in any lone research finding (McGrath, Martin, & Kukla, 1982). Chance or unintended error may have led to erroneous conclusions. One tool for dealing with this problem is meta-analysis. For example, numerous studies, mentioned in chapter 10, examined how violent media affect aggression in viewers (Wood, Wong, & Chachere, 1991). Some found positive results, some negative results, and some no results at all. The different results are due to random error, variations in the independent and dependent variables, and so on. Meta-analysis statistically combines studies to reduce dangers from these chance factors and to allow more confident conclusions.

Meta-analysis cannot rule out a systematic bias across different studies. For example, if 100 studies examined college students delivering electric shock to other students in laboratories, we're not sure whether the results apply to aggression outside the lab. To deal with this problem, researchers use **triangulation**—examining the same problem using different research methods, each having different biases. Field studies suggesting that children who watch more violent TV are more aggressive cannot separate cause and effect, because violence-prone children may choose violent TV shows. Laboratory experiments in which children are randomly assigned to watch violent or nonviolent programs solve that problem but raise questions of artificiality that field studies do not. Surveys of parents can ask about more natural everyday aggression, but are subject to biased parental memory. If all these studies nevertheless point in the same direction, despite opposite strengths and weaknesses, we can make more confident conclusions (Anderson & Bushman, 1997). As discussed in chapter 1, the situation is like that of a detective confronted with several imperfect witnesses: one witness loves the butler and is hard of hearing, one hates the butler but wasn't wearing his glasses, and another has intact vision and hearing but doesn't know the butler well enough to make an airtight identification. If they all agree that he did it, though, the detective can draw a more confident conclusion about the butler's culpability. ■

Triangulation *Examining the same problem using different research methods, each having different biases.*

Thus research methods help overcome a number of problems, including people's biases and limitations in reporting their own social behaviors. As consumers of social science information about how to win friends, influence lovers, pacify potential enemies, and raise happy children, we should all take care before accepting the unsubstantiated opinions of experts.

Summary

Research methods are tools for eliminating bias and seeing things otherwise invisible. They offer some practical recommendations for how to understand the world, including: (1) to look for good descriptions to bolster theoretical explanations, (2) not to trust everything people say about their social motives, (3) to watch out for confounds, and (4) to ask for converging evidence before being too confident about any given conclusion.

How Does Social Psychology Fit into the Network of Knowledge?

In chapter 1, we noted social psychology's close interconnections with other areas of psychology. In later chapters, we've seen numerous connections with *developmental psychology*, observing how adult patterns of aggression, altruism, and love, for instance, grow out of basic predispositions and early learning (see Table 14.1). Connections with *personality psychology* were incorporated into every chapter, as we considered how traits inside the individual continually interact with the social environment. Links to *environmental psychology* showed up in our discussions of heat and aggression, overcrowding, and environmental destruction. In every chapter, we saw connections with *clinical psychology* in the Focus on Social Dysfunction features, which considered topics from mild obsessiveness to paranoia. Likewise, we drew links with *cognitive psychology* in every chapter of this book, as we explored how mental processes of attention, perception, memory, and decision making are intertwined with person–situation interactions. *Physiological psychology* was essential to our discussions of hormonal effects on sexual and aggressive behavior, of genetic influences on altruism, and so on. Given the view of some cognitive psychologists that many of the unique features of the human brain evolved to deal with problems of living in social groups (Pinker, 1997; Tooby & Cosmides, 1992), it makes sense that we human beings devote many of our mental capacities to dealing with other people.

Table 14.1 Social psychology's connections with other areas of psychology.

Area of Psychology	Example of Overlapping Question
Developmental	Does the early attachment between mother and infant influence love relationships in later life?
Personality	What individual differences predict aggressive behavior?
Environmental	What social conditions lead people to recycle?
Clinical	How is paranoia connected to normal group defensiveness?
Cognitive	How does the limited human attention span affect stereotypes?
Physiological	How does testosterone affect human relationships?

Table 14.2 Social psychology's connections with other basic sciences.

Area of Study	Example of Overlapping Question
Genetics	Is altruism linked to common genes shared within families?
Biochemistry	Does testosterone similarly affect male and female behavior?
Sociology	How do groups choose leaders?
Anthropology	Are there universal patterns to human marriage?
Economics	Are there circumstances when people sharing a common resource (such as a forest or an ocean) will restrain their selfish tendencies that lead to overexploitation?
Political Science	How do group processes affect policy decisions in international conflict situations?
Ethology	Do the mating rituals of peacocks shed any light on human courtship?
Ecology	How does the dynamic balance between predators and prey in a forest link with the behavior of students playing a prisoner's dilemma game in a laboratory?

Social psychology is thus centrally linked to all the other areas of brain and behavioral science (Brewer, Kenny, & Norem, 2000).

At a broader level, social psychology has bridges to other disciplines outside psychology's loose boundaries. At the most basic level, research on altruism, aggression, and love has been linked to developments in *genetics* and *biochemistry*. At the aggregate level, research on groups, organizations, and societies weaves social psychology together with the social sciences—*sociology*, *anthropology*, *economics*, and *political science*. At this level, social psychology is also linked to those areas of biological research on complex relationships between groups of animals and their natural environments—*ethology* and *ecology*. Table 14.2 lists some examples of the kinds of questions that link social psychology and other basic sciences.

FOCUS ON Application

Social Psychology's Usefulness for Business, Medicine, and Law

One goal of research is simply to satisfy our curiosity. The human mind craves knowledge about the causes and purposes of human love, self-sacrificial altruism, prejudice, and violence. We want to understand what makes ourselves and others tick. But basic science has always gone hand in hand with application. The discoveries of ancient astronomers gazing at the stars allowed explorers and entrepreneurs to sail around the globe and find their way back to where they started; the discoveries of early biologists curious about the human body and about the tiny animals moving under their microscopes eventually led to modern medicine; and the discoveries of physicists interested in abstract principles of gravity and motion eventually made it possible to land a man on the moon (Boorstin, 1983). Indeed, the philosophical questions that stimulate research in basic science often intrigue us because they deal with puzzling practical problems. The more we can understand about love or friendship or ingroup favoritism, the better chance we have to prevent divorce or loneliness or destructive prejudice.

In every chapter of this textbook, we've spotlighted bridges between social psychology and applied sciences. For example, we saw a number of links with business, as in our feature on honesty in the workplace in chapter 2. Unpleasant relationships on the job can fill our days with misery, damage our bodies, and even disrupt our home lives (Barling & Rosenbaum, 1986). J. Edgar Hoover wasn't the only boss whose employees lived in constant fear of his wrath. Social relationships aren't just the icing on our worklives; they're very often the cake itself. Most jobs require some degree of negotiating, persuading, teaching, disciplining, advising, and cooperating with other people. Hence, there is an inherently close connection between social psychology and business fields such as organizational behavior, marketing, and management. A glance at textbooks in any of these fields reveals considerable overlap with the topics in this textbook. Students who have studied social psychology frequently pursue careers in the business world, and conversely, business students frequently study social psychology as part of their training.

Social psychologists have also built bridges with medicine and other health sciences (Salovey, Rothman, & Rodin, 1998; Snyder, Tennen, Affleck, & Cheavens, 2000). Health psychology interventions were explored in many places throughout this book. Doctors, nurses, and public health officials often find that their persuasive appeals fail to move patients to stop smoking, change unhealthy diets, increase exercise or contraceptive use, or even just take their prescribed medications. Some experts estimate that public health would benefit far more from simple changes in behavior than from dramatic medical discoveries (Matarazzo, 1980). Imagine, for example, the effects on sexually transmitted diseases if all unmarried sexual partners could be convinced to use condoms or the effects on lung cancer if a whole generation of youth could be convinced not to smoke. Without a single advance in medical technology, two of the major health concerns of Western society would practically disappear. Thus, increasing numbers of social psychologists are conducting research on preventive medicine (e.g., Bryan, Aiken, & West, 1999).

A third area in which social psychological principles have been extensively applied is the law (e.g., Ellsworth & Mauro, 1998). We considered these applications in discussing topics such as lie detection, false confessions, and techniques to reduce violence at the societal level. Social psychologists have also conducted research on jury decision making and eyewitness testimony (Wells, 1993; Wells & Leippe, 1981). Obviously, legal argumentation and jury decision making involve attribution, persuasion, and group interaction—processes that social psychologists have studied for decades. In recent years, a number of social psychologists have taken positions teaching in law schools. Increasingly, social psychology students are taking advanced degrees in organizational psychology, health psychology, and legal psychology. ■

In addition to business, medicine, and law, social psychology has obvious implications for education (which involves many of the processes we've discussed throughout this book) and even for engineering (as social communication becomes more and more technologically based). Although social psychological research is often concerned with basic theoretical questions, there are a great number of applications for its theoretical findings. As the pioneering social psychologist Kurt Lewin once said, "There is nothing so practical as a good theory." He would probably be pleased to see the numerous practical applications of the field to which he made such influential theoretical contributions (see Table 14.3).

Summary

Social psychology has bridges to most other disciplines of study, both basic and applied. As we noted in chapter 1, it helps to think of a college education not as a number of disconnected courses but as one long course that provides a set of logical and methodological tools we can use to generate useful knowledge and to answer questions about human nature and our place in the universe.

Table 14.3 Social psychology's connections with applied sciences.

Area of Application	Example of Overlapping Question
Law	How do social pressures within a jury influence the decisions of individual jury members?
Medicine	Can doctors and nurses interact with patients in ways that promote compliance with health recommendations?
Business	Are there ways for management to decrease employee dishonesty?
Education	How do teacher expectancies influence a child's performance in the classroom?
Engineering	How can computer networks be designed to facilitate communication between electronically linked employees?

The Future of Social Psychology

A popular science writer recently suggested that scientists might soon run out of questions to answer. That writer was clearly not familiar with social psychology. Researchers have only begun to understand the complex interactions between person and situation underlying our thoughts and feelings about altruism, racial prejudice, aggression, and group behavior. Indeed, the frontier here is as vast as a great continent, and researchers have so far managed to map only a few intermittent points along the shoreline. As social psychologists explore these questions, they are increasingly joining forces with new integrative disciplines such as cognitive science, evolutionary psychology, and dynamical systems. Cognitive science connects work on social cognition with other research on the workings of the human brain, evolutionary theory provides insights into the ultimate goals of social behavior, and dynamical systems research holds the promise of understanding how the thoughts and motivations of individuals add up to monumental group-level processes from civil rights marches to international conflicts. Because our human ancestors always lived in groups, the eventual integration of the various behavioral and brain sciences will almost certainly have social psychological questions at the fore.

The movement toward a more integrated science of the mind and social behavior isn't only of philosophical interest. It's also laden with immense practical potential. Perhaps the human ingenuity that made it possible to chat with someone on the other side of the globe, to fly from New York to London in an afternoon, and to take close-up photographs of other planets will enable us to solve the great social problems of overpopulation, international conflict, and the destruction of our planet (Oskamp, 2000).

Although such hopes may seem unrealistic now, it's worth keeping in mind that in the few decades since J. Edgar Hoover worried about Communist links to the crowd that marched on Washington, the Cold War between the Soviet Union and the United States has ended and the population explosion has slowed. And when Martin Luther King, Jr., started the fight for civil rights, it still seemed like only a dream that legalized racial discrimination could be erased from U.S. lawbooks. However, the concerted efforts of a committed few made the realization of that dream possible. Perhaps the next century will see advances in the science of social behavior

From individual psychology to society. *Decisions made by single individuals can interact to produce complex, and sometimes unexpected, phenomena at the group level. The civil rights movement provided a grand example of the two-way interaction between individual and society.*

that make it possible for little boys and little girls of different skin colors to walk together in a world free not only of racial intolerance but also of fears of overpopulation, pollution, and warfare. Perhaps the scientific curiosity of your generation will lead to discoveries that one day allow us all to say that we are "free at last!"

CHAPTER 14

Summary

What Ground Have We Covered?

1. We began our investigation of the mysteries of social life with individual motives, feelings, and thoughts. We proceeded to consider how individuals think about, present themselves to, and interact with others. Finally, we explored social processes at the group and global level.
2. The numerous findings of social psychology are best understood not as discrete bits of information but in terms of their implications for broader theoretical perspectives.

Major Theoretical Perspectives of Social Psychology

1. The *sociocultural* perspective focuses on group-level processes such as varying norms across societies.
2. The *evolutionary* perspective focuses on general principles of survival and reproduction that apply across cultures and species.
3. Linking the sociocultural and evolutionary perspectives, we discover common features of human nature underneath sometimes dazzling sociocultural differences.
4. The *social learning* perspective focuses on rewards and punishments in particular environments. Learning processes reflect sociocultural norms and evolved behavioral mechanisms.
5. The *phenomenological* perspective considers how subjective interpretations influence social behavior.
6. The *social cognitive* perspective considers processes involved in noticing, interpreting, judging, and remembering social events. Cognitive scientists and evolutionary psychologists are beginning to search for clues about how evolved brain and behavioral mechanisms are designed to function in the social environment.
7. Examining gender differences and similarities from a variety of perspectives, we see that evolutionary perspectives reveal the biological roots of some sex differences and similarities, sociocultural and social learning perspectives show how sometimes small biological differences can be enhanced by experience, and cognitive perspectives suggest how sex differences sometimes get exaggerated through stereotypes.

Combining the Different Perspectives

1. Our exploration of social life was guided by two broad principles: (1) social behavior is goal oriented, and (2) social behavior represents a continual interaction between person and situation.
2. Several broad motives underlie a wide range of social behavior: (1) to establish social ties, (2) to understand ourselves and others, (3) to gain and maintain status, (4) to defend ourselves and those we value, and (5) to attract and retain mates. These motives are often interdependent and can be subdivided into long-term and immediate subgoals.
3. Studying dysfunctional social behavior can sometimes elucidate normal psychological mechanisms.
4. Some social behaviors serve general, nonsocial motives such as reward seeking. But the search for nonspecific, content-free goals may not be as informative as a search for specific goals aimed at solving particular problems.
5. Person–situation interactions involve six general principles: (1) different people respond differently to the same situation, (2) situations choose people, (3) people choose their situations, (4) different situations prime different parts of the person, (5) people change their situations, and (6) situations change people.

Why Research Methods Matter

1. Research methods are tools that help scientists avoid biased descriptions and explanations.
2. Research methods are the detective tools used by social psychologists. As consumers of scientific results, we should: (1) look for good descriptions to accompany explanations, (2) not trust everything people say, (3) watch for confounds, and (4) ask for converging evidence from different studies and different methods.

How Does Social Psychology Fit into the Network of Knowledge?

1. Social psychology is interconnected with other areas of psychology exploring cognitive and physiological processes, learning and development, individual differences, and disordered behavior.
2. Social psychology links to more molecular sciences such as genetics and molecular biology and to more broadly focused sciences such as ethology, ecology, and other social sciences.

3. Social psychological research has important implications for applied fields such as business, medicine, law, education, and engineering.

The Future of Social Psychology

1. Social psychology increasingly connects with integrative disciplines of cognitive science, evolutionary psychology, and dynamical systems. Because the human mind is designed to promote survival in social groups, social psychological questions are central to an integrated behavioral and brain science.
2. Advances in understanding social behavior could help solve global problems, including overpopulation, international conflict, and environmental destruction.

CHAPTER 14
Key Terms

Proximate explanation *A focus on relatively immediate causes.*

Triangulation *Examining the same problem using different research methods, each having different biases.*

Ultimate explanation *A focus on background or historical causes.*

References

Aaker, D. A., & Myers, J. G. (1987). *Advertising management.* Englewood Cliffs, NJ: Prentice-Hall.

Abalakina-Paap, M., Stephan, W. G., Craig, T., & Gregory, W. L. (1999). Beliefs in conspiracies. *Political Psychology, 20,* 637–647.

Abbey, A. (1982). Sex differences in attributions for friendly behavior: Do males misperceive females' friendliness. *Journal of Personality and Social Psychology, 42,* 830–838.

Abbey, A., Ross, L. T., McDuffie, D., & McAuslan, P. (1996). Alcohol, misperception, and sexual assault: How and why are they linked? In D. M. Buss & N. M. Malamuth (Eds.), *Sex, Power, Conflict* (pp. 138–161). New York: Oxford University Press.

Abelson, R. P. (1981). Psychological status of the script concept. *American Psychologist, 36,* 715–729.

Aberson, C. L., Healy, M., & Romero, V. (2000). Ingroup bias and self-esteem: A meta-analysis. *Personality and Social Psychology Review, 4,* 157–173.

Abu-Lughod, L. (1986). *Veiled sentiments: Honor and poetry in a Bedouin society.* Berkeley: University of California Press.

Acker, M., & Davis, M. H. (1992). Intimacy, passion, and commitment in adult romantic relationships: A test of the triangular theory of love. *Journal of Social and Personal Relationships, 9,* 21–50.

Ackerman, N. W., & Jahoda, M. (1950). *Anti-semitism and emotional disorder: A psychoanalytic interpretation.* New York: Harper.

Adamopolous, J., & Kashima, Y. (1999). *Social psychology and cultural context.* Thousand Oaks, CA: Sage.

Adams, J. (1995). *Sellout: Aldrich Ames and the corruption of the CIA.* New York: Viking.

Adams, R. G. & Bleiszner, R. (1994). An integrative conceptual framework for friendship research. *Journal of Social and Personal Relationships, 11,* 163–184.

Adorno, T. W., Frenkel-Brunswik, E., Levinson, D. J., & Sanford, R. N. (1950). *The authoritarian personality.* New York: Harper and Row.

Affleck, G., Tennen, H., Pfeiffer, C., & Fifield, C. (1987). Appraisals of control and predictability in adapting to a chronic disease. *Journal of Personality and Social Psychology, 53,* 273–279.

Ahlering, R. F., & Parker, L. D. (1989). Need for cognition as a moderator of the primacy effect. *Journal of Research in Personality, 23,* 313–317.

Ahmad, Y., & Smith, P. K. (1994). Bullying in schools and the issue of sex differences. In J. Archer (Ed.), *Male violence* (pp. 70–86). New York: Routledge.

Ainsworth, M. D. S., Blehar, M. C., Waters, E., & Wall, S. (1978). *Patterns of attachment: Assessed in the strange situation and at home.* Hillsdale, NJ: Erlbaum.

Akimoto, S. A., Sanbonmatsu, D. M., & Ho, E. A. (2000). Manipulating personal salience: The effects of performance expectations on physical positioning. *Personality and Social Psychology Bulletin, 26,* 755–761.

Alba, J. W., & Marmorstein, H. (1987). The effects of frequency knowledge on consumer decision making. *Journal of Consumer Research, 14,* 14–25.

Albarracin, D., & Wyer, R. S. (2000). The cognitive impact of past behavior: Influences on beliefs, attitudes, and future behavioral decisions. *Journal of Personality and Social Psychology, 79,* 5–22.

Alcock, J. (1989). *Animal behavior: An evolutionary approach* (4th ed.). Sunderland, MA: Sinauer Associates.

Alcock, J. (1993). *Animal behavior: An evolutionary approach* (5th ed.). Sunderland, MA: Sinauer Associates.

Aldag, R. J., & Fuller, S. R. (1993). Beyond fiasco: A reappraisal of the groupthink phenomenon and a new model of group decision processes. *Psychological Bulletin, 113,* 533–552.

Aldhous, P. (1989). The effects of individual cross-fostering on the development of intrasex kin discrimination in male laboratory mice. *Animal Behavior, 37,* 741–750.

Alicke, M. D. (1985). Global self-evaluation as determined by the desirability and controllability of trait adjectives. *Journal of Personality and Social Psychology, 49,* 1621–1630.

Alicke, M. D., & Largo, E. (1995). The role of the self in the false consensus effect. *Journal of Experimental Social Psychology, 31,* 28–47.

Allee, W. C., Collias, N., & Lutherman, C. (1939). Modification of the social order in flocks of hens by the injection of testosterone propionate. *Physiological Zoology, 12,* 412–440.

Allen, J., Kenrick, D. T., Linder, D. E., & McCall, M. A. (1989). Arousal and attraction: A response facilitation alternative to misattribution and negative reinforcement models. *Journal of Personality and Social Psychology, 57,* 261–270.

Allen, K. M., Blascovich, J., Tomaka, J., & Kelsey, R. M. (1991). Presence of human friends and pet dogs as moderators of autonomic responses to stress in women. *Journal of Personality and Social Psychology, 61,* 582–589.

Allen, M. (1989). The man who broke North Haven's heart. *Yankee, 53,* 52.

Allen, R. W., Madison, D. L., Porter, L. W., Renwick, P. A., & Mayes, B. T. (1979). Organizational politics: Tactics and characteristics of its actors. *California Management Review, 22,* 77–83.

Allen, V. L., & Levine, J. M. (1969). Consensus and conformity. *Journal of Experimental Social Psychology, 5,* 389–399.

Allgeier, A. R., Byrne, D., Brooks, B., & Reeves, D. (1979). The waffle phenomenon: Negative evaluations of those who shift attitudinally. *Journal of Applied Social Psychology, 9,* 170–182.

Allison, S. T., & Kerr, N. L. (1994). Group correspondence biases and the provision of public goods. *Journal of Personality and Social Psychology, 66,* 688–698.

Allison, S. T., & Messick, D. M. (1988). The feature-positive effect, attitude strength, and degree of perceived consensus. *Personality and Social Psychology Bulletin, 14*, 231–241.

Allison, S. T., & Messick, D. M. (1990). Social decision heuristics in the use of shared resources. *Journal of Behavioral Decision Making, 3*, 195–204.

Allison, S. T., Beggan, J. K., & Midgley, E. H. (1996). The quest for "similar instances" and "simultaneous possibilities": Metaphors in social dilemma research. *Journal of Personality and Social Psychology, 71*, 479–497.

Alloy, L. B., & Abramson, L. Y. (1979). Judgment of contingency in depressed and nondepressed students: Sadder but wiser? *Journal of Experimental Psychology, 108*, 441–485.

Alloy, L. B., Abramson, L. Y., & Viscusi, D. (1981). Induced mood and the illusion of control. *Journal of Personality and Social Psychology, 41*, 1129–1140.

Allport G. W., & Postman, L. (1947). *The psychology of rumor.* New York: Henry Holt.

Allport, F. H. (1924). *Social psychology.* Boston: Houghton-Mifflin.

Allport, G. W. (1954). *The nature of prejudice.* Reading, MA: Addison-Wesley.

Allport, G. W., & Kramer, B. M. (1946). Some roots of prejudice. *Journal of Psychology, 22*, 9–39.

Allport, G. W., & Ross, J. M. (1967). Personal religious orientation and prejudice. *Journal of Personality and Social Psychology, 5*, 432–443.

Altemeyer, B. (1981). *Right-wing authoritarianism.* Winnepeg: University of Manitoba Press.

Altemeyer, B. (1988). *Enemies of freedom.* San Francisco: Jossey-Bass.

Altemeyer, B. (1998). The other 'authoritarian personality'. In M. P. Zanna (Ed.), *Advances in Experimental Social Psychology* (Vol. 30, pp. 48–92). New York: Academic Press.

Altman, I., & Haythorn, W. (1967). The ecology of isolated groups. *Behavioral Science, 12*, 169–182.

Alvaro, E. M., & Crano, W. D. (1997). Indirect minority influence: Evidence for leniency in source evaluation and counterargumentation. *Journal of Personality and Social Psychology, 72*, 949–964.

Amabile, T. M., Hennessey, B. A., & Grossman, B. S. (1986). Social influences on creativity: The effects of contracted-for reward. *Journal of Personality and Social Psychology, 50*, 14–23.

Amato, P. R. (1983). Helping behavior in urban and rural environments. *Journal of Personality and Social Psychology, 45*, 571–586.

Ambady, N., & Rosenthal, R. (1992). Thin slices of expressive behavior as predictors of interpersonal consequences: A meta-analysis. *Psychological Bulletin, 111*, 256–274.

Ambady, N., & Rosenthal, R. (1993). Half a minute: Predicting teacher evaluations from thin slices of nonverbal behavior and physical attractiveness. *Journal of Personality and Social Psychology, 64*, 431–441.

American Society for Aesthetic Plastic Surgery (2000). *ASAPS 1999 Statistics on Cosmetic Surgery.* http://www.surgery.org/NewsFlash.asp?NewsID=30.

Amir, Y. (1976). The role of intergroup contact in change of prejudice and race relations. In P. Katz & D. A. Taylor (Eds.), *Towards the elimination of racism* (pp. 245–308). New York: Pergamon.

Ammar, H. (1954). *Growing up in an Egyptian village: Silwa, Province of Aswan.* London: Routledge & Kegan Paul.

Anderson, C. A., (1987). Temperature and aggression: Effects on quarterly, yearly, and city rates of violent and nonviolent crime. *Journal of Personality and Social Psychology, 52*, 1161–1173.

Anderson, C. A., & Bushman, B. J. (1997). External validity of "trivial" experiments: The case of laboratory aggression. *Review of General Psychology, 1*, 19–41.

Anderson, C. A., & DeNeve, K. M. (1992). Temperature, aggression, and the negative affect escape model. *Psychological Bulletin, 111*, 347–351.

Anderson, C. A., & Dill, K. E. (2000). Video games and aggressive thoughts, feelings, and behavior in the laboratory and in life. *Journal of Personality & Social Psychology, 78*, 772–790.

Anderson, C. A., Bushman, B. J., & Groom, R. W. (1997). Hot years and serious and deadly assault: Empirical tests of the heat hypothesis. *Journal of Personality and Social Psychology, 73*, 1213–1223.

Anderson, C. A., Deuser, W. E., & DeNeve, K. M. (1995). Hot temperature, hostile affect, hostile cognition, and arousal: Tests of a general model of affective aggression. *Personality and Social Psychology Bulletin, 21*, 434–448.

Anderson, J. L., Crawford, C. B., Nadeau, J., & Lindberg, T. (1992). Was the Duchess of Windsor right? A cross-cultural review of the sociobiology of ideals of female body shape. *Ethology and Sociobiology, 13*, 197–227.

Anderson, N. H. (Ed.). (1991). *Contributions to information integration theory* (Vols. 1, 2, and 3). Hillsdale, NJ: Erlbaum.

Anderson, S. C. (1993). Anti-stalking laws: Will they curb the erotomanic's obsessive pursuit? *Law and Psychology Review, 17*, 171–191.

Anderson, V. L. (1993). Gender differences in altruism among Holocaust rescuers. *Journal of Social Behavior and Personality, 8*, 43–58.

Andersson, J., & Roennberg, J. (1997). Cued memory collaboration: Effects of friendship and type of retrieval cue. *European Journal of Cognitive Psychology, 9*, 273–287.

Andison, F. S. (1977). TV violence and viewer aggression: A cumulation of study results. *Public Opinion Quarterly, 41*, 314–331.

Anthony, T., Copper, C., & Mullen, B. (1992). Cross-racial facial identification: A social cognitive integration.

Personality and Social Psychology Bulletin, 18, 296–301.

Antill, J. K. (1983). Sex role complementarity versus similarity in married couples. *Journal of Personality and Social Psychology, 45,* 145–155.

Applebome, P. (1983, May 31). Racial issues raised in robbery case. *New York Times,* p. A14.

Applebome, P. (1984, March 22). Black is cleared by new arrest in Texas holdup. *New York Times,* p. A16.

Archer, D., & Gartner, R. (1984). *Violence and crime in cross-national perspective.* New Haven, CT: Yale University Press.

Archer, J. (1994). Introduction: Male violence in perspective. In J. Archer (Ed.), *Male Violence* (pp. 1–22). New York: Routledge.

Archer, R. L. (1984). The farmer and the cowman should be friends: An attempt at reconciliation with Batson, Coke, and Pych. *Journal of Personality and Social Psychology, 46,* 709–711.

Argyle, M. (1957). Social pressure in public and private situations. *Journal of Abnormal and Social Psychology, 54,* 172–175.

Aries, E. J., & Johnson, F. L. (1983). Close friendship in adulthood: Conversational content between same-sex friends. *Sex Roles, 9,* 1183–1197.

Arkes, H. R., Hackett, C., & Boehm, L. (1989). The generality of the relation between familiarity and judged validity. *Journal of Behavioral Decision Making, 2,* 81–94.

Arkin, R. M. (1981). Self-presentational styles. In J. T. Tedeschi (Ed.), *Impression management theory and social psychological research* (pp. 311–333). New York: Academic Press.

Arkin, R. M., & Baumgardner, A. H. (1985). Self-handicapping. In J. H. Harvey & G. Weary (Eds.), *Basic issues in attribution theory and research* (pp. 169–202). New York: Academic Press.

Arkin, R. M., & Baumgardner, A. H. (1988). *Social anxiety and self-presentation: Protective and acquisitive tendencies in safe versus threatening encounters.* Unpublished manuscript, University of Missouri, Columbia.

Armor, D. A., & Taylor, S. E. (1998). Situated optimism: Specific outcome expectancies and self-regulation. In M. P. Zanna (Ed.), *Advances in experimental social psychology.* (Vol. 30, pp. 309–379). New York: Academic Press.

Aron, A., & Aron, E. N. (1994). In A. H. Weber and J. H. Harvey (Eds.), *Perspectives on close relationships* (pp. 131–152). Boston: Allyn & Bacon.

Aron, A., & Westbay, L. (1996). Dimensions of the prototype of love. *Journal of Personality and Social Psychology, 70,* 535–551.

Aron, A., Aron, E. N., & Smollan, D. (1992). Inclusion of other in the self scale and the structure of interpersonal closeness. *Journal of Personality and Social Psychology, 63,* 596–612.

Aron, A., Aron, E. N., Tudor, M., & Nelson, G. (1991). Close relationships as including other in the self. *Journal of Personality and Social Psychology, 60,* 241–253.

Aron, A., Melinat, E., Aron, E. N., Vallone, R. D., & Bator, R. J. (1997). The experimental generation of interpersonal closeness: A procedure and some preliminary findings. *Personality and Social Psychology Bulletin, 23,* 363–377.

Aron, A., Norman, C. N., Aron, E. N., McKenna, C., & Heyman, R. E. (2000). Couples' shared participation in novel and arousing activities and experienced relationship quality. *Journal of Personality & Social Psychology, 78,* 273–284.

Aron, E. N., & Aron, A. (1997). Sensory-processing sensitivity and its relation to introversion and emotionality. *Journal of Personality and Social Psychology, 73,* 345–368.

Aronfreed, J. (1968). *Conduct and conscience: The socialization of internalized control over behavior.* New York: Academic Press.

Aronoff, J., Woike, B. A., & Hyman, L. M. (1992). Which are the stimuli in facial displays of anger and happiness? Configurational bases of emotion recognition. *Journal of Personality and Social Psychology, 62,* 1050–1066.

Aronson, E. (1969). The theory of cognitive dissonance: A current perspective. In L. Berkowitz (Ed.), *Advances in experimental social psychology.* (Vol. 4, pp. 1–34). San Diego, CA: Academic Press.

Aronson, E., Blaney, N., Stephan, C., Sikes, J., & Snapp, M. (1978). *The jigsaw classroom.* Beverly Hills, CA: Sage.

Aronson, E., Turner, J. A., & Carlsmith, J. M. (1963). Communicator credibility and communication discrepancy as determinates of opinion change. *Journal of Abnormal and Social Psychology, 67,* 31–36.

Aronson, E., Wilson, T. D., & Brewer, M. (1998). Experimentation in social psychology. In G. Lindzey and E. Aronson (Eds.), *Handbook of social psychology* (4th ed.) (pp. 99–142). New York: McGraw-Hill.

Aronson, J., Lustina, M. J., Good, C., Keough, K., Steele, C. M., & Brown, J. (1999). When White men can't do math: Necessary and sufficient factors in stereotype threat. *Journal of Experimental Social Psychology, 35,* 29–46.

Asch, S. E. (1955). Opinions and social pressures. *Scientific American, 193,* 31–35.

Asch, S. E. (1956). Studies of independence and conformity: A minority of one against a unanimous majority. *Psychological Monographs, 70,* (9, Whole number 416).

Asch, S. E., & Zukier, H. (1984). Thinking about persons. *Journal of Personality and Social Psychology, 46,* 1230–1240.

Aseltine, R. H., Jr., Gore, S., & Colten, M. E. (1994). Depression and the social developmental context of adolescence. *Journal of Personality and Social Psychology, 67,* 252–263.

Ashmore, R. D., & Del Boca, F. K. (1979). Sex stereotypes and implicit personality theory: Toward a cognitive-social psychological conceptualization. *Sex Roles, 5,* 219–248.

Aspinwall, L. G., & Taylor, S. E. (1993). Effects of social comparison direction, threat, and self-esteem on affect, self-evaluation, and expected success. *Journal of Personality and Social Psychology, 64,* 708–722.

Aune, R. K., & Basil, M. C. (1994). A relational obligations approach to the foot-in-the-mouth effect. *Journal of Applied Social Psychology, 24,* 546–556.

Averill, J. R. (1980). A constructivist view of emotion. In R. Plutchik & H. Kellerman (Eds.), *Theories of emotion* (Vol. 1, pp. 305–340). San Diego, CA: Academic Press.

Averill, J. R. (1983). Studies on anger and aggression. *American Psychologist, 38,* 1145–1160.

Axelrod, R. (1984). *The evolution of cooperation.* New York: Basic Books.

Axelrod, R., & Hamilton, W. D. (1981). The evolution of cooperation. *Science, 211,* 1390–1396.

Axsom, D., Yates, S., & Chaiken, S. (1987). Audience response as a heuristic cue in persuasion. *Journal of Personality and Social Psychology, 53,* 30–40.

Ayres, I., & Siegelman, P. (1995). Race and gender discrimination in bargaining for a new car. *American Economic Review, 85,* 304–321.

Bacon, F. T. (1979). Credibility of repeated statements. *Journal of Experimental Psychology: Human Learning and Memory, 5,* 241–252.

Baer, D., & McEachron, D. L. (1982). A review of selected sociobiological principles: Application to hominid evolution I. The development of group social structure. *Journal of Social and Biological Structures, 5,* 69–90.

Bahr, H. M., & Harvey, C. D. (1979). Correlates of loneliness among widows bereaved in a mining disaster. *Psychological Reports, 44,* 367–385.

Bailey, J. M., Gaulin, S., Agyei, Y., & Gladue, B. A. (1994). Effects of gender and sexual orientation on evolutionarily relevant aspects of human mating psychology. *Journal of Personality and Social Psychology, 66,* 1081–1093.

Baize, H. R., & Schroeder, J. E. (1995). Personality and mate selection in personal ads: Evolutionary preferences in a public mate selection process. *Journal of Social Behavior and Personality, 10,* 517–536.

Ball, A. D., & Tasaki, L. H. (1992). The role and measurement of attachment in consumer behavior. *Journal of Consumer Psychology, 1,* 155–172.

Banaji, M. R., & Greenwald, A. G. (1994). Implicit social cognition: Attitudes, self-esteem, and stereotypes. *Psychological Review, 102,* 4–27.

Banaji, M. R., & Hardin, C. D. (1996). Automatic stereotyping. *Psychological Science, 7,* 136–141.

Bandura, A. (1965). Vicarious processes: A case of no-trial learning. In L. Berkowitz (Ed.), *Advances in experimental social psychology* (Vol. 2, pp. 1–55). New York: Academic Press.

Bandura, A. (1973). *Aggression: A social learning analysis.* Englewood Cliffs, NJ: Prentice-Hall.

Bandura, A. (1977). *Social learning theory.* Englewood Cliffs. NJ: Prentice-Hall.

Bandura, A. (1977). Toward a unifying theory of behavioral change. *Psychological Review, 84,* 191–215.

Bandura, A. (1983). Psychological mechanisms of aggression. In R. G. Geen & E. I. Donnerstein (Eds.), *Aggression: Theoretical and empirical reviews* (Vol. 1, pp. 1–40). New York: Academic Press.

Bandura, A. (1986). *Social foundations of thought and action: A social-cognitive theory.* Englewood Cliffs, NJ: Prentice-Hall.

Bandura, A., Ross, D., & Ross, S. A. (1961). Transmission of aggression through imitation of aggressive models. *Journal of Abnormal and Social Psychology, 63,* 575–582.

Bandura, A., Ross, D., & Ross, S. A. (1963a). Imitation of film-mediated aggressive models. *Journal of Abnormal and Social Psychology, 66,* 3–11.

Bandura, A., Ross, D., & Ross, S. A. (1963b). Vicarious reinforcement of imitative learning. *Journal of Abnormal and Social Psychology, 67,* 601–607.

Bank, B. J., & Hansford, S. L. (2000). Gender and friendship: Why are men's best same-sex friendships less intimate and supportive? *Personal Relationship, 7,* 63–78.

Banks, T., & Dabbs, J., Jr. (1996). Salivary testosterone and cortisol in a delinquent and violent urban subculture. *Journal of Social Psychology, 136,* 49–56.

Bantel, K. A., & Jackson, S. E. (1989). Top management and innovations in banking: Does the composition of the top team make a difference? *Strategic Management Journal, 10,* 107–124.

Barbee, A. P., Cunningham, M. R., Winstead, B. A., Derlega, V. J., Gulley, M. R., Yankeelov, P. A., & Druen, P. B. (1993). Effects of gender role expectations on the social support process. *Journal of Social Issues, 49,* 175–190.

Bargh, J. A., Chen, M., & Burrows, L. (1996). Automaticity of social behavior: Direct effects of trait construct and stereotype activation on action. *Journal of Personality and Social Psychology, 71,* 230–244.

Bargh, J. A., & Chartrand, T. L. (1999). The unbearable automaticity of being. *American Psychologist, 54,* 462–479.

Bargh, J. A. (1996). Automaticity in social psychology. In E. T. Higgins & A. W. Kruglanski (Eds.), *Social psychology: Handbook of basic principles* (pp. 169–183). New York: Guilford.

Bargh, J. A., Raymond, P., Pryor, J. B., & Strack, F. (1995). The attractiveness of the underling: An automatic power (R) sex association and its consequences for sexual harassment. *Journal of Personality and Social Psychology, 68,* 768–781.

Bargh, J. A., & Thein, R. D. (1985). Individual construct accessibility, person memory, and the recall-judgment link: The case of information overload. *Journal of Personality and Social Psychology, 49,* 1129–1146.

Barker, R. G., & Gump, P. V. (1964). *Big school, small school: High school size and student behavior.* Stanford, CA: Stanford University Press.

Barley, S. R., & Bechky, B. A. (1994). In the backrooms of science: The work of technicians in science labs. *Work and Occupations, 21,* 85–126.

Barling, J., & Rosenbaum, A. (1986). Work stressors and wife abuse. *Journal of Applied Psychology, 71,* 346–48.

Barlow, D. H., & Durand, V. M. (1995). *Abnormal psychology: An integrative approach.* Pacific Grove, CA: Brooks/Cole.

Barnett, M. A., Sinisi, C. S., Jaet, B. P., Bealer, R., Rodell, P., & Saunders, L. C. (1990). Perceiving gender differences in children's help-seeking. *Journal of Genetic Psychology, 151,* 451–460.

Baron, R. A. (1989). Personality and organizational conflict: Effects of Type A behavior pattern and self-monitoring. *Organizational Behavior and Human Decision Processes, 44,* 281–296.

Baron, R. A., & Richardson, D. R. (1994). *Human aggression (2nd ed.).* New York: Plenum.

Baron, R. M., & Boudreau, L. A. (1987). An ecological perspective on integrating personality and social psychology. *Journal of Personality and Social Psychology, 53,* 1222–1228.

Baron, R. M., & Misovich, S. J. (1993). Dispositional knowing from an ecological perspective. *Personality and Social Psychology Bulletin, 19,* 541–552.

Baron, R. S. (1986). Distraction-conflict theory: Progress and problems. In L. Berkowitz (Ed.), *Advances in experimental social psychology* (pp. 1–40). Orlando, FL: Academic Press.

Baron, R. S. (2000). Arousal, capacity, and intense indoctrination. *Personality and Social Psychology Review, 4,* 238–254.

Baron, R. S., & Roper, G. (1976). Reaffirmation of social comparison views of choice shifts: Averaging and extremity effects in an autokinetic situation. *Journal of Personality and Social Psychology, 33,* 521–530.

Baron, R. S., Vandello, J., & Brunsman, B. (1996). The forgotten variable in conformity research: Impact of task importance on social influence. *Journal of Personality and Social Psychology, 71,* 915–927.

Barry, B., & Stewart, G. L. (1997). Composition, process, and performance in self-managed groups: The role of personality. *Journal of Applied Psychology, 82,* 62–78.

Bar-Tal, D., & Raviv, A. (1982). A cognitive-learning model of helping behavior development: Possible implications and applications. In N. Eisenberg (Ed.), *The development of prosocial behavior* (pp. 199–217). New York: Academic Press.

Bar-Tal, D., & Saxe, L. (1976). Perceptions of similarly and dissimilarly attractive couples and individuals. *Journal of Personality and Social Psychology, 33,* 772–781.

Bartholomew, R. (1997). Collective delusions: A skeptic's guide. *Skeptical Inquirer, 21,* 29–33.

Bartlett, F. A. (1932). *A study in experimental and social psychology.* New York: Cambridge University Press.

Bartol, K. M., & Martin, D.C. (1986). Women and men in task groups. In R. D. Ashmore & F. K. Del Boca (Eds.), *The social psychology of female-male relations: A critical analysis of central concepts* (pp. 259–310). New York: Academic Press.

Barton, J. (1794). *Lectures on female education.* New York: Gaine.

Bass, B. M. (1985). *Leadership and performance beyond expectations.* New York: Free Press.

Bass, B. M., & Avolio, B. J. (1993). Transformational leadership: A response to critiques. In M. M. Chemers & R Ayman (Eds.), *Leadership theory and research: Perspectives and directions* (pp. 49–80). San Diego, CA: Academic Press.

Bassili, J. N. (1996). Meta-judgmental versus operative indexes of psychological attributes: The case of measures of attitude strength. *Journal of Personality and Social Psychology, 71,* 637–653.

Bastardi, A., & Shafir, E. (1998). On the pursuit and misuse of useless information. *Journal of Personality and Social Psychology, 75,* 19–32.

Bastien, D., & Hostager, T. (1988). Jazz as a process of organizational innovation. *Communication Research, 15,* 582–602.

Bator, R. (1998). *The nature of consistency motivation.* Unpublished manuscript. Arizona State University.

Batson, C. D. (1991). *The altruism question: Toward a social-psychological answer.* Hillsdale, NJ: Erlbaum.

Batson, C. D. (1998). Altruism and prosocial behavior. In D. T. Gilbert, S. T. Fiske, & G. Lindzey (Eds.), *Handbook of social psychology* (4th ed.) (Vol. 2, pp. 282–316). New York: McGraw-Hill/Oxford University Press.

Batson, C. D., & Burris, C. T. (1994). Personal religion: Depressant or stimulant of prejudice and discrimination. In M. P. Zanna & J. M. Olson (Eds.), *The psychology of prejudice: The Ontario Symposium* (Vol. 7, pp. 149–169). Hillsdale, NJ: Erlbaum.

Batson, C. D., Batson, J. G., Griffitt, C. A., Barrientos, S., Brandt, J. R., Sprengelmeyer, P., & Bayly, M. J. (1989). Negative-state relief and the empathy-altruism hypothesis. *Journal of Personality and Social Psychology, 56,* 922–933.

Batson, C. D., Batson, J. G., Singlsby, J. K., Harrell, K. L., Peekna, H. M., & Todd, R. M. (1991). Empathic joy and the empathy-altruism hypothesis. *Journal of Personality and Social Psychology, 61,* 413–426.

Batson, C. D., Duncan, B. D., Ackerman, P., Buckley, T., & Birch, K. (1981). Is empathic emotion a source of altruistic motivation? *Journal of Personality and Social Psychology, 40,* 290–302.

Batson, C. D., & Shaw, L. L. (1991). Evidence for altruism: Toward a pluralism of prosocial motives. *Psychological Inquiry, 2,* 107–122.

Batson, C. D., & Ventis, W. L. (1982). *The religious experience: A social-psychological perspective.* New York: Oxford University Press.

Batson, C. D., Dyck, J. L., Brandt, J. R., Batson, J. G., Powell, A. L., McMaster, M. R., & Griffitt, C. (1988). Five studies testing two new egoistic alternatives to the empathy-altruism hypothesis. *Journal of Personality and Social Psychology, 55,* 52–77.

Batson, C. D., Flink, C. H., Schoenrade, P. A., Fultz, J., & Pych, V. (1986). Religious orientation and overt versus covert racial prejudice. *Journal of Personality and Social Psychology, 50,* 175–181.

Batson, C. D., Naifeh, S. J., & Pate, S. (1978). Social desirability, religious orientation, and racial prejudice. *Journal for the Scientific Study of Religion, 17,* 31–41.

Batson, C. D., Polycarpou, M. P., Harmon-Jones, E., Imhoff, H. J., Mitchener, E. C., Bednar, L. L., Klein, T. R., & Highberger, L. (1997). Empathy and attitudes: Can feeling for a member of a stigmatized group improve feelings toward the group? *Journal of Personality and Social Psychology, 72,* 105–118.

Batson, C. D., Sager, K., Garst, E., Kang, M., Rubchinsky, K., & Dawson, K. (1997). Is empathy-induced helping due to self-other merging? *Journal of Personality and Social Psychology, 73,* 495–509.

Batson, C. D., Turk, C. L., Shaw, L. L., & Klein, T. R. (1995). Information function of empathic emotion: Learning that we value the other's welfare. *Journal of Personality and Social Psychology, 68,* 300–313.

Battaglia, D. M., Richard, F. D., Datteri, D. L., & Lord, C. G. (1998). Breaking up is (relatively) easy to do: A script for the dissolution of close relationships. *Journal of Social and Personal Relationships, 15,* 829–845.

Baum, A., & Davis, G. E. (1980). Reducing the stress of high-density living: An architectural intervention. *Journal of Personality and Social Psychology, 38,* 471–481.

Baumeister, R. F. (1982). A self-presentational view of social phenomena. *Psychological Bulletin, 91,* 3–26.

Baumeister, R. F. (1984). Choking under pressure: Self-consciousness and paradoxical effects of incentives on skilled performance. *Journal of Personality and Social Psychology, 46,* 610–620.

Baumeister, R. F. (1989). The optimal margin of illusion. *Journal of Clinical and Social Psychology, 8,* 176–189.

Baumeister, R. F. (1993). Understanding the inner nature of low self-esteem: Uncertain, fragile, protective, and conflicted. In R. F. Baumeister (Ed.), *Self-esteem: The puzzle of low self-regard* (pp. 201–218). New York: Plenum.

Baumeister, R. F. (1998). The self. In D. T. Gilbert, S. T. Fiske, & G. Lindzey (Eds.), *Handbook of social psychology* (4th ed.) (Vol. 1, pp. 680–740). New York: McGraw-Hill.

Baumeister, R. F., Bratslavsky, E., Muraven, M., & Tice, D. M. (1998). Ego depletion: Is the active self a limited resource? *Journal of Personality and Social Psychology, 74,* 1252–1265.

Baumeister, R. F., Bushman, B. J., & Campbell, W. K. (2000). Self-esteem, narcissism, and aggression: Does violence result from low self-esteem or from threatened egotism? *Current Directions in Psychological Science, 9,* 26–29.

Baumeister, R. F., & Campbell, W. K. (1999). The intrinsic appeal of evil: Sadism, sensational thrills, and threatened egotism. *Personality & Social Psychology Review, 3,* 210–221.

Baumeister, R. F., Hutton, D. G., & Tice, D. M. (1989). Cognitive processes during deliberate self-presentation: How self-presenters alter and misinterpret the behavior of their interaction partners. *Journal of Experimental Social Psychology, 25,* 59–78.

Baumeister, R. F., & Ilko, S. A. (1995). Shallow gratitude: Public and private acknowledgment of external help in accounts of success. *Basic and Applied Social Psychology, 16,* 191–209.

Baumeister, R. F., & Jones, E. E. (1978). When self-presentation is constrained by the target's knowledge: Consistency and compensation. *Journal of Personality and Social Psychology, 36,* 608–618.

Baumeister, R. F., & Leary, M. R. (1995). The need to belong: Desire for interpersonal attachments as a fundamental human motivation. *Psychological Bulletin, 117,* 497–529.

Baumeister, R. F., Muraven, M., & Tice, D. M. (2000). Ego depletion: A resource model of volition, self-regulation, and controlled processing. *Social Cognition, 18,* 130–150.

Baumeister, R. F., & Newman, L. S. (1994). Self-regulation of cognitive inference and decision processes. *Personality and Social Psychology Bulletin, 20,* 3–19.

Baumeister, R. F., & Showers, C. J. (1986). A review of paradoxical performance effects: Choking under pressure in sports and mental tests. *European Journal of Social Psychology, 16,* 361–383.

Baumeister, R. F., Smart, L., & Boden, J. M. (1996). Relation of threatened egotism to violence and aggression: The dark side of high self-esteem. *Psychological Review, 103,* 5–33.

Baumeister, R. F., & Sommer, K. L. (1997). What do men want? Gender differences and two spheres of belongingness. *Psychological Bulletin, 122,* 38–44.

Baumeister, R. F., Stillwell, A. M., & Heatherton, T. F. (1994). Guilt: An interpersonal approach. *Psychological Bulletin, 115,* 243–267.

Baumeister, R. F., Tice, D. M., & Hutton, D. G. (1989). Self-presentational motivations and personality differences in self-esteem. *Journal of Personality, 57,* 547–579.

Baumeister, R. F., Wotman, S. R., & Stillwell, A. M. (1993). Unrequited love: On heartbreak, anger, guilt, scriptlessness, and humiliation. *Journal* *of Personality and Social Psychology, 64,* 377–394.

Baumgardner, A. H. (1990). To know oneself is to like oneself: Self-certainty and self-affect. *Journal of Personality and Social Psychology, 58,* 1062–1072.

Baumgardner, A. H., & Brownlee, E. A. (1987). Strategic failure in social interaction: Evidence for expectancy disconfirmation processes. *Journal of Personality and Social Psychology, 52,* 525–535.

Bavelas, A., Hastorf, A. H., Gross, A. E., & Kite, W. R. (1965). Experiments on the alteration of group structure. *Journal of Experimental Social Psychology, 1,* 55–70.

Beach, L., & Wertheimer, M. (1961). A free-response approach to the study of person cognition. *Journal of Abnormal and Social Psychology, 62,* 367–374.

Beach, S. R. H., Tesser, A., Fincham, F. D., Jones, D. J., Johnson, D., & Whitaker, D. J. (1998). Pleasure and pain in doing well, together: An investigation of performance-related affect in close relationships. *Journal of Personality and Social Psychology, 74,* 923–938.

Beall, A. E. (1993). A social constructionist view of gender. In A. E. Beall & R. J. Sternberg (Eds.), *The psychology of gender* (pp. 127–147) New York: Guilford.

Beaman, A. L., Klentz, B., Diener, E., & Svanum, S. (1979). Self-awareness and transgression in children: Two field studies. *Journal of Personality and Social Psychology, 37,* 1835–1846.

Beauregard, K. S., & Dunning, D. (1998). Turning up the contrast: Self-enhancement motives prompt egocentric contrast effects in social judgments. *Journal of Personality and Social Psychology, 74,* 606–621.

Bechtold, A., Naccarato, M. E., & Zanna, M. P. (1986). *Need for structure and the prejudice-discrimination link.* Paper presented at the annual meeting of the Canadian Psychological Association, Toronto.

Becker, B. J. (1988). Influence again: An examination of reviews and studies of gender differences in social influence. In J. S. Hyde & M. C. Linn (Eds.), *The psychology of gender: Advances through meta-analysis* (pp. 178–209). New York: Academic Press.

Becker, H. S. (1963). *Outsiders.* New York: Free Press.

Becker, T. E., & Martin, S. L. (1995). Trying to look bad at work: Methods and motives for managing poor impressions in organizations. *Academy of Management Journal, 38,* 174–199.

Becoming Barbie. (1995 December 8). *20/20, American Broadcasting Company.*

Bedau, H. A. (1967). *The death penalty in America.* New York: Doubleday.

Beggan, J. K., & Allison, S. T. (1997). More there than meets the eyes: Support for the mere-ownership effect. *Journal of Consumer Psychology, 6,* 285–297.

Belson, W. A. (1978). *Television violence and the adolescent boy.* Westmead, UK: Saxon House, Teakfield.

Bem, D. J. (1967). Self-perception: An alternative explanation of cognitive dissonance phenomena. *Psychological Review, 74,* 183–200.

Bem, D. J. (1972). Self-perception theory. In L. Berkowitz (Ed.), *Advances in experimental social psychology* (Vol. 6, pp. 1–62). New York: Academic Press.

Bendor, J., Kramer, R. M., & Stout S. (1991). When in doubt: Cooperation in a noisy prisoner's dilemma. *Journal of Conflict Resolution, 35,* 691–719,

Ben-Hamida, S., Mineka, S., & Bailey, J. M. (1998). Sex differences in perceived controllability of mate value: An evolutionary perspective. *Journal of Personality & Social Psychology, 75,* 953–966.

Berg, J. H., Stephan, W. G., & Dodson, M. (1981). Attributional modesty in women. *Psychology of Women Quarterly, 5,* 711–727.

Berglas, S., & Jones, E. E. (1978). Drug choice as a self-handicapping strategy in response to noncontingent success. *Journal of Personality and Social Psychology, 36,* 405–417.

Berkowitz, L. (1972). Social norms, feelings, and other factors affecting helping behavior and altruism. In L. Berkowitz (Ed.), *Advances in experimental social psychology* (Vol. 6, pp. 63–108). New York: Academic Press.

Berkowitz, L. (1989). Frustration-aggression hypothesis: Examination and reformulation. *Psychological Bulletin, 106,* 59–73.

Berkowitz, L. (1990). On the formation and regulation of anger and aggression: A cognitive-neoassociationistic analysis. *American Psychologist, 45,* 494–503.

Berkowitz, L. (1993a). *Aggression.* New York: McGraw-Hill.

Berkowitz, L. (1993b). Pain and aggression: Some findings and implications. *Motivation and Emotion, 17,* 277–293.

Berkowitz, L., Cochran, S., & Embree, M. (1981). Physical pain and the goal of aversively stimulated aggression. *Journal of Personality and Social Psychology, 40,* 687–700.

Berkowitz, L., & LePage, A. (1967). Weapons as aggression-eliciting stimuli. *Journal of Personality and Social Psychology, 7,* 202–207.

Berkowitz, L., & Thome, P. R. (1987). Pain expectation, negative affect, and angry aggression. *Motivation and Emotion, 11,* 183–193.

Bernstein, D. A. (1993). Excuses, excuses. *Observer, 6,* 4.

Berntson, G. G., & Cacioppo, J. T. (2000). Psychobiology and social psychology: Past, present, and future. *Personality & Social Psychology Review, 4,* 3–15.

Berry, D. S. (1990). Taking people at face value: Evidence for the kernel of truth hypothesis. *Social Cognition, 8,* 343–361.

Berry, D. S., & Landry, J. C. (1997). Facial maturity and daily social interaction. *Journal of Personality and Social Psychology, 72,* 570–580.

Berry, D. S., & McArthur, L. Z. (1986). Perceiving character in faces: The impact of age-related craniofacial changes on social perception. *Psychological Bulletin, 100*, 3–18.

Berry, D. S., Willingham, J. K., & Thayer, C. A. (2000). Affect and personality as predictors of conflict and closeness in young adults' friendships. *Journal of Research in Personality*, 34, 84–107.

Berscheid, E. (1983). Emotion. In H. H. Kelley, E. Berscheid, A. Christensen, J. Harvey, T. Huston, G. Loevinger, E. McClintock, L. A. Peplau, & D. Peterson (Eds.), *Close relationships* (pp. 110–168). San Francisco: Freeman.

Berscheid, E., Graziano, W., Monson, T., & Dermer, M. (1976). Outcome dependency: Attention, attribution, and attraction. *Journal of Personality and Social Psychology, 34*, 978–989.

Berscheid, E., & Reis, H. T. (1998). Attraction and close relationships. In D. T. Gilbert, S. T. Fiske, & G. Lindzey (Eds.), *Handbook of Social Psychology* (4th ed.) (Vol. 2, pp. 193–281). New York: McGraw-Hill.

Berscheid, E., Snyder, M., & Omoto, A. (1989). The relationship closeness inventory: Assessing the closeness of interpersonal relationships. *Journal of Personality and Social Psychology, 57*, 792–807.

Berscheid, E., & Walster, E. (1974). A little bit about love. In T. Huston (Ed.), *Foundations of interpersonal attraction* (pp. 355–381). New York: Academic Press.

Berscheid, E., & Walster, E. (1978). *Interpersonal attraction* (2nd ed.). Reading, MA: Addison-Wesley.

Bertilson, H. S. (1990). Aggression. In V. J. Derlega, Winstead, B. A. & W. H. Jones (Eds.), *Personality: Contemporary theory and research* (pp. 458–480). Chicago: Nelson-Hall.

Besag, V. (1989). *Bullies and victims in school.* Philadelphia, PA: Open University Press.

Betz, A. L., Skoronski, J. J., Ostrom, T. M. (1996). Shared realities: Social influence and stimulus memory. *Social Cognition, 14*, 113–140.

Betzig, L. (1992). Roman polygyny. *Ethology and Sociobiology, 13*, 309–349.

Bickman, L. (1971). The effect of another bystander's ability to help on bystander intervention in an emergency. *Journal of Experimental Social Psychology*, 7, 367–379.

Bickman, L. (1974). The social power of a uniform. *Journal of Applied Social Psychology, 4*, 47–61.

Biek, M., Wood, W., & Chaiken, S. (1996). Working knowledge, cognitive processing, and attitudes: On the determinants of bias. *Personality and Social Psychology Bulletin, 22*, 547–556.

Biel, A., & Garling, T. (1995). The role of uncertainty in resource dilemmas. *Journal of Environmental Psychology, 15*, 221–233. (A special issue on green psychology.)

Bierly, M. M. (1985). Prejudice toward contemporary outgroups as a generalized attitude. *Journal of Applied Social Psychology, 15*, 189–199.

Biernat, M. (1993). Gender and height: Developmental patterns in knowledge and use of an accurate stereotype. *Sex Roles, 29*, 691–713.

Biernat, M., & Manis, M. (1994). Shifting standards and stereotype-based judgments. *Journal of Personality and Social Psychology, 66*, 5–20.

Biesanz, J. C., Neuberg, S. L., Smith, D. M., Asher, T., & Judice, T. N. (in press). When accuracy-motivated perceivers fail: Limited attentional capacity and the reemerging self-fulfilling prophecy. *Personality and Social Psychology Bulletin.*

Biner, P. M., Angle, S. T., Park, J. H., Mellinger, A. E., & Barber, B. C. (1995). Need state and the illusion of control. *Personality and Social Psychology Bulletin, 21*, 899–907.

Bjorkvist, K., Lagerspetz, K. M. J., & Kaukiainan, A. (1992). Do girls manipulate and boys fight? Developmental trends in regard to direct and indirect aggression. *Aggressive Behavior, 18*, 117–127.

Bjorkvist, K., Osterman, K., & Lagerspetz, K. M. J. (1994). Sex differences in covert aggression among adults. *Aggressive Behavior, 20*, 27–33.

Black, S. L., & Bevan, S. (1992). At the movies with Buss and Durkee: A natural experiment on film violence. *Aggressive Behavior, 18*, 37–45.

Blaine, B., & Crocker, J. (1993). Self-esteem and self-serving biases in reactions to positive and negative events: An integrative review. In R. Baumeister (Ed.), *Self-esteem: The puzzle of low self-regard* (pp. 55–86). New York: Plenum.

Blair, B. G., & Kendall, H. W. (1990). Accidental nuclear war. *Scientific American, 263*, 53–59.

Blair, I. V., & Banaji, M. R. (1996). Automatic and controlled processes in stereotype priming. *Journal of Personality and Social Psychology, 70*, 1142–1163.

Blanchard, F. A., Crandall, C. S., Brigham, J. C., & Vaughn, L. A. (1994). Condemning and condoning racism: A social context approach to interracial settings. *Journal of Applied Psychology, 79*, 993–997.

Blanchard, F. A., Lilly, T., & Vaughn, L. A. (1991). Reducing the expression of racial prejudice. *Psychological Science, 2*, 101–105.

Blanchard, F. A., Weigel, R. H., & Cook, S. W. (1975). The effect of relative competence of group members upon interpersonal attraction in cooperating interracial groups. *Journal of Personality and Social Psychology, 32*, 519–530.

Blanck, P. D., Rosenthal, R., Snodgrass, S. E., DePaulo, B. M., & Zuckerman, M. (1981). Sex differences in eavesdropping on nonverbal cues: Developmental changes. *Journal of Personality and Social Psychology, 41*, 391–396.

Blanton, H., & Buunk, B. P., & Gibbons, F. X., & Kuyper, H. (1999). When better-than-others compare upward: Choice of comparison and comparative evaluation as independent predictors of academic performance. *Journal of Personality and Social Psychology, 76*, 420–430.

Blanton, H., Cooper, J., Skurnik, I., & Aronson, J. (1997). When bad things happen to good feedback: Exacerbating the need for self-justification with self-affirmations. *Personality and Social Psychology Bulletin, 23*, 684–692.

Blascovich, J., & Kelsey, R. M. (1990). Using electrodermal and cardiovascular measures of arousal in social psychological research. In C. Hendrick & M. S. Clark (Eds.), *Review of Personality and Social Psychology: Research methods in personality and social psychology* (Vol. 11, pp. 45–73). Newbury Park, CA: Sage.

Blascovich, J., Ginsberg, G. P., & Howe, R. C. (1975). Blackjack and the risky shift, II: Monetary stakes. *Journal of Experimental Social Psychology, 11*, 224–232.

Blass, T. (1991). Understanding behavior in the obedience experiment: The role of personality, situations, and their interactions. *Journal of Personality and Social Psychology, 60*, 398–413.

Blass, T. (1999). The Milgram paradigm after 35 years. *Journal of Applied Social Psychology, 29*, 955–978.

Blass, T. (2000). *Obedience to authority: Current perspectives on the Milgram paradigm.* Mahwah, NJ: Erlbaum.

Blass, T. (in press). The Milgram paradigm after 35 years: Some things we now know about obedience to authority. *Journal of Applied Social Psychology.*

Bless, H., Bohner, G., Schwarz, N., & Strack, F. (1990). Mood and persuasion: A cognitive response analysis. *Personality and Social Psychology Bulletin, 16*, 331–345.

Bless, H., Clore, G. L., Schwarz, N., Golisano, V., Rabe, C., & Wölk, M. (1996). Mood and the use of scripts: Does a happy mood really lead to mindlessness? *Journal of Personality and Social Psychology, 71*, 665–679.

Bly, B., Pierce, M., & Prendergast, J. (1986, January). Twenty-two rules for successful self-promotion. *Direct Marketing, 48*, 74.

Boaz, T. L., Perry, N. W., Jr., Raney, G., Fischler, I. S., & Shuman, D. (1991). Detection of guilty knowledge with event-related potentials. *Journal of Applied Psychology, 76*, 788–795.

Bobrow, D. G., & Norman, D. A. (1975). Some principles of memory schemata. In D. G. Bobrow & A. G. Collins (Eds.), *Representation and understanding: Studies in cognitive science* (pp. 131–150). New York: Academic Press.

Bodenhausen, G. V. (1990). Stereotypes as judgmental heuristics: Evidence of circadian variations in discrimination. *Psychological Science, 1*, 319–322.

Bodenhausen, G. V., & Lichtenstein, M. (1987). Social stereotypes and information-processing strategies: The impact of task complexity. *Journal of Personality and Social Psychology, 52*, 871–880.

Bodenhausen, G. V., Sheppard, L. A., & Kramer, G. P. (1994). Negative affect and social judgment: The differential impact of anger and sadness. *European Journal of Social Psychology, 24*, 45–62.

Bodenhausen, G. V., & Wyer, R. S., Jr. (1985). Effects of stereotypes on decision making and information-processing strategies. *Journal of Personality and Social Psychology, 48*, 267–282.

Bodenhausen, G. V., Kramer, G. P., & Süsser, K. (1994). Happiness and stereotypic thinking in social judgment. *Journal of Personality and Social Psychology, 66*, 621–632.

Boehm, L. E. (1994). The validity affect: A search for mediating variables. *Personality and Social Psychology Bulletin, 20*, 285–293.

Boen, F., Vanbeselaere, N., Pandelaere, Dewitte, S., Duriez, B., Snauwaert, B., Feys, J., Dierckx, V., & Van Avermaet, E. (in press). Politics and basking-in-reflected-glory. *Basic and Applied Social Psychology.*

Boggiano, A., Harackiewicz, J. M., Bessette, J. M., & Main, D. S. (1985). Increasing children's interest through performance-contingent reward. *Social Cognition, 3*, 400–411.

Bohra, K. A., & Pandey, J. (1984). Ingratiation toward strangers, friends, and bosses. *Journal of Social Psychology, 122*, 217–222.

Bolger, N., & Eckenrode, J. (1991). Social relationships, personality, and anxiety during a major stressful event. *Journal of Personality and Social Psychology, 61*, 440–449.

Bonacich, E. (1972). A theory of ethnic antagonism: The split labor market. *American Sociological Review, 37*, 547–559.

Bond, C. F., & Titus, L. J. (1983). Social facilitation: A meta-analysis of 241 studies. *Psychological Bulletin, 94*, 265–292.

Bond, M. H. (1994). Continuing encounters with Hong Kong. In W. J. Lonner & R. S. Malpass (Eds.), *Psychology and culture* (pp. 41–46). Boston: Allyn & Bacon.

Bond, R., & Smith, P. B. (1996). Culture and conformity: A meta-analysis of studies using Asch's line judgment task. *Psychological Bulletin, 119*, 111–137.

Boninger, D. S., Gleicher, F., & Strathman, A. (1994). Counterfactual thinking: From what might have been to what may be. *Journal of Personality and Social Psychology, 67*, 297–307.

Boninger, D. S., Krosnick, J. A., & Berent, M. K. (1995). Origins of attitude importance: Self-interest, social identification, and value relevance. *Journal of Personality and Social Psychology, 68*, 61–80.

Boorstin, D. J. (1983). *The discoverers.* New York: Random House.

Borden, R. J. (1975). Witnessed aggression: Influence of an observer's sex and values on aggressive responding. *Journal of Personality and Social Psychology, 31*, 567–573.

Borgida, E., Conner, C., & Manteufal, L. (1992). Understanding living kidney donation: A behavioral decision-making perspective. In S. Spacapan, & S. Oskamp (Eds.), *Helping and being helped* (pp. 183–212). Newbury Park, CA: Sage.

Bornstein, G., & Ben-Yossef, M. (1994). Cooperation in intergroup and single-group social dilemmas. *Journal of Experimental Social Psychology, 30*, 52–67.

Bornstein, R. F. (1989). Exposure and affect: Overview and meta-analysis of research, 1968–1987. *Psychological Bulletin, 106*, 265–289.

Boski, P. (1983). A study of person perception in Nigeria: Ethnicity and self versus other attributions for achievement-related outcomes. *Journal of Cross-Cultural Psychology, 14*, 85–108.

Bossard, J. H. S. (1932). Residential propinquity as a factor in marriage selection. *American Journal of Sociology, 38*, 219–224.

Boster, F. J., & Mongeau, P. (1984). Fear-arousing persuasive messages. In R. Bostrom (Ed.), *Communications yearbook* (Vol. 8, pp. 330–375). Beverly Hills, CA: Sage.

Bouchard, T. J. (1984). Twins reared together and apart: What they tell us about human diversity. In S. Fox (Ed.), *The chemical and biological bases of individuality* (pp. 147–184). New York: Plenum Press.

Boulton, M. J. (1994). The relationship between playful and aggressive fighting in children, adolescents, and adults. In J. Archer (Ed.), *Male Violence* (pp. 23–41). New York: Routledge.

Bowers, K. S., & Farvolden, P. (1996). Revisiting a century-old Freudian slip—From suggestion disavowed to the truth repressed. *Psychological Bulletin, 119*, 355–380.

Bowlby, J. (1969). *Attachment and Loss. Vol. 1: Attachment.* New York: Basic Books.

Bowlby, J. (1973). *Attachment and Loss: Vol. II: Separation.* New York: Basic Books.

Bowser, B. P., & Hunt, R. G. (1996). *Impacts of racism on white Americans* (2nd ed.). Thousands Oaks, CA: Sage.

Bradley, G. W. (1978). Self-serving biases in the attribution process: A reexamination of the fact or fiction question. *Journal of Personality and Social Psychology, 36*, 56–71.

Branch, T. (1988). *Parting the waters: America in the King years 1954–63.* New York: Simon & Schuster.

Branscombe, N. R., & Wann, D. L. (1992). Physiological arousal and reactions to outgroup members during competitions that implicate an important social identity. *Aggressive Behavior, 18*, 85–93.

Braver, S. L. (1995). Social contracts and the provision of public goods. In D. A. Schroeder (Ed.), *Social dilemmas: Perspectives on individuals and groups* (pp. 69–86). Westport, CT: Praeger.

Braver, S. L., & Wilson, L. A. (1986). Choices in social dilemmas: Effects of communication within subgroups. *Journal of Conflict Resolution, 30*, 51–62.

Braver, S. L., Linder, D. E., Corwin, T. T., & Cialdini, R. B. (1977). Some conditions that affect admissions of attitude change. *Journal of Experimental Social Psychology, 13*, 565–576.

Brechner, K. C. (1977). An experimental analysis of social traps. *Journal of Experimental Social Psychology, 13*, 552–564

Brehm, J. W. (1966). *A theory of psychological reactance. New York: Academic Press.*

Brehm, J. W. (1999). The intensity of emotion. *Personality and Social Psychology Review, 3*, 2–22.

Brehm, J. W., & Cohen, A. R. (1962). *Explorations in cognitive dissonance.* New York: Wiley.

Brehm, S. S. (1992). *Intimate relationships.* New York: McGraw-Hill.

Brehm, S. S., & Brehm, J. W. (1981). *Psychological reactance.* New York: Academic Press.

Brennan, K. A., & Shaver, P. R. (1995). Dimensions of adult attachment, affect regulation, and romantic relationship functioning. *Personality and Social Bulletin, 21*, 267–283.

Brewer, M. B. (1979). In-group bias in the minimal intergroup situation: A cognitive-motivational analysis. *Psychological Bulletin, 86*, 307–324.

Brewer, M. B. (1988). A dual-process model of impression formation. In T. K. Srull & R. S. Wyer, Jr. (Eds.), *Advances in social cognition* (Vol. 1, pp. 1–36). Hillsdale, NJ: Erlbaum.

Brewer, M. B. (1991). The social self: On being the same and different at the same time. *Personality and Social Psychology Bulletin, 17*, 475–482.

Brewer, M. B. (1997). On the social origins of human nature. In C. McGarty & S. A. Haslam (Eds.), *The message of social psychology: Perspectives on mind in society* (pp. 54–62). Oxford: Blackwell.

Brewer, M. B., & Brown, R. J. (1998). Intergroup relations. In D. T. Gilbert, S. T. Fiske, & G. Lindzey (Eds.), *Handbook of social psychology* (4th ed.) (Vol. 1, pp. 554–594). New York: McGraw-Hill/Oxford University Press.

Brewer, M. B., & Campbell, D. T. (1976). *Ethnocentrism and intergroup attitudes: East African evidence.* New York: Sage.

Brewer, M. B., & Caporael, L. R. (1995). Hierarchial evolutionary theory: There is an alternative and it is not creationism. *Psychological Inquiry, 6*, 31–34.

Brewer, M. B., Kenny, D. A., & Norem, J. K. (2000). Personality and social psychology at the interface: New directions for interdisciplinary research. *Personality & Social Psychology Review, 4*, 2.

Brickner, M. A., Harkins, S. G., & Ostrom, T. M. (1986). Effects of personal involvement: Thought-provoking implications for social loafing. *Journal of Personality and Social Psychology, 51*, 763–770.

Briggs, J. L. (1970). *Never in anger: Portrait of an Eskimo family.* Cambridge, MA: Harvard University Press.

Briggs, S. R., Cheek, J. M., & Buss, A. H. (1980). An analysis of the Self-Monitoring Scale. *Journal of Personality and Social Psychology, 38*, 679–686.

Brigham, J. C. (1971). Ethnic stereotypes. *Psychological Bulletin, 76*, 15–38.

Brigham, J. C., & Malpass, R. S. (1985). The role of experience and contact in the recognition of faces of own- and other-race persons. *Journal of Social Issues, 41*, 139–155.

Brock, T. C. (1967). Communication discrepancy and intent to persuade as determinants of counterarguments. *Journal of Experimental Social Psychology, 3,* 296–309.

Brockner, J., & Chen, Y.-R. (1996). The moderating roles of self-esteem and self-construal in reaction to a threat to self: Evidence from the People's Republic of China and the United States. *Journal of Personality and Social Psychology, 71,* 603–615.

Brown, B. R. (1968). The effects of need to maintain face in interpersonal bargaining. *Journal of Experimental Social Psychology, 4,* 107–122.

Brown, J. D. (1986). Evaluations of self and others: Self-enhancement biases in social judgments. *Social Cognition, 4,* 353–376.

Brown, J. D., Collins, R. L., & Schmidt, G. W. (1988). Self-esteem and direct versus indirect forms of self-enhancement. *Journal of Personality and Social Psychology, 55,* 445–453.

Brown, L. R. (1999). Feeding nine billion. In Brown, L. R., Flavin, C., & French, H. F. (1999). *State of the world: 1999.* (115–132). New York: Norton.

Brown, P., & Levinson, S. C. (1987). *Politeness: Some universals in language use.* Cambridge: Cambridge University Press.

Brown, R. B. (1978). Social and psychological correlates of help seeking behavior among urban adults. *American Journal of Community Psychology, 6,* 425–439.

Browne, A. (1993). Violence against women by male partners. *American Psychologist, 48,* 1077–1087.

Bruder-Mattson, S. F., & Hovanitz, C. A. (1990). Coping and attributional styles as predictors of depression. *Journal of Clinical Psychology, 46,* 557–565.

Bruner, J. S. (1957). On perceptual readiness. *Psychological Review, 64,* 123–152.

Bryan, A. D., Aiken, L. S., & West, S. G. (1996). Increasing condom use: Evaluation of a theory-based intervention to prevent sexually transmitted diseases in young women. *Health Psychology, 15,* 371–382.

Bryan, A. D., Aiken, L. S., & West, S. G. (1999). The impact of males proposing condom use on perceptions of an initial sexual encounter. *Personality & Social Psychology Bulletin, 25,* 275–286.

Bryan, J. H., & Test, M. A. (1967). Models and helping: Naturalistic studies in aiding behavior. *Journal of Personality and Social Psychology, 6,* 400–407.

Bryan, J. H., & Walbek, N. (1970). Preaching and practicing generosity. *Child Development, 41,* 329–353.

Buck, R., & Ginsburg, B. (1991). Spontaneous communication and altruism: The communicative gene hypothesis. In M. S. Clark (Ed.), *Review of personality and social psychology* (Vol. 12, pp. 149–175). Newbury Park, CA: Sage.

Budesheim, T. L., & DePaola, S. J. (1994). Beauty of the beast? The effects of appearance, personality, and issue information on evaluations of political candidates. *Personality and Social Psychology Bulletin, 20,* 339–348.

Bugental, D. B. (2000). Acquisition of the algorithms of social life: A domain-based approach. *Psychological Bulletin, 126,* 187–219.

Bugliosi, V., & Gentry, C. (1974). *Helter skelter.* New York: Bantam.

Building Blocks for Youth (2000). *And justice for some.* Accessed on Internet, at http://www.buildingblocksforyouth.org/justiceforsome/jfs.html

Bukowski, W. M., Hoza, B., & Boivin, M. (1994). Measuring friendship quality during pre- and early adolescence: The development and psychometric properties of the friendship qualities scale. *Journal of Personal and Personal Relationships, 11,* 471–484.

Burger, J. M. (1986). Increasing compliance by improving the deal: The that's-not-all technique. *Journal of Personality and Social Psychology, 51,* 277–283.

Burger, J. M. (1992). *Desire for control: Personality, social, and clinical perspectives.* New York: Plenum Press.

Burger, J. M., & Cooper, H. M. (1979). The desirability of control. *Motivation and Emotion, 3,* 381–393.

Burger, J. M., & Guadagno, R. E. (2000). *Self-concept clarity, responsiveness to false feedback, and the foot-in-the-door procedure.* Unpublished manuscript, Santa Clara University.

Burger, J. M., & Hemans, L. T. (1988). Desire for control and the use of attribution processes. *Journal of Personality, 56,* 531–546.

Burn, S. H. (1996). *The social psychology of gender.* New York: McGraw-Hill.

Burn, S. W. (1991). Social psychology and the stimulation of recycling behaviors: The block leader approach. *Journal of Applied Social Psychology, 21,* 611–629.

Burnkrant, R. E., & Unnava, H. R. (1989). Self-referencing: A strategy for increasing processing of message content. *Personality and Social Psychology Bulletin, 15,* 628–638.

Burns, J. M. (1978). *Leadership.* New York: Harper & Row.

Burnstein, E., & Vinokur, A. (1977). Persuasive argumentation and social comparison as determinants of attitude polarization. *Journal of Experimental Social Psychology, 13,* 315–332.

Burnstein, E., Crandall, C., & Kitayama, S. (1994). Some neo-Darwin decision rules for altruism: Weighing cues for inclusive fitness as a function of the biological importance of the decision. *Journal of Personality and Social Psychology, 67,* 773–789.

Bushman, B. J. (1984). Perceived symbols of authority and their influence on compliance. *Journal of Applied Social Psychology, 14,* 501–508.

Bushman, B. J. (1993). Human aggression while under the influence of alcohol and other drugs: An integrative research review. *Current Directions in Psychological Science, 2,* 148–152.

Bushman, B. J. (1993). What's in a name? The moderating role of public self-consciousness on the relation between brand label and brand preference. *Journal of Applied Psychology, 78,* 857–861.

Bushman, B. J., & Baumeister, R. F. (1998). Threatened egotism, narcissism, self-esteem, and direct and displaced aggression: Does self-love or self-hate lead to violence? *Journal of Personality and Social Psychology, 75,* 219–229.

Bushman, B. J., Baumeister, R. F., & Stack, A. D. (1999). Catharsis, aggression, and persuasive influence: Self-fulfilling or self-defeating prophecies? *Journal of Personality & Social Psychology, 76,* 367–376.

Bushman, B. J., & Stack, A. D. (1996). Forbidden fruit versus tainted fruit: Effects of warning labels on attraction to television violence. *Journal of Experimental Psychology: Applied, 2,* 207–226.

Buss, A. H. (1963). Physical aggression in relation to different frustrations. *Journal of Abnormal and Social Psychology, 67,* 1–7.

Buss, A. H. (1980). *Self-consciousness and social anxiety.* San Francisco: Freeman.

Buss, A. H., & Perry, M. (1992). The aggression questionnaire. *Journal of Personality and Social Psychology, 63,* 452–459.

Buss, D. M. (1987). Selection, evocation, and manipulation. *Journal of Personality and Social Psychology, 53,* 1214–1221.

Buss, D. M. (1989). Sex differences in human mate preference: Evolutionary hypothesis tested in 37 cultures. *Behavioral and Brain Sciences, 12,* 1–49.

Buss, D. M. (2000). *The dangerous passion.* New York: Free Press.

Buss, D. M., & Duntley, J. (1999). The evolutionary psychology of patriarchy: Women are not passive pawns in men's game. *Behavioral & Brain Sciences, 22,* 219–220.

Buss, D. M., & Kenrick, D. T. (1998). Evolutionary social psychology. In D. T. Gilbert, S. T. Fiske, & G. Lindzey (Eds.), *The handbook of social psychology* (4th ed.) (Vol. 2, pp. 982–1026). Boston: McGraw Hill.

Buss, D. M., Larsen, R. J., Westen, D., & Semmelroth, J. (1992). Sex differences in jealousy: Evolution, physiology, and psychology. *Psychological Science, 3,* 251–55.

Buss, D. M., & Schmitt, D. P. (1993). Sexual strategies theory: An evolutionary perspective on human mating. *Psychological Review, 2,* 204–232.

Buss, D. M., et al. (1990). International preferences in selecting mates: A study of 37 cultures. *Journal of Cross-Cultural Psychology, 21,* 5–47.

Buss, D. M., Shackelford, T. K., Kirkpatrick, L. A., Choe, J. C., Lim, H. K., Hasegawa, M., Hasegawa, T., & Bennett, K. (1999). Jealousy and the nature of beliefs about infidelity: Tests of competing hypotheses about sex differences in the United States, Korea, and Japan. *Personal Relationships,* 6: 125–150.

Butler, J. C. (2000). Personality and emotional correlates of right-wing authoritarianism. *Social Behavior & Personality, 2000,* 28, 1–14.

Buunk, A. P. (1980). Extramarital sex in the Netherlands: Motivations in social and marital context. *Alternative Lifestyles, 3,* 11–39.

Buunk, B. (1981). Jealousy in sexually open marriages. *Alternative Lifestyles, 4,* 357–372.

Buunk, B. (1982). Strategies of jealousy: Styles of coping with extramarital involvement of the spouse. *Family Relations, 31,* 13–18.

Buunk, B. P., Angleitner, A., Oubaid, V., & Buss, D. M. (1996). Sex differences in jealousy in evolutionary and cultural perspective: Tests from the Netherlands, Germany, and the United States. *Psychological Science,* 7: 359–363.

Buunk, B. P., & Baker, A. B. (1995). Extradyadic sex: The role of descriptive and injunctive norms. *Journal of Sex Research, 32,* 313–318.

Buunk, B. P., Collins, R. L., Taylor, S. E., VanYperen, N. W., & Dakof, G. A. (1990). The affective consequences of social comparison: Either direction has its ups and downs. *Journal of Personality and Social Psychology, 59,* 1238–1249.

Buunk, B. P., Doosje, B. J., Jans, L. G. J. M., & Hopstaken, L. E. M. (1993). Perceived reciprocity, social support, and stress at work: The role of exchange and communal orientation. *Journal of Personality and Social Psychology, 65,* 801–811.

Buunk, B. P., & Verhoeven, K. (1991). Companionship and support in organizations: A microanalysis of the stress-reducing features of social interaction. *Basic and Applied Social Psychology, 12,* 242–258.

Buunk, B. P., & VanYperen, N. (1991). Referential comparisons, relational comparisons, and exchange orientation: Their relation to marital satisfaction. *Personality and Social Psychology Bulletin, 17,* 709–717.

Byrne, D. (1971). *The attraction paradigm.* New York: Academic Press.

Byrne, D. (1983). Sex without contraception. In D. Byrne and W. A. Fisher (Eds.), *Adolescents, sex, and contraception.* Hillsdale, NJ.: Erlbaum.

Byrne D., & Clore, G. L. (1970). A reinforcement-affect model of evaluative responses. *Personality: An international journal, 1,* 103–128.

Byrne, D., London, O., & Reeves, K. (1968). The effects of physical attractiveness, sex, and attitude similarity on interpersonal attraction. *Journal of Personality, 36,* 259–271.

Byrnes, D. A., & Kiger, G. (1990). The effect of a prejudice-reduction simulation on attitude change. *Journal of Applied Social Psychology, 20,* 341–356.

Cacioppo, J. T., & Petty, R. E. (1982). The need for cognition. *Journal of Personality and Social Psychology, 42,* 116–131.

Cacioppo, J. T., Gardner, W. L., & Berntson, G. G. (1999). The affect system has parallel and integrative processing components: Form follows function. *Journal of Personality and Social Psychology, 76,* 839–855.

Cacioppo, J. T., Klein, D. J., Berntson, G. G., & Hatfield, E. (1993). The psychophysiology of emotion. In M. Lewis & J. M. Haviland (Eds.), *Handbook of emotions* (pp. 119–142). New York: Guilford.

Cacioppo, J. T., Petty, R. E., Feinstein, J. A., & Jarvis, W. B. G. (1996). Dispositional differences in cognitive motivation: The life and times of individuals varying in need for cognition. *Psychological Bulletin, 119,* 197–253.

Cacioppo, J. T., Petty, R. E., Kao, C. F., & Rodriguez, R. (1986). Central and peripheral routes to persuasion: An individual differences perspective. *Journal of Personality and Social Psychology, 51,* 1032–1043.

Cacioppo, J. T., Priester, J. R., & Berntson, G. G. (1993). Rudimentary determinants of attitudes II: Arm flexion and extension have differential effects on attitudes. *Journal of Personality and Social Psychology, 65,* 5–17.

Caldwell, D. F., & O'Reilly, C. A. (1990). Measuring person-job fit with a profile-comparison process. *Journal of Applied Psychology, 75,* 648–657.

Cameron, L. D., Brown, P. M. & Chapman, J. G. (1998). Social value orientations and decisions to take proenvironmental action. *Journal of Applied Social Psychology, 28,* 675–697.

Cameron, P., & Biber, H. (1973). Sexual thought throughout the life-span. *Gerontologist, 13,* 144–147.

Campbell, A. (1995). A few good men: Evolutionary psychology and female adolescent aggression. *Ethology and Sociobiology, 16,* 99–123.

Campbell, A. (1999). Staying alive: Evolution, culture, and women's intrasexual aggression. *Behavioral & Brain Sciences, 22,* 203–252.

Campbell, A., & Muncer, S. (1994). Men and the meaning of violence. In J. Archer (Ed.), *Male violence* (pp. 332–351). New York: Routledge.

Campbell, D. T. (1958). Common fate, similarity, and other indices of the status of aggregates of persons as social entities. *Behavioral Science, 3,* 14–25.

Campbell, D. T. (1965). Ethnocentric and other altruistic motives. In D. LeVine (Ed.), *Nebraska symposium on motivation: 1965* (pp. 283–311). Lincoln: University of Nebraska Press.

Campbell, D. T. (1975). On the conflicts between biological and social evolution and between psychology and oral tradition. *American Psychologist, 30,* 1103–1126.

Campbell, E. Q., & Pettigrew, T. F. (1958). Racial and moral crisis: The role of Little Rock ministers. *American Journal of Sociology, 64,* 509–516.

Campbell, J. D. (1986). Similarity and uniqueness: The effects of attribute type, relevance, and individual differences in self-esteem and depression. *Journal of Personality and Social Psychology, 50,* 281–294.

Campbell, J. D., & Fairey, P. J. (1989). Informational and normative routes to conformity. *Journal of Personality and Social Psychology, 57,* 457–468.

Campbell, J. D., & Tesser, A. (1985). Self-evaluation maintenance processes in relationships. In S. Duck & D. Perlman (Eds.), *Understanding personal relationships: An interdisciplinary approach* (pp. 107–135). Beverly Hills, CA: Sage.

Campbell, J. D., Trapnell, P. D., Heine, S. J., Katz, I. M., Lavallee, L. F., & Lehman, D. R. (1996). Self-concept clarity: Measurement, personality correlates, and cultural boundaries. *Journal of Personality and Social Psychology, 70,* 141–156.

Campbell, M. C. (1995). When attention-getting advertising tactics elicit consumer inferences of manipulative intent. *Journal of Consumer Research, 4,* 225–254.

Cantor, J. R., Zillmann, D., & Einseidel, E. F. (1978). Female responses to provocation after exposure to aggressive and erotic films. *Communication Research, 5,* 395–411.

Cantor, N., & Kihlstrom, J. F. (1987). *Personality and social intelligence.* Englewood Cliffs, NJ: Prentice Hall.

Cantril, H. (1940). *The invasion from Mars. Princeton, NJ: Princeton University Press.*

Caporeal, L. R. (1997). The evolution of truly social cognition: The core configurations model. *Personality and Social Psychology Review, 1,* 276–298.

Caporeal, L. R., & Baron, R. M. (1997). Groups as the mind's natural environment. In J. A. Simpson & D. T. Kenrick (Eds.), *Evolutionary social psychology* (pp. 317–344). Hillsdale, NJ: Erlbaum.

Carducci, B. J., Cozby, P. C., & Ward, D. D. (1978). Sexual arousal and interpersonal evaluations. *Journal of Experimental Social Psychology, 14,* 449–457.

Carducci, B. J., Deuser, P. S., Bauer, A., Large, M., & Ramaekers, M. (1989). An application of the foot in the door technique to organ donation. *Journal of Business and Psychology, 4,* 245–249.

Carli, L. L. (1989). Gender differences in interaction style and influence. *Journal of Personality and Social Psychology, 56,* 565–576.

Carli, L. L. (1990). Gender, language, and influence. *Journal of Personality and Social Psychology, 59,* 941–951.

Carli, L. L., LaFleur, S. J., & Loeber, C. C. (1995). Nonverbal behavior, gender, and influence. *Journal of Personality and Social Psychology, 68,* 1030–1041.

Carlston, D. E., Skowronski, J. J., & Sparks, C. (1995). Savings in relearning: II. On the formation of behavior-based trait associations and inferences. *Journal of Personality and Social Psychology, 69,* 420–436.

Carlyle, T. (1841). *On heroes, hero-worship, and the heroic.* London: Fraser.

Carnegie, D. (1936/1981). *How to win friends and influence people.* New York: Pocket Books.

Carroll, J. L., Volk, K. D., & Hyde, J. S. (1985). Differences between males and females in motives for engaging in sexual intercourse. *Archives of Sexual Behavior, 14*, 131–139.

Carver, C. S., & Glass, D.C. (1978). Coronary-prone behavior and interpersonal aggression. *Journal of Personality and Social Psychology, 58*, 622–633.

Carver, C. S., & Scheier, M. F. (1985). Aspects of the self and control of behavior. In B. R. Schlenker (Ed.), *The self and social life* (pp. 146–174). New York: McGraw-Hill.

Carver, C. S., & Scheier, M. F. (1998). *On the self-regulation of behavior.* Cambridge, MA: Cambridge University Press.

Carver, C. S., Sutton, S. K., & Scheier, M. F. (2000). Action, emotion, and personality: Emerging conceptual integration. *Personality and Social Psychology Bulletin, 26*, 741–751.

Case, R. B., Moss, A. J., and Case, N. (1992). Living alone after myocardial infarction: Impact on prognosis. *Journal of the American Medical Association, 267*, 575–85.

Cashdan, E. (1995). Hormones, sex, and status in women. *Hormones and Behavior, 29*, 345–366.

Caspi, A. (2000). The child is father of the man: Personality continuities from childhood to adulthood. *Journal of Personality & Social Psychology, 78*, 158–172.

Caspi, A., & Bem, D. J. (1990). Personality continuity and change across the life course. In L. A. Pervin (Ed.), *Handbook of personality: Theory and research* (549–575). New York: Guilford.

Caspi, A., & Herbener, E. S. (1990). Continuity and change: Assortative marriage and the consistency of personality in adulthood. *Journal of Personality and Social Psychology, 58*, 250–58.

Caspi, A., Elder, G. H., & Bem, D.J. (1988). Moving away from the world: Life-course patterns of shy children. *Developmental Psychology, 24*, 824–831.

Caughlin, J. P., Huston, T. L., & Houts, R. M. (2000). How does personality matter in marriage? An examination of trait anxiety, interpersonal negativity, and marital satisfaction. *Journal of Personality & Social Psychology, 78*, 326–336.

Cejka, M. A., & Eagly, A. H. (1999). Gender-stereotypic images of occupations correspond to the sex segregation of employment. *Personality and Social Psychology Bulletin, 25*, 413–423.

Cell, C. P. (1974). Charismatic heads of state: The social context. *Behavioral Science Research, 9*, 255–305.

Center for Disease Control (1991). Weapon-carrying among high school students. *Journal of American Medical Association, 266*, 225–253.

Chagnon, N. (1988). Life histories, blood revenge, and warfare in a tribal population. *Science, 239*, 985–992.

Chagnon, N. A., & Bugos, P. E. (1979). Kin selection and conflict: An analysis of a Yanomano ax fight. In N. A. Chagnon & W. Irons (Eds.), *Evolutionary biology and social behavior* (pp.213–238). North Scituate, MA: Duxbury Press.

Chaiken, S. (1987). The heuristic model of persuasion. In M. P. Zanna, J. M. Olson, & C. P. Herman (Eds.), *Social Influence: The Ontario Symposium* (Vol. 5, pp. 3–39). Hillsdale, NJ: Erlbaum.

Chaiken, S., & Eagly, A. H. (1983). Communication modality as a determinant of persuasion: The role of communicator salience. *Journal of Personality and Social Psychology, 45*, 241–256.

Chaiken, S., & Maheswaran, D. (1994). Heuristic processing can bias systematic processing. *Journal of Personality and Social Psychology, 66*, 460–473.

Chaiken, S., & Trope, Y. (Eds.) (1999). *Dual-process theories in social psychology.* New York: Guilford.

Chaiken, S., Giner-Sorolla, R., & Chen, S. (1996). Beyond accuracy: Defense and impression motives in heuristic and systematic processing. In P. M. Gollwitzer & J. A. Bargh (Eds.), *The psychology of action* (pp. 553–578). New York: Guilford.

Chaiken, S., Liberman, A., & Eagly, A. H. (1989). Heuristic and systematic processing within and beyond the persuasion context. In J. S. Uleman & J. A. Bargh (Eds.), *Unintended thought* (pp. 212–252). New York: Guilford.

Chance, S. E., Brown, R. T., Dabbs, J. M., & Casey, R. (2000). Testosterone, intelligence and behavior disorders in young boys. *Personality & Individual Differences, 28*, 437–445.

Chapman, J. G., Symons, C. S., & Caya, M. (1994). The impact of self-attention or consistency between self-reports and behavior. Paper presented at the Convention of the American Psychological Society, July, 1994.

Chatman, J. A. (1991). Matching people and organizations. *Administrative Science Quarterly, 36*, 459–484.

Chatman, J. A., Caldwell, D. F., & O'Reilly, C. A. (1999). Managerial personality and performance: A semi-idiographic approach. *Journal of Research in Personality, 33*, 514–545.

Cheek, J. M., & Briggs, S. R. (1990). Shyness as a personality trait. In W. R. Crozier (Ed.), *Shyness and embarrassment: Perspectives from social psychology* (pp. 315–337). Cambridge: Cambridge University Press.

Cheek, J. M., & Melchior, L. A. (1990). Shyness, self-esteem, and self-consciousness. In H. Leitenberg (Ed.), *Handbook of social and evaluation anxiety* (pp. 47–82). New York: Plenum.

Cheek, J. M., Melchior, L. A., & Carpentieri, A. M. (1986). Shyness and self-concept. In L. M. Hartman & K. R. Blankenstein (Eds.), *Perception of self in emotional disorder and psychotherapy* (pp. 113–131). New York: Plenum Press.

Chemers, M. M. (1997). *An integrative theory of leadership.* Mahwah, NJ: Erlbaum.

Chen, M., & Bargh, J. A. (1999). Consequences of automatic evaluation: Immediate behavioral predispositions to approach or avoid the stimulus. *Personality and Social Psychology Bulletin, 25*, 215–224.

Chen, S., Schechter, D., & Chaiken, S. (1996). Getting at the truth or getting along: Accuracy-versus impression-motivated heuristic and systematic processing. *Journal of Personality and Social Psychology, 71*, 262–275.

Chibnall, J. T., & Wiener, R. L. (1988). Disarmament decisions as social dilemmas. *Journal of Applied Social Psychology, 18*, 867–879

Chin, K., & Lee, L. (1993). Gang violence in Chinatown. (Abstract) *Violent Crime and Its Victims: Proceedings of American Society of Criminology, Phoenix, Arizona, 45*, (p. 96).

Chinese Cultural Connection (1987). Chinese values and the search for culture-free dimensions of culture. *Journal of Cross-Cultural Psychology, 18*, 143–164.

Christensen, D., & Rosenthal, R. (1982). Gender and nonverbal decoding skill as determinants of interpersonal expectancy effects. *Journal of Personality and Social Psychology, 42*, 75–87.

Christensen, P. N., & Kashy, D. A. (1998). Perceptions of and by lonely people in initial social interaction. *Personality and Social Psychology Bulletin, 24*, 322–329.

Christie, R., & Jahoda, M. (1954). *Studies in the scope and method of "The Authoritarian Personality."* Glencoe, IL: Free Press.

Cialdini, R. B. (1995). A full-cycle approach to social psychology. In G. C. Brannigan & M. R. Merrens (Eds.), *The social psychologists: Research adventures* (pp. 52–73). New York: McGraw-Hill.

Cialdini, R. B. (1996). Social influence and the triple tumor structure of organizational dishonesty. In D. M. Messick & A. E. Tenbrunsel (Eds.), *Codes of Conduct* (pp. 44–58). New York: Russell Sage.

Cialdini, R. B. (2001). *Influence: Science and practice* (4th ed). Boston: Allyn & Bacon.

Cialdini, R. B., & Ascani, K. (1976). Test of a concession procedure for inducing verbal, behavioral, and further compliance with a request to give blood. *Journal of Applied Psychology, 61*, 295–300.

Cialdini, R. B., & Baumann, D. J. (1981). Littering: A new unobtrusive measure of attitude. *Social Psychology Quarterly, 44*, 254–259.

Cialdini, R. B., Borden, R., Thorne, A., Walker, M., Freeman, S., & Sloane, L. T. (1976). Basking in reflected glory: Three (football) field studies. *Journal of Personality and Social Psychology, 34*, 366–375.

Cialdini, R. B., Brown, S. L., Lewis, B. P., Luce, C., & Neuberg, S. L. (1997). Reinterpreting the empathy-altruism relationship: When one into one equals oneness. *Journal of Personality and Social Psychology, 73*, 481–494.

Cialdini, R. B., Cacioppo, J. T., Bassett, R., & Miller, J. A. (1978). Low-ball procedure for producing compliance: Commitment then cost. *Journal of Personality and Social Psychology, 36*, 463–476.

Cialdini, R. B., Eisenberg, N., Green, B. L., Rhoads, K., & Bator, R. (1998). Undermining the undermining effect of reward on sustained interest. *Journal of Applied Social Psychology, 28*, 253–267.

Cialdini, R. B., Eisenberg, N., Shell, R., & McCreath, H. (1987). Commitments to help by children: Effects on subsequent prosocial self-attributions. *British Journal of Social Psychology, 26*, 237–245.

Cialdini, R. B., Kallgren, C. A., & Reno, R. R. (1991). A focus theory of normative conduct: A theoretical refinement and reevaluation of the role of norms in human conduct. In M. P. Zanna (Ed.), *Advances in experimental social psychology* (Vol. 24, pp. 201–234). New York: Academic Press.

Cialdini, R. B., & Kenrick, D. T. (1976). Altruism as hedonism: A social development perspective on the relationship of negative mood state and helping. *Journal of Personality and Social Psychology, 34*, 907–914.

Cialdini, R. B., & Richardson, K. D. (1980). Two indirect tactics of image management: Basking and blasting. *Journal of Personality and Social Psychology, 39*, 406–415.

Cialdini, R. B., Kenrick, D. T., & Baumann, D. J. (1982). Effects of mood on prosocial behavior in children and adults. In N. Eisenberg (Ed.), *The development of prosocial behavior.* (pp. 339–359). New York: Academic Press.

Cialdini, R. B., Levy, A., Herman, C. P., Kozlowski, L. T., & Petty, R. E. (1976). Elastic shifts of opinion: Determinants of direction and durability. *Journal of Personality and Social Psychology, 34*, 663–672.

Cialdini, R. B., Schaller, M., Houlihan, D., Arps, K., Fultz, J., & Beaman, A. L. (1987). Empathy-based helping: Is it selflessly or selfishly motivated? *Journal of Personality and Social Psychology, 52*, 749–758.

Cialdini, R. B., Trost, M. R., & Newsom, J. T. (1995). Preference for Consistency: The development of a valid measure and the discovery of surprising behavioral implications. *Journal of Personality and Social Psychology, 69*, 318–328.

Cialdini, R. B., Vincent, J. E., Lewis, S. K., Catalan, J., Wheeler, D., & Darby, B. L. (1975). Reciprocal concessions procedure for inducing compliance: The door-in-the-face technique. *Journal of Personality and Social Psychology, 31*, 206–215.

Cicerello, A., & Sheehan, E. P. (1995). Personal advertisements: A content analysis. *Journal of Social Behavior and Personality, 10*, 751–756.

Cimbalo, R. S., Faling, V., & Mousaw, P. (1976). The course of love: A cross-sectional design. *Psychological Reports, 38*, 1292–1294.

Cioffi, D., & Garner, R. (1996). On doing the decision: The effects of active versus passive choice on commitment and self-perception. *Personality and Social Psychology Bulletin, 22*, 133–147.

Clark, M. S., & Chrisman, K. (1994). Resource allocation in intimate relationships. In A. H. Weber and J. H. Harvey (Eds.), *Perspectives on close relationships* (pp. 176–192). Boston: Allyn & Bacon.

Clark, M. S., & Mills, J. (1993). The difference between communal and exchange relationships: What it is and is not. *Personality and Social Psychology Bulletin, 19*, 684–691.

Clark, M. S., Mills, J. R., & Corcoran, D. M. (1989). Keeping track of needs and inputs of friends and strangers. *Personality and Social Psychology Bulletin, 15*, 533–542.

Clark, M. S., Ouellette, R., Powell, M. C., & Milberg, S. (1987). Recipient's mood, relationship type, and helping. *Journal of Personality and Social Psychology, 53*, 94–103.

Clark, M. S., & Reis, H. T. (1988). Interpersonal processes in close relationships. *Annual Review of Psychology, 39*, 609–672.

Clark, M. S., & Waddell, B. A. (1983). Effects of moods on thoughts about helping, attraction and information acquisition. *Social Psychology quarterly, 46*, 31–35.

Clark, R. D., & Hatfield, E. (1989). Gender differences in receptivity to sexual offers. *Journal of Psychology and Human Sexuality, 2*, 39–55.

Clark, R. D., III (1990). Minority influence: The role of argument refutation of the majority position and social support for the minority position. *European Journal of Social Psychology, 20*, 489–497.

Clark, R. D., III, & Word, L. E. (1972). Why don't bystanders help? Because of ambiguity? *Journal of Personality and Social Psychology, 24*, 392–400.

Clark, R. D., III, & Word, L. E. (1974). Where is the apathetic bystander? Situational characteristics of the emergency. *Journal of Personality and Social Psychology, 29*, 279–287.

Clary, E. G., & Tesser, A. (1983). Reactions to unexpected events: The naive scientist and interpretive activity. *Personality and Social Psychology Bulletin, 9*, 609–620.

Clinton, W. J. (1994). Eulogy delivered at Nixon funeral, April 27, 1994, Yorba Linda, CA.

Clore, G. L., & Byrne, D. (1974). A reinforcement-affect model of attraction. In T. L. Huston (Ed.), *Foundations of interpersonal attraction* (pp. 143–170). New York: Academic Press.

Cocroft, B. K., & Ting-Toomey, S. (1994). Facework in Japan and the United States. *International Journal of Intercultural Relations, 18*, 469–506.

Cody, M. J., Seiter, J., & Montange-Miller, Y. (1995). Men and women in the marketplace. In P. J. Kalbfleish & M. J. Cody (Eds.),. *Gender, power, and communication in human relationships.* (pp. 305–330). Hillsdale, NJ: Erlbaum.

Cohan, C. L., & Bradbury, T. N. (1997). Negative life events, marital interaction, and the longitudinal course of newlywed marriage. *Journal of Personality and Social Psychology, 73*, 114–128.

Cohen, C. E. (1981). Person categories and social perception: Testing some boundaries of the processing effects of prior knowledge. *Journal of Personality and Social Psychology, 40*, 441–452.

Cohen, D. (1996). Law, social policy, and violence: The impact of regional cultures. *Journal of Personality and Social Psychology, 70*, 961–978.

Cohen, D., & Nisbett, R. E. (1997). Field experiments examining the culture of honor: The role of institutions in perpetuating norms about violence. *Personality and Social Psychology Bulletin, 23*, 1188–1199.

Cohen, D., Nisbett, R. E., Bowdle, B. F., & Schwarz, N. (1996). Insult, aggression, and the Southern culture of honor: An "experimental ethnography." *Journal of Personality and Social Psychology, 70*, 945–960.

Cohen, J, & Golden, E. (1972). Informational social influence and product evaluation. *Journal of Applied Psychology, 56*, 54–59.

Cohen, L. L., & Swim, J. K. (1995). The differential impact of gender ratios on women and men: Tokenism, self-confidence, and expectations. *Personality and Social Psychology Bulletin, 21*, 876–884.

Cohen, S. G., & Bailey, D. E. (1997). What makes teams work: Group effectiveness research from the shop floor to the executive suite. *Journal of Management, 23*, 239–290.

Cohen, S., Evans, G. W., Krantz, D. S., & Stokols, D. (1980). Physiological, motivational, and cognitive effects of aircraft noise on children: Moving from the laboratory to the field. *American Psychologist, 35*, 231–243.

Cohn, E. G., & Rotton, J. (1997). Assault as a function of time and temperature: A moderator-variable time-series analysis. *Journal of Personality and Social Psychology, 72*, 1322–1334.

Coker, A. L., Smith, P. H., McKeown, R. E., & King, M. J. (2000). Frequency and correlates of intimate partner violence by type: Physical, sexual, and psychological battering. *American Journal of Public Health, 90*, 553–559.

Cole, D., & Chaikin, I. (1990). *An iron hand upon the people.* Seattle: University of Washington Press.

Collins, B. E., & Hoyt, M. F. (1972). Personal responsibility for consequences. *Journal of Experimental Social Psychology, 8*, 558–593.

Collins, N. L. (1996). Working models of attachment: Implications for explanation, emotion, and behavior. *Journal of Personality and Social Psychology, 71*, 810–832.

Collins, N. L., & Miller, L. C. (1994). Self-disclosure and liking: A meta-analytic review. *Psychological Bulletin, 116*, 457–475.

Collins, R. L. (1996). For better or worse: The impact of upward social comparison on self-evaluations. *Psychological Bulletin, 119*, 51–69.

Colvin, C. R., & Block, J. (1994). Do positive illusions foster mental health? An examination of the

Taylor and Brown formulation. *Psychological Bulletin, 116,* 3–20.

Colvin, C. R., Block, J., & Funder, D.C. (1995). Overly positive self-evaluations and personality: Negative implications for mental health. *Journal of Personality and Social Psychology, 68,* 1152–1162.

Colvin, C. R., Vogt, D., & Ickes, W. (1997). Why do friends understand each other better than strangers do? In W. J. Ickes (Ed.), *Empathic accuracy* (pp. 169–193) NY: Guilford.

Condon, J. W., & Crano, W. D. (1988). Inferred evaluation and the relation between attitude similarity and interpersonal attraction. *Journal of Personality and Social Psychology, 54,* 789–797.

Condry, J. C., & Condry, S. (1976). Sex differences: A study of the eye of the beholder. *Child Development, 47,* 812–819.

Connery, D. S. (1977). *Guilty until proven innocent.* New York: Putnam's Sons.

Connery, D. S. (1995). *Convicting the innocent.* Cambridge, MA: Brookline.

Contreras, J., & Thomas, E. (2000, April 17). The long road home. *Newsweek,* 24–29.

Conway, M., & Giannopolous, C. (1993). Dysphoria and decision making: Limited information use for evaluations of multiattribute targets. *Journal of Personality and Social Psychology, 64,* 613–623.

Conway, M., & White-Dysart, L. (1999). Individual differences in attentional resources and self-complexity. *Social Cognition, 17,* 312–331.

Cook, B. W. (1992*). Eleanor Roosevelt (Vol. 1).* New York: Viking Books.

Cook, S. W. (1978). Interpersonal and attitudinal outcomes in cooperating interracial groups. *Journal of Research and Development in Education, 12,* 97–113.

Cook, S. W. (1985). Experimenting on social issues: The case of school desegregation. *American Psychologist, 40,* 452–460.

Cook, T. D. (1969). Competence, counterarguing, and attitude change. *Journal of Personality, 37,* 342–358.

Cook, W. L. (2000). Understanding attachment security in family context. *Journal of Personality & Social Psychology, 78,* 285–294.

Cook, W. L. (2000). Understanding attachment security in family context. *Journal of Personality & Social Psychology, 78,* 285–294.

Cooley, C. H. (1902). *Human nature and the social order.* New York: Scribners.

Cooley, C. H. (1922). *Human nature and the social order.* New York: Charles Scribner's Sons.

Coon, C. S. (1946). The universality of natural groupings in human societies. *Journal of Educational Sociology, 20,* 163–168.

Cooper, H., & Hazelrigg, P. (1988). Personality moderators of interpersonal expectancy effects: An integrative research review. *Journal of Personality and Social Psychology, 55,* 937–949.

Cooper, J. (1971). Personal responsibility and dissonance: The role of foreseen consequences. *Journal of Personality and Social Psychology, 18* 354–363.

Cooper, J., & Scher, S. J. (1994). When do our actions affect our attitudes? In S. Shavitt & T. C. Brock (Eds.) *Persuasion* (pp. 95–112). Boston, MA: Allyn & Bacon.

Cooper, J., Bennett, E. A., & Sukel, H. L. (1996). Complex scientific testimony: How do jurors make decisions. *Law and Human Behavior, 20,* 379–394.

Cooper, J., Zanna, M. P., & Taves, P. A. (1978). Arousal as a necessary condition for attitude change following induced compliance. *Journal of Personality and Social Psychology, 36,* 1101–1106.

Copeland, C. L., Driskell, J. E., & Salas, E. (1995). Gender and reactions to dominance. *Journal of Social Behavior and Personality, 10,* 53–68.

Copeland, J. T. (1994). Prophecies of power: Motivational implications of social power for behavioral confirmation. *Journal of Personality and Social Psychology, 67,* 264–277.

Corney, R. (1990). Sex differences in general practice attendance and help seeking for minor illness. *Journal of Psychosomatic Research, 34,* 525–534.

Cotterell, N., Eisenberger, R., & Speicher, H. (1992). Inhibiting effects of reciprocation wariness on interpersonal relationships. *Journal of Personality and Social Psychology, 62,* 658–668.

Cottrell, N. B. (1968). Performance in the presence of others: Mere presence, audience, and affiliation effects. In E. C. Simmel, R. A. Hoppe, & G. A. Milton (Eds.), *Social facilitation and imitative behavior* (pp. 91–110). Boston: Allyn & Bacon.

Cottrell, N. B., Wack, D. L., Sekerak, G. J., & Rittle, R. H. (1968). Social facilitation of dominant responses by the presence of an audience and the mere presence of others. *Journal of Personality and Social Psychology, 9,* 245–250.

Cox, C. L., Smith, S. L., & Insko, C. A. (1996). Categorical race versus individuating belief as determinants of discrimination: A study of southern adolescents in 1966, 1979, and 1993. *Journal of Experimental Social Psychology, 32,* 39–70.

Cox, O. C. (1959). *Caste, class, and race: A study in social dynamics.* New York: Monthly Review Press.

Crabb, P. B. (1996a). Answering machines take the "answering" out of telephone interactions. *Journal of Social Behavior & Personality, 11,* 387–397.

Crabb, P. B. (1996b). Video camcorders and civil inattention. *Journal of Social Behavior & Personality, 11,* 805–816.

Crabb, P. B. (1999). The use of answering machines and caller ID to regulate home privacy. *Environment & Behavior, 31,* 657–670.

Crabb, P. B. (2000). The material culture of homicidal fantasies. *Aggressive behavior, 26,* 225–234.

Craig, B. (1985, July 30). A story of human kindness. *Pacific Stars and Stripes*, 13–16.

Cramer, R. E., McMaster, M. R., Bartell, P. A., & Dragna, M. (1988). Subject competence and the minimization of the bystander effect. *Journal of Applied Social Psychology, 18*, 1133–1148.

Crandall, C. S. (1995). Do parents discriminate against their heavyweight daughters? *Personality and Social Psychology Bulletin, 21*, 724–735.

Crawford, C., & Krebs, D. L. (1998). *Handbook of evolutionary psychology: Ideas, issues, and applications.* Mahwah, NJ: Erlbaum.

Crichton, R. (1959). *The great impostor.* New York: Random House.

Crichton, R. (1961). *The rascal and the road.* New York: Random House.

Crocker, J., & Major, B. (1989). Social stigma and self-esteem: The self-protective properties of stigma. *Psychological Review, 96*, 608–630.

Crocker, J., & Schwartz, I. (1985). Prejudice and ingroup favoritism in a minimal intergroup situation: Effects of self-esteem. *Personality and Social Psychology Bulletin, 11*, 379–386.

Crocker, J., Thompson, L. L., McGraw, K. M., & Ingerman, C. (1987). Downward comparison, prejudice, and evaluations of others: Effects of self-esteem and threat. *Journal of Personality and Social Psychology, 52*, 907–916.

Crocker, J., Voelkl, K., Testa, M., & Major, B. (1991). Social stigma: The affective consequences of attributional complexity. *Journal of Personality and Social Psychology, 60*, 218–228.

Croizet, J.-C., & Claire, T. (1998). Extending the concept of stereotype and threat to social class: The intellectual underperformance of students from low socioeconimic backgrounds. *Personality and Social Psychology Bulletin, 24*, 588–594.

Crook, J. H., & Crook, S. J. (1988). Tibetan polyandry: Problems of adaptation and fitness. In L. Betzig, M. Borgerhoff Mulder, & P. Turke (Eds.), *Human reproductive behavior: A Darwinian perspective* (pp. 97–114). Cambridge: Cambridge University Press.

Crosby, F., Bromley, S., & Saxe, L. (1980). Recent unobtrusive studies of black and white discrimination and prejudice: A literature review. *Psychological Bulletin, 87*, 546–563.

Cross, S. E., & Markus, H. R. (1993). Gender in thought, belief, and action: A cognitive approach. In A. E. Beall & R. J. Sternberg (Eds.), *The psychology of gender* (pp. 55–98). New York: Guilford.

Crowne, D. P., & Marlowe, D. (1964). *The approval motive: Studies in evaluative dependence.* New York: Wiley.

Croyle, R. T., & Sandee, G. N. (1988). Denial and confirmatory search: Paradoxical consequences of medical diagnoses. *Journal of Applied Social Psychology, 18*, 473–490.

Croyle, R., & Cooper, J. (1983). Dissonance arousal: Physiological evidence. *Journal of Personality and Social Psychology, 45*, 782–791.

Crozier, W. R. (1979). Shyness as anxious self-preoccupation. *Psychological Reports, 44*, 959–962.

Crutchfield, R. S. (1955). Conformity and character. *American Psychologist, 10*, 191–198.

Cunningham, J., Dollinger, S. J., Satz, M., & Rotter, N. (1991). Personality correlates of prejudice against AIDS victims. *Bulletin of the Psychonomic Society, 29*, 165–167.

Cunningham, M. R. (1986). Levites and brother's keepers: A sociobiological perspective on prosocial behavior. *Humboldt Journal of Social Relations, 13*, 35–67.

Cunningham, M. R. (1989). Reactions to heterosexual opening gambits: Female selectivity and male responsiveness. *Personality and Social Psychology Bulletin, 14*, 27–41.

Cunningham, M. R., Barbee, A. P., Graves, C. R., Lundy, D. E., & Lister, S. C. (1996, August). *Can't buy me love: The effects of male wealth and personal qualities on female attraction.* Paper presented at American Psychological Association convention, Toronto.

Cunningham, M. R., Druen, P. B., & Barbee, A. P. (1997). Angels, mentors, and friends: Tradeoffs among evolutionary, social, and individual variables in physical appearance. In J. Simpson & D. T. Kenrick (Eds.), *Evolutionary social psychology* (pp. 109–141) Hillsdale, NJ: Erlbaum.

Cunningham, M. R., Jegerski, J., Gruder, C. L., & Barbee, A. P. (1995). *Helping in different social relationships: Charity begins at home.* Unpublished manuscript, University of Louisville, Department of Psychology, Louisville, KY.

Cunningham, M. R., Shaffer, D. R., Barbee, A. P., Wolff, P. L., & Kelley, D. J. (1990). Separate processes in the relation of elation and depression to helping. *Journal of Experimental Social Psychology, 26*, 13–33.

Curran, J. (1977). Skills training as an approach to the treatment of heterosexual-social anxiety: A review. *Psychological Bulletin, 84*, 140–157.

Cutrona, C. E. (1982). Transition to college: Loneliness and the process of social adjustment. In L. A. Peplau & D. Perlman (Eds.), *Loneliness: A sourcebook of current theory, research, and therapy.* New York: Wiley-Interscience.

Cutrona, C. E., Cole, V., Colangelo, N., Assouline, S. G., & Russell, D. W. (1994). Perceived parental social support and academic achievement: An attachment theory perspective. *Journal of Personality and Social Psychology, 66*, 369–378.

Czikszentmihalyi, M., Larson, R., & Prescott, S. (1977). The ecology of adolescent activity and experience. *Journal of Youth and Adolescence, 6*, 281–294.

D'Agostino, P. R. (2000). The encoding and transfer of stereotype-driven inferences. *Social Cognition, 18*, 281–291.

D'Agostino, P. R., & Fincher-Kiefer, R. (1992). Need for cognition and the correspondence bias. *Social Cognition, 10*, 151–163.

Dabbs, J. M., Jr. (1996). Testosterone, aggression, and delinquency. In S. Bhasin, H. L. Gabelnick, J. M. Spieler, R. S. Swerdloff, C. Wang, & C. Kelly (Eds.), *Pharmacology, biology, and clinical applications of androgens: Current status and future prospects* (pp. 179–189). New York: Wiley-Liss.

Dabbs, J. M., Jr. (1997). Testosterone, smiling, and facial appearance. *Journal of Nonverbal Behavior, 21,* 45–55.

Dabbs, J. M., Jr. (2000). *Heroes, rogues, and lovers: Testosterone and behavior.* New York: McGraw-Hill.

Dabbs, J. M., Jr., Carr, S., Frady, R., & Riad, J. (1995). Testosterone, crime, and misbehavior among 692 male prison inmates. *Personality and Individual Differences, 18,* 627–633.

Dabbs, J. M., Jr., Frady, R., Carr, T., & Besch, N. (1987). Saliva testosterone and criminal violence in young prison inmates. *Psychosomatic Medicine, 49,* 174–182.

Dabbs, J. M., Jr. Hargrove, M. F., & Heusel, C. (1996). Testosterone differences among college fraternities: Well-behaved versus rambunctious. *Personality and Individual Differences, 20,* 157–161.

Dabbs, J. M., Jr., Jurkovic, G., & Frady, R. (1991). Salivary testosterone and cortisol among late adolescent male offenders. *Journal of Abnormal Child Psychology, 19,* 469–478.

Dabbs, J. M., Jr., & Morris, R. (1990). Testosterone, social class, and antisocial behavior in a sample of 4462 men. *Psychological Science, 1,* 209–211.

Dabbs, J. M., Jr., Ruback, R., Frady, R., Hopper, C., & Sgoutas, D. (1988). Saliva testosterone and criminal violence among women. *Personality and Individual Differences, 9,* 269–275.

Daly, J. A., Hogg, E., Sacks, D., Smith, M., & Zimring, L. (1983). Sex and relationship affect social self-grooming. *Journal of Nonverbal Behavior, 7,* 183–189.

Daly, M., & Wilson, M. (1983). *Sex, evolution, and behavior.* Belmont, CA: Wadsworth.

Daly, M., & Wilson, M. (1988). *Homicide.* New York: Aldine deGruyter.

Daly, M., & Wilson, M. (1990). Killing the competition. *Human Nature, 1,* 83–109.

Daly, M., & Wilson, M. (1994). Evolutionary psychology of male violence. In J. Archer (Ed.), *Male violence* (pp. 253–288). New York: Routledge.

Daly, M., Salmon, C., & Wilson, M. (1997). Kinship: The conceptual hole in psychological studies of social cognition and close relationships. In J. A. Simpson & D. T. Kenrick (Eds.) *Evolutionary social psychology* (pp. 265–296). Mahwah, NJ: Erlbaum.

Damasio, A. R. (1985). Prosopagnosia. *Trends in Neuroscience, 8,* 132–35.

Damasio, A. R., Grabowski, T. J., Bechara, A., Damasio, H., Ponto, L. L. B., Parvizi, J., & Hichwa, R. D. (2000). "Subcortical and cortical brain activity during the feeling of self-generated emotions." *Nature Neuroscience, 3,* 1049–1056.

Danheiser, P. R., & Graziano, W. G. (1982). Self-monitoring and cooperation as a self-presentational strategy. *Journal of Personality and Social Psychology, 42,* 497–505.

Darley, J. M., & Fazio, R. H. (1980). Expectancy confirmation processes arising in the social interaction sequence. *American Psychologist, 35,* 867–881.

Darley, J. M., & Latané, B. (1968). Bystander intervention in emergencies: Diffusion of responsibility. *Journal of Personality and Social Psychology, 8,* 377–383.

Darley, J. M., Fleming, J. H., Hilton, J. L., & Swann, W. B., Jr. (1988). Dispelling negative expectancies: The impact of interaction goals and target characteristics on the expectancy confirmation process. *Journal of Experimental Social Psychology, 24,* 19–36.

Darwin, C. (1872). *The expression of emotions in man and animals.* London: Murray.

Daubman, K. A., Heatherington, L., & Ahn, A. (1992). Gender and the self-presentation of academic achievement. *Sex Roles, 27,* 187–204.

Davidson, K., & Prkachin, K. (1997). Optimism and unrealistic optimism have an interacting impact on health-promoting behavior and knowledge changes. *Personality and Social Psychology Bulletin, 23,* 617–625.

Davidson, O. G. (1996). *The best of enemies: Race and redemption in the new south.* New York: Scribner.

Davidson, R. J., Ekman, P., Saron, C. D., Senulis, J. A., & Friesen, W. V. (1990). Approach/ withdrawal and cerebral assymetry: Emotional expression and brain physiology. *Journal of Personality and Social Psychology, 58,* 330–341.

Davis, J. H. (1969). *Group performance.* New York: Addison-Wesley.

Davis, J. H. (1973). Group decision and social interaction: A theory of social decision schemes. *Psychological Review, 80,* 97–125.

Davis, J. H. (1993). *Mafia dynasty: The rise and fall of the Gambino crime family.* New York: Harper/ Collins.

Davis, J. H., Kerr, N. L., Atkin, R. S., Holt, R., & Meek, D. (1975). The decision processes of 6- and 12-person mock juries assigned unanimous and two-thirds majority rules. *Journal of Personality and Social Psychology, 32,* 1–14.

Davis, K. E., & Todd, M. J. (1985). Assessing friendship: prototypes, paradigm cases and relationship description. In S. Duck & D. Perlman (Eds.), *Understanding personal relationships: An interdisciplinary approach* (pp. 17–38). Beverly Hills, CA: Sage.

Davis, M. (2000, April 8). Tempe teens brawl in "Fight Club." *Arizona Republic,* B1.

Davis, M. H. (1994). *Empathy: A social psychological approach.* Madison, WI: Brown and Benchmark.

Davis, M. H., Conklin, L., Smith, A., & Luce, C. (1996). The effect of perspective taking on the cognitive representation of persons: A merging of self and other. *Journal of Personality and Social Psychology, 70,* 213–226.

Davis, M. H., Morris, M. M., & Kraus, L. A. (1998). Relationship-specific and global perceptions of social support: Associations with well-being and attachment. *Journal of Personality and Social Psychology, 74,* 468–481.

Dawes, R. M. (1980). Social dilemmas. *Annual Review of Psychology, 31,* 169–193

Dawes, R. M. (1989). Statistical criteria for establishing a truly false consensus effect. *Journal of Experimental Social Psychology, 25,* 1–17.

de Waal, F. B. M. (1989). *Chimpanzee politics: Power and sex among apes.* Baltimore: Johns Hopkins University Press.

de Waal, F. B. M. (1996). *Good-natured: The origins of right and wrong in humans and other animals.* Cambridge, MA: Harvard University Press.

Deaux, K., & Hanna, R. (1984). Courtship in the personal column: The influence of gender and sexual orientation. *Sex Roles, 11,* 363–375.

Deaux, K., & LaFrance, M. (1998). Gender. In D. T. Gilbert, S. T. Fiske, & G. Lindzey (Eds.), *The handbook of social psychology* (4th ed., Vol. 1, pp. 788–827). New York: McGraw-Hill.

Deaux, K., & Lewis, L. L. (1984). The structure of gender stereotypes: Interrelationships among components and gender label. *Journal of Personality and Social Psychology, 46,* 991–1004.

Deaux, K., & Major, B. (1987). Putting gender into context: An interactive model of gender-related behavior. *Psychological Review, 94,* 369–389.

Deaux, K., & Stark, B. (1996, May). *Identity and motive: An integrated theory of volunteerism.* Paper presented at the meeting of the Society for the Study of Social Issues, Ann Arbor, MI.

Deaux, K., Reid, A., Mizrahi, K., & Ethier, K. A. (1995). Parameters of social identity. *Journal of Personality and Social Psychology, 68,* 280–291.

DeBono, K. G. (1987). Investigating the social-adjustive and value-expressive functions of attitude: Implications for persuasion processes. *Journal of Personality and Social Psychology, 52,* 279–287.

Deci, E. L. (1971). Effects of externally mediated rewards on intrinsic motivation. *Journal of Personality and Social Psychology, 18,* 105–115.

Deci, E. L., Koestner, R., & Ryan, R. M. (1999). A meta-analytic review of experiments examining the effects of extrinsic rewards on intrinsic motivation. *Psychological Bulletin, 125,* 627–668.

Deci, E. L., & Ryan, R. M. (1985). *Intrinsic motivation and self-determination in human behavior.* New York: Plenum.

DeJong-Gierveld, J. (1980). Singlehood: A creative or lonely experience? *Alternative Lifestyles, 3,* 350–368.

DeLamater, J., & MacCorquodale, P. (1979). *Premarital sexuality: Attitudes, relationships, behavior.* Madison: University of Wisconsin Press.

Deluga, R. J., & Perry, J. T. (1994). The role of subordinate performance and ingratiation in leader-member exchanges. *Group and Organization Management, 19,* 67–86.

DePaulo, B. M. (1982). Social-psychological processes in informal help seeking. In T. A. Wills (Ed.), *Basic processes in helping relationships.* New York: Academic Press.

DePaulo, B. M. (1992). Nonverbal behavior and self-presentation. *Psychological Bulletin, 111,* 203–243.

DePaulo, B. M. (1994). Spotting lies: Can humans learn to do better? *Current Directions in Psychological Science, 3,* 83–86.

DePaulo, B. M., Epstein, J. A., & LeMay, C. S. (1990). Responses of the socially anxious to the prospect of interpersonal evaluation. *Journal of Personality, 58,* 623–640.

DePaulo, B. M., & Fisher, J. D. (1980). The costs of asking for help. *Basic and Applied Social Psychology, 1,* 23–35.

DePaulo, B. M., & Kashy, D. A. (1998). Everyday lies in close relationships. *Journal of Personality and Social Psychology, 74,* 63–79.

DePaulo, B. M., Kashy, D. A., Kirkendol, S. E., Wyer, M. M., & Epstein, J. A. (1996). Lying in everyday life. *Journal of Personality and Social Psychology, 70,* 979–995.

DePaulo, B. M., & Pfeifer, R. L. (1986). On-the-job experience and skill at detecting deception. *Journal of Applied Social Psychology, 16,* 249–267.

DePaulo, B. M., Zuckerman, M., & Rosenthal, R. (1980). Humans as lie detectors. *Journal of Communication, 30,* 129–139.

DePaulo, P. J., & DePaulo, B. M. (1989). Can attempted deception by salespersons and customers be detected through nonverbal behavioral cues? *Journal of Applied Social Psychology, 19,* 1552–1577.

Deppe, R. K., & Harackiewicz, J. M. (1996). Self-handicapping and intrinsic motivation: Buffering intrinsic motivation from the threat of failure. *Journal of Personality and Social Psychology, 70,* 868–876.

Deutsch, L. (1993, August 27). 4 tell jury how they ran from TVs to help Denny. *San Francisco Examiner,* p. A11.

Deutsch, M. (1986). Strategies for inducing cooperation. In R. K. White (Ed.), *Psychology and the prevention of nuclear war* (pp. 162–170). New York: New York University Press.

Deutsch, M., & Gerard, H. B. (1955). A study of normative and informational social influences upon individual judgment. *Journal of Abnormal and Social Psychology, 51,* 629–636.

Deutsch, M., & Krauss, R. M. (1960). The effect of threat upon interpersonal bargaining. *Journal of Abnormal and Social Psychology, 61,* 181–189.

Devine, P. G. (1989). Stereotypes and prejudice: Their automatic and controlled components. *Journal of Personality and Social Psychology, 56,* 5–18.

Devine, P. G., Monteith, M. J., Zuwerink, J. R., & Elliot, A. J. (1991). Prejudice with and without compunction. *Journal of Personality and Social Psychology, 60*, 817–830.

DeVries, D. L., & Slavin, R. E. (1978). Teams-games-tournament (TGT): Review of 10 classroom experiments. *Journal of Research and Development in Education, 12*, 28–38.

DeWeerth, C., & Kalma, A. P. (1993). Female aggression as a response to sexual jealousy: A sex role reversal? *Aggressive Behavior, 19*, 265–279.

Dickey, C. (1991, January 7). Why we can't seem to understand the Arabs. *Newsweek*, p. 26–27.

Diehl, M., & Stroebe, W. (1987). Productivity loss in brainstorming groups: Toward the solution of a riddle. *Journal of Personality and Social Psychology, 53*, 497–509.

Diener, D. M. (2000). Subjective well-being: The science of happiness and a proposal for a national index. *American Psychologist, 55*, 34–43.

Diener, E. (2000). Subjective well-being: The science of happiness and a proposal for a national index. *American psychologist, 55*, 34–43.

Diener, E., Fraser, S. C., Beaman, A. L., & Kelem, R. T. (1976). Effects of deindividuation variables on stealing among Halloween trick-or-treaters. *Journal of Personality and Social Psychology, 33*, 178–183.

Dijker, A. J., & Koomen, W. (1996). Stereotyping and attitudinal effects under time pressure. *European Journal of Social Psychology, 26*, 61–74.

Dijksterhuis, A., & van Knippenberg, A. (1999). On the parameters of associative strength: Central tendency and variability as determinants of stereotype accessibility. *Personality and Social Psychology Bulletin, 25*, 527–536.

Dijkstra, P., & Buunk, B. P. (1998). Jealousy as a function of rival characteristics: An evolutionary perspective. *Personality & Social Psychology Bulletin, 24*, 1158–1166.

DiMento, J. F. (1989). Can social science explain organizational noncompliance with environmental law? *Journal of Social Issues, 45*, 109–133.

Dindia, K., & Allen, M. (1992). Sex differences in self-disclosure: A meta-analysis. *Psychological Bulletin, 112*, 106–124.

Dion, K. L., & Dion, K. K. (1975). Self-esteem and romantic love. *Journal of Personality, 43*, 39–57.

Dion, K. L., Dion, K. K., & Keelan, J. P. (1990). Appearance anxiety as a dimension of social-evaluative anxiety: Exploring the ugly duckling syndrome. *Contemporary Social Psychology, 14*, 220–224.

Dipboye, R. L. (1982). Self-fulfilling prophecies in the selection-recruitment interview. *Academy of Management Review, 7*, 579–586.

Ditto, P. H., & Lopez, D. F. (1992). Motivated skepticism: Use of differential decision criteria for preferred and nonpreferred conclusions. *Journal of Personality and Social Psychology, 63*, 568–584.

Ditto, P. H., Scepansky, J. A., Munro, G. D., Apanovitch, A. M., & Lockhart, L. K. (1998). Motivated sensitivity to preference-inconsistent information. *Journal of Personality and Social Psychology, 75*, 53–69.

Dobash, R. P., Dobash, R. E., Daly, M., & Wilson, M. (1992). The myth of sexual symmetry in marital violence. *Social Problems, 39*, 71–91.

Dobbins, G. H., Long, W. S., Dedrick, E. J., & Clemons, T. C. (1990). The role of self-monitoring and gender on leader emergence: A laboratory and field study. *Journal of Management, 16*, 609–618.

Dodge, K. A. (1982). Social information processing factors in the development of aggression and altruism in children. In C. Zahn-Waxler, M. Cummings, & M. Radke-Yarrow (Eds.), *The development of altruism and aggression: Social and sociobiological origins* (pp. 280–302). New York: Cambridge University Press.

Dodge, K. A. (1986). A social information processing model of social competence in children. In M. Perlmutter (Ed.), *Minnesota symposium on child psychology* (Vol. 18, pp. 77–125). Hillsdale, NJ: Erlbaum.

Dodge, K. A., & Coie, J. D. (1987). Social information processing factors in reactive and proactive aggression in children's peer groups. *Journal of Personality and Social Psychology, 53*, 1146–1158.

Dodge, K. A., & Frame, C. L. (1982). Social cognitive biases and deficits in aggressive boys. *Child Development, 53*, 1146–1158.

Dodge, K. A., Price, J. M., Bachorowski, J. A., & Newman, J. P. (1990). Hostile attributional biases in severely aggressive adolescents. *Journal of Abnormal Psychology, 99*, 385–392.

Doherty, K., & Schlenker, B. R. (1991). Self-consciousness and strategic self-presentation. *Journal of Personality, 59*, 1–18.

Dole, R. (1994). Eulogy delivered at Nixon funeral, April 27, 1994, Yorba Linda, CA.

Dolinski, D. (2000). On inferring one's beliefs from one's attempt and its consequences for subsequent compliance. *Journal of Personality and Social Psychology, 78*, 260–272.

Dollard, J., Miller, N. E., Doob, L. W., Mowrer, O. H., & Sears, R. R. (1939). *Frustration and aggression.* New Haven, CT: Yale University Press.

Donahue, E. M. (1994). Do children use the Big Five, too? Content and structural form in personality description. *Journal of Personality, 62*, 45–66.

Donahue, M. J. (1985). Intrinsic and extrinsic religiousness: Review and meta-analysis. *Journal of Personality and Social Psychology, 48*, 400–419.

Donaldson, S. I., Graham, J. W., Piccinin, A. M., & Hansen, W. B. (1995). Resistance-skills training and onset of alcohol use. *Health Psychology, 14*, 291–300.

Donnerstein, E., & Berkowitz, L. (1981). Victim reactions to aggressive erotic films as a factor in violence against women. *Journal of Personality and Social Psychology, 41*, 710–724.

Doty, R. M., Peterson, B. E., & Winter, D. G. (1991). Threat and authoritarianism in the United States, 1978–1987. *Journal of Personality and Social Psychology, 61*, 629–640.

Doty, R. M., Winter, D. G., Peterson, B. E., & Kemmelmeier, M. (1997). Authoritarianism and American students' attitudes about the Gulf War. *Personality and Social Psychology Bulletin, 23*, 1133–1143.

Dovidio, J. F. (1984). Helping behavior and altruism: An empirical and conceptual overview. In L. Berkowitz (Ed.), *Advances in experimental social psychology* (Vol. 17, pp. 361–427). New York: Academic Press.

Dovidio, J. F. (1993, October). *Androgyny, sex roles, and helping.* Paper presented at the meetings of the Society of Experimental Social Psychology, Santa Barbara, CA.

Dovidio, J. F., Brown, C. E., Heltman, K., Ellyson, S. L., & Keating, C. F. (1988). Power displays between women and men in discussions of gender-linked tasks: A multichannel study. *Journal of Personality and Social Psychology, 55*, 580–587.

Dovidio, J. F., Ellyson, S. L., Keating, C. F., Heltman, K., & Brown, C. E. (1988). The relationship of social power to visual displays of dominance between men and women. *Journal of Personality and Social Psychology, 54*, 233–242.

Dovidio, J. F., Evans, N., & Tyler, R. B. (1986). Racial stereotypes: The contents of their cognitive representations. *Journal of Experimental Social Psychology, 22*, 22–37.

Dovidio, J. F., & Gaertner, S. L. (2000). Aversive racism and selection decisions: 1989 and 1999. *Psychological Science, 11*, 315–319.

Dovidio, J. F., Gaertner, S. L., Validzic, A., Matoka, K., Johnson, B., & Frazier, S. (1997). Extending the benefits of recategorization: Evaluations, self-disclosure, and helping. *Journal of Experimental Social Psychology, 33*, 401–420.

Dovidio, J. F., Kawamaki, K., Johnson, C., Johnson, B., & Howard, A. (1997). On the nature of prejudice: Automatic and controlled processes. *Journal of Experimental Social Psychology, 33*, 510–540.

Dovidio, J. F., Piliavin, J. A., Gaertner, S. L., Schroeder, D. A., & Clark, R. D., III (1991). The Arousal: Cost-Reward Model and the process of intervention: A review of the evidence. In M. S. Clark (Ed.), *Review of personality and social psychology* (Vol. 12, pp. 86–118). Newbury Park, CA: Sage.

Dowd, E. T., Hughes, S., Brockbank, L., Halpain, D., Seibel, C., & Seibel, P. (1988). Compliance-based and defiance-based intervention strategies and psychological reactance in the treatment of free and unfree behavior. *Journal of Counseling Psychology, 35*, 363–369.

Dowd, E. T., Milne, C. R., & Wise, S. L. (1991). The therapeutic reactance scale: A measure of psychological reactance. *Journal of Counseling and Development, 69*, 541–545.

Downs, A. C., & Lyons, P. M. (1991). Natural observations of the links between attractiveness and initial legal judgments. *Personality and Social Psychology Bulletin, 17*, 541–547.

Doyle, A. C. (1887). *A study in scarlet.* In *Beeton's Christmas Annual* (November). London: Ward Lock & Company. (Reprinted in A. C. Doyle (1973), *The complete Sherlock Holmes.* New York: Doubleday)

Doyle, R. (1997, April). By the numbers: Air pollution in the U.S. *Scientific American*, p. 27.

Drigotas, S. M., & Rusbult, C. E. (1992). Should I stay or should I go? A dependence model of relationships. *Journal of Personality and Social Psychology, 62*, 62–87.

Driscoll, R., Davis, K. W., & Lipetz, M. E. (1972). Parental interference and romantic love. *Journal of Personality and Social Psychology, 24*, 1–10.

Driskell, J. E., Hogan, R., & Salas, E. (1987). Personality and group performance. In C. Hendrick (Ed.), *Group processes and intergroup relations* (pp. 91–112). Newbury Park, CA: Sage.

Dryer, D.C., & Horowitz, L. M. (1997). When do opposites attract? Interpersonal complementarity versus similarity. *Journal of Personality and Social Psychology, 72*, 592–603.

Duck, S. (1994). Stratagems, spoils, and a serpent's tooth: On the delights and dilemmas of personal relationships. In W. R. Cupach & B. H. Spitzberg (Eds.), *The dark side of interpersonal communication.* Hillsdale: Erlbaum.

Duckitt, J., & Farre, B. (1994). Right-wing authoritarianism and political intolerance among whites in the future majority-rule South Africa. *Journal of Social Psychology, 134*, 735–741.

Duncan, B. L. (1976). Differential social perception and attribution of intergroup violence: Testing the lower limits of stereotyping of Blacks. *Journal of Personality and Social Psychology, 34*, 590–598.

Dunlap, R. E., & Scarce, R. (1991). The polls: Environmental problems and protection. *Public Opinion Quarterly, 55*, 651–672.

Dunning, D., & Sherman, D. A. (1997). Stereotypes and tacit inference. *Journal of Personality and Social Psychology, 73*, 459–471.

Dunning, D., Leuenberger, A., & Sherman, D. A. (1995). A new look at motivated inference: Are self-serving theories of success a product of motivational forces? *Journal of Personality and Social Psychology, 69*, 58–68.

Dunning, D., Meyerowitz, J. A., & Holzberg, A. D. (1989). Ambiguity and self-evaluation: The role of idiosyncratic trait definitions in self-serving assessments of ability. *Journal of Personality and Social Psychology, 57*, 1082–1090.

Dunning, D., Perie, M., & Story, A. L. (1991). Self-serving prototypes of social categories. *Journal of Personality and Social Psychology, 61*, 957–968.

Dunton, B. C., & Fazio, R. H. (1997). An individual difference measure of motivation to control prejudiced reactions. *Personality and Social Psychology Bulletin, 23*, 316–326.

Durant, W., & Durant, A. (1963). *The age of Louis XIV.* New York: Simon & Schuster.

Dutton, A., & Aron, A. (1974). Some evidence for heightened sexual attraction under conditions of high anxiety. *Journal of Personality and Social Psychology, 30,* 510–17.

Dutton, D. G., & Lake, R. A. (1973). Threat of own prejudice and reverse discrimination in interracial situations. *Journal of Personality and Social Psychology, 28,* 94–100.

Duval, S., & Wicklund, R. A. (1972). *A theory of objective self-awareness.* New York: Academic Press.

Duval, S., Duval, V., & Neely, R. (1979). Self-focus, felt responsibility, and helping behavior. *Journal of Personality and Social Psychology, 37,* 1769–1778.

Dykman, B., & Reis, H. T. (1979). Personality correlates of classroom seating position. *Journal of Educational Psychology, 71,* 346–354.

Eagly, A. H. (1983). Gender and social influence: A social psychological analysis. *American Psychologist, 38,* 971–983.

Eagly, A. H. (1987). *Sex differences in social behavior: A social-role interpretation.* Hillsdale, NJ: Erlbaum.

Eagly, A. H. (1995). The science and politics of comparing women and men. *American Psychologist, 50,* 145–158.

Eagly, A. H. (1997). Sex differences in social behavior: Comparing social role theory and evolutionary psychology. *American Psychologist, 52,* 1380–1383.

Eagly, A. H., Ashmore, R. D., Makhijani, M. G., & Longo, L. C. (1991). What is beautiful is good, but . . . : A meta-analytic review of research on the physical attractiveness stereotype. *Psychological Bulletin, 110,* 109–128.

Eagly, A. H., & Carli, L. L. (1981). Sex of researchers and sex-typed communications as determinants of sex differences in influencability: A meta-analysis of social influence studies. *Psychological Bulletin, 90,* 1–20.

Eagly, A. H., & Chaiken, S. (1993). *The psychology of attitudes.* Fort Worth, TX: Harcourt Brace Jovanovich.

Eagly, A. H., & Chaiken, S. (1998). Attitude structure and function. In D. Gilbert, S. T. Fiske, & G. Lindzey (Eds.), *Handbook of social psychology* (4th ed., Vol. 2, pp. 269–322). Boston: McGraw-Hill.

Eagly, A. H., & Chrvala, C. (1986). Sex differences in conformity: Status and gender role interpretations. *Psychology of Women Quarterly, 10,* 203–220.

Eagly, A. H., & Crowley, M. (1986). Gender and helping behavior: A meta-analytic view of the social psychological literature. *Psychological Bulletin, 100,* 283–308.

Eagly, A. H., Karau, S. J., & Makhijani, M. G. (1995). Gender and the effectiveness of leaders: A meta-analysis. *Psychological Bulletin, 117,* 125–145.

Eagly, A. H., & Steffen, V. J. (1984). Gender stereotypes stem from the distribution of women and men into social roles. *Journal of Personality and Social Psychology, 46,* 735–754.

Eagly, A. H., & Steffen, V. J. (1986). Gender and aggressive behavior: A meta-analystic review of the social psychological literature. *Psychological Bulletin, 100,* 309–330.

Eagly, A. H., & Wood, W. (1991). Explaining sex differences in social behavior: A meta-analytic perspective. *Personality and Social Psychology Bulletin, 17,* 306–315.

Eagly, A. H., & Wood, W. (1999). The origins of sex differences in human behavior: Evolved dispositions versus social roles. *American Psychologist, 54,* 408–423.

Eagly, A. H., Wood, W., & Chaiken, S. (1978). Causal inferences about communicators and their effect on opinion change. *Journal of Personality and Social Psychology, 36,* 424–435.

Eagly, A. H., Wood, W., & Fishbaugh, L. (1981). Sex differences in conformity: Surveillance by the group as a determinant of male nonconformity. *Journal of Personality and Social Psychology, 40,* 384–394.

Earley, P. C. (1989). Social loafing and collectivism: A comparison of the United States and the People's Republic of China. *Administrative Science Quarterly, 34,* 565–581.

Eby, L. T., & Dobbins, G. H. (1997). Collectivistic orientation in teams: An individual and group-level analysis. *Journal of Organizational Behavior, 18,* 275–295.

Echebarria, A., and Valencia, J. F. (1994). Private self consciousness as moderator of the importance of attitude and subjective norm. The prediction of voting. *European Journal of Social Psychology, 24,* 285–293.

Edinger, J. A., & Patterson, M. L. (1983). Nonverbal involvement and social control. *Psychological Bulletin, 93,* 30–56.

Edwards, J. A., & Weary, G. (1993). Depression and the impression formation continuum: Piecemeal processing despite the availability of category information. *Journal of Personality and Social Psychology, 64,* 636–645.

Edwards, J. A., Weary, G., von Hippel, W., & Jacobson, J. A. (2000). The effects of depression on impression formation: The role of trait and category diagnosticity. *Personality and Social Psychology Bulletin, 26,* 462–473.

Edwards, K., & Smith, E. E. (1996). A disconfirmation bias in the evaluation of arguments. *Journal of Personality and Social Psychology, 71,* 5–24.

Efran, M. G., & Patterson, E. W. J. (1974). Voters vote beautiful: The effects of physical appearance on a national election. *Canadian Journal of Behavioral Science, 6,* 352–356.

Efran, M. G., & Patterson, E. W. J. (1976). *The politics of appearance.* Unpublished manuscript, University of Toronto.

Egan, K. J. (1990). What does it mean to a patient to be "in control"? In F. M. Ferrante, G. W. Ostheimer, & B. G. Covino (Eds.),

Patient-controlled analgesia (pp. 17–26). Boston: Blackwell.

Ehrlichmann, H., & Halpern, J. N. (1988). Affect and memory: Effects of pleasant and unpleasant odors on retrieval of happy and unhappy memories. *Journal of Personality and Social Psychology, 55*, 769–779.

Eibl-Eibesfeldt, I. (1973). The expressive behavior of the deaf-and-blind-born. In M. von Cranach & I. Vine (Eds.), *Social communication and movement* (pp. 163–194). New York: Academic Press.

Eibl-Eibesfeldt, I. (1975). *Ethology: The biology of behavior* (2nd ed.). New York: Holt, Rinehart, & Winston.

Eibl-Eibesfeldt, I. (1989). *Human ethology*. New York: Aldine de Gruyter.

Einon, D. (1994). Are men more promiscuous than women? *Ethology and sociobiology, 15*, 131–143.

Eisenberg, N. (1992). *The caring child.* Cambridge, MA: Harvard University Press.

Eisenberg, N., Cialdini, R. B., McCreath, H., & Shell, R. (1987). Consistency-based compliance. When and why do children become vulnerable? *Journal of Personality and Social Psychology, 52*, 1174–1181.

Eisenberg, N., & Fabes, R. A. (1998). Prosocial development. In W. Damon (Ed.), *Handbook of Child Psychology* (5th ed.) (Vol. 3, pp. 701–798). New York: Wiley.

Eisenberg, N., & Miller, P. (1987). The relation of empathy to prosocial and related behaviors. *Psychological Bulletin, 101*, 91–119.

Eisenberg, N., & Shell, R. (1986). Prosocial moral judgment and behavior in children: The mediating role of cost. *Personality and Social Psychology Bulletin, 12*, 426–433.

Eisenberg-Berg, N. (1979). Development of children's prosocial moral judgment. *Developmental Psychology, 15*, 128–137.

Eisenberg-Berg, N., & Hand, M. (1979). The relationship of preschoolers reasoning about moral conflicts to prosocial behavior. *Child Development, 50*, 356–363.

Ekman, P. (1982). *Emotion in the human face* (2nd ed.). Cambridge: Cambridge University Press.

Ekman, P. (1985). *Telling lies: Clues to deceit in the marketplace, politics, and marriage.* New York: W. W. Norton.

Ekman, P. (1994). Strong evidence for universals in facial expressions: A reply to Russell's mistaken critique. *Psychological Bulletin, 115*, 268–287.

Ekman, P., & Friesen, W. V. (1969). The repertoire of nonverbal behavior: Categories, origins, usage, and coding. *Semiotica, 1*, 49–98.

Ekman, P., & Friesen, W. V. (1971). Constants across cultures in the face and emotion. *Journal of Personality and Social Psychology, 17*, 124–129.

Ekman, P., & Friesen, W. V. (1978). *The facial-action coding system.* Palo Alto, CA: Consulting Psychologists Press.

Ekman, P., & O'Sullivan, M. (1991). Who can catch a liar? *American Psychologist, 46*, 913–920.

Elkin, R. A., & Leippe, M. R. (1986). Physiological arousal, dissonance, and attitude change. *Journal of Personality and Social Psychology, 51*, 55–65.

Elliot, A. J., & Devine, P. G. (1994). On the motivational nature of cognitive dissonance: Dissonance as psychological discomfort. *Journal of Personality and Social Psychology, 67*, 382–394.

Elliott, M. et al. (1993). Global Mafia. *Newsweek*, Dec. 13, pp. 22–31.

Ellis, B. J., & Symons, D. (1990). Sex differences in sexual fantasy: An evolutionary psychological approach. *Journal of Sex Research, 27*, 527–555.

Ellis, L. (1986). Evidence of neuroandrogenic etiology of sex roles from a combined analysis of human, nonhuman primate and nonprimate mammalian studies. *Personality and Individual Differences, 7*, 519–552.

Ellsworth, P. C., & Mauro, R. (1998). Psychology and law. In D. T. Gilbert, S. T. Fiske, & G. Lindzey (Eds.), *Handbook of social psychology* (4th ed.) (Vol. 2, pp. 684–732). New York: McGraw-Hill/Oxford University Press.

Emert, C. (2000, September 2). Olympic seal of approval. *San Francisco Chronicle*, pp. D1-D2.

Emmons, R. A. (1989). The personal striving approach to personality. In L. A. Pervin (Ed.), *Goals concepts in personality and social psychology* (pp. 87–126). Hillsdale, NJ: Erlbaum.

Emmons, R. A., Diener, E., & Larsen, R. J. (1986). Choice and avoidance of everyday situations and affect congruence: Two models of reciprocal interactionism. *Journal of Personality and Social Psychology, 51*, 815–826.

Endler, N. S., & Magnusson, D. (1976). *Interactional psychology and personality.* Washington, DC: Hemisphere.

Erber, R. (1991). Affective and semantic priming: Effects of mood on category accessibility and inference. *Journal of Experimental Social Psychology, 27*, 480–498.

Erber, R., & Fiske, S. T. (1984). Outcome dependency and attention to inconsistent information. *Journal of Personality and Social Psychology, 47*, 709–726.

Ericksen, M. K., & Sirgy, M. J. (1989). Achievement motivation and clothing behavior: A self-image congruence analysis. *Journal of Social Behavior and Personality, 4*, 307–326.

Esses, V. M., & Zanna, M. P. (1995). Mood and the expression of ethnic stereotypes. *Journal of Personality and Social Psychology, 69*, 1052–1068.

Essock-Vitale, S. M., & McGuire, M. T. (1985). Women's lives viewed from an evolutionary perspective. II. Patterns of helping. *Ethology and Sociobiology, 6*, 155–173.

Etcoff, N. L., Ekman, P., Magee, J. J., & Frank, M. G. (2000). Lie detection and language comprehension. *Nature, 405*, 139.

Etzioni, A. (1986). The Kennedy experiment: Unilateral initiatives. In R. K. White (Ed.), *Psychology and the prevention of nuclear war* (pp. 204–210). New York: New York University Press.

Evans, G. W., & Lepore, S. J. (1993). Household crowding and social support: A quasiexperimental analysis. *Journal of Personality and Social Psychology, 65*, 308–316.

Evans, G. W., & Saegert, S. (2000). Residential crowding in the context of inner city poverty. In S. Wapner, J. Demick, T. Yamamoto, & H. Minami (Eds.), *Theoretical perspectives in environment-behavior research: Underlying assumptions, research problems, and methodologies.* New York: Kluwer Academic/Plenum Publishers.

Evans, G. W., Hygge, S., & Bullinger, M. (1995). Chronic noise and psychological stress. *Psychological Science, 6*, 333–338.

Evans, G. W., Lepore, S. J., & Allen, K. M. (2000). Cross-cultural differences in tolerance for crowding: Fact or fiction? *Journal of Personality and Social Psychology, 79*, 204–210.

Evans, G. W., Lepore, S. J., & Schroeder, A. (1996). The role of interior design elements in human responses to crowding. *Journal of Personality and Social Psychology, 70*, 41–46.

Evans, G. W., Lepore, S. J., Shejwal, B. R., & Palsane, M. N. (1998). Chronic residential crowding and children's well-being: An ecological perspective. *Child Development, 69*, 1514–1523.

Evans, G. W., Palsane, M. N., & Carrere, S. (1987). Type A behavior and occupational stress: A cross-cultural study of blue-collar workers. *Journal of Personality and Social Psychology, 52*, 1002–1007.

Executive pay (2000, April 17). *Business Week*, 100–112.

Exline, R. V. (1972). Visual interaction: The glances of power and preference. In J. K. Cole (Ed.), *Nebraska symposium on motivation* (Vol. 19, pp. 163–206). Lincoln: University of Nebraska Press.

Fairchild, H. H. (1984). School size, per-pupil expenditures, and academic achievement. *Review of Public Data Use, 12*, 221–229.

Faley, R. H., Knapp, D. E., Kustis, G. A., & Dubois, C. L. Z. (1999). Estimating the organizational costs of sexual harassment: The case of the U.S. Army. *Journal of Business and Psychology, 13*, 461–484.

Farh, J.-L., Dobbins, G. H., & Cheng, B.-S. (1991). Cultural relativity in action: A comparison of self-ratings made by Chinese and U.S. workers. *Personnel Psychology, 44*, 129–147.

Farnham, S. D., Greenwald, A. G., & Banaji, M. R. (1999). Implicit self-esteem. In D. Abrams & M. Hogg (Eds.), *Social identity and social cognition* (pp. 230–248). Malden, MA: Blackwell.

Farrar, E. W. R. (1838). *The young lady's friend; A manual of practical advice and instruction to young females on their entering upon the duties of life after quitting school.* London: John W. Parker.

Farwell, L. A., & Donchin, E. (1991). The truth will out: Interrogative polygraphy ("lie detection") with event-related potentials. *Psychophysiology, 28*, 531–547.

Fast, J. (1970). *Body language.* New York: M. Evans and Company.

Fazio, R. H. (1987). Self-perception theory: A current perspective. In M. P. Zanna, J. M. Olson, & C. P. Herman (Eds.), *Ontario symposium on personality and social psychology* (pp. 129–150). Hillsdale, NJ: Erlbaum.

Fazio, R. H., Jackson, J. R., Dunton, B. C., & Williams, C. J. (1995). Variability in automatic activation as an unobtrusive measure of racial attitudes: A bona fide pipeline? *Journal of Personality and Social Psychology, 69*, 1013–1027.

Fazio, R. H., Sherman, S. J., & Herr, P. M. (1982). The feature-positive effect in the self-perception process. *Journal of Personality and Social Psychology, 42*, 404–411.

Fazio, R. H., Zanna, M. P., & Cooper, J. (1977). Dissonance and self-perception. *Journal of Experimental Social Psychology, 13*, 464–479.

Feagin, J. R., & Feagin, C. B. (1999). *Racial and ethnic relations* (6th ed.). Upper Saddle River, NJ: Prentice Hall.

Feather, N. T. (1998). Reactions to penalties for offenses committed by the police and public citizens: Testing a social-cognitive process model of retributive justice. *Journal of Personality & Social Psychology, 75*, 528–544.

Fehr, B. (1988). Prototype analysis of the concepts of love and commitment. *Journal of Personality and Social Psychology, 55*, 557–579.

Fehr, B., & Russell, J. A. (1991). The concept of love viewed from a prototype perspective. *Journal of Personality and Social Psychology, 60*, 425–438.

Fehr, E., Gachter, S., & Kirchsteiger, G. (1997). Reciprocity as a contract enforcement device. *Econometrica, 65*, 833–860.

Fein, S., & Spencer, S. J. (1997). Prejudice as self-image maintenance: Affirming the self through derogating others. *Journal of Personality and Social Psychology, 73*, 31–44.

Feingold, A. (1990). Gender differences in effects of physical attractiveness on romantic attraction: A comparison across five research paradigms. *Journal of Personality and Social Psychology, 59*, 981–993.

Feingold, A. (1992). Gender differences in mate selection preferences: A test of the parental investment model. *Psychological Bulletin, 112*, 125–139.

Feingold, A. (1992). Good-looking people are not what we think. *Psychological Bulletin, 111*, 304–341.

Feingold, A. (1993). Cognitive gender differences: A developmental perspective. *Sex Roles, 29*, 91–112.

Felson, R. B. (1978). Aggression as impression management. *Social Psychology, 41*, 205–213.

Felson, R. B. (1982). Impression management and the escalation of aggression and violence. *Social Psychology Quarterly, 45*, 245–254.

Felson, R. B., & Tedeschi, J. T. (1993). A social interactionist approach to violence: Cross-cultural implications. *Violence and Victims, 8*, 295–310.

Fenigstein, A. (1979). Self-consciousness, self-attention, and social interaction. *Journal of Personality and Social Psychology, 37*, 75–86.

Fenigstein, A., & Abrams, D. (1993). Self-attention and the egocentric assumption of shared perspectives. *Journal of Experimental Social Psychology, 29*, 287–303.

Fenigstein, A., Scheier, M. F., & Buss, A. H. (1975). Public and private self-consciousness: Assessment and theory. *Journal of Consulting and Clinical Psychology, 43*, 522–527.

Fernald, R. D. (1984). Vision and behavior in an African cichlid fish. *American Scientist, 72*, 58–65.

Ferrante, F. M., Ostheimer, G. W., & Covino, B. G. (1990). *Patient-controlled analgesia.* Boston: Blackwell.

Ferrari, J. R. (1991). A second look at behavioral self-handicapping among women. *Journal of Social Behavior and Personality, 6*, 195–206.

Ferrari, J. R., & Tice, D. M. (2000). Procrastination as a self-handicap for men and women: A task-avoidance strategy in a laboratory setting. *Journal of Research in Personality, 34*, 73–83.

Ferris, T. (1997, April 14). The wrong stuff. *The New Yorker*, p, 31.

Feshbach, S. (1984). The catharsis hypothesis, aggressive drive, and the reduction of aggression. *Aggressive Behavior, 10*, 91–101.

Festinger, L. (1954). A theory of social comparison processes. *Human Relations, 7*, 117–140.

Festinger, L. (1957). *A theory of cognitive dissonance.* Stanford, CA: Stanford University Press.

Festinger, L., & Carlsmith, J. M. (1959). Cognitive consequences of forced compliance. *Journal of Abnormal and Social Psychology, 58*, 202–210.

Festinger, L., Pepitone, A., & Newcomb, T. (1952). Some consequences of de-individuation in a group. *Journal of Abnormal and Social Psychology, 47 (#2 Supp.)*, 382–389.

Festinger, L., Reicken, H. W., & Schachter, S. (1956). *When prophesy fails.* Minneapolis: University of Minnesota Press.

Festinger, L., Schachter, S., & Back, K. (1950). *Social pressures in informal groups.* Stanford, CA: Stanford University Press.

Fiedler, F. E. (1967). *A theory of leadership effectiveness.* New York: McGraw-Hill.

Fiedler, F. E. (1993). The leadership situation and the black box in contingency theories. In M. M. Chemers & R. Ayman (Eds.), *Leadership theory and research: Perspectives and directions* (pp. 1–28). San Diego, CA: Academic Press.

Fiedler, K. (1988). Emotional mood, cognitive style, and behavior regulation. In K. Fiedler & J. P. Forgas (Eds.), *Affect, cognition, and social behavior* (pp. 100–119). Toronto: Hogrefe.

Finch, J. F., & Cialdini, R. B. (1989). Another indirect tactic of (self-) image management: Boosting. *Personality and Social Psychology Bulletin, 15*, 222–232.

Fishbein, H. D. (1996). *Peer prejudice and discrimination: Evolutionary, cultural, and developmental dynamics.* Boulder, CO: Westview Press.

Fisher, J. D., Nadler, A., & Witcher-Alagna, S. (1982). Recipient reactions to aid. *Psychological Bulletin, 91*, 27–54.

Fisher, W. A., Byrne, D., White, L. A., & Kelley, K. (1988). Erotophobia-erotophilia as a dimension of personality. *Journal of Sex Research, 25*, 123–151.

Fishman, P. M. (1978). Interaction: The work women do. *Social Forces, 25*, 397–406.

Fiske, A. P. (1991). The cultural relativity of selfish individualism: Anthropological evidence that humans are inherently sociable. In M. S. Clark (Ed.), *Review of personality and social psychology: Vol. 12, Prosocial behavior* (pp. 176–214). Newbury Park, CA: Sage.

Fiske, A. P. (2000). Complementarity theory: Why human social capacities evolved to require cultural complements. *Personality & Social Psychology Review, 4*, 76–94.

Fiske, A. P., Kitayama, S., Markus, H. R., & Nisbett, R. E. (1998). The cultural matrix of social psychology. In D. Gilbert, S. T. Fiske, & G. Lindzey (Eds.), *Handbook of social psychology* (4th ed., Vol. 2, pp. 915–981). Boston: McGraw-Hill.

Fiske, S. T. (1992). Thinking is for doing: Portraits of social cognition from daguerreotype to laserphoto. *Journal of Personality and Social Psychology, 63*, 877–889.

Fiske, S. T. (1993). Controlling other people: The impact of power on stereotyping. *American Psychologist, 48*, 621–628.

Fiske, S. T., & Cox, M. G. (1979). Person concepts: The effect of target familiarity and descriptive purpose on the process of describing others. *Journal of Personality, 47*, 136–161.

Fiske, S. T., & Neuberg, S. L. (1990). A continuum of impression formation, from category-based to individuating processes: Influences of information and motivation on attention and interpretation. In M. P. Zanna (Ed.), *Advances in experimental social psychology* (Vol. 23, p. 1–74). New York: Academic Press.

Fiske, S. T., & Taylor, S. E. (1991). *Social cognition* (2nd ed.). New York: McGraw Hill.

Fiske, S. T., & Von Hendy, H. M. (1992). Personality feedback and situational norms can control stereotyping processes. *Journal of Personality and Social Psychology, 62*, 577–596.

Fiske, S. T., Neuberg, S. L., Beattie, A. E., & Milberg, S. J. (1987). Category-based and attribute-based reactions to others: Some informational conditions of stereotyping and individuating processes. *Journal of Experimental Social Psychology, 23*, 399–427.

Fitzgerald, L. F. (1993). Sexual harassment: Violence against women in the workplace. *American Psychologist, 48,* 1070–1076.

Fitzgerald, L. F., Shullman, S. L., Bailey, N., Richards, M., Swecker, J., Gold, Y., Ormerod, M., & Weitzman, L. (1988). The incidence and dimensions of sexual harassment in academia and the workplace. *Journal of Vocational Behavior, 32,* 152–175.

Fleming, J. H., & Darley, J. M. (1991). Mixed messages: The multiple audience problem and strategic communication. *Social Cognition, 9,* 25–46.

Fleming, J. H., & Rudman, L. A. (1993). Between a rock and a hard place: Self-concept regulating and communicative properties of distancing behaviors. *Journal of Personality and Social Psychology, 64,* 44–59.

Fletcher, G. J. O., Simpson, J. A., & Thomas, G. (2000). The measurement of perceived relationship quality components: A confirmatory factor analytic approach. *Personality & Social Psychology Bulletin, 26,* 340–354.

Fletcher, G. J. O., Simpson, J. A., Thomas, G., & Giles, L. (1999). Ideals in intimate relationships. *Journal of Personality & Social Psychology, 76,* 72–89.

Flett, G. L., Pliner, P., & Blankstein, K. R. (1989). Depression and components of attributional complexity. *Journal of Personality and Social Psychology, 56,* 757–764.

Flowers, M. L. (1977). A laboratory test of some implications of Janis's groupthink hypothesis. *Journal of Personality and Social Psychology, 35,* 888–896.

Foa, E. B., & Foa, U. G. (1980). Resource theory: Interpersonal behavior as exchange. In K. J. Gergen, M. S. Greenber, & R. H. Willis (Eds.), *Social exchange: Advances in theory and research* (pp. 77–94). New York: Plenum.

Foddy, M. Smithson, M., Schneider, S., & Hogg, M. (1999). *Resolving social dilemmas: Dynamic, structural, and intergroup aspects.* Philadelphia: Psychology Press.

Foley, L. A. (1976). Personality and situational influences on changes in prejudice: A replication of Cook's railroad game in a prison setting. *Journal of Personality and Social Psychology, 34,* 846–856.

Fong, G. T., & Markus, H. (1982). Self-schemas and judgments about others. *Social Cognition, 1,* 191–204.

Ford, C. V. (1996). *Lies! Lies!! Lies!!!: The psychology of deceit.* Washington, DC: American Psychiatric Press.

Ford, T. E. (2000). Effects of sexist humor on tolerance of sexist events. *Personality and Social Psychology Bulletin, 26,* 1094–1107.

Fordyce, W. E. (1988). Pain and suffering: A reappraisal. *American Psychologist, 43,* 276–283.

Forgas, J. P. (1979). *Social episodes: The study of interaction routines.* London: Academic Press.

Forgas, J. P. (1995). The Affect-Infusion Model (AIM). *Psychological Bulletin, 117,* 39–66.

Forgas, J. P., & Bower, G. H. (1987). Mood effects on person perception judgments. *Journal of Personality and Social Psychology, 53,* 53–60.

Forgas, J. P., & Moylan, S. (1987). After the movies: Transient mood and social judgments. *Personality and Social Psychology Bulletin, 13,* 467–477.

Forgas, J. P., Levinger, G., & Moylan, S. (1994). Feeling good and feeling close: Mood effects on the perception of intimate relationships. *Personal Relationships, 2,* 165–184.

Forge, K. L., & Phemister, S. (1987). The effect of prosocial cartoons on preschool children. *Child Development Journal, 17,* 83–88.

Form, W. H., & Nosow, S. (1958). *Community in disaster.* New York: Harper.

Forrest, J. A., & Feldman, R. S. (2000). Detecting deception and judge's involvement: Lower task involvement leads to better lie detection. *Personality and Social Psychology Bulletin, 26,* 118–125.

Forsyth, D. R. (1990). *Group dynamics* (2nd ed.). Pacific Grove, CA: Brooks/Cole.

Forsyth, D. R., Schlenker, B. R., Leary, M. R., & McCown, N. E. (1985). Self-presentational determinants of sex differences in leadership behavior. *Small Group Behavior, 16,* 197–210.

Foster, C. A., Witcher, B. S., Campbell, W. K., & Green, J. D. (1998). Arousal and attraction: Evidence for automatic and controlled processes. *Journal of Personality and Social Psychology, 74,* 86–101.

Foushee, M. C. (1984). Dyads and triads at 35,000 feet. *American Psychologist, 39,* 885–893.

Fox, R. (1992). Prejudice and the unfinished mind: A new look at an old failing. *Psychological Inquiry, 3,* 137–152.

Frable, D. E. S., Blackstone, T., & Scherbaum, C. (1990). Marginal and mindful: Deviants in social interaction. *Journal of Personality and Social Psychology, 59,* 140–149.

Fraley, R. C., & Davis, K. E. (1997). Attachment formation and transfer in young adults' close friendships and romantic relationships. *Personal Relationships, 4,* 131–144.

Frank, F., & Anderson, L. R. (1971). Effects of task and group size upon group productivity and member satisfaction. *Sociometry, 34,* 135–149.

Frank, M. G., & Ekman, P. (1993). Not all smiles are created equal: The differences between enjoyment and nonenjoyment smiles. *Humor, 6,* 9–26.

Frank, M. G., Ekman, P., & Friesen, W. V. (1993). Behavioral markers and recognizability of the smile of enjoyment. *Journal of Personality and Social Psychology, 64,* 83–93.

Frank, R. H., Gilovich, T., & Regan, D. T. (1993). Does studying economics inhibit cooperation? *Journal of Economic Perspectives,* 7, 159–171.

Franzoi, S. L., & Shields, S. A. (1984). The Body Esteem Scale: Multidimensional structure and sex differences in a college population. *Journal of Personality Assessment, 48,* 173–178.

Frazier, P. A., Cochran, C. C., & Olson, A. M. (1995). Social science research on lay definitions of sexual harassment. *Journal of Social Issues, 51*, 21–38.

Fredrickson, B. L., Roberts, T. A., Noll, S. M., Quinn, D. M., & Twenge, J. M. (1998). That swimsuit becomes you: Sex differences in self-objectification, restrained eating, and math performance. *Journal of Personality & Social Psychology, 75*, 269–284.

Freedman, J. L. (1984). Effects of television violence on aggressiveness. *Psychological Bulletin, 96*, 227–246.

Freedman, J. L., & Fraser, S. C. (1966). Compliance without pressure: The foot-in-the-door technique. *Journal of Personality and Social Psychology, 4*, 195–203.

French, J. R. P., Jr., & Raven, B. (1959). The bases of social power. In D. Cartwright (Ed.), *Studies in social power* (pp. 150–167). Ann Arbor, MI: Institute for Social Research.

Frenzen, J. R., & Davis, H. L. (1990). Purchasing behavior in embedded markets. *Journal of Consumer Research, 17*, 1–12.

Frey, D., Schulz-Hardt, S., & Stahlberg, D. (1996). Information seeking among individuals and groups and possible consequences for decision making in business and politics. In E. Witte & J. H. Davis (Eds.), *Understanding group behavior: Small group processes and interpersonal relations* (Vol. 2, pp. 211–225). Mahwah, NJ: Erlbaum.

Fridlund, A. J. (1994). *Human facial expression: An evolutionary view.* San Diego, CA: Academic Press.

Fried, C. B., & Aronson, E. (1995). Hypocrisy, misattribution, and dissonance reduction. *Personality and Social Psychology Bulletin, 32*, 925–933.

Friedmann, E., Katcher, A. H., Lynch, J. J., & Thomas, S. A. (1980). Animal companions and one-year survival of patients after discharge from a coronary care unit. *Public Health Reports, 95*, 307–12.

Friedrich-Cofer, L., & Huston, A. (1986). Television violence and aggression: The debate continues. *Psychological Bulletin, 100*, 364–371.

Frieze, I. H., & Ramsey, S. J. (1976). Nonverbal maintenance of traditional sex roles. *Journal of Social Issues, 32*, 133–141.

Frieze, I. H., Fisher, J. R., Hanusa, B. H., McHugh, M. C., & Valle, V. H. (1978). Attributions of the causes of success and failure as internal and external barriers to acheivement. In J. L. Sherman & F. L. Denmark (Eds.), *The psychology of women: Future directions in research* (pp. 519–552). New York: Psychological Dimensions.

Frijda, N. H. (1986). *The emotions.* Cambridge: Cambridge University Press.

Frijda, N. H. (1988). The laws of emotion. *American Psychologist, 43*, 349–358.

Fritschler, A. L. (1975). *Smoking and politics.* Englewood Cliffs, NJ: Prentice-Hall.

Froming, W. J., & Carver, C. S. (1981). Divergent influences of private and public self-consciousness in a compliance paradigm. *Journal of Research in Personality, 15*, 159–171.

Froming, W. J., Allen, L., & Jensen, R. (1985). Altruism, role-taking, and self-awareness: The acquisition of norms governing altruistic behavior. *Child Development, 56*, 1223–1228.

Froming, W. J., Nasby, W., & McManus, J. (1998). Prosocial self-schemas, self-awareness, and children's prosocial behavior. *Journal of Personality and Social Psychology, 75*, 766–777.

Fry, D. P. (1990). Play aggression among Zapotec children: Implications for the practice hypothesis. *Aggressive Behavior, 16*, 321–340.

Fry, P. S., & Ghosh, R. (1980). Attributions of success and failure: Comparison of attributional differences between Asian and Caucasian children. *Journal of Cross-Cultural Psychology, 11*, 343–363.

Fullerton, H. N., Jr. (1995). The 2005 labor force: Growing, but slowly. *Monthly Labor Review, 118*, 29–44.

Fultz, J., Batson, C. D., Fortenbach, V. A., McCarthy, P. M., & Varney, L. L. (1986). Social evaluation and the empathy-altruism hypothesis. *Journal of Personality and Social Psychology, 50*, 761–769.

Funder, D.C. (1987). Errors and mistakes: Evaluating the accuracy of social judgment. *Psychological Bulletin, 101*, 75–90.

Funder, D.C. (1999). *Personality judgment: A realistic approach to person perception.* San Diego: Academic Press

Furnham, A. (1996). Factors relating to the allocation of medical resources. *Journal of Social Behavior and Personality, 11*, 615–624.

Fussell, P. (1983). *Class.* New York: Ballentine.

Gabbay, F. H. (1992). Behavior-genetic strategies in the study of emotion. *Psychological Science, 3*, 50–55.

Gable, S. L., & Reis, H. T. (1999). Now and then, them and us, this and that: Studying relationships across time, partner, context, and person. *Personal Relationships, 6*, 415–432.

Gabrenya, W. K., Jr., Wang, Y. E., & Latané, B. (1985). Social loafing on an optimizing task: Cross-cultural differences among Chinese and Americans. *Journal of Cross-Cultural Psychology, 16*, 223–242.

Gaertner, S. L., & Bickman, L. (1971). Effects of race on the elicitation of helping behavior. *Journal of Personality and Social Psychology, 20*, 218–222.

Gaertner, S. L., & Dovidio, J. F. (1977). The subtlety of white racism, arousal, and helping behavior. *Journal of Personality and Social Psychology, 35*, 691–707.

Gaertner, S. L., & Dovidio, J. F. (1986). The aversive form of racism. In J. F. Dovidio & S. L. Gaertner (Eds.), *Prejudice, discrimination, and racism* (pp. 61–89). Orlando, FL: Academic Press.

Gaertner, S. L., Dovidio, J. F., Anastasio, P. A., Bachman, B. A., & Rust, M. C. (1993).

The Common Ingroup Identity Model: Recategorization and the reduction of intergroup bias. In W. Stroebe & M. Hewstone (Eds.), *European Review of Social Psychology* (Vol. 4, pp. 1–26). London: Wiley.

Gaertner, S. L., Mann, J. A., Dovidio, J. F., Murrell, A. J., & Pomare, M. (1990). How does cooperation reduce intergroup bias? *Journal of Personality and Social Psychology, 59,* 692–704.

Gagnon, A., & Bourhis, R. Y. (1996). Discrimination in the minimal group paradigm: Social identity of self-interest. *Personality and Social Psychology Bulletin, 22,* 1289–1301.

Gaines, S. O., Panter, A. T., Lyde, M. D., Steers, W. N., Rusbult, C. E., Cox, C. L., & Wexler, M. O. (1997). Evaluating the circumplexity of interpersonal traits and the manifestation of interpersonal traits in interpersonal trust. *Journal of Personality and Social Psychology, 73,* 610–623.

Galanti, G. A. (1993). Reflections on brainwashing. In M. D. Langone (Ed.), *Recovery from cults* (pp. 85–103). New York: Norton.

Galaskiewicz, J. (1985). *Social organization of an urban grants economy: A study of business philanthropy and nonprofit organizations* New York: Academic Press.

Galinsky, A. D., & Moskowitz, G. B. (2000). Perspective-taking: Decreasing stereotype expression, stereotype accessibility, and in-group favoritism. *Journal of Personality and Social Psychology, 78,* 708–724.

Gallup, G., Jr. (1984, March). Religion in America. *The Gallup Report,* Report No. 222.

Gallup. (1997). *Black/White relations in the United States.* Princeton, NJ: Gallup.

Galton, F. (1875). The history of twins as a criterion of the relative power of nature and nurture. *Journal of the Anthropological Institute, 5,* 391–406.

Gangestad, S. W., & Simpson, J. A. (2000). The evolution of human mating: Trade-offs and strategic pluralism. *Behavioral & Brain Sciences, 23.*

Gangestad, S. W., & Snyder, M. (2000). Self-monitoring: Appraisal and reappraisal. *Psychological Bulletin, 126,* 530–555.

Gangestad, S., & Snyder, M. (1985). To carve nature at its joints: On the existence of discrete classes in personality. *Psychological Review, 92,* 317–349.

Gangestad, S. W., & Thornhill, R. (1997). Human sexual selection and developmental stability. In J. A. Simpson & D. T. Kenrick (Eds.), *Evolutionary social psychology* (pp. 169–196). Hillsdale, NJ: Erlbaum.

Gannon, K. M., Skowronski, J. J., & Betz, A. L. (1994). Depressive diligence in social information processing: Implications for order effects in impressions and for social memory. *Social Cognition, 12,* 263–280.

Ganor, S. (1995). *Light one candle.* New York: Kodansha.

Gantner, A. B., & Taylor, S. P. (1992). Human physical aggression as a function of alcohol and threat of harm. *Aggressive behavior, 18,* 29–36.

Gardner, G. T., & Stern, P. C. (1996). *Environmental problems and human behavior.* Boston: Allyn & Bacon.

Gardner, H. (1995). *Leading minds: An anatomy of leadership.* New York: BasicBooks.

Gardner, W. L., Pickett, C. L., & Brewer, M. B. (2000). Social exclusion and selective memory: How the need to belong influences memory for social events. *Personality & Social Psychology Bulletin, 26,* 486–496.

Garrow, D. J. (1986). *Bearing the cross: Martin Luther King, Jr., and the Southern Christian Leadership Conference.* New York: Vintage Books.

Garry, M., & Polaschek, D. L. L. (2000). Imagination and Memory. *Current Directions in Psychological Science, 9,* 6–10.

Gatchel, R. J., Baum, A., & Krantz, D. (1989). *An introduction to health psychology* (2nd ed.). New York: Random House.

Geary, D. C. (2000). Evolution and proximate expression of human paternal investment. *Psychological Bulletin, 126,* 55–77.

Geis, F. L. (1993). Self-fulfilling prophecies: A social psychological view of gender. In A. E. Beall & R. J. Sternberg (Eds.), *The psychology of gender* (pp. 9–54). New York: Guilford.

Geizer, R. S., Rarick, D. L., & Soldow, G. F. (1977). Deception and judgment accuracy: A study in person perception. *Personality and Social Psychology Bulletin, 3,* 446–449.

Geller, E. S. (1992). Applied behavior analysis and social marketing: An integration for environmental preservation. *Journal of Social Issues, 45*(1), 17–36.

Gentry, C. (1991). *J. Edgar Hoover: The man and his secrets.* New York: W. W. Norton.

Gerard, H. B., & Rabbie, J. M. (1961). Fear and social comparison. *Journal of Abnormal and Social Psychology, 62,* 586–592.

Gerbner, G., Gross, L., Morgan, M., & Signorelli, N. (1981). Health and medicine on television. *New England Journal of Medicine, 305,* 901–904.

Gergen, K. J. (1971). *The concept of self.* New York: Holt, Rinehart, & Winston.

Gergen, K. J. (1985). The social constructionist movement in modern psychology. *American Psychologist, 40, 266–275.*

Gergen, K. J., Ellsworth, P., Maslach, C., & Seipel, M. (1975). Obligation, donor resources, and reactions to aid in three cultures. *Journal of Personality and Social Psychology, 31,* 390–400.

Gergen, M. (1990). Beyond the evil empire: Horseplay and aggression. *Aggressive Behaviour, 16,* 381–398.

Gergen, M., & Gergen, K. (1983). Interpretive dimensions of international aid. In A. Nadler, J. D. Fisher, & B. M. DePaulo (Eds.), *New directions in helping* (Vol. 3, pp. 32–348). New York: Academic Press.

Geyer, A. L. J., & Steyrer, J. M. (1998). Transformational leadership and objective performance in banks.

Applied Psychology: An International Review, 47, 397–420.

Giacalone, R. A. (1985). On slipping when you thought you had put your best foot forward: Self-promotion, self-destruction, and entitlements. *Group and Organization Studies, 10*, 61–80.

Giacalone, R. A., & Riordan, C. A. (1990). Effect of self-presentation on perceptions and recognition in an organization. *The Journal of Psychology, 124*, 25–38.

Gibbons, F. X., & Gerrard, M. (1989). Effects of upward and downward social comparison on mood states. *Journal of Social and Clinical Psychology, 8*, 14–31.

Gibbons, F. X., & McCoy, S. B. (1991). Self-esteem, similarity, and reactions to active versus downward social comparison. *Journal of Personality and Social Psychology, 60*, 414–424.

Gibbons, F. X., & Wicklund, R. A. (1982). Self-focused attention and helping behavior. *Journal of Personality and Social Psychology, 43*, 462–474.

Gibbons, F. X., Benbow, C. P., & Gerrard, M. (1994). From top dog to bottom half: Social comparison strategies in response to poor performance. *Journal of Personality and Social Psychology, 67*, 638–652.

Gibbons, F. X., Eggleston, T. J., & Benthin, A. C. (1997). Cognitive reactions to smoking relapse: The reciprocal relation between dissonance and self-esteem. *Journal of Personality and Social Psychology, 72*, 184–195.

Gibson, B., & Sachau, D. (2000). Sandbagging as a self-presentational strategy: Claiming to be less than you are. *Personality and Social Psychology Bulletin, 26*, 56–70.

Gibson, J. J. (1979). *The ecological approach to visual perception.* Boston: Houghton Mifflin.

Gigerenzer, G., & Goldstein, D. G. (1996). Reasoning the fast and frugal way: Models of bounded rationality. *Psychological Review, 103*, 650–669.

Gilbert, D. T. (1991). How mental systems believe. *American Psychologist, 46*, 107–119.

Gilbert, D. T. (1998). Ordinary personology. In D. T. Gilbert, S. T. Fiske, & G. Lindzey (Eds.), *Handbook of social psychology* (4th ed.) (Vol. 2, pp. 89–150). New York: McGraw-Hill/Oxford University Press.

Gilbert, D. T., & Malone, P. S. (1995). The correspondence bias. *Psychological Bulletin, 117*, 21–38.

Gilbert, D. T., Pelham, B. W., & Krull, D. S. (1988). On cognitive busyness: When person perceivers meet persons perceived. *Journal of Personality and Social Psychology, 54*, 733–740.

Gilbert, D. T., Tafarodi, R. W., & Malone, P. S. (1993). You can't not believe everything you read. *Journal of Personality and Social Psychology, 65*, 221–233.

Gilbert, P. (1994). Male violence: Towards an integration. In J. Archer (Ed.), *Male Violence* (pp. 352–389). New York: Routledge.

Giles, H., & Coupland, N. (1991). *Language: Contexts and consequences.* Pacific Grove, CA: Brooks/Cole.

Gilligan, C. (1982). *In a different voice.* Cambridge, MA: Harvard University Press.

Gilmartin, B. G. (1987). *Shyness and love: Causes, consequences, and treatment.* Lanham, MD: University Press of America.

Gilovich, T. (1981). Seeing the past in the present: The effect of associations to familiar events on judgments and decisions. *Journal of Personality and Social Psychology, 40*, 797–803.

Gilovich, T., & Medvec, V. H. (1995). The experience of regret: What, when, and why? *Psychological Review, 102*, 379–395.

Gilovich, T., Medvec, V. H., & Savitsky, K. (2000). The spotlight effect in social judgment: An egocentric bias in estimates of the salience of one's own actions and appearance. *Journal of Personality & Social Psychology, 78*, 211–222.

Giner-Sorolla, R., & Chaiken, S. (1994). The causes of hostile media judgments. *Journal of Experimental Social Psychology, 30*, 165–180.

Giner-Sorolla, R., & Chaiken, S. (1997). Selective use of heuristic and systematic processing under defense motivation. *Personality and Social Psychology Bulletin, 23*, 84–97.

Giving and volunteering in the U.S. (1999). Washington, DC: Independent Sector.

Gladis, M. M., Michela, J. L., Walter, H. J., & Vaughan, R. D. (1992). High school students' perceptions of AIDS risk: Realistic appraisal or motivated denial? *Health Psychology, 11*, 307–316.

Glass, D.C., Singer, J. E., & Friedman, L. N. (1969). Psychic cost of adaptation to an environmental stressor. *Journal of Personality and Social Psychology, 12*, 200–210.

Glickman, S. E., Frank, L. G., Holekamp, K. E., & Licht, P. (1993). Costs and benefits of "androgenization" in the female spotted hyena. In P. Bateson & P. H. Klopfer (Eds.), *Behavior and evolution: Perspectives in ethology* (Vol. 10, pp. 87–117). New York: Plenum.

Godfrey, D. K., Jones, E. E., & Lord, C. G. (1986). Self-promotion is not ingratiating. *Journal of Personality and Social Psychology, 50*, 106–115.

Goethals, G. R., & Zanna, M. P. (1979). The role of social comparison in choice shifts. *Journal of Personality and Social Psychology, 37*, 1469–1476.

Goethals, G. R., Cooper, J., & Naficy, A. (1979). Role of foreseen, foreseeable, and unforeseeable behavioral consequences in the arousal of cognitive dissonance. *Journal of Personality and Social Psychology, 37*, 1179–1185.

Goffman, E. (1959). *The presentation of self in everyday life.* New York: Anchor Books.

Goffman, E. (1961). *Asylums: Essays on the social situation of mental patients and other inmates.* Chicago: Aldine.

Goffman, E. (1963). *Stigma: Notes on the management of spoiled identity.* Englewood Cliffs, NJ: Prentice-Hall.

Gold, R. S., Skinner, M. J., Grant, P. J., & Plummer, D.C. (1991). Situational factors and thought processes associated with unprotected intercourse in gay men. *Psychology and Health, 5,* 259–278.

Goldberg, J. A. (1990). Interrupting the discourse on interruptions: An analysis in terms of relationally neutral, power- and rapport-oriented acts. *Journal of Pragmatics, 14,* 883–903.

Goldstein, J. H. (1986). *Aggression and crimes of violence* (2nd ed.). New York: Oxford University Press.

Goldstein, R. L. (1987). More forensic romances: De Clerambault's Syndrome in men. *Bulletin of the American Academy of Psychiatry and Law, 15,* 267–272.

Gollwitzer, P. M. (1986). Striving for specific identities: The social reality of self-symbolizing. In R. F. Baumeister (Ed.), *Public self and private self* (pp. 143–160). New York: Springer-Verlag.

Gollwitzer, P. M., Heckhausen, H., & Steller, B. (1990). Deliberative versus implemental mindsets. *Journal of Personality and Social Psychology, 59,* 1119–1127.

Gonnerman, M. E., Jr., Parker, C. P., Lavine, H., & Huff, J. (2000). The relationship between self-discrepancies and affective states: The moderating roles of self-monitoring and standpoints on the self. *Personality and Social Psychology Bulletin, 26,* 810–819.

Gonzales, M. H., & Meyers, S. A. (1993). "Your mother would like me": Self-presentation in the personal ads of heterosexual and homosexual men and women. *Personality and Social Psychology Bulletin, 19,* 131–142.

Goodwin, J. S., Hunt, W. C., Key, C. R., & Samet, J. M. (1987). The effect of marital status on stage, treatment, and survival of cancer patients. *Journal of the American Medical Association, 258,* 3125–3130.

Gordon, R. A. (1996). Impact of ingratiation on judgments and evaluations: A meta-analystic investigation. *Journal of Personality and Social Psychology, 71,* 54–70.

Gorsuch, R. L. (1988). Psychology of religion. *Annual Review of Psychology, 39,* 201–221.

Gottlieb, B. H. (1994). Social support. In A. L. Weber & J. H. Harvey (Eds.), *Perspectives on close relationships* (pp. 307–324). Boston: Allyn & Bacon.

Gould, J. L., & Gould, C. L. (1989). *Sexual selection.* New York: Scientific American Library.

Gould, S. J. (1981). *The mismeasure of man.* New York: Norton.

Gouldner, A. W. (1960). The norm of reciprocity: A preliminary statement. *American Sociological Review, 25,* 161–178.

Gracian, B. (1649/1945). *The art of worldly wisdom.* New York: Charles Thomas.

Graybar, S. R., Antonuccio, D. O., Boutilier, L. R., & Varble, D. L. (1989). Psychological reactance as a factor affecting patient compliance to physician advice. *Scandinavian Journal of Behaviour Therapy, 18,* 43–51.

Graziano, W. G., & Eisenberg, N. (1997). Agreeableness: A dimension of personality. In R. Hogan, J. Johnson, & S. Briggs (Eds.), *Handbook of personality psychology* (pp. 795–824). San Diego, CA: Academic Press.

Graziano, W. G., Hair, E. C., & Finch, J. F. (1997). Competitiveness mediates the link between personality and group performance. *Journal of Personality and Social Psychology, 73,* 1394–1408.

Graziano, W. G., Jensen-Campbell, L. A., & Hair, E. C. (1996) Perceiving interpersonal conflict and reacting to it: The case for agreeableness. *Journal of Personality & Social Psychology, 70,* 820–835.

Graziano, W. G., Jensen-Campbell, L. A., Todd, M., & Finch, J. F. (1997). Interpersonal attraction from an evolutionary perspective: Reactions to dominant and prosocial men. In J. A. Simpson & D. T. Kenrick (Eds.), *Evolutionary social psychology* (pp. 141–168). Mahwah, NJ: LEA.

Green, B. L., & Kenrick, D. T. (1994). The attractiveness of gender-typed traits at different relationship levels: Androgynous characteristics may be desirable after all. *Personality and Social Psychology Bulletin, 20,* 244–253.

Green, J. D., & Campbell, W. K. (2000). Attachment and exploration in adults: Chronic and contextual accessibility. *Personality & Social Psychology Bulletin, 26,* 452–461.

Greenberg, J. (1985). Unattainable goal choice as a self-handicapping strategy. *Journal of Applied Social Psychology, 15,* 140–152.

Greenberg, J., & Baron, R. A. (1993). *Behavior in organizations* (4th ed.). Boston: Allyn & Bacon.

Greenberg, J., & Pyszczynski, T. (1985). The effect of an overheard ethnic slur on evaluations of the target: How to spread a social disease. *Journal of Personality and Social Psychology, 21,* 61–72.

Greenberg, J., Pyszczynski, T., & Solomon, S. (1982). The self-serving attributional bias: Beyond self-presentation. *Journal of Experimental Social Psychology, 18,* 56–67.

Greenberg, J., Pyszczynski, T., Solomon, S., Rosenblatt, A., Veeder, M., Kirkland, S., & Lyon, D. (1990). Evidence for Terror Management Theory II: The effects of mortality salience on reactions to those who threaten or bolster the cultural worldview. *Journal of Personality and Social Psychology, 58,* 308–318.

Greenberg, L. (1979). Genetic component of Bee odor in kin recognition. *Science, 206,* 195–197.

Greenberg, M. S., & Westcott, D. R. (1983). Indebtedness as a mediator of reactions to aid. In J. D. Fisher, A. Nadler, & B. M. DePaulo (Eds.), *New directions in helping behavior* (Vol. 1, pp. 113–141). San Diego: Academic Press.

Greenwald, A. G. (1968). Cognitive learning, cognitive response to persuasion, and attitude change. In A. G. Greenwald, T. C. Brock, & T. M. Ostrom (Eds.), *Psycholog-*

ical foundations of attitudes. New York: Academic Press.

Greenwald, A. G. (1980). The totalitarian ego: Fabrication and revision of personal history. *American Psychologist, 35,* 603–618.

Greenwald, A. G., & Banaji, M. R. (1995). Implicit social cognition: Attitudes, self-esteem, and stereotypes. *Psychological Review, 102,* 4–27.

Greenwald, A. G., & Breckler, S. J. (1985). To whom is the self presenting? In B. R. Schlenker (Ed.), *The self and social life* (pp. 126–145). New York: McGraw-Hill.

Greenwald, A. G., McGhee, D. E., & Schwartz, J. L. K. (1998). Measuring individual differences in implicit cognition: The implicit association test. *Journal of Personality and Social Psychology, 74,* 1464–1480.

Gregory, S. W., & Webster, S. (1996). A nonverbal signal in voices of interview partners effectively predicts communication accommodation and social status perceptions. *Journal of Personality and Social Psychology, 70,* 1231–1240.

Gregory, W. L., Burroughs, W. J., & Ainslie, F. M. (1985). Self-relevant scenarios as indirect means of attitude change. *Personality and Social Psychology Bulletin, 11,* 435–444.

Gregory, W. L., Cialdini, R. B., & Carpenter, K. M. (1982). Self-relevant scenarios as mediators of likelihood estimates and compliance: Does imagining make it so? *Journal of Personality and Social Psychology, 43,* 89–99.

Greider, W. (1994, June 16). Nixon's record. *Rolling Stone, p. 40.*

Greiling, H., & Buss, D. M. (2000). Women's sexual strategies: the hidden dimension of extra-pair mating. *Personality & Individual Differences. 28:* 929–963.

Griffitt, W. (1970). Environmental effects on interpersonal behavior: Ambient effective temperature and attraction. *Journal of Personality and Social Psychology, 15,* 240–244.

Griffitt, W., & Veitch, R. (1971). Hot and crowded: Influence of population density and temperature on interpersonal affective behavior. *Journal of Personality and Social Psychology, 17,* 92–98.

Grimes, W. (1997, October 15). In the war against no-shows, restaurants get together. *New York Times,* p. f11.

Gross, J. J., John, O. P., & Richards, J. M. (2000). The dissociation of emotion expression from emotion experience: A personality perspective. *Personality and Social Psychology Bulletin, 26,* 712–726.

Grube, J. A., & Piliavin, J. A. (2000). Role identity, organizational experiences, and volunteer performance. *Personality and Social Psychology Bulletin, 26,* 1108–1119.

Gruner, S. L. (1996, November). Reward good consumers. *Inc.,* p. 84.

Grusec, J. E. (1982). The socialization of altruism. In N. Eisenberg (Ed.), *The development of prosocial behavior* (pp. 139–166). New York: Academic Press.

Grusec, J. E. (1991). The socialization of empathy. In M. S. Clark (Ed.), *Review of personality and social psychology* (Vol. 12, pp. 9–33). Newbury Park, CA: Sage.

Grusec, J. E., & Redler, E. (1980). Attribution, reinforcement, and altruism: A developmental analysis. *Developmental Psychology, 16,* 525–534.

Grusec, J. E., Kuczynski, L., Rushton, J. P., & Simutis, Z. M. (1978). Modeling, direct instruction, and attributions: Effects on altruism. *Developmental Psychology, 14,* 51–57.

Guagnano, G. A., Dietz, T., & Stern, P. C. (1994). Willingness to pay for public goods: Test of a contribution model. *Psychological Science, 5,* 411–415.

Gudjonsson, G. (1992). *The psychology of interrogations, confessions, and testimony.* London: Wiley.

Gudjonsson, G. H. (1988). How to defeat the polygraph tests. In A. Gale (Ed.), *The polygraph test: Lies, truth and science* (pp. 126–136). London: Sage.

Guerin, B. (1993). *Social facilitation.* Paris: Cambridge University Press.

Guerin, B. (1994). What do people think about the risks of driving? *Journal of Applied Social Psychology, 24,* 994–1021.

Guimond, S. (2000). Group socialization and prejudice: The social transmission of intergroup attitudes and beliefs. *European Journal of Social Psychology, 30,* 335–354.

Gully, S. M., Devine, D. J., & Whitney, D. J. (1995). A meta-analysis of cohesion and performance: Effects of level of analysis and task interdependence. *Small Group Research, 26,* 497–520.

Gump, B. B., & Kulik, J. A. (1997). Stress, affiliation, and emotional contagion. *Journal of Personality and Social Psychology, 72,* 305–319.

Guroff, G., & Grant, S. (1981). *Soviet elites: World view and perceptions of the U.S.* (USICA Report No. R-18–81). Washington, DC: Office of Research, United States International Communication Agency.

Gurtman, M. B. (1992). Trust, distrust, and interpersonal problems: A circumplex analysis. *Journal of Personality and Social Psychology, 62,* 989–1002.

Gustafson, R. (1992). Alcohol and aggression: A replication study controlling for potential confounding variables. *Aggressive Behavior, 18,* 21–28.

Gutek, B. A. (1985). *Sex and the workplace.* San Francisco: Jossey-Bass.

Gutentag, M., & Secord, P. F. (1983). *Too many women? The sex ratio question.* Beverly Hills, CA: Sage.

Gutierres, S. E., Kenrick, D. T., & Partch, J. J. (1999). Beauty, dominance, and the mating game: Contrast effects in self-assessment reflect gender differences in mate selection. *Personality & Social Psychology Bulletin, 25,* 1126–1134.

Hackman, J. R. (1992). Group influences on individuals in organizations. In M. D. Dunette & L. M. Hough (Eds.), *Handbook of industrial and organizational psychology,* (2nd ed.) Vol. 3, pp. 212–242).

Palo Alto, CA: Consulting Psychologists Press.

Hackman, J. R., & Morris, C. G. (1975). Group tasks, group interaction process, and group performance effectiveness: A review and proposed integration. In L. Berkowitz (Ed.), *Advances in experimental social psychology* (Vol. 8, pp. 47–99). New York: Academic Press.

Hackman, J. R., & Oldham, G. R. (1980). *Work redesign.* Reading, MA: Addison-Wesley.

Haddock, G., Zanna, M. P., & Esses, V. M. (1993). Assessing the structure of prejudicial attitudes: The case of attitudes toward homosexuals. *Journal of Personality and Social Psychology, 65,* 1105–1118.

Haddock, G., Zanna, M. P., & Esses, V. M. (1994). The (limited) role of trait-laden stereotypes in predicting attitudes toward Native peoples. *British Journal of Social Psychology, 33,* 83–106.

Hakmiller, K. L. (1966). Threat as a determinant of downward comparison. *Journal of Experimental Social Psychology, 2* (Suppl. 1), 32–39.

Hall, J. A. (1984). *Nonverbal sex differences.* Baltimore, MD: Johns Hopkins University Press.

Hall, J. A., & Friedman, G. B. (1999). Status, gender, and nonverbal behavior: A study of structured interactions between employees of a company. *Personality and Social Psychology Bulletin, 25,* 1082–1091.

Hall, J. A., & Halberstadt, A. G. (1986). Smiling and gazing. In J. S. Hyde & M. C. Linn (Eds.), *The psychology of gender: Advances through meta-analysis* (pp. 136–158). Baltimore: Johns Hopkins University Press.

Hamblin, R. L. (1958). Leadership and crises. *Sociology, 21,* 322–335.

Hamermesh, D., & Biddle, J. E. (1994). Beauty and the labor market. *The American Economic Review, 84,* 1174–1194.

Hames, R. B. (1979). Relatedness and interaction among the Ye'kwana. In N. S. Chagnon & W. Irons (Eds.), *Evolutionary biology and human social behavior* (pp. 128–141). North Scituate, MA: Duxbury Press.

Hamilton, D. L. (1981). *Cognitive processes in stereotyping and intergroup behavior.* Hillsdale, NJ: Erlbaum.

Hamilton, V. L., Sanders, J., & McKearney, S. J. (1995). Orientations toward authority in an authoritarian state: Moscow in 1990. *Personality and Social Psychology Bulletin, 21,* 356–365.

Hamilton, W. D. (1964). The genetical evolution of social behavior. *Journal of Theoretical Biology, 7,* 1–52.

Hammock, W. R., & Yung, B. (1993). Psychology's role in the public health response to assaultive violence among young African-American men. *American Psychologist, 48,* 142–154.

Han, S-P., & Shavitt, S. (1994). Persuasion and culture: Advertising appeals in individualistic and collectivistic societies. *Journal of Experimental Social Psychology, 30,* 326–350.

Hansson, R. O., & Slade, K. M. (1977). Altruism toward a deviant in city and small town. *Journal of Applied Social Psychology, 7,* 272–279.

Harackiewicz, J. M., & Manderlink, G. (1984). A process analysis of the effects of performance-contingent rewards on intrinsic motivation. *Journal of Experimental Social Psychology, 20,* 531–551.

Harackiewicz, J. M., Barron, K. E., Carter, S. M., Lehto, A. T., & Elliot, A. J. (1997). Predictors and consequences of achievement goals in the college classroom: Maintaining interest and making the grade. *Journal of Personality and Social Psychology, 73,* 1284–1295.

Harackiewicz, J. M., Sansone, C., & Manderlink, G. (1985). Competence, achievement orientation, and intrinsic motivation: A process analysis. *Journal of Personality and Social Psychology, 48,* 493–508.

Harari, H., Mohr, D., & Hosey, K. (1980). Faculty helpfulness to students: A comparison of compliance techniques. *Personality and Social Psychology Bulletin, 6,* 373–377.

Hardin, G. (1968). The tragedy of the commons. *Science, 162,* 1243–48.

Hare, R. D. (1993). Psychopathy: Below the emotional poverty line. *Violent Crime and Its Victims: Proceedings of American Society of Criminology,* p. 86, 1993.

Hare, R. D., Harpur, T. J., Hakstein, A. R., Forth, A. E., Hart, S. D., & Newman, J. P. (1990). The revised psychopathy checklist: Descriptive statistics, reliability, and factor structure. *Psychological Assessment, 2,* 338.

Hare-Mustin, R. T., & Maracek, J. (1988). The meaning of difference: Gender theory, postmodernism, and psychology. *American Psychologist, 43,* 455–464.

Harkins, S. G., & Jackson, J. M. (1985). The role of evaluation in eliminating social loafing. *Personality and Social Psychology Bulletin, 11,* 457–465.

Harkins, S. G., & Petty, R. E. (1982). Effects of task difficulty and task uniqueness on social loafing. *Journal of Personality and Social Psychology, 43,* 1214–1229.

Harlow, H. F. (1971). *Learning to love.* San Francisco: Albion.

Harlow, R. E., & Cantor, N. (1994). Social pursuit of academics: Side effects and spillover of strategic reassurance seeking. *Journal of Personality and Social Psychology, 66,* 386–397.

Harmon-Jones, E., Brehm, J. W., Greenberg, J., Simon, L., & Nelson D. E. (1996). Evidence that production of aversive consequences is not necessary to create cognitive dissonance. *Journal of Personality and Social Psychology, 70,* 5–16.

Harpur, T. (1993). Cognitive and biological factors contributing to the abnormal perception of emotional material in psychopathic criminals. (Abstract). *Violent Crime and Its Victims: Proceedings of American Society of Criminology, 45,* 86–87.

Harris, M. B. (1992). Sex, race, and experiences of aggression. *Aggressive Behavior, 18,* 201–217.

Harris, M. D. (1977). The effects of altruism on mood. *Journal of Social Psychology, 102*, 197–208.

Harris, M. J., & Rosenthal, R. (1985). Mediation of interpersonal expectancy effects: 31 meta-analyses. *Psychological Bulletin, 97*, 363–386.

Harris, M. J., & Rosenthal, R. (1986). Counselor and client personality as determinants of counselor expectancy effects. *Journal of Personality and Social Psychology, 50*, 362–369.

Harris, R. N., & Snyder, C. R. (1986). The role of uncertain self-esteem in self-handicapping. *Journal of Personality and Social Psychology, 51*, 451–458.

Hart, E. A., Leary, M. R., & Rejeski, W. J. (1989). The measurement of social physique anxiety. *Journal of Sport and Exercise Psychology, 11*, 94–104.

Harter, S. (1993). Causes and consequences of low self-esteem in children and adolescents. In R. Baumeister (Ed.), *Self-esteem: The puzzle of low self-regard* (pp. 87–116). New York: Plenum.

Hartlage, S., Alloy, L. B., Vázquez, C., & Dykman, B. (1993). Automatic and effortful processing in depression. *Psychological Bulletin, 113*, 247–278.

Harvey, J. H., & Omarzu, J. (1997). Minding the close relationship. *Personality and Social Psychology Review, 1*, 224–240.

Harvey, M. D., & Enzle, M. E. (1981). A cognitive model of social norms for understanding the transgression-helping effect. *Journal of Personality and Social Psychology, 41*, 866–888.

Haselton, M. G., & Buss, D. M. (2000). Error management theory: A new perspective on biases in cross-sex mind reading. *Journal of Personality & Social Psychology, 78*, 81–91.

Haslam, N. (1997). Four grammars for primate social relations. In J. A. Simpson & D. T. Kenrick (Eds.), *Evolutionary social psychology* (pp. 297–316). Mahwah, NJ: Erlbaum.

Hass, R. G., & Grady, K. (1975). Temporal delay, type of forewarning, and resistance to influence. *Journal of Experimental Social Psychology, 11*, 459–469.

Hassan, S. (1990). *Combatting cult mind control.* Rochester, VT: Park Street Press.

Hassan, S. (1999). *Free them! Breaking the chains of destructive mind control.* Freedom of Mind Press.

Hassan, S. (2000). *Releasing the bonds: Empowering people to think for themselves.* Freedom of Mind Press.

Hastie, R. (1984). Causes and effects of causal attribution. *Journal of Personality and Social Psychology, 46*, 44–56.

Hastie, R., & Rasinski, K. A. (1988). The concept of accuracy in social judgment. In D. Bar-Tal & A. W. Kruglanski (Eds.), *The social psychology of knowledge* (pp. 193–208). Cambridge: Cambridge University Press.

Hastie, R., & Stasser, G. (2000). Computer simulation methods for social psychology. In H. T. Reis & C. M. Judd (Eds.), *Handbook of research methods in social and personality psychology* (pp. 85–114). New York: Cambridge University Press.

Hastie, R., Penrod, S. D., & Pennington, N. (1983). *Inside the jury.* Cambridge, MA: Harvard University Press.

Hatano, Y. (1991). Changes in the sexual activities of Japanese youth. *Journal of Sex Education and Therapy, 17*, 1–14.

Hatch, J. A. (1987). Impression management in kindergarten classrooms: An analysis of children's face-work in peer interactions. *Anthropology and Education Quarterly, 18*, 100–115.

Hatchett, L., Friend, R., Symister, P., & Wadhwa, N. (1997). Interpersonal expectations, social support, and adjustment to chronic illness. *Journal of Personality and Social Psychology, 73*, 560–573.

Hatfield, E., & Rapson, R. L. (1996). *Love and sex: Cross-cultural perspectives.* Boston: Allyn & Bacon.

Hatfield, E., Sprecher, S., Pillemer, J. T., Greenberger, D., & Wexler, P. (1989). Gender differences in what is desired in a sexual relationship. *Journal of Psychology and Human Sexuality, 1*, 39–52.

Hatfield, E., Traupmann, J., Sprecher, S., Utne, M., & Hay, J. (1985). Equity and intimate relationships: Recent research. In W. Ickes (Ed.), *Compatible and incompatible relationships* (pp. 1–27). New York: Springer-Verlag.

Haugtvedt, C. P., & Petty, R. E. (1992). Personality and persuasion: Need for cognition moderates the persistence and resistance of attitude changes. *Journal of Personality and Social Psychology, 63*, 308–319.

Hawken, P., Lovins, A., & Lovins, L. H. (1999). *Natural capitalism: Creating the next industrial revolution.* Boston: Little Brown.

Hazan, C., & Shaver, P. R. (1987). Romantic love conceptualized as an attachment process. *Journal of Personality and Social Psychology, 52*, 511–524.

Hazan, C., & Shaver, P. R. (1994a). Attachment as an organizational framework for research on close relationships. *Psychological Inquiry, 5*, 1–22.

Hazan, C., & Shaver, P. R. (1994b). Deeper into attachment theory. *Psychological Inquiry, 5*, 68–79.

Hearold, S. (1986). A synthesis of 1043 effects of television on social behavior. In G. Comstock (Ed.), *Public communications and behavior* (Vol. I, pp. 65–133). New York: Academic Press.

Heaven, P. C. L., & Furnham, A. (1987). Race prejudice and economic beliefs. *Journal of Social Psychology, 127*, 483–489.

Heckel, R. V. (1973). Leadership and voluntary seating choice. *Psychological Reports, 32*, 141–142.

Heckhausen, J., & Schultz, R. (1995). A life-span theory of control. *Psychological Review, 102*, 284–304.

Heider, F. (1944). Social perception and phenomenal causality. *Psychological Review, 51*, 358–374.

Heider, F. (1946). Attitudes and cognitive organization. *Journal of Psychology, 21*, 107–112.

Heider, F. (1958). *The psychology of interpersonal relations.* Hillsdale, NJ: Lawrence Erlbaum.

Heilman, M. E. (1995). Sex stereotypes and their effects in the workplace: What we know and what we don't know. *Journal of Social Behavior and Personality, 10*, 3–26.

Heilman, M. E., Block, C. J., & Martell, R. F. (1995). Sex stereotypes: Do they influence perceptions of managers? *Journal of Social Behavior and Personality, 10*, 237–252.

Heine, S. H., Lehman, D. R., Markus, H. R., & Kitayama, S. (1999). Is there a universal need for positive self-regard? *Psychological Review, 106*, 766–794.

Heine, S. H., Takata, T., & Lehman, D. R. (2000). Beyond self-presentation: Evidence for self-criticism among Japanese. *Personality and Social Psychology Bulletin, 26*, 71–78.

Heine, S. J., & Lehman, D. R. (1995). Cultural variation in unrealistic optimism: Does the West feel more invulnerable than the East? *Journal of Personality and Social Psychology, 68*, 595–607.

Heine, S. J., & Lehman, D. R. (1997). Culture, dissonance, and self-affirmation. *Personality and Social Psychology Bulletin, 23*, 389–400.

Hejmadi, A., Davidson, R. J., & Rozin, P. (2000). Exploring Hindu Indian emotion expressions: Evidence for accurate recognition by Americans and Indians. *Psychological Science, 11*, 183–187.

Helgeson, V. S. (1992). Moderators of the relation between perceived control and adjustment to chronic illness. *Journal of Personality and Social Psychology, 63*, 656–666.

Helgeson, V. S., Shaver, P., & Dyer, M. (1987). Prototypes of intimacy and distance in same-sex and opposite-sex relationships. *Journal of Social and Personal Relationships, 4*, 195–234.

Helgeson, V. S., & Taylor, S. E. (1993). Self-generated feelings of control and adjustment to physical illness. *Journal of Social Issues, 47*, 91–103.

Helmreich, R. L., & Collins, B. E. (1967). Situational determinants of affiliative preference under stress. *Journal of Personality and Social Psychology, 6*, 79–85.

Hemphill, J. K. (1950). Relations between the size of the group and the behavior of "superior" leaders. *Journal of Social Psychology, 32*, 11–22.

Hendrick, C., & Hendrick, S. S. (1986). A theory and method of love. *Journal of Personality and Social Psychology, 50*, 392–402.

Hendricks, M., & Brickman, P. (1974). Effects of status and knowledgeability of audience on self-presentation. *Sociometry, 37*, 440–449.

Hendry, J. (1993). *Wrapping culture: Politeness, presentation, and power in Japan and other societies.* Oxford: Clarendon Press.

Henley, N. M. (1973). Status and sex: Some touching observations. *Bulletin of the Psychonomic Society, 2*, 91–93.

Henley, N. M., & Harmon, S. (1985). The nonverbal semantics of power and gender: A perceptual study. In S. L. Ellyson & J. F. Dovidio (Eds.), *Power, dominance, and nonverbal behavior* (pp. 151–164). New York: Springer-Verlag.

Hepworth, J. T., & West, S. G. (1988). Lynching and the economy: A time-series reanalysis of Hovland and Sears (1940). *Journal of Personality and Social Psychology, 55*, 239–247.

Herek, G. M. (1986). The instrumentality of attitudes. Toward a neo-functional theory. *Journal of Social Issues, 42*, 99–114.

Herek, G. M. (2000). The psychology of sexual prejudice. *Current Directions in Psychological Science, 9*, 19–22.

Herek, G. M., & Capitanio, J. P. (1996). "Some of my best friends": Intergroup contact, concealable stigma, and heterosexuals' attitudes toward gay men and lesbians. *Personality and Social Psychology Bulletin, 22*, 412–424.

Herek, G. M., Janis, I. L., & Huth, P. (1987). Decision making during international crises: Is quality of process related to outcome? *Journal of Conflict Resolution, 31*, 203–226.

Hersey, P., & Blanchard, K. H. (1982). *Management of organizational behavior* (4th ed.). Englewood Cliffs, NJ: Prentice-Hall.

Hertwig, R., Gigerenzer, G., & Hoffrage, U. (1997). The reiteration effect in hindsight bias. *Psychological Review, 104*, 194–202.

Hewstone, M. (1989). *Causal attribution: From cognitive processes to cognitive beliefs.* Oxford: Basil Blackwell.

Higgins, E. T. (1987). Self-discrepancy: A theory relating self and affect. *Psychological Review, 94*, 319–340.

Higgins, E. T. (1996). Knowledge activation: Accessibility, applicability, and salience. In E. T. Higgins & A. W. Kruglanski (Eds.), *Social psychology: Handbook of basic principles* (pp. 133–168). New York: Guilford.

Higgins, E. T. (1997). Beyond pleasure and pain. *American Psychologist, 52*, 1280–1300.

Higgins, E. T., & Sorrentino, R. M. (1990). *Handbook of motivation and cognition: Foundations of social behavior* (Vol. 2). New York: Guilford.

Higgins, E. T., Lee, J., Kwon, J., & Trope, Y. (1995). When combining intrinsic motivations undermines interest. *Journal of Personality and Social Psychology, 68*, 749–767.

Higgins, E. T., Rholes, W. S., & Jones, C. R. (1977). Category accessibility and impression formation. *Journal of Experimental Social Psychology, 13*, 141–154.

Higgins, R. L., & Harris, R. N. (1988). Strategic "alcohol" use: Drinking to self-handicap. *Journal of Social and Clinical Psychology, 6*, 191–202.

Hill, K., & Hurtado, A. M. (1993). Hunter-gatherers in the New World.

In P. Sherman & J. Alcock (Eds.), *Exploring animal behavior* (pp. 154–160). Sunderland, MA: Sinauer.

Hill, K., & Hurtado, M. (1996). *Ache life history*. Hawthorne, NY: Aldine-deGruyter.

Hilton, J. L., & Darley, J. M. (1985). Constructing other persons: A limit on the effect. *Journal of Experimental Social Psychology, 21*, 1–18.

Hilton, J. L., & Darley, J. M. (1991). The effects of interaction goals on person perception. In M. P. Zanna (Ed.), *Advances in experimental social psychology* (Vol. 24, pp. 235–267). San Diego, CA: Academic Press.

Hingson, R., & Howland, J. (1993). Promoting safety in adolescents. In S. G. Millstein, A. C. Petersen, & E. O. Nightingdale (Eds.), *Promoting the health of adolescents* (pp. 305–327). New York: Oxford University Press.

Hirt, E. R., Deppe, R. K., & Gordon, L. J. (1991). Self-reported versus behavioral self-handicapping: Empirical evidence for a theoretical distinction. *Journal of Personality and Social Psychology, 61*, 981–991.

Hirt, E. R., Erickson, G. A., & McDonald, H. E. (1993). Role of expectancy timing and outcome consistency in expectancy-guided retrieval. *Journal of Personality and Social Psychology, 65*, 640–656.

Hirt, E. R., McCrea, S. M., & Kimble, C. E. (2000). Public self-focus and sex differences in behavioral self-handicapping: Does increasing self-threat still make it "just a man's game"? *Personality and Social Psychology Bulletin, 26*, 1131–1141.

Hirt, E. R., & Markman, K. D. (1995). Multiple explanation: A consider-an-alternative strategy for debiasing judgments. *Journal of Personality and Social Psychology, 69*, 1069–1086.

Hirt, E. R., McDonald, H. E., & Erickson, G. A. (1995). How do I remember thee? The role of encoding set and delay in reconstructive memory processes. *Journal of Experimental Social Psychology, 31*, 379–409.

Hirt, E. R., Zillman, D., Erickson, G. A., & Kennedy, C. (1992). Costs and benefits of allegiance: Changes in fans' self-ascribed competencies after team victory versus defeat. *Journal of Personality and Social Psychology, 63*, 724–738.

Hochberg, A. (1996, April 19). 1971 school desegregation made friends out of enemies. *All Things Considered*, National Public Radio.

Hochschild, A. (1997, April 14). Mr. Kurtz, I presume? *New Yorker*, pp. 40–47.

Hodgkinson, V. A., & Weitzman, M. S. (1990). *Giving and volunteering in the United States*. Washington DC: Independent Sector.

Hodgkinson, V. A., & Weitzman, M. S. (1994). *Giving and volunteering in the United States*. Washington DC: Independent Sector.

Hoffman, C., & Hurst, N. (1990). Gender stereotypes: Perception or rationalization? *Journal of Personality and Social Psychology, 58*, 197–208.

Hoffman, L. R. (1959). Homogeneity of member personality and its effect on group problem solving. *Journal of Abnormal and Social Psychology, 58*, 27–32.

Hoffman, M. L. (1984). Interaction of affect and cognition in empathy. In C. E. Izard, J. Kagan, & R. B. Zajonc (Eds.), *Emotions, cognitions, and behavior* (pp. 103–131). Cambridge: Cambridge University Press.

Hofling, C. K., Brotzman, E., Dalrymple, S., Graves, N., & Pierce, C. M. (1966). An experimental study in nurse-physician relationships. *Journal of Nervous and Mental Disease, 143*, 171–180.

Hofstede, G. (1980). *Culture's consequences: International differences in work-related values*. Beverly Hills, CA: Sage.

Hofstede, G. (1983). Dimensions of national cultures in fifty countries and three regions. In J. Deregowski, S. Dzuirawiec, & R. Annis (Eds.), *Expiscations in cross-cultural psychology* (pp. 335–355). Lisse: Swets and Zeitlinger.

Hogan, R. (1993). A socioanalytic theory of personality. In M. Page (Ed.), *Nebraska symposium on motivation: Personality—Current theory and research* (pp. 58–89). Lincoln: University of Nebraska Press.

Hogan, R., Curphy, G. J., & Hogan, J. (1994). What we know about leadership: Effectiveness and personality. *American Psychologist, 49*, 493–504.

Hogan, R., & Hogan, J. (1991). Personality and status. In D. Gilbert & J. J. Connolly (Eds.), *Personality, social skills, and psychopathology: An individual differences approach* (pp. 137–154). New York: Plenum Press.

Hogan, R., Jones, W. H., & Cheek, J. M. (1985). Socioanalytic theory: An alternative to armadillo psychology. In B. R. Schlenker (Ed.), *The self and social life* (pp. 175–198). New York: McGraw-Hill.

Hogan, R., Raza, S., Sampson, D., Miller, C., & Salas, E. (1989). *The impact of personality on team performance* (Report to the Office of Naval Research.) Tulsa, OK: University of Tulsa.

Holland, J. L. (1985). *Making vocational choices: A theory of vocational personalities and work environments* (2nd ed.). Englewood Cliffs, NJ: Prentice-Hall.

Holland, J. L. (1997). *Making vocational choices: A theory of vocation personalities and work environments* (3rd ed.). Lutz, FL: Psychological Assessment Resources.

Hollander, E. P. (1993). Legitimacy, power, and influence: A perspective on relational features of leadership. In M. M. Chemers & R. Ayman (Eds.), *Leadership theory and research: Perspectives and directions* (pp. 29–47). San Diego, CA: Academic Press.

Hollingshead, A. B. (2000). Perceptions of expertise and transactive memory in work relationships. *Group Processes and Intergroup Relations, 3*, 257–267.

Holtgraves, T., & Dulin, J. (1994). The Muhammad Ali effect: Differences between African Americans and European Americans in their perceptions of a truthful bragger. *Language and Communication, 14,* 275–285.

Holtgraves, T., & Srull, T. K. (1989). The effects of positive self-descriptions on impressions: General principles and individual differences. *Personality and Social Psychology Bulletin, 15,* 452–462.

Holtgraves, T., & Yang, J-N (1990). Politeness as universal: Cross-cultural perceptions of request strategies and inferences based on their use. *Journal of Personality and Social Psychology, 59,* 719–729.

Homer-Dixon, T. F., Boutwell, J. H., & Rathjens, G. W. (1993, February). Environmental change and violent conflict. *Scientific American,* 38–45.

Hong, Nansook (1998). *In the shadow of the moons: My life in the Reverend Sun Myung Moon's Family.* Boston: Little Brown.

Hong, Y. Y., Chiu, C. Y., & Kung, T. M. (1997). Bringing culture out in front: Effects of cultural meaning system activation on social cognition. In K. Leung, Y. kashima, U. Kim, & S. Yamaguchi (Eds.), *Progress in Asian social psychology* (Vol. 1, pp. 135–146). Singapore: Wiley.

Hong, Y. Y., Morris, M. W., Chiu, C. Y., & Benet-Martinez, V. (2000). Multicultural minds: A dynamic constructivist approach to culture and cognition. *American Psychologist, 55,* 709–720.

Honts, C. R. (1994). Psychophysiological detection of deception. *Current Directions in Psychological Science, 3,* 77–82.

Honts, C. R., Raskin, D.C., & Kircher, D.C. (1994). Mental and physical countermeasures reduce the accuracy of polygraph tests. *Journal of Applied Psychology, 79,* 252–259.

Hoorens, V., & Nuttin, J. M. (1993). Overvaluation of own attributes: Mere ownership or subjective frequency? *Social Cognition, 11,* 177–200.

Hoover, C. W., Wood, E. E., & Knowles, E. S. (1983). Forms of social awareness and helping. *Journal of Experimental Social Psychology, 19,* 577–590.

Hopf, C. (1993). Authoritarians and their families: Qualitative studies on the origins of authoritarian personalities. In W. F. Stone, G. Lederer, & R. Christie (Eds.), *Strengths and weaknesses: The authoritarian personality today* (pp. 119–143). New York: Springer-Verlag.

Hopper, J. R., & Nielsen, J. M. (1991). Recycling as altruistic behavior: Normative and behavioral strategies to expand participation in a community recycling program. *Environment and Behavior, 23,* 195–220.

Hornstein, H. A. (1982). Promotive tension: Theory and research. In V. J. Derlage & J. Grzelak (Eds.) *Cooperation and helping behavior: Theories and research* (pp. 229–248). New York: Academic Press.

Hornstein, H. A., Fisch, E., & Holmes, M. (1968). Influence of a model's feelings about his behavior and his relevance as a comparison other on observers' helping behavior. *Journal of Personality and Social Psychology, 10,* 222–226.

Höss, R. (1960). *Commandant of Auschwitz: The autobiography of Rudolf Höss.* Cleveland, OH: World Publishing Company.

House, R. J., & Shamir, B. (1993). Toward the integration of transformational, charismatic, and visionary theories. In M. M. Chemers & R. Ayman (Eds.), *Leadership theory and research: Perspectives and directions* (pp. 81–108). San Diego, CA: Academic Press.

Hovland, C. I., & Sears, R. (1940). Minor studies in aggression: VI. Correlation of lynchings with economic indices. *Journal of Psychology, 9,* 301–310.

Hovland, C. I., Janis, I. L., & Kelley, H. H. (1953). *Communication and persuasion: Psychological studies of opinion change.* New Haven, CT: Yale University Press.

Hovland, C. I., Lumsdaine, A. A., & Sheffield, F. D. (1949). *Experiments on mass communication.* Princeton, NJ: Princeton University Press.

Howard, D. J. (1990). The influence of verbal responses to common greetings on compliance behavior: The foot-in-the-mouth effect. *Journal of Applied Social Psychology, 20,* 1185–1196.

Howard, D. J. (1995). "Chaining" the use of influence strategies for producing compliance behavior. *Journal of Social Behavior and Personality, 10,* 169–185.

Howard, G. S. (2000). Adapting human lifestyles for the 21st century. *American Psychologist,* 55, 509–515.

Howenstine, E. (1993). Market segmentation for recycling. *Environment and Behavior, 25,* 86–102.

Hsu, F. L. K. (1983). *Rugged individualism reconsidered.* Knoxville: University of Tennessee Press.

Hughes, R. (1987). *The fatal shore.* New York: Knopf.

Hull, C. L. (1934). *Hypnosis and suggestibility.* New York: D. Appleton-Century.

Hull, J., & Bond, C. (1986). Social and behavioral consequences of alcohol consumption and expectancy: A meta-analysis. *Psychological Bulletin, 99,* 347–360.

Hunt, M. (1974). *Sexual behavior in the 1970s.* Chicago: Playboy Press.

Hunt, M. (1990). *The compassionate beast.* New York: William Morrow.

Hunter, J. A., Platow, M. J., Howard, M. L., & Stringer, M. (1996). Social identity and intergroup evaluation bias: Realistic categories and domain specific self-esteem in a conflict setting. *European Journal of Social Psychology, 26,* 631–647.

Huston, T., Ruggiero, M., Conner, R., & Geis, G. (1981). Bystander intervention into crime: A study based on naturally occurring episodes. *Social Psychology Quarterly, 44,* 14–23.

Hyde, J. S. (1990). Meta-analysis and the psychology of gender differences. *Signs, 16,* 55–73.

Hyde, J. S. (1996). Where are the gender differences? Where are the gender similarities? In D. M. Buss & N. M. Malamuth (Eds.), *Sex, power, conflict: Evolutionary and feminist perspectives* (pp. 107–118). New York: Oxford University Press.

Hyde, J. S., & Linn, M. C. (1988). Gender differences in verbal ability: A meta-analysis. *Psychological Bulletin, 104*, 53–69.

Ickes, W. (1993). Traditional gender roles: Do they make, and then break, our relationships. *Journal of Social Issues, 49*, 71–85.

Ickes, W., Patterson, M. L., Rajecki, D. W., & Tanford, S. (1982). Behavioral and cognitive consequences of reciprocal versus compensatory responses to pre-interaction expectancies. *Social Cognition, 1*, 160–190.

Ilgen, D. R., & Hulin, C. L. (2000). *Computational modeling of behavior in organizations: The third scientific discipline.* Washington, DC: American Psychological Association.

Ingham, A. G., Levinger, G., Graves, J., & Peckham, V. (1974). The Ringelmann effect: Studies of group size and group performance. *Journal of Personality and Social Psychology, 10*, 371–384.

Insko, C. A. (1965). Verbal reinforcement of attitude. *Journal of Personality and Social Psychology, 2*, 621–623.

Insko, C. A. (1984). Balance theory, the Jordan paradigm, and the West tetrahedron. In L. Berkowitz (Ed.), *Advances in experimental social psychology* (Vol. 18, pp. 89–140). San Diego, CA: Academic Press.

Insko, C. A., Drenan, S., Solomon, M. R., Smith, R., & Wade, T. J. (1983). Conformity as a function of the consistency of positive self-evaluation with being liked and being right. *Journal of Experimental Social Psychology, 19*, 341–358.

Insko, C. A., Schopler, J., Graetz, K. A., Drigotas, S. M., Currey, D. P., Smith, S. L., Brazil, D., & Bornstein, G. (1994). Individual-intergroup discontinuity in the Prisoner's Dilemma Game. *Journal of Conflict Resolution, 38*, 87–116.

Insko, C. A., Schopler, J., Gratez, K. A., Drigotas, S. M., Currey, K. P., Smith, S. L., Brazil, D., & Bornstein, G. (1994). Interindividual-intergroup discontinuity in the Prisoner's Dilemma Game. *Journal of Conflict Resolution, 38*, 87–116.

Insko, C. A., Schopler, J., Hoyle, R. H., Dardis, G. J., & Graetz, K. A. (1990). Individual-group discontinuity as a function of fear and greed. *Journal of Personality and Social Psychology, 58*, 68–79.

Insko, C. A., Schopler, J., Pemberton, M. B., Wieselquist, J., McIlraith, S. A., Currey, D. P., & Gaertner, L., (1998). Long-term outcome maximization and the reduction of interindividual-intergroup discontinuity. *Journal of Personality & Social Psychology, 75*, 695–711.

Insko, C. A., Smith, R. H., Alicke, M. D., Wade, J., & Taylor, S. (1985). Conformity and group size: The concern with being right and the concern with being liked. *Personality and Social Psychology Bulletin, 11*, 41–50.

Isen, A. M. (1987). Positive affect, cognitive processes, and social behavior. In L. Berkowitz (Ed.), *Advances in experimental social psychology* (Vol. 20, pp. 203–253). New York: Academic Press.

Isen, A. M., & Levin, P. F. (1972). Effects of feeling good on helping: Cookies and kindness. *Journal of Personality and Social Psychology, 21*, 384–388.

Isen, A. M., Shalker, T. E., Clark, M., & Karp, L. (1978). Affect, accessibility of material in memory, and behavior. *Journal of Personality and Social Psychology, 36*, 1–12.

Isenberg, D. J. (1986). Group polarization: A critical review and meta-analysis. *Journal of Personality and Social Psychology, 50*, 1141–1151.

Izard, C. E. (1971). *The face of emotion.* New York: Appleton-Century-Crofts.

Izard, C. E. (1990). Facial expressions and the regulation of emotions. *Journal of Personality and Social Psychology, 58*, 487–498.

Jackson, L. M., & Esses, V. M. (1997). Of scripture and ascription: The relation between religious fundamentalism and intergroup helping. *Personality and Social Psychology Bulletin, 23*, 893–906.

Jackson, S. E. (1992). Team composition in organizational settings: Issues in managing an increasingly diverse work force. In S. Worchel, W. Wood, & J. A. Simpson (Eds.), *Group process and productivity* (pp. 138–173). Newbury Park, CA: Sage.

Jacobs, J. R. (1992). Facilitators of romantic attraction and their relation to lovestyle. *Social Behavior and Personality, 20*, 227–234.

Jacobs, R. C., & Campbell, D. T. (1961). The perpetuation of an arbitrary tradition through several generations of a laboratory microculture. *Journal of Abnormal and Social Psychology, 62*, 649–658.

Jain, S. P., Buchanan, B., & Maheswaren, D. (2000). Comparative versus noncomparative advertising. *Journal of Consumer Psychology, 9*, 201–211.

James, W. (1890). *Principles of psychology.* New York: Henry Holt.

James, W. (1907). *Pragmatism.* New York: Longmans, Green.

Janes, L. M., & Olson, J. M. (2000). Jeer pressure: The behavioral effects of observing ridicule of others. *Personality and Social Psychology Bulletin, 26*, 474–485.

Janicki, M., & Krebs, D. L. (1998). Evolutionary approaches to culture. In C. Crawford & D. L. Krebs (Eds.), *Handbook of evolutionary psychology: Ideas, issues, and applications* (pp. 163–208). Mahwah, NJ: Erlbaum.

Janis, I. L. (1972). *Victims of groupthink.* Boston: Houghton-Mifflin.

Janis, I. L. (1983). *Groupthink: Psychological studies of policy decisions and fiascoes* (2nd ed.). Boston: Houghton Mifflin.

Janis, I. L. (1997). Groupthink. In W. A. Lesko (Ed.), *Readings in social psychology* (3rd edition) (pp. 333–337). Boston: Allyn & Bacon.

Janis, I. L., & Mann, L. (1977). *Decision making: A psychological analysis of conflict, choice, and commitment.* New York: Free Press.

Jankowiak, W. R. (1988). Sex differences in mate selection and sexuality in the People's Republic of China. *Australian Journal of Chinese Affairs, 20,* 63–83.

Jankowiak, W. R., & Fischer, E. F. (1992). A cross-cultural perspective on romantic love. *Ethnology, 31,* 149–155.

Janoff-Bulman, R., & Wade, M. B. (1996). The dilemma of self-advocacy for women: Another case of blaming the victim? *Journal of Social and Clinical Psychology, 15,* 143–152.

Jemmott, J. B., III, Ditto, P. H., & Croyle, R. T. (1986). Judging health status: Effects of perceived prevalence and personal relevance. *Journal of Personality and Social Psychology, 50,* 899–905.

Jensen-Campbell, L. A., & Graziano, W. G. (2000). Beyond the schoolyard: Relationships as moderators of daily interpersonal conflict. *Personality & Social Psychology Bulletin, 26,* 923–935.

Jensen-Campbell, L. A., Graziano, W. G., & West, S. G. (1995). Dominance, prosocial orientation, and female preferences: Do nice guys really finish last? *Journal of Personality and Social Psychology, 68,* 427–440.

Ji, L. J., Schwarz, N., & Nisbett, R. E. (2000). Culture, autobiographical memory, and behavioral frequency report: Measurement issues in cross-cultural studies. *Personality & Social Psychology Bulletin, 26,* 585–593.

Jo, E., & Berkowitz, L. (1994). A priming effect analysis of media influences: An update. In J. Bryant & D. Zillmann (Eds.), *Media effects: Advances in theory and research* (pp. 43–60). Hillsdale, NJ: LEA.

Jockin, V., McGue, M., & Lykken, D. T. (1996). Personality and divorce: A genetic analysis. *Journal of Personality and Social Psychology, 71,* 288–299.

John, O. P., & Robins, R. W. (1994). Accuracy and bias in self-perception: Individual differences in self-enhancement and the role of narcissism. *Journal of Personality and Social Psychology, 66,* 206–219.

Johnson F. L., & Aries, E. J. (1983). Conversational patterns among same-sex pairs of late adolescent close friends. *Journal of Genetic Psychology, 142,* 225–238.

Johnson, B. T., & Eagly, A. H. (1989). The effect of involvement on persuasion: A meta-analysis. *Psychological Bulletin, 106,* 290–314.

Johnson, D. (1993). The politics of violence research. *Psychological Science, 4,* 131–133.

Johnson, D. J., & Rusbult, C. E. (1989). Resisting temptation: Devaluation of alternative partners as a means of maintaining commitment in close relationships. *Journal of Personality and Social Psychology, 57,* 967–980.

Johnson, D. W., & Johnson, R. (1975). *Learning together and alone: Cooperation, competition, and individualization.* Englewood Cliffs, NJ: Prentice-Hall.

Johnson, D. W., & Johnson, R. T. (1994). Cooperative learning in the culturally diverse classroom. In R. DeVillar, C. Fultis, & J. Cummings (Eds.), *Cultural diversity in schools* (p. 57–74). New York: SUNY Press.

Johnson, D. W., Johnson, R., & Maruyama, G. (1984). Goal interdependence and interpersonal attraction in heterogeneous classrooms: A meta-analysis. In N. Miller & M. B. Brewer (Eds.), *Groups in contact* (pp. 187–213). New York: Academic Press.

Johnson, R. W., Kelly, R. J., & LeBlanc, B. A. (1995). Motivational basis of dissonance: Aversive consequences or inconsistency. *Personality and Social Psychology Bulletin, 21,* 850–855.

Joiner, T. E., & Metalsky, G. I. (1996). A prospective test of an integrative interpersonal theory of depression: A naturalistic study of college roommates. *Journal of Personality and Social Psychology, 69,* 778–788.

Joiner, T. E., Alfano, M. S., & Metalsky, G. I. (1992). When depression breeds contempt: Reassurance seeking, self-esteem, and rejection of depressed college students by their roommates. *Journal of Abnormal Psychology, 101,* 165–173.

Joiner, T. E., Jr. (1994). Contagious depression: Existence, specificity to depressed symptoms, and the role of reassurance seeking. *Journal of Personality and Social Psychology, 67,* 287–296.

Jones, E. E. (1979). The rocky road from acts to dispositions. *American Psychologist, 34,* 107–117.

Jones, E. E. (1990). *Interpersonal perception.* New York: Freeman.

Jones, E. E., & Baumeister, R. F. (1976). The self-monitor looks at the ingratiator. *Journal of Personality, 44,* 654–674.

Jones, E. E., & Davis, K. E. (1965). From acts to dispositions: The attribution process in person perception. In L. Berkowitz (Ed.), *Advances in experimental social psychology* (Vol. 2, pp. 220–266). New York: Academic Press.

Jones, E. E., Gergen, K. J., & Jones, R. G. (1963). Tactics of ingratiation among leaders and subordinates in a status hierarchy. *Psychological Monographs,* 77 (3, Whole No. 566): 20.

Jones, E. E., & Harris, V. A. (1967). The attribution of attitudes. *Journal of Experimental Social Psychology, 3,* 1–24.

Jones, E. E., Jones, R. G., & Gergen, K. J. (1963). Some conditions affecting the evaluation of a conformist. *Journal of Personality, 31,* 270–288.

Jones, E. E., & McGillis, D. (1976). Correspondent inferences and the attribution cube: A comparative reappraisal. In J. H. Harvey, W. J. Ickes, & R. F. Kidd (Eds.), *New directions in attribution research* (Vol. 1, pp. 389–420). Hillsdale, NJ: Erlbaum.

Jones, E. E., & Nisbett, R. E. (1972). The actor and the observer: Divergent perceptions of the causes of behavior. In E. E. Jones, D. E. Kanouse, H. H. Kelley, R. E. Nisbett, S. Valins, & B. Weiner (Eds.), *Attribution: Perceiving the causes of behavior* (pp. 79–94). Morristown, NJ: General Learning Press.

Jones, E. E., & Pittman, T. S. (1982). Toward a general theory of strategic self-presentation. In J. Suls (Ed.), *Psychological perspectives on the self* (Vol. 1, pp. 231–262). Hillsdale, NJ: Erlbaum.

Jones, E. E., Rhodewalt, F., Berglas, S., & Skelton, J. A. (1981). Effects of strategic self-presentation on subsequent self-esteem. *Journal of Personality and Social Psychology, 41*, 407–421.

Jones, E. E., & Sigall, H. (1971). The bogus pipeline: A new paradigm for measuring affect and attitude. *Psychological Bulletin, 76*, 349–364.

Jones, E. E., & Thibaut, J. W. (1958). Interaction goals as bases of inference in interpersonal perception. In R. Tagiuri & L. Patrullo (Eds.), *Person perception and interpersonal behavior.* (pp. 151–178). Palo Alto, Stanford University.

Jones, E. E., & Wortman, C. (1973). *Ingratiation: An attributional approach.* Morristown, NJ: General Learning Corporation.

Jones, S. C., & Regan, D. T. (1974). Ability evaluation through social comparison. *Journal of Experimental Social Psychology, 10*, 142–157.

Jones, W. H., & Carver, M. D. (1991). Adjustment and coping implications of loneliness. In C. R. Snyder & D. R. Forsyth (Eds.), *Handbook of social and clinical psychology* (pp. 395–410). New York: Pergamon.

Jones, W. H., Cavert, C. W., Snider, R. L., & Bruce, T. (1985). Relational stress: An analysis of situations and events associated with loneliness. In S. Duck & D. Perlman (Eds.), *Understanding personal relationships: An interdisciplinary approach* (pp. 221–242). Beverly Hills, CA: Sage.

Jones, W. H., Freemon, J. E., & Goswick, R. A. (1981). The persistence of loneliness: Self and other determinants. *Journal of Personality, 49*, 27–48.

Jones, W. H., Hobbs, S. A., & Hockenbury, D. (1982). Loneliness and social skill deficits. *Journal of Personality and Social Psychology, 42*, 682–689.

Jones, W. H., Sansone, C., & Helm, B. (1983). Loneliness and interpersonal judgments. *Personality and Social Psychology Bulletin, 9*, 437–441.

Jorden, D. L. (1993). Newspaper effects on policy preferences. *Public Opinion Quarterly, 57*, 191–204.

Josephs, R. A., Markus, H. R., & Tarafodi, R. W. (1992). Gender and self-esteem. *Journal of Personality and Social Psychology, 63*, 391–402.

Jost, J. T., & Banaji, M. R. (1994). The role of stereotyping in system-justification and the production of false consciousness. *British Journal of Social Psychology, 33*, 1–27.

Jost, J. T., & Burgess, D. (2000). Attitudinal ambivalence and the conflict between group and system justification motives in low status groups. *Personality and Social Psychology Bulletin, 26*, 293–305.

Joule, R. V. (1987). Tobacco deprivation: The foot-in-the-door technique versus the low-ball technique. *European Journal of Social Psychology, 17*, 361–365.

Joule, R. V., Gouilloux, F., & Weber, F. (1989). The lure: A new compliance procedure. *Journal of Social Psychology, 129*, 741–749.

Jourard, S. M., & Rubin, J. E. (1968). Self-disclosure and touching: A study of two modes of interpersonal encounter and their inter-relations. *Journal of Humanistic Psychology, 8*, 39–48.

Judd, C. M., & Krosnick, J. A. (1989). The structural bases of consistency among political attitudes. In A. R. Pratkanis, S. J. Breckler, & A. G. Greenwald (Eds.), *Attitude structure and function* (pp. 99–128). Hillsdale, NJ: Erlbaum.

Judge, T. A., & Bretz, R. D., Jr. (1994). Political influence behavior and career success. *Journal of Management, 20*, 43–65.

Jussim, L. (1991). Social perception and social reality: A reflection-construction model. *Psychological Review, 98*, 54–73.

Jussim, L., Eccles, J., & Madon, S. (1995). Social perception, social stereotypes, and teacher expectations: Accuracy and the quest for the powerful self-fulfilling prophecy. In M. P. Zanna (Ed.), *Advances in Experimental Social Psychology* (Vol. 27, pp. 215–255). New York: Academic Press.

Jussim, L., Nelson, T. E., Manis, M., & Soffin, S. (1995). Prejudice, stereotypes, and labeling effects: Sources of bias in person perception. *Journal of Personality and Social Psychology, 68*, 228–246.

Kacmar, K. M., Delery, J. E., & Ferris, G. R. (1992). Differential effectiveness of applicant impression management tactics on employment interview decisions. *Journal of Applied Social Psychology, 22*, 1250–1272.

Kadlec, D. (1997, May 5). The new world of giving. *Time, 149*, pp. 62–64.

Kahan, D. M. (1997). Social influence, social meaning, and deterrence. *Virginia Law Review, 83*, 349–395.

Kahneman, D., & Tversky, A. (1972). Subjective probability: A judgment of representativeness. *Cognitive Psychology, 3*, 430–454.

Kahneman, D., Knetsch, J. L., & Thaler, R. H. (1991). The endowment effect, loss aversion, and status quo bias. *Journal of Economic Perspectives, 5*, 193–206.

Kahneman, D., Knetsch, J., & Thaler, R. (1986). Fairness and the assumptions of economics. *Journal of Business, 59*, S285–S300.

Kallgren, C. A., Reno, R. R., & Cialdini, R. B. (2000). A focus theory of normative conduct: When norms do and do not affect behavior. *Personality & Social Psychology Bulletin, 26*, 1002–1012.

Kalven, H., Jr., & Zeisel, H. (1966). *The American jury.* Boston: Little, Brown.

Kanazawa, S. (1992). Outcome or expectancy? Antecedent of spontaneous causal attribution. *Personality and Social Psychology Bulletin, 18*, 659–668.

Kaniasty, K., & Norris, F. N. (1995). Mobilization and deterioration of social support following natural disasters. *Contempory Directions in Psychological Science, 4*, 94–98.

Kanter, R. M. (1977). *Men and women of the corporation.* New York: Basic Books.

Kantola, S. J., Syme, G. J., & Campbell, N. A. (1984). Cognitive dissonance and energy conservation. *Journal of Applied Psychology, 69*, 416–421.

Kaprio, J., Koskenvuo, M., & Rita, H. (1987). Mortality after bereavement: A prospective study of 95,647 widowed persons. *American Journal of Public Health*, 77, 283–87.

Karau, S. J., & Williams, K. D. (1993). Social loafing: A meta-analytic review and theoretical integration. *Journal of Personality and Social Psychology, 65*, 681–706.

Karp, D. R., & Gaulding, C. L. (1995). Motivational underpinning of command-and-control, market-based, and voluntarist environmental policies. *Human Relations, 48*, 439–465.

Kashima, Y., & Triandis, H. C. (1986). The self-serving bias in attributions as a coping strategy: A cross-cultural study. *Journal of Cross-Cultural Psychology, 17*, 83–97.

Kashy, D. A., & DePaulo, B. M. (1996). Who lies? *Journal of Personality and Social Psychology, 70*, 1037–1051.

Kassin, S. M., & Kiechel, K. L. (1996). The social psychology of false confessions: Compliance, internalization, and confabulation. *Psychological Science*, 7, 125–128.

Katz, D. (1960). The functional approach to the study of attitudes. *Public Opinion Quarterly, 24*, 163–204.

Katz, I., Wackenhut, J., & Hass, R. G. (1986). Racial ambivalence, value duality, and behavior. In J. F. Dovidio & S. L. Gaertner (Eds.), *Prejudice, discrimination, and racism* (pp. 35–59). Orlando, FL: Academic Press.

Keating, C. F., Mazur, A., & Segall, M. H. (1977). Facial gestures which influence the perception of status. *Sociometry, 40*, 374–378.

Keinan, G. (1987). Decision making under stress: Scanning of alternatives under controllable and uncontrollable threats. *Journal of Personality and Social Psychology, 52*, 639–644.

Kellerman, J., Lewis, J., & Laird, J. D. (1989). Looking and loving: The effects of mutual gaze on feelings of romantic love. *Journal of Research in Personality, 23*, 145–161.

Kellermann, A. L., Rivara, F. P., Rushforth, N. B., Banton, J. B., Reay, O. T., Francisco, J. T., Locci, A. B., Prodzinski, J. P., Hackman, B. B., & Somes, G. (1993). Gun ownership as a risk factor for homicide in the home. *New England Journal of Medicine, 329*, 1084–1091.

Kelley, H. H. (1950). The warm-cold variable in first impressions of persons. *Journal of Personality, 18*, 431–439.

Kelley, H. H. (1967). Attribution theory in social psychology. In D. Levine (Ed.), *Nebraska symposium on motivation* (Vol. 15, pp. 192–240). Lincoln: University of Nebraska Press.

Kelley, H. H. (1973). The processes of causal attribution. *American Psychologist, 28*, 107–128.

Kelley, H. H., & Stahelski, A. J. (1970). Social interaction basis of cooperators' and competitors' beliefs about others. *Journal of Personality and Social Psychology, 16*, 66–91.

Kelley, H. H., Cunningham, J. D., Grisham, J. A., LeFebre, L. M., Sink, C. R., & Yablon, G. (1978). Sex differences in comments made during conflict within heterosexual pairs. *Sex Roles, 4*, 473–492.

Kelly, A. E. (1998). Clients' secret keeping in outpatient therapy. *Journal of Counseling Psychology, 45*, 50–57.

Kelly, A. E., & McKillop, K. J. (1996). Consequences of revealing personal secrets. *Psychological Bulletin, 120*, 450–465.

Kelly, E. L., & Conley, J. J. (1987). Personality and compatibility: A prospective analysis of marital stability and marital satisfaction. *Journal of Personality and Social Psychology, 52*, 27–40.

Kelman, H. C. (1997). Group processes in the resolution of international conflicts. *American Psychologist, 52*, 212–220.

Kelman, H. C. (1998). Social-psychological contributions to peacemaking and peacebuilding in the Middle East. *Applied Psychology: An international review, 47*, 5–28.

Kelman, H. C. (1999). Interactive problem solving as a metaphor for international conflict resolution: Lessons for the policy process. *Peace and Conflict: Journal of Peace Psychology, 5*, 201–218.

Keltner, D., & Ekman, P. (1994). Facial expressions in emotion. In V. S. Ramachandran (Ed.), *Encyclopedia of Human Behavior* (Vol. 2, pp. 361–369). San Diego: Academic Press.

Kemmelmeier, M., & Winter, D. G. (2000). Putting threat into perspective: Experimental studies on perceptual distortion in international conflict. *Personality & Social Psychology Bulletin, 26*, 795–809.

Kenny, D. A. (1994). *Interpersonal perception: A social relations analysis.* New York: Guilford.

Kenny, D. A., & DePaulo, B. M. (1993). Do people know how others view them? An empirical and theoretical account. *Psychological Bulletin, 114*, 145–161.

Kenny, D. A., Albright, L., Malloy, T. E., & Kashy, D. A. (1994). Consensus in interpersonal perception: Acquaintance and the big five. *Psychological Bulletin, 116*, 245–258.

Kenny, R. A., Blascovich, J., & Shaver, P. R. (1994). Implicit leadership theories: Prototypes for new leaders. *Basic and Applied Social Psychology, 15*, 409–437.

Kenny, D. A., & Kashy, D. A. (1994). Enhanced co-orientation in the perception of friends: A social relations analysis. *Journal of Personality and Social Psychology, 67*, 1024–1033.

Kenrick, D. T. (1987). Gender, genes, and the social environment: A biosocial interactionist perspective. In

P. Shaver & C. Hendrick (Eds.) *Review of Personality & Social Psychology* (Vol. 7, 14–43). Newbury Park, CA: Sage.

Kenrick, D. T. (1991). Proximate altruism and ultimate selfishness. *Psychological Inquiry, 2*, 135–137.

Kenrick, D. T., & Cialdini, R. B. (1977). Romantic attraction: Misattribution versus reinforcement explanations. *Journal of Personality and Social Psychology, 35*, 381–391.

Kenrick, D. T., & Funder, D.C. (1988). Profiting from controversy: Lessons from the person-situation debate. *American Psychologist, 43*, 23–34.

Kenrick, D. T., Gabrielidis, C., Keefe, R. C., & Cornelius, J. (1996). Adolescents' age preferences for dating partners: Support for an evolutionary model of life-history strategies. *Child Development, 67*, 1499–1511.

Kenrick, D. T., Groth, G. R., Trost, M. R., & Sadalla, E. K. (1993). Integrating evolutionary and social exchange perspectives on relationships: Effects of gender, self-appraisal, and involvement level on mate selection criteria. *Journal of Personality and Social Psychology, 64*, 951–969.

Kenrick, D. T., & Johnson, G. A. (1979). Interpersonal attraction in aversive environments: A problem for the classical conditioning paradigm? *Journal of Personality and Social Psychology, 37*, 572–579.

Kenrick, D. T., & Keefe, R. C. (1992). Age preferences in mates reflect sex differences in human reproductive strategies. *Behavioral and Brain Sciences, 15*, 75–133.

Kenrick, D. T., Keefe, R. C., Bryan, A., Barr, A., & Brown, S. (1995). Age preferences and mate choice among homosexuals and heterosexuals: A case for modular psychological mechanisms. *Journal of Personality and Social Psychology, 69*, 1166–1172.

Kenrick, D. T., Montello, D. R., Gutierres, S. E., & Trost, M. R. (1993). Effects of physical attractiveness on affect and perceptual judgment: When social comparison overrides social reinforcement. *Personality and Social Psychology Bulletin, 19*, 195–99.

Kenrick, D. T., & Li, N. (2000). The Darwin is in the details. *American Psychologist, 5*, 1060–1061.

Kenrick, D. T., & Luce, C. L. (2000). An evolutionary life-history model of gender differences and similarities. In T. Eckes & H. M. Trautner (Eds.) *The developmental social psychology of gender* (pp. 35–64). Mahwah, NJ.: Erlbaum.

Kenrick, D. T., & MacFarlane, S. (1986). Ambient temperature and horn honking: A field study of interpersonal hostility. *Environment and Behavior, 18*, 179–191.

Kenrick, D. T., Neuberg, S. L., Zierk, K., & Krones, J. (1994). Evolution and social cognition: Contrast effects as a function of sex, dominance, and physical attractiveness. *Personality and Social Psychology Bulletin, 20*, 210–217.

Kenrick, D. T., Nieuweboer, S., & Buunk, A. P. (1995). Age differences in mate choice across cultures and across historical periods. Paper presented at joint meetings of *Society of Experimental Social Psychology* and *European Association of Experimental Social Psychology*. Washington, D.C., October.

Kenrick, D. T., Sadalla, E. K., & Keefe, R. C. (1998). Evolutionary cognitive psychology: The missing heart of modern cognitive science. In C. Crawford & D. Krebs (Eds.), *Handbook of evolutionary psychology: Ideas, issues, and applications* (pp. 485–514). Mahwah, NJ: Erlbaum.

Kenrick, D. T., Sadalla, E. K., Groth, G., & Trost, M. R. (1990). Evolution, traits, and the stages of human courtship: Qualifying the parental investment model. *Journal of Personality, 58*, 97–117.

Kenrick, D. T., & Sheets, V. (1994). Homicidal fantasies. *Ethology and Sociobiology, 14*, 231–246.

Kenrick, D. T., Trost, M. R., & Sheets, V. L. (1996). The feminist advantages of an evolutionary perspective. In D. M. Buss & N. Malamuth (Eds.), *Sex, power, conflict: Feminist and evolutionary perspectives* (pp. 29–53). New York: Oxford University Press.

Kernis, M. H., Cornell, D. P., Sun, C-R., Berry, A., & Harlow, T. (1993). There's more to self-esteem than whether it is high or low: The importance of stability of self-esteem. *Journal of Personality and Social Psychology, 65*, 1190–1204.

Kernis, M. H., Grannemann, B. D., & Barclay, L. C. (1989). Stability and level of self-esteem as predictors of anger arousal and hostility. *Journal of Personality and Social Psychology, 56*, 1013–1023.

Kernis, M. H., Grannemann, B. D., & Barclay, L. C. (1992). Stability of self-esteem: Assessment, correlates, and excuse making. *Journal of Personality, 60*, 621–644.

Kerr, N. L. (1983). Motivation losses in small groups: A social dilemma analysis. *Journal of Personality and Social Psychology, 45*, 819–828.

Kerr, N. L. (1995). Norms in social dilemmas. In D. A. Schroeder (Ed.), *Social dilemmas: Perspectives on individuals and groups* (pp. 31–47). Westport, CT: Praeger.

Kerr, N. L., Atkin, R. S., Stasser, G., Meek, D., Holt, R. W., & Davis, J. H. (1976). Guilt beyond a reasonable doubt: Effects of concept definition and assigned decision rule on the judgments of mock jurors. *Journal of Personality and Social Psychology, 34*, 282–294.

Kerr, N. L., & Bruun, S. E. (1981). Ringelman revisted: Alternative explanations for the social loafing effect. *Personality and Social Psychology Bulletin, 7*, 224–231.

Kerr, N. L., & Bruun, S. E. (1983). Dispensability of member effort and group motivation losses: Free-rider effects. *Journal of Personality and Social Psychology, 44*, 78–94.

Kerr, N. L., Garst, J., Lewandowski, D. A., & Harris, S. E. (1997). That still small voice: Commitment to cooperate as an internalized versus a social norm. *Personality and Social Psychology Bulletin, 23*, 1300–1311.

Kerr, N. L., & Kaufman-Gilliland, C. M. (1994). Communication, commitment, and cooperation in social dilemmas. *Journal of Personality and Social Psychology, 66*, 513–529.

Kerr, N. L., & MacCoun, R. J. (1985). The effects of jury size and polling method on the process and product of jury deliberation. *Journal of Personality and Social Psychology, 48*, 349–363.

Ketelaar, T., & Clore, G. L. (1997). Emotion and reason: The proximate effects and ultimate functions of emotions. In G. Matthews (Ed.) *Cognitive Science perspectives on personality and emotion* (pp. 355–396). Amsterdam: Elsevier.

Ketelaar, T., & Ellis, B. J. (2000). Are evolutionary explanations unfalsifiable? Evolutionary psychology and the Lakatosian philosophy of science. *Psychological Inquiry, 11*, 1–21.

Kiecolt-Glaser, J., Garner, W., Spreicher, C., Penn, G., Holliday, J., & Glaser, R. (1985). Psychosocial modifiers of immunocompetence in medical students. *Psychosomatic medicine, 46*, 7–14.

Kiesler, C. A., & Pallak, M. S. (1975). Minority influence: The effect of majority reactionaries and defectors, and minority and majority compromisers, upon majority opinion and attraction. *European Journal of Social Psychology, 5*, 237–256.

Kiesler, S., Sproull, L., & Waters, K. (1996). A prisoner's dilemma experiment on cooperation with people and human-like computers. *Journal of Personality and Social Psychology, 70*, 47–65.

Kihlstrom, J. F., Cantor, N., Albright, J. S., Chew, B. R., Klein, S. J., & Niedenthal, P. M. (1988). Information processing and the study of the self. In L. Berkowitz (Ed.), *Advances in experimental social psychology* (Vol. 21, pp. 145–178). New York: Academic Press.

Killeya, L. A., & Johnson, B. T. (1998). Experimental induction of biased systematic processing: The directed thought technique. *Personality and Social Psychology Bulletin, 24*, 17–33.

Kim, H. S., & Baron, R. S. (1988). Exercise and the illusory correlation: Does arousal heighten stereotypic processing? *Journal of Experimental Social Psychology, 24*, 366–380.

Kimmel, P. R. (1997). Cultural perspectives on international negotiations. In L. A. Peplau & S. E. Taylor (Eds.), *Sociocultural perspectives in social psychology* (pp. 395–411). New York: Prentice-Hall.

Kinsey, A. C., Pomeroy, W. B., & Martin, C. E. (1948). *Sexual behavior in the human male.* Philadelphia: Saunders.

Kinsey, A. C., Pomeroy, W. B., Martin, C. E., & Gebhard, P. H. (1953). *Sexual behavior in the human female.* Philadelphia: Saunders.

Kipnis, D. (1984). The use of power in organizations and in interpersonal settings. In S. Oskamp (Ed.), *Applied social psychology annual* (Vol. 5, pp. 179–210). Newbury Park, CA: Sage.

Kirkpatrick, L. A., & Hazan, C. (1994). Attachment styles and close relationships: A four year prospective study. *Personal Relationships, 1*, 123–142.

Kirkpatrick, L. A., & Shaver, P. (1988). Fear and affiliation reconsidered from a stress and coping perspective: The importance of cognitive clarity and fear reduction. *Journal of Social and Clinical Psychology, 7*, 214–233.

Kirmani, A. (1990). The effect of perceived advertising cost on brand perceptions. *Journal of Consumer Research, 17*, 160–171.

Kirmani, A., & Wright, P. (1989). Money talks: Perceived advertising expense and expected product quality. *Journal of Consumer Research, 16*, 344–353.

Kissinger, H. (1982). *Years of upheaval.* Boston: Little, Brown.

Kissinger, H. (1994). Eulogy delivered at Nixon funeral, April 27, 1994, Yorba Linda, CA.

Kitayama, S., & Markus, H. R. (1994). *Emotion and culture: Empirical studies of mutual influence.* Washington, DC: American Psychological Association.

Kitayama, S., Markus, H. R., Matsumoto, H., & Norasakkunkit, V. (1997). Individual and collective processes in the construction of the self: Self-enhancement in the United States and self-criticism in Japan. *Journal of Personality and Social Psychology, 72*, 1245–1267.

Kitayama, S., Takagi, H., & Matsumoto, H. (1995). Cultural psychology of Japanese self: I. Causal attribution of success and failure [in Japanese]. *Japanese Psychological Review, 38*, 247–280.

Kivett, V. R. (1978). Loneliness and the rural widow. *The Family Coordinator, 27*, 389–394.

Kleck, R. E., Vaughan, R. C., Cartwright-Smith, J., Vaughan, K. B., Colby, C., & Lanzetta, J. T. (1976). Effects of being observed on expressive subjective and physical responses to painful stimuli. *Journal of Personality and Social Psychology, 34*, 1211–1218.

Klein, W. M., & Kunda, Z. (1993). Maintaining self-serving social comparisons: Biased reconstruction of past behaviors. *Personality and Social Psychology Bulletin, 19*, 732–739.

Klinger, E. (1975). Consequences of commitment to and disengagement from incentives. *Psychological Review, 82*, 1–25.

Klinger, E. (1977). *Meaning and void: Inner experience and the incentives in people's lives.* Minneapolis: University of Minnesota Press.

Knight, G. P., Fabes, R. A., & Higgins, D. A. (1996). Concerns about drawing causal inferences from meta-analysis: An example in the study of gender differences in aggression. *Psychological Bulletin, 119*, 410–421.

Knowles, E. S. (1982). From individuals to group members: A dialectic for the social sciences. In W.

Ickes, & E. S. Knowles (Eds.), *Personality, roles, and social behavior* (pp. 1–25). New York: Springer-Verlag.

Knox, R. E., & Inkster, J. A. (1968). Postdecisional dissonance at post time. *Journal of Personality and Social Psychology, 8*, 319–323.

Knox, R. E., & Safford, R. K. (1976). Group caution at the race track. *Journal of Experimental Social Psychology, 12*, 317–324.

Kobler, J. (1971). *Capone: The life and world of Al Capone. New York: G. P. Putnam's Sons.*

Koestner, R., & McClelland, D.C. (1990). Perspectives on competence motivation. In L. A. Pervin (Ed.), *Handbook of personality: Theory and research* (pp. 527–548). New York: Guilford.

Koestner, R., & Wheeler, L. (1988). Self-presentation in personal relationships: The influence of implicit notions of attraction and role expectations. *Journal of Social and Personal Relationships, 5*, 149–160.

Kohn, A. (1993). *Punished by rewards.* New York: Houghton Mifflin.

Kohnken, G. (1987). Training police officers to detect deceptive eyewitness statements: Does it work? *Social Behaviour, 2*, 1–17.

Kolditz, T. A., & Arkin, R. M. (1982). An impression management interpretation of the self-handicapping strategy. *Journal of Personality and Social Psychology, 43*, 492–502.

Komorita, S. S., & Barth, J. M. (1985). Components of reward in social dilemmas. *Journal of Personality and Social Psychology, 48*, 364–373.

Komorita, S. S., & Parks, C. D. (1995). Interpersonal relations: Mixed-motive interaction. *Annual Review of Psychology, 46*, 183–207.

Komorita, S. S., Hilty, J. A., & Parks, C. D. (1991). Reciprocity and cooperation in social dilemmas. *Journal of Conflict Resolution, 35*, 494–518.

Komorita, S. S., Parks, C. D., & Hulbert, L. G. (1992). Reciprocity and the induction of cooperation in social dilemmas. *Journal of Personality and Social Psychology, 62*, 607–617.

Konrad, A. M., Ritchie, J. E. Jr., Lieb, P., & Corrigall, E. (2000). Sex differences and similarities in job attribute preferences: A meta-analysis. *Psychological Bulletin, 126*, 593–641.

Korda, M. (1975). *Power! How to get it, how to use it.* New York: Random House.

Kors, D. J., Linden, W., & Gerin, W. (1997). Evaluation interferes with social support: Effects of cardiovascular stress reactivity in women. *Journal of Social and Clinical Psychology, 16*, 1–23.

Korte, C., & Kerr, N. (1975). Response to altruistic opportunities under urban and rural conditions. *Journal of Social Psychology, 95*, 183–184.

Kouri, E., Lukas, S., Pope, H., & Oliva, P. (1995). Increased aggressive responding in male volunteers following the administration of gradually increasing doses of testosterone cypionate. *Drug and Alcohol Dependence, 40*, 73–79.

Kowalski, R. M. (2000). "I was only kidding!": Victims' and perpetrators' perceptions of teasing. *Personality & Social Psychology Bulletin, 26*, 231–241.

Kowalski, R. M., & Leary, M. R. (1990). Strategic self-presentation and the avoidance of aversive events: Antecedents and consequences of self-enhancement and self-depreciation. *Journal of Experimental Social Psychology, 26*, 322–336.

Krackow, A., & Blass, T. (1995). When nurses obey or defy inappropriate physician orders: Attributional differences. *Journal of Social Behavior and Personality, 10*, 585–594.

Kramer, R. M., & Brewer, M. B. (1984). Effects of group identity on resource use in a simulated commons dilemma. *Journal of Personality and Social Psychology, 46*, 1044–1057.

Kranzler, D. (1976). *Japanese, Nazis, and Jews: The Jewish refugee community of Shanghai, 1938–1945.* New York: Yeshiva University Press.

Kraut, R. E. (1973). Effects of social labeling on giving to charity. *Journal of Experimental Social Psychology, 9*, 551–562.

Kraut, R. E., & Poe, D. (1980). On the line: The deception judgments of customs inspectors and laymen. *Journal of Personality and Social Psychology, 39*, 784–798.

Kravitz, D. A., & Martin, B. (1986). Ringelmann rediscovered: The original article. *Journal of Personality and Social Psychology, 50*, 936–941.

Krebs, D. (1975). Empathy and altruism. *Journal of Personality and Social Psychology, 32*, 1134–1146.

Krebs, D. (1989). Detecting genetic similarity without detecting genetic similarity. *Behavioral and Brain Sciences, 12*, 533–534.

Krebs, D. L. (1991). Altruism and egoism: A false dichotomy? *Psychological Inquiry, 2*, 137–139.

Krebs, D. L., & Denton, K. (1997). Social illusions and self-deception: The evolution of biases in person perception. In J. A. Simpson & D. T. Kenrick (Eds.), *Evolutionary social psychology* (pp. 21–48). Mahwah, NJ: Erlbaum.

Krebs, D. L., & Russell, C. (1981). Role taking and altruism: When you put yourself in another's shoes will they take you to their owner's aid? In J. P. Rushton & R. M. Sorrentino (Eds.), *Altruism and helping behavior: Social, personality, and developmental perspectives* (pp. 137–165). Hillsdale, NJ: Erlbaum.

Kremer, J., Barry, R., & McNally, A. (1986). The misdirected letter and the quasi-questionnaire: Unobtrusive measures of prejudice in Northern Ireland. *Journal of Applied Social Psychology, 16*, 303–309.

Krosnick, J. A., Betz, A. L., Jussim, L. J., & Lynn, A. R. (1992). Subliminal conditioning of attitudes. *Personality and Social Psychology Bulletin, 18*, 152–162.

Krueger, J., & Clement, R. W. (1997). Estimates of social consensus by majorities and minorities: The case for social projection. *Personality* *and Social Psychology Review, 1*, 299–313.

Krueger, J., & Rothbart, M. (1990). Contrast and accentuation effects in category learning. *Journal of Personality and Social Psychology, 59*, 651–663.

Krueger, J., & Zeiger, J. S. (1993). Social categorization and the truly false consensus effect. *Journal of Personality and Social Psychology, 65*, 670–680.

Kruger, J. S. (1999). *Egocentrism in self and social judgment.* Unpublished doctoral dissertation, Cornell University.

Kruglanski, A. W., & Freund, T. (1983). The freezing and unfreezing of lay-inferences: Effects on impressional primacy, ethnic stereotyping, and numerical anchoring. *Journal of Experimental Social Psychology, 19*, 448–468.

Kruglanski, A. W., & Mayseless, O. (1988). Contextual effects in hypothesis testing: The role of competing alternatives and epistemic motivations. *Social Cognition, 6*, 1–20.

Krull, D. S. (1993). Does the grist change the mill? The effect of the perceiver's inferential goal on the process of social inference. *Personality and Social Psychology Bulletin, 19*, 340–348.

Krull, D. S., & Dill, J. C. (1996). On thinking first and responding fast: Flexibility in social inference processes. *Personality and Social Psychology Bulletin, 22*, 949–959.

Krupat, E. (1985). *People in cities.* New York: Cambridge.

Kukla, A. (1972). Attributional determinants of achievement-related behavior. *Journal of Personality and Social Psychology, 21*, 166–174.

Kulik, J. A., & Mahler, H. I. M. (1987). Effects of preoperative roommate assignment on preoperative anxiety and recovery from coronary-bypass surgery. *Health Psychology, 6*, 525–543.

Kulik, J. A., & Mahler, H. I. M. (1989). Stress and affiliation in a hospital setting: Preoperative roommate preferences. *Personality and Social Psychology Bulletin, 15*, 183–193.

Kulik, J. A., & Mahler, H. I. M. (1990). Stress and affiliation research: On taking the laboratory to health field settings. *Annals of Behavioral Medicine, 12*, 106–111.

Kulik, J. A., Mahler, H. I. M., & Earnest, A. (1994). Social comparison and affiliation under threat: Going beyond the affiliate-choice paradigm. *Journal of Personality and Social Psychology, 66*, 301–309.

Kunda, Z. (1987). Motivation and inference: Self-serving generation and evaluation of evidence. *Journal of Personality and Social Psychology, 53*, 636–647.

Kunda, Z. (1990). The case for motivated reasoning. *Psychological Bulletin, 108*, 480–498.

Kunda, Z., Miller, D. T., & Claire, T. (1990). Combining social concepts: The role of causal reasoning. *Cognitive Science, 14*, 551–577.

Kunda, Z., & Oleson, K. C. (1995). Maintaining stereotypes in the face of disconfirmation: Constructing grounds for subtyping deviants. *Journal of Personality and Social Psychology, 68*, 565–579.

Kunda, Z., & Sanitioso, R. (1989). Motivated changes in the self-concept. *Journal of Experimental Social Psychology, 25*, 272–285.

LaFramboise, T., Coleman, H. L., & Gerton, J. (1993). Psychological impact of biculturalism: Evidence and theory. *Psychological Bulletin, 114*, 395–412.

LaFrance, M., & Mayo, C. (1978). *Moving bodies: Nonverbal communication in social relationships.* Monterey, CA: Brooks/Cole.

Laird, J. D. (1974). Self-attribution of emotion: The effects of expressive behavior on the quality of emotional experience. *Journal of Personality and Social Psychology, 29*, 475–486.

Lambert, A. J., Burroughs, T., Nguyen, T. (1999). Perceptions of risk and the buffering hypothesis: The role of just world beliefs and right-wing authoritarianism. *Personality & Social Psychology Bulletin, 25*, 643–656.

Lamm, H., & Myers, D. G. (1978). Group-induced polarization of attitudes and behavior. In L. Berkowitz (Ed.), *Advances in Experimental Social Psychology* (Vol. 11, pp. 145–195). Orlando, FL: Academic Press.

Lampinen, J. M., & Smith, V. L. (1994, July). *Do source expertise and individual differences affect suggestibility through discrepancy detection or discrepancy resolution?* Paper presented at the meeting of the American Psychological Society, Washington, D.C.

Lancaster, J. B. (1975). *Primate behavior and the emergence of human culture.* New York: Holt, Rinehart, & Winston.

Landau, S. F. (1988). Violent crime and its relation to subjective social stress indicators: The case of Israel. *Aggressive Behavior, 14*, 337–362.

Landau, S. F., & Raveh, A. (1987). Stress factors, social support, and violence in Israeli society: A quantitative analysis. *Aggressive Behavior, 13*, 67–85.

Landis, D., & Brislin, R. W. (1983). *Handbook of intercultural training.* New York: Pergamon.

Lane, C. (1991, January 7). Saddam's Endgame. *Newsweek*, p. 14–18.

Langer, E. J. (1975). The illusion of control. *Journal of Personality and Social Psychology, 32*, 311–328.

Langer, E. J. (1989). *Mindfulness.* Reading, MA: Addison-Wesley.

Langer, E. J. (1989). Minding matters: The consequences of mindlessness-mindfulness. In L. Berkowitz *(Ed.), Advances in experimental social psychology* (Vol. 22, pp. 137–173). San Diego, CA: Academic Press.

Langer, E. J., & Moldoveanu, M. (2000). Mindfulness research and the future. *Journal of Social Issues, 56*, 129–139.

Langer, E. J., & Rodin, J. (1976). The effects of choice and enhanced personal responsibility for the aged: A field experiment in an institutional setting. *Journal of Personality and Social Psychology, 34,* 191–198.

Langer, E. J., Blank, A., & Chanowitz, B. (1978). The mindlessness of ostensibly thoughtful action: The role of placebic information in interpersonal interaction. *Journal of Personality and Social Psychology, 36,* 635–642.

Langlois, J. H., & Roggman, L. A. (1990). Attractive faces are only average. *Psychological Science, 1,* 115–21.

Langlois, J. H., Ritter, J. M., Casey, R. J., & Sawin, D. B. (1995). Infant attractiveness predicts maternal behaviors and attitudes. *Developmental Psychology, 31,* 464–472.

Larrick, R. P., & Blount, S. (1997). The claiming effect: Why players are more generous in social dilemmas than in ultimatum games. *Journal of Personality and Social Psychology, 72,* 810–825.

Larsen, R. J. (2000). Emotion and personality: Introduction to the special symposium. *Personality and Social Psychology Bulletin, 26,* 651–654.

Lassiter, G. D., Koenig, L. J., & Apple, K. J. (1996). Mood and behavior perception: Dysphoria can increase and decrease effortful processing of information. *Personality and Social Psychology Bulletin, 22,* 794–810.

Latané, B. (1996). Dynamic social impact: The creation of culture by communication. *Journal of Communication, 46,* 13–25.

Latané, B., & Bourgeois, M. J. (1996). Experimental evidence for dynamic social impact: The emergence of subcultures in electronic groups. *Journal of Communication, 46,* 35–47.

Latané, B., & Darley, J. M. (1968). Group inhibition of bystander intervention in emergencies. *Journal of Personality and Social Psychology, 10,* 215–221.

Latané, B., & Darley, J. M. (1970). *The unresponsive bystander: Why doesn't he help?* New York: Appleton-Century-Croft.

Latané, B., & L'Herrou, T. (1996). Spatial clustering in the conformity game: Dynamic social impact in electronic groups. *Journal of Personality and Social Psychology, 70,* 1218–1230.

Latané, B., Liu, J. H., Nowak, A., Bonevento, M., & Zheng, L. (1995). Distance matters: Physical space and social impact. *Personality and Social Psychology Bulletin, 21,* 795–805.

Latané, B., Williams, K., & Harkins, S. (1979). Many hands make light the work: The causes and consequences of social loafing. *Journal of Personality and Social Psychology, 37,* 822–832.

Lau, R. R., & Russell, D. (1980). Attribution in the sports pages. *Journal of Personality and Social Psychology, 39,* 29–38.

Laube, J. (1985). Health care providers as disaster victims. In J. Laube & S. Murphy (Eds.), *Perspectives on disaster recovery* (pp. 210–228). Norwalk, CT: Appleton-Century-Crofts.

Laughlin, P. R. (1980). Social combination process of cooperative problem-solving groups at verbal intellective tasks. In M. Fishbein (Ed.), *Progress in social psychology* (Vol. 1, pp. 127–155). Hillsdale, NJ: Erlbaum.

Laughlin, P. R., & Ellis, A. L. (1986). Demonstrability and social combination processes on mathematical intellective tasks. *Journal of Experimental Social Psychology, 22,* 177–189.

Laursen, B., & Bukowski, W. M. (1997). A developmental guide to the organisation of close relationships. *International Journal of Behavioral Development, 21,* 747–770.

Lavine, H., Burgess, D., Snyder, M., Transue, J., Sullivan, J. L., Haney, B., & Wagner, S. H. (1999). Threat, authoritarianism, and voting: An investigation of personality and persuasion. *Personality & Social Psychology Bulletin, 25,* 337–347.

Lazarus, R. S. (1983). The costs and benefits of denial. In S. Breznitz (Ed.), *The denial of stress* (pp. 1–30). Madison, CT: International Universities Press.

Lazarus, R. S., & Folkman, S. (1984). *Stress, appraisal, and coping.* New York: Springer.

Le Bon, G. (1879). Recherches anatomiques et mathematiques sur les lois des variations du volume du cerveau et surs leurs relations avec l'intelligence. *Revue d'Anthropologie,* 2nd series, *2,* 27–104.

Le Bon, G. (1895/1960). *Psychologie des foules (the crowd).* New York: Viking Press.

Leana, C. R. (1985). A partial test of Janis' groupthink model: Effects of group cohesiveness and leader behavior on defective decision making. *Journal of Management, 11,* 5–17.

Leary, M. R. (1986a). The impact of interactional impediments on social anxiety and self-presentation. *Journal of Experimental Social Psychology, 22,* 122–135.

Leary, M. R. (1986b). Affective and behavioral components of shyness. In W. H. Jones, J. M. Cheek, & S. R. Briggs (Eds.), *Shyness: Perspectives on research and treatment* (pp. 27–38). New York: Plenum Press.

Leary, M. R. (1995). *Self-presentation: Impression management and interpersonal behavior.* Madison, WI: Brown & Benchmark.

Leary, M. R., & Baumeister, R. F. (2000). The nature and function of self-esteem: Sociometer theory. *Advances in experimental social psychology, 32,* 1–62.

Leary, M. R., & Kowalski, R. M. (1990). Impression management: A literature review and two-component model. *Psychological Bulletin, 107,* 34–47.

Leary, M. R., & Kowalski, R. M. (1995). *Social anxiety.* New York: Guilford.

Leary, M. R., & Shepperd, J. A. (1986). Behavioral self-handicaps versus self-reported handicaps: A conceptual note. *Journal of*

Personality and Social Psychology, 51, 1265–1268.

Leary, M. R., Tambor, E. S., Terdal, E. S., & Downs, D. L. (1995). Self-esteem as an interpersonal monitor: The sociometer hypothesis. *Journal of Personality and Social Psychology, 68*, 518–530.

Leary, M. R., Tchividjian, L. R., & Kraxberger, B. E. (1994). Self-presentation can be hazardous to your health: Impression management and health risk. *Health Psychology, 13*, 461–470.

Lee, J. A. (1977). A typology of styles of loving. *Personality and Social Psychology Bulletin, 3*, 173–182.

Lee, Y. T., Jussim, L. J., & McCauley, C. R. (1995). *Stereotype accuracy: Toward appreciating group differences.* Washington, DC: American Psychological Association.

Leek, M., & Smith, P. K. (1989). Phenotypic matching human altruism, and mate selection. *Behavioral and Brain Sciences, 12*, 534–535.

Leek, M., & Smith, P. K. (1991). Cooperation and conflict in three-generation families. In P. K. Smith (Ed.), *The psychology of grandparenthood: An international perspective* (pp. 177–194). London: Routledge.

Lefebvre, L. M. (1975). Encoding and decoding of ingratiation in modes of smiling and gaze. *British Journal of Social and Clinical Psychology, 14*, 33–42.

Legrenzi, P., Butera, F., Mugny, G., & Perez, J. (1991). Majority and minority influence in inductive reasoning: A preliminary study. *European Journal of Social Psychology, 21*, 359–363.

Leibman, M. (1970). The effects of sex and race norms on personal space. *Environment and Behavior, 2*, 208–246.

Leippe, M. R., & Elkin, R. A. (1987). When motives clash: Issue involvement and response involvement as determinants of persuasion. *Journal of Personality and Social Psychology, 52*, 269–278.

Leitenberg, H., & Henning, K. (1995). Sexual fantasy. *Psychological Bulletin, 117*, 469–496.

Leith, K. P., & Baumeister, R. F. (1998). Empathy, shame, guilt, and narratives of interpersonal conflict: Guilt-prone people are better at perspective-taking. *Journal of Personality, 66*, 1–37.

Lemly, B. (2000, April, #4). Future tech: Fuel sippers, *Discover, 21.*

Lemyre, L., & Smith, P. M. (1985). Intergroup discrimination and self-esteem in the minimal group paradigm. *Journal of Personality and Social Psychology, 49*, 660–670.

Leo, R. A. (in press). *Police interrogation in America: A study of violence, civility, and social change.* New York: New York University Press,

Lepore, L., & Brown, R. (1997). Category and stereotype activation: Is prejudice inevitable? *Journal of Personality and Social Psychology, 72*, 275–287.

Lepore, S. J., Ragan, J. D., & Jones, S. (2000). Talking facilitates cognitive-emotional processes of adaptation to an acute stressor. *Journal of Personality & Social Psychology, 78*, 499–508.

Lepper, M. R., & Greene, D. (1978). *The hidden costs of rewards.* Hillsdale, NJ: Erlbaum.

Lepper, M. R., Greene, D., & Nisbett, R. E. (1973). Undermining children's intrinsic interest with extrinsic reward: A test of the 'overjustification' hypothesis. *Journal of Personality and Social Psychology, 28*, 129–137.

Lerner, M. J. (1980). *The belief in a just world: A fundamental delusion.* New York: Plenum.

Leung, K. (1988). Theoretical advances in justice behavior: Some cross-cultural inputs. In M. H. Bond (Ed.), *The cross-cultural challenge to social psychology* (pp. 218–239). Newbury Park, CA: Sage.

Leung, K., & Bond, M. H. (1984). The impact of cultural collectivism on reward allocation. *Journal of Personality and Social Psychology, 47*, 793–804.

Leventhal, H., & Cameron, L. (1994). Persuasion and health attitudes. In S. Shavitt & T. C. Brock (Eds.), *Persuasion* (pp. 219–249). Boston: Allyn & Bacon.

Levine, H. (1997). *In search of Sugihara.* New York: Free Press.

Levine, J. M. (1999). Solomon Asch's legacy for group research. *Personality and Social Psychology Review, 3*, 358–364.

Levine, J. M., & Moreland, R. L. (1998). Small groups. In D. T. Gilbert, S. T. Fiske, & G. Lindzey (Eds.), *The handbook of social psychology* (4th ed.) (Vol. 2, pp. 415–469). Boston: McGraw-Hill.

Levine, J. M., & Ranelli, C. J. (1978). Majority reaction to shifting and stable attitudeal deviates. *European Journal of Social Psychology, 8*, 55–70.

LeVine, R. A., & Campbell, D. T. (1972). *Ethnocentrism: Theories of conflict, ethnic attitudes, and group behavior.* New York: Wiley.

Levine, R. V., Martinez, T. S., Brase, G., & Sorenson, K. (1994). Helping in 36 U.S. cities. *Journal of Personality and Social Psychology, 67*, 69–82.

Levy-Leboyer, C. (1988). Success and failure in applying psychology. *American Psychologist, 43*, 779–785.

Lewin, K. (1947). Group decision and social change. In T. M. Newcomb & E. L. Hartley (Eds.), *Readings in social psychology* (pp. 330–344). New York: Henry Holt.

Lewin, K. (1951). *Field theory in social science.* New York: Harper & Row.

Lewin, K. (1951). Intention, will, and need. In D. Rapaport (Ed.), *Organization and pathology of thought* (pp. 95–153). New York: Columbia University Press.

Lewin, K., Dembo, T., Festinger, L., & Sears, P. S. (1944). Level of aspiration. In J. McV. Hunt (Ed.), *Personality and the behavior disorders* (Vol. 1, pp. 333–378). New York: Ronald Press.

Lewin, K., Lippitt, R., & White, R. K. (1939). Patterns of aggressive behavior in experimentally created "social climates." *Journal of Social Psychology, 10*, 271–279.

Lewin, R. (1992). *Complexity: Life at the edge of chaos.* New York: Macmillan.

Lewis, H. S. (1974). *Leaders and followers: Some anthropological perspectives.* Reading, MA: Addison-Wesley.

Lewis, M. (1993). The emergence of human emotions. In M. Lewis & J. M. Haviland (Eds.), *Handbook of emotions* (pp. 223–236). New York: Guilford.

Lewis, M. (2000). *Handbook of emotions.* New York: Guilford.

Leyens, J. P., Camino, L., Parke, R. D., & Berkowitz, L. (1975). Effects of movie violence on aggression in a field setting as a function of group dominance and cohesion. *Journal of Personality and Social Psychology, 32*, 346–360.

Liang, D. W., Moreland, R., & Argote, L. (1995). Group versus individual training and group performance: The mediating role of transactive memory. *Personality and Social Psychology Bulletin, 21*, 384–393.

Liberman, A., & Chaiken, S. (1992). Defensive processing of personally relevant health messages. *Personality and Social Psychology Bulletin, 18*, 669–679.

Liberman, N., & Förster, J. (2000). Expression after suppression: A motivational explanation of post-suppressional rebound. *Journal of Personality and Social Psychology, 79*, 190–203.

Lickel, B., Hamilton, D. L., Wieczorkowska, G., Lewis, A., Sherman, S. J., & Uhles, A. N. (2000). Varieties of groups and the perception of group entitativity. *Journal of Personality & Social Psychology, 78*, 223–246.

Liden, R. C., & Mitchell, T. R. (1988). Ingratiatory behaviors in organizational settings. *Academy of Management Review, 12*, 572–587.

Lieberman, M. A., & Tobin, S. S. (1983). *The experience of old age: Stress, coping and survival.* New York: Basic Books.

Liebrand, W. B., VanRun, G. J. (1985). The effects of social motives on behavior in social dilemmas in two cultures. *Journal of Experimental Social Psychology, 21*, 86–102.

Lightdale, J. R., & Prentice, D. A. (1994). Rethinking sex differences in aggression: Aggressive behavior in the absence of social roles. *Personality and Social Psychology Bulletin, 20*, 34–44.

Lindeman, R., von der Pahlen, B., Ost, B., & Eriksson, C. J. P. (1992). Serum testosterone, cortisol, glucose, and ethanol in males arrested for spouse abuse. *Aggressive Behavior, 18*, 393–400.

Linder, D. E. (1982). Social trap analogs: The tragedy of the commons in the laboratory. In *Cooperation and helping behavior: Theories and research* (pp. 183–205). V. Derlega and J. Grzelak (Eds.), New York: Academic Press.

Lindsay, J. J., & Anderson, C. A. (2000). From antecedent conditions to violent actions: A general affective aggression model. *Personality & Social Psychology Bulletin, 26*, 533–547.

Lindskold, S. (1983). Cooperators, competitors, and response to GRIT. *Journal of Conflict Resolution, 27*, 521–532.

Linville, P. W., Fischer, G. W., & Salovey, P. (1989). Perceived distributions of the characteristics of in-group and out-group members: Empirical evidence and a computer simulation. *Journal of Personality and Social Psychology, 57*, 165–188.

Lippa, R., & Arad, S. (1999). Gender, personality, and prejudice: The display of authoritarianism and social dominance in interviews with college men and women. *Journal of Research in Personality, 33*, 463–493.

Lippmann, W. (1922). *Public opinion.* New York: Harcourt Brace.

Little, B. R. (1989). Personal projects analysis: Trivial pursuits, magnificent obsessions, and the search for coherence. In D. M. Buss & N. Cantor (Eds.) *Personality Psychology: Recent trends and emerging directions* (pp. 15–31). New York: Springer-Verlag.

Locke, V., MacLeod, C., & Walker, I. (1994). Automatic and controlled activation of stereotypes: Individual differences associated with prejudice. *British Journal of Social Psychology, 33*, 29–46.

Locksley, A., Borgida, E., Brekke, N., & Hepburn, C. (1980). Sex stereotypes and social judgment. *Journal of Personality and Social Psychology, 39*, 821–831.

Loftus, E. M., & Ketcham, K. (1994). *The myth of repressed memory: False memories and allegations of sexual abuse.* New York: St. Martin's Press.

Loher, B. T., Vancouver, J. B., & Czajka, J. (1994, April). *Preferences and reactions to teams.* Presented at the 9th annual conference of the Society for Industrial and Organizational Psychology, Nashville, TN.

Lord, C. G., & Saenz, D. S. (1985). Memory deficits and memory surfeits: Differential cognitive consequences of tokenism for tokens and observers. *Journal of Personality and Social Psychology, 49*, 918–926.

Lord, C. G., Lepper, M. R., & Preston, E. (1984). Considering the opposite: A corrective strategy for social judgment. *Journal of Personality and Social Psychology, 47*, 1231–1243.

Lord, C. G., Ross, L., & Lepper, M. R. (1979). Biased assimilation and attitude polarization. *Journal of Personality and Social Psychology, 37*, 2098–2109.

Lord, C. G., Saenz, D. S., & Godfrey, D. K. (1987). Effects of perceived scrutiny on participant memory for social interactions. *Journal of Experimental Social Psychology, 23*, 498–517.

Lord, R. G., De Vader, C. L., & Alliger, G. M. (1986). A meta-analysis of the relation between personality traits and leadership perceptions: An application of validity generalization procedures. *Journal of Applied Psychology, 71*, 402–410.

Lord, R. G., Foti, R. J., & de Vader, C. L. (1984). A test of leadership categorization theory: Internal structure, information processing, and leadership perceptions. *Organizational Behavior and Human Decision Processes, 34,* 343–378.

Lorenz, E. (1963). Deterministic nonperiodic flow. *Journal of the Atmospheric Sciences, 20,* 130–141.

Lorenz, K. (1966). *On aggression.* New York: Harcourt-Brace-Jovanovich.

Losch, M., & Cacioppo, J. (1990). Cognitive dissonance may enhance sympathetic tonis, but attitudes are changed to reduce negative affect rather than arousal. *Journal of Experimental Social Psychology, 26,* 289–304.

Lott, A. J., & Lott, B. E. (1974). The role of reward in the formation of positive interpersonal attitudes. In T. L. Huston (Ed.), *Foundations of interpersonal attraction* (pp. 171–192). New York: Academic Press.

Lott, D. E., & Sommer, R. (1967). Seating arrangements and status. *Journal of Personality and Social Psychology, 7,* 90–95.

Low, B. S. (1998). The evolution of human life histories. In C. Crawford & D. L. Krebs (Eds.), *Handbook of evolutionary psychology* (pp. 131–162). Mahwah, NJ: LEA.

Luginbuhl, J., & Palmer, R. (1991). Impression management aspects of self-handicapping: Positive and negative effects. *Personality and Social Psychology Bulletin, 17,* 655–662.

Luks, A. (1988, October). Helper's high. *Psychology Today,* 39–42.

Lupfer, M. B., Clark, L. F., & Hutcherson, H. W. (1990). Impact of context on spontaneous trait and situational attributions. *Journal of Personality and Social Psychology, 58,* 239–249.

Lydon, J. E., & Zanna, M. P. (1990). Commitment in the face of adversity: A value-affirmation approach. *Journal of Personality and Social Psychology, 58,* 1040–1057.

Lydon, J. E., Jamieson, D. W., & Holmes, J. G. (1997). The meaning of social interactions in the transition from acquaintanceship to friendship. *Journal of Personality and Social Psychology, 73,* 536–548.

Lydon, J. E., Meana, M., Sepinwall, D., Richards, N., & Mayman, S. (1999). The commitment calibration hypothesis: When do people devalue attractive alternatives? *Personality & Social Psychology Bulletin, 25,* 152–162.

Lykken, D., & Tellegen, A. (1996). Happiness is a stochastic phenomenon. *Psychological Science,* 7, 186–189.

Lynn, M., & McCall, M. (1998). *Beyond gratitude and gratuity: A meta-analytic review of the determinants of restaurant tipping.* Unpublished manuscript, Cornell University, School of Hotel Administration, Ithaca, NY.

Lynn, M., & Oldenquist, A. (1986). Egoistic and nonegoistic motives in social dilemmas. *American Psychologist, 41,* 529–534.

Lyubomirsky, S., & Ross, L. (1998). Hedonic consequences of social comparison: A contrast of happy and unhappy people. *Journal of Personality and Social Psychology, 73,* 1141–1157.

Maass, A., & Clark, R. D. (1984). Hidden impact of minorities: Fifteen years of minority influence. *Psychological Bulletin, 95,* 428–50.

Maass, A., Clark, R. D., III, & Haberkorn, G. (1982). The effects of differential ascribed category membership and norms on minority influence. *European Journal of Social Psychology, 12,* 89–104.

Maccoby, E. E., & Jacklin, C. N. (1974). *The psychology of sex differences.* Stanford, CA: Stanford University Press.

MacCoun, R. J., & Kerr, N. L. (1988). Asymmetric influence in mock jury deliberation: Jurors' bias for leniency. *Journal of Personality and Social Psychology, 54,* 21–33.

MacDonald, G., Zanna, M. P., & Holmes, J. G. (2000). An experimental test of the role of alcohol in relationship conflict. *Journal of Experimental Social Psychology, 36,* 182–193.

MacDonald, T. K., Fong, G. T., Zanna, M. P., & Martineau, A. M. (2000). Alcohol myopia and condom use: Can alcohol intoxication be associated with more prudent behavior? *Journal of Personality & Social Psychology, 78,* 605–619.

Mack, D., & Rainey, D. (1990). Female applicants' grooming and personnel selection. *Journal of Social Behavior and Personality, 5,* 399–407.

MacKay, C. (1841/1932). *Popular delusions and the madness of crowds.* New York: Farrar, Straus, and Giroux.

Mackie, D. M., & Goethals, G. R. (1987). Individual and group goals. In C. Hendrick (Ed.), *Group processes* (pp. 144–166). Newbury Park, CA: Sage.

Mackie, D. M., & Worth, L. T. (1989). Cognitive deficits and the mediation of positive affect in persuasion. *Journal of Personality and Social Psychology, 57,* 27–40.

Mackie, D. M., Hamilton, D. L., Schroth, H. A., Carlisle, C. J., Gersho, B. F., Meneses, L. M., Nedler, B. F., & Reichel, L. D. (1989). The effects of induced mood on expectancy-based illusory correlations. *Journal of Experimental Social Psychology, 25,* 524–544.

Macrae, C. N., Bodenhausen, G. V., Milne, A. B., & Jetten, J. (1994). Out of mind but back in sight: Stereotypes on the rebound. *Journal of Personality and Social Psychology, 67,* 808–817.

Macrae, C. N., Bodenhausen, G. V., Milne, A. B., & Wheeler, V. (1996). On resisting the temptation for simplification: Counterintentional effects of stereotype suppression on social memory. *Social Cognition, 14,* 1–20.

Macrae, C. N., Milne, A. B., & Bodenhausen, G. V. (1994). Stereotypes as energy-saving devices: A peek inside the cognitive toolbox. *Journal of Personality and Social Psychology, 66,* 37–47.

Macrae, C. N., Stangor, C., & Milne, A. B. (1994). Activating social stereotypes: A functional analysis. *Journal of Experimental Social Psychology, 30,* 370–389.

Maines, D. R., & Hardesty, M. J. (1987). Temporality and gender: Young adults' career and family plans. *Social Forces, 66,* 102–120.

Maio, G. R., & Esses, V. M. (1998). The social consequences of affirmative action: Deleterious effects on perceptions of groups. *Personality and Social Psychology Bulletin, 24*, 65–74.

Major, B., & Crocker, J. (1993). Social stigma: The affective consequences of attributional ambiguity. In D. M. Mackie & D. L. Hamilton (Eds.), *Affect, cognition, and stereotyping: Interactive processes in intergroup perception* (pp. 345–370). New York: Academic Press.

Major, B., Spencer, S., Schmader, T., Wolfe, C., & Crocker, J. (1998). Coping with negative stereotypes about intellectual performance: The role of psychological disengagement. *Personality and Social Psychology Bulletin, 24*, 34–50.

Major, B., Testa, M., & Bylsma, W. H. (1991). Responses to upward and downward social comparisons: The impact of esteem-relevance and perceived control. In J. Suls & T. A. Wills (Eds.), *Social comparison: Contemporary theory and research* (pp. 237–260). Hillsdale, NJ: Erlbaum.

Malle, B. F. (1999). How people explain behavior: A new theoretical framework. *Personality & Social Psychology Review, 3*, 23–48.

Mandel, D. R., Axelrod, L. J., & Lehman, D. R. (1993). Integrative complexity in reasoning about the Persian Gulf War and the accountability to skeptical audience hypothesis. *Journal of Social Issues, 49*, 201–215.

Mandler, G. (1975). *Mind and body: Psychology of emotion and stress.* New York: W. W. Norton.

Mann, L. (1980). Cross-cultural studies of small groups. In H. Triandis & R. Brislin (Eds.), *Handbook of cross-cultural psychology: Social psychology* (Vol. 5, pp. 155–209). Boston: Allyn & Bacon.

Mann, L. (1981). The baiting crowd in episodes of threatened suicide. *Journal of Personality and Social Psychology, 41*, 703–709.

Mann, T., Nolen-Hoeksema, Burgard, D., Huang, K., Wright, A., & Hansen, K. (1997). Are two interventions worse than none? Joint primary and secondary prevention of eating disorders in college females. *Health Psychology, 16*, 215–225.

Manucia, G. K., Baumann, D. J., & Cialdini, R. B. (1984). Mood influences in helping: Direct effects or side effects? *Journal of Personality and Social Psychology, 46*, 357–364.

Marcus-Newhall, A., Pedersen, W. C., Carlson, M., & Miller, N. (2000). Displaced aggression is alive and well: A meta-analytic review. *Journal of Personality & Social Psychology, 78*, 670–689.

Markman, H. J., Floyd, F., Stanley, S., & Storaasli, R. (1988). The prevention of marital distress: A longitudinal investigation. *Journal of Consulting and Clinical Psychology, 56*, 210–217.

Markus, H. (1977). Self-schemata and processing information about the self. *Journal of Personality and Social Psychology, 35*, 63–78.

Markus, H., & Kitayama, S. (1991). Culture and the self: Implications for cognition, emotion, and motivation. *Psychological Bulletin, 98*, 224–253.

Markus, H., & Nurius, P. (1986). Possible selves. *American Psychologist, 41*, 954–969.

Markus, H., & Wurf, E. (1987). The dynamic self-concept: A social psychological perspective. *Annual Review of Psychology, 38*, 299–337.

Marshall, D. S., & Suggs, R. G. (1971). *Human sexual behavior: Variations in the ethnographic spectrum.* New York: Basic Books.

Martin, C. L. (1987). A ratio measure of sex stereotyping. *Journal of Personality and Social Psychology, 52*, 489–499.

Martin, C. L., & Halverson, C. F., Jr. (1983). The effects of sex-typing schemas on young children's memory. *Child Development, 54*, 563–574.

Martin, K. A., & Leary, M. R. (1999). Would you drink after a stranger? The influence of self-presentational motives on willingness to take a health risk. *Personality and Social Psychology Bulletin, 25*, 1092–1100.

Martin, N. G., Eaves, L. J., Heath, A. C., Jardine, R., Feingold, L. M., & Eysenck, H. J. (1986). Transmission of social attitudes. *Proceedings of the National Academy of Sciences, USA, 83*, 4364–4368.

Martin, R. (1997). "Girls don't talk about garages!" Perceptions of conversations in same- and cross-sex friendships. *Personal Relationships, 4*, 115–130.

Martin, R. G. (1973). *The woman he loved.* New York: Simon & Schuster.

Marwell, G., & Ames, R. (1981). Economists free ride, does anyone else? Experiments on the provision of public goods, IV. *Journal of Public Economics, 15*, 295–310.

Marx, E. M., Williams, J. M. G., & Claridge, G. C. (1992). Depression and social problem solving. *Journal of Abnormal Psychology, 101*, 78–86.

Massing, M. (1996, July 11). How to win the tobacco war. *New York Review of Books*, pp. 32–36.

Matarazzo, J. D. (1980). Behavioral health and behavioral medicine: Frontiers for a new health psychology. *American Psychologist, 35*, 807–817.

Matsunami, K. (1998). *International handbook of funeral customs.* Westport, CT: Greenwood Press.

Matthews, K. A., Scheier, M. F., Brunson, B. I., & Carducci, B. (1980). Attention, unpredictability, and reports of physical symptoms: Eliminating the benefits of unpredictability. *Journal of Personality and Social Psychology, 38*, 525–537.

Matthews, K. A., Woodall, K. L., Engebretson, T. O., McCann, B. S., Stoney, C. M., Manuck, S. B., & Saab, P. G. (1992). Influence of age, sex, and family on Type A and hostile attitudes and behaviors. *Health Psychology, 11*, 317–323.

Mauro, R., Sato, K., & Tucker, J. (1992). The role of appraisal in human emotions: A cross-cultural study.

Journal of Personality and Social Psychology, 62, 301–317.

Mauss, M. (1967). *The gift.* New York: W. W. Norton.

Maxwell, L. E., & Evans, G. W. (2000). The effects of noise on pre-school children's pre-reading skills. *Journal of Environmental Psychology, 20*, 91–97.

Mayer, A. J. (1979). *Madam Prime Minister: Margaret Thatcher and her rise to power.* New York: Newsweek Books.

Mayer, J. D., & Gaschke, Y. N. (1988). The experience and meta-experience of mood. *Journal of Personality and Social Psychology, 55*, 102–111.

Maznevski, M. L. (1994). Understanding our differences: Performance in decision-making groups with diverse members. *Human Relations, 47*, 531–552.

Mazur, A., & Booth, A. (1998). Testosterone and dominance in men. *Behavioral and Brain Sciences, 21*, 353–397.

Mazur, A., Booth, A., & Dabbs, J. M., Jr. (1992). Testosterone and chess competition. *Social Psychology Quarterly, 55*, 70–77.

McAdams, D. P. (1985). Motivation and friendship. In S. Duck & D. Perlman (Eds.) *Understanding personal relationships: An interdisciplinary approach* (pp. 85–105). Beverly Hills, CA: Sage.

McAdams, D. P. (1985). *Power, intimacy, and the life story: Personological inquiries into identity.* Homewood, IL: Dorsey Press.

McAdams, D. P. (1990). *The person.* San Diego, CA: Harcourt Brace Jovanovich.

McAlister, A. L., Ramirez, A. G., Galavotti, C., & Gallion, K. J. (1989). In R. E. Rice & C. K. Atkin (Eds.), *Public communication campaigns* (pp. 291–307). Newbury Park, CA: Sage.

McArthur, L. A. (1972). The how and what of why: Some determinants and consequences of causal attribution. *Journal of Personality and Social Psychology, 22*, 171–193.

McArthur, L. Z. (1981). What grabs you? The role of attention in impression formation and causal attribution. In E. T. Higgins, C. P. Herman, & M. P. Zanna (Eds.), *Social cognition: The Ontario symposium* (Vol. 1, pp. 201–246). Hillsdale, NJ: Erlbaum.

McArthur, L. Z., & Baron, R. M. (1983). Toward an ecological theory of social perception. *Psychological Review, 90*, 215–238.

McCain, B. E., O'Reilly, C. A., III, & Pfeffer, J. (1983). The effects of departmental demography on turnover: The case of a university. *Academy of Management Journal, 26*, 626–641.

McCall, N. (1994). *Makes me wanna holler: A young black man in America.* New York: Random House.

McCann, S. J. H. (1997). Threatening times, "strong" presidential popular vote winners, and the victory margin, 1824–1964. *Journal of Personality and Social Psychology, 73*, 160–170.

McCann, S. J. H. (1999). Threatening times and fluctuations in American church memberships. *Personality & Social Psychology Bulletin, 25*, 325–336.

McCanne, T. R., & Anderson, J. A. (1987). Emotional responding following experimental manipulation of facial electromyographic activity. *Journal of Personality and Social Psychology, 52*, 759–768.

McCarthy, B. (1994). Warrior values: A socio-historical survey. In J. Archer (Ed.), *Male Violence* (pp. 105–120). New York: Routledge.

McCarthy, J. (1952). The master impostor: An incredible tale. *Life, 32*, 79–89.

McCauley, C. (1989). The nature of social influence in groupthink: Compliance and internalization. *Journal of Personality and Social Psychology, 57*, 250–260.

McCauley, C. R. (1995). Are stereotypes exaggerated? A sampling of racial, gender, academic, occupational, and political stereotypes. In Y. T. Lee, L. J. Jussim, & C. R. McCauley (Eds.), *Stereotype accuracy: Toward appreciating group differences* (pp. 215–243). Washington, DC: American Psychological Association.

McClelland, D.C. (1984). *Human motivation.* Glenview, IL: Scott, Foresman.

McClelland, D.C., Atkinson, J. W., Clark, R. A., & Lowell, E. L. (1953). *The achievement motive.* New York: Appleton-Century-Crofts.

McClintock, C. G., Messick, D. M., Kuhlman, D. M., & Campos, F. T. (1973). Motivational basis of choice in three choice decomposed games. *Journal of Experimental Social Psychology, 9*, 572–590.

McConahay, J. B. (1986). Modern racism, ambivalence, and the modern racism scale. In J. F. Dovidio & S. L. Gaertner (Eds.), *Prejudice, discrimination, and racism* (pp. 91–125). Orlando, FL: Academic Press.

McCornak, S. A., & Levine, T. R. (1990). When lovers become leery: The relationship between suspiciousness and accuracy in detecting deception. *Communication Monographs, 57*, 219–230.

McCrae, R. R., & John, O. P. (1992). An introduction to the five-factor model and its applications. *Journal of Personality, 60*, 175–216.

McDaniel, A., & Thomas, E. (1991, September 30). Playing chicken in Iraq. *Newsweek*, p. 40.

McDougall, W. (1908). *Social psychology: An introduction.* London: Methuen.

McDougall, W. (1932). *The energies of men.* London: Methuen.

McFarland, C., Ross, M., & Conway, M. (1984). Self-persuasion and self-presentation as mediators of anticipatory attitude change. *Journal of Personality and Social Psychology, 46*, 529–540.

McFarland, S., Ageyev, V., & Abalakina, M. (1993). The authoritarian personality in the United States and the former Soviet Union: Comparative studies. In W. F. Stone, G. Lederer, & R. Christie (Eds.), *Strengths and weaknesses: The* *authoritarian personality today* (pp. 199–228). New York: Springer-Verlag.

McFarlin, D. B., Baumeister, R. F., & Blascovich, J. (1984). On knowing when to quit: Task failure, self-esteem, advice, and nonproductive persistence. *Journal of Personality, 52,* 138–155.

McGovern, G. (1994, June 16). The last Nixon. *Rolling Stone*, pp. 45.

McGovern, L. P. (1976). Dispositional social anxiety and helping behavior under three conditions of threat. *Journal of Personality, 44,* 84–97.

McGrath, J. E. (1984). *Groups: Interaction and performance.* Englewood Cliffs, NJ: Prentice-Hall.

McGrath, J. E., Martin, J., & Kukla, R. A. (1982). *Judgment calls in research.* Beverly Hills: Sage.

McGrath, P. (1991, January 7). More than a madman. *Newsweek*, pp. 20–24.

McGregor, J. (1993). Effectiveness of role playing and antiracist teaching in reducing student prejudice. *Journal of Education Research, 86,* 215–226.

McGuiness, E., & Ward, C. D. (1980). Better liked than right: Trustworthiness and expertise as factors in credibility. *Personality and Social Psychology Bulletin, 6,* 467–472.

McGuire, A. M. (1994). Helping behaviors in the natural environment: Dimensions and correlates of helping. *Personality and Social Psychology Bulletin, 20,* 45–56.

McGuire, W. J. (1960). Consistency and attitude change. *Journal of Abnormal and Social Psychology, 60,* 345–353.

McGuire, W. J. (1964). Inducing resistance to persuasion: Some contemporary approaches. In L. Berkowitz (Ed.), *Advances in experimental social psychology* (Vol. 1, pp.191–229). San Diego, Academic Press.

McGuire, W. J. (1966). Attitudes and opinions. *Annual Review of Psuchology, 17,* 475–514.

McGuire, W. J. (1986). The myth of massive media impact: Savagings and salvagings. In G. Comstock (Ed.), *Public communication and behavior* (Vol. 1, pp. 173–257). Orlando, FL: Academic Press.

McGuire, W. J., & McGuire, C. V. (1996). Enhancing self-esteem by directed-thinking tasks: Cognitive and affective positivity asymmetries. *Journal of Personality and Social Psychology, 70,* 1117–1125.

McKenna, K. Y. A., & Bargh, J. A. (2000). Plan 9 from cyberspace: The implications of the Internet for personality and social psychology. *Personality & Social Psychology Review, 4,* 57–75.

McKenzie-Mohr, D. (2000). Fostering sustainable behavior through community-based social marketing. *American Psychologist,* 55, 531–537.

McLeod, P. L., & Lobel, S. A. (1992, August). *The effects of ethnic diversity on idea generation in small groups.* Presented at the 52nd annual meeting of the Academy of Management, Las Vegas, Nevada.

McMullen, M. N., & Markman, K. D. (2000). Downward counterfactuals and motivation: The wake-up call and the Pangloss effect. *Personality and Social Psychology Bulletin, 26,* 575–584.

McNulty, S. E., & Swann, W. B., Jr. (1994). Identity negotiation in roommate relationships: The self as architect and consequence of social reality. *Journal of Personality and Social Psychology, 67,* 1012–1023.

McWilliams, S., & Howard, J. A. (1993). Solidarity and hierarchy in cross-sex friendships. *Journal of Social Issues, 49,* 191–202.

Mead, G. H. (1934). *Mind, self, and society.* Chicago, IL: University of Chicago Press.

Mealey, L. (1995). The sociobiology of sociopathy: An integrated evolutionary model. *Behavioral & Brain Sciences, 18,* 523–599.

Medvec, V. H., Madey, S. F., & Gilovich, T. (1995). When less is more: Counterfactual thinking and satisfaction among Olympic medalists. *Journal of Personality and Social Psychology, 69,* 603–610.

Mehrabian, A. (1972). *Nonverbal communication.* Chicago, IL: Aldine.

Meir, E. I., & Hasson, R. (1982). Congruence between personality type and environment type as a predictor of stay in an environment. *Journal of Vocational Behavior, 21,* 309–317.

Meister, A. (1979). Personal and social factors of social participation. *Journal of Voluntary Action Research, 8,* 6–11.

Melamed, B. F., Yurchesson, E., Fleece, L., Hutcherson, S., & Hawes, R. (1978). Effects of film modeling on the reduction of anxiety-related behaviors. *Journal of Consulting and Clinical Psychology, 46,* 1357–1374.

Meleshko, K. G. A., & Alden, L. E. (1993). Anxiety and self-disclosure: Toward a motivational model. *Journal of Personality and Social Psychology, 64,* 1000–1009.

Merton, R. K. (1948). The self-fulfilling prophecy. *Antioch Review, 8,* 193–210.

Messick, D. M., & Brewer, M. B. (1983). Solving social dilemmas: A review. *Review of Personality and Social Psychology, 4,* 11–44.

Messick, D. M., & McClelland, C. L. (1983). Social traps and temporal traps. *Personality and Social Psychology Bulletin, 9,* 105–110

Metcalf, P., & Huntington, R. (1991). *Celebrations of death: The anthropology of mortuary ritual* (2nd ed.). Cambridge, MA: Cambridge University Press.

Meyer, D. E., & Schvaneveldt, R. W. (1971). Facilitation in recognizing pairs of words: Evidence of a dependence between retrieval operations. *Journal of Experimental Psychology, 90,* 227–234.

Michaels, J. W., Blommel, J. M., Brocato, R. M., Linkous, R. A., & Rowe, J. S. (1982). Social facilitation and inhibition in a natural setting. *Replications in Social Psychology, 2,* 21–24.

Michaelsen, L. K., Watson, W. E., & Black, R. H. (1989). A realistic test of individual versus group consensus decision making. *Journal of Applied Psychology, 74*, 834–839.

Mickelson, K. D., Kessler, R. C., & Shaver, P. R. (1997). Adult attachment in a nationally representative sample. *Journal of Personality and Social Psychology, 73*, 1092–1106.

Midlarsky, E., & Nemeroff, R. (1995, July). *Heroes of the holocaust: Predictors of their well-being in later life.* Poster presented at the American Psychological Society meetings, New York.

Mikolic, J. M., Parker, J. C., & Pruitt, D. G. (1997). Escalation in response to persistent annoyance: Groups versus individuals and gender effects. *Journal of Personality and Social Psychology, 72*, 151–163.

Mikula, G., & Schwinger, T. (1978). Affective inter-member relations and reward allocation in groups: Some theoretical considerations. In H. Brandstatter, H. J. Davis, & H. Schuller (Eds.), *Dynamics of group decisions* (pp. 229–250). Beverly Hills, CA: Sage.

Milgram, S. (1963). Behavioral study of obedience. *Journal of Abnormal and Social Psychology, 67*, 371–378.

Milgram, S. (1964). Issues in the study of obedience: A reply to Baumrind. *American Psychologist, 19*, 848–852.

Milgram, S. (1965). Some conditions of obedience and disobedience to authority. *Human Relations, 18*, 57–76.

Milgram, S. (1970). The experience of living in cities. *Science, 167*, 1461–1468.

Milgram, S. (1974). *Obedience to authority: An experimental view.* New York: Harper & Row.

Milgram, S. (1992). Some conditions of obedience and disobedience to authority (pp. 136–161). In S. Milgram, J. Sabini, & M. Silver, (Eds.), *The individual in the social world: Essays and experiments.* New York: McGraw-Hill.

Milgram, S., Bickman, L., & Berkowitz, L. (1969). Note on the drawing power of crowds of different size. *Journal of Personality and Social Psychology, 13*, 79–82.

Milgram, S., Mann, L., & Harter, S. (1965). The lost letter technique of social research. *Public Opinion Quarterly, 29*, 437–438.

Miller, A. G., Collins, B. E., & Brief, D. E. (Eds.). 1995. Perspectives on obedience to authority: The legacy of the Milgram experiments. *Journal of Social Issues, 51* (3).

Miller, D. T. (1976). Ego involvement and attributions for success and failure. *Journal of Personality and Social Psychology, 34*, 901–906.

Miller, D. T. (1999). The norm of self-interest. *American Psychologist, 54*, 1053–1060.

Miller, D. T., & McFarland, C. (1987). Pluralistic ignorance: When similarity is interpreted as dissimilarity. *Journal of Personality and Social Psychology, 53*, 298–305.

Miller, D. T., & Ross, M. (1975). Self-serving biases in attribution of causality: Fact or fiction? *Psychological Bulletin, 82*, 213–255.

Miller, D. T., & Turnbull, W. (1986). Expectancies and interpersonal processes. *Annual Review of Psychology, 37*, 233–256.

Miller, G. F. (1998). How mate selection shaped human nature: A review of sexual selection and human evolution. In C. Crawford & D. Krebs (Eds.), *Handbook of evolutionary psychology: Ideas, issues, and applications* (pp. 87–130). Mahwah, NJ: Erlbaum.

Miller, G. F. (2000). *The mating mind: How sexual choice shaped the evolution of human nature.* New York: Doubleday.

Miller, J. G. (1984). Culture and the development of everyday social explanation. *Journal of Personality and Social Psychology, 46*, 961–978.

Miller, L. C., & Fishkin, S. A. (1997). On the dynamics of human bonding and reproductive success: Seeking windows on the adapted-for human-environmental interface. In J. A. Simpson and D. T. Kenrick (Eds.), *Evolutionary social psychology* (pp. 169–196). Hillsdale, NJ: Erlbaum.

Miller, N. E., & Bugelski, R. (1948). Minor studies of aggression: II. The influence of frustrations imposed by the in-group on attitudes expressed toward out-groups. *Journal of Psychology, 25*, 437–442.

Miller, N., & Brewer, M. B. (1984). *Groups in contact.* New York: Academic Press.

Miller, N., & Zimbardo, P. (1966). Motive for fear-induced affiliation: Emotional comparison or interpersonal similarity? *Journal of Personality, 34*, 481–503.

Miller, P. A., & Eisenberg, N. (1988). The relation of empathy to aggressive behavior and externalizing/antisocial behavior. *Psychological Bulletin, 103*, 324–344.

Miller, P. J., Fung, H., & Mintz, J. (1996). Self-construction through narrative practices: A Chinese and American comparison of early socialization. *Ethos, 24*, 237–280.

Miller, R. S. (1995). On the nature of embarrassability: Shyness, social evaluation, and social skill. *Journal of Personality, 63*, 315–339.

Miller, R. S. (1997). Inattentive and contented: Relationship commitment and attention to alternatives. *Journal of Personality and Social Psychology, 73*, 758–766.

Miller, R. S., & Schlenker, B. R. (1985). Egotism in group members: Public and private attributions of responsibility for group performance. *Social Psychology Quarterly, 48*, 85–89.

Milliken, F. J., & Martins, L. L. (1996). Searching for common threads: Understanding the multiple effects of diversity in organizational groups. *Academy of Management Review, 21*, 402–433.

Mills, J., & Clark, M. S. (1982). Exchange and communal relationships. In L. Wheeler (Ed.), *Review of personality and social psychology* (Vol. 3, pp. 121–144). Beverly Hills, CA: Sage.

Mills, J., & Clark, M. S. (1994). Communal and exchange relationships: Controversies and research. In R. Erber & R. Gilmour (Eds.), *Theoretical frameworks for personal relationships* (pp. 29–42). Hillsdale, NJ: Erlbaum.

Minard, R. D. (1952). Race relationships in the Pocahontas coal field. *Journal of Social Issues, 8*, 29–44.

Mischel, W. (1996). From good intentions to willpower. In P. M. Gollwitzer & J. A. Bargh (Eds.), *The psychology of action: Linking cognition and motivation to action* (pp. 197–218). New York: Guilford.

Mischel, W., & Shoda, Y. (1995). A cognitive-affective system theory of personality: Reconceptualizing situations, dispositions, dynamics, and invariance in personality structure. *Psychological Review, 102*, 246–268.

Mischel, W., Cantor, N., & Feldman, S. (1996). In E. T. Higgins & A. W. Kruglanski (Eds.), *Social psychology: Handbook of basic principles* (pp. 329–360). New York: Guilford.

Mitchell, C. (1999). Negotiation as problem solving: Challenging the dominant metaphor. *Peace and Conflict: Journal of Peace Psychology, 5*, 219–224.

Mitchell, G., & Maple, T. L. (1985). Dominance in nonhuman primates. In S. L. Ellyson & J. F. Dovidio (Eds.), *Power, dominance, and nonverbal behavior* (pp. 49–66). New York: Springer-Verlag.

Moffitt, T. E. (1993). Adolescence-limited and life-course-persistent antisocial behavior: A developmental taxonomy. *Psychological Review, 100*, 674–701.

Moghaddam, F. M., Taylor, D. M., & Wright, S. C. (1993). *Social psychology in cross-cultural perspective.* New York: W. H. Freeman.

Monaghan, E., & Glickman, S. (1992). Hormones and aggressiveness behavior. In J. Becker, S. Breedlove, & D. Crews (Eds.), *Behavioral endocrinology* (pp. 261–285). Cambridge, MA: MIT Press.

Monteith, M. (1993). Self-regulation of prejudiced responses: Implications for progress in prejudice-reduction efforts. *Journal of Personality and Social Psychology, 65*, 469–485.

Monteith, M. J., Sherman, J. W., & Devine, P. G. (1998). Suppression as a stereotype control strategy. *Personality and Social Psychology Review, 2*, 63–82.

Moore, M. M. (1985). Nonverbal courtship patterns in women: Context and consequences. *Ethology and sociobiology, 6*, 237–247.

Moreland, R. L. (1987). The formation of small groups. In C. Hendrick (Ed.), *Group processes* (pp. 80–110). Newbury Park, CA: Sage.

Morganthau, T., & Annin, P. (1997, June 16). Should McVeigh die? *Newsweek*, pp. 20–27.

Morier, D., & Seroy, C. (1994). The effects of interpersonal expectancies on men's self-presentation of gender-role attitudes to women. *Sex Roles, 31*, 493–504.

Morling, B., Kitayama, S., & Miyamoto, Y. (1999, August). *Social practices foster efficacy in the U.S. and relatedness in Japan.* Paper presented at the annual convention of the American Psychological Association, Boston, Massachusetts.

Morris, D. P., Soroker, M. A., & Burruss, G. (1954). Follow-up studies of shy, withdrawn children. I. Evaluation of later adjustment. *American Journal of Orthopsychiatry, 24*, 743–754.

Morris, M. W., & Peng, K. (1994). Culture and cause: American and Chinese attributions for social and physical events. *Journal of Personality and Social Psychology, 67*, 949–971.

Morris, M. W., Podolny, J. M., & Ariel, S. (1998a). *The ties that bind: A cross-national comparison of the determinants of employee obligations to coworkers.* Unpublished manuscript. Graduate School of Business, Stanford University, Stanford, CA.

Morris, M. W., Podolny, J. M., & Ariel, S. (1998b). *Culture and informal work relationships: Cultural norms, social networks, and obligations among employees of North American, Chinese, German, and Spanish operations of a multi-national consumer bank.* Unpublished manuscript. Graduate School of Business, Stanford University, Stanford, CA.

Morris, M. W., Podolny, J. M., & Ariel, S. (2001). Culture, norms, and obligations: Cross-national differences in patterns of interpersonal norms and felt obligations toward co-workers. In W. Wosinska, R. B. Cialdini, D. W. Barrett, & J. Reykowski (Eds.), *The practice of social influence in multiple cultures* (pp. 97–124). Mahwah, NJ: Erlbaum.

Morris, R. (1994). *New worlds from fragments.* Boulder, CO: Westview.

Morris, S. C., III, & Rosen, S. (1973). Effects of felt adequacy and opportunity to reciprocate on help-seeking. *Journal of Experimental Social Psychology, 9*, 265–276.

Morris, S. J., & Kanfer, F. H. (1983). Altruism and depression *Personality and Social Psychology Bulletin, 9*, 567–577.

Morris, W. N., & Miller, R. S. (1975). The effects of consensus-breaking and consensus-preempting partners on reduction of conformity. *Journal of Experimental Social Psychology, 11*, 215–223.

Morrison, J. D. (1993). *Group composition and creative performance.* Unpublished doctoral dissertation, University of Tulsa, Tulsa, OK.

Moscovici, S., & Zavalloni, M. (1969). The group as a polarizer of attitudes. *Journal of Personality and Social Psychology, 12*, 125–135.

Moscovici, S., Lage, E., & Naffrechoux, M. (1969). Influence of a consistent minority on the responses of a majority in a color perception task. *Sociometry, 32*, 365–380.

Moscovici, S., Mucchi-Faina, A., & Maass, A. (1994). *Minority influence.* Chicago: Nelson-Hall.

Moskowitz, G. B. (1993). Individual differences in social categorization: The influence of Personal Need for Structure on spontaneous trait inferences. *Journal of Personality and Social Psychology, 65*, 132–142.

Moskowitz, G. B., & Roman, R. J. (1992). Spontaneous trait inferences as self-generated primes: Implications for conscious social judgment. *Journal of Personality and Social Psychology, 62*, 728–738.

Moskowitz, G. B., Salomon, A. R., & Taylor, C. M. (2000). Preconsciously controlling stereotyping: Implicitly activated egalitarian goals prevent the activation of stereotypes. *Social Cognition, 18*, 151–177.

Mount, M. K., & Muchinsky, P. M. (1978). Concurrent validation of Holland's hexagonal model with occupational workers. *Journal of Vocational Behavior, 13*, 348–354.

Muehlenhard, C. L. (2000). "Categories and sexuality." *Journal of Sex Research, 37*, 101–107.

Mugny, G. (1982). *The power of minorities.* New York: Academic Press.

Mullen, B. (1983). Operationalizing the effect of the group on the individual: A self-attention perspective. *Journal of Experimental Social Psychology, 19*, 295–322.

Mullen, B. (1986). Atrocity as a function of lynch mob composition: A self-attention perspective. *Personality and Social Psychology Bulletin, 12*, 187–197.

Mullen, B., & Copper, C. (1994). The relation between group cohesiveness and performance: An integration. *Psychological Bulletin, 115*, 210–227.

Mullen, B., & Hu, L. T. (1989). Perceptions of ingroup and outgroup variability: A meta-analytic integration. *Basic and Applied Social Psychology, 10*, 233–252.

Mullen, B., & Riordan, C. A. (1988). Self-serving attributions for performance in naturalistic settings: A meta-analytic review. *Journal of Applied Social Psychology, 18*, 3–22.

Mullen, B., Anthony, T., Salas, E., & Driskell, J. E. (1994). Group cohesiveness and quality of decision making: An integration of tests of the groupthink hypothesis. *Small Group Research, 25*, 189–204.

Mullen, B., Atkins, J. L., Champion, D. S., Edwards, C., Hardy, D., Story, J. E., & Vanderklok, M. (1985). The false-consensus effect: A meta-analysis of 115 hypothesis tests. *Journal of Experimental Social Psychology, 21*, 262–283.

Mullen, B., Brown, R., & Smith, C. (1992). Ingroup bias as a function of salience, relevance, and status: An integration. *European Journal of Social Psychology, 22*, 103–122.

Mullen, B., Salas, E., & Driskell, J. E. (1989). Salience, motivation, and artifact as contributions to the relation between participation rate and leadership. *Journal of Experimental Social Psychology, 25*, 545–559.

Mullin, C. (1989). *Error of judgment: The truth about the Birmingham bombers.* Dublin: Poolberg Press.

Munro, G. D., & Ditto, P. H. (1997). Biased assimilation, attitude polarization, and affect reactions to stereotype-relevant scientific information. *Personality and Social Psychology Bulletin, 23*, 636–653.

Munro, R. L., Hulefeld, R., Rodgers, J. M., Tomeo, D. L., & Yamazaki, S. K. (2000). Aggression among children in four cultures. *Cross-cultural Research, 34*, 3.25.

Muraven, M., & Baumeister, R. F. (2000). Self-regulation and depletion of limited resources: Does self-control resemble a muscle? *Psychological Bulletin, 126*, 247–259.

Murdock G. P. (1923/1970). Rank and potlatch among the Haida. In *Yale University publications in anthropology* (Vol. 13). New Haven, CT: Human Relations Area Files Press.

Murdock, G. P. (1949). *Social structure.* New York: MacMillan.

Murray, H. A. (1938). *Explorations in personality.* New York: Oxford University Press.

Murray, S. L., & Holmes, J. G. (1997). A leap of faith? Positive illusions in romantic relationships. *Personality and Social Psychology Bulletin, 23*, 586–604.

Murray, S. L., Holmes, J. G., & Griffin, D. W. (2000). Self-esteem and the quest for felt security: How perceived regard regulates attachment processes. *Journal of Personality & Social Psychology, 78*, 478–498.

Mussweiler, T., & Strack, F. (2000). The use of category and exemplar knowledge in the solution of anchoring tasks. *Journal of Personality and Social Psychology, 78*, 1038–1052.

Myers, D. G. (1975). Discussion-induced attitude polarization. *Human Relations, 28*, 699–714.

Myers, D. G. (1978). Polarizing effects of social comparison. *Journal of Experimental Social Psychology, 14*, 554–563.

Myers, D. G. (2000). The funds, friends, and faith of happy people. *American Psychologist, 55*, 56–67.

Myers, D. G., & Bishop, G. D. (1970). Discussion effects on racial attitudes. *Science, 169*, 778–789.

Myrdal, G. (1944). *An American dilemma: The negro problem and modern democracy.* New York: Random House.

Naccarato, M. E. (1988). *The impact of need for structure on stereotyping and discrimination.* Unpublished masters thesis, University of Waterloo, Ontario.

Nadler, A. (1986). Self esteem and the seeking and receiving of help: Theoretical and empirical perspectives. In B. Maher & W. Maher (Eds.), *Progress in experimental personality research* (Vol. 14, pp. 115–163). New York: Academic Press.

Nadler, A. (1991). Help-seeking behavior: Psychological costs and instrumental benefits. In M. S. Clark (Ed.), *Review of personality and social psychology* (Vol. 12, pp. 290–311). Newbury Park, CA: Sage.

Nadler, A., & Fisher, J. D. (1986). The role of threat to self-esteem and perceived control in recipient reaction to help: Theory development and empirical validation. In L. Berkowitz (Ed.), *Advances in experimental social psychology* (Vol. 19, pp. 81–122). San Diego, CA: Academic Press.

Nadler, A., Maler, S., & Friedman, A. (1984). Effects of helper's sex, subject's sex, subject's androgyny and self-evaluation on males' and females' willingness to seek and receive help. *Sex Roles, 10*, 327–339.

Nail, P. R., MacDonald, G., & Levy, D. A. (2000). Proposal of a four-dimensional model of social response. *Psychological Bulletin, 126*, 454–470.

Nail, P. R., & Van Leeuwen, M. D. (1993). An analysis and restructuring of the diamond model of social response. *Personality and Social Psychology Bulletin, 19*, 106–116.

Nakao, K. (1987). Analyzing sociometric preferences: An example of Japanese and U.S. business groups. *Journal of Social Behavior and Personality, 2*, 523–534.

Nathanson, S. (1987). *An eye for an eye? The morality of punishing by death.* Totowa, NJ: Rowman & Littlefield.

Neely, J. H. (1991). Semantic priming effects in visual word recognition: A selective review of current findings and theories. In D. Besner & G. W. Humphreys (Eds.), *Basic processes in reading: Visual word recognition* (pp. 264–336). Hillsdale, NJ: Erlbaum.

Neidert, G. P., & Linder, D. E. (1990). Avoiding social traps: Some conditions that maintain adherence to restricted consumption. *Social Behaviour, 5*, 261–284.

Nelson, L. J., & Klutas, K. (2000). The distinctiveness effect in social interaction: Creation of a self-fulfilling prophecy. *Personality and Social Psychology Bulletin, 26*, 126–135.

Nelson, L. L, & Milburn, T. W. (1999). Relationships between problem-solving competencies and militaristic attitudes: Implications for peace education. *Peace and Conflict: Journal of Peace Psychology, 5*, 149–168.

Nemeth, C. J. (1986). Differential contributions of majority and minority influence. *Psychological Review, 93*, 23–32.

Nemeth, C. J. (1992). Minority dissent as a stimulant to group performance. In S. Worchel, W. Wood, & J. A. Simpson (Eds.), *Group process and productivity* (pp. 95–111). Newbury Park, CA: Sage.

Nemeth, C. J. (1994). The value of minority dissent. In S. Moscovici, A. Mucchi-Faina, & A. Maass (Eds.), *Minority influence.* Chicago: Nelson-Hall.

Nemeth, C. J., & Wachtler, J. (1974). Creating perceptions of consistency and confidence: A necessary condition for minority influence. *Sociometry, 37*, 529–540.

Nemeth, C. J., Mayseless, O., Sherman, J., & Brown, Y. (1990). Improving recall by exposure to consistent dissent. *Journal of Personality and Social Psychology, 58*, 429–437.

Neuberg, S. L. (1989). The goal of forming accurate impressions during social interactions: Attenuating the impact of negative expectancies. *Journal of Personality and Social Psychology, 56*, 374–386.

Neuberg, S. L. (1996). Social motives and expectancy-tinged social interactions. In R. M. Sorrentino & E. T. Higgins (Eds.), *Handbook of motivation and cognition: The interpersonal context* (Vol. 3, pp. 225–261). New York: Guilford.

Neuberg, S. L., & Fiske, S. T. (1987). Motivational influences on impression formation: Outcome dependency, accuracy-driven attention, and individuating processes. *Journal of Personality and Social Psychology, 53*, 431–444.

Neuberg, S. L., & Newsom, J. T. (1993). Personal Need for Structure: Individual differences in the desire for simple structure. *Journal of Personality and Social Psychology, 65*, 113–131.

Neuberg, S. L., Smith, D. M., Hoffman, J. C., & Russell, F. J. (1994). When we observe stigmatized and "normal" individuals interacting: Stigma by association. *Personality and Social Psychology Bulletin, 20*, 196–209.

Neumann, R. (2000). The causal influences of attributions on emotions: A procedural priming approach. *Psychological Science, 11*, 179–182.

Newcomb, T. M. (1961). *The acquaintance process.* New York: Holt, Rinehart and Winston.

Newcomb, T. M., Koenig, K. E., Flacks, R., & Warwick, D. P. (1967). *Persistence and change: Bennington College and its students after twenty-five years.* New York: Wiley.

Newman, L. S. (1991). Why are traits inferred spontaneously? A developmental approach. *Social Cognition, 9*, 221–253.

"News." (1988). *Stanford Business School Magazine, 56*, 3.

Nezlek, J. B. (1993). The stability of social interaction. *Journal of Personality and Social Psychology, 65*, 930–941.

Niedenthal, P. M. (1990). Implicit perception of affective information. *Journal of Experimental Social Psychology, 26*, 505–527.

Niedenthal, P. M., Tangney, J. P., & Gavanski, I. (1994). "If only I weren't" versus "If only I hadn't": Distinguishing shame and guilt in counterfactual thinking. *Journal of Personality and Social Psychology, 67*, 585–595.

Niemann, Y. F., Jennings, L., Rozelle, R. M., Baxter, J. C., & Sullivan, E. (1994). Use of free responses and cluster analysis to determine stereotypes of eight groups. *Personality and Social Psychology Bulletin, 20*, 379–390.

Nisbett, R. E. (1993). Violence and U.S. regional culture. *American Psychologist, 48*, 441–449.

Nisbett, R. E., & Ross, L. (1980). Human inference. Englewood Cliffs, NJ: Prentice Hall. Norrander, B. (1997). The independence gap and the gender gap. *Public Opinion Quarterly, 61*, 464–476.

Nisbett, R. E., & Wilson, T. (1977). Telling more than we can know: Verbal reports on mental processes. *Psychological Review, 84*, 231–259.

Nisbett, R. E., Polly, G., & Lang, S. (1995). Homicide and regional U.S. culture. In R. B. Ruback & N. A. Weiner (Eds.), *Interpersonal violent behaviors* (pp. 135–151). New York: Springer.

Nixon, R. M. (1978). *RN: The memoirs of Richard Nixon.* New York: Simon & Schuster.

Noel, J.G., Wann, D. L., & Branscombe, N. R. (1995). Peripheral ingroup membership status and public negativity toward outgroups. *Journal of Personality and Social Psychology, 68*, 127–137.

Norenzayan, A., & Nisbett, R. E. (2000). Culture and causal cognition. *Current Directions in Psychological Science, 9*, 132–135.

Norrander, B. (1997). The independence gap and the gender gap. *Public Opinion Quarterly, 61*, 464–476.

Notarius, C., & Markman, H. (1993). *We can work it out: Making sense of marital conflict.* New York: G. P. Putnam's Sons.

Notarius, C., & Pellegrini, D. (1984). Marital processes as stressors and stress mediators: Implications for marital repair. In S. Duck (Ed.), *Personal Relationship, Vol. 5: Repairing Personal Relationships* (pp. 67–88). London: Academic Press.

Novaco, R. W. (1975). *Anger control: The development and evaluation of an experimental treatment.* Lexington, MA: Lexington Books.

Novaco, R. W. (1995). Clinical problems of anger and its assessment and regulation through a stress coping skills approach. In W. O'Connor & L. Krasner (Eds.), *Handbook of Psychological Skills Training: Clinical techniques and applications* (pp. 320–338). Boston: Allyn & Bacon.

Novak, D. W., & Lerner, M. J. (1968). Rejection as a consequence of perceived similarity. *Journal of Personality and Social Psychology, 9*, 147–152.

Nowak, A., & Vallacher, R. R. (1998). *Dynamical social psychology.* New York: Guilford.

Nowak, A., Vallacher, R. R., Tesser, A., & Borkowski, W. (2000). Society of self: The emergence of collective properties in self-structure. *Psychological Bulletin, 107*, 39–61.

Nowak, M. A., & Sigmund, K. (1998). Evolution of indirect reciprocity by image scoring. *Nature, 393*, 573–576.

Nowicki, S., & Manheim, S. (1991). Interpersonal complementarity and time of interaction in female relationships. *Journal of Research in Personality*, 322–333.

Nuttin, J. M., Jr. (1985). Narcissism beyond gestalt and awareness: The name letter effect. *European Journal of Social Psychology, 15*, 353–361.

Nyquist, L. V., & Spence, J. T. (1986). Effects of dispositional dominance and sex role expectations on leadership behaviors. *Journal of Personality and Social Psychology, 50*, 87–93.

O'Brian, M. E., & Jacks, J. Z. (2000, February). *Values, self, and resistance to persuasion.* Poster session presented at the annual meeting of the Society of Personality and Social Psychology, Nashville, Tennessee.

O'Brien, J. A. (1993, September 23). Mother's killing still unresolved, but Peter Reilly puts past behind. *The Hartford Courant*, p. A1.

O'Reilly, C. A., Chatman, J., & Caldwell, D. F. (1991). People and organizational culture: A profile comparison approach to assessing person-organization fit. *Academy of Management Journal, 34*, 487–516.

Oakes, P. J., & Turner, J. C. (1980). Social categorization and intergroup behaviour: Does minimal intergroup discrimination make social identity more positive? *European Journal of Social Psychology, 10*, 295–301.

Oakes, P. J., Haslam, S. A., & Turner, J. C. (1994). *Stereotyping and social reality.* Oxford: Blackwell.

Ofshe, R. J., & Leo, R. A. (1997). The social psychology of police interrogation: The theory and classification of false confessions. *Studies in Law, Politics and Society, 16*, 189–251.

Ogden, C. (1990). *Maggie: An intimate portrait of a woman in power.* New York: Simon and Schuster.

Ogilvie, D. M. (1987). The undesired self: A neglected variable in personality research. *Journal of Personality and Social Psychology, 52*, 379–385.

Oishi, S., Wyer, R. S., & Colcombe, S. J. (2000). Cultural variation in the use of current life satisfaction to predict the future. *Journal of Personality & Social Psychology, 78*, 434–445.

Okimoto, D. I., & Rohlen, T. P. (1988). *Inside the Japanese system: readings on contemporary society and political economy.* Stanford, CA: Stanford University Press.

Olds, J. M., & Milner, P. M. (1954). Positive reinforcement produced by electrical stimulation of the septal area and other areas of the rat brain. *Journal of Comparative and Physiological Psychology, 47*, 419–427.

Oliker, S. J. (1989). *Best friends and marriage: Exchange among women.* Berkeley: University of California Press.

Oliner, S. P., & Oliner, P. M. (1988). *The altruistic personality: Rescuers of Jews in Nazi Europe.* New York: The Free Press.

Oliver, M. B., & Hyde, J. S. (1993). Gender differences in sexuality: A meta-analysis. *Psychological Bulletin, 114*, 29–51.

Olweus, D. (1978). *Aggression in schools.* New York: Wiley.

Olweus, D. (1991). Bully/victim problems among school children: Basic facts and effects of a school-based intervention program. In D. Pepler & K. Rubin (Eds.), *The development and treatment of childhood aggression* (pp. 411–448). Hillsdale, NJ: Erlbaum.

Olzak, S. (1992). *The dynamics of ethnic competition and conflict.* Stanford, CA: Stanford University Press.

Orive, R. (1988). Social projection and social comparison of opinions. *Journal of Personality and Social Psychology, 54*, 953–964.

Osborne, J. W. (1995). Academics, self-esteem, and race: A look at the underlying assumptions of the disidentification hypothesis. *Personality and Social Psychology Bulletin, 21*, 449–455.

Osborne, R. E., & Gilbert, D. T. (1992). The preoccupational hazards of social life. *Journal of Personality and Social Psychology, 62*, 219–228.

Osgood, C. E. (1962). *An alternative to war or surrender.* Urbana: University of Illinois Press.

Oskamp, S. (2000). A sustainable future for humanity: How can psychology help? *American Psychologist, 55,* 496–508.

Ostrom, T. M., & Sedikides, C. (1992). Out-group homogeneity effects in natural and minimal groups. *Psychological Bulletin, 112,* 536–552.

Otta, E., Queiroz, R. D., Campos, L. D., daSilva, M., & Silveira, M. T. (1999). Age differences between spouses in a Brazilian marriage sample. *Evolution and Human Behavior, 20,* 99–104.

Ottati, V., & Lee, Y.-T. (1995). Accuracy: A neglected component of stereotype research.. In Y.-T. Lee, L. J. Jussim, & C. R. McCauley (Eds.), *Stereotype accuracy: Toward appreciating group differences* (pp. 29–59). Washington, DC: American Psychological Association.

Otten, C. A., Penner, L. A., & Altabe, M. N. (1991). An examination of therapists' and college students' willingness to help a psychologically distressed person. *Journal of Social and Clinical Psychology, 10,* 102–120.

Otten, C. A., Penner, L. A., & Waugh, G. (1988). What are friends for: The determinants of psychological helping. *Journal of Social and Clinical Psychology,* 7, 34–41.

Otten, S., & Wentura, D. (1999). About the impact of automaticity in the Minimal Group Paradigm: Evidence from affective priming tasks. *European Journal of Social Psychology, 29,* 1049–1071.

Ovitz and out at Disney (1996, December 13). *New York Daily News,* p. 7.

Ovitz, Hollywood power broker, resigns from no. 2 job at Disney (1996, December 13). *New York Times,* 1.

Owens, L., Shute, R., & Slee, P. (2000). "Guess what I just heard!": Indirect aggression among teenage girls in Australia. *Aggressive Behavior, 26,* 67–83.

Ozer, D. J. (1986). *Consistency in personality: A methodological framework.* New York: Springer-Verlag.

Padilla, A. M. (1994). Bicultural development: A theoretical and empirical examination. In R. G. Malgady & O. Rodriguez (Eds.), *Theoretical and conceptual issues in Hispanic mental health* (pp. 20–51). Malabar, FL: Krieger.

Page, B. I., Shapiro, R. Y., & Dempsey, G. (1987). What moves public opinion? *American Political Science Review, 81,* 23–43.

Paicheler, G. (1976). Norms and attitude change I: Polarization and styles of behaviour. *European Journal of Social Psychology, 6,* 405–427.

Paicheler, G. (1977). Norms and attitude change II: The phenomenon of bipolarization. *European Journal of Social Psychology,* 7, 5–14.

Palmer, C. T. (1993). Anger, aggression, and humor in Newfoundland floor hockey: An evolutionary analysis. *Aggressive Behavior, 19,* 167–173.

Paloutzian, R. F., & Ellison, C. W. (1982). Loneliness, spiritual well-being and the quality of life. In L. A. Peplau & D. Perlman (Eds.), *Loneliness: A sourcebook of current theory, research, and therapy* (pp. 224–237). New York: Wiley.

Pandey, J. (1981). A note on social power through ingratiation among workers. *Journal of Occupational Psychology, 54,* 65–67.

Pandey, J., & Rastagi, R. (1979). Machiavellianism and ingratiation. *Journal of Social Psychology, 108,* 221–225.

Panskepp, J., Siviy, S. M., & Normansell, L. A. (1985). Brain opioids and social emotions. In M. Reite & T. Field (Eds.), *The psychobiology of attachment and separation* (pp. 3–50). London: Academic Press.

Park, B., Judd, C. M., & Ryan, C. S. (1991). Social categorization and the representation of variability information. In W. Stroebe & M. Hewstone (Eds.), *European review of social psychology* (Vol. 2, pp. 211–245). New York: Wiley.

Park, J., & Banaji, M. R. (2000). Mood and heuristics: The influence of happy and sad states on sensitivity and bias in stereotyping. *Journal of Personality and Social Psychology, 78,* 1005–1023.

Parke, R. D., Berkowitz, L., Leyens, J. P., West, S. G., & Sebastian, J. (1977). Some effects of violent and nonviolent movies on the behavior of juvenile delinquents. In L. Berkowitz (Ed.), *Advances in experimental social psychology* (Vol. 10., pp. 135–172). New York: Academic Press.

Parkinson, B., Briner, R. B., Reynolds, S., & Totterdell, P. (1995). Time frames for mood: Relations between momentary and generalized ratings of affect. *Personality and Social Psychology Bulletin, 21,* 331–339.

Parks, C. D., & Vu, A. D. (1994). Social dilemma behavior of individuals from highly individualistic and collectivist cultures. *Journal of Conflict Resolution, 38,* 708–718.

Parks, C. D., Henager, R. F., & Scamahorn, S. D. (1996). Trust and reactions to messages of intent in social dilemmas. *Journal of Conflict Resolution, 40,* 134–151.

Pashler, H. (1994). Dual-task interference in simple tasks: Data and theory. *Psychological Bulletin, 116,* 220–244.

Pataki, S. P., Shapiro, C., & Clark, M. S. (1994). Children's acquisition of appropriate norms for friendships and acquaintances. *Journal of Personal and Personal Relationships, 11,* 427–442.

Patterson, G. R. (1997). Performance models for parenting: A social interactional perspective (pp. 193–226). In J. E. Gruser & L. Kuczynski (Eds.) *Parenting and children's internalization of values: A handbook of contemporary theory.* New York: John Wiley & Sons.

Patterson, G. R., Chamberlain, P., & Reid, J. B. (1982). A comparative evaluation of parent training procedures. *Behavior Therapy, 13,* 638–650.

Patterson, M. P. (1983). *Nonverbal behavior: A functional perspective.* New York: Springer-Verlag.

Paul, L., Foss, M. A., & Galloway, J. (1993). Sexual jealousy in young women and men: Aggressive responsiveness to partner and rival. *Aggressive Behavior, 19,* 401–420.

Paulhus, D. L. (1993). Bypassing the will: The automatization of affirmations. In D. M. Wegner & J. W. Pennebaker (Eds.), *Handbook of mental control* (pp. 573–587). Englewood Cliffs, NJ: Prentice-Hall.

Paulhus, D. L., Martin, C. L., & Murphy, G. K. (1992). Some effects of arousal on sex stereotyping. *Personality and Social Psychology Bulletin, 18,* 325–330.

Pawlowski, B., & Dunbar, R. I. M. (1999). Withholding age as putative deception in mate search tactics. *Evolution & Human Behavior, 20:* 53–69.

Pearce, P. L., & Amato, P. R. (1980). A taxonomy of helping: A multidimensional scaling analysis. *Social Psychology Quarterly, 43,* 363–371.

Pedersen, D., & Van Boven, S. (1997, December 15). Tragedy in a small place. *Newsweek,* pp. 30–31.

Pedersen, W. C., Gonzales, C., & Miller, N. (2000). The moderating effect of trivial triggering provocation on displaced aggression. *Journal of Personality & Social Psychology, 78,* 913–927.

Pelham, B. W. (1991). On confidence and consequence: The certainty and importance of self-knowledge. *Journal of Personality and Social Psychology, 60,* 518–530.

Pelham, B. W. (1993). On the highly positive thoughts of the highly depressed. In R. Baumeister (Ed.), *Self-esteem: The puzzle of low self-regard* (pp. 183–200). New York: Plenum.

Pelled, L. H. (1996). Demographic diversity, conflict, and work group outcomes: An intervening process theory. *Organization Science, 7,* 615–631.

Pelz, D.C. (1956). Some social factors related to performance in a research organization. *Administrative Science Quarterly, 1,* 310–325.

Pemberton, M. B., Insko, C. A., & Schopler, J. (1996). Memory for and experience of differential competitive behavior of individuals and groups. *Journal of Personality and Social Psychology, 71,* 953–966.

Pendry, L. F., & Macrae, C. N. (1994). Stereotypes and mental life: The case of the motivated but thwarted tactician. *Journal of Experimental Social Psychology, 30,* 303–325.

Pendry, L. F., & Macrae, C. N. (1996). What the disinterested perceiver overlooks: Goal-directed social categorization. *Personality and Social Psychology Bulletin, 22,* 249–256.

Pennebaker, J. W. (1982). *The psychology of physical symptoms.* New York: Springer-Verlag.

Pennebaker, J. W., Barger, S. D., & Tiebout, J. (1989). Disclosure of traumas and health among holocaust survivors. *Psychosomatic Medicine, 51,* 577–589.

Pennebaker, J. W., Hughes, C. F., & O'Heeron, R. C. (1987). The psychophysiology of confession: Linking inhibitory and psychosomatic processes. *Journal of Personality and Social Psychology, 52,* 781–793.

Penner, L. A., Dertke, M. C., & Achenbach, C. J. (1973). The flash system: A field study of altruism. *Journal of Applied Social Psychology, 3,* 362–373.

Penner, L. A., & Finkelstein, M. A. (1998). Dispositional and structural determinants of volunteerism. *Journal of Personality and Social Psychology, 74,* 525–537.

Peplau, L. A., Russell, D., & Heim, M. (1979). The experience of loneliness. In I. H. Frieze, D. Bar-Tal, & J. S. Carroll (Eds.), *New approaches to social problems: Applications of attribution theory.* San Francisco: Jossey-Bass.

Perdue, C. W., Dovidio, J. F., Gurtman, M. B., & Tyler, R. B. (1990). Us and them: Social categorization and the process of intergroup bias. *Journal of Personality and Social Psychology, 59,* 475–486.

Perdue, C. W., & Gurtman, M. B. (1990). Evidence for the automaticity of ageism. *Journal of Experimental Social Psychology, 26,* 199–216.

Perloff, R. M. (1989). Ego-involvement and the third-person effect of televised news coverage. *Communication Research, 16,* 236–262.

Perloff, R. M. (1993). *The dynamics of persuasion.* Hillsdale, N.J.: Erlbaum.

Perry, L. C., Perry, D. G., & Weiss, R. J. (1986). Age differences in children's beliefs about whether altruism makes the actor feel good. *Social Cognition, 4,* 263–269.

Pervin, L. A. (1967). Satisfaction and perceived self-environment similarity: A semantic differential study of student-college interaction. *Journal of Personality, 35,* 623–634.

Pervin, L. A. (1992). Traversing the individual-environment landscape: A personal odyssey. In W. B. Walsh, K. H. Craik, & R. H. Price (Eds.), *Person-environment psychology: Models and perspectives* (pp. 71–88). Hillsdale, NJ: Erlbaum.

Pervin, L. A., & Rubin, D. B. (1967). Student dissatisfaction with college and the college dropout: A transactional approach. *Journal of Social Psychology, 72,* 285–295.

Peterson, B. E., Doty, R. M. & Winter, D. G. (1993). Authoritarianism and attitudes towards contemporary issues. *Personality and Social Psychology Bulletin, 19,* 174–184.

Petrie, K. J., Booth, R. J., & Pennebaker, J. W. (1998). The immunological effects of thought suppression. *Journal of Personality and Social Psychology, 75,* 1264–1272.

Pettigrew, T. F. (1958). Personality and sociocultural factors in intergroup attitudes: A cross-national comparison. *Conflict Resolution, 2,* 29–42.

Pettigrew, T. F. (1973). Racism and the mental health of white Americans:

A social psychological view. In C. V. Willie, B. M. Kramer, & B. S. Brown (Eds.), *Racism and mental health* (pp. 269–298). Pittsburgh: University of Pittsburgh Press.

Pettigrew, T. F. (1979). The ultimate attribution error: Extending Allport's cognitive analysis of prejudice. *Personality and Social Psychology Bulletin, 5*, 461–476.

Pettigrew, T. F. (1997). Generalized intergroup contact effects on prejudice. *Personality and Socal Psychology Bulletin, 23*, 173–185.

Pettigrew, T. F. (1998). Intergroup contact theory. *Annual Review of Psychology, 49*, 65–85.

Pettigrew, T. F., & Meertens, R. W. (1995). Subtle and blatant prejudice in western Europe. *European Journal of Social Psychology, 25*, 57–75.

Pettigrew, T. F., & Tropp, L. R. (2000). Does intergroup contact reduce prejudice? Recent meta-analytic findings. In S. Oskamp (Ed), *Reducing prejudice and discrimination. The Claremont Symposium on Applied Social Psychology* (pp. 93–114). Mahwah, NJ: Erlbaum.

Petty, R. E., & Cacioppo, J. T. (1979). Issue involvement can increase or decrease persuasion by enhancing message-relevant cognitive responses. *Journal of Personality and Social Psychology, 37*, 1915–1926.

Petty, R. E., & Cacioppo, J. T. (1984). The effects of involvement on responses to argument quantity and quality: Central and peripheral routes to persuasion. *Journal of Personality and Social Psychology, 46*, 69–81.

Petty, R. E., & Cacioppo, J. T. (1986). *Communication and persuasion: Central and peripheral routes to attitude change.* New York: Springer-Verlag.

Petty, R. E., Cacioppo, J. J., & Goldman, R. (1981). Personal involvement as a determinant of argument-based persuasion. *Journal of Personality and Social Psychology, 41*, 847–855.

Petty, R. E., & Krosnick, J. A. (1996). *Attitude strength: Antecedents and consequences.* Hillsdale, NJ: Erlbaum.

Petty, R. E., & Wegener, D. T. (1998). Attitude change: Multiple roles for persuasion variables. In D. T. Gilbert, S. T. Fiske, & G. Lindzey (Eds.), *Handbook of social psychology* (4th ed.) (Vol. 1, pp. 323–390). New York: McGraw-Hill/Oxford University Press.

Petty, R. E., & Wegener, D. T. (1998). Matching versus mismatching attitude functions: Implications for scrutiny of persuasive messages. *Personality and Social Psychology Bulletin, 24*, 227–240.

Petty, R. E., Wells, G. L., & Brock, T. C. (1976). Distraction can enhance or reduce yielding to propaganda. *Journal of Personality and Social Psychology, 34*, 874–884.

Pfeffer, J. (1998). Understanding organizations: Concepts and controversies. In D. T. Gilbert, S. T. Fiske, & G. Lindzey (Eds.) *Handbook of Social Psychology* (4th ed., Vol. 2, pp. 733–777). New York: McGraw-Hill.

Phillips, D. P. (1985). Natural experiments on the effects of mass media violence on fatal aggression: Strengths and weaknesses of a new approach. In L. Berkowitz (Ed.), *Advances in experimental social psychology* Vol. 19, (pp. 207–250) Orlando, FL: Academic Press.

Phillips, D. P. (1989). Recent advances in suicidology: The study of imitative suicide. In R. F. W. Diekstra, R. Maris, S. Platt, A. Schmidtke, & G. Sonneck (Eds.), *Suicide and its prevention: The role of attitude and imitation* (pp. 299–312). Leiden: E. J. Brill.

Phinney, J., & Devich-Navarro (1997). Variations in bicultural identification among African American and Mexican American adolescents. *Journal of Research on Adolescence, 7*, 3–32.

Pietromonaco, P., & Feldman-Barrett, L. (1997). Working models of attachment and daily social interactions. *Journal of Personality and Social Psychology, 73*, 1409–1423.

Piliavin, J. A., & Callero, P. L. (1991). *Giving blood: The development of an altruistic identity.* Baltimore: Johns Hopkins University Press.

Piliavin, J. A., & Piliavin, I. M. (1972). Effect of blood on reactions to a victim. *Journal of Personality and Social Psychology, 23*, 353–361.

Piliavin, J. A., & Unger, R. K. (1985). The helpful but helpless female: Myth or reality? In V. O'Leary, R. K. Unger, & B. S. Wallston (Eds.), *Women, gender and social psychology* (pp. 149–186). Hillsdale, NJ: Erlbaum.

Piliavin, J. A., Dovidio, J. F., Gaertner, S. L., & Clark, R. D. III (1981). *Emergency intervention.* New York: Academic Press.

Pin, E. J., & Turndorf, J. (1990). Staging one's ideal self. In D. Brisset & C. Edgley (Eds.), *Life as theatre* (pp. 163–181). Hawthorne, NY: Aldine de Gruyter.

Pinel, E. (1999). Stigma consciousness: The psychological legacy of social stereotypes. *Journal of Personality and Social Psychology, 76*, 114–128.

Pinker, S. (1997). *How the mind works.* New York: Norton.

Pittam, J. (1994). *Voice in social interaction: An interdisciplinary approach.* Thousand Oaks, CA: Sage.

Pittman, T. S. (1998). Motivation. In D. T. Gilbert, S. T. Fiske, & G. Lindzey (Eds.) *Handbook of social psychology* (4th ed.) (Vol. 1, pp. 549–590). New York: McGraw-Hill/Oxford University Press.

Pittman, T. S., & D'Agostino, P. R. (1985). Motivation and attribution: The effects of control deprivation on subsequent information processing. In J. H. Harvey & G. Weary (Eds.), *Attribution: Basic issues and applications* (pp. 117–141). New York: Academic Press.

Plagens, P., Miller, M., Foote, D., & Yoffe, E. (1991, April 1). Violence in our culture. *Newsweek*, pp. 46–52.

Platt, J. (1973). Social traps. *American Psychologist, 28*, 641–651.

Pleszczynska, W. K., & Hansell, R. I. C. (1980). Polygyny and decision theory: Testing of a model in lark buntings *(Calamospiza malanocorys). American Naturalist, 116,* 821–830.

Plomin, R., DeFries, J. C., & McClearn, G. E. (1990). *Behavioral genetics: A primer.* New York: W. H. Freeman.

Plous, S. (1985). Perceptual illusions and military realities: A social-psychological analysis of the nuclear arms race. *Journal of Conflict Resolution, 29,* 363–389.

Plutchik, R. (1994). *The psychology and biology of emotion.* New York: HarperCollins.

Pollard, C. A., & Henderson, J. G. (1988). Four types of social phobia in a community sample. *Journal of Nervous and Mental Disease, 176,* 440–445.

Pomazal, R. S., & Clore, G. L. (1973). Helping on the highway: The effects of dependency and sex. *Journal of Applied Social Psychology, 3,* 160–164.

Pomeranz, E. M., Chaiken, S., & Tordesillas, R. S. (1995). Attitude strength and resistance processes. *Journal of Personality and Social Psychology, 69,* 408–419.

Postmes, T., & Spears, R. (1998). Deindividuation and antinormative behavior: A meta-analysis. *Psychological Bulletin, 123,* 238–259.

Pozo, C., Carver, C. S., Wellens, A. R., & Scheier, M. F. (1991). Social anxiety and social perception: Construing others' reactions to the self. *Personality and Social Psychology Bulletin, 17,* 355–362.

Pratkanis, A. R. (2000). Altercasting as an influence tactic. In D. J. Terry & M. A. Hogg (Eds.) *Attitudes, behavior, and social context* (pp. 201–226). Mahwah, NJ: Erlbaum.

Pratto, F. (1996). Sexual politics: The gender gap in the bedroom, the cupboard, and the cabinet. In D. M. Buss & N. M. Malamuth (Eds.), *Sex, power, conflict: Evolutionary and feminist perspectives* (pp. 179–230). New York: Oxford University Press.

Pratto, F., & Bargh, J. A. (1991). Stereotyping based on apparently individuating information: Trait and global components of sex stereotypes under attentional overload. *Journal of Experimental Social Psychology, 27,* 26–47.

Pratto, F., Liu, J. H., Levin, S., Sidanius, J., Shih, M., & Bachrach, H. (1998). *Social dominance orientation and legitimization of inequality across cultures.* Unpublished manuscript, Stanford University.

Pratto, F., Sidanius, J., Stallworth, L. M., & Malle, B. F. (1994). Social dominance orientation: A personality variable predicting social and political attitudes. *Journal of Personality and Social Psychology, 67,* 741–763.

Pratto, F., Stallworth, L. M., Sidanius, J., & Siers, B. (1997). The gender gap in occupational role attainment: A social dominance approach. *Journal of Personality and Social Psychology, 72,* 37–53.

Prentice, D. A., & Miller, D. T. (1993). Pluralistic ignorance and alcohol use on campus: Some consequences of misperceiving the social norm. *Journal of Personality and Social Psychology, 64,* 243–256.

Prentice-Dunn, S., & Rogers, R. W. (1980). Effects of deindividuating situational cues and aggressive models on subjective deindividuation and aggression. *Journal of Personality and Social Psychology, 39,* 104–113.

Prentice-Dunn, S., & Rogers, R. W. (1982). Effects of public and private self-awareness on deindividuation and aggression. *Journal of Personality and Social Psychology, 43,* 503–513.

Price, R. H., & Bouffard, D. L. (1974). Behavioral appropriateness and situational constraint as dimensions of social behavior. *Journal of Personality and Social Psychology, 30,* 579–586.

Priester, J. R., & Petty, R. E. (1995). Source attributions and persuasion: Perceived honesty as a determinant of message scrutiny. *Personality and Social Psychology Bulletin, 21,* 637–654.

Probst, T., Carnevale, P. J., & Triandis, H. C. (1999). Cultural values in intergroup and single-group social dilemmas. *Organizational Behavior and Human Decision Processes, 77,* 171–191.

Pryor, J. B. (1987). Sexual harassment proclivities in men. *Sex Roles, 17,* 269–289.

Pryor, J. B., & Day, J. D. (1988). Interpretations of sexual harassment: An attributional analysis. *Sex Roles, 18,* 405–417.

Pryor, J. B., & Merluzzi, T. V. (1985). The role of expertise in processing social interaction scripts. *Journal of Experimental Social Psychology, 21,* 362–379.

Pryor, J. B., & Stoller, L. (1994). Sexual cognition processes in men who are high in the likelihood to sexually harass. *Personality and Social Psychology Bulletin, 20,* 163–169.

Pryor, J. B., LaVite, C., & Stoller, L. (1993). A social psychological analysis of sexual harassment: The person/situation interaction. *Journal of Vocational Behavior, 42,* 68–83.

Purdon, C. (1999). Thought suppression and psychopathology. *Behaviour Research and Therapy, 37,* 1029–1054.

Purvis, J. A., Dabbs, J. M., & Hopper, C. H. (1984). The "opener": Skilled user of facial expression and speech pattern. *Personality and Social Psychology Bulletin, 10,* 61–66.

Pyszczynski, T. A., & Greenberg, J. (1981). Role of disconfirmed expectancies in the instigation of attributional processing. *Journal of Personality and Social Psychology, 40,* 31–38.

Pyszczynski, T. A., & Greenberg, J. (1987). Toward an integration of cognitive and motivational perspectives on social inference: A biased hypothesis-testing model. In L. Berkowitz (Ed.), *Advances in experimental social psychology* (Vol. 20, pp. 297–340). New York: Academic Press.

Pyszczynski, T. A., Greenberg, J., & Holt, K. (1985). Maintaining consistency between self-serving beliefs and available data: A bias in information evalution. *Personality and Social Psychology Bulletin, 11,* 179–190.

Pyszczynski, T., Greenberg, J., & Solomon, S. (1999). A dual-process model of defense against conscious and unconscious death-related thoughts: An extension of terror management theory. *Psychological Review, 106,* 835–845.

Quattrone, G. A., & Jones, E. E. (1978). Selective self-disclosure with and without correspondent performance. *Journal of Experimental Social Psychology, 14,* 511–526.

Radcliffe-Brown, A. (1913). Three tribes of Western Australia. *Journal of the Royal Anthropological Institute, 43,* 143–194.

Rajecki, D. W., Bledsoe, S. B., & Rasmussen, J. L. (1991). Successful personal ads: Gender differences and similarities in offers, stipulations, and outcomes. *Basic and Applied Social Psychology, 12,* 457–469.

Ramirez, J. M. (1993). Acceptability of aggression in four Spanish regions and a comparison with other European countries. *Aggressive Behavior, 19,* 185–197.

Rapoport, A. (1960). *Fights, games, and debates.* Ann Arbor: University of Michigan Press.

Rapoport, A., Diekmann, A., & Franzen, A. (1995). Experiments with social traps IV: Reputation effects in the evolution of cooperation. *Rationality and Society, 7,* 431–441.

Ratneswar, S., & Chaiken, S. (1991). Comprehension's role in persuasion: The case of its moderating effect on the impact of source cues. *Journal of Consumer Psychology, 18,* 52–62.

Rausch, H. L. (1977). Paradox, levels, and junctures in person-situation systems. In D. Magnusson & N. S. Endler (Eds.), *Personality at the Crossroads* (pp. 287–304). Hillsdale, NJ: Erlbaum.

Rawlins, W. K. (1992). *Friendship matters: Communication, dialectics, and the life course.* New York: Aldine DeGruyter.

Read, S. J., & Marcus-Newhall, A. (1993). Explanatory coherence in social explanations: A parallel distributed processing account. *Journal of Personality and Social Psychology, 65,* 429–447.

Redelmeier, D. A., & Tversky, A. (1990). Discrepancy between medical decisions for individual patients and for groups. *New England Journal of Medicine, 322,* 1162–1164.

Regan, D. T. (1971). Effects of a favor on liking and compliance. *Journal of Experimental Social Psychology, 7,* 627–639.

Regan, P. C. (1998). What if you can't get what you want? Willingness to compromise ideal mate selection standards as a function of sex, mate value, and relationship context. *Personality & Social Psychology Bulletin, 24,* 1294–1303.

Regan, P. C. (1999). Hormonal correlates and causes of sexual desire: A review. *Canadian Journal of Human Sexuality, 8,* 1–16.

Regan, P. C., & Berscheid, E. (1999). *Lust: What we know about sexual desire.* Thousand Oaks, CA: Sage.

Regan, P. C., Snyder, M., & Kassin, S. M. (1995). Unrealistic optimism: Self-enhancement or person positivity? *Personality and Social Psychology Bulletin, 21,* 1073–1082.

Reich, J. W., & Zautra, A. J. (1989). A perceived control intervention for at-risk older adults. *Psychology and Aging, 4,* 415–424.

Reich, J. W., & Zautra, A. J. (1991). Experimental and measurement approaches to internal control in at-risk older adults. *Journal of Social Issues, 47,* 143–158.

Reich, J. W., & Zautra, A. J. (1995). Other-reliance encouragement effects in female rheumatoid arthritis patients. *Journal of Social and Clinical Psychology, 14,* 119–133.

Reich, J. W., & Zautra, A. J. (1995). Spouse encouragement of self-reliance and other-reliance in rheumatoid arthritis couples. *Journal of Behavioral Medicine, 18,* 249–260.

Reich, M. (1971). The economics of racism. In D. M. Gordon (Ed.), *Problems in political economy* (pp. 107–113). Lexington, MA: Heath.

Reid, D. (1984). Participatory control and the chronic-illness adjustment process. In H. Lefcourt (Ed.), *Research with the locus of control construct: Extensions and limitations* (Vol. 3, pp. 361–389). San Diego, CA: Academic Press.

Reif, C. D., & Singer, B. (2000). Interpersonal flourishing: A positive health agenda for the new millennium. *Personality & Social Psychology Review, 4,* 30–44.

Reifman, A., Larrick, R. P., & Fein, S. (1991). Temper and temperature on the diamond: The heat-aggression relationship in major league baseball. *Personality and Social Psychology Bulletin, 17,* 580–585.

Reilly, P. (1995). When will it ever end? In D. S. Connery (Ed.), *Convicting the innocent* (pp. 84–86). Cambridge, MA: Brookline.

Reingen, P. H. (1982). Test of a list procedure for inducing compliance with a request to donate money. *Journal of Applied Psychology, 67,* 110–118.

Reingen, P. H., & Kernan, J. B. (1993). Social perception and interpersonal influence: Some consequences of the physical attractiveness stereotype in a personal selling setting. *Journal of Consumer Psychology, 2,* 25–38.

Reis, H. T., & Wheeler, L. (1991). Studying social interaction with the Rochester Interaction Record. *Advances in Experimental Social Psychology, 24,* 269–318.

Reis, H. T., Senchak, M., & Solomon, B. (1985). Sex differences in the intimacy of social interaction: Further examination of potential explanations. *Journal of Personality and Social Psychology, 48,* 1204–1217.

Reis, H. T., Sheldon, K. M., Gable, S. L., Roscoe, J., & Ryan, R. M. (2000). Daily well-being: The role of autonomy, competence, and relatedness. *Per-*

sonality & Social Psychology Bulletin, 26, 419–435.

Reis, H. T., Wheeler, L., Spiegel, N., Kernis, M. H., Nezlek, J., & Perri, M. (1982). Physical attractiveness in social interaction: II. Why does appearance affect social experience. *Journal of Personality and Social Psychology, 43,* 979–996.

Reisenzein, R. (1983). The Schachter theory of emotion: Two decades later. *Psychological Bulletin, 94,* 239–264.

Reiss, M., & Rosenfeld, P. (1980). Seating preferences as nonverbal communication: A self-presentational analysis. *Journal of Applied Communication Research, 8,* 22–30.

Reno, R. R., & Kenny, D. A. (1992). Effects of self-consciousness and social anxiety on self-disclosure among unacquainted individuals: An application of the Social Relations Model. *Journal of Personality, 60,* 79–94.

Resnick, L. B., Levine, J. M., & Teasley, S. D. (1991). *Perspectives on socially shared cognition.* Washington, DC: American Psychological Association.

Reykowski, J. (1980). Origin of prosocial motivation: Heterogeneity of personality development. *Studia Psychologia, 22,* 91–106.

Rhodewalt, F. (1994). Conceptions of ability, achievement goals, and individual differences in self-handicapping behavior: On the application of implicit theories. *Journal of Personality, 62,* 67–85.

Rhodewalt, F., & Agustsdottir, S. (1986). Effects of self-presentation on the phenomenal self. *Journal of Personality and Social Psychology, 50,* 47–55.

Rhodewalt, F., & Davison, J., Jr. (1986). Self-handicapping and subsequent performance: Role of outcome valence and attributional certainty. *Basic and Applied Social Psychology, 7,* 307–322.

Rhodewalt, F., & Fairfield, M. (1991). Claimed self-handicaps and the self-handicapper: The relation of reduction in intended effort to performance. *Journal of Research in Personality, 25,* 402–417.

Rhodewalt, F., & Hill, S. K. (1995). Self-handicapping in the classroom: The effects of claimed self-handicaps on responses to academic failure. *Basic and Applied Social Psychology, 16,* 397–416.

Rhodewalt, F., & Smith, T. W. (1991). Current issues in Type A behavior, coronary proneness, and coronary heart disease. In C. R. Snyder & D. R. Forsyth (Eds.), *Handbook of social and clinical psychology* (pp. 197–220). New York: Pergamon.

Rhodewalt, F., Morf, C., Hazlett, S., & Fairfield, M. (1991). Self-handicapping: The role of discounting and augmentation in the preservation of self-esteem. *Journal of Personality and Social Psychology, 61,* 122–131.

Rholes, W. S., & Ruble, D. N. (1986). Children's impressions of other persons. *Child Development, 57,* 872–878.

Rholes, W. S., Newman, L. S., & Ruble, D. N. (1990). Understanding self and other: Developmental and motivational aspects of perceiving people in terms of invariant dispositions. In E. T. Higgins & R. M. Sorrentiono (Eds.), *Handbook of motivation and cognition* (Vol. 2, pp. 369–407). New York: Guilford.

Rice, R. E., Gullison, R. E., & Reid, J. W. (1997, April). Can sustainable management save tropical forests? *Scientific American,* pp. 44–49.

Rice, R. W., Instone, D., & Adams, J. (1984). Leader sex, leader success, and leadership process: Two field studies. *Journal of Applied Psychology, 69,* 12–31.

Ridley, M. (1993). *The Red Queen: Sex and the evolution of human nature.* New York: Penguin Books.

Rind, B., & Benjamin, D. (1994). Effects of public image concerns and self-image on compliance. *Journal of Social Psychology, 134,* 19–25.

Ringelmann, M. (1913). Recherches sur les moteurs animés: Travail de l'homme [Research on animate sources of power: The work of man]. *Annales de l'Institute National Agronomique, 2e série—tome XII,* 1–40.

Riordan, C. A., & Tedeschi, J. T. (1983). Attraction in aversive environments: Some evidence for classical conditioning and negative reinforcement. *Journal of Personality and Social Psychology, 44,* 683–692.

Robberson, M. R., & Rogers, R. W. (1988). Beyond fear appeals: Negative and positive persuasive appeals to health and self-esteem. *Journal of Applied Social Psychology,* 277–287.

Roberts, B. W., & Helson, R. (1997). Changes in culture, changes in personality: The influence of individualism in a longitudinal study of women. *Journal of Personality and Social Psychology, 72,* 641–651.

Robinson, M. D., Johnson, J. T., & Shields, S. A. (1995). On the advantages of modesty: The benefits of a balanced self-presentation. *Communication Research, 22,* 575–591.

Rock 'n' ripoff. (1997, November). *Consumer Reports,* p. 7.

Rodin, J. (1986). Aging and health: Effects of the sense of control. *Science, 233,* 1271–1276.

Rodin, J., & Langer, E. J. (1977). Long-term effects of a control-relevant intervention with the institutionalized aged. *Journal of Personality and Social Psychology, 35,* 897–902.

Rodkin, P. C., Farmer, T. W., Pearl, R., & Van Acker, R. (2000). Heterogeneity of popular boys: Antisocial and prosocial configurations. *Developmental Psychology, 36,* 14–24.

Rodriquez, L. J. (1994, July/August). Rekinkling the warrior. *Utne Reader,* pp. 58–59.

Rodseth, L., Wrangham, R. W., Harrigan, A. M., & Smuts, B. B. (1991). The human community as a primate society. *Current Anthropology, 32,* 221–254.

Roese, N. J., & Jamieson, D. W. (1993). Twenty years of bogus pipeline research: A critical review and meta-analysis. *Psychological Bulletin, 114,* 363–375.

Roese, N.J., & Olson, J. M. (1995). *What might have been: The social psychology of counterfactual thinking.* Hillsdale, NJ: Erlbaum.

Rogers, C. R. (1970). *On encounter groups.* New York: Harper & Row.

Rogers, M., Miller, N., Mayer, F. S., & Duval, S. (1982). Personal responsibility and salience of the request for help. *Journal of Personality and Social Psychology, 43,* 956–970.

Rogers, R. W., & Mewborn, C. R. (1976). Fear appeals and attitude change: Effects of a threat's noxiousness, probability of occurrence, and the efficacy of coping responses. *Journal of Personality and Social Psychology, 34,* 54–61.

Rohrer, J. H., Baron, S. H., Hoffman, E. L., & Swander, D. V. (1954). The stability of autokinetic judgments. *Journal of Abnormal and Social Psychology, 49,* 595–597.

Rokeach, M. (1971). Long-range experimental modification of values, attitudes, and behavior. *American Psychologist, 26,* 453–459.

Romer, D., Gruder, C. L., & Lizzadro, T. (1986). A person-situation approach to altruistic behavior. *Journal of Personality and Social Psychology, 51,* 1001–1012.

Romero, A. A., Agnew, C. R., & Insko, C. A. (1996). The cognitive mediation hypothesis revisited. *Personality and Social Psychology Bulletin, 22,* 651–665.

Rose, S., & Frieze, I. H. (1993). Young singles' contemporary dating scripts. *Sex Roles, 28,* 499–509.

Rosen, S., & Tesser, A. (1970). On the reluctance to communicate undesirable information: The MUM effect. *Sociometry, 33,* 253–262.

Rosen, S., Cochran, W., & Musser, L. M. (1990). Reactions to a match versus mismatch between and applicant's self-presentational style and work reputation. *Basic and Applied Social Psychology, 11,* 117–129.

Rosenbaum, M. E. (1986). The repulsion hypothesis: On the nondevelopment of relationships. *Journal of Personality and Social Psychology, 61,* 1156–66.

Rosenblatt, A., Greenberg, J., Solomon, S., Pyszczynski, T., & Lyon, D. (1989). Evidence for Terror Management Theory: I. The effects of mortality salience on reactions to those who violate or uphold cultural values. *Journal of Personality and Social Psychology, 57,* 681–690.

Rosenblatt, P. C. (1974). Cross-cultural perspective on attraction. In T. Huston (Ed.), *Foundations of interpersonal attraction* (pp. 79–99). New York: Academic Press.

Rosenblatt, P. C., & Cozby, P. C. (1972). Courtship patterns associated with freedom of choice of spouse. *Journal of Marriage and the family, 34,* 689–695.

Rosenfeld, H. M. (1966). Approval-seeking and approval-inducing functions of verbal and nonverbal responses in the dyad. *Journal of Personality and Social Psychology, 4,* 597–605.

Rosenthal, A. M. (1964). *Thirty-eight witnesses.* New York: McGraw-Hill.

Rosenthal, R. (1994). Interpersonal expectancy effects: A 30-year perspective. *Current Directions in Psychological Science, 3,* 176–179.

Rosenthal, R., & Jacobson, L. (1968). *Pygmalian in the classroom: Teacher expectation and pupils' intellectual development.* New York: Holt, Rinehart, & Winston.

Rosman, A., & Rubel, P. G. (1971). *Feasting with mine enemy.* New York: Columbia University Press.

Ross, C. E., & Mirowsky, J. (1983). The worse place and the best face. *Social Forces, 62,* 529–536.

Ross, E. A. (1908). *Social psychology.* New York: Macmillan.

Ross, J. R. (1994). *Escape to Shanghai: A Jewish community in China.* New York: Free Press.

Ross, L. (1977). The intuitive psychologist and his shortcomings: Distortions in the attribution process. In L. Berkowitz (Ed.), *Advances in experimental social psychology* (Vol. 10, pp. 174–221). New York: Academic Press.

Ross, L., Greene, D., & House, P. (1977). The "false consensus effect": An egocentric bias in social perception and attribution processes. *Journal of Experimental Social Psychology, 13,* 279–301.

Rosselli, F., Skelly, J. J., & Mackie, D. M. (1995). Processing rational and emotional messages: The cognitive and affective mediation of persuasion. *Journal of Experimental Social Psychology, 31,* 163–190.

Rothbart, M., & Hallmark, W. (1988). In-group-out-group differences in the perceived efficacy of coercion and conciliation in resolving social conflict. *Journal of Personality and Social Psychology, 55,* 248–257.

Rothbart, M., & John, O. P. (1985). Social categorization and behavioral episodes: A cognitive analysis of the effects of intergroup contact. *Journal of Social Issues, 41,* 81–104.

Rothbart, M., Evans, M., & Fulero, S. (1979). Recall for confirming events: Memory processes and the maintenance of social stereotyping. *Journal of Experimental Social Psychology, 15,* 343–355.

Rothbart, M., Fulero, S., Jensen, C., Howard, J., & Birrell, P. (1978). From individual to group impressions: Availability heuristics in stereotype formation. *Journal of Experimental Social Psychology, 14,* 237–255.

Rothbaum, F., Weisz, J. R., & Snyder, S. S. (1982). Changing the world and changing the self: A two-process model of perceived control. *Journal of Personality and Social Psychology, 42,* 5–37.

Rotton J., & Cohn, E. G. (2000). Violence is a curvilinear function of temperature in Dallas: A replication. *Journal of Personality & Social Psychology, 78,* 1074–1081.

Rotton, J. (1983). Affective and cognitive consequences of malodorous pollution. *Basic and Applied Social Psychology, 4,* 171–191.

Rotton, J. (1993). Geophysical variables and behavior: LXXIII. Ubiquitous errors: A reanalysis of Anderson's (1987) "temperature and aggression." *Psychological Reports, 73,* 259–271.

Rouhana, N. N., & Kelman, H. C. (1994). Promoting joint thinking in international conflicts: An Israeli-Palestinian continuing workshop. *Journal of Social Issues, 50*, 157–178.

Rowatt, W. C., Cunningham, M. R., & Druen, P. B. (1999). Lying to get a date: The effect of facial attractiveness on the willingness to deceive prospective dating partners. *Journal of Social and Personal Relationships, 16*, 209–223.

Rowe, D. C. (1996). An adaptive strategy theory of crime and delinquency. In J. D. Hawkins (Ed.), *Delinquency and crime: Current theories* (pp. 268–314). New York: Cambridge University Press.

Ruback, B. R., & Jweng, D. (1997). Territorial defense in parking lots: Retaliation against waiting drivers. *Journal of Applied Social Psychology, 27*, 821–834.

Rubin, M., & Hewstone, M. (1998). Social identity theory's self-esteem hypothesis: A review and some suggestions for clarification. *Personality and Social Psychology Review, 2*, 40–62.

Ruble, D. N., Feldman, N. S., & Boggiano, A. G. (1976). Social comparison between young children in achievement situations. *Developmental Psychology, 12*, 192–197.

Ruble, T. L. (1983). Sex stereotypes: Issues of change in the 1970s. *Sex Roles, 9*, 397–402.

Ruddy, M. G., & Adams, S. R. (1995, July). *Responsiveness to crying: How mothers' beliefs vary with infant's sex.* Poster presented at the American Psychological Society meetings, New York.

Rudman, L. A. (1998). Self-promotion as a risk factor for women: The costs and benefits of counterstereotypical impression management. *Journal of Personality and Social Psychology, 74*, 629–645.

Rudman, L. A., Greenwald, A. G., Mellott, D. S., & Schwartz, J. L. K. (1999). Measuring the automatic components of prejudice: Flexibility and generality of the Implicit Association Test. *Social Cognition, 17*, 437–465.

Rule, B. G., Taylor, B. R., & Dobbs, A. R. (1987). Priming effects of heat on aggressive thoughts. *Social Cognition, 5*, 131–143.

Rumelhart, D. E., & Ortony, A. (1977). The representation of knowledge in memory. In R. C. Anderson, R. J. Spiro, & W. E. Montague (Eds.), *Schooling and the acquisition of knowledge* (pp. 99–136). Hillsdale, NJ: Erlbaum.

Rusbult, C. E., Zembrodt, I. M., & Gunn, L. K. (1982). Exit, voice, loyalty, and neglect: Responses to dissatisfaction in romantic relationships. *Journal of Personality and Social Psychology, 43*, 1230–1242.

Ruscher, J. B., & Fiske, S. T. (1990). Interpersonal competition can cause individuating impression formation. *Journal of Personality and Social Psychology, 58*, 832–842.

Ruscher, J. B., & Hammer, E. Y. (1996). Choosing to sever or maintain association induces biased impression formation. *Journal of Personality and Social Psychology, 70*, 701–712.

Ruscher, J. B., & Hastings, C. T. (1996, October). *Distraction attenuates defensive processing of health risk messages.* Meeting of the Society of Experimental Social Psychology, Sturbridge, MA.

Ruscher, J. B., Fiske, S. T., Miki, H., & Van Manen, S. (1991). Individuating processes in competition: Interpersonal versus intergroup. *Personality and Social Psychology Bulletin, 17*, 595–605.

Rushton, J. P. (1989). Genetic similarity, human altruism and group selection. *Behavioral and Brain Science, 12*, 503–518.

Rushton, J. P., Fulker, D. W. Neale, M. C., Nias, D. K. B., & Esyenck, H. J. (1986). Altruism and aggression: The heritability of individual differences. *Journal of Personality and Social Psychology, 50*, 1192–1198.

Rushton, J. P., Russell, R. J. H., & Wells, P. A. (1984). Genetic similarity theory: Beyond kin selection altruism. *Behavioral Genetics, 14*, 179–193.

Russell, D., Peplau, L. A., & Cutrona, C. E. (1980). The revised UCLA loneliness scale: Concurrent and discriminant validity evidence. *Journal of Personality and Social Psychology, 39*, 472–480.

Russell, J. A. (1991). Culture and the categorization of emotions. *Psychological Bulletin, 110*, 426–450.

Russell, J. A. (1994). Is there universal recognition of emotion from facial expression? A review of the cross-cultural studies. *Psychological Bulletin, 115*, 102–141.

Russell, J. A. (1995). Facial expressions of emotion: What lies beyond minimal universality? *Psychological Bulletin, 118*, 379–391.

Russo, N. F. (1966). Connotations of seating arrangements. *Cornell Journal of Social Relations, 2*, 37–44.

Rutkowski, G. K., Gruder, C. L., & Romer, D. (1983). Group cohesiveness, social norms, and bystander intervention. *Journal of Personality and Social Psychology, 44*, 545–552.

Ryan, C. S. (1996). Accuracy of black and white college students' ingroup and outgroup stereotypes. *Personality and Social Psychology Bulletin, 22*, 1114–1127.

Ryan, C. S., Judd, C. M., & Park, B. (1996). Effects of racial stereotypes on judgments of individuals: The moderating role of perceived group variability. *Journal of Experimental Social Psychology, 32*, 71–103.

Ryff, C. D. (1995). Psychological well-being in adult life. *Current Directions in Psychological Science, 4*, 99–104.

Saarni, C. (1993). Socialization of emotion. In M. Lewis & J. M. Haviland (Eds.), *Handbook of emotions* (pp. 435–446). New York: Guilford.

Sabini, J., & Silver, M. (1982). *Moralities of everyday life.* New York: Oxford University Press.

Sadalla, E. K., & Krull, J. L. (1995). Self-presentational barriers to resource conservation. *Environment and Behavior, 27*, 328–353.

Sadalla, E. K., Kenrick, D. T., & Vershure, B. (1987). Dominance and heterosexual attraction. *Journal of Personality and Social Psychology, 52*, 730–738.

Saenz, D. S. (1994). Token status and problem-solving deficits: Detrimental effects of distinctiveness and performance monitoring. *Social Cognition, 12,* 61–74.

Sagar, H. A., & Schofield, J. W. (1980). Racial and behavioral cues in black and white children's perceptions of ambiguously aggressive acts. *Journal of Personality and Social Psychology, 39,* 590–598.

Sagiv, L., & Schwartz, S. H. (2000). Value priorities and subjective well-being: Direct relations and congruity effects. *European Journal of Social Psychology, 30,* 177–198.

Saks, M. (1977). *Jury verdicts.* Lexington, MA: D.C. Heath.

Sales, S. M. (1973). Threat as a factor in authoritarianism: An analysis of archival data. *Journal of Personality and Social Psychology, 28,* 44–57.

Sales, S. M., & Friend, K. E. (1973). Success and failure as determinants of level of authoritarianism. *Behavioral Sciences, 18,* 163–172.

Salovey, P., & Birnbaum, D. (1989). Influence of mood on health-relevant cognitions. *Journal of Personality and Social Psychology, 57,* 539–551.

Salovey, P., Mayer, J. D., & Rosenhan, D. L. (1991). Mood and helping: Mood as a motivator of helping and helping as a regulator of mood. In M. S. Clark (Ed.), *Review of personality and social psychology* (Vol. 12, pp. 215–237). Newbury Park, CA: Sage.

Salovey, P., Rothman, A. J., & Rodin, J. (1998). Health behavior. In D. T. Gilbert, S. T. Fiske, & G. Lindzey (Eds.), *Handbook of social psychology* (4th ed.) (Vol. 2, pp. 633–683). New York: McGraw-Hill.

Sanbonmatsu, D. M., Akimoto, S. A., & Biggs, E. (1993). Overestimating causality: Attributional effects of confirmatory processing. *Journal of Personality and Social Psychology, 65,* 892–903.

Sanders, G. S. (1981). Driven by distraction: An integrative review of social facilitation theory and research. *Journal of Experimental Social Psychology, 17,* 227–251.

Sandstrom, K. L. (1996). Searching for information, understanding, and self-value: The utilization of peer support groups by gay men with HIV/AIDS. *Social Work in Health Care, 23,* 51–74.

Sanna, L. J. (1998). Self-efficacy and counterfactual thinking. Up a creek with and without a paddle. *Personality and Social Psychology Bulletin, 23,* 654–666.

Sanna, L. J., & Turley, K. J. (1996). Antecedents to spontaneous counterfactual thinking: Effects of expectancy violation and outcome valence. *Personality and Social Psychology Bulletin, 22,* 906–919.

Sanna, L. J., & Turley-Ames, K. J. (2000). Counterfactual intensity. *European Journal of Social Psychology, 30,* 273–296.

Sarason, B. R., Sarason, I. G., & Gurung, R. A. R. (1997). Close personal relationships and health outcomes: A key to the role of social support. In S. Duck (Ed.) *Handbook of personal relationships* (2nd ed.) (pp. 547–573). New York: Wiley.

Sarnoff, I., & Zimbardo, P. (1961). Anxiety, fear, and social affiliation. *Journal of Abnormal and Social Psychology, 62,* 356–363.

Satow, K. L. (1975). Social approval and helping. *Journal of Experimental Social Psychology, 11,* 501–509.

Satterfield, J. M. (1998). Cognitive-affective states predict military and political aggression and risk taking. *Journal of Conflict Resolution, 42,* 667–690.

Saucier, G. (2000). Isms and the structure of social attitudes. *Journal of Personality & Social Psychology, 78,* 366–385.

Savin-Williams, R. C. (1980). Social interactions of adolescent females in natural groups. In H. C. Foot, T. Chapman, & J. R. Smith (Eds.), *Friendship and social relations in children.* London: Wiley.

Saxe, L. (1994). Detection of deception: Polygraph and integrity tests. *Current Directions in Psychological Science, 3,* 69–73.

Scarr, S. (1981). The transmission of authoritarian attitudes in familes: Genetic resemblance in social-political attitudes? In S. Scarr (Ed.), *Race, social class, and individual differences* (pp. 399–427). Hillsdale, NJ: Erlbaum.

Schachter, S. (1951). Deviation, rejection, and communication. *Journal of Abnormal and Social Psychology, 46,* 190–207.

Schachter, S. (1959). *The psychology of affiliation: Experimental studies of the sources of gregariousness.* Stanford, CA: Stanford University Press.

Schachter, S., & Singer, J. E. (1962). Cognitive, social, and psychological determinants of emotional state. *Psychological Review, 69,* 379–399.

Schaller, M., & Cialdini, R. B. (1988). The economics of empathic helping: Support for a mood management motive. *Journal of Experimental Social Psychology, 24,* 163–181.

Schaller, M., & Cialdini, R. B. (1990). Happiness, sadness, and helping: A motivational integration. In E. T. Higgins & R. M. Sorrentino (Eds.), *Handbook of motivation and cognition* (Vol. 2, pp. 265–296). New York: Guilford.

Schaller, M., & Conway, L. G. III (1999). Influence of impression management goals on the emerging contents of group stereotypes: Support for a social-evolutionary process. *Personality & Social Psychology Bulletin, 25,* 819–833.

Schaller, M., Asp, C. H., Rosell, M. C., & Heim, S. J. (1996). Training in statistical reasoning inhibits the formation of erroneous group stereotypes. *Personality and Social Psychology Bulletin, 22,* 829–844.

Schaller, M., Boyd, C., Yohannes, J., & O'Brien, M. (1995). The prejudiced personality revisited: Personal need for structure and formation of erroneous group stereotypes. *Journal of Personality and Social Psychology, 68,* 544–555.

Schank, R. C., & Abelson, R. P. (1977). *Scripts, plans, goals, and understanding.* Hillsdale, NJ: Erlbaum.

Scheier, M. F., & Carver, C. S. (1988). A model of behavioral self-regulation: Translating intention into action. In L. Berkowitz (Ed.), *Advances in experimental social psychology* (Vol. 21, pp. 303–346). San Diego, CA: Academic Press.

Scheier, M. F., & Carver, C. S. (1992). The effects of optimism on psychological and physical well-being. *Cognitive therapy and Research, 16,* 201–228.

Schein, E. (1956). The Chinese indoctrination program for prisoners of war. *Psychiatry, 19,* 149–172.

Schell, J. (1982). *The fate of the earth.* New York: Knopf.

Schelling, T. C. (1968). The life you save may be your own. In S. Chase (Ed.), *Problems in public expenditure analysis.* Washington, DC: The Brookings Institute.

Scherer, K. R., & Wallbott, H. G. (1994). Evidence for universality and cultural variation of differential emotion response patterning. *Journal of Personality and Social Psychology, 66,* 310–328.

Schimel, J., Pyszczynski, T., Greenberg, J., O'Mahen, H., & Arndt, J. (2000). Running from the shadow: Psychological distancing from others to deny characteristics people fear in themselves. *Journal of Personality and Social Psychology, 78,* 446–462.

Schlenker, B. R. (1980). *Impression management: The self-concept, social identity, and interpersonal relationships.* Monterey, CA: Brooks/Cole.

Schlenker, B. R., & Leary, M. (1982a). Audiences' reactions to self-enhancing, self-denigrating, and accurate self-presentations. *Journal of Experimental Social Psychology, 18,* 89–104.

Schlenker, B. R., & Leary, M. (1982b). Social anxiety and self-presentation: A conceptualization and model. *Psychological Bulletin, 92,* 641–669.

Schlenker, B. R., & Trudeau, J. V. (1990). The impact of self-presentations on private self-beliefs: Effects of prior self-beliefs and misattribution. *Journal of Personality and Social Psychology, 58,* 22–32.

Schlenker, B. R., & Weigold, M. F. (1992). Interpersonal processes involving impression regulation and management. *Annual Review of Psychology, 43,* 133–168.

Schlenker, B. R., Dlugolecki, D. W., & Doherty, K. (1994). The impact of self-presentations on self-appraisals and behavior: The power of public commitment. *Personality and Social Psychology Bulletin, 20,* 20–33.

Schlesinger, A. M., Jr. (1978). *Robert Kennedy and his times.* New York: Ballantine Books.

Schmader, T., & Major, B. (1999). The impact of ingroup vs outgroup performance on personal values. *Journal of Experimental Social Psychology, 35,* 47–67.

Schmidtke, A., & Hafner, H. (1988). The Werther effect after television films: New evidence for an old hypothesis. *Psychological Medicine, 18,* 665–676.

Schmitt, B. H., Gilovich, T., Goore, N., & Joseph, L. (1986). Mere presence and social facilitation: One more time. *Journal of Experimental Social Psychology, 22,* 242–248.

Schneider, D. J. (1969). Tactical self-presentation after success and failure. *Journal of Personality and Social Psychology, 13,* 262–268.

Schoenberg, R. J. (1992). *Mr. Capone.* New York: William Morrow.

Schoenrade, P. A., Batson, C. D., Brandt, J. R., & Loud, R. E. (1986). Attachment, accountability, and motivation to benefit another not in distress. *Journal of Personality and Social Psychology, 51,* 557–563.

Schopler, J., & Insko, C. A. (1992). The discontinuity effect: Generality and mediation. In W. Stroebe & M. Hewstone (Eds.), *European review of social psychology* (pp. 121–151). London: Wiley.

Schopler, J., Insko, C. A., Drigotas, S. M., Wieselquist, J., Perberton, M., & Cox, C. (1995). The role of identifiability in the reduction of interindividual-intergroup discontinuity. *Journal of Experimental Social Psychology, 31,* 301–315.

Schroeder, D. A. (1995). An introduction to social dilemmas. In D. A. Schroeder (Ed.), *Social dilemmas: Perspectives on individuals and groups* (pp. 1–14). Westport, CT: Praeger.

Schroeder, D. A. (1995). *Social dilemmas: Perspectives on individuals and groups.* Westport, CT: Praeger.

Schroeder, D. A., Dovidio, J. F., Sibicky, M. E., Matthews, L. L., & Allen, J. L. (1988). Empathy and helping behavior: Egoism or altruism. *Journal of Experimental Social Psychology, 24,* 333–353.

Schroeder, D. A., Penner, L. A., Dovidio, J. F., & Piliavin, J. A. (1995). *The psychology of helping and altruism.* New York: McGraw-Hill.

Schulman, K. A., et al. (1999). The effects of race and sex on physicians' recommendations for cardiac catheterization. *New England Journal of Medicine, 340,* 618–626.

Schulte, B. (1998, March 8). Sleep research focusing on mind's effectiveness. *The Arizona Republic,* p. A33.

Schultz, P. W. (1999). Changing behavior with normative feedback interventions: A field experiment on curbside recycling. *Basic and Applied Social Psychology, 21,* 25–36.

Schulz, R. (1976). Effects of control and predictability on the physical and psychological well-being of the institutionalized aged. *Journal of Personality and Social Psychology, 33,* 563–573.

Schuman, H., Steeh, C., & Bobo, L. (1985). *Racial attitudes in America.* Cambridge, MA: Harvard University Press.

Schur, E. M. (1971). *Labeling deviant behavior: Its sociological implications.* New York: Harper & Row.

Schwartz, B., Tesser, A., & Powell, E. (1982). Dominance cues in nonverbal behavior. *Social Psychology Quarterly, 45*, 114–120.

Schwartz, S. H. (1968). Words, deeds, and the perception of consequences and responsibility in action situations. *Journal of Personality and Social Psychology, 10*, 232–242.

Schwartz, S. H. (1977). Normative influences on altruism. In L. Berkowitz (Ed.), *Advances in experimental social psychology* (Vol. 10, pp. 222–280). New York: Academic Press.

Schwartz, S. H., & Gottlieb, A. (1976). Bystander reactions to a violent theft: Crime in Jerusalem. *Journal of Personality and Social Psychology, 34*, 1188–1199.

Schwartz, S. H., & Gottlieb, A. (1980). Bystander anonymity and reactions to emergencies. *Journal of Personality and Social Psychology, 39*, 418–430.

Schwartz, S. H., & Howard, J. A. (1982). Helping and cooperation: A self-based motivational model. In V. J. Derlega & J. Grelak (Eds.), *Cooperation and helping behavior: Theories and research* (pp. 327–353). New York: Academic Press.

Schwartzwald, J., Bizman, A., & Raz, M. (1983). The foot-in-the-door paradigm: Effects of second request size on donation probability and donor generosity. *Personality and Social Psychology Bulletin, 9*, 443–450.

Schwarz, N. (1990). Assessing frequency reports of mundane behaviors: Contributions of cognitive psychology to questionnaire construction. In C. Hendrick & M. S. Clark (Eds.), *Research methods in personality and social psychology* (pp. 98–119). Newbury Park: Sage.

Schwarz, N. (1990). Feelings as information: Informational and motivational functions of affective states. In R. Sorrentino & E. T. Higgins (Eds.), *Handbook of motivation and cognition* (Vol. 2, pp. 527–561). New York: Guilford.

Schwarz, N., & Clore, G. L. (1983). Mood, misattribution, and judgments of well-being: Informative and directive functions of affective states. *Journal of Personality and Social Psychology, 34*, 513–523.

Schwarz, N., & Clore, G. L. (1988). How do I feel about it? The informative function of affective states. In K. Fiedler & J. Forgas (Eds.), *Affect, cognition, and social behavior* (pp. 44–62). Toronto: Hogrefe.

Schwarz, N., & Clore, G. L. (1996). Feelings and phenomenal experiences. In E. T. Higgins & A. W. Kruglanski (Eds.), *Social psychology: Handbook of basic principles* (pp. 433–465). New York: Guilford.

Schwarz, N., Bless, H., & Bohner, G. (1991). Mood and persuasion: Affective states influence the processing of persuasive communications. In M. P. Zanna (Ed.), *Advances in experimental social psychology* (Vol. 24, pp. 161–197). New York: Academic Press.

Schwarz, N., Bless, H., Strack, F., Klumpp, G., Rittenauer-Schatka, H., & Simons, A. (1991). Ease of retrieval as information: Another look at the availability heuristic. *Journal of Personality and Social Psychology, 61*, 195–202.

Scott, J. P. (1992). Aggression: Functions and control in social systems. *Aggressive Behavior, 18*, 1–20.

Sears, D. O. (1988). Symbolic racism. In P. A. Katz & D. A. Taylor (Eds.), *Eliminating racism: Profiles in controversy* (pp. 53–84). New York: Plenum.

Secord, P. F., Bevan, W., & Katz, B. (1956). The Negro stereotype and perceptual accentuation. *Journal of Abnormal and Social Psychology, 53*, 78–83.

Sedikides, C. (1993). Assessment, enhancement, and verification determinants of the self-evaluation process. *Journal of Personality and Social Psychology, 65*, 317–338.

Sedikides, C., & Anderson, C. A. (1994). Causal perceptions of intertrait relations: The glue that holds person types together. *Personality and Social Psychology Bulletin, 20*, 294–302.

Sedikides, C., & Skowronski, J. J. (1991). The law of cognitive structure activation. *Psychological Inquiry, 2*, 169–184.

Sedikides, C., & Skowronski, J. J. (1997). The symbolic self in evolutionary context. *Personality and Social Psychology Review, 1*, 80–102.

Segal, M. W. (1974). Alphabet and attraction: An unobtrusive measure of the effect of propinquity in a field setting. *Journal of Personality and Social Psychology, 30*, 654–657.

Segal, N. L. (1984). Cooperation, competition, and altruism within twin sets: A reappraisal. *Ethology and Sociobiology, 5*, 163–177.

Segal, N. L. (1991, April). *Cooperation and competition in adolescent MZ and DZ twins during the Prisoners' Dilemma Game.* Paper presented at a meeting of Society for Research in Child Development, Seattle, WA.

Segal, N. L. (1993). Twin, sibling, and adoption methods: Tests of evolutionary hypotheses. *American Psychologist, 48*, 943–956.

Segal, N. L. (2000). *Entwined lives: Twins and what they tell us about human behavior.* New York: Plume.

Seijts, G. H., & Latham, G. P. (2000). The effects of goal setting and group size on performance in a social dilemma. *Canadian Journal of Behavioural Science, 32*, 104–116.

Seligman, C., Becker, L., & Darley, J. (1981). Encouraging residential energy conservation through feedback. In A. Baum, & J. Singer, (Eds.), *Advances in environmental psychology* (Vol. 3, pp. 93–114). Hillsdale, NJ: Erlbaum.

Seligman, C., Fazio, R. H., & Zanna, M. P. (1980). Effects of salience of extrinsic rewards on liking and loving. *Journal of Personality and Social Psychology, 38,* 453–460.

Sell, J., Griffith, W. I., & Wilson, R. K. (1993). Are women more cooperative than men in social dilemmas? *Social Psychology Quarterly, 56,* 211–222

Senneker, P., & Hendrick, C. (1983). Androgyny and helping behavior. *Journal of Personality and Social Psychology, 45,* 916–925.

Servadio, G. (1976). *Mafioso: A history of the mafia from its origins to the present day.* New York: Stein & Day.

Seta, C. E., & Seta, J. J. (1992). Increments and decrements in mean arterial pressure as a function of audience composition: An averaging and summation analysis. *Personality and Social Psychology Bulletin, 18,* 173–181.

Seta, J. J., & Seta, C. E. (1993). Stereotypes and the generation of compensatory and noncompensatory expectancies of group members. *Personality and Social Psychology Bulletin, 19,* 722–731.

Seta, J. J., Crisson, J. E., Seta, C. E., & Wang, M. E. (1989). Task performance and perceptions of anxiety: Averaging and summation in an evaluative setting. *Journal of Personality and Social Psychology, 56,* 387–396.

Shackelford, T. K., & Buss, D. M. (2000). Marital satisfaction and spousal cost-infliction. *Personality & Individual Differences,* 28: 917–928.

Shafer, M., & Crichlow, S. (1996). Antecedents of groupthink: A quantitative study. *Journal of Conflict Resolution, 40,* 415–435.

Shaffer, D. R., Smith, J. E., & Tomarelli, M. (1982). Self-monitoring as a determinant of self-disclosure reciprocity during the acquaintance process. *Journal of Personality and Social Psychology, 43,* 163–175.

Shaffer, D., Garland, A., Vieland. V., Underwood, M., & Busner, C. (1991). The impact of curriculum-based suicide prevention programs for teenagers. *Journal of the American Academy of Child and Adolescent Psychiatry, 30,* 588–596.

Shaffer, J. W., Graves-Pirrko, L., Swank, R., & Pearson, T. A. (1987). Clustering of personality traits in youth and the subsequent development of cancer among physicians. *Journal of Behavioral Medicine, 10,* 441–447.

Sharabany, R. (1994). Intimate friendship scale: Conceptual underpinnings, psychometric properties, and construct validity. *Journal of Personal and Personal Relationships, 11,* 449–469.

Sharpsteen, D. J., & Kirkpatrick, L. A. (1997). Romantic jealousy and adult romantic attachment. *Journal of Personality and Social Psychology, 72,* 627–640.

Shaver, P., Schwartz, J., Kirson, D., & O'Connor, C. (1987). Emotion knowledge: Further exploration of a prototype approach. *Journal of Personality and Social Psychology, 52,* 1061–1086.

Shavitt, S. (1990). The role of attitude objects in attitude function. *Journal of Experimental Social Psychology, 26,* 124–148.

Shaw, J. I., & Steers, W. N. (1996). Effects of perceiver sex, search goal, and target person attributes on information search in impression formation. *Journal of Social Behavior & Personality,* 11: 209–227.

Shaw, M. E., & Wagner, P. J. (1975). Role selection in the service of self-presentation. *Memory and Cognition, 3,* 481–484.

Sheets, V. L., & Bushardt, S. C. (1994). Effects of the applicant's gender appropriateness and qualifications and rater self-monitoring propensities on hiring decisions. *Public Personnel Management, 23,* 373–382.

Sheets, V. L., & Braver, S. L. (1993, April). *Perceptions of sexual harassment: Effects of a harasser's attractiveness.* Paper presented to the Western Psychological Association, Phoenix, Arizona.

Sheets, V. L., & Braver, S. L. (1999). Organizational status and perceived sexual harassment: Detecting the mediators of a null effect. *Personality & Social Psychology Bulletin, 25,* 1159–1171.

Sheldon, K. M. (1999). Learning the lessons of tit-for-tat: Even competitors can get the message. *Journal of Personality & Social Psychology,* 77, 1245–1253.

Sheldon, K. M., & Elliot, A. J. (1999). Goal-striving, need satisfaction, and longitudinal well-being: The self-concordance model. *Journal of Personality and Social Psychology,* 76, 482–497.

Sheldon, K. M., & McGregor, H. A. (2000). Extrinsic value orientation and "the tragedy of the commons." *Journal of Personality, 68,* 383–411.

Shell, R., & Eisenberg, N. (1992). A developmental model of recipients' reactions to aid. *Psychological Bulletin, 111,* 413–433.

Shepher, J. (1971). Mate selection among second generation kibbutz adolescents and adults: Incest avoidance and negative imprinting. *Archives of Sexual Behavior, 1,* 293–307.

Shepperd, J. A. (1993). Productivity loss in performance groups: A motivation analysis. *Psychological Bulletin, 113,* 67–81.

Shepperd, J. A. (1993). Student derogation of the Scholastic Aptitude Test: Biases in perceptions and presentations of College Board scores. *Basic and Applied Social Psychology, 14,* 455–473.

Shepperd, J. A., & Arkin, R. M. (1989). Self-handicapping: The moderating roles of public self-consciousness and task importance. *Personality and Social Psychology Bulletin, 15,* 252–265.

Shepperd, J. A., & Arkin, R. M. (1990). Shyness and self-presentation. In W. R. Crozier (Ed.), *Shyness and embarrassment: Perspectives from social psychology* (pp. 286–314). Cambridge: Cambridge University Press.

Shepperd, J. A., & Arkin, R. M. (1991). Behavioral other-enhancement: Strategically obscuring the link between performance and evaluation. *Journal of Personality and Social Psychology, 60*, 79–88.

Shepperd, J. A., & Socherman, R. E. (1997). On the manipulative behavior of low Machiavellians: Feigning incompetence to "sandbag" an opponent. *Journal of Personality and Social Psychology, 72*, 1448–1459.

Shepperd, J. A., & Taylor, K. M. (1999). Social loafing and expectancy-value theory. *Personality and Social Psychology Bulletin, 25*, 1147–1158.

Shepperd, J. A., Arkin, R. M., & Slaughter, J. (1995). Constraints on excuse making: The deterring effects of shyness and anticipated retest. *Personality and Social Psychology Bulletin, 21*, 1061–1072.

Shepperd, J. A., Ouellette, J. A., & Fernandez, J. K. (1996). Abandoning unrealistic optimism: Performance estimates and the temporal proximity of self-relevant feedback. *Journal of Personality and Social Psychology, 70*, 844–855.

Sherif, M. (1936). *The psychology of social norms.* New York: Harper.

Sherif, M., Harvey, O. J., White, B. J., Hood, W. R., & Sherif, C. W. (1961/1988). *The Robbers Cave experiment: Intergroup conflict and cooperation.* Middletown, CT: Wesleyan University Press.

Sherman, J. W., & Frost, L. A. (2000). On the encoding of stereotype-relevant information under cognitive load. *Personality and Social Psychology Bulletin, 26*, 26–34.

Sherman, J. W., Stroessner, S. J., Loftus, S. T., & Deguzman, G. (1997). Stereotype suppression and recognition memory for stereotypical and nonstereotypical information. *Social Cognition, 15*, 205–215.

Sherman, L. W., & Berk, R. A. (1984). The specific deterrent effects of arrest for domestic assault. *American Sociological Review, 49*, 291–272.

Sherman, L. W., Schmidt, J. D., Rogan, D. P., Gartin, P. R., Cohn, E. G., Collins, D. J., & Bacich, A. R. (1991). From initial deterrence to long-term escalation: Short-custody arrest for poverty ghetto domestic violence. *Criminology, 29*, 821–849.

Sherman, P. W. (1981). Kinship demography, and Belding's ground squirrel nepotism. *Behavioral Ecology and Sociology, 8*, 604–606.

Sherman, S. J., Chassin, L., Presson, C. C., & Agostinelli, G. (1984). The role of the evaluation and similarity principles in the false consensus effect. *Journal of Personality and Social Psychology, 47*, 1244–1262.

Sherrod, D. R. (1974). Crowding, perceived control, and behavioral aftereffects. *Journal of Applied Social Psychology, 4*, 171–186.

Sherwin, B. B., Gelfand, M. M., & Brender, W. (1985). Androgen enhances sexual motivation in females: A prospective, crossover study of sex steroid administration in the surgical menopause. *Psychosomatic Medicine, 47*, 339–351.

Shih, M., Pittinsky, T. L., & Ambady, N. (1999). Stereotype susceptibility: Identity salience and shifts in quantitative performance. *Psychological Science, 10*, 80–83.

Shin, K. (1978). *Death penalty and crime: Empirical studies.* Fairfax, Va: Center for Economic Analysis, George Mason University.

Shiner, R. L. (2000). Linking childhood personality with adaptation: Evidence for continuity and change across time into late adolescence. *Journal of Personality & Social Psychology, 78*, 310–325.

Shotland, R. L., & Straw, M. (1976). Bystander response to an assault: When a man attacks a woman. *Journal of Personality and Social Psychology, 34*, 990–999.

Shulman, S., Elicker, J., & Sroufe, L. A. (1994). Stages of friendship growth in preadolescence as related to attachment history. *Journal of Personal and Personal Relationships, 11*, 341–361.

Shulman, S., Laursen, B., Kalman, Z., & Karpovsky, S. (1997). Adolescent intimacy revisited. *Journal of Youth and Adolescence, 26*, 597–617.

Sicoly, F., & Ross, M. (1979). Facilitation of ego-biased attributions by means of self-serving observer feedback. *Journal of Personality and Social Psychology, 35*, 734–741.

Sidanius, J., Cling, B. J., & Pratto, F. (1991). Ranking and linking as a function of sex and gender role attitudes. *Journal of Social Issues, 47*, 131–149.

Sidanius, J., Levin, S., Liu, J., & Pratto, F. (2000). Social dominance orientation, anti-egalitarianism and the political psychology of gender: An extension and cross-cultural replication. *European Journal of Social Psychology, 30*, 41–67.

Sidanius, J., & Pratto, F. (1993). The inevitability of oppression and the dynamics of social dominance. In P. Sniderman & P. tetlock (Eds.), *Prejudice, politics, and the American dilemma* (pp. 173–211). Stanford, CA: Stanford University Press.

Sidanius, J., & Pratto, F. (1998). *Social dominance: An intergroup theory of social hierarchy and oppression.* New York: Cambridge University Press.

Sidanius, J., & Pratto, F. (1999). *Social dominance: An intergroup theory of social hierarchy and oppression.* New York: Cambridge University Press.

Sidanius, J., Pratto, F., & Bobo, L. (1994). Social dominance orientation and the political psychology of gender: A case of invariance? *Journal of Personality and Social Psychology, 67*, 998–1011.

Siegel, J. M. (1990). Stressful life events and use of physician services among the elderly. *Journal of Personality and Social Psychology, 58*, 1081–1086.

Sigall, H., & Landy, D. (1973). Radiating beauty: The effects of having a physically attractive partner on person perception. *Journal of Personality and Social Psychology, 28*, 218–224.

Sigall, H., & Page, R. (1971). Current stereotypes: A little fading, a little faking. *Journal of Personality and Social Psychology, 18*, 247–255.

Sigelman, C. K., Howell, J. L., Cornell, D. P., Cutright, J. D., & Dewey, J. C. (1991). Courtesy stigma: The social implications of associating with a gay person. *Journal of Social Psychology, 131*, 45–56.

Simon, H. A. (1967). Motivational and emotional controls of cognition. *Psychological Review, 74*, 29–39.

Simon, L., & Greenberg, J. (1996). Further progress in understanding the effects of derogatory ethnic labels: The role of preexisting attitudes toward the targeted group. *Personality and Social Psychology Bulletin, 22*, 1195–1204.

Simonich, W. L. (1991). *Government antismoking policies.* New York: Peter Lang.

Simonton, D. K. (1994). *Greatness: Who makes history and why.* New York: Guilford.

Simonton, D. K. (1997). Foreign influence and national achievement: The impact of open milieus on Japanese civilization. *Journal of Personality and Social Psychology, 72*, 86–94.

Simpson, G. E., & Yinger, J. M. (1965). *Racial and cultural minorities: An analysis of prejudice and discrimination* (3rd ed.). New York: Harper & Row.

Simpson, J. A. (1990). Influence of attachment styles on romantic relationships. *Journal of Personality and Social Psychology, 59*, 971–980.

Simpson, J. A., & Gangestad, S. W. (1991). Individual differences in sociosexuality: Evidence for convergent and discriminant validity. *Journal of Personality and Social Psychology, 67*, 870–883.

Simpson, J. A., & Gangestad, S. W. (1992). Sociosexuality and romantic partner choice. *Journal of Personality, 60*, 31–51.

Simpson, J. A., Gangestad, S. W., Christensen, P. N., & Leck, K. (1999). Fluctuating asymmetry, sociosexuality, and intrasexual competitive tactics. *Journal of Personality & Social Psychology, 76*, 159–172.

Simpson, J. A., Gangestad, S. W., & Lerma, M. (1990). Perception of physical attractiveness: Mechanisms involved in the maintenance of romantic relationships. *Journal of Personality and Social Psychology, 59*, 1192–1201.

Simpson, J. A., & Kenrick, D. T. (1997). *Evolutionary Social Psychology.* Mahwah, NJ: Erlbaum.

Sinclair, L., & Kunda, Z. (2000). Motivated stereotyping of women: She's fine if she praised me but incompetent if she criticized me. *Personality and Social Psychology Bulletin, 26*, 1329–1342.

Sinclair, R. C., & Mark, M. M. (1992). The influence of mood state on judgment and action. In L. L. Martin & A. Tesser (Eds.), *The construction of social judgments* (pp. 165–193). Hillsdale, NJ: Erlbaum.

Sinclair, R. C., Hoffman, C., Mark, M. M., Martin, L. L., & Pickering, T. L. (1994). Construct accessibility and the misattribution of arousal: Schachter and Singer revisited. *Psychological Science, 5*, 15–19.

Sinclair, R. C., Mark, M. M., & Shotland, R. L. (1987). Construct accessibility and generalizability across response categories. *Personality and Social Psychology Bulletin, 13*, 239–252.

Singer, M. T., & Lalich, J. (1995). *Cults in our midst.* San Francisco: Jossey-Bass.

Singh, D. (1993). Adaptive significance of female physical attractiveness: Role of waist-to-hip ratio. *Journal of Personality and Social Psychology, 65*, 293–307.

Singh, D. (1995). Female judgment of male attractiveness and desirability for relationships: Role of waist-to-hip ratio and financial status. *Journal of Personality and Social Psychology, 69*, 1089–1101.

Skinner, B. F. (1938). *The behavior of organisms: An experimental analysis.* Englewood Cliffs, NJ: Prentice Hall.

Slavin, R. E., & Cooper, R. (1999). Improving intergroup relations: Lessons learned from cooperative learning programs. *Journal of Social Issues, 55*, 647–663.

Smith, A. (1776/1976). *The wealth of nations.* Oxford: Clarendon Press.

Smith, C. A., Haynes, K. N., Lazarus, R. S., & Pope, L. K. (1993). In search of the "hot" cognitions: Attributions, appraisals, and their relation to emotion. *Journal of Personality and Social Psychology, 65*, 916–929.

Smith, D. M., Neuberg, S. L., Judice, T. N., & Biesanz, J. C. (1997). Target complicity in the confirmation and disconfirmation of erroneous perceiver expectations: Immediate and longer term implications. *Journal of Personality and Social Psychology, 73*, 974–991.

Smith, D. S., & Strube, M. J. (1991). Self-protective tendencies as moderators of self-handicapping impressions. *Basic and Applied Social Psychology, 12*, 63–80.

Smith, E. E., & Medin, D. L. (1981). *Categories and concepts.* Cambridge, MA: Harvard University Press.

Smith, E. R. (1998). Mental representation and memory. In D. T. Gilbert, S. T. Fiske, & G. Lindzey (Eds.), *Handbook of Social Psychology* (4th ed.) (pp. 391–445). New York: McGraw-Hill.

Smith, E. R., & DeCoster, J. (2000). Dual process models in social and cognitive psychology. *Personality and Social Psychology Review, 4*, 108–131.

Smith, E. R., & Lerner, M. (1986). Development of automatism of social judgments. *Journal of Personality and Social Psychology, 50*, 246–259.

Smith, E. R., & Zárate, M. A. (1992). Exemplar-based model of social judgment. *Psychological Review, 99*, 3–21.

Smith, K. D., Keating, J. P., & Stotland, E. (1989). Altruism reconsidered: The effect of denying feedback on a victim's status to witnesses. *Journal of Personality and Social Psychology, 57*, 641–650.

Smith, M. B., Bruner, J. S., & White, R. W. (1956). *Opinions and personality.* New York: Wiley.

Smith, P. B., & Bond, M. H. (1994). *Social psychology across cultures.* Boston: Allyn & Bacon.

Smith, P. B., & Bond, M. H. (1998). *Social psychology across cultures.* Boston: Allyn & Bacon.

Smith, R. E., & Hunt, S. D. (1978). Attributional processes in promotional situations. *Journal of Consumer Research, 5*, 149–158.

Smolowe, J. (1990, November 26). Contents require immediate attention. *Time*, p. 64.

Sniderman, P. M., & Tetlock, P. E. (1986). Symbolic racism? Problems of motive attribution in political analysis. *Journal of Social Issues, 42*, 129–150.

Snow, D. A., Robinson, C., & McCall, P. L. (1991). "Cooling out" men in singles bars and nightclubs: Observations on the interpersonal survival strategies of women in public places. *Journal of Contemporary Ethnography, 19*, 423–449.

Snyder, C. R., & Forsyth, D. R. (1991). *Handbook of social and clinical psychology*. New York: Pergamon.

Snyder, C. R., & Higgins, R. L. (1988). Excuses: Their effective role in the negotiation of reality. *Psychological Bulletin, 104*, 23–35.

Snyder, C. R., Lassegard, M., & Ford, C. E. (1986). Distancing after group success and failure: Basking in reflected glory and cutting off reflected failure. *Journal of Personality and Social Psychology, 51*, 382–388.

Snyder, C. R., Tennen, H., Affleck, G., & Cheavens, J. (2000). Social, personality, clinical, and health psychology tributaries: The merging of a scholarly "river of dreams." *Personality & Social Psychology Review, 4*, 16–29.

Snyder, M. (1974). Self-monitoring of expressive behavior. *Journal of Personality and Social Psychology, 30*, 526–537.

Snyder, M. (1979). Self-monitoring processes. In L. Berkowitz, (Ed.), *Advances in experimental social psychology* (vol. 12, pp. 86–128). New York: Academic Press.

Snyder, M. (1984). When belief creates reality. In L. Berkowitz (Ed.), *Advances in experimental social psychology* (Vol. 18, pp. 247–304). New York: Academic Press.

Snyder, M. (1987). *Public appearances, private realities: The psychology of self-monitoring*. New York: Freeman.

Snyder, M. (1992). Motivational foundations of behavioral confirmation. In M. P. Zanna (Ed.), *Advances in Experimental Social Psychology* (Vol. 25, pp. 67–114). New York: Academic Press.

Snyder, M., & Cantor, N. (1998). Understanding personality and social behavior: A functionalist strategy. In D. T. Gilbert, S. T. Fiske, & G. Lindzey (Eds.), *The handbook of social psychology* (4th ed.) (Vol. 1, pp. 635–679). Boston: McGraw-Hill.

Snyder, M., & DeBono, K. G. (1985). Appeals to image and claims about quality: Understanding the psychology of advertising. *Journal of Personality and Social Psychology, 49*, 586–597.

Snyder, M., & DeBono, K. G. (1989). Understanding the functions of attitudes. In A. R. Pratkanis, S. J. Breckler, & A. G. Greenwald (Eds.), *Attitude structure and function* (pp. 339–359). Hillsdale, NJ: Erlbaum.

Snyder, M., & Gangestad, S. (1982). Choosing social situations: Two investigations of self-monitoring processes. *Journal of Personality and Social Psychology, 43*, 123–135.

Snyder, M., & Gangestad, S. (1986). On the nature of self-monitoring: Matters of assessment, matters of validity. *Journal of Personality and Social Psychology, 51*, 125–139.

Snyder, M., & Haugen, J. A. (1995). Why does behavioral confirmation occur? A functional perspective on the role of the target. *Personality and Social Psychology Bulletin, 21*, 963–974.

Snyder, M., & Ickes, W. (1985). Personality and social behavior. In G. Lindzey & E. Aronson (Eds.), *Handbook of social psychology* (3rd ed.) (Vol. 2, pp. 883–948). New York: Random House.

Snyder, M., & Omoto, A. M. (1992). Who helps and why? In S. Spacapan & S. Oskamp (Eds.), *Helping and being helped: Naturalistic studies* (pp. 213–239). Newbury Park, CA: Sage.

Snyder, M., & Simpson, J. A. (1984). Self-monitoring and dating relationships. *Journal of Personality and Social Psychology, 47*, 1281–1291.

Snyder, M., & Swann, W. B., Jr. (1976). When actions reflect attitudes: The politics of impression management. *Journal of Personality and Social Psychology, 34*, 1034–1042.

Snyder, M., & Swann, W. B., Jr. (1978). Hypothesis-testing processes in social interaction. *Journal of Personality and Social Psychology, 36*, 1202–12.

Snyder, M., Simpson, J. A., & Gangestad, S. (1984). Personality and sexual relations. *Journal of Personality and Social Psychology, 51*, 181–190.

Snyder, M. L., Stephan, W. G., & Rosenfield, D. (1976). Egotism and attribution. *Journal of Personality and Social Psychology, 33*, 435–441.

Snyder, M., Tanke, E. D., & Berscheid, E. (1977). Social perception and interpersonal behavior: On the self-fulfilling nature of social stereotypes. *Journal of Personality and Social Psychology, 35*, 656–666.

Solano, C., Batten, P. G., & Parish, E. A. (1982). Loneliness and patterns of self-disclosure. *Journal of Personality and Social Psychology, 43*, 524–531.

Solomon, R. L. (1980). The opponent-process theory of acquired motivation: The costs of pleasure and the benefits of pain. *American Psychologist, 35*, 691–712.

Sommers, S. R., & Ellsworth, P. C. (2000). Race in the courtroom: Perceptions of guilt and dispositional attributions. *Personality and Social Psychology Bulletin, 26*, 1367–1379.

Sorrentino, R. M., & Boutillier, R. G. (1975). The effect of quantity and quality of verbal interaction on ratings of leadership ability. *Journal of Experimental Social Psychology, 11*, 403–411.

Sorrentino, R. M., & Field, N. (1986). Emergent leadership over time: The functional value of positive motivation. *Journal of Personality and Social Psychology, 50*, 1091–1099.

Speed, A., & Gangestad, S. W. (1997). Romantic popularity and mate preferences: A peer nomination study.

Personality & Social Psychology Bulletin, 9, 928–935.

Spence, J. T., & Helmreich, R. L. (1978). *Masculinity and femininity.* Austin: University of Texas Press.

Spence, K. W. (1956). *Behavior theory and conditioning.* New Haven, CT: Yale University Press.

Spencer, S. J., Fein, S., Wolfe, C. T., Fong, C., & Dunn, M. A. (1998). Automatic activation of stereotypes: The role of self-image threat. *Personality and Social Psychology Bulletin, 24,* 1139–1152.

Spencer, S. J., Josephs, R. A., & Steele, C. M. (1993). Low self-esteem: The uphill struggle for self-integrity. In R. Baumeister (Ed.), *Self-esteem: The puzzle of low self-regard* (pp. 21–36). New York: Plenum.

Spencer, S. J., Steele, C. M., & Quinn, D. (1999). Stereotype threat and women's math performance. *Journal of Experimental and Social Psychology, 35,* 4–28.

Spokane, A. R. (1985). A review of research on person-environment congruence in Holland's theory of careers. *Journal of Vocational Behavior, 26,* 306–343.

Sprecher, S., & Regan, P. C. (1998). Passionate and companionate love in courting and young married couples. *Sociological Inquiry, 68,* 163–185.

Srull, T. K., & Wyer, R. S., Jr. (1979). The role of category accessibility in the interpretation of information about persons: Some determinants and implications. *Journal of Personality and Social Psychology, 37,* 1660–1672.

Srull, T. K., Lichtenstein, M., & Rothbart, M. (1985). Associative storage and retrieval processes in person memory. *Journal of Experimental Psychology: Learning, memory, and Cognition, 11,* 316–345.

Staats, A. W., Staats, C. K., & Crawford, H. L. (1962). First-order conditioning of meaning and the parallel conditioning of a GSR. *Journal of General Psychology, 67,* 159–167.

Stacy, A., Sussman, S., Dent, C. W., Burton, D., & Flay, B. R. (1992). Moderators of social influence in adolescent smoking. *Personality and Social Psychology Bulletin, 18,* 163–172.

Stangor, C., & Duan, C. (1991). Effects of multiple task demands upon memory for information about social groups. *Journal of Experimental Social Psychology, 27,* 357–378.

Stangor, C., & McMillan, D. (1992). Memory for expectancy-congruent and expectancy-incongruent information: A review of the social and social developmental literatures. *Psychological Bulletin, 111,* 42–61.

Stangor, C., Sullivan, L. A., & Ford, T. E. (1991). Affective and cognitive determinants of prejudice. *Social Cognition, 9,* 359–380.

Stapf, K. H., Stroebe, W., & Jonas, K. (1986). *Amerikaner über Deutschland und die Deutschen: Urteile und Vorurteile.* Köln: Westdeutscher Verlag.

Stark, B., & Deaux, K. (1994). Integrating motivational and identity theories of volunteerism. Poster presented at the annual meeting of the American Psychological Society, Washington, DC. July 2.

Stasser, G. (1992). Information salience and the discovery of hidden profiles by decision-making groups: A "thought experiment." *Organizational Behavior and Human Decision Processes, 52,* 156–181.

Stasser, G., & Titus, W. (1985). Pooling of unshared information in group decision making: Biased information sampling during discussion. *Journal of Personality and Social Psychology, 48,* 1467–1478.

Staub, E. (1974). Helping a distressed person: Social personality, and stimulus determinants. *Advances in experimental social psychology, 7,* 293–341.

Staw, B. M., & Ross, J. (1980). Commitment in an experimenting society. *Journal of Applied Psychology, 65,* 249–260.

Steele, C. M. (1988). The psychology of self-affirmation: Sustaining the integrity of the self. In L. Berkowitz (Ed.), *Advances in experimental social psychology* (Vol. 21, pp. 261–302). New York: Academic Press.

Steele, C. M. (1992, April). Race and the schooling of Black Americans. *The Atlantic Monthly,* pp. 68–78.

Steele, C. M., & Aronson, J. (1995). Stereotype threat and the intellectual test performance of African Americans. *Journal of Personality and Social Psychology, 69,* 797–811.

Steele, C. M., & Josephs, R. A. (1988). Drinking your troubles away II: An attention-allocation model of alcohol's effect on psychological stress. *Journal of Abnormal Psychology, 97,* 196–205.

Steele, C. M., & Josephs, R. A. (1990). Alcohol myopia. *American Psychologist, 45,* 921–933.

Steenbergen, M. R., McGraw, K. M., & Scholtz, J. T. (1992). Adaptation to the 1986 Tax Reform Act. In J. Slemrod (Ed.), *Why people pay taxes* (pp. 21–45). Ann Arbor: University of Michigan Press.

Stein, R. T., & Heller, T. (1979). An empirical analysis of the correlations between leadership status and participation rates reported in the literature. *Journal of Personality and Social Psychology, 37,* 1993–2002.

Steiner, I. D. (1972). *Group process and productivity.* New York: Academic Press.

Stephan, W. G. (1978). School desegregation: An evaluation of predictions made in Brown v. Board of Education. *Psychological Bulletin, 85,* 217–238.

Stephan, W. G., & Finlay, K. (1999). The role of empathy in improving intergroup relations. *Journal of Social Issues, 55,* 729–743.

Stephan, W. G., & Stephan, C. W. (1984). The role of ignorance in intergroup relations. In N. Miller & M. B. Brewer (Eds.), *Groups in contact* (pp. 229–255). New York: Academic Press.

Stephan, W. G., & Stephan, C. W. (1985). Intergroup anxiety. *Social Issues, 41,* 157–175.

Stephan, W. G., & Stephan, C. W. (1996). *Intergroup relations.* Madison, WI: Brown & Benchmark.

Stephan, W. G., Ageyev, V., Coates-Shrider, L., Stephan, C. W., & Abalakina, M. (1994). On the relationship between stereotypes and prejudice: An international study. *Personality and Social Psychology Bulletin, 20,* 277–284.

Stephan, W., Berscheid, E., & Walster, E. (1971). Sexual arousal and heterosexual perception. *Journal of Personality and Social Psychology, 20,* 93–101.

Stern, P. C. (2000). Psychology and the science of human-environment interactions. *American Psychologist, 55,* 523–530.

Stern, P. C., Dietz, T., & Kalof, L. (1993). Value orientations, gender, and environmental concern. *Environment and Behavior, 25,* 322–348.

Sternberg, R. J. (1986). A triangular theory of love. *Psychological Review, 93,* 119–135.

Sternberg, R. J. (1988). Construct validation of a triangular theory of love. Unpublished manuscript.

Sternthal, B., Dholakia, R., & Leavitt, C. (1978). The persuasive effect of source credibility: Tests of cognitive response. *Journal of Consumer Research, 4,* 252–260.

Stets, J. E., & Straus, M. A. (1990). Gender differences in reporting of marital violence and its medical and psychological consequences. In M. A. Straus & R. J. Gelles (Eds.), *Physical violence in American families* (pp. 151–165). New Brunswick, NJ: Transaction.

Stevens, L. E., & Fiske, S. T. (1995). Motivation and cognition in social life: A social survival perspective. *Social Cognition, 13,* 189–214.

Stevens, R., & Slavin, R. (1995). The cooperative elementary school: Effects on student's achievement, attitudes, and social relations. *American Educational Research Journal, 32,* 321–351.

Stewart, J. E. (1980). Defendant's attractiveness as a factor in the outcome of criminal trials: An observational study. *Journal of Applied Social Psychology, 10,* 348–361.

Stewart, J. E. (1985). Appearance and punishment: The attraction-leniency effect. *Journal of Social Psychology, 125,* 373–378.

Stiles, W. B., Lyall, L. M., Knight, D. P., Ickes, W., Waung, M., Hall, C., & Primeau, B. E. (1997). Gender differences in verbal presumptuousness and attentiveness. *Personality and Social Psychology Bulletin, 23,* 759–772.

Stinchcombe, A. L. (1965). Social structure and organizations. In J. G. March (Ed.), *Handbook of Organizations* (pp. 142–193). Chicago: Rand McNally.

Stires, L. K., & Jones, E. E. (1969). Modesty versus self-enhancement as alternative forms of ingratiation. *Journal of Experimental Social Psychology, 5,* 172–188.

Stogdill, R. M. (1974). *Handbook of leadership.* New York: Free Press.

Stone, A. A., Broderick, J. E., Porter, L. S., & Kaell, A. T. (1997). The experience of rheumatoid arthritis pain and fatigue: Examining momentary reports and correlates over one week. *Arthritis Care and Research, 10,* 185–193.

Stone, J., Lynch, C. I., Sjomeling, M., & Darley, J. M. (1999). Stereotype threat effects on Black and White athletic performance. *Journal of Personality and Social Psychology, 77,* 1213–1227.

Stoner, J. A. F. (1961). *A comparison of individual and group decisions involving risk.* Unpublished master's thesis, Massachusetts Institute of Technology.

Storey, A. E., Walsh, C. J., Quinton, R. L., & Wynne-Edwards, K. E. (2000). Hormonal correlates of paternal responsiveness in new and expectant fathers. *Evolution & Human Behavior, 21,* 79–95.

Storms, M. D. (1973). Videotape and the attribution process: Reversing actors' and observers' points of view. *Journal of Personality and Social Psychology, 27,* 165–175.

Stouffer, S. A., Suchman, E., DeVinney, S. A., Star, S., & Williams, R. M. (Eds.). (1949). *The American soldier: Adjustment during army life.* Princeton, NJ: Princeton University Press.

Strack, F., Martin, L. L., & Stepper, S. (1988). Inhibiting and facilitating conditions of the human smile: A nonobtrusive test of the facial feedback hypothesis. *Journal of Personality and Social Psychology, 54,* 768–777.

Strack, S., & Coyne, J. C. (1983). Social confirmation of dysphoria: Shared and private reactions to depression. *Journal of Personality and Social Psychology, 44,* 798–806.

Strickland, B. R., & Crowne, D. P. (1962). Conformity under conditions of simulated group pressure as a function of need for social approval. *Journal of Social Psychology, 58,* 171–181.

Stroessner, S. J., & Mackie, D. M. (1992). The impact of induced affect on the perception of social variability in social groups. *Personality and Social Psychology Bulletin, 18,* 546–554.

Stroh, L. K., Brett, J. M., & Reilly, A. H. (1992). All the right stuff: A comparison of female and male managers' career progression. *Journal of Applied Psychology, 77,* 251–260.

Suedfeld, P., & Tetlock, P. E. (1991). Psychological advice about foreign policy decision-making: Heuristics, biases, and cognitive defects. In P. Suedfeld & P. E. Tetlock (Eds)., *Psychology and social policy* (pp. 51–70). New York: Hemisphere.

Suedfeld, P., Wallace, M. D., & Thachuk, K. L. (1993). Changes in integrative complexity among middle east leaders during the Persian Gulf crisis. *Journal of Social Issues, 49,* 183–191.

Sugarmann, J., & Rand, K. (1994, March 10). Cease fire. *Rolling Stone,* pp. 30–42.

Sullivan, H. S. (1953). *The interpersonal theory of psychiatry.* New York: Norton.

Sullivan, M. J. L., & Conway, M. (1989). Negative affect leads to low-effort cognition: Attributional processing for observed social behavior. *Social Cognition, 7,* 315–337.

Suls, J., Martin, R., & David, J. P. (1998). Person-environment fit and its limits: Agreeableness, neuroticism, and emotional reactivity to interpersonal conflict. *Personality and Social Psychology Bulletin, 24,* 88–98.

Suls, J., Martin, R., & Wheeler, L. (2000). Three kinds of opinion comparison: The triadic model. *Personality and Social Psychology Review, 4,* 219–237.

Summers, A. (1993). *Official and confidential: The secret life of J. Edgar Hoover.* New York: Putnam's Sons.

Sumner, W. G. (1906). *Folkways.* New York: New American Library.

Sussman, S., Dent, C. W., Flay, R. R., Hansen, W. B., & Johnson, C. A. (1986). Psychosocial predictors of cigarette smoking onset by white, black, Hispanic, and Asian adolescents in Southern California. *Morbidity and Mortality Weekly Report Supplement, 36,* 3–10.

Svenson, O. (1981). Are we all less risky and more skillful than our fellow drivers? *Acta Psychologica, 47,* 143–148.

Swann, W. B., Jr. (1984). Quest for accuracy in person perception: A matter of pragmatics. *Psychological Review, 91,* 457–477.

Swann, W. B., Jr. (1990). To be adored or to be known? The interplay of self-enhancement and self-verification. In R. M. Sorrentino & E. T. Higgins (Eds.), *Foundations of social behavior* (Vol. 2, pp. 404–448.). New York: Guilford.

Swann, W. B., Jr., & Ely, R. J. (1984). A battle of wills: Self-verification versus behavioral confirmation. *Journal of Personality and Social Psychology, 46,* 1287–1302.

Swann, W. B., Jr., Hixon, J. G., & De La Ronde, C. (1992). Embracing the bitter "truth": Negative self-concepts and marital commitment. *Psychological Science, 3,* 118–121.

Swann, W. B., Jr., Stein-Seroussi, A., & Giesler, R. B. (1992). Why people self--verify. *Journal of Personality and Social Psychology, 62,* 392–401.

Swann, W. B., Jr., Stephenson, B., & Pittman, T. S. (1981). Curiosity and control: On the determinants of the search for social knowledge. *Journal of Personality and Social Psychology, 40,* 635–642.

Swann, W. B., Jr., Wenzlaff, R. M., Krull, D. S., & Pelham, B. W. (1992). Allure of negative feedback: Self-verification strivings among depressed persons. *Journal of Abnormal Psychology, 101,* 293–306.

Swenson, O. (1981). Are we all less risky and more skillful than our fellow drivers? *Acta Psychologica, 47,* 143–148.

Swim, J. K. (1994). Perceived versus meta-analytic effect sizes: An assessment of the accuracy of gender stereotypes. *Journal of Personality and Social Psychology, 66,* 21–36.

Swim, J. K., & Miller, D. L. (1999). White guilt: Its antecedents and consequences for attitudes toward affirmative action. *Personality and Social Psychology Bulletin, 25,* 500–514.

Swim, J. K., & Sanna, L. J. (1996). He's skilled, she's lucky: A meta-analysis of observers' attributions for women's and men's successes and failures. *Personality and Social Psychology Bulletin, 22,* 507–519.

Swim, J. K., & Stangor, C. (1998). *Prejudice: The target's perspective.* San Diego: Academic Press.

Swim, J. K., Aikin, K. J., Hall, W. S., & Hunter, B. A. (1995). Sexism and racism: Old-fashioned and modern prejudices. *Journal of Personality and Social Psychology, 68,* 199–214.

Swim, J. K., Ferguson, M. J., & Hyers, L. L (1999). Avoiding stigma by association: Subtle prejudice against lesbians in the form of social distancing. *Basic and Applied Social Psychology, 21,* 61–68.

Szymanski, K., & Harkins, S. G. (1987). Social loafing and self-evaluation with a social standard. *Journal of Personality and Social Psychology, 53,* 891–897.

Tajfel, H. (1969). Cognitive aspects of prejudice. *Journal of Social Issues, 25,* 79–97.

Tajfel, H. (1982). Social psychology of intergroup relations. *Annual Review of Psychology, 33,* 1–39.

Tajfel, H., & Turner, J. (1979). An integrative theory of intergroup conflict. In W. G. Austin & S. Worchel (Eds.), *The social psychology of intergroup relations* (pp. 33–47). Monterey, CA: Brooks-Cole.

Tajfel, H., & Turner, J. C. (1986). The social identity theory of intergroup behavior. In S. Worchel & W. G. Austin (Eds.), *Psychology of intergroup relations* (2nd ed., pp. 7–24). Chicago: Nelson-Hall.

Tajfel, H., Billig, M. G., Bundy, R. P., & Flament, C. (1971). Social categorization and intergroup behavior. *Journal of Social Psychology, 1,* 149–178.

Tajfel, H., Sheikh, A. A., & Gardner, R. C. (1964). Content of stereotypes and the inference of similarity between members of stereotyped groups. *Acta Psychologia, 22,* 191–201.

Takahashi, K., Tamura, J., & Tokoro, M., (1997). Patterns of social relationships and psychological well-being among the elderly. *International Journal of Behavioral Development, 21,* 417–430.

Tan, D. T. Y., & Singh, R. (1995). Attitudes and attraction: A developmental study of the similarity-attraction and dissimilarity-repulsion hypotheses. *Personality and Social Psychology Bulletin, 21,* 975–986.

Tanford, S., & Penrod, S. (1984). Social influence model: A formal integration of research on majority and minority influence processes. *Psychological Bulletin, 95,* 189–225.

Tangney, J. P. (1992). Situational determinants of shame and guilt in young adulthood. *Personality and Social Psychology Bulletin, 18,* 199–206.

Tannen, D. (1990). *You just don't understand: Women and men in conversation.* New York: Morrow.

Tax-Smart Charity Gifts. (1998, June 8). *Time, 151*, 221.

Taylor, S. E. (1990). Health psychology: The science and the field. *American Psychologist, 45*, 40–50.

Taylor, S. E., & Brown, J. D. (1988). Illusion and well-being: A social psychological perspective on mental health. *Psychological Bulletin, 103*, 193–210.

Taylor, S. E., Collins, R. L., Skokan, L. A., & Aspinwall, L. G. (1989). Maintaining positive illusions in the face of getting negative information: Getting the facts without letting them get to you. *Journal of Social and Clinical Psychology, 8*, 114–129.

Taylor, S. E., & Crocker, J. (1981). Schematic bases of social information processing. In E. T. Higgins, C. P. Herman, & M. P. Zanna (Eds.), *Social cognition: The Ontario Symposium* (Vol. 1, pp. 89–134). Hillsdale, NJ: Erlbaum.

Taylor, S. E., & Fiske, S. T. (1975). Point of view and perceptions of causality. *Journal of Personality and Social Psychology, 32*, 439–445.

Taylor, S. E., & Fiske, S. T. (1978). Salience, attention, and attribution: Top of the head phenomena. In L. Berkowitz (Ed.), *Advances in experimental social psychology* (Vol. 11, pp. 249–288). New York: Academic Press.

Taylor, S. E., & Gollwitzer, P. M. (1995). Effects of mindset on positive illusions. *Journal of Personality and Social Psychology, 69*, 213–226.

Taylor, S. E., Kemeny, M. E., Reed, G. M., Bower, J. E., & Gruenwald, T. L. (2000). Psychological resources, positive illusion, and health. *American Psychologist, 55*, 99–109.

Taylor, S. E., Klein, L. C., Lewis, B. P., Gruenwald, T. L., Gurung, R. A. R., & Updegraff, J. A. (2000). Biobehavioral responses to stress in females: Tend-and-befriend, not fight-or-flight. *Psychological Review, 107*, 411–429.

Taylor, S. E., Lichtman, R. R., & Wood, J. V. (1984). Attributions, beliefs about control, and adjustment to breast cancer. *Journal of Personality and Social Psychology, 46*, 489–502.

Teenager got doctors' messages, ordered treatment (2000, December 17). *St. Louis Post-Dispatch*. p. A7.

Teger, A. (1980). *Too much invested to quit.* New York: Pergamon.

Tellegen, A., Lykken, D. T., Bouchard, T. J., Wilcox, K. J., Segal, N. L., & Rich, S. (1988). Personality similarity in twins reared apart and together. *Journal of Personality and Social Psychology, 54*, 1031–1039.

Tenbrunsel, A. E., & Messick, D. M. (1999). Sanctioning systems, decision frames, and cooperation. *Administrative Science Quarterly, 44*, 684–707.

Tennen, H., & Herzberger, S. (1987). Depression, self-esteem, and the absence of self-protective attributional biases. *Journal of Personality and Social Psychology, 52*, 72–80.

Terkel, S. (1992). *Race: How blacks and whites think and feel about the American obsession.* New York: Anchor.

Terpstra, D. E., & Baker, D. D. (1986). Psychological and demographic correlates of perception of sexual harassment. *Genetic, Social, and General Psychology Monographs, 112*, 459–478.

Terry, D. J., & Hogg, M. A. (1996). Group norms and the attitude-behavior relationship: A role for group identification. *Personality and Social Psychology Bulletin, 22*, 776–793.

Terry, D. J., & Hogg, M. A. (2000). *Attitudes, behavior, and social context: The role of norms and group membership.* Mahwah, NJ: Erlbaum.

Tesser, A. (1988). Toward a self-evaluation maintenance model of social behavior. In L. Berkowitz (Ed.), *Advances in experimental social psychology* (Vol. 21, pp. 181–227). San Diego, CA: Academic Press.

Tesser, A. (1990). Smith and Ellsworth's appraisal model of emotion: A replication, extension, and test. *Personality and Social Psychology Bulletin, 16*, 210–223.

Tesser, A. (1993). The importance of heritability in psychological research: The case of attitudes. *Psychological Review, 100*, 129–142.

Tesser, A., & Achee, J. (1994). Aggression, love, conformity, and other social psychological catastrophes. In R. R. Vallacher & A. Nowak (Eds.), *Dynamical systems in social psychology* (pp. 95–109). San Diego, CA: Academic Press.

Tesser, A., Campbell, J., & Mickler, S. (1983). The role of social pressure, attention to the stimulus, and self-doubt in conformity. *European Journal of Social Psychology, 13*, 217–233.

Tesser, A., & Smith, J. (1980). Some effects of task relevance and friendship on helping. *Journal of Experimental Social Psychology, 16*, 582–590.

Tessler, R. C., & Schwartz, S. H. (1972). Help-seeking, self-esteem, and achievement motivation: An attributional analysis. *Journal of Personality and Social Psychology, 21*, 318–326.

Tetlock, P. E. (1983). Accountability and complexity of thought. *Journal of Personality and Social Psychology, 45*, 74–83.

Tetlock, P. E. (1983). Policy-makers' images of international conflict. *Journal of Social Issues, 39*, 67–86.

Tetlock, P. E., & Kim, J. I. (1987). Accountability and judgment processes in a personality prediction task. *Journal of Personality and Social Psychology, 52*, 700–709.

Tetlock, P. E., Peterson, R. S., McGuire, C., Chang, S. J., & Feld, P. (1992). Assessing political group dynamics: A test of the groupthink model. *Journal of Personality and Social Psychology, 63*, 403–425.

Tetlock, P. E., Skitka, L., & Boettger, R. (1989). Social and cognitive strategies for coping with accountability: Conformity, complexity, and bolstering. *Journal of Personality and Social Psychology, 57*, 632–640.

Thatcher, M. (1993). *The Downing Street years.* London: HarperCollins.

Thatcher, M. (1995). *The path to power.* London: HarperCollins.

Thibodeau, R., & Aronson, E. (1992). Taking a closer look: Reasserting the role of the self-concept in dissonance theory. *Personality and Social Psychology Bulletin, 18,* 591–602.

Thompson, E. P., Roman, R. J., Moskowitz, G. B., Chaiken, S., & Bargh, J. A. (1994). Accuracy motivation attenuates covert priming: The systematic *re*processing of social information. *Journal of Personality and Social Psychology, 66,* 474–489.

Thompson, H. S. (1994, June 16). He was a crook. *Rolling Stone,* p. 42.

Thompson, J. S., & Thompson, W. C. (1990). Thatcher's leadership. In J. S. Thompson & W. C. Thompson (Eds.), *Margaret Thatcher: Prime minister indomitable* (pp. 3–30). Boulder, CO: Westview Press.

Thompson, L. (1993). The impact of negotiation on intergroup relations. *Journal of Experimental Social Psychology, 29,* 304–325.

Thompson, L., & Fine, G. A. (1999). Socially shared cognition, affect, and behavior: A review and integration. *Personality & Social Psychology Review, 3,* 278–302.

Thompson, L. L., Levine, J. M., & Messick, D. M. (1999). *Shared cognition in organizations: The management of knowledge.* Mahwah, NJ: Erlbaum.

Thompson, M. M., Naccarato, M. E., & Parker, K. E. (1989, June). *Assessing cognitive need: The development of the Personal Need for Structure (PNS) and Personal Fear of Invalidity (PFI) measures.* Paper presented at the annual meeting of the Canadian Psychological Association, Halifax, Nova Scotia.

Thompson, S. C., & Spacapan, S. (1991). Perceptions of control in vulnerable populations. *Journal of Social Issues, 47,* 1–21.

Thompson, S. C., Nanni, C., & Levine, A. (1994). Primary versus secondary and central versus consequence-related control in HIV-positive men. *Journal of Personality and Social Psychology, 67,* 540–547.

Thompson, S. C., Sobolow-Shubin, A., Galbraith, M. E., Schwankovsky, L., & Cruzen, D. (1993). Maintaining perceptions of control: Finding control in low-control circumstances. *Journal of Personality and Social Psychology, 64,* 293–304.

Thompson, S. (1999). Illusions of control: How we overestimate our personal influence. *Current Directions in Psychological Science, 8,* 187–190.

Tibon, S. (2000). Personality traits and peace negotiations: Integrative complexity and attitudes toward the Middle East peace process. *Group Decision and Negotiation, 9,* 1–15.

Tibon, S., & Blumberg, H. H. (1999). Authoritarianism and political socialization in the context of the Arab-Israeli conflict. *Political Psychology, 20,* 581–591

Tice, D. M. (1991). Esteem protection or enhancement? Self-handicapping motives and attributions differ by trait self-esteem. *Journal of Personality and Social Psychology, 60,* 711–725.

Tice, D. M. (1992). Self-concept change and self-presentation: The looking glass self is also a magnifying glass. *Journal of Personality and Social Psychology, 63,* 435–451.

Tice, D. M. (1993). The social motivations of people with low self-esteem. In R. Baumeister (Ed.), *Self-esteem: The puzzle of low self-regard* (pp. 37–54). New York: Plenum.

Tice, D. M., & Baumeister, R. F. (1990). Self-esteem, self-handicapping, and self-presentation: The strategy of inadequate practice. *Journal of Personality, 58,* 443–464.

Tice, D. M., Butler, J. L., Muraven, & M. B., Stillwell, A. M. (1995). When modesty prevails: Differential favorability of self-presentation to friends and strangers. *Journal of Personality and Social Psychology, 69,* 1120–1138.

Tietjen, A. M. (1994). Children's social networks and social supports in cultural context. In W. J. Lonner & R. Malpass (Eds.), *Psychology and culture* (pp. 101–106). Boston: Allyn & Bacon.

Tinbergen, N. (1968). On war and peace in animals and man. *Science, 160,* 1411–1418.

Tindale, R. S., & Davis, J. H. (1983). Group decision making and jury verdicts. In H. H. Blumberg, A. P. Hare, V. Kent, & M. F. Davies (Eds.), *Small groups and social interaction* (Vol. 2, pp. 9–38). Chichester, England: Wiley.

Tindale, R. S., Davis, J. H., Vollrath, D. A., Nagao, D. H., & Hinsz, V. B. (1990). Asymmetrical social influence in freely interacting groups: A test of three models. *Journal of Personality and Social Psychology, 58,* 438–449.

Tindale, R. S., & Kameda, T. (2000). 'Social sharedness' as a unifying theme for information processing in groups. *Group Processes and Intergroup Relations, 3,* 123–140.

Titchener, E. B. (1909). *Elementary psychology of the thought processes.* New York: Macmillan.

Toch, H. (1969). *Violent men: An inquiry into the psychology of violence.* Chicago, IL: Aldine.

Toch, H. (1984). *Violent men.* Cambridge: Schenkman.

Tokayer, M., & Swartz, M. (1979). *The Fugu Plan: The untold story of the Japanese and the Jews during World War II.* New York: Paddington.

Tomkins, S. S. (1970). Affect as the primary motivational system. In M. Arnold (Ed.), *Feelings and emotions* (pp. 101–110). New York: Academic Press.

Tomkins, S. S. (1980). Affect as amplification: Some modifications in theory. In R. Plutchik & H. Kellerman (Eds.), *Emotion: Theory, research and experience: Vol. 1: Theories of emotion* (pp. 141–164). New York: Academic Press.

Tooby, J., & Cosmides, L. (1992). The psychological foundations of culture. In J. H. Barkow, L. Cosmides, & J. Tooby (Eds.), *The adapted mind: Evolutionary psychology and the generation of culture* (pp. 19–136). New York: Oxford University Press.

Torestad, B. (1990). What is anger provoking: A psychophysical study of perceived causes of anger. *Aggressive Behavior, 16*, 9–26.

Tougas, F., Brown, R., Beaton, A. M., & Joly, S. (1995). Neosexism: Plus ça change, plus c'est pariel. *Personality and Social Psychology Bulletin, 21*, 842–849.

Townsend, E. J. (1973). An examination of participants in organizational, political, informational, and interpersonal activities. *Journal of Voluntary Action Research, 2*, 200–211.

Townsend, J. M., & Levy, G. D. (1990). Effects of potential partner's costume and physical attractiveness on sexuality and partner selection: Sex differences in reported preferences of university students. *Journal of Psychology, 124*, 371–76.

Townsend, J. M., & Roberts, L. W. (1993). Gender differences in mate preferences among law students: Diverging and converging criteria. *Journal of Psychology, 127*, 507–528.

Townsend, M. A., McCracken, H. E., & Wilton, K. M. (1988). Popularity and intimacy as determinants of psychological well-being in adolescent friendships. *Journal of Early Adolescence, 8*, 421–436.

Trafinow, D., & Finlay, K. A. (1996). The importance of subjective norms for a majority of people: Between-subjects and within-subjects. *Personality and Social Psychology Bulletin, 22*, 820–828.

Trafimow, D., & Schneider, D. J. (1994). The effects of behavioral, situational, and person information on different attribution judgments. *Journal of Experimental Social Psychology, 30*, 351–369.

Triandis, H. C. (1989). The self and social behavior in differing cultural contexts. *Psychological Review, 96*, 506–520.

Triandis, H. C. (1994). *Culture and social behavior*. New York: McGraw-Hill.

Triandis, H. C. (1995). *Individualism and collectivism*. Boulder, CO: Westview Press.

Triplett, N. (1897–1898). The dynamogenic factors in pacemaking and competition. *American Journal of Psychology, 9*, 507–533.

Trivers, R. L. (1971). The evolution of reciprocal altruism. *Quarterly Review of Biology, 46*, 35–37.

Trivers, R. L. (1985). *Social evolution.* Menlo Park, CA: Benjamin/Cummings.

Trope, Y., & Thompson, E. P. (1997). Looking for truth in all the wrong places? Asymmetric search of individuating information about stereotypes group members. *Journal of Personality and Social Psychology, 73*, 229–241.

Trovillo, P. V. (1939). A history of lie detection. *American Journal of Political Science, 29*, 848–881.

Tuch, S. A. (1987). Urbanism, region, and tolerance revisited: The case of racial prejudice. *American Sociological Review, 52*, 504–510.

Tucker, J. A., Vuchinich, R. E., & Sobell, M. B. (1981). Alcohol consumption as a self-handicapping strategy. *Journal of Abnormal Psychology, 90*, 220–230.

Turke, P. W., & Betzig, L. L. (1985). Those who can do: Wealth, status, and reproductive success on Ifaluk. *Ethology and Sociobiology, 6*, 79–87.

Turner, J. C. (1991). *Social influence.* Pacific Grove, CA: Brooks/Cole.

Turner, J. C., Hogg, M. A., Oakes, P. J., Reicher, S. D., & Wetherell, M. S. (1987). *Rediscovering the social group: A self-categorization theory.* Oxford: Basil Blackwell.

Turner, S. (1978, January 8). The life and times of a pickle packer. *Boston Globe Magazine*, p. 10–00.

Turnquist, L. (2000, August 22). Read this story. *The Oregonian*, pp. D1, D5.

Tversky, A., & Kahneman, D. (1973). Availability: A heuristic for judging frequency and probability. *Cognitive Psychology, 5*, 207–232.

Tversky, A., & Kahneman, D. (1974). Judgment under uncertainty: Heuristics and biases. *Science, 185*, 1124–1131.

Tversky, A., & Shafir, E. (1992a). The disjunction effect in choice under uncertainty. *Psychological Science, 3*, 305–309.

Tversky, A., & Shafir, E. (1992b). Choice under conflict: The dynamics of deferred decision. *Psychological Science, 3*, 358–361.

Tybout A. M., & Yalch, R. F. (1980). The effect of experience: A matter of salience? *Journal of Consumer Research, 6*, 406–413.

Tyler, T. R., & Degoey, P. (1995). Collective restraint in social dilemmas: Procedural justice and social identification effects on support for authorities. *Journal of Personality and Social Psychology, 69*, 482–497.

Tyler, T. R., & Degoey, P. (1995). Trust in organizational authorities: The influence of motive attributions on willingness to accept decisions. In R. Kramer & T. R. Tyler (Eds.), *Trust in organizational authorities* (pp. 331–356). Beverly Hills: Sage.

U.S. Bureau of the Census. (1992). *Statistical abstract of the United States* (112th ed.), Washington, DC: Author

U.S. Bureau of the Census. (1998). International Data Base. Public Website.

U.S. Department of Labor. (1990, March 29). *U.S. Bureau of Labor Statistics News*, 90–154.

U.S. Merit Systems Protection Board. (1988). *Sexual harassment in the federal workplace: An update.* Washington, D.C.: U.S. Government Printing Office.

Udry, J. R., Billy, J. O. G., Morris, N. M., Groff, T. R., & Raj, M. H. (1985). Serum androgenic hormones motivate sexual behavior in adolescent boys. *Fertility and Sterility, 43*, 90–94.

Underwood, B., & Moore, B. (1982). Perspective taking and altruism. *Psychological Bulletin, 91*, 143–173.

Vallacher, R. R., & Nowak, A. (1994). The chaos in social psychology. In R. R. Vallacher & A. Nowak (Eds.), *Dynamical Systems in Social Psychology* (pp. 1–16). New York: Academic Press.

Vallacher, R. R., & Nowak, A. (1997). The emergence of dynamical social psychology. *Psychological Inquiry, 5*, 73–99.

Vallacher, R. R., & Wegner, D. M. (1985). *A theory of action identification.* Hillsdale, NJ: Erlbaum.

Vallacher, R. R., & Wegner, D. M. (1987). What do people think they're doing? Action identification and human behavior. *Psychological Review, 94,* 3–15.

Vallone, R. P., Ross, L., & Lepper, M. R. (1985). The hostile media phenomenon: Biased perception and perceptions of media bias coverage of the Beirut massacre. *Journal of Personality and Social Psychology, 49,* 577–585.

Van Boven, L., Kruger, J., Savitsky, K., & Gilovich, T. (2000). When social worlds collide: Overconfidence in the multiple audience problem. *Personality and Social Psychology Bulletin, 26,* 619–628.

van den Berghe, P. L. (1983). Human inbreeding avoidance: Culture in nature. *Behavioral and Brain Sciences, 6,* 91–123.

van der Dennen, J., & Falger, V. (1990). *Sociobiology and conflict: Evolutionary perspectives on competition, cooperation, violence, and warfare.* London: Chapman and Hall.

van der Plight, J., & Eiser, J. R. (1984). Dimensional salience, judgment, and attitudes. In J. R. Eiser (Ed.), *Attitudinal judgment* (pp. 161–177). New York: Springer-Verlag.

Van Staden, F. J. (1987). White South Africans' attitudes toward the desegregation of public amenities. *Journal of Social Psychology, 127,* 163–173.

Vancouver, J. B., & Ilgen, D. R. (1989). Effects of interpersonal orientation and the sex-type of the task on choosing to work alone or in groups. *Journal of Applied Psychology, 74,* 927–934.

VanDijk, E., & Wilke, H. (2000). Decision-induced focusing in social dilemmas: Give-some, keep-some, take-some, and leave-some dilemmas. *Journal of Personality & Social Psychology, 78,* 92–104.

VanGoozen, S. H. M., Cohen-Kettenis, P. T., Gooren, L. J. G., Frijda, N. H., & VandePoll, N. E. (1995). Gender differences in behaviour: Activating effects of cross-sex hormones. *Psychoneuroendocrinology, 20,* 343–363.

VanLange, P. A. M., Agnew, C. R., Harinck, F., & Steemers, G. E. M. (1997). From game theory to real life: How social value orientation affects willingness to sacrifice in ongoing close relationships. *Journal of Personality and Social Psychology, 73,* 1330–1344.

VanLange, P. A. M., & Liebrand, W. B. (1991). The influence of other's morality and own social value orientation on cooperation in the Netherlands and the U.S.A. *International Journal of Psychology, 26,* 429–449

VanLange, P. A. M., Otten, W., DeBruin, E. M. N., & Joireman, J. A. (1997). Development of prosocial, individualistic, and competitive orientations: Theory and preliminary evidence. *Journal of Personality and Social Psychology, 73,* 733–746.

VanLange, P. A. M., & Rusbult, C. E. (1995). My relationship is better than—and not as bad as—yours is: The perception of superiority in close relationships. *Personality and Social Psychology Bulletin, 21,* 32–44.

VanLange, P. A. M., & Semin-Goosens, A. (1998). The boundaries of reciprocal cooperation. *European Journal of Social Psychology, 28,* 847–854.

VanLange, P. A. M., Van Vugt, M., Meertens, R. M., & Ruiter, R. A. C. (1998). A social dilemma analysis of commuting preferences: The roles of social value orientation and trust. *Journal of Applied Social Psychology, 28,* 796–820.

VanLange, P. A. M., & Visser, K. (1999). Locomotion in social dilemmas: How people adapt to cooperative, tit-for-tat, and noncooperative partners. *Journal of Personality & Social Psychology, 77,* 762–773.

VanVugt, M. (1998). The conflicts in modern society. *Psychologist, 11,* 289–292.

VanVugt, M., & Samuelson, C. D. (1999). The impact of personal metering in the management of a natural resource crisis: A social dilemma analysis. *Personality & Social Psychology Bulletin, 25,* 731–745.

Veblen, T. (1899). *The theory of the leisure class: An economic study of institutions.* New York: MacMillan.

Veitch, R., & Griffitt, W. (1976). Good news, bad news: Affective and interpersonal effects. *Journal of Applied Social Psychology, 6,* 69–75.

Veroff, J. B. (1981). The dynamics of help-seeking in men and women: A national survey study. *Psychiatry, 44,* 189–200.

Vining, J., & Ebreo, A. (1992). Predicting recycling behavior from global and specific environmental attitudes and changes in recycling opportunities. *Journal of Applied Social Psychology, 22,* 1580–1607.

Visser, P. S., & Krosnick, J. A. (1998). Development of attitude strength over the life cycle: Surge and decline. *Journal of Personality and Social Psychology, 75,* 1389–1410.

Vohs, K. D., & Heatherton, T. F. (2000). Self-regulatory failure: A resource depletion approach. *Psychological Science, 11,* 249–254.

von Baeyer, C. L., Sherk, D. L., & Zanna, M. P. (1981). Impression management in the job interview: When the female applicant meets the male (chauvinist) interviewer. *Personality and Social Psychology Bulletin, 7,* 45–51.

von Hecker, U., & Sedek, G. (1999). Uncontrollability, depression, and the construction of mental models. *Journal of Personality and Social Psychology, 77,* 833–850.

Von Hippel, W., Sekaquaptewa, D., & Vargas, P. (1997). The linguistic intergroup bias as an implicit indicator of prejudice. *Journal of Experimental Social Psychology, 33,* 490–509.

Voyer, D., Voyer, S., & Bryden, M. P. (1995). Magnitude of sex differences in spatial abilities: A meta-analysis and consideration of critical variables. *Psychological Bulletin, 117,* 250–270.

Vrij, A. (1993). Credibility judgements of detectives: The impact of nonverbal behavior, social skills, and physical characteristics on impression formation. *Journal of Social Psychology, 133*, 601–610.

Wade, T. J., (2000). Evolutionary theory and self-perception: Sex differences in body esteem predictors of self-perceived physical and sexual attractiveness and self-esteem. *International Journal of Psychology, 35:* 36–45.

Waldrop, M. M. (1992). *Complexity: The emerging science at the edge of order and chaos.* New York: Simon & Schuster.

Walker, S., Richardson D. S., & Green, L. R. (2000). Aggression among older adults: The relationship of interaction networks and gender role to direct and indirect responses. *Aggressive Behavior, 26*, 145–154.

Wallace, M. D. (1979). Arms races and escalations: Some new evidence. In J. D. Singer (Ed.), *Explaining war: Selected papers from the correlates of war project* (pp. 240–252). Beverly Hills, CA: Sage.

Wallach, M. A., Kogan, N., & Bem, D. J. (1962). Group influence on individual risk taking. *Journal of Abnormal and Social Psychology, 65*, 75–86.

Waller, A. L. (1988). *Feud: Hatfields, McCoys and social change in Appalachia, 1860–1900.* Chapel Hill: University of North Carolina Press.

Waller, N. G., Kojetin, B. A., Bouchard, T. J., Jr., Lykken, D. T., & Tellegen, A. (1990). Genetic and environmental influences on religious interests, attitudes, and values: A study of twins reared apart and together. *Psychological Science, 1*, 138–142.

Walter, A. (1997). "The evolutionary psychology of mate selection in Morocco—A multivariate analysis." *Human Nature, 8*, 113–137.

Warburton, J., & Terry, D. J. (2000). Volunteer decision making by older people. *Basic and Applied Social Psychology, 22*, 245–257.

Watanabe, T. (1994, March 20). An unsung "Schindler" from Japan. *Los Angeles Times*, p. 1.

Watkins, A. (1991). *A Conservative coup: The fall of Margaret Thatcher.* London: Duckworth.

Watson, G. (1947). *Action for unity.* New York: Harper.

Watson, T. J. (1990). *Father, son, & co.* New York: Bantam Books.

Watson, W. E., Kumar, K., & Michaelsen, L. K. (1993). Cultural diversity's impact on interaction process and performance: Comparing homogeneous and diverse task groups. *Academy of Management Journal, 36*, 590–602.

Watson, W., Michaelsen, L. K., & Sharp, W. (1991). Member competence, group interaction, and group decision making: A longitudinal study. *Journal of Applied Psychology, 76*, 803–809.

Watt, J. D. (1993). The impact of the frequency of ingratiation on the performance evaluation of bank personnel. *The Journal of Psychology, 127*, 171–177.

Wayne, S. J., & Ferris, G. R. (1990). Influence tactics, affect, and exchange quality in supervisor-subordinate interactions: A laboratory experiment and field study. *Journal of Applied Psychology, 75*, 487–499.

Wayne, S. J., & Liden, R. C. (1995). Effects of impression management on performance ratings: A longitudinal study. *Academy of Management Journal, 38*, 232–250.

Weary, G. (1980). Examination of affect and egotism as mediators of bias in causal attributions. *Journal of Personality and Social Psychology, 38*, 348–357.

Weary, G., Marsh, K. L., Gleicher, F., & Edwards, J. A. (1993). Depression, control motivation, and the processing of information about others. In G. Weary, F. Gleicher, & K. L. Marsh (Eds.), *Control motivation and social cognition* (pp. 255–287). New York: Springer-Verlag.

Webb, E. J., Campbell, D. T., Schwartz, R. D., & Sechrest, L. (1966). *Unobtrusive measures: Nonreactive research in the social sciences.* Chicago: Rand McNally.

Weber, R., & Crocker, J. (1983). Cognitive processes in the revision of stereotypic beliefs. *Journal of Personality and Social Psychology, 45*, 961–977.

Webster, D. M. (1993). Motivated augmentation and reduction of the overattribution bias. *Journal of Personality and Social Psychology, 65*, 261–271.

Webster, D. M., Richter, L., & Kruglanski, A. W. (1996). On leaping to conclusions when feeling tired: Mental fatigue effects on impressional primacy. *Journal of Experimental Social Psychology, 32*, 181–195.

Wechsler, H., Lee, J. E., Kuo, M., & Lee, H. (2000). College binge drinking in the 1990s: A continuing problem: Results of the Harvard School of Public Health 1999 College Alcohol Study. *Journal of American College Health, 48*, 199–210.

Wegner, D. M. (1987). Transactive memory: A contemporary analysis of the group mind. In B. Mullen & G. R. Goethals (Eds.), *Theories of group behavior* (pp. 185–208). New York: Springer-Verlag.

Wegner, D. M. (1994). Ironic processes of mental control. *Psychological Review, 101*, 34–52.

Wegner, D. M. (1995). A computer network model of human transactive memory. *Social Cognition, 13*, 319–339.

Wegner, D. M., & Bargh, J. A. (1998). Control and automaticity in social life. In D. T. Gilbert, S. T. Fiske, & G. Lindzey (Eds.) *Handbook of Social Psychology* (4th edition-Volume 1, pp. 446–496). New York: McGraw-Hill/Oxford University Press.

Wegner, D. M., & Erber, R. (1992). The hyperaccessibility of suppressed thoughts. *Journal of Personality and Social Psychology, 63*, 903–912.

Wegner, D. M., Erber, R., & Raymond, P. (1991). Transactive memory in close relationships. *Journal of Personality and Social Psychology, 61*, 923–929.

Wegner, D. M., Schneider, D. J., Carter, S. III, & Whire, L. (1987). Paradoxical effects of thought suppression. *Journal of Personality and Social Psychology, 58,* 409–418.

Weick, K. E., & Roberts, K. H. (1993). Collective mind in organizations: Heedful interrelating on flight decks. *Administrative Science Quarterly, 38,* 357–381.

Weigel, R. H., Wiser, P. L., & Cook, S. W. (1975). The impact of cooperative learning experiences on cross-ethnic relations and attitudes. *Journal of Social Issues, 31,* 219–244.

Weiner, T., Johnston, D., & Lewis, N. A. (1995). *Betrayal: The story of Aldrich Ames, an American spy.* New York: Random House.

Weinstein, N. D. (1980). Unrealistic optimism about future life events. *Journal of Personality and Social Psychology, 39,* 806–820.

Weinstein, N. D. (1987). Unrealistic optimism about susceptibility to health problems. *Journal of Behavioral Medicine, 10,* 481–500.

Weisfeld, G. (1994). Aggression and dominance in the social world of boys. In J. Archer (Ed.), *Male violence* (pp. 43–69) New York: Routledge.

Weiss, R. S. (1973). *Loneliness: The experience of emotional and social isolation.* Cambridge, MA: MIT Press.

Wells, G. L. (1993). What do we know about eyewitness identification? *American Psychologist, 48,* 553–571.

Wells, G. L., & Leippe, M. R. (1981). How do triers of fact enter the accuracy of eyewitness identification? Memory for peripheral detail can be misleading. *Journal of Applied Psychology, 66,* 682–687.

Wells, P. A. (1987). Kin recognition in humans. In D. J. C. Fletcher & C. D. Michener (Eds.), *Kin recognition in animals* (pp. 395–416). New York: Wiley.

Wenzlaff, R. M., & Wegner, D. M. (2000). Thought suppression. *Annual Review of Psychology, 51,* 93–120.

West, S. G., Gunn, S. P., & Chernicky, P. (1975). Ubiquitous Watergate: An attributional analysis. *Journal of Personality and Social Psychology, 32,* 55–66.

West, S. G., Whitney, G., & Schnedler, R. (1975). Helping a motorist in distress: The effects of sex, race, and neighborhood. *Journal of Personality and Social Psychology, 31,* 691–698.

West, S. G., & Wicklund, R. A. (1980). *A primer of social psychological theories.* Monterey, CA: Brooks/Cole.

Westra, H. A., & Kuiper, N. A. (1992). Type A, irrational cognitions, and situational factors relating to stress. *Journal of Research in Personality, 26,* 1–20.

Weyant, J. (1978). Effects of mood states, costs, and benefits on helping. *Journal of Personality and Social Psychology, 10,* 1169–1176.

Wheeler, L. (1966). Motivation as a determinant of upward comparison. *Journal of Experimental Social Psychology* (Suppl. 1), 27–31.

Wheeler, L., Reis, H., & Nezlek, J. (1983). Loneliness, social interaction, and sex roles. *Journal of Personality and Social Psychology, 45,* 943–953.

White, G. L., Fishbein, S., & Rutstein, J. (1981). Passionate love: The misattribution of arousal. *Journal of Personality and Social Psychology, 41,* 56–62.

White, G. L., & Kight, T. D. (1984). Misattribution of arousal and attraction: Effects of salience of explanation of arousal. *Journal of Experimental Social Psychology, 20,* 55–64.

White, G. M. (1980). Conceptual universals in interpersonal language. *American Anthropologist, 82,* 759–781.

White, H. (1988). Sex differences in vivid memories. *Imagination, Cognition and Personality, 8,* 141–153.

White, L. C. (1988). *Merchants of death.* New York: Morrow.

White, R. K., & Lippitt, R. (1960). *Autocracy and democracy: An experimental inquiry.* New York: Harper & Brothers.

White, R. W. (1959). Motivation reconsidered: The concept of competence. *Psychological Review, 66,* 297–333.

Whitley, B. E., Jr. (1999). Right-wing authoritarianism, social dominance orientation, and prejudice. *Journal of Personality & Social Psychology,* 77, 126–134.

Whyte, G. (1989). Groupthink reconsidered. *Academy of Management Review, 14,* 40–56.

Wicklund, R. A., & Gollwitzer, P. M. (1982). *Symbolic self-completion.* Hillsdale, NJ: Erlbaum.

Widmeyer, W. N. (1990). Group composition in sport. *International Journal of Sport Psychology, 21,* 264–285.

Wiederman, M. W. (1993). Evolved gender differences in mate preferences: Evidence from personal advertisements. *Ethology and Sociobiology, 14,* 331–352.

Wiederman, M. W., & Allgeier, E. R. (1992). Gender differences in mate selection criteria: Sociobiological or socioeconomic explanation? *Ethology and sociobiology, 13,* 115–124.

Wiederman, M. W., & Hurd, C. (1999). Extradyadic involvement during dating. *Journal of Social & Personal Relationships, 16,* 265–274.

Wiederman, M. W., & Kendall. (1999). Evolution, sex, and jealousy: Investigation with a sample from Sweden. *Evolution & Human Behavior, 20,* 121–128.

Wiegman, O., Kuttschreuter, M., & Baarda, B. (1992). A longitudinal study of the effects of television viewing on aggressive and prosocial behaviors. *British Journal of Social Psychology, 31,* 147–164.

Wiersema, M. F., & Bantel, K. A. (1992). Top management team demography and corporate strategic change. *Academy of Management Journal, 35,* 91–121.

Wiggins, J. S., & Broughton, R. (1985). The interpersonal circle: A structural model for the integration of personality research. In R. Hogan & W. H. Jones (Eds.), *Perspectives in*

Personality (Vol. 1, pp. 1–48). Greenwich, CT: JAI Press.

Wilber, K. (1993). *Grace and grit: Spirituality and healing in the life and death of Treya Killam Wilber.* Boston: Shambhala.

Wilder, D. A. (1993). The role of anxiety in facilitating stereotypic judgments of outgroup behavior. In D. M. Mackie & D. L. Hamilton (Eds.), *Affect, cognition, and stereotyping: Interactive processes in intergroup perception* (pp. 87–109). New York: Academic Press.

Wilder, D. A., & Shapiro, P. (1989). The role of competition-induced anxiety in limiting the beneficial impact of positive behavior by an outgroup member. *Journal of Personality and Social Psychology, 56,* 60–69.

Williams, J. E., & Best, D. L. (1990). *Measuring sex stereotypes: A multination study.* Newbury Park, CA: Sage.

Williams, K. D., Bourgeois, M., & Croyle, R. T. (1993). The effects of stealing thunder in criminal and civil trials. *Law and Human Behavior, 17,* 597–609.

Williams, K. D., Harkins, S., & Latané, B. (1981). Identifiability as a deterrent to social loafing: Two cheering experiments. *Journal of Personality and Social Psychology, 40,* 303–311.

Williams, R. B., Jr. (1984, September/October). An untrusting heart. *The Sciences,* pp. 30–36.

Williams, R. M., Jr. (1947). *The reduction of intergroup tensions.* New York: Social Science Research Council.

Williams-Avery, R. M., & MacKinnon, D. P. (1996). Injuries and use of protective equipment among college in-line skaters. *Accident Analysis and Prevention, 28,* 779–784.

Williamson, G., & Clark, M. S. (1989). Effects of providing help to another and of relationship type on the provider's mood and self-evaluation. *Journal of Personality and Social Psychology, 56,* 722–734.

Williamson, G., Clark, M. S., Pegalis, L. J., & Behan, A. (1996). Affective consequences of refusing to help in communal and exchange relationships. *Personality and Social Psychology Bulletin, 22,* 34–47.

Williamson, S., Hare, R. D., & Wong, S. (1987). Violence: Criminal psychopaths and their victims. *Canadian Journal of Behavioral Science, 19,* 454–462.

Willis, R. H. (1965). Conformity, independence, and anticonformity. *Human Relations, 18,* 373–388.

Wills, T. A. (1981). Downward comparison principles in social psychology. *Psychological Bulletin, 90,* 245–271.

Wills, T. A., & DePaulo, B. M. (1991). Interpersonal analysis of the help-seeking process. In C. R. Snyder & D. R. Forsyth (Eds.), *Handbook of social and clinical psychology* (pp. 350–375). New York: Pergammon.

Wilson, E. O. (1992). *The diversity of life.* New York: Norton.

Wilson, E. O. (1975). *Sociobiology: The new synthesis.* Cambridge, MA: Harvard University Press.

Wilson, J. P. (1976). Motivation, modeling, and altruism: A person x situation analysis. *Journal of Personality and Social Psychology, 34,* 1078–1086.

Wilson, M., & Daly, M. (1985). Competitiveness, risk taking, and violence: The young male syndrome. *Ethology and Sociobiology, 6,* 59–73.

Winter, D. D. (2000). Some big ideas for some big problems. *American Psychologist, 55,* 516–522.

Winter, D. G. (1973). *The power motive.* New York: Free Press.

Winter, D. G. (1987). Leader appeal, leader performance, and the motive profiles of leaders and followers: A study of American presidents and elections. *Journal of Personality and Social Psychology, 52,* 196–202.

Winter, D. G. (1996). *Personality: Analysis and interpretation of lives.* New York: McGraw-Hill.

Winter, L., & Uleman, J. S. (1984). When are social judgments made? Evidence for the spontaneousness of trait inferences. *Journal of Personality and Social Psychology, 47,* 237–252.

Wispé, L. (1991). *The psychology of sympathy.* New York: Plenum.

Wittenbrink, B., & Henly, J. R. (1996). Creating social reality: Informational social influence and the content of stereotypic beliefs. *Personality and Social Psychology Bulletin, 22,* 598–610.

Wittenbrink, B., Judd, C. M., & Park, B. (1997). Evidence for racial prejudice at the implicit level and its relationship with questionnaire measures. *Journal of Personality and Social Psychology,* 72, 262–274.

Wolf, S., & Latané, B. (1985). Conformity, innovation, and the psychosocial law. In S. Moscovici, G. Mugny, & E. Van Avermaet (Eds.), *Perspectives on minority influence* (pp. 201–215). Cambridge: Cambridge University Press.

Wolfgang, M. E. (1958). *Patterns in criminal homicide.* Philadephia: University of Pennsylvania Press.

Wong, P. T., & Weiner, B. (1981). When people ask "why" questions, and the heuristics of attributional search. *Journal of Personality and Social Psychology, 40,* 650–663.

Wood, J. V. (1989). Theory and research concerning social comparisons of personal attributes. *Psychological Bulletin, 106,* 231–248.

Wood, J. V., Giordano-Beech, M., & Ducharme, M. J. (1999). Compensating for failure through social comparison. *Personality and Social Psychology Bulletin, 25,* 1370–1386.

Wood, J. V., Giordano-Beech, M., Taylor, K. L., Michela, J. L., & Gaus, V. (1994). Strategies of social comparison among people with low self-esteem: Self-protection and self-enhancement. *Journal of Personality and Social Psychology, 67,* 713–731.

Wood, J. V., Taylor, S. E., & Lichtman, R. R. (1985). Social comparison in adjustment to breast cancer. *Journal of Personality and Social Psychology, 49,* 1169–1183.

Wood, W., Kallgren, C. A., & Preisler, R. M. (1985). Access to attitude-relevant information in memory as a determinant of persuasion.

Journal of Experimental Social Psychology, 21, 73–85.

Wood, W., Lundgren, S., Ouellette, J. A., Busceme, S., & Blackstone, T. (1994). Processes of minority influence: Influence effectiveness and source perceptions. *Psychological Bulletin, 115*, 323–345.

Wood, W., & Stagner, B. (1994). Why are some people easier to influence than others? In S. Shavitt & T. C. Brock (Eds.), *Persuasion* (pp. 149–174). Boston: Allyn & Bacon.

Wood, W., Wong, F. Y., & Chachere, J. G. (1991). Effects of media violence on viewer's aggression in unconstrained social interaction. *Psychological Bulletin, 109*, 371–383.

Woodcock, G. (1977). *Peoples of the coast.* Bloomington: University of Indiana Press.

Woodward, A. L. (1998). Infants selectively encode the goal object of an actor's reach. *Cognition, 69*, 1–34.

Woodzicka, J. A., & LaFrance, M. (in press). Real versus imagined gender harassment. *Journal of Social Issues.*

Wooter, D. B., & Reed, A. (1998). Informational influence and the ambiguity of product experience: Order effects on the weighting of evidence. *Journal of Consumer Psychology*, 7, 79–99.

Word, C. O., Zanna, M. P., & Cooper, J. (1974). The nonverbal mediation of self-fulfilling prophecies in interracial interaction. *Journal of Experimental Social Psychology, 10*, 109–120.

Wortman, C. B. (1975). Some determinants of perceived control. *Journal of Personality and Social Psychology, 31*, 282–294.

Wortman, C. B., & Linsenmeier, J. (1977). Interpersonal attraction and techniques of ingratiation. In B. Staw & G. Salancik (Eds.), *New directions in organizational behavior* (pp. 133–179). Chicago: St. Clair.

Wosinska, W., Dabul, A. J., Whetstone-Dion, R., & Cialdini, R. B. (1996). Self-presentational responses to success in the organization: The costs and benefits of modesty. *Basic and Applied Social Psychology, 18*, 229–242.

Wright, J. C., & Dawson, V. L. (1988). Person perception and the bounded rationality of social judgment. *Journal of Personality and Social Psychology, 55*, 780–794.

Wyer, N., & Sherman, J. W., & Stroessner, S. J. (2000). The roles of motivation and ability in controlling the consequences of stereotype suppression. *Personality and Social Psychology Bulletin, 26*, 13–25.

Wyer, R. S., Jr., Budesheim, T. L., Lambert, A. J., & Swan, S. (1994). Person memory and judgment: Pragmatic influences on impressions formed in a social context. *Journal of Personality and Social Psychology, 66*, 254–267.

Wylie, L., & Forest, J. (1992). Religious fundamentalism, right-wing authoritarianism and prejudice. *Psychological Reports, 71*, 1291–1298.

Wylie, R. (1979). *The self-concept* (Vol. 2). Lincoln: University of Nebraska Press.

Yamagishi, T. (1988a). Seriousness of a social dilemma and the provision of a sanctioning system. *Social Psychology Quarterly, 51*, 32–42.

Yamagishi, T. (1988b). The provision of a sanctioning system in the United States and Japan. *Social Psychology Quarterly, 51*, 264–270.

Yamagishi, T., & Cook, K. S. (1993). Generalized exchange and social dilemmas. *Social Psychology Quarterly, 56*, 235–248.

Yates, S. M., & Aronson, E. (1983). A social psychological perspective on energy conservation in residential buildings. *American Psychologist, 20*, 435–44.

Ybarra, O., & Trafimow, D. (1998). How priming the private self or collective self affects the relative weights of attitudes and subjective norms. *Personality and Social Psychology Bulletin, 24*, 362–370.

Yinger, J. (1995). *Closed doors, oportunities lost: The continuing costs of housing discrimination.* New York: Russell Sage Foundation.

Zaccaro, S. J. (1984). Social loafing: The role of task attractiveness. *Personality and Social Psychology Bulletin, 10*, 99–106.

Zaccaro, S. J. (1991). Nonequivalent associations between forms of cohesiveness and group-related outcomes: Evidence for multidimensionality. *Journal of Social Psychology, 131*, 387–399.

Zaccaro, S. J., & Lowe, C. A. (1985). Effort attributions: Task novelty, perceptual focus, and cue utilization. *Personality and Social Psychology Bulletin, 11*, 489–501.

Zaccaro, S. J., & Lowe, C. A. (1988). Cohesiveness and performance on an additive task: Evidence for multidimensionality. *Journal of Social Psychology, 128*, 547–558.

Zahn-Waxler, C., Robinson, J. L., & Emde, R. N. (1992). The development of empathy in twins. *Developmental Psychology, 28*, 1038–1047.

Zajac, R. J., & Hartup, W. W. (1997). Friends as coworkers: Research review and classroom implications. *Elementary School Journal, 98*, 3–13.

Zajonc, R. B. (1965). Social facilitation. *Science, 149, 269–274.*

Zajonc, R. B. (1968). Attitudinal effects of mere exposure. *Journal of Personality and Social Psychology Monographs, 9* (2, part 2), 1–27.

Zajonc, R. B. (1980). Feeling and thinking: Preferences need no inferences. *American Psychologist, 35*, 151–175.

Zajonc, R. B. (1998). Emotions. In D. T. Gilbert, S. T. Fiske, & G. Lindzey (Eds.), *The handbook of social psychology* (4th ed.) (Vol. 1, pp. 591–632). Boston: McGraw-Hill.

Zajonc, R. B., Heingartner, A., & Herman, E. M. (1969). Social enhancement and impairment of performance in the cockroach. *Journal of Personality and Social Psychology, 13*, 83–92.

Zamaripa, P. O., & Krueger, D. L. (1983). Implicit contracts regulating small group leadership. *Small Group Behavior, 14*, 187–210.

Zander, A. (1985). *The purposes of groups and organizations.* San Francisco: Jossey-Bass.

Zanna, M. P., & Pack, S. J. (1975). On the self-fulfilling nature of apparent sex differences in behavior. *Journal of Experimental Social Psychology, 11*, 583–591.

Zanna, M. T., & Cooper, J. (1974). Dissonance and the pill: An attribution approach to studying the arousal properties of dissonance. *Journal of Personality and Social Psychology, 29*, 703–709.

Zebrowitz, L. A. (1994). Facial maturity and political prospects: Persuasive, culpable, and powerful faces. In R. C. Schank & E. Langer (Eds.), *Beliefs, reasoning, and decision-making* (pp. 315–345). Hillsdale, NJ: Erlbaum.

Zebrowitz, L. A. (1994). Facial maturity and political prospects: Persuasive, culpable, and powerful faces. In R. C. Schank & E. Langer (Eds.), *Beliefs, reasoning, and decision making: Psycho-logic in honor of Bob Abelson* (pp. 315–346). Hillsdale, NJ: Erlbaum.

Zebrowitz, L. A., & Collins, M. A. (1997). Accurate social perception at zero acquaintance: The affordances of a Gibsonian approach. *Personality and Social Psychology Review, 1*, 204–223.

Zebrowitz, L. A., Tenenbaum, D. R., & Goldstein, L. H. (1991). The impact of job applicants' facial maturity, gender, and academic achievement on hiring recommendations. *Journal of Applied Social Psychology, 21*, 525–548.

Zebrowitz, L. A., Voinescu, L., & Collins, M. A. (1996). "Wide-eyed" and "crooked-faced": Determinants of perceived and real honesty across the life span. *Personality and Social Psychology Bulletin, 22*, 1258–1269.

Zeifman, D., & Hazan, C. (1997). Attachment: The pair in pair-bonds. In J. A. Simpson & D. T. Kenrick (Eds.), *Evolutionary social psychology* (pp. 237–264). Mahwah, NJ: LEA.

Zeilik, M. (1994). *Astronomy: The evolving universe* (7th ed.). New York: Wiley.

Zenger, T. R., & Lawrence, B. S. (1989). Organizational demography: The differential effects of age and tenure distributions on technical communication. *Academy of Management Journal, 32*, 353–376.

Zillmann, D. (1983). Transfer of excitation in emotional behavior. In J. Cacioppo & R. E. Petty (Eds.), *Social psychophysiology* (pp. 215–240). New York: Guilford.

Zillmann, D. (1994). Cognition-excitation interdependencies in the escalation of anger and angry aggression. In M. Potegal & J. F. Knutson (Eds.), *Dynamics of aggression: Biological and social processes in dyads and groups* (pp. 45–71). Hillsdale, NJ: Erlbaum.

Zillmann, D., Katcher, A. H., & Milavsky, B. (1972). Excitation-transfer from physical exercise to subsequent aggressive behavior. *Journal of Experimental Social Psychology, 8*, 247–259.

Zimbardo, P. G. (1969). The human choice: Individuation, reason, and order versus deindividuation, impulse, and chaos. In W. J. Arnold & D. Levine (Eds.), *Nebraska Symposium on motivation, 1969* (Vol. 17, pp. 237–307). Lincoln: University of Nebraska.

Zimbardo, P. G. (1977). *Shyness: What it is, what to do about it.* Reading, MA: Addison-Wesley.

Zimbardo, P. G. (1997, May). What messages are behind today's cults? *APA Monitor*, p. 14.

Zorpette, G. (1997, April). A golf cart, it isn't. *Scientific American*, p. 25–26.

Zuckerman, M. (1979). Attribution of success and failure revisited, or: The motivational bias is alive and well in attribution theory. *Journal of Personality, 47*, 245–287.

Zuckerman, M., & Reis, H. T. (1978). Comparisons of three models for predicting altruistic behavior. *Journal of Personality and Social Psychology, 36*, 498–510.

Zuckerman, M., Kieffer, S. C., & Knee, C. R. (1998). Consequences of self-handicapping: Effects on coping, academic performance, and adjustment. *Journal of Personality and Social Psychology, 74*, 1619–1628.

Zuckerman, M., Koestner, R., & Alton, A. O. (1984). Learning to detect deception. *Journal of Personality and Social Psychology, 46*, 519–528.

Zullow, H. M., Oettingen, G., Peterson, C., & Seligman, M. E. P. (1988). Pessimistic explanatory style in the historical record: CAVing LBJ, presidential candidates, and East versus West Berlin. *American Psychologist, 43*, 673–682.

Name Index

A

B

C

D

G

I

J

K

L

M

N

O

P

Q

R

S

T

U

V

W

Y

Z

Subject Index

A

B

C

D

E

F

G

H

I

O

P

Q

R

T

U

V

W

X

Z

Photo Credits

Chapter 1: p. 2 (top), AP/Wide World Photos; **pg. 2 (bottom),** © AP/Wide World Photos; **p. 3,** AP/Wide World Photos; **p. 5,** © Kal Muller/Woodfin Camp; **p. 6 (left)** © Smaril/Liaison Agency; **p. 6 (right)** © Daniel Cox/Liaison; **p. 7:** © Christina Salvador/CORBIS Sygma; **p. 8,** © Liaison Agency; **p. 10,** © AP/Wide World Photos; **p. 12,** AP/Wide World Photos; **p. 13,** © UPI/CORBIS; **p. 14,** Hilmer and Mildred Trost; **p. 16,** © AP/Wide World Photos; **p. 18,** © AP/Wide World Photos; **p. 23,** © Dr. Philip G. Zimbardo; **p. 27,** © 1965 by Stanley Milgram, from the film *Obedience*, distributed by the Pennsylvania State University, Alexandra Milgram; **p. 30 (top),** © Alex Quesada/Woodfin Camp & Associates; **p. 30 (bottom),** © AP/Wide World Photos. **Chapter 2: p. 36 (top),** © Bettmann/ CORBIS; p. **36 (bottom),** © Flip Schulke/CORBIS; **p. 42 (top),** © Dan Budnik/Woodfin Camp & Associates; **p. 43,** © Jeff Persons/Stock Boston; **p. 45 (both),** Dr. Antonio R. Damasio, 2000, October Issue of *Nature Neuroscience, 3* (10), 1049–1056; **p. 48 (left),** © Dr. Fritz Strach; **p. 48 (right),** © Dr. Fritz Strach; **p. 49,** © Orban/Florestier/Liaison Agency; **p. 52,** Indiana Basketball Hall of Fame; **p. 55 (right),** Courtesy of the Krueger Family ; **p. 55 (left),** Courtesy of the Krueger Family; **p. 60 (left),** © James L. Amos/CORBIS; **p. 60 (right),** © Jack Fields/CORBIS; **p. 65,** © Akso Szilvasi/Stock Boston; **p. 68,** © UPI/Corbis. **Chapter 3: p. 74,** © Dirk Halstead/Liaison Agency; **p. 80,** © James Keyser/Timepix; **p. 82 (left),** University of Iowa; **p. 82 (right),** *Detroit Free Press*; **p. 87,** © M. Denora/Liaison Agency; **p. 89,** © AP/Wide World Photos; **p. 95,** © Gerd Ludwig/Woodfin Camp & Associates; **p. 97,** © Terry E. Eiler/Stock Boston; **p. 107,** © CORBIS; **p. 108,** © Bill Horsman/Stock Boston; **p. 110,** © AP/Wide World Photos. **Chapter 4: p. 116,** © AP/Wide World Photos; **p. 117,** © Catherine Karnow/Woodfin Camp & Associates; **p. 118,** © Joseph Schuyler/Stock Boston; **p. 121,** © AP/Wide World Photos; **p. 123,** © Michael Abramson/Woodfin Camp & Associates; **p. 126 (left),** © Dachner Keltner; **p. 126 (right),** © Dachner Keltner; **p. 128 (left),** © Cosmetic Surgery Networkp. **p. 128 (right),** © Cosmetic Surgery Network; **p. 129,** © Hulton Getty/Liaison; **p. 131,** © CORBIS; **p. 135,** © Ron Sherman/Stock Boston; **p. 137,** © Bob Daemmrich/Stock Boston; **p. 141,** © Joan Slatkin/Archive Photos; **p. 142 (left),** © Karin Cooper/Liaison Agency; **p. 142 (right),** © AP/Wide World Photos; **p. 144,** © Karin Cooper/Liaison Agency; **p. 148,** © AP/Wide World Photos. **Chapter 5: p. 152,** © UPI/Corbis; **p. 153,** © A. Ramey/Woodfin Camp and Associates; **p. 159,** © Bobette Gordon; **p. 160,** © A. Ramey/ Stock Boston; **p. 165,** Courtesy American Airlines. Photo: Abrams/Lacagnina/The Image Bank; **p. 167,** Volkswagen of America; **p. 175,** AP/Wide World Photos; **p. 181 (left),** Toyota of America; **p. 181 (right),** Toyota of America; **p. 187 (top),** © UPI/CORBIS; **p. 187 (bottom),** Donald S. Connery; **p. 192,** © Con/Frank Fournier/Woodfin Camp & Associates. **Chapter 6: p. 194,** © AP/Wide World Photos; **p. 195 (both),** Dr. Solomon Asch; **p. 198,** Advertisement reprinted with permission of Bozwell Worldwide, Inc., as agent for the National Fluid Milk Processor Promotion Board; **p. 199,** © 1965 by Stanley Milgram. From the film *Obedience*, distributed by the Pennsylvania State University, Audio Visual Services; **p. 202,** © Cohen/Liaison Agency; **p. 205,** Courtesy of Diners Club International; **p. 212,** © Alan Carey/The Image Works; **p. 218,** USDA; **p. 227 (top),** Steve Hassan; **p. 227 (bottom),** © Pat Greenhouse/*The Boston Globe*. ***Chapter 7:* p. 232,** FDR Library; **p. 233,** © N. Richmond/The Image Works; **p. 238,** Courtesy of the FBI; **p. 240,** © Frank Pedrick/The Image Works; **p. 246,** © Steve Warmowski/*Jornal-Courier*/The Image Works; **p. 250,** © Irven DeVore/Anthro Photos; **p. 251,** AP/Wide World Photos; **p. 253,** © R. Bribiescas/Anthro Photos; **p. 257 (top),** © Philip Gould/ CORBIS; **p. 257 (bottom),** © Nina Leen/Timepix; **p. 259 (bottom),** FDR Library; **p. 259 (top),** FDR Library. **Chapter 8: p. 264 (top),** © CORBIS; **p. 264 (bottom),** © N. Obee/Globe Photos; **p. 267,** © Julie Houck/Stock Boston; **p. 270,** AP/Wide World Photos; **p. 272,** © CORBIS Sygma; **p. 273,** © Willie Hill, Jr./The Image Works; **p. 275,** Victoria & Albert Museum, London, Bridgeman Art Library, London/New York; **p. 276,** © Stephanie Maze/Woodfin Camp & Associates; **p. 280 (left),** Harlow Primate Lab, University of Wisconsin; **p. 280 (middle),** Harlow Primate Lab, University of Wisconsin; **p. 280 (right),** Harlow Primate Lab, University of Wisconsin; **p. 281,** Castle Rock Entertainment (Courtesy Kobal); **p. 285 (left),** David Lundberg Kenrick; **p. 285 (right),** David Lundberg Kenrick; **p. 286,** © Chris Weeks/Liaison Agency; **p. 288 (left),** © Irven de Vore/Anthro Photos; **p. 288 (right),** © Thomas L. Kelly; **p. 291,** © Liaison Agency; **p. 292,** © CORBIS. **Chapter 9: p. 298 (top),** Visas for Life; **p. 298 (bottom),** © CORBIS; **p. 302 (top),** © Michele Burgess/Stock Boston; **p. 302 (bottom),** © N. Richmond/The Image Works; **p. 304,** Visas for Life; **p. 306 (left),** © UPI/ CORBIS; **p. 306 (right),** Rabbi Marvin Tokayer; **p. 309,** Neg. No. 22861 Courtesy Dept of Library Services, American Museum of Natural History; **p. 310,** New York Times Pictures; **p. 311,** Visas for Life; **p. 312 (top),** © Jan Halaska/Photo Researchers; **p. 312 (bottom),** © Myra Miller/Liaison Agency; **p. 318 (left),** © Robert Tur/Robert Clark/Los Angeles News Service; **p. 318 (right),** © Reuters/ CORBIS; **p. 329,** © CORBIS. **Chapter 10: p. 336 (top),** © UPI/CORBIS; **p. 336 (middle top),** © UPI/CORBIS; **p. 336 (middle bottom),** AP/Wide World Photos; **p. 336 (bottom),** AP/Wide World Photos; **p. 338,** AP/Wide World Photos; **p. 344,** © Bob Daemmrich/Stock Boston; **p. 349,** Archive Photos; **p. 350,** © Najlah Feanny/SABA; **p. 352,** © CORBIS Sygma; **p. 355,** David Lundberg Kenricks; **p. 357,** © W. Perry Conway/CORBIS; **p. 359,** © Les Stone/CORBIS Sygma; p. 361, © Culver Pictures; **p. 371,** © UPI/CORBIS; **p. 372,** © H. Barriso, *The Californian*/SYGMA. **Chapter 11:** © A. Ramey/ Woodfin Camp & Associates; **p. 388,** Dr. O. J. Harvey; **p. 390,** © UPI/CORBIS; **p. 392,** © Jeff T. Green/ CORBIS Sygma; **p. 395,** © Jason Szenes/CORBIS Sygma; **p. 396,** © The Burns Collection; **p. 400 (left),** © AP/Wide World Photos; **p. 400 (right),** © AP/Wide World Photos; **p. 411,** © Dr. O. J. Harvey; **p. 413,** © UPI/CORBIS; **p. 414,** © Osha Gray Davidson. **Chapter 12: p. 418,** © Reuters/ CORBIS; **p. 421,** © Ferry/Liaison Agency; **p. 425,** © Gary Walts/Syracuse Newspapers/The Image Works; **p. 428,** © Paul Solomon/Woodfin Camp & Associates; **p. 431,** © Y. Momatiuk & J. Eastcott/ Stock Boston; **p. 436,** © Richard Baker/Katz/SABA; **p. 441,** Archive Photos; **p. 448.** © Robert Maass/ SIPA; **p. 452,** © UPI/CORBIS; **p. 453,** © Richard Baker/Katz/SABA. **Chapter 13: p. 458,** © Richard Lord/The Image Works; **p. 465,** © Michael Siluk/The Image Works; **p. 467,** © Jeffry W.

Myers/Stock Boston; **p. 468,** © AP/Wide World Photos; **p. 470,** © AP/Wide World Photos; **p. 472,** © Jim Sulley/The Image Works; **p. 473,** © AP/Wide World Photos; **p. 474,** © Mike Greenlar/The Image Works; **p. 475 (left),** © George Hall/Woodfin Camp & Associates; **p. 475 (right),** © Kal Muller/Woodfin Camp & Associates; **p. 477,** © Liaison Agency; **p. 482,** © CORBIS Sygma; **p. 487,** © John Ficara/Woodfin Camp & Associates; **p. 488,** © Allan Friedlander/Superstock. **Chapter 14: p. 494 (top),** © AP/Wide World Photos; **p. 494 (bottom),** © AP/Wide World Photos; **p. 495,** © Reuters/Win McNamee/Archive Photos; **p. 498 (left),** © Crochet/Liaison Agency; **p. 498 (right),** © Archive Photos; **p. 499 (left),** © Kent Meireis/The Image Works; **p. 499 (right),** © Lindsay Hebberd/Woodfin Camp & Associates; **p. 502,** © Magnani/Liaison Agency; **p. 507,** © Archive Photos; **p. 509,** AP/Wide World Photos; **p. 510,** AP/Wide World Photos; **p. 511,** © Joshua Bucklan/CORBIS Sygma; **p. 512 (bottom left),** © AP/Wide World Photos; **p. 512 (bottom right),** © AP/Wide World Photos; **p. 512, (top),** © Liaison Agency; **p. 519,** © Archive Photos.